Patricia Paulsen Hughes
3701 Townsend
FW, TX 76110
9246182

Patricia Paulsen Hughes
3701 Townsend
FW, TX 76110

Adapted Physical Education and Recreation

third edition

Adapted Physical Education and Recreation

A Multidisciplinary Approach

Claudine Sherrill

Texas Woman's University

Wm. C. Brown Publishers
Dubuque, Iowa

Book Team

Edward G. Jaffe, *Executive Editor*
Brenda Fleming Roesch, *Editor*
Julie E. Anderson, *Designer*
Kay Dolby, *Design Layout Assistant*
Kevin Campbell, *Production Editor*
Faye M. Schilling, *Photo Research Editor*
Carla D. Arnold, *Permissions Editor*

wcb group

Wm. C. Brown, *Chairman of the Board*
Mark C. Falb, *President and Chief Executive Officer*

wcb

Wm. C. Brown Publishers, College Division

James L. Romig, *Vice-President, Product Development*
David A. Corona, *Vice-President, Production and Design*
E. F. Jogerst, *Vice-President, Cost Analyst*
Bob McLaughlin, *National Sales Manager*
Catherine M. Faduska, *Director of Marketing Services*
Craig S. Marty, *Director of Marketing Research*
Marilyn A. Phelps, *Manager of Design*
Eugenia M. Collins, *Production Editorial Manager*

Aileene Lockhart, Texas Woman's University, *Consulting Editor*

Contents

Part **3**

Adapted Physical Education for Individual Differences 397

Dedicated to my parents, Ivalene and Robert Sherrill, of Logansport, Indiana

Foreword

If a man does not keep pace with his companions, perhaps it is because he hears a different drummer. Let him step to the music which he hears, however measured or far away.

—Henry David Thoreau

Those who dare to teach and lead can never cease to learn! But learn and change we must if we are to continue to grow, progress, and remain current. However, time marches on more rapidly and surely than most of us care to admit. Therefore, to meet needs, satisfy interests, and challenge abilities of every individual each of us is dedicated to serve, teachers and leaders must march to the tune of today's drummer while listening for tomorrow's beat and keeping an eye on past, present, and future happenings.

Each of us must be weary and leery of old wine placed in new bottles—the tried and true couched in new and pseudoscientific terms that are difficult to understand. Confusion results when the obvious is clouded and the simple made complex. Oversimplified approaches that only stress *what* and *how* leave much to be desired; oversophisticated discussions of theory with little regard for sound practice and what goes on in the real world are hollow and inadequate. It is important to know and communicate *why* a particular method or technique is used in a given situation with a particular individual. This requires getting back to basics—fundamentals of the physical, biological, and behavioral sciences comprise the bedrock foundation in this process.

Theory and practice, the old and the new, research evidence and personal experience, the simple and the complex, the innovative and the traditional, the obvious and the subtle—all are necessary in order to understand each person as someone of worth and dignity and to meet each person's specific needs. This book on *adapted and developmental physical education and recreation* tells it like it is and has it all—it is the most complete and current book on this topic yet to be published.

A great deal of lip service is continually given to such current concepts and present-day trends as noncategorical approaches, behavioral objectives, performance goals, mainstreaming, interdisciplinary cooperation, and multiagency teamwork. In this book, these concepts are not only talked about and presented; they are also discussed in terms of practical suggestions, realistic approaches, and functional ways for implementation. Each activity and procedure is important and presented as part of a truly interdisciplinary approach for regular and special physical education, recreation, and related programs for those with various handicapping conditions. This publication blends theory and practice and presents the author's great and varied experience in the field. Claudine Sherrill's thorough treatment of all aspects of these programs enhances each reader's understanding of the field; vision and perspective are projected so that movement with students can be forward and onward.

Discussion and realistic presentations of similarities and differences among specific modalities accentuate the basic team concept. Relationships and interrelationships among different educational, therapeutic, recreational, habilitative, and rehabilitative approaches provide a basis for better service to individuals in school, community, and special programs. This book presents ways to utilize fully the unique contributions of each specialization so as to reduce undesirable overlap and further the interdisciplinary/multiagency concept in action.

The title of this publication—*Adapted Physical Education and Recreation: A Multidisciplinary Approach*—reflects its comprehensive and current nature. In addition to being an excellent textbook for courses in physical education/adapted physical education, recreation/therapeutic recreation, and special education, it is a valuable resource for many other areas—education, occupational therapy, physical therapy, dance therapy, administration, and psychology. *Everyone* working in the field should have a copy as a ready resource for background information in all involved disciplines, practical suggestions in terms of methods and activities, and easily understood discussions of virtually all handicapping conditions. Many examples and personal anecdotes throughout the publication anchor discussions and give added meaning to written and pictorial materials.

Strengths of this publication—there are many—include (a) documentation and illustration with many pictures and other graphic materials throughout each chapter that will be especially appealing to practitioners, students, parents, and volunteers—the book is an excellent resource for these groups; (b) charts and tables that present information in concise, easy-to-understand, practical, and functional ways; (c) selected references at the end of chapters and key resources that are listed in the appendixes are beneficial and current; (d) practical suggestions for implementing programs and activities that are provided and discussed throughout the book; (e) emphasis on *why* as well as *what* and *how* of programming in these areas; (f) research bases for statements and points that are made, along with identification of needed research and voids in many areas; (g) scientific foundations in various areas that are designed to assist in understanding *whys* and *wherefores* of these programs and activities; (h) strong emphasis on each person, regardless of type or severity of handicapping condition, as an individual of worth, dignity, and value; (i) stress on exploratory approaches so that each individual can attain success in terms of his or her own interests, needs, and abilities; (j) treatment and discussion of controversial issues rather than ignoring them; (k) emphasis on developmental sequences and functional abilities rather than particular ages at which certain milestones are reached or when specific skills should be developed; (l) relationships between classroom activities and those in physical education, recreation, and related programs—interrelationships among psychomotor, cognitive, and affective domains; (m) thorough and complete treatment of each individual area and specific topic as well as the entire field.

As motor development, physical proficiency, perceptual-motor function, movement, physical fitness, constructive use of leisure, and lifetime sports continue to receive more emphasis in total function and lifestyle of everyone, including persons with various handicapping conditions, this publication is like an oasis on a desert. Litigation and legislation require *education for all* to be more than words; zero-reject principles mandate schools to meet needs of *all* students regardless of type or severity of handicapping conditions. *Right to treatment* interpretations of laws have implications for physical education, recreation, and related activity areas. *Right to recreation* is implied or directly stipulated through equality of opportunity requirements for all activities in which the nonhandicapped participate. These have all been punctuated by requests of personnel in the field who continue to demand assistance in these areas.

This publication helps to meet these demands and needs. It will be helpful to the neophyte initiating or becoming involved in a program. It will be valuable to the veteran enriching or expanding an ongoing program. Regardless of an individual's background, experience, training, or field of specialization, there is much of value in these pages for him or her. Contents help teachers and leaders provide programs and activities based on the individuality of each participant as he or she strives for maximum degrees of independence.

Recognition of this type of individuality leads to programs, activities, and approaches based on *participant* abilities, interests, and needs. Ultimately, we are helping each to succeed, progress, and achieve so that he or she can stand erect with head high and say—

> Give me pride;
> Give me substance;
> Give me a life of my own
> And I'll stop feeding off yours.
> —Julian Stein

On Being Different

Watching without sight,
Running without legs,
Conversing without voice,
Loving without prejudice,
Ofttimes it is belief that makes it happen . . .
    What's the difference in being different?
Acts which are naive, those deemed grand,
Small, tall, some with, some without,
Some who can, some who can't . . .
    What's the difference in being different?
Thinking, feeling, acting, sharing,
moving, gaming, loving, romping,
You and I, not the same but
yet the same because we are by fate just people . . .
    What's the difference in being different?
Oh for the chance to share my dreams,
to hold hands, to join in happiness,
to play your games, to taste the differences in life,
and not be scorned and turned away . . .
    What's the difference in being different?

—Dave Compton
(July 1975). *Leisurability, 2,* 27.

Preface

This third edition has been revised extensively to encompass the many kinds of knowledge, skill, understanding, and appreciation implicit in the 1980 statement by the American Alliance for Health, Physical Education, Recreation, and Dance (AAHPERD) about competencies needed by regular physical educators and specialists in adapted/developmental physical education. This book reflects the changes in public school programming in response to Public Law 94–142, which requires that all handicapped children and youth ages 3 to 21 receive physical education instruction in the least restrictive environment. For most of these children, the least restrictive placement (according to PL 94–142) is regular, or mainstream, physical education.

The emphasis in this new edition is, therefore, on coping with the increasing individual differences that are confronting all physical educators. Adapted physical education is conceptualized as good instruction in the mainstream as well as separate settings. It implies adapting instruction to the individual needs of students as well as teaching them to adapt and to strive for their own self-actualization. Particular attention is given to early childhood, since this is a new area of endeavor for most physical educators.

The author is a registered therapeutic recreation specialist as well as an adapted physical educator with postdoctoral work in special education. These three disciplines are the main contributors to the multidisciplinary approach. Having taught kinesiology to occupational therapy majors for many years, she is sensitive, also, to the common knowledge base shared by physical educators and therapists in the psychomotor domain. Professionals in all disciplines concerned with the motoric and leisure functioning of children and youth will find this textbook helpful.

Adapted physical education is defined as a comprehensive service delivery system designed to identify and ameliorate problems within the psychomotor domain. Services include assessment, individualized educational programming (IEP), developmental and/or prescriptive teaching, counseling, coordination of related resources/services, and advocacy so as to provide optimal physical education experiences for all children and youth. This textbook prepares undergraduate and graduate students to deliver these services. Conceiving of the field broadly as providing a service delivery system rather than classroom teaching exclusively is consistent with contemporary approaches taken by the other helping professions.

This third edition is responsive to the guidelines for personnel preparation established by the Office of Special Education (OSE, formerly Bureau of Education for the Handicapped, BEH), which funds exemplary training programs in special education, adapted physical education, therapeutic recreation, and related areas. This revision specifically addresses the personnel roles for which undergraduate and graduate students can prepare, the tasks/services they are expected to perform in each role, and the competencies necessary to function as teachers and professional leaders (see Appendix I). These are the target areas on which grant writers focus in describing the excellence of their university training programs.

Approaches to Teaching Adapted Physical Education

Since the early 1970s, three approaches to the teaching of adapted physical education courses have been recognized: (a) categorical, (b) generic/competency, and (c) combined. The oldest of the three, the categorical, followed the medical model in that emphasis was upon categories of handicapping conditions, their nature and needs, and methods of teaching. As the educational model evolved, in contrast to the medical model, emphasis changed from survey of handicapping conditions to awareness of individual differences and competencies needed as generalists and specialists in working with handicapped and/or clumsy students. The generic approach thus stressed such tasks/services as assessment, individualized educational planning, developmental/prescriptive teaching, counseling, and advocacy. Today, most university teachers appear to be using the combined approach, selecting from the categorical and the generic the content that best meets the specific needs of their students.

Organization

This text is organized in three parts, each containing several chapters. This organization permits professors to use any of the three instructional approaches in developing their course outlines: (a) categorical, (b) generic/competency, or (c) combined.

Part 1: A Multidisciplinary Approach

- Emphasizes the generic approach in presenting the historical, legal, humanistic, and developmental foundations of adapted physical education theory
- Draws content from the disciplines of physical education, special education, recreation, and such helping professions as psychology/counseling, physical therapy, and occupational therapy.
- Emphasizes application of principles of biomechanics, exercise physiology, and motor development and learning
- Introduces concepts of sports classification, wheelchair sports, and use of assistive devices as recommended by sports organizations for disabled athletes

Part 2: Assessment and Programming

- Emphasizes the generic approach in applying the achievement-based curriculum (ABC) model and the diagnostic-prescriptive process to meeting the needs of all students
- Stresses assessment, offers descriptions of instruments most often used in adapted physical education, and develops competence in working with reflexes and early childhood movement patterns
- Offers methods and materials in all areas of physical education, including dance, and emphasizes behavior management and humanistic approaches in relation to assessment and the IEP process

Part 3: Adapted Physical Education for Special Populations

- Emphasizes the categorical approach in offering a comprehensive chapter on each of the handicapping conditions (except speech impaired) recognized in PL 94–142
- Provides up-to-date bibliographies to guide students undertaking research on specific handicapping conditions
- Describes fully the activities and competitive events recommended by such sports organizations as National Association of Sports for Cerebral Palsy, Special Olympics, and National Wheelchair Athletic Association

New Chapters in the Third Edition

Many chapters in this book have been completely or partially rewritten to update and/or reorganize content. The overall format has been changed to American Psychological Association (APA) style, which is used in most theses and dissertations and in the *Adapted Physical Activity Quarterly,* the new journal that serves adapted physical education specialists.

New chapters, offering content not in the second edition, include

Chapter 3   The Legal Bases of Adapted Physical Education
Chapter 8   Sports Classifications, Wheelchairs, and Assistive Devices
Chapter 9   Service Delivery and Individualized Educational Programming

New Emphasis on Sports for Individuals with Disabilities

Whereas some authors are undertaking separate books on sports for disabled athletes, this text treats sports and athletics as an integral part of adapted physical education. Over 150 new pages of text on sport for the disabled have been included in this third edition as well as outstanding photographs of disabled athletes in competition.

Pedagogical Devices

This text offers numerous pedagogical devices designed to help students blend theory with practice. Among these are

- *Chapter objectives to guide study*
  Objectives at the beginning of each chapter may form the basis for written assignments or may be used as essay questions on an examination. Or an objective may be assigned to a student who prepares an oral report for class, makes a tape recording or videotape, or develops a slide presentation.

- *Learning activities at the end of each chapter*
  These activities are designed to ensure that practicum experiences supplement classroom theory. Use of these activities works especially well in contract teaching.

- *Subject Index that can be used as a dictionary for looking up spelling of words*
  The subject index can also be used as a testing device. A card for every word in the index is made and color coded (if desired) by chapter. Students randomly draw cards from the stack for a particular chapter and talk or write for 60 seconds on the subject drawn. The subject index can also be used in studying for the final exam; students should be able to spell and discuss every word in the index.

- *Name Index for becoming familiar with authorities in adapted physical education and related disciplines*
  This index can be used the same way as the subject index. Emphasis on learning names (i.e., primary sources) is probably more appropriate for graduate than undergraduate students.

- *Glossary of abbreviations*
  Appendix H allows the reader to quickly look up the meaning of initials and acronyms. This glossary can be used in both studying and testing.

- *Numerous photographs and line drawings*
  Approximately 230 photographs and 170 line drawings enrich the text. Test questions should be drawn from figure captions since these descriptions provide double emphasis of facts.

- *APA format throughout the text*
  Adherence to APA writing style provides a model for students who wish to acquire research and publication skills.

- *Appendixes on prevalence and incidence statistics and medications*
  This material is not available in any other adapted physical education text. Statistics are helpful in preparing term papers and in documenting the need for adapted physical education service delivery. The reference pages on medications are valuable in understanding individual needs of students and working in a multidisciplinary setting.

- *Appendix on history of adapted physical education and sports for disabled athletes*
  Beginning in 1817 with the establishment of the first residential schools in the United States, this chronology of over 100 events includes the initiation of services, enactment of legislation, and formation of organizations.

- *Appendixes on sources of information*
  Appendixes C, D, E, and F acquaint students with the ERIC and MEDLARS computer systems and with over 100 addresses to write for additional information.

- *Bibliography at the end of each chapter to stimulate additional reading*
  Each bibliography includes some research as well as primary and secondary sources of information. Students should be encouraged to demonstrate weekly reading from the bibliography and references section in class discussion and written assignments. Points can be given for number of articles read and quality of reporting on their content.

- *References to reinforce understanding of primary sources*

Acknowledgments

To the many individuals and agencies who shared in this adventure, a heartfelt thank you. I am especially grateful to *Julian Stein,* who served as major reviewer and advisor for the first edition; to *Bill Hillman* and the other members of the National Consortium on Physical Education and Recreation for the Handicapped (NCPERH) who have expressed faith in my ideas and leadership; to *Janet Wessel* of I Can and *Thomas Vodola* of Project Active, whose approaches I integrate and apply in my own way; and to *G. Lawrence Rarick,* whose rare combination of research abilities and humanistic beliefs serves as a model for us all.

To My Students

Most important, I thank my students at the Texas Woman's University, who keep me involved in research and practicum experiences, and the parents who trust us with their children. Each edition brings new students as well as memories of past ones who have shared and grown with me and significantly affected the contents of this book. I wish I could mention all their names, but a few will have to do: Joanne Rowe, J. Randy Routon, Dianne Hurley, Ken Duke, Wanda Rainbolt, Ellen Lubin Curtis-Pierce, Jo Ellen Cowden, Garth Tymeson, Jim Rimmer, Rebecca Reber, Tom Montelione, Jim Mastro, Nancy Megginson, and Rosie Copeland.

To Artists

For her photography and assistance with the many aspects of production, I thank *Rae Allen.* I am indebted also to *Mary Jane Cardenas* and *C. David Mathis,* who provided illustrations for the first edition, to *Molly Pollasch,* who drew the new illustrations for the second edition, and to *Dr. Diann Laing,* who drew the new illustrations for the third edition.

To Special Professionals

For their special assistance in obtaining photographs, I wish to recognize *Dr. Lane Goodwin,* University of Wisconsin at La Crosse; *Dr. George Jurcisin,* of Chillicothe, OH; *Carol Fritze,* director of Special Care School in Dallas; *Richard Ness and Joannie Hill,* Denton State School; and *Nancy Crase,* editor of *Sports 'n Spokes.* Grateful acknowledgment is given also to photographers *Barron Ludlum,* Denton Record Chronicle; *Paul Emert,* Denton State School; and *Jim Estes.* Acknowledgment of persons who contributed specific photographs and of books from which copyrighted figures were taken appear in the Credits section.

Special recognition is extended to *Wynelle Delaney*, DTR, who co-authored Chapter 15, Dance Therapy and Adapted Dance; *Jeff Jones, Carol Mushett*, and *Grant Peacock*, who shared their expertise on cerebral palsy sports, to *Barbara Ross* and *Marsha Ramey*, who assisted with the chapter on mental retardation; to *Charles Buell, Rosie Copeland*, and *James Mastro*, who helped extend my understandings of the blind; to *Ellen Lubin* and *Peter Wisher*, who taught me about the deaf; to *Stan Labanowich*, who convinced me of the value of wheelchair sports, and to *Don Drewry*, who showed me that a double leg amputee can do everything.

To My Role Models

Acknowledgments can be complete only if they extend backward into time to those persons who sparked the initial enthusiasm in teaching and writing: to *Dr. Harry A. Scott* of Teachers College, Columbia University, who spoke of competency-based teaching in the early 1950s; to *Dr. Josephine Rathbone*, also of Teachers College, who instilled in me a deep concern for the right of all persons to efficient and beautiful bodies; and to *Dean Anne Schley Duggan*, Texas Woman's University, who taught me to hear the different drummer and to keep step to the music—however measured or far away.

—Claudine Sherrill

Adapted Physical Education and Recreation

What an individual *can* be, he *must* be. He must be true to his
own nature. This need we may call self-actualization.—Abraham
Maslow

Part 1 A Multidisciplinary Approach

1 Quality Physical Education for All Students

Figure 1.1 Mainstream physical education includes students with a wide range of individual differences. Good teaching implies *adapting* methods and materials to individual needs so that success is built in and self-concept is enhanced.

Chapter Objectives

After you have studied this chapter, you should be able to

1. State the PL 94–142 definition of physical education and discuss contributions of a good program to the cognitive, affective, and psychomotor domains.

2. Identify poor teaching practices and problems that must be eliminated in order for physical education to meet the needs of *all* students.

3. Define *adapted physical education* as (a) an attitude, (b) a service delivery system, and (c) a body of knowledge and discuss the relationship of each to good teaching.

4. Discuss the multidisciplinary bases of adapted physical education in terms of developmental theory and six other areas of knowledge.

5. Differentiate between the terms *adapted* and *adaptive*.

6. State the purpose of adapted physical education and identify goals within each educational domain: (a) affective, (b) psychomotor, and (c) cognitive.

7. Rate your competence in the six tasks that teachers must perform in the implementation of adapted physical education goals and develop a personal learning plan to increase task mastery.

8. Identify and discuss nine major differences between adapted and regular physical education.

9. Relate the content of one or more entries in the bibliography to the content of the chapter.

In physical education every child fails at one time or another—by coming in last on the relay team, by missing the basket or the field goal that would have tied the game, by choking and struggling in the swimming pool. How often must a child fail in order to be labeled clumsy, awkward, uncoordinated, handicapped? How long does a label, once internalized, endure? What effect does it have on the child's growth and development? Most especially, how does failure affect body image and self-concept? Many individuals believe that the improved self-concept that results from a carefully planned progression of successful movement activities is the greatest contribution that physical education can offer the educational process.

Good teaching implies *adapting* the curriculum to individual needs so as to minimize failure and preserve ego strength. In a sense, *all good physical education is adapted physical education.* Regular physical education, sometimes referred to as *mainstream physical education,* includes children with a wide range of individual differences. Some of the children in the mainstream are considered *normal* while others are classified as needing *special education* and identified as having a particular handicapping condition such as mental retardation, orthopedic impairment, or emotional disturbance. Many handicapped children are excellent athletes and can participate successfully in regular physical education. An individual in leg braces may be able, without adaptations, to engage successfully in swimming, gymnastics, or archery. A pupil with a congenital amputation of the arm may be a star soccer player; some have excelled in baseball, basketball, and football! On the other hand, many normal children have problems that require individual attention if physical education is to be a pleasant and self-actualizing experience. Perceptual-motor deficits, low fitness, awkwardness, obesity, asthma, and poor eyesight are but a few of the problems that normal, as well as handicapped, students may exhibit daily.

The integration of handicapped children into as many *mainstream* activities of the school as possible is a current trend. Physical education, art, and music are often the areas of the curriculum in which such integration occurs first. The success of integration depends in large part upon the quality of the regular physical education program and the extent to which it meets individual differences. A sound understanding of regular physical education contributes to the innovation of effective, comprehensive curricular models for handicapped, ill, and disabled individuals.

What Is Physical Education?

Physical education is an *academic subject* similar to reading, arithmetic, and social studies. It is *instructional* and should offer a planned sequence of *new* material each day. Participation should be *required,* as it is in other subjects, or make-ups should be scheduled. The teacher is responsible for lesson plans that include clear statements of behavioral objectives, learning activities, motivational techniques, and evaluation procedures. Physical education is not play, nor is it recess or athletics.

Many different definitions of physical education can be found in textbooks and school curriculum guides, depending upon the philosophy of the writer. Definitions also appear in state law and state education agency (SEA) policies and guidelines.

A definition of physical education appeared for the first time in the federal law PL 94–142, the Education for All Handicapped Children Act. Since legal definitions of terms take precedence over other kinds, the PL 94–142 definition is accepted for use in this textbook. It defines *physical education* as follows:

(i) The term means the development of:
   (A) Physical and motor fitness:
   (B) Fundamental motor skills and patterns; and
   (C) Skills in aquatics, dance, and individual and group games and sports (including intramural and lifetime sports).
(ii) The term includes special physical education, adapted physical education, movement education, and motor development. (20 U.S.C. 1401 [16]) (*Federal Register,* August 23, 1977, p. 42480)

Physical education instruction contributes to development in all three of the commonly recognized domains of behavior: *cognitive* (intellectual skills); *affective* (feelings, opinions, attitudes, beliefs, values, interests, desires); and *psychomotor* (motor and fitness performance). Schema for these domains are widely known and explained in detail in the three well-known taxonomies of educational objectives (Bloom, Krathwohl, and Harrow (see the bibliography at the end of this chapter). Figure 1.2 presents the broad spectrum of behaviors for which the physical educator is responsible.

While the psychomotor domain has traditionally been the focus of physical education instruction, it should be noted that psychomotor behaviors occur within an integrated framework of cognitive-affective-psychomotor interrelationships. *Psychomotor* refers to all *the integrated cognitive-affective-psychomotor behaviors related to the human body and its movement.*

Purpose of Physical Education

The major purpose of physical education instruction is to change psychomotor behaviors, thereby facilitating self-actualization, particularly as it relates to understanding and appreciation of the body (and the self) in motion and at rest. Physical education is not limited to vigorous activities but includes instruction in relaxation, opportunities for creative expression, practice in

Figure 1.2 Behaviors in all three educational domains contribute to physical education knowledge, skills, attitudes, and habits.

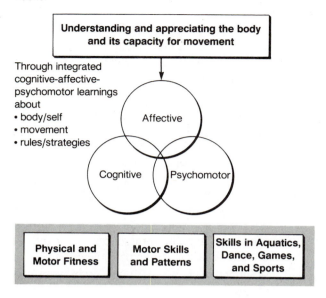

social interaction, and guidance in finding and developing one's leisure self. The outcome of such instruction should be a person who feels good about self, has confidence in movement abilities, and is self-actualizing in the psychomotor domain. What kind of physical education program contributes to these outcomes?

A Model Physical Education Program

Children are taught physical education in classes not larger than 25–30 pupils (the same size as deemed appropriate for other school-based learning activities). Individual needs and interests are identified, and instruction is adapted accordingly. Even a homogeneous class of pupils may be subdivided into ability groupings on the basis of fitness or motor skill. Their teacher views teaching, guidance, and counseling as inseparable processes, and each child is helped to develop interest and skill in activities in which he or she can experience success. Dance and such individual sports as bowling, tennis, and golf are introduced early in the elementary grades.

Warm-up exercises are individualized. Each child, for instance, aspires to a different number of bent-knee sit-ups, depending upon his or her abdominal strength. Children with low strength execute their sit-ups with hands on their thighs, while the more athletically inclined undertake the traditional sit-up with hands clasped behind the neck. In learning racket games, the awkward children use shorter rackets while the better coordinated begin with rackets of standard length.

Children are not expected to conform to the official rules of such games as volleyball and softball. The official rules were never meant for children or for uncoordinated adults. In classes based upon the principle of success, all pupils are not required to stand behind the baseline when they serve a volleyball. All stand at a point on the court where they know they can get the ball over. The well-coordinated children accept the official rule of hitting the ball one time while the less athletic may volley it multiple times. In softball, an inning is played by time rather than by three outs. The pressures inherent in striking out are thereby deemphasized so that equal turns at bat and optimal skill development are possible. The well-skilled athlete can learn and practice official rules in after-school athletic programs or in league play. The instructional period is a time when games are modified in accordance with individual differences. Each child is accepted for what he or she is—awkward, uncoordinated, obese, skinny, or gifted. There must be no doubt in the child's mind which is more important to the teacher—the game or the child. When teaching is based upon the concept of individual differences, children seldom fail. These are the fortunate children!

Poor Teaching Practices

Many physical education settings, however, are antithetical to learning. Such practices as choosing up sides, playing elimination games, and expecting all children to engage in the same activities contribute to failure. Consider the following incidents that occur frequently in classes comprised of normal children.

"What shall we play today?" asks the teacher. "Kickball" is the unanimous choice of the third grade class. Wishing to be democratic and to encourage the development of leadership as well as the ability to follow, Mr. A poses the expected question: "Who wants to be leader?" Nearly everyone's arm rises, and some children chime "I," "I," "I."
    "Billy, you be the leader for team one. Jerry, you can be the leader for team two. Now let's choose up sides quickly." One by one the children are chosen—first Billy's and Jerry's best friends, then their friend's best friends. The skilled children are always among the first to be chosen, and there is much laughter and enthusiasm. Clearly the needs of the majority of the class are being met.
    Now only Jimmy and Darol are left. Skinny or obese, it doesn't really matter—they are different from the others, a little less coordinated, a little slower maturing. Does anyone remember that they were the last boys to be chosen yesterday and the day before that? Mr. A was an outstanding athlete in college and a varsity player on several teams. Never in his life has he been chosen last. How could he possibly understand how it feels?
    Jimmy and Darol stand there, waiting, hoping, trying to smile and act as though they don't care, wanting to cry, just wishing it were over. Everyone staring—or do they even notice? "Oh, well," shrugs Jimmy, "this way I won't have to come up to bat."

Circle dodgeball—the children's favorite. Dodge, twist, jump! At all costs, avoid the ball. Try harder than last time. Won't help. The other kids always try to hit me first. They know I'm easy to put out. And so I join the circle—eliminated again.

Jump rope—got to run in without the rope touching me. Got to concentrate. Got it. 1–2–3–4, I can jump until I miss. Leah and Amy and all my friends make it to 100. 6–7–8 Ooops, miss. And so I go to the end of the file again to wait my turn. 97–98–99–100 . . . and on and on—I'm glad my friends are so good—they've tried to help me—but PE is just a time when I wait a lot for a turn that never lasts very long.

D-O-N-K-E-Y. Another elimination game. Part of the tradition of sports. Each time the kid in front of me makes a basket and I don't, I get a letter on me. I'm not very good. Usually, I get eliminated first. If no one's watching, I can sneak around the fence and have a smoke.

Ann has made an A on every *written* test in physical education she's ever taken. When she hits a ball in tennis class and it fails, as usual, to go where she intended, she knows before the teacher ever tells her that her elbow was bent, the racket face was closed, or that she swung too soon. In fact, Ann knows a lot about tennis—on the verbal level. It's just that her body won't do what her minds says—it never has.

This year, Peter's parents sent a note from their physician to have their son excused from physical education. They are sensitive persons, concerned about their action, worried about the values he'll never derive from guided motor activities. But every day for 6 years, Peter's physical education has started the same way—two laps around the football field. Peter is 5 feet tall, 160 pounds of rounded, squatty body, undeniably obese. He can't run, and each day he dies a little when subjected to the ridicule of his classmates. In the beginning his learning disability was his obesity. Now, more and more, it is his attitude.

Mike tries—he really does—every muscle in his body reveals effort—he's tense, anxious, eager to please. In the agility race he hits his head on the beam he is trying to duck under, trips over the rope he must jump, twists his neck as he tries the required forward roll, and then gamely runs toward the finishing line. The other teams finished seconds ago. The cheering is over. It's quiet. The team tolerates him, hoping they won't have him next time. What is his learning disability—space perception, poor coordination, just plain awkwardness?
    And what does the physical educator say? "Good! All the teams ready? Let's do that relay again! Mike, you exchange places with John." John was on the winning team, and it is only fair to Mike's team to give them a fair chance to win. Does the teacher hear the barely audible slurs? The "Ugh, do we have to have him?" as Mike reluctantly joins the new group.
    The teams are evened up now! Ready—set—go! Kids love relays. They are an integral part of physical education, and everyone must participate—abide by the rules—run the same distance.

These anecdotes describe normal children. They were abstracted from statements of university students asked to recall the physical education experiences from childhood that most influenced their adult attitudes.

Figure 1.3 Awkward children often achieve more success in foot-eye coordination tasks than in hand-eye coordinations.

These adults mostly believed that their physical education had not been adapted to individual needs. They were unaware that many methods exist for ameliorating awkwardness (see Figure 1.3).

Problems To Be Resolved

Let us analyze some of the problems that confront us today and make failure almost inevitable for some students. Some administrators consider physical education of less importance than other academic subjects. The hierarchy of values inherited from the Greeks that some human activities by their nature are intellectually and spiritually more valuable than others still persists. Vestiges of puritan thought linger to make education for play seem less significant than training for work.

Evaluative practices are good indicators of the hierarchy of values that dominate a school system. Should letter grades be given in physical education? Or should we use pass or fail? If letter grades are awarded, should these be figured in the overall grade average? Should a low grade in physical education keep a child off the honor roll? Should failure to complete the four required semesters of physical education in college prevent the senior from graduating?

Conscious or unconscious subscription to a hierarchy of values that recognizes some subjects as intrinsically more valuable than others dictates administrative practices unfavorable to physical education. Some of these practices follow:

1. Scheduling a child into *academic* subjects first and then assigning him or her to physical education in whatever period remains free. It is not uncommon in some schools for teachers to have children from several grade levels at one time on the playground. The less homogeneous the group, the more difficult it is, of course, to adapt activities to individual needs.

2. Allowing physical education classes to have a greater number of students than other classes. The size of a class often determines whether a physical educator teaches children or games!

3. Punishing children by requiring them to stay in the classroom during physical education. Whoever heard of punishing a student by withholding the privilege of participating in a reading or arithmetic activity?

4. Using the physical education class period to set up chairs in the auditorium, clean up the lawn, and perform other tasks unrelated to instructional objectives, or excusing a child so that he or she can make up a test in an academic subject.

5. Providing inadequate facilities and equipment. A community reveals its commitment to good instruction through the amount of space allocated to playfields and indoor instructional areas, the budgetary appropriations, and the sports equipment made available.

Children sometimes fail physical education because of established traditions, customs, and practices that are no longer sound. The lag between what is taught in teacher preparation institutions and the implementation of new ideas in public schools is unjustifiably long. Few institutions in our society are more conservative than schools. Stereotyped notions of physical education impede good teaching. For instance, many schools still cling to the concept of recess as a time of fun and games that has as its main purpose *letting off steam*. Physical educators, ill-prepared to teach dance, aquatics, and individual sports, perpetuate this myth by offering only low-organized games, team sports, and warm-up exercises.

The practice of requiring all physical educators to administer standardized fitness or skill tests also leads to failure. No student should be subjected to a test when both the student and the teacher can predict sub-average performance beforehand. The fetish to have scores recorded for each child, even when statistical treatment of such data strengthens the rationale for additional staff and increased budget, is not justifiable in terms of the influence of failure on self-esteem. Nor is the administration of a battery of diagnostic tests desirable when the child fails more often than succeeds. Testing, like other aspects of physical education, must be individualized!

The domination of public school physical education by team sports competition is another reason for failure. Masculinity is often equated with successful sports participation, and few little boys in our culture admit to not liking team sports. Most coaches are superb teachers. What other faculty members must demonstrate the results of their teaching each Friday night before hundreds of spectators? The pressure to coach is not being criticized here, but rather the lack of concern for—or perhaps the feeling of futility with respect to—the many clumsy, uncoordinated children who could be given alternative physical activities in which they might succeed. Why must all children be subjected to football, basketball, and volleyball, and so few be introduced to aquatics, dance, camping, and the individual sports? The following poem speaks eloquently for the recognition of individual differences and the provision of well-rounded programs of physical education.

I Knew This Kid

I knew this skinny little kid
Who never wanted to play tackle football at all
But thought he'd better if he wanted
His daddy to love him and to prove his courage
And things like that.
I remember him holding his breath
And closing his eyes
And throwing a block into a guy twice his size.
Proving he was brave enough to be loved, and crying
    softly
Because his tailbone hurt
And his shoes were so big they made him stumble.
I knew this skinny little kid
With sky-blue eyes and soft brown hair
Who liked cattails and pussy willows,
Sumac huts and sassafras,
Who liked chestnuts, and pine cones and oily walnuts.
Lurking foxes and rabbits munching lilies,
Secret caves and moss around the roots of oaks,
Beavers and muskrats and gawking herons,
And I wonder what he would have been
If someone had loved him for
Just following the fawns and building waterfalls,
And watching the white rats have babies.
I wonder what he would have been
If he hadn't played tackle football at all.
—James Kavanaugh

Children may fail because of the expectations of adults. John Holt says in one of his many books criticizing American education,

Children fail because they are afraid, bored, and confused. They are afraid, above all else, of failing, of disappointing or displeasing the many anxious adults around them. . . . Even in the kindest and gentlest of schools, children are afraid, many of them a great deal of the time, some of them almost all the time. This is a hard fact of life to deal with. What can we do about it? (Holt, 1964, pp. xiii, 39)

What practices commonly employed in physical education provoke fear? Teacher-imposed objectives guarantee failure for some children while ensuring success for others. Whenever instruction is so structured that all children must attempt the same motor task on the same day and progress at a uniform rate of speed, individual differences are disregarded. The common practice of demonstrating a new skill and then observing each student take a turn creates excessive tension in youngsters who fear ridicule from their peers and criticism from their teacher.

Coping with Failure

So many pupils in regular physical education classes exhibit clumsiness that physical education instruction often seems failure-oriented. How can we prevent failure?

Glasser (1969) believes that there are only two kinds of failure: failure to love and failure to achieve self-worth. These two abilities are so closely related that it is artificial to separate them. To experience success, the child must feel that *someone* cares about his or her performance. In the school context, love may be thought of as social responsibility—caring for others, wishing them success, helping them achieve. Physical education, perhaps more than any area of the curriculum, offers opportunities for experiencing social responsibility—i.e., the capacity for love.

No child who has ever run a relay can doubt that teammates care. The fielder running to catch a fly ball knows that the other players care. Even in the simple dodging and chasing games of early childhood there are ample opportunities for recognition, particularly when a sensitive teacher ensures that everyone has a chance to be *it*. Positive feelings achieved through play are believed to carry over into the classroom setting. Success breeds success. As long as the learning environment is structured so that each student receives some praise and

individual attention, physical education seems conducive to teaching social responsibility and developing self-esteem. The greater the child's feeling of worth, the better he or she can tolerate some of the rejection that may occur at later developmental stages—when seeking new friends, running for office, trying out for the team, and interviewing for jobs.

It is imperative that educators structure the initial years of learning so that the child experiences more successes than failures. Glasser writes in this regard,

A child who has functioned satisfactorily for five years is confident that he will continue to do so . . . this confidence may wane but will still remain effective for about five more years, regardless of how inadequate his school experience is. If, however, the child experiences failure in school during these five years (from ages five to ten), by the age of ten his confidence will be shattered, his motivation will be destroyed, and he will have begun to identify with failure. He will abandon the pathways of love and self-worth and grope blindly toward what seems to him to be the only paths left open, those of delinquency and withdrawal. Although success in school is still possible, with each succeeding year it becomes more difficult and more unlikely. (Glasser, 1969, pp. 26–27)

Good teaching entails adapting the curriculum and instructional environment so that all students have an equal opportunity to participate fully in physical education and experience success (see Figure 1.4). This is the essence of adapted physical education. It may occur in the mainstream, in a separate class, in a 1:1 setting, or in any combination of educational settings. Adapted physical education services may be delivered by a specialist in adapted physical education, a mainstream physical educator with special training, or others with teaching credentials that include adapted physical education courses. Adapted physical education may receive funding from special education resources, regular education resources, or both.

What Is Adapted Physical Education?

Three definitions are needed to fully explain the believing, doing, and knowing components of adapted physical education. First, adapted physical education is an *attitude,* a way of teaching in both mainstream and segregated environments, that is reflected in the beliefs and practices of teachers who adjust learning experiences to meet individual needs and assure optimal success in physical and motor functioning. This definition may be most appropriate for school personnel already in the field, particularly physical education generalists.

Figure 1.4 Sockley is a team game that able-bodied and disabled students can play together. The objective is to sock the tetherball so that it slides down the rope and touches the opponents' flag. The ball slides on a pulley or a loop at the top of the vertical rope.

Adapted physical education is also a *comprehensive service delivery system* designed to identify and ameliorate problems within the psychomotor domain. Services include individualized educational planning, psychomotor assessment, developmental and/or prescriptive teaching, fitness and leisure counseling, coordinating related services and resources, and advocacy for high quality physical education experiences for all human beings. This definition of adapted physical education as a profession seems most appropriate for adapted physical education specialists. There is strong feeling that each of our nation's 16,000 school districts, as well as residential facilities for special populations, should employ one or more adapted physical education specialists to design and/or implement such service delivery systems.

Adapted physical education is the *body of knowledge* that focuses upon identification and remediation of problems within the psychomotor domain in individuals who need assistance in the mainstream and/or specially designed physical education services. This definition is most appropriate for describing what is taught in university courses. The definition pertains to the theory underlying adapted physical education.

Adapted Physical Education as a Discipline

A growing number of persons conceptualize adapted physical education as an academic discipline with a body of knowledge separate from that which comprises regular physical education. As a discipline, adapted physical education is the body of knowledge that focuses upon problems in motor, fitness, and leisure functioning. Adapted physical education does not categorize human beings as handicapped or nonhandicapped, as do eligibility procedures for special education placement. Instead, it analyzes individual differences within the lower ranges of performance in all persons. Additionally, adapted physical education encompasses disabled persons who are or aspire to be gifted athletes and who compete in specially designed sports events, such as wheelchair basketball and soccer, that meet their needs.

Adapted physical education theory pertains primarily to individual differences. These may be *developmental,* as is the case with most clumsy children, or *acquired,* as occurs with spinal cord and head injuries, amputations, and some sensory impairments. All adapted physical education specialists thus are *developmentalists* with strong backgrounds in human growth and development and the neurological bases for normal and abnormal motor functioning. The knowledge base of adapted physical education, however, extends beyond developmental theory and includes the following:

1. Biomechanics, exercise physiology, and motor control theory
2. Assessment, curriculum, instruction, and evaluation theory
3. Self-actualization, self-concept, and motivation theory
4. Social psychology and attitude theory
5. Human relations and communication theory
6. Law, human rights, and advocacy theory

Adapted physical education thus does not draw its knowledge exclusively from physical education. Adapted physical education, as a discipline, merges information from physical education, physical therapy, occupational therapy, counseling and guidance, leisure/recreation services, special education, and other professions as well as from the pure sciences. The beliefs, practices, and knowledge base of adapted physical education are, therefore, *multidisciplinary.*

How Does *Adapted* Differ from *Adaptive*?

Some persons confuse the adjectives *adapted* and *adaptive.* These words should not be used interchangeably. *Adapt* means to make suitable . . . to adjust, accommodate, or modify in accordance with needs. These needs may be developmental or environmental. Educators *adapt* curriculum content, instructional pedagogy, assessment and evaluation methodology, and

physical environment, but they also help students to adapt. Thus, physical education is continuously being *adapted;* it is an active, ongoing process. In contrast, *adaptive* is used to describe behaviors.

Piaget, perhaps the best known of all child psychologists, based his developmental theory upon the concept that *adaptation* is the fundamental characteristic of human life (Phillips, 1969; Piaget, 1962). According to him, there are two types of adaptive behaviors: assimilation and accommodation. Assimilation occurs when an organism incorporates sensory input (like food) into the system and both the food and the person are changed in the process (i.e., the change is interactive). Piaget defines *play* as almost entirely assimilative. Accommodation occurs when sensory input does not change but perceptual motor abilities do (i.e., they mature) and the self becomes more like the environment. Piaget states that imitation is nearly pure accommodation. Behavior is most adaptive when assimilation and accommodation are in balance, but this balance is always temporary in that growth and development consist of continuous adapting (i.e., shifting back and forth between assimilation and accommodation).

In summary, education is *adapted* but behaviors are *adaptive.* Deficits in adaptive behavior are problems of development, maturation, learning, and social adjustment that result in individuals' failure to meet standards of personal independence and social experience expected of their age group and culture. Adapt*ed* physical education thus aims to remediate deficits in adapt*ive* behavior.

Purpose and Goals of Adapted Physical Education

The major purpose of adapted physical education is the same as that of regular physical education: to change psychomotor behaviors, thereby facilitating self-actualization, particularly as it relates to understanding and appreciation of the body and its capacity for movement. These psychomotor behaviors may be primarily cognitive, affective, or psychomotor, as indicated in Table 1.1. In persons with delayed or abnormal motor development, psychomotor problems are typically interwoven with cognitive and social delays and/or deficits. Thus, *failure to play spontaneously* may be as significant a psychomotor problem as impaired sensory input or inability to perform a mature throw. The goals of adapted physical education are presented in Table 1.1. Achievement of these goals occurs through integrated cognitive-affective-psychomotor learnings (see Figure 1.5).

Table 1.1
Goals of Adapted Physical Education Classified According to Domains

Affective Domain Goals

Positive self-concept. To strengthen self-concept and body image through activity involvement; to increase understanding and appreciation of the body and its capacity for movement; to accept limitations that cannot be changed and to learn to adapt environment so as to make the most of strengths (i.e., to work toward self-actualization).

Social competency. To reduce social isolation, to learn how to develop and maintain friendships, to demonstrate good sportsmanship and self-discipline in winning and losing, and to develop other skills necessary for success in the mainstream, including appropriate social behaviors (i.e., how to interact with others—sharing, taking turns, following, and leading).

Fun/tension release. To improve attitude toward exercise, physical activity, and sports, dance, and aquatics so that involvement represents fun, recreation, and happiness; to improve mental health through activity involvement; to learn to release tensions in a healthy, socially acceptable manner; to reduce hyperactivity and learn to relax.

Psychomotor Domain Goals

Motor skills and patterns. To learn fundamental motor skills and patterns; to master the motor skills indigenous to games, sports, dance, and aquatics participation; to improve fine and gross motor coordination for self-care, school, work, and play activities.

Physical and motor fitness. To develop the cardiovascular system, promote ideal weight, increase muscular strength, endurance, and flexibility, and improve posture.

Leisure time skills. To learn to transfer physical education learnings into habits of lifetime sports, dance, and aquatics; to become acquainted with community resources for recreation; to expand repertoire of and/or to refine skills in individual and group games and sports and dance and aquatic activities.

Cognitive Domain Goals

Play and game behaviors. To learn to play spontaneously; to progress through developmental play stages from solitary and parallel play behaviors up through appropriate cooperative and competitive game behaviors. To promote contact and interaction behaviors with toys, play apparatus, and persons; to learn basic game formations and mental operations needed for play; to master rules and strategies of simple games.

Perceptual motor function and sensory integration. To enhance visual, auditory, tactile, vestibular, and kinesthetic functioning; to reinforce academic learnings through games and perceptual-motor activities; to improve cognitive, language, and motor function through increased sensory integration.

Creative expression. To increase creativity in movement and thought. When posed a movement problem, to generate *many* responses, *different* responses, *original* responses. To learn to imagine, to embellish and add on, to risk experimentation, to devise appropriate game strategy, and to create new games, dances, and movement sequences.

Figure 1.5 Severely mentally retarded students can be taught skiing when skills are task analyzed and taught one at a time.

Services in Implementation of Goals

Adapted physical education services can be broken down into specific tasks to be performed by mainstream physical educators and/or adapted physical education specialists. These tasks and related competencies appear in Appendix I. Following is a description of the six services delivered in adapted physical education.

Individualized Educational Planning

Planning entails identifying appropriate physical education goals in accordance with school and community philosophy as well as individual needs. After available instructional time is calculated, the teacher estimates the number of objectives each student can probably achieve within the school year and then selects the specific objectives. Last, the specific adapted physical education services needed to achieve objectives are planned. For students identified by the school system as eligible for special education services, including specially designed adapted physical education, this planning is done by a multidisciplinary team and agreed upon in writing by both school personnel and parents. This written plan, called an individualized educational program (IEP), is required by federal law.

Assessment

Assessment is the combined process of testing, measuring, and evaluating. It is an integral part of the teaching-learning process and occurs continuously. Assessment is needed to determine the best physical education placement for students: mainstream, separate, or combined. Once students are assigned to classes, assessment is needed to determine the *present level of psychomotor functioning;* this serves, then, as the basis for planning. Also, evaluation procedures must be established for periodic determination of the effectiveness of the physical education program.

Developmental and/or Prescriptive Teaching

This is the process in adapted physical education whereby psychomotor behaviors are changed to promote optimal growth and development. With handicapped students, teaching is often called *intervention.* Intervention means interfering with (or coming between, modifying) some undesirable physical, emotional, and/or social behavior to bring about a specific positive change. Each teacher contact with the student directed toward changing behavior is considered an intervention.

Adapted physical education is considered *prescriptive teaching* because the long-term goals and short-term objectives in each student's IEP are agreed upon by a multidisciplinary committee, including one or both parents and (where appropriate) the handicapped student. This agreement constitutes *an educational prescription.*

Adapted physical education is also considered *developmental teaching* because the physical educator adapts the learning activities or interventions to the developmental motor, fitness, or play level of the student. This is generally achieved through *task analysis,* which is defined as the process of breaking down a motor skill (or activity) into its simplest parts. These separate parts are then taught to the student sequentially, from easy to difficult.

Counseling

Physical education adapted counseling (PEAC) is a helping process to facilitate changes in the affective and psychomotor domains. Its purpose is to help the handicapped or clumsy person feel and be more whole, more integrated, and more self-actualizing. Counseling focuses upon reducing discrepancies between ideal self and the actual self in level of motor performance and fitness, use of leisure, and acceptance of body and self (physical appearance, weight, body proportions, missing limbs or parts, or distorted or twisted parts, for example).

Coordination of Resources/Services

In order for physical education to improve quality of life, it must be carried over into daily living activities and leisure. The adapted physical educator therefore identifies community, home, and agency resources that can be utilized by handicapped persons during after-school and weekend hours and then facilitates and coordinates the use of such resources as they relate to psychomotor growth and development (see Figure 1.6).

Advocacy

Advocacy entails defending, maintaining, or promoting the rights of all human beings to high quality physical education experiences and the use of school and community resources. It includes teaching able-bodied persons about the laws that govern human rights and working for stronger legislation. Most important, advocacy involves changing society's attitudes and aspirations in regard to handicapped persons.

Figure 1.6 The adapted physical educator counsels students in understanding and accepting their uniqueness and in finding community recreation resources for further exploration of their potentials. The environment is adapted to assist a student with arthrogryposis (see chapter 22) to learn horseback riding. The adapted physical educator contacted the director of a local stable and provided inservice training for its staff to help them understand and adapt for handicapping conditions.

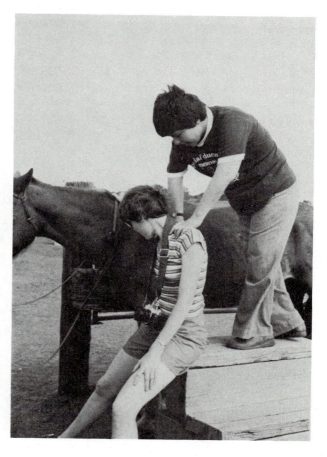

Differences between Adapted and Regular Physical Education

Adapted physical education is more like than unlike regular physical education; however, there appear to be at least nine major differences. Some of these differences are reflected mainly in attitudes of teachers in both mainstream and separate settings, whereas others characterize the school or school district service delivery systems.

Focus on Low Psychomotor Performance

Adapted physical education is mainly concerned with psychomotor performance that is below average (i.e., below the 50th percentile). The adapted physical educator directs his or her energies toward analyzing such performance, identifying the problems, and determining the contributing factors. The instructor then designs specific educational interventions or strategies to ameliorate the problems. The instructor may work with students on a one-to-one basis, in small groups, or in team- or dual-teaching of a large group.

Sports Competition for Disabled Persons

It must not be assumed that low psychomotor performance is synonymous with having a handicapping condition. Many disabled children have the potential of becoming excellent athletes, and sports organizations for disabled persons have evolved that conduct local, state, national, and even international competition. Among these are the National Association of Sports for Cerebral Palsy (NASCP), the United States Association for Blind Athletes (USABA), the National

Figure 1.7 Adapted physical educators in early childhood units must have a strong background in motor development since young handicapped children often perform motorically as infants and toddlers. This Down's syndrome 3-year-old must improve *hand grasp and release* and *visual pursuit and tracking* before ball-handling skills are introduced.

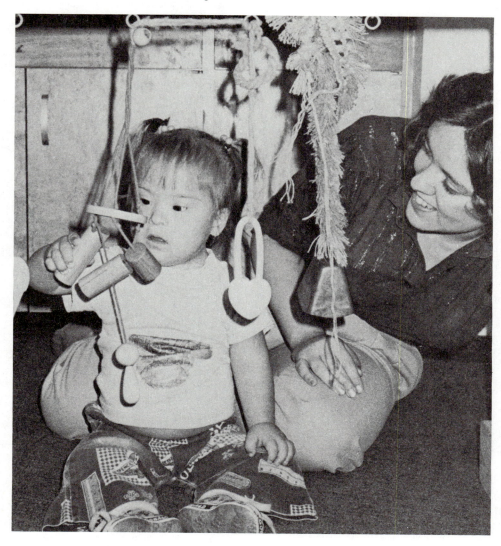

Wheelchair Athletic Association (NWAA), and Special Olympics. Adapted physical educators work with persons who need specially designed sports (e.g., wheelchair basketball and soccer) and/or special classification systems to equalize abilities and ensure fair competition.

Disabled students who aspire to be athletes are generally gifted or at least average in psychomotor functioning. Some can compete equitably with able-bodied peers, particularly in aquatics and individual sports. Adapted physical educators work with mainstream teachers to ensure that disabled students are given this right. Students with average or better motor skills whose handicapping conditions do not permit equitable competition with able-bodied classmates should participate in mainstream physical education when instruction focuses on basic skill development and noncompetitive activities. They must also be afforded opportunities in school to learn and compete in sports specially designed to utilize their particular abilities.

Inclusive of Early Childhood and Postsecondary Ages

Many adapted physical education specialists work in early childhood and infant stimulation units (Figure 1.7). Others provide physical education services for persons 18–21 in vocational education and alternative work/study settings. Still others are employed in community-based and residential programs that offer physical education services for persons over 21.

Self-Actualization as Major Purpose

Self-actualization is making actual, or realizing, all of one's potentialities. It accentuates the positive and stresses continuous striving toward health and optimal development of the self (i.e., one's humanity). Self-actualization theory is derived from the works of Abraham Maslow (1908–1970) and other humanistic psychologists. Adapted physical educators tend to prioritize instructional goals differently from regular physical educators, who stress fitness and motor skills, the unique contribution of their discipline to the total educational process. Most adapted physical education specialists believe that self-actualization, particularly as it relates to self-concept and body image, is the most important goal of movement work with handicapped and/or clumsy students. The rationale for this difference is belief that the self-actualization process is central to a person's feeling that he or she can overcome problems and/or disabilities. Because handicapping conditions (including clumsiness) disrupt the self-actualization process, the teacher must use movement experiences first as a means of learning to understand, accept, and appreciate the body and its capabilities.

Federally Mandated Legislative Base

The administrative and teaching practices in adapted physical education are derived mainly from PL 94–142 and related legislation. In contrast, compulsory physical education for normal students is governed by state law. PL 94–142 defines physical education (as it relates to the handicapped) as a part of special education. *Special education* is defined as

. . . specially designed instruction, at no cost to parents or guardians, to meet the unique needs of a handicapped child, including classroom instruction, instruction in physical education, home instruction, and instruction in hospitals and institutions. (*Federal Register,* August 23, 1977, p. 42480)

This legal definition creates a strong rationale for adapted physical education to be considered a merger of special education and physical education that may evolve into a separate profession.

Multidisciplinary Approach

The multidisciplinary approach addressed in this book particularly applies to this merger between physical education and special education. Additionally, leisure and recreation services are stressed since many physical educators have training and experience in this area. Special emphasis is given also to the use of arts (dance, music, art, and drama) in movement education.

Adapted physical education is a helping profession. It shares the values of such other helping professions as counseling and guidance, psychology, social work, health education, and the various therapies. It can be emphasized in this regard:

The more we study human potential, the more apparent it becomes that the ultimate goal of the helping professions must lie in self-actualization. . . . It demands a forward press, a reaching for the heights, and the fullest possible realization of self for not just a few, but for everybody. (Combs, Avila, & Purkey, 1971, p. 169)

In order to help students achieve self-actualization in the psychomotor domain, adapted physical educators develop knowledge and skills through the study and assimilation of many disciplines.

Emphasis on Services

The emphasis in adapted physical education is on providing a continuum of services rather than simply adapting instruction (instruction is used broadly here as a synonym for curriculum). Much of the work of the adapted physical education specialist is done outside the traditional instructional setting. For instance, time is spent in individual psychomotor assessment, multidisciplinary programming, and home/community follow-up. The six services that adapted physical educators perform are described on page 14.

Educational Accountability

The concept of accountability, when applied to the teaching process, means that a particular program, method, strategy, or intervention can be demonstrated to cause a significant positive change in one or more behaviors. While all teachers are more or less accountable to administrators and parents, the adapted physical educator is expected to maintain written records on each student that document specific progress toward pre-established objectives. To learn more about the accountability movement in education, readers could begin with the works of Lessinger and Turnbull, which are listed at the end of this chapter.

Ecological Orientation

Much of the success of handicapped students in the mainstream depends upon the teacher's skill in removing architectural, attitudinal, and aspirational barriers i.e., facilitating the favorable interrelationships that contribute to social acceptance and good self-concept and, subsequently, to effective learning. Adapted physical education is, therefore, concerned with *ecology* (the science of relationships between organisms and their environments). Adapted physical educators work to change both the human and physical environment to ensure rights as well as opportunities for disabled persons.

The ecological process stresses the mutuality of relationships between handicapped students and their total environment, physical and social, including family, neighbors, and significant others. Not only do adapted physical education specialists adapt the environment, but they also teach coping skills. Operationally defined, *adaptation* is the mode by which persons cope with the environment. Handicapped as well as normal students must learn to adapt to both their physical and social environments. To learn more about ecological teaching approaches, readers may wish to refer to the writings by Barker, Hallahan and Kauffman, Hobbs, Smith, and Weinberg and Wood listed in the bibliography at the end of this chapter.

Learning Activities

1. Write an autobiography or make a tape recording assessing your experiences with persons who are ill, disabled, or handicapped. How do you feel about working with them? Why?

2. Select some handicapping conditions that you know very little about. Find one or more persons with these conditions and volunteer to work with them in physical education activities for a set number of sessions. Keep a journal of your experiences, including changes in how you feel, think, and teach.

3. Interview several parents of normal children (and handicapped children, if available) concerning their perceptions of physical education and anecdotes they can offer illustrating good and bad physical education practices.

4. Interview nonhandicapped (and handicapped, if available) students of various ages concerning their perceptions of physical education and what they like most and least about it. Ask their opinions about how physical education can be improved. On the basis of your interviews, write a *position statement* about the state of physical education in your community.

5. Visit several special education settings—with your class, in small groups, or alone—and observe the behavior of students with various handicapping conditions. Find out what kind of physical education they have and, if possible, observe them in a physical education setting.

6. Invite a public school adapted physical education specialist to speak to your class. Ask him or her to discuss daily tasks performed and the competencies needed to perform these tasks.

References

Combs, A., Avila, D., & Purkey, W. (1971). *Helping relationships: Basic concepts for the helping professions.* Boston: Allyn & Bacon.

Federal Register, May 4, 1977, PL 93–112, the Rehabilitation Act of 1973, Section 504.

Federal Register, August 23, 1977, PL 94–142, the Education for All Handicapped Children Act.

Glasser, W. (1969). *Schools without failure.* New York: Harper & Row.

Gunn, S., & Peterson, C. (1978). *Therapeutic recreation program design.* Englewood Cliffs, NJ: Prentice-Hall.

Holt, J. (1964). *How children fail.* New York: Pittman Publishing Co.

Kavanaugh, J. (1971). *Will you be my friend?* Los Angeles: Nash Publishing Co.

Phillips, J. (1969). *The origins of intellect: Piaget's theory.* San Francisco: W. H. Freeman & Co.

Piaget, J. (1962). *Play, dreams, and imitation in childhood.* New York: W. W. Norton.

Bibliography

Adams, G., & Younger, T. (1984). Personal perspectives on counseling in adapted physical education. *Adapted Physical Activity Quarterly, 1* (3), 185–193.

Barker, R. (1968). *Ecological psychology.* Stanford, CA: Stanford University Press.

Bloom, B. (Ed.). (1956). *Taxonomy of educational goals, Handbook I: Cognitive domain.* New York: David McKay.

Carkhuff, R. (1974). *How to help yourself: The art of program development.* Amherst, MA: Human Resource Development Press.

Carkhuff, R., & Berenson, B. (1976). *Teaching as treatment.* Amherst, MA: Human Resource Development Press.

Combs, A. (1972). *Educational accountability: Beyond behavioral objectives.* Washington, DC: National Education Association.

Eason, R., Smith, T., & Caron, F. (Eds.). (1983). *Adapted physical activity: From theory to application.* Champaign, IL: Human Kinetics Publishers.

Hallahan, D., & Kauffman, J. (1978). *Exceptional children.* Englewood Cliffs, NJ: Prentice-Hall.

Harrow, A. (1972). *A taxonomy of the psychomotor domain.* New York: David McKay.

Hobbs, N. (1975). *The futures of children.* San Francisco: Jossey-Bass.

Krathwohl, D. (Ed.). (1964). *Taxonomy of educational objectives. Handbook II: Affective domain.* New York: David McKay.

Lessinger, L. (1970). *Every kid a winner: Accountability in education.* New York: Simon Schuster.

Maslow, A. (1968). *Toward a psychology of being* (2nd ed.). Princeton, NJ: Van Nostrand.

Maslow, A. (1970). *Motivation and personality* (2nd ed.). New York: Harper & Row.

Rainbolt, W. (1985). Advocacy and coordination of services. *Adapted Physical Activity Quarterly, 2* (1), 1985.

Rogers, C. (1951). *Client-centered therapy.* Cambridge, MA: Riverside Press.

Rogers, C. (1961). *On becoming a person.* Boston: Houghton Mifflin.

Sherrill, C. (1982). Adapted physical education: Its role, meaning, and future. *Exceptional Education Quarterly, 3* (1), 1–9.

Sherrill, C. (Ed.). (1986). *Adapted physical education leadership training.* Champaign, IL: Human Kinetics Publishers.

Smith, J. W. (1975). Health, physical education, recreation, and the ecological spectrum. In A. Lockhart & H. Slusher (Eds.), *Contemporary readings in physical education* (3rd ed.) (pp. 383–391). Dubuque, IA: Wm. C. Brown.

Truax, C. B., & Carkhuff, R. (1967). *Toward effective counseling and psychotherapy: Training and practice.* Chicago: Aldine.

Turnbull, H. R. (1975). Accountability: An overview of the impact of litigation on professionals. *Exceptional Children, 41,* 427–433.

Weinberg, R., & Wood, R. (Eds.). (1975). *Observation of pupils and teachers in mainstream and special education settings: Alternative strategies.* Minneapolis: Leadership Training Institute/Special Education.

2 Multidisciplinary Roots, Practices, and Resources

Figure 2.1

Chapter Objectives

After you have studied this chapter and Appendix G, you should be able to

1. Describe the evolution of adapted physical education in the United States through five different stages of growth.
2. Identify five *personnel roles* of adapted physical education specialists and discuss ways the regular educator can use specialists as resources.
3. Discuss how each of the following forces have contributed to contemporary adapted physical education: (a) research, (b) professional organizations, (c) legislation, (d) litigation, and (e) sports movement for disabled persons.
4. Name several journals that publish research related to adapted physical education and give evidence of familiarity with each.
5. Identify contemporary leaders in adapted physical education, their geographical location, and major contributions.
6. Determine whether such research and demonstration projects as ACTIVE, UNIQUE, I CAN, and PEOPEL are being implemented in school districts near you and what contributions they are making.
7. Differentiate between *legislation* and *litigation,* cite examples of each, and discuss their impact on service delivery to disabled persons.
8. Differentiate between *required* services and *related* services as defined by PL 94–142 and describe some of each.
9. Give definitions for each of the following and discuss how physical educators might interact with specialists in each: (a) recreation, (b) corrective therapy, (c) physical therapy, (d) occupational therapy, (e) dance therapy, and (f) the arts.
10. Identify and discuss trends and issues in multidisciplinary teamwork.
11. Cite and discuss textbooks and journals representative of several disciplines that serve disabled persons.
12. Identify textbooks and/or authors which emphasize the multidisciplinary approach to education of disabled students.

Professionals involved in implementation of PL 94–142 are well aware of the demands in this law for interdisciplinary interaction. From the outset of the service delivery process, the law requires that "the evaluation . . . [be] made by a multidisciplinary team" and then suggests areas for evaluation having implications for the inclusion of a myriad of professionals. The regulations further imply the interaction of groups of personnel at least yearly for the purpose of reviewing and revising each child's IEP (Seaman & Heilbuth, 1986).

The ability to work effectively in a multidisciplinary setting, such as is increasingly expected of physical educators, seems largely dependent upon self-esteem and confidence, openness and security, and good communication skills. These qualities are enhanced by an understanding of one's professional roots in sports, dance, and aquatics (see Figure 2.1), as well as a strong commitment to the discipline's present functioning and future directions. One of the most important skills in multidisciplinary teamwork is interpreting the values of physical education to handicapped pupils and defining one's role and scope in actualizing these values.

History of Adapted Physical Education

Because persons seldom keep abreast of professions other than their own, it is likely that team members may conceptualize physical education as it was in the past. To effectively communicate the present and future status of adapted physical education, it is, therefore, necessary for us to understand our past (see Appendix G). In the United States, adapted physical education seems to have evolved through five stages.

Stage 1, Medically Oriented Gymnastics and Drill

Prior to the 1900s, all physical education was medically oriented and preventive, developmental, or corrective in nature. The physical education curriculum was comprised primarily of that which we know today as gymnastics, calisthenics, body mechanics, and marching or military-like exercise drills. University physical educators were generally *physicians* who applied known principles of medicine to the various systems of exercise. The purpose of physical training (or physical culture, as our profession was called then) was to prevent illness and/or to promote the health and vigor of the mind and body.

Stage 2, Conceptualization of the Whole Child: Education Through the Physical

The gradual transition from medically oriented physical training to sports-centered physical education occurred between the 1890s and the 1930s. Factors influencing this change were (a) the introduction of sports into American culture and subsequently the physical education curriculum; (b) the application of psychological and sociological theory to education, resulting in the conceptualization of the *whole child;* (c) the trend away from medical training as appropriate teacher preparation for physical educators; and (d) the advent of compulsory physical education in the public schools. The famous "battle of the systems" ended with the American system of sports, dance, and aquatics winning over the Swedish and German systems of gymnastics that had previously dominated physical education. Pioneer educators like John Dewey and Edward Thorndike changed our preoccupation with health and physical fitness to concern for the whole child (physical, mental, social, and spiritual).

Teacher preparation programs with degrees specifically in health and physical education (as opposed to medicine) emerged, focusing on the whole child rather than on prevention of illness and/or correction of defects. State legislation making physical education mandatory in the public schools increased the number of students to be taught and brought new problems. What, for instance, should be done if a student were ill, disabled, or handicapped, or lacked the physical stamina to participate in the regular curriculum? The solution was to divide physical education into two branches, *regular physical education* and *corrective, or remedial, physical education.*

Stage 3, Corrective Physical Education

Between the 1930s and the 1950s, both regular and corrective physical education served mostly what are known today as normal students. Assignment to physical education was based upon a thorough medical examination by a physician who determined whether a student should participate in the regular or corrective program. Corrective classes were comprised primarily of limited, restricted, or modified activities related to health, posture, or fitness problems. In many schools students were excused from physical education. In others, the physical educator typically taught several sections of regular physical education and one section of corrective physical education each day. Leaders in corrective physical education continued to have strong backgrounds in medicine and/or physical therapy. Persons preparing to be physical education teachers generally completed one university course in corrective physical education.

Stage 4, Adapted Physical Education

During the 1950s and 1960s, the population served in public school corrective/adapted physical education broadened to include persons with all handicapping conditions. Instrumental in this change was the trend away from residential school placement. This resulted in increased enrollment of handicapped students (particularly the mentally retarded) in the public schools. The values that such children and youth could derive from participation in sports, dance, and aquatics adapted to their special needs were increasingly recognized.

The following definition evolved in the early 1950s:

Adapted physical education is a diversified program of developmental activities, games, sports, and rhythms suited to the interests, capacities, and limitations of students with disabilities who may not safely or successfully engage in unrestricted participation in the vigorous activities of the general physical education program. (Committee on Adapted Physical Education, 1952, p. 15)

This definition was viable throughout the next two decades since adapted physical education teaching practices paralleled the special education procedure of segregating handicapped students in separate classes and/or special schools.

Factors contributing to the changing adapted physical education we know today include (a) research; (b) establishment of a structure within AAHPERD to serve handicapped persons; (c) development of athletic programs for various handicapped groups (see Figure 2.2); and (d) legislation.

Research

Most adapted physical education research in the 1950s and 1960s was on mental retardation and aimed at justifying the provision of physical education programs for mentally retarded students. The classic study by Francis and Rarick (1959) indicated that mildly retarded children aged 7.5 to 14.5 were 2 to 4 years behind their normal peers in motor performance. Stein (1963) focused attention on the motor function and physical fitness of mentally retarded individuals by reviewing 70

Figure 2.2 The Special Olympics movement has had tremendous impact on attitudes concerning the capabilities of mentally retarded persons.

Figure 2.3 Contemporary leaders in adapted and developmental physical education and recreation: *left,* Dr. Julian Stein, Director of Programs for the Handicapped from 1966 to 1981, AAHPERD Headquarters in Reston, VA; *center,* Dr. Lawrence Rarick, renowned researcher in motor performance from the University of California at Berkeley; *right,* Dr. Frank Hayden, first director of Special Olympics.

books and articles relevant to the subject. Hayden (1964) showed that, on the average, retarded children had only 50% of the strength and 30% of the endurance of their nonretarded peers. The powerful influence of these research contributions led, subsequently, to the appointment of Stein as director of the new AAHPER Unit on Programs for the Handicapped and the appointment of Hayden as the first director of Special Olympics (see Figure 2.3).

A national survey conducted by Brace (1966) revealed that nearly one-third of the mentally retarded children in United States elementary schools received no physical education. Rarick et al. (1970) reported that 45% of the educable mentally retarded students in 21 states (sample of 335 schools) received no physical education instruction. The need for improved physical education for handicapped students was thus clearly established.

Figure 2.4 The evolution of wheelchair sports influenced the history of adapted physical education. Pictured here are the Music City (Nashville) Wheelers in competition with the Westland (Detroit) Sparks in the National Wheelchair Basketball Championships, 1980.

Establishment of AAHPERD Structure

In 1965, the Project on Recreation and Fitness for the Mentally Retarded was launched by AAHPERD with a grant from the Joseph P. Kennedy, Jr. Foundation. This project was the forerunner of the *Unit on Programs for the Handicapped,* which served our profession from 1968 to 1984. Dr. Julian Stein directed the project from 1966 to 1981, thereby exerting a strong positive influence on the development of adapted physical education through his personal advocacy as well as through voluminous AAHPERD publications. During these years, the Unit was supported largely by federal grants. When funding was no longer available, AAHPERD began to gradually phase out the program.

Early Athletic Programs and Advocacy

The early development of athletic programs for various handicapped groups contributed to the growth of adapted physical education by increasing public awareness concerning the needs, interests, and abilities of special populations. The first sports organization for disabled persons in the United States was the American Athletic Association for the Deaf (AAAD), in 1945. The National Wheelchair Basketball Association (NWBA), founded in 1949, and the subsequent organization of the National Wheelchair Athletic Association (NWAA) enabled thousands of physically disabled persons to enjoy sports (see Figure 2.4). The Special Olympics movement, initiated by the Joseph P. Kennedy, Jr. Foundation in 1968, consists of year-round training for mentally retarded athletes in several sports, highlighted by seasonal competition at local, district, state, and international levels. Of the many contributions made by this sports movement, perhaps the

Figure 2.5 *left,* Dr. Stan Labanowich, executive director of the National Wheelchair Basketball Association; *right,* Mr. William Hillman, Bureau of Education for the Handicapped (BEH; name changed to Office of Special Education, OSE, in 1980).

greatest is the creation of strong advocates whose belief in athletics for the handicapped carries over into the struggle for quality physical education programming for all children.

Legislation

The strong advocacy of parent and professional groups, coupled with research findings documenting needs, led to legislation for training professional personnel to work with handicapped students. In 1966, the Bureau of Education for the Handicapped (BEH) in the United States Office of Education was created by PL 89–750, an amendment of the Elementary and Secondary Education Act (ESEA) of 1965. The November 1976 issue of *Exceptional Children* describes the history of BEH, which in 1980 became the Office of Special Education (OSE).

In 1967, federal legislation (PL 90–170) was passed that funded training, research, and demonstration projects specifically in physical education and recreation for handicapped individuals. Within the OSE, the advocate for physical education and recreation for handicapped persons since 1968 has been William Hillman (Figure 2.5), a powerful force in graduate training in adapted physical education. Since PL 90–170 and subsequent legislation encompassing physical education for the handicapped are part of special education laws, the mid–1960s can be generalized

as the beginning of the merger of physical education and special education and the beginning of multidisciplinary physical education.

Stage 5, Multidisciplinary Adapted Physical Education

Contemporary adapted physical education was discussed in Chapter 1. This stage began in 1967, with the enactment of PL 90–170, which has funded thousands of graduate assistants in colleges and universities to encourage students to become adapted physical education specialists.

Funding teacher training continues to be a viable way to improve adapted physical education services in the public schools. Today, persons may earn master's and doctoral degrees specifically in adapted physical education. The undergraduate student who completes only one course in adapted physical education and then begins to teach should be acquainted with the *personnel roles* of adapted physical education specialists and know how to use these persons as resources.

The Specialist in the 1980s: Personnel Roles

Specialists work primarily in five roles: direct service delivery, consulting and resource room services, preservice training, in-service training, and administration. Most teachers with master's degrees in adapted physical education work full-time in public or residential schools in *direct service delivery* to severely handicapped students who cannot be placed full-time in regular physical education and in *consulting and resource room* roles in which they assist regular physical educators with students who have psychomotor problems and/or mild handicaps.

Most persons with doctoral degrees in adapted physical education teach in colleges and universities. This is called *preservice training,* meaning they teach students prior to the students' full-time service in a school setting. Almost all persons with expertise in adapted physical education are also involved in *in-service training,* which refers to workshops and concentrated learning experiences directed toward teachers who are already employed. Some adapted physical education specialists work primarily in *administrative roles,* implementing assessment and placement procedures for school districts or residential facilities, and supervising others in direct service delivery. Others direct sports organizations for disabled athletes or agency-sponsored sport and recreation programs.

Figure 2.6 Federally funded research and demonstration projects. From *left,* Dr. Janet Wessel, creator of I CAN curriculum model; Dr. Joseph Winnick, creator of Project UNIQUE; and Dr. Thomas Vodola, creator of Project ACTIVE.

The Regular Physical Educator in the 1980s

The regular physical educator teaches both able-bodied and handicapped students in the mainstream setting, adapting pedagogy, equipment, and environment as needed. Regular educators may also be assigned one or two classes of separate, adapted physical education for students with severe psychomotor problems. Occasionally, they work individually with such students. Regular physical educators are also often involved in Special Olympics, cerebral palsy sports, wheelchair sports, and other special events for disabled persons.

If the school system does not have an adapted physical education specialist, regular physical education teachers perform all of the tasks normally expected of a specialist. To fulfill these responsibilities, they may ask their principals to bring in an adapted physical education consultant for a few days or to fund their participation in workshops, conferences, or courses specifically in adapted physical education. When a school district has 30 to 40 students with severe psychomotor problems, the regular physical educators often band together and ask their administration to employ a full-time adapted physical education specialist.

Forces Contributing to Contemporary Adapted Physical Education

Forces contributing to changes from the 1960s through the 1980s include research, professional organizations, legislation, litigation, and the sports for disabled persons movement.

Research

Research during the past two decades has created a virtual knowledge explosion within adapted physical education. The bibliographies at the end of each chapter of this book list much of the best research on each topic.

Research typically falls into two areas: unpublished, which includes master's theses and doctoral dissertations, and published, which appears in professional journals. All professionals with graduate degrees are expected to engage in research that contributes to the knowledge base of their discipline.

Some research, particularly large scale assessment and curriculum models, is federally funded. These projects have tremendous impact on adapted physical education theory and practice. Their acronyms (like ACTIVE, meaning *All Children Totally Involved Exercising*) make the models easy to remember. To locate the models in the library or to request the school system to buy them, however, the physical educator must learn the researchers' names. Among the models most influential today are those described in the following paragraphs (see Figure 2.6).

Federally Funded Research and Demonstration Projects

Project ACTIVE (*All Children Totally Involved Exercising*)

Researcher
Dr. Thomas Vodola

Center
New Jersey, Township of Ocean School District

Description
Two components: (a) direct service delivery to students with psychomotor problems via a competency-based diagnostic prescriptive teaching and individualized-personalized learning approach and (b) in-service training. Includes battery of tests and seven program manuals, one for each of the following conditions: low motor ability, low physical vitality, postural abnormalities, nutritional deficiencies, breathing problems, motor disabilities or limitations, and communication disorders.

Project UNIQUE

Researchers
Dr. Joseph Winnick and Dr. Frank Short

Center
State University of New York (SUNY) at Brockport

Description
A fitness assessment project designed to determine the best tests for measuring fitness in students with sensory (blind or deaf) or orthopedic impairments. Tests include AAHPERD items and others that can be administered easily in a mainstream setting. Project UNIQUE fitness testing manual (Winnick & Short, 1985) is available.

Project I CAN (*Individualize Instruction, Create Social Leisure Competence, Associate All Learnings, Narrow the Gap between Theory and Practice*)

Researcher
Dr. Janet Wessel

Center
Michigan State University

Description
Consists of three separate programmatic systems: Preprimary Skills, Primary Skills, and Sport, Leisure, and Recreation Skills. Each system includes an observational assessment approach, illustrative goals, objectives, and activities, instructional strategies, and program evaluation materials. Emphasizes an achievement-based curriculum (ABC) model based on five teacher tasks: plan, assess, prescribe, teach, and evaluate.

Project PEOPEL (*Physical Education Opportunity for Exceptional Learners*)

Researchers
Ed Long and Larry Irmer

Center
Phoenix, AZ—Public Schools

Description
A peer teaching model that pairs trained student aides with handicapped students in small (12:12) mainstream high school classes. To qualify, potential aides must complete a one-semester training course.

These and other research studies (both funded and nonfunded) form the bases for adapted physical education practices. To keep abreast of research, persons interested in adapted physical education should read such journals as *Adapted Physical Activity Quarterly, American Corrective Therapy Journal, Research Quarterly for Exercise and Sport, Exceptional Children,* and *Therapeutic Recreation Journal.*

Professional Organizations

Professional organizations work for legislation and educational policy favorable to physical education; conduct conferences at which theory and practice are shared, thus increasing the knowledge base of a profession; and provide collegiality and ethics for their members. The American Alliance for Health, Physical Education, Recreation, and Dance (AAHPERD), specifically, the substructures of the *Therapeutics Council* in ARAPCS and the *Adapted Physical Education Academy* in NASPE; the Council for Exceptional Children (CEC) and the National Therapeutic Recreation Society (NTRS) have all contributed to the evolution of contemporary adapted physical education. In 1985, the ARAPCS and NASPE structures merged into one body under the governance of ARAPCS. This new structure is the Adapted Physical Activity Council. When paying annual AAHPERD membership dues, adapted physical educators should therefore check ARAPCS as one of their two structures. Their official publication is *Able Bodies.*

One organization exists, however, that is exclusively devoted to physical education and recreation for handicapped persons. This is the *National Consortium on Physical Education and Recreation for the Handicapped* (NCPERH), founded in 1975 after 3 years of functioning as a loosely organized national ad hoc committee. The purpose of NCPERH is to promote, stimulate, encourage, and conduct professional preparation and research in physical education and recreation for handicapped persons. As such, this organization has played a major role in shaping the future of adapted physical education, particularly as a graduate specialization and/or profession/discipline. Its membership has been active in promoting legislation and funding favorable to physical education for handicapped persons, in disseminating information about PL 94–142 and Section 504, and in generating a growing knowledge base for adapted physical education through research and demonstration. The newsletter of NCPERH is called *The Advocate*.

Membership is currently open to anyone who is or has been involved in training, demonstration, or research activity related to physical education and recreation for handicapped persons. Membership chairman is Dr. John Hall, Physical Education Department, University of Kentucky, Lexington, KY 40506.

Legislation

Physical education, as well as all school subjects, has been affected tremendously by two federal laws enacted in the 1970s. These were the Education for All Handicapped Children Act (PL 94–142) and Section 504 of the Rehabilitation Act of 1973 (PL 93–112). The rules and regulations for implementing these two laws appear in the *Federal Register,* August 23, 1977, and May 4, 1977, respectively. Whereas PL 94–142 affects school-based instruction primarily, Section 504 influences all aspects of life.

PL 94–142

PL 94–142, enacted in 1975 but not implemented until its rules were printed in the *Federal Register* in 1977, now provides the legal bases for adapted physical education in relation to handicapped children and youth, including the funding of specially designed physical education for students who meet eligibility requirements (i.e., fall within the definitions of handicapping conditions stated in the law). The tremendous impact of this law is the subject of Chapter 3.

The multidisciplinary basis of adapted physical education is established by PL 94–142, as explained in Chapter 1. The law defines specially designed physical education as part of special education; some authors call this special physical education. It should be remembered, however, that adapted physical education is much broader than service delivery to handicapped students; it includes the entire spectrum of individual differences that require adaptations in pedagogy, equipment, or environment for optimal success.

The most important mandate within PL 94–142 is the requirement that physical education services, specially designed if necessary, must be made available to every handicapped student and that these must be free, appropriate, and in the least restrictive environment. PL 94–142 separates *direct services* (i.e., required special education) from *related services* (not required unless proven needed as a *prerequisite* to benefitting from special education). By including physical education as a part of the special education definition, PL 94–142 specifies physical education as a direct and, therefore, required service. This and the process by which students are classified as handicapped and are thus made eligible for services are described fully in Chapter 3.

PL 93–112

PL 93–112, enacted in 1973 but not implemented until its rules were printed in the *Federal Register* in 1977, includes many mandates but is best known for Section 504, often called the "Nondiscrimination Clause." Section 504 states

. . . No otherwise qualified handicapped individual . . . shall, solely by reason of his handicap, be excluded from participation in, be denied the benefits of, or be subjected to discrimination under any program or activity receiving Federal financial assistance.

This means that schools which conduct interscholastic athletics and extraclass activities must provide qualified handicapped students an equal opportunity with the nonhandicapped for participation. Such opportunities must be given in the least restrictive environment. Specifically,

Section 504 states that separation or differentiation with respect to physical education and athletic activities is permissible only if qualified students are also allowed opportunities to compete for regular teams or participate in regular activities. Most handicapped students are able to participate in one or more regular physical education and athletic activities. For example, a student in a wheelchair can participate in a wrestling course. (Stein, 1978, p. 149)

Stein points out also that many practices are made illegal by Section 504, such as barring persons with artificial limbs or one eye or kidney from participating in sports competition. Likewise, athletic events in public places receiving federal funds (almost all do) must be accessible to all spectators, including those in wheelchairs. For information on wheelchair accessibility, contact your school 504 committee or write the American National Standards Institute (ANSI), the government agency responsible for setting wheelchair accessibility standards. For ANSI's address, see Appendix G, 1979 entry. Remember that all facilities do not have to be accessible as long as programs are accessible. Disabled students must have access to at least one swimming pool, gymnasium, and playing field if able-bodied (AB) students are provided opportunities for sports, dance, and aquatics programs.

Accessibility refers to communication (the ability to understand) as well as architecture; hence interpreters for deaf persons must be available as well as braille or tape-recorded signs/directions for blind persons. This type of accessibility should be kept in mind when planning workshops, tournaments, and meets. A person who signs should be placed close to the speaker; professional signers can be employed at hourly rates. The speech or communication science department of a university usually has a list of professional signers and/or can provide guidance in this regard.

The Office of Civil Rights (OCR) is responsible for administering PL 93–112. OCR does not, however, take action until a specific complaint for noncompliance is registered. Most schools, agencies, and universities prefer to handle Section 504 problems rather than have to cope with legal action brought by OCR. Therefore, institutions that receive federal funds designate one of their staff as a 504 compliance officer. This person is the point of contact for students, teachers, parents, or others regarding problems, grievances, and solutions related to an accessible and nondiscriminatory physical, learning, living, and work environment.

Institutions also establish 504 committees or councils, which generally serve as advisory bodies to the 504 compliance officer and as an advocacy bodies for individuals with handicapping conditions. Such committees often conduct handicapped awareness days and programs and architectural needs assessment studies. At least one member of the 504 committee should be from the physical education department to ensure accessibility of its programs and facilities; often physical education majors can obtain valuable experience as student members.

Litigation

In every society, some persons will not obey laws unless the courts require compliance in a lawsuit. The use of the judicial process to force compliance is called *litigation.* Persons who understand due process procedures are in a strong position to negotiate for improved educational programs. Examples of two classic lawsuits are presented here. For further discussion of litigation, consult the writings of Weintraub et al. (1976) or contact your local Association for Retarded Citizens (ARC) or Council for Exceptional Children (CEC). For litigation specifically involving the participation of handicapped students in athletics, see the book by Appenzeller (1983).

The 1954 case of *Brown* v. *Board of Education of Topeka, Kansas,* is often cited as the legal basis for mainstreaming. In this litigation the United States Supreme Court ruled that the doctrine "separate but equal" in the field of public education was unconstitutional and deprived the segregated group (blacks) of rights guaranteed by the Fourteenth Amendment.

The principle of *zero reject,* or free appropriate public education for all children (including the most severely handicapped), has its roots in the 1971 class action suit of *Pennsylvania Association for Retarded Citizens (PARC)* v. *Commonwealth of Pennsylvania.* After several court hearings, it was decided that every child in the state was guaranteed a free, public education and that families would be given notice and the right of due process before administrators made any change in their children's educational status. This case continues to serve as the basis for challenging the constitutionality of excluding severely handicapped children from public school programs.

Full implementation of PL 94–142 and Section 504 will no doubt involve litigation in the years to come. Lawsuits will be filed by parents and parent-professional organizations like ARC, but physical educators may be involved, also. In the final analysis, litigation ensures humanism in education and care of handicapped individuals.

Sports Movement for Disabled Persons

From the 1960s on, several sports organizations for disabled persons were formed. This movement has contributed to changing the nature of adapted physical education and to shifting it away from the medical model. Whereas the medical model of earlier decades emphasized the correction or amelioration of physical defects and/or perceptual-motor problems, the sports movement focused on abilities (i.e., finding or creating sports in which students could participate). Led by disabled persons, sports in the movement were conceptualized as self-actualizing, a means of improving both mental and physical health and of achieving recognition for individual talent and hard work.

No longer are handicapped persons willing to work on motor skills and physical fitness just for the sake of improving locomotion and health. Sports are an integral part of American life, and disabled persons want equal opportunity for learning and competing in sports. They, more than any other force, are helping to define the differences between therapy and education. Most have had years of exercises with various therapists; they

Figure 2.7 Alfred Dore, who weighs 98 pounds, has cerebral palsy and uses a wheelchair, but he can lift 98K (198 pounds). Strength exercises in physical education lead to sports competition.

do not want physical education to simply be more exercise. Instead, they seek opportunities to learn specific sports skills, rules, and strategies (see Figure 2.7).

European countries appear to be far ahead of the United States in providing sports for disabled persons. International competition for deaf athletes, begun in France, has been available since 1924. Shortly before the end of World War II, the Spinal Cord Injuries Centre of the Stoke Mandeville Hospital in England began introducing sports to war veterans in wheelchairs. The first international games for wheelchair users was held in 1952. This undoubtedly influenced United States war veterans in that the National Wheelchair Athletic Association (NWAA) was formed in 1956, and Americans competed in the first Olympic Games for the Disabled held in 1960 in Rome. From that date, international games (designated as Olympics for Paraplegics, or Paraolympics) were held every 4 years, about the same time as the regular Olympics and, where possible, in the same country.

Table 2.1
Chronology of Development of United States Sports Organizations for Disabled Athletes

Date	Organization
1945	American Athletic Association for the Deaf (AAAD)
1949	National Wheelchair Basketball Association (NWBA)
1956	National Wheelchair Athletic Association (NWAA)
1967	National Handicapped Sports and Recreation Association (NHSRA)
1968	Special Olympics, Inc.
1976	United States Association for Blind Athletes (USABA)
1978	National Association of Sports for Cerebral Palsy (NASCP)
1981	United States Amputee Athletic Association (USAAA)

Note: Many other organizations have also been formed, usually to govern a single sport. The magazines *Sports 'N Spokes* and *Palaestra* are excellent sources of further information.

Figure 2.8 Cerebral palsied athletes are part of the national advisory committee of the National Association of Sports for Cerebral Palsy, which meets at the United States Olympic Training Center. Pictured from left to right are Dick Hosty, Ken Wells, Wendy Shugol, and Sal Ficara.

Except for the founding of the National Handicapped Sports and Recreation Association (NHSRA), which governs winter sports, and the creation of Special Olympics, which governs sports for mentally retarded athletes, little happened in the sports movement until the 1976 Olympiad. At that time, the Paralympics concept was broadened to include blind and amputee athletes. In the 1980 Olympiad, the games (with name now changed to International Games for the Disabled [IGD]) included ambulatory cerebral palsied athletes for the first time. In 1984, the IGD included nonambulatory cerebral palsied athletes. The chronology of dates for the founding of United States sports organizations shows the impact of opportunities for international competition.

From the official rule books of the different organizations physical educators can learn the sports events in which students with specific conditions are most likely to succeed. Contemporary adapted physical education emphasizes the teaching of skills, rules, and strategies that can be generalized to present and adult leisure. Local, regional, and national competition is now available to many disabled persons from age 8 and older.

PL 95–606

When the United States Olympic Committee (USOC) was reorganized in the 1970s and plans were made for better promotion and coordination of amateur athletics, sports for disabled athletes were included in the master plan. Specifically, PL 95–606, the Amateur Sports Act of 1978, charged the USOC

to encourage and provide assistance to amateur athletic programs and competition for handicapped individuals, where feasible, the expansion of opportunities for meaningful participation by handicapped individuals in programs of athletic competition for able-bodied individuals. (Article II, 13, p. 2)

Today disabled athletes use the United States Olympic Training Center at Colorado Springs (see Figure 2.8), and sports organizations for disabled athletes are assisted by USOC. New role models are emerging from within the ranks of disabled persons. Contemporary adapted physical education exposes students to these role models and uses a variety of motivation techniques to encourage students to develop lifetime patterns of sports involvement and exercise.

Use of Related Services

Persons who teach children with psychomotor problems often can benefit by using related services. They may confer with professionals in these areas, attend workshops, take courses, or read books and journals in such related services as recreation, physical therapy, occupational therapy, corrective therapy, and the arts. PL 94–142 explains *related services* as follows:

. . . transportation and such developmental, corrective, and other supportive services as are required to assist a handicapped child to benefit from special education. . . . (*Federal Register,* August 23, 1977, p. 42479)

Physical education, as explained in Chapter 1, is a *required, direct service* as opposed to a related service. When educators or parents believe that a child has psychomotor problems that interfere with special education programming, they refer the student to an adapted physical educator for further assessment. The adapted physical educator then decides whether he or she has the necessary skills to work alone with the student or whether specialized assistance of related services personnel are required. The broader the training of adapted physical educators, the more intensive their practicum experiences, and the more varied their reading, the more likely they will be able to deliver services independently. With increasing knowledge and self-confidence, however, comes the desire to approach psychomotor problem solving in an interdisciplinary manner. Thus, adapted physical education and related services personnel interact with each other continuously, developing mutually satisfying *cooperative* relationships and avoiding competition.

Recreation

Many physical educators have a double major in recreation. PL 94–142 explains this profession as follows:

(9) "Recreation" includes:
    (i) Assessment of leisure function;
    (ii) Therapeutic recreation services;
    (iii) Recreation programs in schools and community agencies; and
    (iv) Leisure education. (*Federal Register,* August 23, 1977, p. 42479)

Recreation services for handicapped individuals ideally are delivered by persons with degrees and/or special training in *therapeutic recreation* and *community recreation. Therapeutic recreation* is defined as a process that utilizes recreation services for purposive intervention in some physical, emotional, and/or social behavior to bring about a desired change in that behavior and to promote the growth and development of the individual. Therapeutic recreation specialists are competent in the therapeutic use of such widely diversified program areas as music, dance, art, drama, horticulture, camping, and sports. They are skilled also in leisure counseling and assist persons in making the transition from institutional to community recreation. *Community recreation* is the utilization of all possible community resources (both human and physical) to make the leisure (discretionary or nonwork time) of its citizens rich, varied, satisfying, and self-actualizing. Included among citizens, of course, are handicapped individuals. Both community recreation and therapeutic recreation encompass three types of services: (a) rehabilitation, (b) education, and (c) recreation.

Recreation specialists often refer to the persons they serve as *clients.* The role of the therapeutic recreation specialist varies in degree of control according to the severity of the handicap and the needs of the client. Although recreation is traditionally defined as activities voluntarily pursued during leisure time, rehabilitation often necessitates *prescribed* training to improve specific motor, social, language, and self-care functions.

Prescriptive programming in both rehabilitation and leisure education generally includes: (a) assessment of functions needed for play/recreation; (b) development of long-term goals and short-term objectives; (c) selection of recreation activities and intervention techniques to achieve objectives and goals; (d) program implementation; and (e) evaluation of the program in relation to achievement of the client's goals. As the client progresses through the processes of rehabilitation and leisure education, the programming changes from prescriptive to elective. Clients thus move through a spectrum of play behaviors ranging from dependent and assisted to voluntary and intrinsically rewarding.

Similarities and Differences

The therapeutic recreation specialist is more like than unlike the adapted physical educator. Both are expected to perform the functions of diagnosis, purposive intervention, and evaluation on an independent basis and as coequals on a rehabilitation team. Both work with persons whose individual differences require special assistance.

Traditionally, the adapted physical education specialist has been associated with a school or educational setting, whereas the therapeutic recreation specialist has been associated with a hospital setting or residential facility. The roles of both types of specialists are expanding rapidly. The therapeutic recreation specialist not only works with an individual during his or her period of confinement in a hospital or residential facility, but also provides *follow-up* services in the halfway house setting and in the community.

The therapeutic recreation specialist must, therefore, be knowledgeable about community as well as institutional recreation. Whereas in the past, therapeutic recreation specialists were employed most often in residential facilities for mentally ill and mentally retarded persons, more recently they are expected to be able to work with the aged, alcoholics, drug addicts, the delinquent and criminal, and others who may need long-term recreation and leisure counseling.

The greatest difference between the adapted physical educator and the therapeutic recreation specialist lies in the scope of the program each is qualified to conduct. The adapted physical educator is responsible only for physical activities that lead to increased understanding and appreciation of the body. The therapeutic recreation specialist is responsible for 10 or more widely diversified program areas designed to lead to enriched use of leisure time. Each finds satisfaction in the encouragement of carry-over values and in follow-up procedures to ascertain that the child is using community resources. Leisure time counseling is performed by both specialists, but adapted physical educators generally limit their guidance to sports, dance, and aquatics, whereas the guidance of therapeutic recreation specialists can be as diversified, broad, and extensive as their capabilities permit.

Physical Therapy

PL 94–142 gives only a one-sentence explanation:

(7) "Physical therapy" means services provided by a qualified physical therapist. (*Federal Register*, August 23, 1977, p. 42479)

Traditionally, *physical therapy* has been defined as treatment by using certain physical means such as heat, cold, light, water, electricity, massage, ultrasound, exercise, and functional training. Physical therapists devote much of their time to gait training and wheelchair use (see Figure 2.9).

Many physical therapists work in sports medicine and orthopedic rehabilitation. They use therapeutic exercise to relieve pain, prevent deformity and further disability, develop or improve muscle strength or motor skills, and restore or maintain maximal functional capacities. *Functional training* refers to teaching the patient to use crutches, prostheses, and braces.

Physical therapists work only within a medical model. This means that they carry out an exercise prescription written by a physician. They also work with

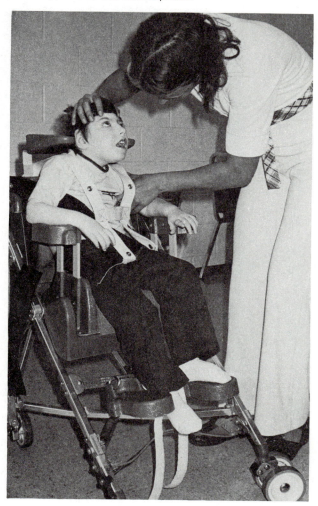

Figure 2.9 The physical therapist often serves as a consultant in the selection and purchase of wheelchairs and special equipment for the multiply handicapped. Here the physical therapist works on correct head positioning of an orthopedically handicapped child with microcephalus.

very sophisticated equipment like that used in functional electrical stimulation (FES) which enables paralyzed individuals to walk or use limbs—actions previously deemed impossible.

Among the best known physical therapy authorities is Berta Bobath, who, with her physician-husband Karel, has developed many of the treatment procedures used with cerebral palsied infants and children. This treatment is based on the *inhibition* of abnormal reflex activity and the *facilitation* of higher level righting and equilibrium reflexes.

Figure 2.10 A revolving plate designed by an occupational therapist allows students who have no arm and hand control to eat independently.

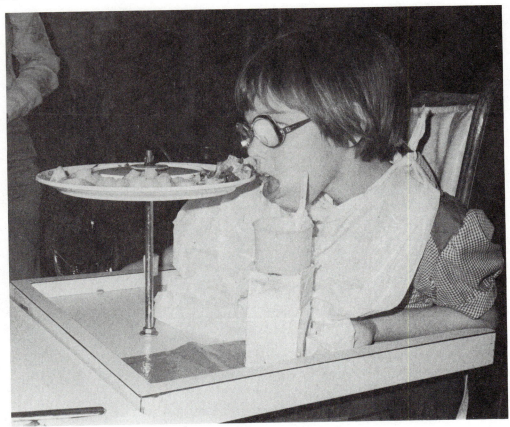

Occupational Therapy

PL 94–142 explains,

  (5) "Occupational therapy" includes:
    (i) Improving, developing or restoring functions impaired or lost through illness, injury, or deprivation;
    (ii) Improving ability to perform tasks for independent functioning when functions are impaired or lost; and
    (iii) Preventing, through early intervention, initial or further impairment or loss of function. (*Federal Register,* August 23, 1977, p. 42479)

The related service that is broadest in scope and most likely to overlap some physical education services, particularly in early childhood programs, appears to be occupational therapy. In its early years this profession focused mainly on activities of daily living (ADL), particularly on the rehabilitation of hand/finger/arm skills relevant to self-care (eating, dressing, grooming), work, and leisure. Often, arts and crafts activities were the medium through which rehabilitation goals were achieved. Historically, occupational therapists have been called upon to fabricate *assistive equipment* like self-help devices and simple splints and braces and to teach use of *orthoses,* devices that enable patients to handle standard objects like spoons and pens without adaptation.

In recent years, however, occupational therapy has broadened to encompass new areas. It is now described as

. . . a bio-psycho-social approach to health care that concentrates on an individual's abilities to perform, maintain, and balance daily occupational roles. Performance of these roles requires mastery of tasks and relationships necessary to actively engage in play, work, and self-maintenance activities. The premise of the profession is that occupation is a major health determinant: the goal-directed use of a person's potential, capabilities, resources, time, energy, interest, and attention will influence the quality of human development and life adaptation. (Lansing & Carlsen, 1977, pp. 211–212)

Whereas *occupation* was once conceptualized as work (vocation or homemaking), it now includes all activity areas of human endeavor: work, play, and self-maintenance (see Figure 2.10).

Of particular interest to physical educators are the many contributions that occupational therapists are making in the area of *sensorimotor integration*. Best known are the works of Jean Ayres, which have popularized the use of the vestibular and tactile sense modalities in developmental therapy. In accordance with Ayres's procedures, many occupational therapists are now using equipment previously thought to belong in gymnasiums: scooter boards, cage balls (called therapy balls in occupational therapy, OT), and balancing apparatus.

Corrective Therapy

Corrective therapy is not mentioned in PL 94–142, but, nevertheless, qualifies as a related service. Its new definition is,

Corrective therapy is the applied science of medically prescribed therapeutic exercise, education, and adapted physical activities to improve the quality of life and health of adults and children by developing physical fitness, increasing functional mobility and independence, and improving psychosocial behavior. The corrective therapist evaluates, develops, implements, and modifies adapted exercise programs for disease, injury, congenital defects, and other functional disabilities. (Purvis, 1985, p. 5)

First organized as the Association for Physical and Mental Rehabilitation in 1946 by therapy aides, physicians, and others who had worked in medical settings in war zones, its membership continues to be known primarily for excellent programs in veterans' hospitals. In 1967, the organization's name was changed to the American Corrective Therapy Association. Every 2 months, it publishes the *American Corrective Therapy Journal*.

The major difference between adapted physical education and corrective therapy is that the latter is usually provided in hospitals, clinics, and centers, whereas adapted physical education occurs in schools. Traditionally, corrective therapy services have been strongest in facilities that serve veterans, but this profession (like others) is broadening its scope.

Some adapted physical educators also hold corrective therapy certification. When persons with such dual training work in school settings, they should refer to themselves and their programs in terms of adapted physical education to avoid confusing co-workers. It should be remembered that corrective therapy, conducted by a nonadapted physical educator, is only a *related service* and cannot substitute for required physical education.

The Arts

Although the arts are not mentioned in the PL 94–142 official definition of related services, they are discussed in the *Federal Register* as follows:

Comment. With respect to related services, the Senate Report states: . . . the list of related services is not exhaustive and may include other developmental, corrective, or supportive services (such as artistic and cultural programs, and art, music and dance therapy) if they are required to assist a handicapped child to benefit from special education. (August 23, 1977, p. 42480)

Dance, although now recognized as a discipline separate from physical education, has traditionally been part of the training of the well-rounded physical educator. Chapter 15 of this book focuses upon the use of dance with handicapped persons.

Many educators believe that the arts (appropriately adapted) are particularly valuable in teaching self-help skills, language, and socialization to handicapped children and youth. An arts-oriented approach to adapted physical education blends music, dance, drama, and the visual/graphic arts with the teaching of movement. The resulting emphasis on movement exploration to a variety of sounds and tempos (music), colors, shapes, textures (art), and thematic ideas (drama) stimulates creative behaviors and builds self-confidence.

The arts for the handicapped movement, along with the concept of Very Special Arts Festivals, which evolved in the 1970s, has attracted many followers. The force behind this movement, an organization called National Committee—Arts for the Handicapped (NCAH), stresses the use of all the arts in education. Also acting as proponents of the arts are several professions, each of which has its own organization: *music therapy* (1950); *dance therapy* (1966); and *art therapy* (1969). By utilizing the expertise of arts educators and therapists, adapted physical educators can enrich learnings about the body and its capacity for creative movement and artistic expression (see Figure 2.11).

Trends and Issues in Multidisciplinary Teamwork

The helping professions, including adapted physical education, have changed tremendously in recent years. As the knowledge explosion continues and the economy of the nation ebbs and flows, we must become increasingly adept in coping with transience. Persons who work

Figure 2.11 Music therapists and adapted physical educators often coordinate efforts in movement exploration activities integrated with music. Here a Down's syndrome child explores what his body parts can do; later he will move his entire body through space, enacting the concepts of *loud* and *soft* as the music therapist provides accompaniment.

in the psychomotor domain with handicapped individuals, regardless of disciplinary affiliation, have much to gain through unification and cooperation. New models of child-centered service delivery systems are replacing traditional unidisciplinary systems.

It is important that prospective adapted physical educators, special educators, occupational therapists, physical therapists, recreators, and related others become acquainted and work together as early as possible in the undergraduate years. These professions have far more commonalities than differences. Each has its earliest roots in medicine; each is extending its role and scope in response to new legislation; and each is dedicated to the self-actualization of handicapped persons.

Professional boundaries between disciplines are becoming more and more ambiguous. To illustrate, a major difference between educators and therapists in the past was that the former worked in schools while the latter were employed by hospitals, clinics, and residential facilities. This is no longer true. Some issues of the *American Journal of Occupational Therapy* focus almost exclusively on public schools (Mitchell &

Lindsey, 1979). Likewise, recreation specialists increasingly are employed by school districts, whereas physical educators once thought that instruction during school hours was theirs alone. Nationwide projects like LEAP (Leisure Education Advancement Project), SELF (Special Education for Leisure Fulfillment), and PREP (Preschool Recreation Enrichment Program) have all demonstrated the efficacy of recreation (leisure education) as a school-based subject.

For further information on these projects, contact William Hillman, Office of Special Education, United States Department of Education, 400 Maryland Ave., SW, Washington, DC 20202, or Hawkins and Associates, 804 D St., NE, Washington, DC 20002.

Some other common ambiguities and misconceptions are the following:

1. Therapists often see themselves as responsible for *individualized* exercise and physical educators for *group* exercise. This is not a valid perception since adapted physical educators, like special educators, work on a one-to-one basis when needed.

2. Cane and crutch-walking procedures and wheelchair transfers were once believed to belong to the therapies but now many public school physical educators teach them. See teacher-training materials by Doolittle (1980), Fait (1978), and Vodola (1976).

3. Recreation specialists often believe that theirs is the major discipline concerned with play, but occupational therapy also considers play a major goal. See any occupational therapy textbook.

4. Sensory integration therapy is conducted by many professionals. Its originator, Jean Ayres, states that it "may be carried out by educators, psychologists, or health-related professionals" (Ayres, 1972, p. ix).

5. Adapted physical educators sometimes assume that physical and occupational therapy curricula do not include content on PL 94–142 and writing IEPs. This is naive. Therapists change their curricula in accordance with new legislation, just as educators do.

These commonalities emphasize the importance of every professional developing as many skills as possible. During economic crises, when job markets narrow, the major criteria for employing adapted physical educators increasingly will be breadth and depth of competence, excellence in work performance, high energy level, and good personality—i.e., the demonstrated ability to get along well with others. Banus, an occupational therapist, effectively discussed the issue of disciplinary boundaries:

We should never permit ourselves to feel boxed in by professional title. . . . One person who informally (outside of an academic program) and thoroughly studies and applies new material may become equally or more competent than the person who originally knew the material but ceased to use it or develop it further . . . with the increase in time and experience after the years of formal education, the pureness of professional knowledge and practice decreases. Only in this way does a profession or a person within a profession develop. (Banus, 1971, p. 520)

Valletutti and Christoplos (1977, 1979) have compiled two excellent volumes on interdisciplinary and multidisciplinary approaches that describe many disciplines and discuss interrelationships. They, too, make a strong case for all professionals to learn as much as possible about helping handicapped children regardless of traditional disciplinary boundaries and territorial protectiveness. Their most significant point pertains to the self-actualizing of all of us:

Interdisciplinary team members should be viewed as *individuals* with insights and skills to contribute to the team rather than as representatives of a discipline. Team membership is thus envisaged as a state of mind and members as *unique contributors* to the whole team process. (Valletutti & Christoplos, 1979, p. 6)

Learning Activities

1. Determine whether your university offers a course of study in special education, occupational therapy, physical therapy, therapeutic recreation, and the like and learn the requirements for a degree in these areas. Organize some multidisciplinary social and professional events for getting acquainted with other persons on your campus who are interested in handicapped individuals. What books do these persons study? What practicum experiences do they have?

2. Organize a panel discussion of students and/or faculty members from different disciplines in which each describes the nature and scope of his or her profession.

3. Write a paper or make a tape recording in which you analyze the similarities and differences among the different disciplines.

4. Arrange to observe representatives of different disciplines in their work settings. Strive to improve your interpersonal communication by asking questions that stimulate exchange of ideas but which are nonthreatening.

5. Invite a resource person to speak to your class about the role of research in shaping and developing a profession. Learn names of journals that publish research pertaining to handicapped persons. Read some of these journals and try applying their content to methodology in working with handicapped students.

6. Request your physical education and/or recreation majors' club to devote a meeting to adapted physical education. Assume responsibility for planning and conducting this meeting.

7. Attempt to locate some handicapped athletes on your campus or in your community. Invite them to do a demonstration on your campus, such as a wheelchair basketball game or Special Olympics event.

References

Appenzeller, H. (1983). *The right to participate: The law and individuals with handicapping conditions in physical education and sports.* Charlottesville, VA: The Michie Co.

Ayres, J. (1972). *Sensory integration and learning disorders.* Los Angeles: Western Psychological Services.

Brace, D. (1968). Physical education and recreation for mentally retarded pupils in public schools. *Research Quarterly, 39,* 779–782.

Committee on Adapted Physical Education. (1952). Guiding principles for adapted physical education. *Journal of Health, Physical Education and Recreation, 23,* 15.

Doolittle, J. E. (1980). Crutch and cane walking. PE 400: Laboratory Exercise 5, course syllabus. University Park: Pennsylvania State University.

Fait, H. (1978). *Special physical education.* Philadelphia: W. B. Saunders.

Federal Register, May 4, 1977, PL 93–112, the Rehabilitation Act of 1973, Section 504.

Federal Register, August 23, 1977, PL 94–142, the Education for All Handicapped Children Act.

Federal Register, November 8, 1978, PL 95–606, The Amateur Sports Act of 1978.

Francis, R. J., & Rarick, G. L. (1959). Motor characteristics of the mentally retarded. *American Journal of Mental Deficiency, 63,* 792–811.

Gunn, S. A., & Peterson, C. A. (1978). *Therapeutic recreation program design: Principles and procedures.* Englewood Cliffs, NJ: Prentice-Hall.

Hayden, F. (1964). *Physical fitness for mentally retarded.* Toronto: Metropolitan Toronto Association for Mentally Retarded.

Lansing, S., & Carlsen, P. (1977). Occupational therapy. In P. Valletutti & F. Christoplos (Eds.), *Interdisciplinary approaches to human services* (pp. 211–236). Baltimore: University Park Press.

Latimer, R. (1977). Physical therapy. In P. Valletutti & F. Christoplos (Eds.), *Interdisciplinary approaches to human services* (pp. 279–305). Baltimore: University Park Press.

Mitchell, M., & Lindsey, D (1979). A model for establishing occupational therapy and physical therapy services in public schools. *American Journal of Occupational Therapy, 33* (6), 361–364.

Purvis, J. (1985). A new description of corrective therapy. *American Corrective Therapy Journal, 39* (1), 4–5.

Rarick, G. L., Widdop, J., & Broadhead, G. (1970). The physical fitness and motor performance of educable mentally retarded children. *Exceptional Children, 36* 508–519.

Seaman, J. A., & Heilbuth, L. (1986). Competencies needed to function in the interdisciplinary area. In C. Sherrill (Ed.), *Adapted physical education leadership training.* Champaign, IL: Human Kinetics Publishers.

Sherrill, C. (Ed.). (1985). *Sport and disabled athletes.* Champaign, IL: Human Kinetics Publishers.

Stein, J. (1963). Motor function and physical fitness of the mentally retarded. *Rehabilitation Literature, 24,* 230–263.

Valletutti, P. J., & Christoplos, F. (Eds.). (1979). *Preventing physical and mental disabilities: Multidisciplinary approaches.* Baltimore: University Park Press.

Valletutti, P. J., & Christoplos, F. (Eds.). (1979). *Preventing physical and mental disabilities: Multidisciplinary approaches.* Baltimore: University Press Park.

Vodola, T. (1976). *Motor disabilities or limitations.* Oakhurst, NJ: Project ACTIVE.

Weintraub, F., Abeson, A., Ballard, J., & LaVor, M. (Eds.) (1976). *Public policy and the education of exceptional children.* Reston, VA: Council for Exceptional Children.

Wessel, J. (Ed.) (1977). *Planning individualized educational programs in special education with examples from I CAN.* Northbrook, IL: Hubbard.

Winnick, J., & Short, F. (1985). *Physical fitness testing of the disabled: Project UNIQUE.* Champaign, IL: Human Kinetics Publishers.

Bibliography

Multidisciplinary/Interdisciplinary

Banus, B. (1979). *The developmental therapist: A prototype of the pediatric occupational therapist* (2nd ed.). Thorofare, NJ: Charles B. Slack.

Combs, A. W., Avila, D., & Purkey, W. (1971). *Helping relationships: Basic concepts for the helping professions.* Boston: Allyn & Bacon.

Ericksen, K. (1977). *Human services today.* Reston, VA: Reston Publishing Co.

French, R., & Jansma, P. (1982). *Special physical education.* Columbus, OH: Charles E. Merrill. (See Chapter 15, The Educational Team Approach.)

Goldenson, R. (Ed.). (1978). *Disability and rehabilitation handbook.* New York: McGraw-Hill.

Nickel, V. (Ed.). (1982). *Orthopedic rehabilitation.* New York: Churchill Livingstone.

Valletutti, P., & Christoplos, F. (Eds.). (1977). *Interdisciplinary approaches to human services.* Baltimore: University Park Press.

Valletutti, P., & Christoplos, F. (Eds.). (1979). *Preventing physical and mental disabilities: Multidisciplinary approaches.* Baltimore: University Park Press.

Wright, B. (1983). *Physical disability—A psychosocial approach* (2nd ed.). New York: Harper & Row.

Adapted Physical Education

Arnheim, D., & Sinclair, W. (1985). *Physical education for special populations*. Englewood Cliffs, NJ: Prentice-Hall.

Auxter, D., & Pyfer, J. (1985). *Adapted physical education and recreation*. St. Louis: C. V. Mosby.

Eason, R., Smith, T., & Caron, F. (Eds.). (1983). *Adapted physical activity*. Champaign, IL: Human Kinetics Publishers.

Fait, H., & Dunn, J. (1984). *Special physical education* (5th ed.). Philadelphia: W. B. Saunders Company.

Kalakian, L., & Eichstaedt, C. (1982). *Developmental/adapted physical education*. Minneapolis: Burgess.

Sherrill, C. (Ed.). (1986). *Adapted physical education leadership training*. Champaign, IL: Human Kinetics Publishers.

Winnick, J. (1979). *Early movement experiences and development: Habilitation and remediation*. Philadelphia: W. B. Saunders.

Therapeutic Recreation

Avedon, E. (1974). *Therapeutic recreation service: An applied behavioral science approach*. Englewood Cliffs, NJ: Prentice-Hall.

Carter, M., Van Andel, G., & Robb, G. (1985). *Therapeutic recreation: A practical approach*. St. Louis: Times Mirror/Mosby College Publishing.

Gunn, S., & Peterson, C. (1978). *Therapeutic recreation program design*. Englewood Cliffs, NJ: Prentice-Hall.

Hutchison, P., & Lord, P. (1979). *Recreation integration*. Ottawa, Ontario, Canada: Leisurability Publications, Inc.

O'Morrow, G. (1980). *Therapeutic recreation: A helping profession* (2nd ed.). Englewood Cliffs, NJ: Prentice-Hall.

Physical Therapy

Bobath, B., & Bobath, K. (1975). *Motor development in the different types of cerebral palsy*. London: William Heinemann Medical Books.

Brunnstrom, S. (1970). *Movement therapy in hemiplegia*. New York: Harper & Row.

Brunnstrom, S. (1972). *Clinical kinesiology*. Philadelphia: F. A. Davis.

Downer, A. (1974). *Physical therapy procedures* (2nd ed.). Springfield, IL: Charles C. Thomas.

Knott, M., & Voss, D. (1963). *Proprioceptive neuromuscular facilitation, patterns, and techniques*. New York: Harper & Row.

Krumhausl, B. (1978). *Opportunities in physical therapy*. Skokie, IL: National Textbook Co.

Pearson, P., & Williams, C. (1972). *Physical therapy services in the developmental disabilities*. Springfield, IL: Charles C. Thomas.

Williams, M., & Worthington, C. (1977). *Therapeutic exercise for body alignment and function* (2nd ed.). Philadelphia: W. B. Saunders.

Occupational Therapy

Ayres, A. J. (1972). *Sensory integration and learning disorders*. Los Angeles: Western Psychological Services.

Ayres, A. J. (1979). *Sensory integration and the child*. Los Angeles: Western Psychological Services.

Cynkin, S. (1979). *Occupational therapy: Toward health through activities*. Boston: Little, Brown.

Fiorentino, M. (1981). *A basis for sensorimotor development—Normal and abnormal*. Springfield, IL: Charles C. Thomas.

Hopkins, H., & Smith, H. (1983). *Willard and Spackman's Occupational Therapy* (6th ed.). Philadelphia: J. B. Lippincott.

Art Education and Therapy

Anderson, F. (1978). *Art for all children*. Springfield, IL: Charles C. Thomas.

Fitt, S., & Riordan, A. (Eds.). (1980). *Dance for the handicapped—Focus on dance IX*. Reston, VA: American Alliance for Health, Physical Education, Recreation, and Dance.

Michel, D. E. (1977). *Music therapy: An introduction to therapy and special education through music* (2nd ed.). Springfield, IL: Charles C. Thomas.

Shaw, A., & Stevens, C. J. (1979). *Drama, theatre, and the handicapped*. Washington, DC: American Theatre Association.

Sherrill, C. (Ed.). (1979). *Creative arts for the severely handicapped*. Springfield, IL: Charles C. Thomas.

3 The Legal Bases of Adapted Physical Education

Figure 3.1 PL 94–142 creates an eligibility system whereby students classified as handicapped through the IEP process can receive individualized training to meet their needs.

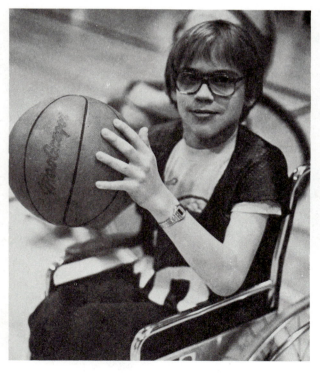

Chapter Objectives

After you have studied this chapter, you should be able to

1. Describe two methods of intervention by the federal government when inequities exist among states in the treatment of minority groups.

2. Cite several resources for learning about law in relation to handicapped persons.

3. Explain the state plan for special education that is required by PL 94–142 and describe the process for becoming involved in its rules and regulations.

4. Note the number of passages that mention physical education in PL 94–142 and the significance of each.

5. Differentiate among the terms *integration, mainstreaming,* and *least restrictive environment.*

6. Name the 11 handicapping conditions recognized in PL 94–142 and define each.

7. Identify the five main components of the written IEP and explain the content of each as it relates to adapted physical education.

8. Explain the PL 94–142 process, including (a) its five phases, (b) regulations relating to dates, and (c) the IEP meeting and participants.

9. Discuss placement criteria in terms of the normal curve for determining eligibility for adapted physical education services.

10. Discuss least restrictive environment and common modifications of regular physical education that should be written on the IEP.

11. Cite six characteristics of good evaluation required by PL 94–142 and relate these to adapted physical education.

12. List strategies that physical educators can use in advocating for needed legislation.

Prior to the enactment of PL 94–142, the Education for All Handicapped Children Act, responsibility for public school education lay primarily with state and local governments. Some states passed laws that ensured quality instruction for its handicapped students, whereas other states did nothing. Some school districts had excellent programs; some had poor ones. Much of this inequity stemmed from lack of fiscal resources; some of it was caused by lack of awareness concerning needs of handicapped students or attitudes of prejudice and bias.

When inequities exist among states in the treatment of minority groups (e.g., blacks, Mexican-Americans, the poor), it has been the practice of the federal government to intervene. Two methods are typically used. The United States Supreme Court may declare an educational practice illegal, as in the doctrines of "separate but equal" that prevailed in the education of black students until the 1954 case of *Brown v. Board of Education of Topeka, Kansas,* and of refusing severely handicapped students free public education, which prevailed before the famous 1971 class action law suit in Pennsylvania. The second method of intervention is enactment of federal laws that mandate equal opportunity and access.

Of the many laws enacted over the years to ameliorate inequities, PL 94–142 is undoubtedly the most important. It is especially relevant to physical education because our field is mentioned in it by name. No other federal law pertaining specifically to public school education has ever mentioned physical education. Unfortunately, this law pertains only to handicapped children and youth; no federal provisions exist to prevent inequities in the education of nonhandicapped students. Thus, PL 94–142 forms the legal bases for about half of the students we serve in adapted physical education, those who can be labeled handicapped through specific eligibility procedures (see Figure 3.1). The legal bases for serving other students with psychomotor problems may be found in state and/or local laws and educational policy or it may be nonexistent.

This chapter presents an introduction to law, human rights, and advocacy theory that forms part of the knowledge base of adapted physical education. Professionals must not only know and apply the law in job performance, but they must actively advocate for it and help others (particularly parents) to understand its impact. Whereas PL 94–142 is popular among persons who believe in equity for all human beings, regardless of cost, many segments of society have repeatedly challenged this law and the related legislation that must be enacted periodically to provide federal money for continued implementation of it. So far, each challenge has been met with floods of visits, telephone calls, and letters to legislators sufficient to assure its retention, but advocates must be ever vigilant. Physical educators must assume an active role in helping to decide how federal (as well as state and local) monies are spent.

Resources for Learning about Law

The *Federal Register,* a daily periodical that is found in most university libraries, is the official government publication for disseminating the rules and regulations that govern implementation of a law. Many university teachers own a copy of the August 23, 1977, *Federal Register,* which serves as the primary source for PL 94–142 theory and practice; for persons who do not own this vital document, direct quotes from the *Federal Register* are included in this chapter. Use of these direct quotes in term papers, research projects, reports to parents and school boards, and letters to legislators is encouraged. Ability to cite the law is *power* in obtaining quality physical education programs for all children.

Several books are particularly good resources:

Appenzeller, H. (1983). *The right to participate: The law and individuals with handicapping conditions in physical education and sports.* Charlottesville, VA: The Michie Co.

Sherrill, C. (Ed.). (1986). *Adapted physical education leadership training.* Champaign, IL: Human Kinetics Publishers.

Weintraub, F., Abeson, A., Ballard, J., & LaVor, M. (1976). *Public policy and the education of exceptional children.* Reston, VA: Council for Exceptional Children.

Each year, since 1979, the United States Department of Education has published an annual report to Congress on the implementation of PL 94–142. This paperback book, usually about 200 pages in length, is the primary source for statistics on number of handicapped students needing and receiving special services, progress made in ensuring free, appropriate education for all children, and trends, issues, and problems pertaining to PL 94–142. The book can be obtained free by contacting your federal legislator or writing the

United States Department of Education, Office of Special Education and Rehabilitative Services, 400 Maryland Ave., SW, Washington, DC 20202.

Journals that frequently carry articles pertaining to PL 94–142 and its implementation include the *Adapted Physical Activity Quarterly* and *Exceptional Children.* Frequently, materials about PL 94–142 can be obtained from the special education director in your school district or from the special education division of the state education agency (SEA). Of these, the state plan is a vitally important resource.

The State Plan for Special Education

PL 94–142 requires every state education agency (SEA) to develop a *state plan* that describes specifically how PL 94–142 will be implemented in that state. This state plan is then submitted to the United States Department of Education every 3 years; this is the official document that enables the state government to receive federal funds (PL 94–142 monies) to supplement the cost of quality education for handicapped students.

Ideally, the state plan should include all of the mentions of physical education that PL 94–142 does. If, however, state education agency personnel are not knowledgeable and/or supportive of physical education, they may neglect writing out procedures for implementing physical education mandates. If the state plan does not include these procedures, then PL 94–142 cannot be enforced in regard to physical education. It is, therefore, imperative that university classes teach physical educators about the state plan and that a copy of it be available for study.

Before a state plan is filed with the federal government, it must be made available to all interested persons, and public hearings must be held to allow individuals and special interest groups to offer input. Input may be agreement or disagreement with changes or pointing out inconsistencies between the state plan and PL 94–142. The dates of these public hearings, by law, are announced in newspapers of the large cities in which they are held; the state education agency (SEA) decides which cities these shall be, but everyone is free to attend and speak. In addition to attending public hearings, physical educators and parents should submit written testimony to the SEA concerning the state plan; deadlines for receiving these letters are also published.

The process for becoming involved in the state plan is outlined in Figure 3.2. It is appropriate for university classes to attend public hearings and write individual letters. Ideally, physical educators take parents of handicapped children to these hearings to speak in favor of PL 94–142 physical education mandates and the

Figure 3.2 The legislative process for influencing the rules and regulations of the state plan. This series of steps occurs once every 3 years. In most states, this is 1985, 1988, and so forth. The resulting 3-year plan governs all aspects of SEA and LEA compliance with PL 94–142.

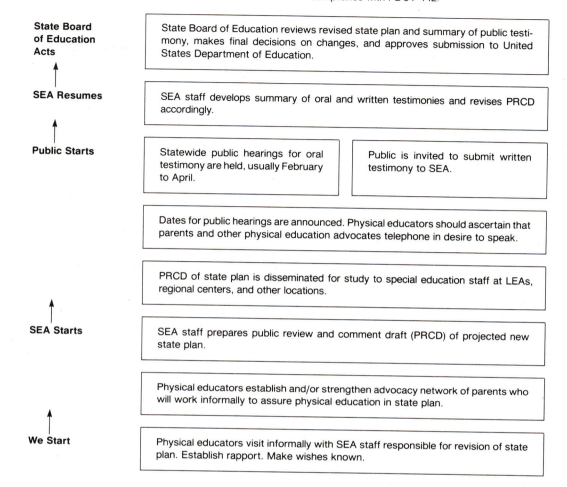

State Board of Education Acts

> State Board of Education reviews revised state plan and summary of public testimony, makes final decisions on changes, and approves submission to United States Department of Education.

SEA Resumes

> SEA staff develops summary of oral and written testimonies and revises PRCD accordingly.

Public Starts

> Statewide public hearings for oral testimony are held, usually February to April.

> Public is invited to submit written testimony to SEA.

> Dates for public hearings are announced. Physical educators should ascertain that parents and other physical education advocates telephone in desire to speak.

> PRCD of state plan is disseminated for study to special education staff at LEAs, regional centers, and other locations.

SEA Starts

> SEA staff prepares public review and comment draft (PRCD) of projected new state plan.

> Physical educators establish and/or strengthen advocacy network of parents who will work informally to assure physical education in state plan.

We Start

> Physical educators visit informally with SEA staff responsible for revision of state plan. Establish rapport. Make wishes known.

values their children have derived from physical education instruction. Only by caring and acting at the state level can PL 94–142 be translated into action without resorting to more extreme alternatives, due process procedures and litigation (actions typically taken only by parents and advocacy organizations).

PL 94–142 and Physical Education

Each passage of the law that mentions physical education is discussed in this section of the chapter, and a direct quotation is provided from the August 23, 1977, *Federal Register.* Readers should attempt to find the comparable passage in their state plans in order to understand specifically how each regulation is interpreted in their states. If the state plan does not include a passage, then physical educators should become involved in the legislative process for changing the state plan.

Physical Education Definition

Page 42480 of the August 23, 1977, *Federal Register* states,

(2) "Physical education" is defined as follows:
(i) The term means the development of:
(A) Physical and motor fitness;
(B) Fundamental motor skills and patterns; and
(C) Skills in aquatics, dance, and individual and group games and sports (including intramural and lifetime sports).
(ii) The term includes special physical education, adapted physical education, movement education, and motor development. (20 U.S.C. 1401 [16]) (*Federal Register,* August 23, 1977, p. 42480)

This definition can be used to differentiate physical education from such related services as occupational and physical therapy. The term *skills,* as used in

PL 94–142, encompasses mental and social (as well as physical) skills needed to learn the rules and strategies of games and sports and the creativity needed in dance and movement education. Nowhere in PL 94–142 is there a definition specifically for adapted physical education. The basic assumption is that adapted physical education is the development of the same abilities as physical education. *Education,* (the learning of new physical, mental, and social skills), *not therapy* (repetition of exercises to correct a condition), is specified.

Physical Education As Part of Special Education

Page 42480 of the August 23, 1977, *Federal Register* states,

(a) (1) As used in this part, the term "special education" means specially designed instruction at no cost to the parent, to meet the unique needs of a handicapped child, including classroom instruction, instruction in physical education, home instruction, and instruction in hospitals and institutions.

Physical education is the only school subject mentioned within this definition. Essentially, this definition makes specially designed physical education a component of special education. This is why adapted physical educators hired to teach separate classes, usually of severely handicapped children, are often salaried by PL 94–142 monies and considered members of the school district's special education staff. In some states, persons taking such positions are required to have separate teacher certification in special education and physical education. A better requirement is a graduate degree or state certification specifically in adapted physical education, the discipline that blends knowledge from these two and related areas pertaining to psychomotor functioning and individual differences.

Physical Education Requirement

Page 42489 of the August 23, 1977, *Federal Register* states,

121a.307 Physical Education
(a) *General.* Physical education services, specially designed if necessary, must be made available to every handicapped child receiving a free appropriate public education.

This passage comprises the legal basis for adapted physical education service delivery for handicapped students. Whether a specially designed program is needed is determined by PL 94–142 eligibility procedures, which are described later in the chapter.

Integration In Regular Physical Education

Page 42489 of the August 23, 1977, *Federal Register* states,

(b) *Regular physical education.* Each handicapped child must be afforded the opportunity to participate in the regular physical education program available to nonhandicapped children unless:
  (1) The child is enrolled full-time in a separate facility; or
  (2) The child needs specially designed physical education, as prescribed in the child's individualized education program.

This passage explains the emphasis throughout the country on ways to successfully integrate handicapped and nonhandicapped students in classroom instruction. Integration is sometimes called *mainstreaming,* or placing the student in the mainstream. The word *mainstreaming* is not a legal term; nowhere does it appear in PL 94–142. It seems to have been coined by the Council for Exceptional Children (CEC), the professional organization to which most special educators and many adapted physical educators belong. Thus, mainstreaming means different things to different people. As used by CEC, mainstreaming is an educational placement philosophy based on the belief that a handicapped student should be educated in the least restrictive environment in which his or her needs can be met. For some children, this is integration; for others, it is partial integration or segregation. Mainstreaming, therefore, cannot be used as a synonym for integration.

In contrast, the word *mainstream* denotes a place, not a process. The words *mainstream* and *regular physical education* can be used interchangeably.

Special Physical Education

Page 42489 of the August 23, 1977, *Federal Register* states,

(c) *Special physical education.* If specially designed physical education is prescribed in a child's individualized education program, the public agency responsible for the education of that child shall provide the service directly, or make arrangements for it to be provided through other public or private programs.

This definition explains why some persons call separate or segregated classes special physical education rather than considering them a part of the adapted physical education placement continuum. *Specially designed physical education,* as defined, does not have to be full-time placement in a separate class. It can refer to specific conditions imposed upon regular class placement, like limited class size, the presence of an assistant for 1:1 instruction, and the availability of wheelchairs and other special or adapted equipment. Just as special education is taught by a certified special education teacher, specially designed physical education should be planned and, when possible, implemented by an adapted physical education specialist.

To receive specially designed physical education under PL 94–142, a student must be declared handicapped in accordance with PL 94–142 definitions. This is done through the individualized education program (IEP) process.

Official Handicapping Conditions

Under PL 94–142, there are 11 official handicapping conditions. These are the same for every state that receives federal monies, although the names of the handicapping conditions may differ (i.e., *visually* *handicapped* might be *blind* or *visually impaired; seriously emotionally disturbed* might be *behavior disorders).* The chapters in section 3 of this book are named according to PL 94–142 terminology. The exception is the orthopedically impaired (OI) category, which is divided into three chapters according to the different sports organizations to which OI persons can belong. No chapters have been written for speech impaired because adapted physical education is obviously not necessary or for the deaf-blind and multihandicapped because these conditions are so severe that a separate textbook is necessary to cover pedagogy.

Table 3.1 contains the PL 94–142 definitions from the *Federal Register*, August 23, 1977, p. 42478:

Table 3.1
PL 94–142 Definitions

Mentally retarded [MR] means significantly subaverage general intellectual functioning existing concurrently with deficits in adaptive behavior and manifested during the developmental period, which adversely affects a child's educational performance.

Orthopedically impaired [OI] means a severe orthopedic impairment which adversely affects a child's educational performance. The term includes impairments caused by congenital anomaly (e.g., clubfoot, absence of some member, etc.), impairments caused by disease (e.g., poliomyelitis, bone tuberculosis, etc.), and impairments from other causes (e.g., cerebral palsy, amputations, and fractures or burns which cause contractures).

Specific learning disability [LD] means a disorder in one or more of the basic psychological processes involved in understanding or in using language, spoken or written, which may manifest itself in an imperfect ability to listen, think, speak, read, write, spell, or do mathematical calculations. The term includes such conditions as perceptual handicaps, brain injury, minimal brain disfunction, dyslexia, and developmental aphasia. The term does not include children who have learning problems which are primarily the result of visual, hearing, or motor handicaps, of mental retardation, or of environmental, cultural, or economic disadvantage.

Seriously emotionally disturbed [ED] means a condition exhibiting one or more of the following characteristics over a long period of time and to a marked degree, which adversely affects educational performance:
(A) An inability to learn which cannot be explained by intellectual, sensory, or health factors;
(B) An inability to build or maintain satisfactory interpersonal relationships with peers and teachers;
(C) Inappropriate types of behavior or feelings under normal circumstances;
(D) A general pervasive mood of unhappiness or depression; or
(E) A tendency to develop physical symptoms or fears associated with personal or school problems.

The term includes children who are *schizophrenic* or *autistic.* The term does not include children who are socially maladjusted, unless it is determined that they are seriously emotionally disturbed.

Visually handicapped [VH] means a visual impairment which, even with correction, adversely affects a child's educational performance. The term includes both partially seeing and blind children.

Deaf [D] means a hearing impairment which is so severe that the child is impaired in processing linguistic information through hearing, with or without amplification, which adversely affects educational performance.

Hard of hearing [HH] means a hearing impairment, whether permanent or fluctuating, which adversely affects a child's educational performance but which is not included under the definition of "deaf" in this section.

Deaf-blind [DB] means concomitant hearing and visual impairments. The combination of which causes such severe communication and other developmental and educational problems that they cannot be accommodated in special education programs solely for deaf or blind children.

Other health impaired [OHI] means limited strength, vitality or alertness, due to chronic or acute health problems such as a heart condition, tuberculosis, rheumatic fever, nephritis, asthma, sickle cell anemia, hemophilia, epilepsy, lead poisoning, leukemia, or diabetes, which adversely affects a child's educational performance.

Speech impaired [SH] means a communication disorder, such as stuttering, impaired articulation, a language impairment, or a voice impairment, which adversely affects a child's educational performance.

Multihandicapped means concomitant impairments (such as mentally retarded-blind, mentally retarded-orthopedically impaired, etc.), the combination of which causes such severe educational problems that they cannot be accommodated in special education programs solely for one of the impairments. The term does not include deaf-blind children.

Note. In 1981, autistic children were officially classified as other health impaired rather than seriously emotionally disturbed.

The PL 94–142 conditions have remained the same since 1977 with one exception. In 1981, by federal law, reference to *autistic* children was deleted from the seriously emotionally disturbed category and placed under the other health impaired category. The legal document indicating this change is *Federal Register,* January 16, 1981, p. 3865 (Volume *46,* [1]).

In order to receive special services (including adapted physical education) funded by PL 94–142 monies, parents must be willing to have their children declared legally handicapped by means of the eligibility process specified in PL 94–142. This process ends with the preparation of an individualized education program (IEP).

Individualized Education Programs (IEPs)

Page 42490 of the August 23, 1977, *Federal Register* states,

As used in this part, the term "individualized education program" means a written statement for a handicapped child that is developed and implemented in accordance with 121a.341–121a.349. (20 U.S.C. 1401[19])

The content that each IEP must contain is also specified on page 42490 of the August 23, 1977, *Federal Register:*

121a.346 **Content of individualized education program.** The individualized education program for each child must include:

(a) A statement of the child's present levels of educational performance;
(b) A statement of annual goals, including short-term instructional objectives;
(c) A statement of the specific special education and related services to be provided to the child, and the extent to which the child will be able to participate in regular educational programs;
(d) The projected dates for initiation of services and the anticipated duration of the services; and
(e) Appropriate objective criteria and evaluation procedures and schedules for determining, on at least an annual basis, whether the short-term instructional objectives are being achieved.

The mandate that physical education be required for all handicapped students necessitates that the IEP include at least a brief description of the student's physical education performance, such as "normal for chronological age," "falls within 30th to 60th percentile for able-bodied students on all tests," or "performs 1 to 2 years below chronological age." Under goals,

again the statement may be brief: "Demonstrate success in regular physical education placement" or "Learn three basic motor skills and 10 games in an adapted physical education placement."

This brevity is necessitated by the fact that all subject matter areas needed by the student must be included in the IEP. Each school district uses a different form, but most special education IEPs are about three to four pages long. Research shows that school districts vary widely on time spent writing IEPs, with a range of from 13 to 150 short term objectives written for each student. The median number of objectives were 22 and 27 in two large-scale studies conducted by the United States Department of Education.

In many school districts, the three-to-four page special education IEP represents a summary of IEPs written by specialists in different areas. The adapted physical educator, for instance, may be expected to write a physical education IEP. Figure 3.3 shows a sample physical education IEP written for a 5-year-old student with mild cerebral palsy. Note that this one-page form includes the five components of an IEP as required by PL 94–142.

PL 94–142 Process

This is sometimes called the IEP or ARD (Admission, Review, Dismissal) Process. It is directed toward finding unserved handicapped children, *admitting* them to the school district's special education program, providing them with special services, *reviewing* their progress at least annually, and subsequently *dismissing* them from special education. The precise roles of the mainstream physical educator and the adapted physical educator are not discussed in PL 94–142 and, thus, vary by school district. In most instances, however, the physical educator is expected to contribute expertise with regard to identification, analysis, and solution of problems in the psychomotor domain.

Five Phases in Process

Table 3.2 depicts five phases of the IEP process: (a) child find (identification of students who may be eligible for special education services, including adapted physical education); (b) initial data collection and pre-IEP meeting; (c) formal admission to special education, including *comprehensive individual assessment* and the official *IEP meeting;* (d) program implementation with annual program review, for the purpose of evaluating the effectiveness of the learning activities in achieving goals and objectives; and (e) dismissal from the special education program into regular education. This last phase may seem idealistic, but it demonstrates PL 94–142 philosophy that students should, if possible, be integrated into regular education.

ADAPTED AND DEVELOPMENTAL PHYSICAL EDUCATION - IEP
Alief Independent School District

Parent Signature of Approval _____ Date _____

Name ___Amy S.___ Date __1-15-80__ School __Washington Elem.__

D.O.B. __7-3-74__ Age __5__ Grade __EC Self-Contained__ Classification __OHI__

ADPE Teacher __C. Pope__ Projected Starting Date of Services __9-1979__

Instructional P.E. Arrangement __1/1 ADPE Specialist 3 times weekly-15 min.__
                               __1/15 Regular PE 2 times weekly - 30 min.__

Physical Abilities/Disabilities __Mild Cerebral Palsy - L. side, hemiplegic__
    __spastic, ambulatory__ Related Services __OT, PT__

PRESENT LEVEL OF PSYCHOMOTOR PERFORMANCE	ANNUAL GOALS
Amy walks independently and climbs stairs with assistance. Uses a wide base of support and carries arms in high guard position. Has developed some protective extension of arms and equilibrium reactions. Amy rolls a 10" ball for distance of 8-10'; hits a suspended swinging ball; throws (RH) with a flinging motion; creeps up an inclined mat and log rolls down; walks a 6" beam with assistance, and balances momentarily on one foot. She is just entering the associative play stage and appears to have had little experience interacting with other children; plays no group games.	1. Develop fundamental movement patterns to age appropriate level. 2. Improve social interaction skills to cooperative play stage. 3. Learn 10+ low organized games. 4. Improve postures in all positions.

SHORT TERM OBJECTIVES	(METHODS/ACTIVITIES)

1. Interact with 3+ classmates each regular PE class
2. Perform a broad jump (2-ft. takeoff and land) for a distance of 8"
3. Maintain balance on one foot for 3-5 seconds
4. Jump down from a height of 10-12"
5. Kick a 10" stationary ball while standing
6. Throw a bean bag 5' using overarm pattern
7. Walk a 5' balance beam (6" wide) on floor unassisted
8. Stand up from supine position in less than 10 seconds
9. Track and catch a 10" ball rolled from 10'
	Command teaching style
	Physical prompts as needed
	Insist on eye contact
	Reinforce-random schedule
	See the following pages of ADPE Guide:
	    Movement Skill-pp.1-9
	    Bean Bag Games - p.22
	
	Note: This section generally refers to school curriculum guide or a favorite book that describes method in detail.

Table 3.2
IEP Process as Required by PL 94–142, Adapted to Show Roles of Mainstream and Adapted Physical Education Instructors

Phase 1 Child find	District-wide screening process for all children in all school subjects. (1) Usually done by mainstream physical education instructor or classroom teacher.	(2) Usually conducted at beginning of school year but can occur anytime. (3) Often informal, resulting from observation and/or conference with parent.	(4) Parent can initiate process instead of teacher.
Phase 2 Initial data collection and pre-IEP meeting	Begins with referral for further testing to determine if adapted physical education/special education services are needed. (1) As result of Phase 1, Child Find, anyone can request special education director to determine pupil's eligibility for special services.	(2) Contact parents for consent to test and/or collect eligibility data. (3) Data collection usually done by mainstream physical education instructor.	(4) Pre-IEP meeting to determine need for more extensive testing. (5) Written report of findings.

Phase 3 Admission to special education, including adapted physical education	**Comprehensive Individual Assessment** Initiated by written report signed by referral committee—see Phase 2.
	
	(1) Special education director assigns persons to do assessment.
	
	(2) Notification of rights to parents.
	
	(3) Obtain parent consent for comprehensive assessment by multidisciplinary team.
	
	(4) Comprehensive individual assessment with psychomotor part done by adapted physical education specialist.
		IEP Meeting
		(1) Procedural safeguards must be observed in planning meeting.
		Consider:
		  (a) Who must be present,
		  (b) Time and place, and
		  (c) Native language.
		(2) Presentation and analysis of assessment data by different team members.
		(3) Agreement on present level of functioning.
			(4) Decision making concerning:
			  (a) Goals and objectives,
			  (b) Services,
			    (i) Educational placement,
			    (ii) Interventions,
			    (iii) et cetera,
			  (c) Dates/timeline,
			  (d) Evaluation plan.
			(5) Write IEP.
			(6) Sign IEP.

Phase 4 Program implementation with annual program review			
Phase 5 Dismissal from special education into full-time regular education			

Regulations Relating to Dates

PL 94–142 requires that an IEP must be in effect *before* a handicapped student can receive special education, including adapted physical education services, or related services. This is because the IEP process is the means by which eligibility for services is determined and educational placement is assigned.

Parental consent is required before comprehensive individual assessment for special education (including adapted physical education) placement can be begun. Once this consent is obtained, most states require that the IEP process be completed in 30 to 60 days.

PL 94–142 also requires that the written IEP must be officially reviewed once each year. Many states require more frequent reviews. The purpose of these reviews is to analyze the student's educational progress and make revisions in the IEP.

Figure 3.4 A normal curve is a mathematical model that shows where 100 or more students will score if given a standardized test. Along the baseline are standard deviation marks ($\pm\sigma$) that divide the curve into 3%, 13%, and 68% areas. Underneath the baseline of the curve is a percentile equivalents scale showing that the 50th percentile is synonymous with the concepts of 0, mean, and average score.

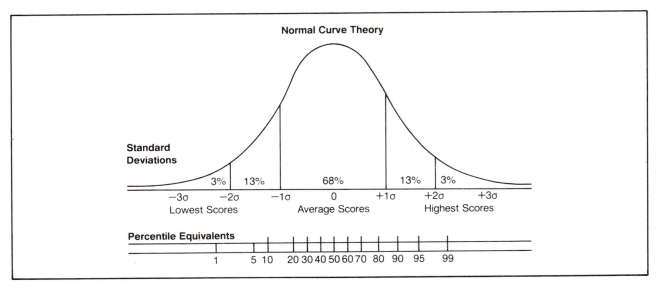

IEP Meeting and Participants

PL 94–142 is very specific about participants in the IEP meeting. It states,

121a.344 Participants in meetings.
(a) General. The public agency shall ensure that each meeting includes the following participants:
  (1) A representative of the public agency, other than the child's teacher who is qualified to provide, or supervise the provision of, special education.
  (2) The child's teacher.
  (3) One or both of the child's parents.
  (4) The child, where appropriate.
  (5) Other individuals at the discretion of the parent or agency. (*Federal Register*, August 23, 1977, p. 42490)

In general, participants in IEP meetings represent four types of roles: (a) parental, (b) administrative, (c) instructional, and (d) diagnostic. Most adapted physical education authorities believe that a physical educator should be present at the IEP meeting to provide input concerning performance and needs in the psychomotor domain. If, however, a physical educator cannot be released from teaching responsibilities to attend, he or she should submit written recommendations to the special education director and, when possible, confer with the parents before the meeting and ask them to serve as advocates for physical education.

The primary purpose of the IEP meeting is to determine for each school subject whether the student should be assigned a regular, special, or combined educational placement. If the school district employs an adapted physical education specialist, this person is typically responsible for assessment and making a recommendation about physical education placement. If no adapted physical education specialist is available, the regular physical educator is expected to perform these tasks or, in some instances, the student is just automatically placed in regular physical education without consideration of needs.

Physical Education Placement Criteria

Several states have adopted criteria or specific guidelines for determining eligibility for adapted physical education services. These are based on the administration of standardized tests for which norms or percentiles are available. This procedure takes the subjectivity out of the placement process and helps ensure appropriate placements when physical educators are excluded from the placement process.

The use of placement criteria is founded in normal curve theory. The normal curve (see Figure 3.4) is based on a mathematical model that shows for every 100 children tested, approximately 68% fall in the middle of the curve designated as +1 or −1 standard deviations from 0, the mean (average score) for the group. These are the students considered to be educationally normal or average. Of the 100 children, approximately 13% score so that they fall in the area between +1 and +2 standard deviations (above average) and 13% fall in the area between −1 and −2 standard deviations (below average). Only 3% fall into the area between

+2 and +3 standard deviations (gifted) and 3% fall into the area between −2 and −3 standard deviations (very delayed or inferior). *Norms* (i.e., statistics that describe test performance of specific groups) are published in evaluation and/or tests and measurement books in order to permit comparing a student's score against the norm (standard) for his or her age group or gender. *Percentiles* are also frequently used to determine a student's performance in relation to average.

Figure 3.4 shows the relationship between percentile, standard deviation areas, and the normal curve. Norms used for adapted physical education placement come from testing large groups of nonhandicapped children to see if the handicapped student performs well enough to succeed within a regular setting with such children.

Among the states that have adopted criteria or specific guidelines for adapted physical education placement are Alabama, Georgia, Minnesota, and Louisiana. The following are those used by Alabama. Georgia's guidelines are almost identical.

a. perform below the 30th percentile on standardized tests of:
  (i) motor development,
  (ii) motor proficiency,
  (iii) fundamental motor skills and patterns,
  (iv) physical fitness,
  (v) game/sports skills,
  (vi) perceptual-motor functioning,
  (vii) posture screening;
b. exhibit a developmental delay of 2 or more years based on appropriate assessment instruments;
c. function within the severe or profound range as determined by special education eligibility standards;
d. possess social/emotional or physical capabilities that would render it unlikely for the student to reach his or her physical education goals without significant modification or exclusion from the regular physical education class.

The Minnesota guidelines have no specific rules on placement according to formal assessment results; however, some general guidelines follow:

a. Developmental age
  (1) 1 to 2 years below chronological age—take a close look at the situation;
  (2) 2 or more years below chronological age—some type of program should be initiated.

b. Percentile rank
  (1) 16th–25th percentile—take a close look at the situation;
  (2) under the 15th percentile—some type of program should be initiated.

The Louisiana criteria are as follows:

a. for students below the age of 6 years:
  (1) evidence a motor deficit by performing at least 1.5 standard deviations below the mean for the student's chronological age;
  (2) demonstrate a motor delay of at least 20% of his or her chronological age when developmental age score is used instead of a standard score.
b. for students ages 6 to 21 years:
  (1) evidence a motor deficit by performing at least 1.5 standard deviations below the mean on a test measuring both fine and gross motor abilities;
  (2) meet less than 70% of the physical education competencies on a test based on the state physical education curriculum.

These criteria pertain to placement of handicapped students in separate or specially designed physical education. Such a placement, by law, can last no longer than a year without formal review. Ideally, with extra help for a year, many students can be returned to regular physical education on a full- or part-time basis.

Placement criteria for adapted physical education services may be different from those used for separate class placement. This author, for instance, believes that any student who consistently scores below the 50th percentile (i.e., the mean) on standardized tests should be provided adapted physical education services. These services may be in the mainstream setting or entail a combined placement of 2 days in a small group adapted physical education setting (like 1:5) and 3 days in regular physical education of normal class size (1:25). If the student meets eligibility requirements for PL 94–142 services, these services should be written into the IEP.

Physical Education Inclusion in IEP

If physical education is not mentioned in the IEP, there is no legal basis for adapted physical education service delivery and/or modifications in the regular physical education program. If a school district has high quality regular physical education instruction with small class sizes, no modifications may be needed. To benefit optimally from instruction, handicapped pupils need approximately the same pupil/teacher ratio in their physical education and classroom settings. The average ratio of number of handicapped students to special education teachers is 18:1, with 12:1 for emotionally disturbed students, 13:1 for mentally retarded students, 17:1 for learning disabled, and 21:1 for other health impaired. Often the class size in regular physical education is the one modification that should be specified. Grading and/or criteria for success is another modification often needed for handicapped students in regular classes.

The most common other modifications of regular physical education that should be written on the IEP are the following:

Changes in equipment and/or availability of special equipment such as wheelchairs

Changes in facilities (air conditioning for severe asthma during high pollen seasons; small rather than large gymnasium for hyperactive, easily distractible students)

Changes in pedagogy (teaching style, motivation techniques, amount of behavior management, task analysis)

Changes in mode of communication (largely gesture or demonstration for mentally retarded, sign language for deaf, verbal instructions for blind)

Changes in class requirements and/or modification of grading system

Another important request to be written into the IEP is instruction by a certified specialist in physical education who has had adapted physical education training rather than by the classroom teacher, coach, or nonspecialist who is utilized in many school districts.

In many instances, these modifications will not be written into IEPs unless parents are taught characteristics of good physical education and refuse to sign their child's IEP until such physical education is written into it. Research is needed to document the differences that such modifications as small class size, instruction by a specialist, and changes in teaching methods, equipment, and facilities make.

Procedural Safeguards

Procedural safeguards are an important part of the IEP process concept. These are due process procedures specified in PL 94–142 to protect the rights of handicapped children and their parents. Among these procedural safeguards are the requirements that parents

sign consent forms prior to assessment activities related to special education eligibility and that parents indicate their approval of the IEP by affixing their signatures.

Least Restrictive Environment Concepts

Whereas much of special education literature uses the term *mainstreaming* to denote a continuum of educational placements, PL 94–142 uses the term *least restrictive environment* to denote the cascade of educational placements that should be available within a school system. The most restrictive placement, as indicated in Figure 3.5, is physical education instruction in a segregated school setting, like residential or day schools, exclusively for mentally retarded, blind, or deaf students. Above this on the cascade (meaning "like a waterfall") are numerous alternative placements.

The least restrictive placement for each student must be determined individually, depending upon the setting in which the student is likely to learn the most—mentally, physically, and socially. Separate one-to-one instruction in a resource room may be the least restrictive environment for a severely disabled student, whereas partial integration in a regular class with a peer tutor may be the least restrictive for a less disabled classmate.

The least restrictive environment also varies in terms of curriculum content and teaching style. For a student in a wheelchair, the regular classroom during a soccer or football unit might be the most restrictive environment, whereas the same classroom during an archery or swimming unit might be least restrictive. For emotionally disturbed students who need externally imposed limits, a movement education setting might be more restrictive (i.e., permitting less learning) than a command-style follow-the-leader class.

In a school or school system large enough to employ two or more physical educators, the optimal organization to permit a continuum of placements seems to be use of one teacher (preferably an adapted physical education specialist) as a resource room specialist who serves PL 94–142 students as well as others with psychomotor problems and temporary disabilities such as broken limbs, sprains, strains, and menstrual pains. This teacher needs a separate gymnasium or movement area that is accessible to wheelchairs, has good lighting, and is insulated against outside sounds. Some

Figure 3.5 (A) Alternative physical education placements cascading upward from most to least restrictive modeled after Deno's (1970) Cascade System of Special Education Service.

(B) Types of partial integration and of assistance that should be prescribed on IEP for students in Level 4 of the Alternative Placements Cascade. Any of the types of assistance can be paired with any of the types of partial integration.

(A) Alternative Placements Cascade

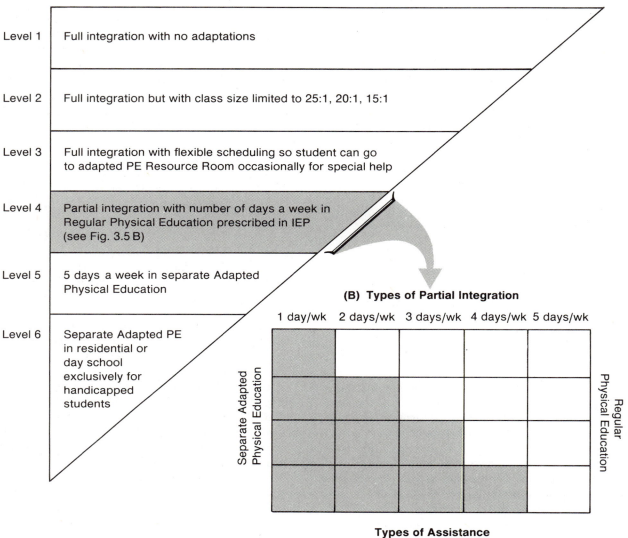

Level 1	Full integration with no adaptations
Level 2	Full integration but with class size limited to 25:1, 20:1, 15:1
Level 3	Full integration with flexible scheduling so student can go to adapted PE Resource Room occasionally for special help
Level 4	Partial integration with number of days a week in Regular Physical Education prescribed in IEP (see Fig. 3.5 B)
Level 5	5 days a week in separate Adapted Physical Education
Level 6	Separate Adapted PE in residential or day school exclusively for handicapped students

(B) Types of Partial Integration

Separate Adapted Physical Education

Regular Physical Education

1 day/wk   2 days/wk   3 days/wk   4 days/wk   5 days/wk

Types of Assistance

- With no assistance
- With occasional tutor
- With peer tutor
- With adult assistance

students are assigned to the resource room teacher on a regular basis at specified times. Blocks of time are left open, however, for the flexible scheduling of:

Students in the mainstream who are having difficulty with a particular skill and need special instruction
Students whose disability (i.e., wheelchair or blindness, for example) makes a particular instructional unit inappropriate
Students temporarily disabled
Teachers who wish assistance in adapting instruction for students
Peer and cross-age tutors who need training in helping handicapped students

Evaluation Procedures

PL 94–142 has also contributed to the improvement of evaluation (sometimes called assessment) procedures, particularly as they pertain to placement. Physical educators, because of their potential role in placement decision making, should know the legal bases for evaluation. The August 23, 1977, *Federal Register,* pages 42496–42497, states,

121a.532 **Evaluation procedures.**
State and local educational agencies shall ensure, at a minimum, that:

(a) Tests and other evaluation materials
    (1) Are provided and administered in the child's native language or other mode of communication, unless it is clearly not feasible to do so;
    (2) Have been validated for the specific purpose for which they are used; and
    (3) Are administered by trained personnel in conformance with the instructions provided by their producer;
(b) Tests and other evaluation materials include those tailored to assess specific areas of educational need and not merely those which are designed to provide a single general intelligence quotient;
(c) Tests are selected and administered so as best to ensure that when a test is administered to a child with impaired sensory, manual, or speaking skills, the test results accurately reflect the child's aptitude or achievement level or whatever other factors the test purports to measure, rather than reflecting the child's impaired sensory, manual, or speaking skills (except where those skills are the factors which the test purports to measure);
(d) No single procedure is used as the sole criterion for determining an appropriate educational program for a child; and
(e) The evaluation is made by a multidisciplinary team or group of persons, including at least one teacher or other specialist with knowledge in the area of suspected disability.

(f) The child is assessed in all areas related to the suspected disability, including, where appropriate, health, vision, hearing, social and emotional status, general intelligence, academic performance, communicative status, and motor abilities.

(20 U.S.C. 1412[5]0)

The United States Department of Education reports that parents lodge more official complaints in regard to placement than any other area. Many of these are related to the evaluation procedures used in decision making. Of particular concern to physical educators is the fact that so few tests in our field have been validated for the specific purpose of placement. The Bruininks-Oseretsky Test of Motor Proficiency, discussed later in this book (see Chapter 11), is one of the few that meets this criterion. Much research is needed in this area. Two pioneer studies that might serve as models are

Broadhead, G. (1982). A paradigm for physical education for handicapped children in the least restrictive environment. *The Physical Educator, 39,* 3–13.
Broadhead, G., & Church, G. (1984). Influence of test selection on physical education placement of mentally retarded children. *Adapted Physical Activity Quarterly, 1* (2), 112–117.

Age Range Covered by PL 94–142

PL 94–142 extended the age limits for free public education to encompass all handicapped persons, ages 3 to 21 years. This provides the rationale for physical educators mastering the multidisciplinary content underlying sensorimotor and play development in infancy and early childhood. Most handicapped 3-year-olds are developmentally delayed, often 2 or 3 years, and function very much like infants and toddlers. It also explains why physical educators should master the multidisciplinary content underlying leisure assessment, education, and counseling: they must be able to address the primary need of students in the 18-to-21-year range which is to learn how to generalize school physical education training into meaningful adult leisure.

Funding of Adapted Physical Education

Whether a school district initiates and maintains a high quality adapted physical education program is often dependent upon funding. It is, therefore, important that physical educators understand methods of public school funding and problems involved in the equalization of educational opportunity for all children.

The funding of public education is primarily the responsibility of local and state education agencies. Quality of education is, therefore, ultimately determined by voters, in terms of amount of school taxes they are willing to pay and decisions the state legislators they elect make in regard to allocation of school monies.

The cost of educating a handicapped child is about $1,000 more each year than that of educating the nonhandicapped. In recognition of this fact, PL 94–142 provides that federal grants be awarded to state education agencies (SEAs). These federal monies must be spent only for the *excess cost* of special education (including adapted physical education) over the average per pupil expenditure in regular education. These are called PL 94–142 flow-through monies because the SEA keeps about 25% of them and distributes the other 75% to local education agencies (LEAs). In 1984, these flow-through monies amounted to about $200 per child. The average excess cost of educating a handicapped child is about $1,000; thus the state and local governments still have to raise about $800 per child or reduce needed services. This helps explain why most educators believe in federal aid to education and vote for legislators who will support it. It reduces by about $200 per child the inequities in the funding of education among communities and states populated by poor, middle class, and rich citizens.

Adapted physical educators employed to serve handicapped students only (usually in separate settings) are often salaried by PL 94–142 flow-through monies. There are, however, many other ways of funding adapted physical educators. A philosophically sound approach is for regular education to contribute toward the salary of adapted physical educators the monies that would be spent on regular physical education if the student had not been placed in a separate setting. Then, special education monies (PL 94–142 and other funds) are applied only toward the excess cost.

Regardless of where the monies come from, if adapted physical education is written into the student's IEP, the school administration must find a way of providing the needed services. The law is clear that related service (physical and occupational therapy) cannot substitute for physical education instruction. The regular physical educator is responsible for teaching handicapped students if no adapted physical education specialist is available. This explains why so many regular physical educators are undertaking graduate work in adapted physical education; they might not wish to become specialists, but they do graduate work because they need additional knowledge to fulfill the expectations of their school systems.

Need for State Laws

PL 94–142 forms the legal basis for adapted physical education only for students declared handicapped by IEP eligibility procedures. Many, many other students have psychomotor problems serious enough to merit adapted physical education intervention. Federal law cannot be passed to improve the general education system for nonhandicapped students since education is not a power given to the United States government by the Constitution.

The only way to ensure high quality physical education, including adapted physical education when needed, for all students is through state legislation. Many states have or are working on legislation that parallels PL 94–142. Physical educators should work actively with state legislators to ensure that the physical education passages in PL 94–142 are included and expanded to include nonhandicapped students in state law.

Advocacy for Needed Legislation

This chapter has emphasized the importance of federal and state laws in shaping contemporary adapted physical education. These laws are not static because implementation depends on funding, which may change annually. Physical educators need to understand the difference between laws that *authorize* and those that *appropriate* monies. PL 94–142 authorized the expenditure of monies for handicapped students. New laws are needed year by year to actually appropriate the money for use.

Following is a list of strategies that physical educators can use in advocating for needed legislation:

1. Get to know your state and federal legislators. Let them know you vote for them specifically because they support legislation favorable to education and/or equal opportunity for handicapped persons.

2. Visit your legislator in his or her office in the Capitol. Get to know the legislator's staff by name and personality; usually, they are the ones responsible for compiling materials, reading and answering letters sent to the legislator, and keeping him or her informed.

3. Make frequent contacts with legislators. The best communication is face-to-face, but telephone calls, telegrams, and letters are crucial when bills are ready for a vote.

4. Do not mail form letters; make contents brief and personal. Be sure to mention the law by name and number and state specifically which passage you wish to retain or change.

5. Develop parent advocacy corps for physical education. Take different kinds of stationary to Special Olympics and other sports practices and ask parents who are waiting to jot letters to their legislators. Offer to speak at meetings of parent groups, inform them about PL 94–142, and ask them to visit, telephone, and write legislators specifically on behalf of physical education.

6. Become a member of parent and other advocacy groups for handicapped persons and encourage them to invite legislators to speak at their meetings. Volunteer to be program chairperson and you can make this happen for sure. Legislators, as well as candidates running for office, are particularly willing to speak during election years.

7. Become personal friends with handicapped persons and encourage them to advocate for physical education. A physical educator and a handicapped adult who believes in physical education make a powerful partnership in facilitating change.

8. When you write to a legislator, be sure to ask for an answer in which he or she states intent to support or not to support your request. When you speak to a legislator, do the same.

9. Invite legislators, with the approval of your administration, to visit your adapted physical education program and/or to be a dignitary in the opening or closing ceremonies of Special Olympics, Cerebral Palsy Sports, or other events.

10. Keep abreast of funding issues, especially which parties and which persons support federal and state funding favorable to education. Find out how your legislator votes on critical issues by reading newspapers or the *Congressional Record* or by telephoning his or her office. Let your legislator know when you approve as well as when you disapprove.

11. Get to know the state directors of physical education and special education and their staff, all of whom are part of the SEA, and encourage them to communicate with legislators.

12. Be sure local and state meetings of physical educators include legislative updates concerning action that may affect adapted physical education. Exhibit bulletin boards showing progress made in implementation of laws. Encourage officers of local and state physical education organizations, as well as members, to maintain close contact with their legislators.

Learning Activities

1. Plan a field trip to the local education agency (LEA) and request the director of special education to explain the implementation of PL 94–142 and the state plan in your own school district.

2. Obtain a copy of the state plan and review it carefully, noting the number of times that physical education is mentioned and which passages parallel those in PL 94–142.

3. Arrange a panel discussion on federal funding of education with particular emphasis on the pros and cons in relation to physical education for handicapped students.

4. Obtain permission to attend IEP meetings conducted in your school district and/or residential facilities for handicapped students.

5. Role play such situations as (a) IEP meeting with a physical educator present, (b) IEP meeting with no physical educator, (c) IEP meeting in which parents advocate strongly for physical education, and (d) other situations.

6. Implement at least three of the strategies listed in this chapter that physical educators can use in advocating for needed legislation.

7. In each learning activity and in class discussion, give evidence of having read several entries in the chapter bibliography.

References

Deno, E. (1970). Special education as developmental capital. *Exceptional Children, 37,* 229–237.

Federal Register, May 4, 1977, PL 93–112, the Rehabilitation Act of 1973, Section 504.

Federal Register, August 23, 1977, PL 94–142, the Education for All Handicapped Children Act.

Bibliography

Appenzeller, H. (1983). *The right to participate: The law and individuals with handicapping conditions in physical education and sports.* Charlottesville, VA: The Michie Co.

Bajan, J., & Susser, P. (1982). Getting on with the education of handicapped children: A policy of partnership. *Exceptional Children, 49* (3), 208–212.

Ballard, J., Ramirez, B., & Weintraub, F. (Eds.). (1982). *Special education in America: Its legal and governmental foundations.* Reston, VA: Council for Exceptional Children.

Budoff, M., Orenstein, A., & Abramson, J. (1981). Due process hearings: Appeals for appropriate public school programs. *Exceptional Children, 48* (2), 180–182.

Buscaglia, L., & Williams, E. (1979). *Human advocacy and PL 94–142.* Thorofare, NJ: Charles B. Slack.

Cowden, J., Wright, J., & Gant, S. (1984). Gary W., et al v. the State of Louisiana: Implications for adapted physical education, recreation, and leisure education. *Adapted Physical Activity Quarterly, 1* (2), 94–104.

Geddes, D. (1981). *Psychomotor individualized educational programs.* Boston: Allyn & Bacon.

Gilliam, J., & Coleman, M. (1981). Who influences IEP committee decisions? *Exceptional Children, 47* (8), 642–644.

Goldstein, S., & Turnbull, A. (1982). Strategies to increase parent participation in IEP conferences. *Exceptional Children, 48* (4), 360–361.

La Vor, M. (1976). Federal legislation for exceptional persons: A history. In F. Weintraub, A. Abeson, J. Ballard, & M. La Vor (Eds.), *Public policy and the education of exceptional children* (pp. 96–111). Reston, VA: Council for Exceptional Children.

Minner, G., Prater, G., & Beane, A. (1984). Provision of adapted physical education: A dilemma for special educators. *Adapted Physical Activity Quarterly, 1* (4), 282–286.

Morgan, D., & Rhode, G. (1983). Teachers' attitudes toward IEPs: A two year follow-up. *Exceptional Children, 50* (1), 64–67.

Peterson, P., & Rabe, B. (1983). The role of interest groups in the formulation of educational policy: Past practice and future trends. *Teachers College Record, 84* (3), 708–729.

Price, M., & Goodman, L. (1980). Individualized educational programs: A cost study. *Exceptional Children, 46* (6), 446–454.

Pugach, M. (1982). Regular classroom teacher involvement in the development and utilization of IEPs. *Exceptional Children, 48* (4), 371–374.

Pyfer, J. (1982). Criteria for placement in physical education experiences. *Exceptional Education Quarterly, 3* (1), 10–16.

Rainbolt, W. (1979). *Federal legislation, physical education, and handicapped people: Questions and answers.* Washington, DC: American Alliance for Health, Physical Education, and Recreation. (AAHPER/IRUC Reprint Services No. 771).

Scanlon, C., Arick, J., & Phelps, N. (1981). Participation in the development of the IEP: Parents' perspective. *Exceptional Children, 47* (5), 373–374.

Sherrill, C. (Ed.). (1986). *Adapted physical education leadership training.* Champaign, IL: Human Kinetics Publishers.

Stein, J. (1977). Individualized educational programs. *Practical Pointers, 1* (6), 8–9.

Stein, J. (1978). Physical education and sports as required by PL 94–142 and Section 504. *American Corrective Therapy Journal, 32,* 145–151.

Stein, J. (1979). The mission and the mandate: Physical education, the not-so-sleeping giant. *Education Unlimited, 1* (2), 10–11.

Wessel, J. (Ed.). (1977). *Planning individualized education programs in special education.* Northbrook, IL: Hubbard.

Wessel, J., & Kelly, L. (1985). *Individualizing instruction: Quality programs for all students.* Philadelphia: Lea & Febiger.

Ysseldyke, J., Algozzine, B., & Epps, S. (1983). A logical and empirical analysis of current practice in classifying students as handicapped. *Exceptional Children, 50* (2), 160–166.

4 Humanism and Adapted Physical Education

Figure 4.1 Warm, subjective, human encounters between physical educators and handicapped persons in a variety of settings are essential to teacher training. There must be quiet times to talk together, to listen, and to feel. *Left,* dance instruction in a leotard is a part of normalization; *top right,* risk recreation activities are as important for disabled persons as they are for the able-bodied; *bottom right,* teachers cheer a mentally retarded cerebral palsied athlete on to victory.

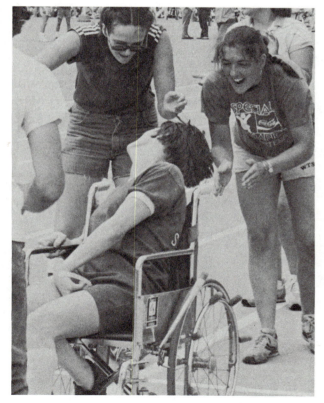

Chapter Objectives

After you have studied this chapter, you should be able to

1. Discuss humanistic philosophy and trace its evolution from the 1950s to the present.

2. Explain each of the following theories and state implications for physical education: (a) normal curve and individual differences, (b) self-actualization, (c) expectancy, (d) attribution, (e) normalization, (f) social learning, and (g) advocacy.

3. Discuss similarities and differences between education and therapy with particular emphasis on adapted physical education.

4. Differentiate between the medical model and the educational model and discuss how each continues to change.

5. Explain the following and cite anecdotes illustrating them from your personal experience: locus of control, Rosenthal effect, self-fulfilling prophecy, perceived competence, sports socialization, role models, semantics, labels.

6. State guidelines for interacting with handicapped students and discuss applications in the physical education setting.

7. Discuss the physical educator's role in working with the family of a handicapped student. Explain the concept of *significant others* and state how significant others' influence may affect the behavior of handicapped students.

8. Discuss problems confronting handicapped persons, with particular emphasis on stigmatization, stereotyping, and prejudice, and suggest solutions. Specifically, how can sports be used to ameliorate problems?

9. Name and describe outstanding disabled athletes who serve as models in sports, dance, aquatics, and/or rich leisure use. Identify factors that may have contributed to their success.

10. Describe your personal philosophy in regard to regular and adapted physical education and identify primary sources for your beliefs.

We deeply believe in and are committed to a philosophy of modern humanism; a way of looking at individuals . . . which supremely values the dignity and worth of all human beings.
—Rosalind Cassidy and Stratton F. Caldwell

Adapted physical education extends the humanistic qualities of prizing, caring, trusting, and respecting to all children and youth, with emphasis on those who are clumsy and/or have disabilities (see Figure 4.1). It honors and exalts all life in a new ethic that accepts diversity and refuses to distance one human being from another. Adapted physical education celebrates individual differences and emphasizes uniqueness.

Implementation of such a philosophy is harder than it seems. Adapted physical educators must be deeply committed persons, willing to stand up for their beliefs against tides of prejudice, ignorance, and stagnated tradition. Sociologically, the handicapped are considered to be a minority group and to possess more or less the same problems as other minorities. Adapted physical educators, therefore, need to learn as much as possible about interpersonal relations and group dynamics. Most important, they must be comfortable with

a continuous process of redefining their beliefs and evolving the philosophy that guides their actions. This philosophy must be flexible and ever growing.

Chapter 3 emphasizes the legal bases for adapted physical education. This chapter presents the humanistic bases. Whereas some school systems and teachers conduct adapted physical education programs because the law requires them to, most become involved with handicapped and clumsy students because of personal beliefs in equal opportunity and access. *Humanism,* broadly defined, encompasses strong belief in equity (which can be rooted either in law or personal values) and understanding of theories pertaining to normal curve and individual differences, self-actualization, expectancy, attribution, normalization, social learning, and advocacy. This chapter contains background information that will contribute to an understanding of humanism in assessment, placement, teaching, and coaching practices.

Humanistic Theory

Humanistic philosophy, as used in this text, has its roots in humanistic psychology, the body of knowledge that pertains to helping persons become fully human (i.e., to realize and develop their human potential). This movement began in the 1950s with the self-actualization theory of Abraham Maslow and the fully functioning self theory of Carl Rogers. These persons and their followers were rebels against the Freudian methods that prevailed in psychiatry as well as the sickness and disease theories that dominated medicine. The 1950s were full of change. This was the era when public schools began serving handicapped students and special education was evolving into a profession. School personnel were developing an educational model to guide service delivery to handicapped students that would soon replace the medical model in which physicians made placement and other decisions.

War veterans were convincing the public that they might be disabled but they were not sick. Observation of handicapped students in the public schools revealed that they, too, were disabled but not sick. Blacks, active in civil rights pursuits, gained access to integrated education in 1954. Everywhere attitudes were changing about the nature of human beings.

Maslow, Rogers, and followers posited that human nature is essentially good and that development (unless delayed, interrupted, or distorted) moves naturally toward a healthy, self-actualizing personality. They were among the first to focus on psychological and physical health rather than on pathology, sickness, and disability, as was then the practice. From their works we derive such guidelines as *It's ability that counts, not disability* (motto of the National Handicapped Sports and Recreation Association) and *Sports by ability, not disability* (motto of the National Association of Sports for Cerebral Palsy).

Humanistic theory is concerned primarily with quality of life. Therapy for the amelioration of defects is not enough. Handicapped persons need education to learn dance, sports, and aquatics skills that, hopefully, will lead to lifetime patterns of active leisure pursuits (see Figure 4.2). About the same time that Maslow and Rogers were making their initial impact, the World Health Organization of UNESCO changed the definition of health away from absence of disease or infirmity to a state of complete physical, emotional, and social well-being. Thus, the medical as well as the educational model, has changed drastically since the 1950s. The desired outcome of education and therapy is the same; only the methods of achieving complete physical, emotional, and social well-being differ.

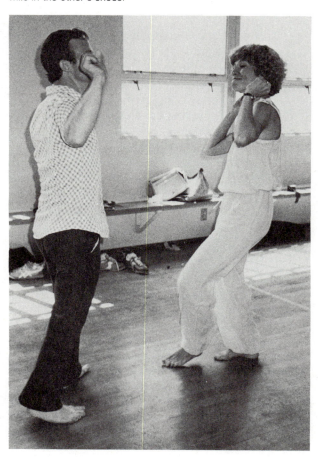

Figure 4.2 Dance, music, and rhythm facilitate getting acquainted and assist with values clarification. Humanism is learning to empathize, to think and feel like another—to walk a mile in the other's shoes.

Therapy uses treatment modalities, one of which is exercise. Typically, therapists do something to or for patients, and the patients' conditions improve.

Educational pedagogies vary widely from teacher-dominated behavior management to facilitation of self-direction and self-responsibility for learning and competence mastery. Humanistic teaching is that which is least restrictive to the individual (i.e., that which enables him or her to be and act most human). In humanism, *human* is conceptualized as a state that embodies the best qualities of personhood; it is not a synonym for *normal,* although some persons use the words interchangeably.

Humanistic theory emphasizes the worth and dignity of all persons and the importance of respecting and valuing individual differences. It encompasses understanding of normalcy, but extends beyond normal curve theory to stress understanding and acceptance of persons who, mathematically, are not normal. Central to humanistic theory, therefore, is knowledge about the normal curve.

Figure 4.3 Theoretical distribution of IQ scores based on normal curve with ten standard deviations to show mentally retarded, normal, and gifted classifications assigned on basis of Wechsler and Stanford Binet test scores.

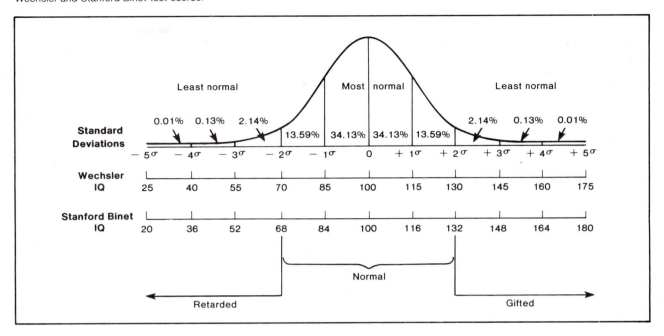

Normal Curve Theory

The word *normal* is used in many ways in our society. In education, however, the word is correctly used only in relation to the normal curve, a model derived by mathematicians that shows statistically how 100 or more persons will place when tested. This mathematical model was first developed for use in intelligence testing and classification of students for appropriate educational placement.

Figure 4.3 depicts the normal curve with five standard deviations below average (the 0 point) and five standard deviations above. *Standard deviation* is a statistical term for points on the baseline where scores are recorded. Note, for instance, the Wechsler IQ Test quotients in Figure 4.3 that begin with the lowest IQs on the left and continue across the baseline with progressively higher IQs. Standard deviations visually divide the curve into areas that are assigned percentages on the basis of how many persons, when tested, fall into each area.

Normal curve theory posits that most persons (specifically 68.26%) fall in the middle of the curve and very few fall at either end. This is true in motor performance and fitness as well as in intelligence testing. The 0 point on the curve is the average score, or mean; Figure 4.3 shows that both the Wechsler and Stanford

Binet average IQ is 100. In normal curve theory, *average* is synonymous with *normal*. Thus, students who score near the middle are considered most normal and those who score at either end are considered least normal.

Normal is, therefore, neither good or bad; it is neither a desirable or undesirable state. It is simply average. In this book, as in most educational texts, *normal* is used as a descriptor for average functioning, appearance, or performance. Whereas regular physical education is most concerned with average performance, adapted physical education focuses on below-average functioning (this may be delayed or abnormal functioning).

Whereas in regular education the normal curve is usually conceptualized as having only three standard deviation areas below and above the mean, it is depicted as having five in special education and adapted physical education. This is because handicapped students, as a group, exhibit more individual differences than the nonhandicapped. The official definition of mental retardation encompasses persons who have IQs below 70, or 68 on standardized tests. Find 70 on the baseline in Figure 4.3 and move your finger to the left to ascertain the standard deviation area in which persons with IQs of 55, 40, 25, or lower would fall.

Another characteristic of the normal curve is that the world population contains approximately the same percentage of persons above and below the mean regardless of the trait or ability being measured. Thus, for every gifted athlete who exists, there is an athlete who is retarded or deficient in motor ability. Most, however, are average. This is what normal means.

Persons average in one characteristic, such as intelligence, are not necessarily average in other abilities. Persons with handicapping conditions, therefore, may place in different normal curve areas for each of their abilities. This is called *intra-individual differences* (*intra* means "within"). In normal curve theory, intra-individual and intragroup differences are often contrasted with *intergroup* differences, meaning between or among several groups.

Humanistic theory requires that teachers assess students to determine present levels of performance and accept the students as worthy human beings regardless of where they fall on the normal curve. Central to humanistic theory also is communication with students to find out where they want to be, what they want to learn, and what goals they wish to undertake first. This is why the IEP meeting (as prescribed by PL 94–142) requires that the student, if appropriate, be present and participate in educational decision making. IEP goals are sometimes written in normal curve language (i.e., to score within plus or minus one standard deviation of the mean of a set of norms on a particular test).

Self-Actualization Theory

Self-actualization theory evolved out of Maslow's hierarchy of human needs, first formulated as a contribution to motivation theory. Maslow posits that each person has five basic needs, which are arranged in order from most to least potent, as follows:

1. Physiological needs (i.e., hunger, thirst, and exercise).
2. Safety needs.
3. Love and belongingness needs.
4. Esteem needs.
5. Self-actualization needs (i.e., the innate drive for becoming all that one has the potential to become).

To determine the personality characteristics that differentiate between self-actualizing and ordinary persons, Maslow made intensive clinical studies of Lincoln, Jefferson, Walt Whitman, Beethoven, William James, Franklin D. Roosevelt, Eleanor Roosevelt, Einstein, and Albert Schweitzer as well as several less well known persons selected by panels as "exceptionally healthy and successful, utilizing their full potential, becoming everything they were capable of."

Among the characteristics that Maslow (1968, 1970) identified as contributing to self-actualization are the following:

1. Positive self-acceptance.
2. Positive acceptance of others in general.
3. Capacity for intimate relationships with other persons.
4. Sense of identity with all humanity.
5. Spontaneity of thought, feeling, and action.
6. Thought processes that are independent, creative, ethical, and democratic.
7. Realistic orientation to life.

These are the personality characteristics that adapted physical educators strive to develop through movement experience. Although these characteristics may seem idealistic and elusive, a standardized test, called the Personal Orientation Inventory (POI), is available to assess values, attitudes, and behaviors relevant to Maslow's concept of the self-actualizing person. This test is well known among counseling and guidance personnel and is described in Buros' *Mental Measurements Yearbook*. Its primary source is

Shostrom, E. L. (1966). *Personal orientation inventory manual.* San Diego, CA: Educational and Industrial Testing Service.

Basic to self-actualization theory is the belief that nondisabled children and youth tend to develop these characteristics without concrete, specific help from teachers. In contrast, the self-actualization process may be delayed, diverted, or even reversed by serious illness or disabilities.

A handicapping condition typically means that there is less of the total self to be actualized (as is the case in blindness, deafness, amputation, mental retardation) and/or that the process of becoming entails conquering various problems (clumsiness, perceptual-motor deficits, health impairments) rather than the self evolving naturally. Adapted physical educators help students to feel good about themselves so that, in turn, the students will become intrinsically motivated to become all that they can be in the areas of fitness, motor skills, sports, dance, and aquatics (see Figure 4.4). Self-actualization in these areas does not occur unless an individual is fully motivated.

Figure 4.4 No variable is more important than the personality of the teacher in working with students who have poor self-concepts and low motivation.

Expectancy Theory

Expectancy theory embodies two basic assumptions: (a) persons will perform as they think others expect them to perform and (b) persons will expect of themselves what others expect of them. This theory, also called Pygmalion theory, takes its name from George Bernard Shaw's play *Pygmalion,* which was made into the famous Broadway play and later became the movie *My Fair Lady.* In *Pygmalion,* an English professor boasts that he can change an ignorant, unkempt young woman from the London slums into a beautiful, polished lady with perfect manners and flawless speech.

Professor Higgins succeeds in achieving this with Eliza Doolittle, changing her from a person who makes a living through selling flowers on the street to a much-sought-after woman of high society. He does not, however, change the way he perceives and treats her, as indicated in Eliza's comments to one of her suitors:

. . . You see, really and truly, apart from the things anyone can pick up (the dressing and the proper way of speaking, and so on), the difference between a lady and a flower girl is not how she behaves, but how she's treated. I shall always be a flower girl to Professor Higgins, because he always treats me as a flower girl, and always will; but I know I can be a lady to you, because you always treat me as a lady, and always will.

—George Bernard Shaw, *Pygmalion*

This passage illustrates clearly the importance of positive thinking, believing, and acting. Just as coaches convey to their athletes the expectation that they will win, so must physical educators demonstrate belief in clumsy and/or disabled persons, helping them to perceive themselves as winners. How perception of oneself influences motivation and success is called the *self-fulfilling prophecy;* persons unconsciously fulfill expectancies held by themselves and others.

Primary sources for expectancy theory are
Martinek, T., Crowe, P., & Rejeski, W. (1982). *Pygmalion in the gymnasium.* West Point, NY: Leisure Press.
Rosenthal, R., & Jacobsen, L. (1968). *Pygmalion in the classroom.* New York: Holt, Rinehart, & Winston.

Rosenthal and followers have conducted so much research on Pygmalion theory that it is also called *Rosenthal theory.* The *Rosenthal effect* (i.e., the outcome of expectancy theory) is said to be operative in classes in which teachers communicate positive expectations to students. In physical education, Thomas Martinek, professor at the University of North Carolina at Greensboro, has spearheaded most of the research: among the most relevant of his studies to adapted physical education is research on the effects of teacher expectation on self-concept.

Martinek and Johnson emphasize that physical educators typically expect more from and appear to care more about their good performers than others:

Within a physical education setting, high achievers have all the advantages—more attention, more praise, more acceptance, more intellectual stimulation, and better self-concept. It follows, then, that the physical education teacher should become sensitized to those behavior mechanisms that mediate expectation which perpetuates success and failure in children. (Martinek & Johnson, 1979, p. 69)

Physical attractiveness, as well as mental, physical, and social performance, has been shown to affect teacher and, later, employer expectations. Persons whose physical disability makes their appearance visibly different from that of peers often are exposed to low expectations and special treatment that sets them still further apart.

Attribution Theory

Attribution refers to the process of making inferences about past, present, or future behaviors and/or events. For instance, most persons *attribute* their success in sports to a combination of physical ability and hard work. Attribution theory is the body of knowledge underlying reasons and/or interpretations that persons give for their behaviors. It helps determine whether students tend to be externally or internally motivated and serves as a basis for decision making in regard to motivation and feedback techniques.

Locus of control is one aspect of attribution. It refers to perceptions concerning whether external or internal factors are controlling one's life. Persons with external locus of control believe that they are controlled by others in the environment, situational factors (such as architectural barriers or inaccessible areas), chance, and/or luck. Many severely handicapped or ill individuals, controlled by others throughout their life spans, become victims of *learned helplessness.* They cease perceiving themselves as competent and/or as able to change or control anything in their lives. In contrast, persons with internal locus of control believe that they control their own destiny; they perceive achievement as the outcome of hard work, sound decision making, and wise utilization of time.

Child development theory emphasizes that locus of control shifts from external to internal as students mature. The degree of this shift depends, however, on child rearing and classroom teaching practices and on such variables as health and disabilities that may prevent independent thought and action. Some persons remain more externally than internally controlled throughout life. This includes many normal persons as well as those with severe mental retardation or emotional disturbance.

Severely physically disabled persons with intact minds typically want to control their own lives just as do able-bodied persons. Humanistic teachers are careful not to do for such persons without first asking for permission or direction. When feeding a disabled person, for instance, it is important to let him or her indicate what he or she wants from the plate and in what order. Before assisting mobility-impaired persons, ask first if they want help and how help can best be given. The movie *Whose Life Is It Anyhow?* is an excellent resource for learning about locus of control.

Because of the tendency of parents and society to overprotect handicapped persons and deny them control of their own lives, it is particularly important in physical education to stress independence, personal control, and responsibility. Remember expectancy theory. Expect persons to assume control over the situational factors in their lives and gradually they will assume that control.

The development of perceived competency is extremely important to self-actualization. Only when persons believe they can cause change in themselves and their environment are they motivated to exert effort.

Normalization Theory

Normalization refers to making available to disabled persons living, learning, and working conditions as close as possible to the norms of able-bodied society. Normalization theory does not mean making disabled individuals normal, as it has sometimes been incorrectly conceptualized, but rather affording them access to the same environment and opportunities their able-bodied peers have. Success in sports competition, especially in events like the Boston Marathon, in which elite wheelchair athletes compete side-by-side with the nondisabled, is believed to be normalizing in the sense that it changes perceptions. Not only does it alter the way that able-bodied persons see the disabled, but it also changes perceptions of disabled persons themselves. Fred McBee, author of *The Continental Quest* and a wheelchair user, described how the 1978 Boston Marathon changed his life. He conveys his feelings as George Murray (Figure 4.5), a wheelchair athlete, finished first in this race—before any of the able-bodied runners:

For his friend, Fred McBee, that day would change his life. . . . He'd seen the gimps come from wheezing through the 40-yard dash in shaking, quaking, rattle-trap wheelchairs, to winning the greatest 26.2 mile race in the world. From a bunch of convalescing cripples out for a little recreation, they'd become muscled, highly fit gimps out for blood. (McBee, 1984a, p. 2)

[McBee earlier explains that only persons in wheelchairs can use such words as *gimps* and *cripples;* they are part of the "in-language" of the wheelchair athlete community, but are never appropriate for an outsider.]

Normalization theory was introduced into the United States from the Scandinavian countries in the late 1960s by Wolf Wolfensberger, who also began the citizen advocacy movement within the National Association for Retarded Citizens. Thus, normalization is often linked with such issues as deinstitutionalization of mentally retarded persons and community, school, and recreation integration. The primary source for normalization theory is *The Principle of Normalization in Human Service,* by Wolf Wolfensberger, published in 1972 by the National Institute on Mental Retardation (NIMR) in Ontario, Canada. The NIMR continues to be the major printer of materials on normalization. Among these materials is a new (1983) assessment instrument called PASSING, the acronym for *Program Analysis of Service System's Implementation of Normalization Goals.* This instrument permits the objective evaluation of services provided by school, recreation, or community programs in terms of normalization theory.

Although initially applied only to mental retardation issues, normalization theory is now widely used in relation to all disabilities in which persons are perceived as looking or behaving differently. Wolfensberger (1972) states that three principles underlie normalization theory:

1. Behavioral and appearance deviancy can be reduced by minimizing the degree to which disabled persons are treated differently from able-bodied persons.
2. Conversely, deviancy is enhanced by treating persons as if they were deviant.
3. To the degree that they are grouped together and segregated from the mainstream of society, individuals will be perceived as different from others and will tend to behave differently.

Social Learning Theory

Social learning theory posits that three groups of variables determine the learning of roles necessary for self-actualization. These include (a) *personal attributes,* which refers to characteristics of the individual; (b) *socializing agents,* which refers to significant others and/or reference groups who exert influence on the individual by teaching and modeling behaviors, beliefs, attitudes, interests, and values; and (c) *socializing situations,* which refers to settings and/or opportunities for learning.

Involvement in sports, as in other forms of social behavior, does not happen naturally. It is determined to a large extent by the social environment in which individuals are reared and subsequently interact as adults. Among the many social systems comprising this environment are the family, school, church, friends, peers, mass media, and sport organizations. The social roles that persons play, who they interact with, and how they interact are influenced by significant others and opportunity set within these systems; so also are their aspirations influenced, with respect to learning the

motor skills and social behaviors indigenous to various sports roles (i.e., team member, competitor, winner). *Socialization* is the term assigned to the process by which persons learn the ways of a given society or social group so that they can function within it.

Sports socialization is the interactional process by which persons acquire the necessary attitudes, values, skills, and knowledge to become athletes and to gain acceptance in sports groups. Youth sports is a dominant trend in American society. Almost every normal child, at one time or another, belongs to an after-school or summer softball, soccer, or football team. Many compete, either in school or out, in swimming, track, gymnastics, and tennis. Essential, therefore, to normalization of handicapped children is making available sports opportunities that are as close as possible to the norms of able-bodied society.

Recent research by Sherrill and colleagues reveals that handicapped persons are still not being given access to equal opportunities for learning and participation in sports in spite of the mandates of PL 94–142. The average ages that top national blind and cerebral palsied athletes had first been exposed to sports instruction were 13 and 18 years, respectively. The average ages for first sports competition were, of course, older. In contrast, most normal children begin sports instruction and competition between the ages of 6 and 10 years, depending on the nature of the sport. Authorities recommend that competition in individual sports like swimming and track begin at about age 6 and that competition in team sports begin at about age 8.

Whereas most normal children are introduced to sports by their parents and siblings, handicapped children are typically given their first sports exposure in school physical education and/or in sports organizations for disabled persons. This fact heightens the responsibility of both regular and adapted physical education teachers to find sports that their students can learn. Both Special Olympics and the National Association of Sports for Cerebral Palsy (NASCP) offer competition in events for severely and profoundly handicapped persons. NASCP, for instance, provides track competition in motorized chairs for persons too disabled to do anything but manipulate a chair through hand movement or breath control.

Role Models

Central to social learning theory is the availability of role models. Whereas, in the past an athlete with a history of disability (like track star Wilma Rudolph, football kicker Tom Dempsey, and baseball player Monte Stratton) received attention enough in the media to be

used as a role model, now numerous elite disabled athletes exist. This book is filled with photos of these persons and, when possible, names are given so that prospective teachers can begin to learn names and background information on disabled athletes. Ablebodied as well as disabled children should be exposed to these great athletes.

Physical education teachers can learn much from becoming personally acquainted with disabled athletes, attending their training sessions and competitive meets, and talking to them and/or their coaches about techniques that work best in teaching and refining sports skills. The pedagogy for teaching physical education to handicapped students remains largely unwritten. Research is badly needed in this area. The best printed sources of information are the official rules manuals of the various sports organizations for disabled athletes and the journals *Sports 'N Spokes* and *Palaestra*.

Following are some vignettes of elite disabled athletes who have served as role models and sources of information to this author. The term *elite* is used in disabled sports, like in able-bodied sports, to denote persons who have achieved success in national and international competition.

James Mastro (Figure 4.6)

Jim, totally blind since about age 18, has recently completed his doctoral degree in adapted physical education at the Texas Woman's University. He is married and has two children. Jim was born with one eye sightless. While fencing with curtain rods in late childhood, he injured the other eye, which, in spite of countless surgeries, gradually became useless.

The former president of the American Beep Baseball Association and an avid goal ball player (see Chapter 25), Jim is best known for international successes in wrestling, shot put, and discus. In 1976, he was an alternate member of the United States Olympic Wrestling Team. He probably would have competed on the first team except that his arm was broken during the last qualifying bout.

During the 1984 International Games for the Disabled (IGD), Jim won a gold medal in wrestling, a gold in shotput for a throw of 12.21 meters, and a silver in discus for a throw of 31.42 meters. Academically, Jim's special interest is sports psychology and socialization. He holds teacher certification in social science and special education. He is the first totally blind (Class B1) person in the United States to earn a doctoral degree in physical education.

Charles Buell (Figure 4.7)

Jim's model and inspiration, Dr. Charles Buell (who is legally [Class B3] rather than totally blind), earned his doctorate in educational psychology from the University of California in Berkeley in 1950. At that time, it was unheard of for blind persons to major in physical education.

Dr. Buell served as the original resource in writing the chapter on blind students in this textbook. Now, over 70 years of age, he continues to train daily and to compete in the annual meet of the United States Association for Blind Athletes. He has received the American Alliance for Health, Physical Education, Recreation, and Dance Honor Award and countless other honors. Like Jim Mastro, he is married to a sighted woman. Dr. Buell's biography served as the topic of the doctoral dissertation by Patricia Whitley (1980); the dissertation can be ordered through university microfilms.

Harry Cordellos (Figure 4.7)

Harry, born with glaucoma and a heart murmur, was partially sighted throughout childhood but so overprotected by parents and teachers that he never engaged in vigorous play. In spite of 14 operations, he was totally blind by age 20. Fortunately, he outgrew his heart problems.

Figure 4.7 *Top*, from left to right, Charles Buell and Harry Cordellos; *top right*, Harry Cordellos performing on one ski; *bottom right*, Janet Rowley throwing discus in the snow.

Today, Harry is best known as a marathoner but he also water skis and competes in USABA swimming and track. His biography, *Breaking Through*, tells how he was finally introduced to sports at age 20 and describes the meaning sport has brought to his life. Harry has run over 100 marathons; he does this with a sighted partner. His best time in the Boston Marathon is 2 hours, 57 minutes, 42 seconds. Harry has run 50 miles in less than 8 hours and has competed in the Iron Man Triathlon in Hawaii (swimming 2.4 miles, biking 112 miles, and running 26.2 miles).

In regard to his introduction to sports via water skiing, Harry says,

He [the instructor] explained a little, but only a little, about water skiing. Then he put the skis and a life jacket on me. I was scared out of my mind, because I didn't know how to swim. But the instructor explained that the jacket would hold me up and that he would be watching every second. If I got into trouble, he would jump in the water right away to help me. He was emphasizing safety and his words helped, but I was still pretty scared.

He handed me the top handle and told me that when I was ready, to yell "hit it." I did what he said and what happened in the next five minutes changed my life forever.

Janet Rowley (Figure 4.7)

Janet Rowley, a blind vocational rehabilitation counselor, holds the world record (4 feet, 6.5 inches), in the high jump, a skill she learned at age 12. In the B2 classification, she can see only shadows and silhouettes. She cannot see the bar as she makes her approach, although she can see the landing pad. In this regard, Janet

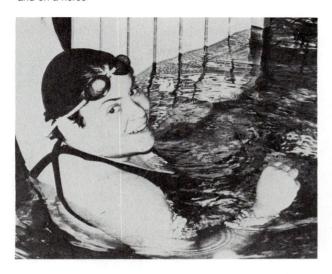 

states, "A lot of mental imagery is involved. In stationary sports, like the shot put, it is basically one motion. In the jump, you have to imagine in your mind what to do." In the 1984 International Games for the Disabled, Janet set a world record of 29.95 meters in the discus and placed third in javelin. She also was a member of the goal ball team.

Wendy Shugol (Figure 4.8)

Wendy, a Class 3 cerebral palsied athlete, recently completed a master's degree in adapted physical education at George Washington University. She teaches special education to orthopedically impaired students and coaches swimming for both able-bodied and disabled athletes in her school district.

Wendy competes internationally in both swimming and horseback riding. As a Class 3 athlete, she competes in 50-meter freestyle and 25-meter back stroke. Like able-bodied athletes, Wendy works out all year long. She owns her own horse and rides frequently.

Wendy's disability is worsened by severe diabetes and associated weight problems. She can take a few steps in her long-leg braces with Lofstrand crutches, but independent walking is no longer functional for her. She uses a wheelchair for daily living activities and is fiercely independent. Naturally, she drives and keeps up her apartment with no outside help. Concerning horseback riding she states,

For one thing, it gives me a tremendous psychological lift, because it is nearly the only sport I can participate in where I am absolutely free. I have four good legs under me and I can keep up with any able-bodied person who happens to be riding with me. On the ground, I'm always lagging behind and asking people to wait up for me. But on a horse, I can go just as fast as any able-bodied person or even pull ahead of them. I might even be a better rider than they are and be able to go faster than they can.

Nancy Anderson (Figure 4.9)

Nancy, a Class 2 cerebral palsied athlete, is the top swimmer in her class in the world. With a 2 classification, she could use a flotation device for competitive swimming, but she manages without one. To the casual observer, she looks like she is drowning, but her long arms generate the speed to complete the 25-meter sprints used in Class 2 competition. Nancy also competes in track and field events and a team game specifically for Class 1 and 2 athletes (bocce) that entails throwing balls at a target ball.

Figure 4.9 Nancy Anderson, a professional writer, receives last minute tips from Coach Marybeth Jones, puts on a nose clip, and mentally prepares to win.

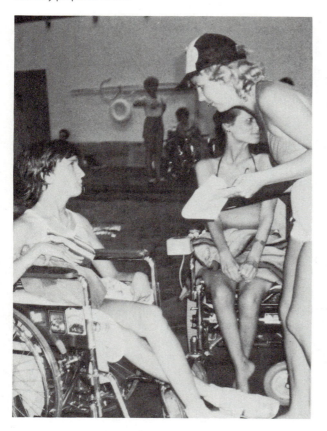

Figure 4.10 On the right, Sharon Rahn Hedrick, winner of the 800 meter wheelchair demonstration at the 1984 Olympic Games.

Figure 4.11 Peter Axelson, engineer and wheelchair user, in the sports he especially enjoys. *Left,* Peter practices a start in the sled called ARROYA, which he designed; *top right,* Peter in flight in the Pterodactyl; *bottom right,* Peter on the hand-bike, cycling with a friend.

Nancy holds a bachelor's degree from Michigan State University and is a professional writer. She owns her own word processer and lives independently in an apartment within a group home complex. Nancy uses a wheelchair for daily living activities; she can take a step or two, with assistance, but does not use crutches. Like other elite athletes, Nancy trains year round.

Sharon Rahn Hedrick (Figure 4.10)

Sharon, who became spinal cord injured as the result of a shooting accident at age 9, won the gold for the women at the 800-meter wheelchair race demonstration at the Los Angeles Olympics in 1984. This was the first time that the Olympics had ever included a wheelchair event. An athlete from Belgium won the comparable 1500-meter event for males (McBee, 1984b).

Sharon, a Class IV NWAA athlete, completed a bachelor's degree in dietetics at the University of Illinois, where she met her husband, also a wheelchair athlete. There, she became known internationally as a wheelchair basketball star. When, in 1977, wheelchair users were permitted for the first time to run the Boston Marathon, Sharon was the only woman to enter. She finished fifth among the wheelchair users, about in the middle of the able-bodied runners. Sharon's life story is told in the September/October 1979 issue of *Sports 'N Spokes* (Geraci, 1979). Concerning the influence of sports, Sharon states,

Without sports I wouldn't be here. I wouldn't have traveled. I wouldn't be the same person. Sports helped me believe there were fewer limitations on things I could do. For me, that means a heck of a lot.

Peter Axelson (Figure 4.11)

Peter, who became spinal cord injured as the result of a climbing accident while a cadet at West Point, dominates the sit-skiing events in winter sports. A Class III/IV athlete, he was first-place winner of the slalom and downhill sit-skiing events at the 1984 National Handicapped Ski Championships conducted by the National Handicapped Sports and Recreation Association.

Peter completed a master's degree in mechanical engineering/design from Stanford University in California and now is president of his own company, Beneficial Designs, Incorporated, a manufacturing and consulting firm that specializes in the design of recreational systems and devices for persons with disabilities. Peter is the designer and creator of the ARROYA, one of the several sit-skis on the market, and has contributed to improved design for the hand-bike and an aircraft called Pterodactyl for wheelchair users; he has also authored several articles for *Sports 'N Spokes*. Peter's life story is told in the September/October 1983 issue of *Sports 'N Spokes* (Taylor, 1983).

In spite of his success in winter sports, Peter's main interest is in integrated recreation (Axelson, 1985). He emphasizes that just because you are in a wheelchair is no reason for your recreation to be centered around wheelchair events. He likes to engage in leisure activities with a wide variety of friends. Cycling, made possible by a hand-bike, is one of Peter's favorite pastimes.

Implications for Teaching

Today, role models can be found within each of the sports organizations for disabled persons as well as in recreation and other areas of life. Geri Jewell, a comedian who has cerebral palsy, is achieving considerable success as a television star; her autobiography, entitled *Geri*, was published in 1984. The governor of Nebraska, Robert Kerrey, has an artificial leg. Forty-one of America's Olympic medalists at the 1984 Los Angeles Games, representing numerous vocations, were on asthma medications or management programs. It is important that prospective teachers become sensitized to the abilities of handicapped persons and begin collecting illustrative materials for sharing with their students.

Books, plays, movies, and videotapes are viable avenues for learning about disabilities. Many new sources are released each year. Materials that are classics should be ready by everyone interested in handicapped persons.

Classics on Disabled Persons

Books, some autobiographical and some fiction, that this author reads over and over again and assigns to her students are the following:

Axline, V. (1964). *Dibs: In search of self*. New York: Ballantine Books. About play therapy and an emotionally disturbed child.

Greenberg, J. (1970). *In this sign*. New York: Holt, Rinehart, & Winston. About a deaf couple, their children, and grandchildren.

Greenfield, J. (1970). *A child called Noah*. New York: Warner Books, Inc. About an autistic child.

Gunter, J. (1949). *Death be not proud*. New York: Harper & Row. About a teenager dying of a brain tumor.

Killilea, M. (1952). *Karen*. Englewood Cliffs, NJ: Prentice-Hall. About a severely handicapped child with cerebral palsy.

Montagu, A. (1971). *The elephant man*. New York: Ballantine Books. About a person with severe, disfiguring handicaps.

Valens, E. (1975). *The other side of the mountain*. New York: Warner Books, Inc. About a ski champion who becomes spinal cord injured.

Many of these books have been made into movies and are available on videotapes that individuals and classes can watch and discuss. Hundreds of similar sources exist; this list represents the favorites of only one person, books she feels have contributed to the development of humanistic philosophy.

Collections by Disabled Persons

Additional excellent sources for learning about humanism in relation to disabled persons are the following:

Eisenberg, M., Griggin, C., & Duval, R. (Eds.). (1982). *Disabled people as second-class citizens*. New York: Springer Publishing Co.

Goffman, E. (1963). *Stigma: Notes on the management of spoiled identity*. Englewood Cliffs, NJ: Prentice-Hall.

Hunt, P. (Ed.). (1966). *Stigma: The experience of disability*. London: Chapman.

Jones, R. (Ed.). (1983). *Reflections on growing up disabled*. Reston, VA: Council for Exceptional Children.

Orlansky, M., & Heward, W. (1981). *Voices: Interviews with handicapped persons*. Columbia, OH: Charles E. Merrill.

Zola, I. (Ed.). (1982). *Ordinary lives*. Cambridge, MA: Apple-wood Books, Inc.

Two especially excellent magazines include writing primarily by disabled persons:

Sports 'N Spokes. A magazine covering wheelchair sports and recreation primarily for those with spinal cord injury, polio, spina bifida, and some congenital defects. Published bimonthly at 5201 North 19th Avenue, Suite 111, Phoenix, AZ 85015.

Disabled USA. A magazine covering all aspects of life and all disabilities. Published periodically by the President's Committee on Employment of the Handicapped, Washington, DC 20210.

Keeping abreast of sources about and/or by disabled persons helps teachers become involved in advocacy. Through advocacy activities, teachers learn skills for changing other persons' opinions, beliefs, and attitudes about handicapped individuals. This is a large part of the adapted physical educator's job.

Advocacy Theory

Broadly defined, *advocacy* is action aimed at promoting, maintaining, or defending a cause. Such action is based on a set of beliefs—i.e., one's philosophy. The two *causes* toward which adapted physical educators direct most of their professional energies are physical education and handicapped individuals.

Advocacy for One's Profession

Not only are physical educators advocates for their own discipline, they are committed to shaping other persons into advocates for physical education. In some instances this commitment involves attempting to change attitudes. In others it entails supporting and reinforcing persons who share similar beliefs. Advocacy for a discipline involves persons in activities that will strengthen it—for instance, public relations, legislation, and research. The best public relations is superb teaching—i.e., an ongoing, live demonstration that physical education can improve quality of living. Other public relations activities include speeches, slide and film presentations, and bulletin board displays. Involvement in legislation begins with careful analysis of candidates for office to determine their attitudes toward both physical education and handicapped persons. It also demands active involvement in politics wherever education and civil rights are involved. Research is advocacy when the problem of a term paper, thesis, or dissertation is to determine the effectiveness of a physical education program in changing a certain behavior. Advocacy for physical education is evidenced also by joining organizations like AAHPERD and working with others toward the common goal of strengthening the profession.

Advocacy for Handicapped Persons

Advocacy for handicapped persons involves functioning on a one-to-one or small-group basis in any of a number of roles: friend, guide, counselor, trustee, foster or adoptive parent, or guardian (see Figure 4.12).

Figure 4.12 Advocacy for handicapped persons involves friendship, taking time to enjoy recreation together, and caring enough to occasionally adapt one's own ability and pace to a slower game.

Such advocacy can be *informal*, like simply becoming friends with handicapped persons on campus or in the community, or *formal*, as part of the *citizen advocacy movement*, which began in the 1970s. In the latter case, the relationship between the interested volunteer and the handicapped person is set up by a *citizen advocacy office*, generally run by a community agency like the Association for Retarded Citizens (ARC).

Wolfensberger has emphasized that an important part of the advocacy mission is implementation of the handicapped person's rights.

Advocates see to it that protégés receive the services to which they are entitled and are accorded the privileges of their citizenship. Pursuit of a protégé's citizenship rights may include such a symbolic act as seeing to it that he can cast his ballot at the polls. Advocate action may necessitate confrontation with agencies and perhaps even legal action. (Wolfensberger, 1972, p. 221)

Figure 4.13 Persons who work with the handicapped must be secure in giving and receiving love. Because of their deficits in language expression, handicapped persons often rely on touch and physical closeness to communicate feelings.

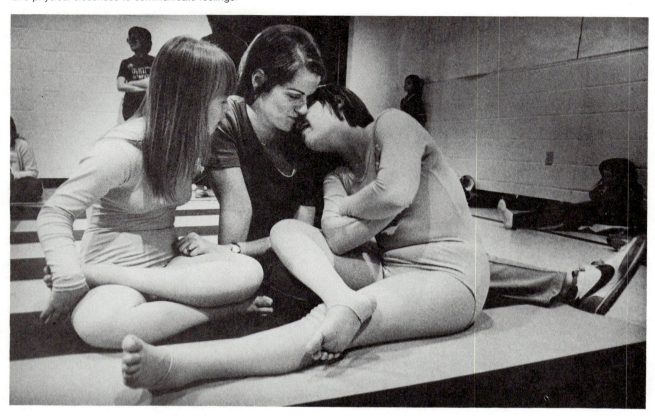

Physical educators are particularly interested in the implementation of handicapped persons' rights to physical education instruction and to use of community recreation resources. Concern in these areas leads to fighting architectural, attitudinal, and aspirational barriers that deny handicapped persons their rights.

Getting Acquainted and Clarifying Beliefs

The best way to learn about handicapped persons, and, thus, to prepare to teach adapted physical education, is to become personally acquainted and closely associated with handicapped persons. As meaningful relationships develop, individuals become increasingly able to interact with one another as *whole persons* rather than as people with problems or disabilities. Through such interactions, physical educators clarify their beliefs concerning handicapped persons and refine their philosophy with regard to advocacy and teaching and/or service delivery. Reference to the following "Guidelines for Interacting with Handicapped Persons" may be helpful in the early stages of getting acquainted.

Guidelines for Interacting with Handicapped Persons
1. Remember that each person who is disabled is different, and no matter what label is attached for the convenience of others, is still a totally "unique" person.
2. Remember that the persons with disabilities are *persons* first and disabled individuals secondly. These persons have the same right to self-actualization as any others—at their own rate, in their own way, and by means of their own tools.
3. Remember that the disabled have the same needs that you have, to love and be loved, to learn, to share, to grow and to experience, in the same world you live in. They have no separate world. There is only *one* world (see Figure 4.13).

4. Remember that the disabled have the same right as you to fall, to fail, to suffer, to decry, to cry, to curse, to despair. To protect them from these experiences is to keep them from life.

5. Remember that only those who are disabled can show or tell you *what is possible for them.* We who love them must be attentive, attuned observers.

6. Remember that the disabled must do for themselves. We can supply the alternative, the possibilities, the necessary tools—but only they can put these things into action. We can only stand fast, be present to reinforce, encourage, hope and help, when we can.

7. Remember that persons with disabilities, no matter how disabled, have a limitless potential for becoming—not what *we* desire them to become, but what is within *them* to become.

8. Remember that all persons with disabilities have a right to honesty about themselves, about you, and about their condition. To be dishonest with them is the most terrible disservice one can perform. Honesty forms the only solid base upon which all growth can take place. And this above all—remember that the disabled need the best *you* possible. In order for them to be themselves, growing, free, learning, changing, developing, experiencing persons—*you* must be all of these things. You can only teach what you are. If you are growing, free to learn, change, develop and experience, you will allow *them* to be.
(Buscaglia, 1975, pp. 19–20)

Problems Confronting Disabled Persons

As physical educators get acquainted with persons who have disabilities, it is increasingly obvious that the problems of disabled persons are the same as those experienced by minority groups in general: stigmatization, stereotyping, and prejudice. Problems of equal opportunity, particularly in regard to access of equipment/facilities, knowledge and skills, friends with whom to train/work out, and availability of coaches, are common to most disabled athletes. Almost all see sports as a means of affirming their competence, thereby seeking to focus attention on their abilities rather than their disabilities.

Stigmatization

Stigmatization refers to special treatment directed toward persons perceived as different. First conceptualized by Goffman (1963), stigma theory defines stigma as an undesired differentness, an attribute that is perceived as discrediting, a failing, a shortcoming, or a handicap. Underlying stigma theory is fear of individuals who are different from oneself, the equating of differentness with inferiority and/or danger, and the belief that persons with stigmata are not quite human and, thus, need not be accorded the same acceptance, respect, and regard that we give others. Most athletes with disabilities, at one time or another, have experienced stigmatization. Many perceive sports as a way of fighting this prejudice and gaining increased acceptance. Illustrative of their beliefs concerning the values of sport in this regard are the following:

A lot of people feel sorry when they see a disabled person. But when they see what a disabled person can do in sports, it helps them understand what he [she] can do in everyday life—things like crossing a street, entering a store, doing a job. I mean, I might not get a job I'm fully qualified for simply because an employer sees me with my crutches. People are MAKING us disabled just by not giving us a chance to extend our abilities. This is our chance to extend our abilities. This is our chance to show what we can do. —Dean Houle, cerebral palsied weightlifter

. . . Part of the motivation for the 1984 International Games for the Disabled is to help bridge the gap of prejudice and ignorance that surrounds the disabled. It [sports] isn't going to be one panacea, but it demonstrates the possibilities and involvement of handicapped people in various factions of life. . . . Each athlete will do the best he/she can. It will be a symbol of ability instead of disability. —Cynthia Good, cerebral palsied horseback rider, Director of Consumer Affairs in the national office of United Cerebral Palsy Associations, Inc.

Stereotyping

Stereotyping refers to conceptualizing and/or treating persons the same without regard for their individuality. Stereotypes are assigned primarily to persons and groups about whom little is known; stereotypes may be good or bad; the problem is that they depersonalize. Generally, stereotypes are learned from authority figures (parents, journalists, textbook writers) and tend to be more rigid than beliefs developed on one's own. The broader the categories used in stereotyping, the less likely they are to be accurate.

Persons with disabilities unanimously indicate the desire to be perceived and treated as individuals rather than globally conceptualized as wheelchair users or paraplegics or blind persons. Yet, much of the public, as well as some professionals, still often perceive all disabled persons to be the same. Many textbooks still refer to CPs rather than to Classes 1–8, to blind rather than Classes B1, B2, and B3, and to spinally paralyzed rather than Classes IA, IB, IC, II, III, IV, V. This book, when appropriate, refers to individuals by their specific sports classifications and/or names. Whereas in the past wheelchair sports evoked mental imagery of spinally paralyzed and amputee athletes, this stereotype is no longer accurate. Approximately half of the cerebral palsied athletes in the United States use wheelchairs, as do many other competitors. In cerebral palsy sports, Class 1, 2, and 6 athletes and Class 3, 4, and 5 athletes are designated as quadriplegic and paraplegic, respectively. The terms *paras* and *quads* no longer can be applied to one specific disability.

Prejudice

Persons with disabilities wish to be judged on self-actualization (i.e., optimal development of sports ability through long, hard training) rather than physical appearance and/or aesthetics of movement. Both stigmatization and stereotyping, however, often lead to discrimination. Research shows that a hierarchy of stigmatized disabilities exists in the minds of both able-bodied and disabled persons. Sensory disabilities are the least stigmatized, then physical handicaps that impair mobility and/or physical attractiveness, and last, mental conditions that affect rationality, self-control, and responsibility.

Persons with less stigmatized disabilities are sometimes prejudiced against individuals who are more stigmatized. Thus, some sensory impaired and physically disabled athletes express considerable prejudice toward Special Olympians. They feel that mentally handicapped persons cannot be athletes in the same sense that physically or sensory impaired individuals can be; moreover, they strongly oppose their Games being held at the same time and place as Special Olympics. Their reasons, of course, are complex. Many, however, are reacting to deep hurts caused by persons mistakenly thinking they are mentally retarded just because they have other disabilities.

The generalization of mental retardation stereotypes and prejudice to other disabilities by the general public is called the *spread phenomenon.* Physical educators should work against the spread phenomenon by teaching parents and children about individual differences within and among disabilities. They should also emphasize that Special Olympics is only for mentally retarded persons. Separate sports organizations exist

for other disabilities. When possible, school systems should integrate sports events for handicapped children into the meets and tournaments of able-bodied children. Except for segregated competition for mentally retarded athletes only, teachers should avoid use of the word *special* in relating to disabled persons.

Labels: The Price of Special Services

An important issue in values clarification is labeling. Ideally, a person should not be assigned such labels as "handicapped," "disabled," "clumsy," or "exceptional." In personal/social relationships, labels are not used.

In the professional setting, however, certain adjectives are used to denote eligibility for special services that, in turn, depend upon the allocation of special monies. These adjectives should be considered objective descriptors of conditions rather than labels.

In this book the terms *handicapped, disabled, impaired, special,* and *exceptional* are used interchangeably and simply connote individual differences that make persons eligible, under law or educational policy, for special education and/or adapted physical education services. The descriptor *handicapped* is used with greater frequency than the others for school-aged children because of its widespread acceptance in legislative and administrative circles. Adults, especially athletes, typically prefer to be called *disabled* rather than handicapped.

Handicap: A Word with Many Meanings

Semanticists point out that words and the way they are used play a large part in interpersonal relations. Words can separate persons or bring them together. This textbook assumes that all human beings have *handicaps* that they seek to *overcome or accept.* Within this semantic framework, many physical and mental attributes can be perceived as handicaps depending upon one's needs, interests, goals, and aspirations. If one aspires to be outstanding in any area of endeavor, possessing only average abilities is a handicap. Short stature, if it prevents one from making the varsity basketball team, may be a handicap. Asthma and other respiratory problems may be a handicap if one desires to socialize but cannot breathe when friends smoke. Finger dexterity becomes a handicap if the time required to type school assignments is so great that it eliminates recreation. Clumsiness, in physical education, is a handicapping condition.

Thus, a handicap is anything that interferes with or prevents achievement of one's goals. Particularly significant to physical educators are psychomotor problems that interfere with social and/or self-acceptance. Adapted physical educators striving toward self-actualization for themselves and others may find these words to be a good philosophy:

God grant me the *serenity* to accept the things I cannot change, the *courage* to change the things I can, and the *wisdom* to know the difference.

—Reinhold Niebuhr

Families and Significant Others

In the ecological approach to service delivery, adapted physical educators work not only with handicapped students but also with parents, siblings, and significant others (peers, teachers, and friends). The only way to teach the whole child is to understand the total social environment in which the child lives. Such desired social outcomes of physical education as self-worth, acceptance by others, and rich, full leisure depend more upon family and neighborhood interactions than on school training. Thus, the teaching-learning process must be a partnership between school and family.

Robinson and Robinson, in an excellent review of the interrelationships between the family and the retarded child, stated,

Thus, the relationship between a retarded child and his family is potentially more complex and ambivalent than the ordinary one, and more intense and prolonged. The parents of most retarded children need at least occasional help in dealing with the family situation, in recognizing and accepting their child's handicaps, and in handling successive day-to-day problems of living both with the retarded child and his normal brothers and sisters. (Robinson & Robinson, 1976, p. 413)

This statement can, of course, be extended to the effects of handicapping conditions other than retardation on a family. Adapted physical educators of the 1980s are spending an increasing amount of time with families, sometimes engaging in formal parent training and other times simply interacting as friends and advocates.

PL 94–142 requires that parents be involved in the IEP process. Parents can, therefore, be powerful forces in assuring that quality physical education is built into the IEP. To do so, however, many parents must be taught the values of physical education and be helped to understand their role as advocates.

Physical educators can help parents become advocates for quality psychomotor training in the following ways: (a) invite them to observe and/or participate in physical education classes, Special Olympics, and other related extraclass activities; (b) show them films and slides of excellent programs; (c) give presentations at meetings of parent-professional organizations like Parent-Teachers Assocation, Association for Retarded Citizens, and Association for Children and Adults with Learning Disabilities; (d) become active members of parent-professional organizations and work side by side with parents in areas of concern other than physical education; (e) become friends who are genuinely interested in them as whole persons rather than just as parents of students with problems. The physical educator must remember that parents have many needs, interests, and priorities, and the more of these the physical educator shares, the more significant will be the relationship.

Working for change becomes a reciprocal process. Physical educators help parents in broad, diverse areas like housing, employment, and civil rights. In return, parents act as advocates for quality physical education. Carl Rogers, the well-known psychotherapist, emphasizes friendship—i.e., a caring, trusting relationship—as an important ingredient of teaching. He states, "In my judgment the *warm, subjective, human encounter* of two persons is more effective in facilitating change than the most precise art or technique growing out of learning theory or operant conditioning" (cited in Buscaglia, 1975, p. 287). Warm, subjective, human encounters between physical educators and parents will lead to quality physical education for handicapped children and youth.

Adapted physical education courses can be enriched by inviting parents, siblings, and handicapped persons to speak and/or participate in discussions about their needs, interests, and concerns. Books like *The Disabled and Their Parents* by Leo Buscaglia offer new insights into service delivery. Case studies, biographies, and autobiographies about handicapped persons also enable physical educators to better understand the persons they teach.

Learning Activities

1. Conduct a class debate (or role play) concerning the pros and cons of integration in physical education and sports competition. Support your position with facts gathered in background reading.

2. Appoint a class committee to locate and establish contact with the local Association for Retarded Citizens (ARC), Association for Children and Adults with Learning Disabilities (ACLD), or similar organization. Invite some members of this organization to speak to your class about advocacy. In return, join their associations and become involved in their activities.

3. Advocate for your profession by updating bulletin boards in your building or on your campus. Stress the values of physical education and recreation for handicapped persons.

4. See if a directory of organizations for handicapped persons is available for your area. If not, develop one. The list of national organizations pertaining to handicapping conditions in Appendix D may give you an idea of the local and regional organizations to look for. Once the directory is complete, contact members of some of the organizations, find out the kind of physical education and recreation in which they engage, and offer to assist with such activities.

5. Conduct a class session on architectural barriers. Simulate handicapping conditions by renting wheelchairs for some of your class members and blindfolding others, for example, and spending half a day moving about the community to learn firsthand how accessible facilities are. Discuss your experiences during the next class session, with emphasis upon improving the status quo.

6. Read books, attend plays, or see movies and videotapes about persons with handicapping conditions. Give reports on these in class and/or role play specific persons.

7. Become involved in a Handicapped Awareness Day. These are often conducted for the entire community by the Mayor's Committee on Employment of the Handicapped. If your university does not have such a day, help to plan and conduct one.

References

Axelson, P. (1985). Facilitation of integrated recreation. In C. Sherrill (Ed.). *Sport and disabled athletes* (pp. 81–92). Champaign, IL: Human Kinetics Publishers.

Buscaglia, L. (1975). *The disabled and their parents: A counseling challenge.* Thorofare, NJ: Charles B. Slack.

Cassidy, R., & Caldwell, S. F. (1975). Humanizing physical education. In A. Lockhart & H. Slusher (Eds.). *Contemporary readings in physical education* (pp. 394–397). Dubuque, IA: Wm. C. Brown.

Geraci, S. (1979). People in sports: Sharon Rahn. *Sports 'N Spokes, 5* (3), 8–10.

Goffman, E. (1963). *Stigma: Notes on the management of spoiled identity.* Englewood Cliffs, NJ: Prentice-Hall.

Maslow, A. (1968). *Toward a psychology of being* (2nd ed.). New York: Van Nostrand Reinhold.

Maslow, A. (1970). *Motivation and personality* (2nd ed.). New York: Harper & Row.

Martinek, T., Crowe, P., & Rejeski, W. (1982). *Pygmalion in the gymnasium.* West Point, NY: Leisure Press.

Martinek, R., & Johnson, S. (1979). Teacher expectations: Effects on dyadic interactions and self-concept in elementary age children. *Research Quarterly, 50,* 60–70.

McBee, F., & Ballinger, J. (1984a). *The continental quest.* Tampa, FL: Overland Press.

McBee, F. (1984b). Wheelers go for the gold. *Sports 'N Spokes, 10* (3), 8–15.

Robinson, N., & Robinson, H. (1976). *The mentally retarded child.* New York: McGraw-Hill.

Taylor, P. (1983). Peter Axelson: Building a better ski sled is only part of the story. *Sports 'N Spokes, 8* (6), 28–30.

Whitley, P. (1980). *Dr. Charles Buell: Leader in physical education for the visually impaired.* Unpublished doctoral dissertation, University of North Carolina, Greensboro.

Wolfensberger, W. (1972). *Normalization.* Toronto: National Institute on Mental Retardation.

Bibliography

Association for Supervision and Curriculum Development. (1967). *Humanizing education: The person and the process.* Washington, DC: National Education Association.

Burns, R. B. (1979). *The self-concept: Theory, measurement, development, and behavior.* New York: Longman.

Buscaglia, L. (1978). *Personhood: The act of being fully human.* New York: Fawcett Columbine.

Buscaglia, L. (1982). *Living, loving, and learning.* Thorofare, NJ: Charles B. Slack.

Cain, L. (1976). Parent groups: Their role in a better life for the handicapped. *Exceptional Children, 42,* 432–437.

Cohen, S. (1977). *Special people.* Englewood Cliffs, NJ: Prentice-Hall.

Corman, L., & Gottlieb, J. (1978). Mainstreaming mentally retarded children: A review of research. In N. R. Ellis (Ed.), *International Review of Research in Mental Retardation,* Vol. 9. New York: Academic Press.

Eisenberg, M., Griggin, C., & Duval, R. (Eds.). (1982). *Disabled people as second-class citizens.* New York: Springer Publishing Co.

Frith, G. (1981). "Advocate" vs. "professional employee": A question of priorities for special educators. *Exceptional Children, 47* (7), 486–492.

Gallager, J., Beckman, P., & Cross, A. (1983). Families of handicapped children: Sources of stress and its amelioration. *Exceptional Children, 50* (1), 10–19.

Gilhool, T. (1976). Changing public policies: Roots and forces. In *Mainstreaming: Origins and implications* (pp. 8–14). Minneapolis: University of Minnesota.

Gliedman, J., & Roth, W. (1980). *The unexpected minority.* New York: Harcourt Brace Jovanovich.

Heshusius, L. (1982). At the heart of the advocacy dilemma. *Exceptional Children, 49* (1), 6–13.

Hunt, P. (Ed.). (1966). *Stigma: The experience of disability.* London: Geoffrey Chapman.

Kleinfield, S. (1979). *The hidden minority: America's handicapped.* Boston: Little, Brown.

Maslow, A. (1970). *Motivation and personality* (2nd ed.). New York: Harper & Row.

Palmer, D. (1983). An attributional perspective on labeling. *Exceptional Children, 49* (5), 423–429.

Rogers, C. (1961), *On becoming a person.* Boston: Houghton Mifflin.

Rogers, C. (1977). *On personal power.* New York: Delacorte Press.

Rosenthal, R., & Jacobsen, L. (1968). *Pygmalion in the classroom.* New York: Holt, Rinehart, & Winston.

Sherrill, C. (Ed.). (1986). *Adapted physical education leadership training.* Champaign, IL: Human Kinetics Publishers.

Sherrill, C., & Ruda, L. (1977). A time to listen to our MR citizens. *Parks and Recreation, 12,* 30–33.

Shontz, F. (1978). Psychological adjustment to physical disability: Trends in the theories. *Archives of Physical Medicine and Rehabilitation, 59,* 251–254.

Silva, J., & Weinberg, R. (Eds.). (1984). *Psychological foundations of sport.* Champaign, IL: Human Kinetics Publishers.

Stubbins, J. (Ed.). (1977). *Social and psychological aspects of disability.* Baltimore: University Park Press.

Tringo, J. (1970). The hierarchy of preference toward disability groups. *Journal of Special Education, 4* (3), 295–305.

Weisz, J. (1979). Perceived control and learned helplessness among mentally retarded and nonretarded children: A developmental analysis. *Developmental Psychology, 15,* 311–319.

Wolfensberger, W. (1972). Normalization via citizen advocacy. In W. Wolfensberger (Ed.), *Normalization.* Toronto: National Institute on Mental Retardation.

Wright, B. (1960). *Physical disability—A psychological approach.* New York: Harper & Row.

Wright, B. (1983). *Physical disability—A psychosocial approach.* New York: Harper & Row.

5 Sensorimotor Development

Figure 5.1 The IEP goal of crawling to a desired toy is implemented for a motorically delayed 2-year-old Down's syndrome infant. The cold, slick mirror provides tactile stimulation to the bare skin as well as visual input. The infant's primary locomotor pattern will continue to be belly crawling and/or a bunny hop movement until he loses the symmetrical tonic neck reflex. Then the IEP goal will be changed to creeping.

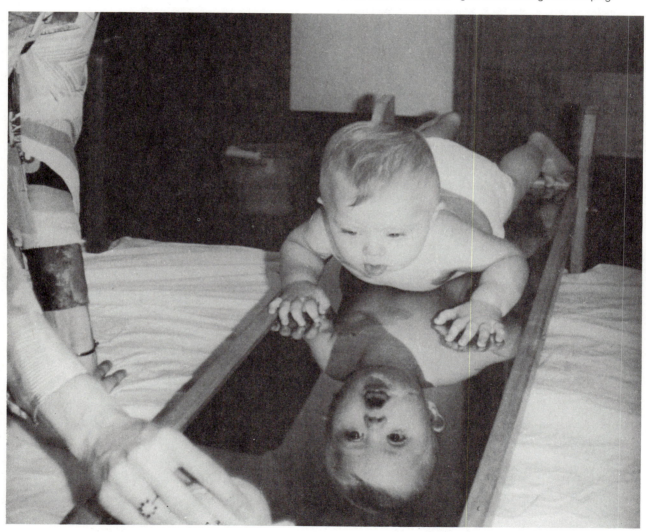

Chapter Objectives

After you have studied this chapter, you should be able to

1. Differentiate between growth and development and give examples of how each affects motor performance.
2. State and explain eight principles of normal development. Discuss how each relates to motor performance.
3. Differentiate between normal, delayed, and abnormal motor development. Give examples of each in relation to the principles of normal development. State which handicapping conditions are most often associated with each.
4. Discuss the dependence of sensorimotor development upon the growth and maturation of the nervous system.
5. Identify 12 major parts of the central nervous system (CNS) and explain the function of each.
6. Discuss the neurological bases of clumsiness, including the model typically used in determining reasons for clumsiness.
7. List and discuss seven characteristics of a mature, intact central nervous system. Demonstrate ability to identify CNS problems when viewing a videotape or film.
8. Differentiate between reflexes and reactions and identify three developmental theories based on levels of CNS functioning.
9. Name 10 sense modalities and discuss their relationship to motor development. Which sense modalities develop earliest and how can sensorimotor training help when working with severely handicapped students?
10. Identify three disorders of muscle tone and demonstrate ability to recognize these. Which handicapping conditions are most often associated with each? What methods can be used to normalize muscle tone?
11. Differentiate between static and dynamic balance and discuss development of the vestibular system in relation to each.
12. Demonstrate familiarity with entries in the bibliography and identify major leaders in sensorimotor development.

An understanding of the broad spectrum of individual differences in physical growth and development is requisite to competent assessment and the development and implementation of IEPs (see Figure 5.1). Optimal multidisciplinary preparation in this area includes courses in genetics, physiology, anatomy, neurology, physiological psychology, motor development, and motor control. This chapter presents the elementary concepts underlying growth and development theory: normal, delayed, and abnormal.

Growth versus Development

The terms *growth* and *development* should not be used interchangeably. Each has its own meaning. Some aspect of physical growth and/or motor development is delayed or abnormal in most handicapped and/or clumsy students.

Growth

Growth refers to an increase in size; changes of most interest to the physical educator are those in the nervous, skeletal, and muscular systems. Most of the growth within the nervous system occurs from the time of conception until age 3 or 4 years, whereas skeletal changes occur primarily in four growth spurts (in utero, 0 to 2 years, 5 to 8 years, and pubertal). Changes in muscle growth can occur at any age, depending upon exercise.

Height, weight, and bone and muscle mass of the entire body as well as the dimensions of individual segments affect motor performance. Growth changes the center of gravity (CG); this in turn affects body balance, as explained by the principle stating the lower the CG, the more stable the object. Young children, with

Figure 5.2 Growth during developmental stages.

Growth in height, weight, limb proportion, circumference

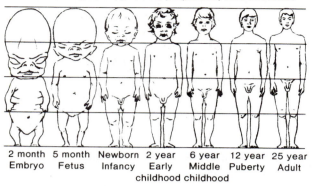

| 2 month Embryo | 5 month Fetus | Newborn Infancy | 2 year Early childhood | 6 year Middle childhood | 12 year Puberty | 25 year Adult |

Developmental Stages

their proportionately larger heads, have a higher CG than older children; thus, toddlers have difficulty with balance. Growth also changes the leverage within the musculoskeletal system. This affects movement in accordance with the principle of leverage: the shorter the bony lever, the more muscular force is needed to move it. Young children with proportionally shorter arms and legs than adults typically do not yet have the muscle strength to throw and kick great distances. Short persons with short arms and/or legs are obviously at a mechanical disadvantage in most sports as opposed to tall persons.

Throughout the life span, many such individual differences (largely determined by heredity) are normal and help to explain variations in motor performance. Pathological conditions like hydrocephalus (large head), Down's syndrome (proportionately shorter arms and legs), and dwarfism that affect size of body parts are examples of abnormalities in growth that affect balance and motor efficiency.

Development

Development is the continual, sequential process by which an individual changes from one life phase to another (see Figure 5.2). Development, thus, refers mainly to changes in function, as in moving through such stages as fetal; embryonic; infant; early, middle, and late childhood; puberty and adolescence; and early, middle, and late adulthood.

Table 5.1
Principles of Normal Development

1. **Continuity.** Development is a continuous process, from conception to death.

2. **Uniform sequence.** The sequence of development is the same in all children, but the rate of development varies from child to child.

3. **Neurological maturation.** Development is intricately related to the maturation of the nervous system. No amount of practice can enable a child to perform a motor task until myelination has occurred.

4. **General-to-specific activity.** Generalized mass activity is replaced by specific responses of individual body parts. The child gains control of large muscle groups before achieving fine finger coordinations.

5. **Cephalocaudal direction.** Gross motor development begins with head control (strength in neck muscles) and proceeds downward.

6. **Loss of reflexes.** Certain primitive reflexes, such as grasp reflex and Moro reflex, must be lost before the corresponding voluntary movement is acquired.

7. **Proximodistal coordination.** Muscle groups near (proximo) midline become functional before those farther away (distal) from midline do. For example, a child learns to catch with shoulders, upper arms, and forearms before catching with fingers. Movements performed at midline (in front of body) are easier than those that entail crossing midline (to left or right of body—i.e., more distant from midline).

8. **Bilateral-to-crosslateral motor control.** *Bilateral* movement patterns (both limbs moving simultaneously, as in arm movements of the breaststroke or reaching for an object at midline) are the first to occur in the human infant, followed by *unilateral* movement patterns (right arm and right leg moving simultaneously or vice versa), followed by *crosslateral patterns* (right arm and left leg moving simultaneously).

Note: Primary sources for these principles are Gesell and Ames (1940) and Illingsworth (1983).

Principles of Motor Development

Normal development is governed by eight principles. When these principles are violated, the child is described as exhibiting abnormal motor development. The *principle of continuity* may be violated in some children who, because of a disability, remain frozen in a particular stage and/or are unable to master motor tasks appropriate to chronological age. The severely disabled person dominated by primitive reflexes who never learns to walk exemplifies *abnormal motor development.* Rate of development (i.e., moving from task

Figure 5.3 The peripheral nervous system. This illustration shows how each of the 31 spinal nerves emerges from the spinal cord by a dorsal (posterior) root and a ventral (anterior) root. The dorsal root transmits sensory messages, whereas the ventral root transmits motor messages. The roots merge after leaving the vertebral area to form a nerve (shown on the right). Nerves are made up of nerve fibers called dendrites and axons.

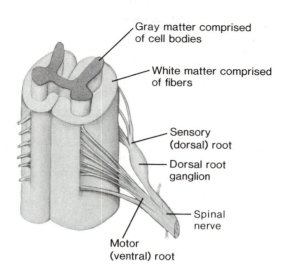

Gray matter comprised of cell bodies

White matter comprised of fibers

Sensory (dorsal) root

Dorsal root ganglion

Spinal nerve

Motor (ventral) root

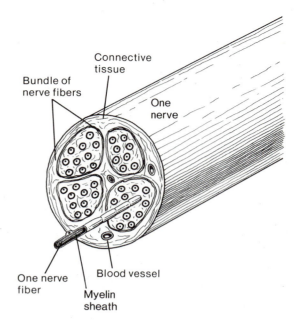

Connective tissue

Bundle of nerve fibers

One nerve

One nerve fiber

Blood vessel

Myelin sheath

to task or stage to stage) varies from child to child; nevertheless, age ranges are designated to indicate normal functioning. When children learn to walk at age 3 or 4 years, as do many with Down's syndrome, this is described as *delayed development*.

The motor development *principle of uniform sequence* specifies that children master tasks/patterns (sit, creep, stand, walk, run) in the same order. Thus, most physical educators believe in stage theory and task analysis. Motor skills can be broken down in numerous components that can then be ordered in a developmental sequence from easy to difficult. Many such sequences appear in the literature to guide physical educators in assessment and instruction. In abnormal development the principle of uniform sequence is violated, as when a child learns to walk but never creeps.

Phylogenetic versus Ontogenetic Development

Motor development is often classified as *phylogenetic* (activities such as creeping, walking, and running that evolve naturally, without instruction, in normal children) and *ontogenetic* (activities that are more or less culturally determined and require instruction and practice even in normal children). The theory of normal motor development holds that phylogenetic activities

occur as the result of *maturation* (as a function of time, without benefit of experience or instruction), whereas ontogenetic activities are believed to result from *teaching/learning/practice*. This classic distinction between maturation and learning does not hold true for abnormal motor development. Many severely handicapped infants and children must be given instruction and repeated practice to learn even the simplest of motor tasks (visual pursuits; grasping and releasing; creeping and walking).

Dependence of Sensorimotor Development upon the Nervous System

Sensorimotor development is intricately related to the growth and maturation of the nervous system. The human infant is born with 10 to 12 billion nerve cells (neurons) organized as a *central nervous system* (brain and spinal cord) and a *peripheral nervous system* (12 pairs of cranial and 31 pairs of spinal nerves). The normal adult has approximately 100 billion neurons. Figure 5.3 shows nerves and depicts the peripheral nervous system.

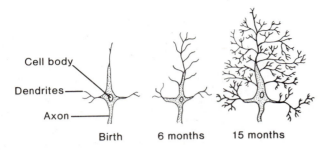

Figure 5.4 Growth of nerve cells (neurons) during infancy. Each nerve cell has three parts: cell body, dendrites, and axon. Cell bodies are located in the brain and spinal cord. Dendrites and axons are the nerve fibers that comprise nerves throughout the body and neural pathways (tracts) inside the spinal cord and brain.

Cell body

Dendrites

Axon

Birth   6 months   15 months

Neuronal Growth and Function

Approximately 3 months before birth, all of the neurons comprising the nervous system are present. Each has a cell body, one axon, and several dendrites. Figure 5.4 shows how the appearance of these cells changes from birth until about 15 months; during this time, the *dendrites* rapidly form many treelike branches that serve to receive impulses from other neurons. Through this process, each neuron becomes interconnected with approximately 10,000 other neurons. The *axon* conducts impulses away from the cell body. The speed and efficiency with which neurons transmit impulses determine, to a large extent, motor control. The junction between two neurons is a *synapse*. From the time that sensory input (visual, auditory, tactile, and the like) is received until a mental or motor response occurs, hundreds (and sometimes millions) of neurons are involved via synaptic link-ups throughout the body.

Prenatal Growth and Development

The preembryotic stage extends from conception to 14 days; during this time, the fertilized egg divides by means of a process called *mitosis* into clusters of cells called blastocysts. The embryonic stage extends from the second to the eighth week; during this time, all of the essential internal and external body parts are formed. The fetal stage extends from the beginning of the eighth week to birth. During this period, *myelination* (development of the covering of nerve fibers) begins and the interconnections between neurons evolve through rapid expansion of dendrites (nerve fibers). The average infant at full-term birth weighs 6 to 8 pounds and is about 50 cm (19.5 inches) long: average head circumference is 34.8 cm (13.75 inches). After birth, the nervous system continues to develop rapidly until age 3 to 4 years.

Development of the Central Nervous System

Just as the body progresses through stages of development (embryo to fetus to infant) so also does the central nervous system (CNS). Beginning as cells called the ectoderm, the CNS evolves into the neural tube that, 28 days after conception (see Figure 5.5), has subdivided into four distinct parts: forebrain, midbrain, hindbrain, and neural tube (spinal cord). Long before birth, these structures evolve into the parts of the CNS with which we are familiar. The hindbrain separates into medulla and pons (the brain stem) and cerebellum. The midbrain expands in size (but its name does not change). The forebrain evolves into several interdependent structures. The innermost of these are the thalamus, hypothalamus, basal ganglia (clumps of cell bodies), and limbic system (a ring of interconnecting pathways and centers in the medial part of each cerebral hemisphere). The outermost is the cerebral cortex, which is smooth before birth, but rapidly develops numerous convolutions (folds, hills, gyri) and depressions (grooves, sulci, fissures). The adult cortex, if unfolded and spread out, would cover about 20 square feet.

Parts of Central Nervous System

Knowing the function of each part of the CNS is essential to understanding individual differences in motor functioning. Following is a simplified explanation of each:

1. Spinal cord—comprised of numerous tracts (pathways), each of which contains nerve fibers carrying impulses to and from the brain. Each tract has a distinct name and function. The name typically indicates the direction in which impulses are carried and the two parts of the CNS connected by the pathway. Illustrative ascending pathways are spinocerebellar and spinothalamic. Illustrative descending pathways are corticospinal and vestibulospinal. The speed and efficiency with which impulses are carried up and down these tracts are major determinants of motor coordination. Spinal cord damage results in muscle weakness or paralysis and lack of sensation (feeling).

2. Medulla—the superior extension of the spinal cord that regulates such vital functions as respiration, heart rate, and blood pressure. Contains nuclei (cell bodies) from which cranial nerves emerge; these nerves relate to sensory systems that originate in the head (vision, audition).

Figure 5.5 Rapid growth of body and brain before birth.

Age	Length	Appearance
4 days		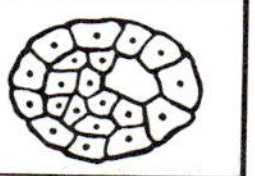
23 days	2 mm	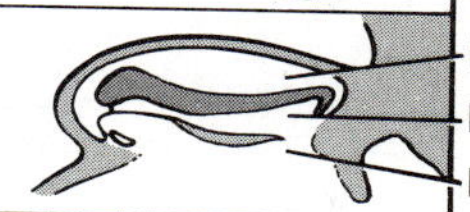 Ectoderm / Mesoderm / Endoderm
28 days	4 mm	
45 days	17 mm	
7 weeks	2.8 cm	
12 weeks	8.8 cm	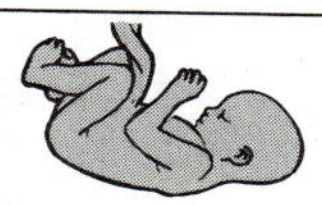
28 weeks	38.5 cm	
First postnatal year+		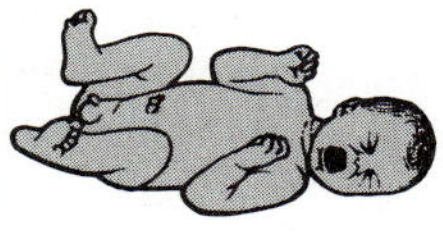

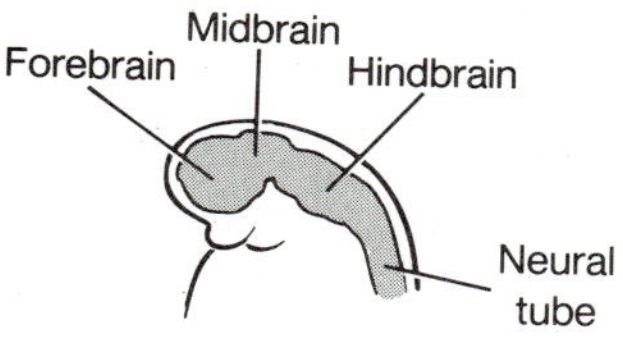

Forebrain / Midbrain / Hindbrain / Neural tube

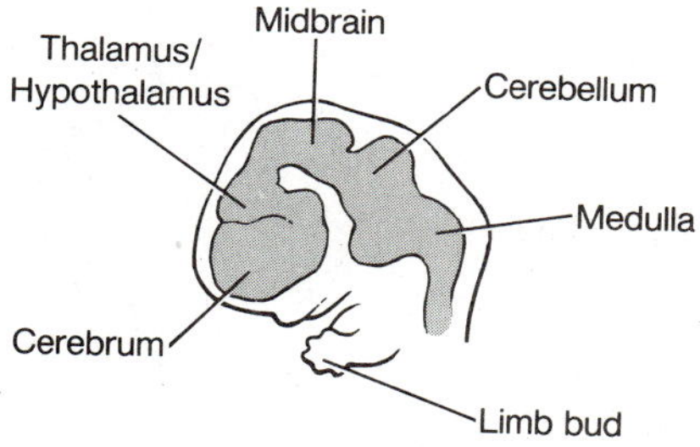

Thalamus/Hypothalamus / Midbrain / Cerebellum / Medulla / Cerebrum / Limb bud

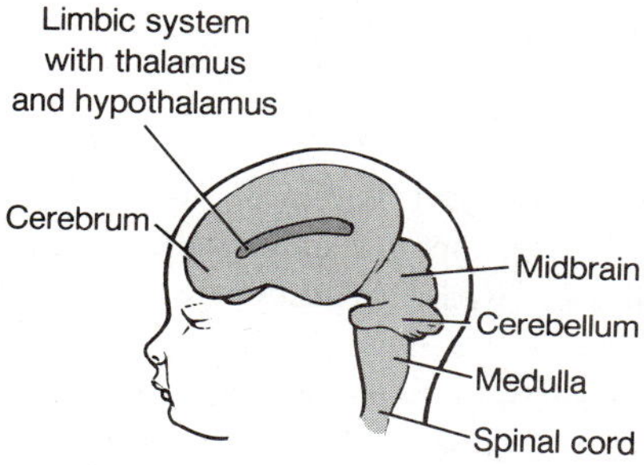

Limbic system with thalamus and hypothalamus / Cerebrum / Midbrain / Cerebellum / Medulla / Spinal cord

3. Pons—(means "bridge") consists mainly of fibers forming a bridge between medulla and cerebellum. Contains nuclei for the vestibular nerve, which is important in the reflex control of head, neck, and eyes, and other nuclei that help regulate coordination and posture.

4. Midbrain—short portion between pons and cerebral hemispheres; oculomotor nerves attach to the front of the midbrain, which is essentially a servomechanism (relay center) for transmitting nerve impulses involved in reflex movements initiated by visual, auditory, and related sensory input.

5. Brain stem—the bundle of nerve tissue that extends upward from the spinal cord to the base of the cerebrum. It includes the medulla, pons, and midbrain. The primary reason for considering these three structures together is the presence in all of them of the *reticular formation* (Figure 5.6), also called the reticular activating system (RAS). This is a complex network of nerve fibers with tiny clumps of cell bodies that connects the brain stem with virtually all other parts of the brain. Its main functions pertain to activation, wakefulness, and arousal; thus, it is believed to play a role in attention, learning, and behavior deficits involving hyperactivity vs. hypoactivity. This role is achieved largely by the RAF filtering incoming sensory impulses and preventing sensory bombardment of the cortex by selectively transferring some sensory impulses upward and inhibiting others. This permits the cortex to focus upon significant stimuli rather than coping with all neural impulses. This function contributes to *sensory integration,* a problem area for many students who exhibit learning deficits. Also important to the brain stem's integrative role is the fact that it contains

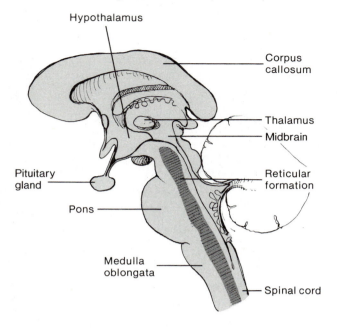

Figure 5.6 Side view of brain stem showing reticular formation. This level of the brain governs most of the primitive reflexes.

Hypothalamus

Corpus callosum

Thalamus

Midbrain

Reticular formation

Pituitary gland

Pons

Medulla oblongata

Spinal cord

all of the centers for the 10 sense modalities except vision and smell (centers that connect directly with the limbic system and cerebral cortex).

6. Cerebellum—(means "little brain") essentially a servomechanism (relay center) for transmitting nerve impulses involved with muscle tone, proprioception (sensory input from muscles, tendons, joints, and vestibular apparatus in inner ear), and reflex postural adjustments in response to proprioceptive input. The cerebellum is important in excitation (activation) and inhibition of muscles, a major determinant in smooth vs. jerky movements. It is also believed to be the structure that, after training and practice of a new motor skill, assumes responsibility for automatic rather than conscious control of motor performance. A major goal of physical education is to motivate students to practice a new skill until it no longer requires motor planning (i.e., conscious thought); at that point the skill becomes subcortical, or reflex, meaning it can be executed at the cerebellar level.

7. Thalamus—(means "little chamber or anteroom") a football-shaped cluster of nerve cells deep within the cerebrum, located immediately above the midbrain. One part acts

as a servomechanism for relaying sensory impulses and the other helps to regulate arousal in relation to activity. Except for smell, each of the senses relays its impulses through the thalamus.

8. Hypothalamus—group of small nuclei underneath the thalamus and close to the pituitary gland. Integrates control of the autonomic nervous system, thereby playing a key role in *homeostatis* (the regulation of balance in internal bodily functions). Among these are regulation of physical growth, heart rate, body temperature, sleep and wakefulness, hunger, dehydration, emotion, and control of stress. This regulation occurs primarily through stimulation of glands which, in turn, release hormones.

9. Basal ganglia—masses of subcortical gray matter (cell bodies) in the interior of the cerebrum, mainly in the corpus callosum area (i.e., near the junction of right and left cerebral hemispheres). Some of the basal ganglia have specific names: globus pallidus, putamen, caudate nucleus, the subthalamic nucleus, and the substantia nigra. The role of these individual structures is not well known, but research is expected to soon provide answers. In general, the basal ganglia help to regulate posture and movement, particularly slow movement. Damage to basal ganglia results in such conditions as athetosis (involuntary, purposeless, slow, repeated motions), tremors of face and hands, and Huntington's chorea.

10. Limbic system—a ring of interconnecting pathways and centers that includes hypothalamus, thalamus, basal ganglia, and other subcortical nuclei that are believed important in control of emotional responses and degree of activity, as in hyperactivity vs. hypoactivity. *Limbus* is Latin for rim or border; the limbic system forms the innermost part of the cerebrum. The limbic system is also considered the evolutionarily old cortex in that it (especially the basal ganglia) is the highest center for motor control in birds and lower animals with little cerebral cortex. It is closely connected to the sense of smell in that the olfactory bulbs and tracts are nearby; evolutionarily, the cerebrum is believed to have begun as a center for smell.

11. Cerebral cortex—(means "bark of tree") anatomically refers to six layers of gray matter (cell bodies) that comprise the outer part of the cerebrum. The cortex performs the higher level

functions: voluntary movement, perception, thought, memory, and creativity. Cortical areas are named according to function: sensory, association, and motor. Sensory areas function in interpretation of impulses from 10 kinds of sensory receptors. Association areas function in analysis of sensory and motor input as well as verbalization, memory, reasoning, judgment, and creativity. Motor areas control voluntary movement; damage to the motor cortex results in spasticity.

12. Corpus callosum—bridge of nerve fibers that connects right and left cerebral hemispheres, thus allowing them to keep in touch with one another. An important function is transfer of learning from one hemisphere to another.

Developmental Milestones

The motor tasks that infants and children are expected to demonstrate at each age are called developmental milestones. Assessment of normal motor behavior is based largely on motor development literature of the 1930s (McGraw, 1935; Shirley, 1933) and observational scales based on this literature. The best known of these instruments are the Bayley Scales of Infant Development (initially called California Infant Scale of Motor Development), for use with children ages 2 to 30 months, and the Gesell Developmental Schedules, for use with children ages 1 month to 6 years. More recently, the Denver Developmental Screening Test (1967), for use with children from 2 weeks to 6 years, 4 months, has been developed along the same format. These assessment approaches all assume that the development of the CNS is intact and continuous and that the appearance (timewise) of these motor milestones is more or less the same for all children.

Developmental theory uses motor milestones to explain the principles of cephalocaudal direction, proximodistal coordination, and bilateral-to-crosslateral motor control. As shown in Figure 5.7, the infant achieves control of the head (cephalus) before achieving control of the lower extremities (generalized to tail [caudo], in professional terminology). The *principle of proximodistal coordination* refers to muscle groups near (proximo) midline (the spinal column) becoming functional before those farther away (distal) from midline. Muscles moving the head, neck, scapula, and trunk become coordinated to permit sitting, crawling, creeping, and standing before muscles of the arms and legs become coordinated enough for throwing, catching, and kicking. The *principle of bilateral-to-crosslateral motor control* explains the early reflexly controlled

Figure 5.7 Developmental milestones in achieving normal walking gait. Note correct terminology for crawl (on belly) versus creep (on hands and knees).

Fetal posture
0 month

Chin up
1 month

Chest up
2 months

Reach and miss
3 months

Sit with support
4 months

Sit on lap, grasp object
5 months

Crawl
6-8 months

Sit alone
7 months

Stand with help
8 months

Stand holding furniture
9 months

Creep
10 months

Walk when led
11 months

Pull to stand by furniture
12 months

Climb stair steps
13 months

Stand alone
14 months

Walk alone
15 months

spreading and closing of both arms (bilateral) simultaneously as well as early voluntary reach activities in which the two arms move together. Developmentally, the infant then moves into the unilateral stage (one arm reach or one leg kick, but without opposition of the other limb for balance). Last, at about 5 to 6 years of age, when the CNS is relatively mature, the child progresses to crosslateral patterns (right arm and left leg or vice versa moving in opposition). This results in good balance.

In adapted physical education, teachers are confronted mostly with delayed or abnormal rather than normal motor development. Mentally retarded children often do not walk alone until ages 2 to 5 years;

many never learn to jump, hop, and skip. Some persons with cerebral palsy never achieve the motor milestones of standing and walking alone. Clumsy students may achieve expected motor milestones, but fail to show good coordination, balance, or agility. Problems in these areas generally relate to integration of reflexes, presence of mature postural reactions, and/or speed and timing with which neural impulses are transmitted.

Neurological Bases of Clumsiness

Clumsiness, like cerebral palsy, can be defined as a group of neuromuscular conditions caused by delayed or abnormal development of the parts of the CNS that control sensorimotor behavior. The severity of the condition(s) typically determines whether the child is called clumsy or cerebral palsied. Without sophisticated laboratory equipment, it is usually difficult to decide whether the problem is primarily sensory, motor, or the central processing that occurs between sensory input and motor output. Often, the problem is in all three; certainly, sound motor functioning cannot occur without intact sensory and central processing systems.

The model typically used in searching for reasons for clumsiness is as follows (see Figure 5.8). Questions typically asked are

1. Is something wrong with the sense organs?
2. Is something wrong with the nerve fibers that carry sensory input?
3. Is something wrong with central processing (i.e., the servomechanisms that relay impulses, the reticular activating system that controls arousal, or the association areas of the cerebral cortex that translate impulses into meaning)?
4. Is something wrong with motor output (i.e., the motor areas of the CNS that activate movement, the nerve fibers that carry motor input to muscles, tendons, and joints, or the motor effectors [endings] within these structures)?

This approach, while interesting, seldom results in specific answers that help in physical education programming.

An alternative approach, used in the therapies and in adapted physical education, entails assessing characteristics of a mature, intact CNS and the developmental level at which problems can occur. Programming then is directed toward specific problems. Table 5.2

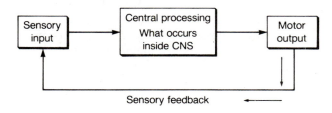

Figure 5.8 Traditional model used in motor development and motor learning to explain processes of sensory input, central processing, and motor output.

Table 5.2
Characteristics of a Mature, Intact Central Nervous System

1. **Reflex integration.** Primitive reflexes are involuntary motor responses to stimuli; reflexes must be fully suppressed or integrated before coordinated, graceful, voluntary movement can occur.

2. **Optimal functioning of reactions.** Reactions are generalized involuntary responses that pertain to static and dynamic balance. Developmentally, reactions replace primitive reflexes.

3. **Freedom from ataxia.** Ataxia is incoordination characterized primarily by irregularity and lack of precision in voluntary motor acts. Ataxic behaviors include over- or undershooting the object when reaching for something or going through an obstacle course; problems include spilling, bumping into things, knocking them over, or stumbling for no apparent reason. In stepping over an object or climbing stairs, persons with ataxia tend to lift their feet too high. An ataxic gait is characterized by irregular steps.

4. **Freedom from athetosis.** Athetosis is involuntary, purposeless, relatively slow, repeated movement that interferes with steadiness, accuracy, and control of one or more body parts.

5. **Freedom from spasticity.** Spasticity is hypertonus (too much muscle tone) that results in reduced range of movement, overly active tonic reflex activity, and stiff, awkward-looking movements. Spasticity occurs only in relation to voluntary movement.

6. **Freedom from associated movements.** The ability to move one body part without associated movements of other parts. This problem is sometimes called *overflow*.

7. **Freedom from sensory input problems.** Visual and auditory problems affect the teaching/learning process in mastering new motor skills and patterns.

Note. The terms *ataxia, athetosis,* and *spasticity,* although used to specify types of cerebral palsy, are not limited to this group of conditions. They also describe clumsy movements and gaits with an infinite variety of etiologies (causes) including brain damage from vehicular accidents, drugs, alcohol, and disease. A person intoxicated with alcohol, for instance, is said to have an ataxic gait; likewise, the toddler just learning to walk evidences developmental ataxia, which disappears with neuromuscular maturation.

Figure 5.9 Developmental levels of CNS at which motor problems occur.

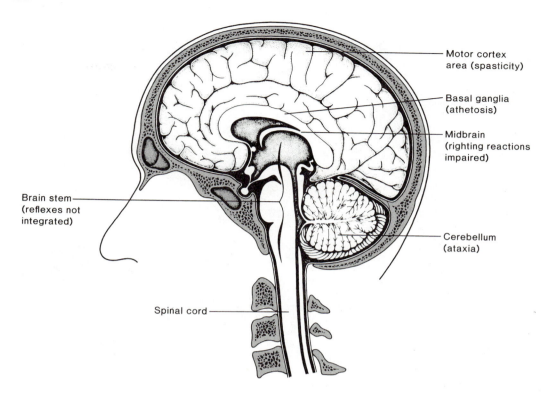

Motor cortex area (spasticity)

Basal ganglia (athetosis)

Midbrain (righting reactions impaired)

Brain stem (reflexes not integrated)

Cerebellum (ataxia)

Spinal cord

presents these characteristics, and Figure 5.9 depicts the developmental levels. Several of these characteristics pertain to the appearance of postural or muscle tone or tonus (i.e., contractile tension within a muscle). Before the CNS matures sufficiently to permit muscles to perform voluntary action (i.e., about 4 months of age), tonus shifts with body position. *Flexor tonus* refers to tension within muscles on the anterior surface of the body that, when mature, will cause flexion movements (i.e., bending, curling). *Extensor tonus* refers to tension within muscles on the posterior surface of the body that will cause extension movements (i.e., straightening, stretching). Persons with delayed or abnormal CNS development may exhibit flexor and extensor tonus abnormalities throughout life.

Developmental Levels in CNS Function

Developmentalists explain the evolution of voluntary movement in terms of CNS function. Newborn infants have no voluntary movement; they are totally controlled by reflexes that originate at the spinal cord and/or brain stem levels.

Reflexes

Infant reflex activity is described as generalized, mass, and diffuse rather than specific. Body parts cannot move separately. In prone position, muscles are dominated by flexor tone; the newborn infant cannot even lift its head (Figure 5.10). In supine position, the extensor muscles all increase in muscle tone. When the positions of the body determine muscle tone in this way, the infant is said to be dominated by reflexes. Until these reflexes are suppressed or integrated at about 4 months of age, the infant cannot roll over or begin to crawl. An important motor development principle is that primitive reflexes must be suppressed or integrated before the corresponding voluntary movement can be achieved. The age at which each reflex is lost is governed by an inborn biological timetable that is more or less the same for all children. This constitutes another example of the motor development principles of continuity and uniform sequence.

Figure 5.10 Domination of flexor tone in prone position is seen in infant about 4 weeks old. *Flexor tone dominance* is normal during the first month of life, after which time extensor muscle tone gradually develops and the body begins to straighten out.

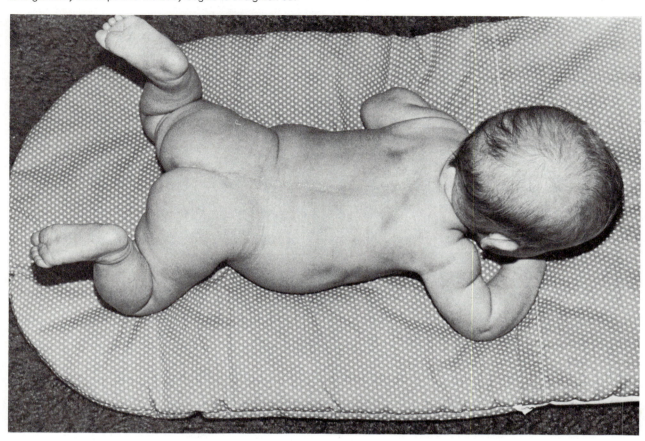

Figure 5.11 Same infant at about 6 months of age, when no longer dominated by flexor tone. Note ability to reach with one arm while the other arm remains motionless. Arms and legs can fully extend. This normal infant will soon be crawling (forward motion on belly). Righting reactions are emerging that permit her to hold her head and neck upright.

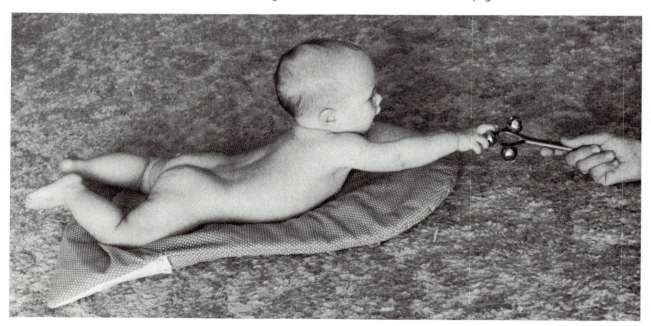

Figure 5.12 Normal infant at 7 weeks of age exhibits no protective extension of the arms. Many adults with severe cerebral palsy have this same problem. When they fall, the arms do not automatically respond with the parachute reaction.

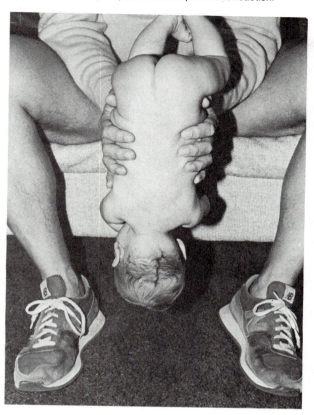

Figure 5.13 Same infant at 16 weeks of age is beginning to show parachute reactions.

Figure 5.14 Same infant at 24 weeks of age showing equilibrium or tilting reactions. These reactions are gradually refined over the next 5 years. Note the compensatory movement and the increased muscle tone on the lowered side.

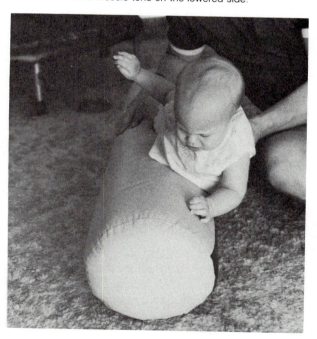

Reactions

As reflexes are suppressed or integrated, postural reactions take their place. Among these are (a) righting reactions that enable the infant to hold the head and neck and later the entire body upright (Figure 5.11); (b) parachute or propping reactions that permit protective extension of the arms or legs when the body is thrown off balance (Figures 5.12 and 5.13); (c) equilibrium or tilting reactions, also protective movements (Figure 5.14); and (d) optical (visual) righting reactions.

Reactions are generalized automatic responses that enable one to support, protect, or right the body or its parts against the pull of gravity. Reactions originate at the midbrain and cortical levels of the CNS. Some older literature uses the terms *reflex* and *reaction* interchangeably; the newer works of such authorities as Mary Fiorentino (occupational therapist), Berta Bobath (physical therapist), and Karel Bobath (physician) use the terms separately to denote different developmental levels of the CNS. Primitive reflexes are responses that are integrated in normal development; reactions remain throughout life, playing an important role in postures and balance.

**Table 5.3
Normal Reflex/Reaction Development**

Level of Development	Level of CNS Maturation	Motor Behaviors
Apedel	Spinal cord and/or brain stem	Prone-lying
Primitive reflexes		Supine-lying
Quadrupedal		Right self, turn over, sit, crawl, creep
Righting reactions	Midbrain	
Bipedal	Cortical	Stand
Equilibrium reactions		Walk

Theories Based on Levels of Function

Several developmental theories are based on levels of CNS functioning. Among these are the reflex testing theory of Mary Fiorentino, the neurophysiological theory of the Bobaths, and the sensory integration theory of Jean Ayres. The three levels of reflex/reaction development that form the basis of the theories of Fiorentino and the Bobaths are presented in Table 5.3.

Ayres, an occupational therapist with a doctoral degree in psychology, emphasizes that assessment and remediation are easier when neural processes are related to level of CNS function. She specifies six levels as important: spinal cord, brain stem with emphasis on reticular formation, cerebellum, basal ganglia, old cortex and/or limbic system, and neocortex. Ayres cautions, however, to remember that in reality several CNS levels function simultaneously in human motor behavior.

In summary, the physical educator who works with handicapped or clumsy students within a multidisciplinary context needs to understand the levels of CNS function in relation to normal, delayed, and abnormal motor development. The elementary facts presented in this book should motivate students who want more information to read such primary sources as

Ayres, A. J. (1972). *Sensory integration and learning disorders.* Los Angeles: Western Psychological Services.

Bobath, K. (1980). *A neurophysiological basis for the treatment of cerebral palsy.* Philadelphia: J. B. Lippincott Company.

Fiorentino, M. (1981). *A basis for sensorimotor development—normal and abnormal.* Springfield, IL: Charles C. Thomas.

These books, respectively, form the bases of sensory integration theory, neurophysiological theory, and reflex/reaction theory. Textbooks used in training physical and occupational therapists are also helpful in increasing understanding of delayed and abnormal motor development.

Myelination

The mature healthy central nervous system is characterized by a multiplicity of synaptic connections and rich neuronal interactions. Early in this chapter, the rapid growth of dendritic networks after birth was offered as one explanation of why CNS functions become increasingly complex. Another explanation lies in myelination.

Approximately 5 months before birth, myelination begins. This is the development of the fatty substance that forms the covering of axons and influences their ability to conduct impulses. At birth, some parts of the nervous system have a moderate amount of myelination (optic tract; motor and sensory roots of the 31 pairs of spinal nerves), but others have none. Myelination continues rapidly from birth until 3 to 4 years of age, when it is mostly complete except for the association areas of the brain. Myelination in these areas is finished between ages 15 to 20 years. Motor milestones such as head lifting from prone, sitting, creeping, standing, and walking cannot be achieved until myelination in the related nerves and spinal tract is completed.

The motor development principles of general-to-specific activity and proximodistal control relate largely to myelination. In early infancy, unpleasant stimuli to a body part does not result in the withdrawal of that part alone; instead, all body parts move in a generalized, mass action. Such *associated movements* are diminished as myelination improves the efficiency of nerve conduction and reflexes are integrated. Until the central nervous system has control over specific movements, the infant is dominated by primitive reflexes.

There appears to be no way to speed up myelination. A characteristic of nerve cell injury and/or disease is *demyelination* (the disintegration of the myelin covering of its fibers) and subsequent loss of motor coordination. *Demyelination* is the cause of multiple sclerosis.

Development of Sensory Systems

Motor development cannot proceed without comparable sensory development. Ten different sense modalities evolve during embryonic and fetal growth: (a) touch and pressure, (b) kinesthesis, (c) vestibular, (d) temperature, (e) pain, (f) smell, (g) taste, (h) vision, (i) audition, and (j) common chemical sense.

Figure 5.15 Sensory receptors. Each sensory input system has distinctly different receptors.

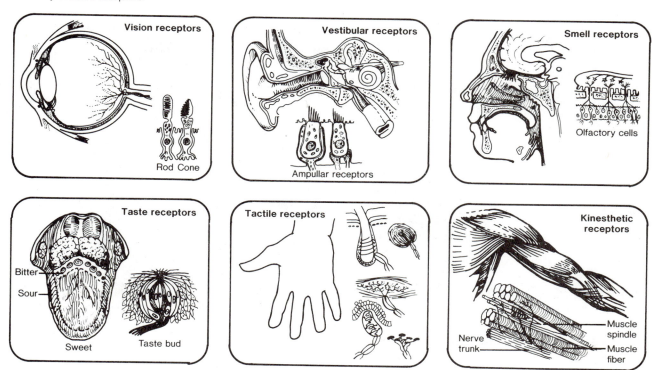

With the exception of the last one, these senses are familiar to all of us. The common chemical sense controls the complex reaction to such activities as peeling an onion (eyes burning, nose sneezing) or eating a hot pepper. Each modality has a special type of end organ (sensory receptor) that is sensitive only to certain stimuli, and each has a separate pathway from the sensory receptor up the spinal cord to the brain. Figure 5.15 depicts some of these sensory receptors.

Like motor development, sensory development is intricately related to the growth and development of the nervous system. The processes of dendritization and myelination help determine the speed and efficiency with which sensory impulses can be transmitted. Sensory systems that mature earliest are touch and deep pressure, vestibular, and kinesthetic. When these systems exhibit delayed or abnormal functioning, motor development and/or learning is affected.

Tactile System

The tactile system is probably the most fully developed sensory apparatus at birth, as is evidenced by the infant's cries signifying discomfort with wet diapers. The tactile system includes six different cutaneous receptors that provide sensory input regarding touch, deep pressure, pain, heat, and cold. In working with severely disabled individuals, attempts are made to stimulate each of these sense modalities (except for pain). Sensory stimulation is commonly used also in infant programs. Swimming or aquatic play, with a variety of water temperatures, is especially stimulating; cold water assists in arousal, whereas warm water has a relaxing effect. Massage, either by hand or vibrator, is used to activate the deep pressure receptors, whereas stroking the skin with the hand or cloths of various textures (silk, velvet, denim, corduroy, terry) stimulates touch receptors. Deep pressure receptors are also stimulated by walking and movement exploration or gymnastic activities in which the weight of the body is taken on different parts.

Need for tactile stimulation varies widely among human beings. Some persons seem impulse-driven to touch everything; they are particularly obvious in stores and museums; among children, they are often the ones who get in trouble for poking at others or pulling pigtails. At the far end of the individual differences spectrum are persons who dislike and avoid touch; if someone accidently brushes against them, a fight may ensue. Students exhibiting these extremes have disorders of tactile reception/perception called *tactile craving* or *tactile defensiveness*. Such disorders are commonly associated with learning disabilities, autistic-like behaviors, mental retardation, and severe emotional disturbances.

Figure 5.16 Ventral suspension is a good test of muscle tone. *Left,* response of normal infant at 1 month of age. Severely handicapped children with *hypotonia* show this same response at all ages. *Right,* Landau reaction in normal infant at 4–6 months, showing elevation of head and an increase in extensor tone of neck and back muscles.

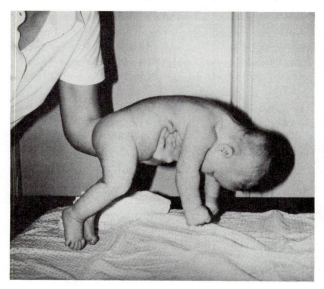 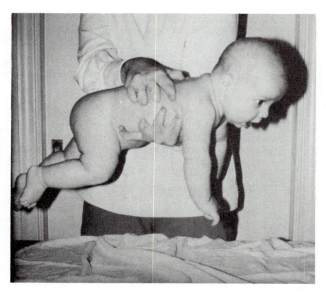

The exact relationship between tactile input and CNS development is not yet known, but sensory integration theorists like Jean Ayres believe that tactile stimulation should be a part of sensorimotor intervention. The theoretical basis for this practice appears to be the belief that tactile stimuli activate or deactivate the reticular formation in the brain stem, the most powerful of the central integrating servomechanisms. The hypothesis that tactile stimulation can contribute to generalized neurological integration and to enhanced perception in other sensory modalities (Ayres, 1972, p. 115) needs further research. Ayres claims that, until age 8 or 9 years, the degree of tactile system integration is one of the best indicators of CNS function.

Kinesthetic System

The kinesthetic system encompasses all of the sensory receptors in the muscles, tendons, and joints that reflexly provide CNS input regarding changes in tension within muscle fibers. Along with the vestibular apparatus in the inner ear, this system regulates muscle and postural tone.

Disorders of muscle tone include (a) hypertonus, (b) hypotonus, and (c) fluctuating tonus. *Hypertonus* is excessive muscle tension, as in spasticity, rigidity, and muscle spasms. *Hypotonus* (see Figure 5.16) is too little tension, as in a muscle group characterized by paralysis or weakness (relaxed, flabby, flaccid). *Fluctuating tonus,* often seen in the athetoid type of cerebral palsy, refers to intermittent increases of postural tone in response to stimulation. Such persons exhibit both hypertonus and hypotonus.

Hypotonia is so common among handicapped infants and children that it has been designated the *floppy infant syndrome* (Dubowitz, 1969). Many mentally retarded infants, especially those with Down's syndrome, are characterized by hypotonia (atonia). The main features associated with hypotonia are (a) bizarre and unusual postures and (b) increased range of movement in joints. Hypotonic infants and/or severely handicapped persons generally lie on their backs, with a froglike posture of the legs (abduction and outward rotation of hips).

Muscle tone is controlled by innervation (i.e., excitation and inhibition stimuli carried to and from the CNS). Normal muscle tone is explained by the principle of *reciprocal innervation.* Simply explained, reciprocal innervation refers to the phenomenon of muscles on one surface contracting while the antagonist muscles on the opposite surface are relaxing. This phenomenon matures with progressive myelination. It contributes to smoothness (grace and coordination) of a movement. Although muscle tone involves continuous activation of the kinesthetic receptors, it is also dependent upon normal function at six levels: (a) the

Figure 5.17 Abnormal asymmetrical tonic neck reflex is often evidenced in trampoline jumps of children with mild brain damage. This reflex is normal from birth to 6 months.

Figure 5.18 Tonic neck reflexes: (A) flexion symmetrical tonic reflex and (B) extension symmetric tonic reflex.

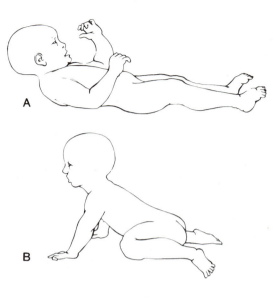

precentral motor cortex, (b) basal ganglia, (c) midbrain, (d) vestibular apparatus, and (e) the spinal cord. Developmental lag and/or injury to any of these affects muscle and postural tone.

The regulation of reciprocal innervation in relation to body postures involves flexion and extension synergies. This terminology is useful in differentiating between normal adult postural tone, in which flexor and extensor muscle tone is in balance, as opposed to reflex domination by flexion or extension synergies, as is evidenced in normal infants up to about 4 months of age and in persons with severe brain damage.

Synergy (combined action) is derived from *syn* (with) and *ergon* (working). Although used in different ways, it can refer to combined action of muscle groups as that caused by the primitive reflexes or to a rehabilitation approach in which specific muscle groups are activated that, in turn, stimulate action of related muscle groups.

The kinesthetic system is responsible for the tonic neck reflexes (both asymmetrical [Figure 5.17] and symmetrical [Figure 5.18]) and other primitive reflexes. As the kinesthetic system matures, these reflexes are integrated and movement becomes increasingly coordinated. Kinesthetic input is essential in all three kinds of human motion: reflexes, reactions,

and voluntary movement. Whether or not kinesthesis results in *conscious* awareness of joint position and movement, however, is still controversial. Neurologically, the kinesthetic sense is subcortical in both structure and function.

Several methods have been proposed for enhancing kinesthesis. Among these are practice of motor skills while blindfolded and coactive movement in which the teacher guides the limbs of the student through a desired pattern. The kinesthetic receptors are activated by changing the tension within muscle, tendon, and joint fibers. Therefore, any movement involving prolonged contraction of extensor muscles against gravity is facilitative. Ayres especially recommends scooter board activities done in prone position with head up to achieve optimal kinesthetic input. Margaret Rood, who was certified in both occupational and physical therapy, recommended the application of pressure to the sites where muscles attach to bones as a means of normalizing muscle tone, thereby reducing hypertonus (i.e., relaxing a muscle); this practice is based on the same theory that underlies neck and back rubs as a means of reducing tension.

In sensorimotor assessment and training, the kinesthetic system always works with the vestibular system. For this reason, the term *proprioception* (proprioceptive input) is frequently used to encompass the combined functioning of the two systems. Moreover, the tactile system is involved also. The term *haptic perception* has been coined by special educators to encompass combined tactile, kinesthetic, and vestibular input.

Sensorimotor Development **95**

Figure 5.19 The vestibular system in the inner ear. This system contains separate parts for static equilibrium (utricle, saccule, vestibule, macula) and dynamic equilibrium (semicircular canals). These parts are connected to the brain stem and cerebellum via the vestibular branch of the eighth cranial nerve.

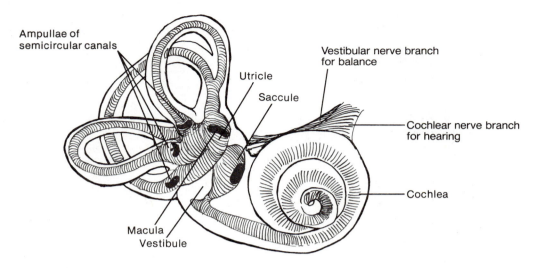

Vestibular System

Balance, which is dependent upon vestibular input from sensory receptors in the inner ear, is the function that most often seems to interfere with good motor performance among students with no known disability. Problems of balance also often characterize the motor functioning of handicapped students. Both perceptual-motor and sensory integration theories, from their inception, have emphasized balance more than any other aspect of physical performance; therefore, this explanation of the vestibular apparatus is more comprehensive than that of the other sensory systems.

Balance (equilibrium) is determined by the vestibular system, which has its sensory receptors in the inner ear. Impulses are carried from this point to the brain stem and cerebellum via the eighth cranial nerve (vestibulo-cochlear), which has two branches: the *vestibular,* which transmits impulses pertaining to equilibrium, and the *cochlear,* which transmits impulses pertaining to hearing. In the brain stem, equilibrium impulses end up in masses of gray matter, called the vestibular nuclei, which are specialized structures within the reticular formation. These relay the impulses (which reflexly change head and neck positions) to the spinal cord via the vestibulospinal and other tracts. Concurrently, they relay vestibular impulses to the nuclei of cranial nerves that innervate the extrinsic eye muscles and such visceral functions as dizziness and nausea. This anatomical sketch of the interrelationships between equilibrium, vision, and viscera helps to explain why, after rapid spinning, it is normal for the eyes to exhibit *nystagmus* (rapid movements) and the student to feel nauseous or dizzy. Motion sickness, which originates in the vestibular system, also involves vision and viscera.

The sense of equilibrium, although entirely reflex in nature, is very complex. Static and dynamic balance have different sensory receptors and are controlled separately; thus, it is possible to have good static balance (stork stand) and poor dynamic balance (walking board) or vice versa.

Static Balance

Organs pertaining to static equilibrium include the vestibule, utricle, saccule, and macula. The vestibule is the bony chamber between the semicircular canals and the cochlea (see Figure 5.19). The membranous labyrinth (tube) inside the vestibule has two parts, the utricle (larger) and the saccule (smaller). The exact function of the saccule is not yet known, so static equilibrium can best be explained in terms of the macula within the utricle. The macula is the structure that contains the hair cells that are receptors for changes in head position (Figure 5.20). The hairs of the hair cells extend upward when the head is in an upright position and downward when the head bends because they terminate in a mass of gelatinous material that is responsive to gravity.

Figure 5.20 Organs for static equilibrium. The macula within the utricle contains the hair cells, which are sensory receptors for static equilibrium. Changes in head position are detected by the macula, as indicated in *A*, head upright, and *B*, head bent and forward.

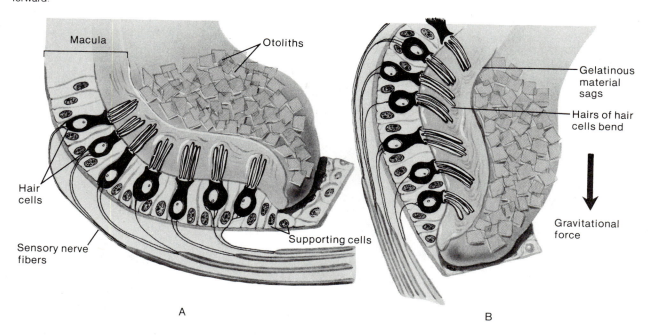

The static equilibrium organs function primarily in maintaining the stability of the head and neck when the body is motionless. This is achieved through the tonic labyrinthine reflexes in early infancy and later by the righting reactions. Any movement of the head and neck stimulates the macula within the labyrinths (vestibular input) as well as the kinesthetic receptors within the muscles, tendons, and joints of the neck; thus, it is impossible, for all practical purposes, to separate static equilibrium and kinesthetic input.

Dynamic Balance

Organs pertaining to dynamic equilibrium include the three bony semicircular canals in the inner ear (see Figure 5.21). At the bottom of each semicircular canal is a swelling called the ampulla, which contains the sensory receptors, each of which is called a crista ampullaris. This structure contains hair cells that extend up into a gelantinous mass and remain upright when the head is motionless. In contrast, when the head moves rapidly, as in falling or in spinning, twirling, or rolling activities, the gelatinous mass moves in the direction of the head movement, thereby bending and stimulating the hair cells. The dynamic equilibrium organs thus function primarily in balancing the head and neck when they are rapidly rotated or moved.

The vestibular system is well developed at birth, as is evidenced by the calming effect of cradling or rocking the infant in arms, crib, or rocking chair. Swings, seesaws, merry-go-rounds, and other playground apparatus owe their popularity to children's natural craving for vestibular stimulation. The use of balance boards, various kinds of balance beams, swinging bridges, and trampolines (all of which have unstable surfaces) in early childhood physical education is based largely on theory that posits that the vestibular system is a coordinating apparatus for all sensory functions (Schilder, 1933). Paul Schilder, the psychiatrist perhaps best known for his classic *The Image and Appearance of the Human Body* (1950), served as one of the major primary sources for Newell Kephart (1960), whose perceptual-motor theory emphasized tumbling, balance beam, and trampoline work.

The popularization of Jean Ayres's vestibular stimulation techniques in conjunction with sensory integration theory has led to the widespread use of vestibular boards and therapy balls (called cage balls by physical educators) to cause momentary loss of balance and subsequent vestibular input to activate compensatory postural adjustments. Persons certified in sensory integration remediation (contact an occupational therapy department for further information) also use spinning and other rapid rotatory movements for vestibular stimulation.

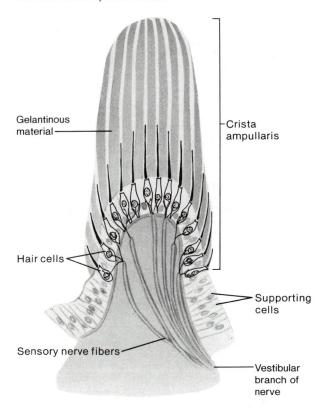

Figure 5.21 Organs for dynamic equilibrium. Within each semicircular canal is a crista ampullaris, which contains the hair cells that detect dynamic motion.

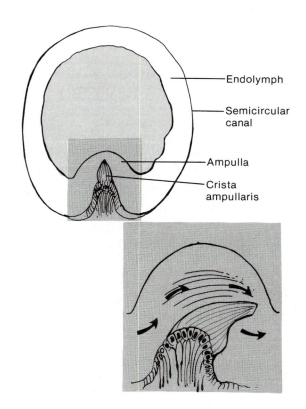

Vestibular Influence on Other Systems

That the vestibular system can excite or inhibit other sensory systems through its influence on brain stem and cerebellar function is well accepted. In summary, the vestibular, kinesthetic, and tactile systems all affect visuomotor performance. Whereas most teachers are knowledgeable about or at least interested in visual input, the physical educator is often the only one who understands and can recognize vestibular, kinesthetic, and tactile dysfunctions. Delayed and abnormal motor development is more closely associated with these systems than with the better known visual and auditory systems. Body image and self-concept are initially formed through movement experiences rooted in the vestibular, kinesthetic, and tactile systems; the child feels good or he or she feels clumsy as a result of movement. Only when mental functioning matures and the child attaches meaning to visual and verbal input are body image and self-concept affected by these systems.

Shift in Dominance of Sensory Systems

The shift in dominance of the sensory systems is, thus, important for physical educators to understand. In normally developing children, the shift from vestibular, kinesthetic, and tactile (VKT) dominance to visual and auditory dominance occurs at about age 7 or 8 years. In children with mental retardation, severe emotional disturbance, learning disabilities, and cerebral palsy, this shift may occur much later. Blindness and/or deafness obviously have great impact on this shift. The physical educator must, therefore, assess which sense modalities comprise the student's strongest channel for motor learning: VKT, visual, verbal, or some combination. Pedagogy should then be directed toward the strong channels of each individual rather than presenting new motor skills to all students in the same way.

Visual and Auditory Systems

Inasmuch as these systems are intricately linked with mental functioning (i.e., the cognitive understanding of what one sees and hears), their discussion perhaps more properly belongs under perceptual-motor theory (see Chapter 11) than sensorimotor development. They are, therefore, only briefly considered here.

After school age is reached, approximately 90% of what the normally functioning child learns comes from visual input. This belief forms the basis of visuomotor theory. The premise has not been subjected to much research, and its validity in terms of children with delayed or abnormal motor development is not known.

Learning Activities

1. View films or videotapes on normal, abnormal, and delayed development to reinforce knowledge of reflexes, reactions, and motor milestones.

2. Obtain permission to film/videotape infants and children of various ages and apply your biomechanics knowledge to analyzing movement.

3. Observe teachers and therapists in a motor development setting with severely handicapped, nonambulatory students and identify abnormal and/or delayed sensorimotor functioning. What methods are being used to ameliorate problems?

4. Make a packet of 3×5" flash cards of new words and names of persons in this chapter. Develop games that can be played with these cards for reinforcing concepts in this chapter.

5. Role play such sensorimotor authorities as Ayres, Bobath, Corbin, Cratty, Fiorentino, and Gesell. Read their books (listed in the bibliography) and develop a panel discussion for role playing their similarities and differences.

References

Ayres, A. J. (1972). *Sensory integration and learning disorders*. Los Angeles: Western Psychological Services.

Bayley, N. (1969). *Manual for the Bayley scales of infant development*. New York: Psychological Corporation.

Bobath, K. (1980). *A neurophysiological basis for the treatment of cerebral palsy*. Philadelphia: J. B. Lippincott.

Dubowitz, V. (1969). *The floppy infant*. London: Spastics International Medical Publications.

Fiorentino, M. (1963). *Reflex testing methods for evaluating CNS development*. Springfield, IL: Charles C. Thomas.

Frankenburg, W., & Dodds, J. B. (1967). The Denver developmental screening test. *The Journal of Pediatrics, 71*, 181–191.

Gesell, A., & Amatruda, C. S. (1949). *Gesell developmental schedules*. New York: Psychological Corporation.

Gesell, A., & Ames, L. B. (1940). The ontogenetic organization of prone behavior in human infancy. *Journal of Genetic Psychology, 56*, 247–263.

Hole, J. (1981). *Human anatomy and physiology* (2nd ed.). Dubuque, IA: Wm. C. Brown.

Illingsworth, R. S. (1983). *The development of the infant and young child*. (8th ed.). Baltimore: Williams & Wilkins.

Kephart, N. (1960). *The slow learner in the classroom*. Columbus, OH: Charles E. Merrill.

Knobloch, H., & Pasamanick, B. (Eds.). (1974). *Gesell and Amatruda's developmental diagnosis* (3rd ed.). New York: Harper & Row.

McGraw, M. (1935). *Growth: A study of Johnny and Jimmy*. New York: Appleton-Century-Crofts.

McGraw, M. (1963). *The neuromuscular maturation of the human infant*. New York: Hafner Publishing Company.

Schilder, P. (1933). The vestibular apparatus in neurosis and psychosis. *Journal of Nervous and Mental Disease, 1* (23), 139–164.

Schilder, P. (1950). *The image and appearance of the human body*. New York: International Universities Press, Incorporated.

Shirley, M. M. (1933). *The first two years: A study of twenty-five babies*. Minneapolis: University of Minnesota Press.

Bibliography

Ayres, A. J. (1974). *The development of sensory integrative theory and practice*. Dubuque, IA: Kendall/Hunt.

Ayres, A. J. (1980). *Sensory integration and the child*. Los Angeles: Western Psychological Services.

Banus, B. (1979). *The developmental therapist* (2nd ed.). Thorofare, NJ: Charles B. Slack.

Bobath, K. (1966). *The motor deficit in patients with cerebral palsy*. London: Spastics International Medical Publications.

Bobath, K. & Bobath, B. (1978). The neurodevelopmental approach to treatment. In P. Pearson & C. Williams (Eds.), *Physical therapy services in the developmental disabilities* (pp. 114–185). Springfield, IL: Charles C. Thomas.

Clark, F., & Shuer, J. (1978). A clarification of sensory integrative therapy and its application to programming with retarded people. *Mental Retardation, 16*, 227–232.

Corbin, C. (1980). *A textbook of motor development* (2nd ed.). Dubuque, IA: Wm. C. Brown.

Cratty, B. J. (1978). *Perceptual and motor development in infants and children* (2nd ed.). New York: Macmillan.

Espenschade, A., & Eckert, H. (1980). *Motor development* (2nd ed.). Columbus, OH: Charles E. Merrill.

Fiorentino, M. (1972). *Normal and abnormal development.* Springfield, IL: Charles C. Thomas.

Fiorentino, M. (1981). *A basis for sensorimotor development—normal and abnormal.* Springfield, IL: Charles C. Thomas.

Garwood, S. G. (1979). *Educating young handicapped children.* Germantown, MD: Aspen Systems Corporation.

Holle, B. (1976). *Motor development in children: Normal and retarded.* St. Louis: C. V. Mosby (Printed by Munksgaard, Copenhagen).

Illingsworth, R. S. (1983). *The development of the infant and young child: Normal and abnormal* (8th ed.). Baltimore: Williams & Wilkins.

Kelso, J., & Clark, J. (Eds.). (1982). *The development of movement control and coordination.* New York: John Wiley & Sons.

Mussen, P. (Ed.). (1970). *Carmichael's manual of child psychology.* New York: John Wiley & Sons.

Paine, R., Brazelton, T. B., Donovan, D., Drorbaugh, J., Hubbell, J., & Sears, E. M. (1964). Evolution of postural reflexes in normal infants and in the presence of chronic brain syndromes. *Neurology, 14,* 1036–1048.

Peiper, A. (1963). *Cerebral function in infancy and childhood.* London: Pitman.

Rarick, G. L. (1961). *Motor development during infancy and childhood.* Madison, WI: College Printing and Typing Co.

Rarick. G. L. (Ed.). (1973). *Physical activity: Human growth and development.* New York: Academic Press.

Ridenour, M. (Ed.). (1978). *Motor development: Issues and applications.* Princeton, NJ: Princeton Book Co.

Stockmeyer, S. (1978). A sensorimotor approach to treatment. In P. Pearson & C. Williams (Eds.), *Physical therapy services in the developmental disabilities* (pp. 186–222). Springfield, IL: Charles C. Thomas.

Williams, H. (1983). *Perceptual and motor development.* Englewood Cliffs, NJ: Prentice-Hall.

Zaichkowsky, L., Zaichkowsky, L., & Martinek, T. (1980). *Growth and development.* St. Louis: C. V. Mosby.

Cognitive and Play Development

Figure 6.1 Balance activities are integrated with cognitive learning (geography) and perceptual-motor practice (form and space perception).

Chapter Objectives

After you have studied this chapter, you should be able to

1. Discuss play theory in relation to normal, abnormal, and delayed development. Include in your discussion 10 major premises of play theory and cite examples of each.

2. Explain stage theory and discuss the role of Piaget and other developmentalists in its evolution. How does understanding of stage theory help in adapted physical education service delivery?

3. Identify five mental operations essential to sound cognitive functioning and discuss each in relation to physical education. Differentiate between *adaptive behaviors* and *mental operations*.

4. Describe Piaget's four stages in cognitive development and cite anecdotes showing how mental operations in each stage can be enhanced through physical education.

5. Discuss the relationship between language development and sensorimotor function. How can physical educators contribute to language development?

6. List 10 stages in toy or object play and discuss each in terms of physical education assessment and programming for (a) young children with and without disabilities and (b) severely handicapped older students.

7. List seven stages in social play development, discuss behavior characteristics of each, and relate these to physical education assessment and programming.

8. Describe six developmental stages in competition and discuss use of competitive vs. cooperative activities for students of different ages and various disabilities.

9. Discuss the development of creative abilities through physical education.

10. Delineate Kohlberg's developmental stages in rules conformity and give examples of the six levels. How do these relate to you as a teacher? How do they relate to your students?

11. Explain self-concept and body image and discuss the development of each. How do handicapping conditions affect development?

12. Explain each of the following: body schema, cathexis, praxis, apraxia, laterality, verticality, bilateral integration, and directionality. How does each relate to physical education assessment and programming?

PL 94–142 emphasizes that physical education includes three areas: physical and motor fitness, fundamental motor skills and patterns, and skills in aquatics, dance, games, and sports. The last of these may be the most important in early development, especially that of severely handicapped children. In infancy and early childhood, these skills are called play and game skills. For the skills to develop normally, mental, social, and moral functioning as well as the sensorimotor system must be intact.

Play has many definitions. It can be used synonymously with recreation and leisure functioning. In infancy and early childhood, however, *play* refers to the spontaneous behaviors (pleasurable) with which children interact with their environment. In normal infants, play is inborn and instinctive. Give them a rattle and they will shake, mouth, and pound it. Put a toy in front of them and they will reach for it. Put them on the floor and, once they have learned to crawl and creep, they will spontaneously move from place to place, exploring their environment.

Normal children progress through easily observable stages of play (see Figure 6.1). From birth until age 2 years, play is mostly sensorimotor, with the child exploring and manipulating his or her environment; almost all of the sense modalities are involved. From 2 to 7 years of age, children develop social skills and elementary understandings of game formations and rules. From 7 years of age on, children develop the mental operations and social and moral understandings that enable them to grasp complex rules and strategies and exhibit good sportsmanship in competitive sports. Moral development, in child growth and development theory, refers to the evolution of behaviors that relate to rules (game and play rules, home and family rules, school rules, society rules), regulations, and laws. In physical education, moral development is closely related to good sportsmanship.

Play Theory

Play theory is so complex that entire books have been written on it. Among the best of these are

Frost, J., & Klein, B. (1979). *Children's play and playgrounds*. Boston: Allyn & Bacon.
Huizinga, J. (1955). *Homo ludens* [Man plays]. Boston: Beacon Press.
Levy, J. (1978). *Play behaviors*. New York: John Wiley & Sons.
Piaget, J. (1962). *Play, dreams, and imitation in childhood*. New York: W. W. Norton & Co.
Wehman, P. (1977). *Helping the mentally retarded acquire play skills: A behavioral approach*. Springfield, IL: Charles C. Thomas.

Play theory is emphasized in the training of occupational therapists, early childhood educators, and recreation and leisure services personnel, but it is often neglected in the undergraduate studies of physical education majors. The reasons for this are not clear except, perhaps, for the fact that play in normal children is spontaneous and physical educators believe it does not have to be taught. Physical educators believe that their subject matter is serious, whereas play is often conceptualized as frivolous and fun (i.e., the opposite of work). If learning is believed to be work rather than play, then physical education games, sports, and fitness activities are treated as work. Exercise physiology reflects this philosophy also through use of such terms as physical work capacity. Students are expected to work at achieving fitness and gaining the skills needed to win at sports; coaches exhort their players to work hard, be serious, and do their best. These beliefs have led some physical educators, especially secondary school teachers, to remain ignorant about play theory. Many physical educators unfortunately believe that play (as well as recreation and leisure) is the exclusive domain of recreators. In disability and illness, however, occupational therapists are often the most knowledgeable about play.

Adapted physical educators, like occupational therapists and recreators, must be concerned with play and must become acquainted with early childhood literature on normal play development. The major premises of play theory are the following:

1. Play, in infancy and early childhood, is the medium through which learning occurs.

2. Sensorimotor development in normal children occurs through play (i.e., spontaneous interactions with the environment).

3. If play behavior is not spontaneous, then it must be taught concurrently with motor skills and patterns.

4. Play, as persons move from childhood into adolescence, becomes more of a mental state than a physical activity. As this occurs, terminology changes from play to playfulness, playful thinking, recreation, and leisure.

5. Play and playfulness are closely related to creativeness. Physical play (spontaneity in moving the body and in exploring the environment in many, new, and different ways) leads to motor creativity. Mental playfulness (spontaneity in generating many, new, and different ideas) leads to mental creativity. Both result in imagination and mental imagery.

6. A broad spectrum of individual differences characterize normal children and adults in the degree to which they possess play behaviors at all ages. In early childhood this is usually measured by observing physical and social play behaviors. In older children and adults this is typically measured in two ways: (a) tests of motor and mental creativity and (b) inventories and rating scales of recreation and leisure behaviors (i.e., beliefs, practices, and preferences).

7. Play and playfulness, regardless of age, are essential to good mental health. They provide the mental flexibility to perceive the world, as well as self, in many different ways, to find alternative ways of thinking, believing, and acting, and to imagine future happenings.

8. Play and playfulness are one medium through which persons adapt to their environment as well as modify the environment to meet their personal needs.

9. Behaviors related to play, playfulness, recreation, and leisure can be changed. If persons of any age exhibit problems or deficits in these areas, education and/or therapy can be used to facilitate change.

10. Play theory does not belong to any one discipline. It is multidisciplinary.

Education versus Therapy

Education refers to techniques that facilitate learning skills, beliefs, attitudes, practices, and habits. Play training, as used by physical educators, recreators, occupational therapists, and regular and special education personnel, is education. From middle childhood on, play training is generally called leisure education. It may be directed toward persons exhibiting normal, delayed, or abnormal play development.

Therapy comes from the Greek word for treatment; its primary aim is not learning, but the application of treatment modalities to make a sick or disabled person well and/or as normally functioning as possible. *Play therapy* is a treatment modality used by psychologists, psychiatrists, social workers, and nurses with psychiatric training. Play therapy was first conceptualized by Freud, who stated that children reveal psychiatric problems in their play; therefore, they can be helped to work through problems by carefully structured play experiences during which the therapist says and does specific things in response to the child's actions. Nondirective therapists, who follow Carl Rogers rather than Freud, use different approaches, usually questions designed to help children solve their own problems and realize increasing control over their lives.

Play therapy most often involves activities using dolls dressed as father, mother, sister, and brother images and sometimes as physicians, nurses, and others in the community. A doll house or a replica of a hospital, school, or community setting is used so that children can *act out* with the dolls such feelings as fear, anxiety, rejection, jealousy, aggression, and hate. Only persons with professional training in psychiatry and play therapy should use the term *play therapy*. Others, regardless of the goals to be achieved through play, use the term *play training* or *leisure education*.

Play Deficits in Handicapped Children

Just as motor development may be normal, delayed, or abnormal, play development is altered by handicapping conditions. Any sensory deficit (visual, auditory, vestibular, and the like) that interferes with sensorimotor development also affects play development, especially from birth through 2 years of age. Thus, most children with congenital blindness or deafness, as well as those with cerebral palsy and/or vestibular dysfunctions, are delayed in play development. If sensorimotor development is delayed (regardless of the reason), as often happens in mental retardation, then play development is delayed also. Abnormal play activity usually characterizes only children with autism or severe emotional disturbance who respond to play objects and apparatus with stereotyped/repetitive movements and/or use them for self-mutilation or injuring others.

A major characteristic of severely handicapped children is that they do not play spontaneously. In spite of the trend toward such children remaining at home with their families, they can best be studied in residential facilities. Ask to visit the units where the most severely disabled persons are housed in any institution.

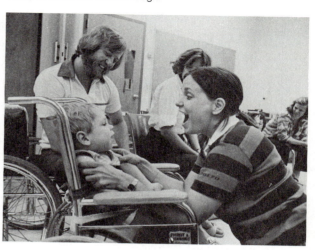

Figure 6.2 Severely handicapped children have to be taught how to play. Often, this begins by teaching them how to laugh. In the game depicted, the teacher has to do something funny every time the child laughs. Later, the child will learn to do something funny to make the teacher laugh.

You will most likely find them sitting, lying, or rocking back and forth, unoccupied, staring into space, or repetitively manipulating some object (i.e., demonstrating autistic-like behaviors). They may be staring at television, but staff will tell you that severely mentally handicapped persons seldom understand television; they just like the changing color and movement on the screen.

This condition does not have to exist. Severely handicapped persons can be taught to play. If they are not taught, play behaviors often never evolve. Imagine an entire life devoid of play! A major goal of adapted physical education is to teach children to play spontaneously. To have motor skills, without play skills, after all is rather meaningless. Unfortunately, many physical educators assigned to work with 3- and 4-year-old handicapped children teach only motor skills or else teach motor skills independently of play skills.

Less severely handicapped students may play spontaneously, but to a lesser extent than nondisabled peers. Upper extremity disabilities may make manipulation of play objects, toys, and table games (cards, checkers, and monopoly, for example) difficult or impossible. Lower extremity disabilities limit play to that which can be done from wheelchairs, scooter boards, crutches, or walkers. Speech problems, such as occur in congenital deafness and severe cerebral palsy, affect the development of social play skills. Mental retardation and learning disabilities prevent engaging in game play that requires fully matured mental operations and intact perceptual abilities. A goal of adapted physical education is to find games and sports that utilize the abilities that such students have and then help them to fully develop their play potential (see Figure 6.2).

Table 6.1
Portion of IEP Relating to Throwing

Present level of performance. Primarily in stage 3, Homolateral throw stage.

Goal. To progress from stage 3 to 4.

Objectives. Given a regulation softball, student will throw a distance of 30 feet, 8 out of 10 times exhibiting the following characteristics: (a) opposition, (b) weight transfer in forward, backward, forward pattern, (c) full rotation of the trunk, etc. *Note that this can be shortened by just writing a, b, c and referring to the assessment form for explanation.*

Service delivery. 5 minutes out of every daily physical education class for 10 weeks will be spent in distance and target throwing games, with a peer tutor present to correct errors and praise strengths. Videotapes will be taken for student to view.

Date for initiating instruction (DII). 1/15/86

Evaluation criteria. See objective. Test given every 2 weeks.

Developmental Stages

Stage theory developed during the 1920s and 1930s, largely through the work of Swiss psychologist Jean Piaget. Today, stages have been described for almost every aspect of infant and child development. Stage theory is based upon the principles of continuity and uniform sequence in normal development. Assuming development is continuous, human beings will progress from one stage to another. There will be, however, some overlap from one stage to another (i.e., the child may possess some characteristics of a lower stage although he or she is mostly functioning in a higher stage). Take, for instance, the overarm throw, as depicted in Figure 6.3. Watch a young child throw; then circle, at the top of page 107, the characteristics he or she exhibits in each stage. It is usually possible to designate the dominant stage.

When chronological age limits are suggested for different stages, it must be remembered that these are only estimates. Although the stages through which all normally developing children pass are uniform, the chronological ages of progression vary widely, particularly when handicapping conditions are present. Occasionally, a child does not pass through stages in the uniform sequence followed by everyone else; this may be an example of abnormal development or, if it seems to make no difference in performance, a chance individual deviation.

Stages are used in adapted physical education, special education, and related areas to assess and describe where handicapped students are within the normal continuum of growth and development. Common understandings, within a school system, of developmental stages facilitate assessment and the writing of goals and objectives for the IEP. This is illustrated in Table 6.1. In the next part of this chapter, developmental stages are described that can assist in assessment and IEP writing for handicapped children.

Cognitive Functioning

Psychomotor learning is closely related to level of cognitive functioning. In order to teach the whole child, the adapted physical educator must obtain information about mental abilities and/or adaptive behaviors. Intelligence can be analyzed into 120 different mental abilities, which in turn can be categorized into five operations. Most authorities concur that these operations are (a) *memory,* retention of what is learned; (b) *convergent production,* finding the one correct or best answer; (c) *divergent production,* discovering many new and different responses in situations where more than one answer is acceptable; (d) *cognition,* encompassing knowing, comprehending, applying, analyzing, and synthesizing; and (e) *evaluation,* reaching decisions about correctness, appropriateness, or adequacy of what is known.

Adaptive behaviors refer to functioning in such broad areas as personal independence, socialization, self-direction, language development, number and time concepts, and physical development. This term is used most often in conjunction with mental retardation, since deficits in mental operations affect adaptive behaviors. Specific adaptive behaviors necessary for teaching children simple games include (a) language development sufficient to understand start and stop cues, purpose of game, and simple rules, (b) mental operations sufficient to understand such game roles as chase/flee or run for safety, and (c) physical development sufficient to run or use wheelchair or scooter board.

Intelligence and Motor Performance

Much adapted physical education research in the 1950s and 1960s focused upon the relationship between intelligence and motor performance in mentally retarded persons. This research indicated that the correlations between IQ and motor performance tests in mildly mentally retarded boys and girls are generally positive, but low (mostly being in the .20s and .30s). Thus, children with mild to moderate mental retardation can often achieve more success in the physical education

Figure 6.3 Four stages in overarm throwing through which children progress. *Stage 1:* **Casting** characterized by: (1) feet remain stationary; (2) no trunk or hip rotation; (3) ball is thrown primarily by elbow extension. *Stage 2:* **Hurling** characterized by: (1) feet remain stationary; (2) preparatory movement involves a rotation of the trunk toward the throwing side; (3) outward rotation and abduction at shoulder joint result in cocking of hand slightly behind head; (4) trunk rotates back to starting position with forward arm swing; (5) angle of release is usually 80–100°. *Stage 3:* **Homolateral throw,** same as stage 2 except (1) child steps into throw (i.e., as right arm throws, right foot steps forward); (2) there is weight shift forward and more pronounced follow-through; (3) angle of release is more horizontal (forward). *Stage 4:* **Crosslateral throw** characterized by (1) opposition (left foot forward as right arm throws); (2) weight transfer in forward-backward-forward pattern; (3) full rotation of trunk to left and right; (4) coordinated involvement of nonthrowing arm in maintaining balance; (5) abduction/outward rotation at shoulder joint in backswing changes to adduction/inward rotation in forward swing and follow through; (6) angle of release is about 45°.

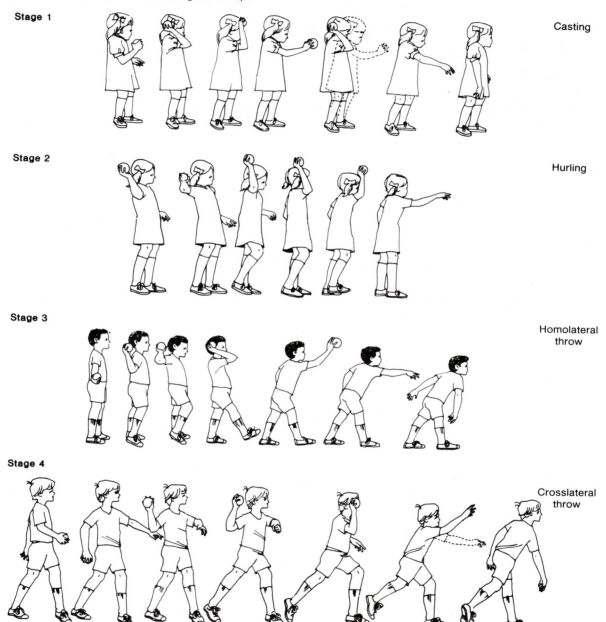

Stage 1 — Casting

Stage 2 — Hurling

Stage 3 — Homolateral throw

Stage 4 — Crosslateral throw

setting than in other academic areas that are highly loaded with intelligence components. Such research favors the integration of children with low mental ability in physical education, but fails to consider such cognitive aspects of physical education as grasping the rules and strategies of game play and understanding movement factors (time, space, force, flow) and mechanical principles.

Stages in Cognitive Development

Classification of handicapped students according to broad stages in cognitive development allows physical educators to predict probable success in instructional units. Jean Piaget, a Swiss psychologist, has hypothesized four major stages of cognitive development:

Stage 1, Sensorimotor Intelligence (0 to 2 Years)

This stage encompasses children's functioning prior to their ability to use symbols—i.e., language. Through use of the sense modalities (primarily the visual, kinesthetic, vestibular, and tactile), infants come to know the world and develop awareness of self, others, and objects. During this stage they begin to recognize objects by color, form, and size and achieve *object permanence,* the understanding that objects continue to exist after they disappear and/or are hidden (Figure 6.4). They also develop spatial relationships. Games like Peek-a-boo and Hide and Seek show when object permanence is understood as well as relationships of objects in space. In this stage, children also acquire the

ability to imitate and play imitation games. They learn that their actions/movements can cause consequences (a cry brings a bottle; a smile causes another person to smile). Some authorities believe that this initial grasp of the relationship between movement and consequence (means and ends) is the beginning of self-concept—i.e., the self as competent or not competent, depending upon the extent to which significant others react to movements.

Stage 2, Preoperational Intelligence (2 to 7 Years)

During this stage, children develop *representation,* the ability to link meaning to objects and subsequently to the symbols (like pictures, written words, and gestures/signs) that represent the objects. Thus, speech takes precedence over movement as a means of expressing thought. Although children progress from parallel to cooperative play during these years, their conceptual framework remains egocentric (I/me-centered).

Thought at this stage primarily focuses on one thing at a time. It is important, therefore, that early childhood physical educators give only one *direction* or *movement suggestion* at a time. Thought is concrete rather than abstract, and thinking is not yet organized according to logical rules.

The mental operations described in Table 6.2 begin to emerge during this stage. Most early childhood games, however, demand only an understanding of the game function, start and stop signals, the baseline or safety zone concept, and the roles of chase/flee, hide/seek, and tag/dodge.

Table 6.2
Emerging Mental Operations That Affect Game and Movement Education Performance in Elementary School Years

Classification is the ability to group things. Children proceed from the ability to match objects that are identical to the ability to group things that are similar and dissimilar. The last skill in the progression is *class inclusion,* the ability to see relationships between parts and wholes and make judgments accordingly.

Seriation (sequencing) is the ability to arrange things according to a dimension along which they differ. For example, in the preoperational stage, the child learns to discriminate the larger and the smaller in a dyad and then a triad. In the operational stage, the child can arrange 10 or more objects from large to small or vice versa.

Number concepts entail the ability to discriminate between and among quantities. For instance, in the preoperational stage, the child can discriminate roughly between a lot and a little. In the concrete operational stage, the child makes increasingly finer discriminations, like differentiating between lines of eight and nine objects.

Conservation refers to understanding of object and quantity permanence and encompasses shape, length, number, and position. Piaget's classic example is filling two identical glasses with identical amounts of water, which, of course, results in equal water heights. Then the water from one glass is poured into a narrower container, causing the water height to rise. If the conservation operation has been acquired, the child will know that the amounts of water continue to be the same irrespective of the perceptual distortion.

Reversibility is the ability to understand and work with opposites (add vs. subtract; right vs. left; move vs. remain stationary). At the preoperational level, children experience difficulty in remembering sequences in reverse order. Likewise, they have problems in determining the correct order of objects when the containers are placed in different positions. During the concrete operational stage the child copes increasingly effectively with opposites as well as time/space relationships encompassing such concepts as near/far, left/right, before/after, and front/behind.

Figure 6.5 Challenging young children to pull different colored valentines from the wall and put them in a basket teaches classification while offering practice in reach-grasp-release.

Stage 3, Concrete Operational Intelligence (7 to 11 Years)

In this stage, children gradually develop the ability to perform such mental operations as classification (Figure 6.5), seriation, numbers, conservation, and reversibility. These operations are necessary for understanding the directions to most of the low organized games children play and for responding to challenges of movement education. Each operation is briefly described in Table 6.2 to show the learning progression that begins in the preoperational stage and continues into the concrete operational stage.

Ability in *classification* is needed before children can successfully engage in team competition (i.e., differentiate between teammates and opponents). It is also essential to game strategies that involve position play. Students must be able to differentiate between offensive and defensive moves and match their use with the situation. The easiest games involving classification are hide and seek, guessing, and retrieval games. In the latter, objects of different colors or shapes are scattered all over the floor and the students are challenged, Who can run and pick up the most blues?

Seriation, usually called *sequencing* in physical education, is the ability to remember sequences as in I'm Going to Grandmother's House. Until children acquire this ability, they cannot remember game rules like what happens in softball after three strikes, after three outs, or when a fly ball is caught.

Until students master number concepts, scoring has little meaning. Likewise, such movement education challenges as "Can you balance on three body parts?" are not understood.

Ability in *conservation* relates to generalization (i.e., understanding that a ball is a ball and can be thrown and caught regardless of its color, size, and shape). Much of perceptual-motor training pertains to object constancy (i.e., an object is the same whether upside down, rotated, or hidden in a background in which it is out of context). Movement education challenges like "How many ways can you move?" or "How many shapes can you make with your body?" help develop conservation. The ability to understand pretend roles like *it* or Mother Witch or Fox and Chickens in What Time Is It, Mr. Fox, also rests in conservation concepts (i.e., people can assume roles, but they have not really changed).

Reversibility is the basic ability needed to play all the early childhood games that involve a quick change of direction of one player (i.e., when tagged) or the entire group (in running away from *it* after a cue word) or a quick change of speed (Red Light, Green Light). Until students develop this mental operation, they cannot change roles within a game (i.e., switch from someone who is fleeing from *it*, after being tagged, to someone who is *it* and now performs a chasing role).

Many physical educators take these mental operations for granted. They evolve with no special training in children without handicapping conditions. Their absence, however, brings chaos when trying to teach the simplest of childhood games. The development of these mental operations is delayed, often by several years, in children with mental retardation and related conditions. Many severely disabled children display mental operations that appear to be frozen at the preoperational level.

Stage 4, Formal Operational Intelligence (11 to 12 Years+)

According to Piaget, children's mental operations begin to acquire adult characteristics at about age 11 or 12. Intelligence becomes increasingly logical and abstract, allowing adolescents to think in terms of ideas rather than things and people. They become capable of problem solving in the scientific sense and can hypothesize and examine alternatives.

Language Development

Essential to the development of mental operations is language functioning. Physical educators working in early childhood settings and/or with severely handicapped persons of all ages cannot assume that students have sufficient language to understand movement concepts and to respond to simple verbal instructions. Adapted physical education personnel work on language development concurrent with psychomotor development.

Many nonverbal handicapped children (particularly the severely mentally retarded and emotionally disturbed as well as the deaf) learn to communicate initially through gesture and sign language. Many perceptual motor theorists believe that language (and perhaps intelligence) is learned through movement. Adapted physical educators should, therefore, understand the sequential development of inner, receptive, and expressive language.

Inner Language

For words to have meanings, they must represent units of experience. *Inner language processes* are those that permit the transformation of experience into symbols. Normally, inner language is developed before the age of 5. Inner language is how one thinks. Persons who speak several languages, for instance, acknowledge that they think only in their native tongue, especially when under duress. Adults with normal hearing whose first exposure to word meanings was the sign language of deaf parents indicate that they think in signs when confronted with difficult mental tasks.

Inner language skills may be developed in the physical education setting through the provision of activities designed to convey the essence or feeling of words pertaining to the self and to space, time, force, and flow. Illustrative of such words are those in Table 6.3.

Receptive Language

Receptive language encompasses comprehension of gestures, postures, and facial expressions; comprehension of the spoken word; and understanding of the symbols or signs used to represent words. Receptive language presupposes integrity of memory, including the ability to remember sequences. Memory may be primarily auditory, visual, or proprioceptive, or a blending of all three.

Table 6.3
Words Representing Inner Language Concepts That Can Be Acquired Through Movement Lessons

Self	Space	Time	Force[a]	Flow

Body parts
Fingers
Hand
Wrist
Elbow
Shoulders
Knee
 	
Body surfaces
Front
Back
Top
Inside
Outside
Bottom
 	
Body movements
Bend
Circle
Grasp
Stretch
Rotate
Release
 	
Body shapes
Curved
Straight/narrow
Straight/wide
Twisted
	Directions
	Forward
	Backward
	Inside
	Outside
	Up
	Down
	Left
	Right
	
	Levels
	High
	Medium
	Low
	
	Size/dimensions
	Large
	Medium
	Small
	Wide
	Narrow
	
	Planes
	Sagittal
	Frontal/vertical
	Horizontal
	
	Pathways (floor or air)
	Slanted
	Straight
	Curved
	Zigzag
		Speed
		Fast
		Medium
		Slow
		Accelerating
		Decelerating
		
		Quantity
		A lot (long)
		A little (short)
		Variable
		
		Rhythm
		Pulse beats
		Accents
		Rhythmic patterns
		  Even
		  Uneven
		Phrases
		
		Numbers
		Concepts
		Sequences
		Processes
			Force
			Strong
			Medium
			Weak
			Heavy
			Light
			
			Qualities
			Sudden, explosive
			Sustained, smooth
			
			Creating force
			Quick starts
			Sustained powerful
			  movements
			Static balances
			
			Absorbing force
			Sudden stops on
			  balance
			Gradual absorption,
			  "give" as in catching
			
			Imparting force
			Rolling
			Throwing
			Kicking
			Striking
				Qualities
				Hyperactive
				Uncontrolled
				Free
				Abandoned
				Exaggerated
				Fluent
				Inhibited
				Restrained
				Bound
				Repressed
				Tied up
				Overcautious
				
				Movement sequences
				Smooth, graceful
				Rough, awkward

[a]Some persons prefer "Effort" or "Weight"

Inner language skills are dependent upon receptive language and vice versa. A child cannot think in a language that has not yet been acquired. The following passage describes the interrelationship between the development of receptive language and inner language skills in Helen Keller at age 7, who was both deaf and blind:

My teacher placed my hand under the spout. As the cool stream gushed over one hand she spelled into the other the word water, first slowly, then rapidly. I stood still, my whole attention fixed upon the motions of her fingers. Suddenly I felt a misty consciousness as of something forgotten—a thrill of returning thought; and knew somehow the mystery of language was revealed to me. I knew then that "w-a-t-e-r" meant the wonderful cool something that was flowing over my hand. That living word awakened my soul, gave it light, hope, joy, set it free! There were barriers still, it is true, but barriers that could in time be swept away.
I left the well-house eager to learn. Everything had a name, and each name gave birth to a new thought. (Keller, 1965, p. 14)

Until age 7, Helen Keller had neither inner language nor receptive language in the ordinary sense. The following passage, however, does show that inner language can develop without vision and audition if the child possesses sufficient intelligence to capitalize upon proprioceptive cues.

I cannot recall what happened during the first months after my illness. I only know that I sat in my mother's lap or clung to her dress as she went about her household duties. My hands felt every object and observed every motion, and in this way I learned to know many things. Soon I felt the need of some communication with others and began to make crude signs. A shake of the head meant "No" and a nod, "Yes," a pull meant "Come" and a push, "Go." Was it bread that I wanted? Then I would imitate the acts of cutting the slices and buttering them. If I wanted my mother to make ice cream for dinner I made the sign for working the freezer and shivered, indicating cold. (Keller, 1965, p. 14)

Figure 6.6 Play apparatus should be used to teach and/or reinforce language concepts. Here Dr. Ellen Lubin Curtis-Pierce, authority in early childhood adapted physical education, uses the London trestle tree apparatus to teach concepts of *up* and *down* while simultaneously working on arm and shoulder strength.

Children vary widely with respect to receptive language skills. The emphasis placed upon *learning to follow directions* reveals that many teachers are not satisfied with the receptive language of their pupils. Physical educators should cooperate with classroom teachers in designing movement experiences that reinforce the meanings of words (see Figure 6.6). Thus, a session on the playground may be built around verbs, nouns, or adverbs. Charades and similar guessing games related to pantomime and facial expressions can be planned to enhance word comprehension. Most important, the child should be taught the names of the things he or she can do, the pieces of apparatus and equipment used, and the games played.

Expressive Language

Expressive language can be verbal or nonverbal. It presupposes integrity of both receptive and inner language. The way a child speaks and writes reveals his or her memory of words, sequences, and syntactic structures. It also lends insight into the child's ability to discriminate between words and letters that sound or look alike.

The thought and memory processes of many persons with severe expressive language deficits are intact. Inability to speak is not an indication of mental retardation, although many persons mistakenly think it is.

Deficits of expressive language constitute the largest disability category recognized by the Office of Special Education. Over 2 million school-age children have language problems severe enough to warrant professional help. Many of these children exhibit inner and receptive language problems as well as difficulties in structuring thoughts into sentences and enunciating words. For this reason, speech therapists, like physical educators, rely heavily upon movement exploration and apparatus work to help preschool children transform experience into symbols and, thus, acquire inner language. The term *presymbolic language* is used by speech therapists to refer to the movement of young children who have not yet mastered the intricacies of speech—i.e., symbolic language.

Table 6.4
Developmental Stages in Toy or Object Play

Stage	Activity	Stage	Activity
1	**Repetitive manual manipulation.** Usually an up-and-down shaking movement of rattles and other noisemakers. May be an autistic behavior or blindism. All repetitive movements of this nature are described as *stereotypic behaviors*.	7	**Personalized toy play.** Occurs first as imitation, usually in conjunction with toy dishes, dolls, and stuffed animals. Pretending to feed toy or rocking it to sleep are early play behaviors. Riding a broomstick horse or using wheel-toys to get from place to place is another example. Child can respond, with gesture, to question, ''What is this toy for?'' These abilities emerge between ages 1 and 2 years.
2	**Oral contacts.** Mouthing of objects; also considered stereotypic behaviors.	8	**Manipulation of movable toy parts.** This includes all the commercial toys (dolls and trucks, for example) with parts that can be turned, pushed, or pulled without coming apart. This manipulation is purposeful, often combined with dramatic play. Also includes door knobs, zippers, velcro fasteners, horns, and bells. These abilities emerge between ages 1.5 and 2.5 years.
3	**Pounding.** Developmentally the first purposeful play movement to appear. It cannot occur until voluntary, one-handed grasp appears, usually about 5 months of age, and child can sit upright with support so at least one hand is free.		
4	**Striking, raking a stationary object.** At about 7 months of age, normal children enjoy raking food pellets or other objects off of a table surface; an ulnar (toward ulna and little finger) raking movement occurs developmentally before the more mature radial (toward radius and thumb) movement. With severely involved older students (especially those with cerebral palsy), striking is easier than throwing.	9	**Separation of toy parts.** This includes putting puzzles (large parts) together and taking them apart; dressing and undressing dolls; connecting and disconnecting cars of a train; building towers with blocks; pinning tail on donkey and body parts on drawing of a person. These skills emerge between ages 2 and 3 years.
5	**Pushing or pulling.** This includes pulling toys by strings and pushing toys on wheels. In normal development, it occurs at about 10 months of age after evolution of pincer grasp (i.e., use of thumb and index finger). In severely involved older students, pushing skills include box hockey and shuffleboard-type games in which a stick is used to push the object. Rolling balls back and forth to a partner is classified as a pushing activity.	10	**Combinational uses of toys.** This refers to dramatic play like tea parties, doctor/nurse, cowboys/Indians in which toys, costumes, and props are used in various combinations. Well developed by ages 3 to 4 years, at which time fine motor activities (drawing, printing, coloring, cutting) begin to assume dominance.
6	**Throwing.** The first two stages, according to child development theory, are called casting and hurling (see Figure 6.3). Casting and hurling are often done from a sitting position. This skill cannot evolve until the child can voluntarily *release* objects; this motor milestone occurs at about 12 months of age.		

Because language deficits affect teaching and learning in the psychomotor domain, adapted physical educators are working more and more closely with speech and hearing personnel. In developing and implementing the IEP, professionals should consider how language functioning is interrelating with cognitive and perceptual motor development. Supplementary reading on this subject in learning disabilities textbooks is recommended.

Developmental Stages in Toy Play

Physical educators often assume that all children are ready for instruction in some kind of ball skills. This is not true of many severely handicapped children. Table 6.4 depicts stages in learning to manipulate play objects (a broader term for toys; *play objects* may be more appropriate for older students). Toy play is largely dependent on normal evolution of voluntary grip (about 5 months) and voluntary release (about 12 months); these abilities are often impaired in cerebral palsied students and others slow to integrate reflexes. Toy play is also dependent on visual integrity; children who are blind are usually delayed in developing object manipulation skills. Throwing a ball is not as motivational for children who cannot see it land as for those reinforced by visual input.

Developmental Stages in Social Play

Children progress through clearly observable developmental play stages/levels that, in turn, determine their readiness for mainstream physical education and/or particular activities. First identified by Parten

Table 6.5
Developmental Stages in Social Play[a]

Stages	Level
Practice play	1. **Autistic or unoccupied.** Plays with own body or with objects, but without apparent purpose. Lies, sits, or wanders about aimlessly. Exhibits stereotyped or repetitive behaviors.
	2. **Onlooker.** Watches others at play, seems interested, follows activity with eyes.
	3. **Solitary play.** Plays alone with definite goal/purpose. Ignores others in close proximity. Reactions to toys/stimuli can be classified as approach or avoidance.
Symbolic play	4. **Parallel play.** Plays independently, but shows awareness and occasional interest in others. Brings toys and/or establishes play space near others.
	5. **Associative play (interactive).** Initiates contacts with others. Interacts on playground apparatus and in "playing house" or other make-believe games. Talks with others. Interactions can be classified as positive or negative and as dyads, triads, and the like.
Rule play	6. **Cooperative play.** Shares toys and apparatus. Participates in simple organized games; understands game formation and base or safety line; knows game goal and can switch roles (chase/flee, tag/dodge, roll/catch). Optimal group size seems to be three to six.
	7. **Cooperative/competitive play.** Engages in progressively more complex, organized games to lead-up games to regulation team sports. Concurrently engages in progression of movement activities demanding self-competition (self-testing), partner competition, and group competition. Individual preferences emerge for team vs. individual vs. no competition.

[a]Stages were identified by Piaget; levels 1 to 6 were first described by Parten; level 7 has been added to denote the entry point for traditional physical education.

(1932), these stages have been subjected to considerable research and guide program planning in such disciplines as early childhood, occupational therapy, special education, and therapeutic recreation. As physical educators begin to work with children under age 6 and/or with severely handicapped children, it is essential that assessment and programming competencies be refined relative to these stages/levels.

While levels 1 to 6 on Table 6.5 were originally evolved to show psychosocial development from ages 0 to 6 and were meant to represent a continuum from least to most mature, it should be noted that persons of all ages and cognitive levels can be classified according to predominant leisure patterns. Some adults, for instance, prefer solitary leisure pursuits (reading, jogging, hobbies), while others prefer to find recreation in a group. It is important that the preferences of handicapped persons as well as their play levels be assessed. Is there a discrepancy between the two? If so, what factors are contributing to the discrepancy?

Traditionally, teachers have assumed that normal children, by age 5 or 6, have reached level 7. Even the simplest of organized games demands some competence in cooperation and/or competition. In contrast, special educators generally cope with tremendous play heterogeneity. The long-term goal of guiding a handicapped pupil from one play level to another often appears on the IEP under adaptive behavior and/or socialization. Rightfully, this goal seems to be an integral part of adapted physical education.

Socialization

Socialization is an important contribution that adapted physical education can make in the affective domain. *Socialization is the process of learning how to behave appropriately in social settings—i.e., how to interact with others.* It entails learning cooperative and competitive behaviors as well as gaining an understanding and appreciation of the rules and laws that govern society. In special education settings, *normalization* is used more or less synonymously with *socialization*.

Developmental Stages in Competition

Children progress through clearly identifiable developmental stages with respect to readiness for competition (see Figure 6.7). The levels on Table 6.6 with the exception of items 4 and 5, are those cited in the *Special Olympics Instructional Manual*. No age groups are associated with the developmental levels, since these levels vary widely and reflect individual differences in personality and temperament as much as maturation.

Figure 6.7 Group games, like cageball, demand social readiness and self-confidence.

Table 6.6
Developmental Stages in Competition

Stages	Level
Self-competition	1. **Nondifferentiated self-competition.** Competes with self against own best performance; makes one's best better.
	2. **Goal-directed, self-competition.** States level of aspiration and tries to attain this specific goal. Teacher or coach may establish goal also.
Individual or dual competition	3. **Organized game competition.** Cooperates with others to achieve a mutual goal, like winning a relay or tagging the most persons.
	4. **Individual competition.** Competes with one opponent in individual sports like track, swimming, bowling, golf, and tennis. Competes against others also in trying to make the best score in fitness, track, and self-testing activities.
	5. **Dual or doubles competition.** Competes in dual sports like doubles in tennis, badminton, and table tennis. Cooperates with partner in doubles tennis, with team in bowling, and in other situations demanding a limited number of interactions.
Team competition	6. **Team competition.** Cooperates with team members while concurrently competing with opponents. The smaller the team, the easier the learning progressions in cooperation and competition.

Although the success of very young children in little league baseball and peewee football has resulted in considerable controversy concerning the age at which one is ready to compete with others, many educators concur that *team competition,* as a school learning experience, *should not be introduced until the third grade* (Figure 6.8). It is doubtful that some handicapped children, particularly the severely retarded, ever acquire the mental and social readiness for team competition.

The rationale for not introducing team competition until the third grade is based primarily upon the social characteristics of children rather than their level of motor skill or their ability to grasp rules and strategy. Each of us has seen beautifully skilled 7- and 8-year-old athletes, already specialized in pitching, catching, or fielding. We have also seen many children sitting on a bench, waiting, and hoping.

Parents who understand the objectives of physical education and the nature and scope of a well-rounded, comprehensive program of activities will not want their children to specialize in team sports at an early age. Aquatics, dance, individual and dual sports (including

Figure 6.8 Ideally team competition should be introduced at about the third grade level, when children are socially and cognitively mature enough to handle complex interactions with teammates and opponents.

Cognitive and Play Development **115**

gymnastics and track), movement exploration, and self-testing activities are every child's educational right to a well-rounded and enriching life. Too much time spent on any one sport deprives an individual of the vital experiences needed to understand and appreciate his or her body and its capacity for an infinite variety of movements.

Creative Abilities

Creativity, like intelligence, is comprised of many factors, each of which is important to self-actualization in handicapped persons. The process of *adapting* entails problem solving, the discovery of alternative ways, and the appreciation of individual differences—i.e., uniqueness. Architectural, attitudinal, and aspirational barriers all constitute problems that demand considerable creativity if handicapped persons are to cope with and/or adapt to their environment.

Research indicates that little relationship exists between creative thinking ability and the generalized ability measured by intelligence tests. The correlations between intelligence and creative thinking in the normal population generally range from .10 to .30. Research also shows low correlations between creativity and motor ability in normal children.

Movement educators have always recognized creativity as an important long-range goal. Creativity can be either verbal (ideas, thoughts, words) or nonverbal (movements, actions, rhythms) (see Figure 6.9). *Motor creativity* refers to the ability to move in many different and unique ways.

Creative experience is closely related to breadth and depth of experience. Developmentally, creativity is preceded by imitation (i.e., "let's pretend" kinds of games) at about 1 year of age. The severely handicapped child confined primarily to a bed or the child who has seldom been taken out of the home for trips to friends' houses, grocery stores, zoos, and the like, is limited in what he or she has seen and heard. Children who have never seen, heard, and smelled real animals, for instance, are lost in movement sessions that involve imitating or portraying animals: dog walk, bear walk, elephant walk, inch worm.

Whereas creativity has its roots in imitation, children must move from this stage to original, imaginative thinking in order to succeed in movement education

Figure 6.9 George Latshaw, internationally known puppeteer, uses creative dramatics to stimulate creativity in thinking and moving during an integrated arts/movement session. The child in long leg braces has spina bifida. The child shaking hands with the puppet has Down's syndrome.

(the problem solving approach to physical education as opposed to follow-the-leader, or command, style). This shift begins to occur in normal human development at about 4 to 5 years of age. At this time, students can be helped to make up stories or to add on to one being told by someone else. Creativity is also partly dependent on the ability to remember sequences and then to put them together in new and different ways. Children must understand reality in order to create fantasy; they must be helped over and over again to understand the difference between what is real and what is pretend or imagined. Games can play an important role in the development of creative abilities.

Many sedentary games like Let's Go To Grandmother's House can be changed to combine large muscle activity, creativity, and memory for sequences. In the traditional Let's Go To Grandmother's House, six to eight persons sit in a circle and the leader begins a story sequence by saying, "I'm going to my grandmother's house and I'm going to take my *dog* (or anything else)." The next person repeats these phrases and adds what he or she is taking, and the game continues until the sequence is too long to be remembered. In physical education, we do not play sedentary games in this way. Instead, we substitute moving across the gymnasium for sitting. Instead of imagining things to take, each child specifies a different way of getting there, and others repeat and add onto the sequence. All the animal walks may be used as well as the steps employed in Red Light, Green Light (baby, giant, umbrella, scissors, crisscross, jumping, hopping, sliding steps). The theme of the game can even be changed from going to grandmother's house to going to the moon or going to the zoo. Instead of being persons, the students can choose to be animals, characters in a popular movie, or heros in history.

The process of changing games enhances creativity. Many handicapped children (particularly those with severe mental retardation, emotional disturbance, and learning disabilities) are characterized by *conceptual rigidity* similar to that exhibited by the normal 2-year-old in the *No* stage (the "terrible twos" say *no* to everything). Such children seem to crave sameness and resist changing game rules and class routines. Deficits in creative abilities can be slowly remediated by teaching children how to change games and by reinforcing mental flexibility. Sources of further information on this topic include elementary school physical education textbooks and the classic book *How to Change the Games Children Play,* by G. S. Don Morris, available through Burgess Publishing Company in Minneapolis.

Moral/Sportsmanship Development

Closely associated with cognitive development is comprehension of the rules and strategies of games and sports. This competence is, however, also a function of social and moral development. Piaget (1932) describes three stages in the consciousness and practice of rules in a game setting like marbles. These stages are useful in classifying handicapped children. While nonhandicapped children generally understand simple game rules by age 4, many handicapped persons show developmental lag behind their peers in readiness for low organized games. This may constitute a real problem in the early grades if the mainstream teacher tries to involve all children simultaneously in the same game, as traditionally has been the practice. Clearly, alternative physical activities must be provided.

From approximately age 4 until adolescence, the normal child tends to regard game rules as sacred and absolute. This characteristic helps to explain the many arguments and confusions that occur in childhood sports, especially when students remember the rules in different ways and/or when the teacher attempts to alter a familiar game structure. Since the underlying philosophy of adapted physical education is to change or adapt games to meet individual needs, it is important to anticipate reactions of the students. They may

balk at game adaptations or perceive them as "special favors" or even as "put downs." Some children would rather fail than feel singled out as needing a particular adaptation. It is essential, therefore, that games be adapted for *all* students rather than for the one or two handicapped. A goal of mainstream physical education is to decrease the conceptual rigidity of children, thereby assisting their movement toward stage 3, when rules increasingly are regarded as relative.

Competitive games thus exemplify for Piaget the advance from a view of morality . . . based on one-sided respect for persons in authority and belief in immutable moral laws comparable to the laws of nature, toward a mature 'autonomous' moral sense, rooted in mutual respect among equals, and capacity for cooperation. (Berlyne, 1973, p. 277)

The movement education approach often focuses upon creating new games from old ones and/or cooperatively agreeing on goal, rule, and penalty variations. Children who are developmentally delayed in internalizing rules experience great difficulty in accepting game changes and/or participating in the process of changing games and creating new activities from old. Students with mental retardation, learning disabilities, and emotional disturbance particularly exhibit *conceptual rigidity* in playground behavior, which is often misinterpreted as bad sportsmanship or stubbornness.

Frequently, children are taught that obeying rules is part of good sportsmanship. It is essential that teachers understand that motivation for obeying rules follows a definite developmental sequence.

Lawrence Kohlberg (1971, 1984) has extended the work of Piaget on moral development and published many papers and books on this subject. Table 6.7 presents his stages.

Kohlberg (1971, 1984) indicates that most elementary school children operate at the lower levels, while junior and senior high students function predominantly at the middle levels.

It can be hypothesized with reasonable certainty that most handicapped students (particularly the MR, ED, and LD) act at the lower levels. This theoretical framework helps to explain why external rewards are probably more important in adapted than in regular physical education. What other implications can be drawn from this discussion? How can training in game rules and strategies be used in socialization and sportsmanship? What teaching methods best achieve these goals?

Table 6.7
Developmental Stages in Rules Conformity

Stages	Level
Premoral	1. **Punishment and obedience.** Right and wrong are determined solely by physical consequences. Children obey rules to avoid punishment.
	2. **Egocentrism.** Right is determined by what satisfies one's personal needs. Some understanding of reciprocity may be present: "You scratch my back and I'll scratch yours." Children conform to receive rewards.
Conventional role conformity	3. **Pleasing others.** Behavior is determined by reinforcement or lack of it from significant others. Children conform to obtain approval.
	4. **Rigid adherence to rules.** In early stages of rules comprehension (ages 4 to 7 years), rules are regarded as sacred and absolute; they cannot be broken by anyone for any reason. From about age 7 on, rules become increasingly relative. Persons conform to avoid censure by authority.
Self-determined morality	5. **Flexible adherence to rules.** Right and wrong are determined by society and reflect strengths and weaknesses of lawmakers. Persons expect the right to help shape rules that affect their daily living and take this responsibility seriously. They usually abide, however, by existing laws while waiting for change to occur. Persons conform to maintain respect of social community.
	6. **Personal ethics and integrity.** Right and wrong are based on personal conscience rather than the laws of society or rules of a game. Persons conform to maintain self-respect and integrity.

Implications for Physical Education Programming

Table 6.8 presents a model that summarizes the many interrelationships that affect physical education programming for handicapped students.

It is possible that many mentally retarded students of elementary and secondary school age whose mental ages remain frozen at the preacademic level can experience greater success in a program of individual sports that stresses competition against the self than through group activities for which they may never achieve readiness. Severely retarded children should not be taught relays or be expected to participate in games that require a set formation. A good measure of readiness is whether the child understands the concept of a circle or line well enough to get into formation without assistance from the teacher. Of course, by continuous drill, children can be trained to stand in a circle, but it is doubtful that they will understand the objective of the game. Many physical education activities other than organized games offer greater potential value to trainable children.

Often, handicapped children are so protected by their parents, siblings, and teachers that they have never engaged in group games. The following quotation from an adapted physical education specialist illustrates this problem.

For several years I had been working with a group of educable mentally retarded children who were segregated from their normal peers on the playground, in the lunchroom, and in nearly all school activities. To offset this, we took the children to the gymnasium of a local university twice a week where they received individual instruction in swimming; trampoline, balance beam, mat, and sidehorse activities; and movement exploration. Many of them became beautiful athletes, and I knew their motor skills were way beyond those of the "normal" children who had received no gymnastics instruction.

Four boys in particular were so good that I decided to confront the school administration with the idea of integrating them into the regular third-grade physical education class. After considerable difficulty, I obtained permission. Since I was the teacher of the "normal" third graders as well as the ungraded retarded children, I anticipated no problems. The four boys felt secure with me and eagerly awaited their extra physical education periods.

First day. Brownies and Fairies. The children were all lined up waiting for the call: "The Brownies are coming." I gave it, and as always the children began running, dodging, tagging, and shouting in joyous manner. I looked out and there in the middle of the confusion was Billy, my best athlete, who could turn flips on the trampoline, outrun, or outthrow any of the "normal" children. He stood frozen, hands over face as if to protect himself, in a stooped posture of fear, eyes closed, teeth clenched, and muscles rigid.

Table 6.8
Assessment and Programming Model: Cognitive-Moral-Play Developmental Channels

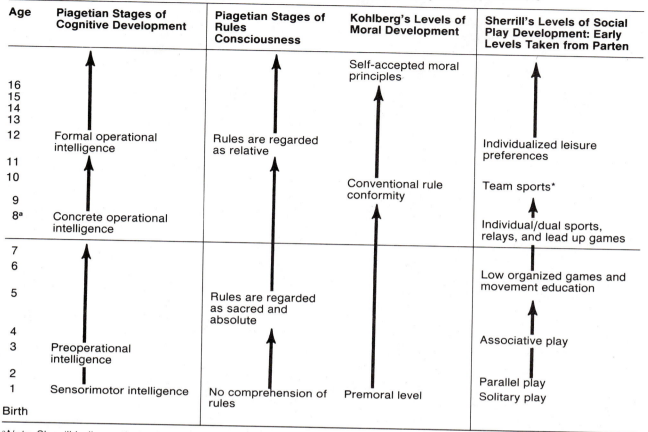

Age	Piagetian Stages of Cognitive Development	Piagetian Stages of Rules Consciousness	Kohlberg's Levels of Moral Development	Sherrill's Levels of Social Play Development: Early Levels Taken from Parten
16			Self-accepted moral principles	
15				
14				
13				
12	Formal operational intelligence	Rules are regarded as relative		Individualized leisure preferences
11				
10			Conventional rule conformity	Team sports*
9				
8ª	Concrete operational intelligence			Individual/dual sports, relays, and lead up games
7				
6				Low organized games and movement education
5		Rules are regarded as sacred and absolute		
4				Associative play
3	Preoperational intelligence			
2				
1	Sensorimotor intelligence	No comprehension of rules	Premoral level	Parallel play / Solitary play
Birth				

ªNote. Sherrill believes that competitive team activities should not be introduced until children enter the concrete operational intelligence stage and show cognitive/moral understanding of rules and strategies. In normal children this occurs around the third-grade level (age 8). Many severely mentally retarded children who remain frozen in the sensorimotor or preoperational intelligence stages never show readiness for competitive team play. Emphasis for them should be on development of lifetime individual sports, dance, and aquatics skills.

It was only then that I realized that Billy had never been in a game with more than 10 children; had never been chased, pursued by a group; had never been exposed to the high intensity of noise that we take for granted in the gymnasium.

A high degree of motor skill is not the only criterion for integrating handicapped children into normal physical education. Special education classes are small, limited in enrollment to fewer than 15 students in most states, and generally ungraded. Many children in special education have not been exposed to large group games and, hence, skip important developmental stages in play. Before they can be integrated into the regular physical education activities of their peers, they must be taken through these developmental stages. After completing such orientation and being integrated, they may still need the support, ego reinforcement, and

counseling of the adapted physical educator in much the same way that a student teacher needs the guidance of the cooperating and supervising teachers.

In analyzing the needs of each individual child in special education, the physical educator should ask these questions:

1. What is the child's mental age? Is the child frozen at a particular developmental stage in play? If so, accept the child as he or she is. Do not try to force the child into activities for which he or she may never be ready. Not all children need group games and relays for self-actualization.

2. In which developmental stage is the child?

3. Has the child skipped any developmental stages? Does the handicap permit the child's being taken back through the developmental stages missed?

4. If the child is frozen at one of the early stages because of mental and/or physical limitations, how can activities be adapted so as not to insult the child's social intelligence?

5. To what extent will the condition affect the speed with which the child can master activities? Does the child have time, within the span of childhood and adolescence, to progress through all of these developmental stages? If not, which ones should be omitted?

6. Am I teaching the child activities with carry-over value for the abundance of leisure time the child is likely to have?

7. Am I acquainting the child with community recreation facilities and resources as part of the physical education program?

8. Am I providing counseling and/or instruction for family members that will reinforce the child's newly developing leisure patterns and enable him or her to gain support (transportation, companionship, expenses) in the use of community resources?

If handicapped children must skip some developmental levels, the least valuable ones are probably oriented toward team competition. The younger children are when lifetime sports are introduced, the more years they have to acquire the skills that will enable them to participate in activities and use community facilities with the nonhandicapped. Awkward children, particularly, should be given instruction in swimming, dance, and individual sports at earlier ages than normal children so they can get a "head start" and thereby compete or even excel in some leisure activities. Such instruction serves to deter loneliness, boredom, and less desirable compensatory behaviors.

Self-Concept and Body Image

The key to helping students progress from one developmental stage to another is making them feel good about themselves and motivating them to strive for self-actualization (i.e., to become the best they can be). Self-concept theory was discussed briefly in Chapter 4. It is important to add to that beginning knowledge base an understanding of developmental theory in relation to self-concept and body image.

Self-concept refers to all of the opinions, attitudes, and beliefs that a person holds about self. The self contains many dimensions (physical, mental, social, moral, and others), and a person may feel good about some dimensions and bad about others. The physical dimensions of self-concept are often called body image.

Body image refers to all of the opinions, attitudes, and beliefs that a person holds about his or her body. These include psychomotor, affective, and cognitive understandings and abilities. Body image development is closely related to sensorimotor development (see Figure 6.10).

Changes in body image and self-concept are not as easy to observe and measure as other characteristics. The reason for this is that body image and self-concept theory is based on *constructs* rather than concepts. *Constructs* are ideas based on hypothesized variables (characteristics, behaviors, conditions) that cannot be observed and measured directly, yet there is widespread agreement on their existence. *Concepts* are ideas based on variables that are real, that have been subjected to considerable observation and testing. A distinction often made between the two terms is that science is based on concepts whereas philosophy and religion are based on constructs. Center of gravity, body mass, reflexes, and motor performance are all concepts. Body image, self-concept, laterality, directionality, and creativity are constructs. A statistical procedure called *factor analysis* is used to analyze constructs and determine the specific factors that comprise them.

Development of Self-Concept

The origin of self-concept is believed to be about 3 months of age, when the infant, held close to the person feeding him or her, begins to perceive the difference between self and not-self. At about 8 months of age this perception matures into recognition of the "I" as a being that can cause things to happen (i.e., smile and the other person smiles back; cry and you get action). In infancy and early childhood it is difficult to separate self-concept from body image, since early feelings about the body and its capacity for movement form the basis of self-concept.

Authorities agree that it is difficult, if not impossible, to measure self-concept before the child is in the first grade. Thus, little is known about this parameter until the child reaches age 5 or 6. Until that time, the self-concept is relatively unstable (i.e., feelings about the self change with the immediate situation).

Factor analysis techniques have shown that self-concept is comprised of many specific factors. Among these are feelings about the self in relation to home and

Figure 6.10 Activities with mirrors help developmentally delayed students gain a better sense of who they are and what their bodies can do.

family; school; ability in games, sports, and recreation; personality and popularity; physical appearance; and life satisfaction and happiness. Good self-concept tests yield scores for each of these factors as well as total score. Initially, self-concept is formed at home and includes only factors relating to home and family. By the second grade, however, the school and other interactions outside of the home have begun to exert a major influence on self-concept formation. By this age, also, children with visible handicapping conditions have come to realize that their appearance is different from that of their peers; this naturally affects self-concept.

Self-concept in childhood shows age trends; then in adolescence it stabilizes, and opinions, attitudes, and beliefs about the self become very difficult to change. Research shows self-concept is highest in the first grade, followed by a steady downward trend from the second through the fourth grades. In the fifth grade (age 10), self-concept begins to change in a more positive direction, but this trend is interrupted by puberty, at which time self-concept plunges to an all-time low in most students. In late adolescence, self-concept finally stabilizes.

Self-concept serves as the directing force in behavior. It usually cannot be changed by teachers, even in early childhood, by short intervention periods. Long-term, intensive programs in which family and school work together are most effective in causing change. Techniques demonstrated effective in improving self-concept are *success-oriented instruction* with lots of praise, *increasing competence* of the child while preserving ego, and increasing number and quality of *peer friendships*.

Development of Body Image

Body image development begins in infancy, probably earlier than does self-concept, and continues throughout life. Early development is considered by some authorities to be synonymous with sensorimotor development. Table 6.9 shows that different terms are applied to body image constructs at different ages.

Cognitive and Play Development **121**

Table 6.9
Terms Used In Different Stages of Body Image Development

Developmental Stage	Body Image Construct
Sensorimotor 0 to 2 years	Body schema
Preoperational 2 to 7 years	Body awareness Self-awareness
Concrete operational 7 to 11 years	Body image Self-concept

Body schema is the diagram of the body that evolves in the brain in response to sensorimotor input. The body schema enables the infant to feel body boundaries, identify body parts, plan and execute movements, and know where the body is in space. Figure 6.11 depicts an adult brain, showing potential that has been developed. The motor projection areas of the brain are topographically organized, with each part controlling specific muscles that, in turn, control body movement. At birth, this capacity to control movement is not yet developed. Remember the motor development principle of general-to-specific activity (i.e., generalized mass activity is replaced by specific responses of individual body parts). Each movement of the body or its parts by the infant or another provides sensorimotor input (kinesthetic, vestibular) to the brain, which causes the body schema to evolve. Likewise, sensory input from the skin, muscles, and joints (touch, pressure, temperature, pain) contributes to the early development of body schema. Figure 6.11 shows that the body schema develops in a cephalocaudal direction with the infant first becoming aware of eating/drinking and then of seeing. Later, the infant gains control of head/neck muscles (turning head from side to side; lifting head), then the hand/finger muscles (grasping/holding toys), then upper extremities, and last the lower extremities. Figure 6.11 shows also that muscle groups responsible for fine muscle control, such as lips and fingers, have a disproportionately large cortical area devoted to them.

Visual input is important in the evolution of body schema. At birth, infants have the ability to briefly fixate on stable objects and to track slow-moving objects through short arcs. Between 0 to 1 month of age, infants have Snellen vision of 20/150 to 20/400. This means that they see at 20 feet what persons with mature vision and normal acuity see at 150 feet. Near vision, however, is better than far vision, and infants begin

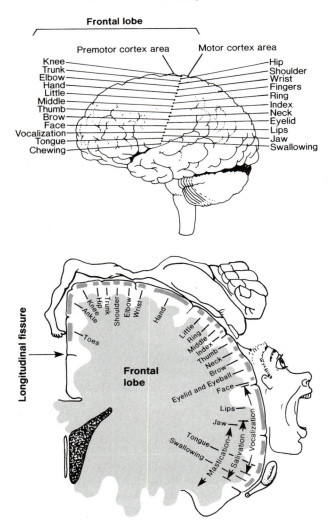

Figure 6.11 *Top*, lateral view of adult brain depicts premotor and motor cortex strips on the frontal lobe. *Bottom*, the diagram of the body that evolves in the brain in response to sensorimotor input. Each voluntary movement is controlled in the same place on the motor strip of every human being.

to visually fixate very early on body parts, especially their hands and feet. Even before their random, generalized movements are brought under control, infants are adding visual images of movement to their body schemas. Visual input is integrated with input from other sensory modalities, and gradually awareness develops of self/not-self at about 3 months of age.

Body schema continues to develop and change throughout the life span. As the child matures, cognitive and affective dimensions are added to the psychomotor parameters. If problems occur, the body schema is affected, motor planning is damaged, and faulty movements occur. Body schema is a neurological entity; it cannot be seen or measured directly. Therefore,

Figure 6.12 Rocking an infant back and forth on a large ball provides proprioceptive feedback for development of laterality and body image.

observable behaviors (thoughts, feelings, movements) relating to the body schema have been given such terms as body ego, body awareness, body percept, body cathexis, body concept, body image, and praxis.

Some body image terms are used interchangeably. Others have been coined to denote a specific dimension of body image. *Cathexis,* for instance, refers to degree of satisfaction or dissatisfaction with various parts or processes of the body and/or self. *Praxis,* the Greek word for action, denotes efficient motor planning and execution of tasks like moving through an obstacle course, imitating movements, and performing angel-in-the-snow. Disturbances of praxis, known as *apraxia,* have been reported in medical literature since 1866.

Body image development follows the principles of normal development. It is a continuous process, with changes occurring in all domains throughout the life span. However, at some ages, development is more concentrated in one domain than in the others. The sequence of body image development seems to parallel Piaget's stages in cognitive development.

Sensorimotor Stage of Development

During the sensorimotor stage (ages 0 to 2 in nondisabled children), infants become aware of their bodies and their capacities for movement. Input from the 10 sensory modalities creates and then reinforces awareness of body boundaries (self/not-self), two sides of the body (laterality), space (verticality and directionality), time (synchrony, rhythm), force, and flow.

Initially, all awareness is internal and primarily proprioceptive and tactile. *Laterality* is, thus, the internal awareness of the two sides of the body (i.e., left/right), whereas *verticality* is the internal awareness of up and down. In accordance with the principle of general to specific activity, the first proprioceptive feedback comes from reflex activity (i.e., generalized mass flexor tone activity in the prone position and extensor tone activity in the supine position). As primitive reflexes are suppressed, voluntary side-to-side and up-down-up movements of the head and limbs provide proprioceptive feedback for continued development of laterality and verticality. External sources of movement like being rocked in the cradle, changed from one position to another (Figure 6.12), or carried in arms or backpack also give proprioceptive feedback.

Thus, laterality develops as well as the capacity to move the two sides of the body *independently* (right arm only, left arm only) and *reciprocally* (right arm with left leg, as in creeping, walking, and other locomotor movements) (see Figures 6.13 and 6.14). Kephart, the foremost perceptual-motor theorist, stresses that laterality must be learned. He states,

It is only by experimenting with the two sides of the body and their relationship to each other that we come to distinguish between the two systems. . . . The primary pattern out of which this differentiation develops is that of balance. (Kephart, 1971, p. 87)

Laterality, a nonverbal entity, thus begins to evolve as children achieve stable sitting, creeping, and standing positions (all of which are dependent upon balance).

Verticality, also a nonverbal entity, is developed similarly as the infant's limbs and body experience the force of gravity. Both laterality and verticality are reinforced by visual input from the environment. Research shows that infants 15 to 20 weeks old can differentiate between four different orientations of the human face. They are consistently more responsive to an "upright face" than to those rotated to the left or right or upside down.

During the sensorimotor period, children also learn to imitate facial expressions, limb movements, and body positions. Visual input is the most important sense modality in imitation, since seeing others motivates the child to locomotion. Needing or wanting an object (food/toy) within the visual field is another reinforcer of imitation. These facts help explain why sensorimotor development is delayed in congenitally blind children.

Motor planning (praxis) also emerges during the sensorimotor period as cognition develops and the child wants to manipulate objects/toys and to move from

Figure 6.13 First stages in development of body image.

4 weeks
or
1 month

Proprioceptive and tactile input from movement of another. First proprioceptive input initiated by self: head and neck muscles.

16 weeks
or
4 months

First awareness of hands. Can voluntarily bring hands to midline. Rolls over, providing proprioceptive input regarding total body in space.

28 weeks
or
7 months

First interest in mirror play.
First awareness of feet.

40 weeks
or
10 months

Laterality is reinforced when balance is maintained in sitting, creeping.
Imitation of movements begins, usually with bye-bye and shaking head yes and no.

Figure 6.14 Later stages in development of body image.

1 year
or
12 months

Proprioceptive input from walking and changing positions from up to down. Competence feeling from casting balls/objects that others must retrieve. Feelings about body as good/bad from toilet training.

1½ years
or
18 months

Understands and can say up, down (first movement concepts).
Is learning names of body parts.
Increased competence from hurling balls/objects.
Retrieves balls for self.

2 years
or
24 months

Has about 300 words in vocabulary.
Can name body parts of doll.
Understands on-off concepts, then in-out, turn around.
Beginning imitative play with dolls, projects feeling about self into doll play.

 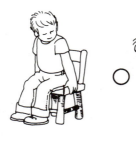 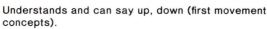

3 years
or
36 months

Understands over-under, front-back, big-little, short-tall/long, high-low.
Copies circles, crosses on paper, but cannot yet draw a person.
Balances on one foot.
Rides tricycle.

Figure 6.15 Self-awareness develops in a definite order: hands, feet, face, and tummy. Infants learn about the body parts they see. Mirrors are needed to learn about the face.

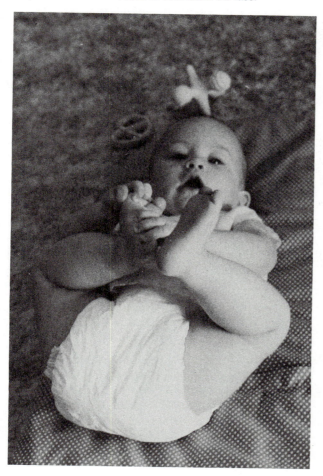

place to place. Early voluntary movement can leave the child feeling competent and loved or clumsy, scorned, and pitied. Thus, body image components in the affective domain begin to interweave with those in the psychomotor domain.

From birth until 2 years of age, children normally acquire a speaking vocabulary of about 300 words. Among these are names of common body parts like hands, feet, face, tummy, nose, eyes, ears, and mouth. Self-awareness develops in a definite order: hands, feet, face, and trunk (Figure 6.15). The emergence of language for body parts and movements reinforces the growing understanding and appreciation of the body.

Preoperational Stage of Development

In this stage, speech develops rapidly (from 300 words at age 2 to several thousand words at age 7) and gradually takes precedence over movement as a means of expression. During this time span, children also begin to perceive themselves as competent and lovable or the opposite. The way they look and move has much to do with such perceptions. Thus, body image development is primarily in the cognitive and affective domains.

The principle of bilateral to unilateral to crosslateral control is evidenced during the preoperational period. At age 2, children's large muscle movements are mostly bilateral. Gradually, children learn *unilateral control:* to move one limb at a time (kicking and trapping soccer-type activities; one-hand throwing and striking movements; imitation games), but typically without the good balance that comes only with arm/leg opposition (see Figure 6.14). By age 7, however, most children have established *crosslateral control;* this is manifested by right arm and left leg (or vice versa) moving forward together in a throw, kick, or strike. *Bilateral integration* is the term given to the ability to perform bilateral, unilateral, and crosslateral movement patterns at will: both limbs, one limb, or right arm and left leg in opposition. This ability is generally measured in body image tests by imitations of movement and angels-in-the-snow sequences. Motor development tests like Bruininks-Oseretsky (see Chapter 11) include more difficult measures of bilateral integration.

Verticality (awareness of up/down) seems to develop primarily between ages 2 and 4, even though it begins with the proprioceptive and visual inputs from pulling oneself upright (about age 12 months), standing, and falling. In spontaneous scribbling, children generally make vertical lines before horizontal lines. Imitation of a vertical stroke occurs between 24 and 30 months of age; imitation of a horizontal stroke occurs between 36 and 40 months. This is consistent with the emergence of one-handed throwing patterns: casting, hurling, underarm throws (back-and-up, forward-down-and-up), overarm throws, and last, sidearm throws, which require horizontal movement. Verticality also helps to explain why preschool children, while learning to bat, typically swing down or up at a ball before developing a mature horizontal swing.

Cognitive awareness of verticality develops at different rates. The words *up* and *down* are in children's speaking vocabularies by age 2 years; some researchers believe these are the first movement commands that children understand. If shown a picture or toy upside down, most 2- and 3-year-olds will direct the teacher to upright it. These same children, however, often fail to recognize familiar figures when the figures are upside down or rotated. This visual perceptual deficit is a problem in rotational or position-in-space constancy.

Directionality is the proprioceptive awareness of the body in space and the understanding of directions (forward, backward, sideward) and surfaces (top, bottom, inside, outside, front, back). This awareness emerges later than laterality, usually about the same time as verticality (i.e., between ages 2 to 4 years). Directionality develops in different stages: first, the body in relation to space and objects in space; then, stationary objects in relation to stationary objects; then, stationary objects in relation to moving objects; and, last, moving objects in relation to moving objects.

Concrete Operational Stage of Development

During this stage, laterality, verticality, and directionality change from proprioceptive entities (as defined in classic perceptual motor literature) to cognitive understandings. Body image and/or perceptual-motor training, in normally developing children, is replaced with games- and fitness-oriented physical education. The body image, like self-concept, fluctuates in childhood and becomes increasingly stable with age. Puberty brings many changes to body image. By the end of the concrete operational stage (about 11 years), however, body image is largely dominated by the affective domain, with children able to designate which body parts and movements they like best and least and why.

Implications for Physical Education Programming

Body image and self-concept have been described in considerable detail in this chapter because most students who need adapted physical education have deficits in these areas. Mentally retarded, learning disabled, and seriously emotionally disturbed children often exhibit delays in these areas. Thus, the physical educator is involved in assessment and programming in the 0 to 2 and 2 to 7 age ranges, regardless of chronological ages of students. Remediation of problems of laterality, verticality, directionality, and bilateral control often appears on IEPs and comprises major physical education goals.

Learning Activities

1. Observe children of several different ages at play in the neighborhood, park, or camp setting. Ask them what their favorite games are. Try to classify them according to cognitive, moral, play, and competitive stages in which they are functioning.

2. Read a book or several articles on the creative process. Make a list of kinds of teacher behavior that might facilitate the development of fluency, flexibility, originality, and elaboration in handicapped as well as normal students in the physical education setting.

3. Conduct a panel discussion, develop a slide show, or write a paper on how such factors as self-concept, body image, attitude toward physical education, play and competition stages, and level of cognitive functioning affect the success of mainstreaming in physical education.

References

Berlyne, D. C. (1973). Cited by Loy and Ingham in G. L. Rarick (Ed.), *Physical activity: Human growth and development* (p. 277). New York: Academic Press.

Keller, H. (1965). *The story of my life.* New York: Airmont Publishing Co.

Kephart, N. (1971). *The slow learner in the classroom* (2nd ed.). Columbus, OH: Charles E. Merrill.

Kohlberg, L. (1971). The cognitive-development approach to moral education. In National Education Association (Ed.), *Values, concepts, and techniques* (pp. 18–35). Washington, DC: Author.

Kohlberg, L. (1984). *The psychology of moral development: The nature and validity of moral stages.* San Francisco: Harper & Row.

Parten, M. (1932). Social participation among preschool children. *Journal of Abnormal and Social Psychology, 27,* 243–269.

Piaget, J. (1932). *The moral judgment of the child.* New York: Harcourt Brace & World.

Bibliography

Anthony, E. J. (1971). The child's discovery of the body. In C. B. Kopp, *Readings in early development for occupational and physical therapy students* (pp. 410–411). Springfield, IL: Charles C. Thomas.

Fisher, S., & Cleveland, S. (1968). *Body image and personality* (2nd ed.). New York: Dover Publications.

Fitts, W. (1972). *The self-concept and performance.* Nashville, TN: Counselor Recordings and Tests.

Fitts, W. (1972). *The self-concept and psychopathology.* Nashville, TN: Counselor Recordings and Tests.

Ford, B., & Ford, R. (1981). Identifying creative potential in handicapped children. *Exceptional Children, 48* (2), 115–122.

Freud, S. (1927). *The ego and the id.* London: Hogarth Press.

Furth, H., & Wachs, H. (1974). *Piaget's theory in practice: Thinking goes to school.* New York: Oxford University Press.

Guilford, J. P. (1967). *The nature of human intelligence.* New York: McGraw-Hill.

Logsdon, B. (1971). *Physical education for children: A focus on the teaching process.* Philadelphia: Lea & Febiger.

Loovis, E. M. (1978). Effect of participation in sport/physical education on the development of the exceptional child. *American Corrective Therapy Journal, 32,* 167–179.

Lowenfeld, V., & Brittain, W. L. (1975). *Creative and mental growth.* New York: Macmillan.

Martens, R. (1975). *Social psychology and physical activity.* New York: Harper & Row.

Morse, W., Ardizzone, J., MacDonald, C., & Pasick, P. (1980). *Affective education for special children and youth.* Reston, VA: Council for Exceptional Children.

Mussen, P. H. (Ed.) (1970). *Carmichael's manual of child psychology* (3rd ed.). New York: John Wiley & Sons.

Oliver, J. (1972). Physical activity and the psychological development of the handicapped. In J. E. Kane (Ed.), *Psychological aspects of physical education and sport* (pp. 187–208). Boston: Routledge & Kegan Paul.

Piaget, J. (1955). *The language and thought of the child.* New York: World Publishing Co.

Rarick, G. L. (Ed.). (1973). *Physical activity: Human growth and development.* New York: Academic Press.

Rarick, G. L. (1980). Cognitive-motor relationships in the growing years. *Research Quarterly for Exercise and Sport, 51,* 174–202.

Shontz, F. (1969). *Perceptual and cognitive aspects of body experience.* New York: Academic Press.

Strain, P. (1982). *Social development of exceptional children.* Rockville, MD: Aspen Systems Corporation.

Stroup, R., & Pielstick, N. L. (1965). Motor ability and creativity. *Perceptual and Motor Skills, 20,* 76–78.

Torrance, E. P. (1962). *Guiding creative talent.* Englewood Cliffs, NJ: Prentice-Hall.

Wehman, P. (1977). *Helping the mentally retarded acquire play skills.* Springfield, IL: Charles C. Thomas.

Williams, H. (1983). *Perceptual and motor development.* Englewood Cliffs, NJ: Prentice-Hall. (See Chapter 10 on self-concept and body awareness.)

Winnick, J. (1979). *Early movement experiences and development habilitation and remediation.* Philadelphia: W. B. Saunders.

Winnick, J. P., & French, R. W. (Eds.). (1975). *Piaget for regular and special physical educators and recreators.* New York: SUNY at Brockport Bookstore.

Wyrick, W. (1968). The development of a test of motor creativity. *Research Quarterly, 39,* 756–765.

Zaichkowsky, L., Zaichkowsky, L., & Martinek, T. (1980). *Growth and development.* St. Louis: C. V. Mosby.

7 Adapting Instruction: Basic Concepts

Figure 7.1 Peer teacher demonstrates hitting piñata for Down's syndrome classmate.

Chapter Objectives

After you have studied this chapter, you should be able to

1. Identify eight behaviors in the creative process and discuss each in relation to adapting instruction to meet individual needs, interests, and abilities. How can these behaviors be assessed and developed in teachers as well as students?

2. Discuss different methods of individualizing instruction and cite examples of each.

3. Explain the concept of *developmental sequences* and apply it to the acquisition of (a) locomotor skills, (b) object skills, (c) movement patterns in sports, (d) play concepts, and (e) games. List the components of each in chronological order and/or from easiest to most difficult.

4. Differentiate between goals and objectives and write examples of each appropriate for inclusion on the physical education IEP.

5. Differentiate between task analysis and activity analysis and apply each to the individualization of instruction.

6. Explain the use of different levels of assistance in teaching: physical, visual, verbal, or a combination of all.

7. Analyze four teaching styles from most to least restrictive and describe each in relation to (a) learning environment, (b) starting routine, (c) presentation of new learning activities, and (d) execution. Relate teaching styles to behaviors that students with various handicapping conditions might exhibit.

8. Discuss behavior management concepts in relation to teaching and describe specific techniques useful in various situations.

9. State illustrative procedures for adapting instruction to problems of (a) strength, endurance, and power, (b) balancing and agility, and (c) coordination and accuracy.

10. Discuss application of exercise physiology to the individualization of instruction. Cite specific examples.

11. Discuss application of kinesiology and biomechanics to the individualization of instruction. Cite specific examples in relation to (a) leverage, (b) force production, (c) stability, and (d) laws of motion.

12. Identify 16 factors that affect the physical education teaching-learning process and discuss their manipulation in adapting instruction.

Good physical education implies *adapting* instruction to the individual needs, interests, and abilities of all students. The ability to adapt is dependent upon personal creativity and a knowledge of the principles of motor development, biomechanics, exercise physiology, and motor learning. Figure 7.1 depicts a creative instructional approach planned by a physical educator and implemented by a peer teacher. Important, also, is a good self-concept and a high level of aspiration for all students (i.e., teachers must believe in themselves, their ability to teach, and the ability of their students to learn).

Creativity

Behaviors in the creative process are presented in Table 7.1. Prospective teachers should be helped to assess themselves on the different behaviors that comprise creativity. Among the standardized instruments that can be used for this purpose are two tests by E. Paul Torrance. *Thinking Creatively with Pictures* yields separate scores for fluency, flexibility, originality, and elaboration. *Thinking Creatively with Words* yields separate scores for fluency, flexibility, and originality. Both can be ordered from Scholastic Testing Service, Incorporated, 480 Meyer Road, Bensenville, IL 60106.

Each test includes several subtests. The best known of the pictorial tests is probably the circles task, in which each person is given a page containing 40 circles, each of which is about the size of a quarter. The task is to create as many different objects or pictures out of these circles as possible in 10 minutes. The test is scored, not only for number of different objects, but for originality or uniqueness of drawings. The best known of the verbal tests is to take a word with multiple meanings (like *head* or *ball*) and think of as many uses as possible. Head,

Table 7.1
Behaviors in the Creative Process[a]

Behavior	Meaning
Cognitive	
1. Fluent thinking: to think of the *most.*	Generation of a quantity, flow of thought, number of relevant responses.
2. Flexible thinking: to take *different* approaches.	Variety of kinds of ideas, ability to shift categories, detours in direction of thought.
3. Original thinking: to think in *novel* or unique ways.	Unusual responses, clever ideas, production away from the obvious.
4. Elaborative thinking: to *add on* to .	Embellishing upon an idea; embroidering upon a simple idea or response to make it more elegant; stretching or expanding upon things or ideas.
Affective	
1. Risk taking: to be *challenged* to.	Expose oneself to failure or criticisms; take a guess; function under conditions devoid of structure; defend own ideas.
2. Complexity: to have *courage* to.	Seek many alternatives; see gaps between how things are and how they could be; bring order out of chaos; delve into intricate problems or ideas.
3. Curiosity: to be *willing* to	Be inquisitive and wonder; toy with an idea; be open to puzzling situations; ponder the mystery of things; to follow a particular hunch just to see what will happen.
4. Imagination: to have the *power* to.	Visualize and build mental images; dream about things that have never happened; feel intuitively; reach beyond sensual or real boundaries.

[a]Adapted from the *Total Creativity Program,* by permission of the author, Frank E. Williams, and the publisher. This program, comprising several volumes, packets, and tape cassettes, is distributed by Educational Technology Publications, 140 Sylvan Avenue, Englewood Cliffs, NJ 07632.

for instance, can refer to a body part, the foam on beer, the position one holds in class, the bathroom, the boss or supervisor, and several other things.

Tests of motor creativity (Wyrick, 1968) have been developed also for use with prospective teachers. Illustrative of the kinds of challenges these present are

1. How many ways can you put a paper cup in a waste basket?
2. How many ways can you move a ball, by striking or hitting only, to a wall?
3. How many ways can you move from one end of a low balance beam to another so that at some time in the moving the hips are higher than the head? The floor and beam may be used in combination.
4. How many different ways can you pick up a hoop or beanbag from the floor?

By engaging in this kind of problem solving behavior, educators can brainstorm ideas for teaching students who cannot learn or perform in expected ways. Try each of these movement challenges, for instance, while pretending to be blind or have an amputation or a severe balance problem. The essence of teaching children who are clumsy and/or handicapped is to *try another way.* Success-oriented physical education is

dependent upon the teacher to keep trying alternative pedagogies as well as different ways of changing games, equipment, and environment until one works.

Fluency and Flexibility

Two traits of creativity, fluency and flexibility, are important in adapting instruction, particularly in schools where teaching supplies and equipment are limited. Conceptualize a movement education session in which you want every student to have a ball or projectile of some kind. It is not necessary that they all have the same kind. How many different kinds can you think of? *Fluency* is your ability to generate a large number of relevant responses. When you thought of different kinds, did you vary your ideas with respect to size, weight, shape, color, texture, and composition? *Flexibility* is your ability to shift categories and think of different kinds. Table 7.2 gives a sampling of the fluent and flexible responses you might have made.

Having thought of numerous alternatives, the next step is to match balls and projectiles up with the abilities of the pupils. A child who has coordination problems needs something big and soft. One with grasp and release problems (cerebral palsy) might do best with a yarn or nerf (sponge rubber) ball. A blind child needs an object with a bell or noisemaker in it, whereas a visually impaired child simply needs a bright color like

Table 7.2
How Creative Are You?

Regulation Round Balls that Vary in Size, Weight, Texture	Homemade Projectiles	Projectiles of Varying Shapes
Baseballs	Beanbags: 3 × 3″, small; 5 × 5″, jumbo	Airplanes (paper, cloth)
Basketballs	Clay	Arrows
Bocce balls	Cork	Balloons
Bowling balls	Felt	Beans
Cage balls: 18″; 24″; 30″; 36″; 48″; 60″; 72″	Foam	Beanbags (soft shots)
Croquet balls	Leather	Clubs
Golf balls	Nerf ball	Coffee can lids (plastic)
Field hockey balls	Nylon sock stuffed	Coins
Lacrosse balls	Paper crumpled into ball	Darts
Marbles	Plastic: ping pong; scoop balls; whiffle balls	Discs
Medicine balls: 4–5 lbs.; 6–7 lbs.; 8–9 lbs.; 11–12 lbs.; 14–15 lbs.	Rubber	Footballs
Playground balls: 5″; 6″; 7″; 8½″; 10″; 13″; 16″	Snowballs	Frisbees
Racketballs	Sponge	Hoops
Rhythm balls: 3¼″	Velcro-covered yarnballs	Horseshoes
Soccer balls		Javelins
Softballs: 9″; 10″; 12″		Lemmi sticks
Table tennis (ping pong)		Paperplate frisbees
Tennis ball		Peas
Tether ball		Pucks: shuffleboard; ice hockey
Volley ball		Rings (quoits): plastic game rings; embroidery hoops; canning rubbers
Water polo ball		Rocks (pebbles)
		Shots: iron or plastic
		Shuttlecocks
		Yardsticks

yellow. Someone in a wheelchair can profit by a string attached to the ball to facilitate recovery, whereas a hyperactive or high-energy student can enjoy a "crazy ball" with unpredictable bounces and great distance capacity.

Next, pretend that you have a class of 10 students, each with a different handicapping condition, but all needing to work on objectives pertaining to throwing. Your assessment records reveal that the students represent all the different stages of throwing ability. Specific objectives to be worked on have been circled on each student's assessment form. In this kind of setting, the more projectiles experimented with by the students the more likely their skills are to generalize from one game or sport to another. The important thing is that the students do not get bored, that each has a maximum number of trials to practice, and that each experiences some success.

Developing throwing skills often takes 5 or 10 minutes of every class period for several weeks. How many different targets can you think of and how will you organize your space for the different kinds of projectiles and targets? Appropriate degree of difficulty is essential to both success and motivation. How can you change projectiles and/or targets to organize stations for students needing easy, medium, or difficult learning progressions? The number of different kinds of targets you conceptualize is a measure of fluency. If your targets are of different colors, sizes, shapes, heights,

widths, and materials, you have demonstrated good flexibility (the ability to think of different categories). If some of your targets make noise or fall down when they are hit, you are more likely to maximize on-task practice time. Have you devised moving as well as stationary targets? Targets that integrate story, television, or movie themes are a measure of originality. If these have a lot of detail, lending themselves to different scoring systems, you have demonstrated elaboration.

At this point, you may be thinking that this is a crazy approach to teaching throwing. This is where the affective behaviors of creativity enter in: to be challenged to take risks, to have courage to try something different, to be willing to toy with ideas, and to have the power to imagine. Teachers with good self-concepts are more concerned with making lessons interesting, exciting, and new than with worrying about what colleagues think of them. Recreation has been defined as the crazy things that persons do to keep from going crazy. Teachers who love their work so much that it seems like recreation do a lot of crazy things. They are generally very creative persons.

So now you have targets! How many different kinds of games can you devise for teaching and practicing throwing? How many different scoring systems can you think of? How many ways can a student experience success? Try applying this process to the teaching of other motor skills. Will it work in the development of specific play and/or social skills?

Individualization

Creative teaching and/or adapting pedagogy, content, and environment to specific needs leads to individualization of instruction. The individualized educational program (IEP) required by PL 94–142 is based on the belief that teachers are creative. Individualization does not mean teaching one-to-one, but changing classroom organization and pedagogical approaches to meet the needs of individuals.

Integration of handicapped students into regular physical education tends to make classes more *heterogeneous* (encompassing wide individual differences). Integration does not necessarily increase heterogeneity with regard to psychomotor abilities, however, since students of normal intelligence have always displayed a wide range of motor abilities. Some handicapped pupils are better in motor ability than their nonhandicapped peers. Integration of MR, LD, and ED children primarily affects heterogeneity in cognitive and affective behaviors—i.e., actual game behaviors (rules, strategies, sportsmanship). Integration of sensory-impaired pupils (blind, deaf, awkward) primarily affects mode of presentation and enhancement of environmental stimuli.

All in all, integration within the gymnasium setting affects group dynamics and interpersonal relationships more than actual motor teaching and learning. With increasing individual differences, problems of classroom management, motivation, and discipline are generally intensified. *Teachers of mainstream physical education must be excellent—more competent in every respect than regular physical educators with students of same or similar ability levels.*

No longer is good physical education a teacher standing in front of the entire class and instructing all students simultaneously on the same skill. With the trend away from ability grouping in all educational settings (not just physical education), the role of teaching is changing from information giver to learning facilitator. Most mainstream physical education seems to function best in classes organized as *learning stations* with an adult teacher aide or a peer or cross-age tutor (physical education honors student from another class) responsible for each station. The mainstream physical educator then moves from station to station, giving attention and assistance to individuals and small groups as needed. Much of the mainstream teacher's work must be completed before class: reviewing students' learning curves and daily assessment data; developing *task cards* for individuals, pairs, and triads and *learning plans* for stations; and teaching (in-servicing) aides and student leaders. Unless building principals allow teachers planning periods for such management tasks, mainstreaming is apt to function less than smoothly.

Figure 7.2 A student who exhibits jumping difficulties during a basketball game rotates out of the game to a *learning station* where he receives individualized help with vertical jumping. Dr. Joanne Rowe assists.

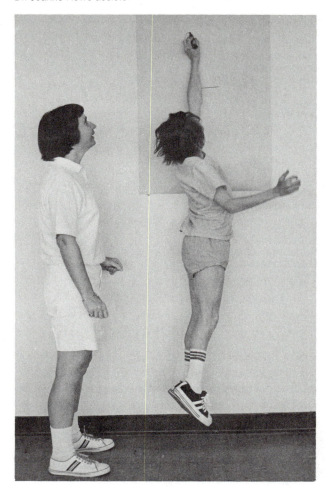

Learning Stations

Learning stations may vary according to number of students assigned, permanency of assignment, nature of learning tasks, and type of teaching style. In an elementary school unit on games, for instance, the largest station may be the playing area for the game itself. Additionally, there should be two or three smaller learning stations (three to six persons in each) with different instructional objectives being implemented at each. A student who experiences a problem pertaining to a skill, rule, strategy, or interpersonal relationship (sportsmanship) during the game goes to the appropriate learning station for help (Figure 7.2). One station may be maintained for motorically gifted students who do not need the game for skill practice as do their peers. Such athletes should have the opportunity for *new learning* of alternative skills/sports. Physical education should be primarily a time of *learning for everyone,* with practice (repetition) and competition occurring mainly after school and during weekends.

In an alternative gymnasium/playing field arrangement, the student might elect (or be assigned) to the same station for several days or weeks. A different sport, dance, or movement education activity is taught at each station. Peers and cross-age tutors can serve as teachers at the stations. Occasionally, a handicapped adult athlete from the community can be recruited to teach a unit at a particular station, thereby serving as a model for handicapped students and facilitating positive attitude change regarding the abilities and competence of handicapped persons.

Still another classroom arrangement is rotation of students from station to station for learning different skills during the same period. Not all students have to rotate around all stations. The *direction* of rotation (counterclockwise), however, should be the same for everyone to avoid confusion. The *time* for changing stations can be the same for everyone (on a set signal) or can vary according to individual differences in learning and completing task cards. For LD, MR, and ED students for whom changing stations may be confusing or impossible without help, *buddies* can volunteer (or be assigned) as partners for the day or the unit.

Task Cards and Learning Materials

Predeveloped learning materials are necessary to individualized and personalized mainstream physical education. These may be task cards that the student picks up as he or she enters class; audiovisuals as individualized learning packages or modules that he or she can carry along; or an infinite variety of materials. Computers are already within the price range of some school districts and increasingly will be used to store IEPs, behavioral objectives, and progressive day-by-day achievements of students. Videotapes can capture trial-by-trial performance and provide immediate personalized feedback for the student as well as assessment data that can be used later by teachers.

The development of task cards and individualized learning materials, like adapting instruction, requires an understanding of individual differences in terms of motor development, biomechanics, exercise physiology, and motor learning. Principles from each of these areas guide the teacher in prescribing appropriate activities for individuals.

Developmental Sequences

A knowledge of developmental sequences is derived from motor development. A developmental sequence is a list of movement patterns presented in the chronological order in which they are acquired by most children (i.e., a developmental sequence states motor

Table 7.3
Developmental Sequence for Acquiring Locomotor Skills

Skill	Approximate Age in Years
Rolling from side to side	.50
Crawling (on belly)	.60
Creeping (hands and knees)	.75
Walk	1.50
Run	1.75
Step (leap) downward	2.00
Vertical jump	2.33
Long jump	3.00
Forward roll	3.00
Hop	3.50
Gallop	3.55
Slide (step, close, step)	4.50
Skip	5.00
Backward roll	6.00

Note. Fall-bend-roll should be taught and practiced before the jump. Teach that falling can be a game.

milestones). Most elementary school physical educators have these lists memorized since the lists are used continuously in determining readiness of a child to learn new skills. The lists also enable a teacher to decide whether motor development is normal, delayed, or abnormal.

Developmental sequences specify the order in which movement patterns should be taught. Table 7.3, for instance, indicates that hopping should be taught before skipping and that vertical jumping should be taught before horizontal jumping. The sequence is more important to remember than the approximate age, since children exhibit wide individual differences in age of learning. Table 7.4 shows that children should be taught to roll a ball before learning to throw and that striking skills should be introduced before catching skills.

Many normal children have acquired the basic movement patterns described in Tables 7.3 and 7.4 before entering school. The goal of elementary school physical education, then, is to help these children refine movement patterns and use the patterns in games and sports. Table 7.5 shows the approximate ages that normal children utilize movement patterns in track and field and gymnastics. In contrast, handicapped children eligible for adapted physical education services usually lag 2 to 3 years behind normal peers in acquisition of motor skills. The older the severely handicapped student becomes, the larger is the lag, with sometimes as much as 6 to 9 years difference in motor functioning of normal and severely handicapped students. Along with motor performance lags are deficits in fitness, play, and social functioning.

A developmental sequence can also be a list of play behaviors listed in the chronological order in which they evolve in most children (see index for developmental stages in toy or object play and developmental stages in social play). Little research has been conducted on the chronological order in which game concepts are mastered, but these, too, should be organized into developmental sequences; then they can be taught sequentially one at a time, the way motor patterns are taught. Following is a hypothesized developmental sequence for play concepts:

1. Peek-a-boo and similar hide/seek games.
2. Follow the leader.
3. Start-stop on cues like Red Light, Green Light.
4. Run-to-change-places games like Under the Parachute and Squirrels in Trees.
5. Run to safety (safe vs. not safe places or people) like Huntsman.
6. Flee (avoiding being tagged) like Chickens and Fox.
7. Tag (learning to tag another).
8. Chase (learning to chase another).
9. Flee-Tag-Chase combinations with a penalty (like going to prison) for being tagged.
10. Flee-Tag-Chase combinations involving changing roles (when tagged, you become a chaser).

Table 7.6 presents a developmental progression (sequence) for teaching and practicing game concepts. Go through elementary school methods textbooks and try putting games in developmental sequences, as in Table 7.6. Think of how many ways the theme of each game can be varied without changing the number of concepts.

Table 7.4
Developmental Sequence for Acquiring Beginning Object Skills

Skill	Approximate Age in Years
Grasping	.50
Pounding	.55
Pushing pellets off table	.65
Releasing	1.00
Throwing[a]	2.00
Striking, downward	3.00
Striking, horizontal	4.00
Catching/trapping large balls	4.00
Catching small balls	6.00

[a]For cerebral palsied and other students who have problems with release, throwing should be moved to the end of the sequence and considered the hardest skill.

Table 7.5
Approximate Ages that Children Utilize Movement Patterns in Sports

Approximate Age	Track and Field Skills	Approximate Age	Gymnastic Skills
		3	Consecutive jumps on trampoline
5	Standing long jump	4	Jump-off dismount from balance beam
6	High jump scissor style	4	Forward walk on beam
7	Running long jump	5	Backward walk on beam
8	Running relays	5	Sideward walk on beam
9	Hurdles	5	Combinations of locomotor movements on trampoline
9	Middle distance runs	5	Combinations of locomotor movements on balance beam
9	High jump straddle style	6	Approach and jump off springboard
10	Long distance runs	7	Front support arm mount
10	Triple jump	7	Squat vault
		7	Straddle vault
		8	Front vault
		8	Flank vault

Knowledge of developmental sequences enhances writing of the individualized educational program (IEP). Specifically, such knowledge facilitates the description of present level of motor performance and the subsequent selection of goals, objectives, and services.

Role of the IEP

The IEP, as explained in Chapter 3, is required only for handicapped children. The mandate is interpreted differently by various school systems, with some believing that IEPs are not needed for handicapped children in the regular physical education program. The physical education portion of the IEPs of pupils in such school districts might simply read, "Regular physical education placement."

This author believes that physical education IEPs should be written for *all students,* with the greatest attention given to those with psychomotor or health problems that may interfere with physical education learning. While this may sound idealistic, it seems the only way to personalize and individualize physical education instruction for all pupils in the mainstream.

We have long recognized the principle of readiness—starting each class where the students are. This principle implies assessment of the level of psychomotor performance—formal or otherwise. The IEP simply extends the practice of determining where the whole class is to determining the needs of the individuals in the class. Likewise, teachers have always written into lesson plans (or at least had in mind) long-range goals and short-term objectives for their students. These have served as the criteria for selecting learning activities (called *services* in the IEP). Good teachers have always subjected their programs to periodic evaluation. *Thus, good physical education teachers have been writing IEPs (at least in their minds) for years.* The concept of the IEP is not really new; the requirement that it be written increases paper work, but developing IEPs for individual students takes no more time than writing lesson plans. Since the fully developed IEP is an annual plan to guide activities for each pupil at the learning stations, it substitutes for lesson plans.

Table 7.6
Developmental Progression I for Teaching Running Game Concepts

Step	Illustrative games
1	**Easiest (one concept)** Flying Dutchman Concepts: Run home on cue. Formation: Line of children holding hands. Start with circle and then break into line. Instructions: Leader pulls line in any direction around the gymnasium. On cue *Flying Dutchman,* all children run to wall or mat designated as home (safety). The term *floor spaces* may be substituted in movement education variations of this game.
2	**Medium (two concepts)** Huntsman Concepts: Follow leader, run home on cue. Formation: File, one student behind the other. Instructions: Teacher moves around the room and says, "I'm going to hunt the monster. Who wants to go on a hunt with me? Get in the file and follow!" This continues, with students joining file and following the leader until cue *bang.* On it, all students run independently to safety zone. Theme can be varied as "I am a police officer. Who wants to chase robbers with me?"
3	**Harder (four concepts)** Chickens and Fox (Run, Children, Run) Concepts: Follow leader, run home on cue, avoid being tagged, penalty. Formation: Scattered, with safety and danger zones clearly marked. Instructions: All children (chickens, rabbits, or whatever) are at home safe with leader. Outside safety zone is a fox or bad person either walking back and forth or pretending to be asleep. Leader says to group, "Let's take a walk" and all walk around danger zone while fox sleeps. Leader or fox can give cue to run home: "Run, chickens, run." Fox tries to tag children before they get home. Fox makes persons who are tagged sit in prison (this introduces penalty concept).
4	**Very hard (five or more concepts)** Simple One-to-One Tag Games See activity analysis in Table 7.8

Note. In writing lesson plans, refer to Game Progression I, step 1, 2, 3, or 4.

Writing Goals and Objectives

Perhaps the most important part of individualizing instruction, and hence of the written IEP, are the long-range goals and short-term objectives. *Goals are broad, global statements for the entire year.* Examples are: (a) Jason will progress from the associative to the co-operative play stage; (b) he will improve his dynamic balance; (c) Kim will learn to bowl; (d) Jean will learn to folk dance; and (e) Bob will improve his cardiovascular endurance.

Goals are broken down into measurable, observable behavioral objectives (sometimes called performance objectives) that can be checked off as students achieve them. Such objectives serve as the basis for *criterion-referenced assessment,* which is continuous and, thus, integrated with teaching. Examples are in Table 7.7.

Objectives are thus specific statements that contain three parts: (a) condition, (b) observable behavior, and (c) criterion level. Writing good objectives is a skill that requires much practice. The following criteria enable you to determine whether or not your objectives are written in behavior terms:

1. Describes learner behavior, not teacher behavior.
2. Describes product, not process (i.e., the terminal behavior, not the learning activity).
3. Includes a verb that specifies a definite, observable behavior.
4. Contains a single learning outcome, not several.
5. Contains three parts: condition, observable behavior, and criterion level.

When working with severely mentally handicapped students, separate objectives may be needed for each part of a complex movement pattern like the jump. Illustrative of this are the following:

1. Given verbal cues, the student can perform the individual parts of a jump 7 of 10 times.
   a. Preliminary crouch with trunk parallel to ground and arms swung backward, as depicted in Figure 7.3.
   b. Take-off from preliminary crouch with arms moving forward and upward, as depicted in Figure 7.3.
   c. Flight with both feet off ground at the same time.
   d. Curl in air in preparation for landing.
   e. Land with arms forward and knees bent without losing balance.

2. Given a verbal cue, the student can perform combinations of the individual parts of a jump 7 of 10 times.
   a. Crouch and take-off.
   b. Crouch, take-off, and fly.
   c. Crouch, take-off, fly, and curl in air.
3. Given a verbal cue, the student can perform a jump in mature form for his or her age 7 of 10 times.

When mastery of a pattern like the jump requires several lessons, *task analysis* assists in the processes of assessment, writing goals and objectives, and selecting instructional activities.

Task Analysis

Task analysis is the process of breaking down a skill or movement into its parts and then ordering these parts into a sequence from easy to difficult. The end process of a task analysis is often called a task or learning sequence. The pedagogy by which a task sequence is taught is forward or backward chaining.

With students whose intellectual and perceptual functions are normal, detailed task analysis is not necessary. Such children learn simple movement patterns by the *whole* as opposed to the *part* method. They see a demonstration, mentally process what they have seen, and then do a fair to good imitation. Further demonstrations accompanied by explanations are all that are necessary. As skills to be learned become more complex, the need for task analysis increases. Thus, normally functioning students learn jumping by the *whole* (nontask analysis) method, but they require the *whole-part-whole* (task analysis) method for learning a tennis serve.

In contrast, severely handicapped students often spend months mastering all of the tasks comprising a simple pattern like jumping. Figure 7.3 presents a task analysis for use in teaching jumping to such children. Before electing to teach by task analysis, try repeatedly to have a student imitate a movement. Often, imitation within a game context (like playing airplanes or jumping jacks or grasshopper) works better than drill. Remember that severely mentally handicapped students may not be able to remember or conceptualize a jumping jack or grasshopper, so bring such things to school. Many students have gotten so excited by watching live grasshoppers, frogs, or toads that they

Table 7.7
Illustrative Short-Term Objectives

Condition	Behavior	Criterion Level
Using the local bowling alley,	Joe will bowl	an average of 130 in 3 consecutive games.
Using 3″ × 3″ bean bags from a distance of 15 feet,	Dave will hit the Project Active wall target (40″ × 60″)	7 of 10 times.
On a 50-item multiple-choice test on fitness,	Bob will score	47, or better on the first trial.
From memory,	Jean will execute in time to music	3 of 4 folk dances without error.

Figure 7.3   Task analysis for teaching jump to severely handicapped students.

| Tasks | 1-2-3-4 | 5-6 | 7 | 8 |

Step	Task
1	Practice crouch without arm movement: down and up, down and up. Emphasize trunk parallel to ground. Play games like run-run-crouch, Simon says crouch.
2	Add attention to feet. Rock forward onto balls of feet with crouch. In crouch position, alternate flat feet with balls of feet to help children remember the difference. Devise games: rock forward and keep balance vs. rock forward and lose balance.
3	Add backward arm swing to crouch. Play games in this position. How many ways can you move forward while in this position?
4	Add forward and upward arm swing. Practice this only in a crouch position to emphasize that its purpose is to generate power to lift off the ground. Play airplane and make engine noise as arms start up, or play jack-in-the-box.
5	Add concept of pushing off with feet to upward arm swing. Push with feet and this causes hip, knee, and ankle extension. Practice this skill while standing on box about 8 inches high so forward thrust results in falling or jumping down and forward. Or begin on low trampoline or bed mattress so forward thrust will carry student to ground.
6	Work on straightening out body, like airplane going in the air. Hold pole with flag over student's head and have student try to touch flag as he or she straightens out. Or focus attention on lifting body over a low rope. In both instances, have body aiming at mat since end of task is usually falling forward. Be sure this falling forward is fun (a game).
7	Add bending to touch toes. Practice from prone position, lying over a bench as well as in air: straight body to bend and touch toes.
8	Practice landing and keeping balance from all kinds of falls and jumps.

Note: Before teaching this task analysis, be sure students know several correct ways to fall.

have performed their first jumps, whereas weeks of routine instruction have failed. This is the result of creative teaching: *fluency* in thinking of how many things jump and/or take off and land and *originality* in devising games, creative drama, or music that might elicit jumping.

In writing a task analysis (like for a jump), think through environmental changes that make learning easier. In a biomechanical context, jumping is purposely losing stability, so think how you can plan violating all of the principles of stability. Jumping also involves overcoming inertia, so consider all the implications of Newton's first law. Child development theorists emphasize that to teach jumping down from a height is easier than teaching jumping up from the floor; this is because losing stability from a height (i.e., the teacher is using gravity to help with learning) is easier. Losing stability from an unstable surface (low trampoline, balancing board, tire, innertube) is easier than losing stability from the floor. Use these biomechanical concepts in teaching a task sequence.

Remember also developmental sequence. What movement patterns must children possess before they are ready to learn jumping? Perhaps the most important one is falling. Children should be taught how to fall, that falling is important in games and creative drama, and that falling is fun. Fall-bend-roll must be mastered before long jumping can be safely taught. Many children learn jumping from land to water before the on-land movement. The task analysis in Figure 7.3 ideally is taught in both environments: swimming pool and gymnasium.

A written task analysis makes lesson plans and IEPs easier to develop. Instead of writing sentences to specify content to be taught, the teacher can simply note, "Task Analysis 1 for Jump, Step 4." In describing present level of performance for the IEP, the teacher can delimit narration to name of the task analysis and number of the step at which the student can succeed. The objective then is to master a certain number of steps before the next PL 94–142 progress review.

Individual steps within a task analysis are taught by a technique called *chaining*. This refers to mastery of a task and then linking it to a task or several tasks previously learned, thereby performing a chain of tasks. Sometimes, a movement pattern can best be taught by *forward chaining* (Figure 7.4), the traditional approach of moving from Step 1 forward through Step 8. Other times it is more efficient to use *backward chaining* (i.e., starting with the last step in the chain and moving backward to Step 1). Backward chaining is particularly effective in movement patterns like

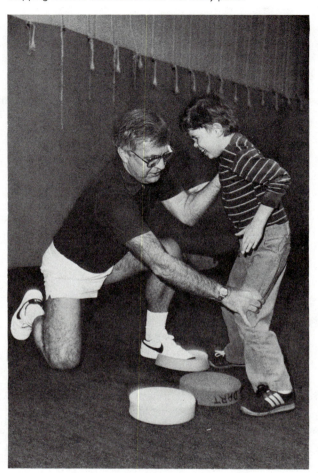

Figure 7.4 Dr. Ernie Bundschuh, University of Georgia, demonstrates forward chaining with severely mentally handicapped child. The simple task of lifting the leg and stepping forward has been broken into many parts.

throwing and striking, in which the last step is dramatic and constitutes a reward within itself (i.e., the noise of a ball hitting a target or striking a bat).

Once the tasks comprising a movement pattern are mastered, new learning progressions can be developed that focus on increasing the height, distance, or speed of the movement. For instance, a second learning progression for jumping might read

1. Jump down from 8-inch step.
2. Jump down from 12-inch step.
3. Jump down from 18-inch bench.
4. Jump down from 24-inch bench.

A third learning progression might read

1. Jump forward 6 inches.
2. Jump forward 12 inches.
3. Jump forward 18 inches.

Figure 7.5 Physical and verbal assistance are almost always needed in teaching severely handicapped children to bat. Note that the target is waist high to make the skill easier. A ball on top of a coffee can is an excellent target because children find the extra noise made on the strike reinforcing.

A fourth learning progression might read

1. Jump over a rope 3 inches high.
2. Jump over a rope 6 inches high.
3. Jump over a rope 12 inches high.

Level of Assistance

In performing a task or sequence of tasks, students require different levels of assistance: physical, visual, verbal, or a combination of these (Figure 7.5). Evaluation and record keeping entail writing next to the task the type of assistance needed. A student might progress, for instance, through the following levels of assistance:

1. *P*—Performs overarm throw with *physical* and verbal assistance.
2. *D*—Performs overarm throw with visual and verbal assistance (i.e., a *demonstration* accompanied by explanation).
3. *C5*—Performs overarm throw with much verbal assistance (i.e., *cues* throughout the sequence).
4. *C1*—Performs overarm throw with minimal verbal assistance (i.e., one or two *cues* only).
5. *I*—Performs overarm throw with no assistance (i.e., *independently*).

These five descriptors of level of assistance can be applied to a single step within a task analysis or a movement pattern or a sequence of movement patterns (i.e., folk dance). Use of initials to represent levels facilitates ease of record keeping and lesson writing.

Physical assistance should always be accompanied by verbal cues. These cues can be spoken, chanted, or sung. Physical assistance should never be called physical manipulation (a medical term often used in therapy and orthopedics). Several learning theorists have created good synonyms for physical assistance. This author likes the term *coactive movement,* taken from the Van Dijk approach from Holland, now widely used throughout the world in working with deaf-blind individuals. In coactive movement, the bodies of the teacher and student move as one, closely touching, in activities like rolling, seat scooting, creeping, knee walking, and upright walking. As the student gets the feel of the task, the distance between the two bodies is gradually increased. The emphasis is then on *mirroring* (i.e., imitating the teacher's movements).

Generalization

The learning of a task sequence is relatively meaningless if generalization does not occur. Generalization refers to the transfer of learning from one piece of equipment to another and from one setting to another. In students with intact intelligence, generalization usually occurs without specific training. When teaching mentally retarded students, however, generalization should be built into task sequences. For example, a learning progression might read

Roll 10-inch rubber ball toward milk cartons.
Roll 10-inch rubber ball toward bowling pins.
Roll bowling ball toward bowling pins.
Roll bocce ball toward target ball.
Roll 10-inch rubber ball toward persons inside a
circle (as in dodgeball).

Such tasks should be practiced on different surfaces (grass, dirt, floor) and in different environments (gymnasium, outdoors, bowling alley). Generalization training can be used to develop creativity in students. The teacher should repeatedly ask, "How many things can we make roll? How many places can we go to roll things? At how many targets can we roll things?"

Table 7.8
Behavioral Requirements of Simple Tag Game: An Activity Analysis Showing Teaching Progression

Cognitive

1. Responds to name.
2. Follows simple directions:
   a. Sit down.
   b. Stay.
   c. Stand up.
   d. Run.
3. Responds appropriately to cues:
   a. Stop, start.
   b. Good, bad.
4. Attends to teacher long enough to grasp game structure and rules.
   a. Visually.
   b. Auditorially.
5. Understands fleeing role.
   a. You (Amy) have a beanbag, squeaky toy, orange, make-believe tail.
   b. Someone (Bob) wants it.
   c. You (Amy) do not want Bob to have object.
   d. You (Amy) run away from Bob when I give cue.
6. Understands chasing role.
   a. Bob chases you when I give cue.
   b. Bob chases you until
      (1) you touch safety base or
      (2) he tags you.
7. Understands concept of safety base.
8. Understands concepts of tagging, penalty, and changing roles.
   a. When tagged, the penalty is you must give Bob the object.
   b. You change roles because you want the object (i.e., you chase Bob or someone else who has object).

Affective

1. Has fun.
   a. Is not frightened by being chased.
   b. Is sufficiently involved that attention does not wander.
   c. Smiles and/or makes joyous sounds.
2. Shows awareness of others.
3. Displays competitive spirit.
4. Tags other person gently.

Psychomotor

1. Performs motor skills.
   a. Runs.
   b. Dodges/ducks.
   c. Tags.
2. Demonstrates sufficient fitness.
   a. Does not become breathless.
   b. Does not develop muscle cramps.

Activity Analysis

Activity analysis is the process of breaking down an activity into the behavioral components requisite for success. In physical education and recreation, the activity to be analyzed is usually a game, sport, or exercise. The process can, however, be directed toward activities of daily living (ADL), leisure, or work. Whereas special educators and physical educators commonly use the terms *task analysis* and *activity analysis* interchangeably, therapeutic recreation specialists and occupational therapists prefer *activity analysis*. This is because they are concerned with the total activity, not just the motor skill and fitness requisites.

Activity analysis typically entails consideration of the three educational domains: cognitive, psychomotor, and affective. Table 7.8 presents an activity analysis for a simple tag game. This type of detailed analysis is needed in teaching games to severely mentally handicapped students. Note the use of a beanbag, squeaky toy, orange, or make-believe tail; a prop is usually necessary with children deficient in pretending skills; otherwise, they simply cannot understand the point of chasing and fleeing.

Prior to being taught the simple tag game described in Table 7.8, children should have learned games involving only one or two concepts: *stop-start,* as in Red Light, Green Light and Musical Chairs and *follow the leader* and *safety-not safety,* as in Flying Dutchman and Huntsman (see Table 7.8). In developmental progressions for teaching games, tag is relatively difficult. Tag involves eight concepts: start-stop, safety-not safety, chasing, tagging, fleeing, dodging, penalty, and changing roles. With severely mentally handicapped students, each concept must be taught and practiced separately, then chains of concepts must be practiced. Task and activity analyses are essential processes in the assessment and instruction of students with mental retardation, emotional disturbance, and learning disabilities. Such analysis may be helpful in adapting instruction to other handicapping conditions also, although application of biomechanical and exercise principles is the basic key to adaptations required by physical disabilities, health impairments, and sensory deficits.

Teaching Styles

Important to the learning success of all students, regardless of handicapping condition, is the teaching style used. Muska Mosston, in 1966, revolutionized physical

Figure 7.6 Sherrill Spectrum of Teaching Styles based on concepts of Muska Mosston (1966, 1981).

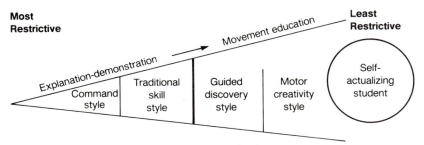

Note: The variables that the teacher manipulates to create different teaching styles are learning environment, starting and stopping routine, presentation mode, and practice or execution mode. See Table 7.9 for suggestions.

education pedagogy by describing seven alternative teaching styles and suggesting that teachers master all styles. Mosston emphasized that teaching style should match the needs of students and, thus, vary from group to group. The ultimate goal, however, was to progressively increase the student's responsibility for his or her learning by moving from the command style to the problem solving (i.e., divergent) style.

Mosston's concept provided the stimulus for Figure 7.6, which is Sherrill's attempt to create a simplified spectrum of teaching styles specifically for use with handicapped students in accordance with the PL 94–142 mandate that students be educated in the least restrictive environment.

Teaching styles to a large extent determine educational environment. The IEP should prescribe the teaching style for which the handicapped pupil is ready. The guiding principle is to facilitate a child's progress from the teaching style and environment that are most restrictive (command style) to least restrictive (motor creativity). Some children, like the severely MR, LD, and ED, who need *optimal structure* and lack the ability to cope with freedom (manage their own behaviors), may remain at the command or traditional skills level throughout their schooling. Others, who have no cognitive, perceptual, or behavior problems, may enter the spectrum at the guided discovery level.

Table 7.9 describes in detail the teaching procedures believed to be optimal within each style. Particular attention is given to the learning environment itself and to starting and stopping protocol. In the mainstream setting, different teaching styles may be in operation at the various learning stations. The same teaching style the child experiences in other subject areas should be used in physical education. For the severely handicapped pupil especially, such *consistency* is imperative.

Students for whom the command teaching style is prescribed usually include those with severe mental retardation, severe learning disabilities, severe emotional disturbance, autism, severe hyperactivity or distractibility, inner or receptive language deficits, and multihandicapping conditions. Four basic principles guide the creation of a learning environment for the command teaching style:

1. Use optimal structure
2. Reduce space
3. Eliminate irrelevant stimuli
4. Enhance the stimulus value of specific equipment or materials

Table 7.10 summarizes the characteristics of most and least restrictive teaching styles for normal students. Remember that what is most restrictive for the normal student may be least restrictive for the severely mentally handicapped student. Restrictive is defined in terms of the environment that permits a student to learn best.

Behavior management is a pedagogy specific to the command teaching style. Because of its effectiveness in working with severely mentally and emotionally handicapped students, it is presented separately.

Table 7.9
Four Teaching Styles from Most to Least Restrictive

Situation	Most Restrictive		Least Restrictive	
	Command Style	*Traditional Skills Style*	*Guided Discovery Style*	*Motor Creativity Style*
Learning Environment	Small space/ Clearly defined boundaries/ Floor spots/ Circles and lines painted on floor/ Equipment always set up in same location/ External stimuli reduced/ Activity stations partitioned off from one another/ Cubicles available	Space increased to normal play area/ Clearly defined boundaries/ No floor spots/ Regulation sports markings painted on floor/ Equipment in different locations/ External stimuli increased/ No partitions/ Cubicles available	Space varies/ Boundaries clearly defined, but space limitations change with each problem/ Imaginary floor spots/ Imaginary floor markings/ Equipment varies and location changes in accordance with problem/ No partitions/ Cubicles available	Determined by student within the limits imposed by school rules and regulations about use of space and equipment
Starting Routine	Goes to assigned floor spots and sits until teacher starts class *or* Goes to assigned space and performs prescribed exercises until teacher starts class, for which, either: Assigned starting place is same all semester *or* Assigned space and/or equipment is rotated so student starts in different place every month.	Student finds own space and sits until teacher starts class *or* Student goes to space of own choice and warms up, and either: Warm-ups may be prescribed as a set routine for each piece of equipment *or* Warm-ups may be created or chosen freely by student	Same as traditional skills approach except that student assumes responsibility for own warm-ups; explores alternative ways of warming up; discovers best warm-ups for self	Determined by student within the limits imposed by school rules and regulations about use of time, i.e., scheduling
Presentation of New Learning Activities	Teacher states behavioral objectives/ Teacher designates student leaders or teacher aides/ Teacher puts students into formation/ Teacher gives directions: one task presented at a time in form of sentences accompanied by demonstrations involving as many students as possible.	Teacher states behavioral objectives/ Students choose own leaders/ Teacher puts students into formation/ Teacher gives directions: several tasks presented at a time in form of sentences accompanied by demonstrations, and either: Teacher prescribes sequences in which they must be practiced *or* Students free to choose sequence in which tasks are practiced.	Teacher states behavioral objectives/ Teacher establishes structure in form of questions designed to elicit either: Increased body awareness *or* Exploration of time, space, force, and flow in relation to movement Teacher offers *no* demonstration; stresses that there is no one correct answer, and reassures pupils that no one can fail/ Teacher provides each student with ball, rope, or prop needed	Student states behavioral objectives/ Student establishes own structure, poses original questions and/ or hypotheses designed to elicit perceptual-cognitive-motor exploration: artistic originality/self-expression; scientific discovery/search for explanations; comic inspiration/invention

Table 7.9 *(Continued)*

Situation	Most Restrictive		Least Restrictive	
	Command Style	*Traditional Skills Style*	*Guided Discovery Style*	*Motor Creativity Style*
Execution	*Student*	*Student*	*Student*	*Student*
	Practices in formation prescribed by teacher/ Waits turn and follows set routine for going to end of file/ Starts on signal/ Moves in unison with peers to verbal cues, drum, or music/ Stops on signal/ Rotates or changes activity on signal; in same direction (CCW)	Chooses own space or formation for practice/ Waits turn but chooses own space and own activity while waiting/ Chooses own time to start/ Moves in own rhythm/ Chooses own time to stop/ Rotates or changes activity when chooses in same direction (CCW)	Finds own space/ Chooses own time to start and stop/ Moves in own rhythm/ Finds movement responses to teacher's questions/ Considers all movement alternatives/ Discovers movement patterns most efficient for self/ Changes activity when teacher poses new question	Finds own space/ Chooses own time to start and stop/ Moves in own rhythm/ Finds movement responses to own questions through creative processes (See table 7.1).
	Teacher	*Teacher*	*Teacher*	*Teacher*
	Moves about room/ Offers individual praise/ Identifies and corrects movement errors by verbal commands and modeling	Moves about room/ Offers individual praise/ Identifies and corrects movement errors by questions which evoke answers from students	Moves about room/ Offers words and phrases of acceptance/ Poses additional questions to individuals/ Acquaints students with names of their movement discoveries	Moves about room/ Offers words and phrases of acceptance/ Mostly observes

Table 7.10
Characteristics of Teaching Styles

Most Restrictive	Least Restrictive	Most Restrictive	Least Restrictive
Teacher dominated	*Student dominated*	*Enhanced stimulus intensity*	*Weakened stimulus intensity*
Assisted movement	*Independent movement*	Bright lights	Normal lighting
Coactive/enactive Shaping/chaining	Self-initiated Exploring/creating	Loud signals Colorful equipment	Soft, quiet signals Regulation colors
Homogeneous grouping	*Heterogenous grouping*	Increased size balls, bases	Regulation size
Much structure	*Little structure*	Memorable texture	Regulation texture
Assigned floor spots Move on cue Drum or musical accompaniment Sameness	Free choice Free choice Own rhythm	Exaggerated teacher gestures and facial expressions	Normal teacher gestures and facial expressions
	Role differentiation	*External motivation*	*Intrinsic motivation*
Reduced space	*Increased space*	Rewards/awards	No external rewards
Decreased stimuli	*Increased stimuli*	Praise	Facilitating/accepting
One instruction No equipment One "it" One base Indoors	Several instructions Lots of balls/props Several "its" Several bases Outdoors	Consistency of teacher	Flexibility of teacher

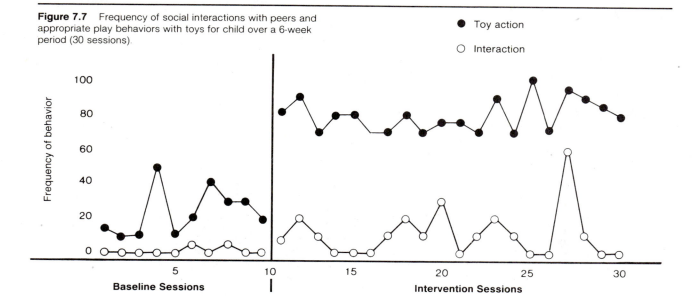

Figure 7.7 Frequency of social interactions with peers and appropriate play behaviors with toys for child over a 6-week period (30 sessions).

● Toy action

○ Interaction

Behavior Management

Behavior management (modification) is used so frequently in special education, particularly with the severely handicapped, that adapted physical educators should be familiar with the basic procedures. A particularly helpful reference is one by Presbie and Brown (1977), who apply behavior management philosophy to the regular physical education program, showing how it too can individualize programming. In a sense, many of us use behavior management techniques every day when we promise ourselves rewards for completing work, losing weight, or other targeted behaviors.

General Procedures

General procedures followed in behavior management include: (a) specify the desired behavior; (b) establish baseline performance by graphing the number of times the behavior normally occurs; (c) apply the intervention; and (d) continue graphing the number of times the behavior occurs to see if the intervention is effective—i.e., the desired behavior increases in frequency.

Figure 7.7 illustrates the kind of graphing procedure used to record changes in play behaviors with toys and social interactions as the result of an *educational intervention*. The intervention in such programs is generally social reinforcement, attention, and praise for showing the desired behavior and no attention otherwise. While such graphing and recording of frequency of behavior are time-consuming, the technique is used in many settings. Whether or not physical educators use the technique, they should understand it to facilitate interpersonal relationships with other staff members.

Figure 7.8 A basic principle of behavior management is *Catch 'em being Good!* Authorities recommend a 5:1 praise/criticism ratio. When teachers issue a criticism or correct a motor skill, they should offer at least five praises around the class before criticizing anyone again.

In Figure 7.8, one severely mentally retarded person was observed for 10 sessions in order to determine baseline performance in regard to interactions with peers and toys. On the IEP, this student's present

Table 7.11
Illustrative Short-Term Objectives Derived from Baseline Observations

Condition	Behavior	Criterion Level
While playing in a room with five to seven other children,	Joe will interact positively by initiating conversation, sharing a toy, or coactively using toys in episodes of at least 3 seconds duration	for an average of 6 episodes per 5-minute observation over 20 sessions.
While playing in a room with tricycle, jungle gym, slide, drums, balls, dolls, and toy cars/trucks,	Joe will interact with toys	for an average of 90 seconds out of each 5-minute observation session over 20 sessions.

level of performance, derived from the graph's baseline, was written as follows: (a) Joe usually has no interactions with peers during play sessions (i.e., he is in the parallel play stage) and (b) Joe interacts with toys for about 20 seconds out of every 5-minute play period; the remainder of the time he stares into space, rocks, or watches others.

Using this baseline information, the teacher described Joe's desired behaviors in the form of short-term objectives, as depicted in Table 7.11. Then, 20 sessions of intervention were conducted during which Joe was given 10-minute, specific lessons on how to interact with peers and toys, followed by 5 minutes of free play. Behaviors tallied and graphed during the free play period (see Figure 7.7) show that Joe's peer interactions varied from 0 to 50, with an average of 7.75; Joe, therefore, achieved the first objective. With regard to the second objective, Joe's toy interactions improved tremendously, but not quite enough to meet the criterion level.

Concepts of Teaching

Behavior management is based on the concepts of *cues* and *consequences,* the actions used by a teacher to change behavior of a student. Behavior management, in its strictest and most effective sense, demands a 1:1 relationship so that virtually every response of the student can have an immediate consequence. Nothing the student says or does is unnoticed.

Cue is the behavioral management term for a command or instruction telling a student what to do. Three rules should be followed in giving cues:

1. Make the cue as brief as possible in the beginning (i.e., "sit" or "stay" or "ready, run").
2. Use the same cue each time.
3. Never repeat a cue until the student makes some kind of response. If correct response is made, reinforce. If no response or wrong one is made, use a correction procedure.

The correction procedure is to say "No, that is not correct; do it this way" and then demonstrate again and/or take the student through the task coactively.

Consequence is the immediate feedback to a behavior that increases or decreases its occurrence (see Figure 7.8). For instance, in aggressive behavior (hitting, kicking, biting, and the like), the consequence should be punishment. In noncompliant behavior (I don't want to; I can't; I don't have to), the consequences should be ignoring the student's words or actions and, if appropriate, coactively taking him or her through the activity.

A consequence can be *reinforcement* (causing a behavior to increase), *punishment* (causing a behavior to decrease), or *timeout* (ignoring inappropriate behavior, removal from a reinforcing environment, or withholding of reinforcers). Rules to be followed in enacting consequences are

1. Give immediate feedback to every response the student makes.
2. Accompany nonverbal reinforcement (food, tokens, hugs) with words or, for deaf students, signs.
3. Reinforce within 2 seconds after a student responds correctly.
4. Ignore inappropriate behavior that affects only the student.
5. Punish inappropriate behavior that hurts others.

Use of consequences to teach or manage behavior is also called *contingency management.* A *contingency* is the relationship between a behavior and the events following the behavior. Giving *tokens* (or points) for correct responses or good behavior is a method of contingency management, providing the tokens are meaningful to the students and can be traded in on things or privileges of real value.

To encourage practice of motor skills, tokens are sometimes given for a set number of minutes or practice trials in which an individual, a team, or an entire class exhibits on-task behavior. *Response cost* is another method of contingency management. In it, points, tokens, or privileges are taken away when students fail to show appropriate behaviors.

Task analysis is also central to teaching by behavior management and keeping a record of the student's progress. The teacher knows precisely what step in a preanalyzed sequence the student is learning, and all attention is focused on that one step until it is achieved.

Table 7.12
Specific Behavior Management Techniques

Technique	Description
Shaping	Refers to reinforcing small steps or approximations of a desired behavior; an analogy might be the praise "You're getting warmer" in the old game of finding a hidden object. Inappropriate or undesired behaviors are ignored.
Chaining	Leading a person through a sequence of responses, as is done in a task-analyzed progression of skills from easy to hard. The sequential mastery of a folk dance with many parts might also be considered chaining.
Backward chaining	Entails starting with the last step in the chain first. For instance, in an overarm throw the backward chain would begin with the release of the ball; then the forward swing of arm and release are practiced; and then the backswing, the foreswing, and the release are practiced. Usually, manual guidance is used in backward chaining.
Prompting	The cue or stimulus that makes a behavior occur. It can be physical, verbal, visual, or some combination of sensory stimuli. In physical education, prompting is usually the behavior management term for physical guidance of the body or limb through a skill.
Fading	The gradual removal of the physical guidance as the person gains the ability to perform the skill unassisted. It can be gradual reduction in any reinforcement that is designed to help the student become increasingly independent.
Modeling	The behavior management term for demonstrating.
Positive reinforcement	An increase in the frequency of a behavior when followed by an event or stimulus the student finds pleasurable. This term should not be confused with *reward*. Although a reward is pleasurable, it does not necessarily increase behavior.
Negative reinforcement	An increase in the frequency of a behavior as a result of removing or terminating something the student perceives as unpleasant, such as being ignored, scolded, or punished by teachers or peers or hearing a loud buzz every time a postural slouch occurs. When students exhibit good behavior because they are intimidated or frightened by the consequence, this is negative reinforcement. In contrast, when students exhibit good behavior because they look forward to the consequence, this is positive reinforcement.
Punishment	The opposite of both positive and negative reinforcement. Punishment is anything that decreases the frequency of a behavior. A spanking, in the behavioral management context, is not punishment unless it decreases undesired behavior.
Extinction	Failure to reinforce (i.e., ignoring a response or behavior). It is a method of decreasing the frequency of a behavior. It can occur unintentionally, as when teachers are too busy or too insensitive to reinforce or it may be done purposely to eliminate a previously reinforced response to make way for the teaching of a new behavior.
Premack technique	A method of reinforcement that involves pairing something a student likes with something the teacher wants him or her to learn or do. The promise of free play when work is done illustrates this technique. It is based on the Premack principle.
Contract teaching	A method of assuring understanding and agreement concerning what is to be learned by student and teacher. A contract is a written document signed by all parties concerned. It lists what is to be learned and the possible consequences of learning and not learning.
Timeout	Withholding of reinforcers, ignoring inappropriate behaviors, or removal from a reinforcing environment. When a game or activity becomes so stimulating to a student that he or she cannot control negative behaviors, there should be a quiet place to go. Timeout can be either required by a teacher or opted by a student.
Good behavior game	Refers to use of a group contingency approach in which all students are affected by the behaviors of each individual. Rules governing good behavior are in writing. The goal of the game is to accumulate points that can be used in buying a pleasant consequence (like free time or a field trip) agreed upon by majority vote. Points are gained by adherring to rules and are subtracted for breaking rules.

Behavior management is data based. In addition to graphing behaviors, records are kept of number of trials required to learn each step and the pass or fail performance for each trial. This system has been called *A Data Based Gymnasium*, by Dr. John Dunn at Oregon State University. Dunn (1985) is one of the foremost authorities in applying behavior management to teaching motor skills to severely mentally retarded students. His book includes numerous task analysis sequences for use in teaching motor skills.

In summary, behavior management pedagogy is based on four general concepts: *cues, consequences, task analysis,* and a *data based gymnasium.* Most authorities consider behavior management the best pedagogical approach for instructing students with severe mental retardation, autism, and emotional disturbance. In the continuum of most to least restrictive teaching styles and environments, behavior management is least restrictive for the severely handicapped, but, strictly applied in its entirety, is most restrictive for most students.

Specific Behavior Management Techniques

Although few physical educators have the pupil-teacher ratio necessary for using behavior management in its entirety, all good teachers use some behavior management techniques. Teaching a complex motor skill to normal students, for instance, requires the techniques of shaping, chaining, and fading. Reinforcement and punishment are integral parts of the structure of every classroom. Table 7.12 presents specific behavior management techniques that are commonly used in physical education.

Adapting Instruction for Physical and Health Problems

Adapting instruction to the needs and interests of students is mostly a matter of common sense and creativity. A knowledge of biomechanical and fitness principles helps also. Adapting may begin during assessment, when it is obvious that a student cannot succeed if the test is administered in the traditional manner, or it may be based upon assessment data and/or the requests (suggestions) of the student. A good rule of thumb is to ask the student what adaptation seems best and to cooperatively make decisions. When an adaptation involves several persons (as in a group game), the concept should evolve from cooperative problem solving.

Students with problems of strength, endurance, power, balance, agility, coordination, and accuracy require adaptations that are based on principles of exercise physiology and biomechanics. Illustrative adaptations follow.

Figure 7.9 Students with cerebral palsy and other conditions of low muscle strength need a lowered basket for optimal success.

Adapting for Problems of Strength, Endurance, and Power

1. Lower the net or basketball goal (Figure 7.9).
2. Reduce the distance the ball must be thrown or served (a) between bases; (b) between serving line and net; (c) between partners.
3. Reduce weight and/or size of ball or projectile. Balloons are probably lightest, whereas medicine balls are heaviest (Figure 7.10).
4. Reduce weight of the bat or striking implement. Shorten the length of striking implement or choke up on the bat.
5. Lower the center of gravity. Games played in a lying or sitting position demand less fitness than those in standing/running position.
6. Deflate air from the ball or select one that will not get away so fast in case student misses a catch and has to chase the ball.
7. Decrease activity time. Reduce the number of points needed to win.
8. Increase rest periods during activity.
9. Utilize frequent rotation in and out of the game or a system for substitution when needed.
10. Reduce the speed of game. Walk rather than run through movements.
11. Consider ambulation alternatives—one inning on scooter boards, one inning on feet.

Figure 7.10 In a task analysis the manipulation of light balls (like balloons) comes before heavy balls. This severely handicapped teenager had so little arm and shoulder strength that shaking a balloon on a string was the first ball-handling activity he was able to master.

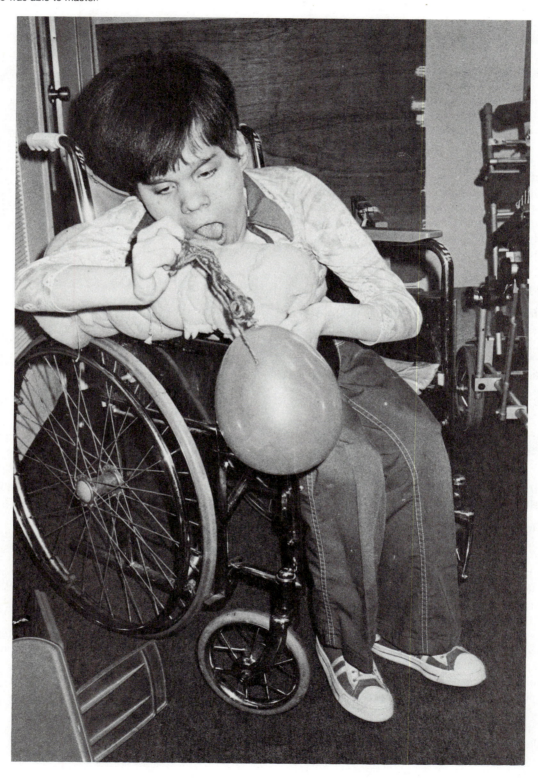

Adapting for Problems of Balance and Agility

1. Lower the center of gravity. On a trampoline, for instance, practice log rolls, creeping, and four-point bounces before trying activities in a standing position. Stress bending the knees (or landing low) when jumping or coming to quick stops.

2. Keep as much of the body in contact with the surface as possible. Flat-footed ambulation is more stable than on tiptoe. Balancing on four or five body parts is more stable than on one.

3. Widen the base of support (distance between feet).

4. Increase the width of lines, rails, or beams to be walked. Note that straight lines are easier to walk than curved ones.

5. Use extended arms for balance. Holding a fishing pole while walking the beam facilitates balance.

6. Use carpeted rather than slick surfaces. Modify surfaces to increase friction. Select footwear (rubber soles) to reduce falls.

7. Learn to fall; practice different kinds of falls; make falls into games and creative dramatics.

8. Provide a barre to assist with stability during exercises or have a table or chair to hold on to.

9. Understand role of visual perception in balance; learn to use eyes optimally.

10. Determine whether balance problems are related to prescribed medications. If there appears to be a relationship, confer with the physician.

Adapting for Problems of Coordination and Accuracy

1. For catching and striking activities, use larger, lighter, softer balls. Balls thrown to midline are easier to catch and strike than those thrown to the right or left. Decrease the distance the ball is thrown and reduce speed.

2. For throwing activities, use smaller (tennis size) balls. If grasp and release is a problem, try yarn or nerf balls and beanbags.

3. Distance throwing is an easier progression than throwing for accuracy.

4. In striking and kicking activities, succeed with a stationary ball before trying a moving one. Increase the surface of the striking implement; choke up on the bat for greater control.

5. Reduce frustration when balls are missed by using backdrops, backstops, nets, and rebounder frame sets. Or attach string to ball for ease of recovery (Figure 7.11).

Figure 7.11 Adapting equipment (like attaching a string to the ball) and using backstops increase easy recovery of ball and maximize time devoted to practicing a skill.

6. Increase the size of target or goal cage to be hit, circumference of basket to be made. Give points for nearness (like hitting backboard) to avoid feeling failure until basket is actually made.

7. In bowling-type games, use lighter, less stable pins. Milk cartons are good.

8. Optimize safety by more attention than normal to glasses protectors, shin guards, helmets, and face masks. Do not remove the child's glasses!

Exercise Physiology in Adaptation

Decreasing the physiological demands of an activity to make it easier for a student has its roots in the principle of overload. This principle states that strength and endurance result when the workload is greater than that to which the student is accustomed. Whereas all students should be pushed to increase their physiological limits once a motor pattern has been acquired, some handicapped students may take much longer than their peers to learn skills. During initial skill learning, the following guidelines (all pertaining to overload) should be followed:

1. Decrease weight being lifted, pushed, pulled, or carried.
2. Decrease the number of repetitions or sets.
3. Decrease the speed of exercise.
4. Decrease the distance covered.
5. Increase rest intervals between activity.
6. Decrease the intensity/type of activity during rest interval.
7. Use any combination of the above.

Exercise physiology principles are further discussed in relation to assessment and teaching in the chapter on fitness. Many clumsy and/or handicapped students, if properly motivated, can develop the same levels of fitness as their peers. If, however, they do not possess the movement patterns and play skills for participation in sports, their fitness needs are more health-related than physical or motor.

Biomechanical Principles in Adaptation

Most of the adaptations made for problems of strength, endurance, power, balance, agility, coordination, and accuracy have their roots in biomechanics. Principles of leverage, force production, and stability and the laws of motion explain adaptations, particularly those that pertain to degree of difficulty.

Leverage

The shorter the lever, the easier it is to move and control. Levers are rigid bars used to impart force or speed. In biomechanics, levers are implements for striking or batting, body parts, or the entire body. Difficulty in using a lever is reduced by shortening it. Thus, we shorten the length of rackets and bats or teach students to choke up on the grip.

Applied to body position in exercise, the shorter the lever being moved, the easier the movement. In sit-ups, for example, the body length is shortened by

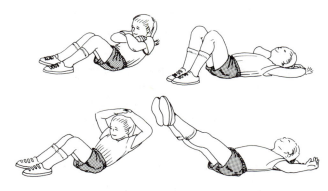

Figure 7.12 Two ways of shortening body length in accordance with the principle of leverage in order to make abdominal strength exercises easier. Top row shows exercises appropriate for weak students; bottom row shows exercises for strong students.

placing arms on thighs or chest, making the exercise easier than the traditional placement of arms behind or over the head (Figure 7.12). Likewise, in push-ups the shortened body position afforded by bending the knees makes bent knee push-ups easier than regulation push-ups. In rotation movements like forward rolls, the tuck position is the shortest lever the body can become and, thus, the easiest for control.

Principles of Force Production

Magnitude of force can be changed by altering (a) leverage, (b) mass of object, (c) weight of object, (d) surface on which object is moving, (e) direction in which object is moving—with or against gravity, and (f) resistance of air or water. In adapted physical education, the concern is often slowing an object so that students will have more success in fielding, catching, trapping, or striking the object. *Mass* of object refers to its total body surface. In general, the larger the ball or projectile, the slower it moves. This is because there is more surface to be affected by gravity (friction) or air resistance. The heavier an object, the slower it moves, but the more strength is needed to control it. Relationships between force, speed, and distance are discussed more fully under the upcoming "Laws of Motion" section.

Clumsy students often have difficulty in getting objects to move in the intended direction. This problem relates either to angle of release or point of application of force. Both are matters of timing or rhythm. It is helpful sometimes to paint a mark on the center of gravity (CG) of an object to help students understand where the implement should hit the ball. Force applied in line with an object's CG results in straight movement unless the object is acted upon by another force, such as the wind. Force applied not in line with an object's CG results in crooked or rotatory movement.

Principles of Stability

These principles are important in helping to maintain balance against the force of gravity. They also can be used to alter the nature of objects to be knocked down or moved in bowling and target games.

1. The lower the center of gravity, the more stable the position. Bending the knees lowers the CG. To make bowling-type games easier, devise objects to be knocked over that are top heavy (i.e., CG is high).

2. The larger the base of support, the more stable the position. Increasing the distance between the feet widens the base. Walking on soles of feet uses a larger base of support than walking on tiptoes or heels. To make bowling-type games easier, devise objects to be knocked over that have a narrow base.

3. The more nearly centered the line of gravity is to the base of support, the more stable the position. Good body alignment thus facilitates balance. Carrying objects anywhere except on the head affects the line of gravity and tends to throw the body off balance. When holding or carrying heavy objects like bowling balls, keep them as close as possible to the body's CG.

4. The larger the mass of a body, the greater is its stability. To make hockey- and shuffleboard-type games easier, reduce the mass of the object to be hit. If tipping over is a problem while sitting, increase the mass of the chair, scooter board, or tricycle by adding weight to it and making it larger.

5. To maintain body balance on a surface that is accelerating or decelerating, widen the stance in the direction the vehicle is moving. Lean opposite the direction of movement. Keep the body weight centered above the base of support. Severely handicapped persons may need to be strapped in a wheelchair to keep weight centered properly.

Laws of Motion

Sir Isaac Newton's three laws of motion explain all adaptations that relate to starting and stopping, accelerating and decelerating, and reacting of surfaces.

Law of Inertia

A body will not move until a force is applied to it, a force sufficient to overcome ground, water, or air resistance. Likewise, a body will move forever if not acted upon by an external force (presence of a barrier that stops it or friction of surface, water, or air).

This law refers to starting and stopping the movement of objects, including the human body. How, for instance, can sprint starts (on foot or in a wheelchair) be made most efficient? How does obesity affect starting and stopping? How does absence of a limb affect starting and stopping (see Figure 7.13).

How does muscle strength affect giving impetus to an external object? How do short arms and legs compare with those of average or long dimensions in force production? With students who lack muscle strength (e.g., muscular dystrophy, cerebral palsy), the teacher makes adaptations in relation to several variables: (a) leverage, (b) mass (amount of surface) of object, (c) weight of object, (d) surface on which object is moving, and (e) resistance of air or water that the object is moving through. Concurrently, the teacher motivates students to increase the strength of their muscles as much as possible and introduces them to strength exercises. Weight reduction programs are initiated for fat students because weak muscles are less able to move heavy limbs than muscles of normal strength.

Law of Acceleration

Velocity of a moving body will remain constant unless acted upon by an external force. Change in speed is inversely proportional to the mass of an object and directly proportional to the amount of force or resistance causing the change. For clumsy children in games requiring retrieval, fielding, catching, or dodging of balls, teachers apply this principle to reduce the speed of the object and make it easier to handle.

Law of Reaction

To every action there is an equal and opposite reaction. This law applies primarily to the surface one pushes or throws against in order to start or stop an object, to increase or decrease its speed, or to determine its direction of movement.

To apply force effectively, whether against the floor (as in locomotor movement) or against an external object (as in pushing, lifting, or pulling), it is easier to have a nonslippery, stationary surface. A balance beam is easier to walk across than a trampoline, bed mattress, or waterbed. A floor or a hard dirt surface is easier to walk or run on than sand or grass. This is because to move the body forward, the feet must exert most of their force backward. In swimming, to move forward in the front crawl, the arms apply force backward.

Figure 7.13 When coaching students with missing limbs, it is important to apply biomechanical principles. Both of these athletes were winners in the International Games for the Disabled.

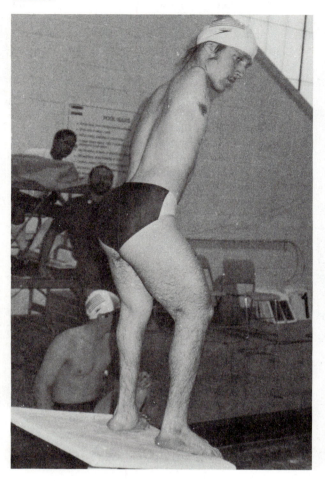

Cooperative Planning

In cooperatively working out adaptations with children, encourage honest appraisal of what they can and cannot do, but *stress abilities in making the adaptations.* Consider adaptations temporary, and plan teaching progressions that facilitate growth from the easy stage toward the more difficult. Utilize motivation and reinforcement techniques, showing that you *care* and you *believe* in the individual's potential to improve. Teach groups that the standard rules of games are not sacred, and encourage creativity in changing games, not only as adaptations for awkward or handicapped students, but because change is fun.

Factors To Be Manipulated

Adapting involves manipulating the factors that affect the teaching/learning process. Some of these factors are

1. *Teaching style,* as discussed earlier in this chapter.
2. *Verbal instructions.* Length of command or verbal challenge, depending upon language development of group; bilingual or unilingual; accompanied by sign language or gesture; loud, soft, or varied; pleasant or stern facial expression and body language; use of certain cue or action words; continuous or intermittent; distance from pupil(s) while talking.

Figure 7.14 Physical guidance through a movement is called the *enactive* or *coactive* method of teaching. Among students with kinesthetic and vestibular problems, it appears to be the most effective method of presenting new skills.

3. *Demonstrations.* By teacher or peers? One person or several simultaneously? How many demonstrations? How often? How long? Best location for demonstrating person or group?

4. *Level of methodology.* Physical guidance through movement (enactive, coactive) (Figure 7.14); demonstration or follow the leader (iconic); verbal instructions (symbolic); or some combination.

5. *Starting and stopping signals.* Discover which works best: voice, whistle, gesture (raising arm), flicker of lights, drum beat, some combination.

6. *Time.* Time of day, season of year.

7. *Duration.* Fixed or variable at each station? For each skill? For taking a test? Number of weeks in instructional period; number of days; number of minutes each day. Amount of activity vs. amount of rest. Massed vs. distributed practices.

8. *Order of learning or trials.* What comes first, middle, and last? What type of rest periods between trials? What type of reinforcements?

9. *Pupil-teacher ratios.* One-to-one or 1:60? Variable or fixed? Remember that teachers can be peers, volunteers, aides.

10. *Size of group.* At each station? In particular games, drills, movement education activities?

11. *Nature of group.* Same or variable for a given period? Ratio of handicapped to nonhandicapped? Homogeneous or heterogeneous in ability level, age, and sex, among others? Predetermined on basis of criteria or random?

12. *Instructional setting.* Indoors or outdoors; temperature; allergen-free; humidity; wind; dust; lighting; acoustics/noise; large vs. small; open vs. partitioned; carpeted vs. wooden floors; concrete vs. abstract (imaginary) boundaries; amount of wall space; availability of mirrors?

13. *Equipment.* A lot or a little; movable or stationary; storage space; safe (good repair) or otherwise; variations in terms of size, shape, texture, and weight?

14. *Architectural barriers and distance of playing area from classrooms.* How difficult is it for an orthopedically handicapped person to travel to and from gymnasium; to get a drink of water; use dressing and bathroom facilities?

15. *Level of difficulty/complexity.* Skill, formation, game rules, game strategies.

16. *Motivation.* Fixed or variable; random or consistent; what kind works best?

Decisions about these factors largely determine the success a student has. Go back over the list and consider how each factor can be manipulated to provide optimal learning conditions for various handicaps, body compositions, age groups, personality types (shy vs. assertive), and ability levels (beginners vs. advanced).

Handicapped Students
in the Mainstream

In contemporary physical education, students with mild or moderate handicapping conditions are mostly in the mainstream. Nevertheless, they, as well as many students not labeled as handicapped, need adapted physical education services. The essence of adapting instruction is individualizing and personalizing. Approaches to achieving this end are dual and team teaching, availability of a resource room, peer and cross-age teaching and modeling, and involvement of parents and volunteers.

Dual and Team Teaching

Mainstream instruction occurs best with dual or team teaching. A growing number of school districts are pairing adapted physical education specialists with regular educators for part or all of the day to assist with individual differences and/or station teaching. This practice is especially desirable in elementary schools or special education units where classroom teachers (rather than physical education specialists) teach motor activities. In such instances, the adapted physical educator may be an *itinerant* teacher moving from regular educator to regular educator or from school to school.

Resource Room

An alternative concept of dual or team teaching is the establishment of a *resource room* or resource learning station where an adapted physical education teacher can always be found (see Figure 7.15). This concept parallels the practice of a nurse's station or an athletic injuries room. Either teachers or students can receive help in the resource room. Some handicapped children may be assigned part-time (2 days a week) to the resource room and part-time (3 days a week) to regular physical education. Other students can float in and out of the resource room for *supplementary* instruction and practice as needed. For instance, the student who finishes academic work before classmates may be rewarded with a *pass* to go "work out" in the adapted physical education resource room. LD, ED, and other students with hyperactive behaviors may be given a pass to the resource room to run laps around the track or shoot baskets until they regain control of themselves and can demonstrate appropriate behavior at their seats.

Figure 7.15 In adapted physical education the gymnasium is often conceptualized as a *resource room* where different skills are taught at *learning stations* in accordance with individual needs.

The resource room should offer facilities for relaxation training and rest as well as activity. It serves as a crisis intervention center for the whole school as well as for the mainstream physical education program.

Peer and Cross-Age Teaching and Modeling

Peer and cross-age teaching is an effective practice in mainstream physical education (see Figure 7.16). Not only does it help the busy teacher in a large class, but it seems to facilitate acceptance of handicapped students. One of the best known models of peer teaching is the PEOPEL (Physical Education Opportunity Program for Exceptional Learners) Project, which originated in Arizona and is now being disseminated through the National Diffusion Network (NDN) and the Office

Figure 7.16 Research shows that children can often teach other children more effectively than adults can. In mainstream physical education well-skilled children are often given special training to qualify as *peer teachers* and then assigned to help handicapped classmates.

of Special Education. In the PEOPEL model, non-handicapped high school students complete a one-semester physical education careers class that provides training for them to work with handicapped peers. They are then assigned to PEOPEL classes, where they serve as peer tutors to provide individualized instruction based upon task-analyzed objectives. Generally, PEOPEL classes are comprised of 12 handicapped students and 12 peer tutors under the supervision of an adult instructor. Statistical research (pretest and posttest design) shows that PEOPEL significantly improves the physical fitness of handicapped students as well as their attitudes toward physical education. It has also facilitated mainstreaming and led to several peer tutors choosing physical education as their university major.

Cross-age tutor programs are effective in many communities in which older students, designated as the honors physical education corps, are released from their schools one or two periods a day to work in elementary schools as physical education teacher aides. Such students generally are required to meet certain criteria and to complete afterschool or weekend training programs. The honors corps often functions as a club (sometimes a subdivision of Future Teachers of America) and meets periodically for in-service training.

A related model is reciprocal teaching (the use of a partner), as explained by Mosston (1981), who notes that even third grade children are capable of observing and correcting one another's movement errors. Research shows that children *learn* through teaching. It is important to allow handicapped as well as nonhandicapped pupils to teach. Success in reciprocal teaching depends largely on preclass organization—the development of task cards or tangible instructions for pairs to follow with regard to learning objectives, principles of good performance, and the like.

Reciprocal and peer teaching generally involve *modeling* (learning through observing and imitating others). Modeling occurs incidentally in mainstream physical education even when reciprocal teaching is not used. A growing body of special education research substantiates that modeling modifies inappropriate behaviors and facilitates interactions among handicapped and nonhandicapped students. It has been shown that normal children are reinforced by being imitated, and they subsequently value the imitator (handicapped) more highly. The reverse may be true also. Modeling appears most effective when there is age and sex similarity.

Parents and Volunteers

Parents and other volunteers, with training similar to that which Project PEOPEL gives high school students, can contribute immeasurably toward individualization and personalization of instruction. They should be assigned to any student who needs help, not just those with handicapping conditions.

The recruitment, training, and supervision of volunteers is an art in itself. Most adapted physical education specialists have considerable experience in this area. Often, a partnership can be worked out with local associations that serve handicapped persons.

Disabled persons, particularly those who are athletes, should be invited to teach instructional units. Such individuals can serve as models for all students, not just handicapped ones.

Learning Activities

1. Conduct an ERIC search at the library to find the most recent publications on mainstreaming and/or use other library techniques to compile a reading list on mainstreaming. Very little has been written on mainstreaming specifically in physical education and recreation, so read about mainstreaming in other fields. Consider how techniques used in other fields can be applied to the physical education setting, and test some of these techniques in a practicum setting to see if they work.

2. Test the ideas (like task cards, learning stations, and peer teaching) in this chapter in your practicum setting and see if you can make them work. Think up some original techniques that might facilitate mainstreaming and test them.

3. Analyze the four teaching styles described in this chapter and practice each style in a role playing setting with your classmates simulating children of different ages and handicapping conditions. If you are successful in the role playing setting, try using the different teaching styles with children. Ascertain that the teaching styles you use are consistent with the ones prescribed in the IEP.

4. Using the format given in this chapter, practice writing behavioral objectives for selected activities for students of various ages and handicapping conditions.

5. Using the format given in this chapter, practice developing IEPs for students of various ages and handicapping conditions.

6. Using the example in this chapter, graph behaviors or scores for yourself or a student over several days.

7. Construct homemade equipment or adapt existing equipment and space to meet the needs of students with special problems of strength, endurance, balance, coordination, and the like.

References

Dunn, J., Morehouse, J., & Fredericks, H. (1985). *Physical education for the severely handicapped: A systematic approach to a data based gymnasium* (2nd ed.). Austin: Pro-Ed Publishers. (Address is 5341 Industrial Oaks Blvd., Austin, TX 78735.)

Mosston, M. (1981). *Teaching physical education* (2nd ed.). Columbus, OH: Charles E. Merrill.

PEOPEL Project Materials, 3839 W. Camelback Road, Phoenix, AZ 85019. Contact Larry Irmer (602–841–3124).

Presbie, R., & Brown, P. (1977). *Physical education: The behavior management approach.* Washington, DC: National Education Association.

Wyrick, W. (1968). The development of a test of motor creativity. *Research Quarterly, 39,* 756–765.

Bibliography

Auxter, D. (1983). Generalization of motor skills from training to natural environments. In R. Eason, T. Smith, & F. Caron, Adapted physical activity (pp. 180–188). Champaign, IL: Human Kinetics Publishers.

Bandura, A. (1971). *Psychological modeling: Conflicting theories.* Chicago: Aldine-Atherton.

Bandura, A. (1977). *Social learning theory.* Englewood Cliffs, NJ: Prentice-Hall.

Barry, N., & Overman, P. (1977). Comparison of the effectiveness of adult and peer models with EMR children. *American Journal of Mental Deficiency, 82,* 33–36.

Bowman, R., & Dunn, J. (1982). Effect of peer pressure on psychomotor measures with EMR children. *Exceptional Children, 48*(5), 449–450.

Burns, R. (1972). *New approaches to instructional objectives.* Dubuque, IA: Wm. C. Brown.

Custer, J., & Osguthorpe, R. (1983). Improving social acceptance by training handicapped students to tutor their nonhandicapped peers. *Exceptional Children, 50*(2), 173–174.

Dunn, J., & French, R. (1982). Operant conditioning: A tool for special educators in the 1980s. *Exceptional Education Quarterly, 3*(1), 42–53.

Dunn, R. (1983). Learning style and its relation to exceptionality at both ends of the spectrum. *Exceptional Children, 49* (6), 496–506.

Folio, M. R., & Norman, A. (1981). Toward more success in mainstreaming: A peer teacher approach to physical education. *Teaching Exceptional Children, 13*, 110–114.

Folsom-Meek, S. (1984). Parents: Forgotten teacher aides in adapted physical education. *Adapted Physical Activity Quarterly, 1*(4), 275–281.

French, R. (1979). The use of homework as a supportive technique in physical education. *The Physical Educator, 36*, 84–89.

Glickman, C., & Wolfgang, C. (1979). Dealing with student misbehavior: An eclectic review. *Journal of Teacher Education, 30*, 7–13.

Horvat, M. (1983). Developing homework assignments and materials for handicapped children in physical education. In M. A. Horvat (Ed.), *Nevada fitness, games, sports, and activities for the handicapped guide* (pp. 208–225). Las Vegas: Nevada State Department of Education.

Jenkins, J., & Jenkins, L. (1981). *Cross-age and peer tutoring: Help for children with learning problems.* Reston, VA: Council for Exceptional Children.

Lavay, B. (1984). Physical activity as a reinforcer in physical education. *Adapted Physical Activity Quarterly, 1*(4), 315–321.

Mager, R. (1962). *Preparing instructional objectives.* Belmont, CA: Fearon Publishers.

Marlowe, M. (1980). Games analysis: Designing games for handicapped children. *Teaching Exceptional Children, 12*, 48–51.

Marlowe, M. (1980). Games analysis intervention: A procedure to increase peer acceptance of socially isolated children. *Research Quarterly for Exercise and Sport, 51*, 422–426.

May, R. (1975). *The courage to create.* New York: W. W. Norton.

Philipp, J. (1969). Comparison of motor creativity with figural and verbal creativity and selected motor skills. *Research Quarterly, 40*(1), 163–173.

Rider, R. A. (1980). Mainstreaming moderately retarded children in the elementary school physical education program. *Teaching Exceptional Children, 12*(4), 150–153.

Salend, S. (1984). Factors contributing to the development of successful mainstreaming programs. *Exceptional Children, 50*(5), 409–416.

Schempp, P., Cheffers, J., & Zaichkowsky, L. (1983). Influence of decision-making on attitudes, creativity, motor skills, and self-concept in elementary children. *Research Quarterly for Exercise and Sport, 54*(2), 183–189.

Stallard, C. (1982). Computers and education for exceptional children: Emerging applications. *Exceptional children, 49*(2), 102–104.

Stein, J. (1979). The mission and the mandate: Physical education, the not so sleeping giant. *Education Unlimited, 1*(2), 10–11.

Strain, P. (1981). *The utilization of classroom peers as behavior change agents.* New York: Plenum.

Torrance, E. P. (1974). *Torrance tests of creative thinking.* Bensenville, IL: Scholastic Testing Service, Inc.

Torrance, E. P. (1977). *Creativity in the classroom* (2nd ed.). Washington, DC: National Education Association.

Torrance, E. P. (1981). *Thinking creatively in action and movement.* Bensenville, IL: Scholastic Testing Service, Inc.

Torrance, E. P., Gowan, J. C., & Khatena, J. (1981). *Creativity: Its educational implications* (2nd ed.). Dubuque, IA: Kendall/Hunt.

Webb, G. (1983). Left/right brains, teammates in learning. *Exceptional Children, 49*(6), 508–515.

Weiss, M. (1983). Modeling and motor performance: A developmental perspective. *Research Quarterly for Exercise and Sport, 54*(2), 190–197.

8 Sports Classifications, Wheelchairs, and Assistive Devices

Figure 8.1 Widespread individual differences exist within cerebral palsy. *Top:* Class 7 and 8 CP athletes play soccer at International Games for the Disabled. *Bottom left,* Class 1 athlete, Mo Gayner, plays defense during IGD wheelchair soccer finals. *Bottom right,* Class 1 athlete Claude Prophete, cheering after the United States wins gold in wheelchair soccer.

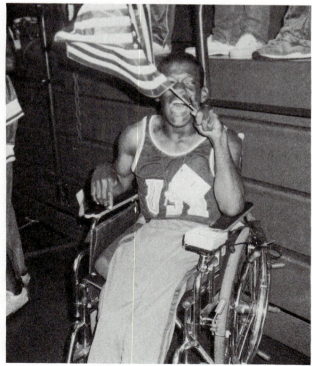

Chapter Objectives

After you have studied this chapter, you should be able to

1. Discuss the sports movement for disabled athletes in relation to the Amateur Sports Act of 1978, the United States Olympic Committee, the Committee on Sports for the Disabled, and planning for the future.

2. Explain the concept of sports classifications and identify and discuss issues in relation to classifications.

3. Identify two principles underlying sports classification theory and discuss their implementation in public schools, including problems to be solved.

4. Explain how sports classification can be used as an assessment approach in public school placement and programming.

5. Identify and discuss parts of a wheelchair.

6. Differentiate between types of wheelchairs and discuss use of each.

7. Operate a wheelchair and assist others in wheelchairs, demonstrating the following: (a) use of brakes, (b) removing armrests and foot plates, (c) maneuvering curbs and stairs, and (d) opening and folding chair.

8. Discuss wheelchair techniques in various sports and adaptations required for different disabilities.

9. Differentiate between orthoses, prostheses, and assistive devices and explain why physical educators need to understand each.

10. Identify different kinds of gaits used with and without crutches or canes when viewed at a sports event or on film and videotape; recognize the stronger leg in each gait, and explain the mechanics of the gait.

11. Explain the normal walking gait of persons at different ages and state points to look for and evaluate.

12. Discuss how gaits associated with various handicapping conditions differ from normal walking gaits and suggest reasons for such deviations; state adaptations in sports and games in relation to the different gaits.

Many opportunities are available in today's society to observe and/or assist with sports for disabled persons. Through such involvement teachers become more aware of individual differences (see Figure 8.1). This chapter presents background information requisite to being a good spectator at events conducted by the various sports organizations for disabled athletes. It also provides introductory content on wheelchairs and assistive devices that will help university students in their volunteer roles at such sports events. More detailed information about each sports organization and the specific events it offers is included in the categorical chapters comprising Part 3 of this book.

Impact of the Sports Movement for the Disabled

The sports movement for disabled persons was described in Chapter 2 as one of the major shapers of contemporary adapted physical education. Seven national organizations sponsor two or more sports of Olympic caliber for disabled citizens and, in accordance with the Amateur Sports Act of 1978, appoint two members each to represent athletes with disabilities on the United States Olympic Committee (USOC), which has its headquarters in Colorado Springs. The USOC structure to which these members belong is the Committee on Sports for the Disabled (COSD). One of the two members from each of the seven organizations, by law, must have a disability; this ensures that disabled persons themselves have a major voice in determining the future of their sports. The COSD meets semiannually. Its goals are (a) enlist increasing support from and involvement by the National Governing Bodies of able-bodied sports, (b) promote more aggressively the concept of sports for handicapped persons, (c) exert more influence internationally on sports and the handicapped, (d) foster more and better research on sports for handicapped individuals, (e) enhance the status of sports for handicapped athletes within the USOC, and (g) obtain a fair share of USOC funds.

Since its inception in 1981, the COSD in partnership with the separate sports organizations has made great strides. The 1984 Olympic Games in Los Angeles featured a wheelchair demonstration (800-m race for women and 1500-m race for men); this was the first time for athletes with disabilities to achieve recognition in the summer Olympic Games. Also for the first time, an athlete in a wheelchair, Neroll Fairhall from New Zealand, met the eligibility requirements to compete in the Olympics. Her sport is archery and her success heralded a new era for persons with disabilities.

Awareness of the sports abilities of disabled persons was also increased in 1984 by the International Games for the Disabled (IGD), in New York City, and the Seventh World Wheelchair Games, in England. These events are held each quadrennium during the same year and, when possible, in the same country as the Olympic Games. Whether these two events should be conducted at the same site or separately is a major issue. IGD serves athletes who are blind or have cerebral palsy, amputations, or les autres conditions. The World Wheelchair Games primarily serve athletes with spinal cord injuries. The World Wheelchair Games were known in the 1960s and the 1970s as the Paraolympics. Today, the International Olympic Committee permits no group to use the word *Olympics* except the mentally retarded population.

Athletes who are mentally retarded or deaf follow a different quadrennium from that used by other athletes. Their events also have contributed to the growing enthusiasm for teaching sports to all children at the earliest age possible. Special Olympics, Incorporated, has held an international meet every 4 years since 1968; this meet is always the year before the Olympics. The international competition for deaf athletes, also conducted every 4 years, is the year after the Olympics. In 1985, the international games for deaf were held for the first time in the United States. Special competencies, other than sign language, are not needed to assist with Special Olympics and athletics for deaf persons. Neither sports organization uses a classification system different from that of regular athletics. Anyone knowledgeable about sports meets who has empathy for disabled persons can thus assist with no special training.

Sports Classifications

This chapter focuses, therefore, on sports organizations that use classification systems to ensure equitable competition. For persons who are blind, cerebral palsied, amputees, spinal cord injured, or les autres, a classification system is important whether they are competing in sports for the disabled or participating in team play in an integrated physical education class.

Assignment of sports classifications to students and use of these classifications in structuring teams is one of the most important principles in adapted physical education. Sports classification theory is emerging as a new area of knowledge. It was ranked by coaches at the 1984 International Games for the Disabled as the sports topic on which research is most needed. Current issues that must be resolved are the following:

1. Should sports classifications be medical or functional?
2. Should sports classifications be specific to each disability (i.e., cerebral palsy, spinal cord injured) or should there be one system broad enough to include all disabilities?
3. Should there be a classification system for each different sport or a general system encompassing several sports?

Principles Underlying Classification Theory

Two basic principles underlie classification theory. First, in individual sports (like track and swimming) only athletes of the same classification compete against each other. Although research is limited, existing evidence shows that sports classification is more important than age or gender when assigning students to heats or events. If a school system does not have two students in a particular classification, then a point system like the handicaps used in golf or bowling should be devised to equalize their competition. Second, in team sports, the teams are scientifically structured with each team having the same number of athletes from each class.

Point System in Team Sports

When disabled students remain in mainstream physical education, fairness in team sports depends on the balance among classifications on each team. A point system can be enacted to ensure equality similar to that used by the National Wheelchair Basketball Association. A numerical value of 1, 2, or 3 points is assigned to each classification. Players on the floor cannot total more than 12 points. This allows each team to use its members as they wish with various combinations of classifications on the floor. This concept can be adapted as appropriate in the school setting.

Medical versus Functional Classification

The medical classification system has been used worldwide for classification of spinal cord injured athletes since the 1940s, when competitive sports were begun in England. Medical classification is anatomically based

Figure 8.2 Medical classification system based on site of spinal cord injury. This system is used by the National Wheelchair Athletic Association.

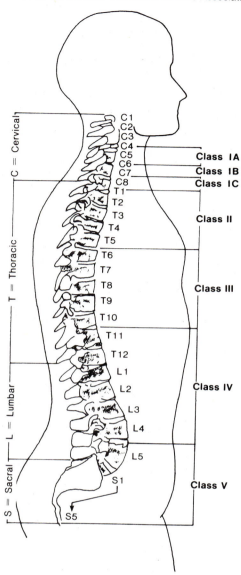

Class IA All cervical lesions with complete or incomplete quadriplegia who have involvement of both hands, weakness of triceps, and with severe weakness of the trunk and lower extremities interfering significantly with trunk balance and the ability to walk.

Class IB All cervical lesions with complete or incomplete quadriplegia who have involvement of upper extremities but less than IA with preservation of normal or good triceps, and with a generalized weakness of the trunk and lower extremities interfering significantly with trunk balance and the ability to walk.

Class IC All cervical lesions with complete or incomplete quadriplegia who have involvement of upper extremities but less than IB with preservation of normal or good triceps, and normal or good finger flexion and extension (grasp and release) but without intrinsic hand function and with a generalized weakness of the trunk and lower extremities interfering with trunk balance and the ability to walk.

Class II Complete or incomplete paraplegia below T1 down to and including T5 or comparable disability with total abdominal paralysis or poor abdominal muscle strength and no useful trunk sitting balance.

Class III Complete or incomplete paraplegia or comparable disability below T5 down to and including T10 with upper abdominal and spinal extensor musculature sufficient to provide some element of trunk sitting balance but not normal.

Class IV Complete or incomplete paraplegia or comparable disability below T10 down to and including L2 without knee extensors or with very weak knee extensors and paralysis of hip abductors.

Class V Complete or incomplete paraplegia or comparable disability below L2 with weak knee extensors.

with IA, IB, IC, II, III, IV, and V classifications assigned according to the spinal cord level of lesion (Figure 8.2). Classification is determined by physicians who observe trunk balance and administer specific muscle strength tests. Medical classification is used by the National Wheelchair Athletic Association (NWAA).

The functional classification system is used by the National Wheelchair Basketball Association (NWBA), the National Association of Sports for Cerebral Palsy (NASCP), the United States Amputee Athletic Association (USAAA), and the United States Association for Blind Athletes (USABA). Each organization has its own system of classification that is based on

function, with classifications assigned on the basis of what individuals can and cannot do in a sports setting. Function does not mean performance. *Function* is capability as judged by certified classifiers who observe an athlete and decide which functional profile best fits their observation. When supplementary information is needed, muscle tests are administered similar to those used in the medical classification system.

Illustrative Functional Classification

The functional classification system can work in public school physical education. It is described here in detail in hopes that innovative teachers and coaches will adapt the system to their school or community size and begin implementing it. The official system used by NASCP is presented as the illustration in Table 8.1 because more school students have cerebral palsy and les autres conditions than any other physical or sensory disability.

Since 1981, the NASCP system has had eight classifications. Classes 1 to 4 are assigned to wheelchair users, and Classes 5 to 8 are assigned to ambulatory athletes. Of the latter, only Class 5 athletes may use assistive devices like canes and crutches. Braces are not considered assistive devices. Table 8.1 presents the functional profile for each classification. If a Class 9 was added for normal students with no coordination or balance problems and a Class 10 was added for gifted athletes, this system could be used in a regular physical education setting that serves both able-bodied and disabled students.

Sports Events for Specific Classifications

Sometimes, physical educators perceive a student as too severely disabled to learn competitive sports. NASCP has demonstrated that virtually all students, assuming that intelligence is intact, can compete if sports are adapted to their abilities. Whereas severely mentally handicapped persons may not understand the purpose and meaning of competition, most physically disabled students are limited only by their teacher's imagination. NASCP, for example, offers competition in motorized chairs in a 60-m dash and the slalom; both tasks require only the ability to move one hand to manipulate the control stick of the chair. Swimming competition for Class 1 and 2 students permits use of buoyancy devices.

Throwing for distance for Classes 1 and 2 utilizes a 5-ounce beanbag called a *soft shot* (Figure 8.3) so as to make the event parallel to the shot put. Calling the projectile a soft shot when working with adolescents and adults is also more humanizing and empathic than referring to it as a beanbag, an implement generally used only by small children. A *soft discus* is another official throwing event. Clubs (Figure 8.3) also are used because they are easier to grasp and throw than balls. For a precision throw, the soft shots are aimed at a ground target so that gravity helps to maximize success. When hand movements are too limited for throwing, feet may be used instead.

Table 8.1
Sport Classifications for Persons with Cerebral Palsy and Les Autres Conditions

Class	Description
1	Uses motorized wheelchair because almost no functional use of upper extremities. Severe involvement in all four limbs, limited trunk control, has only 25% range of motion. Unable to grasp softball.
2	Propels chair with feet and/or very slowly with arms. Severe to moderate involvement in all four limbs. Uneven functional profile necessitating subclassifications as 2 Upper (2U) or 2 Lower (2L), with adjective denoting limbs having greater functional ability. Has approximately 40% range of motion. Severe control problems in accuracy tasks, generally more athetosis than spasticity.
3	Propels chair with short, choppy arm pushes but generates fairly good speed. Moderate involvement in three or four limbs and trunk. Has approximately 60% range of motion. Can take a few steps with assistive devices, but is not functionally ambulatory.
4	Propels chair with forceful, continuous arm pushes, demonstrating excellent functional ability for wheelchair sports. Involvement of lower limbs only. Good strength in trunk and upper extremities. Has approximately 70% range of motion. Minimal control problems.
5	Ambulates without wheelchair but typically uses assistive devices (crutches, canes, walkers). Moderate to severe spasticity of either (a) arm and leg on same side (hemiplegia) or (b) both lower limbs (paraplegia). Has approximately 80% range of motion.
6	Ambulates without assistive devices, but has obvious balance and coordination difficulties. Has more control problems and less range of motion in upper extremities than Classes 4 and 5. Moderate to severe involvement of three or four limbs, with approximately 70% range of motion in dominant arm.
7	Ambulates well, but with slight limp. Moderate to mild spasticity in (a) arm and leg on same side or (b) all four limbs with 90% of normal range of motion for quadriplegia and 90% to 100% of normal range of motion for dominant arm for hemiplegia.
8	Runs and jumps freely without noticeable limp. Demonstrates good balance and symmetric form in performance, but has obvious (although minimal) coordination problems. Has normal range of motion.

Because many Class 2 athletes have more mobility and control with feet than with hands, distance and thrust kicks have been made official events. A 13-inch rubber playground ball (Figure 8.3) is used for the distance kick, whereas a 6-pound medicine ball is used for the thrust kick.

Figure 8.3 Type of projectile influences success of CP athletes. *Top left*, Class 2 lower athlete with no functional arm movements performing distance kick with 13-inch playground ball. *Right*, Class 2 upper athlete almost making bullseye with 5-ounce soft shot. *Lower left*, Class 3 athlete performing club throw for distance.

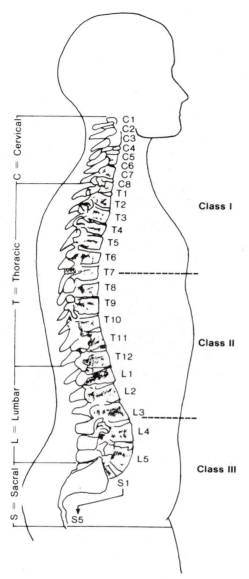

Class I. Complete motor loss at T7 or above or comparable disability that severely limits trunk mobility and balance and arm strength and range of motion.

Class II. Complete motor loss from T8 to L2 or comparable disability (including double leg hip amputee) that limits forward, backward, and sideward trunk mobility and balance.

Class III. Complete motor loss from L3 downward or comparable disability that limits sideward trunk mobility and balance and/or ambulatory speed, balance, and power compared to nondisabled peers. This classification includes persons who ambulate with limp or impaired gait.

New Assessment Approach for Students in Wheelchairs

In 1984, the National Wheelchair Basketball Association adopted a new classification system (Figure 8.4) based upon function in three tests. This same system, created by Horst Strohkendl of West Germany, was used in international competition at the Seventh World Wheelchair Games in 1984 and is now gaining worldwide acceptance.

The system is appropriate for use with any disability. The three tests are simple to understand and easy to administer so that they can be implemented in any school physical education program. For this reason, the three tests are presented on pages 165–67 as a method of classifying all students who wish to engage in wheelchair sports. The concept of able-bodied students learning to use wheelchairs and engaging in competition is explored in Chapter 21. This classification system is broad enough to encompass able-bodied students. Whereas regulation wheelchair basketball competition does not permit involvement of able-bodied athletes, it does allow ambulatory persons with only slight limps to be team members. Most Class III wheelchair basketball players are functional walkers (i.e., they use the chair only for sports).

Figure 8.5 Class I athlete loses balance or leans back on chair to prevent falling. Photo shows person with paraplegia caused by T5 lesion.

Figure 8.6 Class II athlete shows no loss of balance, demonstrates full range of arm motion, and demonstrates good arm and shoulder strength. Photo shows person with paraplegia caused by T11 lesion.

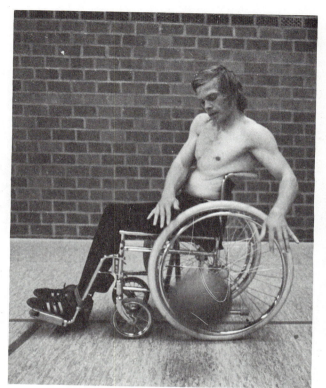

Fail

Pass

Test 1: Assessment of Sitting Stability and Rotation of the Trunk

Purpose
To differentiate between Class I and II athletes.

Instructions
Sit as straight as possible in your chair. Bounce and catch the ball with both hands at the same time while changing the side of the chair after each try. Rotate your trunk as far as possible to each side without losing your balance or leaning back in the chair.

Test Performance
See Figures 8.5 and 8.6.

Performance Expectations

Level of Lesion or Comparable Disability	Performance	Resulting Basketball Classification
T-7 and above, CP classes 1–3	Fail	I
T-8 to L-2, CP classes 4–6, and bilateral hip amputees	Pass	II
L-3 and below, CP classes 7–8, and lower extremity amputees	Pass	III

Functional Profile of Class I
In wheelchair with high back. Poor to nonexistent trunk control and sitting balance. Limited range of motion in arm movements, cannot raise one or both arms above head. Functional limitations in pushing and steering chair; weak, short, choppy arm pushes.

Figure 8.7 Class II athlete cannot perform sit-up by trunk strength alone; must use arm and shoulder thrust. Photo shows person with paraplegia caused by L1 lesion.

Figure 8.8 Class III athlete does sit-up with trunk muscles alone; does not need arm and shoulder muscles. Photo shows person with paraplegia caused by L4 lesion.

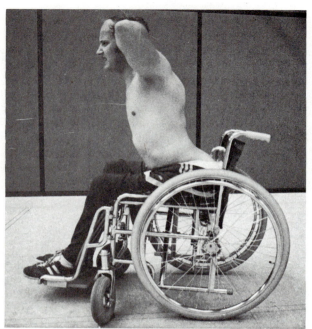

Fail

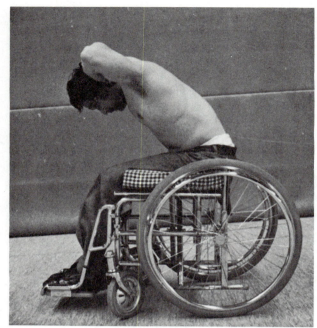

Pass

Test 2: Assessment of Forward/Backward Bending of Trunk

Purpose
To differentiate between Class II and III athletes.

Instructions
Assume a forward bending position (trunk touching thighs) with hands behind neck. Now, raise your trunk to a normal sitting position without removing your hands from behind the neck.

Test Performance
See Figures 8.7 and 8.8.

Performance Expectations

Level of Lesion or Comparable Disability	Performance	Resulting Basketball Classification
T-7 and above, CP classes 1–3	Fail	I
T-8 to L-2, CP classes 4–6, and bilateral hip amputees	Fail	II
L-3 and below, CP athletes 7–8, and lower extremity amputees	Pass	III

Functional Profile of Class II
In wheelchair with regular back height. Fair to good trunk control and sitting balance, but lacks ability to perform forward/backward trunk bending without support from one arm; may show some balance problems when lifting both arms over head with ball or shooting for goal. Normal hand, arm, and shoulder range of motion and strength.

Figure 8.9 Weak Class III athlete in part 1 of test loses balance and leans the trunk and/or arms against wheel or lap for stability. In part 2 of test, can do forward, but not sideward, raising of ball. Photos show person with paraplegia caused by L4 lesion.

Test 3: Assessment of Sideward Bending of Trunk (i.e., Lateral Flexion)

Purpose

To differentiate between functional abilities within Class III.

Instructions

A ball is lying to the side of your wheelchair. Pick up the ball with both hands simultaneously using a sideward bend. Bring the ball over your head and place it on the floor to the other side of your wheelchair. Do this without bending your body forward. Repeat the test to the opposite side.

Test Performance

See Figures 8.9 and 8.10.

Performance Expectations

Level of Lesion or Comparable Disability	Performance	Resulting Basketball Classification
T-7 and above, CP classes 1–3	Fail	I
T-8 to L-2, CP classes 4–6, and bilateral hip amputees	Fail	II
L-3 and below, CP athletes 7–8, and lower extremity amputees	Weak fails, strong passes	III

Functional Profile of Class III

In wheelchair with regular back height. Good to excellent control and balance in all trunk movements, except sideward bending, which varies among athletes. Can pick up ball from any position on floor and dribble with one hand; can steer chair by crossing free arm to grasp opposite wheel.

Figure 8.10 Strong Class III athlete performs side bend and overhead lift of ball with little difficulty. If the hip abductors and knee flexors are not completely paralyzed, some movements of the legs are available to help with balance. Photos show person with paraplegia caused by S1–S2 lesion.

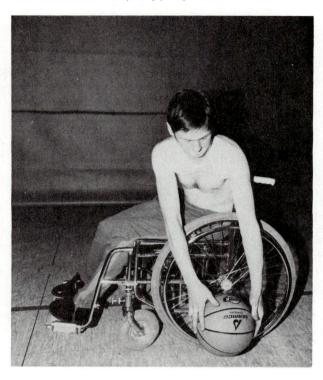 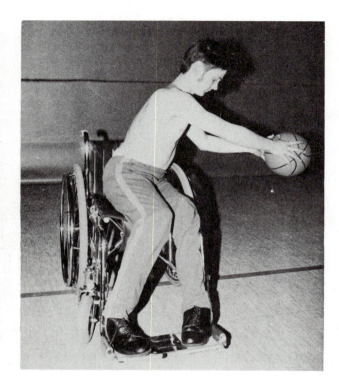

Identification of Parts of Wheelchair

In order to understand similarities and differences among chairs, it is important to be able to identify and discuss the parts of a wheelchair. To master this content and to learn techniques of wheelchair handling and coaching, the reader must have access to wheelchairs.

Definitions of Selected Wheelchair Parts

Drive wheel: Large wheels that serve as the source of thrust. Diameters, numbers of spokes, and other characteristics vary according to function: sports, track, and marathon. Children's and adults' wheels are 20 and 24 inches, respectively, in regular and sports models and larger (usually 27 inches) in racing chairs. In NWBA/NWAA sports, 24 inches is the maximum diameter allowed; international rules permit 26 inches.

Tires: Solid rubber or pneumatic (air) covering of the drive wheel. The regular wheelchair generally comes with rubber tires. Sports chairs and models for outdoor use (track and marathon) have air-filled tires that absorb shock better than solid rubber and provide a more comfortable ride. Like bicycle and auto tires, however, they may have flats. Continuous arm action is needed with air tires because they do not glide as easily as rubber ones; hence, air tires require optimal upper extremity strength. Two types of air tires are available: *clincher,* which has a separate tire and inner tube, and *tubular,* which has the tire sewn around the inner tube.

Handrim: Inner rim on drive wheels that hands grasp in order to propel chair. These range from 12 to 22 inches in regular and sports chairs and are smaller (usually 12 inches) in racing chairs. Handrims may be attached directly to the rim of the wheel or to the spokes or mounted via clips. The diameter of the rim, like a gear, determines the ease of pushing. Large diameters (like lower gears) make starting and acceleration easy. Smaller handrims (like higher gears) are harder to push, but, once inertia is overcome, are preferable for athletes with adequate strength.

Figure 8.11 Parts of wheelchair that physical educators should learn. *Top,* wheel and hub of track chair. *Bottom,* parts of medical model chair.

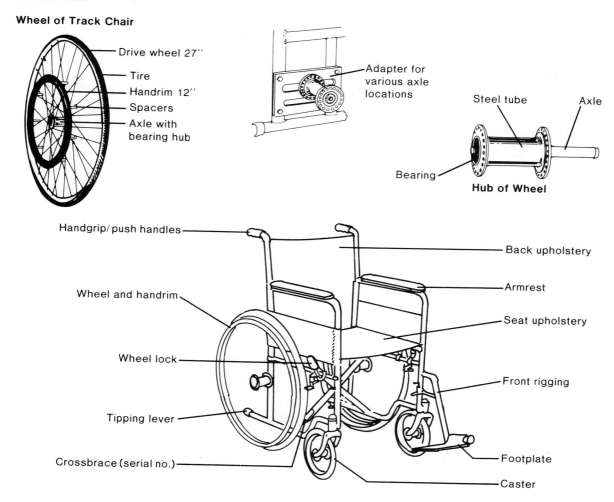

Wheel of Track Chair

- Drive wheel 27''
- Tire
- Handrim 12''
- Spacers
- Axle with bearing hub

- Adapter for various axle locations

- Steel tube
- Axle
- Bearing

Hub of Wheel

- Handgrip/push handles
- Wheel and handrim
- Wheel lock
- Tipping lever
- Crossbrace (serial no.)
- Back upholstery
- Armrest
- Seat upholstery
- Front rigging
- Footplate
- Caster

Projections of handrims: Small handles that make use of handrims easier. Projections are ordered special and used only by persons with minimal arm and hand function (i.e., Class 1 and 2 CP athletes). Also called *spacers.*

Axle: Shaft on which a wheel revolves. Usually refers to drive rather than caster wheel.

Hub: Steel tube that comprises center portion of rear wheel with flanges (heavy rims) at either end. Each rim contains holes for spokes and a central opening for bearings.

Bearing: Outermost part of axle. Bearings affect the rolling resistance of a wheel (i.e., tightening axle toward frame makes wheel revolution more difficult; loosening too much causes wheels to wobble). Bearings may be sealed or not sealed. Teacher should know how to adjust and/or lubricate bearings.

Wheelbase: Distance in inches between front and rear axles. Sports chairs have longer wheelbases than regular chairs (i.e., their caster wheels are further forward).

Front (caster) wheel: Small wheel that performs the function of steering. These are generally 5 inches in diameter. Sports and racing chairs have adjustable caster wheels; the more forward these are positioned, the better their maneuverability. Caster flutter (instability) is lessened by precision sealed bearings (preloaded).

Frame or crossbrace: Supporting metal structure, typically made of stainless steel, steel alloys, aluminum, and titanium. With wear, cracks at or near joints may appear and require repair.

Philosophy of Wheelchair Sports

Adapted physical educators should understand wheelchair selection and develop competency in teaching and coaching wheelchair sports as well as helping students refine skills in activities of daily living (ADL). Ability to prepare disabled persons for wheelchair competition and commitment to the dream of sports for all are characteristics that often distinguish the physical educator from professionals who adhere to the medical model.

The different sports organizations for disabled athletes have widely varying philosophies concerning eligibility for wheelchair competition. The oldest of the organizations, National Wheelchair Basketball Association (NWBA) and National Wheelchair Athletic Association (NWAA), believe that all sports (except swimming) for physically disabled persons should be played in a wheelchair, regardless of the severity of the disability. The chair and the athlete are considered one. Sir Ludwig Guttmann, founder of wheelchair sports, emphasized, "It is no exaggeration to say that the paraplegic and his chair have become one, in the same way as a first class horseman and his mount."

In contrast, the National Association of Sports for Cerebral Palsy (NASCP) and the United States Amputee Athletic Association (USAAA) believe that athletes capable of ambulatory sports, even though slowed by an impaired gait or requiring a prosthesis or assistive device, should be allowed to compete standing up. Many amputees are competent in both wheelchair and ambulatory sports. Cerebral palsied athletes in Classes 1 to 4 compete only in wheelchairs, whereas those in Classes 5 to 8 compete only in ambulatory sports. The one exception to this generalization is for soccer. Class 5 athletes play wheelchair soccer and Class 6 athletes may choose between wheelchair or ambulatory soccer.

In keeping with the goal of lifetime sports participation, physical educators should prepare disabled children and youth for participation in the organization most appropriate to them. NWBA/NWAA serves only persons with permanent physical disability of the lower extremities (i.e., spinal cord injured, spina bifida, polio, or amputation). NASCP serves persons with cerebral palsy, muscular dystrophy, osteogenesis imperfecta, Friedreich's ataxia, dwarfism, and other conditions that affect the total body. Approximately half of these persons use wheelchairs.

Successful wheelchair sports competition depends largely upon the type of chair used. Four types of chairs are described in this chapter: (a) medical model or regular chair, (b) sports chair used for basketball, tennis, soccer, and similar sports, (c) track or racing chair, and (d) motorized chair.

Possible Solutions to Problems

The main problem in implementing a classification system in a school system is too many classifications and too few disabled students. One solution to this problem is to pool all physically disabled students in all schools for instructional units that focus on sports competition. Another solution is to invite adults with handicapping conditions to participate in such instructional units. Research shows, in this regard, that it is more fair for a Class 3 adolescent to compete against a Class 3 adult than for a Class 3 student to compete against students with no disability or with a different classification. Still another solution is to modify the classification system by reducing the number of classifications.

Many physical education activities, of course, do not require classifications to ensure equal opportunity for success. Another solution is to not teach competitive sports or to assign physically disabled students to another class while team sports are being covered. If this option is chosen, then provision should be made for disabled students to learn, in a separate physical education setting, comparable content and skills.

Types of Wheelchairs

Physical educators should be able to identify different types of wheelchairs, state the purpose of each, and discuss similarities and differences. It is important to know also which characteristics of chairs are governed by sports organizations. NWAA/NWBA rules, for instance, dictate size of drive wheels, number of handrims, seat height, and method of securing legs during competition.

Medical Model or Regular Chair

This chair, depicted in Figure 8.12, is the one most commonly prescribed by physicians. Its forebear originated in 1700. King Philip V of Spain is believed to be the first wheelchair user. His chair had wooden wheels, with wooden spokes, adjustable leg rests, and

Figure 8.12 *Left,* medical model or regular chair used by most young children. *Right,* sports chair used in wheelchair basketball.

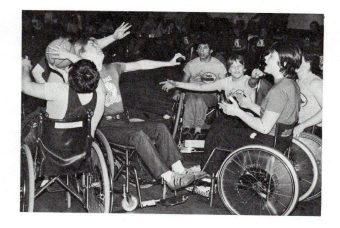

a reclining back. H. A. Everest, one of the founders of Everest & Jennings Wheelchair Manufacturers, is accredited with the design of the contemporary compact foldable chair in the early 1930s, several years after a mining accident made him a paraplegic.

Sports Chair

Originally, sports chair referred to those manufactured specifically for basketball. Now with the proliferation of wheelchair sports (tennis, racketball, soccer, football, softball), the term refers to any chair built to allow optimal maneuverability, quick turning, and rapid acceleration. Over 15 sports wheelchair manufacturers offer distinctly different models. These are reviewed annually in *Sports 'N Spokes,* beginning in 1983.

Sports chairs are built for performance rather than comfort. They often have no handles on the seat back for pushing, no arm rests, and no brakes. Most have rigid frames and do not fold. They can, however, be disassembled easily and quickly for travel. Other differences between the sports and regular models include a lowered seat back, a cushion built into the seat, and a solid front bar for foot placement rather than the traditional folding foot platforms. Axle plates on the drive wheels are adjustable to permit different seat positions. By changing the axle location, the wheelchair's center of gravity is altered and maneuverability is improved.

Sports chairs have some safety factors not found on other types of wheelchairs. *Anti-tip casters* on the kick bar in the rear of the chair reduces the possibility of tipping over. The *roll-bar* (attached underneath the foot platforms) prevents the chair from folding in case of a spill.

Many athletes use the same chair for basketball and track. By purchasing several handrims of different sizes and taking full advantage of adjustable axle and caster plates, the chair can be modified for a specific sports event. Athletes whose major interest is track or marathoning typically use specially constructed chairs.

Track and Racing Chairs

These chairs differ from sports models primarily in size of drive wheels (larger) and handrims (smaller) and in lowered seat position. Since 1975, when Bob Hall gained recognition as the first wheelchair racer to enter the Boston Marathon, chairs have changed drastically to permit greater efficiency in 26.2 mile and even longer runs. Improved pneumatic tires, often with over 100 pounds of air pressure, are used with as little surface on the ground as possible.

Camber, while built into some sports chairs, is a definite necessity in track. *Camber* is a characteristic of the drive wheel, describing a condition in which the bottoms of the wheels are farther apart than the tops.

Figure 8.13 Characteristics of track chair. *Left,* youth track chair with front of seat higher than back. *Right,* drawings showing difference in wheelbase and camber in regular and track chairs.

Regular chair
• Narrow wheelbase
• No camber
• Vertical force applied to handrims

Track chair
• Wide wheelbase
• Much camber
• Diagonal force applied to handrims

The top part of the wheel is closer to the upper body than in the regular chair and is directed toward the arm pit (Figure 8.13). This makes pushing more efficient, lessens the chance that the athlete's arm will bump against the wheel, and permits a natural, relaxed position for the elbows.

Overcoming air resistance in racing is done partly by forward bending of the trunk and partly by adjusting the seat. The front of the seat is kept higher than the rear and the seat back is reclined slightly backward (Figure 8.13). The goal is to minimize the angle of hip flexion and maximize the angle of knee flexion. For athletes with paralyzed or weak trunk and lower back muscles, however, the seat must be steeper to assist them in maintaining a forward trunk bend with thighs to chest.

Motorized Chairs

Motorized chairs (sometimes incorrectly called electric chairs) give severely disabled persons considerable independence. They move at high and low speeds and are generally capable of about 5 miles an hour. Most

can climb inclines of at least 10 degrees. Families/ agencies that can afford to do so provide children who have little arm and shoulder strength/control with motorized chairs as early as age 9 or 10.

In keeping with its motto (Sports by ability . . . not disability), NASCP has designed competitive events (slalom and 60-m dash) in which Class 1 athletes utilize their ability to maneuver a motorized chair. NASCP wheelchair soccer also permits participation in a motorized chair. NWAA/NWBA rules, in contrast, do not allow motorized chairs.

The battery-powered chair is the most commonly used, with two 12-volt batteries that are mounted on a carrier at the back of the chair below seat level. These batteries must be recharged each night in order to supply power for approximately 8 hours of continuous use. Regular automobile batteries are used on most chairs.

Motorized chairs, which must have sturdy frames to support the weight of batteries and other special equipment, are very heavy. Without the batteries, a chair typically weighs 75 to 80 pounds. Folding the chair is impossible without removal of batteries. These problems in portability generally lead users of motorized chairs to purchase a second vehicle (manual) for travel.

Basic Wheelchair Management Skills

Physical educators should experience travel in a wheelchair, both self-propelled and pushed by a friend. Try wheeling about campus, checking buildings, sidewalks, and lawns for architectural barriers. Also, experiment with various track and field activities and make up some games, dances, and rhythmic exercises that can be done from a chair. In learning to maneuver wheelchairs, it is a good idea to use gloves, since hands tend to blister from the vigorous push action. Gloves are allowed in all official NASCP events except weight lifting and field events. Try to achieve the following objectives:

1. Propel wheelchair forward and backward and stop on command.
2. Cover 200 feet in 20 seconds.
3. Perform a complete turn (360 degrees) to the right in 1 minute (repeat to the left).
4. Perform a complete turn to the right without touching the lines of a circle that has a diameter of 6 feet (repeat to the left).

For additional objectives, consult the qualifying times and distances for NASCP and NWAA wheelchair events. Can you perform as well as a Class IA, IB, or IC spinal cord injured person (NWAA) or a Class 2, 3, or 4 cerebral palsied person (NASCP)? What problems do you experience? What adaptations need to be made?

In reality, few wheelchair athletes use the medical model (regular) chair. These chairs are clumsy and slow in comparison with chairs manufactured specifically for sports. Experience with regular chairs, however, will make the physical educator a stronger advocate for the purchase of appropriate wheelchairs for school physical education and athletics. Because practice lags behind knowledge, it may be difficult in some communities to find anything but the regular chair for use in developing beginning teaching competencies.

Handling Brakes

Brakes are used to lock the drive wheels, thereby immobilizing the chair and providing needed stability for making transfers and engaging in field events like throwing and games like shuffleboard. Brakes may be placed partially on to reduce acceleration in going down a steep ramp. Figure 8.14 depicts the two most commonly used types of locks: lever and toggle. Many sports and racing chairs do not have brakes.

Figure 8.14 Locking and unlocking brakes are the first skills to learn in assisting persons who have little arm and hand function. *Top,* toggle type brake. *Bottom,* lever type brake.

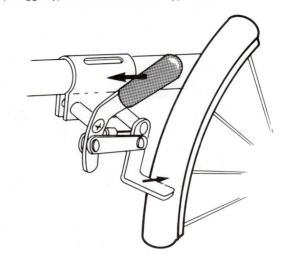

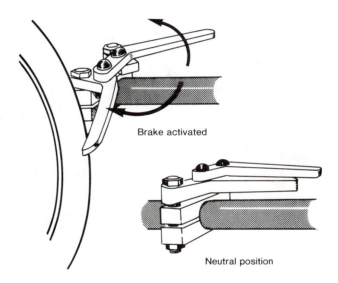

Brake activated

Neutral position

Removing Armrests and Foot Plates

Armrests and foot plates are usually removed before athletes engage in track, field, and other sports events and before transfers to and from the wheelchair are attempted. Armrests are removed by lifting the tubular frames of the arm out of the tubing on the wheelchair (see Figure 8.15). Removable foot plates are swinging

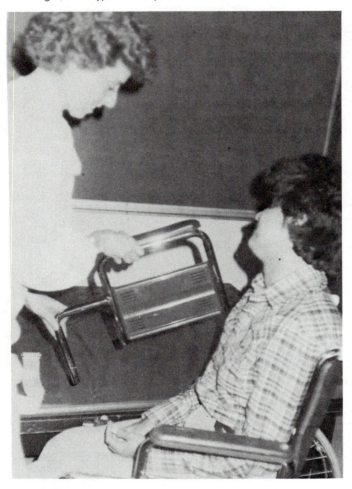

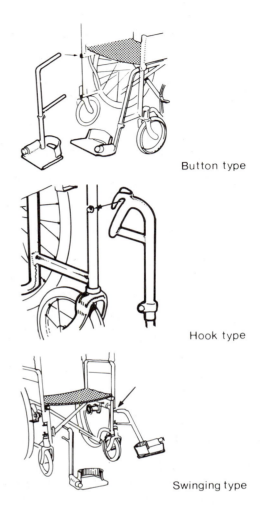

Button type

Hook type

Swinging type

or nonswinging. In the swinging type, the front rigging is released and swung to the side, after which it is removed. In nonswinging foot plates, a button-type or hook-in-place lock is released to permit removal.

Maneuvering Curbs and Stairs

In maneuvering curbs and stairs, the most important thing to remember is the direction the athlete should be facing. The rest (i.e., use of the tipping levers) is common sense. Guidelines for the teacher or assistant to follow are

Descending curb: Turn self and wheelchair backward
Descending steep ramp: Turn self and wheelchair
    backward

Descending stairs: Go down forward with chair tilted
    backward and athlete facing foot of stairs
Ascending curb: Go forward
Ascending stairs: Back up the stairs

In managing stairs, it is best to use two adults, one in back and one in front. The stronger adult should be in back since he or she has the heavier load. The person in back tilts the chair backward and lifts with the handgrips. The person in front lifts the frame (never the footplates, which might accidentally come off).

Folding and Opening the Chair

To open a wheelchair, *push down* on the two seat rails (outermost surfaces of seat). Do not try to open the chair by pulling it apart because this damages the telescoping parts of removable arm rests.

To close the chair, grasp the seat upholstery at its front and back and pull upward. If you intend to lift the folded chair into a vehicle, remove all detachable parts before closing it. The best position to stand while opening or closing a chair is to the side (e.g., facing the wheel).

Wheelchair Sports Techniques

For optimal performance, different types of chairs are needed for different sports. Additionally, chairs must be adapted to accommodate different classes of athletes. Understanding these adaptations makes wheelchair sports a more interesting spectator activity. The best way to learn about adaptations is to visit with coaches and athletes. Very little information has been published (Jones, 1984; McCann, 1981; Spooren, 1981).

Adaptations to Chairs

The more severely handicapped persons are, the higher must be their seat backs. Also, the more severely handicapped, the straighter an athlete must sit to maintain balance. This explains why, in races, some athletes sit up straight and others lean way forward. Of course, if the disability permits, it is more mechanically efficient to lean the trunk forward, decreasing distance between chest and thighs.

Spinal cord injured athletes with high lesions have poor trunk balance. Adaptations to the chair that help to compensate for poor balance include increasing height of seat back, keeping the sidearms on the chair, increasing the sag in the seat to provide better support for the pelvis, and increasing the sag in the seat back to improve lateral stability. Chairs have been so improved that NWAA Class IA athletes (C6 lesion) are now racing marathons (26.2 miles).

Cerebral palsied athletes often exhibit extensor thrust. This is caused by retention of primitive reflexes that cause their legs to straighten out and come off the footrests. Concurrently, their hips tend to slide off the seats and their shoulders thrust backward. To break up this abnormal extensor pattern, straps must be used. Typically, the athlete must have upper and lower legs strapped so that the knees remain bent and the feet remain in contact with the footrests. A seat belt may be used also. It should come from under the seat to hold the thighs down, not from the waist or chest.

Changing the angle of inclination of the seat also helps maintain the hips and trunk in correct position (i.e., flexion). Some sport chairs come with a choice of various rear axle locations that allow for different inclinations of the seat. If the axles do not permit seat adjustments, a wedge-shaped seat cushion can be used (thicker part at front of chair) to keep the knees higher than the hips.

Figure 8.16 Track chair especially designed for Terri Feinstein, international Class 2 athlete, who is a foot pusher.

Most cerebral palsied Class 2 athletes propel their chairs with feet. Foot pushers move backward, whereas foot pullers move forward. Naturally, wheelchairs need to be adapted to these alternative modes of propulsion. Figure 8.16 shows a racing chair constructed especially for a foot pusher. The caster wheels have been reversed so that they lead the chair. The seat is shifted in the direction the athlete looks, and a slight reverse wedge changes the seat inclination to make better use of extensor power.

High Knee Position

Most athletes race with the knees as high as possible and the center of gravity as low as possible. This position permits optimal forward lean of the trunk which, in turn, offers (a) lowered wind resistance, (b) better driving position for arms, and (c) increased trunk stability.

Figure 8.17 Wheelchair arm techniques.

Short propulsion thrusts in ADL activities, basketball, tennis, and most sports except racing. In this technique, the athlete pushes forward and downward (i.e., applies force from A to B) while simultaneously inclining the trunk forward. The handrims are released at point B, the trunk returns to its upright position, and the arms are lifted and repositioned for the next downward and forward push.

Forward, downward thrust | Beginning of recovery | End of recovery

Long duration circular propulsion thrust in track and marathon racing. In this technique, which requires small diameter handrims and correct positioning of the wheelchair seat and back, the athlete maintains hands in contact with the handrims through approximately ¾ of a circle, applying force the entire time. The grip on the handrim is never released, only loosened to allow repositioning. Shoulder joint extension is especially important in providing final propulsive thrust; the lower the seat, the more important the ability of the arms to lift backward.

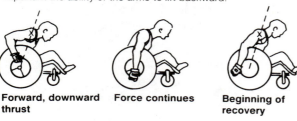

Forward, downward thrust | Force continues | Beginning of recovery

Arm Propulsion

The arm movement is different in track and marathon racing from that in most sports and activities of daily living. Figure 8.17 shows these differences. In athletes with good trunk control, the trunk alternately inclines forward and back during the thrust and recovery phases of the arm thrusts in all sports but track. Class 2 and 3 cerebral palsied athletes (who typically lack trunk control) do not use a forward trunk movement because they must sit straight to maintain balance. Their propulsive thrusts are shorter and choppier than those of Class 4 cerebral palsied athletes, amputees, and spinal cord injured racers.

Track and Road Racing Events

Track distances vary with different disabilities and classifications. For Class 1, 2, and 3 cerebral palsied athletes, the shortest dash is 60 m; for Class 4 athletes the shortest dash is 100 m. The longest CP wheelchair track event is 800 m. For spinal cord injured athletes in NWAA sports, the distances are 60, 100, 200, 400, 800, and 1500 m (the same as for CP sports except for

the 1500 m). Ambulatory CP athletes run 1500 or 3000 m cross country events. Road racing and marathons are extremely popular among wheelchair athletes. In time, specific coaching techniques for each event and sports classification will no doubt be devised.

Slalom

The slalom is a race against time in which athletes follow an obstacle course that has been clearly marked to indicate all maneuvers that are to be made. In both NASCP and NWAA, the slalom is independent of track. Official rule books give specific slalom dimensions. Obstacles are created through the use of ramps and traffic cones. Courses all include the reverse gate maneuver (Figure 8.18).

A *reverse gate* is a 1-meter square with the frontline, endline, and sidelines clearly marked. The task is to enter the 1-meter square facing in one direction, do a 90° turn without touching any line, and leave the square facing in the opposite direction. Touching a line during the maneuver results in a 1-second penalty to total course time. Once outside of the square, the athlete again does a 90° turn so as to progress through the rest of the course in desired direction.

Students in motorized chairs do the slalom as well as less severely disabled athletes. This event is an excellent one for public school physical education. A wide variety of courses can be used with any number of ramps, reverse gates, and cones.

Field

Virtually every field event in which ambulatory athletes compete can be used in wheelchair sports. The major adaptation is in the weight of the object to be thrown. Provision must be made also to tie the chair down or have someone hold it so there is no forward motion during the throw. It is important to determine which movement pattern (overarm, sidearm, underarm, or an innovation) the student does best and to know the best chair placement for this type of throw.

Sports and Games

Almost all regulation sports have been adapted for wheelchairs. The philosophy followed is to change the sport as little as possible so that its integrity is not compromised. This is in accordance with the normalization principle. Students do not want to play baby games; they seek involvement in activities as similar to those of their peers as possible. The major adaptation in tennis and racket games, for instance, is that the wheelchair player is allowed two bounces.

Figure 8.18 Class 1 CP athlete doing a reverse gate in his motorized chair as part of a slalom race.

In wheelchair basketball, the following modifications are made:

1. Five, rather than 3 seconds, are allowed in the lane.
2. When dribbling and holding the ball in the lap, the player can only make two thrusts of the wheels after which he or she must dribble, pass, or shoot.
3. When a player raises his or her buttocks off the chair, a physical advantage foul is called.
4. Fouls in the backcourt by the defensive team result in two shots.
5. A point system determines how many players in each classification may be on the floor.

In wheelchair soccer (the official team game of CP wheelchair athletes), the sport combines elements of indoor soccer and basketball. The game is coed and limited to athletes in Classes 1 to 6. Motorized chairs are used by Class 1 players. The nine players of each team must include four persons from Classes 1, 2, 3, and 6 Lower. The remaining players are made up of any combination of Classes 4, 5, and 6 Upper. The game is played on a regulation basketball court with soccer goals at either end. The ball is a 10-inch rubber playground ball.

Orthoses

Orthoses are braces, splints, or self-help devices that improve function, prevent or correct deformity, relieve pain, or prevent collapse. Corrective shoes, longitudinal arch supports, heel lifts, cervical collars, hand splints, and leg braces are examples of orthoses. The parapodium, a body brace mounted on a platform base, for use in teaching young children with disabilities to stand and walk, is another example. Orthoses are commonly called by abbreviations like AFOs (ankle-foot

Figure 8.19 Illustrative orthoses.

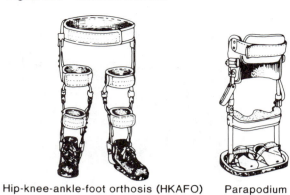
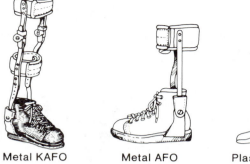

Hip-knee-ankle-foot orthosis (HKAFO) Parapodium Metal KAFO Metal AFO Plastic AFO

Figure 8.20 Front and rear views of a *prosthesis*.

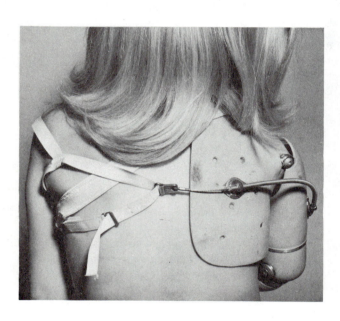
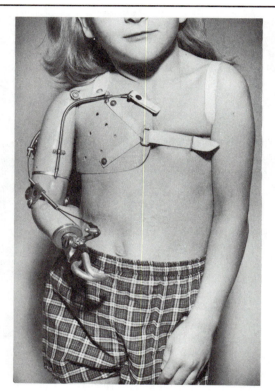

orthoses), KAFOs (knee-ankle-foot orthoses), or HKAFOs (hip-knee-ankle-foot orthoses) (Figure 8.19). They should be worn in physical education unless permission not to is granted by the person who prescribed the orthoses.

Orthoses may be worn by either wheelchair users or ambulatory students. Often, lower limb orthoses are worn inside shoes or under trousers. Orthoses are typically prescribed by a physician and made by occupational therapists or orthotic specialists.

Prostheses

A prosthesis is a substitute for a missing limb (see Figure 8.20). Sports rules for persons with amputations state the activities in which prostheses may be worn. This content is covered in the chapter on orthopedic impairments.

Assistive Devices

Assistive devices may be for upper or lower limbs. Use of a head pointer to give impetus to a ball, a ramp in bocce or bowling-type games, a handle on a bowling ball, and the use of velcro to attach a sports implement to a limb are all assistive devices. In track, assistive devices are canes, crutches, and walkers.

Many wheelchair users also rely upon assistive devices for mobility. Such students should be conceptualized as either functional or nonfunctional walkers. *Functional walkers* do not need a wheelchair unless the sport (e.g., wheelchair basketball) requires it or the terrain is exceptionally hilly and/or rough. *Nonfunctional walkers* can take a few steps with assistive devices when, for instance, making transfers to and from wheelchair and toilet, shower, bed, chair, or car. They lack the function, however, to use walking as an everyday method of locomotion. Often, persons make a decision in adolescence or early adulthood to let themselves become nonfunctional walkers and rely entirely or mostly on the wheelchair. This may occur because weight gain or general lack of fitness makes walking too demanding or because a new place of residence (like a hilly college campus) makes it impossible to get to class on time when using their regular gait.

Rules regarding use of assistive devices in sports vary according to the governing body. The National Wheelchair Athletic Association and National Wheelchair Basketball Association naturally do not permit competition on foot. The United States Amputee Athletic Association permits a choice between assistive devices and wheelchairs in most sports. Associations for cerebral palsied and les autres persons designate Class 5 as the one classification that can use assistive devices in competition.

Physical educators need to learn about crutches and canes for many reasons: (a) because most wheelchair users also rely upon assistive devices part of the time, (b) because many able-bodied students experience temporary disabilities that require use of crutches or canes, (c) because they must teach amputees and Class 5 cerebral palsied students a variety of sports and dance activities, and (d) because they interact with therapists and others who refer to the different kinds of gaits.

Crutches and Canes

The most commonly used types of crutches and canes are axillary and Lofstrand (also called Canadian). Axillary refers to the arm pit area of the body, and axillary crutches are those that fit under the arms. Axillary crutches are used most often by persons with temporary disability, amputees, and severely disabled persons in long leg braces who use a step-to or swing through gait. Most persons with cerebral palsy, les autres conditions, and low-level spinal cord problems use Lofstrand crutches, which have a metal ring that fits around the arm just below the elbow. In Lofstrand crutches, the weight of the body is borne by the hands, whereas in axillary crutches it is borne by the upper arm. Students should never be allowed to run track on axillary crutches because of possible damage to the brachial plexus (a network of nerves near where pressure is being taken).

Students may use one or both Lofstrand crutches in running track or they may use canes. Canes are typically used by persons with hemiplegia (weakness on only one side of the body). Whenever one cane or crutch is used, it is always on the strong side of the body.

Gaits Used with Crutches

At a track meet or training session, a spectator often hears such phrases as, "Look at that three-point gait" or "Isn't that an interesting two-point?" Physical educators do not teach walking on crutches; this is the role of physical therapists. Physical educators are expected to teach track, field, game, and playground skills on crutches. This pedagogy is not yet in writing, so physical educators must be creative in trial and error to determine which techniques work best.

Adapting physical education skills to crutches and canes begins with a basic understanding of walking gaits. These are presented in Figures 8.21 to 8.26. In these figures, the weaker limb (if there is one) is shaded. Except in the three-point and hemiplegic gaits, the stronger leg is advanced first. Knowledge about which leg is stronger is obviously important in coaching track and field.

Gaits without Crutches

In cerebral palsy and les autres sports, Class 6, 7, and 8 athletes run without assistive devices. The gaits exhibited are all impaired in some way. Likewise, mentally retarded persons exhibit a wide range of walking and running patterns in Special Olympics. The lower limb amputee who runs on a prosthesis also has a characteristic gait.

Figure 8.21 Step to, swing to, or drag to gait. This is used by severely handicapped persons who have little or no control of legs. In public schools, the young spina bifida child in long leg braces is the best example. In rehabilitation settings, this is the first gait taught to spinally paralyzed persons with lesions above T10. It is a staccato gait with no follow through in front of the crutches. All the weight is taken by the arms while the legs are lifted and swung or dragged forward. The pattern is lift and drop, lift and drop.

Figure 8.22 Swing through gait. This is the gait used by most amputees and persons with temporary disabilities. The person leans into the crutches, lifting the body off the ground by extending the elbows. The body is swung through the crutches so that the good foot lands in *front* of the crutches. Then the crutches are brought forward and the sequence is repeated.

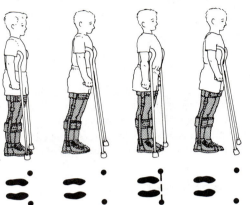

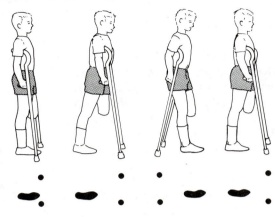

Figure 8.23 Four-point gait. This gait is used by severely involved persons who can move each leg independently. The pattern is (1) advance left crutch, (2) advance right foot, (3) advance right crutch, and (4) advance left foot.

Figure 8.24 Three-point gait. In this gait, both crutches move forward in unison as in the step to and swing through gaits, but the feet move separately. Unlike most gaits, the involved, or weaker, leg takes the first step up to and even with the crutches so it bears only partial body weight as the good leg then steps out in front of the crutches. The pattern is (1) advance both crutches, (2) advance weak leg, and (3) advance strong leg.

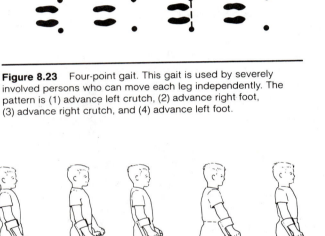

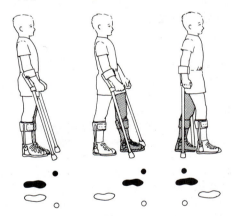

Little research has been conducted on abnormal running gaits. Therefore, abnormal walking gaits are illustrated in this chapter. The basic difference between walking and running, remember, is that running has no period of double support (i.e., both feet on the ground at the same time). Walking gaits are analyzed in terms of stance and swing phases, as depicted in Figure 8.27. It is important to understand that the normal walking gait varies with age. Walking matures as the central nervous system (CNS) develops and myelination is completed. If maturation of the CNS is delayed or frozen or CNS damage occurs, an adolescent or adult may exhibit a gait similar to the normal pattern of a young child. Figure 8.27 depicts normal gaits at different ages.

The art of walking is not perfected until approximately 3 years after the child has taken his or her first step—i.e., some time after age 4 in the normal child. Walking patterns reveal many individual differences

Figure 8.25 Two-point gait. This gait is most like normal walking and running. It is the fastest of the gaits, but requires the most balance because there are only two points of contact with the ground at any time. Whenever a crutch moves, the opposite leg moves in unison. The pattern is (1) advance left crutch and right leg simultaneously and (2) advance right crutch and left leg simultaneously.

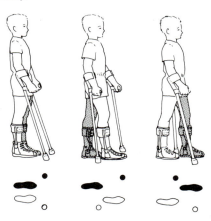

Figure 8.27 Normal gaits at different ages.

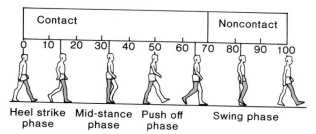

Normal mature walking gait characteristic of children from ages 4–5 years and older. A gait cycle begins with the heel strike of a leg and ends when the heel of the same leg strikes again. Step and stride length relate to height.

First walking pattern showing high guard position of arms, rigid torso, excessive flexion of hip and knee joints, and flat-footed steps.

Figure 8.26 Hemiplegic gait. This gait is similar to the three-point except that one cane is used instead of two crutches. The cane moves first, then the weak leg opposite the cane, then the strong leg. The steps taken with each leg should be equal in length, with emphasis placed on establishing a rhythmic gait. Although used by persons of all ages, this gait is most common in older persons who have had strokes.

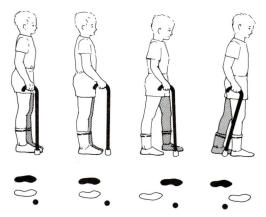

Intermediate walking pattern characteristic of children until age 4 or 5. There is still no trunk rotation and hence no opposition of arm and leg movements. Hip and knee action is still excessive, but heel-toe transfer of weight is beginning to appear.

with each person tending to assume a gait that is efficient for his or her particular body structure. Developmental changes in head, trunk, and limb proportions contribute, in large part, to the transition from immature to mature walking. The proportionately large head and high center of gravity in the toddler, for instance, help to explain the wide base of support. Other factors that may affect the walking pattern include disorders in bilateral integration, such common structural anomalies as uneven length of legs, and deficits in strength and flexibility.

Abnormal gaits that physical educators should recognize appear in Figures 8.28 to 8.31. Figure 8.28 depicts gaits associated with spasticity and ataxia. Although these are commonly seen in cerebral palsy, it should be remembered that many different kinds of disorders of the CNS can cause spasticity and ataxia. Figure 8.29 lumps together gaits in which shuffling or

Figure 8.28 Abnormal gaits associated with spasticity and ataxia.

Scissors gait. Characteristic of quadriplegic spastic cerebral palsy. The legs are flexed and adducted at the hip joint, causing them to cross alternately in front of each other with the knees scraping together. The knees may be flexed to a greater degree than normal, and the weight of the body may be taken primarily on the toes. The gait is characterized by a narrow walking base. Scissoring may be caused by retention of the positive supporting reflex. Toe walking may be caused also by the positive supporting reflex.

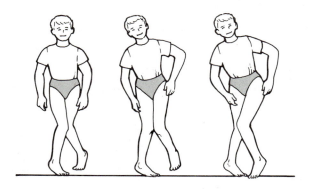

Hemiplegic gait. Characteristic of hemiplegic spastic cerebral palsy. Both arm and leg on the same side are involved. Tends to occur with any disorder producing an immobile hip or knee. Affected leg is rigid and swung from the hip joint in a semicircle by muscle action of the trunk. Individual leans to the affected side, and arm on that side is held in a rigid, semiflexed position.

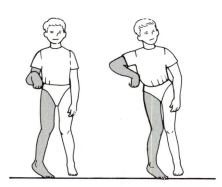

Cerebellar gait. Characteristic of ataxic cerebral palsy, Friedreich's ataxia, and similar les autres conditions. Irregularity of steps, unsteadiness, tendency to reel to one side. Individual seems to experience difficulty in judging how high to lift legs when climbing stairs. Problems are increased when the ground is uneven. Note the similarity between this and the immature walk of early childhood before CNS has matured.

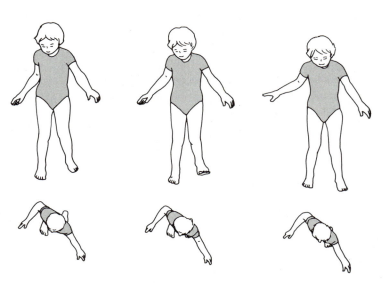

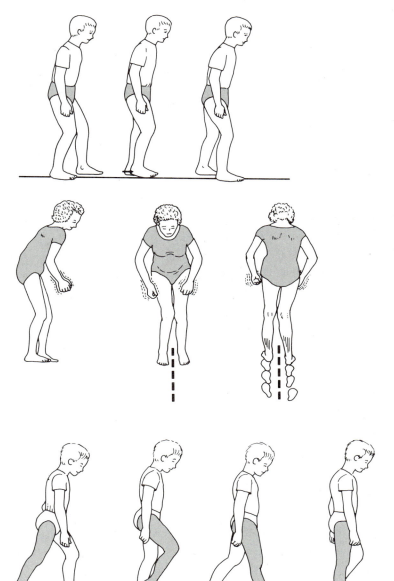

Shuffling gait. Associated with severe mental retardation. Inadequate muscle tonus to lift the foot off the ground during the normal swinging phase of walking. There is excessive flexion at hip, knee, and ankle joints, and the trunk is usually inclined forward. Contact with floor is flat-footed. Usually, there is no opposition of arms and legs.

Propulsion or festination gait. Characteristic of Parkinson's disease, also called *paralysis agitans*. Individual walks with a forward leaning posture and short shuffling steps which begin slowly and become progressively more rapid. This gait also characterizes very old persons with low fitness.

Steppage gait. Also called foot-drop gait and characterized by flopping of the foot on the floor. Knee action is higher than normal, but toes still tend to drag on floor. Caused by paralysis or weakness in the anterior tibial and peroneal muscles. Results in excessive hip and knee flexor work.

Waddling gait. Main deviation from normal is a rolling movement from side to side. This is usually caused by structural problems like bowlegs (genu varum), hip problems and dislocations (coxa vara), knock knees, or one leg longer than the other.

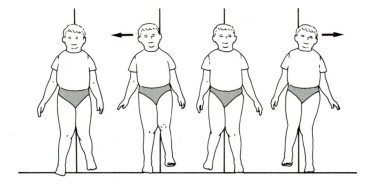

Muscular dystrophy gait. Characterized by awkward side-to-side waddle, sway back (lordosis), arms held in backward position, and frequent falling. Shoulder girdle muscles are often badly atrophied. Calf muscles may be hypertrophied but weak because fat has replaced muscle tissue.

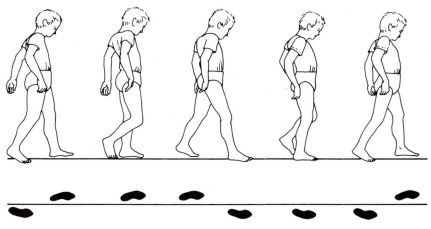

Gluteus maximus lurch. Characterizes polio and other spinal paralysis conditions in which the paralyzed limb cannot shift the body weight forward onto the normal limb. To compensate, the trunk is thrust forward. Once the paralyzed limb is thrown forward in this way, the trunk movement cannot be stopped by the normal braking action of the gluteus. A backward movement of the shoulders is therefore initiated to stop trunk movement. The gait is thus characterized by alternate sticking out of chest (salutation) and pulling back of shoulders.

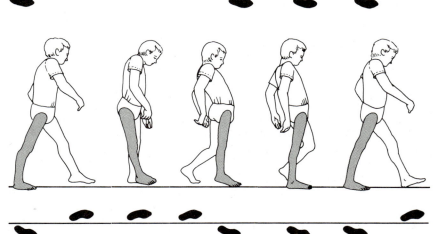

a foot drag of some type occur. These gaits are all characterized by weakness or paralysis of muscles controlling hip, knee, and ankle flexion and extension. Figure 8.30 shows different types of waddling gaits, all of which exhibit abnormal side-to-side movement. Figure 8.31 depicts the Trendelenburg gait, which is caused by weakness of abductor muscles of the hip. The Trendelenburg sign is used in postural assessment to describe persons with hip abductors so weak that they cannot maintain a level pelvis while walking or standing on one foot. A level pelvis (normal) is called a negative Trendelenburg sign. Tilting the pelvis when weight is borne on the affected side is called a positive Trendelenburg sign.

Figure 8.31 Gait characterized by uneven hip height caused by weakness of hip abductor muscles.

Trendelenburg gait. Limp caused by paralysis or weakness of gluteus medius. Pelvis is lower on nonaffected side (i.e., if right gluteus is affected, left hip is lower when standing with weight of body on right leg). In walking, each time the weight is transferred to the right foot, the body leans slightly to the left (the nonaffected side).

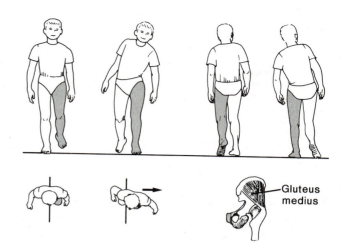

Gluteus medius

Table 8.2
Checklist for Evaluation of Walking in Normal Persons of Different Ages

Directions: Observe the student walking on several different terrains or surfaces (even or uneven), uphill, downhill, and on a level surface. Consider the 11 sets of alternate descriptions and check the one of each set that represents the student's level of performance. Until the child is about age 4 years, most checks will be in the left-hand column. After age 4, the normal child exhibits mature walking. Use findings to write specific behavioral objectives.

Check One	Developmental or Immature Walking	Check One	Mature Walking

	1. Forward lean
	   a. From ground
	   b. From waist and hips
			1. Good body alignment

	2. Wide base of support with heels 5–8″ from line of progression		2. Narrower base of support with heels 2–3″ from line of progression
	3. Toes and knees pointed outward		3. Toes and knees pointed straight ahead
	4. Flat-footed gait		4. Heel-ball-toe transfer of weight
	5. Excessive flexion at knee and hip joints		5. Strong push-off from toes
	6. Uneven, jerky steps[a]		6. Smooth and rhythmical shift of body weight with minimal up-and-down movement of body
	7. Little or no pelvic rotation until second or third year. Body sways from side to side		7. Minimal rotatory action of pelvis (short persons will have more than tall ones)
	8. Rigidity of upper torso		8. Compensatory rotatory action of torso and shoulders inversely related to pelvic rotation
	9. Outstretched arms, also called high guard position		9. Arms swing freely and in opposition with legs
	10. Relatively short stride. In preschool children, the distance from heel to heel is 11–18″		10. Greater length of stride dependent upon length of leg. In the average adult man, the distance from heel to heel is 25–26″
	11. Rate of walking stabilizes at about 170 steps per minute		11. Rate of walking decreases to about 115 to 145 steps per minute

[a]Jerkiness may be caused by a flat-footed or shuffle gait or by excessive stride length.

Learning Activities

1. Get acquainted with students at your university who use wheelchairs and/or assistive devices and ask them to share their knowledge with you. Integrate them into your social group and observe adaptations that they make in sports and other recreational activities.

2. Invite disabled persons to speak to your class concerning use of wheelchairs and/or assistive devices and architectural, attitudinal, and aspirational barriers. When possible, arrange for such persons to receive a consultant's fee or honorarium for sharing their expertise.

3. Attend meets sponsored by various wheelchair sports organizations or the National Association of Sports for Cerebral Palsy. Observe types of wheelchairs in use, wheelchair techniques, and adaptations made.

4. Secure permission to film or videotape disabled persons and apply your biomechanics knowledge to analyzing movement. If possible, involve your kinesiology instructor in this project.

5. Obtain wheelchairs from a local hospital, medical supply company, airport, or other source and practice techniques explained in this chapter.

6. Arrange to visit a school, community agency, or rehabilitation center where several persons are in wheelchairs, secure permission to administer the three NWBA classification tests, and practice assessment skills.

7. Contact the nearest office of United Cerebral Palsy Associations, Incorporated, and find out if staff are involved in the CP sports movement. If so, volunteer your services and, if possible, attend a workshop on classificaton. If not, try to motivate staff to get involved. For further information on classification workshops, contact Bob Bergquist, Physical Education Department, Springfield College, Springfield, MA.

References

Jones, J. A. (Ed.). (1984). *Training guide to cerebral palsy sports*. New York: National Association of Sports for Cerebral Palsy.

McCann, B. C. (1981). Does the track athlete need medical classification. *Sports 'N Spokes, 7*, 22–24.

Spooren, P. (1981). The technical characteristics of wheelchair racing. *Sports 'N Spokes, 7* (4), 19–20.

Bibliography

Gibson, G., Marshall, D., Smith, K., & Winn, O. (1983). The selection of sports wheelchairs. *Sports 'N Spokes, 8* (6), 10–13.

Guttmann, L. (1976). *Textbook of sport for the disabled*. Aylesbury, England: HM & M Publishers.

Higgs, C. (1983). An analysis of racing wheelchairs used at the 1980 Olympic games for the disabled. *Research Quarterly for Exercise and Sport, 54* (3), 229–233.

Hoy, D. (1984). *A wheelchair basketball curriculum*. Edmonton, Canada: University of Alberta.

Labanowich, S. (1978). Psychology of wheelchair sports. *Therapeutic Recreation Journal, 12*, 11–17.

LeMere, T., & Labanowich, S. (1984). The history of sport wheelchairs—Part III. *Sports 'N Spokes, 10* (2), 12–16.

McCann, B. C. (1979). Problems and future trends in classifying disabled athletes. In R. Steadward (Ed.), *Proceedings of First International Conference on Sport and Training of the Physically Disabled Athlete* (pp. 25–35). Edmonton, Canada: University of Alberta.

McCann, B. C. (1980). Medical classification—Art, science, or instinct. *Sports 'N Spokes, 5* (5), 12–14.

Owen, E. (1982). *Playing and coaching wheelchair basketball*. Champaign, IL: University of Illinois Press.

Research and Training Centre for the Physically Disabled. (1983). *Wheelchair track and field introductory coaching manual*. Edmonton, Canada: University of Alberta.

Shaver, L. (1982). *Wheelchair basketball: Concepts and techniques*. Marshall, MN: Southwest State University Press.

Sherrill, C. (Ed.). (1985). *Sport and disabled athletes*. Champaign, IL: Human Kinetics Publishers.

Stein, J. (1986). Personnel training for leadership in sports for athletes with handicapping conditions. In C. Sherrill (Ed.), *Adapted physical education leadership training*. Champaign, IL: Human Kinetics Publishers.

Walsh, C., Hoy, D., & Holland, L. (1982). *Get fit: Flexibility exercises for the wheelchair user*. Edmonton, Canada: University of Alberta.

Part 2 Assessment and Programming

9 Service Delivery and Individualized Educational Programming

Figure 9.1 The capacity to care is the thing which gives life its deepest significance—Pablo Casals. Likewise, it is the thing that gives teaching its deepest significance.

Chapter Objectives

After you have studied this chapter, you should be able to

1. Explain the achievement based curriculum (ABC) model and the diagnostic-prescriptive process and discuss their use in a public school setting.

2. Discuss the following steps in planning a curriculum: (a) prioritizing goals, (b) selecting objectives, (c) calculating instructional time, (d) planning use of time, (e) developing instructional units in relation to available time and (f) decision making about space, equipment, and resources.

3. Differentiate between norm-referenced and criterion-referenced tests and state examples of each.

4. State seven procedures to be followed in assessment and explain each.

5. State criteria for the selection of tests, explain each, and specify reference books that review and/or include copies of tests.

6. Discuss the role of environmental factors in assessment and explain how these can be adapted to ensure that testing is success oriented.

7. Write the services part of the PE-IEP, remembering to include number of minutes per week in each type of setting, the maximum pupil/teacher ratio, and the type of teacher.

8. Differentiate between IEPs and lesson plans and discuss how each can be used to implement the diagnostic-prescriptive process.

9. Contrast behavior management theory with humanistic theory in relation to teaching/counseling.

10. Identify several variables important in teaching/counseling of handicapped and/or clumsy students and discuss each.

11. List 20 principles of motor learning and discuss their application in teaching handicapped and/or clumsy students.

12. Discuss evaluation as it is used in determining pupil gain and program effectiveness.

Adapted physical education, like special education and the other helping professions, provides a continuum of services designed to individualize instruction to meet the needs of all students. Thus, the teacher is conceptualized as a provider or deliverer of services whose work extends beyond the boundaries of the gymnasium (see Figure 9.1).

The curriculum model that guides the delivery of services explained in this chapter appears in Figure 9.2. The model is the same as the well known achievement based curriculum (ABC) model of Janet Wessel, innovator of the I CAN instructional system, except for the addition of counseling. These two processes are integral to teaching clumsy and/or handicapped students, whereas they are incidental in regular physical education.

Adapted physical education service delivery has been influenced by several large-scale, federally funded curriculum models like I CAN. So important are these models that they were introduced in Chapter 2 of this book as evidence of how research changes and shapes a profession. If you have not yet studied these and other models in detail, doing so would make a good project

Figure 9.2 Achievement based curriculum (ABC) model on which I CAN is based (Wessel, 1983). The ABC model has been modified here to include counseling as part of the teaching process.

ABC Implementation Model

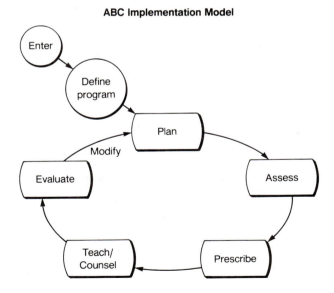

in conjunction with reading this chapter. It is also important to identify models used in your state and to review the curriculum guides of nearby local school districts. Find out also if your state education agency has published an adapted physical education curriculum guide.

Whether or not projects like I CAN and ACTIVE in the United States and PREP in Canada are documented as primary sources, virtually all good adapted physical education follows their procedures. Dr. Thomas Vodola, the innovator of Project ACTIVE, as early as 1965 recommended the TAPE (test, assess, prescribe, evaluate) process as the key to quality service delivery in both regular and adapted physical education. Dr. Janet Wessel, the innovator of I CAN, created an achievement based curriculum (ABC) model that depicts the cyclical nature of service delivery (plan, assess, prescribe, teach, evaluate, repeat). Dr. Patricia Austin, the innovator of PREP, developed an instructional model based on task analysis and individual records showing the level of assistance required by the student for successful performance (physical prompt, visual prompt, verbal prompt, no prompt).

The Diagnostic-Prescriptive Process

Each of these curriculum models embodies the philosophy of PL 94–142 and is helpful in development and implementation of the individualized educational program (IEP). Each also emphasizes a diagnostic-prescriptive process, showing how special education and adapted physical education have evolved the educational model from its predecessor, the medical model. It is important to differentiate educational diagnosis and prescription from medical diagnosis and prescription. Whereas physicians use assessment to diagnose diseases and prescribe treatment, educators test to diagnose problems that interfere with learning and/or successful performance. They also identify strengths so that program planning can emphasize abilities, not disabilities. Educators prescribe interventions, developmental sequences, or programs that are written under the services portion of the IEP.

Table 9.1 describes the diagnostic-prescriptive process. *Diagnosis,* in educational circles, is often called *assessment* because some persons perceive the term diagnosis as more properly belonging to the medical profession. Whatever it is called, the basic principle is individualizing and personalizing physical education.

Table 9.1
Diagnostic-Prescriptive Process

T   **Test** the learner on a formal and informal basis.

A   **Assess** the learner's performance on the basis of
- Background information.
- Test results.
- Informal observation.

P   **Prescribe** educational program in accordance with
- Strengths and weaknesses.
- Learning style.
- Strategies for enhancing self-concept.

E   **Evaluate** the learner's performance at about 9-week intervals, establish new objectives, and prescribe accordingly.

Planning

Before teachers can implement the diagnostic-prescriptive process, however, they must engage in considerable planning in regard to overall goals. Research has shown that physical education can change behaviors in nine general areas. This research has been reviewed by Sherrill (1986), but new studies are being published monthly that document the values of fitness, motor, and leisure instruction.

Prioritizing Goals

Planning begins with prioritizing appropriate physical education goals in accordance with school and community philosophy as well as individual needs of students. Goals are usually prioritized differently for handicapped and/or clumsy students than for normal students. This is because specific needs of the two groups are different.

The Goals of Adapted Physical Education Scale (GAPES) in Table 9.2 enables you and classmates to prioritize goals for adapted physical education, thereby identifying similarities and differences in your philosophy. Read the definitions of each goal very carefully before you check which of each pair of goals you prefer. The technique used in this instrument is *paired-comparison.* You will note that every goal has been paired against each of the other eight goals in round robin tournament fashion. The result is 36 pairs. In each pair, you put a check before the goal you consider most important for handicapped and/or clumsy students. You

Table 9.2

Long-Range Goals of Adapted Physical Education Scale (GAPES), A Paired Comparison Ranking—Form B (Sherrill, 1982)

Let us assume that the *purpose* of adapted physical education is to change psychomotor behaviors (i.e., to remediate or ameliorate specific problems which interfere with success and/or optimal functioning in the regular physical education setting as well as in the home and community). What, then, are our long-range goals which guide program planning? What are our priorities?

The following goals of adapted/developmental physical education are representative of those accepted by educators, parents, and students. In the last section of this table you will be asked to rank these goals using the definitions which follow. Please read these definitions very carefully before beginning the ranking. *Note that all of these goals are to be achieved through movement.*

A. *Positive self-concept:* To develop a positive self-concept and body image through activity involvement; to increase understanding and appreciation of the body and its capacity for movement; to accept limitations which cannot be changed and to learn to adapt environment so as to make the most of strengths (i.e., to work toward self-actualization).

B. *Fun/tension release:* To have fun, recreation, happiness; to release tensions in a healthy, socially acceptable manner; to reduce hyperactivity and learn to relax, to improve mental health and attitude toward exercise and/or physical education.

C. *Creative expression:* To increase creativity in movement and thought. When posed a movement problem, to generate *many* responses, *different* responses, *original* responses. To learn to imagine, to embellish and add on, to risk experimentation, to devise appropriate game strategy, and to create new games, dances, and movement sequences.

D. *Motor skills and patterns:* To learn fundamental motor skills and patterns; to master the motor skills indigenous to games, sports, dance, and aquatics participation; to improve fine and gross motor coordination for self-care, school, work, and play activities.

E. *Play and game skills:* To learn to play (i.e., to progress through developmental play stages from solitary and parallel play behaviors up through appropriate cooperative and competitive game behaviors). To promote contact and interaction behaviors with toys, play apparatus, and persons; to learn basic game formations and mental operations needed for play; to master rules and strategies of simple games.

F. *Physical and motor fitness:* To develop the cardiovascular system, promote ideal weight, increase muscular strength, endurance, and flexibility, and improve postures.

G. *Social competency:* To learn appropriate social behaviors (i.e., how to interact with others—sharing, taking turns, following, and leading). To reduce social isolation, to learn how to develop and maintain friendships, to demonstrate good sportsmanship and self-discipline in winning and losing, and to develop other skills necessary for acceptance by peers in the mainstream.

H. *Leisure-time skills:* To learn to transfer physical education learnings into habits of lifetime sports, dance, and aquatics; to become acquainted with community resources for recreation; to expand repertoire of individual and group games and sports, dance, and aquatic activities and/or to refine skills.

I. *Perceptual motor function and sensory integration:* To enhance visual, auditory, tactile, vestibular, and kinesthetic functioning; to reinforce academic learnings through games and perceptual-motor activities; to improve cognitive, language, and motor function through increased sensory integration.

GAPES: A Paired Comparison Ranking

You are asked to make a choice between two adapted physical education goals. Of each pair presented, please check the goal you see as more important for adapted physical education to achieve. This choice is meant to reflect your opinion of adapted physical education in general and not that of any specific institution. Do not omit any!

Pair			Choices
1	___ Leisure time skills	or	___ Motor skills and patterns
2	___ Play and game skills	or	___ Creative expression
3	___ Leisure time skills	or	___ Creative expression
4	___ Positive self-concept	or	___ Leisure time skills
5	___ Social competency	or	___ Motor skills and patterns
6	___ Social competency	or	___ Positive self-concept
7	___ Fun/tension release	or	___ Social competency
8	___ Perceptual-motor function	or	___ Creative expression
9	___ Physical and motor fitness	or	___ Fun/tension release
10	___ Physical and motor fitness	or	___ Play and game skills
11	___ Play and game skills	or	___ Leisure time skills
12	___ Motor skills	or	___ Play and game skills

Continued on next page

Table 9.2 (Continued)

Pair		Choices		
13	___ Social competency	or	___ Play and game skills	
14	___ Fun/tension release	or	___ Creative expression	
15	___ Play and game skills	or	___ Perceptual motor function	
16	___ Positive self-concept	or	___ Fun/tension release	
17	___ Play and game skills	or	___ Fun/tension release	
18	___ Physical and motor fitness	or	___ Leisure time skills	
19	___ Positive self-concept	or	___ Physical and motor fitness	
20	___ Leisure time skills	or	___ Perceptual motor functioning	
21	___ Social competency	or	___ Physical and motor fitness	
22	___ Social competency	or	___ Creative expression	
23	___ Motor skills and patterns	or	___ Positive self-concept	
24	___ Social competency	or	___ Leisure time skills	
25	___ Motor skills and patterns	or	___ Physical and motor fitness	
26	___ Motor skills and patterns	or	___ Fun/tension release	
27	___ Perceptual motor functioning	or	___ Physical and motor fitness	
28	___ Creative expression	or	___ Physical and motor fitness	
29	___ Perceptual motor functioning	or	___ Motor skills and patterns	
30	___ Fun/tension release	or	___ Leisure time skills	
31	___ Creative expression	or	___ Positive self-concept	
32	___ Motor skills and patterns	or	___ Creative expression	
33	___ Play and game skills	or	___ Positive self-concept	
34	___ Social competency	or	___ Perceptual motor functioning	
35	___ Perceptual motor function	or	___ Positive self-concept	
36	___ Fun/tension release	or	___ Perceptual motor functioning	

may wish to specify the age range and severity of problems of the students to be served in your program.

When done, count and make sure you have 36 checks. Then use the definition page as your tabulation sheet. Go down the list of 36 pairs and place a tally mark in front of the goal definition for each time you have checked it as a preferred goal. The highest number of tallies a goal can receive is 8; the lowest number is 0.

When tallying is completed, identify the three or four goals most important to you. There is not enough time in adapted physical education to work equally on all goals. This process enables you to prioritize use of instructional time. This instrument can be used for prioritizing goals for individual students as well as for the program as a whole. When used as a guide to individual program planning, the goal checked in each pair should reflect needs identified through the assessment process.

Selecting Objectives

After program goals have been selected, they must be broken down into short-term objectives. In many school systems, a curriculum guide is printed that includes philosophy of the program, goals, and objectives; then this process does not have to be repeated year after year.

Illustrative of lists of objectives are those in Table 9.3. Many school systems are computerizing such lists to facilitate the writing of objectives of an IEP. Often on an IEP, the objectives are specified by number (A–1, B–3) rather than writing out the words. In the B–3 example, B refers to the long-term goal (one of the nine) and 3 refers to the specific objective as it is numbered in the curriculum guide.

Once objectives are developed for physical education goals, the teacher must decide how many objectives to select and specifically which ones. Criteria to follow in selecting specific objectives include

1. They are usable/relevant in everyday life.
2. They form the basis for further learning.
3. They are generalizable to many physical education activities.
4. They match assessment data for individual students.

Table 9.3
Illustrative Objectives for Selected Goals as They Might Appear in a Curriculum Guide or an IEP

Goal	Objectives
To demonstrate positive self-concept in relation to fitness, motor, and leisure functioning.	1. To improve score on the physical education portion of a standardized self-concept test (see index for pages on which illustrative tests appear). 2. To demonstrate understanding and appreciation of self by stating accurately one's personal best time, distance, or score on selected tasks like mile run, 50-yard dash, overarm throw, and sit-ups in 30 seconds. 3. To demonstrate belief in ability to improve through hard work by stating high (but realistic) levels of aspiration in terms of targeted personal bests on selected tasks. 4. To demonstrate knowledge of work entailed in improvement by describing minute-by-minute daily practice and/or workout sessions. 5. To demonstrate commitment to change by showing chart kept over several weeks that plots improvement in personal best and/or by showing diary that describes time spent in exercise, games, sports, and dance and/or a diet plan.

To demonstrate functional competence in selected play, game, and dance skills.	1. To progress from the parallel play to the interactive play stage.
	2. To engage successfully in 10 selected games by
	  a. Remaining on task for the entire game without verbal prompting from teacher or peers.
	  b. Following all rules without prompts.
	  c. Not being tagged, made "it", or sent to prison more often than other players.
	3. To demonstrate ability to get into the following formations with nine other students within a count of 10 seconds: single circle, file, line, double circle—two deep, threesomes scattered about the room for squirrels-in-trees game.
	4. To demonstrate appropriate use of the following play objects and apparatus by playing for 3 minutes in response to "Show me how you play with this": ball, racket, tricycle, stall bars, balance beam, minitrampoline.
	5. To demonstrate the ability to portray through movement for 3 minutes each in response to "Show me how this moves": frog, witch, football player, clown, autumn leaf, very old person.

To demonstrate functional competence in selected motor patterns.	1. To progress from Stage 2 to Stage 3 on a selected motor skill developmental sequence. 2. To increase overarm throw distance by 10 feet. 3. To decrease 50-m dash speed by .50 seconds. 4. To demonstrate successfully the first five steps or focal points in a task analysis or learning progression.

To demonstrate functional social competence in play.	1. To be selected by at least 1 of 10 classmates as a first- or second-choice friend on a sociogram.
	2. To select at least one of the same persons on a sociogram who selected him or her.
	3. To demonstrate at least three kinds of positive interacting behaviors during every 20-minute class.
	  a. Initiating conversation.
	  b. Answering questions.
	  c. Asking questions.
	  d. Offering assistance.
	  e. Asking for assistance.
	  f. Congratulating or praising another.
	4. To cope with losing games or failing to achieve desired motor or fitness goal by not crying, pouting, whining, or similar behavior.
	5. To lead group in warm-up or follow-the-leader game, speaking loudly enough to be heard.
	6. To decrease number of behavior problems exhibited during a 20-minute class.

Table 9.4
Calculating Available Instructional Time for the Year

1. *Total number* of instructional weeks available:
   180 day school year = 36 instructional weeks
   230 day school year = 46 instructional weeks
   (Christmas, spring, summer vacations already excluded.) .... __36__ weeks

2. Subtract 2 weeks of the total time available to allow for *cancelled physical education classes* resulting from conference time, psychological testing, swimming schedule, snow days, field trips, voting days (gym in use), holiday assemblies, beginning and end of school, and others. .... __2__ weeks

3. Subtract 2 weeks of the total time available to allow for flex time (unplanned adjustments that need to be made to allow for additional instructional needs). .... __2__ weeks

4. Total weeks available (#1 minus #2 and #3) = ... __32__ weeks (16 each semester)

5. Total days available:
   a. Multiply #4 by the number of physical education classes per week: .... × __5__ days gym/week

   = __160__ days gym/year

   b. Multiply total number of days by the length (minutes) of your physical education class (instructional time—not dressing or set-up time). .... × __30__ minutes gym/day

   = __4,800__ minutes gym/year

Calculating Instructional Time

Before determining number of objectives, the teacher must calculate available instructional time for a specific class and/or child. Table 9.4, based on Wessel's I CAN system, shows how the school calendar is used to do this for the academic year.

Table 9.4 shows that the average student assigned to physical education 5 days a week (30 minutes a day) has 4,800 minutes (80 hours) of instructional time. This is 2,400 minutes (40 hours) a semester, a phenomenally short amount of time for the changing of behaviors.

Planning Use of Time

The next step is to decide how many objectives can be achieved in 2,400 minutes. Remember that handicapped and/or clumsy students typically learn more slowly than their normal peers and that young students learn more slowly than older ones. Wessel estimates that 270 minutes (4.5 hours) are required for a handicapped and/or clumsy preschool child to master one objective. Low skilled students in elementary school and secondary school require about 210 minutes (3.5 hours) and 180 minutes (3 hours), respectively, per each objective. To calculate number of objectives per semester, divide time needed to learn one objective into total instructional time.

Example for elementary school:

$$\frac{2,400 \text{ minutes per semester}}{210 \text{ minutes per objective}} = 11.43 \text{ objectives per semester}$$

Rounding this to 11 objectives per semester, the next decision to be made is how many objectives should be selected from each goal area. Most IEPs seem to include three or four goals, each broken down into three or four objectives. Wessel's time estimates relate mostly to teaching motor and fitness skills; much research is needed on amount of time required to teach rules, strategies, and games. Research is needed also on amount of time required to increase cooperative behaviors and peer interactions and to decrease the many negative behaviors that constitute discipline problems.

Developing Instructional Units

The last step in group planning in relation to time usage is to arrange objectives into instructional units and to specify the beginning and ending date of instruction for each unit. The IEP form, remember, requires a projected date for beginning service delivery. PL 94–142 requires that progress on achievement of objectives must be reviewed for handicapped students every 12 months. Many states require more frequent reviews. This should be considered in determining number of instructional units and duration of each unit. For convenience, let us assume that the periodic IEP review

Table 9.5
Sample Semester Plan for Preschool or Severely Handicapped Child

Instructional Unit		Time in Minutes	Time Spent Each Week, in Minutes	Number of Weeks
1. Running games				
a. Motor skill—running		540	54	
b. Play and game concepts		270	27	
c. Formations		270	27	
d. Social interactions		270	27	
e. Flexible time for self-concept and body image		150	15	
	Total	1,500	150	10
2. Aquatics				
a. Water entry and locomotion		270	67.5	
b. Breathing		270	67.5	
c. Flexible time for self-concept and body image		60	15	
	Total	600	150	4
3. Creative movement/dance				
a. Portraying animals		100	50	
b. Moving to accompaniment		100	50	
c. Abdominal strength		100	50	
	Total	300	150	2

Note. a, b, c refer to specific objectives. If 540 minutes are allocated, 2 objectives can be achieved. If 270 minutes are allocated, 1 objective can be achieved. If less than 270 minutes are allocated, there is not time for completion of one objective.

falls at the same time as the end of a semester (i.e., after about 2,400 minutes of instructional time).

Table 9.5 presents a sample semester plan for a student who requires approximately 270 minutes to achieve an objective (i.e., a preschool child who is slow or a student of any age who is severely mentally handicapped). In 16 weeks, students on this plan are expected to complete seven full objectives and make progress toward five others. Develop some lists of objectives for hypothetical students and then show your competence in prioritizing and organizing these objectives into semester plans. Remember that planning should always be done in units of minutes.

The amount of time required for a student to achieve an objective varies widely. The estimates of 270, 210, and 180 minutes for preschool, elementary, and secondary school students are based on averages. Difficult objectives naturally require more time than easy ones. The art of writing objectives is enhanced by keeping in mind the number of minutes. Flexible time is needed for review and reinforcement of skills, knowledge, rules, and strategies learned in previous units. The planning of instruction is directed primarily toward new learning.

Other Decision Making

Planning also entails decision making about space, equipment, and resources. Size of class is tremendously important, since every student should have maximum on-task time. This means that, in a ball handling unit, every student has a ball; he or she is not standing in a line and waiting for a turn. It means also that every student has a chance to learn sports by practicing as a member of a regulation-size team, not being one of 15 scattered over the softball field. If too many students are assigned to a class in proportion to available space and equipment, selection of objectives and planning of time are obviously affected.

In summary, planning as used in the achievement based curriculum model (see Figure 9.2) refers to decision making in relation to classes. Planning reflects the philosophy of teacher, school, and community. Some of the processes involved in group planning are the same processes used for individualized programming as required in PL 94–142.

Assessment

Assessment refers to testing, measuring, and evaluating (i.e., decision making based on testing and measuring). As such, it is the most important part of the achievement based curriculum (ABC) model. The IEP cannot be written until assessment is completed. Therefore, the first task that physical educators undertake at the beginning of each school year is the testing of individual students and the describing of their present level of educational performance. The next task is writing annual goals, including short-term instructional objectives, for the IEP. In the ABC model, these two tasks combined are considered *assessment,* whereas *evaluation* refers to decision making in terms of the total program and its impact upon the student.

Many authorities use the terms *assessment* and *evaluation* interchangeably. PL 94–142 refers only to evaluation. The newer trend seems to be use of assessment in relation to individuals and evaluation in relation to programs.

Types of Assessment

Good teachers use many types of assessment (see Figure 9.3). Some approaches are informal and unobtrusive, whereas others rely upon standardized tests. With the PL 94–142 requirement that students, if appropriate, attend and participate in their IEP meetings, there is a trend toward involving students in the assessment process. Self-evaluation helps students internalize their needs and become more committed to change.

Assessment of handicapped students specifically for the purpose of determining PL 94–142 eligibility and placement must be completed before instruction begins. The legal procedures that govern this type of assessment should be reviewed in Chapter 4.

All other kinds of assessment and evaluation should be *continuous* with assessment *fully integrated* into the teaching/learning process. Daily recording of scores on a chart is, in fact, an excellent instructional approach. When testing occurs daily, students tend to lose their fear of it.

Observation

Much of assessment is informal and depends on observation. Whenever possible, videotapes should be used to record performance and permit observation by the students. Use of videotapes in conjunction with assessing components of motor performance and quality

Figure 9.3   Good teaching begins with individual assessment.

of movement helps the observational process become more objective. Use of three raters, even when some are students, is more objective than only the teacher observing and assessing performance. Observation is a very difficult skill to learn. When observing, it is essential to know precisely what to look for. This is why so many pictorial movement assessment instruments have been included in this book.

Norm-Referenced Tests

A *norm* is a statistic that describes how large numbers of persons of various ages, abilities, or genders perform on a test. The concept is based on normal curve theory. Most of us are familiar with height-weight norms and various fitness norms that enable us to compare a student with others of his or her same age or gender and decide whether he or she is normal, below average, or above average. Norms are typically used for making placement decisions.

Figure 9.4 Example of how Project ACTIVE scores are plotted on a chart and interpreted through use of norms.

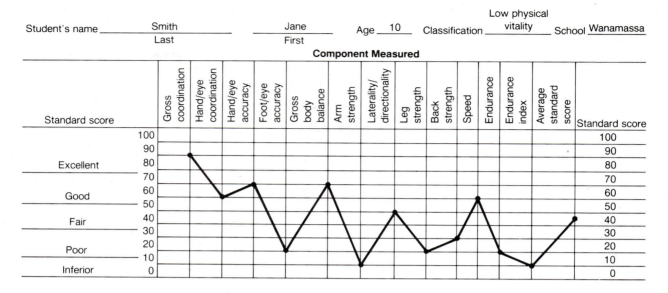

Norms are generally stated as standard scores or percentile ranks that range from 0 to 100, with an average of 50. Figure 9.4, which depicts the Project ACTIVE scores of a 10-year-old girl, shows how norms can be used to identify strengths and weaknesses in relation to one's peers. Using this information, the teacher will develop learning objectives specific to the student's needs. The average standard score of 43 can be used as part of the rationale for this student to receive adapted physical education services. Of the 12 items, she has scored below average (50) on 7.

Norm-referenced tests, while excellent for guiding placement decisions and helping persons assess themselves in relation to peers, do not permit individualization of test instructions and environment. Since most tests are geared toward the abilities of the average child, those who perform below average necessarily fail. Once placement is completed, adapted physical educators therefore often use criterion-referenced tests.

Criterion-Referenced Tests

This type of test is one in which the student's performance is compared against a pre-established criterion or standard. What other students make on the test is not important; only the individual matters. In this book, the assessment instruments showing pictures of children at various developmental stages are criterion-referenced. The criterion is to demonstrate a mature movement pattern or a certain number of components (focal points) of that pattern. The I CAN assessment system is probably the best known of criterion-referenced tests. Figure 9.5 illustrates the I CAN system.

Standardized Tests

Table 9.6 presents a list of the standardized tests used most frequently by physical educators working with handicapped students. Most of these tests are norm-referenced. Each of these tests is discussed in this book. See the index for specific page numbers. It should be noted that several of these tests are part of total instructional systems (i.e., ACTIVE, I CAN, OSU-SIGMA).

New tests that have not yet had time to become well known, but merit attention are the Test of Gross Motor Development (Ulrich, 1985), Peabody Developmental Motor Scales (Folio & Fewell, 1983; Ulrich, 1984), Project UNIQUE fitness tests (Winnick & Short, 1985), and the Movement Patterns Achievement Profile (Evans, 1980), which is for use specifically for preschool handicapped children.

Assessment in adapted physical education is so important that undergraduate students should have experience in administering at least some of these frequently used tests to children. Practice should be followed by interpretation and writing PE-IEPs.

Figure 9.5 Example of I CAN system assessment.

STUDENT/CLASS PERFORMANCE SCORE SHEET   **PERFORMANCE OBJECTIVE: TO ROLL A BALL**

SCORING
Assessment
X = achieved
O = not achieved
Reassessment
⊗ = achieved
∅ = not achieved

ASSISTANCE LEVEL CODE
A = assisted
PA = partially assisted
D = demonstration
V = verbal request
NC = no cue
□ = maintenance target

FOCAL POINTS	STANDARD	TRIALS
1 SIT AND ROLL OR PUSH A BALL a Grasp ball with hands and release	Ball travels arm's length	3 CONSECUTIVE
b Roll or push ball		PRIMARY RESPONSES
2 SIT OR STAND AND ROLL OR PUSH A BALL a Roll or push ball	Ball travels 2 ft.	N - non attending NR - no response UR - unrelated response
b a, above	Ball travels 5 ft.	O - other
3 SIT OR STAND AND ROLL OR PUSH A BALL TO A TARGET a Focus eyes on target		
b Roll or push ball to target	Ball travels 8 ft.	
4 MAINTAIN ACQUIRED LEVEL OF PERFORMANCE a Maintain level after attainment	2 weeks	
b a, above	6 weeks	

(Left margin vertical label: ASSISTANCE LEVEL)

Barbie — focal point columns: 1, 2, 3, 4 — PRIMARY RESPONSES

DATE OR NAME		1a	1b	2a	2b	3a	3b	4a	4b	PRIMARY RESPONSES	COMMENTS
9–24–86	A	X	X	X	X	X	X				Baseline day 1.—15 minute observation period
	PA	X	X	X	X	O	O				
	D	X	X	X	X	O	O				
	V	O	O	O	O	O	O			N	
	NC	O	O	O	O	O	O			N	
9–25–86	A	X	X	X	X	X	X				Baseline day 2.
	PA	X	X	X	X	O	O				
	D	X	X	X	X	O	O				
	V	⊗	O	O	O	O	O			UR	
	NC	X	O	O	O	O	O			UR	
9–26–86	A	X	X	X	X	X	X				Baseline day 3.
	PA	X	X	X	X	O	O				
	D	X	X	X	X	O	O				
	V	X	O	O	O	O	O				
	NC	⊗	O	O	O	O	O				
9–29–86	A	X	X	X	X	X	X				Baseline day 4.
	PA	X	X	X	X	O	O				
	D	X	X	X	X	O	O				
	V	X	⊗	O	O	O	O				
	NC	X	⊗	O	O	O	O				
9–30–86	A	X	X	X	X	X	X				Baseline day 5.
	PA	X	X	X	X	O	O				Maintained previous assessment gains.
	D	X	X	X	X	O	O				Prescribe instructional activities.
	V	X	X	O	O	O	O				
	NC	X	X	O	O	O	O				

Note: If target level for maintenance is not achieved "O" is recorded; place level and letter of focal points that need retention in the "COMMENTS" section.

Table 9.6
Standardized Assessment Tests Most Frequently Used by Physical Educators Working with Handicapped Students (Ulrich, 1985)

Rank	Name
1	Bruininks-Oseretsky Test of Motor Proficiency (Bruininks, 1978)
2	AAHPER Special Fitness Test for Mildly Mentally Retarded (AAHPER, 1976)
3	Brigance Diagnostic Inventory (Brigance, 1978)
4	Hughes Basic Gross Motor Assessment (Hughes, 1979)
5	Project ACTIVE (Vodola, 1976)
6.5	Purdue Perceptual Motor Survey (Roach & Kephart, 1966)
6.5	AAHPERD Health-Related Fitness Test (AAHPERD, 1980)
8	I CAN (Wessel, 1976)
9.5	OSU-SIGMA (Loovis & Ersing, 1979)
9.5	AAHPERD Youth Fitness Test (AAHPERD, 1976)
11	Denver Developmental Screening Test (Frankenburg & Dodds, 1967)
12	AAHPERD Fitness Test for Moderately Retarded (Johnson & Londeree, 1976)

Assessment Procedures

Each time assessment is planned, teachers should adhere to the following procedures:

1. Establish the specific purpose of the assessment.
2. Decide on the specific variables to be assessed.
3. Establish criteria for the selection of tests or data collection protocols.
4. Review all available tests and protocols that purport to assess the variables you selected.
5. Select the tests or protocols to be used and state rationale for selection (i.e., discuss how each meets every criterion).
6. Select the setting for the assessment.
7. Determine environmental factors to be considered and/or adapted.

Purpose of Assessment

Assessment should be directed toward a specific purpose. Among the purposes that entail different decision making processes are the following:

1. *Screening* is used to determine who needs referrals for further testing. Remember Phase 1 (Child Find) of the PL 94–142 IEP process.

The purpose of this phase is for all regular physical educators to screen all students at the beginning of each school year to determine those who may need special help and/or an alternative placement. Often, screening is informal, done primarily through observation.

2. *Placement.* This purpose is also part of the PL 94–142 IEP process. Large amounts of data are collected about the student to determine whether he or she is eligible for adapted physical education services. If the decision is made to place the student in a separate rather than a regular class, the assessment data must clearly show performance below the norms of chronological age-mates and/or inability to learn in a regular setting.

3. *Diagnosis and program planning.* This type of testing is used after placement to identify specific strengths and weaknesses in present level of motor performance. This information, in turn, is used to develop the physical education IEP that guides instruction or intervention. Specifically, this assessment provides information for selecting objectives and prescribing services.

4. *Student progress.* This type of assessment should be continuous with line graphs kept, showing day-to-day or week-to-week progress in relation to specific objectives. Grades are typically based on this type of assessment.

Specific Variables to Be Tested

Research strongly indicates that there is no such thing as general motor ability, a construct held in the 1930s that seems to linger in spite of its outdatedness. Both motor skill performance and physical fitness are multidimensional. It is, therefore, not entirely sound to try to derive a single motor score or quotient for students, regardless of purpose of assessment. Nevertheless, many school systems make placement decisions on the basis of a total score that falls below age norms.

Table 9.7 depicts the specific factors that widely used motor proficiency tests purport to measure. It is obvious that these factors vary widely and that there is little agreement concerning the components of motor proficiency or performance tests. To be useful in program planning and measuring student gains, factors often need to be broken down still further.

The best approach to selecting variables to be tested is to relate them to objectives on the IEP or in an instructional unit. Variables to be tested should be the same as those that will be or are being taught.

Table 9.7
Factors That Widely Used Motor Proficiency Tests Purport to Measure

Hughes Gross Motor Assessment (1979)	Bruininks-Oseretsky Test of Motor Proficiency (1978)	Cratty Six-Category Gross Motor Test (1969)	Project ACTIVE (1976)
1. Static balance, eyes open 2. Elementary ball handling 3. Static balance, eyes closed 4. Leg strength and balance 5. Object control 6. Aiming 7. Dynamic balance	1. Running speed and agility 2. Balance 3. Bilateral coordination 4. Strength 5. Upper-limb coordination 6. Response speed 7. Visual-motor control 8. Upper-limb speed and dexterity	1. Body perception 2. Gross agility 3. Balance 4. Locomotor agility 5. Throwing 6. Tracking	1. Gross body coordination 2. Balance/postural orientation 3. Eye-hand coordination 4. Eye-hand accuracy 5. Eye-foot accuracy

Criteria For Selection of Tests

The universally accepted criteria are validity, reliability, and objectivity. Other criteria may be added, depending upon the purpose of the test and the students with whom it is to be used. All criteria are important, but PL 94–142 mentions only validity. PL 94–142 states that tests must have been validated for the specific purpose for which they are used.

Validity comes from the Latin word for strong. It means well grounded, sound, founded on truth or fact, capable of being justified, supported, or defended. In regard to a test, validity refers to the extent that a test measures what it is supposed to measure. Think of the last final exam you took. Did it measure what the teacher taught? If so, it was valid. Sometimes there is a discrepancy between what teacher and students think has been taught.

Broadly generalizing, there are three kinds of validity. *Content validity* is demonstrated by showing the page number in source materials where test items and/or answers can be found. Often, panels of experts are used to affirm content validity. The other two kinds, criterion and construct, are statistical. *Criterion validity* is the extent to which a test derives the same score/rank as another instrument believed to measure the same thing. *Construct validity* is the extent to which statistics support two constructs: (a) the test discriminates between two groups known to be high and low in the traits being measured and (b) the test items, when subjected to factor analysis, fall into logical clusters.

Reliability is also a statistical concept, usually reported as a correlation, alpha, or Hoyt coefficient. The highest possible coefficient is 1.00; thus, a high reliability might be .80 or .90, depending upon whether the

test measures a variable in the affective or psychomotor domain. Reliability refers specifically to the test generating the same scores in students day after day assuming no instruction is received between test periods.

Objectivity, sometimes called interrater reliability, refers to several scorers or raters each perceiving a student's performance in the same way and giving him or her the same rating or grade.

The availability of norms for a test by which students can be judged against age-mates is an important criterion for tests that yield numerical scores. Tests of this nature are called normative or norm-based. The opposite type of test (criterion-referenced) does not typically yield numerical scores that can be normed.

Reviewing Available Tests

Every professional should maintain a file of tests with pertinent information on each test about variables measured, age range for which the test is appropriate, validity, reliability, and objectivity. Some textbooks include copies of tests. Among the best of these are

Barrow, H., & McGee, R. (1979). *A practical approach to measurement in physical education.* Philadelphia: Lea & Febiger.
Kirkendall, D., Gruber, J., & Johnson, R. (1980). *Measurement and evaluation for physical educators.* Dubuque, IA: Wm. C. Brown.

Most textbooks, however, do not include actual copies of the tests, although they present essential descriptive information. This is because of copyright laws. In most instances, you must write to commercial companies and pay a small charge for sample copies of tests.

The classic reference book in all disciplines for use in reviewing and evaluating tests is the *Mental Measurements Yearbook,* edited by Oscar Buros. This two-volume book, which costs over $100, cannot be checked out of the library; it can be found in the library reference section. The *Mental Measurements Yearbook* is revised every 5 to 10 years and is now in its ninth edition. In spite of its limited title, the book includes reviews of most physical and motor tests. It also includes a list of research studies based on each test, thus being particularly valuable to graduate students.

Selecting Tests

Many tests are available that measure the same things. It is the teacher's responsibility, therefore, to be able to show that the tests he or she is using have higher validity and/or reliability than other possible choices. Moreover, to satisfy PL 94–142, there must be written documentation that the test was validated specifically for the purpose for which it is being used.

Teachers should not make up their own tests by pulling items they like from several different sources. Doing so changes and violates validity and reliability. Normal students are not protected against this practice, and many teachers do make up their own tests. Handicapped students, however, are protected by PL 94–142. Parents who dispute placement and/or assessment results are afforded a legal process whereby justification of the test is mandated.

Teachers who wish to create new tests may do so through enrolling in graduate studies and making the development of new instruments their thesis or dissertation. Properly done, this task requires thousands of hours.

Determining the Setting

Once the purpose of assessment is clarified and tests selected, the teacher must decide which setting will elicit the best performance.

1. Should the test be administered in an individual or group setting?
2. If group, how large? Does everyone take the test at the same time or do some students watch or assist while others perform?
3. Should the setting be formal or informal? Should the students know they are being assessed?

Setting depends largely on the purpose of the assessment. Screening and student progress, as continuous processes, may occur in conjunction with daily instruction. Because testing in relation to placement is a legal process, it may need to be done in a more formal context. The setting for diagnosis and program planning may need to be individualized since students respond to assessment with different degrees of anxiety, frustration, and coping skills.

For young students an informal setting, whenever possible, seems best. The Yellow Brick Road (Kallstrom, 1975), a screening instrument to assess perceptual motor strengths and weaknesses, illustrates a setting that maximizes abilities and minimizes anxiety. The test setting is based on the movie *Wizard of Oz.* Four stations are established for doing the tricks that Oz characters request. In full costume, the cowardly lion gives instructions at one station, the scarecrow at another, the tin man at another, and munchkins at another. A yellow brick road made of contact paper stepping stones provides the structure for getting from one station to another. Periodically, music is played from the movie. Each child carries a ticket for admission to the stations on the way to finding the Wizard. Reinforcement is provided by punching the ticket when the tricks at a station are complete. When the ticket shows four punches, the child is admitted to the reward or free play area that is supervised by the Wizard, who is also in costume.

This gamelike setting can be varied in as many ways as themes exist. What a wonderful way to be tested! For older students, a carnival or field day often achieves the same purpose.

Environmental Factors In Assessment

Students cannot be assessed within a vacuum. How they perform is influenced by hundreds of environmental factors: weather, room temperature, allergens in the air, whether the test administrator smiles or frowns, gender of the test administrator, presence or absence of spectators, and similar factors (see Figure 9.6). Test administrators are likewise influenced by environmental factors, particularly when the assessment is primarily observational. It is important that teachers place themselves where they can see best, where sun is not in their eyes, and where the angle of observation is most favorable.

In regular physical education assessment, the tradition has been to keep all environmental factors constant (i.e., all students use the same test equipment and follow uniform procedures). For some students this practice inevitably results in failure. Assessment, like learning, should be success oriented.

Figure 9.6 Interactions between student, teacher, and the environment all affect assessment outcomes. Here, Dr. Kathryn Yandell assesses catching ability of 4-year-old.

Table 9.8
Test Condition Variables That Can Be Altered to Attain Success-Oriented Assessment

Striking Implement	Trajectory of Object Being Struck	Size of Object Being Struck	Object Direction in Flight	Weight of Object Being Struck	Color of Object Being Struck	Anticipation Location	Speed Object Is Travelling
Hand ↓	Horizontal ↓	Large ↓	Right ↓	Light ↓	Blue ↓	How far must the performer move before striking the object	Slow ↓
Paddle ↓	Vertical ↓	Small	Left ↓	Heavy	Yellow ↓		Fast
Bat	Arc		Center		White		

Note. From *How to Change the Games Children Play* (p. 80) by G. S. D. Morris, 1980, 2nd ed., Minneapolis: Burgess.

A new trend is emerging in which test equipment is altered in accordance with individual needs of students (Morris, 1976). In a test of striking, throwing, or catching ability, for instance, the characteristics of the striking implement and/or object are varied along a continuum from easy to difficult. Table 9.8 describes how eight characteristics can be varied to make a test easier and, thus, success oriented.

Motor performance over several days or weeks is recorded on a profile sheet that describes specific test conditions. Tables 9.9 and 9.10 offer examples of profile sheets. The date recorded in each box in these profile sheets indicates success in 7 of 10 trials, the criterion established in the instructional objectives and written on the physical education IEP.

Can you think of other ways to make assessment success oriented?

Table 9.9
Example of Striking Profile Sheet for Individual Student

| | | Easy ──────────→ Difficult | | |
| | | Color | | |
Size		C_1	C_2	C_3
Easy	S_1	3/15		
	S_2		3/21	
	S_3		3/22	
Difficult	S_4		3/29	4/22

Key for object size
S_1 = Largest ball (18" diameter)
S_2 = Large ball (14" diameter)
S_3 = Small ball (12" diameter)
S_4 = Smallest ball (8" diameter)

Key for object color
C_1 = Blue
C_2 = Yellow
C_3 = White

Note. Adapted from *How to Change the Games Children Play* (p. 81) by G. S. D. Morris, 1980, 2nd ed., Minneapolis: Burgess.

Table 9.10
Example of Catching Profile Sheet for Individual Student

| | | Easy ──────────→ Difficult | | |
| | | Angle of Trajection | | |
Texture		A_1	A_2	A_3
Easy	T_1	3/15		
	T_2		3/21	
	T_3		3/22	
Difficult	T_4			4/22

Key for texture
T_1 = Balloon
T_2 = Nerf ball
T_3 = Rubber ball
T_4 = Softball

Key for angle of trajection
A_1 = Horizontal plane
A_2 = Vertical plane
A_3 = Ball travels in arc

Note. Adapted from *How to Change the Games Children Play* (p. 91) by G. S. D. Morris, 1980, 2nd ed., Minneapolis: Burgess.

Prescribing

Prescribing is the selection of instructional activities based on the assessed needs of students. Prescription entails writing out the content to be taught (i.e., services to be delivered) and stating how much, when, and where, just as a physician states the drug to be taken, time of day, and amount per dose. Within the IEP context, prescribing is the process followed in writing parts *c* and *d* of the IEP:

(c) A statement of the specific special education and related services to be provided to the child, and the extent to which the child will be able to participate in regular educational programs.

(d) The projected dates for initiation of services and the anticipated duration of the services. (*Federal Register*, August 23, 1977, p. 42490)

The IEP

Table 9.11 offers an example of how the services part of the IEP is written. Note the importance of prescribing number of minutes per week in each type of setting, the maximum pupil/teacher ratio, and the type of teacher. PL 94–142 does not say that physical education must be taught by a physical educator. The only way to ensure this is to write it into the IEP.

Lesson Plans

Whereas the IEP is the broad prescription designed to guide several weeks of instruction, the concept of prescription also pertains to the writing of daily lesson plans. Lesson plans should include three parts: introductory activity, lesson body, and summary. The introductory activity is usually a challenge course, game, or dance in which everyone is involved. This serves as a general warm-up and promotes class cohesiveness. The lesson body is specific to the individual. It is usually structured by stations where equipment is set out for work on specific objectives (i.e., throwing station; striking station; tumbling and jumping station; games station). Students may rotate from station to station or stay in the same location. The summary part of the lesson plan is usually 5 minutes of cool down, relaxation, and evaluation. This is the time when tokens, points, and praise are given and goals are set for further learning. This is the time also for motivational speeches designed to encourage students to engage in exercise, sports, and games after school as part of habit-forming homework.

Table 9.11
Example of Services Part of the Physical Education IEP

A. Placement Variables

		60	90
1.	Placement in minutes per week	Adapted PE	Regular PE
2.	Projected dates	9/15–12/21	9/15–12/21
3.	Teacher/pupil ratio	1/5 or less	1/20 or less
4.	Taught by whom	Physical education teacher with 12 credits in adapted physical education	Teacher with physical education degree

B. Services to be Delivered

1. Instruction in skills of creative movement, ball handling, and swimming following task analysis sequences on pages 5 to 15 of selected curriculum guide or book

2. Instruction in games using these skills following the game progression sequences on pages 60 to 80 of selected curriculum guide or book

3. Clubs for throwing instruction that meet specifications of National Association of Sports for Cerebral Palsy

C. Teaching/Management Style

___	Command	___	1:1 behavior management
___	Traditional	X	Individualized token or point system
X	Guided discovery	___	Group contingency system
___	Motor creativity	___	Traditional

D. Adaptations and/or Special Equipment

1. Availability of sports wheelchair for at least 900 minutes during semester

2. Videotape equipment for student to view his or her movement patterns

3. Clubs for throwing instruction that meet specifications of National Association of Sports for Cerebral Palsy

Each part of the lesson plan should focus on the skill, concept, rule, strategy, or self-concept work specified in the student's objectives. There are not enough minutes of instructional time in a semester to permit free play. When free time is awarded as part of a behavior management approach, the freedom should be to choose from among established activities that reinforce learning of objectives, not freedom to engage in social dance, card games, and other activities that are unrelated to physical education objectives.

For students able to read and write, the physical education prescription can be in the form of task cards. These state what skill is to be practiced, under what conditions (i.e., size, weight, and color of ball; distance from target; type of target), and for how many trials. Task cards are kept at stations, stored in individual mail boxes or in files containing clip boards. They may be made of heavy cardboard with string attached for wearing around the neck. Development of task cards is described in more detail by Mosston (1981).

Teaching/Counseling

Teaching/counseling is the process of facilitating learning while building and/or preserving ego strength. It requires skills in listening and communicating as well as instruction and management. Teaching and counseling are inseparable processes when counseling is conceptualized as a helping relationship.

While counseling is a profession that demands specific course work and certification as preparation, all good teachers use counseling techniques (i.e., you do not have to be a counselor to do counseling). In fact, school counselors typically have no training in fitness, motor, and leisure counseling; these are considered the domain of physical education and recreation. To fully help students in these areas, physical educators ideally take course work in counseling.

Theories

Students learn for different reasons. *Behavior management theory* posits that students learn because they clearly understand what the teacher wants and are consistently rewarded for correct responses. *Humanistic theory* posits that students learn because they are responding to a teacher who relates to them with an attitude of acceptance, empathy, concreteness, and personal genuineness. The emphasis is not on telling students what to do, but on guiding them toward making a personal decision to become healthy, fit, happy individuals. Mentally retarded and emotionally disturbed students often learn better by behavior management, but students with intact intelligence tend to

Table 9.12
Illustrative Chart for Tabulating Teacher and Student Behaviors in a Small Group Instructional Setting

Teacher's Name _L. Barnes_   Setting _Gymnasium_
Date _2/14_   Time _9 – 9:30 AM Class_

Place a tally mark for every 3 seconds of the same behavior and for every change of behavior regardless of its duration.

Teacher Behaviors	Student Behaviors	Ann	Joe	Amy
Directions /	Rote response	//	/	//
Information giving LHT /	Analytic response	/		
Questions //	Questions		/	//
Acceptance of students' ideas ///	Acceptance of others' ideas	/	/	
Praise, encouragement LHT LHT /	Praise, encouragement	//	/	
Criticism /	Criticism	/		
Anger, confusion	Silence, confusion			///
Other	Initiating new idea	///	/	
	Other			

Signature of Recorder _L. Gilstrap_
Number of Minutes Behaviors Were Recorded _5_

learn better through humanistic theory. Remember, the overall goal of physical education is not to develop isolated skills and fitness, but also attitudes and habits of vigorous activity that last a lifetime.

Humanistic theory is rooted in counseling skills and the belief that counseling and teaching are inseparable. Specific counseling techniques are described in the chapter on fitness because fitness is the area where most teachers are weakest in the skills of active listening, acceptance, empathy, and cooperative goals setting.

Student-Teacher Interactions

The ways in which teachers interact verbally and non-verbally with students can be classified as helping or nonhelping in terms of facilitating learning and personal commitment to exercise. Table 9.12 presents an illustrative form for recording and studying interactions. In the humanistic gymnasium, students are taught to praise, encourage, and accept each other. This is achieved largely by modeling the behaviors of the teacher.

Other Variables

The most important variable in successful teaching of clumsy and/or handicapped students is class size. Such students need more personalization and individualization than normal peers; this is why they are assigned to adapted physical education. Personalization and individualization, if positive and success oriented, are major contributors to self-concept.

Also important is academic learning time (ALT), also called on-task time. Research shows that individualizing instruction leads to increased ALT (Aufderheide, 1983). The more practice trials a student completes, assuming he or she is paying attention and trying his or her best, the more likely the student is to learn. Increased competence leads to improved self-concept when the competence is acquired in an environment of praise and encouragement rather than criticism and correction.

Principles of Motor Learning/Teaching

Good teaching involves application of the principles of motor learning/teaching. Illustrative of these are the following principles:

1. **Individual differences.** Learners differ in rate of learning, amount of learning, method of learning, and response to external motivation and/or stress. Handicapped children demonstrate more variability in these factors than do normal children; thus, *individualization* of the teaching-learning process is more important for them than for most of their normal peers.

2. **Developmental stages.** Children's thought, play, and movement patterns are bound by the characteristics of the stage in which they are currently operating. Progression to the next

stage is the result of both maturation and learning. Physical educators need, therefore, to plan instruction in accordance with Piagetian (and other) stages of development. See Chapter 6.

3. **Readiness.** Learning proceeds in accordance with neurological maturation. Critical learning periods exist.

4. **Progression.** Motor learning proceeds from simple to complex, large to small, and gross to fine. Learners should be introduced to progressively more difficult tasks. The teacher's ability to task-analyze activities as well as motor skills largely determines the success of handicapped and clumsy children.

5. **Effect.** Learning, for the most part, occurs best when the effect is pleasurable. Success leads to success. Not at all pleasurable are such physical education practices as elimination games, choosing up sides (for the last to be chosen), and competition (for children who generally lose). Reward is a stronger learning reinforcement than punishment.

6. **Maximum involvement.** Learning occurs best when the child is actively and totally involved. Games and movement education activities should be selected on the criterion that every child is moving all (or most) of the time.

7. **Specificity/transfer.** Motor skills should be practiced in gamelike settings under the same space/time factors in which they will be used. For example, softball throws and dashes are more effective when practiced in a diamond formation than in parallel lines (back and forth throwing/running patterns). *Splinter skills* (the ability to perform a motor task in one setting but not in others) often occurs in MR and LD children; this can be avoided by practicing motor skills in a variety of settings with varied equipment; each practice is *specific* and will transfer only to the extent that the next setting is similar.

8. **Attention to relevant cues.** Learning occurs more effectively when the student can attend to relevant cues. This involves not only length of attention span, but also knowledge/ understanding of cues. Many cues are *sensory* rather than verbal, and very young children and MR children seem to benefit more from sensory cues (demonstrations or manual assistance through a movement) than verbal cues. Specific, precise, and near cues are easier to understand

than general, vague, and distant ones. Ideally, presentation of new skills/activities should offer simultaneous input to several senses (concurrent demonstration and verbal instructions).

9. **Goal direction.** Learning occurs best when the student knows and understands the goal or objective. This is related to attending, since knowledge of specific goals allows students to attend to them. Precisely written, measurable behavioral objectives implement this principle in that they clarify learning goals for both student and teacher.

10. **Significant others.** Learning occurs in a social context and is influenced by the presence/ absence of spectators, peers, and teacher; by the sex, age, and personalities of these persons; and by the extent they are perceived to care. Considerable evidence exists that motor skills and activities are better learned at some ages when taught by a peer than by an adult. Evidence also substantiates the importance of the values, leisure patterns, and lifestyle of the home and family setting to what is learned in school.

11. **Motivation.** Learning occurs best when motivation is present. Considerable evidence exists, however, that response to motivation is highly individualized. The physical educator must determine the *conditions* under which each student learns best, the *trial* (when repeated trials are given) during which the child is likely to perform best, and the *reinforcers* that are most effective. Motivation is highly related to the *principle of effect* (i.e., students are more likely to have high motivation when they are succeeding than otherwise).

12. **Knowledge of results (KR).** Learning is more effective when performance is reinforced with *immediate* and *specific* feedback. KR is a type of motivation (see Figure 9.7).

13. **Reward.** Reward is a form of reinforcement and motivation that facilitates learning. In initial skill learning, particularly with MR or young children, *continuous* reinforcement may be necessary. In later stages of learning, *random* reinforcement seems more effective. Rewards may be external (praise, hugs, candy, tokens, points, ribbons) or internal (simply feeling good about oneself).

14. **Exercise/practice.** *Practice,* done in "good form," with attention to relevant cues, and a high level of motivation lead to improvement. Practice without the presence of these conditions

Figure 9.7 Seeing oneself in the mirror reinforces success.

seldom facilitates learning or improves motor performance. "Good form" refers to the form best for the individual and encompasses specificity; the practice must be specific to the speed, distance, force, and rhythm for which the end product is to be used. Some evidence exists that overlearning is the preferred approach to facilitate motor learning in retarded persons.

15. **Drill vs. problem solving.** *Drill* appears to be a faster, more efficient way of learning motor skills that are performed in stable, predictable environments; some examples are individual tasks (not dependent upon another) like volleyball and softball serves, pitching, and bowling. *Problem solving* (movement education tasks) appears better for learning motor skills that are used in changing, unpredictable environments like team games. *Drill* is best with severely handicapped MR and LD children whose cognitive disorders limit problem solving abilities.

16. **Whole vs. part learning.** Simple motor tasks and skills are believed to be learned best by the *whole method*—that is, a demonstration of the skill and the challenge, "Can you do this?" Complex skills are believed to be learned best by the *part method.* In using the part method, it seems best to apply a whole-part-whole approach so that students can conceptualize where the mastery of parts is leading them. In mastery of complex skills, there is some evidence that cognitive mode (holistic or sequential) is specific to the individual. Learning efficiency is increased when method is individualized according to cognitive mode.

17. **Mass vs. distributed practice.** In initial motor learning stages, *distributed* (intermittent) practice is better than massed (continuous), *short* practices are better than long, and *frequent* practices are better than infrequent. With most handicapped children, this implies that several brief physical education periods each day may improve coordination. To implement this concept, classroom teachers can develop motor learning centers within their rooms where individuals can practice at designated times. Such learning centers might diminish hyperactive behavior and reduce classroom stress as well as improve motor performance.

18. **Order of learning.** Initial learnings are retained best, final learning next best, and middle learning worst. This appears related to attention theory in that the first parts of a lesson are generally attended to better than later ones. Since physical educators have traditionally placed review and warm-up first and new skill presentation and practice second, this principle warrants experimentation. Serial order is particularly important with handicapped children like the spastic cerebral palsied, who may fatigue earlier than their normal peers. Time of day, as related to blood sugar levels, affects learning of some children.

19. **Rate of learning.** Beginners make more progress in mastering a motor skill than intermediate or advanced learners. After initial learning, improvement levels off and plateaus may occur. Scores on many trials should be plotted on graphs to show learning curve and document rate and amount of learning during an instructional unit. Much patience and encouragement are needed during plateaus.

20. **Retention.** The more meaningful the skill (or material), the longer it will be retained (remembered). In general, gross motor skills are

retained longer than fine motor skills and other types of material. Overlearning of a skill seems to improve retention. Often, the activities that occur immediately before and after a lesson influence retention as well as learning itself.

Research in motor learning applied to clumsy and/or handicapped persons is just beginning to appear. Scan the *Adapted Physical Activity Quarterly* and other journals for articles related to each of these principles. In which areas of motor learning is research most needed? What can you do?

Evaluation

Evaluation is the continuous process of determining student gain and program effectiveness. Although evaluation should be continuous, the greatest emphasis is usually the last 2 or 3 weeks of an instructional period. This is because of the amount of time needed to write student progress reports and fill in various forms.

Student progress reports should include a description of physical education performance at the beginning of the period, the specific objectives set, charts and graphs showing progress all semester long, and checks showing which objectives are completed and can be discarded. The last part of the student progress report is often the opening section of a new IEP (i.e., statement of present level of motor performance). Thus, the curriculum model perpetuates itself with evaluation leading to modification of the existing program and new planning in light of changes that have occurred.

In regard to the written IEP, evaluation is part *e:*

(e) appropriate objective criteria and evaluation procedures and schedules for determining, on at least an annual basis, whether the short-term instructional objectives are being achieved. (*Federal Register,* August 23, 1977, p. 42490)

When objectives are written in behavioral terms, criteria for evaluation are built in.

Learning Activities

1. Select one of the federally funded curriculum models like I CAN, ACTIVE, or PEOPEL and prepare a 30-minute oral presentation on this model for your class.

2. In a practicum or student teaching setting, implement one of the federally funded curriculum models and write a report on this experience.

3. Given assessment data, age, gender, and handicapping condition, practice writing IEPs.

4. Consider the nine long-range goals of adapted physical education stated in this chapter and write behavioral objectives for each goal. State the test or evaluation approach to be used in determining pupil progress in relation to each goal.

5. Select a test from the list of standardized tests most frequently used by physical educators working with handicapped students, administer it to 10 students, and write your findings in the form of a report.

6. Develop a file of tests with information about validity, reliability, and objectivity on each test. Be sure to include tests in each educational domain: psychomotor, affective, and cognitive.

References

Aufderheide, S. (1983). ALT-PE in mainstreamed physical education classes. *Journal of Teaching in Physical Education, 1,* 22–26.

Bruininks, R. H. (1978). *Bruininks-Oseretsky test of motor proficiency: Examiner's manual.* Circle Pines, MN: American Guidance Service.

Buros, O. (1978). *The eighth mental measurements yearbook.* Lincoln, NE: University of Nebraska Press.

Cratty, B. (1969). *Motor activity and the education of retardates.* Philadelphia: Lea & Febiger.

Evans, J. (1980). *They have to be carefully taught.* Reston, VA: American Alliance for Health, Physical Education, Recreation, and Dance.

Federal Register, August 23, 1977.

Fleishman, E. (1964). *The structure and measurement of physical fitness.* Englewood Cliffs, NJ: Prentice-Hall.

Folio, M. R., & Fewell, R. (1983). *Peabody developmental motor scales and activity cards.* Allen, TX: DLM Teaching Resources.

Hughes, J. (1979). *Hughes basic gross motor assessment manual.* Yonkers, NY: G. E. Miller, Inc.

Kallstrom, C. (1975). *Yellow brick road manual.* Garland, TX: R & K, Inc. Address for ordering is R & K, Inc., PO Box 461262, Garland, TX 75046.

Morris, G. S. D. (1980). *How to change the games children play* (2nd ed.). Minneapolis, MN: Burgess.

Mosston, M. (1981). *Teaching physical education.* Columbus, OH: Charles E. Merrill.

Sherrill, C. (1986). *Adapted physical education leadership training.* Champaign, IL: Human Kinetics Publishers.

Ulrich, D. (1984). Peabody developmental motor scales and activity cards: A review. *Adapted Physical Activity Quarterly, 1* (2), 173–178.

Ulrich, D. (1985). *Standardized motor assessment tests used by adapted physical education teachers.* Unpublished manuscript. Available from author at Physical Education Department, Indiana University, Bloomington, IN 47401.

Ulrich, D. (1985). *Test of gross motor development.* Austin: Pro-Ed Publishers.

Vodola, T. (1973). *Individualized physical education program for the handicapped child.* Englewood Cliffs, NJ: Prentice-Hall.

Vodola, T. (1976). *Project ACTIVE maxi-model: Nine training manuals.* Oakhurst, NJ: Project ACTIVE.

Wessel, J. (1976). *I CAN—Primary skills.* Northbrook, IL: H. Hubbard.

Wessel, J. (1979). *I CAN—Sport, leisure, and recreation skills.* Northbrook, IL: H. Hubbard.

Wessel, J., & Kelly, L. (1985). *Individualizing instruction: Quality programs for all students.* Philadelphia: Lea & Febiger.

Winnick, J., & Short, F. (1985). *Physical fitness testing of the disabled: Project UNIQUE.* Champaign, IL: Human Kinetics Publishers.

Bibliography

American Alliance for Health, Physical Education, Recreation, and Dance. (1976). *Testing for impaired, disabled, and handicapped individuals.* Washington, DC: Author.

Aspy, D. (1972). *Toward a technology for humanizing education.* Champaign, IL: Research Press.

Aspy, D., & Roebuck, F. (1977). *Kids don't learn from people that they don't like.* Amherst, MA: Human Resource Development Press.

Aufderheide, S., Knowles, C., & McKenzie, T. (1981). Individualized teaching strategies and learning time: Implications for mainstreaming. *The Physical Educator, 38* (1), 20–26.

Cheffers, J., Amidon, E., & Rogers, K. (1974). *Interaction analysis: An application to nonverbal activity.* St. Paul: Association for Productive Teaching.

Davis, W. (1984). Motor ability assessment of populations with handicapping conditions: Challenging basic assumptions. *Adapted Physical Activity Quarterly, 1* (2), 125–140.

Ersing, W. (1986). Program models in adapted physical education: Implications for teacher training. In C. Sherrill (Ed.), *Adapted physical education leadership training.* Champaign, IL: Human Kinetics Publishers.

Flanders, N. (1960). *Interaction analysis in the classroom: A manual for observers.* Minneapolis: University of Minnesota.

Hoover, J., & Wade, M. (1985). Motor learning theory and mentally retarded individuals: A historical review. *Adapted Physical Activity Quarterly, 2* (3), 228–252.

Locke, L., & Lambdin, D. (1976). Personalized learning in physical education. *Journal of Physical Education and Recreation, 47,* 32–35.

Lockhart, A. (1980). Practices and principles governing motor learning of children. In C. Corbin (Ed.), *Textbook of Motor Learning* (2nd ed.), (pp. 254–258). Dubuque, IA: Wm. C. Brown.

Morris, G. S. D. (1980a). *How to change the games children play* (2nd ed.). Minneapolis: Burgess.

Morris, G. S. D. (1980b). *Elementary physical education: Toward inclusion.* Salt Lake City, UT: Brighton Publishing Co.

Mosston, M. (1981). *Teaching physical education* (2nd ed.). Columbus, OH: Charles E. Merrill.

Presbie, R., & Brown, P. (1977). *Physical education: The behavior modification approach.* Washington, DC: National Education Association.

Pyfer, J. (1982). Criteria for placement in physical education experiences. *Exceptional Education Quarterly, 3* (1), 10–16.

Rich, S. (1981). *Teaching behaviors in physical education classes for the handicapped.* Unpublished doctoral dissertation, Texas Woman's University, Denton.

Salvia, J., & Ysseldyke, J. (1978). *Assessment in special and remedial education.* Boston: Houghton Mifflin.

Singer, R. (1980). *Motor learning and motor performance* (3rd ed.). New York: Macmillan.

Werder, J., & Kalakian, L. (1985). *Assessment in adapted physical education.* Minneapolis: Burgess.

Wessel, J., & Kelly, L. (1985). *Individualizing instruction: Quality programs for all students.* Philadelphia: Lea & Febiger.

10 Motor Performance, Self-Concept, and Leisure Functioning

Figure 10.1 Success should be achieved in batting a stationary ball before games with moving balls are introduced. Note how batter is applying the *principle of leverage* by choking up on the bat, thereby making it shorter and easier to control.

Chapter Objectives

After you have studied this chapter, you should be able to

1. Use the Milani-Comparetti system to assess nine motor milestones, five primitive reflexes, and 13 postural reactions.

2. Describe the following reflexes, their normal time span and contributions, and the problems that occur when they persist: (a) hand grasp reflex, (b) asymmetrical tonic neck reflex, (c) Moro reflex, (d) symmetrical tonic neck reflex, and (e) foot grasp reflex.

3. Differentiate between righting reactions, parachute reactions, and tilting reactions and discuss the role of each.

4. Discuss pedagogy in relation to reflexes and reactions.

5. Describe the following tests: (a) Brigance Diagnostic Inventory of Early Development, (b) Project ACTIVE Motor Development Test, (c) I CAN Fundamental Skill Test, (d) Test of Gross Motor Development, (e) OSU Scale of Intra Gross Motor Assessment, (f) Denver Developmental Screening Test, (g) Peabody Developmental Motor Scales and (h) Movement Patterns Achievement Profile.

6. Differentiate between developmental, immature, and mature movement patterns and state 10 general characteristics of immature movement patterns.

7. List in correct developmental sequence locomotor movement patterns, the approximate age range when each pattern should be mastered, and teaching suggestions for each.

8. List in correct developmental sequence ball handling patterns, the approximate age range when each pattern should be mastered, and teaching suggestions for each.

9. Use the pictorial assessment instruments to guide observation and assessment of specific characteristics within each developmental stage of movement patterns.

10. Discuss self-concept in relation to pedagogy and identify instruments for assessment of self-concept.

11. Discuss attitude toward physical education, its relationship to self-concept and motor skill, and instruments for assessing attitude.

12. Discuss leisure functioning in relation to pedagogy and identify instruments for assessment of leisure functioning.

Motor performance, self-concept, and leisure functioning are intricately linked in children in our society. Assessment and instruction in physical education should, therefore, focus on all three areas. Pedagogy for teaching motor skills to students with low self-concept is distinctly different from that for students with high self-concept (see Figure 10.1). Whereas persons with intact egos can accept and benefit from correction of motor errors, low self-concept students tend to internalize criticism as further proof of their lack of worth. More personalization, individualization, and praise are needed in adapted than in regular physical education.

This chapter describes instruments for the assessment of primitive reflexes, postural reactions, motor skills and patterns, self-concept, attitudes, and leisure functioning. Many of the assessment approaches are integrated with teaching. The pictorial instruments, for instance, depict the developmental stages through which children progress and list movement components on which to work. A basic assumption of this chapter is that its readers have had a course in elementary school physical education pedagogy and are familiar with many games and movement education activities through which motor skills can be refined. For clumsy students, games, creative drama/dance, and movement education are better approaches than drills to teaching motor skills. Remember that many clumsy and/or handicapped students will never exhibit good form in the traditional sense or look graceful in movement. It is important, therefore, that emphasis be placed on the fun, fitness, and social values of play rather than how a movement looks.

Clumsiness

Clumsiness is failure to show good coordination, balance, and/or agility. Problems in these areas generally stem from neurological deficits that affect integration of reflexes, presence of postural reactions, and/or speed, timing, and sequencing. Such problems are complicated by environmental factors, self-concept, and emotional overlay. Assessment in adapted physical education, therefore, begins with reflexes, reactions, and early motor milestones.

Reflexes

Primitive reflexes are involuntary changes in muscle tone in response to certain stimuli. Whereas in the past, reflexes were associated primarily with infants, research now shows that clumsy persons of all ages occasionally exhibit abnormal reflexes. Adapted physical educators need to understand reflexes for many reasons. The most common orthopedic impairment in the public schools is cerebral palsy; this condition is characterized by retention of primitive reflexes into late childhood and sometimes throughout life. Many learning disabled, emotionally disturbed, and mentally retarded students also exhibit reflex problems.

The best approach to learning about reflexes is probably the study of normal infants. Here, one can see fully developed reflexes at their best and worst, whereas in older students, often only vestiges of such reflexes remain. While these vestiges are sufficient to make movement clumsy, they are often hard to identify and assess. Another approach is to focus on severely handicapped cerebral palsied persons who are dominated by reflex behavior. This can be done by contacting the local office of United Cerebral Palsy Associations, Incorporated, and getting involved in their sports and recreation programs. Books by Bobath (1980) and Fiorentino (1981) offer many illustrations of both normal and cerebral palsied children.

Approximately 30 primitive reflexes dominate the motor behavior of infants. Some assessment approaches, like that of Fiorentino (1973), include all of these reflexes. In extensive observation of clumsy students, this author has found that only about 10 primitive reflexes affect physical education performance. Only these reflexes are covered in this text. While several reflex tests exist, this book describes only one: the Milani-Comparetti System. This one was selected because it is widely used by physical and occupational therapists, is easy to administer, and encompasses essential motor milestones and postural reactions as well as reflexes. The Milani-Comparetti assessment approach covers only five reflexes. The other five reflexes important in physical education performances are described in the chapter on cerebral palsy.

Milani-Comparetti Assessment System

The Milani-Comparetti method of assessing neurologic abnormality was developed in Italy and is used worldwide. It was first reported in medical journals in the United States in the 1960s (Milani-Comparetti & Gidoni, 1967a, b) where it was embraced primarily by followers of the Bobaths, the husband-wife (physician-physical therapist) team responsible for most contemporary treatment and education approaches with cerebral palsied infants and children.

Figure 10.2 shows that the scoring chart is divided into two sections: Spontaneous Behavior and Evoked Responses. Spontaneous behavior encompasses motor milestones in nine areas: four head postures, three body postures, and two active movement sequences. The evoked responses section includes five primitive reflexes and 13 postural reactions (righting, parachute, and equilibrium). Months listed horizontally across the top of the chart show the ages at which responses are normal.

The *content validity* of the approach is based upon the works of such well respected physicians as Bobath (1962), Illingsworth (1960), Paine (1964), and Andre-Thomas and Dargassies (1960). *Construct validity* by the known groups method (Ellison, Browning, Larson, & Denny, 1983) rests on the ability of the Milani-Comparetti (MC) approach to statistically discriminate between normal, transiently abnormal, and abnormal infants ages 6 to 21 months. Interrater reliability has not yet been studied, perhaps because an objective numerical scoring system was not published until 1983.

The numerical scoring system was tested on 999 infants in a program conducted by the Medical College of Wisconsin (Ellison, Browning, Larson, & Denny, 1983). A score of 1 to 5 points is assigned each item on the MC. A score of 5 indicates normal function; 3 to 4 indicates mild to moderate abnormal function; and 1 to 2 indicates severe abnormality. Mean scores for each item for six age ranges are available for infants in six different medical classifications.

For physical educators first learning to use the MC system, it is sufficient simply to use letters to note absence (A) or presence (P) of motor milestones, reflexes, and reactions. It is important also to note appearance of muscle tone: hypotonic, normal, hypertonic, or fluctuating.

Figure 10.2 The Milani-Comparetti Developmental Chart facilitates assessment of achievement of motor milestones (spontaneous behavior) as well as the most important of the many reflexes and reactions.

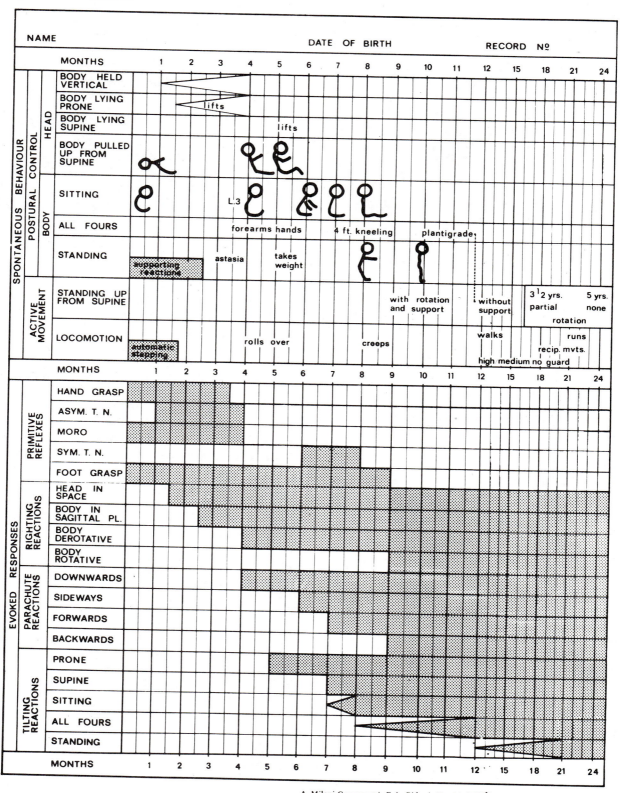

A. Milani Comparetti, E.A. Gidoni: Dev.Med.Child. Neurol. Vol. 9 No 5 Oct 67

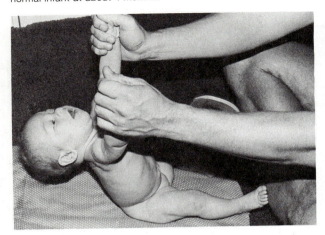 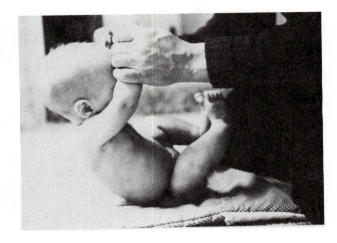

Motor Milestones on Milani-Comparetti Chart

Head Control

Head control is assessed in three positions. As early as 1 month of age, normal infants can hold the head upright when they are held vertically in the air or against someone's chest. The < symbol on the MC Chart denotes growing control from a few seconds at 1 month of age to several minutes at 4 months of age. In contrast, many cerebral palsied adults have difficulty with this task.

In *body lying prone,* infants exhibit three distinct developmental stages:

1.5 mo   Momentary head raise
3.0 mo   Holds head up 45° to 90° with chest up
4.0 mo   Holds head up and props on extended arms

In *body lying supine,* the normal infant lifts the head at about 5 months (note location of word *lifts* on MC Chart). Between 5 and 7 months, this head lifting is observed in conjunction with playing with feet.

In *body pulled up from supine,* the stick figures on the MC indicate the amount of head lag normal at each age when the body is pulled upward by the arms. Figure 10.3 depicts the first two test positions with a normal infant.

Body Control

Body control is assessed in three positions. Stick figures on the MC indicate normal performances.

Five developmental stages are depicted for sitting. These are based on amount of spinal curve and ability to fully extend legs. Independent sitting is achieved between 6 and 8 months. The L3 against the second figure on the MC Chart indicates that the progressive head-to-foot uncurving of the vertebral column has extended downward to the level of the third lumbar segment by the age of 4 months.

All four refers to three developmental stages. *Forearms/hands* denotes a propping position, with head and chest up and weight taken on the forearms. This propping behavior begins between ages 3.5 and 6 months. The *creeping position* is listed as 4-feet kneeling; it begins between 7 and 9 months. *Plantigrade* (Figure 10.4) refers to a bear walk position; infants can assume it between 10 and 12 months of age.

Standing also develops through several stages, the first of which is controlled subcortically by supporting reactions (really a reflex). When the infant loses this reflex, *astasia* (see Figure 10.5) occurs. This is a condition in which weight is taken momentarily, after which the body collapses. When infants take weight on feet at age 5 months, this is finally voluntary movement under cortical control. Independent standing does not occur until about 10 months.

Active Movement

Standing up from a supine lying position is evaluated in terms of amount of trunk rotation and arm assistance. Note four stages on the MC Chart extending from 9 months of age until 5 years. The mature rise to stand requires no trunk rotation and no arm assistance. So important is the rise to stand pattern that it is included on many standardized tests of motor performance and fitness like Project UNIQUE (Winnick & Short, 1985) and Cratty's Six-Factor Gross Motor Test (Cratty, 1969). These tests measure number of seconds

Figure 10.4 Plantigrade is a position in which the weight of body is taken on the hands and feet but there is not yet enough neurological maturation for reciprocal arm or leg creeping movements. Often, the infant rocks forward and backward in plantigrade and appears to be playing or doing tricks.

Figure 10.5 Earliest standing progression. *Left,* supporting reaction elicited by top of foot rubbing against table. *Right,* same infant in *astasia* as supporting reaction weakens and is lost. Any weight bearing that occurs before about 5 months of age is reflex in nature (i.e., under subcortical control). Many severely handicapped children remain frozen in the astasia stage throughout life.

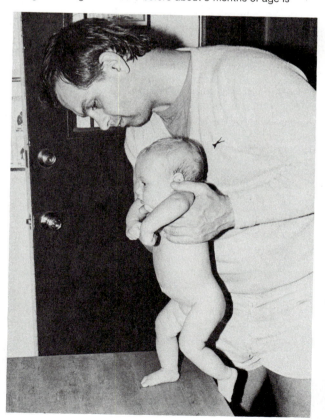

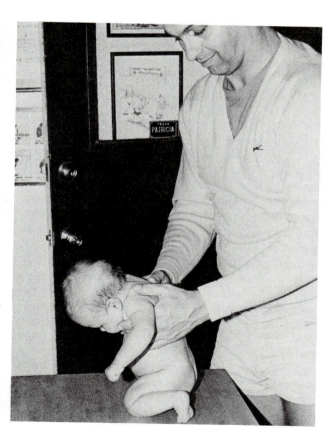

required to rise from a supine position (arms at sides, palm down) rather than the quality of the movement pattern. The test item is often called *scramble* because the task is to scramble to one's feet as fast as possible.

Locomotion is evaluated in five stages, each clearly marked on the MC Chart. *Rolling over,* the first locomotor task that infants master, begins between 4 and 6 months. *Creeping* (hands and knees forward motion) begins between 8 and 9 months. *Walking* begins at 12 months, with evaluation covering the position of the arms (high, medium, and no guard). *Running* and reciprocal arm movements begin at about 21 months.

Reflexes on the Milani-Comparetti Chart

All reflexes are good and serve a definite purpose during the months that their presence is normal. If, however, a reflex persists beyond its normal time span, it interferes with and/or delays the appearance of motor milestones. The following descriptions of reflexes, therefore, include contributions of reflexes as well as problems caused by abnormal persistence. The shaded areas on the MC Chart indicate the months during which each reflex is normal.

Hand Grasp Reflex

Description
Flexion of fingers in response to object being drawn across palm or hypertension of wrist.

Normal Time Span and Contributions
Normal during first 4 months. Tactile stimulation by object in hand is the beginning of eye-hand coordination and visual body awareness.

Persistence
Interferes with development of voluntary grasp; compromises tactile sensory input.

Asymmetrical Tonic Neck Reflex (ATNR)

Description
On guard fencing position activated by rotation or lateral flexion (tilt) of head that stimulates stretch receptors in neck muscles. A brain stem reflex causing increased extensor tonus of limbs on chin side and increased flexor tonus in limbs on head side (Figure 10.6).

Normal Time Span and Contributions
Normal from 4 to 6 months. Helps break up flexor and extensor pattern dominance so that each side of body can function separately.

Figure 10.6 Abnormal asymmetrical tonic neck reflex is often evidenced in trampoline jumps of children with mild brain damage. This reflex is normal from birth to 6 months.

Persistence
1. Prevents learning to roll from supine to prone and vice versa since extended arm gets in the way.
2. Interferes with maintaining head in midline independent of limb movement, which, in turn, impairs normal hand-eye coordination development. Associated problem is loss of visual fixation (inability to keep eyes on ball when limbs are moving).
3. Prevents independent flexing of limb to bring it toward midline as in playing with object or feeding self. Each time shoulder or elbow flexes, head turns to opposite side and vice versa. Helps explain why persons bend their elbow in tennis forehand drive; as head rotates to left to see ball, right elbow flexes.
4. Causes one arm to bend or collapse in the beginning forward roll position if head tilts or rotates even slightly.
5. In sports positions that involve a rotated head, such as softball batting or tennis stance, prevents or compromises the bat or racquet crossing midline and, thus, properly following through.
6. In severe conditions, may contribute to scoliosis, subluxed or dislocated hips, or wind-swept lying position.

Failure of this reflex to become integrated explains much of the clumsiness physical educators observe, especially in relation to ball activities. Many of the verbal cues that physical educators give (Keep your eye on the ball; don't bend your elbow; remember to follow through) are not commands that can be consciously implemented. Thus, bright, but clumsy, students often think and sometimes respond, "I know what I'm doing wrong, but my body won't do what my mind tells it."

Moro Reflex

Description

The body stiffens and arms and legs involuntarily spread and close in response to loud noise, unstable lying/sitting surface, or falling movement (Figures 10.7 and 10.8).

Figure 10.7 The Moro reflex, generally elicited by a sensation of losing balance, must be inhibited before the child shows unilateral control of the arms, as in the *propping reactions* which prevent falls while learning to sit. Retention of this reflex into childhood interferes with the many automatic, compensatory arm movements used daily to maintain equilibrium during locomotor activities.

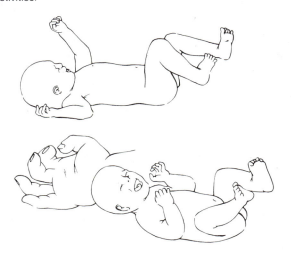

Figure 10.8 The Moro reflex elicited by this fearsome visual stimulus and loud noise was accompanied by a quick sucking in of breath that makes the chest appear almost deformed.

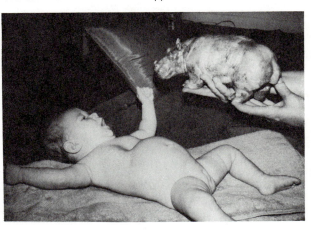

Normal Time Span and Role

Normal during first 4 months. Contributes to development of extensor and abductor strength of upper extremities, including fingers; serves as precursor to propping and parachute reactions.

Persistence

Interferes with learning to sit and using the arms for balance.

Symmetrical Tonic Neck Reflex (STNR)

Description

Flexion and extension movements of the head influence muscle tone distribution in relation to upper and lower body. Head flexion increases flexor tone of upper body and extensor tone of lower body; head extension does the opposite (Figures 10.9 and 10.10). Predominant upper body muscle tone is always that of the head and neck.

Normal Time Span and Contribution

Normal from 4 to 6 months. Contributes to achievement of such important motor milestones as lifting and supporting upper body on arms and rising to four-point creeping position.

Persistence

1. Prevents reciprocal flexion and extension movement of legs needed in creeping (i.e., with head up, child is frozen in bunny hop position).
2. Compromises ability to do certain stunts, exercises, and animal walks with head up. Makes holding head up difficult in regulation push-up position, in prone scooter board activities in which legs are extended, and in wheelbarrow races.

Figure 10.9 Tonic neck reflexes: (*A*) flexion symmetrical tonic neck reflex and (*B*) extension symmetric tonic reflex.

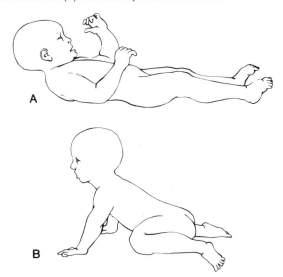

3. Compromises ability to do exercises, stunts, gymnastics, and synchronized swimming that require head held down in tucked position with knees simultaneously tucked to chest. Explains why ''tuck position'' is difficult to maintain as head changes position from flexion to extension (i.e., why persons come out of their tuck too soon).

4. Compromises sitting position. Head down helps activate extensor thrust in lower extremities; increases high guard position of arms. Head up contributes to good sitting posture, but increases difficulty of hand and arm activities that entail flexion like lifting arm for overarm throw.

5. Looking down at ground or balance beam compromises distribution of muscle tone; helps to explain gait of toddler with arms in high guard and abnormally stiff leg action and/or tendency to toe walk.

Figure 10.10 Symmetrical tonic neck reflex in Down's syndrome infant. When head is up, weight is taken on arms (extended elbows) and legs seem frozen in flexion. Baby cannot learn to creep until this reflex is lost.

Foot Grasp Reflex

Description
Flexion of toes (clawing motion) in response to deep pressure stimulation of soles of feet, as in standing.

Normal Time Span and Contributions
Normal during first 9 months.

Persistence
Interferes with balance in walking and standing. Often seen in conjunction with positive supporting reflex (increased extensor tone that results in toe walking).

Reactions on the Milani-Comparetti Chart

Reactions are generalized postural responses that occur at the midbrain and cortical levels of the CNS. Reactions take the place of reflexes in righting or protecting the body against the pull of gravity. As indicated on the MC Chart, reactions all persist beyond 24 months of age. In fact, most authorities agree that reactions remain throughout life, playing an important role in vestibular function. In delayed motor development such as that characterizing mentally retarded children, the problem seems to be primarily delay in appearance of postural reactions rather than abnormal retention of reflexes (Molnar, 1978).

Righting Reactions

The righting reactions normally appear between 1.5 and 9 months of age. Elicited only from a lying position, they enable the infant to hold the head and later the entire body upright.

Head in Space Righting: The ability to lift the head from a prone lying position (Figure 10.11). This reaction appears at about 1.5 months of age. This should not be confused with voluntary head lifting, which is under cortical rather than midbrain control. Voluntary head lifting in order to see or reach for something does not occur until 3 or 4 months of age.

Body in Sagittal Plane Righting: Often called the *Landau reaction* (Figure 10.12). It is the ability to lift the head and arch the back when held in a prone position in space. Any increase in extensor tone of the spine and hips in response to upward head movement shows this reaction at work. It first appears at about age 2.5 months.

Figure 10.11 Down's syndrome babies are *hypotonic* and exhibit *delayed motor development*. Here, a 7-month-old is showing *head in space righting reaction*, which normally appears at about 1.5 months of age. The infant can hold this lift only a few seconds.

Figure 10.12 Body in sagittal plane righting (also called Landau reaction to test of ventral suspension). *Left,* response of normal infant at 1 month of age. Severely handicapped children with hypotonia show this same response at all ages. *Right,* Landau reaction in normal infant at 4–6 months.

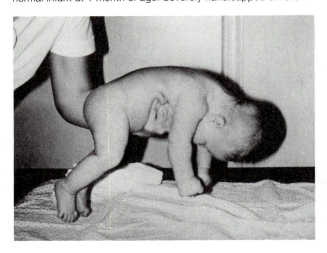 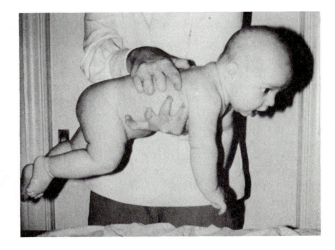

Figure 10.13 *Left,* body derotative reaction not present. *Top left,* front and, *lower left,* back views of reflexive rolling in normal infant from birth until about 4 months. Note rotation of the head results in the entire body following as a single unit. *Right,* appropriate body derotative reaction showing mature or segmental rolling.

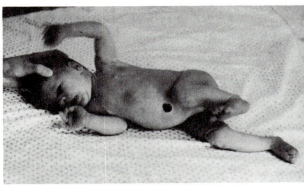

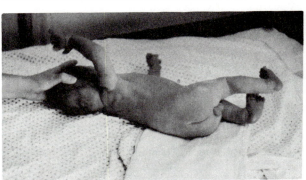

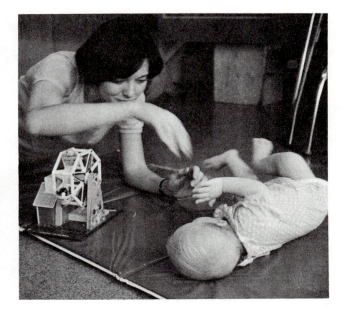

Body Derotative: The ability to perform mature segmental rolling from supine to prone instead of the log roll in response to head being turned (Figure 10.13). In mature rolling, which appears at about age 4 months, the child turns the head first, then the shoulders, then the pelvis, and last the legs.

Body Rotative: The ability to rise to a stand from either a prone or supine lying position (Figure 10.14). It first appears at 9 months of age.

Motor Performance, Self-Concept, and Leisure Functioning **221**

Figure 10.14 Body rotative reaction in immature rise to stand that utilizes trunk rotation and arm assistance. Pictured are film tracings of a 17-year-old girl with cerebral palsy who demonstrates body rotative pattern of normal 9-to-12-month-old infant. The mature rise to stand requires no trunk rotation and no arm assistance.

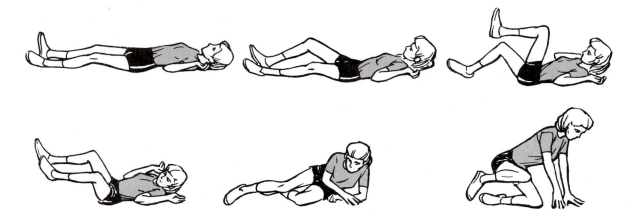

Figure 10.15 Forwards parachute reaction is tested from any position that might result in a head-first fall. Arms should automatically move toward floor to break the fall and protect the head. *Left*, child exhibits appropriate reaction. *Right*, forwards parachute is not yet present.

Parachute Reactions

Sometimes called propping reactions, these are protective extensor movements of legs or arms that occur (through subcortical activation) whenever the body is thrown off balance. They first appear between 4 and 9 months of age. Testing parachute reactions requires no equipment except, possibly, for the forwards parachute.

Downwards Parachute: This is the only reaction involving legs. When the body is extended vertically, feet down, in the air, the legs react by automatically extending, abducting, and outwardly rotating. This first appears at about 4 months of age. In contrast, cerebral palsied persons (put in this position) show scissoring of the legs.

Sideways Parachute: Tested in a sitting position. In response to a sideward push, the arm that is closest to the floor automatically abducts and extends to prevent a fall. This first appears at 6 months of age.

Forwards Parachute Tested from any position that might result in a fall, head first (Figure 10.15). A forward fall automatically activates arm flexion forward toward the floor and wrist and finger extension. This first appears at 7 months of age.

Backwards Parachute Tested from a sitting position. In response to a push that would cause a backward fall, arms extend backward toward the floor and wrist and fingers extend. This first appears at 9 months of age.

Tilting Reactions

Sometimes called equilibrium reactions, these are compensatory movements of the spine that prevent falls. They first appear between 5 and 12 months of age. Whereas the midbrain controls righting and parachute reactions, the cerebral cortex controls tilting reactions. These are the movements associated with vestibular function and called balance by most persons. Prone, supine, sitting, and all-fours tilting reactions are usually tested on a vestibular board or large ball. Standing tilting reactions are tested by standing on any unstable surface. The examiner focuses attention on the spinal curvature needed to maintain balance. The concavity of this curve should be always uphill. There should be increased muscle tone on the side nearest the floor. Tests and practice on unstable surfaces should emphasize very slow shifts in position. If shifts are too fast, protective extension movements are elicited instead of those described in Figures 10.16 and 10.17.

Figure 10.16 Tilting reactions normally begin to appear around the sixth month and gradually are perfected over the next 5 years. Prone and supine equilibrium should be tested and facilitated before the others. A large ball, bolster, or tilt board can be used.

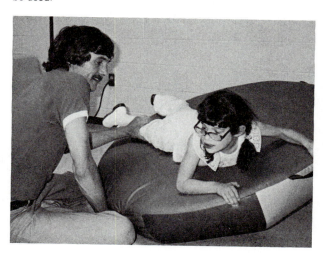
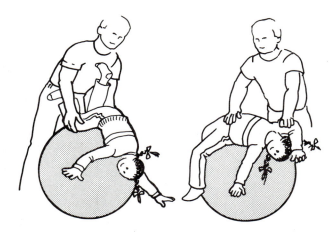

Figure 10.17 Tilting reactions.

| Backward tilt | Level | Forward tilt |

Forward tilt should result in extension/hyperextension of head, neck, and trunk and in adduction of scapulae. *Backward tilt* should result in flexion of head, neck, and trunk and abduction of scapulae.

| Backward tilt | Level | Forward tilt |

Sideward tilt should result in rotation of the head and trunk toward the uptilting side. There is also flexion and abduction of the limbs on the uptilting side; the opposite characterizes limbs on the downtilting side.

| Backward tilt | Level | Forward tilt |

Forward tilt on all fours results in symmetrical extension tonic neck reflex posture.

Standing tilts elicit increased muscle tone on the downhill side.

Application of the Milani-Comparetti System

According to test constructors, assessment of the functions listed on the Milani-Comparetti Chart should not take over 5 minutes. Teachers can fill in the information on the basis of observation of the student over several days. Many of the tests used to ascertain reactions are also used as learning activities. When possible, evaluation of this kind should be multidisciplinary.

Figure 10.18 presents an example of the Milani-Comparetti Chart filled in and the written report accompanying it for the 9-year-old girl depicted in Figure 10.19. This girl (fictitious name, Kay) was born with athetoid cerebral palsy affecting all four limbs. Athetosis, remember, is involuntary movement caused by damage to the basal ganglia that interferes with steadiness, accuracy, and control. Kay's intelligence quotient is above 90 (i.e., low average). She is in the fourth grade of a public school in which she is mainstreamed into first-grade spelling and mathematics classes. The rest of the school day, she is in a self-contained class for multihandicapped students. Kay receives adapted physical education on a 1:1 basis three times a week, 30 minutes a day. She also receives physical, occupational, speech, and music therapy in 30-minute sessions.

Special equipment is needed to help Kay function independently. She lacks the arm strength and control to maneuver a manual wheelchair, so a motorized chair is required. Kay is nonverbal, so a head pointer is essential to her pointing out words on a Bliss symbol board, typing, and doing art work. Figure 10.18 shows that all five primitive reflexes are present: hand grasp, asymmetrical tonic neck, Moro, symmetrical tonic neck, and foot grasp. Knowledge of this guides the physical educator in selecting which throwing, striking, and kicking patterns to teach Kay.

Also present is the crossed extensor reflex (not covered by the MC Chart). This reflex adversely affects kicking a ball from a standing position and other reciprocal leg movements. In this reflex, fluctuation in muscle tone and/or movement of one leg reflexly affects the other. Figure 10.19 shows Kay's problems in trying to kick. When one leg is lifted to kick the ball, a strong extensor spasm affects the support leg and causes loss of balance. This reflex explains much of the awkwardness in young children learning to kick as well as problems in neurologically impaired students.

Figure 10.18 Milani-Comparetti evaluation for 9-year-old girl with athetoid cerebral palsy affecting control of head and all four limbs. An *A* on the chart indicates absence of a response, and a *P* indicates presence of a response. Note that absence is interpreted as bad under spontaneous behaviors and under righting, parachute, and tilting reactions, but as good in relation to primitive reflexes. The circled areas indicate the body positions that were attained. To interpret, the Spontaneous Behavior section indicates the actions Kay could perform independently. She could lift her head from prone or supine lying and when being pulled up into a sit-up position. She could not, however, maintain the head in an upright position when her body was vertical. She could sit independently only if the arms and legs were placed in the proper support position. Four-point kneeling could be maintained only momentarily. Kay could do no independent standing or locomotor activities. The Evoked Responses section indicates that all five reflexes were still present and that all reactions except *body derotative* were absent (i.e., Kay could do mature segmental rolling but otherwise totally lacked head and neck control and body equilibrium).

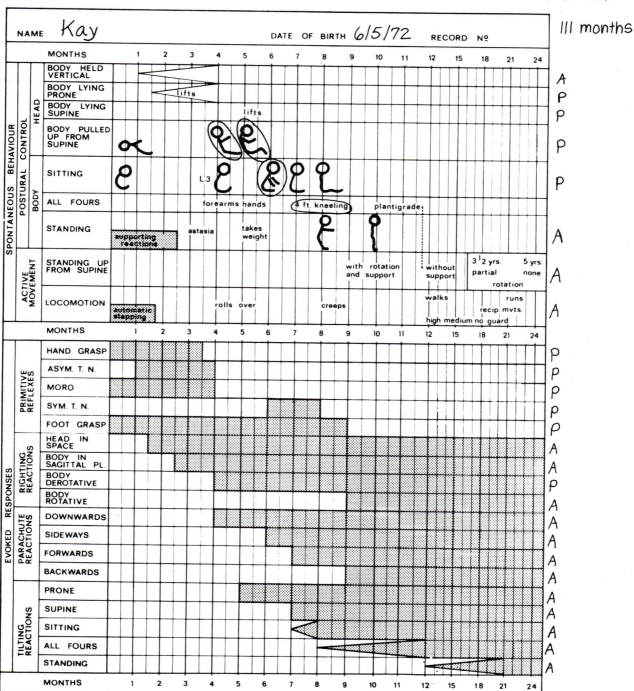

A. Milani Comparetti, E.A. Gidoni: Dev.Med.Child. Neurol. Vol. 9 No 5 Oct 67

Figure 10.19 *Top left,* 9-year-old with no arm/hand control using head pointer to touch symbols on a communication board during a conversation with friend. *Right,* crossed extensor reflex interfering with kicking; this child should be taught kicking only from a sitting position. *Bottom left,* one of several correct ways to position a CP child so head can be maintained in upright posture.

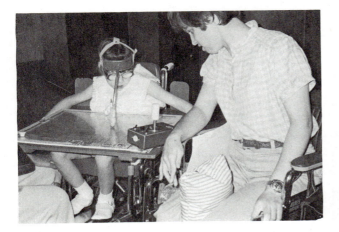

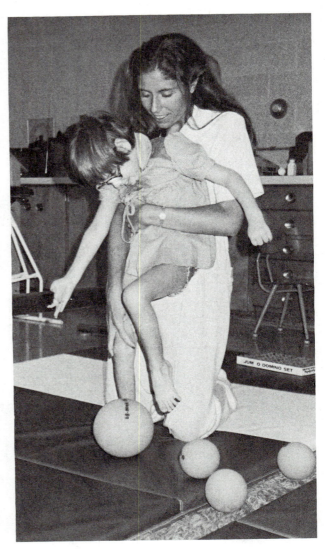

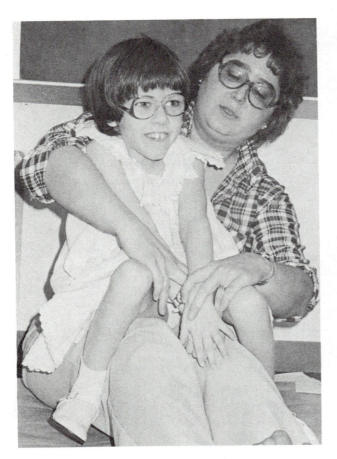

In teaching object control to persons with tonic neck reflexes, position in relation to the target is very important. With the ATNR present, for instance, it may be best to place the throwing arm side to the target rather than facing it. The best throwing pattern for Kay is arm extended sideward at shoulder height and pointed toward the target with most of the movement coming from wrist flexion. Because of presence of the hand grasp reflex, release is very difficult. Therefore, bean bags are used rather than balls. Overall, striking activities offer Kay more success than throwing ones. Adaptations to pedagogy should be based on knowledge of which reflexes and reactions are present. Much research is needed in this area.

Pedagogy in Relation to Reflexes and Reactions

Physical education for young children with abnormal reflexes is guided by the neurophysiological treatment approach of Bobath (1980). This approach rests on two principles:

1. Inhibition or suppression of abnormal reflex activity.
2. Facilitation of righting, parachute, and equilibrium reactions in their proper developmental sequence.

The first principle is achieved primarily through correct positioning and the proper selection of activities. With severely disabled children, correct positioning is achieved through specially designed wheelchairs and strapping of body parts. Maintaining the head in midline is especially important since head rotation and flexion/extension elicit the asymmetrical and symmetrical tonic neck reflexes, respectively. Velcro ties are often used to prevent undesirable head movement. With less severely disabled students, ball handling and other physical activities should be taught utilizing a developmental progression in which all tasks are performed with head straight forward. Targets and/or balls to be hit off tees should be placed at eye level or, in the case of floor targets, far enough away so the student does not drop the head to look downward. As long as therapists are striving to inhibit or suppress abnormal reflex activity, physical educators should cooperate. Often, however, this goal is re-evaluated at age 7 or 8 years when it becomes evident that it may not

be achievable. When this occurs, the emphasis may change to finding ways the student can utilize reflex activity to his or her advantage. For instance, a side position to the target with head rotated to the right, thereby eliciting the ATNR, may make it easier to release objects with the right arm.

The second principle is achieved primarily through exercises, stunts, and games that follow the natural developmental sequence whereby students gain the strength and coordination needed to attain a proper balance between mobility and stability (i.e., voluntary control over purposeful movement as well as maintenance of a set posture against the pull of gravity). Figure 10.20 presents the exercise sequence first recommended by Margaret Rood in the 1950s and still followed by many therapists today. The scientific rationale for these and similar exercises is presented by Shirley Stockmeyer, a physical therapist who teaches at Boston University. Stockmeyer (1972) rather than Rood has done most of the writing in relation to the sensorimotor approach innovated by Rood and, more recently, expanded and popularized by Jean Ayers.

The Rood mobility-stability model emphasizes many exercises and positions common to physical educators, such as the supine tuck and hold, modified log roll, swan, and creeping. Whereas regular physical educators have used these exercises primarily to develop abdominal and back extensor strength, therapists believe the exercises facilitate sensory integration and neurological maturation. Whatever the rationale, the tasks in Figure 10.20 have stood the test of time and should be incorporated into physical education programming for awkward students.

The sensory integration approach of Ayres (1972) is also appropriate for physical education directed toward inhibiting abnormal reflexes and stimulating normal postural reactions. Ayres believes that activities that activate the vestibular, tactile, and kinesthetic sense modalities contribute to CNS integration. Illustrative of these activities are those in Figure 10.17, which can be done on balance (vestibular) boards, bolsters, large cage balls, or apparatus having an unstable surface. By repeatedly reacting to loss of balance, the student has optimal opportunities to develop

Figure 10.20 Rood's developmental approach for severely handicapped children. Margaret Rood, both an occupational and a physical therapist, believes that motor patterns are developed from fundamental reflex patterns present at birth that are utilized and gradually modified through sensory stimuli. Many contemporary movement approaches are based on Rood's concepts. Rood's eight motor patterns can serve as IEP goals for severely handicapped, nonambulatory children.

(A) *Total supine flexion position* simulates position in womb and normal motor control from birth to 4 weeks; the tonic labyrinthine reflex is integrated by putting child in this position. Alternately holding this position and relaxing in bent knee supine lie is excellent abdominal and trunk exercise for all ages.

(B) *Roll over* with arm and leg on same side flexed is recommended for children dominated by the primitive tonic reflexes.

(C) *Pivot prone* position, involving extension of the neck, trunk, shoulders, hips, and knees, is the first *stability* pattern of total body against gravity. Ability to maintain this position shows that the tonic labyrinthine reflex and the symmetrical tonic neck reflex have been integrated.

(D) *Neck co-contraction* facilitates head control by utilizing labyrinthine righting reflex to align head. This is strengthened by having child lift head to look at various objects.

(E) *Prone-on-elbows* position is a prerequisite to crawling activities. This pattern helps inhibit the symmetrical tonic neck reflex. It also facilitates strength development by co-contraction of muscles on opposite surfaces of neck, shoulder girdle, and shoulder joints.

(F) *Creeping position* involves co-contraction of muscles on opposite surfaces of trunk and lower extremities; i.e., static strength development of muscle groups for stability against pull of gravity.

(G) *Standing* progresses from a static bilateral posture to the ability to shift weight and move body parts (thereby changing center of gravity) without losing balance.

(H) *Walking* entails periods of double and single foot support against the pull of gravity. Rotatory action of the trunk and pelvis, which develops at age 2–3, contributes to growing stability in locomotor activities.

normal postural reactions. Additionally, Ayres emphasizes scooter boards, playground apparatus like the merry-go-round that spins, and various kinds of go-carts that take the child through space. It is interesting that these are the activities that normal children engage in on their own as though in response to some internal drive.

Students who exhibit reflex and reaction problems (i.e., clumsiness) are often assigned to adapted physical education classes that emphasize sensorimotor or perceptual motor training. In such classes, most activities center on body image and balance. This type of programming is discussed in the next chapter.

Other Tests Covering Reflexes

New tests developed for use by physical educators and special educators are beginning to include assessment of reflexes. Illustrative of these are the Brigance Diagnostic Inventory and the Peabody Developmental Motor Scales, both of which are described later in this chapter.

Table 10.1
Motor Patterns Included on Most Frequently Used Instruments

Item	Brigance	ACTIVE	I CAN TGMD	OSU-S	Denver
Pedal tricycle or wheel toys	X				X
Creep		X			
Walk	X	X			
Heel-to-toe walk	X				X
Stair/ladder climb	X	X		X	X
Balance, one foot	X	X			X
Balance beam	X				X
Run	X		X	X	
Vertical jump	X	X	X		X
Long jump	X		X	X	X
Leap			X		
Hop	X	X	X	X	X
Skip	X	X	X	X	
Gallop			X		
Slide			X		
Kick	X	X	X	X	X
Bounce and catch	X	X	X		X
Catch thrown ball	X	X	X		X
Throw	X	X	X	X	X
Strike		X	X	X	
Rhythms	X	X	X		

Note. Test of Gross Motor Development (TGMD) by Ulrich is included with I CAN, since Ulrich created a standardized numerical scoring system for I CAN items (except for rhythms).

Movement Patterns and Tests

Because many educators have not been taught to recognize reflexes and reactions, most instruments for assessing movement patterns take a biomechanical or task analysis approach. The physical educator who works with clumsy and/or handicapped students needs to use both types of assessment approaches.

Movement pattern assessment instruments most frequently used by physical educators working with handicapped students (Ulrich, 1985) include the following, listed from most to least often mentioned: Brigance Diagnostic Inventory, Project ACTIVE, I CAN, OSU-SIGMA, and Denver Developmental Screening Test. Table 10.1 contrasts the movement patterns assessed by each. These instruments are described briefly on the pages that follow. Additionally, three other, newer instruments are described that seem especially promising: Test of Gross Motor Development, Peabody Motor Development Scales, and Movement Patterns Achievement Profile.

Brigance Diagnostic Inventory of Early Development (IED)

Purpose
To assess children whose developmental levels range from birth to 7 years of age in major developmental domains: preambulatory motor skills and behaviors, gross motor skills and behaviors, fine motor skills and behaviors, self-help skills, prespeech, speech and language skills, general knowledge and comprehension, readiness, basic reading skills, manuscript writing, and math. The IED is useful in making diagnostic/referral decisions, defining strengths and weaknesses on a wide variety of tasks, and developing instructional objectives.

Description
A criterion-referenced instrument comprised of skill sequences arranged developmentally from easy to difficult. The teacher checks each item within a skill sequence that the student can perform; methods of assessment are flexible and include observing the child and interviewing the parents or knowledgeable others. The number of items comprising each skill sequence varies.

Within the gross motor domain are 13 skill sequences and 115 items, as follows: standing, 18; walking, 19; stairs and climbing, 16; running, 8; jumping, 5 plus distances to discriminate between age groups; hopping, 2 with levels (attempts, 1 hop, 2 hops, distance of 1 m, distance of 2 m) specified to discriminate between age groups; kicking, 4; balance board, 11; catching, 8; rolling and throwing, 6 plus distances specified and number of successful beanbag tosses into a wastebasket; ball bouncing, 4; rhythm, 6; and wheel toys, 8.

Scoring
After placing a check on each item the child can do, the teacher records the corresponding developmental age on a bar graph that depicts selected ages in months from birth to 7 years. The developmental age is obtained from the numbers (e.g., 1.6, 3.0, 4.0, 5.0, 6.0 for wheel toys) written in front of selected items in the skill sequence.

Curriculum
No curriculum is presented, but test items are written in behavioral format so that they can serve as IEP objectives. The assessment system thus eliminates the writing of objectives. For example, the teacher can write only *B-11A,3* on the IEP and everyone using the Brigance Inventory knows this refers to the following: *by date, when requested to do so and with demonstration by examiner if necessary, student will bounce a playground ball with one hand a distance of 2 m (6 feet 8 inches) and catch it with both hands.*

Validity
Content validity by documenting motor development books from which skill sequences and developmental ages were taken.

Reliability
None stated.

Primary Sources
Brigance, A. (1978). *The Brigance diagnostic inventory of early development.* Worburn, MA: Curriculum Associates, Inc.

Address for Ordering
Curriculum Associates, Inc., 5 Esquire Road, North Billerica, MA 01862.

Project ACTIVE Motor Ability Test, Level 2

Purpose
To assess children, ages 4 to 8 years, on five motor ability factors.

Descriptions
Norm-referenced test comprised of 23 items organized under five factors as follows: gross body coordination, 5; balance/postural orientation, 8; eye and hand coordination, 6; eye-hand accuracy, 2; foot-eye accuracy, 2.

Scoring
See manual. Different system used for each factor. Highest possible score is 88 points. Scores are yielded for separate factors and total test.

Validity
Content validity affirmed by panel of experts. This test is almost exactly the same as the Basic Motor Fitness Test for Emotionally Disturbed and Mentally Handicapped (Hilsendager, Jack, & Mann, 1968).

Reliability
Test-retest coefficients for separate factors range from .39 to .94 for several samples of neurologically impaired and communication handicapped children.

Similar Tests
Level 1 motor ability test has same items as Level 2, but a different scoring system; it uses rating scales to assess developmental level at which student is performing the item. *Level 3* motor ability test, recommended for ages 8 to 11 years, assesses the same five factors as Level 2 but uses different items for the first three factors.

Primary Sources
Hilsendager, D., Jack, H., & Mann, L. (1968). *Basic motor fitness test for emotionally disturbed and mentally handicapped.* Philadelphia: Temple University.

Vodola, T. (1973). *Individualized physical education program for the handicapped child.* Englewood Cliffs, NJ: Prentice-Hall.

Vodola, T. (1976). *Project ACTIVE maxi-model kit.* Oakhurst, NJ: Township of Ocean Park.

Address for Ordering:
VEE, Inc., PO Box 2093, Neptune City, NJ 07753, or Project ACTIVE, Township of Ocean School District, 163 Monmouth Road, Oakhurst, NJ 07755.

I CAN Fundamental Skills Test

Purpose
To assess motor performance of ambulatory students of any age for the purpose of selecting and implementing instructional objectives.

Description
Criterion referenced, with student performance score sheets available for locomotor and rhythmic skills (run, leap, horizontal jump, vertical jump, hop, gallop, slide, skip, move to even beat, move to uneven beat, move to musical accent) and object control skills (underhand roll, underhand throw, overhand throw, kick, bounce, catch, underhand strike, overhand strike, forehand strike, backhand strike, sidearm strike). No chronological ages are associated with performance. Testing involves observing students and checking the skill levels at which they are performing.

Scoring
For most skills, four or five levels are stated. Illustrative of levels are the following for the horizontal jump:
1. With assistance.
2. Without assistance.
3. Mature pattern.
4. Jump for distance.

Once the skill level is determined, the teacher checks specific focal points within that skill level which the student can do. *Focal point* is a synonym for *task,* and the points are listed in task analysis format.

Validity

Content, with skill analyses taken from motor development texts. The I CAN tests form the basis for the more sophisticated Test of Gross Motor Development (Ulrich, 1985), which has been subjected to extensive validation work.

Reliability

None reported on I CAN, but refer to work of Ulrich.

Curriculum

Comprehensive curricular materials are available.

Primary Sources

Wessel, J. (1976). *I CAN: Locomotor and rhythmic skills.* Northbrook, IL: Hubbard.

Wessel, J. (1976). *I CAN: Object control.* Northbrook, IL: Hubbard.

Wessel, J., & Kelly, L. (1985). *Individualizing instruction: Quality programs for all students.* Philadelphia: Lea & Febiger.

Address for Ordering

Hubbard Scientific Co., PO Box 104, Northbrook, IL 60062.

Test of Gross Motor Development (TGMD)

Purpose

To identify children ages 3 to 10 years who are significantly behind their peers in the execution of 12 gross motor skill patterns.

Description

Two subtests are designed to assess different aspects of gross motor development: locomotion and object control. The results of the test provide both criterion- and norm-referenced interpretations. National representative norms are provided for both subtests and a gross motor development composite for children ages 3 to 10 years. The examiner is required to judge the presence or absence of 3 or 4 motor behaviors in each of 12 gross motor skills: run, gallop, hop, leap, horizontal jump, skip, slide, two-hand strike, stationary bounce, catch, kick, and overhand throw. Each skill is illustrated in the test manual.

Validity

Content validity was established by having three content experts judge whether the specific gross motor skills selected represented skills that are frequently taught to young children. Construct validity was established by testing the hypothesis that gross motor development would improve significantly across age levels. It was also supported by testing the hypothesis that mentally handicapped children would score significantly lower than nonhandicapped children of similar age. The test was also validated for instructional sensitivity. The results indicate that the test is sensitive to formal instruction in gross motor development.

Reliability

Test-retest reliability coefficients for the 12 gross motor skills ranged from .84 to .99. Interscorer reliability estimates for the skills ranged from .79 to .98 for 10 raters. The reliability of mastery decisions was reported for handicapped and nonhandicapped samples using the total test score. Individuals who scored at or above 85% test mastery level were classified as masters of gross motor development, while those not achieving this level were classified as nonmasters. The proportion of students classified consistently across two testing occasions was calculated. The result for the handicapped group was .87, while the nonhandicapped group was .89.

Primary Sources

Ulrich, D. A. (1984). The reliability of classification decisions made with the objectives-based motor skill assessment instrument. *Adapted Physical Activity Quarterly, 1,* 52–60.

Ulrich, D. A. (1985). *The Test of Gross Motor Development.* Austin, TX: PRO-ED.

Ulrich, D. A., & Ulrich, B. D. (1984). The objectives-based motor skill assessment instrument: Validation of instructional sensitivity. *Perceptual and Motor Skills, 59,* 175–179.

Ulrich, D. A., & Wise, S. L. (1984). The reliability of scores obtained with the objectives-based motor skill assessment instrument. *Adapted Physical Activity Quarterly, 1,* 230–239.

Address for Ordering

PRO-ED Publishing Co., 5341 Industrial Oaks Blvd., Austin, TX 78735.

Ohio State University Scale of Intra Gross Motor Assessment (OSU-SIGMA)

Purpose

To assess the qualitative aspects of 11 basic motor skills of children ages 2.5 to 14 years.

Description

Criterion referenced, with four levels of development specified for each motor skill. Specific criteria are stated for each level, with Level 1 designated as least mature. Teacher observes student in natural or test setting and rates performance of each skill as Level 1, 2, 3, or 4. The skills assessed are walking, stair climbing, running, throwing, catching, long jumping, hopping, skipping, striking, kicking, and ladder climbing.

Validity

Content validity by 11 experts who rated test, using 5-point Likert-type scale, on understandability and usefulness and by documentary analysis of the literature.

Reliability

None reported on student performance. Objectivity of scorers, however, was reported under this general heading with 13 judges viewing and rating the videotaped performance two times (1 week apart) of 12 children, ages 2.5 to 14 years. Resulting data, analyzed by Scott's Pi, produced test-retest scorer reliabilities ranging from .50 to 1.00 and intrajudge agreement ranging from .67 to 1.00.

Curriculum Available

Performance-based curriculum related to SIGMA (Loovis & Ersing, 1979).

Primary Sources

Ersing, W., Loovis, M., & Ryan, T. (1982). On the nature of motor development in special populations. *Exceptional Education Quarterly, 3* (1), 64–72.

Loovis, M. (1975). *Model for individualizing physical education experiences for the preschool moderately retarded child.* Unpublished doctoral dissertation, Ohio State University.

Loovis, M., & Ersing, W. (1979). *Assessing and programming gross motor development for children* (2nd ed.). Loudonville, OH: Mohican.

Address for Ordering

Mohican Publishing Co., PO Box 295, Loudonville, OH 44842.

Denver Developmental Screening Test

Purpose

To identify developmental delays in children from birth to age 6 years in four areas: gross motor, fine motor-adaptive, language, and personal-social.

Description

Norm referenced, with charts showing the age at which 10, 25, 50, 75, and 90% of children can perform specific tasks. Total test includes 105 items. The gross motor portion includes 31 items: lifts head momentarily from prone position; lifts head up 45 degrees from prone position; lifts head up 90 degrees from prone position; raises body to chest up, arm support position; holds head steady; rolls over; shows no head lag in pull to sit; bears some weight on legs in momentary stand; sits without support; stands holding on; pulls self to stand; gets to sitting position; walks holding on furniture; stands momentarily; stands alone well; stoops and recovers; walks well; walks backwards; walks up steps; kicks ball forward; throws ball overhead; balances on one foot 1 second; jumps in place; pedals tricycle 10 feet or more; broad jumps; balances on one foot 5 seconds; balances on one foot 10 seconds; hops on one foot two or more times; walks heel-to-toe; catches bounced ball from 3 feet; and walks backward heel-to-toe.

Scoring

Items are scored on pass, fail, refusal, or no opportunity to observe.

Validity

Criterion referenced, with the following tests: Stanford-Binet IQ Test, .85; Revised Yale Developmental Schedules, .95; Cattell Infant IQ Scale, .97; and Bayley Infant Mental Scale, .89.

Reliability

Test-retest reliability coefficients ranging from .66 to .93.

Primary Sources

Frankenburg, W., Camp, B., & Van Natta, P. (1971). Reliability and stability of the Denver developmental screening test. *Child Development, 42,* 1315–1325.

Frankenburg, W., Camp, B., & Van Natta, P., (1971). Validity of the Denver developmental screening test. *Child Development, 42,* 475–485.

Frankenburg, W., & Dodds, J. (1967). The Denver developmental screening test. *The Journal of Pediatrics, 71,* 181–191.

Sewell, J. (1980). *Changes in motor performance of young handicapped children.* Unpublished master's thesis, Texas Woman's University, Denton.

Address for Ordering

Ladoca Project and Publishing Foundations, Inc., East 51st Avenue and Lincoln St., Denver, CO 80216.

Peabody Developmental Motor Scales (PDMS)

Purpose

To measure both gross and fine motor development of children from birth through 83 months. Scales are recommended for (a) developmental screening, (b) information on which motor tasks have been mastered, which skills are developing, and which skills are not yet in the behavior repertoire, and (c) determining unique motor strengths and weaknesses.

Description

Norm referenced, with the gross motor scale containing 170 items with 10 items at each of 17 age levels. Gross motor items are classified into five categories: (a) reflexes, (b) balance, (c) nonlocomotor, (d) locomotor, and (e) receipt and propulsion of objects. The fine motor scale consists of 112 items in four skill categories: (a) grasping, (b) hand use, (c) eye-hand coordination, and (d) manual dexterity.

Scoring

Each item is scored as 0, 1, or 2. A *0* indicates that the child could not or would not attempt the item or that the attempt does not show that the skill is emerging. A *1* indicates that the student's performance shows a clear resemblance to the item criterion, but does not fully meet it. A *2* indicates that the student performs at criterion level.

Validity

Content validity by review of other validated motor development tests. Construct validity by known groups method. Criterion-related validity by determining similarity between PDMS performance and that of Bayley Scales of Infant Development (Bayley, 1969), but no correlations were cited.

Reliability

Test-retest reliability for 38 children on gross and fine motor skills, respectively, were .95 and .80. Interrater reliabilities for gross and fine motor scores were .97 and .94.

Curriculum Available

File is available including 170 activity cards for gross motor and 112 activity cards for fine motor development. Each card is matched to a test item and provides a behavioral objective and four instructional strategies.

Primary Sources

Folio, M. R., & Fewell, R. (1983). *Peabody developmental motor scales.* Allen, TX: DLM Teaching Resources.

Address for Ordering

DLM Teaching Resources, PO Box 4000, One DLM Park, Allen, TX 75002.

Movement Patterns Achievement Profile (MPAP)

Purpose

To assess movement patterns of children ages 2½ to 5 years.

Description

Two levels (i.e., two tests) comprise the instrument. Level 1 was designed to assess able-bodied children and those with mild handicapping conditions such as language disorders, auditory impairments, mental retardation, and/or combinations of these. Level 2 was specifically designed for physically handicapped or lower functioning mentally retarded children. Test items are presented in task analysis format.

Items in Level 1 include walking, running, jumping forward, jumping downward, ascending stairs, descending stairs, climbing ladder, descending ladder, catching, throwing, static balance, dynamic balance, rolling a ball, and body image. The total score possible for Level 1 is 130 points or 125 total points for children with hearing impairments.

Items in Level 2 are the same as those in Level 1 except that crawling [sic, creeping] is added and running is omitted. The total score possible for Level 2 is 94 points.

Scoring

On the Level 1 test, 11 items are scored from 0 to 10 points and 1 item each is scored 0 to 9, 0 to 6, and 0 to 5 points. On the Level 2 test, 1 item (creeping) is scored 0 to 10 points, 1 item is scored 0 to 8, 7 items are scored 0 to 7, 2 items are scored 0 to 6, and 3 items are scored 0 to 5. The number of points for each item depends upon the number of steps in its task analysis.

Validity

Content validity based on independent ratings of seven experts and construct validity based on factor analysis.

Reliability

Test-retest reliability coefficients for individual items range from .46 to .87 with a mean of .73.

Primary Sources

Evans, J. (1980). *They have to be carefully taught: A handbook for parents and teachers of young children with handicapping conditions.* Reston, VA: American Alliance for Health, Physical Education, and Recreation.

Evans, J., & Baizley, J. (1976). *The effects of a movement program on the development of motor patterns and skill of young handicapped children.* Research project funded by Manitoba Medical Service Foundation, Inc. Winnipeg, Canada: Society for Crippled Children and Adults.

Address for Ordering

AAHPERD Publications, 1900 Association Drive, Reston, VA 22091—entire test is in book by Evans (1980).

Developmental, Mature, and Immature Patterns

In most assessment approaches, a distinction is made between developmental, mature, and immature movement patterns. It is important that physical educators understand each.

Developmental movement patterns are those which are normal for a particular age group but which will not be acceptable in later years. Books that serve as primary sources in this area are

McClenagan, B., & Gallahue, D. (1978). *Fundamental movement.* Philadelphia: W. B. Saunders.

Wickstrom, R. (1983). *Fundamental motor patterns* (3rd ed.). Philadelphia: Lea & Febiger.

This chapter includes several pictorial assessment instruments (e.g., Figures 10.31, 10.32, 10.34) based upon the concepts of developmental movement patterns and progression through stages.

Mature movement patterns are those which are mechanically efficient. Usually they conform more or less to "good form" for adults. It should be remembered, however, that "good form" encompasses many individual differences. Little is known about "good form" for an amputee, a paraplegic, or a dwarf. Obviously, the movement patterns of adults with structural divergencies cannot be judged by the same criteria as movement patterns of able-bodied athletes.

Immature movement patterns are those that fail to meet the criteria of mechanical efficiency and economy of energy. In other words, the movement pattern does not produce the end result expected of a person of a certain age with a certain amount of instruction. The person's scores are consistently below the norms. Mechanical efficiency is closely related to optimal perceptual-motor functioning and total fitness.

Each time a teacher identifies a motor pattern as immature, he or she has an obligation to analyze *why* so that specific remediation can be built into the educational prescription.

Task Analysis and Instruction

On the pages that follow, each movement pattern is analyzed in detail, and checklists are provided for identifying the aspects of each movement pattern that are mature rather than developmental or immature. These checklists can be used as step-by-step guides in helping students to refine their natural movement patterns.

Motor assessment should be integrated with teaching. It should also be continuous, and learning curves should be plotted to show progress over many days (trials).

Sports and dance skills related to the basic locomotor patterns presented in this chapter are analyzed also. If a child can jump, for instance, to what extent can he or she transfer that knowledge and skill to track and field and gymnastics events? Which of a child's natural movement patterns, when refined, offer the greatest potential for success among peers? *The specialist in adapted physical education looks first at the strengths of the child.*

These strengths are recorded in the IEP as the *present level of motor performance*. The physical educator then analyzes the movement patterns in terms of how they can be improved. The list below presents *general problems* that should be identified. These problems may occur in all movement patterns.

General Characteristics of Immature Movement Patterns

1. **Inconsistency.** Exhibition of greater trial-to-trial inconsistency than more proficient peers show. Variation from trial to trial in preferred hand or foot, balance, force, rhythm, and other motor characteristics.
2. **Perseveration.** Inability to stop at the appropriate time and/or to perform a prescribed number of movements without overflow. For example, when dribbling a ball, the child may continue the dribbling action of the hand after the ball is no longer within reach.
3. **Mirroring.** Inability to transpose right-left visual cues to own body; failure to separate own directional movements from those of a leader. Evidenced when child is imitating the movement of someone facing him or her.
4. **Asymmetry.** Deficit in bilateral coordination evidenced when two limbs are supposed to contribute equally to force production or balance.
5. **Loss of dynamic balance.** Inability to maintain postural control of the body in relation to gravity. Evidenced by bumping into objects as well as by frequent shifts of position.
6. **Falling after performance.** An idiosyncracy exhibited after completion of a specified motor task. May be a compensatory measure to control perseveration or reduce loss of balance.
7. **Extraneous motions.** Excessive and/or irrelevant motions that tend to disrupt the temporal organization of a skill. The movement of the limbs may exceed the normal ranges for efficiency; they may be held in unusual positions, or additional movements may be added to the skill sequence.
8. **Inability to maintain rhythm or pattern.** Tendency to progressively accelerate or diminish the pace until child's movements do not match those of the leader. Or inability to maintain self-imposed rhythm of a task such as hopping or jumping in a repetitive manner.
9. **Inability to control force.** Inability to generate the correct amount of force to execute a motor task. Usually pertains to distance or height. Child throws, kicks, strikes, or jumps with too much force or too little. Relates to problems of balance and maintenance of rhythm.
10. **Inappropriate motor planning.** A catch-all category for problems of sequencing related to the interaction of rhythm and force in complex tasks. The delay or prematurity of a motor response, as in swinging too late or too early; the misapplication of force, as in failure to strike the center of the ball or to apply the right amount of force at the right time.

These 10 points, adapted from a speech by Haubenstricker and Seefeldt (1973), can be made into a checklist.

Rolling

Developmentally, the first locomotor movement pattern that appears is rolling, the ability to turn the body from side to side. It evolves during infancy as follows:

2 months old—roll from side to back.
4 months old—roll from back to side.
6 months old—roll from back to back or abdomen to abdomen by means of partial turns with rest periods between them.

Immature rolling occurs when, after 4 months of age, the child continues to roll as a single unit—i.e., cannot rotate one segment at a time. The primitive

Figure 10.21 Mature or segmental rolling normally begins at about 4 months of age after the asymmetrical tonic neck reflex is lost.

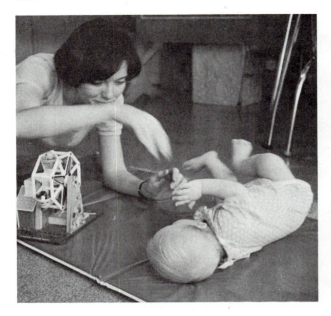

Figure 10.22 Criteria recommended by Rathbone for the evaluation of creeping are (1) the spine should appear loose (flexible) throughout; (2) the shoulders should be on the same level as the hips; (3) the knees should point straight ahead or slightly outward; (4) the pelvis should not swing strongly from side to side; (5) the feet should remain in contact with the floor; (6) the head should bend and twist away from the forward moving arm.

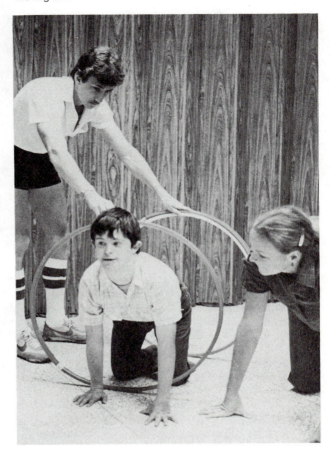

neck-righting reflex must be lost before *mature rolling* can occur. In mature (segmental) rolling, the child turns the head first, then the shoulders, then the pelvis, and last the legs. The muscles of the abdomen and posterior trunk are prime movers for this rotatory action (see Figure 10.21). A person with severe motor involvement may be unable to perform any locomotor movements other than variations of the log roll.

Physical education programming should include many different kinds of rolls on varied surfaces. Rolling *down* a padded inclined board is easier than rolling on a level surface. *Doggie rolls* (with limbs flexed) are easier than log rolls (with limbs extended). Most normal children can do forward rolls by age 3 and backward rolls by age 6 or 7. Backward rolls should be learned and practiced on an inclined surface before on a level one.

Crawling and Creeping

The terms *crawling and creeping* are sometimes used interchangeably, but child growth and development theorists make a definite distinction between the two patterns. *Crawling* is primarily an arm action that pulls the body along the floor while the abdomen and legs drag along behind. This pattern appears between the fourth and ninth months but may be skipped altogether. *Creeping* is a locomotor pattern in which the weight of the body is distributed equally to the hands and knees. Most authorities believe that the evaluation

of crawling and creeping should be based primarily upon the presence of *opposition*—i.e., a crosslateral pattern.

Mature creeping occurs in normal children at about 9 months of age. In order to assume the four-point creeping position, the child must have lost the symmetrical tonic neck reflex (STNR).

Physical educators have long recognized the value of creeping in the development of trunk muscles and arm and shoulder strength. Rathbone (1959) was stressing the importance of creeping exercises in the early 1930s, introducing thousands of teachers to the Klapp Creeping System from Germany (see Figure 10.22). She recommended creeping as one of the best abdominal exercises as well as for relief of menstrual cramps.

Figure 10.23 Scooter board activities are fun for all ages. Their primary value, however, is as a lead-up to creeping for severely handicapped children. Scooter boards facilitate development of head, neck, and upper back extensor strength as well as reciprocal arm action.

If a child cannot creep, his or her limbs can be patterned through creeping movements. There are many exercises that can be done in the stationary four-point position to facilitate the development of strength and balance. To succeed in creeping, a child must be able to balance on three body parts. In mature creeping, the body balances on left hand and right knee while the other two body parts move, and vice versa. Scooter board activities can be used as a leadup to creeping (Figure 10.23).

Walking

Assessment of walking was covered in the chapter on sports classifications because many gaits are normal, depending upon handicapping condition. The section that follows, therefore, focuses on teaching and/or re-refining walking patterns. Many of the suggestions offered are also applicable to running.

Body Alignment in Walking versus Running

A forward lean rather than good body alignment often characterizes the walk. To heighten proprioceptive awareness, students should practice body leans of different degrees and learn which is appropriate for walking and other locomotor activities. *Forward lean,* a term used also in teaching running, is the line between foot contact of the extended rear leg and the center of gravity. The lean should be from the ground so that the whole body is involved, not just the hips and waist. Forward lean can be discussed in terms of the hands of a clock. Thus, in walking, the body should be in 12 o'clock position. In the mile run, the lean is about 10°, about one-third of the way between 12 and 1 o'clock. In middle distance runs, the lean increases to between 15° and 18°, or halfway between 12 and 1 o'clock. In sprinting, the lean is greatest, about 25° to 30°, or at 1 o'clock. Only by practicing walks and runs does the pupil learn to discriminate between good and poor postural alignment.

Figure 10.24 Walking, in a hypotonic Down's syndrome child, is facilitated by having a cart filled with weights to push. The cart provides needed stability while it also creates motivation to practice the movement pattern. The use of creative dramatics—with the physical educator telling a story about a little girl taking her doll for a walk—helps to integrate movement and language development.

Figure 10.25 The spina bifida child's first experience in walking is on crutches. Young children seldom practice for the mere sake of practice. The physical educator must be skillful in the use of a wide variety of motivational techniques.

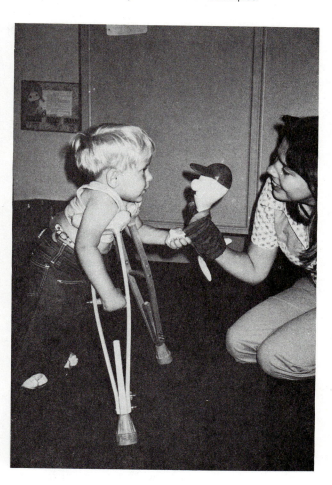

Heel-Toe Transfer of Weight

Further observation should ascertain that the heel strikes the ground first, after which the body weight is transferred sequentially along the outer border of the foot to the metatarsal area and the toes. The step ends with a push off or thrust of the flexor muscles of the big toe. The person unable to demonstrate this heel-ball-toe action may require physical therapy and/or concentrated exercises aimed at strengthening or stretching particular muscles. *Simplified tap dance or games* requiring the child to tap different parts of the foot to the floor are recommended. If the main difficulty is the push off, running in sand and other toe curling exercises like picking up marbles are helpful.

Shuffling the Feet

In slow walking, a characteristic of many persons with handicapping conditions, both feet may be on the floor as much as 30% of the time. If the period of double support exceeds this, the person is described as having a shuffling gait (see Figure 10.24). The seriousness of this problem can be determined by observing the person's attempts to step over bamboo poles, rungs of a ladder, or other low obstacles placed 12 to 18 inches apart on the floor. In some cases, shuffling is a result of laziness or poor concept formation rather than muscle tonus inadequate to lift the foot off of the floor. If it is believed that the latter is the cause, exercises should be administered to strengthen the flexors of the hip, knee, and ankle, which contract to facilitate the swinging phase. Sometimes, as in spina bifida, muscle paralysis results in shuffling (see Figure 10.25).

Table 10.2
Running Classifications

1. Moves wheelchair forward with arms
2. Moves wheelchair forward with feet
3. Moves wheelchair backward with feet
4. Uses a cane
5. Uses crutches
6. Partner assists
7. Guide wire or rope assists
8. Uses walker or similar device
9. Uses no assisting device

Note. Adapted from *Project UNIQUE Test Manual* by J. Winnick and J. Silva, 1979, Brockport: NY, SUNY.

Running

Running demands more balance than walking because the weight of the entire body is supported on one foot at a time. Unlike walking, there is no period of double support in running. Running also differs from walking by having a nonsupport phase, a time when the body is actually in flight or "sailing through the air."

Running can be done in many different ways; see Table 10.2. In mainstream physical education, all running patterns (including wheelchairs) are incorporated into games, relays, and fitness testing and training. Figure 10.26 depicts use of a guidewire.

Severely and profoundly retarded children who lack the concept of running should be introduced to it by walks down hills steep enough to quicken the pace to a run. In early stages of learning they may have a rope around the waist and be pulled into a running gait. Patient teaching is required also to convey the concepts of starting, stopping, and staying in a lane.

Less involved children will need special instruction related to running on the balls of the feet, lifting the knees, and swinging the arms. To facilitate running on the balls of the feet, practice can be up short, steep hills or steps. Jumping and hopping activities also tend to emphasize staying on the balls of the feet. Possible solutions to inadequate knee lift include riding a bicycle, particularly uphill; running up steep hills or steps; and running in place with knee action exaggerated to touch the outstretched palms of hands. Correction for swinging arms across the body or without vigor include practice in front of a mirror and running with a baton or small weight bar.

Observation of the running pattern during low organized games is one of the best ways of predicting game leadership; the fast runners can subsequently be

Figure 10.26 Guide wire or rope-assisted running for a blind child also provides a socialization experience when a sighted child runs lengths of the gymnasium at the same time. Fitness is seldom improved by such running unless it is continued for at least 12 minutes.

divided equally among the teams. The teacher can also observe agility and changes of level and combined movement patterns of running, tagging, and dodging. Stop and start running games like Red Light, Green Light are particularly good in teaching body control. Characteristics of developmental vs. mature running are listed in Table 10.3.

Dashes are often used as track events. The reaction time of severely MR, LD, and ED children to the starting signal may make running times inaccurate. In such instances the stop watch should not be started until the child has passed the 5-yard line—i.e., he or she should run 55-yard dashes. Children must be taught also not to slow down as they come to the finish line.

Table 10.3
Checklist for Evaluation of Running

Directions: Observe the student running at full speed in a variety of situations—games, track events, etc. Consider the 13 sets of alternate descriptions and check the one of each that represents the student's level of performance. Most normal children exhibit mature runs by ages 7 or 8. Use findings to write specific behavioral objectives.

Check One	Developmental Running	Check One	Mature Running
	1. Short running stride		1. Increased length of stride

	2. Exaggerated leg and foot movements
	  a. Toeing out of foot of recovery leg
	  b. Outward rotatory movement of recovery knee especially obvious from back view
	  c. Foot of recovery leg crosses midline in back just before it swings forward
			2. Minimal rotatory leg movements
			  a. Toes point straight ahead
			  b. Knees point straight ahead

	3. Knee not lifted high in the air in forward swing		3. Knee of recovery leg swung forward higher and faster. Thigh should be more or less horizontal to ground at end of knee lift
	4. Low heel kick-up as leg is swung forward (as viewed from rear)		4. Heel brought closer to the buttock on knee lift
	5. Mechanically inefficient push-off—less extension in rear leg		5. Increase in extension and velocity of driving leg—i.e., rear leg when it pushes off
	6. Support phase relatively long—this is because driving leg moves more slowly		6. Decrease in amount of time spent in ground contact—only 1/60 to 3/60 second
	7. Forward foot contacts ground at point ahead of the body's center of gravity		7. Forward foot contacts ground at point directly under the body's center of gravity; knee bends slightly immediately after foot touches ground
	8. Little forward lean early in sprint		8. Forward lean between 25° and 30° early in sprint; less later
	9. Excessive up-and-down movement of body		9. Minimal amount of body rise
	10. Limited range of arm movement		10. Hand swings as high as chin on forward swing; elbow reaches as high as shoulder on backswing
	11. Excessive bending and rigidity in arm movement at elbows		11. Elbows maintained in 90° angle with tendency to straighten on downward part of backswing and to bend on forward swing
	12. Arms tend to swing across trunk toward the midline		12. Minimal shoulder rotation
	13. Arms not working in true opposition to legs		13. Arms working in opposition to legs

Table 10.4
Comparison of Three Types of Runs

Characteristics	Sprint	Middle Distance Run	Long Distance Run
Foot plant	Land high on ball of foot; heel does not touch	Land lower on ball of foot than in 50-yard dash; heel does not touch	Land low on ball of foot, drop to heel
Knee action	Lift knee high and straight forward	Lift knee less high than in 50-yard dash	Lift knee slightly as compared to other runs
	Thigh should be more or less horizontal to ground at end of knee lift	Thigh should be less horizontal, about 70° to 80° at end of knee lift	Thigh is less horizontal at end of knee lift than in other runs
	Less rear kick than in other kinds of runs	More rear kick than in sprint	More rear kick than other runs
Forward body lean	Lean between 25° and 30°—about 1 o'clock	Lean between 15° and 18°—about halfway between 12 and 1 o'clock	Lean about 10°—about one-third of way between 12 and 1 o'clock
Arm action	Pump arms vigorously with hands reaching chin level or higher	Use slightly less vigorous arm action	Swing arms naturally at about shoulder level

Likewise, in softball they must be coached to overrun first base and not to slow down as they approach home plate.

Children should be helped to understand the concept of speed. Any child with number concepts up to 15 can understand running a 50-yard dash in 9 vs 13 seconds (decimals can be omitted in early learning). In track meets, emphasis can be placed on self-competition by pinning cards with the children's best times on their backs. As they finish a dash, they are told whether or not they beat their own time. Ribbons can be awarded to children who beat their own times rather than (or in addition to) children who beat others. An alternative technique is recording the child's expressed level of aspiration and making awards for meeting or surpassing this estimate.

The physical educator should be able to evaluate the different kinds of runs: (a) jogging; (b) sprinting; (c) middle distance runs—880 yards and up; and (d) long distance runs—mile and over for children. The 440-yard dash can be classified as either a sprint or a middle distance run depending upon the circulorespiratory endurance of the students. Table 10.4 shows that each type of run varies with respect to foot plant, knee action, forward body lean, and arm action. These four components are generally the ones on which pupils need the most practice.

To understand the mechanics of running, children should be taught the meanings of such words as forward lean, driving leg, recovery leg, center of gravity, and striding. *Forward lean* is the line between foot contact and center of gravity. Forward lean is greatest early in the sprint when the runner is accelerating rapidly and levels off after the point of maximum speed is reached. Many coaches believe that forward lean cannot be taught. It is a direct result of forward acceleration and, to some degree, of air resistance. The *driving leg* is the one that extends and pushes against the ground. The *recovery leg* is the one in which the high knee lift is important. The *center of gravity* is the point in the pelvis below which the recovery foot should try to land. The rate of striding is dependent upon four factors: (a) speed of extension of driving leg; (b) speed with which recovery leg is brought through; (c) length of time body is in air; and (d) landing position of the recovery foot in relation to the center of gravity.

Illustrative of the many running patterns that physical educators seek to improve are those of the 13-year-old cerebral palsied, mentally retarded boy depicted in Figure 10.27. He is confined to a walker cart comprised of a stabilizing strap around his chest and a canvas sling in which he sits.

Ascending and Descending Stairs

Exploration of space includes stairsteps if they are available. Even before children begin to walk they ascend stairs using a pattern strikingly similar to creeping movements on a level surface. The criteria used in the evaluation of creeping apply to this early method of ascending the stairs.

Figure 10.27 Two running patterns exhibited within a 50-yard dash at a local Special Olympics meet by a 13-year-old mentally retarded boy with spastic cerebral palsy. Note toward the end of the dash how he begins to use his arms to increase forward momentum.

Gait Pattern #1

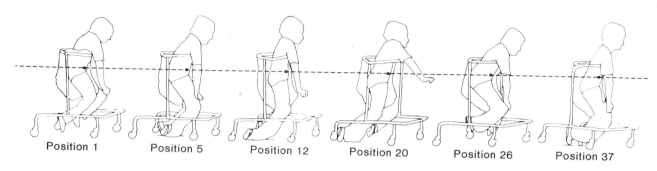

Position 1　　Position 5　　Position 12　　Position 20　　Position 26　　Position 37

Gait Pattern #2

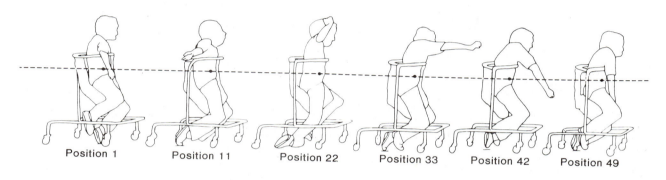

Position 1　　Position 11　　Position 22　　Position 33　　Position 42　　Position 49

Figure 10.28 Thirteen-year-old child with Down's syndrome descends stairs in immature fashion, leading with the same foot and marking time on each rung. This movement pattern is exhibited in the normal child at about 28 months of age. Descending is more difficult than ascending.

Climbing stairs and ladders progresses through two stages, each of which is performed first with help and later independently. *Stage 1* is leading with one foot and marking time until the trailing foot is on the same step or rung in a period of double support. The lead foot is generally the preferred or dominant foot. *Stage 2* is the mature foot-over-foot pattern, the weight supported on alternate feet on each step.

Descending stairs and ladders follows the same developmental pattern but occurs several months later (see Figure 10.28). Sinclair reports that 89% of her 3-year-old subjects could ascend stairs using a foot-over-foot pattern, but only 12% could use the mature pattern in descending. Almost a year later, at age 4, most of the children exhibited a foot-over-foot pattern in descending.

Since contemporary architecture seems to provide fewer and fewer steps for practice of ascending and descending skills, it may be desirable to purchase or construct staircases, ramps, and ladders scaled down to the small child's leg and foot size (see Figure 10.29). Commercially available staircases provide steps that are 2, 4, 6, and 8 inches high, with 4 inches being the recommended height. The practice steps also vary in width

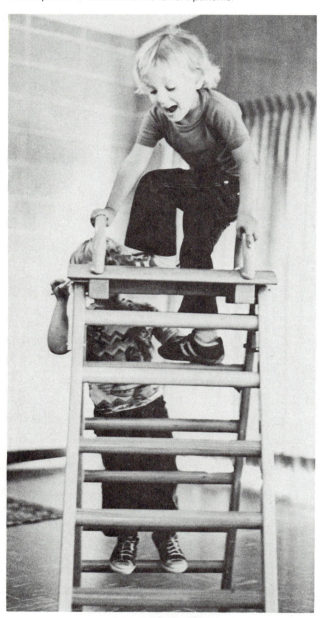

Figure 10.29 Play apparatus should be designed so that children practice progressively more difficult kinds of climbing, balancing, and jumping. Such climbing facilitates the same reciprocal arm and leg action as used in creeping and facilitates development of crosslateral movement patterns.

with the following dimensions commonly used: (a) 32 × 32 × 2; (b) 36 × 36 × 4; and (c) 40 × 40 × 6.

Characteristics of the mature ascending pattern are

1. Slight forward lean from ankle joints, not the hips.
2. Center of gravity balanced directly above forward foot.
3. Placement of entire foot on each step.
4. Reliance upon knee extension rather than plantar flexion at ankle joint for most of power.
5. Handrails not used.
6. Eyes straight ahead rather than looking down.

Characteristics of the mature descending pattern are

1. No forward or backward lean.
2. Center of gravity balanced approximately over center of base of support.
3. Handrails not used.
4. Eyes straight ahead rather than looking down.

Leaping

The earliest form of a jump is really a leap, for it involves a one-foot take-off and a transfer of weight to the opposite foot. Leaping, however, is generally associated with dance and movement exploration. It is usually characterized by a forward-backward stride, a one-foot take-off, a period of flight or nonsupport, elevation during the flight, and a transfer of body weight in the air so that the child takes off on one foot and lands on the other. Sideward leaps are used in tests of dynamic balance and agility and in some dances.

Children usually attempt their first leaps at about age 2. These may be called "step-down jumps" since they almost always involve stepping down from a height. Thus, an excellent screening technique is placing the child on a 12- to 18-inch height and instructing him or her to jump off. The responses, from least mature to most mature, may be any of the following:

1. Refuses to jump—just stands—cries.
2. Sits down and scoots off of the height.
3. Squats or stoops and then jumps down.
4. Steps down from an upright position.
5. Jumps down using a two-foot take-off and a two-foot landing.

Table 10.5
Comparison of Leap, Jump, and Hop

	Leap	Jump	Hop
Takeoff	Always a one-foot takeoff	May be either two-foot or one-foot takeoff	Always a one-foot takeoff
Flight	Weight always transferred from one foot to the other	Weight always transferred to two feet	Weight never transferred
Landing	Always a one-foot landing	Always a two-foot landing	Always a one-foot landing on same foot

Jumping

Considerable confusion exists in the literature with respect to the definitions of jump, hop, and leap. Kephart's indiscriminate use of the word *jump* in the Purdue Perceptual-Motor Survey is particularly misleading. Table 10.5 clarifies the three terms.

The following list of motor skills shows the natural developmental progression from a leap to a jump to a hop. The observer should check the developmental stage at which the child is presently functioning.

Developmental Stages

1. Step-down from height.
2. Vertical jump (two-foot take-off and two-foot landing).
3. Jump-down from height with two-foot landing.
4. Modified running long jump (really a leap) with a one-foot take-off, transfer of weight in air, and one-foot landing.
5. Regulation standing long jump with two-foot take-off.
6. Jump down with one-foot take-off and two-foot landing.
7. Modified running long jump with a one-foot take-off and a two-foot landing.
8. Jump over an object with a two-foot take-off and a two-foot landing.
9. Hop.
10. Regulation running long jump with a one-foot take-off and two-foot landing.

Figure 10.30 Three-year-old improves kinesthetic awareness of up and down as a lead-up to jumping.

Often, children have trouble learning to jump because they lack kinesthetic awareness of up and down. Figure 10.30 presents a technique for ameliorating this problem.

The best test of jumping skill is to observe which pattern comes naturally rather than to demonstrate a particular kind of jump that is then imitated by the child. The child should be tested first while standing on a bench 12 to 18 inches high and later while standing on a level surface. The challenge posed may be, How many different ways can you make your body cross over this line on the floor? Children with known neurological problems like cerebral palsy may need a horizontal bar or rope to hold onto for balance while attempting jumping tasks.

Figure 10.31 Developmental stages in standing long jump.
Stage 1: **Immature jump** at about 28 months characterized by
(1) incomplete crouch; (2) difficulty in using both feet and arms
simultaneously; (3) arms are used for balance during flight but do
not contribute to forward momentum; (4) feet lead in flight and
landing phases rather than arms. *Stage 2:* **Elementary school
age jump** characterized by (1) forward body lean; (2) arms
initiate takeoff; (3) body does not fully straighten out during flight;
(4) insufficient trunk flexion during flight downward; (5) unsteady
landing. *Stage 3:* **Mature childhood jump** characterized by
(1) trunk parallel to ground in preliminary crouch; (2) angle of
takeoff is 45°; (3) body fully extended during upward flight with
arms stretched upward; (4) full trunk flexion during flight
downward; (5) steady landing with arms forward. *Stage 4:* Mature
athletic jump is not pictured. This jump characterizes high-level
performance in competition.

Stage 1

Stage 2

Stage 3

Well-coordinated children can perform the standing long jump from a two-foot take-off and with a two-foot landing at about age 3. No significant differences appear in the long-jumping abilities of boys and girls until about age 8, at which time boys begin to excel.

Standing Long Jump (Broad Jump)

Since the standing long jump is included in almost all tests of fitness as a measure of leg power, the characteristics of the immature vs. the mature movement patterns are listed in the checklist in Table 10.6 (see also Figure 10.31).

Jump Used as a Dismount

The term *dismount* used in gymnastics is a jump from a piece of apparatus down to the floor. Dismounts are used to end routines on the balance beam, the even parallel bars, the uneven parallel bars, the horse, and the buck. Judged for their aesthetic appearance and mechanical efficiency, dismounts may involve difficult movements such as handsprings and cartwheels or simple jumps downward using a two-foot take-off and land.

No knowledge is more important to a child than how to get off a piece of gymnastic apparatus or play equipment safely. The first skill that should be taught on a balance beam is the *jump-off dismount*. Children who feel secure about their jumping ability will no longer fear falling. Only then should locomotor movements (walks, runs, skips) on the balance beam be introduced.

Table 10.6
Checklist for Evaluation of Standing Long Jump

Directions: Observe the student performing several broad jumps. Consider the 18 sets of alternate descriptions and check the one of each set that represents the student's present level of performance. Most normal children exhibit mature jumps by ages 7 or 8 years. Use findings to write specific behavioral objectives

	Check One	Developmental or Immature	Check One	Mature
Preliminary crouch		1. Little or no crouch		1. Assume preparatory crouch with hips, knees, and ankles in deep flexion
		2. Trunk not parallel to ground		2. Trunk is almost parallel to ground
		3. No backward-upward swing of arms		3. Weight moves forward as arms swing backward-upward
		4. No return movement of arms; no weight shift forward		4. Weight continues to move forward as arms swing forward-downward
		5. Insufficient shoulder joint flexion—arms not lifted high enough		5. Crouch phase ends when arms are in line with trunk
Takeoff		6. Takeoff begins with *simultaneous* extension at hip, knee, and ankle joints		6. Takeoff beings with *successive* initiation of extension at hip, knee, and ankle joints
		7. Takeoff angle is more than 45°		7. Takeoff is approximately 45°
		8. Arm swing not coordinated with leg movements		8. Arms swing forward-upward as heels are lifted
Flight upward		9. Incomplete body extension at takeoff		9. Body is in full extension at beginning of flight
		10. Arms never fully flexed overhead to form single long lever with trunk		10. Arms are flexed at shoulder joint and elbows extended. Arms are in line with trunk to form single long lever
		11. Knee and hip flexion occur simultaneously		11. Lower legs flex first during flight
Flight downward		12. Incomplete hip flexion during flight		12. Hip joint flexion begins when knee flexion reaches 90°
		13. Forward arm action not coordinated well with knee and hip extension		13. As knees come forward and knee joint extends, arms and trunk reach forward
		14. Incomplete knee extension at end of flight		14. Knees are fully extended at end of flight
Landing		15. Toes contact ground first		15. Heels touch ground before toes
		16. Incomplete spinal and hip flexion at moment of contact		16. Trunk and thighs are almost touching at moment of contact
		17. Center of gravity too far backward at moment of contact resulting in unsteady landing		17. Instantaneous flexion of knees when heels contact ground
		18. Hands touch the floor		18. Arms reach forward-upward to help maintain balance.

Vault

Jumping becomes a sports skill when it is used in gymnastics as a means of getting over a piece of apparatus. There are many different kinds of apparatus the student can *vault* over: (a) a low beam about thigh or hip high; (b) a tumbling bench; (c) a vaulting box; (d) a horse; or (e) a buck.

Instead of demonstrating standard vaults and expecting the student to imitate, the teacher should observe the different movement approaches explored by the student in attempts to get over the apparatus. Which of the following movement patterns offer the student the most success?

1. *Squat vault.* Weight taken equally on both arms, knees are pulled upward, tucked to chest, and then continue forward. Body passes over box in a squat position.
2. *Straddle vault.* Weight taken equally on both arms, and legs are abducted in wide stride semisitting position. Hands are on inside and legs on the outside. Body passes over box in this straddle position.
3. *Flank vault.* Initially done with both arms on the box. Standard flank vault is performed with one arm. While arms support weight of body, both legs are lifted simultaneously over the box. The side of the body passes over the box. Sometimes called a side vault.
4. *Front vault.* Same as flank vault except that the front of the body passes over the box.

The beginning vault is often a combined side-front vault with both hands on the box and the knees bent as the legs pass over. Most elementary school textbooks recommend that the squat vault be taught first. The law of individual differences rules that *all* children should not be introduced to the same progression of vaults nor tested on a single movement pattern selected by the teacher. When allowed to discover their own ways of getting over, first-grade children can succeed at vaulting. A beatboard or springboard is necessary to attain the height necessary for propulsion of the body over the box.

Jumping on a Springboard, Beatboard, or Minitramp

The movement patterns used on the springboard, beatboard, minitramp, and diving board are similar. For better transfer of learning, the child should have experience on all four pieces of apparatus. If the budget allows the purchase of only one, the beatboard is recommended.

The following questions serve as guides for observation and evaluation of the natural movement pattern of the child when challenged to run up the board, jump once on the end of the board, and then land on the mat.

1. Does the child run slowly, with hesitancy, or at an appropriate speed?
2. How long is the child's approach—i.e., how many steps does he or she take prior to reaching the beatboard?
3. Does the child run flat-footed or on the balls of the feet?
4. Does the child slow down or stop before executing the jump on the end of the board?
5. Does the child use a two-foot take-off from the board?
6. Which foot is the last to push off before the two-foot take-off is initiated?
7. Does the child gain maximum height in his or her jump?
8. Is the amount of forward lean mechanically efficient so the child falls neither forward nor backward?
9. Does the child bend at hip, knee, and ankle joints upon landing in order to absorb the shock?
10. Does the child have trouble maintaining balance upon landing?

Specific tasks that the child can be asked to perform while jumping are

1. Clap hands overhead, behind back, in front of body.
2. Land beyond a certain line or marker on the mat.
3. Assume a tuck position in the air.
4. Assume a pike position in the air.
5. Assume a straddle position in the air.
6. Assume a hurdle position in the air.
7. Assume a laterally flexed position in the air.
8. Make a turn in the air.
9. Land with feet together, feet apart, one foot in front of the other.
10. Land with arms in various positions.
11. Land and immediately perform a forward roll.

Jump Used as Mount

The term *mount* used in gymnastics is a jump from a beatboard, springboard, or minitramp up onto a piece of apparatus. Mounts are used to begin routines on the balance beam, the even parallel bars, the uneven parallel bars, the horse, and the buck.

Some of the easiest mounts that can be practiced on various pieces of apparatus are

1. Straight arm support mount.
   a. Short approach.
   b. Double-leg take-off.
   c. Both hands on top of beam or bar.
   d. Jump to push-up position with both arms straight.
   e. Thighs supported against beam.
   f. Head high.
   g. Back arched.
   h. Toes pointed.
2. Crotch seat mount.
   a. Perform straight arm support mount.
   b. Swing one leg sideward (abduction).
   c. Continue swing until body straddles beam.
   d. Hands grip beam behind.
   e. Toes pointed.
   f. Good body alignment.
3. Squat mount.
   a. Perform straight arm support mount.
   b. Simultaneously tuck knees to chest.
   c. End squatting with arms on outside.
   d. Head up.

Children need practice jumping up onto things as well as jumping down. If no apparatus can be improvised, they may jump (two-foot take-off) *up* the stairs, *up* on automobiles tires, *up* on street curbs, *up* on rocks, and so on.

Jumping on a Trampoline

The trampoline is used widely with exceptional children. Kephart, Getman, Cratty, and others have recommended the trampoline as one of the best means of improving laterality (i.e., the kinesthetic awareness of right and left requisite to the maintenance of balance and good body alignment). This objective can be achieved only if the child is subjected to extensive problem solving and challenged to transfer what he or she knows about locomotor and nonlocomotor movements to the enigmatic surface of the trampoline.

Emphasis should not be on the learning of such traditional skills as the seat drop during early lessons, but rather upon motor fluency and originality. The child may attempt rolls, animal walks, rope jumping, turns in the air, and other stunts. The teacher who is capable of maintaining silence, accepting a child as he or she is, and observing closely will find the trampoline an extremely valuable diagnostic aid. The problems that a child exhibits on the trampoline are the same as those the child has overcome and/or learned to compensate for when on the ground.

Hopping

Hopping is the most difficult of the basic locomotor skills. Sinclair (1973) reported that only 28% of her 3-year-old subjects could hop; 71% of the 4-year-old children could hop; and 96% of the 5-year-old children could hop. Not until age 5 could the children hop equally well on the preferred and nonpreferred foot. Sinclair's subjects had no known perceptual-motor problems.

Children with neurological deficits that affect balance may never learn to hop. Cratty (1967) reported that only 25% of the children with Down's syndrome whom he tested could hop in square or circular patterns. The children with moderate mental retardation could hop on one foot in succession, and only 5% of them could hop in square or circular patterns. The performance of mildly mentally retarded children approached that of normal children, although games such as hopscotch were decidedly difficult for almost half of them.

Before challenging a child to perform a task that may be unrealistic for his or her capabilities, the teacher should test for static balance. Can he or she stand motionless with all weight on one leg? For how many seconds? On which leg is this task easier? If the child fails the test of static balance, what are the reasons? Inadequate leg strength, poor body alignment, faulty proprioception, or deficits in the vestibular system?

Cratty reported that approximately 75% of children with Down's syndrome whom he tested in Los Angeles could not maintain their balance on one foot for more than a few seconds. Most of these children found it almost impossible to balance on one foot with eyes closed. Only two-thirds of the moderately mentally retarded children could maintain their balance on one foot for more than 5 seconds without vision. Approximately 70% of the mildly mentally retarded children could maintain their balance on one foot with arms folded across their chests, and about one-half of them could maintain the balance position on one foot with their eyes closed. Mildly mentally retarded children seem to improve significantly in their ability to balance between the chronological ages of 8 and 14 years.

Few tests of hopping are standardized and yield numerical scores. The best known is that included in the Purdue Perceptual Motor Survey (Roach & Kephart, 1960). The following items comprise the test.

Hop 1/1. The child is asked to stand with feet together, then to hop on the right foot, lifting the left, and next to alternate, hopping first on the right and then on the left.

Hop 2/2. This task is the same as the foregoing except that the child hops twice on the right foot, twice on the left, and so on.

Table 10.7
Percentage of Boys Able to Hop Three Patterns

Age	3L,3R %	2L,2R %	3L,2R %
6½	23	16	7
7	35	19	10
7½	48	38	18
8	63	53	31

Note. From ''An Evaluation of Performance on Rhythmic Hopping Patterns'' by J. F. Keogh and P. Pedigo, 1967, sponsored by the National Institute on Child Health and Human Development (Grant HD09059–03), UCLA. Unpublished paper.

Hop 2/1. The child is asked to hop twice on the right foot, once on the left, twice on the right, and so on.

Hop 1/2. The child is asked to hop once on the right foot, twice on the left, and so on.

Performance on these tasks is evaluated in accordance with the following 4-point scale:

4—The child performs all tasks easily.
3—The child can alter sides symmetrically.
2—The child can hop on either foot at will; can alternate, but cannot maintain a rhythm.
1—The child can perform only symmetrically.

Applying Kephart's concept of hopping alternately from one foot to another without breaking the rhythm, Keogh and Pedigo established the norms in Table 10.7 for boys on three hopping patterns.

Rhythmic Two-Part Motion

Developmentally, the average child does not learn how to combine basic locomotor movements until about age 3. The *gallop* is the first combination to be mastered. Sinclair reported that 76% of her 3-year-olds and 92% of her 4-year-olds could gallop. Most of her children succeeded in galloping before they could hop.

Since the gallop is a combination of the walk and the leap, it seems reasonable to introduce the skill at the time the child refines his or her leap. This may be the first skill learned in a forward-backward stride position with the same foot leading throughout. The teacher who is concerned with the establishment of dominance should observe which foot is the lead one and whether the same foot is used consistently in this role. Sinclair observed that most children learned to lead with their nonpreferred foot much later than with their preferred foot.

The *slide* is identical to the gallop except that it is executed sideward rather than forward and, hence, requires a better defined sense of laterality. Approximately 34% of Sinclair's 3-year-olds and 77% of her 4-year-olds could slide. In the early years, children seem to have a preferred side in sliding. There is a tendency for beginners to err by rotating the head, trunk, pelvis, or hip in the direction of the slide rather than to truly lead with the shoulder. The importance of moving sideward as a means of improving balance and laterality was emphasized by Kephart, who noted that this is one of the few skills that teach lateral transfer of weight rather than forward-backward transfer.

In elementary school folk dances executed in a circle, the slide is one of the easiest and most popular steps. The pattern traditionally used is seven slides to the right with a transfer of weight to the opposite foot on the eighth count, followed by seven slides to the left and a transfer of weight. This sequence should be practiced early.

Skipping is a combination of walk and hop in an uneven rhythm. It is learned after the leap, jump, and hop are mastered. Approximately half the 4-year-olds can skip, and by the first grade, almost all children can skip. Boys generally experience more difficulty than girls. Mastery seems to progress through two or three stages: (a) a type of shuffle on one foot alternated with a walk on the other; (b) a skip on one foot alternated with a walk on the other; and finally (c) a skip alternately performed by both feet. As in all locomotor patterns, the arms work in opposition to the legs.

Rathbone listed skipping along with hanging by the arms and balancing as the three forms of physical activity that are especially important in childhood. She stated, "Skipping will help to lift the body high, to extend it. It will also set a pattern of joyousness, which, in itself, encourages elevation. The adult who discourages a child from skipping and hopping about is harming his body as much as his spirit" (Rathbone, 1959, p. 5).

Throwing

Developmentally, throwing begins with the emergence of voluntary grasping and holding behaviors. This occurs at about 7 months of age, when the infant begins to play with (manipulate) cubes and pellets. At about the same time, the infant begins to reach with one hand and transfer objects from hand to hand.

At about 11 months the child is able to voluntarily release objects. The child begins to "cast a ball imitatively" and to offer the ball to his or her mirror image at about 12 months of age. Not until 15 months does the child gain the fine muscle control to release a tiny pellet—i.e., drop it into a cup.

At about 1½ years of age, the child progresses from *casting* to *hurling.* The child also begins to follow directions like "Put the ball on the table. . . . Go get the ball. . . . Give the ball to me." Hemiplegic persons, as

Figure 10.32 Four stages in overarm throwing through which children progress. *Stage 1:* **Casting** characterized by (1) feet remain stationary; (2) no trunk or hip rotation; (3) ball is thrown primarily by elbow extension. *Stage 2:* **Hurling** characterized by (1) feet remain stationary; (2) preparatory movement involves a rotation of the trunk toward the throwing side; (3) outward rotation and abduction at shoulder joint result in cocking of hand slightly behind head; (4) trunk rotates back to starting position with forward arm swing; (5) angle of release is usually 80–100°. *Stage 3:* **Homolateral throw,** same as stage 2 except (1) child steps into throw (i.e., as right arm throws, right foot steps forward); (2) there is weight shift forward and more pronounced follow-through; (3) angle of release is more horizontal (forward). *Stage 4:* **Crosslateral throw** characterized by (1) opposition (left foot forward as right arm throws); (2) weight transfer in forward-backward-forward pattern; (3) full rotation of trunk to left and right; (4) coordinated involvement of nonthrowing arm in maintaining balance; (5) abduction/outward rotation at shoulder joint in backswing changes to abduction/inward rotation in forward swing and follow through; (6) angle of release is about 45°.

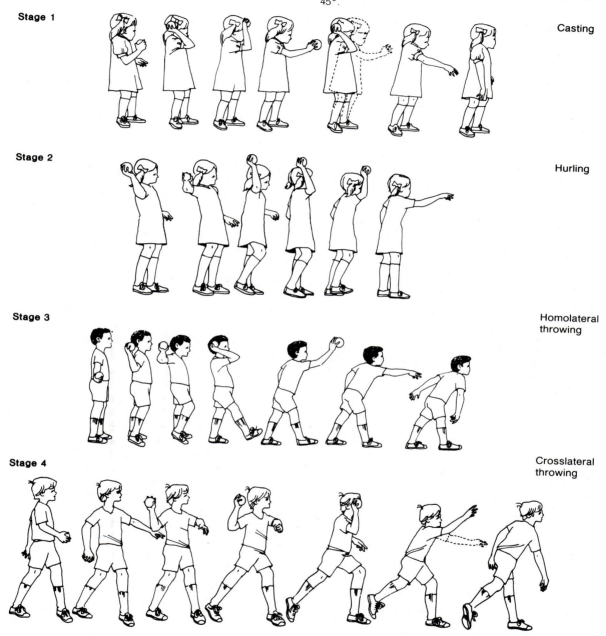

Stage 1 — Casting

Stage 2 — Hurling

Stage 3 — Homolateral throwing

Stage 4 — Crosslateral throwing

well as the cerebral palsied, may show considerable delay in mastering ball handling skills because of difficulties with the grasp and release pattern. Yarn or nerf (rather than rubber) balls are recommended for such persons, who may remain frozen in the casting and hurling stages for many years.

Figure 10.32 presents the four stages through which normal children progress from ages 1 through 6 and up. Tennis balls, bean bags, and yarn balls are generally used with young children. For the IEP, recording the stage in which the child is functioning is easier than describing the specific behaviors.

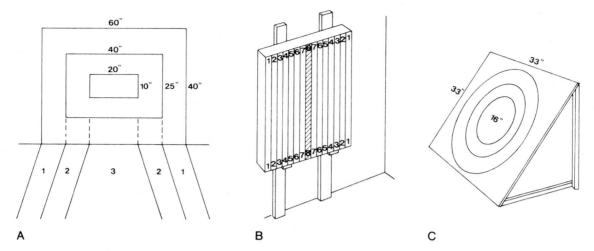

Figure 10.33 Targets recommended for accuracy throwing. (A) Target used for both throwing and kicking by Dr. Thomas Vodola in Project Active assessment and teaching; softball-size whiffleball is thrown from minimum distance of 10 feet. (B) Vertical target throw with tennis ball aimed toward *8 space* used by Dr. Lawrence Rarick; for horizontal target throw, the target is rotated so parallel divisions (4.8 inches each) run horizontally. (C) Rarick ball toss for accuracy target in which a soccer ball is thrown underhand (two hands) from distances of 6, 9, 12, 15, and 18 feet.

The mature throw is characterized by *opposition* (left foot forward when right arm throws), *weight transfer* in forward-backward-forward pattern, *hip and spinal rotation,* a *smooth follow-through,* and a *45° angle of release.* Many persons believe that velocity of throw is one of the best measures of maturity. Two-year-olds may throw as slowly as 8 feet per second, while 12-year-olds throw 50 to 80 feet per second.

Both target and distance throws should be practiced. Children should be given many trials every day. Warm-up exercises are important before throws. Figure 10.33 shows targets used by Vodola and Rarick.

Rolling or Pushing

The first ball handling activity to be executed with a partner is usually rolling an 8- to 10-inch playground ball back and forth while sitting widestride on the floor. For children whose orthopedic impairment prohibits floor sitting, a long table can be used with partners sitting in chairs at either end. In this adaptation, a pushing rather than rolling pattern may be used.

From rolling in the sitting position, the child progresses to rolling and fielding balls in the standing position. He or she also begins rolling balls toward wall targets, bowling pins, and similar targets. For the severely handicapped, a long cord on the ball facilitates recovery. Through rolling, children have their first visual tracking activities, and *watching the ball move* should be stressed.

Catching

Catching entails a *reach, bend, pull* movement pattern. It also presupposes integrity of the visual tracking system. It is a more difficult task to master than throwing, and early learning of throwing and catching should probably occur separately at different stations.

The principle of specificity should guide the teaching of catching in that large balls demand movement patterns different from small balls. Catching lessons should involve practice with all sizes of balls coming in different flight patterns (horizontal vs. vertical) at different speeds. Little transfer of learning from one kind of catch to another occurs.

Visual acuity, which is poor in infants and improves up to age 8 or 9 years, affects catching. Many Down's syndrome children, for instance, are near-sighted (myopic). *Astigmatism* causes blurring of the ball. Poor binocular fusion (*integration*) is manifested in double vision (*diplogia*) and functional blindness in one eye (*amblyopia*). Many CP and MR persons have *strabismus* (cross eyes), which also affects visual acuity and tracking.

Practice in visual tracking of a suspended ball is a good lead-up activity for catching as well as striking and kicking skills. A tether ball apparatus can be used or a homemade system of balls of different sizes, shapes, and colors suspended at different heights. Simply tracking a moving object is boring, so the activity should entail touching, striking, kicking, or catching the object being tracked. Developmentally, *horizontal tracking* is believed to occur before vertical tracking, and *near-to-far* tracking is successful before far-to-near.

Figure 10.34 Catching a small ball. *Stage 1:* **Immature hand scoop** characterized by (1) initial eye focus on thrower but inability to track ball from far to near; (2) avoidance reaction often shown by closing eyes or turning head as ball approaches; (3) arms stiffly extended in front of body with hands waist high or higher; (4) rigid stationary position of feet and body; (5) hand action is a poorly timed scooping pattern which often misses ball. *Stage 2:* **Successful beginner coordination** characterized by (1) initial eye focus on thrower followed by attention to own motor response and ball's actual arrival; (2) arms semiflexed (forearms in supination) with fingers forward and palms up; (3) as ball contacts hands, forearms rotate to facilitate gripping ball; (4) entire body flexes (gives with the ball) on receipt. *Stage 3:* **Mature catch** characterized by (1) eyes track ball continuously through entire flight; (2) child runs to meet the ball, aligning his body with flight trajectory; (3) arms reach for ball with forearms in midposition, thumbs on top, fingers pointing toward ball; (4) as ball contacts hands, shoulder joint adducts and wrist and fingers flex to grasp ball; (5) the "give with ball" begins immediately upon contact and occurs over greatest possible distance for optimal shock absorption.

Stage 1   Immature hand scoop

Stage 2   Beginner coordination

Stage 3   Mature catch

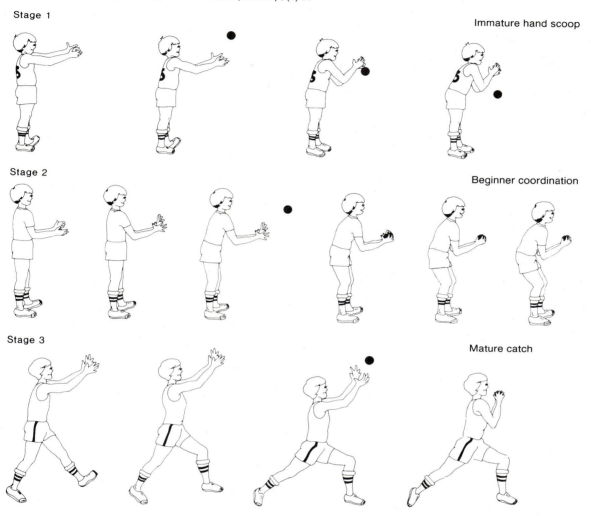

Visual tracking should be practiced with *ground balls; straight trajectory balls* coming to knee, waist, shoulder, and head; and *fly balls* coming with curved trajectories. Research shows that, in far-to-near tracking for catching, young children attend to the thrower rather than to the flight of the ball. Developmentally, the child next is able to attend both to the source of the flight and his or her own motor response. Only with much practice does the child achieve the ability to visually monitor the entire flight and make discriminatory judgments with respect to velocity.

Figures 10.34 and 10.35 present stages in catching that can be used in describing present level of performance and writing objectives for the IEP. Remember that catching problems are *visuomotor,* and work with other team members in the development of comprehensive visual perception programs.

Figure 10.35 Catching a large ball. *Stage 1:* **Passive arm cradle** in normal 2- or 3-year-old girl characterized by (1) making arm cradle, often with adult help, before ball is tossed; (2) rigid stationary position of feet and body; (3) no response until after ball has landed in cradle; (4) pull toward chest. *Stage 2:* **Stiff-arm clapping motion** characterized by (1) extending arms and spreading fingers; (2) rigid stationary position of feet and body; (3) clapping response when ball touches either hand; (4) control gained by forearm pull toward chest. *Stage 3:* **Initial eye-hand control** characterized by (1) eyes track ball from far to near, with most attention given to the source of flight and own motor response; (2) body moves to position self in line with trajectory of ball; (3) arms outstretched while running to meet the ball; (4) hands only contact the ball; (5) ball is pulled toward chest. *Stage 4:* **Mature basketball catch** characterized by (1) eyes track ball continuously through entire flight; (2) body moves to position self in line with trajectory of ball; (3) arms, hands, and fingers are relaxed until time to contact ball; (4) catch accomplished by simultaneously stepping toward ball, partially extending arms, and spreading fingers; (5) follow-through is a slight flexion at shoulder and elbow joints.

Stage 1: Passive arm cradle

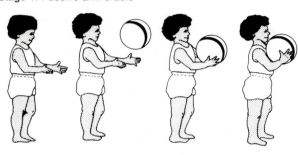

Stage 2: Stiff arm clapping

Stage 3: Initial eye-hand control

Stage 4: Mature catch

Striking and Kicking

Striking and kicking are similar motor learning processes in that each demands relatively sophisticated *visuomotor* skills. Practice should begin with stationary objects of different sizes, weights (see Figure 10.36), and colors in optimal lighting conditions (never facing the sun). If balance is a problem, a barre or chair should be provided to hold on to for stability. When success with stationary balls is consistent, practice progresses to balls suspended at different heights. Only when success is possible does the teaching progress to moving balls.

A ball-tossing apparatus that can be regulated for speed is probably more important in adapted physical education than for the tennis or softball team. If a sharing arrangement cannot be worked out, purchase is of high priority. Homemade systems of pulleys with suspended balls moving horizontally or vertically at different speeds can be created also.

Learning to control the direction balls are sent is important. See Chapter 11, Perceptual-Motor Functioning, Games, and Sports, for ideas regarding timing and body positioning in relation to the arriving ball.

The principle of leverage (*the shorter the lever, the easier it is to achieve accuracy and control*) should be applied in selecting bats, rackets, and other striking implements. Hitting a balloon or yarn ball with the hand creates a shorter lever for beginners than use of an implement. Thus, balloon volleyball and movement exploration activities comprise an excellent first teaching progression.

Adapted games using field or ice hockey, croquet, and golf concepts in which a ball or puck on the floor is given impetus are sometimes easier for clumsy persons to master than throwing, catching, and striking games. This may be particularly true of CP and brain-damaged persons with grasp and release problems.

Most important individual differences should be honored within game situations. In softball and kick-ball, there is no reason everyone coming up to bat (or kick) should use the same size ball. Nor should all the children have to bat (kick) a moving ball. Using balls of variable sizes not only influences the success of the batter but gives better practice and more success options to the fielders. Likewise, there is no reason why all children must operate under the 3-strike rule; some need 5, 7, or 10 strikes. If success still does not occur, the batting tee offers a last chance, since the experience of running bases is too valuable to justify exclusion from it.

Self-Concept

Self-concept, what persons think and/or feel about their appearance, abilities, disabilities, and relationships with others, is the frame of reference through which they interact with the world. Self-concept, in early childhood and among many persons of all ages, is related to what individuals can do with their bodies and how they think others perceive their movement competence.

Self-concepts of handicapped and/or clumsy students are often lower than those of able-bodied peers. Inherent in low self-concept are expectations of failure, fear of letting teammates down during a crucial play, dread of being teased or singled out from others for correction and/or help with skills, and a growing reluctance to participate. It becomes increasingly easier to sit and watch others play and/or compete than to risk failure. Thus, many clumsy students may profess a desire to sit out or keep score when, deep inside, they long to participate and to be part of the group.

Before such students can be taught basic movement patterns, games, and sports in the traditional skill-oriented manner, they must be helped to change negative feelings about the self and taught methods of coping with the stresses related to fear of failure and lack of understanding and acceptance by others. Until they believe in themselves and trust in teachers and peers, it is unlikely that students with low self-concepts will put forth their best efforts in learning skills, rules, and strategies. As indicated in Chapter 6, low self-concept becomes increasingly a problem with age, often reaching its peak in adolescence. The factors related to low self-concept are many, and teachers should learn as much about their students' homes and school backgrounds as possible in an effort to identify and ameliorate causes.

Assessment of Self-Concept

Because pedagogy for teaching physical education to students with low self-concepts is different from that of students with no problems in the affective domain, adapted physical education assessment should include tests of self-concept and related measures. Many standardized tests exist for this purpose. Following are two tests and descriptions of two others.

Piers-Harris Children's Self-Concept Scale The Way I Feel About Myself

Purpose
To assess self-concept of students in Grades 3 to 12. Can be used in lower grades if items are read to the child. Factor analysis shows the test measures six factors: (a) behavior, (b) intellectual and school status, (c) physical appearance and attributes, (d) anxiety, (e) popularity, and (f) happiness and satisfaction.

Description
Consists of 80 brief statements to which the student responds with yes or no.

Scoring
Scores range from 1 to 80, with 1 point given for each response that shows good self-concept. Means range from 47.79 to 60.40 on different studies on normal children reported in test manual. Raw score for 52nd percentile is 54; raw score for 41st percentile is 50; raw score for 31st percentile is 46.

Validity
Construct validity based on factor analysis and known groups methods with all items discriminating between students with high and low scores on the total test. Criterion validity with Lipsitt Children's Self-Concept Scale (.68), with various teacher ratings (.06 to .43), and with various peer ratings (.26 to .49).

Primary Sources
Piers, E., & Harris, D. (1964). Age and other correlates of self-concept in children. *Journal of Educational Psychology, 55* (2), 91–95.

Smith, M. (1979). Prediction of self-concept among learning disabled children. *Journal of Learning Disabilities, 12,* 664–669.

Address for Ordering
Counselor Recordings and Tests, Box 6184, Acklen Station, Nashville, TN 37212.

Copy of the Test
Here is a set of statements. Some of them are true of you and so you will circle them YES. Some are not true of you and so you will circle them NO. Answer every question even if some are hard to decide. There are no right and wrong answers. Only you can tell us how you feel about yourself, so we hope you will mark them the way you really feel inside.

*1. My classmates make fun of me.	Yes/No
2. I am a happy person.	Yes/No
*3. It is hard for me to make friends.	Yes/No
*4. I am often sad.	Yes/No
5. I am smart.	Yes/No
6. I am shy.	Yes/No
7. I get nervous when the teacher calls on me.	Yes/No
8. My looks bother me.	Yes/No
9. When I grow up I will be an important person.	Yes/No
10. I get worried when we have tests in school.	Yes/No
11. I am unpopular.	Yes/No
12. I am well behaved in school.	Yes/No
13. It is usually my fault when something goes wrong.	Yes/No
14. I cause trouble to my family.	Yes/No
*15. I am strong.	Yes/No
16. I have good ideas.	Yes/No
17. I am an important member of my family.	Yes/No
*18. I like being the way I am.	Yes/No
*19. I am good at making things with my hands.	Yes/No
20. I give up easily.	Yes/No
21. I am good in schoolwork.	Yes/No
22. I do many bad things.	Yes/No
*23. I can draw well.	Yes/No
24. I am good in music.	Yes/No
25. I behave badly at home.	Yes/No
26. I am slow in finishing my schoolwork.	Yes/No
27. I am an important member of my class.	Yes/No
28. I am nervous.	Yes/No
29. I have pretty eyes.	Yes/No
30. I can give a good report in front of the class.	Yes/No
31. In school I am a dreamer.	Yes/No
32. I pick on my brother(s) and sister(s).	Yes/No
33. My friends like my ideas.	Yes/No
34. I often get into trouble.	Yes/No
35. I am disobedient at home.	Yes/No
36. I am unlucky.	Yes/No
37. I worry a lot.	Yes/No
38. My parents expect too much of me.	Yes/No
39. I usually want my own way.	Yes/No
40. I feel left out of things.	Yes/No
*41. I have nice hair.	Yes/No
42. I often volunteer in school.	Yes/No
43. I have a pleasant face.	Yes/No
44. I sleep well at night.	Yes/No
*45. I hate school.	Yes/No
*46. I am among the last to be chosen for games.	Yes/No
47. I am sick a lot.	Yes/No
48. I am often mean to other people.	Yes/No
49. My classmates in school think I have good ideas.	Yes/No
*50. I am unhappy.	Yes/No
51. I have many friends.	Yes/No
52. I am cheerful.	Yes/No
53. I am dumb about most things.	Yes/No
*54. I am good-looking.	Yes/No
55. I have lots of pep.	Yes/No
56. I get into a lot of fights.	Yes/No
*57. I am popular with boys.	Yes/No
58. People pick on me.	Yes/No
59. My family is disappointed in me.	Yes/No
*60. I wish I were different.	Yes/No

61. When I try to make something, everything seems to go wrong.   Yes/No
62. I am picked on at home.   Yes/No
*63. I am a leader in games and sports.   Yes/No
*64. I am clumsy.   Yes/No
*65. In games and sports I watch instead of play.   Yes/No
66. I forget what I learn.   Yes/No
67. I am easy to get along with.   Yes/No
68. I lose my temper easily.   Yes/No
*69. I am popular with girls.   Yes/No
*70. I am a good reader.   Yes/No
71. I would rather work alone than with a group.   Yes/No
72. I dislike my brother (sister).   Yes/No
73. I have a bad figure.   Yes/No
74. I am often afraid.   Yes/No
75. I am always dropping or breaking things.   Yes/No
76. I cry easily.   Yes/No
77. I am different from other people.   Yes/No
78. I think bad thoughts.   Yes/No
79. I can be trusted.   Yes/No
80. I am a good person.   Yes/No

*Items that appear in Cratty Self-Concept Test.

Cratty Self-Concept Scale

Purpose
To estimate how children in Kindergarten through Grade 6 feel about their general physical appearance and their ability to perform physical skills.

Description
Consists of 20 brief questions to which the student responds with yes or no.

Scoring
Scores range from 1 to 20, with 1 point given for each response that shows good self-concept. Mean scores range from 14.1 to 15.7 for K to 6, with no significant differences between grades or genders. Cratty defines *high self-concept* as 16 and over and *low self-concept* as 14 and under.

Validity
Content validity with all items but one reworded from the Piers-Harris Self-Concept Scale. Construct validity by method of known groups with every item discriminating between students with high and low scores on the total test.

Reliability
Test-retest reliability of .82 for 288 children.

Primary Sources
Barrow, H., & McGee, R. (1979). *A practical approach to measurement in physical education* (3rd ed.). Philadelphia: Lea & Febiger.
Cratty, B. (1974). *Motor activity and the education of retardates* (2nd ed.). Philadelphia: Lea & Febiger.
Cratty, B., Ikedo, N., Martin, M., Jennett, C., & Morris, M. (1970). *Movement activities, motor ability, and the education of children*. Springfield, IL: Charles C. Thomas.

Copy of the Test
1. Are you good at making things with your hands?   Yes/No
2. Can you draw well?   Yes/No
3. Are you strong?   Yes/No
4. Do you like the way you look?   Yes/No
5. Do your friends make fun of you?   Yes/No
6. Are you handsome/pretty?   Yes/No
7. Do you have trouble making friends?   Yes/No
8. Do you like school?   Yes/No
9. Do you wish you were different?   Yes/No
10. Are you sad most of the time?   Yes/No
11. Are you the last to be chosen in games?   Yes/No
12. Do girls like you?   Yes/No
13. Are you a good leader in games and sports?   Yes/No
14. Are you clumsy?   Yes/No
15. In games, do you watch instead of play?   Yes/No
16. Do boys like you?   Yes/No
17. Are you happy most of the time?   Yes/No
18. Do you have nice hair?   Yes/No
19. Do you play with younger children a lot?   Yes/No
20. Is reading easy to you?   Yes/No

Note: From *Movement Activities, Motor Ability, and the Education of Children* by B. Cratty et al., 1970, Springfield, IL: Charles C. Thomas. Used by permission of Charles C. Thomas and the author.

Martinek-Zaichkowsky Self-Concept Scale (MZSC)

Purpose
To assess self-concept of children in Grades 1 to 8. Factor analysis shows that the test measures five factors: (a) satisfaction and happiness, (b) home and family relationships and circumstances, (c) ability in games, recreation, and sports, (d) behavioral, personal, and social characteristics in school, and (e) personality traits and emotional tendency.

Description
Consists of 25 pairs of pictures, one in each pair depicting good self-concept and one depicting bad. The student points to the picture that shows how he or she feels inside.

Scoring
Scores range from 1 to 25, with 1 point given for each picture pointed to that depicts good self-concept.

Validity
Construct validity based on factor analysis. Criterion validity with Piers-Harris Self-Concept Scale ($r = .49$) and with Coopersmith Self-Esteem Inventory ($r = .56$).

Reliability
.75 to .92 for Grades 1 to 4 by Hoyt Estimate of Reliability.

Primary Sources

Karper, W., & Martinek, T. (1982). Differential influence of various instructional factors on self-concepts of handicapped and nonhandicapped children in mainstreamed physical education classes. *Perceptual and Motor Skills, 54,* 831–835.

Karper, W., & Martinek, T. (1983). Motor performance and self-concept of handicapped and nonhandicapped children in integrated physical education classes. *American Corrective Therapy Journal, 37,* 91–95.

Martinek, T., & Zaichkowsky, L. D. (1977). *Manual for the Martinek-Zaichkowsky Self-Concept Scale for Children.* Jacksonville, IL: Psychologists and Educators, Inc.

Address for Ordering

Psychologists and Educators, Inc., Jacksonville, IL 62650. L. Zaichkowsky. School of Education, Boston University, Boston, MA 02215.

Tennessee Self-Concept Scale

Purpose

To assess self-concept of persons age 12 or over and having at least a sixth-grade reading level.

Description

Consists of 100 self-descriptive statements, each of which is rated on a 5-point scale. Two forms are available: Clinical and Research (C & R) Form and Counseling Form. Both forms use the same test booklet, but different scoring systems are used.

Scoring

Scoring is complicated, and test manual is required for instructions. Separate scores are calculated on physical self, moral-ethical self, personal self, family self, social self, and self-criticism. These are summed to derive scores on identity (who he or she is), self-satisfaction (how he or she accepts self), and behavior (how he or she acts).

Validity

Content validity affirmed by 7 clinical psychologists used as judges to classify items. Construct validity by factor analysis and known group methods with items discriminating between groups known to be high and low on certain psychological dimensions.

Reliability

Test-retest reliabilities ranging from .65 to .92 on the different scales for 60 college students.

Primary Sources

Fitts, W. (1965). *Manual for Tennessee Self-Concept Scale.* Nashville: Counselor Recordings and Tests.

Address for Ordering

Counselor Recordings and Tests, Box 6184, Acklen Station, Nashville, TN 37212.

Assessment of Attitude toward Physical Education

Attitude toward movement and/or physical education is closely associated with attitude toward self. It is normal to feel negative toward situations and activities in which one expects to do poorly. Use of standardized tests helps identify the specific aspects of physical education that are most and least meaningful. Such tests also help to pinpoint areas of greatest anxiety. Two illustrative instruments follow that are appropriate for adapted physical education.

Simon and Smoll Attitude Toward Physical Activity Scale (SATPA)

Purpose

To measure attitudes in children, from Grade 3 on and adults. Has been shown to be statistically equivalent with Kenyon's (1968) Attitude Toward Physical Activity Scale.

Format

Semantic differential, using eight bipolar adjective pairs (good-bad, worthless-worthwhile, pleasant-unpleasant, bitter-sweet, nice-awful, sad-happy, clean-dirty, and steady-nervous) to show multidimensional feelings toward physical activity. See sample item with 7-point range between each adjective pair. The same measurement approach is applied to six attitude subdomains: social experience, health and fitness, thrill and risk, beauty in human movement, tension release, and long and hard training.

Scoring

A separate score, ranging from 8 (1 point for each of eight adjective pairs) to 56 is derived for each attitude subdomain. Total score ranges from 48 (very bad attitude) to 336 (very good attitude).

Validity

Criterion-related, with Kenyon's (1968) Attitude Toward Physical Activity Scale, with Hoyt equivalence reliabilities for able-bodied adults ranging from .79 to .90 (Schultz & Smoll, 1977) and for cerebral palsied adults ranging from .69 to .82 (Cooper, 1984).

Reliability

Internal consistency reliability coefficients of .80 to .89 and test-retest *rs* of .44 to .62 for children (Simon & Smoll, 1974).

Average Scores

Means for each subdomain are as follows:

Subdomain	Simon & Smoll	Politino	Cooper
	AB children, ages 9–11, (N=992)	ED children ages 8–13 (N=80)	Adult CP athletes (N=165)
Social exper.	48	38	48
Health/fitness	46	41	47
Beauty	45	36	47
Tension release	43	36	46
Thrill	38	31	42
Training	38	32	41
Composite	—	212	271

Primary Sources

Cooper, M. (1984). *Attitudes toward physical activity and sources of attraction to sports of cerebral palsied athletes.* Unpublished doctoral dissertation, Texas Woman's University, Denton.

Kenyon, G. S. (1968). A conceptual model for characterizing physical activity. *Research Quarterly, 39,* 96–105.

Politino, V. (1980). *Attitudes toward physical activity and self-concept of normal and emotionally disturbed children.* Unpublished doctoral dissertation, Southern Illinois University, Carbondale.

Schutz, R., & Smoll, F. (1977). Equivalence of two inventories for assessing attitudes toward physical activity. *Psychological Reports, 40,* 1031–1034.

Simon, J., & Smoll, F. (1974). An instrument for assessing children's attitudes toward physical activity. *Research Quarterly, 45,* 407–415.

Copy of the Test

There are six scales to which the student must respond. The first two scales are presented here. The ideas for the other four scales are given, and the teacher need only photocopy the same bipolar adjective scale to go with each idea.

Samples from SATPA (two of the six scales)

What Does the Idea in the Box Mean to You?

PHYSICAL ACTIVITY AS A SOCIAL EXPERIENCE
Physical activities which give you a chance to meet new people and be with your friends.

Always think about the idea in the box.

good	1 2 3 4 5 6 7	bad
of no use	1 2 3 4 5 6 7	useful
not pleasant	1 2 3 4 5 6 7	pleasant
bitter	1 2 3 4 5 6 7	sweet
nice	1 2 3 4 5 6 7	awful
happy	1 2 3 4 5 6 7	sad
dirty	1 2 3 4 5 6 7	clean
steady	1 2 3 4 5 6 7	nervous

What Does the Idea in the Box Mean to You?

PHYSICAL ACTIVITY FOR HEALTH AND FITNESS
Taking part in physical activities to make your health better and to get your body in better condition.

Always think about the idea in the box.

good	1 2 3 4 5 6 7	bad
of no use	1 2 3 4 5 6 7	useful
not pleasant	1 2 3 4 5 6 7	pleasant
bitter	1 2 3 4 5 6 7	sweet
nice	1 2 3 4 5 6 7	awful
happy	1 2 3 4 5 6 7	sad
dirty	1 2 3 4 5 6 7	clean
steady	1 2 3 4 5 6 7	nervous

PHYSICAL ACTIVITY AS A THRILL BUT INVOLVING SOME RISK
Physical activities that are dangerous. They also can be exciting because you move very fast and must change directions quickly.

PHYSICAL ACTIVITY AS THE BEAUTY IN HUMAN MOVEMENT
Physical activities which have beautiful movements. Examples are ballet-dancing, gymnastics-tumbling, and figure skating on ice.

PHYSICAL ACTIVITY FOR THE RELEASE OF TENSION
Taking part in physical activities to get away from problems you might have. You can also get away from problems by watching other people in physical activities.

PHYSICAL ACTIVITY AS LONG AND HARD TRAINING
Physical activities that have long and hard practices. To spend time in practice you need to give up other things you like to do.

PEOPEL Physical Education Attitude Survey (Modified from Wear's Physical Education Survey)

Directions: We are interested in knowing your opinions about PE classes. Please answer each question by marking the box which best expresses your feelings on each statement. The questions refer only to PE CLASSES and NOT to after-school sports activities.

The results of this survey will not affect your grade in any way.

	Agree Strongly	Agree	No Opinion/Don't Know	Disagree	Disagree Strongly
1. If the school has to drop some classes, PE should be one of them.—	☐	☐	☐	☐	☐
2. Playing together in PE helps students learn to get along with each other.	☐	☐	☐	☐	☐
3. The time spent in dressing for and participating in PE could be better spent in other activities.—	☐	☐	☐	☐	☐
4. Playing hard in PE activities and games helps to work off emotional tension/frustration (such as unhappiness, anger, etc.).	☐	☐	☐	☐	☐
5. A student's body is usually strong enough without the physical exercise in PE.—	☐	☐	☐	☐	☐
6. I would only take PE if I had to.—	☐	☐	☐	☐	☐
7. It is important that students learn and improve physical skills such as running, jumping, shooting baskets, or hitting a ball.	☐	☐	☐	☐	☐
8. Students would be better off emotionally if they did NOT play games and sports in PE.	☐	☐	☐	☐	☐
9. PE does more harm to students than it does good.—	☐	☐	☐	☐	☐
10. Schools do NOT place enough importance on PE.	☐	☐	☐	☐	☐
11. Playing games and sports with other students in PE is fun.	☐	☐	☐	☐	☐
12. There should be NO MORE than two class periods of PE during the week.—	☐	☐	☐	☐	☐
13. It is harder to make friends in PE classes than in other classes.—	☐	☐	☐	☐	☐
14. Students are organized into teams for many PE activities. Belonging to these teams is usually a good experience.	☐	☐	☐	☐	☐
15. Playing games and sports in PE does NOT help students become more physically fit.—	☐	☐	☐	☐	☐
16. PE is important in helping students learn about good health.	☐	☐	☐	☐	☐
17. The extra physical strength gained from PE helps students perform their daily tasks better.	☐	☐	☐	☐	☐
18. PE helps students develop mentally, emotionally, and socially.	☐	☐	☐	☐	☐
19. PE encourages students to compete with each other. This often makes them dislike one another.—	☐	☐	☐	☐	☐
20. I would advise most people to take PE.	☐	☐	☐	☐	☐
21. Physical education classes do NOT make you feel better physically.—	☐	☐	☐	☐	☐
22. Participating in games and sports helps students learn new activities to use in their spare time.	☐	☐	☐	☐	☐

Scoring: A statement followed by a dash (—) is scored 1, 2, 3, 4, 5. All other statements (no —) are scored 5, 4, 3, 2, 1.

Pedagogy In Relation to Low Self-Concept

Teaching practices that enhance self-concept generally also contribute to improvement of attitude toward movement and/or physical education. Ideally, the practices that follow would be used with all students; large class sizes and various other factors, however, often make the practices impractical for regular physical education. This is why they are described here as critical to effective teaching in adapted physical education.

1. Conceptualize individual and small group counseling as an integral part of physical education instruction. Remember, the characteristics of a healthy counseling relationship are active listening, empathy, acceptance, willingness to become involved in another person's problems, and commitment to helping that person change in the way he or she chooses, which may or may not be the way you would choose. Listening to a student, asking questions to draw him or her out, and taking the initiative in following up when the student seems to withdraw are ways of showing one cares. Essential to the improvement of self-concept is the feeling that other persons genuinely care.

2. Teach students to care about each other and show that they care. This is sometimes called *social reciprocity* and begins with the facilitation of one-to-one relationships, followed by increasingly complex social structures. *Reciprocity* is an interaction in which persons positively reinforce each other at an equitable rate, thereby increasing the probability of continuing interactions. Reinforcement can be by facial and gestural expressions or by verbal praise and cheering for one another. Students typically model the teacher's behavior in relation to the handicapped and/or clumsy child. Therefore, the teacher must model encouragement, positive expectation, faith that the student really is exerting his or her best effort, and day-by-day acceptance of motor and social outcomes.

3. Emphasize social interaction and helping one another rather than individual performance. Plan lots of partner work. When necessary, assign partners who will bring out the best in one another rather than allowing chance to determine class twosomes. Match students up with the same care used by computerized dating services; remember, the creation of a friendship is often more valuable than any other factor in enhancing self-concept. Show awareness of emerging friendships and praise students for behaviors that help and support each other.

4. Stress the importance of genuineness and honesty in praise. Accept, but do not praise, motor attempts that are obviously unsuccessful. Instead provide such input as "Hey, this isn't like you. Tomorrow will be better" or "What's wrong? Let's try another way of throwing the ball!" or "I can tell you are upset by your performance today. You seem to be trying very hard and still not reaching your goal. How can I help?" Apply the same kind of sports psychology strategies to disabled students as you do to the able-bodied. In the real world of sport and competition, it is not effort that counts, but success. Therefore, structure lessons so as to build in success.

5. Build in success through the use of task and activity analysis. Also important is identifying the student's unique learning style. Does he or she learn best through visual or auditory input or a combination of the two? Or must he or she learn kinesthetically through trial and error, trying alternative ways until one works? Motor planning and subsequent performance is enhanced in most students by having students talk aloud as they perform, giving themselves step-by-step directions. Remember, in many clumsy students, the mind grasps what is to be done motorically, but the body simply does not do what the mind wills. Therefore, do not repeatedly tell students what they are doing wrong. Ask questions, and let them tell you. When possible, videotape or film and provide opportunities for watching and analyzing one's motor performance. Expect students to set their own goals, but provide counseling in terms of realistic levels of aspiration.

6. Increased perceived competence (Harter, 1978; Hedrick, 1985) in relation to motor skill and fitness increases self-concept. There is no substitute for success in beginning to feel good about oneself. Perceived competence, in turn, enhances intrinsic motivation to persevere. Competence, however, is typically perceived in terms of a reference group. It is important to help students compare their efforts, successes,

and failures against others of similar abilities and disabilities rather than the population as a whole. This is often more difficult than it sounds because many disabled students have not yet learned to accept themselves as they are, and they still model after the average performer in the mainstream. Yearning to be normal and, thus, to perform motorically as normal people leads to anger and depression, which ultimately must be worked though.

7. Convey that you like and respect disabled students as human beings, for themselves as whole persons, not just for their motor skills and fitness. The bottom line is that many clumsy students will remain clumsy in spite of best efforts of self, teacher, and peers. This is the rationale for separate instructional settings and sports organizations like the National Association of Sports for Cerebral Palsy and Special Olympics, giving students realistic reference groups for forming opinions about themselves and setting leisure-time use goals. Clumsiness and low skill do not have to be reasons for disliking and avoiding physical education. Too often, physical educators have equated skill with fun. The emphasis, instead, should be on use of sports classfications to equalize abilities and counseling to find and accept a realistic reference group for oneself. Movement is intrinsically fun and satisfying when one does not feel different from everyone else and embarrassed by that difference.

8. Stress movement education and motor creativity rather than sports competition in the early stages of working with students with low self-concept. Many clumsy students can excel in fluency, flexibility, originality, and elaboration, largely because *try another way* is an intrinsic part of their lifestyles. Such students can find much satisfaction in choreographing original aerobic exercise, dance, gymnastics, and synchronized swimming routines. Likewise, clumsy students may be adept at creating new games and/or changing rules, strategies, and skills in existing ones. The teacher who truly values individual differences conveys this to students who, in turn, learn to value themselves as the "different drummers in the physical education world." In this regard, the words of Henry David Thoreau remain timely:

If a man does not keep pace with his companions, perhaps it is because he hears a different drummer. Let him step to the music which he hears, however measured or far away.

9. Enhance self-concept by leisure counseling directed toward identifying the physical activities in which one would like to engage and barriers to be overcome in achieving desired leisure lifestyle. Disabled students should be helped to see the relationship between physical education instruction and present, as well as future, use of leisure time. Activities to be learned and practiced during class time ideally should be selected by the student rather than the teacher. Because many disabled adults are unable to find full-time employment, it is especially important that they be taught early that leisure can be meaningful. Wholesome attitudes toward leisure contribute to good self-concept in persons who have an abundance of leisure time.

Assessment of Leisure Functioning

Adapted physical education assessment and programming should include leisure functioning. Ideally, adapted physical education specialists, as part of their multidisciplinary training, should complete courses in leisure counseling and leisure education. If they have not done so, physical educators need to ask administrators to employ persons who do have the expertise to select and administer tests of leisure functioning. Following are descriptions of some of the commonly used assessment instruments in the many varied areas of leisure functioning.

Leisure Diagnostic Battery (LDB) of Perceived Freedom in Leisure

Purpose
To assess five components of recreation and leisure functioning. Separate test forms are available for (a) adults and youths, ages 9 to 15 years, and (b) normal cognitive functioning and mild mental retardation.

Description of Youth Battery for Normal Cognitive Functioning
Five scales, including 95 items, that are summed to yield score of perceived freedom in leisure. A 3-point scale is used with each item to indicate extent that item describes self. Each scale can be used separately as follows:

1. Playfulness Scale—20 items that measure sense of humor, manifest joy, and social, cognitive, and physical spontaneity. Alpha coefficient of .97.
2. Perceived Leisure Competence Scale—20 items that measure extent one sees personal abilities in leisure to be adequate; encompasses cognitive, physical, social, and general competence. Alpha coefficient of .89.
3. Perceived Leisure Control Scale—17 items that measure beliefs regarding attribution (i.e., whether recreation and leisure are under personal control or

dominated by significant others, fate, and luck). A measure of individual's sense of freedom to control leisure process and outcomes. Alpha coefficient of .88.

4. Leisure Needs Scale—20 items that measure ability to satisfy 10 intrinsic needs (relaxation, surplus energy, compensation, catharsis, optimal arousal, gregariousness, status, creative expression, skill development, and self-image) via recreation and leisure experiences. Alpha coefficient of .90.
5. Depth of Involvement in Leisure Scale—18 items that measure degree to which one can become absorbed in leisure experiences (i.e., ability to center attention and use personal resources in leisure experiences). Alpha coefficient of .88.

Validity
Grounded in sociopsychological and leisure theory (Csikszentmihalyi, 1975; Ellis, 1973; Iso-Ahola, 1980; Lieberman, 1977; Weiner, 1974) with thorough documentation of conceptual bases and empirical evidence of extent that LDB results reflect theoretical structure. Construct validity (Ellis & Witt, 1982). Pilot testing reported with several disabilities.

Reliability
Cronbach's alpha coefficients ranged from .80 to .90 for the separate scales, with .96 for total measure (95 items) based on 200 youths, ages 10 to 14 years, from public schools in two cities. Test-retest reliabilities for 84 youths ranged from .77 to .82, with overall r of .89.

Primary Sources
Csikszentmihalyi, M. (1975). *Beyond boredom and anxiety.* San Francisco: Josey Bass.
Ellis, M. (1973). *Why people play.* Englewood Cliffs: Prentice-Hall.
Ellis, G., & Witt, P. (1982). *Leisure diagnostic battery: Theoretical and empirical structure.* Denton, TX: North Texas State University.
Ellis, G., & Witt, P. (1984). The measurement of perceived freedom in leisure. *Journal of Leisure Research, 16*(2), 110–123.
Howe, C. (1984). Leisure assessment instrumentation in therapeutic recreation. *Therapeutic Recreation Journal, 18*(2), 14–24.
Iso-Ahola, S. (1980). *The social psychology of leisure and recreation.* Dubuque, IA: Wm. C. Brown.
Lieberman, J. (1977). *Playfulness: Its relationship to imagination and creativity.* New York: Academic Press.
Weiner, B. (Ed.). (1974). *Cognitive views of human motivation.* New York: Academic Press.

Address for Ordering
Dept. of Recreation and Leisure Studies, North Texas State University, Denton, TX 76203.

Leisure Activities Blank (LAB)

Purpose
To collect information from persons, age 15 years or older, about past and future involvement with selected leisure activities.

Description
120 closed-ended items.

Validity
Construct validity verified by factor analysis.

Reliability
Internal consistency of .69 to .93, with a median of .82 and a split-half reliability of .76 to .94, with a median of .85.

Primary Sources
McKechnie, G. E. (1975). *Manual for the leisure activities blank.* Palo Alto, CA: Consulting Psychologists Press.

Address for Ordering
Consulting Psychologists Press, Inc., 577 College Ave., Palo Alto, CA 94306.

Sutton-Smith and Rosenberg Play and Games List

Purpose
To determine preferred play and game activities and categories of play.

Description
One hundred eighty games, pastimes, and activities, each of which is checked as *like* or *dislike.* Students are asked to mark only the games that they currently play. Games can be categorized as masculine/feminine and/or broken down into 16 categories, among which are imitative and make-believe (cowboys and cowgirls, space travellers, dressing-up), leader games (Simon says, Redlight), chasing games (tag, hide and seek, statues), games of individual skill (hopscotch, jump rope, four square), skilled pastimes (swimming, skating, camping), and major sports (bowling, soccer, track and field).

Validity
None given.

Reliability
Test-retest of .89 reported by Marlowe et al. (1978).

Primary Sources
Marlowe, M., Algozzine, B., Lerch, H., & Welch, P. (1978). The games analysis intervention as a method of decreasing feminine play patterns of emotionally disturbed boys. *Research Quarterly, 49*, 484–490.
Sutton-Smith, B., & Rosenberg, B. (1961). Sixty years of historical change in the game preferences of American children. *Journal of American Folklore, 74*, 17–46.
Sutton-Smith, B., & Rosenberg, B. (1963). Development of sex differences in play choices during preadolescence. *Child Development, 34*, 119–126.

Address for Ordering
Dr. Brian Sutton-Smith, University of Pennsylvania Graduate School of Education C1, Philadelphia, PA 19104.

Leisure Satisfaction Scale (LSS)

Purpose
To measure degree of contentment in relation to six aspects of leisure experiences and situations: psychological, physiological, social, relaxational, educational, and aesthetic; to measure positive perceptions or feelings that result from engaging in leisure activities/experiences.

Description
Long form comprised of 51 closed-ended items; short form comprised of 24 items, 4 for each subscale. Each item is answered on a true-false scale.

Validity
Content validity as judged by a group of experts. Construct validity by factor analysis on data from 347 individuals.

Reliability
Alpha coefficients of .95 and .93 for long and short forms, respectively.

Primary Sources
Beard, J., & Ragheb, M. (1980). Measuring leisure satisfaction. *Journal of Leisure Research, 11,* 20–32.
Ragheb, M., & Beard, J. (1980). Leisure satisfaction: Concept, theory, and measurement. In S. E. Iso-Ahola (Ed.), *Social psychological perspectives on leisure and recreation* (pp. 329–353). Springfield, IL: Charles C. Thomas.

Address for Ordering
Entire test appears in sources listed above. Charles C. Thomas, Publishers, 301–327 E. Lawrence Ave., Springfield, IL 62717.

Leisure Ethic Scale

Purpose
To measure the degree of positive or negative affect associated with leisure; specifically, to measure attitudes toward leisure.

Description
Ten statements, each of which is rated on a 4-point Likert-type scale (completely disagree, moderately disagree, moderately agree, completely agree).

Scoring
All items are scored 4 points for completely agree to 1 point for completely disagree except item 5, which is reversed. Possible scores range from 13 (worst attitude) to 37 (best attitude).

Validity
Criterion validity with high correlations with other leisure scales and peer ratings.

Reliability
Test-retest correlations of .82, .59, .87, and .85 for 1 to 5 weeks.

Primary Sources
Crandall, R., & Slivken, K. (1980). Leisure attitudes and their measurement. In S. E. Iso-Ahola (Ed.), *Social psychological perspectives on leisure and recreation* (pp. 261–284). Springfield, IL: Charles C. Thomas.
Slivken, K. (1978). *Development of a leisure ethic scale.* Unpublished master's thesis, University of Illinois.

Address for Ordering
Entire test appears in sources listed above. Charles C. Thomas, Publishers, 301–327 E. Lawrence Ave., Springfield, IL 62717.

Pedagogy in Relation to Leisure Functioning

Public Law 94–142 includes recreation as a related service that may be prescribed on the IEPs of handicapped students if such services are necessary for them to benefit from special education, including adapted physical education. *Recreation* is defined in the law as including assessment of leisure function, therapeutic recreation services, recreation programs, and leisure education. In Chapter 6 of this text, the importance of play in cognitive and social development was stressed. Also noted was the fact that severely handicapped infants and children do not play spontaneously, as do their able-bodied peers.

Deficits in leisure functioning are common among disabled persons. If students do not understand leisure and do not have positive attitudes toward the use of free time, it is doubtful that they will benefit optimally from instruction in motor skills and fitness. Therefore, physical education should be integrated with leisure education, with emphasis on the generalization of gymnasium skills to after-school and weekend leisure. Leisure education may also be taught as a separate subject and infused in other curricular areas.

Only a small part of leisure education pertains directly to physical education. The taxonomy of leisure education includes nine major categories:

100   Games
200   Sports
300   Nature activities
400   Collection activities
500   Craft activities
600   Art and music activities, including dance
700   Education, entertainment, and cultural activities
800   Volunteer activities
900   Organizational activities

The adapted physical educator should assume responsibility for helping students acquire the attitudes, knowledge, skills, and habits necessary for optimal leisure functioning, both as participants and as spectators, in games, sports, and dance. Without such competencies, most persons lead entirely passive lives without sufficient vigorous exercise to maintain physical and mental health.

Basic movement patterns, regardless of level of skill reached, should be taught within a games/sports/dance context. Adapted physical education classes should include some kind of daily examination of use of leisure time. Such questions should be posed as (a) What did you do after school yesterday? (b) What games did you play? (c) With whom? (d) Where? (e) For how long? (f) What do you plan to do today after school? this weekend? this summer? Barriers to leisure involvement should be examined also and plans made for removing them.

Common barriers to leisure involvement include (a) accessibility to areas and facilities, (b) communication problems, (c) decision-making deficits, (d) lack of motivation, (e) health and/or fitness constraints, (f) lack of knowledge and skill needed for participation, (g) no one with whom to exercise and/or play, (h) monetary constraints, (i) travel or mobility problems, and (j) insufficient time. Many of these barriers relate to lack of knowledge about community resources and opportunities. One goal of adapted physical education instruction should be acquainting students with such resources and reinforcing their use before graduation. Another goal is helping students find friends who share common leisure interests. Such friends may be same-age peers or volunteers.

For further information, the following sources are recommended:

Bender, M., Brannan, S., & Verhoven, P. (1984). *Leisure education for the handicapped: Curriculum goals, activities, and resources.* San Diego, CA: College-Hill Press.

Joseph P. Kennedy, Jr. Foundation. *Let's Play-to-Grow.* Materials available from 1350 New York Avenue, NW, Suite 500, Washington, DC 20005.

Wehman, P., & Schleien, S. (1981). *Leisure programs for handicapped persons: Adaptations, techniques, and curriculum.* Baltimore: University Park Press.

Wuerch, B. & Voeltz, L. (1982). *Longitudinal leisure skills for severely handicapped learners, the Ho'Onanea curriculum component.* Baltimore: University Park Press.

Learning Activities

1. Interview several parents concerning the ages at which their children first performed the locomotor tasks listed in this chapter.

2. Observe normal and handicapped preschool children at play. What differences, if any, are evident in their motor performance?

3. Observe one child at play in a gymnasium or on a playground for 30 minutes. Record the number of different locomotor and nonlocomotor movement patterns the child uses. Record the number of times the child changes level and/or direction. Compare your tabulations with those of others in your class. Using this information, participate in a discussion on motor creativity with emphasis on fluency.

4. Use the checklists in this chapter to practice the evaluation of locomotor movement patterns and related skills: walking, running, ascending and descending stairs, leaping, standing long jump, trampoline jump, and hop.

5. Observe children vaulting over various pieces of apparatus. Which movement patterns offer them the most success: squat vault, straddle vault, flank vault, front vault? Teach one of these vaults to a group of beginners, and make a list of the movement problems or errors exhibited in their first several attempts.

6. Observe children in ball handling activities and classify them according to developmental stages.

References

Andre-Thomas, C., & Dargassies, S. (1960). *The neurological examination of the infant.* London: National Spastics Society/Heinemann.

Bobath, K. (1962). An analysis of the development of standing and walking patterns in patients with cerebral palsy. *Physiotherapy, 48,* 144.

Bobath, K. (1980). *A neurophysiological basis for the treatment of cerebral palsy.* London: National Spastics Society/Heinemann.

Cratty, B. J. (1967). *Developmental sequences of perceptual motor tasks.* Long Island, NY: Educational Activities.

Cratty, B. J. (1969). *Motor activity and the education of retardates.* Philadelphia: Lea & Febiger.

Corbin, C. (1980). *A textbook of motor development.* Dubuque, IA: Wm. C. Brown.

Ellison, P., Browning, C., Larson, B., & Denny, J. (1983). Development of a scoring system for the Milani-Comparetti and Gidoni method of assessing neurological abnormality in infancy. *Physical Therapy, 63,* (9), 1414–1423.

Fiorentino, M. (1973). *Reflex testing methods for evaluating CNS development* (2nd ed.). Springfield, IL: Charles C. Thomas.

Fiorentino, M. (1981). *A basis for sensorimotor development—Normal and abnormal.* Springfield, IL: Charles C. Thomas.

Haubenstricker, J., & Seefeldt, V. (1974). *Sequential progression in fundamental motor skill of children with learning disabilities.* Speech given at International Conference of the Association for Children with Learning Disabilities, Houston, TX.

Illingsworth, R. S. (1960). *The development of the infant and young child, normal and abnormal.* Edinburgh: Livingstone.

Milani-Comparetti, A., & Gidoni, E. (1967). Pattern analysis of motor development and its disorders. *Developmental Medicine and Child Neurology, 9,* 625–630.

Molnar, G. (1978). Analysis of motor disorder in retarded infants and young children, *American Journal of Mental Deficiency, 83,* 213–221.

Paine, R. S. (1964). The evolution of infantile postural reflexes in the presence of chronic brain syndromes. *Developmental Medicine and Child Neurology, 6,* 345.

Rathbone, J. (1959). *Corrective physical education* (6th ed.). Philadelphia: W. B. Saunders.

Rood, M. (1956). Neurophysiological mechanisms utilized in the treatment of neuromuscular dysfunction. *American Journal of Occupational Therapy, Part 2, 10* (4), 220–225.

Shaffer, K. (1982). *Utilization of abnormal reflexes to develop ball skills in cerebral palsied children.* Unpublished master's thesis, Texas Woman's University, Denton.

Sinclair, C. (1973). *Movement of the young child.* Columbus, OH: Charles E. Merrill.

Stockmeyer, S. (1972). A sensorimotor approach to treatment. In P. Pearson & C. Williams (Eds.), *Physical therapy services in the developmental disabilities* (pp. 186–222). Springfield, IL: Charles C. Thomas.

Winnick, J., & Short, F. (1985). *Physical fitness testing of the disabled: Project UNIQUE.* Champaign, IL: Human Kinetics Publishers.

Bibliography

American Alliance for Health, Physical Education, and Recreation. (1972). *Special Olympics instructional manual.* Washington, DC: Author.

Arnheim, D., & Pestolesi, R. (1973). *Developing motor behavior in children.* St. Louis: C. V. Mosby.

Burnett, C., & Johnson, E. (1971). Development of gait in childhood. *Developmental Medicine and Child Neurology, 13,* 196–215.

Connolly, K. (Ed.). (1973). *Mechanisms of motor skill development.* New York: Academic Press.

Corbin, C. (1980). *A textbook of motor development* (2nd ed.). Dubuque, IA: Wm. C. Brown.

Evans, J. (1980). *They have to be carefully taught: A handbook for parents and teachers of young children with handicapping conditions.* Reston, VA: American Alliance for Health, Physical Education, Recreation, and Dance.

Flinchum, B. (1975). *Motor development in early childhood.* St. Louis: C. V. Mosby.

Gallahue, D. (1976). *Motor development and movement experiences for young children.* New York: John Wiley & Sons.

Gallahue, D. (1982). *Understanding motor development in children.* New York: John Wiley & Sons.

Geddes, D. (1974). *Physical activities for individuals with handicapping conditions.* St. Louis: C. V. Mosby.

Gordon, N., & McKinlay, I. (Eds.). (1980). *Helping clumsy children.* New York: Churchill Livingstone.

Harter, S. (1978). Effectance motivation reconsidered: Toward a developmental model. *Human Development, 21,* 32–64.

Hedrick, B. N. (1985). The effect of wheelchair tennis participation and mainstreaming upon the perceptions and competence of physically disabled adolescents. *Therapeutic Recreation Journal, 19,* (2), 34–46.

Keogh, J. (1980). A movement developmental framework and a perceptual-cognitive perspective. In G. Brooks (Ed.), *Perspectives in the academic discipline of physical education* (pp. 211–233). Champaign, IL: Human Kinetics Publishers.

Knobloch, H., & Pasamanick, B. (Eds.). (1974). *Gesell and Amatruda's developmental diagnosis* (3rd ed.). New York: Harper & Row.

McClenaghan, B., & Gallahue, D. (1978). *Fundamental movement: A developmental and remedial approach.* Philadelphia: W. B. Saunders.

Rarick, L. (Ed.). (1973). *Physical activity: Human growth and development.* New York: Academic Press.

Ridenour, M. (Ed.). (1978). *Motor development: Issues and applications.* Princeton, NJ: Princeton Book Co.

Roberton, M. A. (1975). *Stability of stage categorizations across trials: Implications for the stage theory of overarm throw development.* Unpublished doctoral dissertation, University of Wisconsin, Madison.

Roberton, M. A., & Halverson, L. E. (1977). The developing child—His changing movement. In B. Logsdon (Ed.), *Physical education for children* (pp. 24–67). Philadelphia: Lea & Febiger.

Sinclair, C. B. (1973). *Movement of the young child.* Columbus, OH: Charles E. Merrill.

Thomas, J. (1984). *Motor development during childhood and adolescence.* Minneapolis: Burgess.

Vodola, T. (1976). *Motor disabilities or limitations: An individualized program.* Oakhurst, NJ: Project ACTIVE.

Watkinson, E. J., & Wall, A. E. (1982). *PREP—The PREP play program: Play skill instruction for mentally handicapped children.* Ontario: Canadian Association for Health, Physical Education, and Recreation.

Wessel, J. (1976–1980). *I CAN: Individualized physical education curriculum materials.* Northbrook, IL: Hubbard.

Whiting, H. T. A. (1969). *Acquiring ball skill.* Philadelphia: Lea & Febiger.

Wickstrom, R. L. (1983). *Fundamental motor patterns* (3rd ed.). Philadelphia: Lea & Febiger.

Williams, H. (1983). *Perceptual and motor development.* St. Louis: C. V. Mosby.

Zaichkowsky, L., Zaichkowsky, L., & Martinek, T. (1980). *Growth and development: The child and physical activity.* St. Louis: C. V. Mosby.

11 Perceptual-Motor Functioning, Games, and Sports

Figure 11.1 Movement exploration uses kinesthetic, vestibular, and visual sensory input to increase body awareness.

Chapter Objectives

After you have studied this chapter, you should be able to

1. Briefly discuss the history of perceptual-motor theory and identify some of its leaders. Analyze changing beliefs over the years, particularly with respect to the use of perceptual-motor activities to improve cognitive functioning.

2. Define perception and explain its four components: awareness, discrimination, organization, and cue selection. Discuss these components in terms of normal and abnormal functioning of the 10 sense modalities.

3. Describe the following tests: (a) Sherrill Perceptual-Motor Screening Test, (b) Purdue Perceptual-Motor Survey, (c) Bruininks-Oseretsky Test of Motor Proficiency, (d) Southern California Perceptual Motor and Postrotatory Nystagmus Tests, and (e) Hughes Basic Gross Motor Assessment.

5. Analyze similarities and differences between Frostig, Kephart, Ayres, and Sherrill in terms of perceptual-motor factors to be assessed, method of assessment, and programming for remediation.

6. Explain how practice in basic game and dance formations can contribute to perceptual motor learning.

7. Discuss developmental stages in drawing, game formations, and directions of movement in sport and how these are interrelated.

8. Describe how perceptual-motor training occurs in everyday game and play activities. State perceptual-motor goals and objectives achieved through ball handling activities.

Systematic efforts to unravel the mysteries of how patterned motion is accomplished are seen in studies which go by different names; motor learning, sensory-motor learning (sensori-motor, sensori neuromotor); psycho-motor learning (psycho-motor); menti-motor learning (ideo-motor); neuro-muscular learning (neuro-motor); perceptual-motor learning (perceptuo-motor, visuo-motor, tactual-motor). What do all of these terms imply? Definitions, when given at all, are usually so diverse, contradictory, and imbricated as to render them confusing. . . . What's in a name? Regardless of the one chosen, those who would understand learning of any sort must remember that so far as is presently known *the ingredients of learning are intricate, multi-dimensional, delicately integrated and basically inseparable.*

—Aileene Lockhart

Foundations of Perceptual-Motor Theory

The practice of formally assessing perceptual-motor strengths and weaknesses has a relatively short history beset with controversy, misunderstanding, and competition. From the 1930s onward, several disciplines endeavored to develop techniques for assessing perceptual-motor development and identifying associated dysfunctions. Leaders in the fields of medicine, optometry, clinical psychology, physical therapy, and occupational therapy all contributed substantially to the evolution of evaluation techniques in the perceptual-motor domain before most physical educators became interested in the movement.

Authorities outside our discipline, such as Kephart, Frostig, and Barsch, were primarily interested in perceptual-motor training because of its hypothesized relationship to cognitive learning and academic achievement. Hallahan and Cruickshank (1973) point out that, between 1936 and 1970, perceptual-motor training was the most popular method of education of LD children. It was used widely also with mentally retarded pupils. *In the 1980s this is no longer true.*

Perceptual-motor activities like angels-in-the-snow, balance-beam walking, trampoline bouncing, chalkboard exercises and games, obstacle courses (see Figure 11.1), and tracking small suspended swinging balls still endure. The reasons for using them, however, differ from those cited in the 1960s. Among most educators today, these activities are simply a part of the normal developmental sequence for helping children mature motorically and gain the play skills so important to social acceptance and good self-concept in the early years. There seems to be a definite relationship between clumsiness and learning problems among LD, MR, and ED children, but *one does not cause the other.*

Hallahan and Cruickshank have done probably the most complete analysis of perceptual-motor research, between 1936 and 1970. Their book should be required reading for physical educators. They trace the origins of perceptual-motor theory to Alfred A. Strauss and

Heinz Werner, German psychologists who migrated to the United States in the 1930s to escape Hitler. Both eventually settled in Michigan, where they conducted the pioneer research on brain-injured, mentally retarded children that formed the basis for almost all early LD practices. Some of the people influenced by Strauss and Werner were William Cruickshank, a special educator who applied their research specifically to CP and brain-injured persons; Newell C. Kephart, an educational psychologist, whose classic book *The Slow Learner in the Classroom* (1960) still serves as the guide for most perceptual-motor practitioners; and Gerald Getman, an optometrist, who popularized the importance of vision in learning. Ray Barsch, a special educator in the neighboring state of Wisconsin, built upon Strauss and Werner theory in his *Movigenics Curriculum,* which was based on the development of spatial movement patterns as the physiological bases of learning. Marianne Frostig, a developmental psychologist in Los Angeles, whose *Test of Developmental Vision* and prolific writing/speaking on perceptual-motor remediation dominated the 1950s and 1960s, also regards the works of Strauss and Werner as important to her orientation.

Individually, these perceptual-motor theorists who all believed that perceptual-motor activities led to improved reading skills and cognition might not have made a great impact on education. In 1964, however, they all (with the exception of Getman) became part of the Professional Advisory Board of the newly formed Association for Children with Learning Disabilities. Collectively they exerted tremendous influence on teaching practices. Parents especially came to believe in their theories. Physical educators therefore cannot afford to be ignorant of perceptual-motor principles and practices. These remain controversial, and the best approach seems to be *open-mindedness.* Hallahan and Cruickshank stated in this regard,

Although no persuasive empirical evidence has been brought to the fore in support of perceptual-motor training, neither has there been solid negative evidence. Owing to the lack of satisfactory research studies with proper methodological controls, it is injudicious to decide wholeheartedly that perceptual-motor training deserves or does not deserve approval. The ultimate acceptance or rejection of these theorists and their procedures ought to depend upon systematic, empirical investigations yet to be done. This is not to imply obsolescence of former theories or practices in perceptual-motor training. On the contrary, new experimentation may well find itself drawing upon, refining, and expanding ideas from the past. (Hallahan & Cruickshank, 1973, p. 216)

Perceptual-Motor Training

Kephart, Getman, Barsch, and Frostig all held similar beliefs concerning the nature of perceptual-motor training. Each undoubtedly influenced the other, although, as authors, each sought to create unique training models and to emerge as a leader in his or her own right. Today, the works of Kephart and Frostig remain viable, largely because they developed assessment instruments that are still in use. Frostig's Developmental Test of Visual Perception (1963) is a paper-pencil test that is widely used by elementary school teachers but has little relevance for physical educators. The Purdue Perceptual Motor Survey (Roach & Kephart, 1966) takes its name from Purdue University in Indiana, where Kephart taught during most of his professional career. It is one of the 10 most frequently used assessment instruments in adapted physical education (Ulrich, 1985). The constructs upon which this test was based continue to guide early childhood physical education, especially that pertaining to body image and balance. These constructs were introduced in Chapter 6 of this book as requisite to understanding the play and cognitive development of children.

Contributions of Kephart

A review of Kephart's theory, with emphasis upon the perceptual-motor activities he recommended, provides an understanding of perceptual-motor training as most authorities conceptualize it. Kephart and followers believed that this type of training would improve academic abilities. In contrast, today's physical educators believe these activities are important in improving movement skills. Research has not shown perceptual-motor training to be more effective than other forms of physical education in enhancing motor development.

Newell C. Kephart's theory is presented in *The Slow Learner in the Classroom,* published in 1960 and revised in 1971. Kephart, like Piaget, is a developmentalist. Whereas Piaget established the sensory-motor stage as 0 to 2 years of age, Kephart emphasized that movement is the basis of the intellect without clarifying an age span for which the assumption is most true. Under the motor bases of achievement, Kephart discussed infant motor explorations, reflex and postural adjustments, laterality, directionality, body image, motor generalization, and motor learning. The terms *laterality* (internal awareness of two sides of the body) and *directionality* (understanding of directional concepts in relation to self and space) were coined by Kephart and continue to influence theory and practice.

Figure 11.2 Balance beam work was popularized by Kephart as an integral part of perceptual-motor training.

Most of the items contained in the Purdue Perceptual Motor Survey are presented in *The Slow Learner in the Classroom* as training activities. Kephart used the term *slow learner* to denote clumsy children, not mentally retarded ones. His greatest emphasis in perceptual-motor training was on balance. To improve balance, Kephart emphasized that students must be exposed to many and varied activities that make them lose balance. Only by struggling to regain balance does a child improve. Hence, Kephart recommended locomotor activities and stunts on walking boards (i.e., low balance beam) (see Figure 11.2), balance boards, trampoline, and bedsprings and mattress. Kephart believed that laterality was largely a matter of balance (i.e., without internal awareness of two sides of the body, one can hardly balance), so these activities are now widely accepted as contributing to the development of laterality.

In regard to body image and the ability to move one or more body parts without overflow (i.e., differentiation), Kephart recommended use of an angels-in-the-snow sequence including unilateral, bilateral, and crosslateral movements. He also stressed the importance of follow-the-leader activities in which the teacher performed an arm movement and then the students imitated it from memory. In such imitations, students were taught not to mirror activities, but to use the same body parts (R and L) as the demonstrator. Kephart's idea of an obstacle course was two chairs and a broomstick; with these, he created problem solving situations that required squeezing through, stepping over, and ducking under.

Kephart believed that stunts and games entailing forward, backward, and sideward movements were important also to body image development. Specifically, he recommended the duck walk, rabbit hop, crab walk, measuring worm, and elephant walk. Today, physical educators continue to emphasize all of these except the duck walk, which is believed injurious to knee joints.

Kephart stressed the practice of rhythmic patterns as important in remediating kinesthetic and tactual problems. In this regard, he recommended the use of bongo drums and the child learning to imitate even and uneven rhythms, first using one side of the body and then alternating right and left sides. Theorists later named this *bilateral motor coordination* because it combines ability to make right-left discriminations with ability to imitate rhythmic patterns and gestures.

In regard to hand-eye coordination, Kephart focused most of his attention on perceptual-motor match, ocular control, and form perception. This part of his theory was primarily visual motor. It emphasized use of chalkboard activities like drawing circles simultaneously with both arms and drawing lines to connect dots. Also important were tasks that required that the student fixate eyes on a small object and then follow its movement. Most of today's striking activities that use a ball suspended on a string come from Kephart's marsden ball tasks. The marsden ball, named after the optometrist who conceived the idea in the 1950s, is a soft object about the size of a tennis ball, suspended by a string from overhead. The child stands about an arm's length from the ball and tries to touch it as the teacher swings it from side to side and forward and backward. Physical educators tend to conceptualize this activity as individual, dual, or team tetherball and to vary the size of the balls in accordance with students' skill levels.

Figure 11.3 Perceptual motor training, as advocated by Cratty, emphasized the integration of problem solving with movement tasks. Here, Dr. Gail Webster, Northern Illinois University, challenges a child to find New Mexico and do a forward roll on top of it.

Work on form perception was primarily tracing and copying crosses, circles, rectangles, diamonds, and other shapes. Whereas Kephart conceived this as a paper-pencil activity, physical educators have generalized it to large shapes and patterns on the floor that form paths to be followed in practicing locomotor activities. Likewise, various shapes are used on walls so that form perception is taught concurrently with target throwing. The copying tasks on the Purdue Perceptual Motor Test come directly from the Bender-Gestalt Test (Bender, 1938).

Contributions of Cratty

Although many physical educators have subscribed to perceptual-motor training at one time or another, few have contributed to theory and practice through writing or research. Bryant J. Cratty, a physical education professor at the University of California at Los Angeles, thus stands out as the major contributor. Throughout the 1960s and 1970s, Cratty published about 30 books on this topic; many are cited in the bibliographies of this text. He also developed a test (the Six-Category Gross Motor Test, 1969) to measure body image and perceptual motor function (Knapczyk & Liemohn, 1976).

In these books, Cratty described games that incorporated concepts of perceptual-motor match, ocular control, and form perception. He stressed that academic learning would not improve as the result of Kephart-like activities unless numbers, letters of the alphabet, and words were woven into floor and wall grids (patterns) and emphasized. Thus, Cratty called attention to the principle of specificity. Cratty emphasized that movement is not the sole basis of the intellect. If properly planned and conducted, however, movement can contribute to problem solving skills and academic learning (see Figure 11.3).

Contributions of Ayres

Whereas perceptual-motor theorists focus upon enhancement of voluntary movement (i.e., that controlled by the cerebral cortex), A. Jean Ayres believes

Figure 11.4 Rolling down a ramp on a scooter board and then grabbing balls with either arm is a sensory integration task recommended by Ayres.

that motor training should be directed toward the subcortical levels of the brain. Her book, *Sensory Integration and Learning Disorders,* published in 1972, has been a powerful influence in switching adapted physical educators' attention from perceptual-motor to sensory integration theory. A. Jean Ayres is a professor of occupational therapy at the University of California at Los Angeles; her doctoral degree is in neurodevelopmental psychology.

One of Ayres' earliest research studies was a factor analysis of perceptual-motor dysfunction (Ayres, 1965). On the basis of her analysis, she hypothesized that perceptual-motor dysfunctions can be classified into five syndromes: (a) problems of vestibular and bilateral integration, (b) apraxia, (c) tactile defensiveness, (d) left hemisphere dysfunction, and (e) right hemisphere dysfunction. Primarily through work with learning disabled students, Ayres came to believe in the 1970s that these were sensory integration rather than perceptual-motor problems.

Sensory integration theory emphasizes that activities for clumsy children should enhance tactile, kinesthetic, and vestibular function (all of which are controlled at the subcortical level) before focusing on vision and audition. Instead of starting clumsy children where they are and working to improve locomotor and object control patterns, Ayres believes in moving backward phylogenetically to reflexes and postural reactions. Like Kephart, she emphasizes balance (i.e., vestibular function). Her vocabulary and training practices are rooted in neurology, whereas Kephart had little formal training in neurophysiology.

Ayres recommends many activities that help develop basic motor patterns. Among these are scooter boards and therapy balls. Not only are scooter boards used on level surfaces, but Ayres recommends building ramps that students can ride down on their scooter boards (Figure 11.4). Sensory integration theory is well accepted in the therapies and adapted physical education. Some persons are still using the terms *perceptual-motor* and *sensorimotor* as synonyms. The difference lies primarily in whether training is directed at the subcortical or cortical levels. Perception demands cognitive ability (i.e., sufficient intelligence and developmental maturity to mentally process what one is seeing, hearing, and feeling).

Perceptual-Motor Functioning, Games, and Sports **271**

Contributions of Williams

Many physical educators have studied perception and attempted to apply perceptual theories to physical education instruction. Illustrative of these is Harriet Williams, physical education professor at the University of South Carolina and author of *Perceptual and Motor Development* (1983). Much of Williams' early work pertained to the perception of moving objects by children of various ages. She has shown that the ability to quickly and accurately judge moving objects in space does not mature until approximately 12 years of age. Williams' writing pertains most to visual and auditory processes. She differentiates between intrasensory vs. intersensory integration, whereas Ayres and other developmentalists have focused upon sensory integration as a global concept.

Intrasensory integration refers to maturation within (intra) one sensory system. This is the approach often taken in school-based perceptual-motor training, in which emphasis is primarily on improvement of visual development, particularly as it relates to reading. Sometimes, two or three systems (visuomotor or tactile-kinesthetic-visual) are theoretically considered as one for the purpose of improving reading and writing skills. When this occurs, the emphasis is usually on intrasensory integration. Remediation is directed toward the separate functions within the system: awareness and/or acuity, localization, discrimination, memory, and figure-ground.

Intersensory integration is defined by Williams (1983, p. 162) as the ability to use or integrate several sources of sensory integration simultaneously to help in adapting to the environment and/or to solve problems. There are three levels of intersensory functioning: (a) a low-level automatic level of integration, which is inborn and manifested by reflex integration and sound postural reactions; (b) a higher order of integration that primarily involves cognitive discrimination of shapes, sizes, colors, and sounds; and (c) a cognitive/conceptual level of integration, which involves transfer of ideas or concepts across different sense modalities.

A major contribution of Williams is the positing of intrasensory and intersensory development theory and the construction of a test battery to evaluate this development (Williams, Temple, & Bateman, 1979). Whereas Williams' research, had it been conducted in the 1960s and 1970s, might have been considered part of perceptual-motor theory, the trend today is to focus on motor control. In the 1980s, perceptual-motor theory seems slowly to be giving way to new ideas and concepts. In order for our knowledge base to continue to grow, physical educators need to understand perception and its role in motor control.

Perception

Perception is defined as the basic, immediate discriminatory behavior that relates individuals to their surroundings. The process of perception includes *awareness, discrimination, organization,* and *cue selection. Awareness* is neurological feedback that something is happening.

In order for a state of mental awareness to exist, four prerequisites are necessary.

1. A stimulus capable of initiating a response from some part of the nervous system.
2. A sensory receptor or sense organ that can react to the stimulus.
3. An ascending pathway (tract) for conducting the impulse arising in the sensory receptor to the brain.
4. A region within the brain capable of translating impulses into sensations. The four regions primarily responsible for translating electrical impulses into sensations are (a) cerebral cortex; (b) thalamus; (c) hypothalamus; and (d) cerebellum.

Discrimination is the ability to differentiate between stimuli, including the acuity with which a child can discriminate between sounds, tempos, colors, forms, joint positions, or degrees of muscular tension. *Organization* refers to the capacity to organize stimuli into a meaningful whole. *Cue selection* refers to the ability to attend to relevant cues and block out irrelevant stimuli. Special educators often refer to perception as *decoding,* the ability to obtain meaning from sensory stimuli—i.e., receptive understanding of words, pictures, gestures, joint position, and muscle tension. Problems of perception can then be categorized as dysfunctions of auditory, visual, and proprioceptive decoding.

Memory

Memory is involved in the assessment of perceptual problems. Some persons have good awareness, discrimination, organization, and cue selection but exhibit short- or long-term memory deficits. It is difficult to determine whether errors are problems of perception or memory. *Closure* is often involved also. Closure is the ability to recognize (remember) an item or experience when only part of it is presented.

Visual Perception

Visual perception has been broken down also into such discrete attributes as discrimination, figure-background phenomena, depth perception, object constancy, phi phenomenon, and retinal inhibition. A child will not have disturbances of all of the attributes. *Discrimination* refers to the ability to differentiate visually between different forms, sizes, weights, heights, colors, textures, distances, speeds, and rhythms. Young children tend to rely first upon color and later upon forms or shapes of objects for identification and classification. Other discriminative abilities normally develop sequentially with increasing maturity.

Visual figure-background phenomena refers to the ability to identify and focus attention upon a single object or figure in a cluttered and/or complex background. Children who become so confused during a tag game that they cannot locate *it* and individuals who cannot follow the serial path of a golfball or baseball are illustrative of persons with figure-background problems. The ability to differentiate visually between a selected object and a complex background develops slowly and does not reach peak performance until adolescence.

Depth perception refers to the ability to judge distances and to discriminate between the spatial dimensions of near and far. It is also called *stereopsis*. Children who exhibit unreasonable fear of walking a high beam or jumping into a swimming pool may have problems of stereopsis. *Object constancy* refers to the ability to identify an object regardless of the direction it points, the shape it assumes, and the hue it is colored. A chair, for instance, must be perceived as a chair whether it is big or little, wooden or upholstered, red or green, rightside up or upside down. *Phi phenomenon,* sometimes called autokinetic movement, refers to the erroneous perception of movement when an object is actually stationary. This phenomenon may occur when the child focuses upon the same object, like the page of a book, for a prolonged period of time. In such instances, the words seem to float about. *Retinal inhibition* occurs when a person appears to be looking directly at an object and gives no evidence of seeing it. Difficulties in attending to visual cues fall into this category.

Auditory Perception

Auditory perception also can be broken down into several different factors. *Auditory discrimination* refers to the ability to distinguish between different frequencies (pitches), intensities, and tonal qualities (timbre) of sounds. *Auditory figure-background phenomenon* implies the ability to distinguish relevant sounds (usually words) from background of noise and confusion. *Directionality of sound* refers to the ability to determine the direction from which auditory stimuli are emanating. *Temporal perception* refers to the ability to discriminate between fast and slow, even and uneven, accented and unaccented as well as to recognize variations in rhythm such as 4/4, 3/4, or 6/8.

Haptic Perception

Haptic perception encompasses kinesthetic, vestibular, and tactile input. The haptic receptors are located throughout the body in (a) skin and deeper underlying tissue; (b) muscles and tendons, which attach muscles to bone; (c) skeletal joints and connecting ligaments between all moveable bones; (d) blood vessels; and (e) hair cells located in the semicircular canals, utricle, saccule, and cochlea of the inner ear. The simultaneous input of these receptors is integrated in the parietal area of the brain into information about the body, its environment, and their interrelationships. Specifically, the haptic system provides two major kinds of information. In the first category, the *touch-pressure sense modality* gives information about the environment as (a) surface texture; (b) surface area or size, shapes, borders, angles, and openings; (c) qualities of consistency such as hard, soft, resilient, or viscous; (d) temperature; (e) pressure; and (f) pain. In the second category, *the kinesthetic and vestibular sense modalities* provide information about the body itself: (a) dynamic movement patterns of the trunk, arms, legs, mandible, and tongue; (b) static limb positions or postures; (c) linear and rotatory directions of movement of the skull, limbs, and body as a whole; (d) the location of the body in relation to external objects; (e) weight of resistance to gravity; (f) the relative weights of external objects that are being pushed, pulled, lifted, or lowered; and (g) the relationship of the body to gravitational pull.

Tactile Perception

Dysfunctions of the touch-pressure sense modalities include failure to (a) identify the presence of pressure on the skin; (b) locate the exact point on the skin where touch is made; (c) differentiate two or more stimuli that are applied simultaneously; (d) indicate the direction of an object moving over the skin; and (e) register sensitivity to pain and temperature. Most tests of tactile perception involve the fingers. *Finger localization,* the ability to identify without vision which finger is touched by the examiner, is considered a valid measure of body image as well as a perceptual ability.

The ability to recognize objects by touch and to distinguish shapes, letters, or numbers drawn on the skin requires the integration of sensations from a series of points on the skin's surface. To test discrimination of surface textures, it is generally best to allow the child to rub or pull the stimulus object through the fingers. Little information about subtle differences in textures can be obtained merely by touching. Often it is difficult to distinguish between language deficits and poor tactile discrimination. Before the latter is tested, it is important to ascertain that the child knows the meaning of such adjectives as thick, thin, smooth, rough, wet, and dry.

Disorders of tactile perception include tactile defensiveness and finger agnosia. *Tactile defensiveness* is an imbalance in the tactile system. It is manifested by pupils who avoid touch and dislike tight or even normal-fitting clothing and by pupils who crave touch. *Finger agnosia,* also called Gerstmann's syndrome, is the specific inability to recognize, identify, differentiate, indicate, and orient the individual fingers of either hand.

Proprioception

The kinesthetic and vestibular sense receptors can be grouped together as proprioceptors. Proprioception includes sensations pertaining to balance, position, and movement. The vestibular apparatus in the inner ear registers stops, starts, and changes in direction related to static and dynamic balance. The kinesthetic receptors in the joints are believed most vital to the perception of space and movement. These joint receptors discharge at a given rate for a given angle of a joint. It has been found that subjects can detect the bending of a single joint as little as a fraction of $1°$. In this regard, it is known that persons detect the angles of joints, not the length of muscles.

Awareness of position and movement of the joints seems to depend solely upon joint receptors. The amount of information that is obtained from muscles and tendons is limited. Specifically, muscle receptors register stretch, and tendon receptors register strain. Receptors in joints, muscles, tendons, ligaments, and skin all contribute to perception of muscular effort required to resist and/or overcome gravity and to impart force to an external object. Kinesthetic perception is not a general ability. It is comprised of many different factors, each of which must be taught and measured separately.

Screening Procedures

Children with deficits in perceptual-motor functioning often fail to receive needed help because of weaknesses in diagnostic and referral procedures. The tests reviewed in this chapter, for instance, are generally administered after a child is referred to the adapted physical educator. Who is responsible for initial identification? Upon what basis is referral made? In most school systems the assignment to adapted physical education is made by the special education coordinator or school principal. In some states, assignment comes from a committee that reviews recommendations made by the classroom teacher. Seldom is the adapted physical educator expected to screen all pupils in a school system; nor is there sufficient time for in-depth observation of all children.

It is important, therefore, that the adapted physical educator assume initiative in preparing materials to help colleagues identify children who may benefit from perceptual-motor training. The following checklist developed specifically for use by classroom teachers may help to meet this need. It lists characteristics commonly exhibited by children with learning disabilities and/or mild neurological damage and has proven successful as a screening device for identifying perceptual-motor awkwardness. It is recommended that this checklist be filled out for each child early in the year. The Sherrill Screening Checklist and Purdue Perceptual Motor Survey are helpful screening instruments.

Perceptual-Motor Screening Checklist

This checklist is to be completed by the classroom teacher, speech therapist, or physical education instructor. The observations should be made during regular class periods without the knowledge of the student being observed. The observation should be over a period of time sufficient for an objective view of the student. *Pupils with more than 10 items checked should be subjected to thorough study and quite possibly assigned to adapted physical education.*

Sherrill Perceptual-Motor Screening Checklist

___ 1. Fails to show opposition of limbs in walking, sitting, throwing.
___ 2. Sits or stands with poor posture.
___ 3. Does not transfer weight from one foot to the other when throwing.
___ 4. Cannot name body parts or move them on command.
___ 5. Has poor muscle tone (tense or flaccid).
___ 6. Uses one extremity much more often than the other.
___ 7. Cannot use arm without "overflow" movements from other body parts.
___ 8. Cannot jump rope.
___ 9. Cannot clap out a rhythm with both hands or stamp rhythm with feet.
___ 10. Has trouble crossing the midline of the body at chalkboard or in ball handling.
___ 11. Often confuses right and left sides.
___ 12. Confuses vertical, horizontal, up, down directions.
___ 13. Cannot hop or maintain balance in squatting.
___ 14. Has trouble getting in and out of seat.
___ 15. Approaches new tasks with excessive clumsiness.
___ 16. Fails to plan movements before initiating task.
___ 17. Walks or runs with awkward gait.
___ 18. Cannot tie shoes, use scissors, manipulate small objects.

19. Cannot identify fingers as they are touched without vision.
20. Has messy handwriting.
21. Experiences difficulty tracing over line or staying between lines.
22. Cannot discriminate tactually between different coins or fabrics.
23. Cannot imitate body postures and movements.
24. Demonstrates poor ocular control; unable to maintain eye contact with moving objects; loses place while reading.
25. Lacks body awareness; bumps into things; spills and drops objects.
26. Appears excessively tense and anxious; cries or angers easily.
27. Responds negatively to physical contact; avoids touch.
28. Craves to be touched or held.
29. Overreacts to high-frequency noise, bright lights, odors.
30. Exhibits difficulty in concentrating.
31. Shows tendency to fight when standing in line or in crowds.
32. Avoids group games and activities; spends most of time alone.
33. Complains of clothes irritating skin; avoids wearing coat.
34. Does not stay in assigned place; moves about excessively.
35. Uses either hand in motor activities.
36. Avoids using the left side of body.
37. Cannot walk sideways to either direction on balance beam.
38. Holds one shoulder lower than the other.
39. Cannot hold a paper in place with one hand while writing with the other.
40. Avoids turning to the left whenever possible.
41. Cannot assemble puzzles that offer no difficulty to peers.
42. Cannot match basic geometric shapes to each other visually.
43. Cannot recognize letters and numbers.
44. Cannot differentiate background from foreground in a picture.
45. Cannot identify hidden figures in a picture.
46. Cannot catch balls.

Purdue Perceptual Motor Survey

Purpose
To identify children, ages 6 to 10 years, who do not possess perceptual-motor abilities necessary for acquiring academic skills by the usual instructional methods (i.e., this was designed to be a screening instrument, not a test).

Description
Thirty items organized under five headings: balance and postural flexibility, body image and differentiation, perceptual-motor match, ocular control, and form perception. Of these, only the first two sections include physical education type movements. These are

Balance and Postural Flexibility
1. Walking board forward.
2. Walking board backward.
3. Walking board sideward.
4. Jumping (including jump, hop forward, skip, hop in place 1/1, 2/2, 2/1, and 1/2).

Body Image and Differentiation
1. Identification of nine body parts: shoulders, hips, head, ankles, ears, feet, eyes, elbows, mouth.
2. Imitation of 17 arm movements categorized as unilateral, bilateral, and crosslateral.
3. Obstacle course (chair and 3-foot broomstick) entailing three tasks: going over, going under, and going between.
4. Strength tests in prone position from Kraus-Weber: (a) raise chest and hold 10 seconds and (b) raise legs and hold 10 seconds.
5. Angels-in-the-snow sequence including 10 tasks (R arm only, R leg only, L arm only, L leg only, both arms, both legs, L arm and L leg, R arm and R leg, R arm and L leg, L arm and R leg).

Scoring
See test manual. Different system used for each of 30 items, but score ranges from 1 to 4 on each.

Validity
Criterion-related against teachers' ratings of 297 children; coefficient was .65.

Reliability
Test-retest *r* of .95 on 30 children (Seaman & DePauw, 1982). For 88 mildly mentally retarded children, ages 8 to 10 years, test-retest coefficients for specific items were identification of body parts, .75; imitation of movement, .51; obstacle course, .64; and angels-in-the-snow, .35 (Sherrill, 1985).

Primary Sources
Roach, E., & Kephart, N. (1966). *The Purdue perceptual-motor survey.* Columbus, OH: Charles C. Merrill.

Seaman, J., & DePauw, J. (1982). *The new adapted physical education.* Palo Alto, CA: Mayfield Publishing Co.

Sherrill, C. (1985). *Reliability coefficients for selected body image items performed by mentally retarded children.* Unpublished manuscript, Texas Woman's University, Denton.

Address for Ordering
Charles E. Merrill Publishing Co., 1300 Alum Creek Drive, Columbus, OH 43216.

Assessment of Perceptual-Motor Function

Tests that include measures of both gross and fine motor proficiency obviously assess perceptual-motor function. For many years the Lincoln-Oseretsky Motor Development Scale (Sloan, 1955) was the best known instrument of this nature. With the enactment of PL

94–142, however, there was a need for tests validated specifically for use in school placement and physical education programming. The Bruininks revision of the Lincoln-Oseretsky Scale met this need. Today, it is the most frequently used assessment instrument in adapted physical education (Ulrich, 1985). Other frequently used tests are those by Ayres (1968, 1975) and Hughes (1979). Following are descriptions of these tests.

Bruininks-Oseretsky Test of Motor Proficiency (BOTMP)

Purpose
To assess motor performance of children from 4.6 to 14.6 years of age. Validated specifically for use in placement of students.

Description
Two forms are available: short and long.

Short Form
Norm referenced, with 14 items assessing eight factors: (a) running speed and agility, (b) balance, (c) bilateral coordination, (d) strength, (e) upper-limb coordination, (f) response speed, (g) visual-motor control, and (h) upper-limb speed and dexterity.

Long Form
Same as short form, except with 46 items.

Scoring
Total test scores, subtest scores, and gross motor and fine motor composite scores can be derived.

Validity
BOTMP is a revision of the well known Lincoln-Oseretsky Test of Motor Proficiency. Content and construct validity is confirmed by similarity between factor analysis studies of BOTMP and works of Cratty (1967), Fleishman (1964), Guilford (1958), Harrow (1972), and Rarick, Dobbins, and Broadhead (1976).

Reliability
For short form: Test-retest *rs* ranging from .81 to .89 for 126 children. For long form: Test-retest *rs* ranging from .80 to .94. For the separate subtests, *rs* ranging from .15 to .89.

Primary Sources
Bruininks, R. H. (1978). *Bruininks-Oseretsky test of motor proficiency manual.* Circle Pines, MN: American Guidance Service.

Bruininks, V., & Bruininks, R. (1977). Motor proficiency of learning disabled and nondisabled students. *Perceptual and Motor Skills, 44,* 1131–1137.

Beitel, P. A., & Mead, B. (1980). Bruininks-Oseretsky test of motor proficiency: A viable measure for 3–5 year old children. *Perceptual and Motor Skills, 51,* 919–923.

Broadhead, G., & Bruininks, R. (1982). Childhood motor performance traits on the short form Bruininks-Oseretsky Test. *The Physical Educator, 39,* 149–155.

Address for Ordering
American Guidance Service, Circle Pines, MN 55014.

Bruininks-Oseretsky Test Items
(*Denotes items on short form)

Factor: Running Speed and Agility
Subtests: 1 on both long and short forms

*30-yard shuttle run

Factor: Balance
Subtests: 8 on long form, 2 on short form
  1. Standing on preferred leg on floor for 10 seconds
  *2. Standing on preferred leg on balance beam for 10 seconds
  3. Standing on preferred leg on balance beam—eyes closed—for 10 seconds
  4. Walking forward on line on floor, 6 steps
  5. Walking forward on balance beam, 6 steps
  6. Walking forward heel-to-toe on line on floor, 6 steps
  *7. Walking forward heel-to-toe on balance beam, 6 steps
  8. Stepping over response speed stick on balance beam

Factor: Bilateral Coordination
Subtests: 8 on long form, 2 on short form
  *1. Tapping feet alternately while making circles with fingers, 90 seconds
  2. Tapping—Foot and finger on same side synchronized, 90 seconds
  3. Tapping—Foot and finger on opposite side synchronized, 90 seconds maximum
  4. Jumping in place—leg and arm on same side synchronized, 90 seconds
  5. Jumping in place—leg and arm on opposite sides synchronized, 90 seconds
  *6. Jumping up and clapping hands
  7. Jumping up and touching heels with hands
  8. Drawing lines and crosses simultaneously, 15 seconds

Factor: Strength
Subtests: 3 on long form, 1 on short form
  *1. Standing long jump
  2. Sit-ups, 20 seconds
  3. Knee push-ups, 20 seconds—for all girls and boys under age 8
     Full push-ups—for boys age 8 and over

Factor: Upper-Limb Coordination
Subtests: 9 on long form, 2 on short form
  1. Bouncing a tennis ball 5 times and catching it with both hands
  2. Bouncing a tennis ball 5 times and catching it with preferred hand
  *3. Catching a tennis ball 5 times with both hands tossed from 10 feet
  4. Catching a tennis ball 5 times with preferred hand tossed from 10 feet
  *5. Throwing a tennis ball overhand at an eye-height target 5 feet away (1 practice and 5 trials)
  6. Touching a swinging ball with preferred hand, 5 trials
  7. Touching nose with index fingers—eyes closed, 90 seconds
  8. Touching thumb to index fingers—eyes closed, 90 seconds
  9. Pivoting thumb and index finger, 90 seconds

Factor: Response Speed
Subtest: 1 on both long and short forms

Stopping a falling stick with preferred thumb. The teacher holds the response speed stick against the wall and then drops it.

Factor: Visual-Motor Control
Subtests: 8 on long form, 3 on short form
 1. Cutting out a circle with preferred hand
 2. Drawing a line through a crooked path with preferred hand
 *3. Drawing a line thorough a straight path with preferred hand
 4. Drawing a line through a curved path with preferred hand
 *5. Copying a circle with preferred hand
 6. Copying a triangle with preferred hand
 7. Copying a horizontal diamond with preferred hand
 *8. Copying overlapping pencils with preferred hand

Factor: Upper-Limb Speed and Dexterity
Subtests: 8 on long form, 2 on short form
 1. Placing pennies in a box with preferred hand, 15 seconds
 2. Placing pennies in two boxes with both hands
 *3. Sorting shape cards with preferred hand
 4. Stringing beads with preferred hand
 5. Displacing pegs with preferred hand
 6. Drawing vertical lines with preferred hand
 *7. Making dots in circles with preferred hand
 8. Making dots with preferred hand

To administer the Bruininks-Oseretsky Test of Motor Proficiency, it is imperative to have a copy of the test manual. The items are described here largely to show tasks that students should be able to perform. Many of these items, particularly those pertaining to balance and upper-limb coordination, appear on many other physical education tests. They should be considered in writing instructional objectives and selecting learning activities. Remember, these tasks can be mastered through participation in games as well as through drill.

The tests of A. Jean Ayres are often used also in assessment. Portions of her work that are especially applicable to physical education follow.

Southern California Perceptual Motor Test (SCPMT)

Purpose
To measure six aspects of sensory integration of children 4 to 8 years old.

Description
Originally published as a separate test (Ayres, 1968), this test is now part of the Southern California Sensory Integration Tests (Ayres, 1980). The SCPMT contains six subtests: imitation of postures, crossing midline of body, bilateral motor coordination, right-left discriminations, standing balance—eyes open, and standing balance—eyes closed.

Validity
Construct validity by factor analysis. Content validity by similarity of subtests to those comprising other published tests: Berges and Lezine (1965), Head (1926), Fleishman (1964), Sloan (1955), and Roach and Kephart, (1966).

Reliability
Test-retest coefficients on 239 children ranging from .16 to .69 for individual subtests.

Primary Sources
Ayres, A. J. (1968). *Southern California perceptual-motor tests.* Los Angeles: Western Psychological Services.

Ayres, A. J. (1980). *Southern California sensory integration tests manual* (2nd ed.). Los Angeles: Western Psychological Services.

Berges, J., & Lezine, I. (1965). *The imitation of gestures.* London: Heinemann Medical Books.

Fleishman, E. (1964). *The structure and measurement of physical fitness.* Englewood Cliffs, NJ: Prentice-Hall.

Head, H. (1926). *Aphasia and kindred disorders of speech.* Cambridge: Cambridge University Press.

Roach, E., & Kephart, N. (1966). *Purdue perceptual-motor survey.* Columbus, OH: Charles E. Merrill.

Sloan, W. (1954). *The Lincoln-Oseretsky motor development scale.* Chicago: Stoelting.

Address for Ordering
Western Psychological Services, 13081 Wilshire Blvd., Los Angeles, CA 90025.

SCPMT Items
 1. Imitation of 12 postures. Nine postures involve arm movements only, and three involve finger movements only. One of the latter (pivoting thumb and index finger) is same as BOTMP item. Amount of time required to assume posture is important, with 3 seconds as the goal and 10 seconds as the cut-off point.
 2. Crossing Midline of Body. Eight imitations involving touching the hand to ear or eye as follows:
R hand to R ear
R hand to L eye
L hand to R eye
L hand to L ear
L hand to R ear
L hand to L eye
R hand to R eye
R hand to L ear
 3. Bilateral Motor Coordination. Eight imitations involving touching palms of hands to thighs in smooth, rhythmical motions.
Illustrative of these are
R hand to L thigh, L hand to right thigh, repeat once
L hand to L thigh, pause, right hand to right thigh quickly twice
 4. Right-Left Discrimination. Ten responses, each within 3 seconds, to such commands as
Show me your right hand
Touch your left ear
Take this pencil with your right hand
Now put it in my right hand
 5. Standing Balance: Eyes Open. Entails standing on one foot with arms folded across chest for maximum of 180 seconds. Same leg position as BOTMP. Done on preferred and nonpreferred foot.
 6. Standing Balance: Eyes Closed. Same as item 5 except eyes closed.

Test of Vestibular Function: Southern California Postrotatory Nystagmus Test (SCPNT)

Purpose
To measure vestibular function.

Description
The child sits cross-legged on a board that turns freely on a ball bearing device that is attached to another board. The latter board rests on the floor. The child is passively rotated to his or her left 10 times in 20 seconds and then abruptly stopped. The period during which the child's eyes move back and forth involuntarily following stopping is timed to the nearest second.

Scoring
Examiner uses stop watch to time number of seconds of nystagmus movement. The range for most normal children is 9 to 11 seconds, but this varies by age and gender. See examiner's manual for norms, means, and standard deviations.

Validity
Theoretical bases appear to be drawn from neurophysiological literature that indicates relationship between nystagmus and vestibular function.

Reliability
Test-retest correlation for 42 children is .83.

Primary Sources
Ayres, A. J. (1975). *Southern California Postrotatory Nystagmus Test*. Los Angeles: Western Psychological Services.
Gorman, D. R., & Pyfer, J. (1981). Postrotatory nystagmus responses following controlled vestibular stimulation among adult, normal child, learning disabled child and emotionally handicapped child populations. *American Corrective Therapy Journal, 35,* 11–20.
Kantner, R. M., Clark, D. L., Allen, L. C., & Chase, M. F. (1976). Effects of vestibular stimulation on nystagmus response and motor performance in the developmentally delayed infant. *Physical Therapy, 56,* 414–421.
Stilwell, J. M., Crowe, T. K., & McCollum, L. W. (1978). Postrotatory nystagmus duration as a function of communication disorders. *American Journal of Occupational Therapy, 32,* 222–228.

Basic Gross Motor Assessment (BGMA) Hughes, 1979, 1981

Purpose
To evaluate minor motor problems in children, ages 5 years, 6 months, to 12 years, 5 months. Author emphasizes that the purpose is not to detect developmental delay in motor performance.

Description
Includes eight subtests: (a) static balance, modified stork stand; (b) stride jump, (c) tandem (heel-toe) walk as a measure of dynamic balance, (d) hopping, (e) skipping, (f) target toss (6 bean bags aimed at specific floor targets), (g) yo-yo (manipulating ball suspended by string from a container up and into the container) as a measure of object control, and (h) ball handling skills (catch, throw, dribble) using a 6- or 7-inch diameter ball. Norm referenced, using a 0–3 scoring system for each subtest as follows:

> 0 = three observed difficulties or unable to perform test
> 1 = two observed difficulties
> 2 = one observed difficulty
> 3 = no difficulty

Some subtests are scored on several dimensions, so total perfect possible score is 57. Norms are available for total motor score and 19 individual item scores.

Validity
Content validity affirmed by panel of six authorities. Construct validity, including both factor analysis and statistical discrimination between known groups (normative sample and special education children referred by teachers for evaluation of suspected motor difficulties).

Reliability
Test-retest reliability of .97 on 48 students. Interrater reliability of .97. Internal consistency coefficients for each age level ranged from .59 to .79, with a median value of .71.

Primary Sources
Hughes, J. (1979). *Hughes basic gross motor assessment manual.* Yonkers, NY: G. E. Miller, Inc.
Hughes, J., & Riley, A. (1981). Basic gross motor assessment. *Physical Therapy, 61* (4), 503–511.

Address for Ordering
G. E. Miller, Inc., PO Box 266, 484 S. Broadway, Yonkers, NY 10705.

Integrated Testing/Teaching Approach

All physical education is by nature perceptual-motor education. The principle of specificity applies to perceptual-motor learning, creating a strong rationale for physical educators to apply perceptual-motor constructs to the learning of sports, dance, and aquatics movements. (See Table 11.1.)

Behavioral Objectives to Guide Testing/Teaching

The Sherrill Perceptual-Motor Tasks for Physical Education (SPMTPE) is designed for both testing and teaching. The approach is criterion-based rather than normative. The 10 items are written as behavioral objectives with subtasks that are more or less developmentally sequenced. They should be used as checklists

Table 11.1
Perceptual-Motor Factors That Widely Used Tests Purport to Measure

Frostig Developmental Test of Visual Perception (1963)[a]	Kephart-Roach Purdue Perceptual-Motor Survey (1966)	Ayres Southern California Perceptual-Motor Tests (1965–69)	Sherrill Perceptual-Motor Tasks for Physical Education (1976)
1. Eye-motor coordination a. Keeping pencil between two horizontal or curved lines b. Connecting dots or figures	1. Balance and posture a. Walking board b. Hopping and jumping	1. Imitation of postures; reproduction of 12 arm and hand movements	1. Identification of body parts
2. Figure-ground a. Overlapping outlines b. Embedded figures	2. Body image and R-L discrimination a. Identification of body parts b. Imitation of movement c. Obstacle course d. Kraus-Weber e. Angels-in-the-snow	2. Crossing midline of body; using right or left hand to touch designated ear or eye	2. Right-left discriminations
3. Form constancy, overlapping and embedded forms	3. Perceptual-motor match a. Chalkboard activities b. Rhythmic writing	3. Bilateral motor coordination; rhythmic tapping using palms of hands on thighs	3. Changing positions in space
4. Position-in-space figures like stars, chairs, ladders in different positions in space	4. Ocular control; ocular pursuits	4. Right-left discrimination; identification of right and left dimensions of various objects	4. Crossing the midline
5. Spatial relations; reproducing designs or figures by connecting dots appropriately	5. Form reproduction; drawing simple geometric figures on blank paper	5. Standing balance, eyes open	5. Imitation of movements
		6. Standing balance, eyes closed	6. Imitation of sports movements
			7. Visual tracking
			8. Static balance
			9. Dynamic balance
			10. Lateral dominance

[a]Note that all items on this test are paper–pencil rather than movement oriented.

in determining specific strengths and weaknesses in identification of body parts, right-left discriminations, changing positions in space, crossing the midline, imitation of movements, moving objects in space, visual tracking, static balance, dynamic balance (see Figure 11.5), and lateral dominance. Success (motor output) in these tasks depends on the integrity of proprioceptive and tactual input and central processing. Some children fail to make adequate motor responses because of auditory and/or visual deficits in understanding and remembering test instructions. To identify such children, the instructions for implementing the following behavioral objectives are either auditory or visual.

I. **Major task: identification of body parts.**
   Other tasks: auditory discrimination; memory; and sequencing.
   A. Given opportunities to touch body parts and surfaces after the teacher has called their names, students can
      1. Touch body parts one by one in response to such one-word directions as "elbow," "wrist," "chin," "waist."

Figure 11.5 Tiltboards, like the homemade one pictured, are used to improve dynamic balance and thereby enhance vestibular functioning.

2. Touch two body parts simultaneously.
3. Touch five body parts in the same sequence as they were named by the teacher.
4. Do all of the above with eyes closed.

II. **Major task: right-left discriminations with body parts.**

Other tasks: auditory discrimination; memory; and sequencing.

A. Given opportunities to touch body parts and surfaces after the teacher has called out the instructions, the student can
1. Use the right hand to touch parts named on right side.
2. Use the right hand to touch parts named on left side (this involves crossing the midline and should be more difficult than item 1).
3. Use the left hand to touch parts named on the left side.
4. Use the left hand to touch parts named on the right side.

B. Given opportunities to position a bean bag shaped like a *b*, the student can make a *p;* a *q;* a *b;* and a *d*.

C. Given opportunities to touch body parts of a facing partner, the student can follow verbal instructions without demonstrations. The student can
1. Use the right hand to touch body parts on the right side of partner.
2. Use the right hand to touch body parts on the left side of partner.

III. **Major task: changing positions in space.**

Other tasks: auditory discrimination; memory; and sequencing.

A. Given opportunities to identify his or her body position in relation to fixed objects, the student can
1. Stand in front of, in back of, to the right of, and to the left of a chair or a softball base.
2. Run to first base on a softball diamond.

3. Demonstrate where the right fielder, the left fielder, and the center fielder stand on a softball diamond.
4. Put specified body parts on top of diamonds, squares, circles, and other shapes on the floor.
5. Climb over a rope or horizontal bar or duck under it.

B. Given opportunities to follow verbal directions in warm-ups without the benefit of demonstration, the student can
1. Assume the following basic exercise positions: supine lying; hook lying; prone lying; long sitting; hook sitting; cross-legged sitting; kneel; half-kneel; squat; half-squat.
2. Demonstrate the following different foot positions in response to commands: wide base; narrow base; forward-backward stance; square stance; closed stance; open stance.
3. Perform a specific exercise seven times, use the eighth count to return to starting position, and stop precisely on the stop signal.

IV. **Major task: crossing the midline.**
Other tasks: auditory discrimination; memory; and sequencing.
A. Given opportunities to move the right arm across the midline in response to verbal instructions with no demonstration, the student can
1. Draw lines from left to right and from right to left on the chalkboard.
2. Draw geometrical shapes or write numbers or letters on the far-upper or lower-left corners of the chalkboard.
3. Throw a ball diagonally to a target on the far left.
4. Field a ball on the ground that is approaching the left foot.
5. Perform a backhand drive in tennis.
6. Catch a ball that rebounds off the wall to the left.
7. Toss a tennis ball vertically upward in front of left shoulder.

V. **Major task: imitation of movements.**
Other tasks: visual discrimination; memory; and sequencing.
A. Given opportunities to imitate the arm and leg movements of the teacher in an Angel-in-the-Snow sequence, the student can
1. Imitate bilateral movements.
   a. Move both arms apart and together while legs remain stationary.
   b. Move both legs apart and together while arms remain stationary.
   c. Move all four limbs apart and together simultaneously.
   d. Move any three limbs apart and together simultaneously while the fourth limb remains stationary.
2. Imitate unilateral movements.
   a. Move the right arm and right leg apart and together simultaneously while the left limbs remain stationary.
   b. Move the left arm and left leg apart and together simultaneously while the right limbs remain stationary.
3. Imitate crosslateral movements.
   a. Move the right arm and left leg apart and together simultaneously while the other limbs remain stationary.
   b. Move the left arm and right leg apart and together simultaneously while the other limbs remain stationary.

B. Given opportunities to imitate the arm movements of the teacher as depicted in Figure 11.6, without verbal instructions, the student will not mirror movements and can
1. Start and stop both arms simultaneously.
2. Correctly imitate six of nine arm movements.

C. Given opportunities to imitate the arm movements of the teacher who is holding a racquet, the student can correctly imitate, while holding a racquet, 6 out of 11 arm movements in Figure 11.6.

VI. **Major tasks: imitation of ball movements; aim; and force.**
Other tasks: visual discrimination; memory; and sequencing.
A. Given opportunities to imitate the movements of the teacher, without verbal instructions, the student with a tennis ball can
1. Imitate the teacher's movements precisely, using the right arm when the teacher does.
2. Toss the ball into the air to exactly the same height as the teacher tosses the ball.

Figure 11.6 Arm positions that children should be able to imitate. The top seven positions are used in the Purdue perceptual motor survey. These positions should be incorporated into follow-the-leader activities with dramatic themes like imitating airplanes or robots. They may also be used as a test of body image and right-left discriminations.

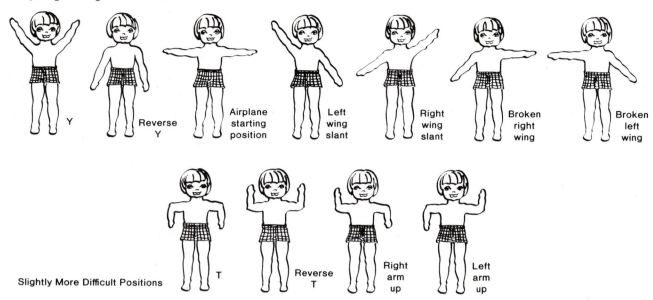

Y   Reverse Y   Airplane starting position   Left wing slant   Right wing slant   Broken right wing   Broken left wing

Slightly More Difficult Positions   T   Reverse T   Right arm up   Left arm up

3. Bounce the ball so it lands on the floor in precisely the same place as does the teacher's (in front of right foot, to the left side of left foot, and so on).
4. Bounce the ball so that it rises to the same height as the teacher's before it is caught.
5. Throw the ball so that it touches a wall target in relation to the student precisely as the teacher's throw related to himself or herself.

VII. **Major task: visual tracking.**
Other tasks: visual discrimination; memory; and sequencing.
  A. Given opportunities to track with both eyes a small hand mirror that the teacher is moving about 20 to 24 inches from his or her face, the student can
    1. Track the mirror from left to right.
    2. Track the mirror as it circles in a clockwise direction, then in a counterclockwise direction.
    3. Track the mirror as it moves in a large figure eight.
  B. Given opportunities to track flying bean bags (easier than flying balls), the student can
    1. Run or move the body so that the bean bag hits some part of him or her as it falls.

2. Run or move the body so that he or she catches 7 of 10 bean bags before they fall.
3. Run or move the body so that he or she strikes the bean bag with some kind of a racquet, paddle, or bat before it falls.
  C. Given opportunities to track ground balls being rolled toward him or her, the student can
    1. Stop those balls coming to the right.
    2. Stop those balls coming to the midline.
    3. Stop those balls coming to the left.

VIII. **Major task: static balance.**
Other tasks: visual or auditory.
  A. Given opportunities to explore static balance, the student can
    1. Balance on one foot with eyes open for 20 seconds.
    2. Balance on tiptoes with eyes open for 20 seconds.
    3. Balance on a stick, a rock, or a log with one foot.
    4. Perform a knee scale.
    5. Balance while maintaining a squatting position.
    6. Assume a tripod balance or head stand.
    7. Repeat each of the above with eyes closed.

IX. **Major task: dynamic balance.**
   Other tasks: visual or auditory.
   A. Given opportunities to explore dynamic balance, the student can
      1. Walk a straight line in heel-to-toe fashion.
      2. Jump backward five times and stop without losing balance.
      3. Walk a balance beam while holding a 10-pound weight in one arm.
      4. Alternate walking and squatting on a balance beam.
      5. Turn completely around three times while walking a beam.
      6. Do six kangaroo jumps with a rubber playground ball held securely between the legs.
      7. Maintain balance on a tiltboard or stabilometer.

X. **Major tasks: lateral dominance.**
   Other tasks: visual or auditory.
   A. Given opportunities to explore movement possibilities with bean bags, balls, ropes, bats, pencils, and other implements, the student can:
      1. Demonstrate more skill with the preferred hand than the nonpreferred hand.
      2. Exhibit a consistent preference for one hand over the other.

The behavioral objective approach to perceptual-motor appraisal results in a concrete list of things the student can and cannot do that should serve as the basis for developing long-term educational prescriptions. It is important that the physical educator identify the sense modality through which the child seems to learn best: visual, auditory, or haptic (tactile and proprioceptive input). Deficits should be noted also since they are sometimes as handicapping as real blindness or deafness.

Perceptual-Motor Training in Physical Education

Perceptual-motor training in adapted physical education should not duplicate that in the classroom. The objectives may be identical, but the activities differ. In the classroom, children usually sit at desks or stand in designated places. They trace, draw, connect dots, or use scissors to make shapes. The emphasis is upon eye, hand, or eye-hand movements to teach concepts about space. In the physical education setting, children practice purposeful movement of the entire body; they learn that shapes can be dynamic or static. The emphasis is upon making shapes with their own bodies and working together with a group to make the shapes or formations requisite for playing games or performing dances.

Game Formations and Perception

If the educational prescription for a child calls for a great amount of structure, limited space, and the reduction of external stimuli, then activities using the traditional circle and line formations are ideal. The principle of structure is implemented by an understanding of formations, the ability to move smoothly from one formation to another, and skill in maintaining proper spatial relationships within the formation. Several sessions can be devoted to learning the names of formations, following instructions, and studying the similarities between shapes made in the classroom and formations used on the playground. Young children should achieve success in small groups (four to eight pupils) before they are challenged to become part of a larger circle or line. Several variations of each formation should be explored so that a group in a circle, for instance, can respond easily to such commands as facing in or out, facing clockwise (CW) or counterclockwise (CCW), facing a partner, standing behind a partner, or standing side-by-side with a partner. Formations may be painted on the floor or temporarily marked by rope or cord to help severely involved children in their early efforts at conceptualizing shapes, getting in the correct position, and staying there.

Before games and dances are introduced, shape (form) perception should be stressed through small-group circle and line activities that do not require a partner. The class should be broken down into several groups with four to eight children in each for the following shape perception activities.

1. Follow the verbal instruction of the teacher: single circle; facing in; facing out; facing in; facing CCW; facing in; facing CW; facing CCW.

2. When the groups can respond successfully to one instruction at a time, give a sequence to be remembered and carried out.
   Example A:
   single circle, facing CCW;
   walk eight steps forward;
   then do four jumps backward;
   repeat the sequence, facing CW.
   Example B:
   single circle, facing in;
   walk four steps forward;
   single circle, facing out;
   walk four steps forward;
   single circle, facing in;
   eight slides CCW;
   single circle, facing out;
   eight slides CW.

3. When a sequence of locomotor activities using different formations is mastered, add to it tasks using a ball, rope, hoop, or scarf.

Example A:

single circle, facing in;

stand in place, bouncing ball to self four times;

single circle, facing CCW;

walk forward, dribbling ball four times;

single circle, facing out;

stand in place, tossing ball into air and catching it four times;

single circle, facing CCW;

do something original with the ball four times.

Example B:

single circle, facing in, with colorful scarf in each hand;

touch toes and stretch arms upward four times;

single circle, facing out, arms up;

single circle, facing in, arms down;

repeat three times;

single circle, facing CCW;

walk forward eight steps while performing large arm circles.

4. Each group is seated with a deck of specially made cards. Each card depicts a different formation. The leader shuffles the deck, someone draws, and the group jumps up and makes designated formation. The shuffling and drawing continue until all cards are used.

5. Formations or shapes are projected onto the wall by use of an opaque or slide projector. The group makes the formation that appears on the wall. Words can be projected rather than diagrams and pictures.

6. Teacher holds up artificial fruit or vegetable, such as apple, orange, grape, banana, ear of corn, or hot red pepper. Group forms large or small circle or rectangle in keeping with shape of object being shown.

7. Each child has a stretch rope (see Figure 11.7). The teacher shows a cardboard shape and/or names a shape, and the child makes this shape with the stretch rope.

8. Each child has one hand holding a long, continuous stretch rope shared by the group. When the name of a formation is called, the rope is stretched into the correct shape.

9. Each group has a list or diagram of four or five shapes that have duplicates hidden about the play area. The rules of a scavenger hunt are followed. When all the duplicate cards are found, the group carries them to the teacher and demonstrates ability to get into each formation.

10. Each group has a long and a short bamboo pole representing the hands of a clock. On command, the poles are moved to show different times of day. Bodies lying on the floor can be substituted for the hands of a clock or made into the arrow on a compass.

Table 11.2 on pages 286–87 enumerates the play formations with which children should become familiar. Circles, lines, and scattered formations are most appropriate for the primary grades. Files, shuttles, longway sets, and squares are introduced in the intermediate grades. The illustrative games and dances cited for each formation offer a high degree of structure with emphasis upon the skills of listening and following instructions. Unless an educational prescription calls for the explanation-demonstration instructional approach, most physical educators prefer the freedom of the scattered formation in which children can develop motor creativity through problem solving.

Most children with learning disabilities, however, seem to need repeated drill in order to approach normalcy with respect to spatial awareness, right-left discriminations, and directional understandings. Drill, or perceptual-motor training, should be a means, not an end. The classroom teacher uses drill as one way of improving reading and writing skills. The physical educator views drill as lead-up activity requisite to success in games and dance. It is believed that success in play builds self-confidence, which, in turn, carries over into the classroom and contributes to academic achievement.

Developmental Stages in Game Formations and Directions of Movement

Learning formations and directions of movement, whether through the explanation-demonstration approach or the problem-solving approach, should parallel the developmental stages in reproducing such forms on paper, blackboards, walls, floors, sand, air, or water. The ability of young children to get into a formation is related to the degree to which they have grasped the *concept* of the formation requested. If the ability to draw a shape can be used as a measure of the child's grasp of the concept, it is important to note the following developmental stages in drawing:

1. Looks at writing implements; may hold them; watches others make marks with them.

2. Crude scribbling, seemingly at random, without producing any coherent design.

3. Rudimentary space perception evidenced by coloring within the general outlines of a figure.

4. Ability to stay within a design; accurate drawing of figures.

5. The reproduction of more complex designs, and drawing pictures of objects.

6. Prints numbers and letters.

7. Acquires handwriting skills, with decreasing amounts of visual monitoring of movements needed—i.e., can write without the need of constantly watching his or her moving hand. (Cratty & Martin, 1969, p. 67)

Children begin scribbling sometime after the 12th month, initially producing randomized dots and lines. No conclusive evidence is available as to whether horizontal, vertical, or lateral lines are produced first. The first shape that a child learns to reproduce is a circle; this is also the formation in which the child plays his or her earliest games.

The ability to draw a circle appears at about age 3. The ages at which a child can reproduce different forms while looking at sample drawings follow:

Age 4—Can draw circles and squares fairly accurately but may not close the circles. Unable to draw rectangles, triangles, or diamonds.

Age 5—Can draw closed circles, squares, and rectangles fairly well.

Age 6—Can draw previously learned shapes with greater accuracy, but still has not mastered triangles and diamonds.

Age 7—Can draw triangles and diamonds with reasonable accuracy.

Counterclockwise Direction Predominates

The direction in which the child draws a circle is important to note also. Preschoolers generally begin a circle on the upper right hand portion of the paper and proceed clockwise, the direction of rotation least often used in dance and sport activities. From age 6 upward, most children draw circles in a *counterclockwise* direction, the traditional direction of movement in folk dancing, in jogging, and in rotating from station to station in the gymnasium. The counterclockwise direction is used more often than the clockwise in drawing squares, rectangles, and triangles among individuals with mature movement patterns. Elementary school physical education should provide many opportunities for exploring different shapes or forms that the body can assume and for experimenting with counterclockwise and clockwise locomotor movements and nonlocomotor movements of the limbs, head, and trunk.

Table 11.2
Basic Game and Dance Formations

Formation	Drills or Movement Exploration	Games	Dances
Single circle	Facing in Facing out Facing counterclockwise (CCW) Facing clockwise (CW) With *It* in the middle With *It* as part of the circle When part of the circle, *It* may be described as assuming a 1 o'clock, 3 o'clock, 6 o'clock position	Parachute activities Hot Potato Cat and Rat Duck, Duck, Goose Mickey Mouse (Spaceman) With *It* in Middle Circle Call-Ball Catch the Cane	Farmer in the Dell Hokey-Pokey Loopty Loo Did You Ever See a Lassie? Go In and Out the Windows Captain Jinks Cshebogar
Double circle When boys and girls are partners, the girl is traditionally on the boy's right X O Boy Girl	Both facing in (also called Two Deep) Both facing out Facing partner Facing in, side by side Facing out, side by side Facing CCW, side by side Facing CW, side by side Boy rotates CCW, girl remains stationary Girl rotates CCW, boy remains stationary Grand right and left, girl rotates CCW while boy rotates CW	Two Deep Caboose Dodgeball Run for Your Supper	How D'Ye Do, My Partner Seven Steps Hot Cross Buns Pop Goes the Weasel Skip to My Lou Bleking American Schottische Patticake Polka
Single line or row XXXXX Usually has teacher or *It* in front, sometimes called teacher ball formation	Side by side Straight vs. crooked Curved Staggered	Mother, May I? Red Light, Green Light Fire Engine (Beef Steak) Midnight Old Mother Witch Chinese Wall Pom-Pom-Pull Away Teacher Ball	Technique classes in modern dance, ballet, tap dance
Double line XXXXX XXXXX	Side by side Two deep, all facing front Two deep, all facing back Two deep, facing partner, no space between Two deep, back to back, with space between	Brownies and Fairies Crows and Cranes Steal the Bacon Line Dodgeball Volleyball Newcomb	Crested Hen (three pupils) I See You (any number) Troika (three pupils)

While much research has been conducted on the ability of young children to reproduce shapes with a pencil or crayon, little information is available concerning developmental stages in moving the entire body or parts of the body in one direction or another. The difficulty so often experienced in teaching an allemande left followed by a grand right and left reveals the need for more problem solving with respect to directions.

If the selection of physical education formations is made upon the basis of a child's readiness and/or the criterion of probable success, many questions must be asked. Which direction of movement is easier for a child: counterclockwise or clockwise? Is preference for direction similar to right- and left-handedness? If so, we should accept children's continued preferences for directions and when possible, place them where they can use the preferred direction.

Direction in Singing Games and Dance

In singing games and folk and square dance, it is worth noting the traditional direction of moving when boys and girls are directed to change partners, which entails rotating in different directions. The girls, who traditionally are on the outside, rotate counterclockwise while the boys rotate clockwise. Some dances, like the American schottische, call for the two partners to each step hop in an individual circular or diamond floor pattern and then return to one another. In such instances the girl step hops in a clockwise pattern and the boy step hops in a counterclockwise pattern.

Table 11.2
Basic Game and Dance Formations (continued)

Formation	Drills or Movement Exploration	Games	Dances
Scattered or random formation within set boundaries	Within walls of room Within rectangular area Within circular area Within triangular area Within alleys or lanes	Squirrel in the Tree Hide and Seek Huckleberry Beanstalk Keep Away Tag	Social or fad dancing Creative dance
Single file or column X X X X X	Each child behind the other Straight vs. crooked *It* in front of file Everyone in file facing forward Everyone in file facing backward Everyone in file facing alternately forward and backward Everyone in file facing diagonally right or left	Basketball shooting games H-O-R-S-E Twenty-one Over and Under Relay Running Relays Ball Handling Relays	
Double file or longways set XX XX XX XX XX	Each child and a partner behind the leading couple Girl traditionally on the right of boy Lead or head couple move Last or rear couple move All couples facing forward All couples facing backward All partners facing each other, same as zigzag line	Three-legged Relay Partner Relay Tandem Relays	A Hunting We Will Go London Bridge Bumps-a-Daisy Paw Paw Patch Virginia Reel
Shuttle formation drill and relays; object is shuttled back and forth from file to file	Two files, facing one another XXXXX XXXXX Two files, diagonally facing same goal like a basket O X X X X	Can shuttle object and go to end of own file *or* Shuttle object and go to end of the other file	Good use of space in continuous practice of locomotor skills
Square or quadrille, comprised of four couples OX X O O X XO	Girl on right of boy, standing side by side facing partner Facing opposite First couple out to the right (CCW) Circle all Swing partner Swing opposite		Most square dances, such as Arkansas Traveler Texas Star Dive for the Oyster Red River Valley Take A Little Peek

In many folk dances, performing a waltz step, two step, or polka with a partner requires that the couple move about the circle in a counterclockwise direction and less often in a clockwise direction. Although the direction of the circle is counterclockwise, the couple is making clockwise turns.

Anyone who has taught folk or square dance knows that instructions concerning direction of movement are more often misunderstood than any other aspect of the lesson. One reason for this is frequent incorrect use of the terms *right* and *left* in lieu of clockwise and counterclockwise. It should be remembered that whenever partners facing each other in a closed position perform in synchrony, the boy is moving with his left foot while the girl is moving with her right or vice versa. When standing in a double circle, facing partners, boys must move to their left as girls move to their right in order to perform together a series of steps, like eight slides, in a counterclockwise direction. It is obvious that the teacher who persists in telling students to move to the *left* or *right* will eventually be confronted with bedlam. *Instructions pertaining to floor patterns—i.e., moving in circular, triangular, or rectangular paths—must be given in terms of counterclockwise and clockwise.*

Perception in Volleyball: Visual Pursuit and Game Rotation

The lead-up games to volleyball, which are begun at about the third-grade level, can be used to reinforce right-left discriminations and to provide practice in visual pursuit and/or tracking. For most children, these lead-up games represent their initial experience in tracking large objects that move through a predictable low-high-low arc and in catching and/or striking balls that *descend* rather than ascend (like a bouncing ball) or approach horizontally (like a thrown ball).

Newcomb, the best-known lead-up game to volleyball, substitutes throwing and catching various objects over a net for volleying. It is based upon the assumption that tracking and catching a descending ball are prerequisites to tracking and striking (volleying). Certainly, catching and throwing are more familiar skills than volleying and serving. *Visual tracking* is an important contribution of volleyball at the elementary grade level. Children should not be rushed into the mastery of the relatively difficult skills of volleying and serving. Nor should individual differences be ignored and all children forced to use the same skills in a game setting. When a volleyball approaches, each child should have options: to catch the ball and return it across the net with a throw or to volley it across. Likewise, the child whose turn it is to serve may choose to put the ball into play with a throw from behind the baseline or a serve from any place on the right hand side of the court. Thus, in the early stages of learning the serve, some children may be only three giant steps behind the net while others may have the coordination and arm and shoulder strength to achieve success from behind the baseline. *Balloons* can be substituted for volleyballs with the very young or very weak.

Badminton, tennis, and deck tennis also emphasize visual pursuit skills; they should be introduced at the same time as other net games. Any kind of racquet can be used; the shorter the handle, the better for beginning players. *Large yarn balls* can be substituted for shuttlecocks.

Team games teach spatial awareness through *position play*. Playing a particular position on the court and rotating from position to position reinforces the concepts of right, center, and left and of front and back. Following is a progression for teaching right-left discriminations as they relate to volleyball, newcomb, group badminton, tennis, and deck tennis. Starting with a small number of children on a team and gradually increasing the number of team members is educationally sound, whereas assigning 8 to 10 elementary school children to a team is not. Socially, children must learn to relate to and work with one or two friends before being thrown into larger impersonal game settings. The average class needs a net for every six beginning players; this is not a budgetary problem for the creative teacher who uses strings with crepe paper (or rag) streamers as substitutes.

Rotation in volleyball depends upon the child's ability to make right-left discriminations; ability to walk or move sideward, backward, and forward; and comprehension of clockwise as a direction. The teacher who cares about transfer of learning and wishes to save children with directional deficits embarrassment on the playground will use the concept of rotation in the classroom. They will have the child sitting in the *RB* (right back) chair stand, recite, and then allow everyone to rotate in a clockwise position so a new child is *RB* and preparing to recite.

Perception in Softball

A child's success or lack of success in softball, kickball, and baseball may be an excellent indicator of perceptual-motor efficiency, especially with respect to right-left discriminations, crossing the midline, and visual pursuits. No other physical activity offers richer opportunities for perceptual-motor training.

First, the understanding of the diamond and the positions of the players on the field requires the ability to make right-left discriminations. The concept of infield vs. outfield offers a new dimension of spatial awareness. The expectation that each player *cover* a particular area of the field and *back up* other players is based upon spatial awareness. Bases are run in a *counterclockwise* direction. Pitches are described as inside, outside, high, low, and curved to the right or left. A batter who misses the ball is told that he or she swung too early or too late. Decision making by a fielder as to where to throw the ball is based upon visual memory of sequences. Is there a player on third base? On first and third? On all of the bases? Where should the ball be thrown first? The batter must make decisions with respect to directions also. If there is a runner on third base, where should the batter hit the ball? If there are runners on first and second base, where should the ball be hit? And *ad infinitum*.

Figure 11.8 offers suggestions for teaching children three sets of terms that are applicable to any sport that entails use of a bat or racquet—square stance, open stance, and closed stance. The different types of stances are seen in golf also. Opportunities for practicing each of the situations depicted should be provided within the structure of the classroom, where distractions are minimal. Knowledge gained in the classroom can be applied later in problem solving during a game situation. For instance, when the ball goes to the right instead of over the net in a tennis game, can the child reason why? When the golf ball goes to the left into a sandtrap instead of straight down the fairway, does the student know what caused the directional deviation?

Figure 11.8 Variations in batting which should be practiced in the classroom with a yarn or paper ball.

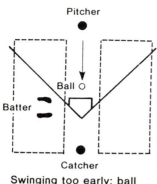

Swinging too early: ball has not yet arrived at the plate; if hit, it will probably go to the left.

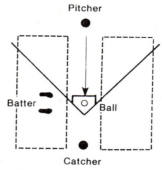

Correct timing of swing: ball is directly over plate; when hit, it will probably go toward the shortstop.

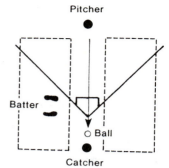

Swinging too late: ball has already passed over the plate; if hit, it will probably go to the right.

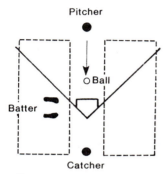

Square stance: best for beginners.

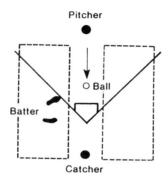

Open stance: if hit, the ball will probably go to the left.

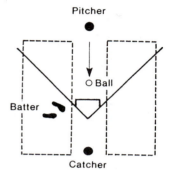

Closed stance: if hit, the ball will probably go to the right.

Learning Activities

1. Develop a file of perceptual-motor tests.
2. Administer each of the tests described in this chapter to at least one pupil, preferably the same child. Write a report presenting the findings of the tests and make an educational diagnosis in the form of several conclusions about specific perceptual-motor strengths and weaknesses.
3. Invite the special education coordinator in your community to the class to describe the specific perceptual-motor tests and evaluation procedures currently being used in the public schools.
4. Observe how an educational diagnostician or other specialist collects data for a child's files.
5. Refer to the bibliography of films with perceptual-motor implications on pp. 138–139 of the AAHPERD Publication *Foundations and Practices in Perceptual-Motor Learning—A Quest for Understanding* and/or to similar bibliographies. Order and view some of the films.

References

Ayres, A. J. (1965). Patterns of perceptual-motor dysfunction in children: A factor analytic study. *Perceptual and Motor Skills, 20*, 335–368.

Ayres, A. J. (1972). *Sensory integration and learning disorders*. Los Angeles: Western Psychological Press.

Bender, L. (1938). *Bender gestalt test*. New York: American Orthopsychiatric Association, Inc.

Bender, L. (1938). *Bender gestalt test*. New York: American Orthopsychiatric Association, Inc.

Cratty, B. J. (1969). Cratty six-category gross motor test. In B. J. Cratty, *Perceptual-motor behavior and educational processes* (pp. 220–241). Springfield, IL: Charles C. Thomas.

Cratty, B. J., & Martin, M. M. (1969). *Perceptual-motor efficiency in children*. Philadelphia: Lea & Febiger.

Frostig, M. (1963). *Marianne Frostig developmental test of visual perception* (3rd ed.). Palo Alto, CA: Consulting Psychologists Press.

Hallahan, D., & Cruickshank, W. (1973). *Psychoeducational foundations of learning disabilities*. Englewood Cliffs, NJ: Prentice-Hall.

Knapczyk, D., & Liemohn, W. (1976). A factor study of Cratty's body perception test. *Research Quarterly, 47*, 678–682.

Lockhart, A. (1964). What's in a name? *Quest, 2*, 9–13.

Roach, E., & Kephart, N. (1966). *The Purdue perceptual-motor survey*. Columbus, OH: Charles E. Merrill.

Rood, M. (1954). Neurophysiological reactions as a basis for physical therapy. *Physical Therapy Review, 34*, 444–449.

Williams, H., Temple, I., & Bateman, J. (1979). A test battery to assess intrasensory and intersensory development of young children. *Perceptual and Motor Skills, 48*, 643–659.

Bibliography

American Alliance for Health, Physical Education, and Recreation. (1968). *Perceptual-motor foundations: A multidisciplinary concern*. Washington, DC: Author.

American Alliance for Health, Physical Education, and Recreation. (1971). *Foundations and practices in perceptual-motor learning*. Washington, DC: Author.

Ayres, A. J. (1972). *Sensory integration and learning disorders*. Los Angeles: Western Psychological Services.

Barsch, R. H. (1968). *Enriching perception and cognition*. Seattle: Special Child Publications.

Benton, A. L. (1969). *Right-left discrimination and finger localization*. New York: Hoeber.

Birch, H., & Lefford, A. (1967). Visual differentiation, intersensory integration and voluntary motor control. *Monographs of the Society for Research in Child Development, 32*, 1–87.

Brown, J. W. (1972). *Aphasia, apraxia, and agnosia*. Springfield, IL: Charles C. Thomas.

Bryant, P. (1974). *Perception and understanding in young children*. New York: Basic Books.

Capon, J. (1975). *Perceptual-motor lesson plans*. Alameda, CA: Front Row Experience.

Carterette, E., & Friedman, M. (Eds.). (1978). *Perceptual ecology*. New York: Academic Press.

Cratty, B. J. (1978). *Perceptual and motor development in infants and children* (2nd ed.). New York: Macmillan.

Dember, W., & Warm, J. (1979). *Psychology of perception* (2nd ed.). New York: Holt, Rinehart, & Winston.

Geert, P. (1983). *The development of perception, cognition, & language: A theoretical approach*. Boston: Routledge & Kegan Row.

Gibson, E. (1969). *Principles of perceptual learning and development*. New York: Appleton-Century-Crofts.

Goodman, L., & Hammill, D. (1973). The effectiveness of the Kephart-Getman activities in developing perceptual-motor and cognitive skills. *Focus on Exceptional Children, 4*, 1–10.

Hallahan, D., & Cruickshank, W. (1973). *Psychoeducational foundations of learning disabilities*. Englewood Cliffs, NJ: Prentice-Hall. (see Chapters 5 and 6)

Hanson, M. (1973). *A factor analysis of selected body-image tests appropriate for use with the mentally retarded*. Unpublished doctoral dissertation, Texas Woman's University, Denton.

Keogh, J. F. (1978). Movement outcomes as conceptual guidelines in the perceptual-motor maze. *Journal of Special Education, 12*, 321–330.

Kephart, N. (1960). *Slow learner in the classroom*. Columbus, OH: Charles E. Merrill. (2nd ed. in 1971).

Kidd, A. H., & Rivoire, J. (Eds.). (1966). *Perceptual development in children*. New York: International Universities Press.

Liemohn, W., & Knapczyk, D. (1984). An analysis of the Southern California perceptual motor tests. *Research Quarterly for Exercise and Sport, 55* (3), 248–253.

Maslow, P., Frostig, M., Lefever, D., & Whittlesey, J. (1964). The Marianne Frostig developmental test of visual perception, 1963 standardization. *Perceptual and Motor Skills, 19*, 463–499.

Montgomery, P., & Richter, E. (1977). *Sensorimotor integration for developmentally handicapped children*. Los Angeles: Western Psychological Services.

Moore, J., Guy, L., & Reeve, T. (1984). Effects of the Capon perceptual-motor program on motor ability, self-concept, and academic readiness. *Perceptual and Motor Skills, 58* (3), 711–714.

Pick, A. (Ed.). (1979). *Perception and its development*. Hillsdale, NJ: Lawrence Erlbaum Associates.

Pick, H., & Pick, A. (1970). Sensory and perceptual development. In P. Mussen (3rd ed.), *Carmichael's manual of child psychology* (pp. 773–847). New York: John Wiley & Sons.

Provine, R., & Westerman, J. (1979). Crossing the midline: Limits of early eye-hand behavior. *Child Development, 50*, 437–441.

Reid, G. (1981). Perceptual-motor training: Has the term lost its utility? *Journal of Health, Physical Education, Recreation, and Dance, 52* (6), 38–39.

Schiffman, H. R. (1976). *Sensation and perception*. New York: John Wiley & Sons.

Shontz, F. C. (1969). *Perceptual and cognitive aspects of body experience*. New York: Academic Press.

Thomas, J., Chissom, B., Stewart, C., & Shelley, F. (1975). Effects of perceptual motor training on preschool children: A multivariate approach. *Research Quarterly, 46*, 505–513.

Walk, R., & Pick, H. (1981). *Intersensory perception and sensory integration*. New York: Plenum.

Walk, R., & Pick, H. (Eds.). (1978). *Perception and experience*. New York: Plenum.

Watkins, E. (1976). *The Watkins Bender-Gestalt scoring system: Norms, interpretation, and scoring manual for normal subjects and subjects with learning disabilities*. San Rafael, CA: Academic Therapy Publications.

Williams, H., & DeOreo, K. (1980). Perceptual-motor development. In C. Corbin (Ed.), *A textbook of motor development* (2nd ed.), (pp. 135–196). Dubuque, IA: Wm. C. Brown.

Williams, H. (1983). *Perceptual and motor development*. Englewood Cliffs, NJ: Prentice-Hall.

Ziviani, J., Poulsen, A., & O'Brien, A. (1982). Correlation of the Bruininks-Oseretsky test of motor proficiency with the Southern California sensory integration tests. *American Journal of Occupational Therapy, 36* (8), 517–523.

12 Postures

Figure 12.1 Instructor requests student to select the body type picture that most closely resembles his own as part of posture counseling. (See Rowe and Caldwell in references.)

Chapter Objectives

After you have studied this chapter, you should be able to

1. Discuss assessment techniques for postures and body typing.
2. Explain normal postural development with implications for strength and flexibility training at different ages.
3. State posture training guidelines and contrast old and new approaches to ameliorating posture problems.
4. Identify the most common postural problems and explain which muscle groups (extensors, flexors, abductors, and adductors) are abnormally weak or tight in relation to each. Apply this to activity selection.
5. Discuss scoliosis and kyphosis as orthopedic problems that require cooperative program planning among physician, teacher, and family. State procedures for initiating and/or facilitating this cooperation.

The expression of the face balks account,
But the expression of a well-made man appears not only in his face,
It is in his limbs and joints also, it is curiously in the joints of his hips and wrists,
It is in his walk, the carriage of his neck, the flex of his waist and knees, dress does not hide him,
The strong sweet quality he has strikes through the cotton and broad-cloth,
To see him pass conveys as much as the best poem, perhaps more,
You linger to see his back, and the back of his neck and shoulder-side.

—Walt Whitman

Each person's postures are expressions of his or her thoughts, feelings, and moods. Postures are affected by height, weight, fitness, body type, body image, and self-concept, all of which are aspects of posture training. Figure 12.1 depicts a lesson in which a mentally retarded adolescent is learning about body types. Physical education is the only subject in the curriculum that focuses upon the body as an instrument of expression. Through the appraisal of the postures of school children and the subsequent amelioration of problems of body alignment, the physical educator makes a unique contribution to personality development, peer acceptance, and vocational success.

Each person possesses not one but many postures. Any position is a posture, and one individual assumes thousands of static and dynamic postures each day—standing, walking, running, sitting, sleeping, stooping, climbing, and ad infinitum. The appraisal of body alignment is based, therefore, upon careful observation of many postures.

Group Screening

Screening for postural deviations should be completed early in the semester. Whenever possible, students should be kept unaware that they are being so screened.

Instead, they may think they are practicing selected locomotor skills or engaging in movement exploration. Ideally, they are moving in a circle and responding to changes in direction while the teacher observes from the center of the circle. Their movements should be natural, spontaneous, and relaxed. Prior to beginning the circular activity, it is desirable to group the students informally according to body build. To facilitate this process, four or five students representing different body types are selected as leaders. The students are then requested to stand behind the person with the body type most similar to their own. The resulting files are structured into a circle, and screening begins.

One of the most efficient procedures is to group the students into quartiles. First identify the 25% of the class who have the best postures and the 25% who have the worst postures. Then place the remaining students in the upper and lower middle quartiles.

Approximately 1 week later repeat the screening procedures without reviewing your notes. Compare the names of the students assigned to each quartile with those assigned previously. Schedule individual posture examinations for those students who fell into the lowest quartile during both screening sessions.

Identical procedures may be used in the classroom when the students are unaware that their sitting postures are being evaluated. The way a student sits at a desk, the tilt of the head, the distance of eyes from paper, and whether or not the feet touch the floor—all have significance in determining postural fitness. Postures, like movement patterns, are unique to the individual. Family similarities appear in postures as well as in faces. Genetic predispositions toward body build, weight, height, and level of energy have as great an influence on postures as do environmental factors.

Figure 12.2 Posture score sheet.

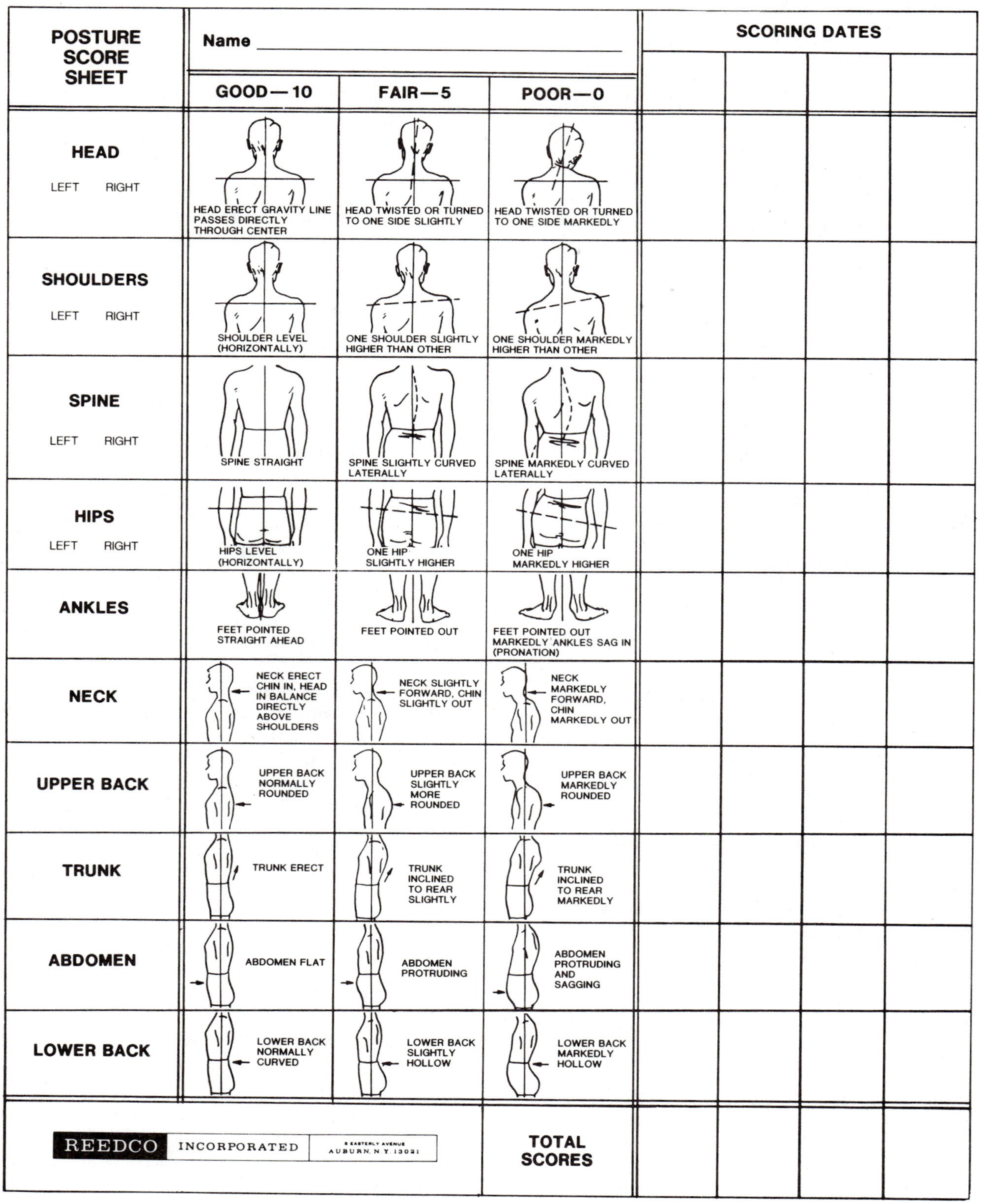

POSTURE SCORE SHEET	Name _____			SCORING DATES			
	GOOD—10	FAIR—5	POOR—0				
HEAD LEFT RIGHT	HEAD ERECT GRAVITY LINE PASSES DIRECTLY THROUGH CENTER	HEAD TWISTED OR TURNED TO ONE SIDE SLIGHTLY	HEAD TWISTED OR TURNED TO ONE SIDE MARKEDLY				
SHOULDERS LEFT RIGHT	SHOULDER LEVEL (HORIZONTALLY)	ONE SHOULDER SLIGHTLY HIGHER THAN OTHER	ONE SHOULDER MARKEDLY HIGHER THAN OTHER				
SPINE LEFT RIGHT	SPINE STRAIGHT	SPINE SLIGHTLY CURVED LATERALLY	SPINE MARKEDLY CURVED LATERALLY				
HIPS LEFT RIGHT	HIPS LEVEL (HORIZONTALLY)	ONE HIP SLIGHTLY HIGHER	ONE HIP MARKEDLY HIGHER				
ANKLES	FEET POINTED STRAIGHT AHEAD	FEET POINTED OUT	FEET POINTED OUT MARKEDLY ANKLES SAG IN (PRONATION)				
NECK	NECK ERECT CHIN IN, HEAD IN BALANCE DIRECTLY ABOVE SHOULDERS	NECK SLIGHTLY FORWARD, CHIN SLIGHTLY OUT	NECK MARKEDLY FORWARD, CHIN MARKEDLY OUT				
UPPER BACK	UPPER BACK NORMALLY ROUNDED	UPPER BACK SLIGHTLY MORE ROUNDED	UPPER BACK MARKEDLY ROUNDED				
TRUNK	TRUNK ERECT	TRUNK INCLINED TO REAR SLIGHTLY	TRUNK INCLINED TO REAR MARKEDLY				
ABDOMEN	ABDOMEN FLAT	ABDOMEN PROTRUDING	ABDOMEN PROTRUDING AND SAGGING				
LOWER BACK	LOWER BACK NORMALLY CURVED	LOWER BACK SLIGHTLY HOLLOW	LOWER BACK MARKEDLY HOLLOW				
REEDCO INCORPORATED 8 EASTERLY AVENUE AUBURN, N.Y. 13021			**TOTAL SCORES**				

Individual Examination

Students identified as needing special guidance and counseling with respect to postures are scheduled for an individual examination. The whole child must be considered, including the child's anxiety about being singled out as different, and the child's thoughts and feelings about his or her physical self. The general procedures used in posture counseling parallel those described under fitness counseling. Unless the teacher plans to schedule relatively frequent follow-up conferences, the individual examination should not be conducted.

Figure 12.2 presents one of the many forms that can be filled out during the examination. The form is identical to that used in the New York Posture Test with the exception of three omissions: feet, side view of shoulders, and side view of chest. The New York State Fitness Test, which includes the Posture Test, can be obtained by writing to the State Education Department, Division of Health, Physical Education, and Recreation, Albany, NY 12224.

Posture Grid

The room in which the posture examination is administered should have a grid comprised of 2-inch squares on the wall (see Figure 12.3). The vertical lines are at right angles to the horizontal lines and extend all the way to the floor. These lines provide reference points for ascertaining the correct alignment of body parts. Footprints should be painted on the floor in front of the grid to facilitate correct standing positions.

Some individuals prefer a posture screen comprised of vertical and horizontal strings hooked onto a frame so as to make 2-, 4-, or 6-inch squares that serve as reference points. The student stands behind the screen and is viewed through it.

Posture Photographs

Photographs of students whose postural fitness warrants individual examination are recommended for the following reasons:

1. To enable students to see themselves as others see them and to serve as a motivational device toward positive change.
2. To orient parents and the public to the broad objectives of physical education.
3. To serve as a measure against which postural change can be estimated.
4. To supplement school files, thereby improving the permanent record of the whole child.

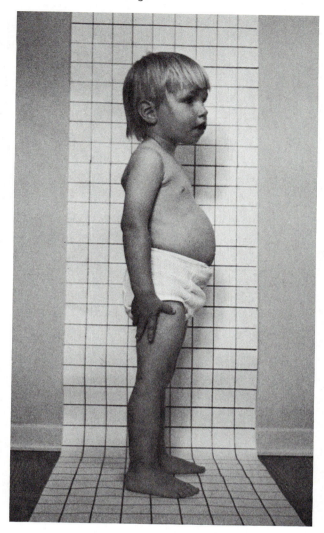

Figure 12.3 Two-year-old stands in front of posture grid. His posture is normal for his age.

The following procedures are recommended in photographing postures:

1. Two students standing in front of the grid can be photographed simultaneously and the resulting snapshot divided.
2. Only back and side views of the student are essential.
3. The students should be barefoot. Swimming trunks or shorts are recommended for boys. Pants and bra or a two-piece swimming suit are recommended for girls. Long hair should be pulled back to reveal the ear lobe.

Figure 12.4 Seven body types differing on somatotype dimensions.

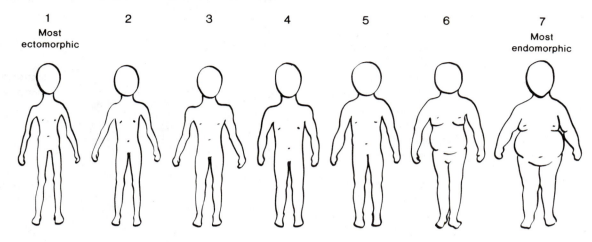

4. The back should be bare, with a black dot placed on each spinous process. An ordinary magic marker makes the dot. Dots should be made with student standing. Changes of position during the procedure should be avoided.

5. Polaroid cameras have the advantage of instantaneous film development. If the snapshot is not good, a second one can be taken immediately.

6. Students must be assured that pictures will be held in confidence. Often it is more valuable to give the pictures to the student for further study than to file them.

Body Typing

Posture evaluation begins with the classification of each student with respect to body type or build. This procedure, called *somatotyping,* enables the physical educator to determine the student's limitations in sports, dance, and aquatics and thus to offer scientific guidance in helping the student develop lifetime leisure skills.

William H. Sheldon (1954) is credited with refining somatotype techniques. He identified three basic body types and photographed 4,000 men, classifying them in accordance with the characteristics of each body type. This research showed that no one meets the qualifications for any one body type, but that each individual is comprised of components of all three types.

A somatotype classification is comprised of three numbers, such as 236 or 171. Each digit ranges from 1 to 7, with 1 representing the lowest degree of a characteristic (Figure 12.4).

The first digit in the series indicates what degree of *endomorph* body build characteristics are present. These characteristics are roundness and softness of the body; breasts and buttocks well developed; high square shoulders and short neck; and predominance of abdomen over thorax.

The second digit indicates what degree of *mesomorph* body build characteristics are present. These characteristics are solid, well-developed musculature; bones usually large and covered with thick muscle; forearm thickness and relative largeness of wrist, hand, and fingers; large thorax and relatively slender waist; broad shoulders and well developed trapezius and deltoid; buttocks exhibit muscular dimpling; and abdominal muscles prominent and thick.

The third digit indicates what degree of *ectomorph* body build characteristics are present. These characteristics are small bones and thin muscles; linearity, fragility, and delicacy of body; limbs relatively long, trunk short, and shoulders narrow; shoulders droop and predisposed toward winged scapulae; abdomen and lumbar curve flat; thoracic curve relatively sharp and elevated; and no bulging of muscle at any point.

A predominantly endomorphic person commonly has a somatotype of 721, 731, or 631. For such persons, physical education should emphasize the management of obesity. Strenuous activities such as contact sports, weight lifting, and pyramid building are contraindicated, particularly during periods of rapid growth. Their joints are more subject to trauma than those of other pupils, either from cumulative daily gravitational stresses or sudden traumas. Almost always, during childhood and adolescence, physiological age is not commensurate with chronological age. The endomorph is predisposed to such postural deviations as knock-knees, pronated feet, flat feet, sagging abdomen, round shoulders, and round back. Physical education for obese youngsters is discussed in Chapter 17.

A predominantly mesomorphic person commonly has a somatotype of 171, 172, 272, or even 372. For success in contact sports, the pupil requires a certain amount of cushioning by fat. A 2, 3, or 4 rating in endomorphy is therefore desirable for athletes. Football players typically have somatotypes of 273, 371, or 471; baseball players tend to have 262, 263, or 462; while tennis players and long-distance runners may be classified as 153 or 154. Mesomorphs are better adapted structurally, organically, and neurologically to meet stress than other body types. They seldom exhibit severe posture deviations. Their major problem seems to be a substantial gain in weight after age 30.

A predominantly ectomorphic person commonly has a somatotype of 217, 227, or 236. The 217 extreme seldom succeeds in athletic endeavors; such a person is characterized by muscle flaccidity, a floppiness of movement, and looseness at joints that predisposes him or her to many postural problems that do not respond to exercise. A predominantly ectomorphic person simply lacks potential to persist in movement long enough for the principle of overload to be operative; he or she fatigues easily and is sometimes described as having *asthenia.* He or she can be helped best by a "slowing down" program of physical education that provides instruction in relaxation and supervised rest. Less extreme ectomorph types often excel in activities like cross-country running in which they set their own pace. They tend to have too little body padding to engage safely in contact sports. Likewise, they chill easily and require shorter swimming periods and outdoor play sessions than their peers.

Body Image Testing

Several body image tests have been designed to determine the extent to which persons recognize their own body types (Darden, 1972; Gottesman & Caldwell, 1966; Rowe & Caldwell, 1963). In most of these, the pupil is presented with seven pictures, each differing from the other quantitatively on somatotype dimensions, as shown in Figure 12.1. The pictures are presented in random order, and the child is requested to select the one that most resembles himself or herself. In other instances, he or she is asked "Which drawing is most like you?" and "Which drawing would you rather be like?" Regardless of the approach used, instruction geared toward understanding and appreciating body types is valuable.

Normal Postural Development

Figure 12.5 depicts nine stages in the development of normal postures. At birth, the entire spinal column of the infant is flexed in a single C curve. Only when the extensor muscles of the neck and back are sufficiently strengthened by random kicking and wiggling do the cervical and lumbar curves begin to appear. The cervical curve develops at about 4 to 5 months of age, while the lumbar curve begins to develop sometime after the child learns to walk. Toddlers and young children with disabilities that prevent upright locomotion characteristically have *flat backs.* This condition is normal during the months when the child is gaining confidence in walking and running activities. If flat back persists beyond the toddler stage, it is considered a postural deviation.

The normal preschool child tends to develop an exaggerated lumbar curve, which may persist throughout grade school. This condition is caused by the imbalance in the strength of the abdominal muscles and the hip flexors. It is normal for the abdominal musculature of the preschool child to be too weak to maintain the pelvis in a neutral position.

The resulting lordosis characterizes the young child's postures until sufficient abdominal strength is developed to counteract the downward pull of the hip flexors. Lordosis, therefore, is normal in a young child and should not be labeled as a posture deviation until adolescence. The degree of lumbar curvature should, however, lessen from year to year.

In the adult, four curves are readily discernible in the spinal column. Viewed from the side these are

1. Concave—cervical spine comprised of 7 vertebrae.
2. Convex—thoracic spine comprised of 12 vertebrae.
3. Concave—lumbar spine comprised of 5 vertebrae.
4. Convex—sacral spine comprised of 5 sacral vertebrae fused in adulthood and called the sacrum.

Erect, extended carriage results when the thoracic and sacral flexion curves are in balance with the cervical and lumbar hyperextension curves. Whenever one curve increases, the other curves tend to increase also to compensate for the imbalance.

Figure 12.5 Normal postural development from infancy through age 2.

(A) Spinal column is flexed in single C curve; arms and legs are flexed—birth to 2 months.

(B) Reflex stretching out of arms (Moro) until about 6 months, at which time protective extensor (parachute) reaction appears.

(C) Extensor tone increases, reinforced by random limb movements, and cervical curve begins to appear.

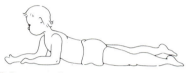

(D) Early sitting with head control shows strong cervical extensor muscles—about 6 months.

(E) Prone-on-elbows crawling position, combined with labyrinthine and optical righting reflexes, reinforces development of cervical curve.

(F) Creeping further strengthens abdominal and lumbar spine muscles—8 months.

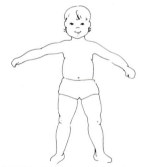

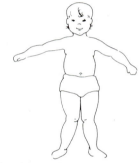

(G) Early standing with support shows flat back posture.

(H) Lumbar curve appears as back muscles are further strengthened by walking, with wide base stance—about 14 months.

(I) Knock knees is normal in early walking, especially in endomorphic body types.

When a posture problem becomes evident, it is important to analyze the imbalance of the muscle groups by considering these questions:

1. Muscles on which surface are too tight—i.e., stronger than their antagonists? Which stretching exercises are indicated?

2. Muscles on which surface are too loose—i.e., weaker than their antagonists? Which strengthening exercises are indicated?

3. What role is gravity playing in the muscle imbalance?

Usually, strength exercises are chosen for amelioration of posture problems. The principle of *reciprocal innervation* should be remembered: When muscles on one surface are being strengthened, muscles on the antagonistic surface are being stretched simultaneously. Regardless of the type of exercise selected, both surfaces are affected.

Contraindicated Exercises

Figure 12.6 depicts exercises that students with certain kinds of posture problems should not do. *Contraindicated* is a medical term meaning there is an indication against (contra) prescription of such exercises. The exercises shown may make tight muscles even tighter, as in push-ups and the swan, or they may lead to stretching and tearing a tight muscle group, as in straight-leg toe touches.

Posture Training Guidelines

Once the present level of postural fitness is assessed and annual goals written to include posture training, short-term objectives are developed. These objectives can be broken down into behaviors. Illustrative target behaviors for improving walking postures are (a) keeps head and trunk erect with eyes generally focused straight ahead; (b) swings arms in opposition with normal range of motion; (c) uses regular, rhythmic, heel-ball-toe

Figure 12.6 Exercises that are contraindicated when certain posture problems are present. (*A*) Straight leg lift and hold should not be used when persons have weak abdominal muscles and/or lordosis. (*B*) Straight leg sit-ups should not be used when persons have weak abdominal muscles. (*C*) Push-ups should not be used when persons have round shoulders. (*D*) The swan should not be used when persons have lordosis. (*E*) Deep knee bends and the duck walk are contraindicated for most students because of the strain put on the knee joints. (*F*) Straight leg toe touch and bear walk should not be used when persons have hyperextended knees.

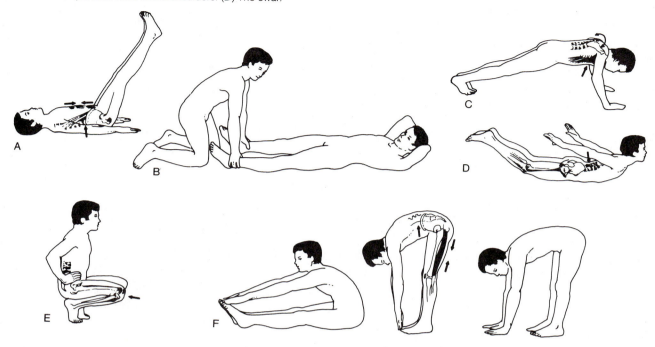

transfer of weight; and (d) maintains normal support base—i.e., heels, 2 to 3 inches from line of progression.

For many years, individualized, prescribed exercises were the accepted practice in posture training and body mechanics activities. These exercises were often boring and, if not rigidly adhered to, no improvement occurred. Moreover, if performed incorrectly, such exercises could actually injure the child. The trend now is away from isolated exercises and toward gamelike activities that utilize muscle groups in therapeutically sound ways. This chapter, therefore, includes only a few exercises for each condition.

General physical education programming designed to achieve posture training objectives emphasizes use of the kinesthetic, vestibular, and visual sense modalities in such activities as body awareness or proprioceptive training, body image work, static and dynamic balance tasks, and body alignment activities in front of mirrors. Whenever possible, videotape feedback is provided. Emphasis is placed on sports, dance, and aquatics activities that demand full extension of the trunk, head, neck, and limbs—i.e., reaching toward the sky, lifting the chest, stretching upward. Dance, gymnastics (free exercise and balance beam routines), trampolining, and swimming typically reinforce extension, correct body alignment, and good balance. Relaxation training is used to teach and/or reinforce understanding of tightness/tension in muscle groups vs. looseness/nontension.

Behavior Management in Posture Training

Posture problems can be corrected by behavior management techniques (Johnson, Catherman, & Spiro, 1981; O'Brien & Azrin, 1970; Rubin, O'Brien, Ayllon, & Roll, 1968; Tiller, Stygar, Hess, & Reimer, 1982). Among the types of apparatus used for correcting posture are the following:

1. A portable apparatus worn on the back at about the level of the second thoracic vertebra which emits a 550-cps tone at an intensity of 55 decibels whenever the wearer slouches (Rubin, O'Brien, Ayllon, & Roll, 1968). Twenty-five adults, ages 18 to 49 years, showed mean reduction of 86% in slouching.

2. A vibrotactile posture harness designed to detect slouching and energize a vibrotactile stimulator on the shoulder whenever slouching occurred. There was no auditory signal, just tactile; harness was not detectable by associates (O'Brien & Azrin, 1970). Eight adults showed mean reduction of 35% in slouching.

3. Foam helmet training device with a mercury switch and buzzer that emits noise whenever the head deviates from upright position used in conjunction with a vest containing a buzzer system that makes noise whenever torso inclines abnormally (Tiller, Stygar, Hess, & Reimer, 1982). Used with one moderately retarded female, age 20 years, in 4 months of training (200 steps each session).

4. Music played during the duration of appropriate posture for 9-year-old cerebral palsied boy with mental retardation who needed physical support of orthopedic chair and straps for good posture. Johnson, Catherman, and Spiro (1981) reported that response-contingent music is more effective than physical support alone in teaching a multiply handicapped child good posture.

Forward Head and Neck

Normally, the head is balanced above the cervical vertebrae in such a way that minimal muscle effort is required to resist the pull of gravity. When the earlobe is no longer in alignment with the tip of the shoulder (acromion process), forward head and neck is diagnosed.

In its *mildest form,* the head tends to droop forward. The normal posterior concavity of the cervical spine increases so slowly that most persons are unaware that forward head and neck is developing. In the mild stage, the best ameliorative exercise is practice in discriminating between good and poor alignment.

In more *severe cases,* usually accompanied by round back, the cervical spine hyperextends to whatever degree is necessary to compensate for the forward droop of the head and the increasing dorsal convexity of the thoracic spine (Figure 12.7). This results in adaptive shortening and tightening of the cervical extensors, mainly the upper trapezius and splenius capitis and cervicis (Figure 12.8). This tightness is accentuated in the area of the seventh cervical vertebrae, where a layer of fat tends to accumulate. The combined prominence of the seventh cervical vertebra and excess adipose tissue is called a *dowager's hump.* The neck flexors tend to stretch, sag, and become functionally worthless. This hyperextension of the neck is sometimes called cervical lordosis.

In mild forms of cervical lordosis, both the neck flexors and extensors are weak. Gravity, rather than an

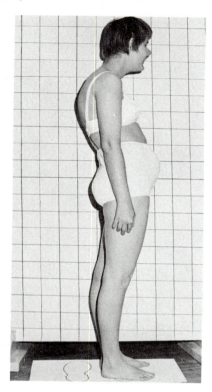

Figure 12.7 Severe degree of forward head and neck causes compensatory dorsal and lumbar curves.

imbalance of muscular strength, is primarily responsible for the forward position. In the severe form, the flexors and extensors remain weak, but the neck extensors have adaptively shortened and tightened, giving the false impression of strength. In mild forward head and neck, the extensors primarily need strengthening exercises. Flexibility is not a problem. As the condition becomes progressively severe, the muscles may feel stiff, tense, and sore. The emphasis in exercise shifts to flexibility, particularly stretching the cervical extensors.

Ameliorative Exercises

1. *Chin to shoulder touch.* Attempt to align head and neck with other segments of the body. Rotate slowly to the left until chin touches shoulder. Repeat to opposite side.

2. *Lateral flex with ear touch.* Attempt to align head and neck with other segments of the body. Laterally flex to the left until ear touches shoulder. Repeat to opposite side.

3. *Circling.* Circle the head as slowly as possible counterclockwise and then clockwise.

Figure 12.8 Cervical extensors adaptively shorten and tighten as forward head and neck becomes severe.

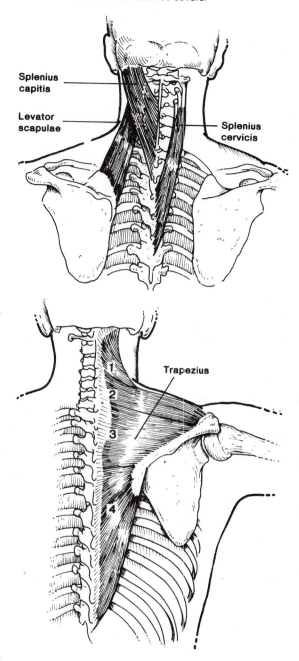

Figure 12.9 The intervertebral disk. (*A*) Flexion of the spine permitted by shift of fluid. (*B*) Compression of the disk occurs when noncompressible fluid of nucleus expands the elastic annulus. (*C*) Normal extended position with annulus fibers held taut; internal pressure is indicated by arrows. (*D*) Section of vertebrae. (*E*) Cross section of intervertebral disk.

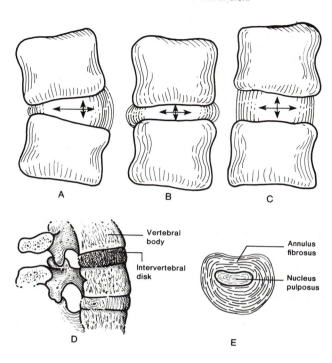

Over a long duration of time, the head tilt causes an adaptive shortening and tightening of the neck muscles on the side of the tilt. Tight muscles on the right side may be stretched by lateral flexion exercises to the left, and vice versa. A slow static stretch and hold is more effective than rhythmic exercises.

Kyphosis

Translated literally, *kyphos* means a sharp angulation. Increasing backward convexity in the thoracic region results in the condition commonly known as humpback, hunchback, Pott's curvature, or round upper back. Increased backward convexity in the lumbar region results in the condition known as flat back or lumbar kyphosis. For the purposes of this book, use of the term *kyphosis* is limited to the postural deviation of round upper back. The condition is rarely found among normal children in the public school setting.

True kyphosis is associated with disease of the intervertebral disks or of the epiphyseal area of the vertebrae. The intervertebral disk (Figure 12.9) is the fibrocartilage padding between vertebral bodies. The disk is comprised of two parts: the outer annulus fibrosus, known for its strength and elasticity, and the

Excessive Head Tilt

If the top of the head is tilted toward the right, the deviation of right tilt (RT) is recorded. The symbol LT is used for the opposite condition. A head habitually held in a tilted position is often symptomatic of vision or hearing impairments. Almost always the individual is unaware of the tilt and needs exercises for improving proprioception.

inner nucleus pulposus, which contains fluid that absorbs shock in locomotor movements and maintains the separation of the vertebral bodies. The nucleus pulposus has all the characteristics of a hydraulic system.

Any degenerative disease of the intervertebral disk is characterized by changes in pressure that cause pain. In old age, the fluid content of the nucleus pulposus decreases and the annulus fibrosus becomes progressively less elastic. These changes limit motion of the back. Any prolonged inactivity seems to contribute to degeneration of the intervertebral disks. Severely and profoundly retarded individuals whose mobility is limited often exhibit kyphosis at a young age.

Lordosis

Lordosis, also called sway or hollow back, is an exaggeration of the normal posterior concave curve in the lumbar region. It not only affects the five lumbar vertebrae, but also throws the pelvis out of correct alignment (Figure 12.10).

Figure 12.10 Pelvic tilts. (A) Normal pelvic tilt (neutral position) in good posture. The buttocks are tucked in. Anterior and posterior muscles are equal in strength. (B) Anterior pelvic tilt causes lordosis and protruding abdomen. The anterior iliac spines are rotated downward by tight hip flexors. The posterior sacrum is rotated upward by tight lumbar extensors.

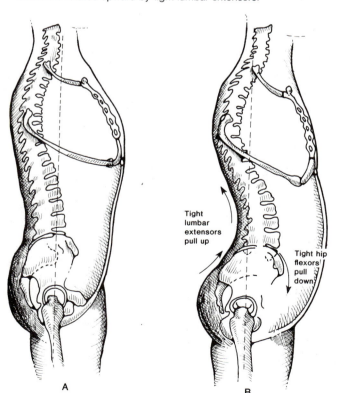

Tight lumbar extensors pull up

Tight hip flexors pull down

A

B

Lordosis has many possible causes: genetic predisposition; weak abdominal muscles, which allow the pelvis to tilt downward anteriorly; weak gluteal muscles and hamstrings, which cannot counteract this anterior tilt; overly tight lumbar extensors, which contribute to an anterior tilt; over-developed hip flexors, which cause anterior tilt; and, on rare occasions, occupations like professional dance.

In true lordosis the following characteristics will probably be present:

1. Anterior tilt of pelvis.
2. Tight lower back muscles, tight lumbodorsal fascia, tight hip flexors, tight iliofemoral (Y) ligaments, weak abdominals, weak hamstrings, and weak gluteals.
3. Knees may be hyperextended.
4. Compensatory kyphosis may develop to balance the increased concavity; if so, the pectorals and anterior intercostals may be tight also.
5. Upper body tends to shift backward as a compensatory measure. This shifts the weight of the body from the vertebral bodies onto the neural arches, bringing the spinous processes closer together than normal and sometimes pinching nerves.
6. Lower back pain.
7. Faulty functioning of internal organs, including those of digestion, elimination, and reproduction.
8. Predisposition toward dysmenorrhea and menstrual pain.
9. Increased incidence of back strain and back injuries.

Correction of lordosis, at least in the early stages, is largely a matter of increasing proprioceptive awareness so that the student can feel the difference between an anterior and a posterior tilt. Alternate anterior and posterior pelvic tilts should be practiced while lying supine, kneeling, sitting, standing, and performing various locomotor activities. Activities like the backbend, which emphasize hyperextension of the lumbar spine, are contraindicated.

Weak abdominals almost universally accompany lordosis. For this reason, strength exercises for the abdominals should be undertaken along with stretching exercises for the tight lumbar extensors. This dual purpose is accomplished to some extent without special effort in accordance with the principle of reciprocal innervation.

Ameliorative Exercises

1. Bicycling motion of legs while lying supine with back flattened to maintain contact with the floor.
2. Paint the rainbow. From a supine position, do a straight leg lift. Then continue the leg movement in an arc (like a rainbow) over the body until toes pass your forehead and reach the floor.
3. Angry cat exercise. From a hands and knees creeping position, alternate rounding the back like an angry cat with flattening the back.
4. Cross sitting forward bend. From a cross sitting position with hands clasped behind neck, bend forward so that head approaches floor without lifting buttocks. Maintain a slow stretch for several seconds.

In all exercises and activities, whether for posture correction or not, *avoid arching the back*. Particularly watch the tendency to hyperextend the lumbar spine when performing abdominal exercises and other movements from a supine position.

Flat Back

Flat back is a decrease or absence of the normal anteroposterior curves. It is the opposite condition from lordosis. The posterior concavity of the lumbar curve is decreased—i.e., the normal posterior concavity is gradually changing toward convexity.

Characteristics of flat back include

1. The pelvic inclination is less than normal, with the pelvis held in a more or less continuous posterior tilt.
2. Back appears too flat, with little or no protrusion of the buttocks.
3. Lower back muscles are weak.
4. Hip flexors, especially the psoas major, are weak and elongated.

Flat back is associated with the debutante slouch seen so often in fashion magazines in which young women pose languidly with hips thrust forward and upper back rounded. Such models are usually flat chested and so thin that the abdomen cannot protrude. It is sad that the fashion world sometimes chooses to present this image to the American public rather than one of good body alignment with normal busts, hips, and buttocks in gracefully curved balance. Flat back is also characteristic of the body build of young toddlers who have not been walking long enough to develop the lumbar curve.

Ameliorative Exercises

1. Alternate anterior and posterior pelvic tilts from a hook lying position to increase proprioceptive awareness.
2. Hyperextension of the lumbar spine to strengthen back muscles.
3. Prone lying trunk lifts and hold.
4. Prone lying leg lifts and hold.

Scoliosis

Scoliosis is a lateral curvature of the spine. (See Figures 12.11 to 12.14.) Although the condition begins with a single curve, it usually consists of a primary curve and a compensatory curve in the opposite direction.

Figure 12.11 Right total scoliosis with 80° curve in 16-year-old. Curve was first noticed at age 6.

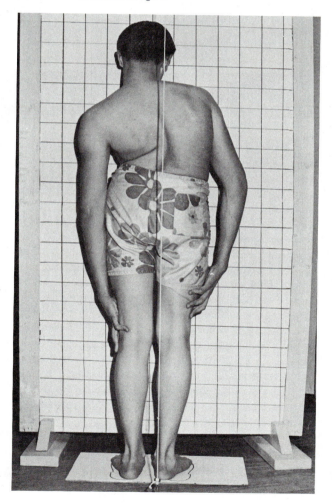

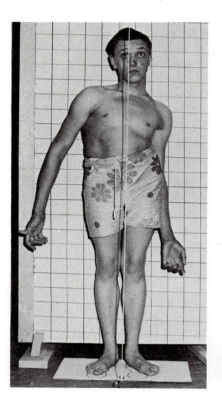

Figure 12.12 In right total scoliosis, the right shoulder is high and carried forward.

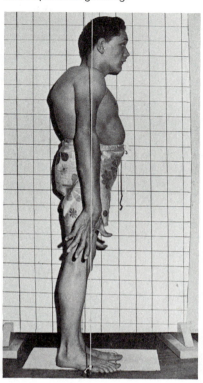

Figure 12.13 Right (convex) side of right total scoliosis shows back hump and bulging rib cage. Muscles on this side require strengthening.

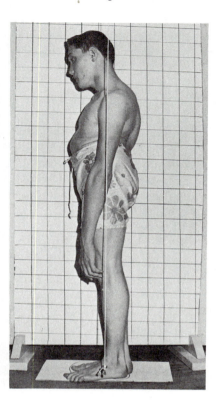

Figure 12.14 Left (concave) side of right total scoliosis reveals muscles which need stretching.

Usually appearing in early childhood, scoliosis may arrest itself without treatment. Often, however, it becomes progressively debilitating. *It is more serious than any of the other common posture deviations and should be referred to a physician. Often it is considered an orthopedic handicap.*

Lateral curves are described in their early stages as C curvatures and in their later stages as S curvatures. They are classified also as functional, transitional, and structural curves. The structural curve is a permanent one that can be corrected only by surgery; it is usually an S curve. The functional curve is one in which the bony tissues are still pliable and the involved muscles are still flexible. Physicians classify the severity in terms of the number of degrees that the major or primary curve deviates from normal. A mild scoliosis is 15 to 35°; moderate is 35 to 75°; and severe is 75 to 150°.

Keynote Positions

When certain *keynote positions* (see Figures 12.15 and 12.16) are assumed, the functional curve straightens out for the duration the position is held. A functional curve can be ameliorated by therapeutic exercise, and most physicians choose to combine prescribed exercises with bracing and/or surgery.

Keynote positions may be used as diagnostic devices or as corrective exercise. Among the most common keynote positions are the following:

1. Adam's position (Figures 12.15 and 12.16)—relaxed forward bending held for several seconds from a standing posture. The knees are straight so that the flexion occurs from the hips and spinal column.
2. Hanging with both arms from a horizontal bar.
3. Symmetrical arm raise from a standing position. The individual with a total left curve flexes the right arm at the shoulder joint to whatever height is necessary to straighten the spine. The other arm is maintained in a position of abduction. In some cases, raising both arms and/or raising one leg sideways may help the curve to disappear.

Figure 12.15 Sixteen-year-old with right total scoliosis in Adam's position. If the curve were not structural, it would disappear in this keynote position.

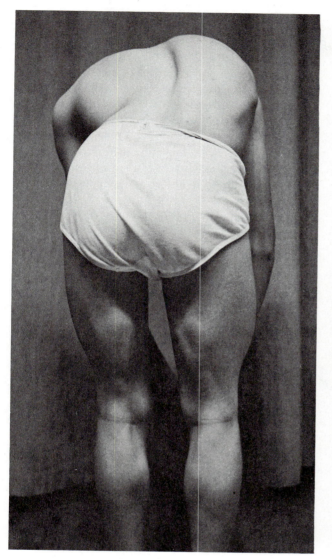

Figure 12.16 Permanent scoliotic hump prominent in Adam's position. Boy lacks lumbar flexibility to touch toes without bending knees.

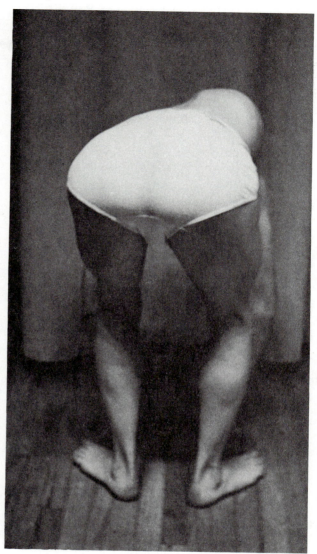

If the lateral curve is not temporarily obliterated by any of these positions, it can be assumed that scoliosis is in a transitional or structural stage. In such instances, the physical educator should insist that the child be examined by a physician. No corrective exercises should be undertaken without a permission slip from the parents and a medical clearance from the physician. Ideally, the physician will prescribe specific exercises to be practiced under the supervision of adapted physical education personnel.

Lateral curves are named in terms of the direction of their convexity. Among right-handed persons, the most common type of scoliosis is the *total left curve*.

Explanation of Rotation in Normal and Lateral Curvatures

Kinesiologically, rotation of the trunk is defined in the direction which the anterior vertebral bodies move. If the trunk rotates to the right, the vertebral bodies are turned to the right. Normally, any rotation of the trunk to the right is accompanied by a slight amount of lateral flexion to the right. In scoliosis, the rule with respect to the normal rotation of vertebral bodies reverses itself. Thus, scoliosis is a condition in which the vertebral bodies rotate toward the convexity of the curve and the spinous processes toward the concavity. This occurs partly because the bodies are less firmly bound together by strong ligaments than the spinous processes.

Characteristics of Left Curve

In the total left lumbar curve to the convex side, the following characteristics may be observed:

1. Spinous processes deviate from midline, rotating toward the concavity of the curve.
2. Left shoulder is higher than the other shoulder. Left shoulder may also be carried forward. In appraisal of the asymmetry of the shoulders, check the inferior angles of the scapula to see if one is carried lower than the other, abducted further away from the spinal column, or winged away from the rib cage. Also check the angle between the neck and the shoulder on both sides of the body.
3. The head may be tilted to one side.
4. There is a lateral displacement of the trunk toward the side of convexity since the thorax is no longer balanced directly over the pelvis.
5. Posteriorly, the ribs usually bulge out on the convex side of the curve; rib cage tends to lose its flexibility.
6. Right hip is usually higher than the other and the right iliac crest more prominent. Said in another way, when there is a lateral pelvic tilt, the convexity of the spine is toward the lower hip.
7. Contour of the waistline is affected with the notch on the concave side greater than that on the convex.
8. Right leg may be longer than left. In other words, a long leg will push the hip to a higher level and contribute to curvature on the opposite side.
9. Side bending tends to be freer to the right (concave side) than to the left.
10. Forward flexibility of the spine may be limited as a natural protective mechanism of the body against further deformity.
11. Muscles on the concave side become increasingly tight while those on the convex side are stretched and weakened.

Ameliorative Exercises

Principles for planning ameliorative exercises for a child with functional scoliosis include

1. Work on improvement of body alignment in front of a mirror before undertaking specific exercises for scoliosis.
2. Use keynote positions (with exception of Adam's position) as corrective exercises. When a position is identified in which the curve is temporarily obliterated, spend as many seconds as comfortable in it; rest and repeat.
3. Emphasize swimming and other activities that encourage development of the trunk without placing the strain of weight-bearing on the spine.
4. Avoid forward flexibility of spine unless prescribed by a physician.
5. Use breathing and chest expansion exercises to maintain flexibility of chest and prevent further distortion of thorax.
6. If you tend to be conservative and wish to avoid controversial practices, use only symmetrical exercises that develop left and right sides equally. Exercises for strengthening the back extensors are recommended.
7. If you are willing to use activities that authorities are about equally divided on, try such *asymmetrical* exercises as
   a. Hang facing outward from stall bars and swing legs in.
   b. Hang from stall bars with right hand only (for left total curve). Right side is to the stall bars, and left hand is used whenever needed for balance.
   c. Kneel on right knee, with leg extended to side, right arm curved above head. Laterally flex trunk several times to the left. The purpose of most asymmetrical exercises is to stretch muscles on the concave side and/or to strengthen muscles on the convex side. Generally, exercises prescribed by physicians are asymmetrical in nature.
8. Encourage the student with scoliosis to participate in regular physical education classes and athletic competition.

Scoliosis is more prevalent in girls and among ectomorphic body types, but it is not confined to either. About 75% of the known cases are idiopathic; about 12.5% are congenital anomalies; and the other 12.5% result from paralysis or paresis of muscles on one side of the spinal column. Many persons with poliomyelitis suffer from scoliosis.

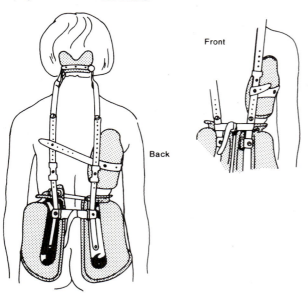

Figure 12.17 Milwaukee brace fitted to a right thoracic, left lumbar scoliotic curve. Developed in 1945 by Blount and Schmidt of Milwaukee, this brace is successful in preventing further curvatures in about 70 percent of the cases. It is generally worn 23 hours a day over a long undershirt, and children can run and play in it with few restrictions.

Front

Back

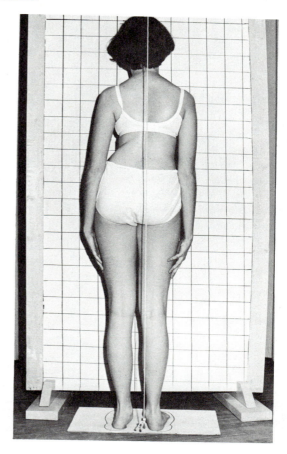

Figure 12.18 Right dorsal scoliosis with 65° curve. This 18-year-old has worn a Milwaukee brace and had Harrington instrumentation and spinal fusion. Further correction is not feasible.

Among the kinds of treatments used are the Milwaukee brace (see Figure 12.17), Harrington instrumentation and spinal fusion, and various kinds of body casts.

Students with severe scoliosis or kyphosis in the Milwaukee brace (see Figure 12.18) should have a well-rounded physical activity program rather than exercise alone. Cailliet stated in this regard:

Just as exercises alone are of limited value in either correcting or controlling scoliosis, applying a Milwaukee brace without exercises is of limited value. . . . The brace permits almost unlimited activities, excluding only contact sports for the safety of other children and very active sports such as tumbling on a trampoline, horseback riding, and strenuous gymnastics. . . . (Cailliet, 1975, pp. 72, 75)

Uneven Shoulder Height

When the two shoulders are of unequal height, the higher one is recorded as LH (left high) or RH (right high). To ascertain the unevenness of shoulders, it is best to use a horizontal line on the wall behind the student. Other techniques that may be used include

1. If the head is not tilted, the distance between the shoulders and ear lobes on the right and left side may be sighted and compared.
2. The level of the inferior angles of the scapulae may be compared. The inferior angles are at about the level of the seventh thoracic spinous process.

3. The level of the two clavicles may be compared.

Whenever a high shoulder is recorded, a lateral spinal curve convex on the same side should be suspected (see Figure 12.19). If scoliosis is not found, shoulder asymmetries are not a problem. *In normal development the dominant side of the body has a slightly depressed shoulder and slightly higher hip.* This should not be confused with scoliosis.

Uneven Hip Height

When two hips are of unequal height, the higher one is recorded as LH or RH. Traditionally, the anterior superior iliac spines serve as the anatomical landmarks for judging asymmetry. A string may be stretched between these two points.

Differences in hip height may be caused by scoliosis, uneven leg length, or the habit of standing on one leg for long periods of time. To determine leg lengths,

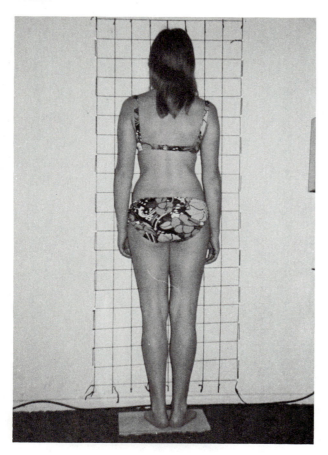

Figure 12.19 Left shoulder high and some evidence of a beginning left scoliotic curve. Note unevenness of waistline notches.

the student lies in a supine position. The length of each leg is recorded as the distance from the anterior superior iliac spine to the medial ankle bone.

Round Shoulders

Round shoulders is a forward deviation of the shoulder girdle in which the scapulae are abducted with a slight lateral tilt. This brings the acromion processes (shoulder tips) in front of the normal gravitational line. Round shoulders should not be confused with round back (kyphosis). They are distinctly different problems.

Synonyms for round shoulders are abducted scapulae, forward deviation of the shoulder girdle, protraction of scapulae, and separation of scapulae. Kinesiologically, the condition results when the strength

of the abductors (pectoralis minor and serratus anterior) becomes greater than that of the adductors (rhomboids and trapezius III). To determine the extent of the forward deviation, the distance between the vertebral borders of the scapulae is measured. In the adult, the normal spread is 4 to 5 inches, depending upon the breadth of the shoulders.

The incidence of round shoulders is high among persons who work at desk jobs and, hence, spend much of their time with the shoulders abducted. Athletes often exhibit round shoulders because of overdevelopment of the anterior arm, shoulder, and chest muscles resulting from sports and aquatics activities, which stress forward movements of the arms. This tendency may be counteracted by engaging in an exercise program designed specifically to keep the posterior muscles equal in strength to their antagonists. Perhaps the easiest way to do this is to swim a few laps of the back crawl each day. Certainly, the well-rounded athlete who enjoys many different activities is less likely to develop round shoulders than is one who specializes almost exclusively in tennis, basketball, or volleyball.

The following segmental analysis demonstrates the compensatory changes in alignment of body parts that result from round shoulders.

Head and neck out of alignment and displaced forward.

Thoracic spine. Increasing convexity that tends to negate the effectiveness of the upward pull of the sternocleidomastoid and scaleni muscles, which normally maintain the upper ribs and sternum in a high position. The weak back muscles are elongated by the increased convexity of the spine.

Chest. Lowered position. Whereas persons with good postures lead with the chest, this individual leads with the shoulders. The failure of the anterior muscles to exert their usual effect on the sternum and ribs results in a lowered position of the diaphragm which, in turn, affects breathing.

Shoulder joint. Increased inward rotation of the humeral head.

Arms. Arms are carried more forward than usual with palms facing toward the rear (Figure 12.20), whereas normally only the little finger of the hand can be seen from the rear. The elbows may be held out close to the body.

Lumbar spine. Lordosis may develop to compensate for increased convexity of thoracic spine.

Knees. Knees may hyperextend to compensate for the change in the lumbar curve.

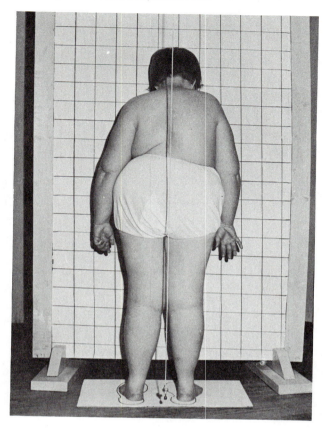

Figure 12.20 Round shoulders can be detected from a rear view by the palms of the hands. This child also has mild scoliosis, knock knees, and pronated feet.

With the alignment of almost all the body segments altered, the entire body slumps, creating the impression of general fatigue. This posture is assumed temporarily in times of extreme mental depression or bereavement, revealing the unity of mind and body. Mentally ill persons who have been institutionalized several years often assume the round-shouldered postures of defeat.

Ameliorative Exercises

Exercises for round shoulders should simultaneously stretch the tightened anterior muscles and strengthen trapezius III and the rhomboids. So many exercises for round shoulders are recommended in textbooks that it is difficult to evaluate their respective effectiveness in accomplishing these goals. The four that appear to be most effective, in rank order from best to good, are

1. Pull resistance. Sit on chair facing the wall with pulleys, with the arms extended sideward at shoulder height and the hands grasping the handles. Slowly move the arms backward, keeping them at shoulder height.

2. Prone lateral raise of weights. Assume a prone position on a bench. The hands grasp dumbbells on the floor to each side of the body. The weights are lifted toward the ceiling as far as possible, keeping the arms straight. Hold. (Chin should remain on the bench.)

3. Push against wall. Sit cross-legged with the head and back flat against the wall. The arms are bent at shoulder height with the palms facing the chest, fingertips touching, and elbows against the wall. Keeping the head and spine against the wall, press the elbows back with as much force as possible.

4. Head resistance. Lie on back, arms out to side, palms down, knees flexed, and feet spread. Raise hips and arch back so that shoulders are off mat, supporting weight on feet, hands, and back of head in a modified wrestler's bridge.

Winged Scapulae

Also called projected scapulae, winged scapulae refers to a prominence of the inferior angles of the scapulae. The scapulae are pulled away from the rib cage and the vertebral borders are lifted. Since the serratus anterior is the muscle that normally holds the inferior angle of the scapula close to the rib cage, it is believed to be weak when winging occurs.

Winged scapulae are normal in preschool and elementary school children (Figures 12.21 and 12.22) since the serratus is slower in developing than its antagonists. Since the serratus anterior is a prime mover for upward rotation and abduction, it is strengthened by hanging, climbing, and other activities executed above the head. Many girls in our society do not outgrow winged scapulae as do boys. This postural deviation is often a part of the debutante slouch described earlier. Winged scapulae often accompany round shoulders. They are associated also with congenital anomalies and postural conditions in which the ribs protrude.

Figure 12.21 Winged scapulae is normal in preschool child. Atrophied right leg has not yet affected shoulder height.

Figure 12.22 Winged scapulae in predominantly ectomorphic preadolescent.

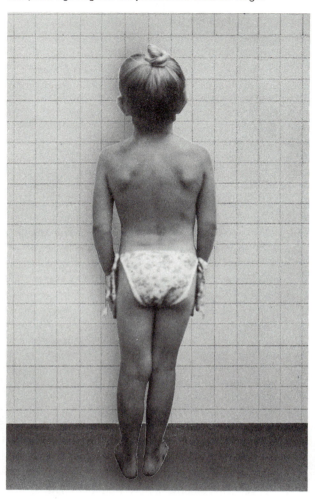

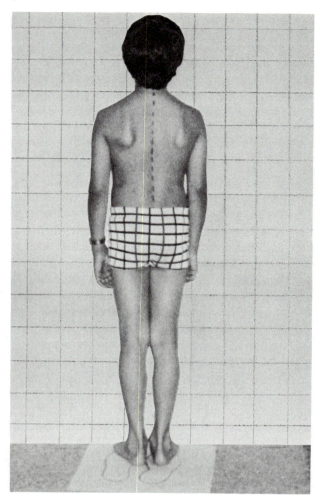

Deviations of the Chest

Asthma, other chronic upper respiratory disorders, and rickets may cause changes in the rib cage with resulting limitations in chest flexibility and improper breathing practices. These changes are designated as functional, transitional, and structural depending upon their degree of severity. Congenital anomalies, of course, do account for some chest deviations.

Hollow Chest

The most common of the chest deviations, this term denotes the relaxation and depression of the anterior thorax that normally accompanies round shoulders and/or kyphosis. Specific characteristics of hollow chest are concave or flattened appearance of anterior thoracic wall, depressed (lowered) ribs, low sternum, tight intercostal and pectoral muscles, limited chest flexibility, and habitually lowered diaphragm that limits its movement in breathing.

Hollow chest can be traced to the failure of the neck and pectoral muscles to exert their usual lifting effect on the ribs and sternum. The neck muscles are elongated and weak. The pectoral muscles are excessively tight and strong.

Barrel Chest

The barrel chest is characteristic of persons with severe chronic asthma who become hyperventilated because of their inability to exhale properly. Over a period of years, the excess air retained in the lungs tends to expand the anteroposterior dimensions of the thorax so that it takes on a rounded appearance similar to that of full inspiration.

Specific characteristics of barrel chest are

1. Thoracic spine extends.
2. Sternum is pushed forward and upward.

3. Upper ribs (second through the seventh) are elevated and everted. Eversion of the ribs is defined as the inner surfaces rotating to face downward. This occurs when the lower border of the rib turns forward.

4. Costal cartilages tend to straighten out when the ribs elevate.

5. Lower ribs (8th through the 10th) move laterally, thus opening the chest and widening the subcostal angle.

6. Floating ribs are depressed and spread.

7. Diaphragm is habitually depressed, which in turn displaces the internal organs in the direction of the abdominal wall.

8. Abdomen protrudes in response to organs pressed against the weakened abdominal wall.

Barrel chest is normal for infants and preschool children. The lateral widening of the thorax from side to side so that it no longer resembles a barrel occurs normally as a result of the vigorous play activities of young children. Severely handicapped persons who cannot engage in physical activities often have chests that remain infantile and underdeveloped.

Funnel Chest

The opposite of barrel chest, this condition is an abnormal increase in the lateral diameter of the chest with a marked depression of the sternum and anterior thorax. The sternum and adjacent costal cartilages appear to have been sucked inward.

Funnel chest, also called *pectus excavatum,* is usually a congenital anomaly. It appears in many severely retarded persons. It may be caused also by rickets or severe nasal obstruction—i.e., enlarged adenoids.

Pigeon Chest

Also called chicken breast, or *pectus carinatum,* this condition takes its name from the abnormal prominence of the sternum. The anteroposterior diameter of the thorax is increased as a result of the forward displacement of the sternum. The deviation is rare, caused by rickets during the early growth period. It may also be congenital.

Abdominal Weakness

Abdominal weakness is classified as mild, moderate, or severe or first, second, and third degree. Abdominal protrusion is normal in the young child (Figure 12.23) and usually accompanied by lordosis. Participation in the vigorous activities of the elementary school years should result in a flat, taut abdomen in adolescence and

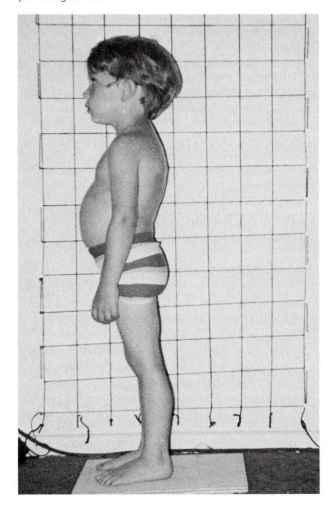

Figure 12.23 Good posture for a normal preschooler includes a protruding abdomen

early adulthood. The *lower part of the abdomen* contracts reflexly whenever the body is in complete extension, as in most locomotor activities. The emphasis upon extension in modern dance and ballet contributes particularly to abdominal strength, as does swimming the front crawl and other strokes executed from an extended position. The *upper part of the abdomen* works in conjunction with the diaphragm, gaining strength each time breathlessness in endurance-type activities forces the diaphragm to contract vigorously in inhalation. Abdominal exercises in a physical education class are a poor substitute for natural play activities. They are not recommended so long as the child derives pleasure from running, jumping, climbing, hanging, and skipping.

When a lifestyle changes from active to sedentary, regardless of the reason, abdominal exercises should become part of the daily routine. In middle and old age, the upper abdominal wall may become slightly rounded but the musculature below the umbilicus should remain flat and taut.

Because the abdominal wall of the child normally protrudes, it is important to evaluate strength upon the basis of performance tests rather than upon appearance alone.

Visceroptosis is the term used when an abdominal protrusion is severe and the viscera (internal organs) drop down into a new position. The stomach, liver, spleen, kidneys, and intestines may all be displaced, resulting in adverse effects upon their various functions. This condition occurs mainly in adults.

Principles in Teaching Exercises

1. Teach abdominal exercises that will simultaneously stretch the tight lumbar extensors and hip flexors.
2. Use the supine hook rather than straight leg lying position to eliminate the action of the strong hip flexors.
3. Avoid hyperextension of the spine.
4. Avoid prone-lying exercises like the swan and the rocking chair.
5. Eliminate the possibility of breath holding during exercise by requesting the students to count, sing, whistle, or hum. Incorrect breathing tends to build up intra-abdominal pressure, which may result in a hernia.
6. Include lots of twisting movements of the trunk.
7. Gradually build tolerance for endurance-type exercises that cause vigorous breathing, which in turn strengthen the upper abdominal wall.
8. Use locomotor activities that emphasize extension of the spine. Skipping and swimming are especially good.
9. Take advantage of the extensor reflex elicited in the creeping position.
10. Use the upside-down positions in yoga for training the extensor muscles. The neck stand is preferred to the head stand.

Exercises in the Creeping Position

1. Crosslateral creeping. As the right arm moves forward, the left knee should move forward.
2. Crosslateral creeping combined with blowing a ping pong ball across the floor.
3. Crosslateral creeping combined with pushing an object like a bottle cap or toy automobile with the nose.
4. Angry cat. Alternate (a) humping the back and letting the head hang down with (b) extending the spine with the head held high.
5. In static creeping position, move the hips from side to side.

Ideally, creeping exercises are performed in front of a mirror so the student can improve proprioceptive awareness and the instructor can ascertain that the spine is not hyperextended. *It is important also to use knee pads when creeping exercises are undertaken.*

Exercises in the Supine Hook Position

1. Abdominal pumping (Mosher exercise). Arms in reverse T. The *reverse T arm position* is used to prevent lumbar hyperextension. Arms are abducted and elbows bent at a right angle. Hands reach upward above the head. Retract abdominal wall strongly, pulling the anterior pelvis upward and depressing the thorax.
2. Curl down or reverse trunk curl. Knees and hips are flexed and knees are drawn toward chest, so curl commences at the lower spinal levels. Obliques are more active in reverse curls than in regular trunk curls. First ⅓ of curl is most valuable.
3. Sit-up with trunk twist for maximal activity of oblique abdominals. Feet should not be held down because holding them activates the unwanted hip flexors.
4. Double leg raise and hold. Then lower legs slowly to starting position. Watch for arching of back just before the feet touch the floor. May also be done with *soles of feet together and knees apart:* this lessens pull of psoas even more.
5. Paint-the-rainbow-type activity. Head touching wall, bring legs up to touch wall with knees.
6. Double knee raise and patticake.
7. Alternate ballet legs. From bent knee position, raise knees to chest and then lift legs alternately as done in the synchronized swimming stunt by the same name. To make this more difficult, legs can be adducted and abducted in this position.
8. Double knee circling. Keep heels close to thighs. Arms in reverse T. Flex the hips until the thighs are vertical. Keeping the shoulders flat, make circles with the knees.

   More difficult variation: Flex knees toward the chest, straighten legs to vertical, and make circles with both feet. Keep the shoulders flat and the heels together.
9. Alternate leg circling. Retract the abdominal wall and flex both knees to chest. Extend one leg and then the other in reciprocal leg circling or bicycle motion. Return the flexed legs to the chest and then lower to the floor.

   Vary the difficulty by changing the size of the circles, the number completed before resting, and the speed of the performance. Most difficult is making small circles at slow speed just above the floor. Right foot makes clockwise circles

Figure 12.24 Mild to moderate bowlegs is normal in infancy and corrects itself, usually by 2 years of age. Children then tend to develop knock knees, which is most obvious at ages 3–4 years. This condition also corrects itself.

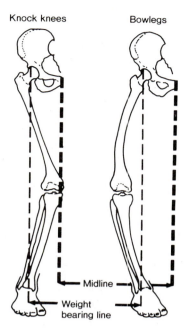

Knock knees   Bowlegs

Midline

Weight bearing line

Figure 12.25 Anatomy of the hip joint. The acetabulum is a cup-shaped hollow socket that is formed medially by the pubis, above by the ilium, and laterally and behind by the ischium. Around the circumference of the hip socket is a fibrocartilaginous ring that serves to deepen the socket and assure stability of the joint. Three ligaments reinforce the joint. Of these, the most often injured is the iliofemoral (Y) ligaments. These are the ligaments that are stretched when students do splits or turn the legs outward in ballet positions.

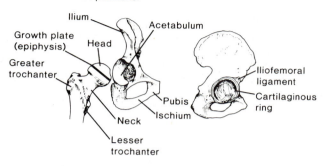

Ilium
Acetabulum
Growth plate (epiphysis)   Head
Greater trochanter
Iliofemoral ligament
Pubis
Cartilaginous ring
Ischium
Neck
Lesser trochanter

The exercises cited earlier are helpful in relieving *menstrual pain*. They may also lessen the discomfort of constipation and/or the accumulation of gas (flatus) in the digestive tract.

Alignment of Lower Extremities

A quick screening device to judge the overall alignment of the legs is the game known as Four Coins. The challenge is, "Can you put a coin between your thighs, your knees, your calves, and your ankles and simultaneously hold all the coins in place?" If the body parts are well proportioned and correctly aligned, this task should present no problem. When the student stands with feet together and parallel, the medial aspects of the knees and ankles should be touching their opposites. Figure 12.24 depicts developmental changes in hips and leg alignment. It is normal for infants and toddlers to have bowlegs and for preschool children to have knock-knees. These conditions normally correct themselves.

Individual differences in the alignment of the legs and in locomotor patterns are largely dependent upon the hip joint. Students who toe inward or outward in their normal walking gait, for instance, usually have nothing wrong with their feet. The origin of the problem usually can be traced to an imbalance of strength in the muscles that rotate the femur at the hip joint.

Hip Joint Problems

The hip joint is formed by the articulation between the head of the femur and the acetabulum of the pelvis. Figure 12.25 depicts its anatomy. How the head fits into

while left foot makes counterclockwise circles. Both legs make clockwise circles. Both legs make counterclockwise circles. Describe figure eight with one foot or both together.

10. Drumming. Feet are used like drum sticks, alternately beating the floor.

11. Alternate knee and elbow touch in opposition. Hands behind neck. Each time try to reach farther with the elbow and less far with the opposite knee.

12. Supine bent knee lower trunk twist. Arms in reverse T. Raise both knees until the thighs are vertical. Keep shoulders flat and lower knees toward the mat on one side, return to a vertical position. Repeat to other side and return. Legs should not be allowed to fall; must be controlled throughout the movement.

Regardless of type, abdominal exercises should accomplish the following purposes:

1. Relieve congestion in the abdominal or pelvic cavities; this includes expelling gas and improving local circulation.

2. Retrain the upper abdominal wall to increase its efficiency in respiration.

3. Retrain the lower abdominal wall to improve its efficiency with respect to holding the viscera in place.

Figure 12.26 Angulation of the neck of the femur explains coxa valga and vara.

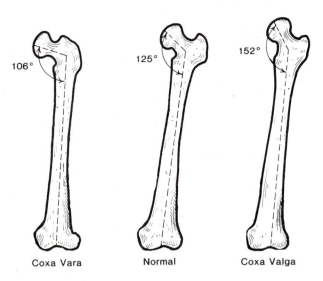

Coxa Vara   Normal   Coxa Valga

Figure 12.27 Bowlegs in early childhood is almost always accompanied by coxa vara. The horizontalization of the femoral neck limits the action of the gluteus medius, the abductor responsible for maintaining hip joint stability during locomotion. The result is a waddling gait in which the shoulders incline toward the weight-bearing foot. Exercise cannot correct this gait because it is caused by a structural abnormality.

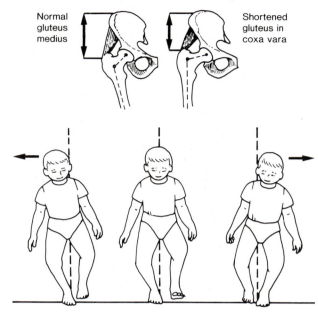

Normal gluteus medius   Shortened gluteus in coxa vara

the acetabulum determines function and stability. Important to the understanding of several problems is the angulation of the neck of the femur, depicted in Figure 12.26. Hip joint problems affect leg alignment and gait. Several of these are discussed in the chapter on orthopedic impairments.

Abnormal positioning of the femoral head within the acetabulum is called *coxa vara* (decreased angulation) or *coxa valga* (increased angulation). Both cause waddling gaits. Neither condition can be corrected by exercise. Casting, bracing, and surgery are used.

Coxa Vara

The decreased angulation in coxa vara may result in the affected leg becoming shorter. Outward rotation and abduction are limited. The cause is either congenital or acquired. When congenital, coxa vara is usually accompanied by bowlegs (Figure 12.27). When acquired, the condition usually first appears in adolescence. It may be called either *slipped femoral epiphysis* or adolescent coxa vara and is more common in males than females. The epiphysis (growth center) of the femoral head slips down and backward, changing the angulation of the femoral neck.

Coxa Valga

In contrast, coxa valga malpositions in normal children are associated with upward, anterior dislocations of the hip. The condition is almost always congenital and is often called *congenital dislocation of the hip* (CDH) rather than coxa valga. This is the fourth most common

orthopedic birth defect. The affected leg is longer, and both inward and outward rotation are limited. Many severely disabled nonambulatory persons develop coxa valga between ages 2 and 10; in this condition, the head of the femur is usually displaced upward (like CDH) and posteriorly (unlike CDH).

Bowlegs (Genu Varum)

Although the Latin term *genu*, meaning "knee," emphasizes the capacity for knees and ankles to touch simultaneously, bowing can occur in the shaft of the femur as well as the tibia. *Varum* refers to inward bowing. One or both legs may be affected.

The legs of infants are often bowed. The natural pull of the peroneal muscles on the shaft of the tibia during the first months of walking tends to straighten out the bow. In this instance, an imbalance in strength between two muscle groups works to the toddler's advantage. By the age of 2 years or so, the tibials have gained sufficient strength to offset the pull of the peroneals, and any bowing that remains may become structural.

Persistent or late-appearing bowlegs may be caused by such pathological conditions as renal or vitamin D resistant rickets and growth disorders that affect the epiphyseal plates. Illustrative of the latter is

Blount's disease, or *tibia vara,* an outward bowing of the tibia caused by retardation of growth of the medial epiphyseal plate at the top of the tibia. Blount's disease usually occurs between 1 and 3 years of age and is corrected by surgery. Pathological conditions that are often complicated by bowed legs include *arthrogryposis* and *osteogenesis imperfecta* (see index for page numbers giving further information).

In adulthood, bowing is structural and exercises are not beneficial. Many individuals with mild to moderate conditions have strong muscles and are not impaired noticeably by this deviation. Bowlegs tend to shift the weight toward the lateral border of the foot and to maintain the foot in a supinated position (see Figure 12.24).

Functional bowlegs is sometimes confused with the structural condition. In functional bowlegs, the curve appears as a result of hyperextending the knees and inwardly rotating the femurs. If the patellae face inward, it is likely that the apparent bowlegs are a functional adaptation that can be eliminated by strengthening the outward rotators of the hips and relaxing the knees so that correct leg and thigh alignment is possible.

Toeing Inward

Toeing inward (pigeon toes) is usually caused by an imbalance in the strength of the muscles that serve as prime movers for hip rotation. When the inward rotators, *gluteus minimus* and *gluteus medius,* are stronger than the outward rotators, the student toes inward (see Figure 12.27).

Ameliorative Exercises

1. Develop proprioceptive awareness of the different foot positions through movement exploration on all kinds of surfaces.
2. Stretch the tight inward rotators by doing activities that emphasize outward rotation. Ballet techniques are especially effective.
3. Strengthen the weak outward rotators by doing activities that emphasize outward rotation.
4. Avoid inward rotation movements.

Toeing Outward

Toeing outward occurs when the posterior group of muscles on the sacrum called "the six outward rotators" (see Figure 12.28) is stronger than the prime movers for inward rotation. Since toeing outward is a way of widening the stance and improving the balance, it may be observed in toddlers just learning to walk, the aged, blind persons, and others who are unsure of their footing.

Ameliorative Exercises

1. Develop proprioceptive awareness of the different foot positions through movement exploration on all kinds of surfaces.
2. Stretch the tight outward rotators by doing activities that emphasize inward rotation.
3. Strengthen the weak inward rotators by doing activities that stress inward rotation.
4. Avoid outward rotation movements.

Knock-Knees (Genu Valga)

The Latin word *valgum* can mean either knock-knees or bowlegs, but is used in most adapted physical education references as knock-knees, referring specifically to the bending outward of the lower legs so that the knees touch, but the ankles do not.

Knock-knees occurs almost universally in obese persons. In the standing position, the gravitational line passes lateral to the center of the knee rather than directly through the patella as is normal. This deviation in the weight-bearing line predisposes the knee joint to injury. Knock-knees is usually accompanied by weakness in the longitudinal arch and pronation of the feet (see Figure 12.28).

No treatment or exercises are recommended for knock-knees in children younger than age 7 because developmentally this is a normal condition. In severe knock-knees, physicians often prescribe ⅛-inch heel-raise on medial border and/or use of a night splint. In severe cases that persist, surgery (osteotomy) is used.

The gait is altered by *increased lateral sway* to position the body weight directly over the weight-bearing foot and by *inward rotation at the hip* to prevent the knees from striking each other while passing.

Ameliorative Exercises

1. Stretch the muscles on the lateral aspect of leg (peroneal group) by doing supination exercises (inversion and adduction of foot).
2. Strengthen the tibials by doing supination exercises; this also helps to strengthen longitudinal arch.
3. Strengthen outward rotators of the hip joint by doing activities that stress outward rotation.

Figure 12.28 Knock knees elongates tendons on medial side and tightens tendons on lateral side. Lateral muscles of lower leg tighten, pulling outer border of foot upward and forcing weight onto inner border.

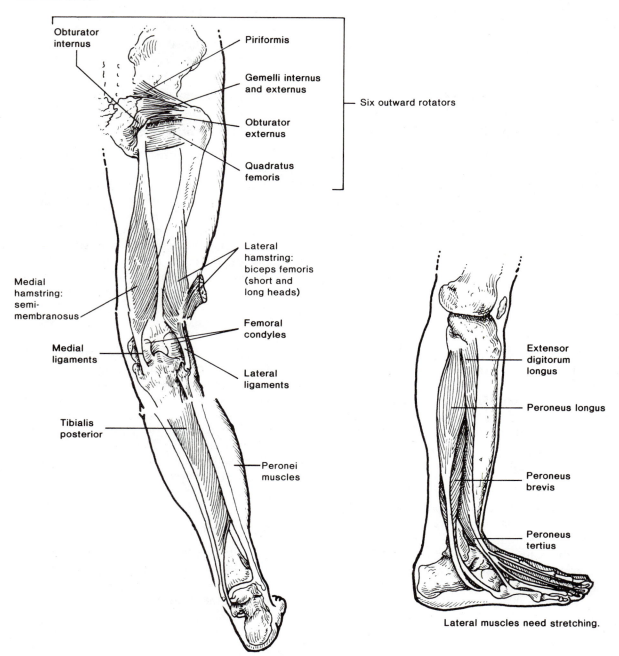

Posterior muscles need strengthening.

Lateral muscles need stretching.

Hyperextended Knees

Also called back knees or *genu recurvatum,* hyperextended knees is a deviation in which the knees are pulled backward beyond their normal position. This posture problem can be identified best from a side view (see Figure 12.29).

Hyperextension of the knees tends to tilt the pelvis forward and contribute to lordosis, thereby throwing all of the body segments out of alignment. It occurs more often in children than in adults and in ectomorphs than in other body types. In young children, hyperextended knees may be symptomatic of anxiety and tension. It is observed frequently when a new motor skill is being attempted. When a child poses for posture pictures, he or she may thrust the knees backward when "freezing" for the camera. In most instances, hyperextended knees is not a habitual posture, but one that appears now and then and can be best prevented by verbal reminders to maintain good body alignment.

This condition is usually caused by knee extensor weakness or muscle imbalance. When muscles are too weak to hold the knee in correct alignment, it is stabilized by the posterior ligamentous capsule, which, not being designed for this purpose, gradually yields. Back knees can also be caused by tight calf muscles, Achilles tendon contractures, and bony abnormalities that fix the foot in a plantar flexion (equinus) position and consequently affect stance and gait. In cerebral palsy, back knees often result from surgical overcorrection of knee flexion deformities. In spinal cord injuries and polio, the knees are sometimes surgically placed in recurvatum to permit independent walking as an alternative to wheelchair locomotion.

Severe cases of back knees are usually treated by prescription of a knee-ankle orthosis that holds the foot in slight dorsiflexion and the knee in flexion. Specific exercises should not be done in physical education unless medically prescribed. In mild/moderate back knees the emphasis should be on developing kinesthetic awareness of correct knee alignment and avoiding exercises and activities that put stress on the weak knee joint. Contraindicated activities include touching the toes from a standing position, deep knee squats, and duck and bear walks.

Tibial Torsion

The tibia is twisted and the weight-bearing line is shifted to the medial aspect of the foot. The deviation is often more marked in one leg than in the other, with the affected foot toeing inward and pronating. Tibial

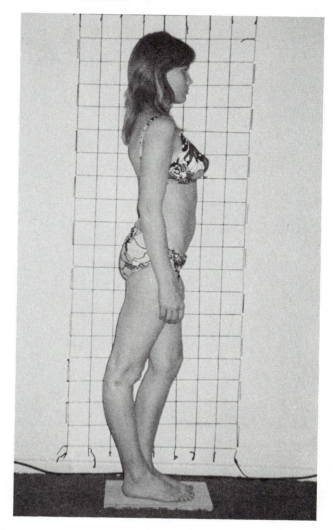

Figure 12.29 Right knee in hyperextension after knee surgery following an automobile accident. Malalignment of legs contributes to lordosis.

torsion often accompanies knock-knees, flat feet, and pronated feet. Congenital anomalies of the foot may be accompanied by twisting of the lower end of the tibia. Congenital tibial torsion is usually corrected in infancy by plaster casts, braces, splints, and/or surgery.

Deviations of the Feet

Poor alignment in any part of the body affects the weight-bearing function of the feet. Obesity increases the stress on the joints. Abnormal formation of bones

Figure 12.30 Medial torsion of left tibia in young adolescent with surgically corrected clubfoot.

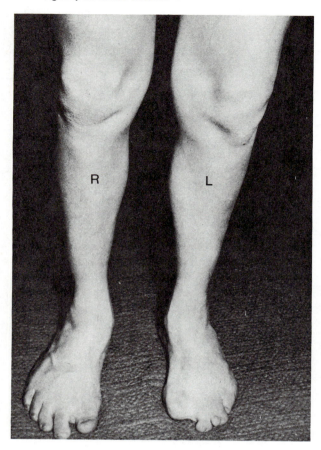

Figure 12.31 Normal bone structures affect alignment of the leg and foot and determine capacity for correct foot placement during gait. Joints are named for the two bones that touch. Thus, the ankle joint is the talotibial joint. The talocalcaneal and talonavicular joints are the sites of varus (inward) and valgus (outward) foot deformities.

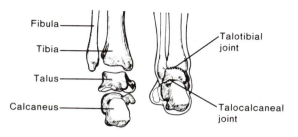

Figure 12.32 Club foot shoes with lateral side of shoes and heels raised to correct varus deformity.

as in clubfoot (see foot in Figure 12.30) also affects alignment, as does weak or paralyzed leg and foot muscles resulting from spinal cord injury or neuromuscular conditions like cerebral palsy. Figure 12.31 depicts bones of the foot that often get out of alignment.

Club Foot

Talipes equinovarus, or congenital club foot, is the most common of all orthopedic defects, with an incidence of one out of approximately 700 births. *Talipes* comes from two Latin words, *talus,* meaning ankle or heel, and *pes,* meaning foot. *Equinovarus* (stemming from *equus,* meaning horse, and *varus,* meaning bent in) is an adjective specifying a position in which the entire foot is inverted, the heel is drawn up, and the forefoot is adducted. This forces the child to walk on the outer border of the foot. Although bracing, casting, and surgery may correct club foot, the child reverts to supinated walking when especially tired or upon first awakening.

Children who have undergone casting and splinting for club foot are generally required to wear *corrective shoes.* Extremely expensive, these shoes are often unattractive high-top leather shoes with many laces (Figure 12.32). Many children, sensitive about this prescription, refuse to wear their corrective shoes as they grow older. Or they may ask to wear tennis shoes, at least in physical education, in order to be like their friends. Permission should be tactfully denied unless written instructions from the physician indicate that the child need not wear the corrective shoes during physical education.

Talipes equinovarus varies in degrees of severity. Changes in the tendons and ligaments result mostly from contractures. The Achilles and tibial tendons are always shortened, causing a tendency to walk on the toes or forefoot. Bony changes occur chiefly in the talus, calcaneus, navicular, and cuboid. Tibial torsion is usually present.

Several other types of talipes are recognized; Figure 12.33 illustrates these.

Talipes cavus—hollow foot or arch so high as to be disabling.

Talipes calcaneus—contracture of foot in dorsiflexed position.

Figure 12.33 Abnormalities of foot alignment. Varus positions are frequently seen in hemiplegic spastic cerebral palsy and in uncorrected congenital bone and joint defects. Valgus positions are seen in association with flat and/or pronated feet. The cavus position is rare.

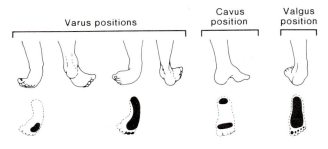

Varus positions | Cavus position | Valgus position

Figure 12.34 The Denis-Browne splint used to correct club foot and other problems.

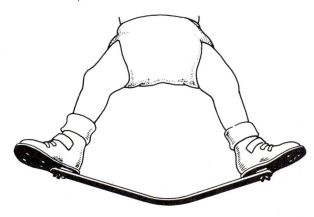

Talipes equinus—contracture of foot in plantar-flexed position.

Talipes varus—contracture of foot with toes and sole of foot turned inward.

Talipes valgus—contracture of foot with toes and sole of foot turned outward.

Just as *talipes equinovarus,* the most common form, is a combination of two types, so any two types can coexist as calcaneovarus, calcaneovalgus, or equinovalgus.

Metatarsus varus is a frequent congenital defect similar to club foot except that only the forefoot or metatarsal area is affected. The treatment for talipes and *metatarsus varus* is similar, beginning preferably within the first 2 weeks of life with casting that may continue for many months. The weight of a cast prevents normal mobility of the infant and may delay the accomplishment of such motor tasks as rolling over, standing alone, and walking.

The Denis-Browne splint is used for correcting club foot and other defects (Figure 12.34). It may be worn nights only or both day and night. Although it does not permit standing, the splint allows vigorous activities that utilize crawling, creeping, and scooter boards.

Among students who do not have pathological problems are many individual differences in foot functioning and gait. Assessment should begin with movement exploration to ascertain that the student has full range of ankle and foot motion and can do the following in both nonweight-bearing and weight-bearing positions: (a) plantar flexion and dorsiflexion at the ankle joint; (b) supination, pronation, and circumduction at the talonavicular and talocalcaneal joints, (c) flexion, extension, abduction, and adduction of the toes.

The two joints of the foot where most of the movements occur, and subsequently the deviations, are the *talonavicular* and *talocalcaneal* joints. In the former, the talus is transferring the weight of the body to the forward part of the foot, and in the latter it is transferring the weight to the back part of the foot. How this weight is transferred determines the presence or absence of foot problems.

Normally, the weight of the body in locomotor activities is taken on the outer border of the foot and then transferred via the metatarsal area to the big toe, which provides the push-off force for forward movement. When this sequence occurs, the foot is maintained in slight supination, which is considered the "strong position" of the foot. All locomotor activities should be performed in this slightly supinated position, which forces the weight of the body to be taken on the outer border of the foot.

Kinesiologically, supination is a combination of adduction and inversion (turning the soles of the feet inward). The same muscles that act as prime movers for inversion (supination) are responsible for maintenance of a strong longitudinal arch. They are the tibialis anterior and the tibialis posterior. Almost all foot exercises involve strengthening and tightening of these two muscles of the lower leg.

Longitudinal Arch

The longitudinal arch extends from the calcaneus to the distal end of the first metatarsal. The height of longitudinal arches appears to be determined genetically and bears little relationship to strength. A low arch can be as strong or stronger than a high arch, which tends to be vulnerable to injury.

The longitudinal arch is held in place primarily by the three "bowstring" ligaments. They are the long plantar ligament, the plantar calcaneo-cuboid ligament, and the spring ligament (also called plantar calcaneonavicular ligament). These ligaments are named for the two bones to which they attach.

Figure 12.35 Medial view of foot illustrating pain centers and structures that support the longitudinal arch. Pain centers are (A) under metatarsal-phalangeal joints, (B) insertion of plantar ligaments to calcaneus, (C) under navicular, and (D) mid-dorsum, where shoelaces tie.

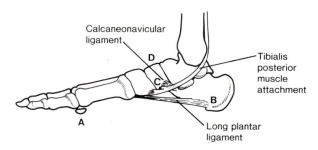

Figure 12.36 Assessment of severity of flatfoot. (A) *Feiss line method:* arrow shows approximate location of navicular bone in normal foot on left and third degree flatfoot on right. (B) *Helbing's sign method:* arrow denoting straight Achilles tendon on left shows normal foot; arrow showing Achilles tendon flaring inward on right shows flatfoot. Note in both (A) and (B) that flatfoot is accompanied by pronation.

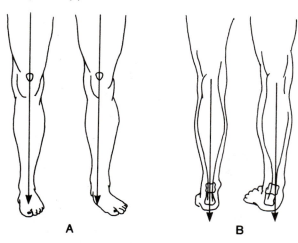

Fallen Arches

Fallen or broken arches, in the layperson's language, are sprains of the ligaments that normally provide support for the longitudinal arch. These sprains are classified as traumatic or static. *Traumatic arch sprain* is caused by violent stretching of one or more ligaments. *Static sprain* is the term given to arches that are more or less permanently lowered because the ligaments are too elongated to maintain the tarsals and metatarsals in their respective positions. The condition cannot be traced to a particular injury. Instead, it is the result of continuous stress on the longitudinal arch like, for instance, that imposed by obesity. For persons with these problems, arch supports and adequate strapping should be prerequisites for participation in physical education. In addition, the student should practice prescribed foot exercises daily for strengthening the tibials and improving alignment of the foot.

Pain Centers

Examinations of the feet should include questions concerning pain or discomfort in the following "pain centers" (Figure 12.35) of the foot: sole of foot under metatarsal-phalangeal joints; sole of foot close to the heel where the plantar ligaments attach to the calcaneus; under surface of navicular; mid-dorsum, where shoelaces tie; and outer surface of sole of foot, where most of weight is borne. These areas should be inspected closely for thicknesses and other abnormalities.

Flatfoot (Pes Planus)

Flatfoot may be congenital or postural. The black race is predisposed to congenital flatfoot. If the muscles of the legs and feet are strong and flexible and the body is in good alignment, the congenital flatfoot is not considered a postural deviation.

Infants are born with varying degrees of flatfeet. Strong arches develop as the natural consequence of vigorous kicking and strenuous locomotor activities.

Faulty body mechanics and improper alignment of the foot and leg may create an imbalance in muscle strength, which in turn prevents maintenance of the longitudinal arch in the correct position. The result is an orthopedic problem rather than one that can be corrected by exercise alone. The physician often prescribes special shoes.

To evaluate the severity of flatfoot, the *Feiss line* (Figure 12.36) method is used. This entails drawing an imaginary line from the medial malleolus to the metatarsophalangeal joint of the big toe. The distance that the navicular (scaphoid) is from the Feiss line determines whether the condition is first, second, or third degree as follows:

First degree—navicular 1 inch below line.
Second degree—navicular 2 inches below line.
Third degree—navicular 3 inches below line.

The *Helbing's sign* (Figure 12.36) may also be used to evaluate the severity of flatfoot. It is defined as a medial turning inward of the Achilles tendon as viewed from behind.

Ameliorative Exercises

1. Strengthen the tibials by supination exercises like patticake, with feet together, apart.

2. Strengthen and tighten other muscles, ligaments, and tendons on the medial aspect of the foot by inversion exercises.

3. Stretch the tight muscles, ligaments, and tendons on the lateral aspect of the foot.

Pronation

Of all of the postural foot defects, pronation is the most common and the most debilitating. It is defined variously as taking the weight of the body on the inner border of the foot, rolling inward on the ankles, and combined eversion and abduction. Eversion, which is the kinesiological term for turning the sole of the foot outward, occurs when the lateral muscles of the lower leg (peroneals) are tighter than the tibials. This deviation occurs mainly in the talonavicular and talocalcaneal joints.

The inward rotation of the tarsal bones often causes a stretching of the bowstring ligaments and the subsequent dropping of the tarsals so that flatfoot is a related disorder. The student tends to toe outward and to complain of pain in the longitudinal arch and in the calf muscles (gastrocnemius and soleus). The Feiss line and the Helbing's sign described earlier are used also for diagnosis of pronation.

Pronation may occur in early childhood as well as other growth periods. In affluent areas, well over 10 to 20% of the children may wear corrective shoes designed to ameliorate the condition of pronation (Figure 12.37). In these shoes the medial border is built up in such a way as to force the weight of the body to be taken on the outer border of the foot. The shoes are prescribed by physicians. Children who wear corrective shoes should not change to tennis shoes for physical education activity, nor should they go barefooted without the permission of their orthopedist.

Ameliorative Exercises

1. Begin with nonweight-bearing exercises and do not add weight-bearing exercises until indicated by orthopedist.

2. Emphasize toe-curling exercises to strengthen the flexors of the toes.

3. Emphasize plantar flexion and inversion.

4. Avoid dorsiflexion exercises and maintenance of foot in dorsiflexion for long periods of time.

5. Avoid eversion movements.

6. In picking up marbles and other objects with the toes, stress a position of inversion, such as
   a. Pick up marbles with toes.
   b. Deposit into box across the midline, which forces the foot into inversion.

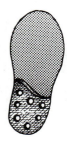

Figure 12.37 Thomas heel shoes used to correct flat foot and other alignment problems. The medial border of the shoe is extended forward and is raised.

7. In relay activities for correction of pronation, make sure objects held by toes of right foot are passed to the left to ensure inversion.

Calluses

A callus is a thickening of the skin that results from undue pressure, friction, or irritation, usually caused by poorly fitted shoes. Calluses become painful when the underlying tissue or periosteum is bruised. They may occur anywhere on the body, but the most frequent source of pain is under the metatarsal heads.

The pain of calluses is relieved by inserting pads in the shoe that shift the weight of the body to another part of the foot. Calluses may be softened with lanolin and buffed down by an emery board, but the best treatment is prevention through wearing only properly fitted shoes.

Papillomas

The term *papilloma* refers to any benign skin tumor. On the sole of the foot, the most common type is the *plantar wart,* which tends to grow inward. Surgical excision, chemotherapy, and X rays are the most common treatments. Weight-bearing activities are painful during the weeks following the removal of a plantar wart, but with proper padding, highly motivated students will wish to continue participating in physical education.

Dermatitis

Dermatitis in the metatarsal area is usually a fungus infection such as athlete's foot. The use of talcum powder and lamb's wool between the toes tends to relieve itching and pain.

Syndactylism

Extra toes, the absence of toes, or the webbing of toes all affect mechanical efficiency in locomotor activities (see Figure 12.38), but a child with good coordination

Figure 12.38 Absence of big toe affects balance and locomotor efficiency.

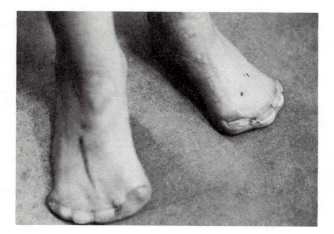

Figure 12.39 Bunion limits flexion of big toe.

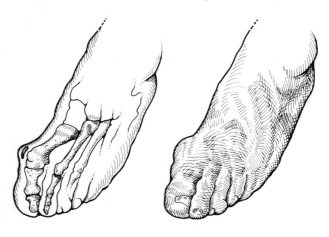

can learn to compensate well enough to achieve recognition as an outstanding athlete. An example is Tom Dempsey, stellar kicker for the Philadelphia Eagles of the National Football Conference, who has part of his kicking foot missing.

Webbing of toes is usually corrected surgically, and extra toes may be removed to facilitate purchase of shoes. The most debilitating defect is absence of the big toe, which plays a major role in static balance and in the push-off phase of locomotor activities.

Hallux Valgus

Hallux is the Latin word for big toe and *valgus* is a descriptive adjective meaning bent outward. Hence,

hallux valgus is a marked deviation of the big toe toward the four lesser toes. This adduction at the first metatarsophalangeal joint causes shoes to exert undue pressure against the medial aspect of the head of the first metatarsal, where a bursa (sac of synovial fluid) is present in the joint. Several changes in this bursa may occur as a result of the pressure exerted by the shoe. If the bursa enlarges, it is called a *bunion* (Figure 12.39), the Greek word for turnip. This phenomenon happens so often that the terms *bunion* and *hallux valgus* are used as synonyms. If the bursa becomes inflamed, it is called *bursitis*. If the irritation results in a deposit of additional calcium on the first metatarsal head, this new growth is called an *exostosis*.

Learning Activities

1. Photograph the back and side views of the postures of selected persons in the following age ranges: (a) under 6, (b) 6 to 11, (c) 12 to 16, (d) 17 to 30, (e) 31 to 59; and (f) over 60. Note the postural characteristics of each age group and suggest, where appropriate, specific activities for improvement of postures.

2. Have someone photograph or videotape some of your postures. Analyze each segment of your body in terms of good alignment and write a report describing your posture deviations and recommended activities.

3. Visit a nursing home or center for the aged and observe the postural characteristics of its residents.

4. Develop a collection of slides or "closeup" photographs of feet that depict deviations.

5. Use ink or poster paint to make footprints of persons of different ages, beginning with a toddler. Note the developmental changes in the longitudinal arch.

6. Develop a 10-point scale for judging body mechanics and use it in a group-screening situation to assign the pupils to quartiles. If other raters are assisting, compare your ratings with theirs. Discuss similarities and differences.

7. Teach and/or lead your class in several exercises or activities for each posture deviation.

References

Cailliet, R. (1975). *Scoliosis: Diagnosis and management.* Philadelphia: F. A. Davis.

Darden, E. (1972). A comparison of body-image and self-concept variables among sport groups. *Research Quarterly, 43,* 7–15.

Gottesman, E. G., & Caldwell, W. E. (1966). The body-image identification test: A quantitative projective technique to study an aspect of body-image. *The Journal of Genetic Psychology, 108,* 19–33.

Johnson, C. M., Catherman, G. D., & Spiro, S. H. (1981). Improving posture in a cerebral palsied child with response-contingent music. *Education and Treatment of Children, 4* (3), 243–251.

O'Brien, F., & Azrin, N. H. (1970). Behavioral engineering: Control of posture by informational feedback. *Journal of Applied Behavior Analysis, 3,* 235–240.

Rowe, A. S., & Caldwell, W. E. (1963). The somatic apperception test. *The Journal of General Psychology, 68,* 59–69.

Rubin, H., O'Brien, T., Ayllon, T., & Roll, D. (1968). Behavioral engineering: Postural control by a portable operant apparatus. *Journal of Applied Behavior Analysis, 1,* 99–108.

Sheldon, W. H. (1954). *Atlas of man: A guide for somatotyping of adult males at all ages.* New York: Harper & Row.

Tiller, J., Stygar, M. K., Hess, C., & Reimer, L. (1982). Treatment of functional chronic stooped posture using a training device and behavior therapy. *Physical Therapy, 11,* 1597–1600.

Whitman, W. (1938). I sing the body electric (1885). *Complete poetry and selected prose and letters* (p. 89). London: The Nonesuch Press.

Lindsey, R., Jones, B. J., & Whitley, A. V. (1974). *Body mechanics—posture, figure, fitness.* Dubuque, IA: Wm. C. Brown.

Lowman, C. L., & Young, C. H. (1960). *Postural fitness.* Philadelphia: Lea & Febiger.

MacEwen, G. D. (1974). *Spinal deformity in neurology and muscular disorders.* St. Louis: C. V. Mosby.

Mueller, G. W., & Christaldi, J. (1966). *A practical program of remedial physical education.* Philadelphia: Lea & Febiger.

Phelps, W., Kiphuth, R., & Goff, C. (1956). *The diagnosis and treatment of postural defects* (2nd ed.). Springfield, IL: Charles C. Thomas.

Rathbone, J., & Hunt, V. V. (1965). *Corrective physical education* (7th ed.). Philadelphia: W. B. Saunders.

Scranton, P., Clark, M., & McClosky, S. (1978). Musculoskeletal problems in blind children. *Journal of Bone and Joint Surgery, 60-A* (3), 363–365.

Sherrill, C. (1980). Posture training as a means of normalization. *Mental Retardation, 18,* 135–138.

Steindler, A. (1977). *Kinesiology of the human body under normal and pathological conditions.* Springfield, IL: Charles C. Thomas.

Stoker, B. (1977). *The postural characteristics of the severely mentally retarded.* Unpublished master's thesis, Texas Woman's University, Denton.

Vodola, T. (1976). *Postural abnormalities: An individualized program.* Oakhurst, NJ: Project ACTIVE.

Wessel, J. (1976). *Health/Fitness: Posture—I CAN training program.* Northbrook, IL: Hubbard.

Bibliography

Basmajian, J. (Ed.). (1984). *Therapeutic exercise* (4th ed.). Baltimore: Williams & Wilkins.

Daniels, L., & Worthington, C. (1977). *Therapeutic exercise for body alignment and function* (2nd ed.). Philadelphia: W. B. Saunders.

Davies, E. (1958). *The elementary school child and his posture patterns.* New York: Appleton-Century-Crofts.

Houser, E. (1962). *Curvatures of the spine.* Springfield, IL: Charles C. Thomas.

Keim, H. (1972). *Scoliosis.* Summit, NJ: Ciba Pharmaceutical Co.

Kudlac, R. (1978). *Scoliosis: Its incidence in nonambulatory mentally retarded persons.* Unpublished master's thesis, Texas Woman's University, Denton.

13 Fitness for Fully Living

Figure 13.1 The 1980 AAHPERD health-related fitness test item to assess the flexibility of the lower back and hamstrings entails one slow maximal reach and stretch.

Chapter Objectives

After you have studied this chapter, you should be able to

1. Contrast health-related vs. physical or motor fitness and discuss tests for assessing each.
2. Discuss the meaning of fitness for severely handicapped nonambulatory students vs. ambulatory handicapped students vs. normal students. State appropriate assessment techniques and fitness goals for each.
3. Identify factors contributing to low fitness and discuss how these can be ameliorated through adapted physical education programming.

4. Discuss counseling techniques as they relate to fitness and other physical education goals.
5. Demonstrate ability to use norms in writing IEPs, and contrast use of norms with criterion-referenced testing approaches.
6. Identify 12 principles of fitness teaching and discuss their application to specific handicapping conditions. Explain how they can be implemented in coordinated home, school, and community fitness programs.

We must take immediate steps to ensure that every American child be given the opportunity to make and keep himself physically fit . . . fit to learn, fit to understand, to grow in grace and stature, to fully live.

—John F. Kennedy

Fitness in the physical education setting too often has been interpreted narrowly as fitness to play, to excel in athletics, and to score in certain percentiles on tests of strength and endurance. Physical fitness must encompass fitness for sitting as well as for running, for reading and writing as well as for playing, for white collar jobs as well as those that are more physically demanding. Neuromuscular relaxation is as important a part of physical fitness as is cardiovascular endurance.

Types of Fitness

Two types of fitness are recognized: health-related and physical or motor. Table 13.1 presents the factors believed to comprise health-related fitness and the tests used to measure them (see Figures 13.1 and 13.2). *Health-related fitness* refers to those aspects of physiological and psychological functioning that are believed to offer protection against such degenerative diseases as obesity and coronary heart disease (the nation's number one killer). *Physical or motor fitness* refers to the traditional concept of optimal strength, endurance, flexibility, power, agility, and balance for sports functioning or, in the case of many handicapped persons, for daily living activities.

In severely handicapped persons, physical fitness encompasses the functioning of the postural reflex mechanism—i.e., muscle tonus, adequate strength to

Table 13.1
AAHPERD Health-Related Fitness Test (1980)

1. *Cardiovascular function*
   Mile run (1609.76 m.) or 9-minute run or 1.5-mile run
2. *Body composition*
   Amount of fat determined by sum of triceps and subscapular skinfolds taken by caliper
3. *Strength/endurance*
   Bent-knee sit-ups in 60 seconds
4. *Lower back/hamstrings flexibility*
   Sit and reach—one slow maximal stretch

Figure 13.2 The mile or 1.5 mile run-walk is considered the best activity for developing cardiovascular fitness. Note that the artificial leg on man to left does not prevent such training.

lift the head, roll over, sit, and creep, and maintenance of sufficient range of motion (flexibility) to prevent contractures. It is disconcerting that fitness is so poorly understood that special educators often rank fitness as the least important competency area for teachers of severely mentally retarded persons.

The official recognition of health-related fitness by our profession in 1980 constitutes a giant step forward in educating the American public concerning the relevancy of physical education goals to their everyday lives. Let us hope that the next step will be the recognition of developmental fitness with attention to the needs of infants and children, both normal and handicapped. Attitudes toward fitness as well as habits conducive to it are probably well established in early childhood before formal instruction is ever offered.

Factors Contributing to Low Fitness

Numerous factors contribute to low fitness: (a) obesity; (b) underweight; (c) asthma and other chronic respiratory problems; (d) susceptibility to infectious diseases, including the common cold; (e) poor nutrition; (f) inadequate sleep; (g) a lifestyle that does not encompass physical exercise; (h) a repugnance toward perspiration, dirt, wind, and other environmental factors surrounding physical activity; (i) fear of failure and/or embarrassment; and (j) a genetic predisposition toward low fitness. Persons who are mentally ill, emotionally disturbed, or who use alcohol, drugs, and other mood modifiers excessively are generally characterized by low physical fitness since mind and body contribute equally to a state of well-being.

Children should not be compelled to engage in a program of fitness conditioning that has no *personal* meaning, nor should they be subjected to fitness tests that they are destined to fail. One of the great tragedies of the physical fitness emphasis is the universal testing and evaluation of all children, using identical fitness tasks and norms as though individual differences do not exist in the public schools. Teachers should adapt fitness tests to the needs of individual pupils.

Fitness Counseling

Individuals with subliminal fitness need special physical education programs designed to change their attitudes toward exercise, to support them in attempts to increase pain tolerance, and to raise their level of fitness as quickly as possible. These objectives can be accomplished best when implemented in groups of not more than 10 students. Low physical fitness deserves a guidance and counseling approach as much as does low mental and emotional fitness. For this reason, the school

psychologist or a specialist trained in group therapy techniques should work closely with the physical educator in shaping attitudes and modifying behavior. Time should be allocated for individual conferences and small-group therapy sessions during which the reasons for low fitness are explored and alternative methods of developing strength and circulorespiratory endurance are analyzed.

Adapted physical educators should have some academic background in guidance and counseling. In addition to theoretical knowledge, they must be careful listeners and good observers. The most important attribute of a would-be counselor is belief in the worth and dignity of every human being. Questions that teachers should consider before extending their role to fitness counseling are as follows:

How do we look upon others?
Do we see each person as having worth and dignity in his or her own right?
Do we treat individuals as persons of worth, or do we subtly devalue them by our attitudes and behavior?
Is our philosophy one in which respect for the individual is uppermost?
Do we respect every individual's capacity and right to self-direction, or do we basically believe that the lives of others would be best guided by us?
To what extent do we have a need and a desire to dominate others?
Are we willing for people to select and choose their own values, or are our actions guided by the conviction (usually unspoken) that they would be happiest if they permitted us to select their values, standards, and goals?

The primary purpose of fitness counseling is to change attitudes toward the body and its capacity for strength, flexibility, and circulorespiratory endurance. When attitudes are changed, new habits of exercise result. The fact that so large a proportion of the American public remains unfit demonstrates that physical educators in the past have been relatively unsuccessful in shaping and changing attitudes.

The teacher's attitudes—rather than knowledge, theories, and techniques—are the most important determinants of attitude change and behavior modification on the part of the student. Students cannot cope with problems of obesity, awkwardness, and low fitness until they can objectively analyze the causal factors and resultant consequences. In many instances, they lack faith in their ability to change themselves and suffer from poor self-concepts. They may feel defeated, hostile, or misunderstood; they seldom feel good about themselves. It is necessary, therefore, to change the attitude toward self before modifying attitudes toward exercise and fitness.

Some of the roles that a physical educator may play in fitness counseling include:

1. Listener. This role is essentially passive, with the teacher's comments limited to "Hmm," "Yes," "Uh-huh." It may be beneficial to a student in desperate need of emotional catharsis, but contributes neither to improved self-concept nor attitude change. Nevertheless, we have all seen students who were so angry, wound up, or upset that they required only a sympathetic listener until they calmed down sufficiently to relate to another person.

2. Interpreter. In this role the teacher attempts to clarify and objectify the student's feelings by restating the student's words in a different way, more clearly and objectively. For example:
Student: I know the students are always laughing at me because I am so clumsy and awkward. No one wants me on the team. I don't have many friends.
Teacher: You resent the fact that your classmates seem to judge you upon the basis of your athletic ability and not for what you are.

3. Reflector. The teacher responds with reflective statements that convey an understanding and acceptance of the student's attitudes and feelings. This involves learning to perceive the world as the student sees it and to perceive the student as the student sees him- or herself. This role may be conceived as empathizing with or adopting the student's frame of reference.

During a counseling session, the teacher's attitude and responses should make it easier for a student to listen to himself or herself. When the student perceives that the teacher thinks he or she is worth listening to, self-respect is heightened. When another self (the teacher) can look upon the student's obesity or awkwardness or lack of fitness without shame or emotion, the student's capacity to look at himself or herself objectively grows. Realization that whatever attitude the student expresses is understood and accepted leads to a feeling of safety and the subsequent courage to test new ideas and try different methods of improving fitness.

Fitness counseling may encompass several stages: (a) initial collection of data; (b) establishing rapport; (c) listening with appropriate responses; (d) providing support and reinforcement in the exercise setting; and (e) continuous evaluation and follow-up. Facts about the student's fitness are gathered through observations, interviews, and various tests. The greater the data accumulated about an individual, the more insight the teacher has. When the team approach to fitness counseling is implemented, the physical educator may have access to achievement scores in other areas, indices of self-concept, intelligence quotient, psychological evaluations, and information about family background. There appears to be a trend toward faculty from many different disciplines sitting down together to share perceptions about a particular child and to recommend remediation. The individual with low fitness frequently has multiple problems. The team approach ensures that the person will be treated as a *whole* rather than by bits and pieces.

To understand fitness problems in their true perspective, the teacher needs information about the student's life experiences, values, and perceptions of what is meaningful in life. Requesting the student to prepare an autobiography may meet this need. The tendency to write only about fitness and athletic ability in an autobiography for the physical education teacher can be counteracted by suggesting that such questions as the following be answered:

1. What makes you unique and different from every other human being?
2. What have been the most meaningful events in your life?
3. Which human beings have touched your life significantly?
4. What things in your life have happened that you would change if you could?
5. What do you intend to be doing 10 years from now?
6. What will you be like when you are middle aged?

In some instances, negative feelings about the self and/or fitness may be too embarrassing, intimate, or difficult for the student to approach in a face-to-face situation. Writing out responses to such questions as the following facilitates communication:

1. How do you feel about your fitness (or weight or failing a test or whatever)?
2. How do you think others feel about your fitness?
3. How do you think others think you feel about your fitness?
4. How do you think others should feel about your fitness?

It is important to note whether the student interprets *others* as peers, parents, teachers, or a combination. The student's responses tend to present an accurate picture of the *significant others* who may covertly or overtly be shaping his or her attitudes.

Rapport between two persons begins at the moment of face-to-face contact. It is essential, therefore, that the very first conference with a student convey feelings of acceptance and understanding and a belief in the student's self-actualizing potential. Counseling sessions should be held in a quiet setting where the teacher is free from interruption. All sessions should be conducted in private with assurance that information will be kept in confidence. Two feelings are most important for optimal growth and positive change: (a) I exist, therefore I am lovable; and (b) I am competent. Early conferences may be devoted to getting acquainted, finding common interests and values, and sharing ideas. An invitation to go fishing, take a walk, or eat out may contribute to the establishment of rapport more readily than formal interviews or conferences. Only when the child feels lovable and competent is he or she ready for preplanned regular counseling sessions.

Every word spoken by a teacher in a counseling setting carries some meaning to the student. Likewise, shifts in postures, hand gestures, slight changes in tone, pauses, and silences convey acceptance or nonacceptance. It is recommended that over 50% of the teacher's responses in a counseling session fall into the reflection category. The teacher sets the limits on how long a session may last, but the student may determine how short it can be. In other words, a student should feel free to terminate a session whenever he or she wishes.

Concurrent with the fitness counseling sessions, the student should be provided with adapted physical education, either of an individual or small group nature. In some respects, fitness counseling is similar to dance or play therapy in that movement experiences frequently provide the basis for discussion. Sometimes an adapted physical education lesson will turn into a counseling session and vice versa.

Successes and failures in the gymnasium are accepted with equanimity. Neither praise nor blame is offered. The teacher uses words primarily to reflect what the student is feeling in a manner similar to that employed in the counseling session. On some occasions, the teacher may imitate the movement of the student, using this technique to reflect how the student looks to another and to reinforce the belief that others can accept the student and his or her movement as the best of which he or she is capable at the moment. Imitation of movements, performed without words, shows willingness to suffer what the student is suffering, to feel as he or she feels, to perform through his or her body, and to walk in his or her shoes.

Success in counseling is dependent upon the skill of the teacher in the following functions: (a) seeing the student as a co-worker on a common problem; (b) treating the student as an equal; (c) understanding the student's feelings; (d) following the student's line of thought; (e) commenting in line with what the student is trying to convey; and (f) participating completely in the student's communication. The teacher's tone of voice is extremely important in conveying willingness and ability to share a student's feelings.

As fitness counseling proceeds, the student should grow in self-acceptance. The following criteria may serve as one basis for evaluation: (a) the student perceives himself or herself as a person of worth, worthy of respect rather than criticism; (b) the student perceives his or her abilities and characteristics with more objectivity and greater comfort; (c) the student perceives himself or herself as more independent and more able to cope with problems; (d) the student perceives himself or herself as more able to be spontaneous and genuine; and (e) the student perceives himself or herself as more integrated, less divided. Self-acceptance implies the desire and ability to change what can be changed, to accept what cannot be changed, and the wisdom to know the difference. Fitness counseling will not be 100% successful. Some students will remain obese. Many will continue in lifestyles devoid of exercise. But the physical educator will have the experience of viewing fitness through others' eyes and experiencing what others feel as they attempt to cope with movement problems. The insights that result may well lead to the creation of new and more effective techniques for building physical fitness.

Fitness Testing

Long- and short-term goals in the IEP must be based on assessment. With the handicapped, this assessment begins with careful observation and recording of anecdotal data. Some of the criteria addressed include (a) alertness—i.e., sufficient fitness to take in and respond to the surrounding world; (b) energy enough to keep up with peers (handicapped and normal) in play as well as school work; (c) ability to stay awake (in spite of prescribed medications) and to concentrate; (d) freedom from pain, discomfort, and breathlessness during movement; and (e) sufficient health to enjoy life, relax, laugh, and behave in age-appropriate ways.

Mainstreaming of handicapped children with their normal peers can be facilitated greatly by attending to criteria for health-related fitness. Numerous researchers have shown, for instance, that even among nonhandicapped children *peer acceptance* is related to motor *performance*.

Table 13.2 summarizes the physical fitness tests used most often in the public schools for both normal and handicapped students. Since most teachers know how to administer the AAHPER Youth Fitness Test, procedures are not included in this book. Test manuals giving instructions as well as normative data are listed in the Bibliography.

A brief chronology of the evolution of physical fitness testing for normal and handicapped children follows to help readers find primary sources and understand relationships.

Table 13.2
Factors of Physical Fitness for Normal and Handicapped Students and Test Items Used to Measure Them

AAHPER Physical Fitness, Rev. (1975) Ages 10 to 17[a]	Two AAHPER Fitness Tests for Retarded; EMR, Ages 8 to 18 (1968) TMR, Ages 6 to 19 (1976)	Project ACTIVE Level II Physical Fitness Test for MR, LD, and ED Pupils (1978)	Project UNIQUE for Blind, Deaf, Orthopedically Impaired (1979)[b] Ages 10 to 18
1. *Cardiovascular function* 1- or 1.5-mile for time 600-yard run-walk 9- or 12-minute run-walk	300-yard run-walk	1. *Cardiovascular fitness* 200-yard dash, age 11 and below 8-minute run, ages 12 to 13 12-minute run, ages 14 and above	1. *Cardiorespiratory function* 1- or 1.5-mile for time 9- or 12-minute run-walk
2. *Abdominal strength/ endurance* Bent-knee sit-ups for 60 seconds	Same for EMR; 30 seconds for TMR	2. *Abdominal strength/ endurance* Modified sit-ups (curl-ups) no limit	2. *Dynamic strength/ endurance* Bent-knee sit-ups, 60 seconds Timed leg-raise Timed prone trunk-raise
3. *Arm and shoulder strength/endurance* Pull-ups or flexed arm hang	Flexed arm-hang for both boys and girls	3. *Arm and shoulder strength* Static arm hang for time beginning in flexed arm position and continuing as straight arm hang	3. *Static muscular strength* Flexed arm-hang Pull-ups Grip strength, R and L
4. *Explosive leg strength* Standing broad jump (best of three trials)	Same	4. *Explosive leg power* Standing broad jump (best of three trials)	4. *Explosive muscular strength* Standing broad jump 50-meter/yard dash Softball throw for distance/speed
5. *Speed and explosive leg strength* 50-yard dash	Same		5. *Flexibility* Sit and reach
6. *Speed and change of direction* Shuttle run between two parallel lines 30 feet apart	Same for EMR; eliminated for TMR		6. *Static balance* Modified stork stand
			7. *Agility* Rise to stand, mat creep Shuttle run, same as AAHPER
	Softball throw for distance		8. *Percent body fat* Calipers measure of triceps, abdominal and subscapular areas.

[a]Buell (1973) indicated all norms on this test were appropriate for blind and partially sighted except 50-yard dash, long-distance runs, shuttle run, and softball throw.
[b]Structure of this test based on factor analyses of Rarick; 1980 AAHPERD Health Related Fitness; and 1975 AAHPER Physical Fitness Tests.

Chronology of Fitness Testing

1958 Original AAHPER Youth Physical Fitness Test presented to the field by Paul Hunsicker.

1964 Hayden Physical Fitness Test for Mentally Retarded published in Canada with norms for pupils ages 8 to 17 on eight items: (a) hang time, (b) medicine ball throw, (c) speed back lifts, (d) speed sit-ups, (e) vertical jump, (f) floor touch, (g) back extension, and (h) 300-yard run.

1965 First AAHPER Fitness Test Manual published with norms for pupils ages 10 to 17.

1965 Dissertation on motor performance and fitness of elementary school children completed by Margie Hanson, currently AAHPERD Consultant on Elementary School Physical Education in Reston, VA. Norms are presented for about 30 test items for children ages 6 and up.

1966 Julian Stein, former director of AAHPERD Programs on the Handicapped in Reston, VA, completed 442-page dissertation entitled "Physical Fitness in Relation to Intelligence Quotient, Social Distance, and Physique of Intermediate School Mentally Retarded Boys," now considered a classic in the field.

1968 AAHPER/Kennedy Foundation Special Fitness Test for the Mentally Retarded (EMR) published with norms for pupils ages 8 to 18.

1968 Basic Motor Fitness Test for Emotionally Disturbed and Mentally Handicapped Children at Buttonwood Farms Project, Pennsylvania, reported by Hilsendager, Jack, and Mann.

1973 Buell Adaptation of 1965 AAHPER Fitness Test for *blind and partially seeing* pupils ages 10 to 17 published.

1975 Revised AAHPER Youth Fitness Test Manual published.

1976 AAHPER Motor Fitness Testing Manual for the Moderately Mentally Retarded published with norms for children ages 6 to 19. Developers were Leon Johnson and Ben Londeree at the University of Missouri.

1978 Project ACTIVE (Thomas Vodola) Motor Ability and Physical Fitness norms published for normal, mentally retarded, learning disabled, and emotionally disturbed individuals. This test was based on 1968 Hilsendager, Jack, and Mann battery.

1979 Project UNIQUE (Joseph Winnick of New York) funded by Bureau of Education for the Handicapped to develop norms for blind, deaf, and orthopedically impaired youth ages 10 to 18.

1980 AAHPERD Health-Related Fitness Test published.

1985 Fitness Test for Disabled published (Project UNIQUE).

1985 Fitness norms for Special Olympians published (Roswal, Dunleavy, & Roswal, 1985). Norms based on 2,084 Special Olympians.

Administration of the Health-Related Fitness Tests

Administration of this test demands the purchase of skinfold calipers and the sit and reach flexibility apparatus. This latter can be constructed fairly easily in the school shop. *Lange calipers* are sold by Cambridge

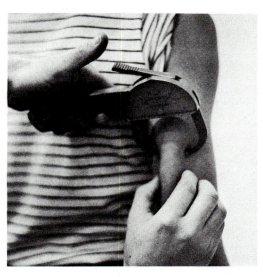

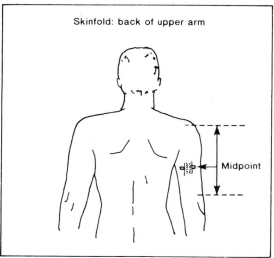

Figure 13.3 Triceps skinfold measure of body fat taken by Lange caliper *(top)* is part of 1980 AAHPERD health-related fitness test. The sketch *(bottom)* shows the midpoint of the back upper arm as a standard place to make the measurement.

Skinfold: back of upper arm

Midpoint

Scientific Industries, 527 Poplar Street, Cambridge, MD 21013, and an increasing number of other companies. *Harpenden calipers* are sold by H. E. Morse Co., 455 Douglas Avenue, Holland, MI 49423.

Body Fat Measurements

Skinfold calipers are used to determine body fat, considered the most important component of *body composition*. Specific anatomic landmarks (see Figures 13.3 to 13.5) are the skinfold sites. Different combinations of sites are recommended by various authorities. The 1980 AAHPERD Health-Related Fitness test uses triceps and subscapular measures. Winnick, in Project

Figure 13.4 Subscapular skinfold measure of body fat taken by Lange caliper is part of 1980 AAHPERD health-related fitness test.

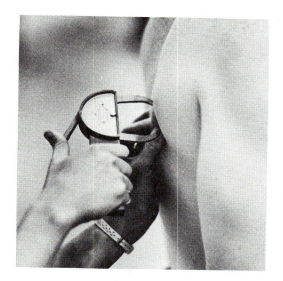

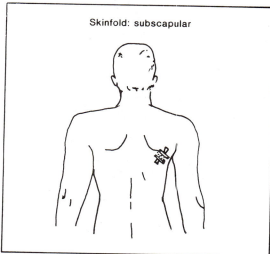

Skinfold: subscapular

Figure 13.5 Abdominal (suprailiac) skinfold measure of body fat taken by Lange caliper and used by Rarick and Winnick in combination with the two AAHPERD measures for more definitive assessment of handicapped students.

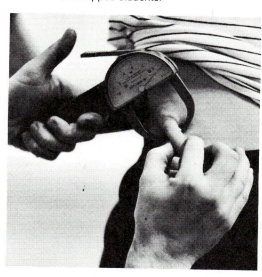

Table 13.3
Criteria for Interpreting Skinfold Caliper Measures[a]

Site	Range	Sex
Triceps and abdominal	6 to 20 mm	Males
Triceps and abdominal	7 to 28 mm	Females
Subscapular	Slightly lower	Males and females

[a]Skinfold measures should generally follow the figures reported here.

UNIQUE, uses triceps, subscapular, and abdominal skinfold measures in accordance with the Rarick protocol. Rarick (1980) states that these three measures along with body weight and bi-iliac breadth are common definers of the body fat factor in normal children ages 6 to 10 and in EMR and TMR mentally retarded children of similar ages.

Many mathematical equations and conversion tables are described in exercise physiology books for use in interpreting percent of body fat from caliper readings. For the public school teacher who is using the test primarily as a screening device to separate the overweight from the normal, the criteria in Table 13.3 indicate normal ranges for students ages 10 to 18.

When testing time is so limited that three measures on each student seem an impossible task, the *triceps measure* can be used alone. Table 13.4 states criteria indicating obesity at ages 5 to 30.

If a teacher does not have calipers and cannot arrange to borrow some, *height* and *weight* measures can be used to screen weight problems as well as growth abnormalities. *It should be understood, however, that height-weight tables are not accurate indicators of weight problems.* Several researchers have reported that ideal weights given on standard weight tables have correlation coefficients of only *.67 with calculated percent body fat.* This explains why our profession (AAHPERD) is strongly recommending the purchase and use of skinfold calipers.

Table 13.4
Minimum Triceps Skinfold Thickness Indicating Obesity (mm)

Age (Years)	Males	Females
5	12	14
6	12	15
7	13	16
8	14	17
9	15	18
10	16	20
11	17	21
12	18	22
13	18	23
14	17	23
15	16	24
16	15	25
17	14	26
18	15	27
19	15	27
20	16	28
21	17	28
22	18	28
23	18	28
24	19	28
25	20	29
26	20	29
27	21	29
28	22	29
29	23	29
30	23	30

Height-weight measures, while not accurate as screening devices, do heighten motivation in training programs. The criterion for overweight is generally considered 10 to 20% above ideal weight, and the criterion for obesity is believed to be 20% and over. An understanding of height-weight measures is also essential to the adapted physical educator who is reading research on growth and development of handicapped persons. Bruininks (1974), in his review of physical development of mentally retarded persons, cites well over 30 studies from 1883 to 1974 that have used height-weight and other simple anthropometric measures. Much of this research was conducted by physicians. The 1980s appear to be the first decade in which calipers are in widespread use; thus, the physical educator must know both the old and the new.

Cardiovascular Fitness Testing

In order to scientifically plan an exercise program, it is necessary to know both the resting and the maximum heart rate. Resting heart rate is obtained by counting the pulse after a person has been in a sitting position for 5 or more minutes. While several laboratory methods exist for calculating maximal heart rate (treadmill, bicycle ergometer), the most practical one for public school personnel is to count the heart beat after an all-out 12-minute or 1.5-mile run. For children under age 13 or handicapped persons (for whom motivation over long periods of time is a problem), a 9-minute or 1-mile run is recommended. In cases of severe cognitive disorders, where it is doubtful that the student grasps the concepts of speed/distance/endurance, a 600- or 300-yard run may be substituted as a last resort. Hence, these are the items included on both the AAHPERD Health-Related and Physical/Motor Tests.

Persons unknowledgeable about heart function (parents, principals, and sometimes even students) may worry about these test items. Such concerns must be alleviated. Often, inviting in a guest speaker from the American Heart Association or a cardiologist will help achieve this goal. Table 13.5 presents maximal heart rates for males and females, ages 4 to 33. Research shows that the maximal heart rates of children exceed those of adults and that children physiologically are capable of the same all-out running efforts as adults. Corbin's (1980) synthesis of research on cardiovascular fitness is especially excellent reading for anxious persons.

After maximum heart rate is determined, the teacher needs to determine the intensity, duration, and frequency of exercise needed to improve cardiovascular endurance in each individual. These decisions comprise the cardiovascular exercise prescription and vary according to age, weight, and general fitness level. For simplification, exercise *intensity* (work load) can be designated as light, moderate, or heavy, as indicated in Table 13.6.

Duration refers to time and pacing of an exercise session. It can be continuous, in which 15 to 60 minutes of continuous walking, running, swimming, and the like of a particular intensity are prescribed (as in *aerobic exercise* programs). Or it may be *intermittent* as in interval training (maximum speed for a set distance followed by rest period of set time; both repeated for several bouts).

Frequency generally refers to number of exercise sessions a week. For persons of very low fitness (or with chronic heart or lung problems) whose initial programs

Table 13.5
Maximal Heart Rates: Ages 4 to 33

		Age Groups						
	Sex	*4 to 6*	*7 to 9*	*10 to 11*	*12 to 13*	*14 to 15*	*16 to 18*	*20 to 33*
Maximum heart rate[a]	M	203 ± 2.2 7.0	208 ± 2.4 8.4	211 ± 2.3 8.1	205 ± 4.1 17.7	203 ± 4.1 12.8	202 ± 3.1 9.2	194 ± 1.6 10.3
Maximum heart rate[a]	F	204 ± 5.0 13.2	211 ± 2.0 7.5	209 ± 2.5 8.8	207 ± 2.8 10.0	202 ± 2.0 6.6	206 ± 2.5 7.7	198 ± 1.5 9.9

[a]Numbers represent mean, standard error of the mean, and standard deviation.

Table 13.6
Illustrative Exercise Intensities for Person of Average Fitness Weighing 154 Pounds (70 kg)

Intensity	Heart Rate (bpm)	VO₂ (Liters/ Minute)	Calories per Minute
Light	100	1.0	5
Moderate	135	2.0	10
Heavy	170	3.0	15

VO_2 refers to maximum oxygen uptake.

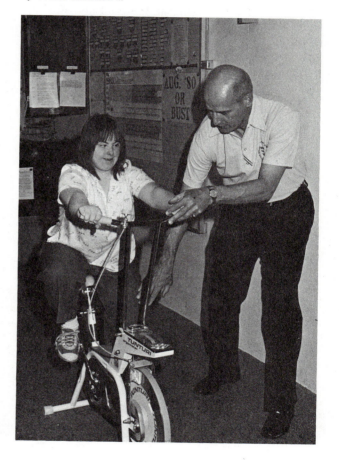

Figure 13.6 Work on the bicycle ergometer is one of the best ways to increase aerobic fitness. Here Dr. Lane Goodwin, director of one of the largest undergraduate adapted physical education programs in the country, works with a Down's syndrome adolescent.

are restricted to 5 to 15 minutes per session, frequency may refer to times per day. The lower the intensity and shorter the duration that can be endured, the more frequent the sessions need to be.

Procedures for assessing other factors of fitness are not covered here since most teachers have administered the other tests that are recommended (see Table 13.2). Fitness assessment should be continuous (rather than at the beginning and end of instructional units). Each day's performance may be graphed (or at least noted) as part of the interrelated assessment/motivation/teaching/learning process.

Administration of Physical Work Capacity Tests

Physical work capacity on a bicycle ergometer or treadmill is considered the best test of cardiovascular fitness (see Figure 13.6). The former seems to be used most often with the handicapped as well as with children. With paraplegics and lower limb amputees arm pedaling replaces leg motion.

Physical working capacity (PWC) is the maximum level of metabolism (work) of which a person is capable. The PWC is used as a measure of *aerobic capacity*. It is expressed in terms of *maximum oxygen uptake* (liters/minute and ml/kg/minute) and *maximum work* on a bicycle ergometer to bring the heart rate to 170 beats per minute (kg/170).

The ml/kg/minute for normal children ages 4 to 15 ranges from about 46.0 to 60.0. Rimmer and Rosentswieg (1982) found the maximum oxygen uptake (VO_2) of learning-disabled boys ages 8 to 10 to be only 40.0. The ml/kg/minute for normal adolescents and adults ages 14 to 30 ranges from about 40.0 to 60.0. Coleman et al. (1976) found the VO_2 of institutionalized EMR and TMR men ages 16 to 24 to be only 31.7.

The kg/170 for normal persons ages 14 to 30 ranges from about 865 to 968. Coleman et al. (1976) found that 37 EMR and TMR males ages 16 to 25 had a kg/170 of only 754.1, which was 75 to 80% of that of nonhandicapped persons.

While there are few laboratory studies of fitness among different handicapped groups, a growing body of research substantiates the low cardiovascular fitness of handicapped persons. This, coupled with other high-risk factors like obesity and physical inactivity, make many handicapped persons prime candidates for heart disease.

Teaching for Fitness

A common misconception is that physical education activities automatically develop muscular strength and endurance. Thus, two laps around the field at the close of each class period or 3 minutes of calisthenics at the beginning seldom have the effect desired. The same amount of exercise executed faithfully each day will contribute to the maintenance of whatever level of strength and circulorespiratory endurance already exists, but it will *not improve* fitness.

Fitness lessons should include scientifically planned warm-up, training, and cool-down activities conducted in accordance with the principles of fitness training.

Principles to Guide Fitness Teaching

1. **Individual differences.** Every student's exercise prescription and/or IEP should be different, based on specific assessment data, motivation level, and activity preferences. Persons become fit quicker when allowed to choose between several exercises/activities (categorized by the teacher as equivalent in work load).

2. **Overload/intensity.** Increases in strength and endurance result when the *work load* is greater than that to which the student is accustomed. Technically, overload refers only to amount of work or stress, although some persons conceptualize it as encompassing amount of energy (intensity) also. Overload/intensity can be achieved in the following ways:
   a. Increase the number of pounds being lifted, pushed, or pulled. This results in progressive resistance exercises.
   b. Increase the number of repetitions, sets, or type of exercise performed.
   c. Increase the distance covered.
   d. Increase the speed with which the exercise is executed.
   e. Increase the number of minutes of continuous all-out effort.
   f. Decrease rest interval between active sessions.
   g. Increase intensity/type of activity during rest/relaxation phases.
   h. Use any combination of the above.

3. **Frequency.** Training sessions (particularly those of all-out effort) should be scientifically spaced so that there is time for physiological homeostasis to occur—i.e., muscles to rest. Too frequent practices tend to result in chronic fatigue, muscle stress, and motivation problems.

4. **Specificity/transfer.** Values gained from exercises done in one position or at one speed will not transfer or benefit the person in other positions or at alternative speeds. Exercises are highly specific; thus, strength exercises particularly need to be done at many joint angles, many intensities. Warm-ups should use the same movements and positions that will be used later in the game or training exercise.

5. **Active/voluntary movement.** Outcome is most effective when the exercise is *active* (done by the student) rather than passive (done by a therapist or teacher). In the case of severely handicapped children with little or no movement capacity of a particular body part, the teacher should encourage all-out effort of the student to at least initiate the movement, which then can be assisted by the teacher. The student should be actively concentrating and assisting in coactive movement.

6. **Progressive resistance.** Stress or overload should be increased gradually but consistently over a long period of time. Amount of resistance (weight) to be added should be determined scientifically.

7. **Recovery/cool down.** Students with dyspnea (breathlessness/breathing difficulty) should not lie or sit down immediately after high intensity exercise. This tends to subvert return of blood to the heart and causes dizziness. *Cool down* should entail continued slow walking or mild activity.

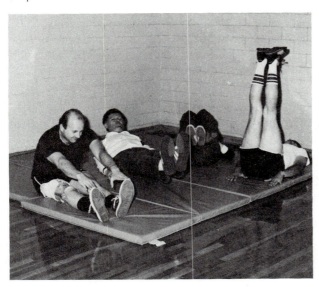

Figure 13.7 Adherence to the principle of individual differences is illustrated at this teaching station for development of abdominal strength. From left to right, first person has artificial leg and is completing a straight-leg sit-up; second person, with high fitness, is performing the straight-leg lift and hold, which would be contraindicated for persons with lesser strength; third and fourth persons are performing easy progression leg lifts adapted to their fitness levels

8. **Warm-up.** A few minutes of warm-up exercises using movements specific to the game or training to follow should precede high-intensity exercise sessions or competitive games. Research shows warm-up is particularly important for persons with chronic respiratory or cardiovascular conditions. Warm-ups should emphasize stretching (extension) exercises and facilitate range of motion.

9. **Static stretch.** Slow static stretches are generally more effective in increasing range of motion (flexibility) than ballistic (rhythmic bouncing) exercises. Note ballistic type exercises are contraindicated (not recommended) by some handicaps; for instance, in spastic cerebral palsy they elicit the abnormal stretch reflex.

10. **Contraindication.** Physical educators should know what exercises/activities are contraindicated (not recommended) for each individual (see Figure 13.7). If correct postural alignment cannot be maintained during execution of an exercise, it is usually too difficult a progression and is therefore contraindicated.

11. **Adaptation.** Physical educators should know how to task analyze exercises into easy, medium, and difficult progressions and ascertain that each student is doing the progression best for him or her. A biomechanical principle often used in adapting exercises is *leverage*; the shorter the lever, the easier the exercise. For instance, straight leg lifts from a supine position to develop or assess abdominal strength are very difficult since the body (as a lever) is in its longest position. By doing bent knee leg lifts, the body lever is shortened and the exercise is made easier.

12. **Motivation.** Persons who wish to be physically fit must be willing to pay the price. They must be motivated to tolerate boredom, fatigue, and discomfort. Fitness does not come easily.

Warm-up Exercises

A *warm-up* is a preparatory activity engaged in immediately before a game, fitness test, or all-out performance of any kind for the purpose of improving performance and preventing injury by increasing muscular temperature, circulation, range of joint mobility, and producing a condition of readiness. The physiological basis for warm-ups lies primarily in the fact that the effectiveness of muscular contractions depends upon temperature. The internal body temperature at rest is 37° C, or 98.6° F. During exercise of high intensity and long duration, deep muscle temperature rises 1 to 2° C. This increase usually occurs during the first 30 minutes of exercise and then plateaus. An increase in body temperature does not occur easily, however, because the temperature control system of the human body is highly effective.

Warm-ups may be classified as active or passive and as specific or general. Active warm-ups entail exercise of some kind, while passive warm-ups encompass hot showers, diathermy, and massage. Specific warm-ups are those in which the movements imitate the ensuing activity. General warm-ups are those that utilize several muscle groups that are not necessarily the ones that will be exercised in ensuing activities. Specific warm-ups are recommended over general warm-ups.

Specific warm-ups, which generally employ a forward-backward stride, are used to *stretch* muscles that will be used later in the physical education period. *Perhaps jogging and follow-the-leader locomotor activities are the best specific warm-up since success in most motor activities depends upon running speed and agility in executing quick stops, starts, turns, and dodges.* For a throwing and catching game, the best warm-ups are throwing and catching, with gradually increasing speed and force of throw.

General warm-ups, so often conducted as calisthenics at the beginning of a class period, offer little or no contribution to the objectives of physical education. The image of mass drill in jumping jacks, side stretches, and toe touches has indeed hurt our profession.

It has become increasingly evident over the years that physical fitness can be increased only through application of the overload principle. Not all children need to engage in programs for building strength, circulorespiratory endurance, and flexibility. The activities in this chapter are recommended primarily for individuals with subminimal fitness. Children with adequate fitness should engage in maintenance programs and concentrate on development of leisure skills.

Progressive Resistance Exercises (DeLorme Program)

Progressive resistance exercises (PRE) are used widely in rehabilitative settings as well as athletics. The relatively high incidence of knee injuries among athletes and the subsequent surgery and rehabilitation have served to acquaint many persons with progressive resistance exercises. The postoperative patient is encouraged to undertake a regimen of knee extension exercises as soon after surgery as pain tolerance allows. Designated as quadriceps femoris progressive resistance exercises, extension of the leg at the knee joint is first executed without external weights. As the strength of the muscle group increases, progressively heavy weights are strapped to the foot.

The PRE technique, based upon knowledge of the individual's pain tolerance, entails the following three procedures:

1. Determine maximal resistance that can be lifted *10* times (10 RM).
2. Then plan four exercise sessions weekly comprised of 30 repetitions executed as follows:
   a. Ten repetitions at ½ 10 RM (half the maximal resistance determined in procedure 1).
   b. Ten repetitions at ¾ 10 RM (three-fourths the maximal resistance determined in procedure 1).
   c. Ten repetitions at 10 RM (the maximal resistance determined in procedure 1).
3. Increase the 10 RM (maximum resistance that can be lifted 10 times) each week.

The 10–20 Repetitions Sequence

Another weight training technique uses the heaviest weight that can be lifted 10 times (10RM). The number of repetitions increases over a 10-day period in accordance with the plan outlined in Table 13.7.

Table 13.7
10–20 Repetitions Sequence

	First 3 days	4th day	5th day	6th day	7th day	Last 3 days
First progression	10	12	14	16	18	20
Second progression	Same as above, but with a heavier weight.					

For individuals with less strength, a 5–10 repetitions sequence can be patterned after the 10–20 series. This technique can be applied to any kind of weight lifting program. Among the kinds of weights successfully used with exceptional children are

1. Teddy bears and other stuffed animals filled with 7, 10, and 15 pounds, respectively, of aquarium sand.
2. Fireplace logs.
3. Sacks of potatoes, cat sand, dry dog food, or flour found in grocery stores—1, 5, 10, 25, 50, and 100 pound bags are usually available.
4. Plastic bottles filled with sand.
5. Back packs such as those used on hiking and camping trips.
6. Dumbbells.
7. Universal gym.
8. Homemade weights from tin cans, cement, and wooden dowels or broomsticks.

Interval Training

Developed originally to condition long distance runners and swimmers, interval training can be adapted to any physical activity. It is especially beneficial for children with asthma and/or low fitness. The basic objective is to exercise for short periods of time with a rest interval between exercise periods in order to develop greater energy potential for a particular motor activity.

The interval training prescription (ITP) should be planned for each student individually or for small homogeneous groups rather than for the class as a whole. A typical ITP for 1 day might resemble that in Table 13.8. After the first 2 weeks, training only twice weekly will result in significant gains in circulorespiratory endurance.

In order to plan the ITP, the following terms must be understood:
1. *Set*—Term that encompasses both the work interval and the rest interval. An ITP may have any number of sets.

Table 13.8
Interval Training Prescription (ITP) for Running

Day 1	Repetitions	Distance Each Work Interval	Amount of Time Each Rest Interval	Total Distance per Set
Set 1	4	220 yards	Depends on heart recovery rate	½ mile
Set 2	8	110 yards	Depends on heart recovery rate	½ mile

2. *Work interval*—Also called a bout. A prescribed number of repetitions of the same activity under identical conditions. Traditionally, the work has been walking, running, or swimming a prescribed number of yards at optimum or near optimum speed *in an effort to raise the heart rate to 180 beats per minute.* If the heart rate does not reach this level after 2 or 3 work intervals, the student should be encouraged to run faster. For variety, work intervals may entail performing an optimum number of squat thrusts, sit-ups, or push-ups within a prescribed number of seconds.

3. *Rest interval*—The number of seconds or minutes between work intervals during which the student catches his or her breath and prepares for the next repetition. During the rest period the student should walk rather than sit, lie, or assume a stationary position. Prescribing a light activity like walking, arm circles, or toe touches may be psychologically beneficial in that it keeps the mind off the impending exhaustion and provides structure. The number of seconds comprising the rest interval depends on individual heart recovery rate. *The next repetition should not be begun until the heart rate drops to 120 beats per minute.* If the heart rate does not recover within the rest interval, the student should be excluded from further interval training for the remainder of the day.

    If taking the pulse rate is not feasible, the time of the rest interval should initially be approximately twice the amount of time consumed by the work interval.

4. *Repetitions*—The number of times the work interval is repeated under identical conditions. The amount of effort exerted in each repetition should be kept more or less constant.

5. *Target time*—The best score that a student can make on the prescribed activity. Target times are usually determined for the 110-, 220-, and 440-yard dashes and/or any other activities to be included in the ITP. Target times are generally not determined until the first 2 weeks of training are completed. The target time is then used as a motivational device to encourage all-out performance.

6. *Level of aspiration*—A statement made by the student of the score he or she thinks he or she can attain in a particular activity. This is also a motivational device.

All-out effort is often motivated after the first few weeks by prescribing the speed of the sprint as follows:

One repetition of 660 yards in 2:03
Six repetitions of 220 yards in 0:33
Six repetitions of 110 yards in 0:15

Older children may be guided in developing individualized exercise sessions comprised of sets that reflect their own levels of aspiration. Presumably, if the child states the number of seconds in which he or she can run 110 yards six times consecutively, he or she will be more motivated to accomplish the goal (level of aspiration) established by him- or herself than one imposed by an adult.

In keeping with the overload principle, the exercise sessions become increasingly more demanding each week. Early in the semester many of the work intervals may be relatively slow runs continued for long distances. As the semester progresses, the long runs are gradually replaced with shorter, faster sprints. *For adolescents and adults, a total workout distance of over 1.5 miles must eventually be achieved for maximum circulorespiratory benefits.* Research is needed to provide comparable information about elementary school children, particularly those with asthma and other respiratory problems.

The following list of procedures may help the adapted physical education specialist in planning each ITP:

1. Test each student individually to determine his or her maximum running time for 110, 220, and

Table 13.9
Sample ITP Card for Pupils of Similar Ability

Day 5	Repetitions	Activity	Rest Interval	Evaluation		Ruda Rowe Stokes
Set 1	4 reps	Runs 220 yards	Walk for 60 seconds between sprints	Easy	Medium	Hard
Set 2	6 reps	Squat thrusts for 10 seconds	Head circling for 20 seconds between bouts			
Set 3	4 reps	Crab walk for 10 seconds	Movement of choice for 20 seconds between bouts			
Set 4	8 reps	Run 110 yards	Walk for 30 seconds between sprints			

440 yards. If a track is not available, adjust these distances in accordance with the space available on your playground.

2. Upon the basis of these preliminary scores, organize the students into small homogeneous groups. If the class is small, each child may work with a single partner of like ability.

3. Develop specific behavioral objectives for each small group. Whenever possible, let the group participate in the development of objectives. Give each child a written copy of the objectives.

4. Explain the principle of interval training to the group and establish a card file where the students may pick up their individualized ITPs at the beginning of each physical education period. This procedure serves as a substitute for roll call and enables the students to begin exercise immediately upon entering the room.

5. An ITP card for three children of similar ability appears in Table 13.9. On the right-hand side of the card, the students check whether each set was easy, medium, or difficult after its completion. These checks help the teacher to determine the extent to which the degree of difficulty (strenuousness) should be changed on the next ITP. On the back of the card the students may record their individual scores or write comments.

6. Apply the principle of overload in developing new cards for each session. Older students can develop their own ITPs.

7. Retest periodically to determine if behavioral goals are being met and to regroup students if necessary.

Circuit Training

Circuit training develops selected aspects of fitness as the student moves from station to station, performing a different fitness task at each station, and completes the circuit a prescribed number of times. Ideally, the task performed at each station uses different groups of muscles, thereby developing different aspects of fitness.

For adolescents and adults, from 6 to 10 stations are recommended, depending upon available space and equipment. For elementary school children, from two to six stations may be attempted.

The amount of time at each station varies, but initially is relatively brief. Thirty seconds at each station, with 10 seconds for rotation, has been found satisfactory. Thus, a circuit can be completed in approximately 2½ minutes. As the semester progresses, the amount of time at each station can be extended or the number of completed circuits increased. The intensity of the work demanded should be increased gradually in keeping with the overload principle.

Procedures to be followed in teaching and preparing students for circuit training are:

1. Ascertain that the students know how to perform the fitness tasks.

2. Divide the class into squads, preferably homogeneous groupings, and assign each squad to a different starting point on the circuit.

3. Practice the mechanics of rotating in a counterclockwise direction from station to station.

4. Develop an individualized circuit training plan for each student. Among the many ways individualized circuits can be developed are Methods A and B, described below.

Method A for Adolescents and Adults

This method is the least structured in that each student rotates from station to station at his or her own rate of speed and finishes the circuit training portion of the class at a different time. Specific directions should be given with respect to where to go and what to do when the circuit is completed. This method is not recommended for young children, nor for individuals who need structure.

Procedures for Method A are as follows:

1. Test every student, allowing several trials at each station. Each trial should be for a set time period such as 30 seconds, during which the fitness task is performed as many times as possible. Record the student's best score at each station, as illustrated in Table 13.9.
2. Base each student's individualized circuit upon one-half of his or her best test performance at each station. To illustrate: one circuit for Litty will consist of four runs, each 20 yards long; 3 pull-ups; 14 bent-knee sit-ups; 9 squat thrusts; and 10 bend, twist, and touch tasks.
3. Determine the number of seconds required for Litty to go through the prescribed circuit three times.
4. Establish the *target time* as two-thirds of the actual time required to complete three circuits.
5. In the exercise sessions that follow, encourage Litty to bring her circuit time down to her target time. When this goal is accomplished, the number of circuits may be increased, the number of seconds at each station increased, or an entirely new circuit comprised of different fitness tasks begun. If the goal is not achieved in several weeks, the target time may be reset or a new circuit begun.

Method B for Children

This method is structured so that all students begin and end the circuit at the same time. Rotation occurs only on signal, and students give an all-out performance at each station until the signal to stop sounds. The objective is to compete against oneself, making a higher score than the previous turn at the station. This method is recommended for elementary school children and individuals who need structure.

Procedures for Method B are as follows:

1. Assign each student a home station, where his or her score card is kept. Prior to starting the circuit the student may check previous scores. At the completion of the circuit the new scores are recorded. To assist in fast, efficient recording, a shoe bag can be attached to the wall with each child's card in a different compartment. Ideally, each card is a different color or in some way made easily identifiable.
2. Determine the number of seconds required for the group to change stations and keep this factor constant by calling, "Rotate -1-2-3-4-5-6-7-8-9-10." On your last count, all students should be ready to begin the next fitness task.
3. For young students or those who have problems with handwriting, a recorder may work at each station. Immediately upon completion of the circuits, children tell the recorder their scores. It is important that this be done quietly and that each child's score be kept confidential. At no time should circuit training become competition with others. Students who cannot remember all their scores until home station is reached can carry score cards with them from station to station. Sometimes instead of recording a numerical score, the process is simplified by writing a + if the student's score was improved and a 0 if it was not.

Aerobics

Aerobics is a progressive physical conditioning program that stimulates circulorespiratory activity for a time period sufficiently long to produce beneficial changes in the body. The originator of the now widely used aerobics exercise program is Kenneth H. Cooper, a physician and major in the United States Air Force Medical Corps, who currently directs The Aerobics Center at 12100 Preston Road in Dallas, Texas. Based upon a longitudinal study of the circulorespiratory fitness of over 5,000 adult male subjects, Cooper (1968) stresses two underlying principles: (a) if the exercise is vigorous enough to provide a sustained heart rate of 150 beats per minute or more, the training effect benefits begin about 5 minutes after the exercise starts and continue as long as the exercise is performed; and (b) if the exercise is not vigorous enough to produce or sustain a heart rate of 150 beats per minute, but is still demanding oxygen, the exercise must be continued considerably longer than 5 minutes, the total period of time depending on the oxygen consumed.

The aerobics exercise program can be divided into three phases: (a) evaluation of circulorespiratory fitness by means of the 12-minute run test; (b) a period of progressive conditioning that extends over several weeks; and (c) maintenance of optimal fitness by earning a specific number of points for exercise each week. The points are based upon the amount of oxygen consumption per minute during the exercise as illustrated in Table 13.10.

Table 13.10
Points Awarded on the Basis of Time and Oxygen Requirements for the 1-Mile Run

Time in Minutes	Points	Oxygen (mls/kg/min)
14½–20	1	7
12–14½	2	14
10–12	3	21
8–10	4	28
6½–8	5	35
6½ or less	6	42

Table 13.11
Fitness Categories Based upon Distance Covered in 12-Minute Run-Walk

Fitness Category	Distance Covered	Oxygen Consumption
I Very poor	Less than 1.0 mile	28.0 ml or less
II Poor	1.0–1.24 miles	28.1–34 ml
III Fair	1.25–1.49 miles	34.1–42 ml
IV Good	1.50–1.74 miles	42.1–52 ml
V Excellent	1.75 miles or more	52.1 ml or more

Evaluation of Aerobic Fitness

Prior to undertaking an aerobics training program, individuals who are unaccustomed to exercise and who may already have circulorespiratory problems should be examined by a physician. After a medical examination, fitness for aerobic training is evaluated by the distance covered in a 12-minute run-walk. Students are classified into five categories of fitness as depicted in Table 13.11.

Progressive Aerobic Conditioning

The fitness classification of the student determines the number of weeks of conditioning that will be required in order to work up to the maintenance phase of 30 points per week. The following guidelines can be used in this regard: (a) very poor category—16 weeks; (b) poor category—13 weeks; and (c) fair category—10 weeks. For students in these three categories, conditioning begins with the accumulation of 10 points a week during the first 2 to 3 weeks, after which an additional 3 to 5 points are required each week until the sum of 30 is reached. Students who score in the good and excellent fitness categories do not participate in the program of progressive conditioning. They go directly to the maintenance phase, earning 30 points each week.

Maintenance of Optimal Aerobic Fitness

The most efficient way to earn 30 points is to jog 1½ miles in 12 minutes four times a week. For covering 1½ miles in 12 minutes, 7½ points are awarded. The following activities, each worth 5 points, create a basis for developing an individualized maintenance program:

Bicycling 5 miles in less than 20 minutes
Running 1 mile in less than 8 minutes
Swimming 600 yards in less than 15 minutes
Handball played for a total of 35 minutes
Stationary running for a total of 12½ minutes

For individual sports enthusiasts, one set of singles tennis games earns 1½ points; nine holes of golf earn 1½ points; water or snow skiing for 30 minutes earns 3 points; and ice or roller skating for 15 minutes earns 1 point. For the bicycle rider who enjoys leisurely pedaling, at least 30 minutes of cycling is required to earn 1 point.

Jogging and Hiking

Jogging, hiking, and performing walk-runs all contribute to fitness if the principle of overload is applied from day to day. These activities are particularly successful when correlated with social studies and/or related to a trip across the state, the United States, or another continent. Individual mileage sheets, superimposed upon maps, can be kept by the students. Merit badges or certificates for achievement may be awarded for the completion of every 50-mile distance.

Hiking is one of the few activities in which a severely handicapped student can participate. It can be done in braces, on crutches, or in a wheelchair. The rehabilitation of most individuals with cardiovascular disease includes daily walks of increasingly long duration and at progressively faster speeds. The exercise plan presented in Table 13.12 has been successful with secondary school youths whose level of fitness initially was too low to enjoy other forms of physical education.

Jogging, or cross-country track, is becoming increasingly popular with all age groups. When motivated by an adult who will run with them, many first and second grade children can jog a mile or further with less discomfort than the adult who accompanies them. Every child, no matter how poor his or her motor coordination, can find pleasure in leisurely running. The *scout's pace* can be used in early stages of training as follows: jog 110 yards, walk 55 yards, jog 110 yards, walk 55 yards, ad infinitum. The scout's pace can also be interpreted as meaning run as far as you can, then walk until breath is restored, after which running is resumed.

Table 13.12
A 14-Week Run-Walk Program

Week	Distance in Miles	Time Goal Minutes	Points for Aerobics Fitness Plan
1	1	20:00	
2	1	18:00	5
3	1	16:00	5
4	1	15:00	5
5	1½	27:00	7½
6	1½	26:00	7½
7	1½	25:00	7½
8	1	14:25	10
9	2	33:00	10
10	2	32:00	10
11	1½	21:40	15
12	2	28:50	20
13	2	28:30	20
14	2½	36:00	25

Continuity Exercises Based Upon Rope Jumping

Procedures in developing a continuity exercise program that utilizes the interval approach include

1. Make a tape recording that establishes a cadence of 80 jumps per minute—i.e., one every ¾ second.
2. Test the students to determine how long they can jump without a rest interval.
3. Upon the basis of individual scores, assign the students to homogeneous groups, each of which has a leader.
4. Develop a sequence of continuity exercises for each group, giving the leaders the written instructions.
5. Assuming that the class can be divided according to exercise capabilities into three groups—easy, medium, and difficult—illustrative sequences appear in Table 13.13.
6. Each group has approximately one-third the floor space with its leader in front. All groups exercise simultaneously to the tape recording or to a piece of music, but each group is doing its own thing based upon its abilities. The groups that finish first go to preestablished stations, where students work on skills.
7. The principle of overload is applied in changing the sequence from week to week. Whenever possible, use contemporary music—i.e., the top 10 songs of the day. Integrating popular music

Table 13.13
Illustrative Sequences Individualized to Meet Capabilities

Easy Sequence	Medium Sequence	Difficult Sequence
1. Rope jump 1 minute	1. Rope jump 3 minutes	1. Rope jump 4 minutes
2. Rest 60 seconds	2. Rest 30 seconds	2. Rest 20 seconds
3. Rope jump 30 seconds	3. Rope jump 1½ minutes	3. Rope jump 2 minutes

with exercise encourages students to perform the routines outside the school day, since certain tunes are heard repeatedly over radio and television.

8. When push-ups, sit-ups, and other exercises are being performed, encourage optimum class involvement by asking the students to call out the cadence count in military fashion.

Astronaut Drills

The drills traditionally used in football practice can be adapted to meet the fitness needs of children as well as to reinforce concepts pertaining to body positions and body parts. Many football teams employ only three signals or verbal cues in their grass drills, *go*, *front*, and *back*. The correct response to each cue follows:

1. *Go*—run in place with vigorous high knee action. Maintain top speed.
2. *Front*—drop to prone lying position and assume a ready position to ensure quick response to the next cue.
3. *Back*—drop to supine lying position and assume a ready position to ensure quick response to the next cue.

These cues are given in various orders, challenging the student to persist in continuous motion. The principle of overload is applied through progressively increasing the duration of time spent in the *go* position. After students have mastered these cues, others might be added: right side lie, left side lie, squat, long sit, and so on.

Obstacle or Challenge Courses

Perhaps no activity is as popular with elementary school pupils as following a leader through an obstacle course. Apparatus for these courses can be purchased commercially or constructed by teachers and parents. Homemade obstacle courses are often built around a theme. Assigning pieces of equipment novel names creates the mood for themes built around space travel, a jungle trek, a western outpost, or an Indian village.

Seldom is a class small enough that all students can move through an obstacle course simultaneously. Congestion and confusion should be prevented by assigning not more than two students to each piece of apparatus and by having them stand at their assigned apparatus while awaiting the signal *go* rather than all standing in a file behind the leader. Thus, only 14 students can move efficiently through a seven-piece obstacle course at any given time. The flexible teacher will post a time schedule listing each student's name and stating the time at which he or she is excused from regular class activities to go through the obstacle course.

Learning Activities

1. Develop a slide presentation, flannel board talk, videotape, or film designed to instruct the lay person on the specific components of fitness. Use it with at least one group.

2. Make a tape recording or write a paper elaborating upon the meaning of "Fitness for What?" as it pertains to you personally.

3. Experiment with the concept of level of aspiration by recording the scores you think you will make on several fitness tests, taking the tests and recording your actual scores, and subtracting to obtain your discrepancy scores. Read some research studies on level of aspiration, particularly as it relates to self-concept.

4. Decide which is your favorite test for each of the components of fitness. State the criteria for your decision.

5. Learn to take pulse rate and blood pressure. Practice recording these parameters before and after various kinds of exercises.

6. Administer each of the tests described in this chapter to at least five persons. Combine their scores with those collected by your classmates for the same age range and sex. Compute the mean, median, and standard deviation.

7. Select a person with low fitness and write an exercise prescription of several weeks' duration to meet the person's special needs.

8. Conduct a mini-lesson demonstrating your understanding of three of the training techniques described in this chapter.

References

Bruininks, R. (1974). Physical and motor development of retarded persons. In N. R. Ellis (Ed.), *International Review of Research in Mental Retardation.* (pp. 209–261). New York: Academic Press.

Colemen, A. E., Ayoub, M., & Fredrich, D. (1976). Assessment of physical work capacity of institutionalized mentally retarded males. *American Journal of Mental Deficiency, 80,* 629–635.

Cooper, K. (1968). *Aerobics.* New York: M. Evans Co., Inc.

Corbin, C. (1980). *A textbook of motor development* (2nd ed.). Dubuque, IA: Wm. C. Brown.

Rarick, L. (1980). Cognitive-motor relationships in the growing years. *Research Quarterly, 51,* 180–181.

Rimmer, J., & Rosentswieg, J. (1982). The physical working capacity of learning disabled children. *American Corrective Therapy Journal, 36,* 133–134.

Roswal, G. M., Dunleavy, A., & Roswal, P. (1985). Normative health related fitness data for Special Olympians. In C. Sherrill (Ed.), *Sport and disabled athletes* (pp. 231–238). Champaign, IL: Human Kinetics Publishers. For several privately printed books concerning tests and norms, contact Dr. Glenn Roswal, Department of HPERD, Jacksonville State University, Jacksonville, AL 36265.

Bibliography

Allen, J. (1980). Jogging can modify disruptive behaviors. *Teaching Exceptional Children, 12,* 66–70.

American Alliance for Health, Physical Education, and Recreation. (1976). *AAHPER youth fitness test manual.* Washington, DC: Author.

American Alliance for Health, Physical Education, and Recreation. (1976). *Special fitness test manual for the mildly mentally retarded.* (2nd ed.). Washington, DC: Author. First edition, 1968.

American Alliance for Health, Physical Education, Recreation, and Dance. (1980). *Health related physical fitness test manual.* Washington, DC: Author.

American College of Sports Medicine (Ed.). (1980). *Guidelines for graded exercise testing and exercise prescription* (2nd ed.). Philadelphia: Lea & Febiger.

Astrand, P., & Rodahl, C. (1977). *Textbook of work physiology.* New York: McGraw-Hill.

Bar-Or, Oded (1983). *Pediatric sports medicine for the practitioner.* New York: Springer-Verlag.

Buell, C. (1973). AAHPER youth fitness test adaptation for the blind. In *Physical education and recreation for the visually handicapped.* Washington, DC: American Alliance for Health, Physical Education, and Recreation.

Cooper, K. (1982). *The aerobics program for total well-being: Exercise-diet-emotional balance.* New York: M. Evans & Co., Inc.

Corbin, C., Dowell, L., Lindsey, R., & Tolson, H. (1978). *Concepts in physical education* (3rd ed.). Dubuque, IA: Wm. C. Brown.

Cox, R., & Nelson, J. (Eds.). (1980). *Symposium papers: Exercise physiology—exercise and heart disease and analysis of body composition.* Washington, DC: American Alliance for Health, Physical Education, and Recreation Research Consortium.

Cundiff, D. (Ed.). (1979). *Implementation of aerobic programs.* Washington, DC: American Alliance for Health, Physical Education, Recreation, and Dance.

Davis, G., Kofsky, P., Kelsy, J., & Shephard, R. (1981). Cardiorespiratory fitness and muscular strength of wheelchair users. *Canadian Medical Association Journal, 125* (12), 1317–1323.

deVries, H. (1980). *Physiology of exercise* (3rd ed.). Dubuque, IA: Wm. C. Brown.

Falls, H. (1980). Modern concepts of fitness. *Journal of Physical Education and Recreation, 51,* 25–27.

Falls, H., Baylor, A., & Dishman, R. (1980). *Essentials of fitness.* New York: Saunders College/Holt, Rinehart & Winston.

Fleishman, E. A. (1964). *The structure and measurement of physical fitness.* Englewood Cliffs, NJ: Prentice-Hall.

Godfrey, S. (1974). *Exercise testing in children.* Philadelphia: W. B. Saunders.

Hayden, F. J. (1964). *Physical fitness for the mentally retarded.* Ontario: Toronto Association for Retarded Children.

Jackson, A., & Coleman, E. A. (1976). Validation of distance runs for elementary school children. *Research Quarterly, 47,* 86–94.

Johnson, L., & Londeree, B. (1976). *Motor fitness testing manual for the moderately mentally retarded.* Washington, DC: American Alliance for Health, Physical Education, and Recreation.

Johnson, W., & Buskirk, E. (Eds.). (1974). *Science and medicine of exercise and sport* (2nd ed.). New York: Harper & Row.

Katch, F., & McArdle, W. (1977). *Nutrition, weight control, and exercise.* Boston: Houghton Mifflin.

Londeree, B., & Johnson, L. (1974). Motor fitness of TMR vs. EMR and normal children. *Medicine and Science in Sports, 6,* 247–252.

Marmis, C., Montoye, H. J., Cunningham, D. A., & Kozar, A. J. (1977). Reliability of the multi-trial items of the AAHPER youth fitness test. *Research Quarterly, 40,* 240–245.

Miller, D., & Allen, T. E. (1979). *Fitness: A lifetime commitment.* Minneapolis: Burgess.

Pollock, M., Miller, H. S., Linnerud, A. C., Laughridge, E., Coleman, E., & Alexander, E. (1974). Arm pedaling as an endurance training regimen for the disabled. *Archives of Physical Medicine Rehabilitation, 55,* 418–424.

Pollock, M., Wilmore, J. H., & Fox, S. M. (1978). *Health and fitness through physical activity.* New York: John Wiley & Sons.

Rarick, G. L., Widdop, J. H., & Broadhead, G. (1970). The physical fitness and motor performance of educable mentally retarded children. *Exceptional Children, 36,* 509–519.

Sharkey, B. (1979). *Physiology of fitness.* Champaign, IL: Human Kinetics Publishers.

Sorani, R. (1966). *Circuit training.* Dubuque, IA: Wm. C. Brown.

Sorensen, J. (1979). *Aerobic dancing.* New York: Rawson, Wade.

Stein, J. (1985). Physical fitness of children and youth with handicapping conditions. *Adapted Physical Activity Quarterly, 2* (1), 1–7.

Tu, J., & Rothstein, A. (1979). Improvement of jogging performance through application of personality specific motivational techniques. *Research Quarterly, 50,* 97–103.

Wilmore, J. (1976). *Athletic training and physical fitness.* Boston: Allyn & Bacon.

Winnick, J., & Short, F. (1984). The physical fitness of youngsters with spinal neuromuscular conditions. *Adapted Physical Activity Quarterly 1,* (1), 37–51.

Winnick, J., & Short, F. (1984). Test item selection for the Project UNIQUE physical fitness test. *Adapted Physical Activity Quarterly 1* (4), 296–314.

Winnick, J., & Short, F. (1985). *Physical fitness testing of the disabled: Project UNIQUE.* Champaign, IL: Human Kinetics Publishers.

Note: For research concerning fitness and specific handicapping conditions, see Bibliographies of chapters in Part 3 of this text.

14 Relaxation and Reduction of Hyperactivity

Figure 14.1 Concentrating on body parts.

Chapter Objectives

After you have studied this chapter, you should be able to

1. Describe assessment techniques for determining hypertension.
2. In mini-teaching lessons, demonstrate ability to use the following approaches to teaching relaxation: imagery, deep body awareness, Jacobsen techniques, static stretching exercises, yoga, and Tai Chi.
3. State behavioral objectives for relaxation training and indicate a method of evaluating whether these objectives are being met.

Instruction and practice in relaxation are integral parts of a comprehensive adapted physical education program. Relaxation instruction is sometimes combined with body image training, particularly with young students (see Figure 14.1). Children must be able to recognize body parts before relaxation of body parts can be learned. Relaxation, defined physiologically, is a neuromuscular accomplishment that results in a reduction of muscular tension. Tension is the amount of electrical activity present in a muscle. The shortening of muscle fibers is attended by an increase of electrical voltage. Shortening, contracting, and tightening are synonyms in the sense that each implies increased muscle tension. The release of tension within a muscle is attended by a decrease of electrical voltage, which is expressed in microvolts or millivolts. Complete muscle relaxation is characterized by electrical silence—i.e., zero action potentials.

Neuromuscular tension is a positive attribute. No movement can occur without the development of tension in the appropriate muscle groups. Unfortunately, however, many persons maintain more muscles in a state of tension than is necessary for the accomplishment of motor tasks. Such excessive neuromuscular tension is known as *hypertension,* not to be confused with arterial hypertension. The purpose of relaxation training is to prevent or reduce hypertension.

Not all persons need relaxation training. Individual differences in tension should be assessed, and only students who exhibit abnormal signs should be assigned to relaxation and slowing down activities in lieu of the vigorous activities that traditionally comprise the program.

Signs of Hypertension

Excessive neuromuscular hypertension is identified by the presence of certain signs.

Hyperactivity: Inability to remain motionless for set period of time; wriggles in chair; shifts arm or leg; plays with hair; scratches, rubs or picks at skin; makes noises with feet; drums fingers on desk top or doodles with pen; chews gum, pencil, or fingernails; fails to keep place in line or any set formation.

Facial expression: Lines in face seldom disappear; eyes frequently shift focus; lips quiver or seem abnormally tight; cheek muscles show tension; immobile expression, such as frozen smile or incessant frown; eye tic.

Breathing: Unconscious breath holding; shallow, irregular breaths; hyperventilation.

Skin: Nervous perspiration; irritations caused by picking; hives, eczema.

Voice: Two opposite patterns, the more common of which is talking too much, louder than usual, faster than usual, and with higher pitch; deep sighs indicating excessive respiratory tension; crying.

These signs are characteristic of persons on the verge of emotional breakdowns, but they also appear in times of great stress such as final examination period, death or severe illness in family, impending divorce of parents, and/or incessant bickering among family members. Certain prescribed drugs, such as diet pills, and also those consumed illegally, result in overt signs of hyperactivity. Constant physical pain or discomfort is sometimes evidenced in signs of hypertension.

When the problems causing hypertension are not resolved over long periods of time, the sufferers slip into a state of *chronic fatigue*. They often experience insomnia. When they do sleep, they typically awake unrested. Symptoms of chronic fatigue are (a) increase of tendon reflexes; (b) increase of muscle excitability; (c) spastic condition of smooth muscles exhibited in diarrhea and stomach upsets; (d) abnormal excitability of heart and respiratory apparatus; (e) tremors; (f) restlessness; and (g) irritability. In this stage, many persons seek the help of a physician; generally they complain of feeling tired all of the time. They know they are not really sick, but neither do they feel well.

Hypertension in Children

In the past, hypertension has been associated more with adults than children. It is now recognized that many hyperactive youngsters, especially those with learning disabilities, exhibit signs of neuromuscular hypertension that can be ameliorated through relaxation training. Likewise, many essentially *normal* persons are simply highstrung just as others are slow moving and easy going. Levels of hypertension seem to be largely determined by heredity and reinforced by the environment.

Pupils who need training in tension reduction may feel guilty about the hypertension, particularly if they have been led to believe that they are different from others in the household. Many children deny that they feel tense. Others, accustomed to hypertension, do not realize that conditions of less tension exist.

Testing for Excess Tension

Awareness of residual hypertension can be developed by instructing pupils to lie on their backs and release all tensions. The teacher lifts one body part at a time and then lets go. The degree of hypertonus present is recorded as *negative, slight, medium,* or *marked* on the right and left sides for the muscles of the wrist, elbow, shoulder, ankle, knee, hip, and neck. Hypertonus is detected by such *unconscious* muscular responses as

1. Assistance: student assists teacher in lifting the body part.
2. Posturing or set: student resists gravity when teacher removes support.

3. Resistance: student tenses or resists the action of the teacher in lifting the body part.
4. Perseveration: student continues a movement after the teacher starts it.

The presence of residual hypertension can be assessed also through electromyography. It is now being used in several programs of relaxation therapy for children with learning disabilities. The electromyometer, like any electromyographical apparatus, records the amount of electrical activity present in the muscle fibers. Biofeedback in the form of sound and a digital readout reinforces attempts to reduce tension, making the apparatus effective both as a teaching and an evaluation device.

Teaching Relaxation

Techniques of teaching relaxation vary with the age group, the nature of the handicapping condition, and the number of class sessions to be spent. Each of the techniques described in this section aims at lowering the tension, i.e., the electrical activity of skeletal muscles. With the exception of the Jacobson techniques, few have been subjected to scientific research. Although their effectiveness may not be substantiated statistically, the various techniques each have strong proponents and seem worthy of exploration. Imagery, deep body awareness, the Jacobson techniques, static stretching exercises, yoga, and Tai Chi are considered. Breathing exercises are also important in relaxation training.

Imagery

The *imagery* (see Figure 14.2) or ideational approach is well received in the primary grades. Poems and short stories are excellent to help children become rag dolls flopping, ice cream melting, merry-go-rounds stopping, balloons slowly deflating, icicles melting, faucets dripping, salt pouring from a shaker, bubbles getting smaller, and snowflakes drifting downward. For greatest effectiveness, the children must be drawn into discussions of what relaxes them and be encouraged to make up their own stories and poems. It is also enlightening to ask children to develop lists of their favorite *quiet* things and *slow* activities. Focus may be directed toward enacting things that start out fast, gradually decrease in speed, and eventually become motionless.

Illustrative of some ideational approaches used to elicit relaxed movements follow:

You are a soft calico kitten lying in front of the warm fireplace. The fire is warm. You feel so-o-o good. First you stretch your right arm—oh, that feels good. Then you stretch your left arm. Then you stretch both legs. Now you are relaxed all

over. The fire is so warm and your body feels so relaxed. This must be the best place in the whole world—your own little blanket in front of your own fire. You are so-o-o relaxed that you could fall asleep right now. You are getting sleepy now—maybe you will fall asleep now.

You are the tail of a kite that is sailing gently high, oh so-o-o high in the light blue sky. The kite goes higher and so do you—very slowly and very gently in the soft breeze. Now you are going to the right. Oh the breeze is warm and ooh so soft—it is blowing so gently that you can feel it only if you think real hard. Can you feel the soft, warm breeze blowing you to the left? It is so-o-o gentle and so-o-o soft.

You are becoming a puppet. The change starts in your feet. Slowly each part of your body becomes lifeless and is completely relaxed, as if it were detached from you.

Let's make believe we are a bowl full of jello! Someone has left us out of the refrigerator and we begin to dissolve slowly away. Our arms float down and our body sinks slowly into the bowl.

Older children, no longer able to assume magically the feeling-tone of an animal or object, continue to find relaxation in the mood of certain poems and stories read aloud. They may lie in comfortable positions in a semidarkened room while listening and attempt to capture the essence of the words through consciously releasing tensions. Instrumental music may be substituted for reading if the group desires.

Deep Body Awareness

To facilitate deep body awareness, the teacher begins the class with everyone in a comfortable supine position (see Figure 14.3). The teacher then directs everyone's attention to specific parts of the body, asking them to analyze and verbalize the sensations they are experiencing. If pupils seem reluctant to share aloud their feelings, the teacher may offer such additional guidance as

1. Which parts of your arm are touching the floor? Is the floor warm or cool, smooth or rough, clean or dirty?

2. How long is your arm from the tip of the middle finger to shoulder joint? From tip of the middle finger to elbow? From tip of the middle finger to wrist crease? How heavy is your arm? How heavy is each of its parts?

3. Can you feel the muscles loosening? If you measured the circumference of your upper arm, how many inches would you get?

Figure 14.3 Two Down's syndrome girls participate in a deep body awareness relaxation activity at the close of their physical education class. This constitutes a "cool-down" time to help them make the transition from strenuous motor work to quiet academic learning.

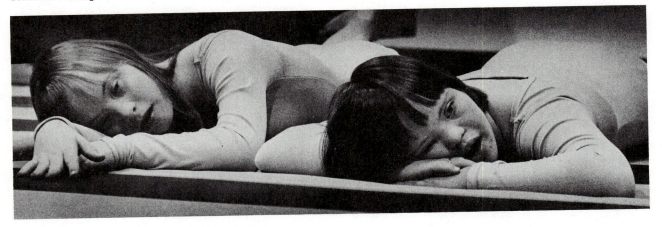

4. Can you feel the blood pulsating in veins and arteries?

5. Can you feel the hairs on your arm? The creases in your wrist? The finger nails? The cuticles? Any scars?

6. What other words come to mind when you think about *arm*?

The underlying premise in deep body awareness is that pupils must increase kinesthetic sensitivity before they can consciously control it. They must differentiate between parts of a whole and be able to describe these parts accurately. As deep body awareness is developed, each pupil discovers which thoughts and methods of releasing tension work best for him or her personally.

Jacobson Techniques

Most widely known of the techniques of neuromuscular relaxation are those of Edmund Jacobson, a physician and physiologist who began his research in tension control at Harvard University in 1918. His first two books, *Progressive Relaxation* and *You Must Relax,* were published in 1920 and 1934, respectively. Jacobson's work had a profound influence on Josephine Rathbone, the foremost pioneer in corrective physical education, who taught relaxation as an integral part of correctives (see Rathbone's books in bibliography; they continue to be excellent primary sources).

Jacobson's techniques, known originally as a system of *progressive conscious neuromuscular relaxation,* are referred to as *self-operations control* in his later books (see bibliography). The progression of activities is essentially the same. He suggests three steps

for learning to recognize the sensations of *doing* and *not doing* in any specific muscle group: (a) tension followed by relaxation against an outside resistance such as the teacher pushing downward on a limb that the student is trying to lift; (b) tension within the muscle group when no outside resistance is offered, followed by release of the tension; and (c) release of tension in a resting muscle group that has not been contracted.

Jacobson recommends that relaxation training begin in a supine position with arms at the sides, palms facing downward. The mastery of *differential control* of one muscle group at a time begins with hyperextension at the wrist joint only. All other joints in the body remain relaxed while the pupil concentrates on bending the hand backward. The resulting tension is felt in the back upper part of the forearm.

Self-operations control outlined by Jacobson is a slow procedure. Each class session is 1 hour long. During that time a particular tension, like hyperextension of the wrist, is practiced only three times. The tension (also called the control sensation) is held 1 to 2 minutes, after which the pupil is told to *go negative* or completely relax for 3 to 4 minutes. After the completion of three of these tension and relaxation sequences, the pupil lies quietly with eyes closed for the remainder of the hour. Session 2 follows the same pattern except that the tension practiced is bending the wrist forward so as to tense the anterior muscles of the forearm. Every third session is called a zero period in that no tension is practiced. The entire body is relaxed the whole time.

In all, seven sessions are recommended for learning to relax the left arm. During the fourth session the tension created by bending the elbow about 35° is practiced. During the fifth session the tension created in the back part of the upper arm when the palm presses downward against a stack of books is practiced. The sixth session is a zero period. The seventh session calls for progressive tension and relaxation of the whole arm.

Detailed instructions are given for proceeding from one muscle group to the next. The completion of an entire course in relaxation in the supine position requires the following amount of time: left arm, 7 days; right arm, 7 days; left leg, 10 days; right leg, 10 days; trunk, 10 days; neck, 6 days; eye region, 12 days; visualization, 9 days; and speech region, 19 days. Then the same order and same duration of practices are followed in the sitting position. While Jacobson indicates that the course can be speeded up, he emphasizes that less thoroughness results in reduced ability to recognize tension signals and turn them off.

Static Stretching Exercises

To illustrate the efficacy of static stretching, try these experiments, holding each position for 60 or more seconds.

1. Let the head drop forward as far as it will go. Hold this position and feel the stretch on the neck extensors.
2. Let the body bend at the waist as in touching the toes. When the fingertips touch the floor, hold, and feel the stretch in the back extensors and hamstrings.
3. Do a side bend to the left and hold.
4. Lie supine on a narrow bench and let your head hang over the edge.
5. Lie on a narrow bench and let the arms hang down motionless in space. They should not be able to touch the ground.

When the pupil learns to release tension in these static positions, relaxation is achieved. Yoga, because it is based upon such static stretching, is often included in instructional units on relaxation.

Yoga

Yoga is a system of physical, mental, and spiritual development that comes from India, where it dates back several centuries before Christ. The word *yoga* is derived from the Sanskrit root *yuji,* which means to join or bind together. Scholars recognize several branches of yoga, but in the United States the term is used popularly to refer to a system of exercises built upon held positions or postures and breath control. More correctly, we should say *Hatha Yoga* rather than yoga when teaching aspects of this system to our students. In the word *Hatha,* the *ha* represents the sun (expression of energy) and the *tha* represents the moon (conservation of energy). In yoga exercises, these two are always interacting.

Hatha Yoga offers exercises particularly effective in teaching relaxation and slowing down the hyperactive child. The emphasis upon correct breathing in Hatha Yoga makes it especially valuable in the reconditioning of persons with asthma and other respiratory problems. Moreover, the nature of Hatha Yoga is such that it appeals to individuals whose health status prohibits participation in vigorous, strenuous physical activities.

Hatha Yoga, hereafter referred to as yoga, can be subdivided into two types of exercises: *asanas* and *pranayanas.* Asanas are held positions or postures like the lotus, the locust, and cobra poses. Pranayanas are breathing exercises. In actuality, asanas and pranayanas are interrelated since correct breathing is emphasized throughout the assumption of a particular pose. Several of the asanas are identical or similar to stunts taught in elementary school physical education. The yoga *bent bow* is the same as the human rocker. The *cobra* is similar to the swan and/or the trunk lift from a prone position to test back strength. The *plough pose* resembles the paint-the-rainbow stunt.

Differences between yoga and physical exercise as it is ordinarily taught are

1. Exercise sessions traditionally emphasize movement. *Yoga is exercise without movement.*
2. Exercises usually involve several bounces or stretches, with emphasis upon how many can be done. Yoga stresses a *single, slow* contraction of certain muscles followed by a general relaxation. Generally, an asana is not repeated. At the very most, it might be attempted two or three times.
3. Exercises usually entail some pain and discomfort since the teaching progression conforms to the overload principle. In yoga, the number of repetitions is not increased. The duration of time for which the asana is held increases in accordance with ease of performance.
4. Exercises ordinarily stress the development of strength, flexibility, and endurance. Yoga stresses relaxation, balance, and self-control.

In summary,

The gymnast's object is to make his body strong and healthy, with well-developed muscles, a broad chest, and powerful arms. The yogi will get more or less the same results; but they are not what he is looking for.

He is looking for calm, peace, the remedy for fatigue; or, better still, a certain immunity to fatigue.

He wants to quiet some inclination or other of his, his tendency to anger, or impatience—signs of disturbance in his organic or psychical life. He wants a full life, a more abundant life, but a life of which he is the master. (Dechanet, 1965, p. 18)

Tai Chi

Tai Chi Chuan, pronounced *tie jee chwahn* and called Tai Chi for short, is one of the many slowing-down activities found to be successful with hyperactive children. An ancient Chinese system of exercise, it is practiced by an increasing number of adults in the United States. In large metropolitan areas on the east and west coasts, instruction from masters, usually listed in the telephone directory, is available. Tai Chi is used by many dance therapists.

Tai Chi is a series of 108 specific learned patterns of movements called *forms* that provide exercise for every part of the body. The forms have colorful names which tend to captivate children: Grasp Bird's Tail Right, Stork Spreads Wings, Carry Tiger to Mountain, Step Back and Repulse Monkey, Needle at Sea Bottom, High Pat on Horse, Parting with Wild Horse's Mane Right. The 108 forms are based upon 37 basic movements; thus, there is much repetition in the execution of a series of forms.

Tai Chi is characterized by extreme slowness, a concentrated awareness of what one is doing, and absolute continuity of movement from one form to another. The same tempo is maintained throughout, but no musical accompaniment is provided. All movements contain circles, reinforcing the concepts of uninterrupted flow and quiet continuity. All body parts are gently curved or bent, allowing the body to give into gravity rather than working against it, as is the usual practice in western culture. No posture or pose is ever held. As each form is approximately completed, its movement begins to melt and blend into the next form. This has been likened to the cycle of seasons when summer blends into autumn and autumn into winter.

Although instruction by a master is desirable, Tai Chi is simple enough that it can be learned from a pictorial text. Movements can be memorized by repeatedly performing forms 1 to 20 in the same order without interruption. One form should never be practiced in isolation from others. Later, forms 21 to 57 are learned as a unity as well as forms 58 to 108. This approach is especially beneficial for children who need practice in visual perception, matching, and sequencing. Its greatest strength, however, lies in the principle of slowness. Each time the sequence of forms is done, day after day, year after year, the goal is to perform it more slowly than before.

For persons who feel disinclined to memorize and teach preestablished forms, the essence of Tai Chi can be captured by restructuring class calisthenics as a follow-the-leader experience in which flowing, circular movements are reproduced as slowly as possible without breaking the continuity of the sequence. For real relaxation to occur, the same sequence must be repeated daily.

Suggestions for Reducing Hyperactivity

The etiology of hyperactivity is generally unknown. An accepted behavioral characteristic of many brain-injured children, it is manifested also by many children with no known handicaps. One has only to observe a new litter of kittens or puppies to note substantial differences in levels of activity, energy, and aggressiveness. What keeps children keyed up? How can hyperactivity be channeled into productivity? How can hyperactivity be reduced?

A common misconception is the belief that regular physical education provides an outlet for releasing excessive nervous tensions and letting off steam. This may be true on some days for a few of the better coordinated youngsters who find satisfaction in large motor activities. It is not a valid supposition when physical education is an instructional setting in which pupils are introduced daily to new learning activities. Hyperactive children have just as much trouble listening to the physical educator and conforming to the structure of the play setting as they experience in the classroom. The mastery of a new motor skill, or even the practice of an old one, is no more relaxing than reading or learning to play the piano.

Once a skill is refined and is performed without conscious thought, it can become a channel for releasing tensions. Simple repetitive activities like jogging and swimming laps may serve this purpose for some individuals, just as knitting, gardening, or playing the piano is soothing to others. A good physical education program, however, devotes little of its time allotment to such repetitive activities. *Letting off steam* simply is not an objective of the regular physical education program.

Hyperactive children need vigorous physical activity, as do all pupils. Whereas normal children typically make the transition from play to classroom work without special help, hyperactive children require a longer period of time and assistance in making the adjustment. *This is not a reason for excusing them from physical education.* It does call for recognition of individual differences and the availability of a quiet, semidark area where children can lie down and practice the relaxation techniques they have been taught before they return to the classroom. Large cardboard boxes that children can creep into and hide are recommended for the primary grades. When a place free from noise cannot be found, earphones with music or a soothing voice giving relaxation instruction can be used to block out distractions. The use of this quiet space should not be limited to a particular time of day or to certain children. All persons, at one time or another, need a retreat where they can go of their own accord, relax, and regain self-control.

If several children appear to be especially hyperactive during a physical education period, the teacher should end the vigorous activity early and devote the last 10 minutes or so to relaxation training. Changes of weather, particularly the onset of rain, seem to heighten neuromuscular tensions. Examinations, special events, and crises carried by the news media may have pupils so keyed up that the best physical education for the entire class is rest and relaxation. Certainly physical educators should ask themselves at the beginning of each period, "Do the pupils need slowing down or speeding up? Is any one child especially keyed up? Which activity can that child be guided into before a discipline problem occurs?"

Hyperactivity can be reduced only if the causes are eliminated. The following adaptations seem to help the hyperactive child retain self-control in the activity setting.

1. Decrease the space. If outdoors, rope off boundaries. If indoors, use partitions.

2. Decrease the noise by arranging for smaller classes and using yarn balls and beanbags rather than rubber ones. Use verbal stop and start signals instead of a whistle. Do not tell the children to be quiet; inhibiting their natural inclination to shout, run, jump, and throw only raises tension levels.

3. Structure the activities so that the children do not have to wait in lines and take turns. Good physical education implies maximal involvement of all the children all the time. Each pupil should have his or her own ball, rope, or piece of apparatus.

4. Designate certain spaces such as learning stations and use the same direction of rotation each period. If necessary, rope or partition off these stations to minimize distractions.

5. Deemphasize speed by stressing accuracy and self-control.

6. Avoid speed tests. This approach necessitates a whole new look at measurement and evaluation in physical education. On a paper-pencil test, do not count questions that are not answered as wrong. Instead, send the child home with a similar test and instruction to repeatedly practice taking it until he or she can answer all questions accurately within a set time limit. This may require 10 trials for some children and 50 for others. Learning to cope with speed tests, however, should take place in a nonthreatening situation.

7. Avoid relays based upon the team or individual who can finish the fastest. Instead, experiment with different concepts: Who can go the slowest? Who can use the most interesting movement pattern? Who can be the most graceful? Who can be the most original? Who can create the funniest movement pattern?

8. Build in success. Even a hyperactive child will remain motionless to hear himself or herself praised. Much of the residual neuromuscular tension that characterizes certain children stems from failure and fear of failure. After success in a new motor skill has been achieved, stop the pupil while he or she feels positive about the effort and direct attention to something new.

Learning Activities

1. Observe several children in classroom and physical education settings, and compare signs of hypertension present in each.

2. Visit a day care center or residential facility for the mentally ill and observe signs of hypertension in the patients. If relaxation training or dance therapy is provided for the patients, arrange to observe sessions.

3. Conduct at least two mini-lessons in which you demonstrate your competence in teaching such relaxation techniques as imagery, deep body awareness, Jacobson self-operations control.

References

Dechanet, J. M. (1965). *Yoga in ten lessons.* New York: Cornerstone Library.

Bibliography

Anneberg, L. (1977). *A study of the effect of different relaxation techniques on tactile deficient and tactile defensive children.* Unpublished master's thesis, University of Kansas, Lawrence.

Belcher, V. (1980). *Anxiety and tension reduction in movement therapy with short-term hospitalized psychiatric patients.* Unpublished master's thesis, Loyola Marymount University.

Benson, H. (1975). *The relaxation response.* New York: Avon Books.

Bernstein, D. A., & Borkevec, T. D. (1973). *Progressive relaxation: A manual for therapists.* Champaign, IL: Research Press.

Bhatara, V. L., Arnold, E., Lorance, T., & Gupta, D. (1979). Muscle relaxation therapy in hyperkinesis: Is it effective? *Journal of Learning Disabilities, 12,* 182.

Brena, S. F. (1971). *Yoga and medicine.* New York: Julian Press.

Carter, J., Lax, B., & Russell, H. (1979). Effects of relaxation and EMG training on academic achievement of educable mentally retarded boys. *Education and Training of Mental Retardation, 14,* 39–41.

Cautela, J., & Groden, J. (1978). *Relaxation: A comprehensive manual for adults, children, and children with special needs.* Champaign, IL: Research Press.

Cole, E. (1978). *Swimming and hyperactivity: The influence of water temperatures.* Unpublished master's thesis, Texas Woman's University, Denton.

Cratty, B. J. (1972). *Physical expressions of intelligence.* Englewood Cliffs, NJ: Prentice-Hall.

Frederick, A. B. (1979). *Relaxation: Education's fourth R.* Washington, DC: ERIC Clearinghouse on Teacher Education.

Gail, L. (1978). *Relaxation in expressive therapies and movement therapy: A focusing and socialization process.* Unpublished master's thesis, Lesley College.

Girdano, D., & Everly, G. (1979). *Controlling stress and tension: A holistic approach.* Englewood Cliffs, NJ: Prentice-Hall.

Goldstein, K. (1978). *T'ai Chi Ch'uan: A related form of dance/movement therapy.* Unpublished master's thesis, Lesley College.

Harvey, J. R. (1979). The potential of relaxation training for the mentally retarded. *Mental Retardation, 17,* 71–76.

Herman, P. (1980). *The effects of yoga on the development of kinesthesis of preschool children.* Unpublished master's thesis, University of Kansas, Lawrence.

Hittleman, R. (1969). *Introduction to yoga.* New York: Bantam Books.

Hopkins, L. J., & Hopkins, J. T. (1976). Yoga in psychomotor training. *Academic Therapy, 11,* 461–464.

Jacobson, E. (1970). *Modern treatment of tense patients.* Springfield, IL: Charles C. Thomas.

Klein, S. A., & Deffenbacher, J. L. (1977). Relaxation and exercise for hyperactive impulsive children. *Perceptual and Motor Skills, 45,* 1159–1162.

Koeppen, A. S. (1974). Relaxation training for children. *Elementary School Guidance and Counseling, 9,* 14–21.

Maisel, E. (1972). *Tai Chi for health.* New York: Holt, Rinehart, & Winston.

Rathbone, J. (1969). *Relaxation.* Philadelphia: Lea & Febiger.

Rathbone, J., & Hunt, V. (1965). *Corrective physical education* (7th ed.). Philadelphia: W. B. Saunders.

Steinhaus, A. (1964). Facts and theories of neuromuscular relaxation. *Quest* (Monograph III), 3–14.

Tegner, B. (1973). *Kung fu and Tai Chi: Chinese karate.* Ventura, CA: Thor Publishing Co.

15 Dance Therapy and Adapted Dance

with coauthor Wynelle Delaney, DTR

Figure 15.1 Anne Riordan, chairperson of Programs for the Handicapped for the National Dance Association, AAHPERD, demonstrates modern dance skills and creative compositional abilities of severely mentally retarded adolescents and physically disabled persons.

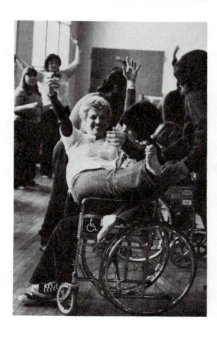

Chapter Objectives

After you have studied this chapter, you should be able to

1. Discuss the similarities and differences between dance therapy and adapted dance.
2. State guidelines for children's dance and apply them in planning an adapted dance program (as one-third of their regular physical education programming) for selected handicapped children.
3. Develop behavioral objectives for adapted dance and indicate a method of evaluating whether these objectives are being met.
4. Explain Sherrill's theoretical model of dance and indicate how each level contributes to development in the affective domain.
5. Develop modules or mini-lessons that show your understanding of rhythmic body action, spontaneous dance, dramatic play-acting and character dancing, movement exploration, improvisation, creativity through dance, communication through dance, and dance as an art form.
6. Contrast the values of creative dance vs. singing games, folk dance, and square dance. Discuss each in relation to selected handicapping conditions.
7. Discuss the values of tap dance and how it can be adapted to all levels of severity.

One of the wonders of human movement, and specifically of the dance experience, is its changing, amorphous, and quick-silver nature. It is process, not permanent fixed product. The same is true of the child, a human changeling hung between his beginning and his becoming, suspended in his being for a very brief and special time. It is beautifully apparent that dance and the child are natural companions. If, as Merleau Ponty suggests, our bodies are our way of having a world, the child is busily at home in his own body forming and shaping his own world, its inner and outer hemispheres. He is making himself up as he goes along.

—Nancy W. Smith

Perhaps no part of the physical education curriculum is as important to the handicapped child as creative rhythmic movement boldly and imaginatively taught. It can be enjoyed by the nonambulatory in beds and wheelchairs, by other health-impaired persons who need mild range-of-motion exercise, and by the thousands of youngsters who find greater fulfillment in individual and dual activities than in team sports. Whereas much of physical education focuses upon cooperation, competition, and leadership-followership, creative dance offers opportunities for self-discovery and self-expression. It is axiomatic that children must understand and appreciate their bodies and their capacities for movement before they can cope with the external demands of the world. The additional barriers to self-understanding and self-acceptance imposed by a handicapping condition intensify the need for carefully guided nonthreatening movement experiences designed to preserve ego strength, increase trust, and encourage positive human relationships. Gesture, pantomime, dance, and dance-drama can substitute for verbal communication when children lack or mistrust words to express their feelings.

Distinction Between Adapted Dance and Dance Therapy

It is important to differentiate between dance as a therapeutic experience, dance therapy as a profession, and adapted dance. Prior to the formation of the American Dance Therapy Association, Incorporated, in 1966, little distinction between terms was made. Dance conducted with handicapped persons (whether the condition was physical or mental) was typically called dance therapy. Today the use of the term *dance therapy* is restricted to dance/movement conducted by persons who are registered as dance therapists with the American Dance Therapy Association, Incorporated (ADTA). In this sense, dance therapy is like physical therapy and occupational therapy. Dance specialists and others who are not registered therapists may use dance with handicapped populations and/or for therapeutic purposes, but they may not ethically describe their work as dance therapy. So what do we call dance designed to meet the educational and artistic needs of persons with special needs?

Adapted Dance/Dance for Handicapped

Adapted dance is a term appropriate to denote rhythmic movement instruction and/or experiences that are modified to meet the needs of persons who have significant learning, behavioral, or psychomotor problems that interfere with successful participation in programs of regular dance in education and art. *Adapt* means to make suitable, to adjust, to accommodate, or modify in accordance with needs. These needs may be developmental or environmental. Dance specialists may *adapt* curriculum content, instructional pedagogy, assessment and evaluation approaches, and physical environment; the essence of this process of adapting is personal creativity.

Adapted dance is a broader and more contemporary term than dance for the handicapped. Paralleling the definition of adapted physical education, adapted dance focuses upon the identification and remediation of problems within the psychomotor domain in individuals who need assistance in mainstream dance instruction and/or specially designed educational and artistic experiences. The use of adapted dance is not limited to handicapped persons, but encompasses such special populations as the aged, juvenile delinquents and criminals, substance abusers, pregnant women, and our nation's many obese and/or unfit citizens. It also provides specialized help for clumsy persons for whom dance instruction, in the presence of the graceful and the beautiful, is often a nightmare.

Adapted dance, like adapted physical education, is first and foremost an attitude that refuses to categorize human beings into special populations such as the aged or the mentally retarded and instead celebrates individual differences. *Adapted dance* is conceptualized especially for persons (whatever the reason) who are not comfortable and/or successful in the regular dance setting. The purpose of adapted dance, like adapted physical education, is to facilitate self-actualization, particularly as it relates to understanding and appreciation of the body and its capacity for movement. The resulting changes in psychomotor behavior eventually permit full or partial integration in regular dance as a joyous, fulfilling experience.

Adapted dance can be education, art, or recreation. It can also be therapeutic, but it is not therapy. The foremost pioneer in adapted dance, particularly in exploring its potential as a performing art, is Anne Riordan (see Figure 15.1), in the Modern Dance Department at the University of Utah (Fitt & Riordan, 1980). In a film titled *A Very Special Dance,* marketed by the National Dance Association, Riordan demonstrates dance as both education and art with disabled persons who are members of the performing group called SUNRISE.

Dance Therapy

The official ADTA definition of *dance therapy* is as follows:

Dance therapy is the psychotherapeutic use of movement as a process which furthers the emotional and physical integration of the individual. Dance therapy is distinguished from other utilizations of dance (for example, dance education) by its focus on the nonverbal aspects of behavior and its use of movement as the process for intervention. Adaptive, expressive, and communicative behaviors are all considered in treatment, with the expressed goal of integrating these behaviors with psychological aspects of the person. Dance therapy can function as a primary treatment modality or as an integral part of an overall treatment program. (American Dance Therapy Association, circa 1975)

This explanation stresses the use of dance/movement as nonverbal psychotherapy requiring a therapeutic contract between therapist and client. Thus, *dance therapy* is a specific treatment modality used in mental illness and emotional and behavioral problems. Dance therapy is not prescribed for other handicapping conditions (like mental retardation and orthopedic impairment) unless the individual has emotional problems that require nonverbal psychotherapy.

Adapted Dance in the Physical Education Curriculum

Dance is an integral part of physical education. As such, it must be given the same amount of time and emphasis in the curriculum as other program areas. Table 15.1 presents guidelines for children's dance.

The emphasis, at least for normal children, is clearly upon guided discovery and motor creativity. Most handicapped children can benefit from the same kinds of dance experiences as their peers. The exceptions are pupils whose educational prescriptions indicate that they cannot yet cope with freedom in a group setting or that they lack the mentality and/or readiness for problem solving. Children whose understanding of language is too inadequate to comprehend the verbal challenges of movement exploration fare best in simple, repetitive activities.

Inherent in the nature of singing games, folk and square dance, ballet, and tap dance is perceptual-motor training. The teaching style used is drill—i.e., demonstration-explanation-imitation. Success is largely dependent upon visual and auditory perception, memory

Table 15.1
Guidelines for Children's Dance

Movement-Centered Dance Activities

The following movement-centered activities are basic to children's dance development and, when adapted to age level, should form the major part of the dance curriculum from early through middle childhood and beyond. It is upon the success of these experiences, especially the first four, that satisfactory and satisfying dance learnings will depend.

Experiences evolving from the use of the movement elements of space, time, force, and the development of an awareness of sequential changes in body shape.

Movement exploration, improvisation, investigation, and invention, using dance ideas such as those evolving from experiences with movement elements, from imaginary and literary sources, from properties of various kinds, or from music and other types of sound accompaniment.

Experiences with movement that help to synchronize it with musical structure, such as pulse, accent, phrasing; the development of sensitivity to the quality of musical sounds and the ability to relate to them in many different ways.

Experiences with basic locomotor and nonlocomotor movements; making combinations of these movements; discovering and learning traditional dance steps.

The organizing of movement into dances of various complexities.

The relating of dance movement to other curriculum experiences, such as art, music, science, social studies, and language arts—wherever and whenever appropriate.

Of the many kinds of "learned" dances, certain ones help to motivate movement in early childhood. Some of these are known as action or movement songs, others as singing games or song dances. These should be included in a comprehensive dance curriculum.

Traditional folk dance patterns are best left for the middle childhood years, where they will be learned quickly and danced with satisfaction if based upon earlier learnings. Further experiences that might be included in the dance program for the middle childhood years are the following.

Experiences with movement, arrived at through exploration, that can be used to increase body strength, flexibility, and precision.

Experiences in ethnic and popular "fad" dance patterns.

Opportunities for performing dances for schoolmates other than regular classmates and possibly for outsiders, such as parents.

Sharing and reacting to other children's dances.

Audience-Centered Dance Activities

The following audience-centered experiences should expose the child to dance as a performing art, helping him or her to understand and appreciate its ramifications. Children of all ages can participate as an audience to their aesthetic and artistic advantage.

Seeing pictures and slides of dance.

Seeing films of concert dance artists.

Seeing and discussing lecture-demonstrations by professional and semiprofessional dancers, with active participation when possible.

Seeing concert or theatre dance programs appropriate to age level and experience.

Participating in other enriching experiences, such as dramatic performances, music concerts, museum exhibits, or book and science fairs.

for steps and sequences of steps, and the ability of the body to do what the mind wills. The elements of time, space, force, and flow are established by the instructions. Structure is reinforced by the tempo of the music, the formation in which the dancers stand, and the spatial relationships between couples. The emphasis is upon correct imitation rather than creative discovery. The pupil knows exactly what is expected of him or her and finds security in performing the same steps as everyone else. The competent teacher ensures success by breaking the parts of a dance down to a level commensurate with the students' skills. A dance for moderately and severely retarded children might involve nothing more than following the leader in the execution of simple rhythmic activities in an AB or ABA form. The nature of the dance experiences provided a child should depend upon his or her educational prescription (see Figure 15.1). Whenever possible, all the activities in Table 15.1 should be included.

Creative dance is a term used primarily in early childhood education and the elementary schools. It implies a movement exploration approach to self-discovery, creativity, and nonverbal communication. The instructional environment is one of problem solving; there is no demonstration and no imitation. The content is a variety of movement experiences through which the child learns to manipulate the elements of force, space, time, and flow. Since dance is independent of other art forms, these movement experiences do not necessarily involve music nor accompaniment to sounds. The concept of *rhythmic movement* in creative dance relates to the natural rhythm of the body and the universe and not to the ability to keep time with externally imposed accompaniment.

Creative dance is the first form of dance to which children should be exposed. It is probably more valuable in the curriculum of children with handicapping conditions than any other form. Like sports, creative dance can be individual, dual, or group, depending upon readiness to interact, trust, and share with others. Just as games are considered lead-up activities to regulation sports, creative dance can serve as the foundation for modern or contemporary dance.

Modern dance, also called contemporary dance, is one of the fine arts. It presupposes an understanding and appreciation of the body as a tool for self-expression and the ability to manipulate force, space, time, and flow in movement. Beginning courses in modern dance are replications of the content and experiences of *creative dance*. Once this background is gained, instruction in modern dance generally focuses upon the improvement of technique (movement skills) and/or choreography (creativity skills). Just as some persons engage in sports for the joy of moving, some pupils dance because it is inherently satisfying. Others, like highly skilled athletes, seek excellence in public performance.

Movement Elements

Both creative and modern dance focus upon the movement elements. Sally Fitt (Fitt & Riordan, 1980) has proposed an excellent model for relating movement elements to dance instruction for handicapped students. *The element of space* can be broken down into several factors:

1. Direction of body movement: right, left, forward, backward, sideward, up, down, in, out, over, under.
2. Level of movement: high, low, medium or of body position: lie, sit, squat, kneel, stand.
3. Dimension of movement: large, small, wide, narrow, tall, short.
4. Path of movement: direct (straight) or indirect (curved, zigzag, twisted, crooked).
5. Focus of eyes: constant, wandering, near, far, up, down, inward, outward.

The element of shape pertains to the different shapes that the body can assume. Dance therapists using the concepts of effort-shape devised by Rudolph Laban (1960) refer frequently to *shaping*. Developmentally, children are said to demonstrate *horizontal shaping* at ages 4 to 5; *vertical shaping* at ages 5 to 6; *sagittal shaping* at ages 6 to 7; two shaping combinations at ages 8 to 12; and three shaping combinations in adolescence and maturity.

1. *Horizontal shaping* is the ability to shape in the horizontal plane with widening and narrowing (spreading and enclosing) movements. The horizontal plane includes all rotatory movements—i.e., turning toward or away from a stimulus.
2. *Vertical shaping* is the ability to shape in the vertical plane with rising and sinking (ascending and descending) movements.
3. *Sagittal shaping* is the ability to shape in the sagittal plane with forward and backward (advancing and retreating) movements.

The element of time can be broken down into the following factors:

1. Tempo or rate of speed of movement: fast, slow, accelerating, decelerating.
2. Rhythm: even or uneven, referring to regularly or irregularly timed movements.

Table 15.2
Questions to Elicit Specific Behavioral Traits Through a Study of the Element of Space

I. Self-discovery
  A. *Space*
    1. Can you define space?
      a. Own inner, outer boundaries, top, bottom boundaries
      b. Others
      c. Shared
    2. Do you understand spatial factors as they relate to movement?
      a. Direction—Can you make your body go up, down, forward, backward, sideward?
      b. Level—Can you move through space on a low, medium, or high level?
      c. Dimension—How large a movement can you make with your arms?
      d. Path—Can you walk in a direct pathway? an indirect pathway?
      e. Focus—Can you maintain continuous focus with a moving object?
    3. Can you execute movements for traversing space?
  B. *Direction*
    1. What locomotor movements enable the body to go up and down?
      a. Jump?
      b. Hop?
      c. Leap?
    2. What locomotor movements can be used to go forward and backward?
      a. Animal walks?
      b. Human walk?
      c. Run?
      d. Jump?
      e. Hop?
      f. Gallop, skip?
      g. Leap?
      h. Schottische, polka, and the like?

  C. *Other spatial factors*
    1. Locomotor and nonlocomotor factors applied to each of spatial factors.
    2. Can you execute movements in each of the planes: horizontal, vertical, sagittal?
    3. Are you aware of specific joints and body parts in space?
II. Nonverbal communication
  A. *Movement*
    1. How can movement be used to show possession of space or of objects in space?
    2. Can you guess what space belongs to another by his or her movements?
    3. Can he or she guess the boundaries of your space?
    4. How might you show possession of space if you were
      a. Male or female lion with a litter of cubs?
      b. Softball player sharing the field with other players?
      c. Dog guarding a bone?
      d. Automobile driver on a busy freeway?
      e. Standing in line at a cafeteria?
    5. What kind of communication movements can you make when
      a. Someone invades your space?
      b. You wish to share your space with a friend?
      c. You wish to share the space of a stranger?
      d. You are frightened to explore a new space?
      e. You are depressed or lonely in your space?
  B. *Other factors*
    1. How does the color (hue) and lightness or darkness of a space affect your movements?
    2. How does the size of a space affect your feeling-tone and your movements?
    3. How does sound (noise or quiet) in a space affect your movements?
    4. How do you move if you are lost in space vs. confident of your directions?

The element of force (effort). Dance educators seem to prefer the term *force* to denote such qualities of movement as heavy, light, tensed, relaxed, strong, weak. Laban (1960) used the term *weight* defined as the measurable degree of strength used in the action. Dance therapists who adhere to effort-shape concepts prefer the term *effort,* which is defined as the way kinetic energy is expended in space, force, and time.

The element of flow is sometimes separated from force to describe free vs. bound movement. *Flow* also refers to the ease with which transitions are made from one movement sequence to another. The element of *flow* may be especially important in working with hyperactive, labile, or emotionally disturbed children since it can be associated with precise feeling states that lend insight into problems of self-control. Flow can be judged on a 7-point continuum ranging from hyperactive, uncontrolled, free, abandoned, exaggerated, and fluent at one extreme to inhibited, restrained, bound, repressed, tied-up, and overcautious at the other extreme.

In creative dance, activities are designed to give experience in the manipulation of these movement elements and their inherent factors. The term *creative dance* is somewhat of a misnomer if creativity is defined as fluency, flexibility, originality, and elaboration. Dance experiences may be shaped to contribute to self-discovery, nonverbal communication, or creativity. It is important that the educator emphasize one of these at a time rather than attempt to accomplish all objectives simultaneously. Tables 15.2 and 15.3 depict the vast differences in the movement problems to be solved under each objective.

Table 15.3
Questions to Facilitate Development of Motor Creativity

A. *Fluency*
   How many different ways can you move in space?
B. *Flexibility*
   1. Is your fluency all in one category or do you shift easily using all possible categories: direction, level, dimension, path, focus?
   2. Do you use different categories of locomotor movements, such as body upside down vs. right side up; body weight on one limb vs. two, three, or four limbs; and others?
C. *Originality*
   How many of your movements are novel in the sense that no one else thinks of them?
D. *Elaboration*
   1. Do you experiment with variations of locomotor movements, such as performing them with toes pointed in vs. toes pointed out?
   2. Do you embellish your movements with extra identifiable details?

E. *Risk taking*
   Do you have the courage to risk using your body in new ways in space?
F. *Complexity*
   Are you challenged to group movements together in new sequences, to experiment with various forms, to create an orderly composition out of chaos?
G. *Curiosity*
   Are you willing to devote time and energy to exploring all possible movement alternatives?
H. *Imagination*
   Do you have the power to visualize movement sequences beyond the limits of your performing ability?

Self-discovery aims at developing an understanding and appreciation of the body and its capabilities. The acquisition of information about movement elements, the development of language skills, and improved motor coordination are all implied as the pupil is guided toward the correct answer to each question. The emphasis, however, should be on the joy of movement and discovery of what the body can do, not on the acquisition of skills that can be measured and graded. It seems best to avoid grading children's early attempts at movement. The physical educator must remain ever aware that some handicapped children, particularly those with brain damage, have special problems in the perception and subsequent manipulation of space and time factors.

Children may understand and appreciate their bodies and derive great satisfaction from exploration of space but still be unable to use movement to convey their needs, wishes, feelings, and moods to others. In contrast, some severely handicapped persons like Helen Keller became adept at nonverbal communication with only limited movement capabilities. The mastery of sign language and pantomime broadly interpreted can be dance education. The use of gesture as expressive movement can be traced back to Dalcroze (1923), but dance specialists have not typically focused upon the communicative aspects of dance in education. In the last two decades the increasing incidence of emotionally disturbed persons and the evolution of dance therapy as a new profession have led to a reexamination of dance as a means of helping individuals relate to one another and communicate meaningfully without words.

The traits that researchers claim comprise creativity have little to do with communication, skill in movement, or understanding of self. Ideally, dance experiences leading to self-discovery and increased skill in communication will foster fluency, flexibility, originality, and elaboration, but the number of outstanding dance performers who lack creativity cannot be denied. Clearly, the traits of creativity must receive special attention in early childhood. Learning-disabled pupils may appear more creative than their peers because perceptual deficits force them to see the world in a different perspective. Perhaps this is a strength that can be built upon. The child confined to a wheelchair may have a beautiful creative mind capable of choreography if his or her imaginative powers are sharpened by many and varied opportunities to view dance and study movement elements.

Rhythm Skills

Dance is an independent art form. It can exist without music, accompaniment, costumes, scenery, or props. Traditionally, however, a major objective in dance education has been to teach children to relate movement effectively to accompanying sounds and to music. Too often this objective has been implemented by encouraging children to listen to a piece of music, a song, or a poem and then to develop movement sequences that fit the accompaniment. This approach tends to *turn off* those pupils with problems of auditory perception and timing. Many handicapped children do not respond naturally to pulse beats or to the time intervals between the beats. With such children it is advisable to separate instruction in dance from that in music until success is achieved in one or the other.

Sound rhythms initially should follow the tempos of the children, not vice versa, as is the traditional practice. The teacher should beat the drum to the tempo established by the child, thereby assuring that the child's first attempts to move with accompaniment are successful. Every effort should be made to determine the natural rhythm of the child—whether fast, slow, or medium tempo; 4/4 or 3/4 phrases; the rhythmic pattern or the underlying beat; whether the child responds to accents; and whether transitions from one tempo to another are made. During this period of observation the child should be encouraged to make up his or her own accompaniment: with a song, a nursery rhyme, a verse, hand clapping, foot stamping, or a tambourine, drum, or jingle bells. Only when the child gives evidence of moving in time to his or her own accompaniment should the next stage be introduced—conforming to an externally imposed rhythm.

Elements of Rhythm

Rhythmic structure in dance has four aspects: *pulse beats, accents, rhythmic patterns,* and *musical phrasing.*

1. *Pulse beat,* the underlying beat of all rhythmic structure, can be taught as the sounds of walk or run; the ticking of a clock, watch, or metronome; the tapping of a finger; the clapping of hands; or the stamping of feet. The beats can occur in fast, medium, or slow tempos and in constant or changing rates of speed.

2. *Accent* is an emphasis—i.e., an extra loud sound or extra hard movement. Syllables of words are accented, and beats of measures are accented.

3. *Rhythmic pattern* is a short series of sounds or movements superimposed on the underlying beat and described as even or uneven. Illustrative of *even* rhythmic patterns are the walk, run, hop, jump, leap, step-hop, schottische, and waltz. Illustrative of *uneven* rhythmic patterns are the gallop, slide, skip, two-step, polka, and bleking. In rhythmic patterns the duration of time between beats varies. The simplest patterns for children are as follows:

   a. *Uneven* long-short patterns as in the gallop, skip, and slide in 6/8 tempo:

   b. *Even* twice as fast or twice as slow walking patterns in 4/4 tempo:
   Walk, ♩ ♩ ♩ ♩   4 steps to a measure

   Run, ♫ ♫ ♫ ♫   8 steps to a measure

   Slow walk, ♩ ♩   2 steps to a measure

4. *Musical phrasing* is the natural grouping of measures to give a temporary feeling of completion. A phrase must be at least two measures long. It is the expression of a complete thought or idea in music. Phrasing may help to determine the *form* of a modern dance composition, and children should be guided in the recognition of identical phrases within a piece of music. One movement sequence is created for each musical phrase; identical phrases may suggest identical movement sequences.

Some children require no special help in movement to music. They do not need adapted dance. Others who have grown up in homes without music or who have central nervous system deficits affecting temporal perception must be provided a carefully designed progression of experiences broken down into parts so small that success is ensured. A succession of units might include

1. Creative movement without accompaniment in which an idea, feeling, or mood is expressed.

2. Creative movement, with the child encouraged to add sound effects.

3. Creative movement interspersed with discovery activities in which the child can beat a drum, clash cymbals, or use other rhythmic instruments as part of a dance-making process. No instructions are given on how to use the instruments; they are simply made available along with the freedom to incorporate sounds as the child wishes.

4. Creative movement accompanied by the teacher or another pupil using a variety of interesting sounds that fit the child's dance-making.

5. Discussions concerning what kind of accompaniment best supports the theme or idea of different movement sequences; through problem-solving the child tells the teacher what kind of accompaniment he or she wants; the idea is tried, and the child evaluates whether it worked or not.

6. Introduction of the concept that a dance can be repeated over and over again; it has some kind of *form*—at least a beginning and an end—and both movements and accompaniment must be remembered so that they can be reproduced.

At this point the pupils learn the difference between dancing—i.e., moving for pleasure—and making a dance. They are helped to see their creation as an art product that may endure like a painting or a musical composition. They take pride in organizing their movement sequences into an integrated whole and comparing their dance-making process and products with those of dance artists on the various films that can be rented. Since handicapped children typically become adults with an abundance of leisure, it is extremely important that spectator appreciation of modern dance and ballet be developed concurrently with their first attempts at dance making. Perhaps a performing group from a local high school or college can be invited in to demonstrate dance compositions. It is futile to expect children to retain excitement about dance making (choreography) unless they are exposed to the art products of others and led to believe that dance is a significant part of the cultural-entertainment world.

Only when dance experiences in which movement is primary and accompaniment is secondary prove successful should the study of rhythmic skills be introduced to children known to be weak in temporal perception. These pupils typically will be off the beat as often as on it. They are likely to accent the wrong beat of a measure. And they may find the recognition of musical phrases hopelessly frustrating. Dance researchers have not yet designed studies to investigate the learning problems of these pupils. There seems to be some feeling among dance educators that any pupil can keep in time with the music if he or she tries hard enough. Such is not the case! Just as reading specialists are seeking alternative approaches to teaching their subject, dance educators must devise ways in which the rhythmically disabled and retarded pupil can find success. Murray (1953) stressed that calling attention to inaccurate response and creating tensions through continuous drill do not solve the problem. Nothing is sadder than a child concentrating so hard on tempo that the joy of movement is lost. The child who does not keep time to the music truly may be hearing a different drum beat.

Similarities between Adapted Dance and Dance Therapy

Both the dance educator and the dance therapist rely heavily upon the medium of creative dance to accomplish certain objectives. Dance education can be therapeutic just as dance therapy can be educational. Certainly, the adapted physical educator who uses creative dance as a means of helping handicapped children to understand and appreciate their bodies and their movement capabilities is engaged in a therapeutic endeavor. But the work should not be considered as dance therapy anymore than as physical therapy or occupational therapy. Since the incorporation of the American Dance Therapy Association, Inc., in May of 1966, dance therapy has gained increasing recognition as an independent profession.

Dance educators, therapists, and artists may use similar approaches in working with handicapped persons. The unique professional preparation of each of these specialists, however, enables them to accomplish different objectives. Dance therapists, with a strong background in psychology, may label their activities as rhythmic body action, spontaneous dance, dramatic play, fantasy action, movement exploration, improvisation, or relaxation. They generally avoid the word *teach* since therapy implies affective rather than cognitive behavioral changes.

Dance can be an art form, an educational experience, or a therapeutic tool. It is readily adaptable to widely diversified needs, ages, and objectives.

The places where dance lives—space, time, energy, motion, are so broad and general that it has a spectrum which will stretch to enormous distances to encompass feeling and emotion. At one end is dance as an art form and at the other end is dance in the classroom as an exercise in learning experience.

—Bella Lewitzky
California Institute of the Arts at Valencia

A Theoretical Model of Dance

Figure 15.2 attempts to depict dance activities that comprise the spectrum of feeling and emotion. Dance therapy forms the base of the spectrum, for it emphasizes rhythmic, expressive movement as a means of establishing initial contact with human beings who have lost the capacity to relate effectively to others. It aims to provide safe, nonjudgmental experiences in body action, which lead to increased trust and improved communication. In the middle of the spectrum are experiences that may be either adapted or regular dance. At the top of the theoretical model is dance as an art form, the vision of most dance educators as they guide their pupils toward creativity, motor skill, and communication.

Rhythmic body action, a term used more in dance therapy than in education, was coined by Marian Chace (n.d.) in her classic definition of dance therapy as "a specific use of rhythmic body action employed as a tool in the rehabilitation of patients in present-day institutions." Note that this definition is no longer the official one (see p. 356).

Rhythmic body action may be nothing more than rocking back and forth, clapping, or stamping. It may involve the entire body or only parts. Broadly defined, the term "rhythmic body action" can encompass all authentic dance experiences. In therapy with deeply disturbed, withdrawn, depressed, or catatonic patients, rhythmic body action in a circle is often a first step toward socialization. The movements in the initial stages of dance therapy are similar to the warm-up techniques used in dance education—arm and leg swings,

Figure 15.2 A theoretical model of dance in the spectrum of feeling and emotion.

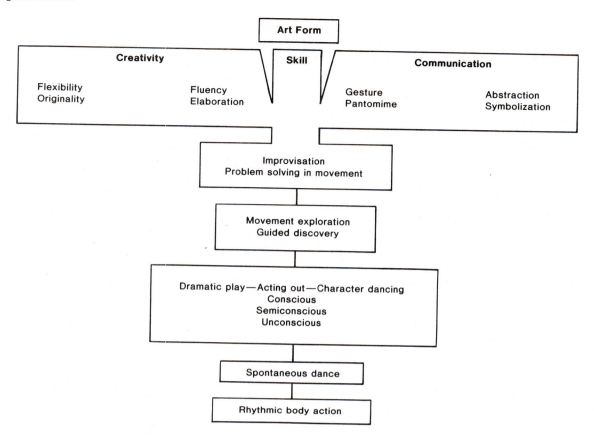

stretches, and eventually total body involvement through locomotor activities. The purpose is different, however, since the therapist uses this approach to help the patient to relate to the group, to assay his or her loneliness through moving in unison with others, rather than to increase muscle flexibility and prevent injury. Rosen summarizes the desired outcomes of rhythmic body action:

In a group, the patient learns that his individualized ways of moving are acceptable, and he learns to accept others and their individualized patterns; he learns to move in harmony and unison with others, to follow and to lead; and as he participates in all the varied movement experiences of the group, he becomes more and more capable of functioning as a part of it. If he is permitted he will dance out spontaneously the compelling impulses of his life and he will feel gratification and pleasure in the experience of being able to express them so vividly, with his body. (Rosen, 1957, p. 61)

Spontaneous dance, a term given therapeutic connotations by Bender and Boas (1941) in their work with disturbed children at Bellevue Hospital in New York, refers to locomotor and nonlocomotor activities initiated by the children themselves in a play setting. The inhibitions and resistance of patients may be overcome by encouraging them to execute cartwheels, somersaults, runs, leaps, and skips. Movement seems to stimulate children into expressing deeply buried fantasies and personal conflicts. Bender and Boas noted that the children talked through and explained their fantasies while engaged in movement, unaware that they were providing data for the psychologists and therapist. Spontaneous dance is seen also as a natural response to a jukebox or other music source. Even severely retarded children seem to derive great benefits from spontaneous dance.

The therapist may use spontaneous dance as a setting for evaluating the needs of a child. Persons trained in effort-shape record the characteristics of a patient's movements in signs that appear as follows:

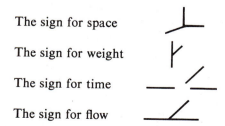

The sign for space

The sign for weight

The sign for time

The sign for flow

North (1972) described the use of these signs and their many variations in the assessment of personality as it is revealed through spontaneous movement behavior. Excellent quantified rating scales appear in her book for separate appraisal of the patient's use of space, weight, time, flow, and selected combinations of these movement elements.

Dramatic play and *character dancing* provide opportunities for emotional catharsis. The acting out and/or living through old (or someone else's) real-life situations gives a sense of how it feels to fit within such situations. Children can also attempt to become that which they fear or admire or do not understand. They can experience living the character in a story or a life-plot in a nonthreatening environment.

Characterization of stories provides opportunities for older children to regress in a socially acceptable manner and to receive help in distinguishing between real and make-believe worlds. Bunzel (1948), who employed the technique of inventing stories that patients interpreted through movements, noted the frequency of requests for roles that seemed to fulfill wish-dreams.

. . . the pretty daughter of a beautiful mother asked to play Cinderella in a story which she helped to develop. Surprisingly enough other members of the group agreed and after the performance, for the rest of the year, this girl was brought more and more into the foreground, where she found recognition and firm support. (Bunzel, 1948, p. 180)

Character dancing, as used in dance therapy, entails the assumption of the role of an imaginary character like, for instance, a giant. The main objective of character dancing is to provide socially acceptable outlets for controlled regression and sublimation of aggressive and erotic drives. Patients are given an opportunity to project aggressive and hostile feelings onto a make-believe character and to practice shifting from one behavior to another as in portraying such opposites as *a mean giant* and *a nice giant*.

Courtney (1968) uses the term *fantasy-action* as a special kind of dramatic play that enables children to identify with fantasized objects in order to work experimentally toward mastering the future. Through the fantasy-action, children attempt within an imaginary world to solve real-life experiences with which they have not yet learned to cope.

Movement exploration is used similarly by the dance therapist and the dance educator. It is guided discovery in helping the child to find self and test his or her movement effectiveness against reality. The child must exhibit readiness for understanding and accepting self and must be helped to realize that he or she is loved for what he or she is, not for what he or she can do.

Free exploration, invention, and improvisation (see Figure 15.3) are used interchangeably in children's dance. This technique allows children to create without

Figure 15.3 Movement improvisation in which the teacher contributes to IEP goals of improving both body image and balance.

regard for a plot or story line; it implies spontaneous, intuitive problem solving—movement and thought inseparable in the evolution process. In dance therapy, improvisations are used primarily to provide opportunities to fantasize in a socially acceptable manner and to release aggressive, hostile, or erotic feelings in a safe, nonjudgmental environment. In dance education, practice in improvisation is thought to develop skills in choreography (dance making).

Pantomime and mimetic dance activities in the therapeutic setting help patients to establish contact with reality and provide practice in the selection of appropriate movements for expressing specific emotions or feelings. Mimetic dance activities also serve as an effective way of motivating patients to act out or talk about ideas and experiences associated with the past. Greater personal involvement is necessary in pantomime than in the other dance therapy activities.

Dance therapists focus primarily upon the development of communication and socialization skills, whereas dance educators seek simultaneously to perfect motor skills, to elicit creativity in choreography, and to increase the communicative quality of dance as an art form. Adapted physical educators may identify more easily with dance therapists than with dance teachers. Associate membership is open to them in the American Dance Therapy Association, Inc., and an increasing number of workshops are available for learning about therapeutic relationships and the dance.

Ideas from Dance Therapy

The following pages written by a registered dance therapist offer specific ideas that the adapted physical educator can test in the school setting. In those parts of the country where dance therapists are available, they may be employed to work cooperatively with the adapted physical educator or to provide consultant services. It should be remembered that people who use dance therapeutically are not dance therapists unless they have received the special extensive training that qualifies them to meet the registry standards of the American Dance Therapy Association, Inc.

Through the therapeutic use of rhythmic and expressive movements, children gain better perspective about themselves, their own ideas, and their feelings. They come to know their bodies better. They gain skill and control as they move through space. They find ways to use body action constructively; insight is gained into the meanings implied in their body action; and a more accepting self-body-image is developed.

Therapeutic dance encourages and fosters children's faith in their own ideas and in their own ways of expressing these ideas. A sense of personal worth begins to emerge. Children begin to like themselves better as they come to believe in their own ideas and begin to realize that their ideas do count, are worth listening to and watching, and can be shared. Positive group relationships develop through sharing and experimenting with ideas. Opportunities begin to occur for gaining appreciative understanding of other people's ideas and their ways of expressing them.

Working with the expression of feelings is interwoven in various ways into dance, both indirectly in body action at the nonverbal level and directly with words and action at a conscious level. It is usually characteristic of dance therapy techniques that emotional tensions are worked with indirectly by centering attention on how the muscles can be used—such as hard or fast, or slow or easy ways—rather than by speaking directly to the children's feeling-states. When children express their tensions in forceful moving-out behavior, activities are centered around aggressive-moving circle *dances* or controlled slow-motion-aggressive-pantomime. At other times, fast running, challenging ways of jumping-falling-rolling-pushing-spinning, or tug-of-war can facilitate the reduction of tensions. When tensions seem high, and forceful moving-out action seems contraindicated because the children's behaviors are expressed in depressed, turned-in movements, the action moves into gently paced rocking, swaying, swinging, controlled slow rolling, or tension-relaxation muscle isolation movements. On other occasions, when the children's tension levels are not high, activities focus on feelings directly at a conscious level. Only then do the children experiment with the different ways that feelings can be expressed through movement.

Activities Used with Children in Dance Therapy

Some of the activities used in helping children become aware of their bodies and how their muscles work include the following:

1. Stretches, contractions, relaxations: individually, with partners, and in moving circle-dance action.

2. Opposites movements: experimenting with such movements as tall-short, wide-narrow, fast-slow, stiff-floppy, open-closed, heavy-light, high-low.

3. Feeling the floor different ways with bodies: by rolling across the floor stretched out full length at varying speeds and levels of muscle tension; rolling around in tight curled-up balls; doing front and back somersaults; crumpling body movements to effect collapsing to the floor; free falls sideward-forward-backward.

4. Exploring movement through space: making different shapes and patterns; creating geometric patterns; *writing* imaginary letters and numbers with their bodies stationary and/or traveling.

5. Using different traveling styles across the floor: running, jumping, walking, and creeping; variations within each style; working individually, with partners, and with groups of different sizes.

6. Muscle isolation: using specific parts of the body in movement patterns while the rest of the body remains immobile; or following the action of the specific set of muscles leading a movement pattern; immobilization of body parts by playing *freeze* and *statue* games that stop movement in midaction; continuing on in movement retaining the *frozen* or *statue* position; having partners arrange each other's bodies into shapes or *statues*.

7. Reflection movement patterns of others (Figure 15.4): moving in synchrony with a partner's movements as though looking in a mirror; moving on phrase-pattern behind a partner as though echoing his or her movements; moving in opposite patterns to partner's; reflecting similar or complementary movement patterns, yet different.

Children's ideas can be encouraged to emerge in a variety of ways. At times emphasis is upon verbalization of abstract ideas and at other times the focus is on body movement expression. Many times verbal and physical expression are combined. The following activities are some of the experiments and experiences that children seem to enjoy.

Figure 15.4 Reflecting the movement patterns of others.

1. Single word or object stimulus:
    a. "How many different ideas can the word 'beach' remind you to think about?" "What kinds of ideas come to you when you hear the word 'beach'?"
    b. "How many different ways can you pretend to use a popsicle stick?"
2. Imaginary props. "Without telling us what it is, think of one particular thing or object you could use in three different ways. Show us how you would use it. After you have finished using it three different ways, call on us and we will try to guess what objects you were using." Sometimes, after the child has completed his or her turn, and the object has been guessed, the other children contribute ideas orally on how the object could also be used. Stress is placed on being creatively supportive of each other's ideas.
3. Word cues. Words written on slips of paper are drawn in turn; the child translates the word into pantomime or dance movement. As the other children think they recognize the word cue, they join in with the movement in their own ways and

within their own framework of understanding. When the action is stopped, verbal comparison is made of the meanings the children gave to their movement interpretations. Observations and comments are shared about the different ways used to express the same word-meaning in movement. Movement can then resume with the children's sharing of each other's movement styles. The word cues are usually presented in categories:

a. *Doing*—chopping, hiding, twisting, carrying, hurrying, touching, dropping, sniffing, bouncing, flying, planting, pushing.
b. *People*—old person, mailcarrier, maid, nurse, airplane pilot, cook, police officer, doctor, hunted criminal, firefighter, mother, baby.
c. *Muscle isolation dances*—shoulder dance, head dance, knee dance, hip, hand, elbow, foot, leg, knee, back, finger.
d. *Feelings*—ashamed, surprised, sad, stuck-up, angry, worried, greedy, jealous, happy, excited, in love, afraid, disgusted.
e. *Animals*—bee, horse, alligator, lion, snake, spider, elephant, crab, butterfly, worm, monkey, gorilla, mouse.

f. *Mime dramas*—underwater adventure, a scary time, at the beach, at a bus stop, going on a picnic, climbing a mountain, a visit to the zoo, on a hike outdoors, an afternoon in the park, a baseball game.

g. *A happening story*—a siren blowing, red light flashing, thick fog, whistle blowing, fire burning, animal sounds, gun firing, child crying, dream happening, rushing water.

4. Different ways over and under a rope. As a rope is gradually raised or lowered, the children use as many different ways as they can to move over or under the rope without touching it.

5. Idea box. Sometimes a box is kept in which the children put various objects they find or like—e.g., leaves, crayon bits, combs, brushes, tiny statues, clothespins, buttons, pictures, paper clips, rubber discs. Periodically, an object is taken from the box to *play around* with. The different ideas the children think up about the object can be taken into creative movement, creative storytelling, or creative dramatics.

6. Stories. Sometimes stories are read to the children so they can make up their own endings and/or think about the possible alternative endings that can be used. The stories and the possible endings can be translated into dramatic action, either in part or total.

When feelings are focused on directly and at a conscious level, children can experiment with different ways feelings can be expressed through movement. The following activities illustrate some of the ways children can purposefully work with feelings or feeling-tones.

1. Descriptive mime or *dance* movements to a stimulus word indicating a specific feeling—e.g., see item 5, "Idea box," in the preceding list.

2. Descriptive mime, *dance,* or story evolving from a spontaneous sound made by the child reflecting the feeling-tone of that sound.

3. Feeling-tones in music. As music is played, the children respond in their own movement styles to the feeling-quality they *hear* in the music. When the action is finished, the children compare their responses with each other, noting differences in responses to the same music. They also *try on* each other's feeling responses or movement styles as the music is played again.

4. Stories *danced* to feeling-quality of the music. Turns are taken as individuals, pairs, or several children dance a story they have planned around the feeling-quality in the music. Sometimes the same music is chosen for all the children; other

times the different groups of children choose different music. When the *danced* story is finished, the children who watched attempt to relate their observations and interpretations of the story to the dancers. After everyone has had a chance to interpret, the performer(s) describe their own story. When it seems appropriate, children share together some of the movement qualities presented in the stories.

5. Feeling-tones in colors. Lightweight fabrics of different colors are placed around the floor in order of child's color preference; talk about what a specific color "makes you think about"; list ideas on paper; try on some of the ideas in movement. List ideas about what kinds of feelings might be reflected in a specific color. Experiment and show through movement how one can move to express the feelings listed, in pairs, groups, or individually. Continue on from one color fabric to another. The single feeling-action can be enlarged into pantomime or dramatizations of a story idea woven around the feeling.

6. Baseball game (or alternate sport) in different movement styles. All players work together to reflect a specific feeling in their movement styles as they "play" the game.

a. *Sad*—the batter waits sadly for the ball to be thrown, the pitcher sadly throws the ball, the batter sadly hits at the ball. If he misses, everyone is sad and says so or makes sounds accordingly. The ball is sadly put back into play. If the ball is hit, the batter sadly runs to the base as the pitcher or players sadly go after the ball and try to throw the runner out. Such mood continues throughout the play around the bases until the runner sadly makes a run or is thrown out.

b. *Happy*—follows the same format as above. The batter is happy when he misses the ball or when he is thrown out. The pitcher is happy when the batter makes a base run or a home run.

c. *Laughing-angry*—this type of contradictory expressive behavior becomes challenging and hilarious. Different combinations of contradictory feelings/sounds demand special awareness of how one uses expressive action. This also comes close to the reality of the mixed communication many people use in less exaggerated fashion in everyday life.

Figure 15.5 Soft nylon has a relaxing and quieting effect.

Figure 15.6 Experiencing the spatial structure of soft floating fabric.

Materials Used in Dance Therapy with Children

Soft materials are used in all three of the above areas for stimulating a variety of safe activities that are imaginative and self-structuring. Two-and-a-half-yard lengths of nylon fabrics of different hues aid in reducing tension and hyperactivity and in relaxing tight muscles (see Figure 15.5). In response to the floating, smooth quality of the colorful nylon, children move rhythmically, stretching, turning, reaching, and covering themselves in various ways. Their actions seem to reflect a sensuous enjoyment and an aesthetic awareness as the fabrics float and move across their bodies.

Paradoxically, the soft fabrics can become a factor in spatial structuring as well (see Figure 15.6). At times, when children feel extremely tense and seem to have a need for containment, being wrapped completely immobile in the full width of the fabric by either turning when standing or rolling when lying down will have a relaxing and quieting effect. Without speaking directly to such needs, children will ask for this kind of containment by suggesting familiar activities that have included it in other movement contexts. Nylon fabrics also provide an intermediary focus for children who find it difficult to relate directly to other persons. Spin-arounds, with partners holding opposite ends of the fabric, aid in keeping distance yet staying together. Wrap-up spin-outs allow a moment's closeness with access to quick and immediate freedom from nearness. Imaginative play and imagery are stimulated by using the fabric as clothing, costumes, bedding, housing, or light-shields to put a color glow in a darkened room. Aggressiveness is accommodated by wrapping a soft yarn ball inside one end of the fabric and throwing it as if it were a comet streaming through space. *Dodge*

fabric has aggressive moments of fun and beauty combined when one or several fabrics are loosely wadded into a ball and thrown at a moving human target. The floating open of the fabric(s) while traveling in space sometimes creates unusual beauty. Children also like to lie down and be covered completely with one fabric at a time in layering fashion. As the layers of fabric increase, children typically comment on the constant change of color and the increasing dimness.

Soft, stretchy, tubular knit fabrics that are approximately 3 yards long have soothing, protecting properties. The tubular fabrics make excellent *hammocks* on which to lie and be swung (see Figures 15.7 and 15.8). When persons alternate in lifting ends of the fabric, causing the body to roll from side to side, a special sensation of being moved in space is felt. An interesting sensation of directional change is experienced when running and bouncing forward into a tautly stretched fabric that *gives* and then bounces the person off backwards. Stretch-tube fabrics lend themselves well to nondirected dramatic play and fantasy-action. They become roads, rivers, roofs, ghosts, hooded persons, Roman togas, stuffed sausages, pickles, grass, tunnels. Playing inside stretch-tube fabrics adds further dimension to their use. It is a way for children to shield themselves from direct observation and physical touch contact with other persons while at the same time being able to look out through the fabric and see the persons. When working inside, the fabrics can become an open-ended tunnel to explore, or a closed and safe haven for being swung, rolled, dragged gently around the floor, or for pretending all alone in fantasy-action. Inside the fabrics can also become a place to experiment with making different shapes and forms by bending and extending body parts against the softly resilient material. When lying outside on the fabric, and being swung gently, spontaneous pantomimes of *dreams*

Figure 15.7 Experiencing the sensation of directional change in a different way.

Figure 15.8 Learning trust as the hammock descends.

Figure 15.9 Yarn balls permit safe release of aggressive tensions.

are easily evoked. These *dreams* come from children's unconscious urges and needs, and the expressive body action accompanying the dream fantasies allows for safe catharsis and emotional release of tensions reflected in the dream content. The fabrics offer opportunity for rocking and swaying when children need comforting and relaxing, without those needs being openly or directly addressed. *Games* experienced earlier when the children were simply exploring the use of the fabrics can be repeated when the need for comforting arises.

Yarn balls about 6 inches in diameter permit many varieties of throwing activities for imaginative play as well as safe release of aggressive tensions (Figure 15.9). The teacher's imaginative thinking about different ways to throw, jump with, and bat the ball stimulates alternative ways of thinking and also encourages children to risk expressing their own ideas. Warm-up stretches are executed by using different body positions to transfer the ball to the next recipient. One-to-one synchronization of full body action occurs when partners try to support a ball between them with various parts of their bodies while traveling across the room. Yarn balls can be used aggressively for *bowling* or dodge ball. They can also be kept rolling around the floor by being hand-batted vigorously back and forth. More structured and functionally demanding activities are done with rhythmically synchronized toss, catch, and rolling games. Isolations of body parts can be experienced by bouncing the ball off different parts of the body or by contacting the ball with a specific body part before releasing and passing it on to another person. In dramatic play and fantasy action the balls become various kinds of foods, jewels, rocks, rockets, bombs, and the *equipment* for pretend games of baseball, kickball, touch football, and bowling.

Principles upon Which Dance Therapy Is Based

With modification, the techniques of dance therapy are applicable to persons of most ages and with most disabilities, because dance therapy focuses upon qualities of nonverbal communication in everyday life. Marian Chace (n.d.), one of the major pioneers in the evolution of dance therapy as a profession, influenced persons who studied with her toward acceptance of principles that she felt were basic to dance therapy and common to all forms of therapy. She believed that the dance therapist keeps things simple by leading out from what is happening inside the patient rather than imposing the action from the outside. The therapist allows time for things to happen within the on-going action rather than trying to *do* a lot. Chace recommended that the dance therapist work toward enriching experiences in a nonjudgmental, neutral way, without moralizing. This is best accomplished by working *with* the patient rather than *on* him or her. It is essential that the dance therapist be secure and able to listen to what is going on at the verbal level and yet see subtle nonverbal cues. The therapist should emanate friendliness, yet remain neutral and resist being caught up in his or her need to be liked by the patient. Patients must be helped to relate to persons who are genuine and truthfully warm. They need relationship space that allows them to give back warmth without feeling threatened by the therapist's needs.

Therapeutic Tools

The *therapeutic tools* used by the dance therapist could be thought of as rhythm, touch, verbalization, space, and people. Activities are simply the media for the use of therapeutic tools.

It is the *movement of the patient,* rather than that of the therapist, that is used as a means of establishing the therapeutic relationship. By tuning in and sharing a patient's movements, the therapist can very clearly and quickly relate to the patient. They can *speak* to each other in movement. The therapist then works toward transcribing patients' movements into reality-oriented and functional expressions since patients are unable to do this for themselves. The therapist also tries to influence change in patients' distorted body-images through muscular action.

Basically, it is the rhythmical quality of expressive movement that enables the patient to use body action in safe ways that hurt no one. Open use of aggressive movements has less therapeutic value than rhythmic action that focuses on body awareness. For optimal results, expressive movement must be under the patient's conscious rather than unconscious control. Rhythmic action also affords an area for relating that is outside both the patient and the dance therapist. It offers the satisfaction of sharing movement and minimizes destructiveness of action. There is no need felt for the movement to be realized in its destructive form. This leaves the patient free to go on to other things, with pathological urges released rhythmically, constructively, and safely, for the moment.

All therapeutic body movement is geared toward getting in touch with as much of the skin's surface as possible. It is through tactile stimulation and muscular contraction that the patient regains contact with his or her body surface and comes to understand its boundaries. Direct touch by the therapist is used to reinforce the patient's growing ability to distinguish between himself or herself and others.

Verbalization between the therapist and patient is geared to the meaning of muscular action rather than the feeling-tone behind the action. The patient comes to realize that his or her movement qualities are reality-based and that he or she is capable of purposive movement. Verbalization is not for telling the patient what to do, but for helping him or her to know where he or she is going and why.

Space is an extension and reflection of body image, so the use of space is important. A patient who is manic and hyperactive perceives his or her own space zone as wide and scattered and having tremendous force and power. The dance therapist then uses movements far away from the patient, coming in only tentatively as the patient will allow. The patient already feels that they are *together* even though they are actually far apart. If a patient is frozen or constricted in movement, the space zone is small and constricted. The dance therapist then moves in quite closely, but with care and awareness, because a constricted space is generally a supercharged zone. The dance therapist also uses space to encourage a *coming forward.* Such dance movements can provide safe areas for hostile body action that might have been used out of control. *Going forward* movements can provide safe areas for a withdrawn person to learn that he or she can come out and not be hurt, nor will he or she hurt anybody.

The ultimate goal of the dance therapist is for patients to work in a group. Group work reduces one-to-one identifications and increases opportunities for patients to assume responsibility for their own growth and not stay dependent upon the therapist.

Learning Activities

1. Obtain a list of members and registered dance therapists from the American Dance Therapy Association, Inc., and invite those residing near your school to serve as guest speakers. Learn about graduate training in dance therapy and standards for registration.

2. Discuss similarities and differences between dance therapy and dance education.

3. Conduct several mini-lessons with children to demonstrate your competence in teaching creative dance. Do not try to conduct dance therapy until you complete advanced training.

4. Demonstrate your competence in teaching folk or square dance to both ambulatory and wheelchair pupils.

5. Demonstrate your ability to compose simple foot movement routines that might be considered adapted tap dance; teach a routine to music to one or more groups.

References

American Dance Therapy Association. (circa 1975). Annual proceedings and other materials available through the national office.

Bender, L., & Boas, F. (1941). Creative dance in therapy. *American Journal of Orthopsychiatry, 2,* 235–245.

Bunzel, G. (1948). Psychokinetics and dance therapy. *Journal of Health, Physical Education, and Recreation, 19,* 180–181, 227–229.

Chace, M. (n.d.). *Dance alone is not enough.* From mimeographed materials distributed by St. Elizabeth's Hospital and Chestnut Lodge in Washington, DC.

Courtney, R. (1968). *Play, drama, and thought: The intellectual background to dramatic education.* London: Cassell & Co., Ltd.

Dalcroze, E. (1923). *The eurythmics of Jacques-Dalcroze.* London: Constable & Company.

Fitt, S., & Riordan, A. (Eds.) (1980). *Dance for the handicapped—focus on dance IX.* Reston, VA: American Alliance for Health, Physical Education, Recreation, and Dance.

Laban, R. (1960). *The mastery of movement* (2nd ed.). London: MacDonald & Evans.

Lewitzky, B. (n.d.). Philosophical statement. In B. Schiff (Ed.), *Artists in the schools* (p. 124). Washington, DC: National Endowment for the Arts.

Murray, R. L. (1953). *Dance in elementary education.* New York: Harper & Row.

North, M. (1972). *Personality assessment through movement.* London: MacDonald & Evans Ltd.

Rosen, E. (1957). *Dance in psychotherapy.* New York: Teachers College, Columbia University.

Smith, N. W. (1973). Prologue. In G. Andrews Fleming (Ed.), *Children's dance* (pp. 5–6). Washington, DC: American Association for Health, Physical Education, and Recreation.

Bibliography

American Association for Health, Physical Education, and Recreation. (1974). *Dance therapy: Focus on dance VII.* Washington, DC: Author.

American Dance Therapy Association. Annual proceedings. Published each year. Write to ADTA for cost and titles of back issues still available.

Bartenieff, I., & Davis, M. A. (1963). *Effort-shape analysis of movement: The unity of expression and function.* New York: Albert Einstein College of Medicine.

Barton, B. (1982). Aerobic dance and the mentally retarded. *The Physical Educator, 39* (1), 25–29.

Bernstein, P. L. (1972). *Theory and methods in dance-movement therapy.* Dubuque, IA: Kendall/Hunt.

Bornell, D. (1979). *Movement is individuality.* San Pedro, CA: GSC Athletic Co.

Boswell, B. (1982). *Adapted dance for mentally retarded children: An experimental study.* Unpublished doctoral dissertation, Texas Woman's University, Denton.

Brown, O. (1980). *A comparison of the attention span of hyperactive and nonhyperactive children while performing to live and recorded dance instructions.* Unpublished doctoral dissertation, Texas Woman's University, Denton.

Canner, N. (1968). *. . . And a time to dance.* Boston: Beacon Press.

Caplow-Lindner, E., Harpaz, L., & Samberg, S. (1979). *Therapeutic dance/movement: Expressive activities for older adults.* New York: Human Sciences Press, Inc.

Chace, M. (1964). Dance alone is not enough. . . . *Dance Magazine, 38,* 46–47, 58–59.

Chaiklin, H. (Ed.). (1975). *Marian Chace: Her papers.* Columbia, MD: American Dance Therapy Assn.

Chambliss, L. (1982). Movement therapy and the shaping of a neuropsychological model. *American Journal of Dance Therapy, 5,* 18–27.

Chapman, A., & Cramer, M. (1973). *Dance and the blind child.* New York: American Dance Guild, Inc.

Cole, I. L. (1978). *Dance therapy with a nonverbal, autistic child: A documentation of process.* Unpublished doctoral dissertation, Texas Woman's University, Denton.

Costonis, M. (Ed.). (1977). *Therapy in motion.* Urbana, IL: University of Illinois Press.

Crain, C. (1981). *Movement and rhythmic activities for the mentally retarded.* Springfield, IL: Charles C. Thomas.

Crain, C., Eisenhart, M., & McLaughlin, J. (1984). The application of a multiple measurement approach to investigate the effects of a dance program on educable mentally retarded adolescents. *Research Quarterly for Exercise and Sport, 55* (3), 231–236.

Delaney, W. (1976). *Dance therapy: Selected materials for professional preparation.* Unpublished master's thesis, Texas Woman's University, Denton.

Eddy, J. (1982). *The music came from deep inside: Professional artists and severely handicapped children.* New York: McGraw-Hill.

Espenak, L. (1981). *Dance therapy, theory, and applications.* Springfield, IL: Charles C. Thomas.

Fitt, S., & Riordan, A. (Eds.). (1980). *Dance for the handicapped—focus on dance IX.* Reston, VA: American Alliance for Health, Physical Education, Recreation, and Dance.

Harris, C. G. (1979). Dance for students with orthopedic conditions. *AAHPERD Practical Pointers, 2,* 1–22.

Hecox, B., Levine, E., & Scott, D. (1975). A report on the use of dance in physical rehabilitation: Everybody has the right to feel good. *Rehabilitation Literature, 36,* 11–16.

Hill, K. (1976). *Dance for physically disabled persons.* Washington, DC: American Alliance for Health, Physical Education, and Recreation.

Jentsch, A. (1974). Wheelchair square dancing for severely retarded multiple handicapped. In J. Stein (Ed.), *The best of challenge* (Volume 2), Washington, DC: American Alliance for Health, Physical Education, and Recreation.

Klaf, C. (1957). *Rhythmic activities for handicapped children.* Unpublished doctoral dissertation, University of Southern California, Los Angeles.

Lefco, H. (1977). *Dance therapy: Narrative case histories of therapy sessions with six patients.* Chicago: Nelson-Hall Co.

Leventhal, M. (1965). *A dance-movement experience as therapy with psychotic children.* Unpublished master's thesis, University of California, Los Angeles.

Leventhal, M. (Ed.). (1980). *Movement and growth: Dance therapy for the special child.* New York: New York University.

Ohwaki, S. (1976). An assessment of dance therapy to improve retarded adults' body image. *Perceptual and Motor Skills, 43,* 1122.

Robins, F., & Robins, J. (1968). *Educational rhythmics for mentally and physically handicapped children.* New York: Association Press.

Rosen, E. (1974). *Dance in psychotherapy.* New York: Dance Horizons.

Schattner, R. (1967). *Creative dance for handicapped children.* New York: John Day.

Schmais, C. (1976). What is dance therapy? *Journal of Health, Physical Education, and Recreation, 47,* 39.

Sherrill, C. (Ed.). (1979). *Creative arts for the severely handicapped.* Springfield, IL: Charles C. Thomas. Includes several chapters on dance for handicapped and dance therapy.

Sherrill, C., & McBride, H. (1984). An arts intervention model for severely handicapped children. *Mental Retardation, 22,* (6), 316–320.

Shoop, T. (1974). *Will you, won't you join the dance?* Palo Alto, CA: National Press Books.

Siegel, E. (1984). *Dance-movement therapy: A psychoanalytic approach.* New York: Human Sciences Press, Inc.

Szyman, R. (1976). Square dancing on wheels. *Sports N' Spokes, 2,* 5–7.

16 Aquatics for Handicapped Students

Figure 16.1   Although the child is orthopedically impaired, he is not handicapped in the water. (Photos by Judy Newman.)

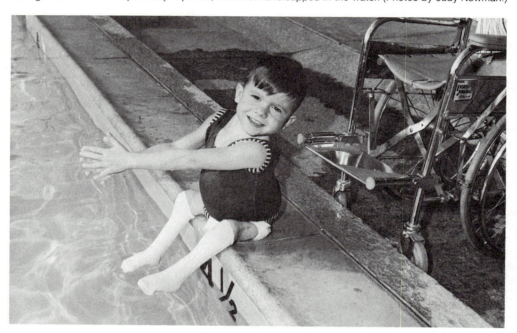

Chapter Objectives

After you have studied this chapter, you should be able to

1. State behavioral objectives for teaching swimming to children of different ages with selected handicapping conditions and indicate a method for determining whether these objectives are being met.

2. Apply task analysis to teaching swimming and discuss activities for achieving selected goals.

3. Analyze how swimming contributes to perceptual-motor development. State specific perceptual-motor problems that can be remediated through swimming and determine specific teaching techniques.

4. Analyze how swimming contributes to fitness and posture. State specific problems in these areas that can be remediated through swimming and indicate specific teaching techniques.

5. Discuss administrative aspects of an aquatics program for the handicapped in such varied settings as camp, school, or YMCA-YWCA—mainstream vs. separate classes.

Advantages Offered by Aquatics

A mother speaks of her dyslexic son in a poignant account of learning to cope with learning disabilities:

He might not be able to manage a tricycle, but he had the freedom of a large safe beach where he could run for a mile if he felt inclined. Beach balls eluded him—he could neither throw nor catch—but there was the warm sand to mess with, and the water itself. The big moment of Mike's young life came at three-and-a-half, when he learned to swim. . . . The beach baby turned into a water rat. By five he could safely swim out of his depth, and by six he not only had a crawl stroke, but was so at home in the water that he literally did not seem to know if he was on it or under it. (Clarke, 1973, p. 9)

At the end of the book Mike had graduated from Harvard University with a doctoral degree. He still could not "read, write, nor talk too good either." But he had persevered in learning to compensate for his weaknesses and to utilize fully his strengths. Like other boys, he longed for athletic success, tried out for teams, failed. He was especially awkward in baseball and handball. As an adult, he recalled the pleasure derived from swimming and its contribution to the maintenance of some ego strength throughout a childhood characterized by very few successes.

Aquatics, perhaps more than any other aspect of the physical education program, appeals to persons with all kinds of conditions (see Figure 16.1). Even those so severely involved as to be bedfast experience satisfaction in water play. The discipline of physical therapy has long recognized the rehabilitative values of exercises executed in water. As early as 1937, Charles Lowman, an orthopedic specialist, published a book on hydrotherapy. Many public schools have Hubbard tanks, where physical therapists work with orthopedically handicapped children.

Therapeutic exercise underwater is especially valuable for the nonambulatory pupil whose body parts lack the strength to overcome the force of gravity. In the pool, the force of gravity is greatly minimized, permitting some range of movement to limbs that have none when not immersed in water. Children who require crutches and/or braces to walk on land can often ambulate in water.

The methods of teaching the nine regulation swimming strokes to children with physical and mental deficits are similar to those traditionally employed with all beginners. If the primary purpose of swimming in the adapted physical education program were to develop skill, this chapter would be unnecessary. The progression of competencies for earning American Red Cross swimming certificates seems quite adequate. The following pages focus upon adapting swimming instruction to the needs of preschool children and/or any individual whose mastery of aquatic skills appears frozen at the prebeginner level. The content has been tested on children with learning disabilities and/or mental retardation who participate in a year-round aquatic program at the Texas Woman's University.

Over the years, three prebeginner swimming certificates have evolved. Initially, the levels of competency that the certificates represent were named after fish: minnows, crappies, and dolphins. The children were not as enamoured of these appellations as were the adults who created them. First of all, many of them had never seen real fish, alive or dead, and to them the names were meaningless. Some of the pupils did report first-hand knowledge of fish, but remembered the unpleasant odor more than the beauty of movement. Said one, "I don't want to be a fish—ugh—they stink." Still

Table 16.1
Beginning Competency Levels of Swimming for Children

Level I, Explorer Movement Exploration in Water	Level II, Advanced Explorer Movement Exploration in Water	Level III, Floater Prebeginning Swimming
1. Enter and leave water alone	1. Put face in water	1. Blow bubbles (10 seconds)
2. Walk across pool holding rail	2. Blow bubbles (5 seconds)	2. Bracketing on front with kick
3. Walk across pool holding teacher's hand	3. Touch bottom or toes with hands	3. Change of position: stand; front-lying with support; stand
4. Stand alone	4. Retrieve objects from bottom	4. Prone float
5. Walk across pool pushing kickboard	5. Assume horizontal position with teacher's help	5. Change of position: stand; back-lying with support; stand
6. Jump or hop several steps alone	6. Hold onto kickboard pulled by teacher	6. Back float
7. Walk and do breaststroke arm movements	7. Jump into water without help	7. Flutter kick using board
8. Do various locomotor movements across the pool	8. Take rides in back-lying position	8. Jellyfish float
9. Blow bubbles through plastic tube	9. Change of level: squat to stand; stand to squat	9. Perform breaststroke arm movements
10. Blow ping-pong ball across pool	10. Play follow-the-leader type water games	10. Swim one-half width any style
	11. Demonstrate bracketing on back with kick	11. Perform at least one stunt like stand or walk on hands, front somersault, back somersault, tub, surface dive

another problem arose with respect to self-concept; heavily muscled boys, particularly from economically deprived areas, had no intention of being "sissy minnows" regardless of their dependence upon the teacher in the water.

The three certificates subsequently were designated as Explorer, Advanced Explorer, and Floater in accordance with the levels of competency achieved. These certificates were printed on cards of the same size and shape as the standard Red Cross certificates. Originally, they came in different colors, but after the year that one little girl with Down's syndrome sobbed all through the awards ceremony because her card was not white like her boyfriend's, it was decided to make the cards uniform in color as well as size, shape, and format.

The motor tasks required for passing each certificate are listed in Table 16.1. The major achievement at the Explorer level is to release the teacher's hand and perform basic locomotor movement patterns independently at a distance several feet away from the side of the pool. It is not necessary to put the face in the water to earn Explorer status. Many youngsters initially are so terrified of the water that several lessons are required before they will loosen their deathlike grips on the teachers. Many additional lessons pass before enough courage is developed to let go the side of the pool and walk independently. Nevertheless, *all* students who earn the Explorer certificate take as much pride in it as their peers do in the Red Cross achievement cards.

The Advanced Explorer certificate represents two major accomplishments: putting the face in the water and willingness to lift the feet from the pool bottom, thereby assuming a horizontal position with the help of the teacher. At this level also the child begins to experiment with somersaults, standing on his or her head, walking on hands, and other stunts that are not based upon the ability to float.

Earning the third and final prebeginner certificate, Floater, is dependent upon the ability to relax sufficiently to float for several seconds. At this level children usually begin to swim. Navigation is more often under the water than on top, and underwater swimming can be used to fulfill the requirement of one-half width. Long before the pupils learn to swim recognizable strokes they become proficient in many basic stunts of synchronized swimming. They develop creative routines to music that are weird combinations of walks, runs, jumps, hops, standing in place and stroking with arms, and regulation synchronized swimming stunts.

The water can be viewed as simply another medium for refining movement patterns and exploring time-space-self relationships. The Texas Woman's University aquatics program is coordinated with lessons in movement exploration conducted in the gymnasium. Virtually every activity learned out of water is attempted also in the swimming pool. The movement exploration teaching style described in Chapter 7 (guided discovery and motor creativity) establishes the framework in which learning occurs. The three most important objectives of the program are (a) to improve self-concept, (b) to increase self-confidence, and (c) to develop courage. Secondary to these goals, the teacher concentrates upon dimensions of body image: (d) identification of body parts; (e) improvement of proprioception; and (f) development of such inner language concepts as bent vs. straight, vertical vs. horizontal, pike vs. tuck; back layout vs. front layout; and pull phase (application of force) vs. recovery phase. As a technique for enhancing self-concept, children are drilled on the *names* of the stunts and skills they learn to perform. As they acquire a vocabulary that enables them to share their successes with others, children seem to demonstrate increased motivation for undertaking new aquatic adventures. Moreover, this emphasis on vocabulary in the swimming setting reinforces words learned in the classroom and the gymnasium, thereby contributing to transfer of learning and reducing development of splinter skills.

Differences between Movement Exploration and Regular Swimming Instruction

Some of the differences between a movement exploration program in the water and regular swimming instruction are explicit in the following principles for guiding movement explorations:

1. The teacher is in the water with the children rather than on deck (see Figure 16.2). Physical contact between teacher and pupil is based upon the needs of the learner for security and affection. Although independence in the water is the ultimate goal, it is not rushed.

2. The teacher avoids mentioning tasks like putting the face underwater which the pupil interprets as unpleasant. Instead, gamelike situations are devised that induce the child to attempt the task without conscious realization of what he or she is doing. The following anecdote demonstrates teaching:

> I had been in the water with Charles for about twenty minutes and had had no success with anything I had tried to teach him. I was particularly concerned with getting him to put his entire face and head in the water. I finally decided to make a game out of it, so I borrowed the small inner tube from one of the other instructors. Without any type of explanation I placed the inner tube between Charles and myself and ducked under water and came up with it around my neck. Charles was delighted and asked me to do it again. After repeating it I asked him if he would like to put his head through the inner tube. Without answering my question, he completely submerged his body and came up with the inner tube around his neck. I was more than pleased and had him repeat it five or six times. Then I asked him to submerge without coming up under the inner tube. I received a very blunt "no." He told me he could not put his head under water and he did not wish to try. We continued using the inner tube for the remainder of the hour.

3. As few words as possible are used in teaching. Cue words like "up," "down," "pull," "recover," and "kick 2–3–4" are substituted for sentences. A well-modulated voice helps convey the meaning of instructions. A *high* voice can be used for up movements and *low* (pitch) voice for down movements. The voice can be loud and forceful during the pull phase and soft and gentle during the recovery phase.

4. Corrections and modifications of movements are generally made by moving the child's limbs through the desired pattern of movement rather than by the explanation-demonstration technique. Some persons refer to this as the *kinesthetic* method of teaching since such input is proprioceptive.

5. Acceptance of the child is shown through frequent mirroring of his or her movements. Teacher and pupil take turns *following the leader* with precise imitation of postures, arm movements, and kicks.

6. Synchronized swimming, jumping, and diving are introduced much earlier than usual in swimming instruction. Emphasis is upon the combination of stunts and locomotor movements—i.e., creating sequences (routines) and remembering and executing sequences developed by others.

Aquatics for Handicapped Students   **377**

Figure 16.3   Comparison of bilateral and crosslateral strokes.

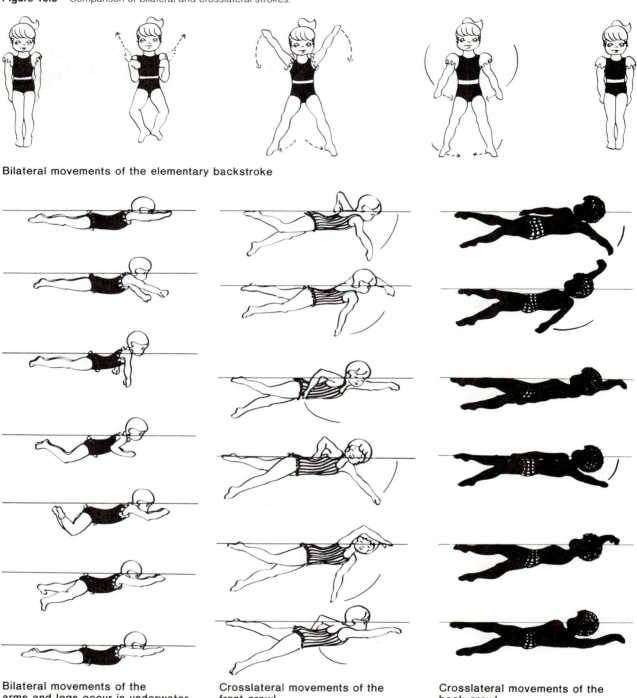

Bilateral movements of the elementary backstroke

Bilateral movements of the arms and legs occur in underwater swimming and the breaststroke

Crosslateral movements of the front crawl

Crosslateral movements of the back crawl

7.   Another difference between movement exploration in the water and regular swimming instruction is flexibility on the part of the teacher in modifying requirements in accordance with individual differences. Testing is planned upon the basis of the strengths of an individual, not preestablished competences that are thought to meet the needs of all beginner swimmers.

8.   Bilateral, unilateral, and crosslateral movement patterns are encouraged in that order, reflecting an understanding of child growth and development. Thus, the breaststroke and the

elementary backstroke are the first real swimming strokes to be introduced. The bilateral movements of the breaststroke usually appear in underwater swimming without the benefit of instruction. Figure 16.3 allows for a comparison of the simplicity of bilateral strokes with the relative complexity of crosslateral strokes.

The bilateral movements of the elementary backstroke are similar to those in angels-in-the-snow and jumping jacks. Land drill is used before the children shower or after they dry and dress to ensure transfer of learning. Drill in the water can be facilitated by suspending a hammock from the ceiling, using flotation devices, and lying on a table under the water.

Figure 16.3 shows bilateral movements of the arms and legs in underwater swimming and the breaststroke and in the elementary backstroke as well as the more difficult crosslateral swimming strokes. Six kicks of each leg are coordinated with every cycle of arm movements. As the right arm pulls, for instance, the right leg kicks *up*, down, *up*. The emphasis in the flutter kick is on the up beat! It is essential that arm strokes and leg kicks be practiced in a horizontal rather than a standing position. Equally important, the teacher should demonstrate new skills in the horizontal position.

No stroke is more difficult to master than the front crawl. Although the rhythm of the flutter kick may come naturally to a few students, it is a nightmare for many others. Land drills to music in 3/4 time with a strong accent on the first beat in every measure may contribute to relaxed, effective kicking in the water; if not, the practice can be justified for its contribution to abdominal strength. Both in land drills and in the water there is a tendency to collaborate with the force of gravity and accentuate the downbeat; this error must be avoided. Devising some kind of contraption 12 to 18 inches above the floor to be kicked on each upbeat may focus the pupil's attention on the desired accent.

The flutter kick warm-up exercise should begin in the position depicted in Figure 16.4 rather than with both legs on the floor since at no time during the crawl stroke are the legs motionless and in the same plane. With poorly coordinated pupils it is best to leave the arms motionless in the starting position until the rhythm of the kick is mastered. The verbal cues *right-arm-pull* or *left-arm-pull* can be substituted for *kick-2-3* even though the arms do not move. The first progression for this exercise is lying on the floor; the next progression for this exercise is lying on a bench with arms and legs hanging over.

When a pupil demonstrates no progress in the flutter kick over a period of weeks, it can be safely assumed that the desired movement is not *natural* for him or her and that an alternate method of kicking should

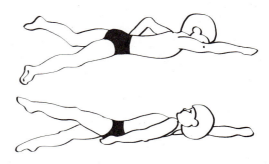

Figure 16.4 Ready position for flutter kick warmup.

be substituted. In such instances the front crawl can be modified into the *trudgeon stroke* by substituting the scissors kick for the flutter kick.

The American Red Cross teaches nine basic strokes. The student's ability to perform one or two of these strokes really well is the criterion for success in a program for handicapped persons. Which stroke the child chooses makes no difference whatsoever as long as he or she feels safe in the water and enjoys swimming. One of the purposes of movement exploration is to guide the student toward discovery of this stroke for himself or herself.

Activities for the Explorer

Washcloth Games

Each child is supplied with a washcloth, and the swimming pool is compared with the bathtub at home. The teacher's relaxed patter of questions usually elicits the desired exploration of the water.

1. What do you do with a washcloth? Don't tell me; show me!

2. What part do you wash first? Did you wring the cloth out before you started to wash? Don't you wring it out first at home?

3. Did you wash behind your ears? The back of your neck? Your elbows? Your knees? Your ankles? What about the soles of your feet? Are they clean?

4. Do you like to have someone wash your back? If you do, you can find a partner and take turns washing each other's back.

5. Can you play throw and catch with your partner by using the washcloth as a ball?

6. What happens if you miss the catch? Can you pick the washcloth off the bottom of the pool with your toes? With some other part of your body?

7. Let's play steal each other's washcloth. To begin, each of you must fold your washcloth and put it neatly over your shoulder or on top of your head. When I say go, move around stealing as many washcloths as you can but don't forget to protect your own. When I say stop, everyone must have one hand on the railing before I count to 10; then we will determine who is the winner.

Sponge Games

Every pupil with a sponge

1. Do you see something at the bottom of the pool? That's correct! There are plates, saucers, bowls, glasses, and cups. Guess what your job is? That's correct! Recover the dishes any way you wish, wash them with your sponge, and set the table on the deck. Whoever finishes the most place settings wins.

2. Have you ever scrubbed down walls? Each of you find your very own space on the wall and let's see you scrub! Have you ever washed a car? Let's pretend the wall is a car! What else can we pretend the wall is? Does anyone know how to scrub the floor? Let's see!

3. See this big innertube. Let's use it to shoot baskets with our sponges. Can you make your sponge land inside the innertube?

4. What other target games can we invent with the sponges?

5. Dodge or catch. This game is played like dodgeball except that the child has the option of dodging or catching. Occasionally, someone may get hit full in the face with a wet sponge. Although a sponge cannot hurt, some children feel threatened by this activity; hence, the participants should be volunteers.

All the sponges in the water

1. Who can get his bucket filled with water first? The only method of getting water in the bucket is squeezing out sponges.
   a. Individual game. Who can recover the most sponges, squeeze them out, and toss them back in the water?
   b. Partner game. One pupil remains in the water recovering sponges and handing them to his or her partner on deck, who squeezes the sponges and tosses them back into the water.

2. Sponges of different colors are floating in the water. Children all have one hand on the pool railing. On the signal *go* they respond to the teacher's question, "Who can recover a blue sponge and put it on the deck first?" A yellow sponge? A pink sponge?

3. Sponges of different shapes or sizes are floating in the water. Same instructions as before.

4. Who can recover two sponges and put one under each of his or her feet? How many of you are standing on sponges? Can you walk across the pool on the sponges?

Parachute Games

In the water a large sheet of clear plastic makes the best parachute; round table cloths and sheets can also be used. All of the parachute activities played on land can be adapted to the water. "Who can run under the parachute?" invariably gets the face in the water. "Who can climb over the parachute?" leads to taking turns riding on the magic carpet that is pulled through the water by classmates.

Blowing Games

These can be played either in or out of the water; they are important lead-up activities to rhythmic breathing.

1. Each child has a clear plastic tube 12 to 18 inches long. Plastic tubing can be purchased in any hardware store. Who can walk along with the plastic tube in a *vertical* position and blow bubbles in the water? Who can walk along with the plastic tube in a *horizontal* position and blow bubbles in the water?

2. Who can blow a ping-pong ball across the water? A toy sailboat? A small sponge?

3. On the side of the pool are many balloons that need blowing up. The object is to blow up a balloon while you walk or run across the pool. Who can make the most trips back and forth and thus blow up the most balloons? You may take only one balloon each trip.

4. Inflatable air mattresses and rafts provide ample practice in blowing for several children. Teams of three or four pupils may cooperate in blowing up a mattress with the promise that they may play on it in the water after it has been sufficiently inflated.

5. A yarnball or ping-pong ball is suspended from a string. Each child has one. Who can keep the ball in motion the longest by blowing?

Self-Testing Activities for the Explorer

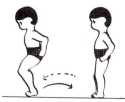

Horizontal or long jump

1. Who can jump forward across the pool? Who can jump backward? Sideward? How many different ways can you jump? Can you carry something heavy as you jump?

Vertical jump and reach

2. How high can you jump? A pole with flags of various colors provides incentive for progressively increasing the height of the jump. Which flag did you touch when you jumped?

Cable jump

3. Can you jump over a stick, a scarf, or a rope? In which nursery rhyme does someone jump over a candlestick?

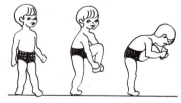

Greet the toe

4. Can you greet your toe? Can you hop while holding one foot?

Jump and tuck

5. Can you jump up and touch your knees? Can you jump up and touch your toes?

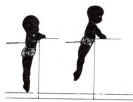

Straight arm support lean

6. Stand in the water facing the side of the pool with both hands on deck. How many times can you lift your body up almost out of the water with your arms alone? This is like a push-up on land. Can you lift your body upward and maintain a straight arm support?

Aquatic sprint

7. How many seconds does it take you to run across the pool? How many widths of the pool can you run in 3 minutes?

Bracketing with back lean

8. Can you hang on the pool railing (gutter) and arch your back? Can you do this with the soles of your feet on the wall instead of the floor? Can you do this with only one arm?

Matching locomotor movements to lines and forms

9. Can you walk a straight line drawn on the floor of the pool? A circular line? A zigzag line? Can you march on the line? Can you hop on it? Can you do these movements backward? Sideward?

Airplane or single-foot balance

10. How many different ways can you balance on one foot? Can you do an arabesque? A pirouette?

Aquatics for Handicapped Students **381**

Activities for the Advanced Explorer

Advanced explorers are learning to put their heads under water and to change level from up to down and vice versa. They are also experimenting with all of the possible ways to enter the water. They are not yet secure about a horizontal position in the water, but will assume it when the teacher's hand is in contact with some part of their bodies.

Towel Games

1. Taking rides. A child who trusts the teacher enough to hold his or her hands and allow the feet to rise from the bottom, thereby assuming a horizontal position in the water, can be taken on *rides*. These rides can be as dramatic as the child's (or the teacher's) imagination, with sound effects for a train, rocket ship, or whatever. The teacher talks to the child, continuously maintaining eye contact and pulling him or her along while walking backward. The next step in the development of trust is to convince the child to hang onto a towel or kickboard while the teacher pulls on the other end. Thus, the rides across the pool continue, but the child is progressively farther away from the teacher.

2. Individual tug of war. Every two children share one towel, each holding onto one end. A line on the bottom of the pool separates the two children, and the object is to see who can pull the other over the line first. As balance and body control in the water improve, teammates can be added until group tug of war is played. Only one teammate should be added to each side at a time.

3. Catch the snake. A rope about 6 feet long has a towel tied onto the end. The teacher or an agile child pulls the rope around the pool. The object is to see who can *catch the snake* first. The winner then becomes the runner who pulls the snake around the pool.

4. Beater goes round. Children stand in a single circle, facing inward. The *beater* stands on the outside of the circle, facing counterclockwise and holding a small hand towel (one not big enough to hurt when child is hit with it). A second child is running counterclockwise in front of the *beater*, trying to avoid being hit by the towel. He or she can be safe by ducking in front of any player in the circle after he or she has run around at least one-half of the circle. The player whom he or she ducked in front of must now run to avoid being beaten.

5. Tag with towels on pool bottom as safety rests.

6. Over and under relay using towels instead of a ball.

Exploration of Body Shapes Used in Aquatics

The terms *tuck*, *pike*, and *layout* are used in synchronized swimming, diving, and gymnastics. The Advanced Explorer learns to assume these shapes on land, in shallow water, and in the air. Movement exploration on the trampoline and the springboard in the gymnasium reinforce learning in the pool area. This aspect of aquatic training is designed specifically to improve proprioceptive awareness. The following questions elicit desired responses:

Tuck positions

1. In how many different ways can you assume a tuck position on land? In the water? In the air?

Pike positions

2. In how many different ways can you assume a pike position on land? In the water? In the air?

Layout positions

3. How many ways can you assume a layout position on land? In the water? In the air? Can you do back layouts? Front layouts? Side layouts?

Curved positions

4. In how many ways can you make your body curved on land? In the water? In the air? Can you combine a front layout with a curve? A back layout with a curve? A side layout with a curve?

It is anticipated that early attempts at assuming tuck, pike, and layout positions in the water will result in sinking to the bottom. Many children accidentally discover floating while concentrating upon body shapes. Those who do not discover floating gain valuable practice in breath control and balance.

Exploration of Ways to Enter the Water

Many children prefer a session of jumping and/or diving to swimming. In the beginning they may wish to have the teacher hold one or both hands and jump with them. Others prefer the teacher to be standing or treading water and awaiting their descent with outstretched arms. Participation in some kind of creative dramatics that demands a jump into the water often subtly evokes the desired response in children who have previously demonstrated fear and reluctance. Themes that have been particularly successful in motivating children to enter the water are (a) playing firefighter and sliding down the fire pole; (b) carrying lighted candles through a dark cave or perhaps the ancient Roman catacombs; (c) going on an African safari; (d) imitating Mary Poppins by opening an umbrella in flight; and, of course, (e) emulating spacetravelers through various trials and tribulations. In response to how many different ways can you enter the water feet-first, children may demonstrate the following:

1. Climb down the ladder. Most efficient method is facing ladder with back to water.
2. Sitting on edge of pool, scoot off into water: (a) freestyle (any way you wish); (b) in tuck position; (c) in pike position; and (d) with one leg straight, one bent.
3. Kneeling or half kneeling, facing water.
4. Kneeling or half kneeling, back to the water.
5. Squatting, facing water.
6. Squatting, back to water.
7. Standing, facing water using (a) step off; (b) jump and kneel in air before contacting water; (c) jump and tuck in air; (d) jump and clap hands; (e) jump and turn; (f) jump and touch toes; (g) hop; (h) leap; (i) arabesque; and (j) pike drop forward (camel walk position).
8. Standing, back to water, using: (a) stepoff; (b) jump; (c) hop; and (d) pike drop backward.

Stages in learning to dive

In response to how many different ways can you enter the water head-first, children discover the various stages in learning to dive. They may also lie on the side and do a log roll into the water or accidently perform a front somersault.

Self-Testing Activities for the Advanced Explorer

Frog jump

1. Can you jump like a frog under the water?

Jack-in-the-box

2. Can you squat in water over your head and then jump up and yell *boo* like a jack-in-the-box?

Dog walk when four limbs touch pool bottom; lame dog walk when three limbs touch bottom.

3. Can you do a dog walk with your head under water? A lame dog walk?

Mule kick

4. Can you do a mule kick in the water?

Seal walk

5. Can you do a seal walk under the water?

Camel walk

6. Can you do a camel walk under water? This is also called a wicket walk.

Egg sit followed by V sit

7. Can you do an egg sit at the bottom of the pool? Can you do an egg sit near the surface and sink downward?

Human ball bounce

8. Can you do five bent knee bounces at the bottom of the pool? Pretend you are a ball being dribbled.

Coffee grinder

9. Can you do the coffee grinder stunt at the bottom of the pool?

Knee scale

10. Can you do a balancing stunt under water with one knee and both hands touching the bottom? Can you lift your arms and do a single knee balance?

Bracketing

Bracketing (Figure 16.5) is the term for holding onto the gutter (rail) of the pool with one or both hands and allowing the feet to rise from the bottom of the pool so that the body is in a horizontal position.

Retrieving Objects from the Bottom of the Pool

Advanced Explorers learn about spatial relationships within a new context as they open their eyes under water and see objects *through* the water. In the earliest stages of underwater exploration they may hold both of the teacher's hands and submerge together. Under water, the student and teacher may establish eye contact, shake hands, and mirror each other's hand and arm movements. Later, the student can be challenged to retrieve all sorts of things from the bottom. Practice in form, size, weight, and color discrimination can be integrated with the instructions for retrieval of objects.

Figure 16.5 Bracketing on the front and back.

Activities for the Floater

The Floater is comfortable in the water and can do almost anything but swim a coordinated stroke for 20 yards to qualify for the Red Cross Beginner card. The Floater is probably more competent in underwater swimming than performing strokes near the surface. This is the period during which the following tasks are mastered: (a) horizontal to vertical positioning; (b) floating; (c) bobbing; (d) front to back positioning and vice versa; and (e) simple stunts in synchronized swimming.

Horizontal to Vertical Positioning

At this level, the Floater demonstrates ease in moving from a horizontal position to a vertical one. The degree of difficulty of this task varies with amount of buoyancy, specific gravity, and absence or paralysis of limbs. Simple sequencing is introduced as depicted in Figure 16.6.

Floating

In order to teach floating to persons with varying body builds and/or amputations of one type or another, it is important for the physical educator to have some understanding of the following terms: *buoyancy, specific gravity,* and *center of buoyance* (CB).

Buoyancy is the quality of being able to float. The buoyancy of a human being depends upon the amount of water that each body part is able to displace and the weight of the body part itself. The larger the surface of the body part, the more water it will displace. For instance, the typical woman with wide pelvis and well-rounded buttocks displaces more water than the average man with his characteristic narrow hips and flat buttocks. The lighter the weight of the body part, the less upward force is required to buoy it up. Thus, if a

Figure 16.6   Simple sequencing.

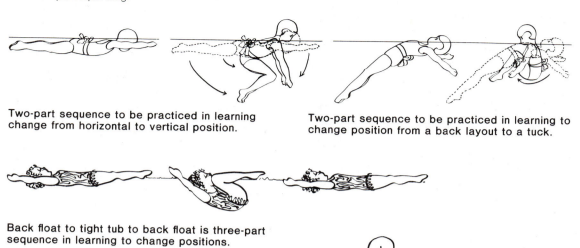

Two-part sequence to be practiced in learning change from horizontal to vertical position.

Two-part sequence to be practiced in learning to change position from a back layout to a tuck.

Back float to tight tub to back float is three-part sequence in learning to change positions.

A five-part sequence in changing position.

cork and a marble of the same surface area are dropped into water, the cork will float and the marble will sink. Adipose tissue (fat) weighs less than muscle and bone tissue. Thus if two persons of equal surface areas try to float and one individual is fat while the other is heavily muscled, the fat person will be buoyed upward more easily than the person with well-developed musculature. Buoyancy is explained by *Archimedes' principle,* which states: a body submerged in a liquid is buoyed up by a force equal to the weight of the displaced liquid.

The *specific gravity* of a human being is its weight compared to the weight of an equal amount of water as shown in this formula:

$$\text{Specific gravity} = \frac{\text{Weight of body}}{\text{Weight of equal amount of water}}$$

After full inspiration, the specific gravity of most adult human beings is slightly less than 1. This means that most adults can float with head above the surface of the water when their lungs are filled with air. After exhalation, the specific gravity of most adults is approximately 1.02. Only when the specific gravity is above 1.02 do individuals experience difficulty in floating.

The *center of buoyance* (CB) of a human being in water is similar in function to the center of gravity (CG) when the body is not immersed in fluid. Both are areas where weight is concentrated; both serve as fulcrums about which the body rotates.

The CB, for most persons, is located in the thoracic cavity. The more obese an individual is, the lower his or her CB is. The CB is defined as the center of

Figure 16.7   Effects of buoyancy on floating explain why there are many correct ways.

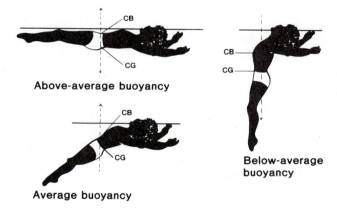

Above-average buoyancy

Average buoyancy

Below-average buoyancy

gravity of the volume of the displaced water before its displacement. If an object were of uniform density, its CB and CG would coincide; this is not the case with living creatures, human or fish.

In the water, the body can be likened to a first-class lever which, like a see-saw, totters back and forth around its fulcrum (CB) until balance is achieved. Only when the CB and the CG are in the same vertical line can a person float without motion.

Figure 16.7 shows that there is no one correct way to float. Each person must experiment until he or she discovers the position in which CB and CG are aligned vertically. The following hints may help pupils cope with problems of buoyancy.

Below-Average Buoyancy

Men, as a whole, have less buoyancy than women. Black students have less buoyancy than white students. Buoyance can be increased by raising the CG and hence the CB. This can be done by extending the arms overhead, by bending the knees so that heels almost touch the buttocks, or by assuming a tuck or jellyfish floating position. It also helps to hyperventilate, keeping the lungs filled with air, and exhaling as seldom as possible.

No attempt should be made to lift the feet and legs and attain a horizontal position since they will only drop downward again, building up enough momentum as they do so to pull the entire body under. Many persons who believe themselves to be *sinkers* could float if they started in the vertical rather than the horizontal position.

Above-Average Buoyancy

The obese person experiences many problems of balance for which he or she must learn to compensate. The alternate arm stroke on the back crawl, for instance, must be performed twice as fast as normal to prevent the body from rolling over. The hips, legs, and feet are often above water level so that no kick is possible.

The most anxiety-ridden experience, however, for the obese beginning swimmer is changing position from a horizontal position to a vertical stand. Try as he or she may, it is not easy to make the legs drop and the shoulders and trunk come forward so that the CG and CB are aligned over the feet.

Amputations

Amputations affect the location of the CG and the CB, which in turn affect buoyancy and balance. The loss of a limb causes displacement of the CG and CB to the opposite side. Thus, a pupil who has lost a right leg or arm has a tendency to roll to the left where the weight of the body is centered. Most persons with amputations or paralysis of muscles in limbs, whether congenital or acquired, can become excellent swimmers. Extensive movement exploration is recommended to enable each handicapped person to discover the floating position and swimming strokes that best serve his or her needs. Most pupils with severe orthopedic disabilities seem to prefer swimming on the back. Specifically, the following strokes are suggested:

1. Loss of both legs—back crawl or breaststroke.
2. Loss of one leg—back crawl, elementary backstroke, or sidestroke.
3. Loss of both arms—any kick that can be done on the back. This person has exceptional difficulty in changing from horizontal layout position to a stand.

4. Loss of one arm—sidestroke or swimming on back with legs providing most of the power and the one arm finning.
5. Loss of one leg and one arm—sidestroke with leg on the bottom; arm will create its own effective finning action.

Bobbing

Bobbing is similar to several vertical jumps in place except that all the power comes from the arms. It can be done in either shallow or deep water, but traditionally is associated with water over the head.

Down phase in bobbing   Up phase in bobbing

Bobbing consists of two phases. In the *down phase,* both arms are raised simultaneously upward, causing the body to descend. The breath is exhaled. When the feet touch the bottom of the pool, the arm movement ends. The *up phase* is then initiated by both arms pressing simultaneously downward. This action pushes the body upward. The arm movements in bobbing are different from all others the child has encountered. The concept of displacing water—i.e., pushing in the direction opposite from that which you wish to go—should be explained.

Bobbing accomplishes several goals: (a) improves rhythmic breathing; (b) increases vital breathing capacity—i.e., tends to hyperventilate the swimmer; (c) heightens proprioceptive awareness; and (d) serves as a warm-up activity. Bobbing is recommended especially for asthmatic children. Variations of bobbing are

1. Progressive bobbing. The down phase is identical to that of bobbing in place. The up phase, however, is modified by using the legs to push the body off the pool bottom at approximately a 65° angle. The arm movement is basically the same. Progressive bobbing is a survival skill in that it can be used as a means of locomotion from the deep end of the pool to the shallow.
2. Bobbing on one leg.
3. Bobbing in a tuck position. Down phase: arms pull upward, legs extend so that feet touch the

bottom. Up phase: arms press downward, tuck knees to chest so that full tuck is achieved at height of up phase.

4. Seesaw bobbing with a partner. To begin, partners face each other and hold hands. Then a rhythm is established in which one person is up while the other is down, as in partner-jumping on a trampoline.

Finning and Sculling

After the pupil masters a float, several sessions in movement exploration should focus upon the arms and hands. Such problems as the following can be posed for the back layout, front layout, tuck, and pike positions.

1. In the back layout position, how many different ways can you place your arms?

2. Which positions of the arms make floating easier? More difficult?

3. How many different kinds of movements can you perform with your arms in each position?

4. Which of these movements seem to make you sink? If you do sink, which of these movements can help your body rise to the surface of the water?

5. Which movements of the arms propel the body through the water head first?

6. Which movements of the arms enable you to execute the following changes of position?
(a) prone float to stand; (b) prone float to back float; (c) back float to stand; and (d) back float to prone float.

7. If you move only one arm, what happens? Can you propel the body directly to the right by using one arm only? Directly to the left?

8. In what other ways can you propel the body directly to the left? Directly to the right?

9. In how many different ways can you *push* the water away from you? *Pull* the water toward you?

Given sufficient time and encouragement, the pupil eventually discovers finning and sculling for himself or herself. Ideally, creative dramatics should be combined with movement exploration so that the child can tell the teacher and/or peers which emotions are being expressed by particular arm and hand movements. Variations of charades can be played in the water; the low organized game of trades offers opportunities for pantomime; and/or the pupils may *act out* the feeling that a particular musical composition conveys. When *finning* and *sculling* are discovered, the teacher should introduce the names of these movements and explain their usefulness in changing positions in the water. Movement exploration can then focus upon how many different ways the pupil can fin or scull.

Finning

Finning is defined as a series of short pushes with the palms of the hands against the water in the *opposite* direction to the one in which the pupil wishes to move. Each push is followed by a quick bent arm recovery under the surface of the water.

Sculling

There are many different recognized types of *sculling*. In the standard scull, the hands are at the hips close to the body. Movement at the shoulder joints is limited to inward and outward rotation of the arms that seem to be initiated by the hands in their execution of tiny figure eight motions close to the surface of the water.

The motion of the hands and wrists consists of an inward and outward phase, each of which is performed with equal force. The palms move toward midline during the inward phase and away from midline during the outward phase so that the water is alternately scooped toward the hips and then pushed away. The thumbs are up during the inward phase and down during the outward phase. If the child does not discover sculling for himself or herself, the movement should be introduced in the classroom and mastered before it is attempted in water. Sculling, for many swimmers, is a difficult pattern to learn through imitation.

Synchronized Swimming

The regulation stunts usually taught in units on synchronized swimming are similar to those performed in tumbling and gymnastics. Executing stunts in the water improves proprioception, enhances body awareness, and provides practice in the imitation of movements. The stunts described on the following pages can be mastered early in beginning swimming. The primary prerequisites are a feeling of ease in the water, the ability to scull while floating, and a keen sense of where the body is in space. Research at the Texas Woman's University has demonstrated that many slow learners can be taught to execute simple synchronized swimming stunts long before they achieve skill and endurance in regulation strokes.

All stunts are begun from either the front layout position or the back layout position, as depicted in Figures 16.8 and 16.9. Whereas skilled performers are

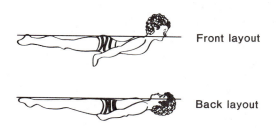

Front layout

Back layout

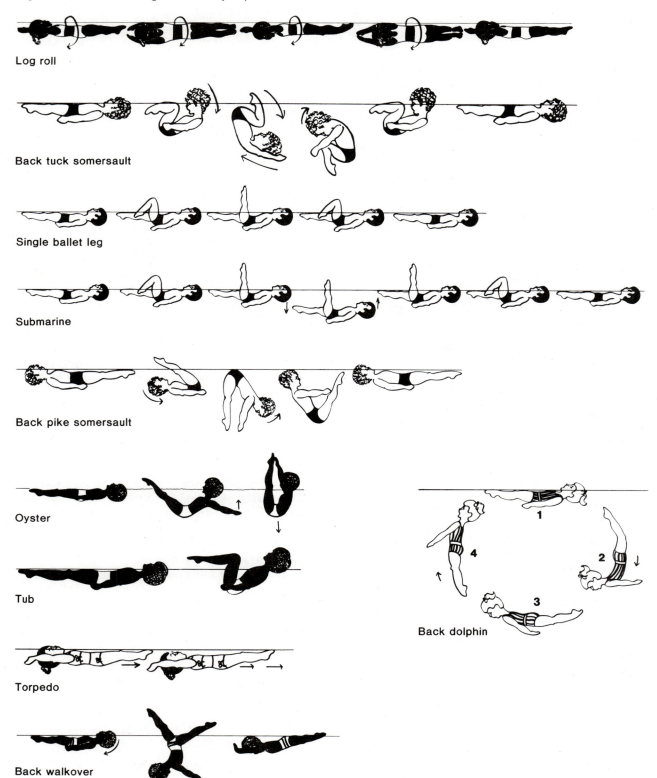

Figure 16.8 Stunts that begin in a back layout position.

Log roll

Back tuck somersault

Single ballet leg

Submarine

Back pike somersault

Oyster

Tub

Torpedo

Back walkover

Back dolphin

Figure 16.9 Stunts that begin in a front layout position.

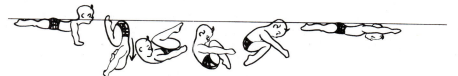

Front tuck somersault

Flying porpoise

Porpoise

Front pike somersault

Front walkover

concerned with the aesthetic appearance of a stunt, the adapted physical educator does not worry about *good form*. The stunts are introduced in a manner similar to other tasks in movement exploration. Very few verbal directions are posed; on some occasions a casual demonstration motivates the pupil to attempt new positions in the water. The stunts that follow are listed in order of difficulty under their respective starting positions. Stunts in which the body is carried in a tuck position are easier than those executed in the pike or layout positions.

Stunts That Begin in a Back Layout Position

Tub. Can you change from a back layout position to a tuck position with the thighs perpendicular to the surface of the water? In this position, can you use sculling to revolve the body around in a circle?

Log rolling. Can you roll the extended body over and over while keeping the legs motionless? This is identical to the stunt by the same name on land.

Back tuck somersault. Can you perform a backward roll in a tuck position?

Oyster, clam, or pike up. Can you drop your hips as you simultaneously hyperextend and inwardly rotate the arms at the shoulder joints? When you are touching your toes in a pike position, can you sink to the bottom?

Back pike somersault. Can you assume a pike position with trunk under the water but parallel to the surface? Can you perform a backward roll in this pike position? Which part of this stunt is like the oyster?

Torpedo. Can you scull with your hands overhead so that your body is propelled in the direction of your feet? Submergence of the head and shoulders is optional.

Back dolphin. Can you maintain a back layout position as your head leads your body around in a circle under the surface of the water? Can you perform this same stunt with one knee bent?

Single ballet leg. Can you scull across the pool with one leg perpendicular to the surface of the water and the other leg extended on the surface of the water?

Submarine. While performing a single ballet leg, can you submerge the entire body up to the ankle of the perpendicular leg and then rise to the surface?

Back walkover. Can you start a back dolphin but do *the splits* with the legs while they are above the surface of the water? This stunt ends in a front layout.

Stunts That Begin in a Front Layout Position

Front tuck somersault. Can you perform a forward roll in a tuck position?

Flying porpoise. Can you stand on the bottom, push off, and do a surface dive that looks like a flying porpoise?

Porpoise. Can you bend at the waist so that the trunk is almost perpendicular to the bottom while the thighs remain parallel to the water? From this position can you raise both legs until the entire body is vertical and then submerge?

Front pike somersault. Can you assume a pike position identical to the beginning of a porpoise? From this position can you do a forward roll?

Front walkover. Can you assume a pike position identical to the beginning of a porpoise? As the legs come out of the water, they do *the splits* so that you finish in a back layout position.

Rolling in the Water

Methods of rolling from back to front and vice versa in the water each have names within synchronized swimming circles. These terms are used by the adapted physical educator in order to teach children names for the stunts that they can perform, thereby improving their communication skills.

Half log roll. Changing from back to front float or from front to back float.

Log roll. Beginning from a back layout position with arms overhead, there are three ways to execute the log roll: (a) reach arm across body; (b) cross one arm over the other; or (c) cross one leg over the other.

Corkscrew. Log roll from sidestroke position to prone float or to same side on which you started. If sidestroke is on the left, a complete roll to the left is executed.

Reverse corkscrew. If sidestroke is on the left, a complete roll to the *right* is executed.

Marlin. (a) Start in *back layout* position, arms in T position, palms down; (b) roll onto right side, moving R arm to sidestroke position and L arm to side for *side layout* position; (c) continue roll onto front layout position, with both arms in T position; (d) roll onto L side, moving L arm to sidestroke position and R arm to side for *side layout* position; and (e) finish in *back layout* position with arms in T position.

Administrative Aspects of an Aquatics Program

Few teachers of handicapped students have the opportunity to design their own pool, but a community or school committed to serving *all* persons will implement adaptations recommended by a specialist. These may include construction or purchase of the following:

1. Nonskid surface for floors and decks.
2. Handrails in the shower room.
3. Several ways to turn the water off and on in the shower room, such as a button on the floor as an alternative for persons who have no use of their arms. Ideally, the water in the shower room should turn itself off automatically.
4. Doors into the locker room and the pool wide enough to allow wheelchairs through.
5. Ramps as well as stairsteps; a movable ramp for entrance into the swimming pool; ladders that telescope up and down. (See Figure 16.10.)
6. Flashing red and green lights at the deep and shallow ends respectively; a metronome or radio playing at the shallow end.

Figure 16.10 Use of chairlift for multiply handicapped student.

7. Floating buoys extended across the pool to warn of deep water; a change in the texture (feel) of the tile along the gutter; the depth of the pool written in braille in the tile every several feet.

8. A horizontal line on the wall that is the same height as the depth of the water below it; this line allows children to compare their heights with the line on the wall to ascertain that the water will not be over their heads if they jump into the pool at a certain point; the line on the wall or the wall itself may be color coded in terms of depth of the water.

9. A large storage cabinet with good ventilation to house the sponges, candles, rubber toys, ping-pong balls, and other accessories to movement exploration not used in ordinary swimming.

10. Hooks on the wall or plans for storage of inner tubes and other flotation devices needed in adapted physical education.

The depth of the pool determines its expense in large part. The Olympic size pool that provides for progressively deeper water is not recommended for the handicapped, nor for any group of children when instruction is the primary purpose of the pool. There is a definite trend toward building two or three separate pools rather than the multipurpose structure of the past.

The instructional pool needs a depth of only 3½ to 4 feet of water. Separate pools are constructed for diving, advanced synchronized swimming, and scuba diving.

Several public schools are now purchasing the porta-pool, which can be moved from school to school every several weeks. At the end of the day's instruction, a roof is pulled over the pool and securely locked in lieu of having to provide fencing and other safety measures. Nursery schools and special education units would do well to purchase the aluminum tank type pool sold by Sears and other commercial companies. Such pools are less expensive than trampolines and other pieces of playground apparatus.

The temperature of a swimming pool is normally maintained between 78° and 86°. While this temperature is invigorating, it is not geared to the needs of the beginning swimmer, who is partially out of the water when not in a horizontal position. Moreover, cold water tends to produce hypertonus and to heighten the spasticity of children with cerebral palsy.

To facilitate relaxation of muscles in the water and ensure an optimum learning environment, the temperature of water for adapted physical education instruction should be in the low 90°s. Increasing the temperature of the water causes two problems in the management of a pool: (a) the chlorine evaporates in 90° water and (b) the windows in the pool steam up from the evaporated water. Increasing chlorine count is easy enough, but the complaints of the swimmers about the chlorine hurting their eyes appears unavoidable. Sunlamps or infrared lamps built into the ceiling tend to control evaporation.

While the use of flotation devices has been criticized in conjunction with instruction for the nonhandicapped person, they are recommended highly in the adapted physical education setting. Their most important contribution is allowing independence in the water so that the severely involved person does not have to hold onto the teacher for support. In other cases, flotation devices serve as substitutes for missing or paralyzed limbs. They can help immeasurably in ensuring a proper head position when the child has poor control of cervical muscles. Cork slabs, styrofoam pieces, and small inflated tubes can be attached to disabled limbs to promote buoyancy.

Swim fins are recommended especially for children with spastic cerebral palsy since they tend to minimize the exaggerated stretch reflex and provide additional power in the kick. Individuals with amputations of upper or lower extremities may use swim fins as substitutes for limbs. Only by continuous experimentation can the teacher determine the type of flotation device and/or substitute limb that is best for a particular pupil. Considerable creativity is often required in solving problems of where and how to attach such devices to the body.

Figure 16.11 Sample information sheet to be filled in by physician.

Name _____

Medical Diagnosis _____

Diagnosis in laymen's terms _____

_____

Which part of the body, if any, is involved:

____ Right arm   ____ Left arm   ____ Neck

____ Right leg   ____ Left leg   ____ Trunk

Other_____

What specific exercises or movements do you recommend for the involved parts?

_____

Do you recommend learning to float or swim in any particular position?

____ Front   ____ Right side   ____ Head out of water

____ Back   ____ Left side   ____ Head used normally in rhythmic
                                               breathing

Should any special precautions be taken?

____ Needs to wear nose clip   ____ Should *not* dive

____ Needs to wear ear plug   ____ Needs to wear glasses

____ Should *not* hold breath   ____ Should *not* hyperventilate

____ Should *not* put head under water

   I recommend that this person participate in regularly scheduled swimming lessons adapted to his special needs as indicated on this sheet.

_____   _____
Date   Name of Physician

Health Examination

Written approval of both the physician and the parents should be on file prior to the beginning of swimming instruction. Most physicians prefer to use their own form but are willing to fill out supplementary information sheets (Figure 16.11).

Maintenance of close rapport with local physicians is essential to good adapted physical education. A thank-you mailed to the physician after receipt of the supplementary sheet contributes to good rapport. Likewise, it is worthwhile to develop a mimeographed sheet describing the similarities and differences between swimming in the adapted physical education setting and the regular class. Adaptations such as increased pool temperature, availability of ramps and flotation devices, and individualized or small-group instruction should be explained.

Conditions for Which Swimming or Diving Is Contraindicated

Swimming is universally recommended for individuals with all kinds of disabilities, with the exception of the following conditions: infectious diseases in the active stage—i.e., the child still has an elevated temperature; chronic ear infections, also the months during which tubes are in the ears; chronic sinusitis; allergies to chlorine or water; skin conditions such as eczema and ringworm; open wounds and sores; osteomyelitis in the active stage; inflammation of joints, as in rheumatoid arthritis; severe cardiac conditions; and venereal diseases.

Physicians will sometimes prescribe hydrotherapy for individuals with some of these conditions. Girls who wear internal tampons should be encouraged to participate fully in regularly scheduled instruction during their menstrual periods. Pregnant women generally swim until the sixth or seventh month, depending upon the philosophy of the obstetrician.

Diving may be contraindicated for individuals with arrested hydrocephalus, hemophilia, or anomalies of the face or head that affect normal breathing. Children with spastic cerebral palsy should not be taught to dive unless instruction is requested specifically by the parents and endorsed by the physician.

Time of Day for Swimming Instruction

The practice of waiting 1 or 2 hours after eating before engaging in swimming instruction is no longer viewed as valid except in the case of training for competitive swimming. Hence, swimming may be scheduled whenever it is convenient. It is perhaps better to conduct instruction after lunch than immediately before, when the level of blood sugar characteristically reaches its daily low.

Classroom teachers report that swimming early in the day tends to exert a quieting influence upon hyperactive children. A procedure should be created whereby a pupil may request a pass to report to the swimming teacher in lieu of a regularly scheduled class when the child feels exceedingly aggravated or in special need of *letting off steam*.

Undressing, Showering, and Dressing

Assisting young children and severely involved individuals with dressing procedures is an integral part of teaching swimming to the handicapped. Extreme care should be given to drying the skin and hair of children with Down's syndrome since they are especially susceptible to upper respiratory infections.

Moisturizing cream or oil should be applied to dry skin immediately after swimming. The characteristic dry, rough skin of many children could be softened by regular applications of cream.

If land drill is planned prior to entrance in the water, the preliminary shower should be eliminated. At no time should a child in a wet suit be out of the pool for more than a few seconds.

Teachers must observe their swimmers closely for blueness of lips, teeth chattering, goose bumps, and other evidence of chilling. Children tend to chill more quickly than adults; the thinner the child, the shorter the time in the water he or she can endure. In accordance with the principle of individual differences, *all* pupils should not be scheduled for instructional periods of identical lengths. Children in wet suits should *not* be allowed to sit on the edge of the pool with a towel draped about them in hopes that they will magically warm up and return for additional instruction. A child who professes to be too cold to remain in the pool should be expected to dry off and dress fully. Activities should be planned for individuals who leave the pool early, and the dressing room should be supervised at all times.

Learning Activities

1. Work a set number of hours in an aquatics program for children.
2. Find a nonswimmer who is afraid of the water. Take him or her through the Explorer, Advanced Explorer, and Floater competency levels described in this chapter. Keep a chronological log in case-study style of the teaching techniques used and the learner's responses.
3. Visit your local American Red Cross and YMCA offices and find out about the services they offer handicapped persons.
4. Complete the Red Cross certificate on teaching swimming to handicapped persons.

References

Clarke, L. (1973). *Can't read, can't write, can't takl too good either.* New York: Walker & Company.

Bibliography

American Alliance for Health, Physical Education, and Recreation. (1969). *A practical guide for teaching the mentally retarded to swim.* Washington, DC: Author.

American National Red Cross. (1975). *Swimming for the handicapped—instructor's manual* (rev. ed.). Washington, DC: Author.

Annand, V. (Ed.). (1976). Special issue on aquatics. *Therapeutic Recreation Journal, 10,* 33–76.

Brabant, J. (1983). Scuba diving for the disabled. *Sports 'N Spokes, 9,* (4), 9–11.

Bradley, N., Fuller, J., Pozos, R., & Willmers, L. (1981). PFDs: Personal flotation devices. *Sports 'N Spokes, 7* (1), 23–25.

Bradtke, J. (1979). Adaptive devices for aquatic activities. *AAHPERD Practical Pointers, 3,* 1–15.

Bundschuh, E. L., Williams, W. C., Holliingsworth, J., Gooch, S. & Shirer, C. (1972). Teaching the retarded to swim. *Mental Retardation, 10,* 14–17.

Canadian Red Cross Society. *Manual for teaching swimming to the disabled.* National Office, 95 Wellesley Street E, Toronto 5, Canada.

Cordellos, H. (1976). *Aquatic recreation for the blind.* Washington, DC: American Alliance for Health, Physical Education, and Recreation.

Grosse, S., & Gildersleeve, L. (1984). *The Halliwick method: Water freedom for the handicapped.* Milwaukee: Milwaukee Public Schools. (To purchase, write S. Grosse, 7252 W. Wabash Ave., Milwaukee, WI 53223.)

Grosse, S., & McGill, C. (1979). Independent swimming for children with severe physical impairments. *AAHPERD Practical Pointers, 3,* 1–15.

Grutzmacher, J. (1960). *An evaluation of three experimental methods of teaching swimming to blind and partially seeing children.* Unpublished doctoral dissertation, Ohio State University.

Holt, L. E., Joiner, L. M., Holt, A., & Shafter, A. (1970). Silvia versus Red Cross methods in teaching swimming to EMR children. *American Journal of Mental Deficiency, 74,* 483–487.

Keith, C. A. (1972). *The effect of swimming upon self-concept and selected motor fitness components in educable mentally retarded children.* Unpublished doctoral dissertation, University of Southern Mississippi.

Lowman, C. L., & Roen, S. (1952). *Therapeutic use of pools and tanks.* Philadelphia: W. B. Saunders.

Marshall, K. (1969). *The relationship between participation in a program of planned aquatic activities and changes in self-concept of orthopedically handicapped.* Unpublished doctoral dissertation, Texas Woman's University, Denton.

Moran, J. (1971). *The effects of the front crawl swimming stroke on trainable mentally retarded children.* Unpublished doctoral dissertation, University of Utah.

Nerger, J. A. (1977). *Development of beginning swimming techniques for visually impaired children.* Unpublished master's thesis, Texas Woman's University, Denton.

Newman, J. (1976). *Swimming for children with physical and sensory impairments.* Springfield, IL: Charles C. Thomas.

Padden, D. (1959). Ability of deaf swimmers to orient themselves when submerged in water. *Research Quarterly, 30,* 214–225.

Patrick, G. (1975). *Behavior modification techniques in aquatics.* Washington, DC: American Alliance for Health, Physical Education, Recreation, and Dance. (1900 Association Drive, Reston, VA 22091, IRUC reprint order #290.)

Piper, C. (Ed.). (1983). *Aquatics.* Topeka, KS: Jostens Publications.

Priest, L. (Ed.). (1977). *Adapted aquatics.* Garden City, NY: Doubleday.

Reynolds, G. D. (Ed.). (1973). *A swimming program for the handicapped.* New York: Association Press.

Richards, B. (1973). *The effect of drownproofing on the water survival of educable mentally retarded boys.* Unpublished master's thesis, University of Wisconsin, Whitewater.

Special Olympics, Inc. (1981). *Special Olympics swimming and diving sports skills instructional program manual.* Washington, DC: Author.

Stewart, J. B., & Basmajian, J. V. (1978). Exercises in water. In J. Basmajian (Ed.), *Therapeutic Exercise* (3rd ed.) (pp. 275–280). Baltimore: Williams & Wilkins.

Torney, J., & Clayton, R. (1981). *Teaching aquatics.* Minneapolis: Burgess.

Wilson, K. (1980). *Aquatics for the multiply handicapped: Six case studies.* Unpublished master's thesis, Texas Woman's University, Denton.

Wright, J. (1977). *Changes in self-concept and cardiovascular endurance of mentally retarded youth in a Special Olympics swimming program.* Unpublished master's thesis, Texas Woman's University, Denton.

Part 3 Adapted Physical Education for Individual Differences

17 Other Health Impaired Conditions

Figure 17.1 Students classified as *other health impaired* generally look normal but have chronic or acute health problems that adversely affect their educational performance.

Chapter Objectives

After you have studied this chapter, you should be able to

1. Define the term *other health impaired* (OHI) in relation to PL 94–142, cite examples of OHI conditions, and state the incidence of each.

2. Discuss the following topics in relation to OHI conditions: excuses from physical education, contraindication of vigorous activity, role of physician and other multidisciplinary team members, expectancy theory in relation to physical education programming, side effects of medication, and behavior management.

3. Explain each OHI condition included in the chapter, discuss its causes and/or biochemical bases, and state characteristics, behaviors, or symptoms. Remember the wide range of individual differences within each condition as you do this.

4. Synthesize information from this text and related readings into illustrative statements of present level of psychomotor functioning for hypothesized students with each OHI condition and develop physical education IEPs for these students.

5. Discuss integration of students with mild, moderate, and severe degrees of each condition into regular physical education and interscholastic athletics. When is integration the least restrictive environment? What classroom and teacher characteristics/behaviors are most facilitative? What adaptations, if any, should be made in grading systems for OHI students in regular physical education? In assessment and evaluation?

6. Discuss adapted physical education in terms of special individual or small group exercise, diet, and counseling programs that some OHI students may need. Explain the importance of involving families and significant others in such programming.

7. Design illustrative lesson plans for special individual or small group exercise, diet, and counseling programs for hypothesized students. In each, state specifically how instructional and environmental variables should be adapted.

8. Discuss available and needed research on physical education and athletics concerning each OHI condition. In which journals and books is such research found? What other sources (like theses and dissertations) can be used?

Special education funding is available for conditions specified under PL 94–142 as *other health impaired* (OHI). Legislation defines this term as "limited strength, vitality, or alertness due to chronic or acute health problems which adversely affect a child's educational performance" (*Federal Register,* August 23, 1977, p. 42478 [see Figure 17.1]). While many persons interpret *educational performance* as referring exclusively to the cognitive domain, several innovative physical educators have enlisted the aid of local physicians in diagnosing and classifying children with disorders like obesity, asthma, and heart disease as *other health impaired*. In this way they have made students who need adapted physical education programming eligible for such services under special education funding. In other instances, funds have been obtained for special exercise programs from voluntary agencies like the Lung Association or Heart Association.

Whether funding is available or not, physical educators need to understand and adapt programming for health impaired conditions. These conditions occur frequently among normal students as well as among the handicapped. They comprise the major reason why students request to be excused from physical education.

Incidence of OHI Conditions

PL 94–142 cites 11 examples of OHI conditions (see Chapter 3, p. 45, cited from *Federal Register*). The incidence of these per 1,000 persons in the general population is given in Table 17.1. Each of these conditions, with implications for physical education, is discussed

Table 17.1
Incidence Per 1,000 Persons of OHI Conditions Cited In PL 94–142

Condition	Incidence
Cancer	250
Heart condition	120
Diabetes	10
Epilepsy	5
Asthma	3–6
Rheumatic fever	2
Sickle cell anemia	2[a]
Hemophilia	.10
Nephritis (kidney disease)	—[b]
Lead poisoning	—[b]
Tuberculosis	—[b]

[a]Two per 1,000 blacks.
[b]Statistics not available.

in this chapter. Autism, which in 1981 was officially changed from the seriously emotionally disturbed category to OHI conditions, has an incidence of 5 per 10,000; it also is included in this chapter.

Numerous other OHI conditions that are common in the school age population include *obesity,* with an incidence of 10 to 20 per 1,000; *cystic fibrosis,* with an incidence of 1 per 1,000; *anemia,* with an incidence of 2 per 1,000; and such problems as menstrual disorders and teenage pregnancy. State educational policy generally requires that OHI conditions be officially diagnosed by a physician. An important role of the physical educator therefore is to refer students who request excuses from physical education to a physician who, in turn, will prescribe the type of instruction appropriate to the condition.

Anorexia nervosa, bulimia, and alcohol and drug abuse may be considered OHI conditions in some states. Because they are officially recognized by the American Psychiatric Association as mental disorders, they are discussed in this book in the chapter on serious emotional disturbances.

Excuses from Physical Education

Contemporary physical education philosophy does not condone excuses from physical education, even from physicians. The problem of medical excuses nevertheless still exists in communities in which there is no adapted physical education program and/or school personnel have not established rapport with physicians and educated them concerning the nature and scope of adapted physical education.

PL 94–142, strictly interpreted, makes excuses from physical education illegal. Remember, the law states, *Physical education services, specially designed if necessary, must be made available to every handicapped child receiving a free appropriate public education* (*Federal Register,* August 23, 1977, p. 42489). There is no law, of course, to protect nonhandicapped students from excuses when OHI conditions require program adaptations.

Central to the philosophy of no excuses from physical education is belief that classes should be *instructional* and thus treated as other instructional areas within the curriculum. Some physical educators violate this principle by conducting classes in which students do nothing but jog or perform repetitive exercises. In contrast, English classes do not require that students do all their reading and writing in class, nor do math and other academic classes require all work to be done in class. Music, art, and vocational education classes do not repeat the same activities day after day. Until physical educators assume responsibility for teaching *new* content daily and developing attitudes, knowledge, and habits conducive to healthy living, there will continue to be problems with medical excuses. Class is the place where one learns a wide variety of activities to keep physically fit and develops attitudes that lead to after-school exercise; class is *not* the place where one fulfills his or her daily need for exercise.

Central also to the philosophy of no excuses are teachers trained in adapted physical education who know how to individualize instruction to meet the needs of each student. The availability of a resource room, separate from the gymnasium, facilitates implementation of adapted physical education programming, as do flexible scheduling, testing procedures, and grading practices.

When Vigorous Activity Is Contraindicated

A basic principle of adapted physical education is modifying type, duration, and intensity of activity to meet individual needs. Physical education can include instruction in relaxation, mild rhythmic exercise on land or in water, accuracy tasks, like archery, dart shooting, and other activities done from a stationary position. Occasionally, the best physical education is teaching respect for the body's limits by permitting a nap or lie-down in a darkened room conducive to optimal rest.

Acute, or active, infection in any part of the body contraindicates vigorous exercise. This includes the common cold and respiratory infections in which the body temperature is elevated. Many of the OHI conditions described in this chapter have an acute or active stage; in most cases the student will be hospitalized or homebound during these days. If, for any reason, a student with a fever is in school, he or she should be learning relaxation techniques or sedentary physical activities.

Migraine and other severe headaches also contraindicate vigorous exercise. These are usually symptomatic of other conditions, and the student should be referred to a physician. Severe sunburn or injuries sustained in child abuse or fights may necessitate activity adaptation.

McArdle's syndrome is a rare neuromuscular condition in which skeletal muscle phosphorylase is deficient or absent. Exercise is contraindicated in this condition because the pathology causes muscle cramps, tenderness, and swelling to result from even mild exercise.

Among students able to attend school some type of physical education is appropriate, except for these exceptions, almost all of the time. When students request excuse from physical activity, their feelings should not be taken lightly. This is one of the most important reasons for scheduling an individual conference and beginning a counseling or helping relationship. Remember, *behavior is caused,* and it is essential to discover reasons why a student wants to be excused.

Role of the Physician

The role of the physician thus is no longer to write excuses for physical education. Nevertheless, the physician remains a very important part of the educational team, particularly in programming for OHI students. Rather than send written forms to be filled out, the physical educator should visit with the physician by telephone or in person. Advice should be solicited concerning recommended type, duration, and intensity of exercise. This should be in conjunction with the physical educator's description of his or her training in adapting exercise and of the many, varied activities available to students.

The rapport that physical educators have with physicians is different from that of professionals (physical and occupational therapists, some therapeutic recreation personnel, dance therapists) who follow the medical model. In these professions, workers seek exercise or activity prescriptions from physicians and are bound by ethics to follow them. Physical educators, like other special educators, adhere to an educational model in which placement and instructional decisions are made by educational teams, not a single physician. The physician may be a member of the multidisciplinary team. Many persons still do not know about this since the switch from a medical to an educational model did not begin until the 1950s and still is not fully implemented in some school systems.

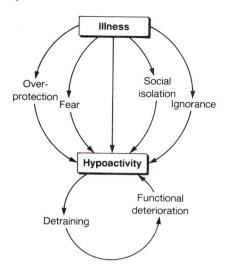

Figure 17.2 Direct and indirect links between illness and hypoactivity.

Basic Concepts in OHI Programming

Many of the conditions described in this chapter traditionally have been considered illnesses or diseases. The trend is away from this concept toward use of the term *condition.* Persons in the OHI classification may have periods of acute illness, but most of the time they *manage* their condition through use of prescribed medications and healthful living practices (i.e., well-balanced diets and regular sleeping, eating, and exercise habits). It is important, therefore, that teachers and parents not treat such persons as though they are ill. Remember expectancy theory; treat persons as ill or diseased and they will begin to assimilate your beliefs and actions into their self-concepts and behaviors. Treat them as healthy, intelligent persons who are managing their problems as best they can, and students will strive to fulfill this image.

In programming, stress abilities, not disabilities. Emphasize that you believe in students and their right to equal opportunity for instruction, recreation, and competition. Acquaint them with role models who have succeeded in sports despite OHI conditions.

Work with parents to minimize overprotection and with peers to ensure optimal acceptance and respect. Educate all concerned that regular exercise, except during episodes of acute illness, is as essential for OHI students as for nonhandicapped peers. Figure 17.2 depicts direct and indirect links between perceived illness and decreased exercise. One goal of adapted physical education is to break the vicious circle of illness to detraining and/or sedentary lifestyle to functional deterioration. This entails time spent in individual or small group counseling and helping as well as instruction in physical activities that are attractive to the students.

Many persons with OHI conditions have to be first convinced that they can engage in vigorous activities without ill effects. Table 17.2 presents reasons given for hypoactivity. These may be valid, but, in most instances, properly used medications and a positive mental state can prevent fears from materializing. Often, learning how much medication to take is accompanied by bad experiences, and some students give up before management of their condition is learned.

Most persons with OHI conditions, before they become physically fit, experience considerable discomfort in initial attempts to exercise and diet. They need to know that this is true of all persons and not specific to their health impairment. Exercise is not intrinsically pleasurable. Attitudes have to be inculcated that exercise is fun as well as necessary to healthy functioning. Unfortunately, persons with such conditions as asthma, obesity, and heart disease may require more time to become fit than peers without health impairments. They have a tendency to lose faith in their ability to achieve goals and/or become bored. Teacher and peer counseling is effective in counteracting this.

OHI conditions are often complicated by multiple health problems, many of which stem from hypoactivity. Obesity, for instance, is more common in persons with OHI conditions than in the general population. Almost all medications used to manage conditions have side effects. These vary widely from depression and extreme mood swings to fluid retention, weight gain, and general irritability. Both students and teachers need to understand side effects and work together in managing them. Maintaining good mental health is an essential goal.

Persons with OHI conditions fluctuate more from day to day in how they feel than able-bodied peers. They have good days and bad days, both mentally and physically. The inability to predict health and vitality from one day to the next causes anxiety and depression in some persons, who feel that their lives are controlled externally by unexplained variables. Every effort should be made in physical education programming to permit students to control their lives. This includes opportunities to make decisions about which activities should be learned and duration and intensity of practice. Teaching/learning contracts are helpful in this regard.

Behavior Management and Increasing Self-Control

Behavior management can be externally controlled or self-controlled. Information about locus of control, attribution, and most effective motivators should guide the physical educator in planning individualized programs. Physical education goals should be developed

Table 17.2
Causes of Hypoactivity in Pediatric Condition, as Stated by Parents or Patients

Condition	Cause of Hypoactivity
Bronchial asthma	Fear of post exercise attack
Diabetes mellitus	Danger of hypoglycemic crisis
Epilepsy	Fear of seizure and injury
Heart diseases	Fear of "heart attack"
Hemophilia	Fear of injury and bleeding
Obesity	Inhibition, social discrimination, low fitness
Innocent murmur	Fear of "heart attack"

cooperatively by student and teacher, shared with parents, and (when appropriate) with physician. Friends and peer counselors are important to involve also so that the student receives continuous and consistent positive reinforcement for exercise.

Emphasis should be placed on giving the student increasing responsibility for planning, implementing, and evaluating his or her activity program. The goal is to develop lifetime habits of physical activity, not just to participate fully in physical education class. Just as students do homework for language arts and math and receive credit toward their grades for homework, physical educators should encourage and reward after-school involvement in jogging, sports, dance, and aquatics.

Obesity

Obesity, to be eligible for special education funding, must be declared an *other health impairment* or *orthopedic handicap* by a physician and shown to affect the student's educational performance. Often more crippling than the loss or disability of body parts (see Figure 17.3), obesity affects 10 to 15% of school-age children in the United States. Moreover, one out of four girls and one out of five boys will be at least 10% overweight by the time they reach 20 years of age.

In the elementary grades, the classroom teacher periodically records the height and weight of each child. Later, the physical education specialist assumes responsibility for the classification of students into height-weight categories and the referral of the obese to their family physician. What criterion should be used in making decisions about who should be referred?

Most teachers use reference tables based upon desirable body weights for certain combinations of age, sex, and height factors. All such tables are subject to controversy. Children who are 10 to 20% above their

Figure 17.3 Obesity, when classified as either an *other health impaired* condition or an *orthopedic handicap*, is eligible for special education funding. Such children often need adapted physical education more than mentally retarded, blind, and deaf students.

Figure 17.4 The major endocrine glands, which help to regulate body fat and growth, are the pituitary, thyroid, and adrenal glands. Note that the adrenal glands are located above each kidney; this explains the derivation of their name: *ad* (toward) + *renal* (kidney).

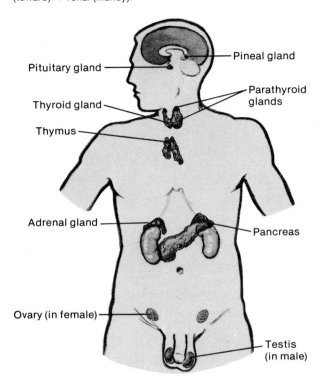

desired weight are considered *overweight*. Persons over 20% of their desired weight are *obese*, and those over 50% of their desired weight are *superobese*. This decision-making process is a screening technique since the clinical diagnosis of obesity is based upon many variables not considered in height-weight tables. Clinical judgment takes into account somatotypes, distribution of fat, muscle development, and sexual maturation as well as actual weight, height, age, and sex. No clinical tool for measuring obesity or estimating total body fat, not even the popular skin-fold thickness caliper measurements, is a reliable substitute for the physician's clinical judgment.

Causes of Obesity

Causes of obesity in childhood can be endocrine, medication-induced, or nonendocrine. Typically, the physician rules out endocrine and medication-induced etiologies before delving into other possible causes.

Endocrine Obesity

The endocrine system consists of glands (Figure 17.4) which secrete hormones, thereby controlling body activities and maintaining homeostasis. Amount of hormone secretion is regulated by either impulses from nerve fibers or releasing factors secreted by the hypothalamus (the part of the brain responsible for growth of body cells). Disorders of endocrine function result in several clinical obesity subtypes. Illustrative of these are the following:

1. *Hypothalamic obesity* manifested in syndromes in which the genitalia are markedly undeveloped and the weight is concentrated about the breasts, hips, and abdomen.

2. *Pituitary obesity*, generally designated as Cushing's syndrome. *Hirsutism*, or excessive hair growth, occurs in about 25% of the cases. Other characteristics are menstrual irregularities, acne, irregular fat distribution with adipose tissue concentrated around the breasts and abdomen, a ruddy, moon-shaped face, and a *buffalo hump*.

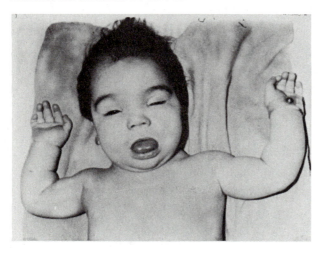

3. *Thyroid obesity,* including cretinism (Figure 17.5), juvenile hypothyroidism, and myxedema. These clinical types are often puffy and myxedematous (swelling of tissues), but not actually fat.
4. *Adrenocortical obesity,* caused by malfunction of the adrenal cortex, the outer covering of the adrenal glands. Hypersecretion of the cortex in childhood causes sexual precocity—i.e., the early development of secondary sexual characteristics. Appearance is similar to that of Cushing's syndrome.

Less than 10% of childhood obesity can be ascribed to one of these clinical types. Of these disorders, however, many are complicated by mental retardation and other abnormalities. The adapted physical educator therefore is confronted with endocrine obesity more often than is the regular physical educator.

Medication-Induced Obesity

Medications used to manage such chronic conditions as severe asthma, arthritis, leukemia, and nephritis tend to cause obesity as one of their side effects. The result is appearance similar to that of Cushing's syndrome. This is because the medications (cortisone, prednisone, and other adrenocortical steroids) are related to the adrenocorticotrophic hormone (ACTH) secreted by the pituitary gland, which, in turn, regulates secretions of the adrenal glands. The ACTH-related medications are the miracle drugs of the twentieth century; children, as well as adults, who require them on a daily basis may exhibit many side effects like mood swings, depression, increased appetite, and insatiable hunger for sweets. Neither the mechanisms of the drugs nor the side effects are yet well understood. In addition to *cushingoid obesity,* long-term reliance on the steroids may also cause growth retardation, osteoporosis (softening of bones), and hypertension.

Nonendocrine Obesity

Nonendocrine causes of obesity include (a) habits of overeating in relation to energy output, (b) familial and genetic patterns, (c) environmental influences, (d) metabolic sluggishness, and (e) psychogenic effects. Obesity is seldom traced to a single cause. The interaction between hereditary and environmental factors, complicated by a vicious circle of emotional problems stemming from and contributing to fatness, must be explored skillfully.

Familial patterns of fat distribution are often apparent. Fat may be centralized or localized about the hips, thighs, breasts, chest, or abdomen. Before planning weight reduction regimes, it is advisable to obtain information about the total body weights and patterns of fat distribution of parents, grandparents, and siblings. Even with stringent dieting, it is difficult to change the prominence of such body parts as hips and buttocks, which may be genetically predisposed to heavy padding. Children should be helped to understand that losses in weight do not necessarily slim down desired body parts. Body build is determined by the bony skeleton, not by adipose tissue. Goal setting must be realistic.

Studies show that in families with parents of normal weight, only 8 to 9% of the children are obese. When one parent is obese, 40% of the children are likewise. When both parents are obese, this percentage doubles. Eating patterns learned early in childhood and passed down from generation to generation seem to be as much a factor as genetic predisposition. The leisure time attitudes, interests, and practices of family and neighborhood also affect the balance between food intake and energy expenditure. Some ethnic and cultural values also contribute to obesity: (a) a fat baby is a healthy one; (b) the amount of food on the table is indicative of economic status; (c) it is impolite to refuse dessert or a second helping; (d) a good host or hostess always has something in the pantry or refrigerator; (e) new neighbors should be welcomed with gifts of food; and (f) desserts, rather than fruits and less fattening foods, are traditionally the proper refreshments for social functions.

Table 17.3
The Caloric Cost of Various Activities

Activity	Caloric Cost	
	Per Minute	*Per Hour*
Walking slowly (2.6 mph)	1.92	115
Walking moderately fast (3.75 mph)	3.58	215
Walking very fast (5.3 mph)	9.42	565
Running	13.33–21.67	800–1,300
Swimming	5.0–16.67	300–1,000
Rowing	16.67–21.67	1,000–1,300
Cycling	2.5–10.0	150–600

(Running, Swimming, Rowing, Cycling: depending on speed)

Weight Reduction Programs

The physical educator who wishes to introduce a weight reduction program into his or her school must be conscious of working, not only with the *whole* child, but with the entire family and ethnic group. Perhaps the most successful weight reduction classes are part of the extracurricular program organized to include both parents and children.

Whether curricular or extracurricular, weight reduction programs should be engaged in voluntarily and supported by sympathetic counseling. The approach must be nonthreatening and nonchastising. Fat children often have emotional problems that perpetuate habits of overeating. Many psychologists believe that eating is a form of oral gratification to which persons unconsciously regress when they feel unloved or insecure. Such persons tend to nibble continuously, not because they are hungry, but to meet hidden needs and drives. The fat child must be reassured that he or she is loved and accepted for what he or she is. This is difficult when one realizes that the child does not easily separate the self from the body. Criticism of excessive body weight is often internalized as criticism of self. Many obese persons have built up elaborate defense mechanisms to preserve ego strength. It should not be assumed that they will be receptive to offers to help with weight loss, nor that they will admit openly to dissatisfaction with their bodies.

Long-Term Management of Obesity

Long-term management of obesity has been likened to that of alcoholism and drug abuse. The problem can be solved temporarily, but never cured. Of the many persons who make rapid and large weight losses, only 10% achieve lifetime weight control. Steiner states in this regard,

Obesity is more preventable than curable, particularly if the weight gain starts early in life and becomes excessive or progressive beyond adolescence. In our experience most early and excessive weight gainers remain obese into adulthood. Out of 200 children who were obese under the age of 9 years, 74 percent of the boys and 70 percent of the girls remained obese at age 18 years regardless of the type of diet or medication used to manage the obesity. (Steiner, 1970, p. 23)

Much research has been conducted in which persons are subjected to vigorously controlled weight reduction programs. Although temporary success is usually achieved, most of the obese persons regain lost pounds within a period of 3 years. Clearly, only the symptoms of obesity are being treated in most management programs, and the underlying causes of weight gain have not been eliminated.

Implications for Physical Education

The obese child can often be helped by a combination of diet control, exercise, drugs, and counseling. One therapeutic approach without the others is generally futile and serves only to disappoint the pupil. Hence, the physical educator must work as part of a team that never loses sight of the *whole* child nor the child's role in the family setting.

The goal of most weight reduction programs is to achieve a new balance between food intake and energy output. A pound of body weight is the equivalent of 3,500 calories. In order to lose an average of 2 pounds a week over a long duration of time, the dieter must take in 1,000 fewer calories a day. This deficit can be created partially through exercise, as demonstrated by Table 17.3.

The exact caloric count for an activity depends upon body weight, but these approximations give an idea of the caloric loss that can be expected through exercise. The well proportioned physical educator often does not realize how unpleasant vigorous exercise can be for obese persons. A consideration of the physical characteristics of the obese pupil leads to realistic program planning.

1. *Distended abdomen.* This results in anatomical differences in the position of the stomach and the length of the intestinal tract, thereby affecting vital processes. It also creates excessive pressure on the diaphragm, which leads to difficulty in breathing and the consequent accumulation of carbon dioxide, which helps to explain patterns of drowsiness. The distended abdomen makes forward bending exercises difficult or impossible.

2. *Mobility of rolls of fat.* The bobbing up and down of breasts, abdomen, and other areas where excessive fat is deposited is uncomfortable and often painful during locomotor activities.

3. *Excessive perspiration.* Layers of fat serve as insulation, and the obese person more quickly becomes hot and sweaty than the nonobese.

4. *Galling between the thighs and other skin areas that rub together.* After perspiration begins, continued locomotion causes painful galling or chafing somewhat similar to an abrasion. Such areas heal slowly because of continuous irritation and sometimes become inflamed.

5. *Postural faults.* Obese children are particularly vulnerable to knock knees, pronation, flatfeet, sagging abdomen, drooped shoulders, and round back. These postural deviations all affect mechanical efficiency in even simple locomotor activities.

6. *Skeletal immaturity.* The growth centers in the long bones of obese adolescents are particularly susceptible to injury, either from cumulative daily gravitational stress or sudden traumas from such strenuous or heavy activities as contact sports, weight lifting, and pyramid building.

7. *Edema.* Obese persons seem to retain fluids more readily than nonobese. This causes swelling of ankles, breasts, and wrists, particularly during the menstrual period.

8. *Broad base in locomotor activities.* The combination of knock knees, tendency toward galling between thighs, and pronation result in a slow, awkward gait with feet often shoulder width apart.

9. *Fear of falling.* Added weight makes falling from heights both painful and dangerous.

10. *Excessive buoyancy in water.* The inability to keep most of the body submerged makes the mastery of standard swimming strokes difficult.

The truly obese child finds any exercise more vigorous than walking almost impossible. Physicians recommend that a 1,200 calorie regimen designed to cause a weight reduction of approximately 2 pounds a week be supplemented by a daily walk of at least 1 mile. Physical education for the obese pupil should be scheduled immediately after lunch and offer sufficient time for the completion of a mile-long walk. A pedometer fastened to the pupil's belt enhances record keeping.

In a weight reduction program, the primary purpose of the physical educator is to change attitudes toward exercise and to develop habits of regular daily activity that will endure beyond the program itself. What will make walking pleasurable? An opportunity to socialize with a friend, the chance to take a dog for an outing, the freedom to walk to an agreed upon destination across town? Many individual sports—golf, archery, the discus and javelin throws, horseshoes, and croquet—are walking activities in which the obese can find success. Any throwing or striking activity in which balls or projectiles must be repeatedly recovered can be adapted into games with motivational point systems. Oftentimes, the walk to a community bowling alley or batting range is more valuable in terms of caloric expenditure than the sport itself. Some obese children have developed such power in batting that their slowness in getting to base is not a real handicap. In some schools the obese pupil is given a turn at bat and a friend runs the bases for him or her.

The need for socialization through play is the same for obese children as for others with disabling conditions. Walking and exercising done in conjunction with a special weight reduction program should not substitute for physical education activities with peers even though the obese child's participation may be limited to score keeping or umpiring. Others must learn to accept the obese child just as they would an amputee.

Like other orthopedically handicapped pupils, the obese child should be allowed privacy in dressing and showering if it is requested. Standard gymnasium costumes may be impossible to find, and long pants may be more appropriate than shorts.

Figure 17.6 Exercises for dysmenorrhea. (*A*) *Billig pelvic stretch*. Place forearm, elbow, and palm of hand against wall at shoulder height; place other hand against posterolateral pelvis and push pelvis forward and sideward toward wall while strongly contracting gluteal and abdominal muscles; relax and repeat eight times to each side. (*B*) *Knee-chest position*. Lie as indicated for several minutes with knees as close to chest as possible. For variation, combine with abdominal pumping or extend legs alternately backward very slowly. (*C*) *Mosher* *abdominal pumping*. Alternately contract and relax abdominal muscles slowly but forcefully enough that on contraction pelvis flattens against floor and on relaxation pelvis moves upward. Coordinate deep breathing with tensing and relaxing and massage area if it seems to relieve pain. (*D*) *Golub stretch and bend*. Perform exercise in two parts as shown, lifting leg as high as possible on stretch phase while maintaining rest of body in good alignment. At end of each upward stretch, relax momentarily in good standing posture with arms extended at shoulder height; then repeat to opposite side.

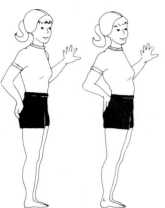

A. Bellig pelvic stretch

B. Knee-chest position

C. Mosher abdominal pumping

D. Golub stretch and bend

The heavier a child is, the more important it is that certain activities be avoided. These include tasks that involve lifting his or her own weight such as chinning and rope climbing, and those that entail lifting external weights such as weight training, serving as the base of a pyramid, and couple tumbling stunts. The sympathetic teacher can devise many adaptations to draw the pupil into the group and foster the development of favorable attitudes toward fitness.

The use of successive contracts, specifying specific goals and rewards after the loss of each 5 or 10 pounds, has been found an effective motivational technique in weight reduction. The pupil is free at all times to revise the contract to allow more food and less exercise, but few take advantage of this option. This contract is a means of involving the child in his or her own decision making, yet reinforcing the successes.

Research has shown that adapted physical education programs conducted specifically for obese students have been successful in reducing the prevalence and degree of obesity (Johnson, 1968). Special camps for obese children have also been shown effective (Rohrbacher, 1973).

Menstrual Problems

Girls sometimes use menstrual problems as an excuse not to suit up and participate in physical education. A healthy approach to solving this problem is *modeling* (setting a good example) by the female physical educator, who should point out that she always suits up, regardless of her period, and that in the real world women are expected to show up for work every day and be optimally productive. All girls should be required to dress for activity and to engage in some kind of mild activity. Nowdays most girls (using internal tampons) swim during their periods and engage in normal or strenuous exercise. *Task cards* with special abdominal exercises designed to alleviate pain can be given to girls who prefer mild activity on these days (see section on abdominal relaxation in Chapter 12, Postures).

Dysmenorrhea (painful menstruation) does occur in some girls early in the menstrual cycle, usually before the blood begins to flow freely. This pain is often partly caused by an accumulation of gas (flatus) or by constipation. Exercises that relieve flatus, such as the bent-knee creeping position/movement, and several yoga techniques also ameliorate menstrual pain (see Figure 17.6). Severe or continued pain that cannot be relieved by aspirin and exercise signals the need to see a physician. *Menorrhagia* (excessive flow) is not normal and contraindicates exercise. The student should lie in a supine position with legs propped up and should see a physician as soon as possible.

Teenage Pregnancy

In many states, pregnancy in young adolescents is categorized as an *other health impaired condition* and included within the special education administrative domain. Infants born to extremely young mothers, as well as middle-aged ones, are considered high risk (more likely to have problems). Maintaining a high level of health and fitness, with optimal prenatal care, in teenage pregnant girls generally necessitates school-based or private agency assistance.

Most physicians concur that pregnant girls should engage in regular daily exercise up until the time of delivery. Activities recommended include archery, badminton, bowling, dancing, golf, jogging, swimming, and tennis—practically all the individual and dual sports. Swimming after the first 30 weeks of pregnancy should be approved by the physician since it is somewhat controversial. Special exercises for pregnancy are available through physicians and described in several books. These are generally more enjoyable when done with others and with musical accompaniment.

The intensity and duration of exercise are highly specific to the individual and depend largely on the state of health and fitness before pregnancy. When persons have previously been sedentary, exercise programs must be progressive. Whenever possible, pregnant women in their 20s who have previously borne children should be brought in to lead exercises and serve as models. With some girls, it is motivational to have their husbands (or boyfriends) engage in the exercise programs with them.

Individual or group exercise is just as important after arrival of the baby as before. If the lifestyle before pregnancy did not include exercise, it would be good if motherhood were to cause increased awareness of the importance of a family exercising together.

Cancer

Cancer, a condition of unknown etiology in which body cells multiply in an abnormal manner and cause tumors, is second only to accidents as a cause of death in children ages 1 to 15 years. Most children who develop cancer, however, do not die; they continue to attend school while undergoing treatment. The incidence in children under 15 years is approximately 13 per

Table 17.4
Incidence of Various Types of Cancer in Childhood

Type	Relative Incidence (%)
Leukemias	33.8
Lymphomas, including Hodgkin's disease	10.6
CNS tumors	19.2
Adrenal glands and sympathetic nervous system	7.7
Muscle, tendon, fat cancers	6.7
Kidney cancer (Wilms' tumor)	6.0
Bone cancer	4.5
Eye cancer	2.7
Other	1–2.0

Note. In contrast, cancer of the lung, breast, colon, and skin is most common in adults.

100,000. Each year about 7,000 new cases are diagnosed within this age range. Table 17.4 indicates the incidence of the various types of childhood cancer.

For the population as a whole, it is estimated that one in every four persons will have cancer. Cancer, the second greatest cause of death in adults, affects more persons in middle and old age than in youth.

Management of Cancer

Cancer is treated by chemotherapy (drugs), radiation therapy, and surgery. Estimates are that of every six persons with cancer, two will be saved, one will die but could have been saved if proper treatment had been received, and three cannot be saved with current knowledge. These estimates are for the total population, not children and youth whose chances for recovery are considerably higher. Over half of the cancer fatalities are over age 65.

Side effects of treatment are sometimes more difficult to manage than cancer itself. Radiation treatments are painless, but the side effects may include hair falling out, nausea, vomiting, and weight loss. The side effects of chemotherapy are similar, with additional problems like anemia and associated decreased exercise tolerance, easy fatigability, and heightened susceptibility to respiratory infections. Often, low blood cell counts caused by chemotherapy result in the need for periodic blood transfusions.

No physical education research has yet been published in relation to childhood cancer. The psychological effects of physical exercise and the importance of continued involvement in peer activities form the major rationale for keeping students with cancer in regular physical education, adapting instruction as needed.

Cardiovascular Problems

Broadly speaking, there are two types of cardiovascular problems: congenital heart disease and acquired cardiovascular disorders. Over 25 million Americans have some form of cardiovascular disorders. An additional 30 to 40 thousand infants are born with heart disease each year. Moreover, the incidence of death from cardiovascular disease in the United States is higher than in any other country in the world.

Heart disease is the number one cause of death in United States citizens ages 25 and over. It ranks sixth as a cause of death in the 15- to 24-year age range. Although not a leading cause of death among children, acquired cardiovascular disorders are believed to begin in childhood. A major role of physical education, therefore, is to teach the values of physical activity in reducing the incidence of heart disease and to develop attitudes and habits conducive to healthy cardiovascular function.

Values of Physical Activity

The values of physical activity should be universally known and understood, even by mentally retarded children. Handicapped adults who can serve as models of fitness should be found in the community, and/or films should be shown of such persons as Harry Cordellos, blind marathon runner and swimmer, and Pete Strudwick, who runs without feet. Cardiovascular benefits of strenuous physical activity include the following:

1. A slower heart rate. The normal heart beats about 72 times a minute or 103,680 times a day. If the resting heart beat can be dropped to 60 times a minute, the heart only beats 86,400 times a day—quite a difference.

2. Lower blood pressure. Ideally, in adults, systolic blood pressure should be around 130 and diastolic should be in the 70s.

3. Increased cardiac output (liters of blood ejected by heart per minute). Five liters per minute is normal for an average adult man at rest; in a well-trained athlete this can be increased to 42 liters per minute.

4. Improved blood circulation with improved transport of oxygen (and hemoglobin) to cells.

5. Decreased serum lipids (fatty substances) in blood.

6. Improved maximum oxygen (O_2) consumption. The minimal threshold standard for optimal fitness for men ages 20 to 40 seems to be an *oxygen uptake* (aerobic capacity) of 38 to 45 milliliters (ml) of oxygen per kilograms (kg) of body weight per minute.

Table 17.5
Risk Factors in Cardiovascular Disease

Factors that can be altered
1. Hypertension (high blood pressure)
2. Elevated serum cholesterol levels
3. Cigarette smoking
4. Diet
5. Physical inactivity
6. Body fatness
7. Diabetes
8. Emotional stress

Factors that cannot be altered
1. Heredity
2. Age
3. Sex
4. Race

Risk Factors in Heart Disease

Physical educators are concerned with preventive education and exercise for all persons as well as with meeting the needs of students with cardiovascular disorders. Much of the fitness thrust in physical education strives to achieve these goals.

The three greatest risk factors in acquired heart disease that can be altered by changed lifestyles are (a) hypertension (high blood pressure), (b) elevated serum levels in blood, and (c) cigarette smoking. Table 17.5 shows the other risk factors. Handicapped and nonhandicapped students alike need to be taught these factors and encouraged to develop lifestyles that minimize them. Among handicapped persons, *obesity* and *physical inactivity* are particularly acute. Teachers should be aware of their roles as models—i.e., that children learn more from appearance and actions than from words. It is important also to engage in family education rather than focus exclusively on students.

Acquired Cardiovascular Disorders

Coronary heart disease (also called atherosclerosis) causes over 50% of the deaths from acquired disorders. It is a slow, progressive, degenerative condition in which the inside linings of the arteries become thickened by deposits of fats and other materials. (See Figure 17.7.) This narrows the passageway for blood circulation. Eventually, one of the vessels supplying the heart becomes blocked. The result is a heart attack (myocardial infarction).

Figure 17.7 Coronary heart disease results when one or more of these coronary arteries (blood vessels of the heart) develops a condition that interferes with the delivery of an adequate supply of blood (and hence oxygen) to the structures of the heart.

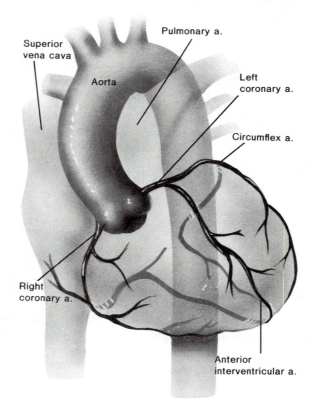

Superior vena cava

Aorta

Pulmonary a.

Left coronary a.

Circumflex a.

Right coronary a.

Anterior interventricular a.

Table 17.6
Cardiovascular Disorders and Percentage of Deaths

Disorder	% of All Deaths
Coronary artery disease (atherosclerosis)	56
Stroke	20
Hypertension (high blood pressure)	7
Myocardial degeneration	5
General arteriosclerosis	4
Rheumatic fever	2
Other cardiovascular diseases	5

Table 17.6 gives the names of the other acquired heart disorders and the percentage of deaths caused by each. Approximately 1 of 10 Americans has heart disease. Children and youth are thus familiar with heart disease in that many of their parents, relatives, and adult friends have it.

Rheumatic Fever

Acquired heart disease in children and adolescents is often the result of rheumatic fever. This disease is a chronic inflammation caused by an allergic reaction to the antibodies that the body produces to fight streptococcus bacteria.

About 500,000 youths ages 5 to 19 have rheumatic heart disease. Rheumatic fever and rheumatic heart disease are separate entities. Of every 100 persons with a streptococcus infection, approximately 1 to 3 will develop rheumatic fever. Of the youngsters who have rheumatic fever, only half will develop rheumatic heart disease.

Characteristics

In recent years there has been a tendency to overdiagnose rheumatic fever. To combat this problem, the American Heart Association has derived five criteria for use in making a valid diagnosis. At least one of the following criteria, along with laboratory evidence based upon a throat culture, must be present to confirm a diagnosis of rheumatic fever.

1. *Arthritis*—manifested in tenderness, swelling, heat, and redness in one or more joints. Aching of joints without these symptoms is not indicative of rheumatic fever.

2. *Infection of heart muscle*—often diagnosed by the presence of heart murmurs. It is cautioned, however, that about 60% of all children have benign heart murmurs. Three types of inflammation may occur:

   a. *Myocarditis*—inflammation of the wall of the heart often resulting in enlargement of the heart. When the acute phase of the inflammation is over, the heart usually returns to its normal size and frequently recovers completely.

   b. *Pericarditis*—inflammation of the outer lining of the heart.

   c. *Endocarditis*—inflammation of the valves and/or the inner lining of the heart. This is the most dangerous side effect in that scar tissue causes the valves to become either *stenotic* or *regurgitant*. The mitral and aortic valves are affected most frequently. Regurgitant valves cause the condition popularly known as *leakage of the heart* in that they permit blood to leak into the chamber it has just left. Stenosis, or narrowing of the valves, often does not occur until several years after the first attack.

3. *Chorea*—also known as St. Vitus Dance. Rheumatic inflammation of a part of the brain that results in tics, motor awkwardness, and tremors. It should be noted that chorea is caused by numerous other factors besides rheumatic fever.

4. *Skin rash*—may appear only from 24 to 48 hours.

5. *Subcutaneous nodules*—seen only in more severe cases of rheumatic fever, these are nontender, hard lumps that may appear over the elbows, knees, shins, backs of the forearms, or wrists.

Management of Disease

In the past, the main form of treatment was strict bed rest for 2 or 3 months followed by a 6- to 9-month period of convalescence in which activity was limited. The judicious use of steroids now enables pupils to get up in a few days and return to school in 2 or 3 weeks. No activity restrictions are necessary other than exclusion from competitive sports for 2 or 3 months. The introduction of exercise early in the therapeutic regime, even when severe heart damage is suspected, is recommended to avoid the physical and psychological problems of prolonged invalidism.

Once students have had rheumatic fever, they are increasingly susceptible to recurrences of inflammation. Each new attack brings the possibility of permanent heart damage. Since the initial flareup of rheumatic fever often does not injure the heart, prevention of subsequent attacks is all important. This is accomplished through daily ingestion of penicillin tablets or monthly intramuscular injections over a period of years. Streptococcus never becomes resistant to penicillin, so the dosage remains essentially the same as the child grows into adulthood. The age at which the daily medication can cease is controversial, ranging between 20 and 40, but there is agreement that the individual should be free of all rheumatic symptoms for at least 5 years.

Individuals who have had valvular heart disease of any kind are urged to take large doses of appropriate antibodies before dental work or surgery regardless of their age. Adults who have had rheumatic heart disease are especially susceptible to pericarditis, myocarditis, and endocarditis throughout their lifetimes. Because of the amount of bacteria normally present in the mouth, dental work poses a particular threat.

Implications for Physical Education

Every child who has had rheumatic fever is different. Half of them never develop heart disease and hence have no activity restrictions. The other half vary tremendously with respect to degree and duration of disability. Many children have grown up believing that they have heart disease only to learn in adulthood that physicians can no longer detect symptoms of cardiac imperfection. As a whole, persons with cardiovascular problems probably impose more restrictions on themselves than necessary.

No child who is able to walk to school and/or a distance of a block or so should be excused from physical education. In severe cases of rheumatic heart disease, physical education may be limited only to walking and relaxation exercises, but some type of regular activity is essential to *total* rehabilitation. The physical education program for a pupil with a history of rheumatic heart disease is similar to the progressive reconditioning plan followed by the middle-aged after a coronary attack. If, however, there is severe valvular involvement, physical exercise will contribute little to improved cardiovascular function.

Whereas exercise is almost always emphasized in the rehabilitation of an adult after a heart attack, it may be contraindicated in children whose hearts are pumping against the narrowed aortic valve or leaking mitral valve so characteristic of rheumatic fever heart disease. In such cases the primary objective of physical education is to develop interest and skill in such lifetime sports as fishing, archery, and leisurely hikes. No attempt is made to work on cardiovascular fitness through exercise. In rheumatic heart disease, as in other cardiovascular conditions, the work tolerance of each pupil must be determined individually. The classifications denoting severity of disability and the general guidelines for planning exercise are applicable to all kinds of heart disease.

Congenital Heart Defects

Congenital heart disease is approximately 20 times more frequent in childhood than acquired cardiovascular disorders. The incidence of congenital heart defects is 6 to 10 per 1,000 live births. While many of these infants will die during their first year, an ever-increasing number are being kept alive. It is estimated that 75 to 80% can be helped by surgery. Ideally, this surgery is undertaken before age 6 so that the child can start school with a normal or near-normal heart and few exercise restrictions. In the case of the blue baby, however, surgery may be done during the first few weeks of life.

Neill and Haroutunian (1977), reporting on 2,639 patients ages 10 to 29 years seen in their cardiac clinic, indicate that 73% had congenital malformations, 7% had rheumatic heart disease, 2% had arrhythmias, another 2% had systemic hypertension, and 16% had essentially normal hearts. These current statistics confirm prevalence estimates of congenital defects in the generations born since refinement of heart surgery techniques.

Once a congenital defect has been corrected by surgery, the chances are good that the child will have no exercise restriction. Many participate in strenuous high level competitive sports. The pupil should be allowed the freedom to decide how hard to play, since sensations are usually a reliable guide to exercise tolerance. The psychological problems stemming from parental overprotection and preoperative anxieties and fears are generally greater than residual physiological limitations.

Physical educators should be familiar with the most prevalent congenital heart defects in that they appear in children's files rather frequently. Table 17.7 lists

Table 17.7
Most Frequent Congenital Heart Defects (%)

Defect	Abbreviation	%
Ventricular septal defect	VSD	21
Tetralogy of Fallot	TOF	20
Pulmonic stenosis	PSV	10
Atrial septal defect	ASD	9
Aortic stenosis, valvar	ASV	7
Coarctation of aorta	COA	6
Single ventricle and tricuspid atresia	SIV TAT	4
Patent ductus	PDA	4
Mitral insufficiency, stenosis	MIC	4
Endocardial cushion defect	ECD	3
Transposition	TGV	2
All other		10
		100

From Neill and Haroutunian, 1977, p. 720.

these defects and the approximate percentage of each in terms of total number of defects. A brief review of the anatomy of the heart and the physiology of normal blood circulation enhances understanding of the medical terms used in relation to congenital heart defects. This review is afforded by Table 17.8 and Figure 17.8.

Definitions of Terms

A review of the basic terms used in heart disease helps to make sense of the congenital disorders.

Septal refers to septum, meaning a dividing wall between two chambers. In the heart there is an atrial septum and a ventricular septum.

Patent is from the Latin word *patens*, meaning wide open or accessible.

Ductus arteriosus is a tubelike passageway in the fetus between the aorta and the main pulmonary artery.

Tetralogy is a group or series of four.

Great vessels are the aorta and pulmonary artery.

Stenosis means constriction or narrowing of a passageway.

Coarctation means tightening or shriveling of the walls of a vessel; compression.

Atresia means pathological closure of a normal anatomical opening, or congenital absence of the opening.

Table 17.8
Review of Blood Flow in Pulmonary and Systemic Circulation

	Collecting Chamber for Blue Blood	Valve	Pumping Chamber	Valve	Artery	Circulation	Venus Return	Collecting Chamber for Pink Blood
Pulmonary Circulation	Right atrium	Tricuspid	Right ventricle	Pulmonary	Pulmonary	Lungs	Pulmonary veins	Left atrium
Systemic Circulation	Left atrium	Mitral	Left ventricle	Aortic	Aorta	Total body	From head and arms via superior vena cava; from trunk and legs via inferior vena cava	Right atrium

Figure 17.8 Diagram showing four chambers of the normal heart and physiology of pulmonary and systemic circulation.

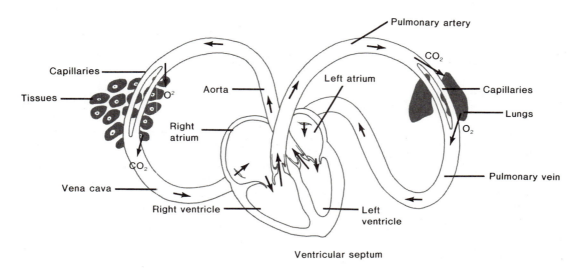

Shunt is a hole in the septum between the atria or the ventricles that permits blood from the systemic circulation to mix with that of the pulmonary circulation or vice versa.

Cyanosis is blueness resulting from deficiency of oxygen in blood.

This book focuses only on the three most common congenital defects. These account for over 50% of all problems.

Ventricular Septal Defect

Small openings (holes) in the septum often close spontaneously during the first or second year of life. Many small and even medium-sized openings that do not close are harmless and can be ignored completely. Some shunting occurs in any septal defect. The severity of the problem depends upon the effect that the shunt has on pulmonary circulation and the extent that the amount of oxygen normally circulated throughout the body is decreased. (See Figure 17.9.)

Figure 17.9 Ventricular septal defect, the most prevalent congenital heart condition, is caused by an opening in the *ventricular septum* which permits abnormal shunting of blood from the left to right side of heart. In minor cases, the heart compensates by hypertrophying, and the cardiac function is relatively normal except for a loud heart murmur.

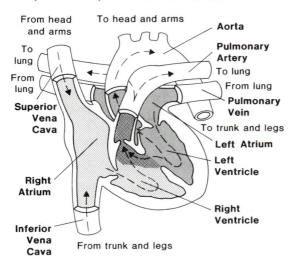

Figure 17.10 Tetralogy of Fallot, which causes *blue babies*, may result in hypoxic spells characterized by breathlessness, hyperventilation, increased cyanosis, and loss of consciousness. While waiting for the physician, the child should be held upright, against the teacher's shoulder, with the knees tucked up to the chest.

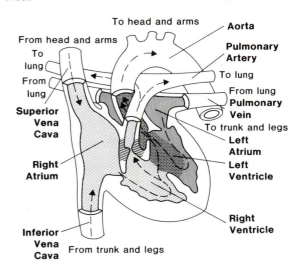

Ventricular septal defects can now be repaired in open heart surgery with a mortality risk of less than 5%. The surgeon may either suture the sides of the defect together or insert a plastic patch over the hole.

Tetralogy of Fallot

This combination of four abnormalities is the most common of the congenital heart defects that produce cyanotic or *blue babies* (Figure 17.10). The abnormalities are (a) ventricular septal defect; (b) pulmonary stenosis; (c) enlarged right ventricle; and (d) an abnormal positioning of the aorta so that it *overrides* both the right and left ventricles. These abnormalities cause interrelated malfunctioning in which *unoxygenated* blood from the right ventricle is forced through the left ventricle and circulated throughout the body. The unoxygenated blood is bluish in color. If enough of it mixes with the pink blood in the systemic circulation, the infant becomes cyanotic.

Tetralogy of Fallot can be corrected through surgical repair, but the mortality rate is still 5 to 25%. Whenever possible, corrective surgery is not undertaken until the child is 4 or older.

Stenosis and Coarctation

Both of these terms refer to a narrowing or constriction of a valve or the area near it, resulting in decreased flow of blood. This congenital narrowing is relatively frequent in the pulmonary and aortic valves. If the constriction is great, the muscle wall of the affected ventricle hypertrophies as it repeatedly exerts the extra effort required to push the blood through the valve. *Pulmonary stenosis* (Figure 17.11) leads to right heart failure, with the increased pressure backing up into the veins of the body. Edema is a side effect. *Aortic stenosis* (Figure 17.11) leads to left heart failure, with the pressure building up in the left atrium and the lungs. Insufficient blood is pumped to the brain and other vital organs of the body including the heart itself. Symptoms of severe aortic stenosis are breathing difficulty, chest pain, and fainting.

Implications for Physical Education

Many handicapped children (particularly deaf-blind and multihandicapped) have heart defects. Approximately 40% of Down's syndrome children are so affected, mostly with minor septal defects. Metabolic and nutritional diseases, especially those involving the deficiency or excess of thyroid hormones, are generally

Figure 17.11 Pulmonic and aortic stenosis. Shading indicates the stenotic valve. (A) Narrowed pulmonary valve, which decreases blood flow from the right ventricle into the pulmonary artery and lungs where carbon dioxide is released and oxygen taken in. (B) Narrowed aortic valve, which decreases blood flow from left ventricle into the aorta and thus interferes with coronary blood flow.

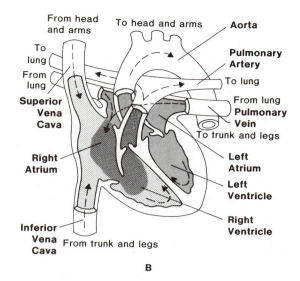

A

B

complicated by heart disease, as are the muscular dystrophies, rheumatoid arthritis, and other musculoskeletal diseases.

Few children die of congenital heart disease after age 5. The prevailing teaching philosophy is well expressed as follows:

It is rare that a child with congenital heart disease requires any restrictions other than those imposed by him alone. The major possible exception is the child with aortic stenosis. A recent review of the natural history of this disease indicates that the possibility of sudden death is a hazard. Yet, most of the deaths occurred in severely affected patients. The greatest risk was during the first year of life and after the first three decades. We are not convinced that there is any proof that the child with mild aortic involvement requires restriction of his activities. . . . The child with moderate or severe disease probably should not be allowed to participate in competitive sports. However, in most of these children, the obstruction will have been relieved by operation long before they have developed a deep interest in athletic activities. (Adams & Moss, 1969, pp. 605–606)

Guidelines for Handicapped Students

1. The individualized physical education program for a student with cardiac involvement should be developed in a multidisciplinary setting. Physician, parents, classroom teacher, physical education specialist, and pupil should all provide input.

2. Activities described in Chapter 14 on relaxation and reduction of hyperactivity should be taught as well as breathing exercises and games.

3. If the pupil already knows how to swim and relaxes easily in water, aquatic activities are excellent since the water minimizes the pull of gravity on the body. In contrast, perhaps no activity is more demanding than swimming the width of the pool when one is a beginner!

4. In order to determine the appropriate amount of exercise, the pulse rate should be taken before and after a new sequence is tried. The pulse rate rises normally during the exercise, but it should return to resting rate in no more than 3 minutes after cessation of movements. If it does not, the sequence should be made easier before the next attempt.

5. Exercises performed in a back lying position are the least demanding of all activities. Each student should be encouraged to establish his or her own cadence rather than conform to the pace set by a teacher. He or she should also assume increasing responsibility for the number of repetitions and the duration of rest periods.

6. The guided discovery and motor creativity teaching styles can be used to facilitate a growing understanding of the body and an appreciation of abilities and limitations.

7. Guidance in establishing a realistic level of aspiration for various activities should be provided. Emphasis should be upon competition against self rather than others. Recreational activities that encourage competition against self should be taught. The student should be introduced to community facilities where these are conducted.

Guidelines for All Students

All able-bodied students should be encouraged to exercise at 60 to 90% of their maximum heart rate at least 15 minutes a day, 3 to 5 times a week as a means of preventing heart disease. When persons do not do this of their volition, an exercise prescription may be used as motivation. Unless the physical educator has special training in exercise physiology and cardiac rehabilitation, the prescription should be written by a physician.

Table 17.9 presents recommendations for an exercise prescription for adults who wish to maintain and/or improve cardiovascular function. This program is designed to burn about 300 calories per workout. It has been used successfully in 20-week training periods with sedentary (but healthy) men.

Cardiac Rehabilitation

Principles of cardiac rehabilitation apply to persons of all ages. With special training in exercise physiology, adapted physical educators should be able to develop and/or implement exercise prescriptions for persons of low fitness, including those recovering from heart attacks. Such programs begin with a medical examination, including an exercise stress test, administered or supervised by a physician. Many physical educators learn to give stress tests in exercise physiology courses. In the case of cardiovascular disease, however, it is essential to have electrocardiographic monitoring capacity and emergency equipment like the DC cardiac defibrillator available. Cardiovascular rehabilitative training should not be begun until a signed release from the physician and the student (or client) is on file.

The aerobic exercise phase of cardiac rehabilitation begins about 8 to 12 weeks after a heart attack or coronary bypass surgery. With regard to intensity and duration of prescribed exercise,

Table 17.9
Recommendations for Exercise Prescription for Healthy Adults

Frequency	3–5 days/week
Intensity	60–90% of maximum heart rate
	50–80% of maximum oxygen uptake
Duration	15–60 minutes (continuous)
Mode (activity)	Run, jog, walk, bicycle, swim, or endurance sport activities
Initial level of fitness	High = higher work load
	Low = lower work load

Note. These recommendations can be applied to athletes as well as sedentary persons. The prescription will differ in that the athlete will require more frequent and exhausting bouts of work, and the sedentary person a more conservative regimen with more interval work.

The usual procedure is to recommend that the patient maintain his or her highest conditioning heart rate at 80–85 percent of the measured maximal or symptomatic heart rate on the exercise test for 15–20 minutes 3 times a week . . . preliminary data on patients with coronary atherosclerotic heart disease indicate that this level of intensity, duration, and time of conditioning does provide measurable benefits in 6–12 weeks. (Gilbert, 1978, p. 559)

Stress testing is repeated periodically and the exercise prescription revised accordingly.

Persons in cardiac rehabilitation programs demonstrate achievement at the 6 MET capacity before transferring from an individualized program having continuous heart monitoring to a group program. *MET* is a term often used in exercise prescriptions; it is the basal oxygen requirement of the body sitting quietly—i.e., a measure of energy consumption. One MET equals 3.5 milliliters of oxygen per kilogram of body weight per minute. Table 17.10 illustrates how the MET is used in an exercise prescription.

Most adapted physical educators, however, are concerned primarily with the management of heart disease in children and youth. Compared to the growing body of knowledge on adults, little has been published on children, normal or handicapped.

Respiratory Problems

Most of us take breathing for granted. We squeeze air out of our lungs 20,000 times a day and seldom think about the phenomenon of respiration. Yet respiratory diseases are the fastest rising causes of death in the United States. This section is about persons who struggle to breathe. They may have *asthma, chronic obstructive pulmonary diseases,* or *cystic fibrosis.* The symptoms are similar in all conditions, and exercise is

Table 17.10
Unsupervised Walking Program

Exercise tolerance test information: A patient is stopped by 3+ angina (heart rate 130) after 2.5 minutes at 3 mph on a 10% upgrade on the treadmill. Angina and ST segment depression began at 2.5 mph at a heart rate of 120.

First exercise prescription: 2.5 mph at 10% upgrade = 6 METS = 21 ml O_2/kg min. This is the angina threshold. Train at 75% of 6 METs = 4.5 METs = walking at 3.0–3.5 mph on level ground, daily.

Period	Intensity (METs)	Intensity (ml O_2/kg min)	Equivalent exercise
Warm up	2–3	7–11	Walk ¼ mile in 7.5 min (2 mph)
Training	4–5	14–18	Walk 1 mile in 20 min (3 mph)
Cool down	2–3	7–11	Walk ¼ mile in 7.5 min (2 mph)

Subsequent exercise prescriptions: Using the same warm-up and cool-down patterns, alter the training period as follows:

1. Walk 2 miles in 40 minutes daily for 3 weeks (4.5 METs for twice the duration).
2. Walk 2 miles in 35 minutes daily for 3 weeks (approx. 7 METs for nearly the same duration).
3. Retest. If the patient completes the 4 mph stage at 10% grade on the treadmill with 3 mm ST depression (28 ml O_2/kg min, 8 METs) and develops 1+ angina at the 3.5 mph stage, the patient should then:
4. Walk 2 miles in 35 minutes, increasing to 3 miles in 51 minutes within 3 weeks.
5. Increase to 3 miles in 45 minutes for 3 weeks.

vital for the maintenance of respiratory fitness. It is estimated that almost half of the chronic diseases suffered by children under age 17 are respiratory in nature. Asthma, hayfever, and other allergies account for approximately 33% of all chronic diseases in this age group. Bronchitis, sinusitis, and related conditions cause 15.1%. Cystic fibrosis, although rare, results in death from chronic lung disorders. The physical activities for these children are the same as those for children with asthma.

Emphysema is primarily a disease of middle and old age, but its origins can often be traced to asthma and chronic bronchitis in earlier years. Over a million persons in this country lead restricted lives because of emphysema. The fastest growing cause of total disability in the United States, it is surpassed only by heart disease.

Asthma

Asthma is a chronic lung disease similar to other *health impaired conditions* (diabetes, epilepsy, and the like). Management depends largely on medication and avoidance of stimuli that trigger attacks. Attacks are characterized by spasms of the bronchial tubes (see Figure 17.12), swelling of their linings, and excessive secretion of mucus, all of which cause coughing, wheezing, dyspnea (breathing difficulty), and a feeling of constriction in the chest.

Prevalence

In the United States, asthma is the leading chronic disease in the age group below 18. Approximately 6 million Americans suffer from asthma, most of whom are under age 15. The incidence of asthma is slightly higher among boys than girls. Many children seem to *grow out of* asthma during puberty; thus, the greatest concentration of asthmatic children is in elementary school.

Children with asthma tend to be multiply handicapped in that they frequently suffer also from hayfever, various allergies, sinus trouble, and upper respiratory infections. They are prone also to weight problems and low fitness.

Causes of Asthma

The etiology of asthma has now been traced to *deficient homeostatic function* at the cellular level; specifically, an abnormality in the beta adrenergic receptors of the lungs. These receptors serve to maintain balance between the nerve fibers that release epinephrine (adrenalin) and those that liberate acetylcholine. Any alteration of this balance causes changes in the tonus of the bronchial tube linings. The resulting deficient homeostasis increases irritability of the bronchii to all kinds of stimuli.

Within the broad spectrum of individual differences, asthmatics may be hypersensitive to cigarette smoke, changes in weather, changes in body temperature, air pollutants, and other stimuli too numerous to name. Because infection affects homeostasis, it is a major precipitator of bronchial constriction and other asthmatic symptoms.

Multiple factors interact to produce the symptoms of asthma. The tendency to develop allergic sensitivities is clearly inheritable. Persons with asthma may manufacture a special type of antibody, which has been termed *reaginic, homocytotropic, skin sensitizing, or immunoglobulin E (IgE). These antibodies, called reagins,* are responsible for positive skin tests. Although allergies to specific pollens, molds, foods, and animals frequently are present, *asthma is no longer considered fundamentally an allergic disease.*

Figure 17.12 Diagram of the lungs showing bronchial tubes.

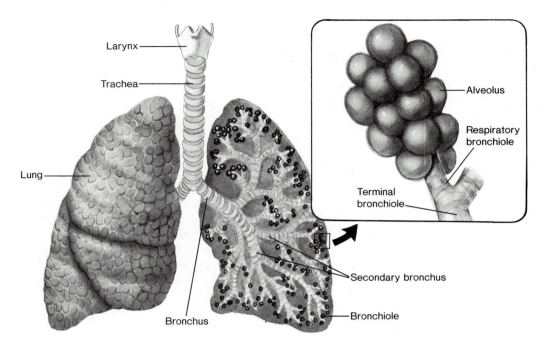

Larynx

Trachea

Lung

Bronchus

Alveolus

Respiratory bronchiole

Terminal bronchiole

Secondary bronchus

Bronchiole

Asthma Attacks

While asthma is chronic and always present, *attacks* occur only occasionally. A brief look at normal respiration helps to explain the extreme difficulty with exhalation during an asthmatic attack (see Table 17.11). During both inspiration and expiration in asthma, more and more muscular effort is needed to move air through the constricted passageways. Because of the difficulty and prolongation of the expiratory phase, normal deflation of the lungs cannot occur before the next inhalation begins. The lungs therefore remain in a state of maximum expansion. Because of the growing oxygen deficit, the child tries to take in more and more air, thereby compounding the problem of exhalation.

Asthmatic attacks progress through three stages: (a) coughing, (b) dyspnea, and (c) severe bronchial obstruction. The third stage should be prevented whenever possible by use of medication, cessation of exercise, or removal of allergens.

A hacking, nonproductive cough constitutes the first warnings of an impending attack. In this stage the bronchial tubes are secreting mucus, which accumulates and obstructs the passage of air. The coughing is caused by the reflex action of the smooth, involuntary muscles of the bronchioles in an attempt to remove the accumulating mucus. Treatment should begin at this point to prevent the onset of the next stage.

Table 17.11
Phenomena of Normal Breathing

Inhalation	Exhalation
Bronchial tubes widen.	Bronchial tubes narrow.
Diaphragm contracts and descends. Contraction of the diaphragm pulls down on the central tendon, and up on the sternum and ribs, thereby increasing vertical diameter of thorax.	Diaphragm ascends as a result of its elastic recoil action when it relaxes.
Abdominal muscles relax (return to normal length).	Abdominal muscles shorten, particularly in forced exhalation.
Upper ribs are elevated.	Ribs are depressed.
Thoracic spine extends.	Thoracic spine tends to flex.

Dyspnea occurs when the linings of the bronchioles swell, thus narrowing the air passages. The diminished flow of air through the bronchioles results in increasing shortness of breath. Wheezing is caused by the movement of the air in and out of the constricted bronchial tubes and in and through the accumulated mucus. During this stage the pattern of breathing is markedly altered, with difficulty experienced in *exhalation* and resultant gasping for air.

Normally, the discomfort during this stage is intense. The student cannot breathe in a lying position so he or she sits or paces until medication takes effect. While inhalators bring more-or-less immediate relief, most medications taken by mouth require several minutes. Intellectually, the asthmatic may be well aware of the need to relax and control himself or herself, but the ability to do so in the absence of oxygen is lessened. The tenser he or she becomes, the more difficult it is to exhale. As the medication begins to dilate the bronchioles, the attack subsides, usually with much coughing and spitting of mucus.

If the treatment does not prove effective, *severe bronchial obstruction* results in so little passage of air that the child becomes cyanotic and may die if emergency measures are not taken. Breathing during this stage may become inaudible, wheezing may cease, and the fatigued respiratory center in the medulla may no longer function normally. An asthmatic attack seldom progresses this far. If it does, the child should be rushed to the nearest hospital.

Exercise and Asthma

In the middle 1970s new research findings were published on exercise-induced asthma (EIA) that are now influencing physical education practices. It was found that short-term exercise of less than 4 minutes facilitated breathing (bronchodilation), while longer-term exercise resulted in bronchoconstriction. EIA occurs in persons of all ages but is more common in children, appearing in 85% of boys and 65% of girls with severe asthma. EIA is elicited most often in running activities and least often in swimming.

Screening tests are recommended to determine whether an asthmatic person falls in the EIA classification. If he or she does, special pre-exercise medication like *cromolyn sodium* is prescribed to prevent or reduce EIA in competitive exercise. *Warm-up* activities prior to competition have been found important also. Hard exercise (75% or greater of maximum oxygen uptake) is more likely to produce EIA if not preceded by warm-up.

Children with EIA should participate in regular strenuous exercise, within the guidelines of pre-exercise medication and warm-ups. Guiding the EIA child into the *best* kind of activity for his or her condition is important—i.e., dashes are preferable to long-distance runs, and games like baseball, softball, and volleyball are more fitting than those that demand continuous running. The newly accepted principle for EIA children is *intermittent exercise*—no more than 5 minutes of vigorous activity followed by 5 minutes of rest; then another 5 minutes of vigorous activity and another 5 minutes of rest; and so forth. Swimming remains the exercise of choice.

Implications for Physical Education

The Committee on Children with Handicaps of the American Academy of Pediatrics issued a formal statement on the asthmatic child and participation in physical education:

Physical activities are useful to asthmatic children. The majority of asthmatic children can participate in physical activities at school and in sports with minimal difficulty, provided the asthma is under satisfactory control. All sports should be encouraged, but should be *evaluated on an individual basis for each asthmatic child,* depending on his tolerance for duration and intensity of effort. Fatigue and emotional upheaval in competitive athletic contests appear to be predisposing factors in precipitating asthmatic attacks in some instances. This may depend to some extent on the duration and severity of the disease. *As a general rule, every effort should be made to minimize restrictions and to invoke them only when the condition of the child makes it necessary.* (American Academy of Pediatrics, 1982)

The decision to modify the regular physical education program should be shared cooperatively by physician, child, parents, and physical educator. Before a group conference for this purpose is called, the physical educator should take the initiative in acquainting the physician with the nature and scope of the physical education activities. Without such orientation, many pediatricians do not have adequate background to evaluate specific sports, dance, and aquatics activities as strenuous, moderate, or mild. Nor will they know that the physical educator has special training in adapting activities to the needs of asthmatic students.

The medications that students with severe asthma take every few hours have increased in effectiveness over the years. Students who experience breathing problems in physical education are not yet properly managing their asthma and need to be referred to a specialist for further study. Often, considerable time is required to determine the best drug for a particular person and to experiment with different dosages; likewise, time is needed to learn to manage both the environment and stresses related to feeling different from peers. Should the asthmatic student want to give up and resume a sedentary lifestyle, the physical educator must inspire the faith and courage to return to the physician once again and to keep trying alternatives.

Asthma can be managed so students can participate in vigorous activities of their choice. The Asthma and Allergy Foundation of America began a national scholarship program in 1984 in recognition of this fact. Awards ranging from $1,000 to $10,000 are given to high school students with asthma who excel in both competitive sports and academics.

In recognition of the importance of role models, this same organization is disseminating information about the many asthmatic athletes of Olympic caliber.

Of the 597 members of the 1984 United States Olympic Team, 11% were involved in an aggressive screening and counseling asthma outreach program. Among these athletes were medal-winning cyclists Alexei Grawal, Bill Nitts, and Steve Hegg; sprinter Jeannette Bolden; swimmer Nancy Hogshead; rowing medalist Ginnie Gilder; and many others. The new message is that persons with asthma can excel in competitive sports. For an excellent pamphlet on asthma and exercise, write to Exercise and Asthma, Asthma and Allergy Foundation of America, 1302 18th Street NW, Suite 303, Washington, DC 20036.

The greatest challenge to physical educators is helping asthmatic students overcome initial barriers. Many, in the beginning, are overweight and have very low fitness. The breathlessness and severe discomfort they experience are not caused by asthma, but by their low fitness. The nature of their condition is such, however, that it takes longer to achieve fitness than non-asthmatic peers. There is no doubt more discomfort also.

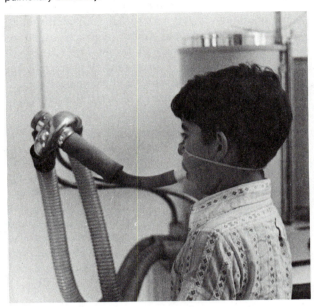

Figure 17.13 Child exhales into spirometer as test of pulmonary efficiency.

Screening

Information that should be obtained about the asthmatic student before beginning an exercise program includes (a) age; (b) type of asthma; (c) season during which asthma is most severe; (d) number of attacks during each of the previous 3 months; (e) specific allergens or conditions that seem to precipitate asthma; (f) specific dosage of tablets or number of times inhalators and/or suppositories have been used during the last 10 days; and (g) a measure of pulmonary efficiency. The two tests used most often to measure pulmonary efficiency are the FEV_1 (forced expiratory volume for 1 second) and the MBC (maximal breathing capacity). Both require laboratory apparatus such as a spirometer (Figure 17.13) or respirometer.

To determine MBC, the student is asked to breathe as hard and fast as possible into a hose for a certain number of seconds. The volume of the expired air is collected and measured. The MBC is the number of liters of air per minute that can be moved by breathing as deeply and rapidly as possible. Normal values on the MBC range from 43 to 155 liters for males and 41 to 123 liters for females. Asthmatic persons have lower MBC values than individuals free of lung disease.

The FEV_1 is the number of cubic centimeters of air forcefully exhaled in the first second after a deep inspiration. Normal FEV_1 values range from 500 to 4,500 cubic centimeters for boys and from 350 to 3,400 cubic centimeters for girls. Any disease that causes bronchial obstruction and resistance in the airways reduces FEV_1.

Special Asthma Exercise Programs

Many school systems, often with help from the local lung association, have started special exercise programs for asthmatic children. These programs teach understanding of the respiratory system, stress breathing exercises and games, and attempt to build self-confidence in movement. They are intended as *supplements* to the regular physical education program.

Asthmatic children must be taught the kinesiology of respiration. They should understand the difference between costal and diaphragmatic breathing and be able to feel the muscles of inspiration and forced expiration. Persons with asthma typically overwork the upper chest, using the intercostal muscles more than the diaphragm.

The diaphragm is a dome-shaped structure that separates the thoracic and abdominal cavities. The top of the dome, called the central tendon, is the part of the diaphragm that descends during inspiration and ascends during expiration. Surrounding the central tendon are the muscle fibers that attach the diaphragm to the circumference of the thoracic outlet. The diaphragm should be the principal muscle of inspiration. In normal quiet breathing it should be the only respiratory muscle in action.

Diaphragmatic breathing is sometimes called abdominal breathing since the abdomen can be seen alternately protruding in inhalation and flattening in exhalation. In normal expiration no muscle contraction is required. Exhalation depends, in large part, upon the ability of the diaphragm to relax and be carried upward by its elastic recoil action. The phrenic nerve, which innervates the diaphragm, is extremely susceptible to nervous tension. Hence, any coughing, wheezing, or anxiety-producing conditions increase the tonus of the diaphragm, which in turn tenses the pectorals, the three scaleni, and the trapezius. The result is distension of the chest similar to that felt when the breath is held for a long time. The discomfort of the distension cannot be relieved because the fully contracted diaphragm cannot relax and ascend, thereby helping to push air out of the thoracic cavity. In normal respiration the diaphragm may move from 1 to 7 centimeters; during an asthmatic attack it may move up and down only a fraction of a centimeter or not at all. A person who relies more and more upon costal breathing gradually loses the flexibility of the lower chest muscles.

The main value of special asthma exercise programs is the opportunity for persons with similar problems to talk together, share solutions, and provide reinforcement for one another. The best qualified teacher to conduct such programs is one who has had formal training in both physical education and counseling. The trend of the 1980s, encouraged by the American Lung Association, is family exercise programs, camping trips, and other activities that permit sharing at all levels. School nurses are excellent resources in helping to locate the local branch of the American Lung Association. In most cities this organization offers numerous activities. It also provides, usually at no cost, speakers and films.

Breathing Exercises

Breathing exercises are no longer considered a viable approach to the management of asthma. They may be used in chronic obstructive lung disease, cystic fibrosis, muscular dystrophy, and other very severe conditions that cannot be managed by medication and environmental controls. In such instances, they are commonly associated with hospitalization and inability to exercise in normal ways. Research, with one or two exceptions, has repeatedly indicated no significant values accruing from breathing exercises. Games are more effective in improving expiration and also help to clear mucus from passageways.

Games to Improve Expiration

In ordinary expiration, no muscles are used. In vigorous exhalation, the following muscles contract: internal and external obliques, transversus abdominis, transversus thoracis, serratus posterior inferior, and posterior portions of the intercostals. Since the abdominal muscles participate vigorously in laughing, coughing, panting, and singing, games based upon these activities can be developed.

Games Using Abdominal Muscles

Laugh-In
Circle formation with *it* in center. *It* tosses a handkerchief high into the air. Everyone laughs as loudly as possible as it floats downward, but no laughter must be heard after the handkerchief contacts the floor. Anyone breaking this rule becomes the new *it*. For variation, pupils can cough instead of laugh.

Laugh Marathon
Each pupil has a tape recorder. The object is to see who can make the longest playing tape of continuous laughing.

Guess Who's Laughing
All pupils are blindfolded. One, who is designated as *it*, laughs continuously until classmates guess who is laughing.

Red Light, Green Light Laughing
This game is played according to traditional rules except that laughing accompanies the running or is substituted for it.

All games designed to improve exhalation should be played in erect standing or running postures since the spine and pelvis must be stabilized by the lumbar extensors in order for the abdominal muscles to contract maximally.

Blowing Activities

Blowing activities are especially valuable in emphasizing the importance of reducing residual air in the lungs. Learning to play wind instruments is recommended strongly. Swimming offers a recreational setting for stressing correct exhalation. Games found to be especially popular follow:

Snowflakes
Equipment: A 1-inch square of tissue paper for each child. *Procedure:* Two teams with each child having one piece of paper. Each participant attempts to keep the paper above the floor after the whistle is blown. When the paper touches the floor the participant is disqualified. The winner is the team in which a player keeps the tissue in the air for the longest time.

Ping Pong Relay

Equipment: One ping pong ball for each team. *Procedure:* Two teams with one-half of the players of each team behind lines 50 feet apart. A player blows the ping pong ball across the floor to his or her team member, who blows the ball back to the starting line. The relay continues until each player has blown the ball. The team that finishes first is the winner.

Under the Bridge

Equipment: One ping pong ball for each team. *Procedure:* Teams with players standing in single file with legs spread. The last player in the file blows the ball forward between the legs of his or her team members with additional blowing provided by the other players to move the ball quickly to the front. If the ball rolls outside the legs of the players, the last player must retrieve the ball and blow it again. When the ball reaches the front, the first player in the file picks up the ball, runs to the end of the file, and blows the ball forward again. The team finishing first is the winner.

Balloon Relay

Equipment: One balloon for each player. One chair for each team placed on a line 95 feet from the starting line. *Procedure:* Children on the teams line up in single file behind the starting line. Upon the signal to start, the first player of each team runs to the opposite line, blows up his or her balloon, places it on the chair, and sits on the balloon until it breaks. He or she then returns to the starting line and tags the next player, who proceeds in the same manner.

Blow Out the Candle

Equipment: A candle is placed on the floor between every two children. *Procedure:* Opponents lie on the floor on opposite sides 8 feet from the candle. Players attempt to blow out the candle from the greatest distance possible. The child who blows out the candle at the greatest distance is the winner.

Ping Pong Croquet

Equipment: Ping pong balls and hoops made of milk cartons taped to the floor. *Procedure:* Each player crawls and blows the ping pong ball through the series of hoops, positioned on the floor in the same manner as in a game of croquet. The ball must be moved and controlled entirely by blowing. The hands may not touch the ball at any time. The players who finish first are the winners. Several playing areas may be provided to accommodate more players.

Figure 17.14 Blowing exercises: (A) self-competition in candle blowing and (B) self-competition in bottle blowing.

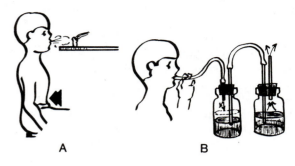

Self-Competition in Candle Blowing

Equipment: Movable candle behind a yardstick placed opposite the mouth (Figure 17.14). *Procedure:* Child attempts to blow out lighted candle set at gradually lengthened distances on the yardstick.

Self-Competition in Bottle Blowing

Equipment: Two half-gallon bottles, half filled with water and connected with three rubber hoses and two glass pipes. See Figure 17.14. *Procedure:* Child attempts to blow water from one bottle to another, first from sitting position and then standing position.

Pursed Lip Breathing Contests

This can be competition against self or others. Emphasize a short inspiration through the nose and long expiration through gently pursed lips, making a whistling or hissing noise. This is called *pursed lip breathing.* Try timing the expiration phase with a stop watch or metronome. Expiration should be at least twice as long as inspiration.

The Physical Education Environment

Since so many asthmatic persons are sensitive to pollens and dust, physical education should be conducted indoors at least during the seasons of peak incidence of attacks. Ideally, the room should be air conditioned and entirely dust-free. The humidity should be maintained as low as possible.

Changes in weather, particularly cold, dry air, predispose persons to attacks. Alterations in body temperature, specifically becoming overheated, seem to cause wheezing. A cold, wet towel on the forehead and/ or the back of the neck between activities will help to maintain uniform body temperature.

When the chalkboard is in use, asthmatic students should be stationed as far away from it as possible. Nylon-covered, allergen-free mats containing foam rubber as filler are recommended.

Most persons with asthma are extremely sensitive to cigarette smoke. Even if a cigarette is not burning, residual fumes can trigger an attack.

Whereas all children become thirsty during vigorous physical activity, they are generally encouraged to wait until the end of the period to get a drink of water. In contrast, forcing fluids is an essential part of the total exercise program for asthmatic students. As tissues become drier during exercise, the mucus thickens and is more difficult to cough up. More than three or four consecutive coughs should be avoided since coughing itself dries out the mucus membranes. The only means of thinning this mucus is through fluids taken by mouth or intravenously. Four or five quarts of water a day are recommended. Cold drinks are contraindicated since they may cause spasms of the bronchial tubes; hence, hot drinks and fluids at room temperature are recommended. The physical educator should ascertain that fluids are taken periodically throughout the exercise session.

Antihistamines are not desirable for asthmatic students because they tend to dry out the mucus in the airway. If, because of hay fever or other allergies, the student is taking antihistamines, it is even more important that fluid intake be increased.

Posture Problems

In chronic asthma, permanent deformities of the chest may result—kyphosis, barrel chest, pigeon chest, and Harrison's sulcus. These defects can be traced to an actual shortening of the muscle fibers of the diaphragm and intercostals. When maintained in the lowered position characteristic of inspiration, the diaphragm affects the position and function of the viscera, which are pushed against the abdominal wall. The asthmatic typically experiences difficulty in flattening the abdomen, which, along with the chest, may become permanently distended.

Psychological Problems

In the past, some persons believed that psychological problems caused asthma This etiology is not valid. Asthma is a chronic lung disease that, like all illnesses and handicaps, complicates the life of both the asthmatic person and the family. Different persons cope with illnesses in different ways, and some handle stress better than others.

The psychological phenomenon known as a *reaction formation* is common among asthmatics. In order to prove their worth to others, they tend to establish unrealistically high levels of aspiration and then totally exhaust themselves in all-out effort to accomplish such goals. When it appears that they cannot live up to their own or the perceived expectations of others, an asthmatic attack often occurs, thereby adding more stress. "I could have made the deadline if I hadn't gotten sick!" "I would have won the match if I hadn't started wheezing." The physical educator will find many asthmatic children eager to play, despite parental restrictions, and unwilling to withdraw from a game even when they evidence asthmatic symptoms. Many do not impose limitations upon themselves, refusing to accept the inevitability of an attack. Like all children, they want to be *normal*. The following memories of asthmatic adults lend some insight into the phenomenon of reaction formation.

I can remember going out to play with the kids in the neighborhood. I never thought about my asthma. I was highly competitive . . . loved to run . . . had to win. The asthma never came while I was playing. Oh, maybe a little wheezing, but I ignored that. But invariably in the middle of the night, after an unusually hard day of play, I would awake gasping . . . terrified . . . unable to breathe.

Of course, this roused up the whole family and we were all exhausted the next day.

My parents used to find me sitting and holding a neighborhood cat . . . stroking and loving it. My nose would be running and my eyes half swollen and filled with tears. It wasn't any special cat, just any animal I could find. They wouldn't let me have a pet at home because I was so allergic to them. The first thing I did after college was to buy a cat and start taking weekly injections to build up tolerance. I still take pills.

I never took a test in high school that I didn't stay up all night beforehand studying. By the time everyone else woke up, I'd have diarrhea, stomach cramps, a headache . . . and be literally convinced I didn't know enough to make an A. But I always made it to school. If I accidentally fell asleep or something prevented me from learning the material, I'd wake up with asthma and be in bed for a week. The whole time I was in bed I'd worry about not taking the test and this would make me sicker. Then my mouth and nose would break out with fever blisters and I would be too ashamed of my appearance to return to school until it healed. I'd catch up on my studies and make A's on the next round of tests. I always felt like the teachers wouldn't like me if I didn't make A's.

The reaction formation in the asthmatic person creates a vicious circle in which stress precipitates coughing, wheezing, and dyspnea. The inability to breathe, particularly in a young child, results in helplessness, frustration, and anxiety which, in turn, intensifies the asthmatic problem. The asthmatic child wants his or her parents to awaken and keep him or her company during an attack, yet the child experiences considerable emotional conflict about such dependency. Should an attack occur in the physical education class, the asthmatic child likewise has mixed feelings. He or she wants attention and an offer of help, yet dislikes himself or herself for seeking solicitousness. The more the child worries about what others think, the worse the asthma becomes. Once an attack begins, the child cannot will it to stop. Nor can he or she *consciously* bring on an attack. The interplay of physiological and psychological etiological factors in asthma is so enigmatic that they remain little understood.

Occasionally, childhood asthma cannot be managed efficiently in the school and home environment. In such instances the child is typically referred to such treatment centers as CARIH, the Children's Asthma Research Institute and Hospital, in Denver, Colorado. CARIH is the largest hospital in the western hemisphere that treats asthmatic children and the only center whose staff conducts research exclusively on asthma and allergic diseases.

Chronic Obstructive Pulmonary Diseases

Chronic obstructive pulmonary diseases (COPD), including chronic bronchitis and pulmonary emphysema, now constitute the fastest growing chronic disease problem in America. The death rate has doubled every 5 years over the past 20 years.

Chronic bronchitis is defined as a recurrent cough characterized by excessive mucus secretion in the bronchii. The three stages are (a) *simple,* in which the chief characteristic is mucoid expectoration; (b) *mucopurulent,* in which the sputum is intermittently or continuously filled with pus because of active infection; and (c) *obstruction,* in which there is narrowing of the airways in addition to expectoration. This is the stage at which the complications of emphysema and/or heart failure occur. The three stages may merge one into the other and span a period of 20 or more years.

Pulmonary emphysema is a destruction of the walls of the alveoli of the lungs. This destruction results in overdistention of the air sacs and loss of lung elasticity. Emphysema is a Greek word that means literally to inflate or puff up. Like the asthmatic, the person with emphysema has difficulty expelling air. Whereas the normal person breathes 14 times a minute, the emphysematous person may breathe 20 to 30 times a minute and still not get enough oxygen into the bloodstream. The characteristic high carbon dioxide level in the blood causes sluggishness and irritability. The heart tries to compensate for lack of oxygen by pumping harder, and possible heart failure becomes an additional hazard.

Emphysema is more common among men than women. Over 10% of the middle-aged and elderly population in America is believed to suffer with emphysema. The specific etiology is still under study, but smoking and air pollution are considered the most potent causal factors.

Patients with COPD tend to restrict their activities more and more because of their fear of wheezing and dyspnea. This inactivity results in muscle deterioration, increased shortness of breath, and increasing inactivity—a vicious cycle! The activities recommended for the asthmatic child are suitable also for individuals with bronchitis and emphysema.

Cystic Fibrosis

Cystic fibrosis, a childhood disease that was not recognized as a separate entity from bronchopneumonia until 1936, is included in this section because 90% of persons with cystic fibrosis die from chronic lung disorders. The physical education program for a child with cystic fibrosis is similar to that of asthmatic students.

It is estimated that 1 child in every 1,000 is born with cystic fibrosis. The cause of the disease is unknown, but research strongly suggests transmission through a recessive gene. There are approximately 10 million carriers of this gene in the United States. If two carriers happen to bear offspring, there is a 1-in-4 chance that their infant will have cystic fibrosis and a 2-in-4 chance that the child will be a carrier.

Cystic fibrosis accounts for almost all the deaths in childhood from chronic nontuberculosis pulmonary disease. Although the life span of cystic fibrosis patients is increasing, many still succumb before age 10 and 80% before age 30.

The child with cystic fibrosis looks and acts essentially normal. In most cases, no one, save the parents and physician, is aware of the disease until the final stage. No cure is known, and treatment revolves around prevention and/or control of pulmonary infection, maintenance of proper nutrition, and prevention of abnormal salt loss. Many students perform well above average in tests of muscle power, endurance, and agility despite moderately severe respiratory disease as judged by clinical and chest X-ray scoring.

The primary disorder in cystic fibrosis is the abnormal secretion of the membranes that line the internal organs. Normal mucus is thin, slippery, and clear. In cystic fibrosis the mucus is thick and sticky, creating two major problems. First, it clogs the bronchial tubes, interfering with breathing, and it lodges in the branches of the windpipe, acting as an obstruction. The resulting symptoms resemble those in asthma, bronchitis, and emphysema. Second, it plugs up the pancreatic ducts, preventing digestive enzymes from reaching the small intestine and causing malnutrition. Commercially prepared pancreatic extracts must be taken to substitute for the enzymes no longer present in the digestive tract. In some severe cases the intestinal tract is obstructed completely by an accumulation of the thick, puttylike material. The sweat glands also produce an unusually

Figure 17.15 Hospital treatment for persons with asthma, cystic fibrosis, and similar conditions consists largely of special medications via a bronchodilator, chest physiotherapy done by a respiratory therapist, and postural drainage. The major purpose is to facilitate coughing to clear mucus from the clogged bronchial tubes.

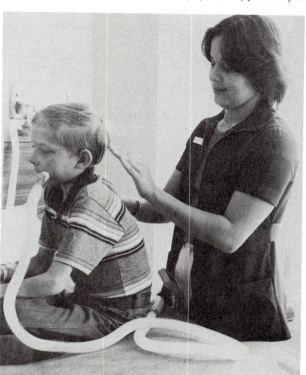 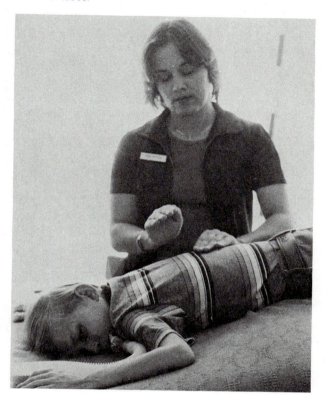

salty sweat. Excessive loss of sodium chloride in perspiration is an ever-present danger. Many sufferers take salt tablets regularly as part of their general management program.

In addition to regular breathing exercises, the cystic fibrosis child undergoes daily aerosol therapy. A nebulizer or inhalator may be used to relieve broncho spasms.

Treatments for Severe Conditions

Persons with severe asthma, chronic obstructive lung disease, and cystic fibrosis generally spend some time each year in the hospital or at home convalescing from attacks that were complicated by colds, flu, or other respiratory illness. Special treatment in hospitals includes postural drainage and thumping by a respiratory therapist. This, as well as intermittent positive pressure breathing (IPPB), is used with persons having all kinds of severe respiratory disorders.

Postural Drainage

Postural drainage is an activity in which the child lies in various positions that enable gravity to help the cough drain the bronchial tree of accumulated mucus. The bronchodilator is used before the child assumes 10 different positions. The teacher, therapist, or parent taps the child's upper torso with his or her fingers, as depicted in Figure 17.15. Each of the positions is designed to drain a specific area of the bronchial tree; hence, the benefit derived from the position depends upon the amount of congestion present. Not all positions are required each session.

Intermittent Positive Pressure Breathing (IPPB)

In IPPB, the student breathes into a plastic mouth piece that is attached to a machine which forces a measured amount of medication through the lungs under a controlled level of pressure (Figure 17.16). Bronchodilators and other kinds of medication can be put in the positive pressure machine. IPPB may be prescribed on a daily basis or used only in times of pulmonary crises.

IPPB is believed to produce a lowered alveolar PCO_2, decreased outward filtration of plasma from the pulmonary capillary membrane, decreased residual volume, increased intrapulmonary mixing, more uniform aeration, increased cough efficiency, and decreased bronchial resistance.

Figure 17.16 Young adolescent with cystic fibrosis undergoes intermittent positive pressure breathing therapy several times each day during her frequent hospital confinements. Note characteristic stunting of physical growth caused by several years of drug therapy.

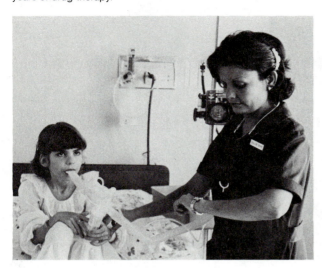

Figure 17.17 Muscle contractions during seizures are tonic or clonic. They may affect all parts of the body.

Tonic stage

Clonic stage

Similar effects are obtained through the use of an aerosal or hand nebulizer. Additional information about available equipment can be obtained through the local lung association.

Convulsive Disorders

Approximately 2 million persons in the United States have epilepsy. This is roughly 1 out of every 150 to 200 persons. Most of these individuals are on medications that are almost 100% effective in preventing seizures. They live completely normal lives, and friends seldom know about their condition.

Terminology

The terms *epilepsy, seizure disorders,* and *convulsive disorders* are used interchangeably to denote a chronic condition of the central nervous system that is characterized by recurrent seizures. This condition is not a disease, but rather an upset in the electrical activity of neurons within the cerebral cortex.

A *seizure* is a sudden change in consciousness or behavior characterized by involuntary motor activity and caused by abnormal electrical activity of cortical neurons. Synonyms for seizure are *convulsion* or *fit*. Muscle contractions caused by epilepsy are called *clonic* (jerky or intermittent) or *tonic* (continuous, stiff, or rigid) (Figure 17.17).

Biochemical Explanation

Seizures are caused by abnormalities in cell membrane stability. Normally, the cell membrane maintains equilibrium between sodium outside the cell and potassium inside the cell (see Figure 17.18). The balance controls *depolarization,* the cellular process that permits electrical current to be transmitted down the nerve fiber and carry messages to other nerve fibers. Epileptic cells are unable to maintain the normal balance; therefore, depolarization occurs too easily and too frequently. The resulting abnormal discharge of electrical activity spreads to the normal neurons, causing them to discharge also so that soon an entire area of the brain is involved.

Seizures are designated as *focal* or *generalized,* depending on how much of the brain is involved. *Focal* seizures are focused, or localized, in one specific area of the brain such as, for instance, the motor strip of the right frontal lobe. The synonym for focal is *partial*. *Generalized seizures* involve the entire cerebral cortex (both hemispheres).

Age at Time of First Seizure

The age of onset of the first seizure helps to explain why so many physical educators must cope with this problem. Twenty percent of all persons with epilepsy have their first seizure before age 10. These are usually children with known or suspected neurological damage

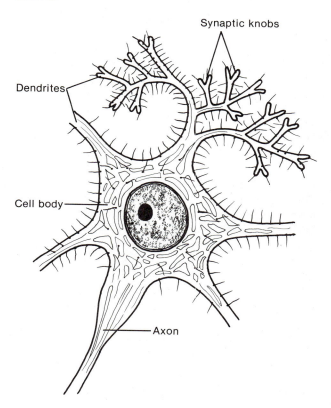

Figure 17.18 Neurons within the cerebral cortex have synaptic knobs that release neurotransmitters that cause an increase in membrane permeability to sodium and thus trigger nerve impulses. Problems in synaptic transmission sometimes result in seizures.

Synaptic knobs

Dendrites

Cell body

Axon

Table 17.12
Two Commonly Used Classification Systems in Epilepsy: A Comparison of Terms

International Classification System (Gastaut, 1970)	Traditional Clinical Classification System
I. Partial seizures	
A. Without impairment of consciousness	Focal epilepsy Motor (Jacksonian) or sensory
B. With impairment of consciousness	Psychomotor or temporal lobe epilepsy
II. Generalized seizures	
A. Absence	Petit mal
B. Tonic-clonic	Grand mal
C. Tonic only	Limited grand mal
D. Clonic only	
E. Myoclonic	Atypical petit mal *or* minor motor seizures *or* Lennox-Gastaut syndrome
F. Atonic	
G. Akinetic	
H. Infantile spasms	Jackknife or Salaam seizure
III. Unilateral seizures	
IV. Unclassified seizures	

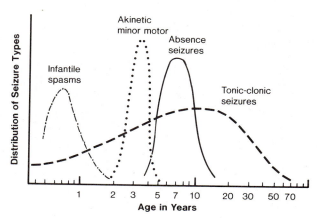

Figure 17.19 Ages at which various seizure types occur most often.

that results in multiple handicaps. Cerebral palsy, mental retardation, and learning disabilities often are complicated by convulsive disorders. Thirty percent of persons with epilepsy have their first seizure in the second decade, while 20% convulse initially in the third decade. The final 30% have their first seizure after age 40.

Type of Seizures

Classification of seizures varies according to whether traditional clinical symptomology serves as its basis or the international classification system adopted by the World Health Organization in 1970. The Epilepsy Foundation of America favors the latter (Gastaut, 1970), but textbooks have been slow to embrace the new system. Table 17.12 presents a comparison of the two systems. A nationwide effort is underway to educate physicians to the new terms and convince them to discard such words as grand mal, petit mal, and Jacksonian. Different types of seizures have their first incidence at certain ages (see Figure 17.19).

Partial Seizures

Of the many kinds of partial seizures, the Jacksonian is most common. Clonic (jerky) contractions begin in one part of the body, usually a hand or foot, and from that point spread up the limb until all of the muscles are involved. This is sometimes called *march epilepsy* because the contractions march up the limb. The student usually does not lose consciousness, although impairment of speech and other responses may occur.

Psychomotor epilepsy (sometimes called *auto-matism*) is characterized by unexplainable short-term changes in behavior that the pupil later does not remember. Automatic activity is carried on while the student is in a state of impaired consciousness. One child may have temper tantrums, suddenly exploding for no reason, hitting another student, provoking a fight, or throwing things about the room. Another may have spells involving incoherent chatter, repetition of meaningless phrases, and inability to answer simple questions. Still another has episodes of sleepwalking or wakes the family at night with hysterical, unexplainable sobbing. Psychomotor attacks also may be confused with daydreaming or not paying attention in class.

Generalized Seizures

Absence seizures (previously called petit mal) account for about 8% of all epilepsy. Their symptoms are so subtle that the inexperienced observer seldom notices the seizure. There is an impairment of consciousness, never more than 30 seconds, in which the student seems dazed. The eyes may roll upward. If the person is talking at the time, there is a momentary silence and then continuation, with no loss of unity in thought. These seizures are rare before age 3 and often disappear after puberty. They are more common in girls than in boys.

Tonic-clonic seizures (previously called grand mal) are the most dramatic and easily recognized. They have three or four stages.

1. *Aura.* This is a warning or premonition of the attack, that is always the same for a particular person. An aura may be a certain smell, flashing of lights, vague feeling of apprehension, a sinking feeling in the abdomen, or a feeling of extraordinary rapture. Only about 50% of the persons have auras.

2. *Tonic phase. Tonic* means constant, referring to the continuous contraction of muscles. The person straightens out, becomes stiff, utters a cry, and loses consciousness. If there is a tonic contraction of respiratory muscles, the person becomes cyanotic. Fortunately this phase seldom lasts more than 30 seconds.

3. *Clonic phase. Clonic* refers to intermittent contraction and relaxation of muscles. The clonic phase persists from a few seconds up to 2

or 3 minutes. The tongue may be bitten as the jaws work up and down. The sphincters around the rectum and urinary tract relax, causing the person to urinate or defecate into his or her clothing.

4. *Sleep or coma phase.* After a period of brief consciousness or semiconsciousness, during which the person complains of being very tired, he or she lapses into a sleep that may last several hours. Upon awakening, the person is either very clear or is dazed and confused. Usually, there is no memory of the seizure.

Occasionally, seizures occur that are entirely clonic or tonic.

Myoclonic seizures are brief, sudden, violent contractions of muscles in some part or the entire body. Often, these are manifested by sudden head jerk, followed by jerking of arms and legs, and the trunk bending in upon itself. There may be a loss of consciousness, but the duration of a myoclonic seizure is much briefer than that of tonic-clonic or tonic or clonic only types.

Atonic seizures are similar to absence seizures except that there is momentary diminution or abolition of postural tone. The student tends to sag or collapse.

Akinetic seizures (also called sudden drop attacks) cause the student to suddenly lose muscle tone and plummet to the ground, momentarily unconscious. These seizures may be sometimes purposely aborted. Sudden falling asleep (narcolepsy) may be a form of akinetic seizure.

Infantile spasms (also called jackknife seizures) are usually characterized by a "doubling up" motion of the entire body, although they may be less generalized and manifested only by head dropping and arms flexing. Infantile spasms typically occur between 3 and 9 months of age, after which other types of seizures may replace them. This problem is associated with severe mental retardation. Infantile spasms should not be confused with the generalized seizures that many normal infants and children (5 to 10%) have in conjunction with illness and high fever; these are called *febrile seizures* and typically are a once-in-a-lifetime happening.

Unilateral seizures are those in which only one side of the brain is involved and, therefore, only one side of the body. These may be of any type.

Unclassified seizures are those that do not meet the criteria for any one type or those that are mixed types. About 35 to 40% of epilepsy is a combination of absence and tonic-clonic seizures.

Etiology

The etiology of epilepsy falls within two broad classifications: (a) idiopathic (genetic or endogenous) and (b) acquired (symptomatic or exogenous). *Idiopathic* means the cause is unknown, and 80% of all epilepsy remains unexplainable. There appears to be a genetic predisposition toward epilepsy, but this is subject to controversy. In general, the epileptic parent has 1 chance in 40 of giving birth to an epileptic child. The incidence is increased if both parents are epileptic. *Acquired* epilepsy can be traced directly to birth injuries, brain tumors, anoxia, lead poisoning, cerebral abscesses, and penetrating injuries to the brain.

Factors That Aggravate Seizures

1. Changes in alkalinity of the blood (see Figure 17.20). These changes are very subtle and minute. High alkalosis favors seizures. High acidity inhibits seizures. Diet therapy is used frequently. Acid-producing diets, high in fat content—such as cream, butter, eggs, and meat—have successfully produced a quieting effect. This kind of diet is called a *ketogenic diet* (high in fat). The ability of persons with epilepsy to metabolize fat is disturbed as in diabetes. They can metabolize fat down to ketone bodies (acidosis), but have difficulty with further metabolism to CO_2 and H_2O. The accumulation of acid products in the blood as a result of exercise is believed to help prevent seizures.

2. Alcoholic beverages. An excessive intake lowers threshold.

3. In women, menstrual periods. Many girls and women have seizures only around their periods. Edema aggravates the onset of seizures. One of the side effects of ovarian (esterogenic) hormones is to encourage retention of salt (sodium) in the body. This retention of sodium binds water within the tissue, obvious through the swelling of breasts, nasal membranes, ankles, fingers, and possibly even a gain in weight.

4. Psychogenic stimulus. Anger, fright, bad news, and other high stress factors may precipitate seizures.

5. Hyperventilation, or overbreathing, precipitates absence seizures. Holding the breath as long as possible, as in distance underwater swimming, is a common form of hyperventilation that is contraindicated. Breath-holding lowers the carbon dioxide content of the blood, which normally acts as a stimulant for the respiratory center in the brain. Some forms of hyperventilation, such as voluntary forced breathing exercises, increase the alkalosis of the blood, thereby lowering the seizure threshold. Bobbing in swimming, blowing a wind instrument, and singing may cause hyperventilation. Dizziness and/or feeling faint are warning signals.

6. Chronic recurrent head trauma such as might occur in boxing or soccer (when the ball is given impetus with the head). This factor is controversial in that some physicians report that their patients have participated regularly with no ill effects in boxing, soccer, and other sports in which the head repeatedly was subjected to blows.

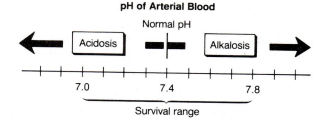

Figure 17.20 Most factors that aggravate seizures relate to electrolyte balance in the cellular fluids, especially the balance between acidosis and alkalosis in the pH of arterial blood.

Seizures and Exercise

Seizures seldom, if ever, occur while a student is engaging in vigorous physical activity. In the cool-down period immediately after a game, usually in the locker room, a number of *first* seizures occur. No one knows why. Up to that point the pupil has been completely *normal,* and nothing in the medical history explains the sudden onset of a convulsive disorder. Since many first seizures appear in the adolescent years, it is understandable why the physical educator should become involved in helping the pupil make necessary social and medical adjustments.

Social Problems

The social problems in epilepsy are greater than the medical ones. The student regaining consciousness after a first seizure does not remember anything that happened. He or she is self-conscious and embarrassed about being stared at by a cluster of classmates. Who wouldn't be? Adolescence in our culture is a time of particular sensitivity, and most teenagers with convulsive disorders confess that their greatest hang-up is what friends think. On the other hand, the peer group that has witnessed the seizure has undergone a terrifying, traumatic experience. It is probably the first seizure they have seen, and they are eager to talk about it and share perceptions. Individual responses are as variable as human beings themselves, but many persons are reluctant to continue dating or even socializing with a person who has seizures. Some states still have legislation that persons with epilepsy cannot marry and/or have children. Driver's licenses, if issued, have restrictions. Employment opportunities are reduced, and insurability under workmen's compensation is a problem.

Medication

Phenobarbital and dilantin, the drugs used most often in controlling *tonic-clonic seizures,* were not introduced until 1912 and 1938, respectively. Perhaps new generations will be increasingly free of prejudice. Today, it is relatively rare for a person to have seizures in public. Teachers who work with children from low-income families see many seizures, almost always caused because a prescription is not filled on time. Often the problem is carelessness or ignorance rather than lack of money. When taken regularly according to directions, modern medications are almost completely effective in preventing seizures.

The period of time required to determine correct dosages varies with individuals. Hence, the first few months after an initial seizure may be especially troublesome, with too little medication resulting in seizures and too much causing drowsiness and other side effects. During this time the pupil may have many absences from school, with the subsequent problems of lowered grades and inability to keep up with social activities. Once the correct dosage is decided upon, the medical problem is essentially eliminated.

Physical educators who work in residential facilities for mentally retarded persons know that seizures are fairly common occurrences among the institutionalized population. It is estimated that approximately one-third of mentally retarded persons in residential facilities have convulsive disorders.

Classroom Management

Should a seizure occur during class, the physical educator should clear the area around the student. No attempt should be made to hold the body down or restrain limbs. Ascertain that the mouth and nose are clear and permitting breathing. Lying in a prone position is probably best. The seizure should be allowed to run its normal course, with everyone remaining calm and accepting.

Implications for Physical Education

The American Medical Association (1968, 1974) recommends that students with epilepsy participate fully in school physical education and athletics. Reversing its initial stand, this association now indicates that collision (football, ice hockey, lacrosse) sports and contact (basketball, soccer, wrestling) sports can be played by the medically balanced student. Boxing should be avoided as well as activities like heading the ball in soccer, which involve repeated insults to the head.

Activities that might result in a fall (cycling, horseback riding, rope- or tree-climbing, parallel bars, trampoline, balance beam, mountain climbing) should always be done with a partner or group. Likewise, swimming and other water sports should not be engaged in alone. In some students, a specific activity, for unknown reasons, may precipitate seizures. If this occurs *repeatedly,* then that one activity should be restricted.

Livingston, a physician at Johns Hopkins Hospital, points out that the emotional disturbances of children excluded from the sports of their peers are more difficult to handle than medical problems. He allows his patients to participate in all sports but diving, prohibiting it not because of the possibility of head injuries but because of the obvious complications associated with a seizure underwater. Livingston states,

Over the past 33 years I have observed at least 15,000 young children with epilepsy, many of whom have been under my personal care during their entire scholastic careers. Hundreds of these patients have played tackle football, some have participated in boxing, lacrosse, wrestling, and other physical activities which render the participant prone to head injuries. I am not cognizant of a single instance of recurrence of epileptic seizures related to head injury in any of these athletes. (Livingston, 1969, p. 1917)

Students whose seizures are under control are no different from their peers. They need good supervision when enrolled in beginning swimming, but so do all children! Likewise, they need a gymnastics teacher who is competent in spotting techniques. Again, this does not make them different from their peers, who also need a good spotter when undertaking activities on the high balance beam, parallel bars, and trampoline. Most important, persons with epilepsy need the acceptance and belonging that team membership ensures.

Diabetes

A disturbance resulting in insufficient insulin in the bloodstream, *diabetes mellitus* affects approximately 8 million persons in the United States. It is the second most frequent cause of blindness and the most common cause of irreversible blindness. Diabetes now ranks eighth in the causes of death in this country. It occurs most frequently in persons over 40, bringing with it such severe complications as renal diseases, cardiovascular disease, blindness, and amputations.

According to the American Diabetes Association, for every 10,000 persons in the community there will be 1 diabetic under age 20, 10 diabetics between ages 20 and 40, 100 diabetics between ages 50 and 60, and 1,000 diabetics over age 60. Females are more likely to have diabetes than males, and there seems to be a direct relationship between obesity and the onset of diabetes in middle age. All ethnic groups are affected, but the highest incidence occurs among Jewish persons.

Although the discovery of insulin in 1921 by Canadians Banting and Best completely transformed the outlook for persons with diabetes, further medical progress has been slow. The cause of diabetes is still unknown. The major factors in the management of diabetes continue to be diet, insulin, and exercise.

Biochemical Explanation

Diabetes is a disorder of the Islets of Langerhans, the part of the pancreas that secretes insulin, a hormone that causes a decrease in the level of blood glucose (sugar). Insulin and another hormone secreted by the pancreas (glucagon) work together to maintain a relatively constant blood sugar level regardless of what is eaten. When protein metabolism is disturbed, a drop in blood sugar causes *hypoglycemia*. Diabetes also contributes to abnormal fat metabolism resulting in an increase in ketone bodies (acids) in the blood. Ketones are normally excreted in the urine; this is why daily urine tests are used in the management of diabetes. When ketone bodies accumulate excessively, they can result in a diabetic coma (called ketoacidosis or acidosis).

Types of Diabetes

Traditionally, diabetes has been classified into two types: (a) juvenile and (b) adult or maturity-onset. Approximately 85% of the known diabetics fall in the latter classification. Synonyms for these categories are as follows:

Juvenile	**Adult**
Ketoacidosis-prone	Ketoacidosis-resistant
Insulin-dependent	Noninsulin-dependent

Individuals who develop diabetes before age 20 generally have the juvenile type. Such persons almost always require insulin, whereas individuals in the other category rely primarily upon diet therapy and oral hypoglycemic drugs. Little or no insulin is manufactured by the pancreas of the juvenile sufferer, who may go rather quickly into diabetic coma, which can result in death if not treated adequately. In contrast, adult diabetes is less dramatic. The pancreas is capable of manufacturing some insulin even though the amount is insufficient for body needs.

Recognition of Symptoms

Many diabetic persons remain undiagnosed. Physical educators should recognize symptoms and encourage a visit to a physician.

The most common symptoms of diabetes are constant thirst, frequent urination, extreme hunger, drowsiness and fatigue, dryness of mouth, lips, and skin, visual disorders, rapid weight loss, itching of the genitals, and skin problems that do not heal readily. Urine tests are used for screening, but the blood glucose tolerance test is the most accurate diagnostic technique. These tests, of course, are administered initially by the physician.

Daily Urine Tests

Once the condition is diagnosed, the student is expected to test his or her urine one or more times daily. In severe diabetes, urine tests may be prescribed as often as four times a day: morning, before breakfast; noon, before lunch; afternoon, before supper; and bedtime, around 9 P.M. In mild cases controlled by diet alone, urine is tested once a day or less.

The purpose of the urine test is to ascertain the amount of sugar in the urine. A negative test, or one in which no sugar is apparent, is desired. The physical educator should be sensitive enough to associate fluctuations in a pupil's moods with the disheartening experience of an occasional positive urine test. It is important also in terms of body image and self-concept that urine and urination be assigned positive connotations. Counseling should be provided for youngsters who have been taught that certain bodily functions and/or parts are dirty or bad. Allowing a diabetic pupil to perform urine tests on classmates in a lecture-demonstration setting may lead to increased understandings among peers.

Insulin Reaction or Hypoglycemia

Insulin reaction, or shock, may be caused by delaying or skipping meals, overexercising, or accidentally injecting too much insulin. Each of these practices can result in *hypoglycemia,* or low blood sugar, which in turn can lead to convulsions similar to epileptic seizures or unconsciousness. Early symptoms of insulin shock include (a) shakiness or trembling, (b) nervousness, (c) nausea, (d) headache, (e) fatigue, (f) excessive perspiration, and (g) hunger. If these symptoms are recognized in time, the reaction can be prevented by drinking fruit juice or carbonated drinks or by eating candy, corn syrup, or honey. Many people carry Lifesavers for such occasions.

Characteristics of insulin reaction include (a) sluggish thinking, (b) muscle weakness, (c) drowsiness, (d) blurred or double vision, (e) unconsciousness and/or convulsions. Occasionally, a person in insulin shock is mistakenly charged with alcoholic intoxication. If the person is conscious, eating something with sugar should end the reaction. If not, the person should receive an injection of *glucagon,* which will cause the liver to break down liver glycogen (Figure 17.21) and release free glucose into the bloodstream. A coach taking students on an overnight trip may wish to require that a diabetic bring along glucagon as an emergency precaution.

William F. Talbert, who has had diabetes since age 10, tells of having an insulin reaction during a finals tennis match with Pancho Gonzalez, then the amateur champion.

I took the first set from the fiery Californian but lost the next two. In the fourth set my game collapsed completely as I double-faulted, sprayed shots wildly out of court and stumbled about. My old doubles partner, Gar Mulloy, rushed out on the court after I had lost three games in succession to Pancho.

"Drink this, Willie," Gar commanded. He put a glass of sugared water into my hand and I downed it greedily. It was the answer. Gar had realized that I was losing control of my functions and going into insulin reaction through rapid burning of sugar. In a reversal of form that baffled Pancho and the gallery, I took twelve of the next fourteen games to win the match and the Southampton trophy. (Talbert, 1971, p. 27)

Another description of an insulin reaction comes from the parents of a 6-year-old boy:

I found him sobbing on the edge of his bed at five in the morning. I thought he was having a nightmare. He couldn't tell me what was wrong. He lay looking at his hands like someone on an LSD trip finding minuscule meanings in the texture of his skin. Then I noticed that he was unsteady when he went for a drink of water, and I knew. It was insulin reaction.

We were frantic—preparing orange juice, jelly on bread, cookies, ice cream—but he cried hysterically and pushed away the food. We tried to force him; he fell and bumped his head.

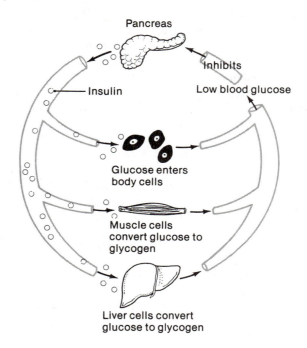

Figure 17.21 Normally the pancreas secretes the right amount of insulin to promote diffusion of glucose (sugar) cells, particularly those of skeletal, heart, and smooth muscles and of fat tissue. Insulin also stimulates muscle and liver cells to convert glucose to glycogen, which is essential to the synthesis of proteins and fats.

Pancreas

Inhibits

Insulin — Low blood glucose

Glucose enters body cells

Muscle cells convert glucose to glycogen

Liver cells convert glucose to glycogen

We panicked. We felt the insulin reaction was too far gone. We injected glucagon—a hormone that rapidly raises the blood sugar level.

In a few minutes his head was clear and he began to eat some of the sweets. But none of us was ever the same again. (Brandt, 1973, p. 36)

Since insulin reaction can occur anytime that physical activity is more strenuous than the amount of insulin injected can handle, it is imperative that the physical educator be able to recognize symptoms and give immediate treatment. It should be emphasized that *over-exercising* is not the problem. Rather it is the inability to judge ahead of time the amount of food and/or insulin needed for the forthcoming exertion.

Coma or Ketoacidosis

Less common, but more severe in possible consequences, is the diabetic coma, more properly called *ketoacidosis.* This is caused by an increase in acids (ketone bodies) resulting from too rapid breakdown of fat in the bloodstream. Before the discovery of insulin, ketoacidosis ended in death for most diabetic children and many adults. It can still result in death, and anyone in a coma should be rushed to the hospital. There the coma is treated with large doses of insulin and intravenous fluids to reduce the characteristic dehydration.

Warning symptoms of an impending diabetic coma include extreme thirst, loss of appetite, nausea, vomiting, abdominal pain, leg cramps, nervousness, and dimness or blurring of vision. Persons with diabetes sometimes are temporarily blinded by ketoacidosis. In cases of *diabetic retinopathy* (disease of the retina characterized by hemorrhages within the eye), irreversible blindness may result. Hence, many persons must live with the fear of an unexpected coma from which they may emerge totally blind. Once a person lapses into unconsciousness, the following signs are present: labored breathing, rapid pulse, lowered blood pressure, fruity odor to breath, dry skin, and flushed face.

Some of the causes of diabetic coma are (a) insufficient insulin; (b) neglecting to take injection; (c) onset of infection or mild illness; (d) diarrhea, vomiting, and mild stomach upsets; (e) overeating or excessive drinking of alcoholic beverages; and (f) emotional stress. Pregnancy also must be a time of extra precaution. Essentially, any deviation from *regular* eating, sleeping, and exercise patterns holds some danger. Even a mild cold complicates a diabetic's metabolism. Insulin needs may be increased by as much as one-third when the individual runs a fever.

Management of Diabetes

Good diabetic control is based upon proper diet, exercise, and insulin. Changes in any one of these necessitates adjustments in the others.

The diabetic diet should be characterized by (a) regularity of food intake from day to day; (b) regularity in mealtime; (c) exclusion of refined sugars; and (d) mild to moderate restriction of carbohydrates. If a meal is missed, the insulin dosage must be reduced.

Since most persons with diabetes tend to be overweight, the diet is generally low in calories. Food exchanges are figured with precision, and emphasis is placed upon weight control. To maintain the blood sugar at a constant level, five or six small meals daily are recommended in lieu of the traditional large meals.

One milligram of standard USP insulin contains 33 units. The average diabetic child requires approximately 20 to 30 units on a day filled with normal physical activity. Sedentary children may require as many as 40 to 80 units a day. Traditionally, persons with diabetes have been taught to change their insulin dosage in accordance with anticipated exercise. *The newer practice is to modify food intake rather than alter insulin dosage.* Thus, persons looking forward to strenuous or prolonged activity (athletic competition, hiking or cycling trip, marathon) should increase food intake rather than decrease insulin. This should be done *before* the exercise, ideally not fewer than 3 hours before warming up. For regular exercise, a 1 to 1.5 hour interval is usually sufficient.

The nature of food intake before and during strenuous exercise is important. Meals before exercise should contain higher than normal carbohydrate content. Fluids containing sugar should be ingested at least once an hour during periods of prolonged exercise.

Also important in preventing exercise-induced hypoglycemia is adjusting site of insulin injection to type of activity. When the exercise is primarily lower limb, as in track, insulin should be injected into the arm. When both upper and lower extremities are involved, the preferred injection site is the abdomen.

Implications for Physical Education

Regular exercise is tremendously important in the control of diabetes. The rationale for this lies in the fact that exercise helps to burn sugar, thereby influencing the amount of sugar the body will use or tolerate. A daily consistent exercise plan not only lessens the insulin requirement for persons with diabetes, but can also be used to help with weight reduction. With the exception of the physician, perhaps no one is more important in the management of diabetes than the physical education teacher. Positive attitudes toward vigorous physical activity must be developed early. Lifetime sports must be taught and the use of community recreation resources encouraged.

Since insulin injections are made to parts of the body not generally exposed to public view, the physical educator may be the only teacher aware of the condition. With the growing incidence of drug abuse, the physical educator's role in the locker room and shower area takes on greater responsibility. He or she may see the sites of injections and be forced to investigate whether the pupil is diabetic or taking illegal drugs. The physical educator is also in a position to evaluate the inevitable growth of scar tissue and to comment upon changing the site of injections. Insulin may be injected into the buttocks, upper arms, outer sides of thighs, and lower part of the abdomen. The site of injection should be changed frequently to minimize the breakdown of tissue.

Kidney and Urinary Tract Disorders

Approximately 3% of American school children have some history of a kidney or urinary tract disorder. Moreover, urinary-genital malformations account for 300,000 of the common birth defects in the United

Figure 17.22 The kidneys are located in the posterior abdomen at the junction of the thoracic and lumbar vertebrae. (A) The urinary tract consists of the ureter (the tube connecting kidneys with bladder), the bladder, and the urethra. The kidneys and urinary tract together are often called the *renal tract* or *renal system.* (B) One of the million nephrons inside the kidneys.

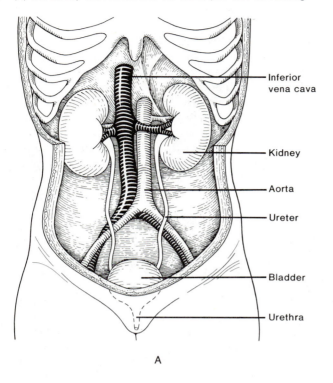

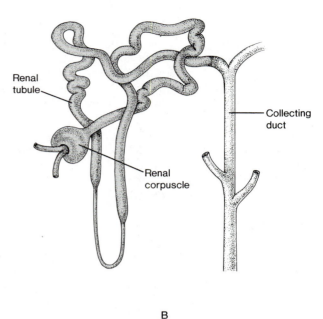

A

B

States, sharing second place in prevalence with congenital blindness and congenital deafness. Only mental retardation afflicts more newborn infants. *Vigorous exercise is contraindicated when kidney infection is present,* and the physician who has not been oriented to the possibilities of an adapted program often excuses the child from physical education.

Biochemical Explanation

Normal functioning of the kidneys is required to excrete urine and to help regulate the water, electrolyte, and acid base content of the blood (i.e., to maintain homeostasis within the body). Problems of fluid retention (edema) and fluid depletion (dehydration) relate largely to the ability of the kidneys to alter the acidity of urine. Urination gets rid of body wastes like urea (an end product of protein metabolism). Renal failure often results in death by uremic poisoning.

Kidney and urinary disorders are many and varied. When both the kidneys and the urinary tract (Figure 17.22) are involved, problems are often referred to as *renal disorders.* PL 94–142 lists *nephritis* as one of its

11 examples of other health impairments. Nephritis (also called Bright's disease) is inflammation of the kidneys. The name is derived from *nephron,* the functional unit within the kidneys (Figure 17.22). Each kidney is comprised of about 1 million nephrons, each of which helps filtrate substances from the blood and, subsequently, changes some of the resulting filtrate into urine and reabsorbs the remainder. This process results in about 45 gallons (180 liters) of filtrate every 24 hours; only about 3 liters of this is voided as urine. The ability of the renal system to reabsorb the rest and maintain the balance between all its contents is obviously vital to life. Many disorders, too numerous to name and discuss, can occur. There are approximately 55,000 kidney-related deaths each year.

Management of Renal Disorders

As last resort treatments, dialysis and kidney transplants are becoming increasingly successful and affordable. Many congenital disorders are corrected through surgery, as are kidney stones and urinary tract obstructions. Routine management of less severe conditions includes antibiotics to treat infections, drugs to control hypertension, low-salt and other modified diets, and iron supplementation to control anemia.

Implications for Physical Education

The child with nephritis will probably be in and out of the hospital many times. Each time he or she returns to school the fitness level is low because the child has been confined to a hospital room without appreciable exercise. Most physicians concur that children with kidney and urinary tract disease need moderate exercise. They are adamant, however, that such children should not be subjected to physical fitness tests nor to actual physical stress of any kind.

Particularly susceptible to renal disorders are persons with spina bifida, spinal cord injuries, and amputations. Further detail on management of urinary problems appears in the chapter on orthopedic handicaps.

Hemophilia

The term *hemophilia* encompasses at least eight different bleeding disorders that are caused by the lack of any 1 of 10 different clotting factors in the blood. Although only 1 in 10,000 persons is afflicted in the United States, the physical educator who has one hemophiliac child is likely to have several since it is an inherited disorder. Historically, it has been said to appear only in males and to be transmitted through females. Recently, however, a type of hemophilia in women has been identified.

Contrary to popular belief, outward bleeding from a wound does not disable most hemophiliacs; rather internal bleeding does. A stubbed toe, a bumped elbow, a violent sneeze, or a gentle tag game can be fatal. Each causes bleeding beneath the surface of the skin that is manifested by discoloration, swelling, and other characteristics of a hematoma. The hemophiliac child tends to have many black and blue spots, swollen joints, and considerable limitation of movement. Minor internal bleeding may be present much of the time. When internal bleeding appears extensive, the child is rushed to the hospital for transfusions.

Over a period of years, repeated hemorrhages into joints, if untreated, result in hemophilic arthritis. To minimize joint bleeding, the afflicted body part is frequently splinted. Pain is severe, and the hemophiliac may avoid complete extension. This tendency, of course, results in such orthopedic complications as contractures. Hemophiliac children should be allowed to engage in regular physical education and should be expected to establish their own limitations. As in so many other handicaps, the problems of peer group acceptance, parental overprotection, and social isolation are more intense than the unpredictable episodes of bleeding that halt the usual routine of life. Swimming, creative dance, rhythmic exercises on heavily padded mats, and such individual sports as fishing, shuffleboard, and billiards or pool offer much satisfaction. Catching activities generally are contraindicated.

Sickle-Cell Disease (Anemia)

Although discovered by physician James Herrick in 1910, *sickle-cell disease* did not receive widespread attention until the early 1970s. At that time, 1 of every 400 black Americans was believed to have the disorder.

Sickle-cell disease is an inherited blood disorder that takes its name from the sickle-shape the red blood cells assume when the oxygen content of the blood is low. Persons with the disease are anemic, suffer crises of severe pain, are prone to infection, and often have slow-healing ulcers of the skin, especially around the ankles. Many do not live to adulthood.

Regular exercise should not be curtailed, but tests and activities of cardiovascular endurance are contraindicated. Under intense exercise stress, particularly at altitudes above 10,000 feet, where the oxygen content of the air is decreased, persons with sickle-cell anemia may collapse. They should also avoid becoming overheated since the normal evaporation of perspiration cools the skin and may precipitate an attack.

The disease develops at the time of conception, but symptoms do not usually appear until the child is 6 months or older. The first symptoms are pallor, poor appetite, early fatigue, and complaints of pain in the back, abdomen, and the extremities. The child may not evidence sickle-cell anemia until he or she catches a cold or has an attack of tonsillitis; then he or she reacts worse than the normal child.

The course of the disease is marked by a sequence of physiological crises and complications that can be recognized, predicted, and treated, but not prevented. The crisis results from spasms in key blood vessels. The child experiences agonizing pain in certain muscles and joints, particularly those of the rib cage, and may run a high fever. Some crises are severe enough to require hospitalization. As the child grows older and learns limitations, the attacks become less frequent.

Anemia

Anemia is a condition of reduced oxygen-carrying capacity of the blood caused by deficiency in either red blood cells or hemoglobin, the oxygen-carrying pigment within the red blood cells. Mild anemia is not easily recognizable, but more severe conditions are characterized by loss of color in cheeks, lips, and gums; lowered activity level because of limited amount of oxygen available to burn calories; and increased heart and breathing rates.

Anemia, often a characteristic of chronic debilitating conditions like leukemia, kidney disease, and lead poisoning, can also occur independently. *Cooley's anemia*, a genetic disorder most common in persons whose descendents are from Italy, Greece, Turkey, and surrounding areas, affects approximately 9 of every 10,000 United States citizens (i.e., it is almost twice as common as autism and Down's syndrome). Symptoms begin to appear at 1 or 2 years of age, and medical treatments (blood transfusions and drug therapy) are needed throughout life. *Iron deficiency anemia,* caused by insufficient daily intake of iron or excessive loss of iron through hemorrhaging, is even more common than Cooley's anemia. Students with severe mental retardation, cerebral palsy, and disorders that affect chewing/swallowing processes or food intake are at particularly high risk.

Symptoms of anemia, regardless of the cause or type, include irritability, lethargy, and increased fatigability because of high cardiac output. Students with anemia, however, can perform well at low and moderate exercise intensities. In spite of this, many tend to adopt sedentary life styles. Hypoactivity contributes more to their lack of fitness than pathological limitations. Students with anemia should not be excused from regular physical education; rather, they should be encouraged to participate fully, with adaptations made in regard to fitness testing expectations and standards.

Lead Poisoning

The three most common environmental hazards to children's health are metal pollution (lead, mercury, zinc), air pollution (including cigarette smoke), and low-level radiation. Of these, the most research has been done on lead.

Lead poisoning is a leading cause of health impairments in children ages 1 to 4 years. Elevations in blood/lead concentration are associated with cognitive and behavioral difficulties. Approximately 600,000 children under 6 years of age have elevated blood/lead levels; this has been estimated at 5 to 8% of all preschool children.

Approximately 600,000 tons of lead are released by the smelting industry into the environment annually, much of which is carried by winds and deposited in soil where children play. This lead fallout, as well as that caused by lead gasoline, is now the leading cause of lead poisoning. In earlier decades, the main routes of exposure were ingestion of paint or paint dust, milk formulas from improperly soldered cans, and tainted drinking water. The federal Lead Poisoning Prevention Act of 1971 permits large scale screening of preschool children to identify those at risk, but little else has been done (except in individual communities) to cope with this problem.

Physical educators working in blighted urban areas can expect as many as 40% of their students to carry significant lead burdens, which cause subtle health and behavior problems. Characteristics of mild lead poisoning are listlessness, lethargy, irritability, clumsiness, and anemia, all of which contribute to developmental delay. Severe and/or persistent lead poisoning, without treatment, typically results in seizures, coma, and eventual death. Even with treatment, mental retardation and epilepsy often occur. Lead poisoning is treated by such drugs as edetate calcium disodium and penicillamine, which can be taken either orally or by intramuscular injection. Most important, however, is removal of students from lead-tainted environments.

Tuberculosis

Tuberculosis, although no longer a common cause of death, still ranks within the top 10 reportable diseases. The incidence of reported tuberculosis is about the same as that of infectious hepatitis, measles, and rubella. Among causes of death, tuberculosis ranks 19th. The decreasing incidence of this disease is due to a vaccine that is about 80% effective in disease prevention.

Tuberculosis, although often conceptualized as a lung disease, can affect any tissue in the body. Tuberculosis is an infectious disease caused by bacteria (i.e., the tubercle bacillus) and characterized by the formation of tubercles (little swellings). In this country, bone and joint tuberculosis is more likely to come to the attention of physical educators than the other types. Of the skeletal sites of tuberculosis, the most common is the spine, followed by hip and knee.

Pott's disease, or tuberculosis of the spine, is a disorder that often results in kyphosis (round upper back). This inflammation of the vertebral bodies occurs most often in children and young adults. Pott's disease is characterized by the formation of little tubercles on the vertebral bodies. Destruction and compression of the vertebral bodies affects the spinal cord and adjacent nerves to the extent that movement becomes extremely painful. The characteristic kyphotic curvature is called a *gibbus,* meaning hump. The condition of having a humpback is *gibbosity.* A medical synonym for Pott's disease is *tuberculous spondylitis.*

Tuberculosis remains a common cause of meningitis (infection of covering of brain) during early childhood. The consequences of this disease, even with the best treatment, are severe, with some degree of intellectual deficit occurring in about 20% of children, as well as hearing and vestibular defects. Seizures, hydrocephalus, spasticity, ataxia, and incoordination are common outcomes also.

Autism

Autism is a severely incapacitating condition that typically appears during the first 3 years of life and is characterized by severe communication and other developmental and educational problems. Although originally placed under the category of seriously emotionally disturbed in PL 94–142, research showing that not all autistic persons had such disturbance led to a legal reclassification in 1981 (see *Federal Register,* volume 46, no. 1, January 15, 1981, p. 3865). Autism is now legally defined as an *other health impaired condition.*

Used in psychiatry to mean withdrawn and self-absorbed, autism comes from the Greek word *autos,* meaning self. Kanner (1943) was the first person to describe autistic children as a group. Since then, a growing body of literature has resulted in much controversy. The causes of autism remain unknown, and the values of various therapeutic techniques are highly speculative.

Childhood autism denotes an extremely heterogenous chronic condition. It may occur by itself or in association with other disorders that affect brain function. About 40% of persons with autism have IQs below 50; only 30% have IQs of 70 or above. IQ testing, however, is extremely difficult with tremendous variability manifested in different kinds of tasks. In general, autistic persons perform lowest in abstract or symbolic thought and highest on tasks requiring visual-spatial or manipulative skills. Among the common characteristics of autism are

1. Withdrawal from or failure to become involved with people.
2. Muteness or inability to use speech for communication.
3. Unusual bodily movements and peculiar mannerisms.
4. Abnormal response to one or more types of sensory stimuli, usually sound.
5. Pathological resistance to change manifested by observance of rituals, excessive preoccupation with certain objects without regard for their accepted functions, and emotional outbursts when sameness of environment is threatened.
6. Lack of appropriate play.
7. Isolated areas of high-level functioning within the context of otherwise mentally and socially retarded behaviors.

The incidence of autism is 2 to 4 cases per 10,000 with approximately three times more males affected than females. Recent research shows that the condition is modifiable, especially by behavior management techniques. About one-third of persons with autism are able to make adequate social adjustment by adulthood and live and work fairly independently; the other two-thirds remain severely handicapped. Intellectual function and ability to develop language skills appear to be the critical factors in remediation.

Early research indicated that the motor development of autistic children was normal, but recent studies indicate inadequate motor control and delayed acquisition of motor skills. Reid, Collier, and Morin (1983) reported that autistic students were within normal ranges of height and weight, but scored below norms on physical fitness measures of estimated body fat, grip strength, abdominal strength, and flexibility. Morin and Reid (1985) noted that autistic adolescents performed motorically about the same as matched mentally retarded counterparts.

Pedagogy found effective with autistic students in public school settings has primarily involved one-to-one instruction utilizing behavior management techniques. The student-teacher ratio in physical education should be the same as that in other school subjects, and similar environmental controls and methods should be used. Because autistic students are typically unresponsive to social stimuli and social rewards, primary reinforcers like food are more often used than in other developmental disabilities. Sensory stimulation like music and tickling have shown some promise as substitutes for food. An important goal is to help autistic students to respond increasingly to stimuli in the environment rather than continuing to block out almost all input. Swimming pool activities have been found successful in this regard (Killian, Joyce-Petrovich, Menna, & Arena, 1984).

Psychologists and dance/movement therapists recommend intervention that is almost exactly opposite of that favored in most special education circles. Obviously, there are no easy answers. It seems prudent to understand and experiment with therapeutic approaches as well as behavioral ones.

Bettelheim (1967) and many psychotherapists emphasize that the major objective in working with autistic children is to provide an environment of potentially positive valence in which nothing is forced on them. For years they have functioned mechanically. As such children begin to consciously act, they must be reassured that it is they alone who have power over their own behavior: eating, moving the bowels, playing, or talking. This helps to explain why often the first positive acts are the reverse of the teacher's wishes. For example, a large number of autistic children give up toilet training in their first steps toward wellness. For even this, they must receive encouragement—but not too much lest they feel pushed. The role of the teacher in such cases is to subtly encourage the child into defiance.

Some physical educators, accustomed to praising children for positive acts, may find such approaches difficult to implement. The importance of seeking further training in psychology cannot be overemphasized. The autistic child is fragile. Progress can be inhibited for months because one unknowledgeable staff member scolds such a child for dirtying his or her pants or expresses too much enthusiasm over a small achievement.

Aberrant motor behavior displayed by autistic children includes rocking, head rolling and banging, and tapping or twiddling with the fingers. These acts often constitute the sum of the autistic child's experience and maximum ability for dealing with reality. Thus, it is important that the teacher not interfere. Bettelheim has recommended that however difficult a symptom is to accept, the adult must communicate respect for the child's means of coping with the world. Whenever possible, the adult seeks to help the child improve on these spontaneous idiosyncrasies rather than drop them. For instance, a child who twiddles only his or her fingers may be encouraged to twiddle objects. It is important to help autistic children form a body image through movement therapy that utilizes rhythms, vocalizations, and body actions on a primitive sensory-motor level. The progress of autistic children is very slow. Kalish (1968), for instance, describes sessions with a child over a period of 3 years. Several months of this time were spent simply in establishing rapport and building trust. Initially, the 5-year-old tolerated little or no physical contact. She hovered in one corner of the room and occupied herself with perseverative head movements. Occasionally, she would burst out of her corner, jump up and down three or four times in a stylized ritual, and then return to the corner. Never did she stray more than a few feet from this spot. Kalish described her method of establishing contact as follows:

My first approach to her was to make use of the diagonal spatial path from the opposite corner of the room. Moving tentatively and in an indirect line, but toward Laura, I tried to incorporate her finger and hand rhythms into my feet and body movements. I did not venture past "her" side of the center of the room. Taking my cues from her, I would suddenly jump up and down, using her timing and return to the corner.

For many sessions, she gave only a fleeting glance, but as she seemed to get "used" to my presence, her glance was more sustained looking, at a distance. I moved closer to her corner, then back to my own, until now we shared all the space in the room, sometimes together and sometimes separately. (Kalish, 1968, p. 56)

Approximately 2 years later, after sessions were increased to three or four times a week, Laura was willing to sit on the therapist's lap and able to concentrate on movement patterns in a mirror. She was still unable to imitate movements, but was making definite progress toward this end. One of the most significant changes was her interest in the mirror. It seemed as though Laura was discovering her body for the first time.

Adler, another dance therapist, has developed a beautiful 29-minute film depicting work with an autistic child. The film "Looking At Me" can be rented through University of California Extension Media Center, 2223 Fulton Street, Berkeley, CA 94720. Adler, like Kalish, is concerned with helping the autistic child establish self-identity. Her philosophy is summarized in the following paragraph:

I am impressed with the simplicity of Ronald Laing's statement: "the sense of identity requires the existence of another by whom one is known." But of course, the difficulty is—How to know another and How to let another know you. My premise, at this point, is, if the other is a severely disturbed child, my "meness" can only be effective in developing her identity if it is genuinely reflective of what she knows best—her tiny, perseverative intensely physical world. Therefore, at this time, in my own evolution, I am deeply invested in providing an opportunity for a disturbed child to BE—to BE herself literally, with all of her "bizarre" and "crazy" mannerisms and expressions, I begin there, by reflecting her world, primarily on a body level. I try to "speak" her language by moving with her, as she moves in space. In the beginning, there is much direct imitation, which by definition means delayed response on my part. However, as she permits my presence, and as the trust develops, I find that the one-sidedness falls away and a more mutual dialogue begins to creep into being: we become synchronous. (Adler, 1968, p. 43)

Movement or dance therapy appears to be a viable way to work with autistic children who characteristically are mute or severely retarded in language development. Even after learning to talk, they stubbornly reverse pronouns to avoid using "I." A typical verbal exchange might be: Teacher: "Do you want to jump on the trampoline?" Child: "You want to jump," meaning "I want to jump." The physical educator should not try to correct this speech pattern. The avoidance of "I" is believed to be either a denial of selfhood or an absence of awareness of self, while the substitution of "you" shows some awareness of the selfhood of others. Autistic children, like normal 2-year-olds, also avoid the word *yes,* responding negatively to both invitations and commands whether they mean it or not.

Theories vary as to whether autistic children do not relate to human beings or simply do so negatively. Characteristically, the persons they treat as nonexistent feel rejected and find it difficult to work with autistic children over a period of months. Objectives that might be accomplished through physical education activities remain largely unexplored.

Learning Activities

1. Go through this chapter and write every word with which you are unfamiliar on notecards, alphabetize these, and write definitions on the backs of the cards. Develop word- and quiz show-type games that use these cards to reinforce your memory of definitions.

2. Identify the organizations and/or agencies related to each OHI condition and write or telephone national, state, and local offices for additional information. Ask if they have an official position statement on sports participation and what sports events they sponsor.

3. Identify outstanding persons at local, state, and national levels who have OHI conditions and discuss how these persons can be used as role models for disabled students. Make a scrapbook of newspaper clippings about possible role models.

4. Invite persons with OHI conditions to speak to your class and/or visit camp or recreation programs designed specifically for children with such conditions.

5. Role play IEP meetings or other situations in which controversial issues, including proper physical education placement and involvement in interscholastic competition, are debated. Assign roles representing parents and various members of the multidisciplinary team.

References

Adams, F., & Moss, A. (1969). Physical activity of children with congenital heart disease. *American Journal of Cardiology, 24*, 605–606.

Adler, J. (1968). The study of an autistic child. *American Dance Therapy Association Proceedings* (Third Annual Conference). Baltimore: ADTA.

American Academy of Pediatrics, Committee on Sports Medicine (August, 1982). *The asthmatic child and his participation in sports and physical education.* Mimeographed.

American Medical Association. (1968). The epileptic child and competitive school athletics. *Pediatrics, 42,* 700.

American Medical Association (1974). Epileptics and contact sports: Position statement. *Journal of American Medical Association, 229,* 820–821.

Bettelheim, B. (1967). *The empty fortress.* New York: Macmillan.

Brandt, N. (1973). Your son has diabetes. *Today's Health, 51*(6), 34–37, 69–71.

Gastaut, H. (1970). Clinical and electroencephalographic classification of epileptic seizures. *Epilepsia, 11,* 102–113.

Gilbert, C. A. (1978). Exercise and the heart. In J. Basmajian (Ed.), *Therapeutic exercise* (3rd ed.) (pp. 548–564). Baltimore: Williams & Wilkins.

Johnson, L. (1968). *An experimental study of the obese individual in physical education.* Unpublished doctoral dissertation, West Virginia University, Morgantown.

Kalish, B. (1968). Body movement therapy for autistic children. *American Dance Therapy Association Proceedings* (Third Annual Conference). Baltimore: ADTA.

Kanner, L. (1943). Autistic disturbances of affective contact. *Nervous Child, 2,* 217–250.

Killian, K., Joyce-Petrovich, R., Menna, L., & Arena, S. (1984). Measuring water orientation and beginner swim skills of autistic individuals. *Adapted Physical Activity Quarterly, 1*(4), 287–295.

Livingston, S. (1969). Letter to the editor. *Journal of American Medical Association, 207.*

Morin, B., & Reid, G. (1985). A quantitative and qualitative assessment of autistic individuals on selected motor tasks. *Adapted Physical Activity Quarterly, 2* (1), 43–55.

Neill, C., & Hartoutunian, L. (1977). The adolescent and young adult with congenital heart disease. In A. J. Moss, F. H. Adams, & G. C. Emmanouilides (Eds.), *Heart disease in infants, children, and adults* (2nd ed.) Baltimore: Williams & Wilkins.

Reid, G., Collier, D., & Morin, B. (1983). The motor performance of autistic individuals. In R. Eason, T. Smith, & F. Caron (Eds.), *Adapted physical activity* (pp. 201–218). Champaign, IL: Human Kinetics Publishers.

Rohrbacher, R. (1973). Influence of special camp program for older boys on weight loss, self-concept, and body image. *Research Quarterly, 44,* 150–157.

Steiner, M. M. (1970). *Clinical approach to endocrine problems in childhood.* St. Louis: C. V. Mosby.

Talbert, W. F. (February–March, 1971). Double challenge for a champion. *World Health,* 25–27.

Bibliography

American Academy of Pediatrics. (1978). Cardiac evaluation for participation in sports. *The Physician and Sports Medicine, 6,* 102.

American College of Sports Medicine (Ed.). (1980). *Guidelines for graded exercise testing and exercise prescription* (2nd ed.). Philadelphia: Lea & Febiger.

Bar-Or, O. (1983). *Pediatric sports medicine for the practitioner.* New York: Springer-Verlag.

Berg, K. (1979). The insulin-dependent diabetic runner. *Physician and Sports Medicine, 7*(11), 71–79.

Boshell, B. R. (1979). *The diabetic at work and play* (2nd ed.). Springfield, IL: Charles C. Thomas.

Campaigne, B., Gilliam, T., Spencer, M., & Gold, E. (1984). Heart rate holter monitoring of 6- and 7-year old children with insulin dependent diabetes mellitus, cardiovascular and short term metabolic response to exercise: A pilot study. *Research Quarterly for Exercise and Sport, 55*(1), 69–73.

Cole, I. L. (1978). *Dance therapy with a nonverbal, autistic child: A documentation of process.* Unpublished doctoral dissertation, Texas Woman's University, Denton.

Cole, I. L. (1982). Movement negotiations with an autistic child. *Arts in Psychotherapy, 9*(1), 49–55.

Corbin, C. (1980). Cardiovascular fitness of children. In C. Corbin (Ed.), *A textbook of motor development* (2nd ed.) (pp. 107–114). Dubuque, IA: Wm. C. Brown.

Costill, D. L., Cleary, P., Fink, W. J., Foster, C., Ivy, J. L. & Witzmann, F. (1979). Training adaptations in skeletal muscle of juvenile diabetes. *Diabetes 28,* 818–822.

Delacato, C. (1976). *The ultimate stranger: The autistic child.* Garden City, NY: Doubleday.

Diabetes and exercise: A round table. (1979). *Physician and Sports Medicine, 7*(3), 49–71.

Dreisbach, M., Ballard, M., Russo, D., & Schain, R. (1982). Educational intervention for children with epilepsy: A challenge for collaborative service delivery. *Journal of Special Education, 16*(1), 111–121.

Dunlap, G., Kaegel, R. L., & Egel, A. L. (1979). Autistic children in school. *Exceptional Children, 45,* 552–559.

Engle, M. E. (Ed.). (1981). *Pediatric cardiovascular disease.* Philadelphia: F. A. Davis.

Evans, H. (1979). *Lung diseases of children.* New York: American Lung Assn.

Exercise and asthma: A round table. (1984). *Physician and Sports Medicine, 12*(1), 59–77.

Fine, A. H., Feldis, D., & Lehrer, B. (1982). Therapeutic recreation and programming for autistic children. *Therapeutic Recreation Journal, 16,* 6–11.

Fitch, K. (1975). Exercise-induced asthma and competitive athletics. *Pediatrics* (Supplement), *56,* 844–846.

Frazee, R., Brunt, D., & Castle, R. (1984). Exercise tolerance level of a young child with congenital heart disease associated with asplenia syndrome. *Adapted Physical Activity Quarterly, 1*(4), 322–326.

Kalish, B. (1976). *Body movement scale for autistic and other atypical children.* Unpublished doctoral dissertation, Bryn Mawr College.

Kern, L., Koegel, R., Dyer, K., Bleu, P., & Fenton, L. (1982). The effects of physical exercise on self-stimulation and appropriate responding in autistic children. *Journal of Autism and Developmental Disorders, 12*(4), 399–419.

Lin-Fu, J. (1979). Lead exposure among children—A reassessment. *New England Journal of Medicine, 300,* 731–732.

Livingston, S. (1972). *Comprehensive management of epilepsy in infancy, childhood, and adolescence.* Springfield, IL: Charles C. Thomas.

Ludvigsson, J. (1980). Physical exercise in relation to degree of metabolic control in juvenile diabetics. *Acta Paediatrica Scandinavica* (Suppl. 283), 45–48.

Marley, W. P. (1977). Asthma and exercise: A review. *American Corrective Therapy Journal, 31,* 95–102.

Morton, A., Fitch, K., & Hahn, A. (1981). Physical activity and the asthmatic. *Physician and Sports Medicine, 9*(3), 51–64.

Moss, A. J., Adams, F. H., & Emmanouilides, G. C. (Eds.). (1977). *Heart disease in infants, children, and adolescents* (2nd ed.). Baltimore: Williams & Wilkins.

Needleman, H. (1979). Deficits in psychologic and classroom performance of children with elevated dentine lead levels. *New England Journal of Medicine, 300,* 695–698.

Persson, B., & Thorin, C. (1980). Prolonged exercise in adolescent boys with juvenile diabetes mellitus. Circulatory and metabolic responses in relation to perceived exertion. *Acta Paediatrica Scandinavica* (Suppl. 283), 62–69.

Rutter, M. (1978). Diagnosis and definition of childhood autism. *Journal of Autism and Childhood Schizophrenia, 8,* 139–146.

Spooner, F., & Dykes, M. (1982). Epilepsy: Impact upon severely and profoundly handicapped persons. *The Journal of the Association for the Severely Handicapped, 7*(3), 87–96.

Steele, S. (1983). *Health promotion of the child with long term illness* (3rd ed.). Norwalk, CT: Appleton-Century-Crofts.

Watters, H., & Watters, W. (1980). Decreasing self-stimulatory behavior with physical exercise in a group of autistic boys. *Journal of Autism and Developmental Disorders, 10*(4), 379–387.

Williams, H. E., & Phelan, P. D. (1975). *Respiratory illness in children.* Oxford: Blackwell Scientific Publications.

Wing, L. (Ed.). (1976). *Early childhood autism* (2nd ed.). New York: Pergamon Press.

Winnick, J. (1977). Physical activity and the asthmatic child. *American Corrective Therapy Journal, 31,* 148–151.

18 Learning Disabilities

Figure 18.1 An alternative to beam walking is a Cratty floor grid on which every letter of the alphabet and every number can be found. Here an LD boy leads his teacher in walking out the number 8.

Chapter Objectives

After you have studied this chapter, you should be able to

1. Define the term *learning disabilities* and discuss behaviors commonly associated with it.

2. State four principles for controlling hyperkinesis and discuss the application of each in a physical education setting.

3. Discuss specific techniques to be used in the amelioration of each of the following: distractibility, dissociation, perseveration, social imperception, immature body image, poor spatial orientation, and apraxia.

4. Discuss assessment of LD students, problems that may occur, and adaptations that might be helpful. Relate this to perceptual-motor deficits that may be manifested in listening, thinking, talking, reading, or arithmetic and indicate how such deficits may affect testing motor performance.

5. Given behaviors of hypothesized LD students, including statements of their present level of psychomotor functioning, develop physical education IEPs.

6. Discuss integration of students with various combinations of LD problems into regular physical education and interscholastic athletics. What conditions must be present to make integration the least restrictive placement?

7. Re-read the chapter on perceptual-motor training and relate its contents to LD students of different ages and constellations of problems. Describe specific perceptual-motor activities you would weave into lesson plans.

8. Discuss available and needed research on physical education and athletics for LD students. Does such research take into consideration class size, motivation theory, social acceptance, and similar variables?

Thomas Edison, Woodrow Wilson, Winston Churchill, Albert Einstein, Walt Disney, and Mickey Mantle all manifested learning disabilities severe enough to disrupt their early schooling. Each at one time or another was labeled a failure because of specific deficits in language or mathematical processes. The discrepancy between estimated intellectual potential and actual academic achievement has long baffled parents and educators.

Numerous terms have been used to describe the underachieving pupil with normal or better intelligence: word-blind, dyslexic, aphasic, brain-injured, neurophrenic. With the recognition in the 1960s that the *whole* child was not handicapped by a specific disability, the terminology switched from adjectives to such prepositional phrases as *with learning disabilities* and *with minimal brain dysfunction*. The founding of the Association for Children with Learning Disabilities (ACLD) in 1964 contributed greatly to the standardization of terminology and the mobilization of efforts directed toward legislation for this group. In 1980 the name of this organization changed to ACLD, Inc. (An Association for Children and Adults with Learning Disabilities). The purpose of ACLD, as cited in its early literature, revealed a broad definition of learning disabilities: "to advance the education and general well-being of children with adequate intelligence who have learning disabilities arising from perceptual, conceptual, or subtle coordinative problems, sometimes accompanied by behavior difficulties."

The year 1968 marks the official recognition of learning disabilities as an educational category with independent funding by the United States Office of Education. At this time also the definition of learning disabilities was delimited as follows:

Children with special (specific) learning disabilities exhibit a disorder in one or more of the basic psychological processes involved in understanding or in using spoken or written language. These may be manifested in disorders of listening, thinking, talking, reading, writing, spelling, or arithmetic. They include conditions which have been referred to as perceptual handicaps, brain injury, minimal brain dysfunction, dyslexia, developmental aphasias, etc. They do not include learning problems which are due primarily to visual, hearing, or motor handicaps, to mental retardation, emotional disturbance, or to environmental disadvantage. (Education of Handicapped Children, 1968, p. 14)

This definition, although decidedly different from the earlier ACLD concept, is now widely accepted. With only a few words changed, it is the official PL 94–142 definition.

Prevalence

It is conservatively estimated that 1.8 million children between the ages of 3 and 21 in the United States have learning disabilities severe enough to warrant special educational services. This represents approximately 42% of all handicapped children receiving special education. Less conservative estimates indicate that one out of every five school children has learning problems of neurological origin that interfere with optimal success in the normal classroom. Unfortunately, in some communities the LD label has become an umbrella under which all educational enigmas fall.

The prevalence of learning disabilities is far greater among boys than girls. The ratio seems to range from 15:1 to 25:1.

Characteristics of Children with Learning Disabilities

No two children with learning disabilities exhibit the same constellation of strengths and weaknesses. Yet, in spite of their heterogeneity, LD children display certain behaviors more often than do the normal population. Among these are disordered or hyperkinetic behavior, distractibility, dissociation, perseveration, social imperception, immature body image, poor spatial orientation, and nonspecific awkwardness or clumsiness. Learning disabled children often exhibit many perceptual-motor problems (reread Chapter 11). From the 1930s through the 1970s, perceptual-motor activities (such as the one shown in Figure 18.1) were commonly used in both academic and physical education classes for learning disabled students. Today, perceptual-motor training is controversial. This chapter, therefore, focuses on the many problems LD students may exhibit in addition to perceptual-motor deficits.

Hyperkinesis

The hyperactive child manifests disorders of listening, thinking, reading, writing, spelling, or arithmetic primarily because he or she cannot sit still long enough to complete a task. Such children are forever wiggling, shuffling their feet, swinging their legs, doodling, pinching, chewing gum, gritting their teeth, and talking to themselves or others. They seem never to tire, and require unbelievably little sleep. They have been described as

being up by 5:05 A.M., into the kitchen by 5:08 A.M., having the pans out of the cupboard by 5:09 A.M., mixing the flour and sugar on the floor by 5:11 A.M., walking through it in bare feet by 5:15 A.M., turning attention to the living room drapes by 5:18 A.M., and inadvertently knocking over a table lamp at 5:20 A.M. This wakens all members of the family, who individually and collectively descend on the first-floor scene, and thus begins another day of tension, discipline, and frustration. (Cruickshank, 1967, p. 34)

Hyperactivity may be worse on some days than others. Classroom teachers have been known to send the child to the playground on such days: "You take him . . . I can't teach him a thing in the classroom." Hyperactive children may display *catastrophic reactions* to unexpected stimuli like a sharp noise, a scary incident in a movie, or a playful jab from a teammate. They tend to fall apart, to sob uncontrollably, to scream, or to display sudden outbursts of anger or physical aggression.

Hyperactivity should not be confused with individual differences in energy, impulse control, and enthusiasm. All toddlers exhibit problems with impulse control. This is evidenced when children of different ages are asked, "How slowly can you draw a line from this point to that point?" Or, "How slowly can you walk across the room?" Or, "How slowly can you do tasks in the Bruininks-Oseretsky tests?" The older the normal child is, the more easily he or she can slow down the pace and consciously determine the tempo. Impulse control may be related to hyperactive behavior, but it is not the same thing.

Hyperactivity is a medical problem. It is usually recognized and referred to a physician long before the child enters school. Most physicians use medication as a last resort in the management of hyperactivity. Nevertheless, large numbers of LD youngsters are so uncontrollable that drugs are prescribed: ritalin (methylphenidate), dexedrine, benzedrine, and methedrine, all of which are stimulants. Research has demonstrated that these stimulant drugs slow down the LD child, increase the attention span, and enable the child to concentrate on one thing at a time. The use of stimulants in the management of hyperactivity is analogous to the prescription of insulin for the diabetic. Both conditions involve deficits in body chemistry for which drugs must compensate. In the LD child, insufficient amounts of serotonin, epinephrine (adrenalin), and norepinephrine, which control the activity centers in the brain, are circulating in the body. The concentrations of these substances within the body generally change with age, and the deficit normally corrects itself in the middle school or junior high years. Medications cannot correct the physiological deficit; they simply compensate for it until the body chemistry changes of its own accord. Hyperactivity normally ceases to be a problem at about the time of puberty, and medication is stopped. Children do not become addicted to the drugs used in the management of hyperactivity, and there are no withdrawal problems. The main side effects are depressed appetite and sleeplessness.

What educational adaptations must be implemented for the hyperactive child? How do these affect physical education instruction? Numerous approaches have been proposed, several of which are controversial. It is essential, however, that the instructional practices in physical education be consistent with those used by other teachers. If, for instance, the classroom environment is highly structured, then the physical education program must be also.

Principles for Controlling Hyperkinesis

The concepts of Cruickshank (1967) and Strauss and Lehtinen (1947) continue to shape the educational prescriptions of hyperactive children. According to them, a good teaching environment is based upon four principles:

1. Establishment of a highly structured program.
2. Reduction of environmental space.
3. Elimination of irrelevant auditory and visual stimuli.
4. Enhancement of the stimulus value of the instructional materials themselves.

The principle of *structure,* as applied to the physical education setting, requires the establishment of a routine that is repeated day after day and leaves nothing to chance. For instance, the pattern of activities will follow the same sequence each period: sitting on prescribed floor spots while waiting for class to begin; warm-ups always done in the same area and facing the same direction; introduction and practice of new skills; participation in games or dances; return to floor spots and sitting or lying during *cool-down* period of relaxation and discussion. If instructional stations are used, a certain piece of apparatus is always located in the same space and the pupils always mount it from the same direction. Rotation from station to station is always in the same direction, traditionally counterclockwise. Characteristically, after warm-ups each pupil goes to his or her assigned station to start instruction, and rotation always proceeds from this same spot. Identical start, stop, and rotation signals contribute also to structure since the child knows precisely which response is appropriate for each signal.

Moreover, the composition of each squad or team is structured in much the same fashion as are groups for play therapy or psychotherapy. A balance is maintained between the number of hyperactive and sluggish children so that one behavioral extreme tends to neutralize the other. The proportion of aggressors and nonaggressors is weighted, as are natural leaders and followers. A genuine attempt, often demanding much trial and error, is made to determine which combination of human beings learn together most efficiently. It

must be emphasized that the success of this structure is based upon ease of learning; it is totally unrelated to winning and losing and has little to do with level of skill.

The principle of *space reduction* suggests the use of lane markers and partitions to delimit the vast expanse of play area considered desirable for normal children. Special emphasis must be given to boundaries and the penalties incumbent upon stepping out of bounds for LD children. The major value of low organized games may be learnings about boundaries, baselines, and space possession and utilization.

Space reduction necessarily limits the size of the squads, which rotate from station to station. Most elementary school children function best in groups of six to eight; LD children often require still smaller groups for optimal learning. It should be remembered that these may be pupils confined to individual cubicles in the classroom. The child who lacks readiness for group activities in the classroom will seldom display success in group games on the playground.

The principle of *extraneous stimuli control* demands the maintenance of a neat, clean, well-ordered play area. No balls or equipment are in sight unless they are required for the game in progress. Cruickshank (1967) recommends that wall, floor, and furniture be the same color; that transparent window panes be replaced by opaque glass; and that wooden doors enclose all shelves. Several authorities have challenged the extremity of these measures, but all concur that extraneous visual and auditory stimuli that distract children should be eliminated.

When several squads are each practicing different motor tasks, often on different pieces of apparatus, the attention of the pupil may be diverted by children at other stations. It is not uncommon for the LD child to respond to the attractiveness of another station by roaming about, losing his or her own squad, forgetting the name of his or her partner, and becoming generally disoriented. Again, partitions to eliminate the extraneous visual stimuli from other stations prevent many such problems. Similar distractions are present when physical education is held out-of-doors: cars in the nearby street, neighborhood animals, leaves rustling on the trees, birds flying overhead, weeds among the grass where the ball is rolling, even the wind and sun. The severely hyperactive pupil should be scheduled only for indoor physical education, where environmental variables can be more easily manipulated and controlled.

The principle of *instructional stimulus enhancement,* as applied to the physical education setting, implies the extensive and concentrated use of color to focus and hold the pupil's attention on a particular piece of apparatus, a target, or a ball. Sound may be used similarly. Wall-to-wall mirrors in which children can see and learn to evaluate their motor performance seem to increase concentration also.

The principles of structure, space reduction, stimuli control, and instructional stimulus enhancement form the basis of a sound physical education program for LD children. Freedom is increased gradually in accordance with the pupil's ability to cope.

Social incentives and extrinsic rewards based upon Skinnerian principles of reinforcement for nonhyperactivity are recommended also. For instance, every child who stays within the space boundaries of his or her station for the allotted time period may be rewarded with a red chip, paper money, or piece of candy just before the whistle blows for rotation to the next station. Stars are pasted on charts for children who stay in line and take their turn at the proper time. Sometimes contracts are made in which pupils specify what they will do in expectation of a certain reward. There is little time for writing out a contract for physical education as is done in the classroom. Therefore, prefabricated contracts of different colors that require only the signatures of teacher and pupil may be readied ahead of time. The child may refuse a contract or select from several that specify varying lengths of concentration on particular activities. Contracts may also give structure to endurance-type activities that require walking, running, or swimming certain distances.

For additional techniques of coping with hyperkinesis, reread Chapter 14, Relaxation and Reduction of Hyperactivity.

Distractibility

Distractibility is the inability to concentrate attention on any particular object or person in the environment. Some pupils are distracted by any movement, sound, color, or smell and lack the ability to block out irrelevant stimuli as do normal persons. Admonishing such pupils to *pay attention* is useless. They would if they could. Instead, such a pupil reacts to

the grinding of the pencil sharpener, to the colors of dozens of shirts and dresses which surround him, to the movement of the child next to him across the aisle, to an announcement on the intercommunication system, to the leaves on the tree blowing in the wind outside the room, to the movement of the goldfish in the aquarium, to another child who just sneezed, to the teacher's whispers to yet a third child, to the footsteps of a group of children walking past his room in the hall, to the crack at the top of his desk into which his pencil point will just fit, to the American flag hanging in the front of the room, to the Thanksgiving Day decorations on the walls, to dozens and dozens of other unessential things in the room which prevent him from writing his name on the top line! It

isn't that he refuses to cooperate with the teacher's request to "start here." It is that he simply cannot refrain from reacting to the unessential stimuli in his environment. This is, we think, the result of a neurological impairment. The difficulty which he experiences in carrying out the simple request of the teacher occurs again and again each day as one learning opportunity after another is presented to him. (Cruickshank, 1967, p. 33)

Principles 3 and 4 discussed under hyperkinesis relate to distractibility also. Refer also to the writings of Hallahan and Cruickshank (1973) in the Bibliography.

Dissociation

Another characteristic of the LD child is *dissociation,* the inability to perceive things as a whole. Dissociation can be social, visual, or auditory. LD children are sometimes criticized for displaying poor judgment when, in fact, they lack the ability to see the whole and hence respond to relatively unimportant details within the whole. The old adage *He can't see the forest for the trees* seems apropos.

Visual dissociation is especially a problem in learning to read and write. To form the letter *m,* for instance, a child must be able to bring together three distinct lines:

$$ | \eta \eta = m $$

If the three separate lines are conceptualized but never synthesized into a meaningful whole, the child's *m* may look like this.

$$ \setminus \eta \, ^7 $$

Visual dissociation is apparent also in poor performance on pegboards, puzzles, and other assembling tasks. Tests of body image that require the pupil to draw a person or himself or herself often reveal unconnected body parts. The tendency of so many children to touch, stroke, feel, and paw at the teacher has been related to their inability to see whole; tactile contact lends reassurance that the adult is really there. The child's need in this regard can be minimized by the teacher taking the initiative in physical contact, putting an arm around the child's shoulder, patting him or her, and reinforcing visual cues.

Auditory dissociation is evidenced when sounds are heard and recognized but cannot be synthesized into a meaningful whole. The child understands individual words but fails to grasp the meaning of the entire sentence. The child can follow instructions when given one task at a time, but cannot anticipate the outcome. Sometimes, unaware that a task is finished, the child continues to wait for the next instruction.

The whole-part-whole teaching methodology with as little verbalization as possible helps to cope with dissociation. The child on the trampoline for the first time, for instance, must get the *feel* of the whole before he or she cares much about proper use of arms and landing in shoulder-width stride. Beginning instruction in throwing and striking activities should focus upon the target to be hit, not on the stance, grip, backswing, release, and follow through.

LD children characteristically have little faith in forearms, hands, and fingers—the body parts held responsible for awkward handwriting—and generally perform better when not self-conscious about sequential and correct use of such parts.

In the warm-up portion of the period, it seems better to use locomotor activities that demand the integrated working together of the whole body rather than calisthenics that emphasize the movement of parts. Thus, runs, hops, jumps, animal walks, log rolls, and tumbling activities are preferable to arm flinging, side bending, toe touching, and head circling.

Practice in getting into different game and dance formations can be used to teach pupils to see themselves as parts of a whole. Creative dance, swimming, and gymnastics in which individuals or partners devise an original stunt or movement sequence and then combine it with those of others reinforce understandings of parts vs. wholes. Even a pyramid can be taught as a whole comprised of parts. In movement exploration, children should be helped to combine isolated stunts into routines or set sequences. The teacher is forever challenging, "What two or three movements can you combine to make a whole composition?"

Children who dissociate often experience difficulty with *sequencing*, the ability to remember and/or put parts together in the correct order. Physical education offers innumerable opportunities for practice in sequencing. Folk and square dance, for instance, are based on the ability to remember and perform sequences of steps in the correct order. Routines on gymnastic apparatus also teach sequencing. Memory of the instructions for a low organized game is still another example.

For additional information on coping with dissociation, reread Chapter 11, Perceptual-Motor Functioning, Games, and Sports.

Perseveration

Perseveration is more apparent in LD children than in peers of the same age. Often interpreted as stubbornness, this is the inability to shift easily from one idea or activity to another. Perseveration is present when a pupil

1. Continues to grind on and on long after a pencil is sharpened.

2. Continues to bounce the ball after the signal for stopping has been given.

3. Continues to laugh or giggle after everyone else stops.

4. Repeats the same phrase over and over or gets *hung* on one topic of conversation.

Perseveration is the opposite of distractibility, and it is uncanny that the LD child seems to be always at one extreme or the other of the continuum, never in the middle. Perseveration contributes to a behavioral rigidity, which is evidenced in games when the pupil refuses to adapt rules or to test a new strategy.

To minimize perseveration, the physical educator should plan a sequence of activities in which each is distinctly different from the other in formation, starting position, basic skills, rules, and strategies. A circle game, for instance, might be followed by a relay in files. In circuit training, a station stressing arm and shoulder strength might be followed by one emphasizing jumping activities. Games based upon stop-and-go concepts reinforce the ability to make transitions from one activity to another. Illustrative of these are Red Light, Green Light; Musical Chairs; Cakewalks; Statues; and Squirrels in the Trees.

Social Imperception

Inadequacies of social perception—namely, the inability to recognize the meaning and significance of the behavior of others—contribute to poor social adjustment.

LD children often seem to have difficulty in making and keeping friends of their own age. The problems of hyperactivity, distractibility, dissociation, and perseveration are complicated further by their inability to deal with abstractions and double meanings. They become the butt of jokes when they cannot share the multiple meanings of such words as "screw," "ball," "grass," "pot," and "head." Moreover, much of the humor in our society is abstract and entirely lost on them. Because they fail to comprehend the subtleties of facial expression, tone of voice, and body language, they do not realize that they are angering, antagonizing, or boring others until some kind of explosion erupts. Then they retreat with hurt feelings, wondering why the others *blew up all of a sudden* or told them *to get out and leave them alone.*

The aspect of physical education perhaps most helpful in remediating social imperception is dance, with its inherent concern for body language and nonverbal communication. Games can be devised also to help children learn to cope with imagery and find delight in *make believe.* The often cruel give and take of childhood dramatic play can be cushioned by imposing time and space limitations on such activities. With severely involved children, play should seldom—if ever—be left unstructured. It is far better to delimit the activity with "You may play cowboys and Indians with John and Chris in Room 121 for 20 minutes" than to allow the group interaction to continue indefinitely, ultimately ending with a fight of some kind. In schools that have daily recess, the teacher should specify ahead of time names of persons who have permission to play together, the space on the playground they may occupy, and the equipment they may use. Freedom is given to children with social imperception only in small degrees as they demonstrate increasing ability to cope in social situations.

Immature Body Image

As normal children mature, they become conscious of their own bodies, internalize their perceptions, and acquire what is called a *body image*. This, like other acquisitions in the affective domain, is a theoretical construct. It is difficult to define and even harder to measure.

Authorities seem to agree, however, that certain traits comprise an immature body image. Among these are (a) finger agnosia, (b) inability to identify body parts and surfaces, (c) inability to make right-left discriminations on self and others, (d) difficulty in distinguishing between male and female body types and body proportions, and (e) problems in matching own somatotype and body parts to those of others. These deficits are thought to stem from brain damage, specifically in the nondominant hemisphere, which in the average right-handed person is on the right. Lesions here are known to alter recognition of body parts and awareness of corporeal (body) and extracorporeal space.

Of the many body image deficits, *finger agnosia* has received the most attention. The inability to identify fingers is revealed in self-drawings and finger localization tests. In Benton's test, which has a reliability of .91, the child identifies single fingers that have been tactually stimulated. The task is performed both with the hands visible and hidden from sight. Large numbers of children fail this test and reveal problems in their drawings. The following description of a 6-year-old with high average intelligence is typical.

. . . He made the drawing after being instructed to draw a picture of himself and quickly drew all of the figure except the fingers. When he came to the point of wanting to put on fingers, he became confused, looked at the examiner's hands and then at his own mittens in an attempt to adapt them to the situation. Finally, in a mood of desperation, he placed his hand on the paper in the appropriate position and traced around two of his fingers; he repeated this procedure on the other side, thus putting fingers at the end of both arms. From this performance and on the basis of other evidence, we concluded that this boy had a finger agnosia. He was unable, except by highly devious routes, to visualize his own fingers. (Johnson & Myklebust, 1967, p. 237)

Remediation of immature body image problems through physical education involves the use of finger plays, action songs, dances, games, and exercises that refer to body parts. Finger play, sometimes called *handies,* are especially popular with young children.

Opportunities should be provided for children to see themselves in the mirror, on videotape, and in moving pictures. Games should be devised in which older pupils estimate the length and/or the circumference of body parts and then compare their estimations with actual measurements. Activities leading to an understanding of body types should be taught also. Pictures or slides of different body types can be exhibited on the wall and the children taught to recognize a body type similar to their own. The different shapes of faces and dimensions of limbs can be approached in the same manner. Instruction pertaining to body parts can be correlated with a study of grooming, hair styling, clothes selection, postures, and body language.

Movement exploration can reinforce learnings about body parts.

1. Can you bounce the ball with your elbow? Your foot? What other body parts?
2. Can you cross the rope and land on one hand and one foot simultaneously? On both hands simultaneously?
3. Can you hold onto your ankles with your hands and walk? Can you keep your right elbow on your left knee as you walk?
4. Can you grasp the ball with just your thumb and index finger? With all your fingers? With your palm?
5. How many activities can you do with your buttocks in contact with the floor? With the front surface of your thigh in contact with the floor?
6. In swimming, how many different body parts can you use in pushing off from the side?

Much research is needed to determine the relationship between participation in certain activities and changes in body image. Conclusive evidence is not available for recommending one kind of program over another.

Poor Spatial Orientation

Closely allied to body image deficits are disturbances in spatial orientation. LD children are described as *lost in space*. They typically lose their way enroute to a destination and show confusion when given north-south-east-west and right-left directions. Moreover, they experience difficulty in estimating distance, height, width, and the other coordinates of space. As a result, they are forever bumping into things and misjudging the space requirements in such tasks as stepping through geometric forms, ducking under a low rope, and squeezing through a narrow opening.

Problems in recognizing and naming right and left body parts may stem from deficits in laterality, visual and auditory perception, or receptive and expressive language. The ability to make *right-left discriminations* on oneself and to follow instructions using these terms does not normally stabilize until age 6 or 7. Whereas laterality pertains only to subjective, or self, space, right-left discriminations extend to objective, or external, space. Many normal children are in the upper elementary grades before they can project the directions of right-left from themselves to another person and from object to object. Individuals with learning disabilities, despite special training, seem to experience difficulty with right-left discriminations throughout life.

Problems in *crossing the midline* relate to the proprioceptive awareness of right and left. This deficit is often revealed in chalkboard activities in which a child draws a horizontal line from his or her right side to midline and then switches the chalk to the left hand for continuation of the line. The child seems to lack the ability to shift weight from side to side so that such hand switching is unnecessary. Inadequate follow-through and change of weight in sports activities illustrate midline problems. The discrepancy between fielding or striking a ball on the preferred side as opposed to the nonpreferred shows that some midline difficulty is normal.

Physical education activities for problems of laterality, right-left discriminations, and crossing the midline are similar in that all pertain to balance and the establishment of crosslateral movement patterns.

Balance beams and boards and the trampoline can be used specifically for this purpose. Sideward beam walking is considered more valuable than other tasks because of the shifting of weight from side to side. For balance beam and trampoline training to contribute toward improved proprioception, movement problems must be posed that necessitate frequent postural adjustments. Unlike regular physical education, training to improve spatial orientation should focus upon movement exploration rather than mastery of traditional gymnastic skills.

Whereas laterality pertains only to self (subjective) space, *directionality* is a theoretical construct that refers specifically to external (objective) space. Directionality is the ability to locate oneself in relation to a fixed or moving point outside the body. It develops through the process of perceptual-motor matching and presumes integrity of vision and audition. Directionality is the validation of proprioceptive awareness of right-left, up-down, front-back-side, and other directional concepts with visual, auditory, and tactual feedback and vice versa. Later, the child learns to generalize about the spatial relationships of one external object to another. Reading, for instance, is partially a matter of perceiving spatial relationships between letters, words, and lines. Rotations and reversals of letters are believed to be problems of directionality. Reversals of *b, d, p,* and *q* seem to indicate deficits in proprioceptive awareness of right and left, while reversals of *m, w, n,* and *u* seem to indicate problems with up and down directions. The perceptual-motor matching skills inherent in directionality pertain also to the perception and reproduction of geometric forms in body movement, art activities, and handwriting.

Figure-background constancy is the ability to pick a simple object or figure out of a cluttered, complex background. Symmetrical figures are more easily found than asymmetrical. Deficits in figure-background constancy are either reversals or forced responsiveness. *Reversal* is a situation wherein the background stimuli take precedence over the foreground stimulus. *Forced responsiveness* is an equally strong reaction to all factors in the environment and the inability to select objects from this environment for special attention. This problem is illustrated by children who respond well in a flashcard drill showing they know a word, but become confused in reading a book because they cannot discriminate the desired word from the others on the page. The problem is apparent in paper-pencil tests or games of embedded figures that ask, Can you find the hidden objects?

On the playground, balls and teammates may blend together or float in and out of focus. Confusions pertaining to near-far, front-back, and high-low suggest figure-background problems. These are often confounded further by dissociation since distinguishing a foreground stimulus from background clutter may also entail recognition of a part from its whole.

Figure 18.2 Masking tape figures on wall help children with figure-background problems.

To minimize such problems, balls, play apparatus, and floor patterns should be brightly colored to contrast with the background. Balance beams and mats should be a different color from the floor. Masking tape figures on walls and floors (see Figure 18.2) should utilize reds and blues, colors that have been shown to be children's favorites. Basketball backdrops and goal cages should stand out boldly against less relevant stimuli.

Visual and auditory games that stress the locations of objects and sounds may be directed toward remediation of figure-background problems. Illustrative of these are such guessing games as I Bet You Can't See What I See, Who's Got My Bone?, Huckleberry Beanstalk, and Hot and Cold. Scavenger hunts also demand the ability to isolate relevant stimuli from the background.

Nonspecific Awkwardness or Clumsiness (Apraxia)

The child with learning disabilities is typically uncoordinated and inaccurate in motor responses. There may be a discrepancy as great as 4 years between motor skills level and chronological age. This, of course, affects peer acceptance and self-concept. Louise Clarke, the mother of a boy with learning disabilities, devoted several passages to this difficulty in her excellent book:

There was a new area of incompetence too. Mike's school was very big on athletics. All the men teachers directed at least one sport, and starting in the second grade there was a great deal of talk about who made what team.

Mike did not make any.

Mr. Klein, the athletic director, was openly contemptuous, and the best Mike got from any of the male staff was amused tolerance. He wanted very much to make a team, and during vacations he and his father threw balls back and forth, or his father would throw them for him to bat. It was an endless exercise. . . .

Mike never did get the knack of it. He would miss catches by fractions of inches, but near-misses do not count in games. His batting was so erratic that his father . . . could not field them half the time. (Clarke, 1973, p. 20)

Mike, like most other learning disabled children, seemed to have trouble only in hand-eye coordination and balance. He was an excellent swimmer, winning many ribbons in competitive events from grade school on. Moreover, his strength, cardiovascular endurance, and running speed enabled him to perform well on fitness tests. Having completed a PhD in science at Harvard University in his 20s, Mike recalled his physical education experiences and stated,

My hand-eye coordination was never very good and it still isn't. But I wouldn't tell dyslexics to stay away from sports, just the competitive sports that put a premium on hand-eye coordination, like baseball or handball. Anything where the margin of error is small. Tennis and squash allow for a margin of error. They demand coordination, but you can get away with it; you don't have to hit the ball everytime at dead center of the racquet. (Clarke, 1973, p. 132)

Parents are generally more concerned about awkwardness in fine motor tasks than in gross motor activity. Typically, the LD child displays problems in cutting with scissors; handwriting; coping with buttons, snaps, and zippers; tying shoes; using knife, fork, and spoon; lacing and sewing activities; pegboard games; and other tasks demanding manual dexterity. The correlation between fine motor and gross motor activities is low.

Little, if any, evidence exists to show that training in gross motor activities will carry over into manipulative skills and vice versa. *A motor development program therefore should entail practice on the specific skills in which the child is weak. Remediation directed primarily toward the improvement of coordination, however, should not be substituted for a broad comprehensive program of sports, dance, and aquatics.*

Competitive Play and Game Choices

Among the several authorities who question whether LD children can function optimally in integrated physical education programs is Angie Nall, who stated,

LD children can easily participate in a daily physical education program of big motor activities if there is a very small group of children, sufficient supervision so that those who need it may have a one-to-one supervision, and if there is no competition in the group. These children cannot take noise and react with negative behavior. It is, therefore, difficult to work with them in a gymnasium. Competition means someone must lose. These children have lost so many times in their lives that one more loss merely compounds the problem. (Nall, 1972)

The game choices of LD children have been studied by Cratty, Ikeda, Martin, Jennett, and Morris (1970) and by Trammell (1974). Both investigations used modifications of the Sutton-Smith Play and Game List (see Chapter 10). Cratty et al. compared the percentage of children with and without movement problems who indicated a liking for 37 games. His sample of 293 elementary school children ranged in age from 5 through 12. He concluded that clumsy children tend to avoid vigorous, active games, particularly those involving direct contact such as football, wrestling, and boxing. He noted also that boys with movement problems seemed to prefer some type of fantasy play in which "pretend" bravery could be evidenced (spaceman, cowboy, cops and robbers). This was not true of boys of the same age representing the normal population.

Trammell (1974) used chi-square values to determine significant differences in the preferences for 120 games, 27 of which were classified as competitive. The subjects were 197 children classified as LD under special education legislative provisions in Texas and 197 children not so classified. The ages ranged from 8 through 12. It was concluded that LD children were more like normal children in game choices than unlike them. Of 120 games, there were only 18 on which normal and LD boys disagreed enough to yield a significant difference. LD and normal girls were even more alike than the boys. Of 120 games, there were only 9 in which the two groups disagreed enough to cause a significant difference.

All other differences between LD and normal boys and girls were in the degree to which games were liked or disliked. Particularly significant was the fact that both groups professed to like such competitive games as football, basketball, and baseball.

Learning Activities

1. Read biographies or autobiographies of persons believed to have had learning disabilities, such as Thomas Edison, Albert Einstein, and Walt Disney, and discuss the impact of such disabilities on their lives. Identify friends and acquaintances who may have LD conditions that are not diagnosed and give anecdotes of behaviors that seem to confirm your suspicions.

2. Attend meetings of the local chapter of the Association for Children and Adults with Learning Disabilities (ACLD) and discuss values of physical education with parents. Offer to present a slide show or program on PL 94–142, physical education, and learning disabilities.

3. Engage in a debate concerning (a) the value of perceptual-motor training vs. traditional physical education for young LD children,

(b) the advisability of LD students engaging in competitive athletics, or (c) integration vs. separate physical education for extremely hyperactive students.

4. Create games and physical activities designed to ameliorate such problems as hyperactivity, dissociation, social imperception, and poor spatial orientation.

5. Observe LD students at play in a nonstructured setting like recess or lunch period and compare their behaviors with those demonstrated in a highly structured physical education class. Create a record keeping system (i.e., tally different behaviors) for making observation as objective as possible.

References

Clarke, L. (1973). *Can't read, can't write, can't takl too good either.* New York: Walker & Company.

Cratty, B., Ikeda, N., Martin, M., Jennett, C., & Morris, M. (1970). Game choices of children with movement problems. In B. Cratty (Ed.). *Movement abilities, motor ability, and the education of children* (pp. 45–85). Springfield, IL: Charles C. Thomas.

Cruickshank, W. (1967). *The brain-injured child in home, school, and community.* Syracuse: Syracuse University Press.

Education of Handicapped Children, "Notes and Working Papers . . ." (1968). (Prepared for the Subcommittee on Education of the Committee on Labor and Public Welfare, United States Congress, p. 14). Washington, DC: Government Printing Office.

Johnson, D. J., & Myklebust, H. R. (1967). *Learning disabilities.* New York: Grune & Stratton.

Nall, A. (1972). Personal correspondence with director of Angie Nall School-Hospital, Beaumont, TX.

Strauss, A. A., & Lehtinen, L. (1947). *Psychopathology and education of the brain-injured child.* New York: Grune & Stratton.

Trammell, C. (1974). *A comparison of expressed play interests of children with language and/or learning disabilities and normal children.* Unpublished master's thesis, Texas Woman's University, Denton.

Bibliography

Algozzine, B., & Ysseldyke, J. (1983). Learning disabilities as a subset of school failure: The oversophistication of a concept. *Exceptional Children, 50*(3), 242–246.

Arnheim, D., & Sinclair, W. (1979). *The clumsy child* (2nd ed.). St. Louis: C. V. Mosby.

Ayres, A. J. (1965). Patterns of perceptual-motor dysfunction in children: A factor analytic study. *Perceptual and Motor Skills, 20,* 335–368.

Ayres, A. J. (1972). *Sensory integration and learning disorders.* Los Angeles: Western Psychological Services.

Ayers, A. J. (1978). Learning disabilities and the vestibular system. *Journal of Learning Disabilities, 11,* 18–29.

Benyon, S. (1968). *Intensive programming of slow learners.* Columbus, OH: Charles E. Merrill.

Broadhead, G. (1972). Gross motor performance in minimally brain injured children. *Journal of Motor Behavior, 4,* 103–111.

Broxterman, J., & Stebbins, A. (1981). The significance of visual training in the treatment of learning disabilities. *American Corrective Therapy Journal, 35,* 122–125.

Bruininks, V., & Bruininks, R. (1977). Motor proficiency of learning disabled and nondisabled students. *Perceptual and Motor Skills, 44,* 1131–1137.

Coleman, J., Keogh, J., & Mansfield, J. (1963). Motor performance and social adjustment among boys experiencing serious learning difficulties. *Research Quarterly, 34,* 516–517.

Cowden, J., Eason, R., & Wright, J. (1983). A comparison of two sensory motor intervention programs for elementary children diagnosed as specific learning-disabled. In R. Eason, T. Smith, & F. Caron (Eds.). *Adapted physical activity* (pp. 236–243). Champaign, IL: Human Kinetics Publishers.

Cratty, B. (1985). *Active learning: Games to enhance academic abilities* (2nd ed.). Englewood Cliffs, NJ: Prentice-Hall.

deQuiros, J. B., & Schrager, O. L. (1978). *Neurological fundamentals in learning disabilities.* Novato, CA: Academic Therapy Publications.

Eason, B. L., & Smith, T. L. (1979). Effects of chromatic targets on a throwing task for subjects referred for learning disability. *Perceptual and Motor Skills, 48,* 229–230.

Elstein, A. E. (1977). *Effects of physical education on the physical fitness, social adjustment, and self-concept of learning disabled students.* Unpublished doctoral dissertation, Temple University.

Fleisher, L., Soodak, L., & Jelin, M. (1984). Selective attention deficits in learning disabled children. *Exceptional Children, 51*(2), 136–141.

Geddes, D. (1980). Future directions: Physical activity for LD children. *Academic Therapy, 16,* 5–9.

Gruber, J. J. (1969). Implications of physical education programs for children with learning disabilities. *Journal of Learning Disabilities, 2,* 44–50.

Gubbay, S. (1975). *The clumsy child: A study of developmental apraxic and agnosic ataxia.* Philadelphia: W. B. Saunders.

Hallahan, D., & Cruickshank, W. (1973). *Psychoeducational foundations of learning disabilities.* Englewood Cliffs, NJ: Prentice-Hall.

Hayes, M. L. (1974). *The tuned-in, turned-on book about learning disabilities.* San Rafael, CA: Academic Therapy Publications.

Hayes, M. L. (1975). *Oh dear, somebody said "learning disabilities."* San Rafael, CA: Academic Therapy Publications.

Johnson, R., & Rubison, R. M. (1983). Physical functioning levels of learning disabled and normal children. *American Corrective Therapy Journal, 37,* 56–60.

Maloy, C. F., & Sattler, J. M. (1979). Motor and cognitive proficiency of LD and normal children. *Journal of School Psychology, 17,* 213–218.

Myers, P., & Hammill, D. (1976). *Methods for learning disorders* (2nd ed.). New York: John Wiley & Sons.

Pyfer, J., & Carlson, B. R. (1972). Characteristic motor development of children with learning disabilities. *Perceptual and Motor Skills, 35,* 291–296.

Rimmer, J., & Rosentswieg, J. (1982). The physical working capacity of learning disabled children. *American Corrective Therapy Journal, 36,* 133–134.

Sherrill, C. (1980). Physical education for learning disabled students in the public schools. *ACLD Newsbriefs, 130,* 6–7.

Sherrill, C., & Pyfer, J. (1985). Learning disabled students in physical education. *Adapted Physical Activity Quarterly, 2*(4), 283–291.

Stamps, L., Eason, B., & Smith, T. (1983). Discriminatory response time and heart rate differences between gifted and learning disabled children. In R. Eason, T. Smith, & F. Caron (Ed.). *Adapted physical activity* (pp. 226–229). Champaign, IL: Human Kinetics Publishers.

Trammell, C. (1974). *A comparison of game preferences of learning disabled with normal children.* Unpublished master's thesis, Texas Woman's University, Denton.

19 Mental Retardation

Figure 19.1 Special Olympics has demonstrated the potential of mentally retarded persons to the world. *Top,* Eunice Kennedy Shriver, the founder of Special Olympics, provides encouragement. *Bottom,* action from the Little Stanley Cup game, a feature event of the International Special Olympics floor hockey tournament in Toronto, Ontario.

Chapter Objectives

After you have studied this chapter, you should be able to

1. State the three criteria for educational diagnosis of mental retardation and discuss each part in relation to physical education programming.

2. Identify several different clinical types (i.e., syndromes) associated with mental retardation and describe characteristics/behaviors associated with each. What implications, if any, do these have for physical education programming? What research is available to assist in answering this question?

3. Discuss assessment of fitness of students with varying levels of mental retardation (mild, moderate, severe, and profound) and describe differences in procedures between testing such students and those of average intelligence. Specifically, what adaptations must be made?

4. Discuss motor development (normal, abnormal, and delayed) and motor ability in terms of different levels of mental retardation and various syndromes. What are the implications for physical education programming?

5. Given level of mental retardation, chronological age, and present level of psychomotor functioning for hypothesized students, write physical education IEPs.

6. Discuss integration of students with mild, moderate, severe, and profound degrees of mental retardation into regular physical education. What conditions must be present to make integration the least restrictive placement? What instructional and environmental adaptations will likely need to be made in the regular physical education setting?

7. Apply principles of motor learning to teaching new activities and/or games to students with varying levels of mental retardation severity.

8. Describe Special Olympics programming and discuss conditions that contribute to a good year-round program.

9. Discuss available and needed research on physical education and athletics for mentally retarded students. Cite research contributions of such authorities as Larry Rarick, Bryant Cratty, John Dunn, Julian Stein, and Frank Hayden.

Mental retardation is perhaps the best known of all handicapping conditions because Special Olympics has given it so much visibility (see Figure 19.1). *Mental retardation* refers to (a) significantly subaverage general intellectual functioning existing concurrently with (b) deficits in adaptive behavior and (c) manifested during the developmental period. The three parts of this definition warrant analysis.

Subaverage general intellectual functioning refers to performance that is two or more standard deviations below average on a standardized intelligence test. On the Stanford-Binet and the Wechsler scales, the two most widely used intelligence tests, this represents IQs of 68 and 70, respectively. Because of the many inaccuracies in intelligence testing, a diagnosis of mental retardation is never made on subaverage intellectual functioning alone.

Deficits in adaptive behavior refer to problems of maturation, learning, and/or social adjustment that result in the individual's failure to meet standards of personal independence and social responsibility expected of his or her age and cultural group. Adaptive behavior is measured by such standardized instruments as the Vineland Social Maturity Scale, the Gesell Developmental Schedules, and scales similar to that depicted in Table 19.1.

Adaptive behavior is becoming increasingly important as a criterion for mental retardation and for educational classification. Discrepancies between adaptive behavior and measures of intellectual functioning have led to such terms as the "6-Hour Retarded Child," used to designate the child who performs normally except during the 6 hours each day that he or she is in school.

Developmental period (see Figure 19.2), the third part of the definition, specifies that the subaverage intellectual functioning and deficits in adaptive behavior are severe enough that they are identified within the first 18 years of life.

Table 19.1
Levels of Adaptive Behavior Used in Classification of Mental Retardation

	Preschool Ages 0–5 Maturation and Development	School Age 6–21 Training and Education	Adult Age 21 and Over Social and Vocational Adequacy
Level I, mild	Can develop social and communication skills; minimal retardation in sensorimotor areas; often not distinguished from normal until later age.	Can learn academic skills up to approximately sixth-grade level by late teens; can be guided toward social conformity; "educable."	Can usually achieve social and vocational skills adequate to minimum self-support but may need guidance and assistance when under unusual social or economic stress.
Level II, moderate	Can talk or learn to communicate; poor social awareness; fair motor development; profits from training in self-help; can be managed with moderate supervision.	Can profit from training in social and occupational skills; unlikely to progress beyond second-grade level in academic subjects; may learn to travel alone in familiar places.	May achieve self-maintenance in unskilled or semi-skilled work under sheltered conditions; needs supervision and guidance when under mild social or economic stress.
Level III, severe	Poor motor development; speech is minimal; generally unable to profit from training in self-help; little or no communication skills.	Can talk or learn to communicate; can be trained in elemental health habits; profits from systematic habit training.	May contribute partially to self-maintenance under complete supervision; can develop self-protection skills to a minimal useful level in controlled environment.
Level IV, profound	Gross retardation; minimal capacity for functioning in sensorimotor areas; needs nursing care.	Some motor development present; may respond to minimum or limited training in self-help.	Some motor and speech development; may achieve very limited self-care; needs nursing care.

Figure 19.2 During growth from a fertilized egg into an infant, many genetic disorders can occur. Every normal human cell contains 46 chromosomes within its nucleus. Within each chromosome are hundreds of genes linked together to form the long threadlike strands of genetic material called DNA (deoxyribonucleic acid), which directs growth and development.

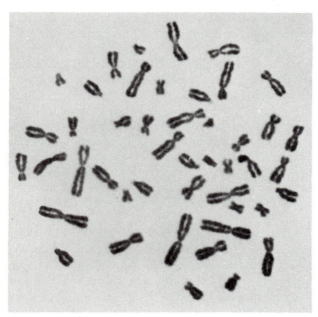

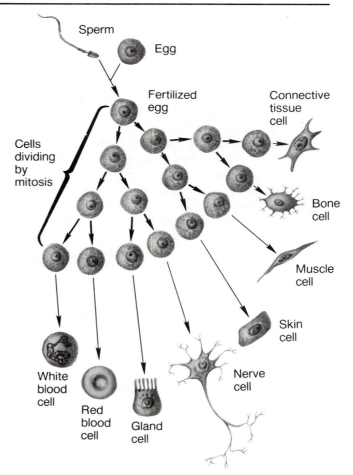

Table 19.2
Estimates of Retardation by Level

1980 Census	All Ages (millions)
General population	215
Retarded population: 3% of general population. This can be broken down as follows:	6.45
Mild (IQ 53+) about 89%	5.74
Moderate (IQ 36–52) about 6%	.39
Severe (IQ 20–35) about 3.5%	.23
Profound (IQ 0–20) about 1.5%	.10

Prevalence

Approximately 6.5 million Americans meet these criteria and are regarded as mentally retarded. Table 19.2 presents a breakdown by level of retardation.

In the average community, for every 1,000 school-age children there are approximately 25 mildly retarded, 4 moderately retarded, and 1 severely or profoundly retarded. The incidence of mild retardation varies with socioeconomic and cultural levels. Poverty areas have roughly twice as many as middle-class neighborhoods. The incidence of severe and profound retardation is remarkably stable for all income groups. Most retarded children live at home and attend public schools. The quality of their physical education instruction varies widely, reflecting the philosophy of administrators and school board and the initiative of their teachers.

Less than 10% of all retarded persons are institutionalized. Generalizations about institutionalized populations are

1. Most of the residents have IQs under 35. This reflects the nationwide trend toward providing institutional care only for persons who cannot be integrated back into the community.
2. The medical classifications are primarily *unknown causes and prenatal influence.* The clinical type that occurs most frequently is Down's syndrome.
3. Approximately one third to one fourth of the residents have convulsive disorders.
4. Over one third of the residents have obvious motor dysfunctions. Most prevalent of these is spasticity.
5. Approximately one third to one fourth are multihandicapped by sensory impairment. Visual deficits occur with the greatest frequency.

It is obvious that physical education and recreation program planning in residential facilities and public schools must serve vastly different groups. The range of individual differences within mental retardation is probably far greater than within the so-called normal population.

Medical Classifications and Etiologies

The American Association on Mental Deficiency (AAMD) recognizes 10 medical classifications of mental retardation (Grossman, 1984). Within several of these classifications are *clinical types* such as Down's syndrome, microcephalus, and hydrocephalus (conditions that involve certain anatomical, physiognomical, or pathological features that permit easy identification). Most retarded persons, however, cannot be distinguished from the normal population by their physical appearance. Nor is the cause of their retardation known. Hence, the AAMD classifications for the great majority of retarded persons are "other conditions" and "environmental influences." The AAMD categories of mental retardation are as follows:

1. *Other conditions.* Includes cases in which there is
   a. No evidence of a physical cause or structural defect.
   b. No history of subnormal functioning in parents and siblings.
   c. No evidence of an associated psychosocial factor.
2. *Environmental influences.* Includes retardation resulting from neglect, sensory deprivation, severe deficits of special senses, and other indications of adverse environmental conditions.
3. *Chromosomal abnormality.* Includes all kinds of physical aberrations, most common of which is Down's syndrome (Figure 19.3), which ranks fourth as a cause of mental retardation among institutionalized populations. Approximately 10% of such populations have Down's syndrome.
4. *Unknown prenatal influence.* Approximately 17% of the retardation in institutionalized populations is attributed to congenital cerebral defects, unknown prenatal influences, and primary cranial anomalies.
   a. Cerebral malformation including the partial or complete absence of a part of the brain (anencephaly).
   b. Craniofacial anomalies of unknown origin, including microcephalus (Figure 19.4), Apert's syndrome (Figures 19.5 and 19.6), Cornelia de Lange syndrome (Figure 19.7), Laurence-Moon-Biedl syndrome, and different kinds of craniostenosis (narrowing of cranium).

Figure 19.3 The chromosomal abnormality most common is Down's syndrome, in which every cell has 47 chromosomes instead of 46. The karyotype on the right was made by photographing a cell nucleus under an electron microscope. Then, the chromosomes were cut out of the photograph, matched up in pairs, and numbered. Although there are several kinds of Down's syndrome, the usual problem is in chromosome 21. This affects all aspects of development and function.

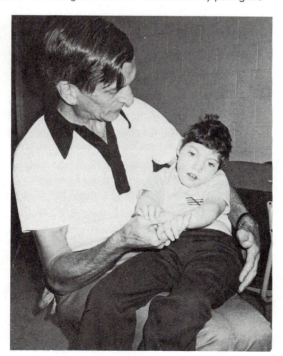

Figure 19.4 Microcephalus (abnormally small head) is a frequent occurrence in mental retardation syndromes. Here the teacher is working on head and neck control by pulling the nonambulatory child to a sitting position. This exercise is repeated many times, with verbal encouragement to hold the head in alignment with the body.

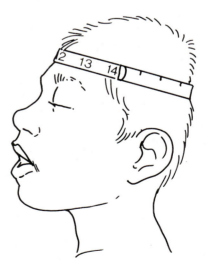

Figure 19.5 Apert's syndrome—illustrative of cerebral malformation of unknown prenatal influence. *Left,* characteristics are craniostenosis (premature closure of cranial sutures), bulging of eyes, and defective formation of facial bones. Severity of mental retardation varies. *Right,* ball-handling activities must be adapted to hands of child with Apert's syndrome.

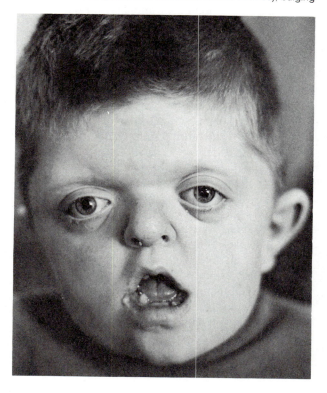

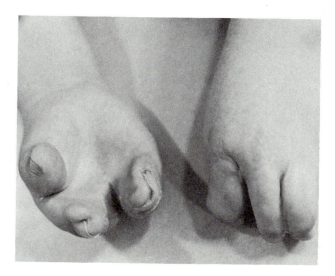

Figure 19.6 Same boy as in figure 19.5 after several surgeries on face. Now 5 years older, the boy can shoot baskets, dribble, and throw and catch. He remains nonverbal and functions cognitively at Piaget's sensorimotor level.

Figure 19.7 Nine-year-old with Cornelia de Lange syndrome looks and functions like a toddler. This syndrome is characterized by very small stature, bushy eyebrows, long and curly eyelashes, and generalized hairy skin. The muscle tone is often hypertonic.

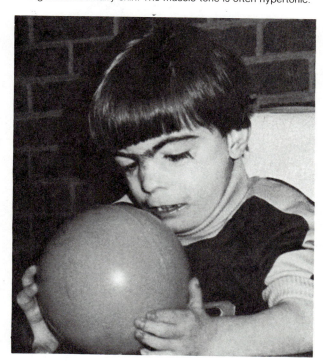

c. Spina bifida and other disorders related to faulty closure of the neural tube.
d. Hydrocephalus (Figures 19.8 and 19.9).
e. Other.

5. *Gestational disorders*. Includes low birth weight (2,500 gm, or 5 pounds 8 ounces), premature birth, and postmature birth (exceeding normal time by 7 days).

6. *Trauma or physical agents*. Includes injuries to the brain before, during, or after birth. *Anoxia* or *hypoxia* (insufficient oxygen) may result in brain injury as a side effect of poisoning, shock, convulsions, and severe anemia.

7. *Infection and intoxication*.
   a. Prenatal and maternal infections that affect the child in utero, such as rubella (German measles) and syphilis.
   b. Postnatal cerebral infections—i.e., encephalitis.
   c. Cerebral damage caused by toxic agents (drugs, poisons, maternal disorders like diabetes and malnutrition).

8. *Metabolism or nutrition*. Includes disorders caused by metabolic, nutritional, endocrine, or growth dysfunctions. Listed in order of their incidence among institutionalized retarded populations are the following:
   a. Unspecified.
   b. Phenylketonuria (PKU).
   c. Hypothyroidism (cretinism).
   d. Galactosemia.

9. *Postnatal gross brain disease*. Includes neoplasms and hereditary conditions in which there are combined lesions of the skin and nervous system. Although rare, the following physical characteristics are easily identified in a visit to any state residential facility.
   a. Cafe-au-lait spots on the skin, named because their color is that of *coffee with cream*. These are particularly symptomatic of *neurofibromatosis* (von Recklinghausen's disease).
   b. Port wine stain on face and/or scalp symptomatic of *Sturge-Weber-Dimitri's* disease. The port wine stain is caused by an *angioma* (a growth comprised of dilated blood vessels).

Figure 19.8 Severe hydrocephalus (abnormal accumulation of cerebrospinal fluid in the ventricles of the brain) makes correct body alignment difficult.

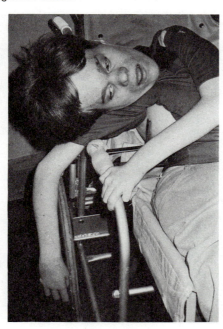

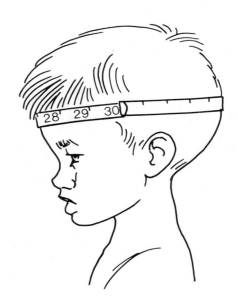

c. Butterfly-shaped rash extending from cheeks to forehead, head, and neck with nodules varying in size from a pinhead to a pea. This rash is evident in *tuberous sclerosis,* a condition characterized by nodules throughout the central nervous system and tumors of various organs.

10. *Following psychiatric disorder.* Includes retardation following psychosis or other psychiatric disorder when there is no evidence of cerebral pathology.

Fitness and Mental Retardation

The most widely used tests of fitness for mentally retarded individuals are those developed by Hayden (1964), AAHPER/Kennedy Foundation (1968), Johnson and Londeree (1976), and the Project ACTIVE (1978) battery based on the test of Hilsendager, Jack, and Mann. These tests are described in the chapter on fitness. All use more or less the same items as for normal children. Modifications are made most often on the cardiovascular item, with the distance or time of run-walk reduced. The more retarded a person is, the less likely he or she will understand the concepts of speed and endurance. Most severely retarded persons simply won't "keep going" in run-walks unless

Figure 19.9 Sometimes, hydrocephalus can be corrected through a surgical procedure called *shunting.* Left, the ventriculo-peritonial (VP) shunt involves inserting a tube into the ventricles. This tube has a one-way valve that lets fluid flow out of the brain and into another tube that is threaded just under the skin down to the abdomen, where it is reabsorbed by the blood vessels in the membranes surrounding internal organs. A less-often used procedure is to thread the tube into the heart instead of the abdomen. Children with shunts typically have no activity restrictions except avoidance of blows to the head. Right, shunting is not always successful, and teachers must adapt activities accordingly. This hydrocephalic student enjoys repeatedly batting a ball suspended from the ceiling by a string. Note placement of mirror so student can receive visual input.

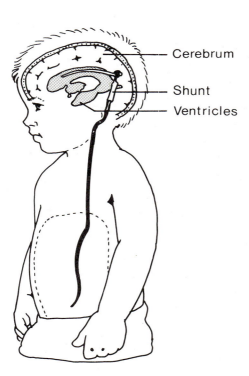

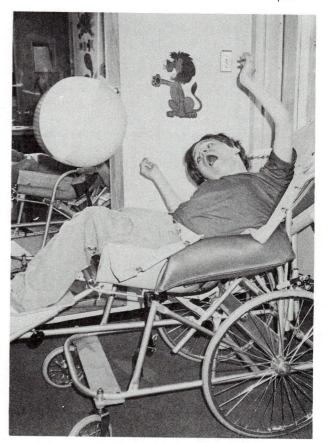

Table 19.3
Frequency of Obesity in an Institutionalized Mentally Retarded Population (Ages 14–40+) by Level of Retardation and Sex

Level of Retardation	Males			Females		
	Total N	N Obese	% Obese	Total N	N Obese	% Obese
Profound	116	35	30.2	104	38	36.5
Severe	96	48	50.0	47	28	59.6
Moderate	97	53	54.6	42	26	62.0
Mild	34	19	55.9	19	14	73.7
Total	343	155	45.2	212	106	50.0

Note. Obesity was defined as 20% body fat for men and 30% body fat for women as measured by Lange skinfold calipers and determined by formulae of Jackson and Pollock. From Rimmer, Radcliffe, Kelly, & Ness, 1980.

paired off with a buddy who tandem-moves with him or her and/or chases. Moreover, most profoundly retarded persons do not run well; some cannot run at all.

Illustrative of programming concepts that work is a 3-month walking program conducted by Ross (1975) 5 days a week, 45 minutes a day, for 22 profoundly retarded institutionalized females ages 18 to 24. The same walk-run path was used every day, and it was necessary to maintain a 1:1 pupil-teacher ratio to keep the students on the path, going the correct direction, and moving as fast as possible. The group significantly increased walking speed from 1.24 to 1.44 miles during 45 minutes. (Remember that persons of good fitness cover 1.5 miles in 12 minutes.) When time does not permit daily walk-runs within the school day, physical educators should encourage families to start home programs. Not only do retarded persons desperately need exercise, but they benefit greatly from the persons and places they see while walking.

One of the best sources of ideas for fitness teaching is AAHPERD's *Best of Challenge* series (see Bibliography). Illustrative of the ideas presented is the micro-pacing track, a small circular track with several lanes built around a 10- to 20-foot rotating steel arm, to which an adult tricycle is attached. The teacher or a pupil with good fitness rides the tricycle while the students run after and try to beat it. The lanes and circle form the necessary structure for class management.

The stationary bicycle (or, if funds permit, a bicycle ergometer) in the classroom or home permits exercise in all kinds of weather. Ideally, such rides should continue until the heart rate reaches 150, but many weeks of conditioning are needed to achieve this since the muscles wear out long before the heart rate substantially increases. In using the bicycle ergometer to assess cardiovascular fitness of adult EMR and TMR males, Coleman, Ayoud, and Friedrich (1976) found that their fitness was 20 to 30% below that of normal peers.

The chapter on fitness stressed the risk factors associated with heart disease. The lifespans (as well as quality of life) of many retarded persons are substantially reduced by cardiovascular and/or cardiorespiratory problems. Small wonder when implementation of exercise programs is so difficult! Moreover, fitness is complicated by obesity in many retarded persons.

Table 19.3 shows that obesity, as determined by the skinfold calipers technique in 555 institutionalized persons, characterized from 30.2 to 73.7% of the population. Weight control programs comprise an important part of adapted physical education.

Motor Ability and Performance

Most mentally retarded infants and young children are developmentally delayed. Those with severe/profound retardation tend to be *multihandicapped* by such conditions as cerebral palsy, hydrocephalus/spina bifida, or sensory impairments. When physical disability is not present, the delayed motor development seems related to *a subtle but specific disturbance in the evolution of infant reflex behavior.* In developmental delay (unlike cerebral palsy), primitive reflexes do not seem to persist beyond the expected age, but the appearance of postural adjustment reactions (propping and equilibrium) is greatly delayed (Molnar, 1978).

Physical educators in early childhood units may have several children who do not yet walk. The mean age of walking in mentally retarded children is reported as 4.2 years for Down's syndrome children and 3.2 years for other types. For such children, physical education should emphasize vestibular stimulation or

Table 19.4
Similarity of Motor Ability Factor Structures for Normal, EMR, and TMR Persons (Rarick, 1979)

Similarity of Factor Structures for Normal and EMR Children Ages 6–10		Similarity of Factor Structures Across 7 Groups of TMR Persons Ages 6–26	
Factor	*Common Definers*	*Factor*	*Common Definers*
1. Body fat (dead weight)	Weight, three skinfolds (abdominal, subscapular, triceps)	1. Body fat (dead weight)	Weight, three skinfolds (triceps, subscapular, abdominal)
2. Fine visual-motor coordination	Minnesota manipulative, ring stacking	2. Fine visual-motor coordination	Minnesota manipulative
3. Gross limb-eye coordination	Target throw vertical	3. Upper limb-eye coordination	Target throw horizontal, target circle
4. Strength-power	Knee flexion and extension	4. Arm strength	Elbow flexion and extension
5. Leg power-coordination	35- and 150-yard dashes, scramble	5. Leg power-coordination	Bicycle with and without resistance
6. Balance	Railwalk forward and backward	6. Balance	Railwalk side and back
		7. Spinal flexibility	Lateral spinal extension

Note. Common definers identify the tests in which groups were most similar. Tables derived from factor analysis of scores on 47 physical and motor tests administered to 406 normal and EMR children and 453 TMR persons. Research supported by the Bureau of Education for the Handicapped, Washington, DC

balancing activities (adjustment to changing equilibrium while being held or while on a water bed, moon walk, tilt board, and therapy [cage] ball, for example). Almost no physical education research is available to assist us in curriculum planning for children under age 6.

The major researcher in physical education for mentally retarded children ages 6 and up is Lawrence Rarick, professor emeritus at the University of California at Berkeley. His works form our knowledge base with regard to motor ability (see Bibliography). Among the most important facts are

1. The factor structure of motor ability is similar for normal, EMR, and TMR children, ages 6 to 10, and for boys and girls, except that performance level markedly favors boys. Table 19.4 presents the factors that should serve as the basis for curriculum planning.

2. The greater the intellectual deficit in retarded persons, the more pronounced is the motor deficiency. One does not cause the other, but they go together.

3. Mildly retarded children are 2 to 4 years behind their normal peers on most measures of motor performance. With increasing age, the problem becomes greater. It is not known whether this motor discrepancy is the result of inequitable instruction and experience or reflects limited learning capabilities. Rarick (1980) found that

EMR boys were .96 standard deviation below the average motor performance of normal peers, meaning that 87% of the normal boys were better than the EMRs. EMR girls were 1.83 standard deviations below the average performance of normal peers, meaning that 95% of the normal girls were better than the EMRs.

4. The greatest difficulty in teaching motor tasks lies in *attention and comprehension* rather than execution once the task is understood. This implies that demonstrations should accompany verbal instructions, and careful attention should be given to task analysis in introducing new skills.

5. The relationship between motor performance and intelligence in retarded persons generally ranges between .10 and .30. The motor tasks that correlate highest with intelligence are balance items and tests of fine visual-motor coordination.

6. Motor development programs should provide great variability in the practice of skills. For instance, an overarm throw should be practiced with many different projectiles of varying size, weight, shape, and color (see Table 7.2), in many different places, with varied targets, distances, and wind conditions. Such variable practice results in development of a motor schema that facilitates transfer to a similar but unfamiliar task.

Physical education programming is affected by levels of retardation. The term *retarded* should never be used without specifying the level as mild, moderate, severe, or profound since individual differences within this special population are far greater than differences within the normal population. It should be emphasized also that *mildly retarded persons are more like the normal in motor performance than like the lower levels of retardation.* Since 89% of all retardation falls within the mild classification, most retarded pupils can participate in regular physical education and athletics. Their success will depend largely on class size and the excellence of the mainstream physical educator. Programming for pupils with mild retardation is, therefore, primarily a matter of facilitating attitudinal changes among regular educators and normal peers.

In contrast, the provision of movement experiences for more severely retarded children demands an understanding of realistic expectations for motor performance at each combination of age and level. The following pages suggest ideas for programming the average retarded student within each level. Individual differences should be kept in mind and each pupil encouraged to achieve optimally. With good physical education, particularly in early childhood, retarded persons in the future may accomplish motor feats as yet undreamed of.

Physical Education for Mildly Retarded (EMR) Students

Most special educators believe that mildly mentally retarded children approximate their normal peers in height, weight, and motor coordination. Rarick (1980) and many physical educators disagree, citing research that shows that most mildly retarded pupils are inferior in motor performance to their normal peers. Children with mild retardation should be integrated as early as possible into the regular physical education and athletic program. Any pupil, whether retarded or normal, who deviates more than one standard deviation from the mean on fitness or skill tests should receive adapted physical education instruction in addition to the regularly scheduled program.

Approximately 80% of the mildly retarded population marry and rear children. Almost all of them find employment, usually in blue collar jobs, which demand high levels of fitness. Their jobs, like those of millions of Americans, allow for a growing abundance of leisure time. It is estimated that the average work week by the year 2000 will drop to 30 hours or fewer and that 3-day weekends will be the rule rather than the exception.

As a part of physical education, high level retarded persons must be introduced to community recreation facilities and helped to earn money to take advantage of bowling alleys, golf driving ranges, skating rinks, and swimming pools. Habits of using such facilities should be well established before graduation. They must be guided also in the selection of lifetime sports suited to their body build, motor coordination, and level of fitness. The acquisition of skills in lifetime sports should be a high priority.

Because they are likely to be deficient in verbal communication, high level retarded students should be provided with socially acceptable means for nonverbal expression of creativity, frustration, anger, hostility, and elation. They can be taught to sublimate emotions into physical activity—dance, jogging, shadow boxing, riflery, or golf. Repeated failure experiences in life and in school may leave them with a low frustration tolerance. Sports that involve striking, hitting, and kicking offer alternatives to drug and alcohol abuse, overeating, and other acts harmful to themselves or others. Students must be taught that sports and dance activities can be mood modifiers.

About the same percentage of high level retarded can achieve success in team sport competition as do normal children. They play by regulation rules and derive all the values associated with athletics. Leisure counseling should help graduating students find opportunities for continued team sport participation within the community recreation structure and/or make the transition to individual sports that are available.

Physical Education for Moderately Retarded Students

Students within the 36 to 52 IQ range have entirely different physical education needs from mildly retarded and normal individuals. In planning physical education activities for lower level retarded students, *social or mental age is more important than chronological age. Social age is determined by adaptive behavior.* Mental age, as used in special education literature, is generally based upon Stanford-Binet IQ scores. Depending upon chronological age and IQ, *the moderately retarded student has a mental age between 2 and 7 years.*

Estimates of the highest possible level of adaptive behavior functioning (social maturity) for the moderately retarded student by the AAMD lend insight into the kinds of instruction that are appropriate for each chronological and mental age.

Moderate Retardation, 3 to 9 Years Old

With a mental age somewhere between 2 and 5 years, this student is making his or her first attempts at locomotor movements. Generally, after chronological age 3 he or she learns to walk alone, run, negotiate stairs, and pass an object to another. Between chronological ages 6 and 9 he or she may learn to jump and later to balance on one foot briefly. Often the student needs to hold on to a bar, chair, or rope when attempting balance activities. The student may climb up and down stairs, but does not alternate feet. He or she can throw a ball or bean bag, but lacks the hand-eye readiness for catching.

Essentially, this student functions motorically and socially like a preschooler. He or she seems to profit most from a follow-the-leader approach using simple homemade apparatus. The student is in the *parallel play stage,* and a major goal is teaching him or her to interact socially with other students. The best teaching occurs on a one-to-one ratio with the teacher verbally motivating and manually helping the student to discover ways his or her body can move. Few words are needed, and the important verbal cues and phrases of praise are repeated over and over. Hand clapping, hugs, and gestures help to reinforce verbal praise. Swimming instruction—i.e., movement exploration in the water—should be begun. The student is not yet ready for low organized games and does not understand formations.

Moderate Retardation, 9 to 12 Years Old

The child may learn to hop, gallop, and then to skip. He or she learns to ascend a short flight of stairs, alternating feet, without support, before mastering descending tasks of the same nature. He or she appears to grasp the concept of throwing an object at a target, sometimes achieving success in hitting it. The child makes the first fairly successful attempts at climbing trees and jungle gyms and at riding a tricycle.

He or she moves into the *associative play* stage, beginning to interact with other children in simple make-believe play such as *House* and *Hospital.* Play interests are similar to his or her mental age, which ranges from 3 to 5 years.

The student should be introduced to his or her first low organized games. Flying Dutchman, Musical Chairs, and Catch My Tail are examples of activities that have proven appropriate for this group. In Flying Dutchman, a line of children holding hands is walked in any direction. When the verbal cue "Flying Dutchman" is called out by the teacher, the children drop hands and run back to a mat that has been established as home base. Musical Chairs can be played

without modification, but the students may need help in finding their chairs. In Catch My Tail, one corner of a scarf is tucked into the back of the belt of one student, who runs about the room with the others trying to grab the scarf.

Examples of games not usually successful are Chicken, Come Home, Cat and Rat, Dodge Ball, and relays. In Chicken, Come Home, and similar activities, the students cannot remember which role they are playing or which direction to run. Only a few seem to understand the concepts of tagging, dodging, and catching. In Cat and Rat there seems to be no idea about who is chasing whom, that one should get away, or that the circle should either help or hinder the players. In Dodge Ball they fail to grasp the idea of the game and wander away from the circle. These students can be forced through the motions of a relay but have no idea of its purpose, of winning and losing, or of belonging to a team.

Moderate Retardation, 12 to 15 Years Old

He or she may master the locomotor movement generally practiced in the primary grades: run, hop, gallop, skip, and simple dance steps. The young adolescent learns to go up and down stairs, alternating feet, without hesitation. He or she is partially successful in jump rope activities and may learn to use skates and a sled. Although consistency in throwing and hitting a target improves, the adolescent still lacks readiness for catching activities.

He or she begins to participate spontaneously in group activities and seems to enjoy simple low organized games. *His or her physical education needs are similar to those of children in the primary grades, but he or she is socially mature enough to react negatively to baby games. Names of games and stunts must sometimes be changed to assure their acceptance* (see Figure 19.10). In striving to be like other persons of the same age, the young adolescent demonstrates interest in the popular team sports and social dance. He or she can be introduced to the concepts of competition but tends to be frozen at the *I* stage of development.

Moderate Retardation, 15 Years Old and Up

Sometime between middle and late adolescence, motor behavior stabilizes. Although mental age falls between 4 and 7 years, his or her social and recreational interests approximate those of the average young teenager. The moderately retarded student performs better in individual events like track, swimming, and gymnastics than in team sports. He or she enjoys social dance and keeps abreast of new fad steps.

Figure 19.10 Level of social maturity is more important than mental and chronological age in selecting games and recreational activities for the mentally retarded. Even students with IQs below 30 rebel at playing "baby games."

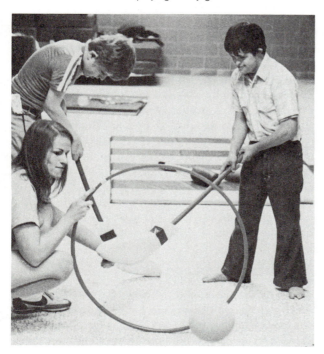

Down's Syndrome

About 1 of every 600 or 700 children—15,000 per year—is born with Down's syndrome (see Figure 19.11). *In public school classes for moderately retarded pupils, they make up 30 to 40% of the students.* In state residential facilities, they comprise approximately 10% of the population. Because they closely resemble each other in facial features and body structure, children with Down's syndrome are recognized more easily than any other clinical type. Their characteristics and special needs should be understood by the physical educator.

Almost nothing was known about this syndrome until 1959, when it was demonstrated that these children have 47 chromosomes in each cell rather than the normal 46. The extra chromosome is in the 21st chromosomal pair; thus, the term *trisomy 21* is often used. Since 1959, three distinct types of Down's syndrome have been discovered: (a) the standard trisomy, (b) translocation, and (c) mosaicism. The cause of this chromosomal abnormality is still unknown. High-risk parents are those who carry chromosomal defects themselves; those exposed to genetically damaging agents such as a virus, repeated X-rays, or chemical exposure; and women of advanced child-bearing age. At age 25 a woman has a risk of 1 in 1,000 of bearing

Figure 19.11 Child with Down's syndrome learns to catch.

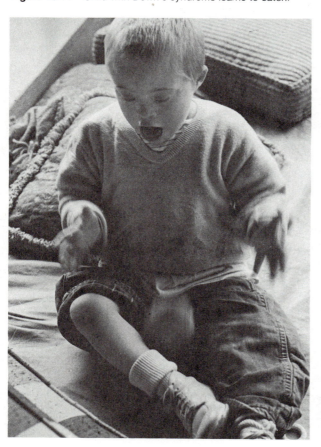

an infant with Down's syndrome; at age 35, a risk of 1 in 250; at age 40, a risk of 1 in 100; and at age 45, a risk of 1 in 50. It is believed that genetic counseling and prenatal screening will all but eliminate chromosomal abnormalities in the next few decades.

Students with Down's syndrome are so different from other retarded individuals that physical educators must study their characteristics separately. From an anatomic point of view, newborn infants with Down's syndrome are unfinished. All of the systems in the body show gross deficiencies in growth and development. Not only is the physical growth abnormally slow, but it ceases altogether at an early age, thereby resulting in stunted growth or dwarfism. Few persons with Down's syndrome ever exceed a height of 5 feet. In addition to dwarfed stature and short, broad hands and feet, the person is recognized by almond-shaped slanting eyes, which are often close-set and strabismic; a flattening of the bridge of the nose; and a large tongue that protrudes frequently from the abnormally small mouth. Protrusion of the tongue is probably due to the smallness of the oral cavity rather than the size of the tongue. This latter characteristic is a definite health problem in that it induces mouth breathing and contributes to susceptibility to upper respiratory infections. The skin lacks elasticity, hangs loosely, and tends to be rough. Hair is straight, fine, and sparse. With regard to dental health, persons with Down's syndrome are known to have small teeth in abnormal and maloccluded alignment.

Congenital heart disorders are common. Approximately 40 to 60% reveal a heart murmur and evidence of septum defect. The circulatory system is immature, with arteries remaining narrow and thin and the vascular tree having fewer branches than normal. It is interesting to note that a large percentage have "systolic heart murmur" written on their school records, but no medical restrictions on physical activity are generally stated. For legal protection, it is recommended that the physical educator be particularly cautious in working with this group and insistent upon having current health clearance forms on file.

Newborn infants with Down's syndrome, like most severely neurologically involved babies, exhibit an extreme degree of *muscular hypotonia*. This fact has led to coinage of the term *floppy babies*. The muscular flabbiness decreases with age, but never completely disappears. The abdomen of the adolescent and the adult generally protrudes like that of a small child. Almost 90% have umbilical hernias in early childhood, but the condition often corrects itself. This finding suggests that abdominal exercises be selected and administered with extreme care. Straight-leg lifts and holds are contraindicated. Other postural and/or orthopedic problems commonly associated with Down's syndrome are dorsolumbar kyphosis, dislocated hips, funnel-shaped or pigeon-breasted chest, and club feet.

The lax ligaments and apparent looseness of the joints lead some authors to describe persons with Down's syndrome as "double-jointed." The characteristic structural weakness of ligaments perhaps affects the function of the foot most. Many children have badly pronated and/or flat feet and walk with a shuffling gait. Daily foot exercises are recommended. Adapted tap dance (foot stamping and the like) utilizes muscles of the feet and lower legs optimally.

Assessment of the differences in tactual, spatial, and kinesthetic skills of familial, brain damaged, and Down's syndrome children have shown the latter to be the most perceptually handicapped. Persons with Down's syndrome are especially deficient on nonvisual tasks that require the interpretation of tactual, kinesthetic sensations. They seem poorest in tactile and fine motor discriminations and highest on visual tasks. Vision, however, is often impaired by strabismus, myopia, and astigmatism. Auditory discrimination has received little attention, but most persons with Down's syndrome are able to perform folk and square dances in time to the music.

Balance is one of the abilities in which persons with Down's syndrome are most deficient (Figure 19.12). In this area they tend to perform 1 to 3 years behind other

Figure 19.12 Preadolescent with Down's syndrome exhibits balance deficits.

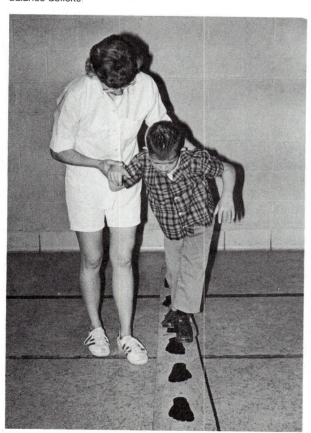

persons with the same level of retardation. Many persons with Down's syndrome cannot balance on one foot for more than a few seconds, and most cannot maintain balance at all with eyes closed. In general, basic movements are awkward. The gait is conspicuously infantile until about age 6. Many walk with a broad base through life. Students with Down's syndrome show severe impairment in perceptual-motor functioning when they attempt to perform accuracy tasks such as hopping or jumping prescribed floor patterns. Only about 50% can jump with both feet simultaneously one or more times. Only about one-fourth can hop on one foot and/or jump backward.

Persons with Down's syndrome show marked variability in learning capacities. Generally, the large majority, whether institutionalized or not, fall into the moderately retarded category. Recent observations, however, have revealed that those who remain in their natural home settings often function at a higher level than others. Characterized by a good memory, many can acquire a large vocabulary, read at the primary level, and learn to spell well. Seagoe (1964) tells the story of a boy with Down's syndrome who read at the seventh-grade level and kept a daily diary using Spanish as well as English over a period of years. Students with Down's syndrome often give the impression of knowing more than they do because of their astounding gift of mimicry.

The IQ of individuals with Down's syndrome tends to drop slowly during early adolescence so that many initially are enrolled in the highest level special education classes and later are transferred to lower groups. During puberty, marked changes in the intellectual status may occur; persons with Down's syndrome may become less attentive, slower, and more difficult to teach than before. The cause of such deterioration is unknown, although new research suggests Alzheimer's disease.

The social maturity of persons with Down's syndrome is consistently greater than their mental ages would lead one to expect. They are described as mannerly, responsible, cooperative, scrupulous, cheerful, and gregarious. Although usually cooperative, persons with Down's syndrome may exhibit extreme stubbornness. They like routine and may resist changes. This trait, similar to perseveration and conceptual rigidity in the brain damaged, makes the person with Down's syndrome seem similar to the normal 2-year-old who is frozen at the "No" stage. Stubbornness appears to be a CNS deficit and should be dealt with accordingly rather than punished.

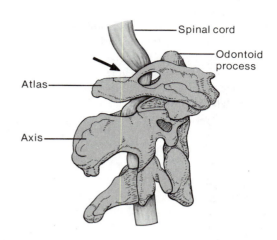

Figure 19.13 Atlantoaxial instability may contribute to a dislocation of the atlas, which may injure the spinal cord. It may be caused by either forceful forward or backward bending of the head.

Atlantoaxial Instability

Atlantoaxial instability is an orthopedic problem present in approximately 17% of persons with Down's syndrome. Atlantoaxial refers to the joint between the first two cervical vertebrae known as atlas and axis, respectively. Instability indicates that the ligaments and muscles surrounding this joint are lax and the vertebrae can slip out of alignment easily. Forceful forward or backward bending of the neck, which occurs in gymnastics, swimming, and other sports events, may dislocate the atlas, causing damage to the spinal cord (Figure 19.13).

Since 1983, Special Olympics has required a physician's statement that indicates absence of this condition in persons with Down's syndrome (DS) as a prerequisite for unrestricted participation in Special Olympics. This statement must be based on X-rays, the cost of which is typically covered by health insurance or medicaid. Enforcement of this requirement by school administrators would be prudent also, since contemporary physical education practice favors vigorous activity for DS children, often in an integrated setting. If this medical clearance is not on file, physical educators should restrict DS students from participation in gymnastics, diving, butterfly stroke and diving start in swimming, high jump, pentathlon, soccer, and any warm-up exercise placing pressure on the head and neck muscles. This restriction should be temporary, with a time limit set for obtaining the X-rays. If DS students are diagnosed as having atlantoaxial syndrome, they are permanently restricted from these activities; there are, however, many other physical education activities in which they can safely engage.

Physical Education for Severely and Profoundly Retarded Students

Children whose IQs fall below 35 are totally dependent. In accordance with PL 94–142, many of these children attend public schools. Physical growth and development are so slow that these youngsters may function as infants during their first 6 or 7 years. They are confined to cradles and playpens, and only with patient, persevering training are they taught purposive movement. The highest level severely retarded child seldom learns to walk alone steadily before age 6. The highest level profoundly retarded individual may not do so until age 9 or so. The average performance is much below this estimate, and some profoundly retarded persons never become ambulatory.

Table 19.5 on page 470 compares typical responses of profoundly and severely retarded males in four activities with approximately a 1:15 teacher/pupil ratio.

These are the children who do not play spontaneously. Even after some locomotor skills are mastered, they may lie or sit for hours, perseveratively rocking back and forth, and giving little evidence of environmental awareness.

Sensory-Motor Training and Assessment

Sensory-motor training is the earliest form of physical education provided for most severely and profoundly retarded children. Webb recommends improving four areas of behavior: (a) level of awareness, (b) movement, (c) manipulation of environment, and (d) posture and locomotion. The Glenwood Awareness, Manipulation, and Posture (AMP) Index can be used to assess progress in conjunction with the training (Webb & Koller, 1979). It is available through Glenwood (Iowa) State Hospital-School. Table 19.6 on page 471 summarizes techniques of sensory-motor training.

Level of Awareness

Activities are designed to help children recognize pleasant and unpleasant stimuli, to remember past exposures to them, and to exercise discrimination in anticipating or avoiding future contacts. Specifically, *avoidance reactions* (crying or turning away) are evoked in response to uncomfortably hot and cold water, vigorous toweling of skin, restraints such as splint jacket or weights on legs, taps from a rubber hammer, and extreme tastes such as alum or lemon. *Approach reactions* (smiling or turning toward a visual or auditory stimulus) are encouraged in response to bell ringing, music, a human voice, and various colorful objects. Response to cuddling by drawing closer is another important approach reaction. Children are drilled also on such discriminatory reactions as responding to name, obeying simple verbal and/or gesture commands, and turning toward objects as they are named. All responses at this level are nonverbal since the child has not yet acquired speech.

Movement

As the child becomes increasingly aware of sensory stimuli, he or she must be trained to make progressively more adequate motor adjustments. Externally imposed motion promotes discriminatory reactions as the child learns the difference between movement and no movement. At first, all purposive movement must be initiated by the teacher, who carries, rocks, rolls, bounces, and swings the child. Eventually, the child begins to offer active assistance when the limbs are manipulated or the body moved. As independent movement is achieved, the child is led through the following teaching progression: roll to side; roll from front to back; roll completely over; roll in a barrel; roll over such obstacles as firm pillows and inner tubes; rock on a rocking chair or horse; bounce on a bed, jump-up seat, or trampoline; and swing in a hammock or suspended seat. These activities are continued until sufficient muscle strength is developed to allow sitting and standing without external support.

Manipulation of Environment

Whereas the normal infant reaches for objects, grasps and plays with them, and eventually learns to get attention by throwing them on the floor, the severely or profoundly retarded child will evidence these behaviors only after training. Manipulation of environment implies lessons in reaching, grasping, releasing, throwing, holding, passing from hand to hand, rubbing, squeezing, tasting, pounding, shaking, taking apart, and reassembling. It also includes socialization experiences, beginning with response to mirror image and extending to communication with others through sounds, gestures, or words. Self-help skills are emphasized, and the child is taught to manipulate eating utensils, to assist in dressing him- or herself, and to cooperate in bathing and toilet activities. The practice of these tasks can be made into games, and the child's work becomes inseparable from play.

Table 19.5
Comparison of Motor Responses of Severely and Profoundly Retarded Persons

Activities/Tasks	Responses of Profoundly Retarded Males Ages 10–32 (Mental Age 0–2)	Responses of Severely Retarded Males Ages 14–20 (Mental Age 2–5)
Bean bag/Free play; carry on head; step and hop over one bag; toss bean bag into container; toss bean bag to instructor.	This group preferred to chew or eat the bean bags. The free play consisted primarily of releasing the bag as soon as it was placed in the hand. The students were manually manipulated through each movement on a one-to-one basis. The shape of the bean bag appeared to make little difference, but occasionally a student would reach for a certain color. Pleasure was derived mainly from attention of the teacher rather than the activity itself.	The majority of severely retarded boys were more creative with the bean bags than were the profoundly retarded boys. There was less tendency to chew the bag and a better concept of throwing. Free play consisted of the students bringing the bag to the teacher to play with them on a one-to-one basis. Several observed the demonstrations and attempted to imitate the teacher. Coordination was more highly developed than in the other group, but much manual assistance was required in the foot work.
Rope and yarn/Hop on one or both legs; hop over rope; use vertical and horizontal space; crouch down and stretch tall with rope in hand; curl up on floor and stretch long; grip rope and follow instructor.	The profoundly retarded group did not follow instructions. Individuals were manipulated through the movements by two instructors. Curling and crouching were accepted far more readily than stretching. Walking out floor patterns seemed to be simply a matter of follow-the-leader with no real awareness of the patterns.	The severely retarded group copied demonstrations, often adapting them to their own abilities. Although most attempted to hop, there was little success. This group had some concept of what was beneath their feet and enjoyed being led through and around objects. They preferred to hold the instructor's hand rather than a rope.
Cage ball/Roll ball to students on a one-to-one basis; small group activities in a circle—sit and kick ball to each other, sit and push ball to each other; repeat from a standing position.	The ball appeared to be irritating to a number of the profoundly retarded children. They turned away from it or attempted to push it away. Others grinned as they pushed it away, indicating that they recognized the teacher's pleasure at their correct response. A few attempted to tease the teacher by pushing the ball the opposite way and watching the teacher for a reaction. None of the students used their feet to kick the ball without constant reminders. The students remained in the circle, but did not interact with their peers. Essentially the activity was a one-to-one exchange with the teacher.	The severely retarded children performed the activities with little effort. Their attention span, however, was short. The teacher had to repeatedly call out names to get responses to the ball and to close gaps in the circular formation. The group appeared to grasp the concept of the circle and playmates but preferred to roll the ball to the teacher rather than their peers. Compared to other daily lessons, the cage ball activities were especially successful.
Universal gym and mat/Press weights with legs; push and pull weights with arms; sit up on inclined board; log roll; forward roll; creeping activities on mat.	On a one-to-one basis, approximately half the profoundly retarded group would perform what was requested to some degree. They enjoyed raising the weights and letting them drop with a loud bang. The noise appeared to be exciting to them and the center of the entire activity. The heights and weights of the adult students made mat work extremely fatiguing for the instructors. Many of the students were so large that they could not be safely manipulated by the two instructors. Four of the 30 pupils could do the mat activities. The group was too large for implementation of goals.	With a few exceptions, all of the severely retarded children learned to perform simple presses and pulls on the universal gym. These students also enjoyed making loud noises with the weights but would lower them slowly and quietly when under the direct surveillance of the instructor. About half of the 25 pupils performed all the mat activities with the teacher's help. Others attempted the activities only after repeated urging. Most of the pupils expressed more fear and distress than enjoyment of the mat activities.

Note. Barbara Ross, an adapted physical educator, wrote these descriptions of group activities comparing the responses of profoundly and severely retarded males. Activities for the two groups were conducted separately. The sizes of the profoundly retarded and severely retarded groups were 30 and 25, respectively. Two or three teachers worked together in handling groups of this size.

Table 19.6
Techniques of Sensory Motor Training for Severely/Profoundly Mentally Retarded Persons

Goal	Action	Materials Required
Increasing awareness by stimulating sense modalities	1. Toweling, brushing, icing, stroking, tapping, contact with textures	1. Towels, brushes (light), ice bags, textured fabrics
	2. Applying restraints for short periods, promoting body awareness by cuddling and holding tightly	2. Sand bags, splint jackets, strong gentle arms
	3. Following flashlight, hanging ball, colored toys, camera flashes	3. Flashlight, ball hanging from ceiling, blocks, balls, dolls, camera with flash
	4. Calling name of child; naming objects used, nearby persons, and actions; shaking ball, rattle; presenting music and commands	4. Wrist and ankle bells; noisemakers; tape recorders; nursery rhymes and records with varying loudness, pitch, and tempo
	5. Exposing child to extreme tastes	5. Sweet, sour, bitter, salty substances (honey, lemon, alum, salt)
	6. Exposing child to extreme odors	6. Pungent substances (coffee, cinnamon, vinegar), scented candles, incense, aerosol sprays
	7. Exposing child to extreme temperatures	7. Two basins with warm and cold water, ice bags, heating pads
	8. Mirror play	8. Full mirror, small mirrors which can be moved horizontally
	9. Wind movements	9. Fans to create wind tunnels, blowing air, fanning
	10. Vibration	10. Hand vibrators, mattress vibrators
Improving movement	1. Rolling	1. Mats with rough, smooth, hard, soft surfaces
	2. Rocking	2. Rocking chairs and horses, large beach balls
	3. Bouncing	3. Air mattress, trampoline, jump-up seat
	4. Swinging	4. Hammocks, suspended seats
	5. Coactive movements	5. Manual guidance of body or limbs (Chapter 10)
Improving manipulation	1. Reaching	1. Toys with various textures, colors, and sounds, water play, sticky clay, sand, finger paint, punching balls
	2. Grasping	2. Same as 1, yarn balls, nerf balls
	3. Holding	3. Same as 1 and 2
	4. Releasing	4. Small balls
	5. Throwing	5. Balls, praise, food treats, affection
	6. Responding to social cues	6. Same as 5
	7. Developing relationship to one person	7. Individual teacher
Developing posture and locomotion	1. Lifting head while prone	1. Chest support
	2. Sitting	2. Rubber tube
	3. Crawling and creeping	3. Crawler, scooter board, creep up padded stairs, inclined mats
	4. Standing	4. Standing tables, human support
	5. Riding tricycle	5. Tricycle with or without seat support and feet straps
	6. Walking	6. Parallel bars, human support, pushing weighted cart, coactive movement
	7. Stair climbing	7. Practice stairs

Note. Adapted from Webb, 1969.

Table 19.7
Basic Movement Performance Profile—Texas Adaptation of Fait Instrument

1. **Walking**
   0—makes no attempt at walking
   1—walks while being pulled
   2—walks with toe-heel placement
   3—walks with shuffle
   4—walks with heel-toe placement and opposite arm-foot swing

2. **Pushing (wheelchair)**
   0—makes no attempt to push wheelchair
   1—makes some attempt to push wheelchair
   2—pushes wheelchair once with arms only
   3—pushes wheelchair with continuous motion for 10 feet
   4—pushes wheelchair carrying adult occupant continuously for 10 feet

3. **Ascending stairs (up 4 stair steps)**
   0—makes no attempt to walk up stairs
   1—steps up 1 step with assistance
   2—walks up 4 steps with assistance
   3—walks up 4 steps; two feet on each step
   4—walks up 4 steps; alternating one foot on each step

4. **Descending stairs (down 4 stair steps)**
   0—makes no attempt to walk down stairs
   1—steps down 1 step with assistance
   2—walks down 4 steps with assistance
   3—walks down 4 steps, two feet on each step
   4—walks down 4 steps, alternating one foot on each step

5. **Climbing (4 rungs; first choice, ladder of a slide; second choice, step ladder)**
   0—makes no attempt to climb ladder
   1—climbs at least 1 rung with assistance
   2—climbs 4 rungs with assistance
   3—climbs 4 rungs, two feet on each rung
   4—climbs 4 rungs, alternating one foot on each rung

6. **Carrying (folded folding chair)**
   0—makes no attempt to lift chair from floor
   1—attempts but not able to lift chair from floor
   2—lifts chair from floor
   3—carries chair by dragging on the floor
   4—carries chair 10 feet

7. **Pulling (wheelchair)**
   0—makes no attempt to pull wheelchair
   1—makes some attempt to pull wheelchair
   2—pulls wheelchair once with arms only
   3—pulls wheelchair with continuous motion for 10 feet
   4—pulls wheelchair carrying adult occupant continuously for 10 feet

8. **Running**
   0—makes no attempt to run
   1—takes long walking steps while being pulled
   2—takes running steps while being pulled
   3—jogs (using toe or flat of foot)
   4—runs for 25 yards, with both feet off the ground when body weight shifts from the rear to front foot

9. **Catching (bean bag tossed from 5 feet away)**
   0—makes no attempt to catch bean bag
   1—holds both arms out to catch bean bag
   2—catches bean bag fewer than 5 of 10 attempts
   3—catches bean bag at least 5 of 10 attempts
   4—catches bean bag at least 8 of 10 attempts

10. **Creeping**
    0—makes no attempt to creep
    1—will assume hands and knees position
    2—creeps with a shuffle
    3—creeps alternating hands and knees
    4—creeps in a crosslateral pattern with head up

11. **Jumping down (two-foot take-off and landing from 18-inch folding chair)**
    0—makes no attempt
    1—steps down from chair with assistance
    2—steps down from chair
    3—jumps off chair with two-foot take-off and lands with assistance
    4—jumps off chair with two-foot take-off and lands while maintaining balance

Posture and Locomotion

Training begins with lifting the head while in different lying positions. Motivational devices like the smell of a food treat or the sound of a bell are often required to elicit a head-lifting response, particularly from a prone position. Children who lack the muscular strength to sit without support are strapped into correct sitting position for a few minutes each day. Various kinds of apparatus on wheels or rollers facilitate the first attempt at creeping, standing, and walking. The teacher must repeatedly guide the limbs through the desired movement patterns in an attempt to elicit kinesthetic and vestibular feedback that enables the child to remember and reproduce particular movements. For optimal results, this work should be done in front of a mirror to facilitate visuo-motor integration. Sound effects should be used also to reinforce positive attempts.

Basic Movement Training and Assessment

Severely and profoundly retarded persons may spend their lifetimes acquiring basic locomotor movements. It is doubtful that running, jumping, and other motor skills can be taught except on a one-to-one basis, with the teacher repeatedly moving limbs through desired movement patterns. A review of Chapter 10, Motor Performance, Self-Concept, and Leisure Functioning, will help with the development of a sequential progression for teaching motor patterns normally acquired during ages 1 to 6.

Several schools use the Basic Movement Performance Profile (BMPP) as the basis for curriculum planning (see Table 19.7).

First developed by Fait (1972) and colleagues at the Mansfield Training School, the BMPP has been revised and standardized by Ness (1974) at the Denton

Table 19.7   (continued)

12. **Throwing (overhand softball, three attempts)**
0—makes no attempt to throw
1—grasps ball and releases in attempt to throw
2—throws or tosses ball a few feet in any direction
3—throws ball at least 15 feet in air in intended direction
4—throws ball at least 30 feet in the air in intended direction

13. **Hitting (volleyball with plastic bat)**
0—makes no attempt to hit ball
1—hits stationary ball fewer than 3 of 5 attempts
2—hits stationary ball at least 3 of 5 attempts
3—hits ball rolled from 15 feet away fewer than 3 of 5 attempts
4—hits ball rolled from 15 feet away at least 3 of 5 attempts

14. **Forward roll**
0—makes no attempt to do forward roll
1—puts hands and head on mat
2—puts hands and head on mat and pushes with feet and/or knees in an attempt to do roll
3—performs roll, but tucks shoulder and rolls to side
4—performs forward roll

15. **Kicking (soccer ball)**
0—makes no attempt to kick stationary ball
1—pushes stationary ball with foot in attempt to kick it
2—kicks stationary ball several feet in any direction
3—kicks stationary ball several feet in intended direction
4—kicks ball rolled from 15 feet away in direction of roller

16. **Dynamic balance (4-inch beam with shoes on)**
0—makes no attempt to stand on beam
1—stands on beam with assistance
2—walks at least 5 steps with assistance
3—walks at least 5 feet without stepping off beam
4—walks at least 10 feet without stepping off beam

17. **Hanging (two hands on horizontal bar)**
0—makes no attempt to grasp bar
1—makes some attempt to hang from bar
2—hangs from bar with assistance
3—hangs from bar for at least 5 seconds
4—hangs from bar for at least 10 seconds

18. **Dodging (a large cage ball rolled from 15 feet away)**
0—makes no attempt to dodge ball
1—holds up hands or foot to stop ball
2—turns body to avoid ball
3—dodges ball at least 5 of 10 attempts
4—dodges ball at least 8 of 10 attempts

19. **Static balance (standing on one foot with shoes on)**
0—makes no attempt to stand on one foot
1—makes some attempt to stand on one foot
2—stands on one foot with assistance
3—stands on one foot for at least 5 seconds
4—stands on one foot for at least 5 seconds with 5 pounds of weight in the same hand as elevated foot

20. **Jumping (standing long jump, three attempts)**
0—makes no attempt to jump
1—jumps with a one-foot stepping motion
2—jumps from crouch with two-foot take-off and landing at least 1 foot
3—jumps from crouch with two-foot take-off and landing at least 2 feet
4—jumps from crouch with two-foot take-off and landing at least 3 feet

State School. It has a reliability coefficient of .94, derived by the test-retest method using 60 profoundly retarded adults.

Profoundly retarded residents at the Denton State School scored from 25 to 65 of 80 possible points on the BMPP. The only tasks that 90% of the residents could perform without training were walking and pushing a wheelchair. The next easiest were walking up and down stair steps. Catching was easier than throwing, a finding contradictory of normal early childhood development. The most difficult tasks, on which none of the residents scored a 4, were walking 10 feet on a 4-inch walking board, hanging from a horizontal bar, dodging a cage ball, standing on one foot, and long jumping. After the administration of the BMPP, individualized physical education prescriptions should be devised to help each student develop the basic movement patterns he or she lacks.

Fitness, Rhythms, and Games

The mastery of skills beyond running and jumping is probably less important than the maintenance of a minimum level of fitness. Far too many severely and profoundly retarded persons spend so much time sitting that their muscles tighten and contort trunks and limbs into unusable shapes. But how do you motivate such persons to run or even walk sufficient distances to develop minimal circulovascular endurance? How do you persuade them to do a repeated number of sit-ups, toe touches, or arm circles?

The teacher of these persons must possess abundant energy and a high level of fitness. They will generally run only so long as the teacher runs too. This is true of most other exercises. If there is no model to imitate, they will not respond to movement instructions—possibly because they cannot remember even simple exercises without visual stimuli.

By adolescence, a few (but not many) can begin to enjoy simple games and dance activities such as Drop the Handkerchief; Duck, Duck, Goose; Musical Chairs; and Did You Ever See a Lassie? Most severely and profoundly retarded children continue to respond best on a one-to-one basis. Ball handling (rolling, bouncing, chasing, and retrieving), water play, and repetitive activities such as swinging arms and stamping feet are effective. Interesting music with a strong beat generally elicits rhythmic movement that bears some resemblance to social dance.

Background music seems also to improve response to exercise sessions, and some experiments have shown that retarded persons can be conditioned to perform a certain exercise each time the same melody is heard. Most training centers provide for 5 to 10 minutes of exercise at regularly scheduled times each day, so that the children respond appropriately as they do to meal, bath, and bed time. For best results, exactly the same exercises to the same music should be executed daily at the designated times. Severely retarded persons are not bored by repetition. On the contrary, it provides them with security and a sense of well-being.

Operant conditioning, or *shaping,* is used to reinforce learning through the immediate rewarding of each correct response. The reward is generally eatable, such as M&M candy or cereal, but may be a hug, pat, or words of praise. In operant conditioning, one teacher is needed for each child, as illustrated in the following example of a fifth lesson on the toe touch exercise.

Teacher turns on music and flips slide projector on to automatic. Red slides begin to show.
Child rises from chair and stands on specified floor marking.
Teacher puts M&M in child's open mouth and says "Good girl."
Child makes slight forward motion as though intending to touch toes.
Teacher puts M&M in child's mouth and says "Good girl"; manually pushes child down to the correct position.
Child's fingers touch floor at end of down phase.
Teacher puts M&M in child's mouth and says "Good girl."
Child extends to starting position.
Teacher puts M&M in child's mouth and says "Good girl." Turns off music and slide projector. Allows child to wander off. Then repeats entire sequence.

As conditioned responses grow stronger, fewer M&Ms are given so that eventually only one reward is required at the completion of the toe touch. Later, the child may progress to a series of eight toe touches before the reward is received. The success of operant conditioning depends upon the teacher's ability to break an exercise down into a sequence of very small tasks and the consistency in rewarding each success. The initial tasks must be so simple that success is inevitable. For instance, rising from a chair might be broken down into the following tasks, each of which is rewarded separately: puts one or both feet on floor; bends forward slightly; positions hands on arm rest for balance; lifts buttocks from chair; takes weight on one or both feet; lifts head; extends trunk; and extends knees. In accordance with the principle of individual differences, the type of reward may vary with each child.

Posture Training

As severely retarded persons are integrated into school and community life, normalized appearance becomes increasingly important. Postures play an important part in this process. The most frequently occurring dynamic posture problems among severely handicapped adults are shuffling gait, too little arm swing, uneven gait, and forward tilt of head and trunk. The most common static posture problems are flatfeet, protruding abdomen, forward head and neck, feet pointed out and pronated, and lordosis.

Several training strategies appear more effective in ameliorating posture problems in mentally retarded children than do traditional exercise routines: (a) peer and cross-age modeling; (b) behavior management techniques; (c) body awareness activities; (d) relaxation training; and (e) sociodrama, role playing, and counseling. Of these, the natural peer and cross-age modeling that occurs in integrated school/community settings may (with continuous verbal reinforcement) be the most effective. Mentally retarded children in large residential facilities are exposed primarily to poor postures; it seems reasonable to believe that they grow up subconsciously mimicking the movement behaviors around them. The use of sociodrama, role playing, and counseling in posture training recognizes the fact that postures reflect the thoughts, feelings, and moods of human beings. Concentration upon physical characteristics is incomplete without concomitant attention to self-concept and social relationships.

The Special Olympics Program

Special Olympics is an international program of physical fitness, sports training, and competition for mentally retarded children and adults. Ideally, it is a *year-round program* that involves some athletic competition for all persons ages 8 and over regardless of how low their skill level may be. The Special Olympics dream was conceived and implemented in 1968 by the Joseph P. Kennedy, Jr. Foundation.

Positive, successful experiences in sport are believed to contribute to improved self-concept and to carry over into the classroom, home, and sheltered workshop. Hence, Special Olympics are organized so that everyone can be a winner. Meets are arranged to give competitors the feeling of being an athlete rather than a retarded person. The Special Olympics oath, repeated before engaging in competition, reinforces this feeling:

Let me win
But if I cannot win
Let me be brave in the attempt.

Daily physical education instruction is the most important aspect of Special Olympics. Ideally, the program culminates each spring in local and state meets where individuals have an opportunity to exhibit the skills that they have been practicing all year. For many Special Olympians, the meet represents a first time to win an award, to have a picture in the newspaper, to receive recognition at a school assembly, and to have parents and neighbors observe.

Official Special Olympics sports include aquatics, athletics (i.e., track and field), basketball, bowling, gymnastics, floor and poly hockey, figure and speed skating, alpine and cross country skiing, soccer (six-a-side), softball, and volleyball. These sports, which have been demonstrated as appropriate for mentally retarded persons, should be taught in school physical education programs. Individual sports, particularly aquatics, track and field, and bowling, should be taught before team sports. Following are the official Special Olympics track and field events:

50-meter dash	100-meter dash
200-meter run	400-meter run
400-meter walk	Mile run
4×100-meter relay (400 meter)	Shot put (men 5.44 kg, woman 4 kg)
Pentathlon (includes 100-meter dash, 400-meter run, shot put, running long jump, high jump)	Softball throw
	25-meter wheelchair race
	Wheelchair relay
	30-meter wheelchair slalom
High jump	4 × 25 (100-meter)
Standing long jump	wheelchair relay

Since 1981, Special Olympics, Inc., has conducted a comprehensive training program for volunteer coaches. Sports skills instructional program manuals are available for the official sports. Each manual includes long-term goals, short-term objectives, checklists of levels 1 and 2 skills assessment, a task analysis and teaching suggestions for every skill, and other information. Through training clinics conducted by their state organization, teachers can obtain these manuals and become certified as Special Olympics coaches. Certification must be renewed periodically.

Many rule and policy changes were made by Special Olympics, Inc., in 1984–1985 to make its sports program more consistent with sports for able-bodied persons. Sports like frisbee-disc, which do not have national governing bodies (NGBs), were eliminated, and rules of all other sports are now the same as those of the NGBs. Special Olympians no longer receive participation ribbons. First through eighth place awards are given for all competitive events; the first three are medals and the last five are ribbons. These changes were all in accordance with the principle of normalization.

New sports may become Special Olympics official sports as they gain widespread acceptance and meet the criteria established for the health and safety of the participants. Also, at all levels of Special Olympics other sports are practiced as well as other recreational activities so that the participants have a broad range of activities from which to choose and can find one or more to suit their individual abilities and preferences. Demonstration clinics are held at the games, sometimes led by well-known athletes, to teach the children new skills in sports such as football, gymnastics, and basketball, for example.

Because there is a great range of athletic ability among retarded persons, competition takes place in several divisions based upon ability as well as age and sex. The range of abilities encompassed by each division is left to the discretion of meet directors rather than predetermined by national norms. Assignment to a division is based upon actual performance in an event as recorded on the entry form by the coach or teacher. This requirement demands that all athletes be tested beforehand in the events they wish to enter. Special educators as well as physical educators should know how to assess performance in these activities. Only after the scores of all pupils have been submitted does the meet director determine who belongs in which division under each age group. Competition within each division is separate for males and females.

In 1985, age groups for Special Olympics individual sports competitions (summer) were changed to include the following:

Youth	Ages 8 to 11
Junior	Ages 12 to 15
Senior	Ages 16 to 22
Sub-masters	Ages 23 to 29
Masters	Ages 30 years and over
Open age group	Reserved for situations in which rules require a minimum of three competitors in each division

Team and winter sports competitions now include the following age groups:

Junior	Ages 15 years and under
Senior	Ages 16 to 29
Masters	Ages 30 years and over
Open age group	Same as above

In order to compete in state meets, Special Olympians must be at least 12 years old and must have won first, second, or third place in their event in a sanctioned area meet. A division consists of a minimum of three and a maximum of eight competitors or teams. If there are not enough competitors or teams to make a division, then two divisions can be combined.

The pageantry and color of Special Olympics are as exciting to many athletes as the sports events. The opening ceremonies of a meet may include such highlights as the lighting of a Special Olympics torch, a parade of the athletes and/or of a band and local dignitaries, the raising of the American flag and the Special Olympics flag, a release of doves or balloons, the Special Olympics oath repeated in unison, and group warm-up exercises led by a visiting professional athlete. The closing ceremony is equally impressive, with a final parade of the athletes, extinguishing of the Special Olympics flame, lowering of flags, and friendship songs. Most state meets are organized so as to provide competitors with an overnight experience. Special educational events include sports clinics and the opportunity to meet famous athletes and government figures.

Special educators, physical educators, and community recreation personnel must work cooperatively to make the year-round Special Olympics program a success. Information on establishing, developing, and becoming involved in such a program can be obtained by writing to the state director or to Mrs. Eunice Kennedy Shriver, Special Olympics, Inc., Joseph P. Kennedy, Jr. Foundation, 1350 New York Avenue, NW, Suite 500, Washington, DC 20005. (A brochure and list of state directors are available from the Kennedy Foundation upon request.)

Learning Activities

1. Become involved as a Special Olympics volunteer coach who works regularly with athletes. Obtain the Special Olympics sports skills instructional manuals and use these to guide your coaching. If possible, attend a training clinic and complete certification as a Special Olympics coach.

2. Attend Special Olympics local and state meets as a spectator or official volunteer. Become acquainted with parents of at least 10 Special Olympians and ask them about the school physical education their offspring are receiving.

3. Become involved in the implementation of the Joseph P. Kennedy, Jr. Foundation, Let's Play to Grow, and/or other recreation programs.

4. Attend meetings of the local chapter of the Association for Retarded Citizens (ARC) and volunteer your services to their various projects.

5. Develop a friendship with a mentally retarded person of your age or older and, once a week, do something of a social or recreational nature together, just the two of you!

6. Visit a group home and/or a residential facility for mentally retarded persons. Discuss the exercise, diet, and physical recreation aspects of the lives of the persons living there and do something to enhance these aspects.

7. Work on your assessment skills by administering selected tests to several mentally retarded students. Write your findings as a report and recommend physical education activities based on these findings.

References

Coleman, E., Ayoud, M. M., & Friedrich, D. W. (1976). Assessment of physical work capacity of institutionalized mentally retarded males. *American Journal of Mental Deficiency, 80*, 629–635.

Fait, H. F. (1972). *Special physical education.* Philadelphia: W. B. Saunders, pp. 208–209.

Grossman, H. J. (Ed.). (1984). *Manual on terminology and classification in mental retardation.* Washington, DC: American Association on Mental Deficiency.

Molnar, G. (1978). Analysis of motor disorder in retarded infants and young children. *American Journal of Mental Deficiency, 83*, 213–221.

Ness, R. (1974). *The standardization of the basic movement performance profile for profoundly retarded institutionalized residents.* Unpublished doctoral dissertation. North Texas State University, Denton.

Rarick, G. L. (1980). Cognitive-motor relationships in the growing years. *Research Quarterly for Exercise and Sport, 51*, 174–192.

Ross, B. (1975). *Changes in profoundly mentally retarded adult females during a walking program.* Unpublished master's thesis, Texas Woman's University, Denton.

Seagoe, M. V. (1964). *Yesterday was Tuesday, all day and all night.* Boston: Little, Brown.

Webb, R., & Koller, J. (1979). Effects of sensorimotor training on intellectual and adaptive skills of profoundly retarded adults. *American Journal of Mental Deficiency, 83*, 490–496.

Bibliography

American Alliance for Health, Physical Education, and Recreation. (1971–1977). *The best of challenge vol. I, 1971; vol. II, 1974; vol. III, 1977.* Washington, DC: Author.

American Alliance for Health, Physical Education, and Recreation. (1972). *Special Olympics instructional manual—from beginners to champions.* Washington, DC: Author.

Beasley, C. B. (1982). Effects of a jogging program on cardiovascular fitness and work performance of mentally retarded adults. *American Journal of Mental Deficiency 86*, 609–613.

Beuter, A. (1983). Effects of mainstreaming on motor performance of intellectually normal and trainable mentally retarded students. *American Corrective Therapy Journal, 37*(2), 48–52.

Birrer, R. (1984). The Special Olympics: An injury overview. *Physician and Sports Medicine, 12*(4), 95–97.

Broadhead, G., & Church, G. (1984). Influence of test selection on physical education placement of mentally retarded children. *Adapted Physical Activity Quarterly, 1*(2), 112–117.

Bruininks, R. (1974). Physical and motor development of retarded persons. In N. R. Ellis (Ed.), *International review of research in mental retardation* (Vol. 7, pp. 209–261). New York: Academic Press.

Bundschuh, E., & Cureton, K. (1982). Effect of bicycle ergometer conditioning on the physical work capacity of mentally retarded adults. *American Corrective Therapy Journal, 36*(6), 159–163.

Byde, R., & McClenaghan, B. (1984). Effects of selected types of feedback on the anticipation timing task with moderately mentally retarded children. *Adapted Physical Activity Quarterly, 1*(2), 141–146.

Cooke, R. (1984). Atlantoaxial instability in individuals with Down's syndrome. *Adapted Physical Activity Quarterly, 1*(3), 194–196.

Corman, L., & Gottlieb, J. (1978). Mainstreaming mentally retarded children: A review of research. In N. R. Ellis (Ed.), *International review of research in mental retardation* (Vol. 7, pp. 251–257). New York: Academic Press.

Cowie, V. (1970). *A study of the early development of mongols.* New York: Pergamon Press.

Cratty, B. (1974). *Motor activity and the education of retardates* (2nd ed.). Philadelphia: Lea & Febiger.

Dixon, J. (1979). The implications of attribution theory for therapeutic recreation service. *Therapeutic Recreation Journal, 13*, 3–11.

Drowatzky, J. N. (1971). *Physical education for the mentally retarded.* Philadelphia: Lea & Febiger.

Dummer, G. (1985). Teacher training to enhance motor learning by mentally retarded persons. In C. Sherrill (Ed.), *Adapted physical education leadership training.* Champaign, IL: Human Kinetics Publishers.

Dunn, J., Morehouse, J., & Fredericks, H. D. B. (1985). *Physical education for severely handicapped: A systematic approach to a data based gymnasium.* Austin: Pro-Ed Publishers.

Fredericks, H. D. B. (1980). *The teaching research curriculum for moderately and severely handicapped: Gross and fine motor.* Springfield, IL: Charles C. Thomas.

Gearheart, B., & Litton, F. (1979). *The trainable retarded* (2nd ed.). St. Louis: C. V. Mosby.

Hackett, L. C. (1970). *Movement exploration and games for the mentally retarded.* Palo Alto, CA: Peek Publications.

Hardman, M., & Drew, C. (1977). The physically handicapped retarded individual: A review. *Mental Retardation, 15*, 43–48.

Haring, N. (Ed.) (1977). *Developing effective individualized education programs for severely handicapped children and youth.* Washington, DC: United States Office of Education, Bureau of Education for the Handicapped.

Haskins, J. (1976). *A new kind of joy: The story of Special Olympics.* New York: Doubleday.

Hayden, F. (1964). *Physical fitness for the mentally retarded.* Ontario: Toronto Association for Retarded Children.

Hayden, F. (1974). Physical education and sport. In J. Wortis (Ed.), *Mental retardation and developmental disabilities* (pp. 213–229). New York: Brunner/Mazel.

Heitman, R., & Justen, J. (1980). Locus of control and social reinforcement in the motor performance of educable mentally retarded students. *Education and Training of the Mentally Retarded, 15,* 204–208.

Hsu, P., & Dunn, J. (1984). Comparing reverse and forward chaining instructional methods on a motor task with moderately mentally retarded individuals. *Adapted Physical Activity Quarterly, 1*(3), 240–246.

Johnson, L., & Londeree, B. (1976). *Motor fitness testing manual for the moderately mentally retarded.* Washington, DC: American Alliance for Health, Physical Education, and Recreation.

Joseph P. Kennedy, Jr. Foundation. (1977). *Let's play-to-grow for families, for schools, for communities.* Materials available from 1350 New York Avenue, NW, Suite 500, Washington, DC 20005.

Leighton, J. (1966). The effect of a physical fitness developmental program on self-concept, mental age, and job proficiency in the mentally retarded. *Journal of the Association for Physical and Mental Rehabilitation, 20,* 4–11.

Levy, J. (1974). Social reinforcement and knowledge of results as determinants of motor performance among EMR children. *American Journal of Mental Deficiency, 78,* 752–758.

Londeree, B., & Johnson, L. (1974). Motor fitness of TMR vs. EMR and normal children. *Medicine and Science in Sports, 6,* 247–252.

Loovis, M. (1975). *Model for individualizing physical education experiences for the preschool moderately retarded child.* Unpublished doctoral dissertation, Ohio State University.

Mills, A., & Barnes, L. (1984). A world of winners: International Special Olympics. *Palaestra, 1*(1), 6–10.

Moon, M. S., & Renzaglia, A. (1982). Physical fitness and the mentally retarded: A critical review of the literature. *Journal of Special Education, 6*(3), 269–287.

Moran, J., & Kalakian, L. (1977). *Movement experiences for the mentally retarded or emotionally disturbed child* (2nd ed.). Minneapolis: Burgess.

Mori, A., & Masters, L. (1980). *Teaching the severely mentally retarded adaptive skills training.* Germantown, MD: Aspen Systems Corporation. Includes three chapters on physical education.

Polloway, E., & Smith, J. D. (1983). Changes in mild mental retardation, programs, and perspectives. *Exceptional Children, 50*(2), 149–159.

Rarick, G. L. (1978). Adult reactions to the Special Olympics. In F. L. Smoll & R. E. Smith (Eds.), *Psychological perspectives in youth sports* (pp. 229–246). New York: Halsted Press.

Rarick, G. L., Dobbins, D. A., & Broadhead, G. D. (1976). *The motor domain and its correlates in educationally handicapped children*. Englewood Cliffs, NJ: Prentice-Hall.

Rarick, G. L., Widdop, J., & Broadhead, G. (1970). The physical fitness and motor performance of educable mentally retarded children. *Exceptional Children, 36,* 509–519.

Robinson, N., & Robinson, H. (1976). *The mentally retarded child* (2nd ed.). New York: McGraw-Hill.

Roswal, G., Roswal, P. & Dunleavy, A. (1985). Normative health-related fitness data for Special Olympians. In C. Sherrill (Ed.), *Sport and disabled athletes* (pp. 231–238). Champaign, IL: Human Kinetics Publishers.

Rynders, J., Johnson, R., Johnson, D., & Schmidt, B. (1980). Producing positive interaction among Down's syndrome and nonhandicapped teenagers through cooperative goal structuring. *American Journal of Mental Deficiency, 85,* 268–273.

Sherrill, C. (1980). Posture training as a means of normalization. *Mental Retardation, 18,* 135–138.

Songster, T. (1985). Sport for mentally retarded athletes: International perspectives. In C. Sherrill (Ed.), *Sport and disabled athletes* (pp. 73–80). Champaign, IL: Human Kinetics Publishers.

Sontag, E., Certo, N., & Button, J. (1979). On a distinction between the education of the severely and profoundly handicapped. *Exceptional Children, 45,* 604–616.

Special Olympics, Inc. (1981 on). *Sports skills instructional program manuals*. Contact state Special Olympics office or Special Olympics, Inc., 1350 New York Avenue, NW, Suite 500, Washington, DC 20005.

Staugaitis, S. (1978). New directions for effective weight control with mentally retarded people. *Mental Retardation, 16,* 157–162.

Stein, J. (1966). *Physical fitness in relation to intelligence quotient, social distance, and physique of intermediate school mentally retarded boys.* Unpublished doctoral dissertation, George Peabody College for Teachers.

Ulrich, D. (1983). A comparison of the qualitative motor performance of normal, educable, and trainable mentally retarded students. In R. Eason, T. Smith, & F. Caron (Eds.), *Adapted physical activity* (pp. 219–225). Champaign, IL: Human Kinetics Publishers.

Wehman, P. (1977). *Helping the mentally retarded acquire play skills*. Springfield, IL: Charles C. Thomas.

Wehman, P., Berry, G., Karan, O., Renzaglia, A., & Schutz, R. (1978) Developing a leisure skill repertoire in SVH and profoundly handicapped persons. *AAESPH Review, 3*(3), 162–172.

Wright, J. (1977). *Changes in self-concept and cardiovascular endurance of mentally retarded youth in a Special Olympics swimming program.* Unpublished master's thesis, Texas Woman's University, Denton.

Wysocki, B. A., & Wysocki, A. C. (1973). The body image of normal and retarded children. *Journal of Clinical Psychology, 29,* 7–10.

20 Serious Emotional Disturbances

Figure 20.1 The emotionally disturbed child must be taught how to channel aggression.

Chapter Objectives

After you have studied this chapter, you should be able to

1. Contrast the terminology and definitions of severe emotional disturbance used by PL 94–142, the CEC, and the American Psychiatric Association. What is the major application and value of each?

2. Discuss changes in the diagnosis and treatment of emotional disturbance during the past decade. How have these affected attitudes toward persons with mental disorders?

3. Explain each of the following: (a) organic mental disorders, (b) substance use disorders, (c) schizophrenic disorders, (d) affective disorders, (e) personality disorders, and (f) the diagnostic categories specific to childhood and adolescence. Indicate behaviors that teachers should call to the attention of school counselors.

4. Differentiate between anorexia nervosa and bulimia and discuss each in relation to eating habits, exercise, and body image disturbances.

5. Differentiate between movement disorders associated with mental disorders and those not so associated.

6. Discuss the use of sports, dance, and aquatics as vehicles for the amelioration of different kinds of behavior and mental disorders.

7. State eight suggestions for working with schizophrenic and/or overly aggressive students.

8. Discuss depression and suicide in school-aged students and techniques for coping with these problems.

9. Discuss available and needed research on physical education, exercise, and mental health in school-aged students. Which research exists pertaining specifically to emotional disturbance, motor development, and physical education?

10. Explain why autism was not covered in this chapter. On which pages is it described?

The monkey bars, crisscrossing up and down, forward and backward, intrigued him. There was no question that his jiggler pointed in their direction. But what if he got caught in the middle of all that iron? What if he couldn't get out?

He walked over cautiously and touched the closest bar. It was cold. A sinister chill ran through him. But the jiggler pointed in that direction again. This time he touched a bar warmed by the sun. This felt different, more inviting, but he was still afraid. It looked like a wonderful toy to climb over and swing from. And it looked like an awful monster that could tangle you up, crush you, and kill you.

Theodore Isaac Rubin

Playground and gymnasium settings can be terrifying to a child, as depicted so well by Rubin, a practicing psychiatrist in Brooklyn, whose book should be read by all teachers interested in childhood schizophrenia. In the passage above, he describes Jordi, an 8-year-old boy with a diagnosis of schizophrenic reaction-type, mixed, undifferentiated, chronic. Like most emotionally disturbed children today, Jordi lives at home and attends a day school. Jordi is afraid of almost everything and carries a jiggler (a doorknob tied to a string) for security. Only when he learns to play stoop ball does he give up the jiggler. Later, it is his skill in stoop ball that gives him enough confidence to respond affirmatively to an invitation to participate in a handball game—one of his first efforts to relate to the peer group.

Prevalence

Prevalence of severe emotional disorders varies widely because of differing definitions and diagnostic criteria. In the adult United States population, one of six persons at some time in life will have problems severe enough to require professional help. It is commonly believed that handicapped persons have more problems than the nonhandicapped (Bishop, 1980).

The diagnosis of mental disorders is difficult, and most psychiatrists prefer not to attach a label. The prevalence of behavior disorders in the school population ranges from 2 to 22%, depending upon the criterion of behavior disorders used. The ratio of boys to girls is approximately 4:1. The United States Department of Education estimates very conservatively that approximately 2% of the school-age population is so severely emotionally disturbed that special education provisions are required. This includes over 1 million pupils between ages 5 and 19. This estimate as well as the PL 94–142 definition of severely emotionally disturbed have been strongly criticized as excluding many students who need professional help.

Suicide increasingly is a problem of childhood and adolescence. Suicide ranks third as the leading cause of death in the 15 to 24 age bracket. Statistics for all age groups combined reveal that over 25,000 suicides occur each year. Approximately 2 million persons in this country have made one or more attempts at suicide.

Delinquency, a legal term reserved for youngsters whose behavior results in arrest and court action, is another manifestation of emotional problems. The crime rate among young persons has increased steadily during the past decade. It is estimated that youthful offenders account for 61% of all auto thefts, 54% of larcenies, 55% of burglaries, and 33% of robberies. Long before their initial arrest, many delinquents are described by classroom teachers as defiant, impertinent, uncooperative, irritable, bullying, attention seeking, negative, and restless. Other delinquents are seen as shy, lacking in self-confidence, hypersensitive, fearful, and excessively anxious.

Definitions

Definitions of severe emotional disturbance come from several sources. The three most frequently used are PL 94–142, the Council for Exceptional Children (CEC), and the American Psychiatric Association.

PL 94–142 Terminology

The term used in determining eligibility for special education services is *seriously emotionally disturbed.* This term means

a condition exhibiting one or more of the following characteristics over a long period of time and to a marked degree, which adversely affects educational performance:
(A) An inability to learn which cannot be explained by intellectual, sensory, or health factors;
(B) An inability to build or maintain satisfactory interpersonal relationships with peers and teachers;
(C) Inappropriate types of behavior or feelings under normal circumstances;
(D) A general pervasive mood of unhappiness or depression; or
(E) A tendency to develop physical symptoms or fears associated with personal or school problems. (*Federal Register*, August 23, 1977, p. 42478)

Originally, this PL 94–142 definition included *autism.* Since 1981, however, autistic children have been included instead in the official definition of *other health impaired.*

CEC Terminology

Many special educators use the term *behavior disorders* rather than emotional or mental illness. In 1962, the Council on Exceptional Children formed the Council for Children with Behavioral Disorders (CCBD). This organization publishes a quarterly journal called *Behavioral Disorders* and exerts much influence on special education practices.

American Psychiatric Association Terminology

The nomenclature of mental disorders is established by the American Psychiatric Association in a book entitled *Diagnostic and Statistical Manual of Mental Disorders,* which is published approximately every 10 years. The third edition (1980) made drastic changes in terminology that rendered many textbooks out of date. For example, the age-old classification of mental disorders into neuroses, psychoses, and personality or character disorders was discarded. The first two of these terms no longer appear in its glossary.

The *Diagnostic and Statistical Manual of Mental Disorders (DSM-III)* identifies 16 diagnostic categories, discusses each, and states criteria for medical diagnosis. Among these are (a) disorders usually first evident in infancy, childhood, or adolescence, (b) organic mental disorders, (c) substance use disorders, (d) schizophrenic disorders, (e) affective disorders, (f) psychosexual disorders, and (g) personality disorders. Conditions previously lumped together as psychoses and neuroses now each have their own specific categories. Readers who still feel they must lump together conditions are told to use the terms *psychotic disorders* and *neurotic disorders;* lumping, however, is strongly discouraged. This new official recognition of the specificity of mental disorders reflects the knowledge explosion of the last decades, specifically in regard to diagnosis and treatment.

All of the disciplines that adhere to the medical rather than the educational model use *DSM-III* as their primary source. This includes therapeutic recreation personnel, occupational and physical therapists, and many others with whom adapted physical educators work. Within the multidisciplinary context, it is therefore important to be familiar with at least some of the content of *DSM-III*. New knowledge, published as research, also typically appears under specific rather than general classifications.

The *DSM-III* also serves as the primary source for differentiating between sanity and insanity in court cases and for labeling certain behaviors as normal vs.

abnormal. Most state laws are consistent with theory evolved by the American Psychiatric Association; this theory changes, of course, as knowledge about human behavior expands. For instance, masturbation and homosexuality were once considered evil and abnormal behaviors that would lead to insanity. *DSM-III* does not mention masturbation among psychosexual disorders. It states that homosexuality itself is not a mental disorder (p. 282), but that homosexual feelings and practices that lead to persistent distress are a psychosexual disorder.

Classic Mental Disorders

Of the 16 *DSM-III* diagnostic categories, the ones most common in our society are described in this section. Children and youth, as well as adults, may be diagnosed as having these disorders. The behaviors are essentially the same regardless of age.

Organic Mental Disorders

This category encompasses psychological abnormalities associated with transient or permanent dysfunction of the brain. By tradition, disorders related to aging of the brain or damage of the brain from injuries (war, vehicle, and the like) or ingestion of drugs, alcohol, and other substances fall into this category. Alzheimer's disease (degeneration of the brain that results in premature aging) is illustrative of aging disorders, as is dementia senility. Substance-related damage is differentiated from substance use disorders that have not yet resulted in actual brain damage.

Substance Use Disorders

DSM-III states that, in our society, use of substances like coffee, tobacco, alcohol, and caffeine soft drinks to modify mood or behavior under certain circumstances is generally considered as normal and appropriate (p. 163). There are, however, widespread cultural and religious variations in what is considered appropriate.

When more or less regular substance use results in behavioral changes that negatively affect work and leisure productivity, social functioning, or happiness/welfare of family or friends, substance use is labeled a mental disorder. Substance use disorders may be manifested as either *abuse* or *dependence*. Substances may be either legal (coffee, tobacco) or illegal (marijuana, cocaine, amphetamines). Likewise, they may be medically prescribed to control a chronic health problem or available on the open market. The nature of the substance is not relevant; the diagnostic criteria include inability to reduce or stop use and episodes of overuse.

Table 20.1
Types of Schizophrenic Disorders Specified in *DSM-III*

1. *Disordered type:* characterized by marked incoherence and dull, silly, or inappropriate affect, but no delusions.
2. *Catatonic type:* characterized by marked psychomotor disturbance that may range from stupor to purposeless hyperactivity. Catatonic rigidity is the maintenance of a rigid posture against efforts to be moved. Catatonic posturing refers to assumption of inappropriate or bizarre postures.
3. *Paranoid type:* characterized by delusions and/or hallucinations.
4. *Undifferentiated type:* characterized by prominent delusions, hallucinations, incoherence, or grossly disorganized behavior. Meets criteria for more than one type of schizophrenia or for none.
5. *Residual type:* characterized by such chronic signs as social withdrawal, eccentric behavior, dull affect, and illogical thinking, but without prominence of delusions or hallucinations.

Schizophrenic Disorders

This includes numerous conditions, all characterized by deterioration from previous level of functioning and psychotic features and episodes. *DSM-III* defines *psychotic* as a term indicating gross impairment in reality testing. The psychotic features vary from person to person, but generally include disturbances in thought processes, perception, and affect (i.e., emotions or feelings). The person tends to withdraw from and/or distort reality. Distortions include *hallucinations* (perceiving things that do not exist) and *delusions* (interpreting ideas and events in unrealistic, inappropriate ways).

Although the word *schizophrenia* is derived from *schizein* (to split) and *phren* (mind), schizophrenic disorders are no longer described as split personalities, as they used to be. Table 20.1 summarizes the five types of schizophrenia described in *DSM-III*.

Of the mental conditions that require hospitalization, schizophrenic disorders are the most common. Half of all mental patients are schizophrenic. Moreover, 1 of every 100 persons in the world suffers from schizophrenia at some time or another. In the United States, more than a quarter of all hospital beds are filled with patients who have schizophrenia.

DSM-III states that the onset of schizophrenia is usually adolescence or adulthood. Nevertheless, estimates of childhood schizophrenia range from 100,000 to 500,000. There are approximately 4,000 psychotic children in state hospitals, close to 2,500 in residential treatment and day care centers, and at least 3,000 schizophrenic children in day care clinics.

Affective Disorders

These encompass the manic and depressive syndromes and thus are disturbances of mood. They may be bipolar disorders (i.e., characterized by mood shifts from mania to depression and vice versa) or unipolar (usually characterized by episodes of extreme depression). Manic episodes are defined as presence (for at least 1 week) of such behaviors as hyperactivity and restlessness, decreased need for sleep, unusual talkativeness, distractibility manifested as abrupt, rapid changes in activity or topics of speech, inflated self-esteem, and excessive involvement in such high risk activity as reckless driving, buying sprees, sexual indiscretions, and quick business investments. Depressive episodes include loss of interest or pleasure in all or almost all usual activities, too much sleep or insomnia, poor appetite and significant weight loss, low self-esteem, chronic fatigue, diminished ability to think, concentrate, and make decisions, and recurrent thoughts of death and suicide.

Personality Disorders

This broad category characterizes persons whose personality traits are inflexible and maladaptive and cause significant impairment in social, leisure, or vocational functioning. Individuals with personality disorders are grouped into three clusters: (a) persons who appear odd or eccentric, (b) persons who appear antisocial, erratic, or narcissistic, and (c) persons who appear anxious or fearful, as manifested by compulsive, dependent, or passive-aggressive behaviors.

Socially maladjusted and behaviorally disordered children as well as juvenile delinquents fall into this diagnostic category. The term *personality disorders,* however, is not typically assigned until adolescence or adulthood because of the plasticity of childhood behavior.

Disorders in Students

DSM-III separates mental disorders first evident in infancy, childhood, or adolescence from the other 15 diagnostic categories. Table 20.2 lists the conditions included. Although such problems as substance use and schizophrenia often appear in childhood, they are excluded from this diagnostic category because symptoms are the same regardless of age. This section describes disorders not covered elsewhere in the book that affect physical education teaching/learning.

Table 20.2
Disorders Usually First Evident in Infancy, Childhood, or Adolescence

1. Mental retardation
2. Attention deficit disorders
3. Conduct disorders
4. Anxiety disorders
5. Attachment, schizoid, identity, and other disorders
6. Eating disorders, including anorexia nervosa
7. Stereotyped movement disorders
8. Stuttering, bed wetting, sleep terror, and other disorders
9. Pervasive developmental disorders, including autism
10. Specific developmental disorders pertaining to learning and academic success (e.g., reading)

Attention Deficit Disorders

Signs are developmentally inappropriate inattention, impulsivity, and hyperactivity. Onset is about 3 years of age, but the disorder is often not diagnosed until problems occur at school. The disorder is 10 times more common in boys than girls and seems to appear more often in some families than others (i.e., there appears to be a genetic predisposition). Other predisposing factors are mental retardation, convulsive disorders, and some forms of cerebral palsy and other neurological disorders. The PL 94–142 category of learning disabilities has a high prevalence of attention deficit disorders. *DSM-III* estimates that 3% of prepubertal United States children exhibit this disorder.

Conduct Disorders

This is characterized by repetitive and persistent behaviors that violate the basic rights of others and/or the norms and rules of society. Children in this category are divided in four subtypes. *Undersocialized* children are unable to establish a normal degree of affection, empathy, or bond with others; there is typically a lack of concern for anyone but self and little or no guilt is felt. *Socialized* types of conduct disorders show social attachment to some persons, but are unduly callous or manipulative toward individuals to whom they are not attached. *Aggressive* types are those who exhibit any kind of physical violence; this includes theft, property damage, and intimidation or harm of persons and/or animals. *Nonaggressive* types are characterized by absence of violence. Nonaggressive behaviors include lying, truancy, running away, and substance use.

Conduct disorders are more prevalent in children of adults who have mental disorders, particularly those in the substance user category. With the exception of the undersocialized type, conduct disorders are more common in males than females, with the prevalence ratios ranging from 4:1 to 12:1.

Anxiety Disorders

This category includes students who exhibit abnormal and persistent fears and/or unrealistic worries. After 18 years of age this condition is called *agoraphobia*. It also includes students who persistently shrink from contact with strangers (avoidant disorders). Initial learning in swimming, gymnastics, and other physical education activities causes some students considerable anxiety. It is important to determine whether these behaviors are specific to the gymnasium or part of a generalized pattern.

Attachment, Schizoid, Identity, and Other Disorders

This broad category includes behaviors not otherwise classifiable that pertain to immature emotional functioning and poorly developed social responsiveness. Disturbances in this category are not due to autism, mental retardation, or physical disabilities. *Schizoid* should not be confused with schizophrenia. Schizoid disorders are defects in the ability to form social relationships accompanied by lack of concern about social isolation; the condition is relatively rare and should be differentiated from normal individual differences in social reticence. *Identity disorders* (which are associated mostly with adolescence) pertain primarily to self-concept, friendship patterns, and gender orientation.

Eating Disorders

This category includes gross disturbances in eating behaviors. Most common are anorexia nervosa and bulimia. Although these may occur at any age, their first manifestation is almost always in childhood or adolescence.

Anorexia nervosa is a condition characterized by significant weight loss, refusal to maintain normal body weight, disturbance of body image, and intense fear of becoming obese. In females, it is accompanied by amenorrhea (cessation of menstrual periods). The disorder occurs primarily in females (95%). The prevalence rate for females in the 12- to 18-year-old age range is about 1 of every 250. This condition leads to death by starvation in about 15–21% of the treated

Table 20.3
Movement Disorders Not Associated with Mental Illness

1. Choreiform. Random, irregular, nonrepetitive dancelike movements.
2. Dystonic. Slow, twisting movements interspersed with prolonged states of muscular tension.
3. Athetoid. Slow, irregular, writhing movements.
4. Myoclonic. Brief, shocklike muscle contractions that affect one muscle or its parts, but not entire muscle groups.
5. Spasms. Stereotypic movements that affect groups of muscle. Slower and more prolonged than tics.

cases. Hospitalization is generally required to prevent starvation. The major diagnostic criterion is permanent weight loss of at least 25% of original body weight.

Bulimia is a condition characterized by recurrent episodes of binge eating (the consumption of huge quantities in 2 hours or less), awareness that the eating pattern is abnormal, fear of being unable to stop eating voluntarily, and depressed mood following eating binges. The disorder is more common in females than males and typically begins in adolescence or early adulthood. Persons with bulimia are usually within a normal weight range, but they exhibit frequent weight fluctuations because of alternating binges and fasts. They try to control weight by dieting, self-induced vomiting, or the use of laxatives and medicines. Bulimia is seldom totally incapacitating, although it may affect social, leisure, and vocational functioning. Unlike anorexia nervosa, it does not result in death when untreated. It is, in fact, very much like alcohol and substance abuse.

Stereotyped Movement Disorders

This category includes persons with tics, stereotypic movement patterns (often called blindisms or autistic-like movements), and Tourette's syndrome. They may be independent disorders or coexist with such handicapping conditions as deaf-blindness, blindness, autism, and severe mental retardation.

Tics are defined by *DSM-III* as involuntary rapid movements of related skeletal muscles or involuntary production of noises or words. Tics should be differentiated from other kinds of movement disorders (choreiform, dystonic, athetoid, myoclonic, spastic) that are not encompassed by this diagnostic category (see Table 20.3).

Stereotypic movement refers to voluntary habits or mannerisms that appear to be pleasurable. This category includes rocking, head banging, repetitive hand movements, bizarre posturing, and other movements.

Tourette's syndrome is a condition characterized by multiple vocal tics and the presence of involuntary, repetitive, rapid, purposeless movements of multiple muscle groups. Its onset is typically between 2 and 13 years of age, and its duration is usually lifelong, although there may be periods of remission.

Prevalence varies from 1 to 5 per 10,000 (i.e., about the same as Down's syndrome or autism). The disorder affects three times as many males as females. Vocalizations in Tourette's syndrome are described as clicks, grunts, yelps, barks, sniffs, coughs, and words.

About 60% of persons with this condition experience an irresistible urge to utter obscenities. The symptoms are heightened by stress, but disappear during sleep and sometimes during daytime activities that are particularly absorbing.

Implications for Physical Education

Sports, dance, and aquatics are often viewed as vehicles for the amelioration of behavior disorders. Team membership can be made meaningful enough that a youngster will curb unsocialized behaviors. The physical educator soon learns to help aggressive children express their hostility in socially acceptable ways (see Figure 20.2): punching a bag, jumping, leaping,

Figure 20.2   Tetherball is a group activity in which hostility can be released in socially acceptable ways.

throwing, pushing, and pulling. Offensive strokes like the smash and skills like the volleyball spike can be practiced when tension is especially great. It sometimes helps to paint faces on the balls and punching bags. The teacher can join in stomping empty food cans, paper cups turned upside down, and balloons. The making of noise itself relieves tension.

It is important that children learn that it is acceptable to take out aggressions on things but never on persons or animals. Thus, boxing or wrestling against other children is contraindicated for some emotionally disturbed children who have not yet mastered control of their emotions. Aggressive children often can be developed into good squad leaders. Always they demand special attention—a personal "Hello, John" at the *first* of the period and the frequent use of their names throughout the class instruction.

More difficult to cope with are withdrawing and overanxious behaviors. Most authorities concur that children should not be forced to participate in activities that they fear or intensely dislike. Swimming, tumbling, and apparatus seem to evoke withdrawal reactions more often than do other physical education activities. In normal children, these fears gradually subside when it becomes obvious that the peer group is having fun. Coaxing, cajoling, and reasoning accomplish little other than giving the child the extra attention he or she may be seeking. In the case of actual behavior disorders, psychotherapy and other specialized techniques are generally needed. The physical educator should work cooperatively with the school psychologist in strengthening the child's self-confidence and feelings of worth.

Placement of Emotionally Disturbed Students

Although most emotionally disturbed (ED) children live at home and are educated in public schools, some (especially within the 16- to 21-year old age range) are hospitalized and receive treatment similar to adult mental patients. An excellent hospital education and treatment program is described by Northcutt and Tipton (1978), who emphasize the importance of structure. At the time of initial hospital placement, ED adolescents are typically confused, anxious, delusional, and angry. Hospitalization is a last resort, generally indicating the need for vigorous use of antipsychotic drugs (chemotherapy) and, for perhaps 5% of the patients, electroshock therapy.

During this initial stage, formal education is typically limited to recreation classes. These provide a wide range of activities including rhythmic exercise, dance, yoga, and arts and crafts. Emphasis is upon success and immediate reward. These classes are mostly taught by therapeutic recreation or physical education personnel with strong backgrounds in psychology. During the first weeks in the hospital, however, the major thrust is determining which medications should be prescribed and how much; equally important is control of medication side effects that may include drowsiness, listlessness, muscle stiffness, nausea, blurred vision, and others.

When students can concentrate on simple structured tasks and are no longer dangerous to selves or others, they are moved to the intermediate unit, which offers more freedom. Additionally, the intermediate unit provides scheduled small group instruction (8 to 10 students) in academic subjects, including physical education, art, and music. Emphasis at this stage is more on learning to assume responsibility for behavior (attending classes on time, managing anger and aggression, and acting appropriately) than on learning subject matter. A token economy and other behavior management techniques are used.

Within a few months, the student moves to the day school, which is as much as possible like a regular public school. The major difference is that classes are individualized and self-paced by the students. Emphasis is placed on their independently setting and achieving goals. Most adolescents are hospitalized for less than 1 year.

Successful mainstream reentry is obviously dependent upon public school personnel adherring to the same education principles as hospital personnel. Chief among these is minimizing stress and ensuring success. The techniques that follow are appropriate for either hospital or school personnel. The disciplines of therapeutic recreation and dance therapy emphasize working with mental disorders more than does physical education. Thus, persons from these fields make excellent consultants.

Techniques for Working with Schizophrenic Students

Wolman (1970) cites four principles that guide work with schizophrenic students: (a) graded reversal of deterioration; (b) constructive progress; (c) education toward reality; and (d) directive guidance. Under the first principle, he emphasizes, *We do not remove, take apart, or take away whatever neurotic defenses the schizophrenic child possesses. We build upon what we find.* It is essential that the child not feel disapproval and not be criticized for acting like a baby. The growth process is likened to the normal child's transition from a nipple to a cup. The nipple is not taken away, but the cup is made as attractive as possible. For a while, the child uses both and then gradually rejects the nipple. The principle of constructive progress implies the addition of new, more mature, and tempting elements to life. Since the schizophrenic child is afraid of growing up, he or she must be lured and/or bribed into accepting adolescence and adulthood.

Schizophrenic students typically are trying to escape reality through withdrawal. Therefore, no therapeutic procedure is more important than reality testing. This necessitates acquainting the student with the physical and social environment and shifting his or her attention from the inner world of fantasy toward the real world of happenings. Since the normal child's world centers about play, physical education is tremendously important in this process. When the child tries to attribute monsterlike qualities to playground apparatus or magical powers to a jiggler or ball, as Jordi does in the opening paragraph, the physical educator must convince the child of the true nature of the things about him or her. It is wrong to *play along* with the fantasy of an emotionally disturbed person. Likewise, the educator should not *play along* with hallucinations or ask questions pertaining to them, thereby appearing to be interested. Recommended responses to hallucinations are, "You know that is not true" or "That doesn't make sense."

Directive guidance, the fourth principle, emphasizes the importance of telling students the difference between right and wrong rather than hoping they will learn for themselves in a laissez-faire environment. Schizophrenic children, to become whole, must become well-adjusted adults in a *given* society. They must believe in the value of rules and laws and be capable of accepting the power figures in our society: umpires, police officers, teachers, and administrators. Helping children to understand the structure of games and the importance of rules and penalties in facilitating good play is often a first step toward wellness.

Schizophrenic children do not respond well to firm discipline, as do normal children. They are terrified by external power, both real and imagined.

A schizophrenic child becomes more paranoid when treated with firmness. He considers it proof of his paranoid ideas. But a loving, soothing attitude of a familiar, affectionate adult will bring him back to normal behavior. (Wolman, 1970, p. 20)

Whereas normal children may feel hostile to authority figures, they can do so without acting out and without excessive guilt. In schizophrenic children, even small bits of criticism may elicit destructive behavior. The physical educator should understand that hostility is basically a protective reaction of the organism to danger. The schizophrenic feels much more endangered by criticism and/or even helpful suggestions than can be imagined. Yet such students must be given firm limits. An important part of their reality testing is the growing knowledge that there are adults who do not get angry when they misbehave. The physical educator must combine friendliness and warmth with consistent enforcement of limits. Should a temper tantrum occur, it is better not to try to talk over the noise. A child driven by panic or rage is out of contact with reality, and reasoning will not help. Sometimes there is no alternative but physical restraint to stop aggressive behavior.

The following suggestions may help the teacher in working with schizophrenic and/or overly aggressive students.

1. Avoid conflict with the child that might cause temper tantrums. Overlook minor transgressions. Each temper tantrum is a step backward.

2. If the child becomes aggressive, try to distract him or her. Get the child interested in some new toy or game.

3. Should a child strike or bite you, do not become ruffled or angry. In a cool, calculated manner, say something like "Ouch, that hurt! What in the world did I do to cause you to bite me?"

4. Do not show fear or confusion about the child's behavior. Schizophrenic students tend to be extrasensitive to the feelings of teachers and may use such information to manipulate the adult. Never say, for instance, "I just don't understand you" or "I don't know what to do with you."

5. Do not use threats or physical violence or abandonment. Do not punish the child, since punishment reinforces paranoid beliefs.

6. Reward good behavior and structure the situation so as to avoid bad behavior.

7. Create situations for learning to relate socially to others in movement exploration (see Figure 20.3), dance, and individual and dual sports before pushing the child into the complex human relationships of team sport strategy.

8. Structure play groups and/or class squads very carefully, ascertaining that a balance is maintained between the number of aggressive and the number of passive children. The school psychologist may help the physical educator with this endeavor.

Techniques for Working with Depressed Children and Adolescents

Extreme depression can characterize any age group. Depressive symptoms are present in approximately 40% of the adolescent suicide attempts. The incidence of suicide is rising among young children as well as teenagers, where it is already the third leading cause of death in this country.

The depressed child typically reveals social withdrawal (Figure 20.4), loss of initiative, a decrease in appetite, and difficulty in sleeping. Such children generally have a self-depreciating attitude, believe that they are bad, and wish to punish themselves. Suicide,

Figure 20.3 Sharing a piece of tubular jersey during a guided movement exploration lesson helps two children to begin to relate to each other socially in a nonthreatening setting.

Figure 20.4 Depressed persons tend to withdraw. Here, Dr. Karen DePauw guides a rhythmic activity and encourages involvement.

truancy, self-destructive behaviors like head banging and disobedience may all be behavioral equivalents of depression.

More than anything else, depressed persons need to be kept active. Yet they often refuse to participate in physical activity. They have no desire to learn new skills since life is not worth living and they intend to kill themselves anyway. Some depressed persons will sit for days, crying and thinking of methods of suicide. Whereas most of us are inclined to sympathize with anyone who cries, it is best to display a rough, noncommittal exterior. For instance, the patient may be asked, "Do you play golf?" The typical response is a self-depreciating, "I'm not any good" or "I'm not good enough to play with so-and-so." Instead of trying to build up the patient's ego, as a teacher might do with a well person, it is best to agree and make a statement like "That's probably true!" In other words, the teacher should mirror or restate the patient's thoughts rather than contradict him or her. Psychologists concur that praise and compliments serve only to make the truly depressed person feel more unworthy. They feel guilty when others say good things about them and/or are nice to them.

Severe depression is often treated by electric shock therapy (EST) and antidepressant medications. The teacher or therapist cooperates with the psychiatric staff by maintaining a full schedule of physical activities for the depressed patient, who generally follows instructions but will not engage in recreational activities voluntarily. One of the greatest problems of depressed patients is learning to recognize and cope with the anger that they turn inward toward themselves, thereby causing the state of depression. If they can be made angry by an external force and helped to express this anger outwardly instead of repressing it, a major goal is accomplished. Situations must be devised to make them angry enough to risk standing up for themselves, a first step back to self-respect and self-love. In one situation this was accomplished by awaking five severely depressed patients before dawn and insisting that they were scheduled for a 6 AM swimming class. Without breakfast, they were ushered into an ice cold outdoor pool and told they must stay in the water. In addition to these unpleasantries, the therapist scolded and ridiculed them. Typically, the depressed person submits to such a program, but if the unpleasantries are intense enough, there may be mild protests. When these are autocratically ignored, real anger can sometimes be evoked. Whatever techniques are used, the teacher or therapist must work closely with the psychiatric staff.

Serious Emotional Disturbances **489**

Each depressed person is uniquely different from others, and no single approach can be recommended. Physical education and recreation personnel should remember, however, that their primary role is to engage the patient in activity, not to listen to sad stories and self-criticism. Other staff members are employed specifically to listen and conduct verbal therapy.

Adapting the Public School Program

Students whose problems are so severe that they meet PL 94–142 eligibility requirements for special services probably need separate, adapted physical education instruction in a class not larger than 12 students. Within special education the average pupil-teacher ratio across the country varies from 12:1 to 21:1, depending upon the nature of the disability. The special education average pupil-teacher ratio is lower for ED classes (12:1) than for any other disability except for severely multiply handicapped children. Small class size in physical education, as in special education, is probably the single most important criterion for success.

Behavior management techniques comprise the major pedagogy in most schools. Research by Vogler and French (1983) explains in detail the use of a behavior management strategy called the *Good Behavior Game.* This technique primarily focuses upon helping students understand and conform to on-task behavior. Tokens in the form of frowny faces are given to class squads (six students in size) for each student who is not on task. Squads with the fewest tokens are rewarded with free time.

In addition to group management techniques, there must be individual time for sharing with students. Teachers who work with ED children should undertake graduate work in counseling and psychology to increase the effectiveness of their communication skills. Although teacher-imposed structure is important, the goal should be helping the student to manage increasing freedom and assume responsibility for his or her actions.

Learning Activities

1. Read biographies, autobiographies, and novels about mental disorders (*I Never Promised You a Rose Garden,* by Joanne Greenberg; *Sybil,* by Flora R. Schreiber; *Dibs,* by Virginia Axline; *The Savage God: A Study of Suicide,* by A. Alvarez; and *The Bell Jar,* by Sylvia Plath). Give book reports in class or create some method of sharing. Do such books encompass exercise and physical activity? How?

2. Invite a school counselor or psychologist to class to discuss common problems in the public schools and responsibilities that teachers have in working with mental health personnel.

3. Visit a halfway house or residential facility for persons with severe emotional disturbance. Observe group therapy, exercise, and recreation sessions.

4. Invite a recreation specialist who is employed in a facility for emotionally disturbed persons to speak to your class.

5. Enroll in courses in counseling and psychology to broaden your knowledge base about treatment approaches.

References

American Psychiatric Association. (1980). *Diagnostic and statistical manual of mental disorders* (3rd ed.). Washington, DC: Author.

Bishop, D. (Ed.). (1980). *Behavioral problems of the disabled: Assessment and management.* Baltimore: Williams & Wilkins.

Northcutt, J., & Tipton, G. (1978). Teaching severely mentally ill and emotionally disturbed adolescents. *Exceptional Children, 45*(1), 18–23.

Rubin, T. I. (1962). *Jordi, Lisa, and David.* New York: Macmillian.

Vogler, E. W., & French, R. (1983). The effects of a group contingency strategy on behaviorally disordered students in physical education. *Research Quarterly for Exercise and Sport, 54*(3), 273–277.

Wolman, B. B. (1970). *Children without childhood.* New York: Grune & Stratton.

Bibliography

Allen, J. (1980). Jogging can modify disruptive behaviors. *Teaching Exceptional Children, 12,* 66–70.

American Alliance for Health, Physical Education, and Recreation. (1976). *Physical education, recreation, and related programs for autistic and emotionally disturbed.* Washington, DC: Author.

Baker, A. (1979). Cognitive functioning of psychotic children: A reappraisal. *Exceptional Children, 45,* 344–348.

Bandura, A. (1973). *Aggression: A social learning analysis.* Englewood Cliffs, NJ: Prentice-Hall.

Bloom, R., & Hopewell, L. (1982). Psychiatric hospitalization of adolescents and successful mainstream reentry. *Exceptional Children, 48*(4), 352–357.

Brown, B. J. (1976). The influence of a physical education program on the basic motor fitness of emotionally disturbed children. *American Corrective Therapy Journal, 30,* 15–20.

Byers, E. S. (1979). Wilderness camping as a therapy for emotionally disturbed children: A critical review. *Exceptional Children, 45,* 628–637.

Dozier, J. E., Lewis, S., Kersey, A. G., & Charping, J. W. (1978). Sports group: An alternative treatment modality for emotionally disturbed adolescents. *Adolescence, 13*(15), 483–488.

Dunlap, G., Kaegel, R. L., & Egel, A. L. (1979). Autistic children in school. *Exceptional Children, 45,* 552–559.

Dunn, J., & French, R. (1982). Operant conditioning: A tool for special physical educators in the 80s. *Exceptional Education Quarterly, 3*(1), 42–53.

Ertel, D., & Voyat, G. (1982). Sensorimotor analysis of early onset childhood psychosis. *Teachers College Record, 84*(2), 433–447.

Ferdinande, R., & Colligan, R. (1980). Psychiatric hospitalization: Mainstream reentry planning for adolescent patients. *Exceptional Children, 46,* 544–548.

Forness, S. (1981). Concepts of learning and behavior disorders: Implications for research and practice. *Exceptional Children, 48*(1), 56–64.

Gallagher, P. (1979). *Teaching students with behavior disorders.* Denver: Love Publishing Co.

Gruber, J., & Noland, M. (1977). Perceptual-motor and scholastic achievement relationships in emotionally disturbed elementary school children. *Research Quarterly, 48,* 68–73.

Hersen, M., Eisler, R., & Miller, P. (Eds.). (1983). *Progress in behavior modification.* New York: Academic Press.

Hewett, F. (1980). *The emotionally disturbed child in the classroom* (2nd ed.). Boston: Allyn & Bacon.

Hilsendager, D., Jack, H., & Mann, L. (n.d.). *Basic motor fitness test for emotionally disturbed and mentally handicapped.* Philadelphia: Temple University. (See Project ACTIVE materials.)

Hilsendager, D., Jack, H., & Mann, L. (1968). The buttonwood farms project. *Journal of Health, Physical Education, and Recreation, 39,* 46–48.

Jansma, P. (1972). *Behavior modification principles applied to male adolescents by a physical educator in a mental hospital.* Unpublished doctoral dissertation, University of Wisconsin, Madison.

Kauffman, J., & Lewis, C. D. (Eds.). (1974). *Teaching children with behavior disorders: Personal perspectives.* Columbus, OH: Charles E. Merrill.

Knoblock, P. (1983). *Teaching emotionally disturbed children.* Hopewell, NJ: Houghton Mifflin.

Konopka, G. (1983). Adolescent suicide. *Exceptional Children, 49*(5), 390–394.

Lowry, T. (Ed.). (1974). *Camping therapy: Its uses in psychiatry and rehabilitation.* Springfield, IL: Charles C. Thomas.

Mann, L., Hilsendager, D., & Jack, H. (1973). *A comparison of three methods of physical education programming for emotionally disturbed children.* Final Report, USOE Grant No. OEG-0-70-3557(607).

Marlowe, M., Algozzine, B., Lerch, H. H., & Welch, P. D. (1978). The games analysis intervention as a method of decreasing feminine play patterns of emotionally disturbed boys. *Research Quarterly, 49,* 484–490.

Moran, J., & Kalakian, L. (1977). *Movement experiences for the mentally retarded or emotionally disturbed child* (2nd ed.). Minneapolis: Burgess.

Noland, M., & Gruber, J. (1976). Relationships between selected personality and motor variables in emotionally disturbed children. *Research Quarterly, 47,* 741–749.

Parker, R. (1975). The comprehensive evaluation in recreation therapy scale: A tool for patient evaluation. *Therapeutic Recreation Journal, 9*(4), 143–154.

Pfeffer, C. (1981). Suicidal behavior of children. *Exceptional Children, 48*(92), 170–172.

Poindexter, H. B. (1969). Motor development and performance of emotionally disturbed children. *Journal of Health, Physical Education, and Recreation, 40,* 69–71.

Politino, V. (1979). *Attitudes toward physical activity and self-concept of normal and emotionally disturbed children.* Unpublished doctoral dissertation, Southern Illinois University, Carbondale.

Rider, B. A. (1973). Perceptual motor dysfunction in emotionally disturbed children. *American Journal of Occupational Therapy, 26*(6), 316–320.

Romananczk, R. G. (1975). Increasing isolate and social play in severely disturbed children: Intervention and postintervention effectiveness. *Journal of Autism and Childhood Schizophrenia, 5,* 57–70.

Rosen, E. (1974). *Dance in psychotherapy.* New York: Dance Horizons.

Stott, D. (1978). Association of motor impairment with various types of behavior disturbance. *Journal of Learning Disabilities, 11,* 147–154.

Swanson, H. L., & Reinert, H. (1979). *Teaching strategies for children in conflict.* St. Louis: C. V. Mosby.

21 Orthopedic Impairments

Figure 21.1 Wheelchair square dance.

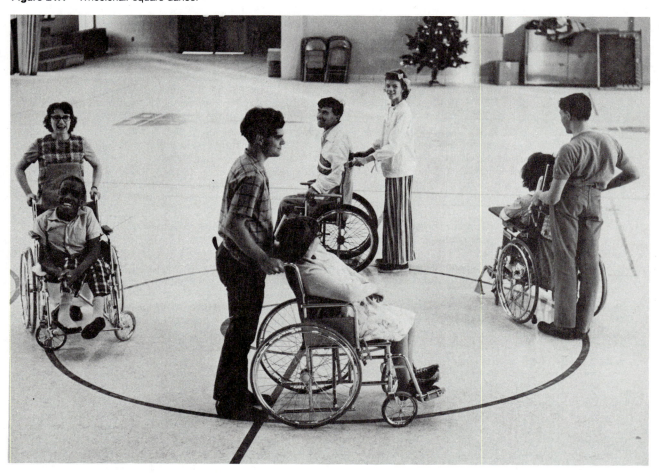

The handicapped child has a right:

1. To as vigorous a body as human skill can give him.
2. To an education so adapted to his handicap that he can be economically independent and have the chance for the fullest life of which he is capable.
3. To be brought up and educated by those who understand the nature of the burden he has to bear and who consider it a privilege to help him bear it.
4. To grow up in a world which does not set him apart, which looks at him, not with scorn or pity or ridicule—but which welcomes him, exactly as it welcomes every child, which offers him identical privileges and identical responsibilities.
5. To a life on which his handicap casts no shadow but which is full day by day with those things which make it worthwhile, with comradeship, love, work, play, laughter, and tears—a life in which these things bring continually increasing growth, richness, release of energies, joy in achievement. (White House Conference, 1933)

Chapter Objectives

After you have studied this chapter, you should be able to

1. Discuss the importance of physical educators understanding the eligibility requirements, classification systems, and competitive events of the different sports organizations. Indicate your knowledge of each of these for the NWAA, NWBA, and USAAA. (Review Chapter 8 for information on NWBA.)

2. Discuss the inclusion of wheelchair sports in the curriculum of a regular (but integrated) physical education program.

3. Identify the four most common congenital orthopedic conditions, describe each, and discuss physical education programming.

4. Define *osteochondroses,* discuss the most common types, and state recommendations for physical education.

5. Differentiate between slipped femoral epiphysis (adolescent coxa vara), dysplasia, subluxation, luxation and pathological dislocation of the hip (coxa valga). Discuss each in relation to physical education.

6. Explain trauma (including thermal injuries) and disease as causes of orthopedic disabilities. State examples of each, describe rehabilitation, and discuss physical education programming.

7. Differentiate between congenital and acquired amputations, give examples of each, and discuss fitting of prostheses, rehabilitation, and physical education programming.

8. Identify and describe the nine USAAA sports classifications and discuss sports in relation to each.

9. Identify and describe the five NWAA sports classifications and discuss sports in relation to each.

10. Differentiate between physical education, occupational therapy, and physical therapy goals for persons with different levels of spinal cord injury.

11. Discuss fitness (both assessment and programming) in relation to orthopedic disabilities.

12. Given age, gender, and a description of psychomotor functioning of hypothesized orthopedically impaired students, write physical education IEPs. Substantiate your choice of placement as integration, partial integration, or separate.

13. Discuss available and needed research on physical education and athletics for OI students.

. . . But I, that am not shaped for sportive tricks,
Nor made to court an amorous looking-glass;
I, that am rudely stamp'd, and want love's majesty
To strut before a wanton ambling nymph;
I, that am curtail'd of this fair proportion,
Cheated of feature by dissembling nature,
Deform'd, unfinish'd, sent before my time
Into this breathing world, scarce half made up,
And that so lamely and unfashionable
That dogs bark at me as I halt by them;
Why, I, in this weak piping time of peace,
Have no delight to pass away the time,
Unless to spy my shadow in the sun,
And descant on mine own deformity;

King Richard III

This quotation from Shakespeare offers some insight into the problems of body image and self-concept experienced by handicapped students. In a society that holds physical attractiveness in high esteem, the orthopedically different person is confronted with unattainable goals. He or she can be taught that beauty comes from within. This truism does not, however, alleviate loneliness or the teasing to which the ugly or awkward child is subjected.

Philosophy

Much of the harassment experienced by such children occurs during free play. It could be minimized if supervised physical education were provided and non-handicapped children were taught acceptance of individual differences. It is ironic indeed that high level athletes equate their abilities with those of other competitors through carefully structured systems of handicaps in golf, bowling, and other sports, whereas pupils in physical education are treated as though individual differences do not exist.

In physical education, *why* must all students

1. Score the same number of points for a basket or goal regardless of their height, weight, and motor coordination?
2. Cover the same distance in a relay?
3. Stand on the same starting line?
4. Have the same number of safeties in tag games?
5. Have the same number of serves in volleyball, tennis, and badminton?
6. Have the same number of strikes in softball and baseball?
7. Have the same tempo of music in folk dance?

Students should be taught to sit down together, appraise individual and team strengths and weaknesses, and devise systems of handicaps that give everyone a fair chance at winning. The presence of physically handicapped students in a classroom can lead to new insights in the utilization of human resources and the implementation of democratic beliefs (Figure 21.1). By adult standards, students may be cruel in their honest assessment of potentials and their uninhibited curiosity about physical defects. This openness is balanced by an uncanny sense of fair play and concern for one another's welfare. The first principle in integrating a physically different student into the normal group is to guide the pupils in the solution of their own problem: How can we change the game so that everyone can play an approximately equal amount of time, experience challenge, and have fun? The problem solving should not focus exclusively upon the integration of one person, but, rather, the wise utilization of the diversified talents of each group member.

This chapter describes only those conditions which render students eligible for sports participation under the aegis of the National Wheelchair Athletic Association (NWAA), the National Wheelchair Basketball Association (NWBA), the National Handicapped Sports and Recreation Association (NHSRA), and the United States Amputee Athletic Association (USAAA). Many persons who do not use wheelchairs for daily living activities engage in sports competition as members of these organizations. Since a major purpose of school physical education is to teach activities

for leisure-time use that hopefully will carry over into adulthood, the physical educator needs to learn as much as possible about these organizations and the sports they govern.

Until the late 1970s, *wheelchair sports* was a generic term that applied to all persons with a *significant, permanent, physical disability of the lower extremities that prevents full participation with able-bodied peers* (wording paraphrased from the NWAA handbook). This concept still applies to wheelchair basketball, which in 1984 adopted a new classification system based on assessment of functional abilities rather than anatomical site of lesion (see Chapter 8). For other activities, however, NWAA wheelchair sports now include mostly persons with limps caused by orthopedic defects and/or muscular weakness (paresis) or paralysis caused by spina bifida, spinal cord injuries, or polio. Lower limb amputees may compete in the open division of NWAA sports, but since 1981 they have had their own organization, which provides competition for persons with either upper or lower limb defects.

Persons no longer eligible for NWAA wheelchair sports are those with cerebral palsy and other locomotor disabilities (les autres) like muscular dystrophy, multiple sclerosis, osteogenesis imperfecta, and dwarfism. The National Association of Sports for Cerebral Palsy (NASCP), founded in 1978, conducts both wheelchair and ambulatory sports for these persons and is working toward the formation of a United States organization specifically for les autres. Cerebral palsy and les autres conditions are therefore covered in separate chapters in this book.

The term *wheelchair sports* should therefore be preceded by NWAA, NASCP, or USAAA to denote the population served. These organizations limit their sports to persons with normal intellectual functioning. Special Olympics offers wheelchair activities for mentally retarded persons. The widespread association of the word *special* with mental retardation makes this word unacceptable to most persons with other disabilities. Teachers should therefore avoid calling sports events and/or physical education for physically disabled individuals Special Physical Education or Special Events Day.

The basic philosophy underlying this chapter and several others in this book is that *disabled students should receive at least part of their physical education in the mainstream* (see Figure 21.2). Within that setting, however, instruction should be adapted to individual differences with game rules changed to permit equal opportunities for success among all students. Classification systems should be used when students are placed on teams to ensure equal distribution of abilities. School physical education should be for the learning of skills, rules, strategies, and habits, not competition per se. Only when game rules are adapted can learning for all students occur.

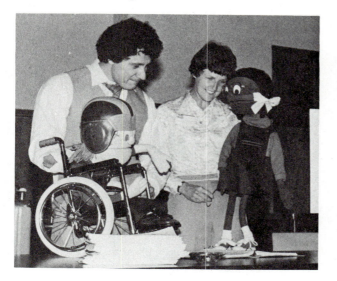

Figure 21.2 Puppets and dolls with disabilities can be used to facilitate understanding of wheelchairs and architectural barriers in the mainstream setting.

Figure 21.3 Randy Snow, wheelchair tennis champ, conducts workshops around the country to emphasize that many individual sports can be adapted for mobility-impaired persons. The opponent can be either ambulatory or nonambulatory.

All schools with an enrollment of 300 or more should have at least two sports wheelchairs as part of their permanent physical education equipment. These chairs should be used in both mainstream and separate adapted physical education by both disabled and able-bodied students. In team sports practice and competition, one chair can be integrated within each team; who is in the chair is relatively unimportant since all students can benefit from exposure to wheelchair sports. The orthopedically impaired student, however, has no opportunity to develop locomotor sports skills generalizable to adulthood unless wheelchairs are provided. Wheelchairs can be integrated into all physical education instruction: dance, individual sports (see Figure 21.3), relays, challenge courses, and adventure activities. Equal learning opportunity for orthopedically impaired and able-bodied students can be ensured only through the provision of wheelchairs. This aspect of instruction should therefore be written into the IEP.

As this chapter is studied, remember that many students who do not own wheelchairs and who do not need them for everyday living should receive wheelchair instruction. This includes all students with a limp or impairment that slows running speed and thus places them at a disadvantage when participating with able-bodied peers. All such students are eligible for NWAA, NWBA, or USAAA competition and have the right, as do able-bodied peers, to learn skills in school that prepare them for competition in interscholastic and/or club sports.

The alternative to providing wheelchair instruction is to limit the physical education curriculum to upper extremity activities done from a stationary position (archery, riflery, table tennis, horseshoes,

bowling), swimming, and horseback riding. No student should be forced to sit on the sidelines or serve as score-keeper or official because an activity in which he or she cannot participate fully is being taught. During such units as basketball, football, and soccer, if wheelchair integration is not deemed appropriate, students with orthopedic problems should be rotated into separate, adapted physical education.

Terminology

Persons who use prostheses, wear braces, maneuver wheelchairs, or ambulate with the aid of crutches or canes bear many labels: crippled, disabled, impaired, handicapped. Each has a personal preference as to what he or she wishes to be called and should be asked about that preference. Some authors assign slightly different meanings to each term, but this practice seems merely to be playing with words. The Office of Special Education, Department of Education, Washington, DC recognizes a category designated *orthopedically impaired* (OI). In this chapter, this term will be used interchangeably with related labels to denote a person of normal intelligence who has been deprived of part or full use of his or her limbs and whose condition is more or less static and incurable. OI persons are further described as *ambulatory* or *nonambulatory*, depending upon their independence in locomotor activities. Particular orthopedic handicaps are described as *congenital* and/or *chronic* or as *acquired* and/or *acute*. Some disabilities, such as growth disorders, are temporary, although most are permanent.

Congenital Conditions

Congenital and/or chronic conditions are birth defects. When abnormalities of structure or function are apparent at birth, they are called *congenital*. When they appear later in life but are genetically caused, they are termed *chronic*. The etiology of birth defects is often unknown. It is estimated that 20% are hereditary, 20% are environmental in the sense that viral, parasitic, or bacterial infections of the pregnant mother affected the fetus, and 60% result from an interaction of hereditary and environmental factors.

The four most common congenital orthopedic defects, in order of their frequency of occurrence, are *club foot; cleft lip* and/or *cleft palate; spina bifida;* and *congenital dislocation of the hip.* The need for adapted physical education depends upon the extent to which the condition was corrected in infancy and early childhood. Bracing, casting, and surgical techniques have advanced so much that the casual observer often cannot detect birth defects. Conceivably, the psychological effects of spending months in casts and braces, of hospitals and surgery at so young an age, and the oversolicitous attitudes of parents and siblings may leave the child more handicapped than the original defect. Certainly, the life experiences of such pupils have been grossly different from those of normal children, and mild emotional disturbances, feelings of inferiority, and overcompensation are fairly common. It is recommended that all prospective teachers read *Of Human Bondage,* as an introduction to this chapter. It is W. Somerset Maugham's semiautobiographical novel about the effects of a club foot on normal growth and development.

Acquired Conditions

Acquired and/or acute conditions are those which arise from trauma, disease, or disorders of growth and development. *Trauma* encompasses conditions stemming from motor vehicle accidents, falls, fires, firearms, and explosives. Each year accidents injure and disable approximately 10 million Americans, of whom 40,000 to 50,000 are children. Almost one half of these accidents occur in the home, with *falls* causing the most injuries among the total population and *fires* resulting in the most among persons ages 1 through 44. Burns are discussed in detail in this chapter because they are the number one cause of disability under the broad category of trauma and often result in amputations. *Disease,* as a cause of orthopedic handicaps, includes cancer, poliomyelitis, osteomyelitis, and many others. *Disorders of growth and development,* sometimes called the *osteochondroses,* may occur in over 50 anatomical sites.

Temporary Orthopedic Problems

Since adapted physical education philosophy emphasizes *no excuses* from physical education, it is essential that the teacher understand problems and adapt for them. Some problems, such as growth disorders, last 1 or 2 years and arrest themselves. Others only temporarily affect physical education because they are corrected by surgery or bracing.

Growth Disorders

The physical educator working with junior high or middle school youngsters is confronted with a high incidence of *osteochondroses* or growth plate disorders. Such diagnoses as *Perthes' disease, Osgood-Schlatter disease, Kohler's disease, Calve's disease, and Scheuermann's disease* all fall within this category and demand adaptations in physical education.

An osteochondrosis is an abnormality of an *epiphysis* (growth plate) in which normal growth or ossification is disturbed. The etiology is generally unknown, although trauma is sometimes suspected. The terms *osteochondrosis, osteochondritis juvenilis, apophysitis,* and *growth plate disorders* are all used interchangeably.

A brief review of the growth and development of bones contributes to an understanding of the osteochondroses. Skeletal growth in the fetus consists of the transformation of hyaline cartilage and fibrous membranes into bone by the processes of endochondral and intramembranosus ossification. This transformation is not complete at the time of birth. Throughout childhood cartilage is slowly being replaced by bone (see Figure 21.4). Moreover, existing bone continues to grow in diameter and length until adult skeletal dimensions are reached.

The growth plate is the structure responsible for longitudinal growth of the immature bone, which has the following identifiable parts:

1. *Diaphysis*—a primary center of ossification in the embryo; the shaft of the long bone in the child.
2. *Metaphysis*—the end of the diaphysis which constitutes the most recently formed bone.
3. *Bony epiphyses*—secondary centers of ossification at the ends of long bones. In the immature skeleton these are pieces of bone separated from the end of the bone by cartilage. In adulthood the epiphyses fuse with the diaphysis.
4. *Apophysis*—a bony projection without an independent center of ossification.

Figure 21.4 Growth cartilage at the hip joint where Perthes Disease occurs. The line of dots represents germinal cells. They are laying down cartilage which is later replaced by bone.

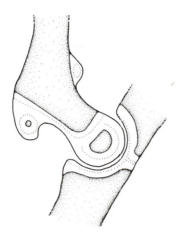

Figure 21.5 Common sites of osteochondroses.

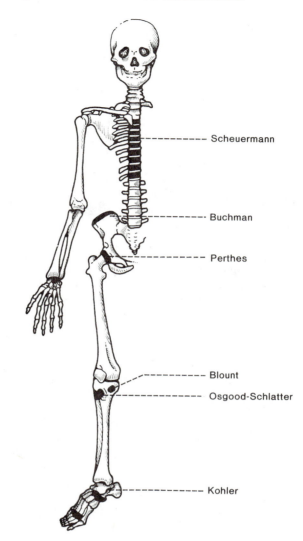

The growth plate, a cartilaginous disc between the epiphysis and the metaphysis, traditionally has been designated the *epiphyseal plate*. Newer sources, however, refer to the *growth plate* or *metaphyseal growth plate* since the metaphysis, not the epiphysis, contributes to new bone growth. Sometime before age 25, at a date which is specific for each bone, the metaphyseal cartilage ceases to proliferate, and closure takes place between the diaphysis and the epiphysis. Normally this closure occurs from 1 to 3 years earlier in girls than in boys.

Disorders of the growth plate include premature closure, delayed closure, and interruption in the growth process. Stature is considered the best guide of growth plate activity, although skeletal maturity itself is generally determined by X-rays of the carpal bones. Bone growth and subsequent closure are affected by heredity, diet, hormones, general health status, and trauma. Ill health and malnutrition generally delay skeletal maturity, whereas trauma affects a single growth plate closure. Obese children are particularly susceptible to disorders of the growth plate.

Some of the most common sites of growth plate disorders are depicted in Figure 21.5 and included in the following list:

Bony Part Affected	Name of Disorder
Tibial tuberosity	Osgood-Schlatter
Calcaneal apophysis	Sever
Vertebral epiphyses	Scheuermann
Capital femoral epiphysis	Perthes (Legg-Calve-Perthes)
Tibia, proximal epiphysis	Blount
Tarsal, navicular	Kohler
Secondary patellar center	Sinding-Larson
Iliac crest	Buchman

Over 71% of the osteochondroses are found at the first four sites. The pathology in all of the osteochondroses is similar (see Figure 21.6). For unknown reasons, cells within the bony center of the epiphysis undergo partial *necrosis* (death), probably from interference with the blood supply. The *necrotic* tissue is removed by special cells called osteoclasts, and the bony center is temporarily softened and liable to deformation of shape, which may become permanent. In time, new healthy bone cells replace the dead tissue, and the bone texture returns to normal.

This cycle of changes may take as long as 2 years, during which time the youngster must be kept off the affected limb. Enforcing the rule of no weight bearing on an athletic child is not easy since the child experiences no symptoms of illness and only occasional pain

Figure 21.6 The cycle of changes in osteochondritis: (1) normal epiphysis before onset; (2) the bony nucleus undergoes necrosis, loses its normal texture, and becomes granular; (3) the bone becomes fragmented; (4) if subjected to pressure, the softened epiphysis is flattened; (5) normal bone texture restored, but deformity persists. The cycle occupies about 2 years.

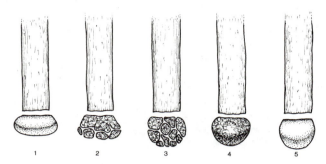

in the involved area. The primary danger in osteochondroses is not in the present, but rather in the deformity, limp, and predisposition to arthritis that may occur if rules are not followed.

Scheuermann's Disease

Juvenile kyphosis, or *Scheuermann's disease,* is a disturbance in normal vertebral growth. It results from *epiphysitis,* inflammation of an epiphysis, and/or *osteochondritis,* inflammation of cartilage, either of which may cause fragmentation of vertebral bodies. One or several vertebrae are involved. The etiology is generally unknown, and the condition has been likened to Perthes' disease in that it seems to have an active phase during which exercise, particularly forward flexion, is contraindicated. The student should be protected from all flexion movements by a hyperextension brace, which places the weight on the neural arches rather than the defective vertebral bodies. Although the student experiences some discomfort, the pain is not great enough to impose limitation of natural movement; sometimes the condition is painfree. In such instances it may be difficult to prevent the student from engaging in physical activity. Unfortunately, if bracing and nonactivity are not enforced, the resulting kyphotic hump may be both severe and persistent. When X-rays reveal the healing of fragmented areas, the student may participate in physical education classes with no restrictions. Occasionally, the student will continue to wear a back brace, body jacket, or cast for a number of months after the disease is arrested.

Perthes' Disease

Perthes' disease, the destruction of the growth center of the hip joint, occurs between ages 4 to 8 years. Its incidence is 1 per 18,000, and approximately four to five times more boys than girls are affected. Typically, the condition lasts 2 to 4 years, during which the child may need adapted physical education—most likely in the mainstream setting. Adapting is needed in choice of activities that can be done while wearing a splint and/or using a wheelchair. If the hip joint is not protected (i.e., kept in nonweight-bearing status) during the body's natural repair process, the femoral head becomes flattened and irregular (*coxa plana*), which makes joint surface incongruent and leads to hip joint degenerate arthritis.

Slipped Femoral Epiphysis (SFE)

Another hip joint growth disorder involves a slipping or dislocation of the femur. This condition occurs during adolescence, shortly before or during the pubertal growth spurt. The incidence is 2 to 13 per 100,000. SFE is more common in males (2.2 to 1) than females and in blacks than whites. Like the other growth disorders, the cause is not known. The condition occurs more often in obese than normal-weight teenagers. The growth center typically slips down and backward; this is probably because the angulation between the growth center and the femur changes during adolescence from horizontal to a more vertical plane. This makes slippage easier. This condition is sometimes called *adolescent coxa vara.* Once diagnosed, SFE is usually corrected surgically. Upon return to school, students are usually restricted from vigorous weight-bearing physical education for about a year. Adaptation entails arranging for swimming and/or upper extremity sports and exercises in place of the regular curriculum.

Problems Corrected by Surgery

Many problems discussed in the chapter on postures may be severe enough to qualify as orthopedic impairments. Among these are scoliosis and congenital defects of the feet, legs, and hips. In most states, educational policy requires that OI conditions be diagnosed by physicians before special education money can be used on adapted physical education and other services. If the movement restrictions and/or limp caused by such conditions *adversely affect the child's [physical] education performance* (PL 94–142, *Federal Register,* 1977, p. 42478), in the physician's opinion, then eligibility procedures for PL 94–142 monies should be begun.

Congenital defects of the feet, legs, and hips are generally corrected by surgery, bracing, or casting in infancy or early childhood. In spite of the correction, the gait may continue to be impaired so that students do not have a fair chance in competitive activities with peers. Most such students remain in mainstream physical education and instruction is adapted accordingly.

Club Foot

Talipes equinovarus, or congenital club foot, is the most common of all orthopedic defects, with an incidence of 1 of approximately 700 births.

Figure 21.7 Surgically corrected feet of preadolescent boy with talipes and toe deformities.

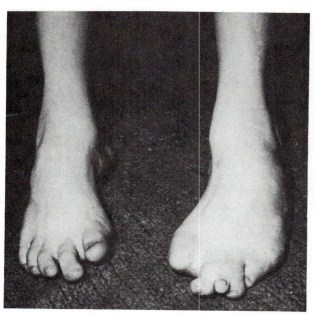

Figure 21.7 depicts the club foot of a preadolescent boy who has undergone several operations and spent months in casts and braces. He is an enthusiastic athlete and in the starting lineup of his Little League baseball team. His slight limp is noticeably worse during cold winter days and rainy seasons, when he can hardly walk the first hour or so after awakening. As the day wears on, his gait becomes almost normal, enabling him to run fast enough to hold his own in athletic feats with peers.

Congenital Dislocation of the Hip

Congenital dislocation of the hip (CDH) encompasses various degrees of *dysplasia,* or abnormal development, of the acetabulum and/or head of the femur. This same condition appears also in certain blood lines of German Shepherds. In humans it is more common among girls than boys and usually occurs in one hip rather than both. Its incidence is approximately one to three per 1,000 births.

The terms *subluxation* and *luxation* are synonyms for dislocation, describing the position of the femoral head in relation to a shallow, dysplasic acetabulum (Figure 21.8). In subluxation the femur is only partially displaced, whereas in luxation the femoral head is completely dislocated above the acetabulum rim. These aberrations often are not recognized until the child begins to walk. Nonsurgical treatment involves repositioning, traction, and casting. In the majority of cases in which the child is above age 3, surgical reduction (repositioning) is used. After age 6, more complicated operative procedures such as osteotomy and arthroplasty are applied.

Reference to congenital hip dislocation on a child's record usually means that he or she has undergone long periods of hospitalization and immobilization in splints

Figure 21.8 Hip joint problems. (*A*) Normal position of femoral head. (*B*) Anterior upward subluxation. (*C*) Anterior upward dislocation in coxa valga. (*D*) Downward dislocation in coxa vara.

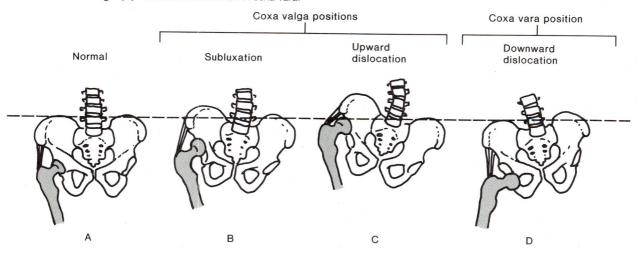

or casts extending from waist to toes. Generally, the child has had fewer opportunities to learn social and motor skills through informal play than have normal peers. As in other congenital anomalies, any problems the child manifests are more likely to be psychological than physical.

Pathological Dislocation of the Hip

Dislocation of the hip is a problem commonly associated with students unable to stand because of severe paralytic or neurological conditions (polio, spina bifida, cerebral palsy). The incidence of dislocation in severely disabled nonambulatory persons is 25%. The average age of dislocation is 7 years, but the range of frequent occurrence varies from 2 to 10 years. Like CDH, the condition is corrected by surgery.

Pathological dislocation may occur at any age. In most cases, the head of the femur becomes displaced upward and posteriorly (note this is different from slipped femoral epiphysis). Pathological dislocation appears mostly in persons with coxa valga (increased neck-shaft angle of femur). Coxa valga is present in most normal infants before weight bearing begins; the gradual change in neck-shaft femoral angle accompanies normal motor development. Childhood coxa valga and associated hip dislocation thus sometimes characterize delayed or abnormal motor development.

Scoliosis

Lateral curvature of the spine is discussed fully in the chapter on postures. Severe conditions are treated by surgery, casting, and braces. As in Scheuermann's disease, vigorous forward flexion of the trunk may be contraindicated. Otherwise, there are seldom restrictions imposed on regular physical education. This condition does not cause a limp, so wheelchair activities are not indicated.

Trauma and Osteomyelitis

Other temporary problems include trauma injuries and disease that may result in a limp. These typically require several weeks of adapted physical education (i.e., assignment to stations where activities that the sound limbs can do are being taught) as well as supplementary physical therapy. *Exercises done to rehabilitate a limb should not substitute for physical education.*

Trauma Injuries

Temporary trauma injuries include contusions (crushed limbs), strains, sprains, dislocations, and fractures. These types of musculoskeletal injuries are studied intensively by physical educators in courses on first aid, health emergency care, and athletic injuries; therefore, they are not discussed here. The prospective adapted physical educator, although sometimes not interested in athletics per se, can learn much by serving as the assistant to the university athletic trainer.

Osteomyelitis

Osteomyelitis is frequently a childhood disease. It is caused by staphylococcus, streptococcus, or pneumococcus organisms. Even with the best medical treatment, it may result in permanent disability. The bones most often affected are the tibia, femur, and humerus. The symptoms are similar to those of an infected wound: (a) pain and tenderness, particularly near the end of the bone in the metaphyseal region; (b) heat felt through the overlying skin; (c) overlying soft tissues feel hard (indurated); and (d) neighboring joints may be distended with clear fluid. Generally, a good range of joint movement is retained, although the child begins to limp from the acute pain. Pus forms and finds its way to the surface of the bone, where it forms a *subperiosteal abscess*. If treatment is not begun, the abscess eventually works its way outward, causing a *sinus* (hole) in the skin over the affected bone from which pus is discharged continuously or intermittently. This sinus is covered with a dressing that must be changed several times daily.

Although only a single limb is typically affected and the child appears otherwise healthy and energetic, *the physical educator should remember that exercise is always contraindicated when any kind of infection is active in the body.* The medical treatment is rest and intensive antibiotic therapy, often accompanied by surgery to scrape the infected bone and evacuate the pus.

In its early stages, osteomyelitis is described as *acute.* If the infection persists or reoccurs periodically, it is called *chronic.* Since chronic osteomyelitis may linger for years, the physical educator should confer with the physician about the nature of an adapted program.

Permanent Orthopedic Conditions

To enhance understanding of specific physical education pedagogy, permanent conditions are discussed in this chapter either in relation to amputee sports or

NWAA sports. Students with congenital and acquired amputations may participate in amputee sports and some NWAA sports. Students with severe thermal injuries may be eligible for amputee or les autres sports. Students with neuromuscular conditions like spina bifida, spinal cord injuries, and polio that result in paralysis or paresis (weakness) participate in NWAA sports. This chapter organization is designed to emphasize the importance of exposing students to sports that can be used in their leisure and of introducing them to sports organizations that govern competition.

Amputee Sports and Physical Education

Most school-age children and youths with amputations participate in regular physical education. With properly fitted prostheses, they typically can keep up with classmates, although supplementary adapted physical education may be needed. Typically, there is only one student with an amputation in the school, and the extent of his/her participation depends largely on attitudes of parents, teachers, and classmates. Attitudes (and subsequently participation) are affected by many factors, among which are time of occurrence (congenital or acquired) and degree of severity (number of limbs missing and level of amputation).

Prevalence of Amputations

Approximately 311,000 amputees reside in the United States. Of these, 7% are under age 21, 58% are between ages 21 and 65, and 35% are over 65 years. Among school-age persons there are more upper extremity amputees than lower. This is reversed in the general population, probably because war injuries more commonly affect legs than arms.

Degree of Severity

The number of limbs missing and the level of the amputation determine, to a large extent, motor performance. Compared with other lower extremity disabilities, amputees are considered minimally handicapped unless both femurs are amputated at the hip joint (bilateral hip amputee). With the exception of these persons, for instance, all amputees are in Class III (least disabled) in wheelchair basketball; this means their abilities are equivalent to Class 7 and 8 cerebral palsied athletes and Class V spinal cord injured persons who can walk, but with a limp.

Congenital Amputations

Occasionally, a child is born with one limb or a part of the arm or leg bones missing. These skeletal anomalies, known as *congenital amputations* or *limb deficiencies,* are often associated with the thalidomide babies born after World War II. Most such conditions, however, have unknown etiology. There are two types of limb deficiencies: *dysmelia* (absence of arms or legs) and *phocomelia* (absence of middle segment of a limb, but with intact proximal and distal portions). In the latter, hands or feet are attached directly to shoulders or hips, respectively. In phocomelia (*phoco* means seal-like and *melos* means limb), the hand or foot is often removed surgically within the first few months after birth. Absence of the fibula, with a congenitally deformed foot, is also a common condition that is corrected surgically.

Joey Lipski, world class swimmer and track star, is illustrative of a person with dysmelia. Born without arms, he does not wear prostheses in competition. Joey learned to swim at age 8 and at age 15 set world records for his classification in the 100-meter freestyle event (2:05.6) and in the 50-meter backstroke (57.0). He runs the 100-meter dash in 19.5 seconds and the 200-meter event in 41.42 seconds.

Karen Farmer, world class athlete in discus, javelin, and shot put, was born with a club foot and missing fibula. These were surgically removed when she was 18 months old, and a prosthesis was fitted soon afterward. Her shot put and discus records are 10.02 and 32.36 meters, respectively. Almost all of Karen's competitive experience has been against able-bodied athletes; she attends Washington State University on an athletic scholarship and says she has never found a sport she couldn't master.

Age of prosthetic fitting is obviously very important in subsequent development of motor skills. Upper extremity prostheses are fitted when the child develops good sitting balance, usually between 8 and 10 months of age. Lower extremity prostheses are fitted when the child begins to pull up to a stand, usually between 10 and 15 months. As the child grows, the prostheses must be periodically replaced: every 15 to 18 months for an upper extremity prosthesis and about every 12 months for a lower extremity prosthesis.

Figure 21.9 Canadian Arnie Boldt, world champion high jumper.

Acquired Amputations

Of the various disabilities that can result from trauma and disease, the elective amputation is the most dramatic. Not only does the child suffer anxieties about no longer being *whole,* but efficient use of prosthetic devices demands much effort.

The etiologies of acquired amputations in children in order of incidence are trauma, cancer, infection, and vascular conditions like gangrene. Under trauma, the leading causes of amputation are farm and power tool accidents, vehicular accidents, and gunshot explosions. Most of these occur in the age group from 12 to 21. Children who lose limbs because of malignancy are also primarily within this age group.

Arnie Boldt (Figure 21.9), the one-legged world champion high jumper, is illustrative of a person with an acquired amputation. Raised on a farm, he lost his lower leg in a farm accident at 3 years of age. Much of his competitive experience has been against able-bodied athletes.

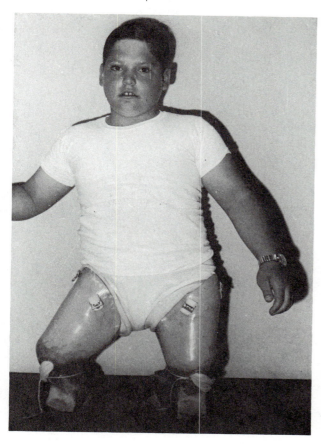

Since 1964, immediate postsurgical prosthetic fitting has gradually become the trend. In most cases, prostheses are fitted in less than 30 days after the amputation. This practice offers several advantages. First, particularly in a person with cancer, a prosthesis and early ambulation contributes to a positive psychological outlook. Second, amputation stumps in children do not usually shrink and there is no physical reason for delaying fitting. Third, phantom pain has become almost nonexistent because of improved surgical techniques. Fourth, edema (swelling) is best controlled and wound healing facilitated by an immediate postsurgical socket.

In modern hospital settings the patient is provided training in use of the prosthesis by physical therapists and occupational therapists. Ideally, this training includes exposure to playground equipment and recreational activities. If the amputee does not appear secure in class activities utilizing gymnastic and playground equipment, the adapted physical educator may need to supplement the hospital training (see Figure 21.10).

Thermal Injuries

Approximately 300,000 Americans annually suffer disfiguring injuries from fires. Another 12,000 die each year. The mortality rate is greatest among persons under age 5 and over age 65. No other type of accident permanently affects as many school-age children. Many thermal injuries result in amputations. As more persons are kept alive, physical educators must become increasingly adept at coping with all aspects of thermal injuries.

During past decades children with more than 60% of their skin destroyed seldom survived. Now, increasing numbers of individuals are returning to society scarred and horribly disfigured. What kind of physical education should be provided for the young child with extensive scar tissue? How can the physical educator help such children find social acceptance? What are the effects of disfiguring thermal injuries upon self-concept? An account (Rothenberg & White, 1985) of a child with third degree burns over 90% of his body helps to answer these questions.

Thermal injury can be caused by fire, chemicals, electricity, or prolonged contact with extreme degrees of hot or cold liquids. Children who have sustained disfiguring thermal injuries, upon entering school, frequently recognize for the first time that they are deviates from the *normal*. They have been known to describe themselves as monsters. Typically they have no hair on scalp, no eyebrows or eyelashes, and scar tissue covers the face.

Scar tissue is an inevitable outcome of severe burns. Wound coverage is attained by the growth of scar tissue from the periphery to the center of the wound. Thick scar tissue forms *contractures* across joints, limits range of motion, causes scoliosis of the spine, and shortens underlying muscles. The severity of hypertrophic scarring (Figure 21.11) and scar contracture may be decreased by early splinting, pressure, and therapeutic exercise.

Jobsts (Figure 21.12), elastic supports made to fit a specified portion of the body, may be prescribed as a means of reducing scar hypertrophy. The purpose of the jobst is to apply constant pressure to the healed areas that are presenting signs of thickening scar tissue. The elastic supports achieve the best results when worn 24 hours daily. Therefore, as the child is returned to the classroom, he or she is expected to wear these supports under clothing.

Isoprene splints or *braces* may be applied to areas where the jobsts do not provide adequate pressure to the scar tissue. The elastic face mask does not apply

Figure 21.11 Hypertrophic scarring of healed burn on lateral aspect of trunk 2 years after burn occurred.

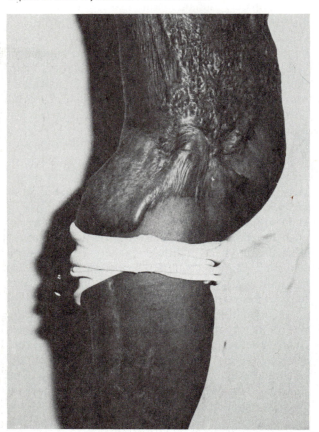

Figure 21.13 Jobsts elastic face mask and isoprene splint applied to the junction of the nose and cheek.

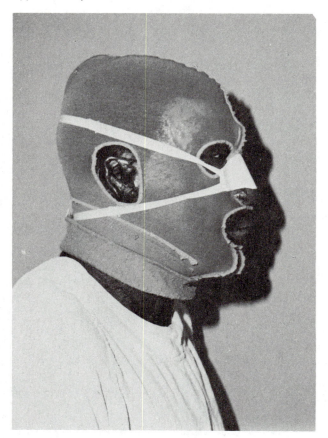

Figure 21.12 Jobsts elastic support jackets applied to arm and hand.

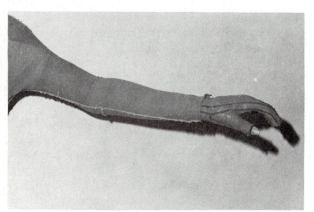

significant pressure to the junction of the nose and cheek, which frequently fills with scars (Figure 21.13). The isoprene splints require frequent removal for cleansing of the splint and application of lotion to prevent skin dryness. There are various types of hand splints for abduction of the thumb that a child may be required to wear during daily activities. The pupil wearing such splints should be encouraged to use the hands normally in physical education activities and should be given no restrictions. Hence, the child is encouraged to increase pain tolerance. The physical educator may need to assist the child in proper cleaning and reapplication of the splint after vigorous exercise.

Several years of rehabilitation are required for severely burned children. They must not be excused from physical education because they are wearing jobsts, braces, or splints. Each pupil must learn the tolerance of new skin tissue to such elements as direct sunlight and chlorine in freshwater pools. They must expose themselves to the sun for a progressively longer period each day. The physical educator may wish to confer with a specialist in thermal injuries.

The young tissue of healed burns is delicate. It quickly becomes dry when exposed to sunlight for an extended period of time. Full thickness burns have a tendency to dry and irritate easily because of the absence or impairment of sweat ducts, hair follicles, and sebaceous glands. Itching occurs with drying and irritation of healed burn wounds. Frequent applications of a lanolin lotion are recommended.

Indoor physical education is preferable to activities in the direct sunlight. Since contractures are a major problem, emphasis should be upon flexibility or range of motion exercises. Dance and aquatic activities are recommended especially. For the many thermal injuries that result in amputations, other adaptations include those in the following section.

Adaptations for Burns and/or Amputations

The only adaptations recommended pertain to dressing and shower rules. Girls and boys should be allowed to wear long pants or the type of clothing in which they feel most comfortable. Shower rules should be waived. The amputee who is sensitive about changing clothes in the locker room should be given a place of his or her own, and classmates should be encouraged to allow the desired privacy.

The general attitude among physicians is that an amputee can do anything if the prosthesis is well fitted.

Athletic activity is possible for the amputee and there are numerous examples of those who have competed successfully in many sports—both as amateurs and as professionals. When strenuous activities are planned, it is recommended that the limb maker check the limb to make certain that the anticipated hard use can be tolerated. Special exercises are given to help the amputee acquire the balance, coordination, and ability to run rapidly that are prerequisites for sports. (Epps & Vaughn, 1972, p. 129)

Balance is probably the one aspect of motor performance that gives the amputee the most trouble. The unilateral lower limb amputee should be taught to use the sound limb for kicking balls while the prosthetic limb maintains the weight of the body. In ascending stairs, the child should be taught to lead with the sound limb; in descending, to lead with the prosthesis in the stable extended position. The bilateral above-knee amputee (Figure 21.14) has more difficulty with steps and often requires a railing and crutch. He or she typically climbs and descends stairs in a sideward manner. The unilateral upper-limb amputee finds that the weight of a bowling ball or tennis racquet in its descent throws him or her off balance because the prosthetic arm may

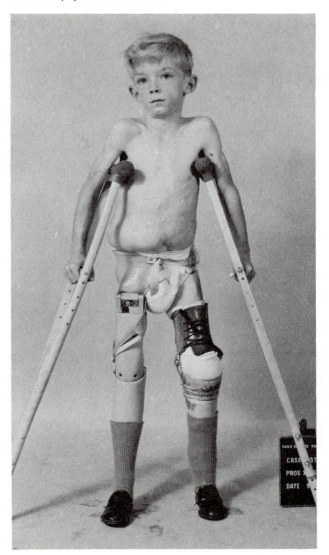

Figure 21.14 The bilateral above-knee amputee may require months of physical rehabilitation.

not compensate in accordance with the principle of opposition. This problem, at least in bowling, can be overcome by developing a scissors step, crossing the leg on the good arm side over the other, and taking the weight of the ball in stride.

Amputees swim without their prostheses. Fins may be strapped to the arm or leg stumps as needed. For water skiing and/or activities in salt water, an old pair of artificial legs are used since salt water may cause the new ones to crack.

Figure 21.15 Therapeutic horseback riding was initiated in England in the 1950s. The first established program in the United States began in 1968 when the Cheff Center in Augusta, Michigan opened. This double-leg amputee was taught riding by a Cheff Center graduate. Note the specially made saddle.

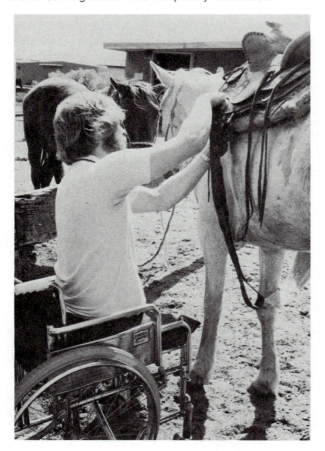

Amputees also often ride without prostheses. Specially made saddles and other equipment may be needed (see Figure 21.15).

In addition to guiding the amputee in sports, dance, and aquatic activities, the physical educator should recognize any gait deviations that may develop and refer the pupil back to the physical therapist and/or the prosthetist. Most gait deviations result from problems with the alignment or fit of the prosthesis.

Amputee Sports Classifications and Rules

By the time children with amputations reach adolescence, many want opportunities for vigorous competition against others with comparable disabilities. To ensure fair competition when amputees pit their strengths against one another, the United States Amputee Athletic Association (USAAA) enforces a strict

Table 21.1
Sport Classifications for Persons with Amputations

Nine General Classifications for Amputations

Class A1 = Double AK	Class A7 = Double BE
Class A2 = Single AK	Class A8 = Single BE
Class A3 = Double BK	Class A9 = Combined
Class A4 = Single BK	lower plus
Class A5 = Double AE	upper limb
Class A6 = Single AE	amputations

Note. Abbreviations used are as follows: *AK*, above or through the knee joint; *BK*, below knee, but through or above ankle joint; *AE*, above or through elbow joint; *BE*, below elbow, but through or above wrist joint.

classification system with nine classifications used for such sports as swimming. These are presented in Table 21.1. (See Figures 21.16 to 21.18.)

Figure 21.16 United States Amputee Athletic Association Classifications A1 to A4. *Top left,* Class A1, double above knee. *Top right,* Class A2, single above knee. *Bottom left,* A3, double below knee. *Bottom right,* A4, single below knee.

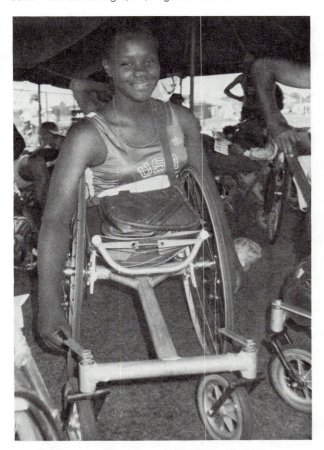

Figure 21.17 United States Amputee Athletic Association Classifications A5 to A7. *Top left,* Class A5, double above elbow. *Top right,* Class A6, single above elbow. *Bottom left,* Class A7, double below elbow.

Figure 21.18 United States Athletic Association Classification A9. Even with combined lower plus upper limb amputations, many sports are possible.

Figure 21.19 Running gait of A2 amputee. Note structure and composition of prosthesis is such that it is difficult to distinguish from real leg. (From Dr. Bea Gordon and Dr. Sue Gavron.)

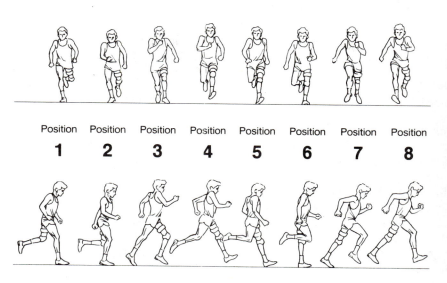

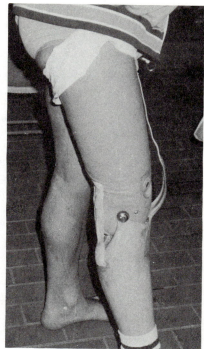

Position 1 Position 2 Position 3 Position 4 Position 5 Position 6 Position 7 Position 8

In field and track events, fewer classifications are used. In field, double arm amputees compete together in one class whether the amputation is above or below the elbow, and single arm amputees likewise form one class. More severely involved lower extremity amputees use wheelchairs, whereas less involved ones throw from a standing position. A similar classification system is used in track.

In volleyball, a point system is used similar to that in wheelchair basketball to ensure equal distribution of abilities on opposing teams. Persons are assigned 1, 2, 3, or 4 points depending upon two criteria: A1 to A9 classifications and muscle strength scores determined by certified testers. At all times, players on the floor must total 13 or more points. Like regular volleyball, six players comprise a team.

Option of Sitting or Standing Rules

Lower limb amputees have the option in many sports of using a wheelchair or standing/walking/running/jumping. Some sports are organized primarily by sitting rather than standing rules. Sitting volleyball encompasses Classes A1 to A9, whereas only athletes in A2 to A4 and A6 to A9 are eligible for standing volleyball. Traditionally, basketball has been played in wheelchairs. At the International Games for the Disabled, however, a demonstration game was played with amputees standing. Although the able-bodied athletes beat the amputees, hopes were high among American athletes that standing basketball would become an official event.

Whether track events should be in wheelchairs or ambulatory is highly controversial at this time, with the current rules mostly favoring wheelchair competition for lower limb amputees. In A4 events, which are ambulatory, competitors are required to wear prostheses and use both legs in running; hopping is not allowed. Physical educators who permit students with lower limb amputations to compete in races against able-bodied peers should study the pros and cons of this controversy carefully. Cinematographical research is helpful in the study of gaits (see Figure 21.19). Many physicians believe that ambulatory activities of this nature put too much stress on the good leg and predispose the athlete to eventual injury and/or degenerate arthritic disease.

Use of Prostheses and Orthoses

Regulations concerning prostheses and orthoses are important. In air pistol, air rifle, and swimming, for instance, prostheses and orthoses are not permitted. In archery, the draw may be made with a prosthesis or orthosis, and a releasing aid may be used by Classes A6, A8, and A9. These classes may also receive help with loading arrows into the bow. In field and most track events, the wearing of a prosthesis is optional. In volleyball, lower limb prostheses and orthoses are permitted, but not upper limb. In lawn bowling, Classes A5 and/or A7 may use prosthesis or orthosis if they wish. In table tennis, however, these are not allowed. Persons who are unable to perform a regulation serve because of their disability are allowed to bounce the ball on the table and then smash it across the net. Obviously, there is much to be learned in order to help amputee students prepare for high-level competition against other amputees.

Amputee Sports Governing Bodies

In the United States, summer sports are governed by the United States Amputee Athletic Association (USAAA) and winter sports are conducted under the auspices of the National Handicapped Sports and Recreation Association (NHSRA). Annual national as well as regional competitions are held. Every 4 years, as close to the Olympic Games as possible, international competition governed by the International Sports Organization for the Disabled (ISOD) is held. Amputees also compete in NWBA basketball and in the open category of NWAA events such as track, field, swimming, table tennis, and archery. Many amputees are also becoming marathoners, tennis and racketball players, snow and water skiers, and competent participants in an ever-expanding variety of sports.

NWAA Sports

The National Wheelchair Athletic Association offers competition for persons with spina bifida, spinal cord injuries, postpolio, and other spinal neuromuscular conditions in the following sports: air weapons (pistol and rifle), archery, athletics (track, field, marathoning), fencing, slalom, swimming, table tennis, and weight lifting. These, therefore, are the sports that should be taught (along with dance, basketball, and other wheelchair activities) in school physical education if students are to develop skills, attitudes, and habits that can be generalized into current and adult leisure.

Separate organizations govern such wheelchair sports as basketball, bowling, scuba diving, road racing (marathoning), tennis, racquetball, softball, quad rugby, and horseback riding. Addresses of these organizations appear in the appendix. The monthly magazine *Sports 'N Spokes* carries articles, with numerous photographs, on wheelchair sports, primarily in regard to the successes of persons with spinal neuromuscular conditions. At present this magazine is a better sourcebook for pedagogy than any textbook available. Also essential to developing pedagogy specific to spinal neuromuscular conditions are the official rulebooks of the organizations that govern wheelchair sports.

Students, age 16 and over, compete with adults in NWAA sports, wheelchair basketball, tennis, and racket sports. Adult sports have been available since the 1950s, and most major cities have one or more wheelchair basketball teams. An important responsibility of the physical educator is helping high school

youth make contact with this team as well as other groups sponsoring appropriate activities. Introduction of younger students to adult wheelchair athletes helps them find role models and begin to visualize themselves as self-actualizing persons capable of learning almost any sport they wish.

Junior wheelchair competition is also available for children ages 8 through 15. Several large cities, usually through the cooperation of sports organizations, school systems, and municipal parks and recreation associations, are offering annual competitions open to youths throughout the United States. Illustrative of these are the Junior Orange Bowl Sports Ability Games in Coral Gables, Florida, begun in 1982, and the Milwaukee Mail-A-Graphic Bowling, Track, and Field Meets. The first national junior wheelchair championship conducted by NWAA was held at the University of Delaware in July 1984. Increasing local and regional sports opportunities are available throughout the country. It is important that the physical educator be sure students are entered in the appropriate meets. It should be remembered that Special Olympics are only for mentally retarded persons. Meets for physically disabled students of average or better intellectual functioning should not use the words *special* or *olympics*.

Students with spinal neuromuscular conditions should receive physical education instruction involving upper extremity sports skills in regular physical education. Most students with spina bifida and spinal cord injuries, however, need concurrent separate adapted physical education to master wheelchair sports and dance activities. When such students participate in squad or team activities, either in regular or separate physical education, a classification system should be enacted to ensure fair distribution of abilities among the teams.

Paralysis and paresis (weakness) caused by spinal neuromuscular conditions can range from almost total to minimal disability. This broad spectrum of individual differences has led to a medical classification system based on site of spinal cord lesion and individual muscle strength testing. In NWAA adult competition, muscle testing is done by special certified physicians and physical therapists; therefore, this section describes only classification by spinal cord lesion, the system most often used in youth sports.

Figure 21.20 depicts the seven levels of spinal cord functioning that are needed for totally fair competition. The higher an injury occurs, the more muscles are paralyzed. Function is classified according to the region of the spine and/or the spinal nerves affected. There are 31 pairs of spinal nerves. Each nerve emerges from the spinal cord via sensory (dorsal) and motor (ventral) roots that unite, leaving the spinal column through the intervertebral foramen between each two vertebrae. At this point each nerve divides into many

Figure 21.20 NWAA classification for wheelchair sports.

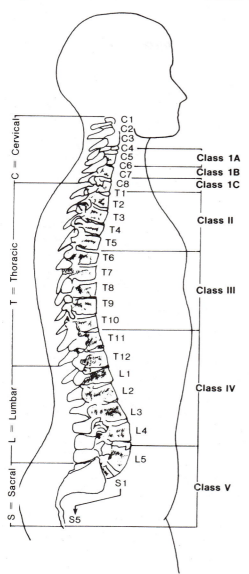

Class IA. All cervical lesions with complete or incomplete quadriplegia who have involvement of both hands, weakness of triceps and with severe weakness of the trunk and lower extremities interfering significantly with trunk balance and the ability to walk.

Class IB. All cervical lesions with complete or incomplete quadriplegia who have involvement of upper extremities but less than IA with preservation of normal or good triceps and with a generalized weakness of the trunk and lower extremities interfering significantly with trunk balance and the ability to walk.

Class IC. All cervical lesions with complete or incomplete quadriplegia who have involvement of upper extremities but less than IB with preservation of normal or good triceps and normal or good finger flexion and extension (grasp and release) but without intrinsic hand function and with a generalized weakness of the trunk and lower extremities interfering significantly with trunk balance and the ability to walk.

Class II. Complete or incomplete paraplegia below T1 down to and including T5 or comparable disability with total abdominal paralysis or poor abdominal muscle strength and no useful trunk sitting balance.

Class III. Complete or incomplete paraplegia or comparable disability below T5 down to and including T10 with upper abdominal and spinal extensor musculature sufficient to provide some element of trunk sitting balance but not normal.

Class IV. Complete or incomplete paraplegia or comparable disability below T10 down to and including L2 without knee extensors or very weak knee extensors and paralysis of hip abductors.

Class V. Complete or incomplete paraplegia or comparable disability below L2 with weak knee extensors.

branches that go to specific muscles. Damage to either the spinal cord or its nerves results in complete or incomplete paralysis. Incomplete paralysis is also called paresis (weakness).

Although there are only seven cervical vertebrae, there are eight cervical nerves. Damage to these, as well as the first thoracic nerve, results in *quadriplegia,* meaning all four limbs and trunk are involved. Damage to the fifth cervical vertebrae (C5) or above makes a person dependent upon portable respirators and other apparatus to maintain vital life functions. Such persons are therefore seldom seen outside of a hospital setting. Sports classifications begin with C6 or incomplete

C5 lesions. This is the highest level lesion that permits learning of manual wheelchair skills. NWAA, unlike cerebral palsy sports, does not offer motorized chair activities.

Sports activities for persons with quadriplegia are conducted within three classifications: 1A, 1B, and 1C. Although persons in these classifications are severely handicapped, there are many sports activities they can learn. Much of their physical education success depends upon the provision of a properly fitted high-back sports chair. In youth sports, the three quadriplegia classifications are grouped together and considered as one Junior (J)1.

Table 21.2
Goals for Persons With Quadriplegia

NWAA Class	Spinal Cord Level	OT Goals Self-Care & ADL SKills	PT Goals Wheelchair & Ambulation Skills	PE & R Goals Sports, Dance, & Aquatics Skills
—	Incomplete C5	Type, feed self Use assistive devices	Push on flat surface Manipulate brakes Stand at tilt table	Power chair activities, games, dance Basic sport skills Swimming wth flotation devices
IA	C6	Drink Wash, shave Brush hair Dress upper half Sit up/lie down in bed Write, draw Crafts, hobbies	Push on sloping surface Turn wheelchair Remove armrests/ footplates Transfer chair to bed, chair to car Stand in bars	Manual chair activities, games, and dance 60-, 100-, 200-, 400-, 800-m track events 400- and 800-m track relay Slalom Pentathlon Club throw, 2-k shot put, discus Weight lifting 25-yard front and back freestyle, breast, and butterfly—no flotation devices 75-yard individual medley (3×25) 100-yard distance freestyle Archery, air weapons, table tennis Sit-skiing (snow events) Marathon and road racing
IB	C7	Turn in bed Dress lower half Skin care Bladder and bowel control Crafts, hobbies	Wheel over uneven surface Bounce over small elevations Pick up objects from floor Negotiate curbs Perform almost all transfers Swing-to in bars Drive automobile with manual controls	Same as IA, except 100-, 200-, 400-, 800-, 1500-m track events Shot put, discus, javelin (no club) Swimming same, except 100-yard individual medley (4×25) with butterfly as fourth stroke
IC	C8	Same as IB, except more finger control	Same as IB, except more finger control	Same as IB, except 200-yard distance freestyle

Persons with damage to the 12 thoracic nerves, five lumbar nerves, and first and second sacral nerves and/or comparable levels of the spinal cord have *paraplegia,* meaning the trunk and lower extremities are involved. The last three sacral nerves (S3, 4, 5) are irrelevant to skeletal muscle innervation. Paraplegia is divided into four classifications for adult NWAA sports and two for youth sports. For youth age 15 and under, Classes II and III form the J2 classification. These persons have good transfer skills (from wheelchair to car, floor, or another chair) and those with lower level lesions can walk with crutches. Classes IV and V form the J3 classification. Although these persons compete in wheelchairs, most of their activities of daily living (ADL) are done on crutches or with a cane. Some can walk and run independently.

ADL, Ambulation, and Sports Skills

Tables 21.2 and 21.3 show activities of daily living, ambulation (wheelchair and nonwheelchair), and sport skills that persons with quadriplegia and paraplegia can learn. These tables also show the differing goals of physical educators, physical therapists, and occupational therapists. The activities listed under physical education are meant to serve as guides in writing IEPs and planning curriculum for students with spinal neuromuscular conditions.

Table 21.3
Goals for Persons With Paraplegia

NWAA Class	Spinal Cord Level	OT Goals Self-Care & ADL Skills	PT Goals Wheelchair & Ambulation Skills	PE & R Goals Sports, Dance, & Aquatics Skills
II	T1 to T5	Trunk, leg, foot Vocational rehabilitation	Do wheelies (see Figure 21.21) Transfer chair to floor Walk in bars or with walker	Same as IC, except 3-k shot put 50-yard front and back freestyle, breast
III	T6 to T10	Same as above	Swing-to on crutches Transfer chair to crutches Use stairs	Same as II, except 400- and 1600-m track relay 50-yard butterfly 400-yard distance freestyle Class 1 wheelchair basketball Snow skiing (upright with special apparatus)
IV	T11 to L2	————	All gaits on crutches All transfers	Same as III, except 200-yard individual medley Wheelchair tennis, racketball 500-yard distance freestyle Class 2 wheelchair basketball
V	L3 and below	————	Functional walking without crutches—may use cane, braces	Same as above, except Class 3 wheelchair basketball

Figure 21.21   Learning to do wheelies and to maneuver the chair over obstacles are prerequisite to competing in NWAA obstacle courses as well as to coping with street curbs and other architectural barriers.

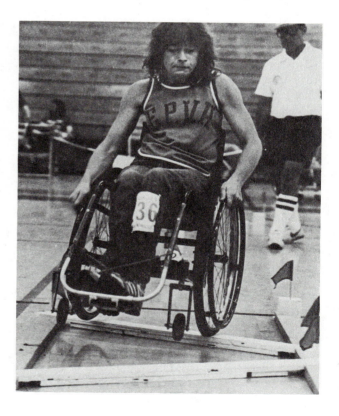

Fitness and Spinoneuromuscular Conditions

A relatively substantial amount of literature on adult fitness has been amassed, but much work is still needed. Published research on adults is based largely on standard upper extremity laboratory equipment. Whereas prior to the 1980s the life span of persons with spinoneuromuscular conditions was shortened by respiratory infections, pneumonia, and other illnesses, longevity and causes of death (heart and vascular disease) are now about the same as for the able-bodied. Obviously, disabled persons need vigorous training regimes, as do the able-bodied. This training, however, must be adapted to obtain maximum benefits from arm exercise since legs and, often, trunk muscles are paralyzed. Bicycles using arm cranking rather than foot pedaling are generally employed to obtain training effects in the lab. Sprints and distance racing in wheelchairs can be used in the field as well as weight training.

If persons in wheelchairs are active in work and leisure, their lives probably demand a greater level of fitness than is needed by the general population. Making wheelchair transfers demands a tremendous amount of arm and shoulder strength, as does overcoming architectural barriers. The heart rate of wheelchair users, because the work load is concentrated on a smaller muscle mass, is higher than in persons with equivalent oxygen intake who are walking (Davis, Kofsky, Kelsey, & Shephard, 1981).

Many persons in wheelchairs are sedentary; reasons for this include (a) lack of employable skills, (b) depression, (c) anger about their situation, (d) nonsupportive family and friends, (e) fear of unknown and/or of rejection, and (f) insufficient leisure training and opportunities. Such sedentary persons have been shown to have 50% less maximum oxygen uptake than wheelchair athletes who regularly train vigorously (Zwiren & Bar-Or, 1975). Wheelchair athletes, however, have significantly lower maximum oxygen uptake than able-bodied athletes (Gass & Camp, 1979; Zwiren & Bar-Or, 1975). One reason for this may be the characteristic loss of vasomotor regulation below the lesion level; this causes poor blood flow to active muscles, inefficient venous return, and poor stroke volume. Another reason may be local muscle fatigue, caused by so much energy cost on so little muscle mass.

Muscle strength of adult wheelchair users has been measured primarily by isokinetic tests on the Cybex II apparatus and static strength tests on upper arm cable tensiometers and hand grip dynamometers. As in the able-bodied population, there are significant differences between genders. Moreover, among males, there is a significant strength difference between Class II and Class III, IV, and V persons (Kofsky, Shephard, Davis, & Jackson, 1985).

These same researchers report a significant difference between genders in aerobic power, as predicted by a submaximum arm ergometer test (Kofsky, Shephard, Jackson, & Keene, 1983). In this measure also, among males, there is a significant aerobic power difference between Class II and Class III, IV, and V persons. This research is reviewed to emphasize the importance, both in research and teaching, of considering classifications rather than lumping all wheelchair users together.

To date, the only published fitness research on youth is that of Winnick and Short (1984) in conjunction with Project UNIQUE. Their subjects included 141 youths, ages 10 to 17 years, with spinoneuromuscular conditions classified into NWAA Classes II, III, IV, and V. On 11 tests (triceps, abdominal, and subscapular skinfolds, right and left hand grip strength, arm hang, pull-ups, 50-yard dash, shuttle run, long distance run, and softball distance throws), there were significant gender differences only on the softball throw. This favored males. There were no significant test differences between NWAA classes. Norms, based on these subjects, and testing procedures appear in a Project UNIQUE manual (Winnick & Short, 1985).

Comparisons were made also between neurospinally disabled and able-bodied students. These showed the disabled students to be inferior on all measures compared. Moreover, the normally expected improvements from age to age did not appear in the disabled youth.

Spina Bifida

The incidence of spina bifida per 1,000 live births ranges from 1.1 to 4.2. (See Figure 21.22.) As a congenital orthopedic impairment, it ranks second only to cerebral palsy in prevalence in the adapted physical education setting. *Spina bifida* is a defect in the spinal column caused by failure of one or more vertebral arches (posterior part of vertebrae) to close before birth (see Figure 21.23). The defect takes the form of a sac (tumor) caused by protrusion of the spinal cord and cerebrospinal fluid through the opening. While several terms are used to designate the degree of severity, the most common condition is myelomeningocele (MM). The derivation of this word is *myelo-* (prefix denoting spinal cord), *meningo-* (referring to membrane or covering of spinal cord), and *cele* (from kele meaning tumor). Thus, MM and spina bifida are often used interchangeably.

MM children whose conditions are not complicated by multiple handicaps can become excellent swimmers by reliance upon strong arm strokes. Typically, they are limited out of the water by long leg and back braces, crutches, or wheelchairs. The adapted physical educator should request information from the

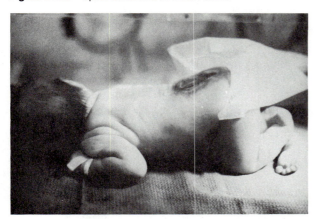

Figure 21.22 Spina bifida in a newborn infant.

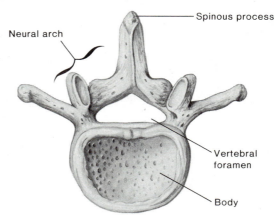

Figure 21.23 Parts of a single vertebra viewed from the top.

Neural arch

Spinous process

Vertebral foramen

Body

Table 21.4
Relationship between Location of Spina Bifida, Loss of Muscle Control, and Type of Ambulation[a]

Approximate Location of Vertebral Defect	Point Below which Control Is Lost	Prognosis for Ambulation	Equipment Used for Ambulation	NWAA Classification
12th thoracic	Trunk	Nonambulatory	Wheelchair, standing brace	Probable Class IV
1st lumbar	Pelvis	Exercise ambulation	Wheelchair, long leg braces, and crutches	
3rd lumbar	Hip	Household ambulation	Long leg braces and crutches	Probable Class V
5th lumbar	Knee	Community ambulation	Short leg braces and crutches	

[a]Table supplied by Dennis Brunt, who has his doctoral degree in adapted physical education and is certified also in physical therapy.

parents in the application and removal of long leg and back braces, since the child is certain to need bathroom facilities at one time or another. Unless the physician advises otherwise, the braces should be removed for rest periods, training in relaxation, and passive range of motion exercises.

Children with myeloceles can enjoy all the physical education activities possible from a wheelchair. They can often excel in upper limb sports like archery, rifle shooting, and bowling. Their physical education programming is similar to that of other children in wheelchairs. Whether or not they need the wheelchair for ambulation, MM children should be taught wheelchair sports so that they can engage (if they choose) in the vigorous competition available through disabled sports organizations. Those in long and short leg braces have been known to complete the 600-yard walk-run, to master sport skills like dribbling and basketball shooting, and to engage in other mainstream physical education activities with their peers.

The higher the location of MM on the spinal column, the more nerves are affected and, consequently, the greater the muscular involvement. Table 21.4 shows that MM in the lowermost part of the back generally permits walking with crutches and leg braces, whereas MM in the upper lumbar region or higher involves more or less complete trunk and pelvic paralysis and resulting inability to ambulate independently. Thus, spina bifida persons are eligible for wheelchair sports.

Spina bifida children are fitted with braces and crutches (see Figure 21.24) as soon as they are ready to walk, often at ages 2 to 3. Learning to ambulate seems very frustrating for many of them, and games should be devised to encourage practice in ambulation as well as strengthening of the upper limbs. While many of these preschoolers seem to cry a lot, this is not from pain. Physical educators should avoid being manipulated by MM children, many of whom are very bright and simply prefer being sedentary to learning new movement patterns.

Figure 21.24 In the least involved type of spina bifida, the child can ambulate with Lofstrand or forearm crutches and short leg braces. Dr. Ken Duke is accompanying the child to a sports activity.

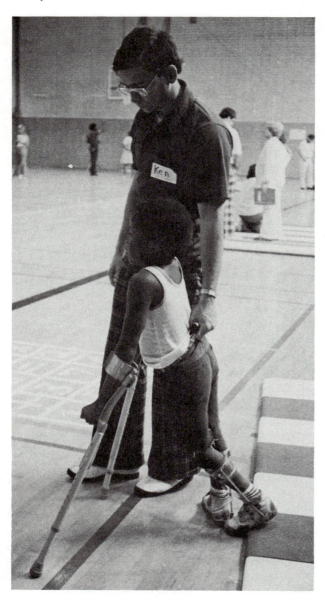

Figure 21.25 A surgically corrected spina bifida in a severely handicapped child with concurrent hydrocephalus. Surgery is usually done during the first few hours of life.

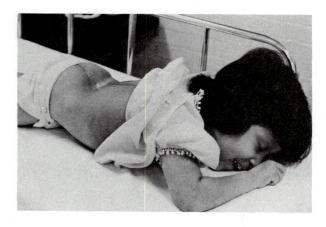

Figure 21.26 Catheterization as a means of withdrawing urine from the bladder is used by persons with spina bifida, spinal cord injuries, and other conditions that cause urinary incontinence. The catheter is lubricated and then inserted into the penis about 6 inches or into the female opening about 3 inches. Parents can generally instruct teachers in the correct procedure.

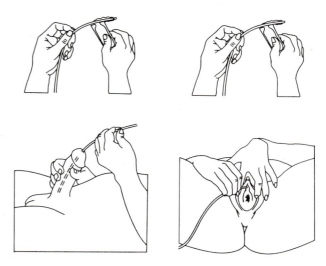

Many MM children are multihandicapped. Approximately 90% have *hydrocephalus* (Figure 21.25) (increased amount of cerebrospinal fluid in ventricles of brain), which is generally relieved surgically by the *shunting* procedure. Although usually correctable, hydrocephalus may cause some brain damage, with resulting mental retardation and/or perceptual motor and attention disorders. In some children, the hydrocephalus eventually arrests itself, whereas in others, repeated surgical intervention is needed. In infancy and the preschool years, hydrocephalus and complications of its treatment appear to be the major cause of death.

Most MM children have little or no control of their bladder. This problem, called *incontinence*, requires the use of special procedures for controlled urination. The most common procedure seems to be *catheterization*, the inserting of a catheter (tube) through the urethra into the bladder for the withdrawal of urine at set intervals. Figure 21.26 illustrates this procedure for both sexes. In early childhood, catheterization must be done by the teacher or an aide, but later students learn to perform this simple, nonsterile procedure for themselves. Alternatives to catheterization are the Credé maneuver (exerting manual pressure on the lower abdomen to initiate urination) or the wearing of a urinary bag. Whatever the procedure, frequent emptying of the bladder is extremely important. Retention of urine leads to urinary and kidney infections, a major cause of illness and death among persons with spina bifida.

Other problems likely to be experienced by persons with spina bifida are obesity, skin lesions, and deformities of the spine and lower extremities. Approximately 50% of MM children become obese; this increases to 95% in MM children who spend most of their time in wheelchairs. Skin lesions often result from rubbing of braces against the back or from bruises and injuries to lower limbs. Since MM persons lack sensation, they may rub areas open in seat scooting or other activities involving contact between body parts and a surface. Once a lesion occurs, poor circulation seems to slow healing. Wrinkled socks may cause blisters also. Deformities of the spine (lordosis, scoliosis, and kyphosis) and foot defects (talipes) often occur with spina bifida. These problems can sometimes be prevented (at least partially) by attention to positioning, emphasis on good body alignment, and exercise.

Spina bifida children are more likely to need full-time adapted physical education placement in early childhood than later. During the first few years in school, physical education should stress movement exploration, creative dance, rhythms, and swimming.

Appraisal of nonlocomotor movement capabilities lends insight into program planning. The answers to the following questions can be derived from movement exploration in a dance or aquatic setting.

1. What body parts can the person bend and straighten? What *combination* of body parts can he or she bend and straighten? When performed rhythmically, bending and straightening become swinging.

2. What body parts can the person stretch? In which directions can he or she stretch?

3. What body parts can the person twist? What *combination* of body parts can he or she twist? Can he or she twist at different rates of speed? Can he or she combine twists with other basic movements?

4. What body parts can the person circle? What *combination* of body parts can he or she circle?

5. Can the person rock forward in the wheelchair and bend over to recover an object on the floor? If lying or curled up on a mat, can the person rock backward and forward? Can this rocking movement provide impetus for changing positions? For instance, when sitting on a mat, can he or she rock over to a hands and knees creeping position?

Figure 21.27 Scooterboard activities offer young spina bifida children easy mobility while building arm and shoulder strength.

6. Does the person have enough arm strength to lift and replace the body in the wheelchair in a bouncing action? Can he or she relax and bounce on a mattress, a trampoline, or a moon walk?

7. What body parts can the person shake? What combination of body parts? Can he or she shake rhythm instruments?

8. Can the person sway from side to side? Can he or she sway back and forth while hanging onto a rope or maintaining contact with a piece of apparatus?

9. Can the person push objects away from the body? Does he or she have the potential to succeed in games based upon pushing skills like box hockey and shuffleboard? Can he or she maneuver a scooter board? (See Figure 21.27.) A tricycle? A wagon? Can he or she walk while holding onto or pushing the wheelchair? Can he or she push off from the side of the swimming pool? Can some part of his or her body push off from a mat?

10. Can the person pull objects toward him or her? In which directions can he or she pull? Can the person use a hand-over-hand motion to pull himself or herself along a rope, bar, or ladder? Can he or she manipulate weighted pulleys?

11. Can the person change levels? For instance, can he or she move from a lying position to a sitting, squatting, or kneeling position or vice versa? How does the person get from a bed, sofa, chair, or toilet to the wheelchair and vice versa?

12. Can the person demonstrate safe techniques for falling? When the person loses balance, in which direction does he or she usually fall?

Spinal Cord Injuries

The incidence of spinal cord injuries is 10,000 to 12,000 each year. Approximately 85% of these injuries are sustained by males, with the peak age-range being 15 to 28 years. The causes of spinal cord injuries are estimated as follows: 40% vehicular accidents, 20% falls, and 40% gunshot wounds, sporting accidents, industrial accidents, and agricultural accidents in order of decreasing incidence. Although spinal cord injuries are rare compared to spina bifida, persons with these injuries are highly visible. The accident typically stuns the whole community, especially when it occurs in high school youths.

The widespread popularity of wheelchair basketball has also contributed to awareness of the general public concerning the disability. Many spinal cord injured (SCI) persons are war veterans, as depicted in the movie *Coming Home,* which illustrates a T11-L2 injury (i.e., Class IV). An excellent way to learn about capabilities associated with damage at different levels is to watch videotapes of such films as *Whose Life Is It Anyway* (depicting an architect with a C4-5 level injury caused by an automobile accident) and *The Other Side of The Mountain* (depicting an athlete with a C5-6 level injury caused by a skiing accident). Books and plays on which these films are based may be read also.

The most common injury is the middle-to-low cervical lesion (C5-6). Refer to Table 21.2 and note that this quadriplegic condition is a NWAA Class 1A. The easiest way to visualize the C5-6 injury is to remember that there is little or no hand control without adaptive devices, there is absence or great weakness of the triceps (elbow extensors), and there is almost no trunk control and mobility. Persons with this injury generally use a motorized chair for activities of daily living. In relearning how to swim, they initially need flotation devices, but have the ability to swim independently. With a properly fitted high-back manual sports chair, they can engage in many sports activities. Some have completed marathons (26.2 miles).

The second most common site of injury is the thoracolumbar junction (T12-L1), which is a NWAA Class IV. These persons can learn all gaits and typically use Lofstrand (forearm) crutches for activities of daily living. They can learn almost any wheelchair sport and, with special apparatus, can stand while snow skiing.

About 50% of SCI persons sustain complete severing of the spinal cord. When this occurs, there is total loss of the following:

1. All voluntary movement below the lesion level.
2. All sensation below the lesion level.
3. Normal sensation and control of bladder, bowel, and sexual functioning.
4. Normal control of sympathetic nervous system, which can affect temperature control, heart rate, blood pressure, and other vital functions.

Especially important to these persons is understanding that their sexual desire is not lost and that many alternative ways of making love are possible.

If incomplete severing occurs, then any combination of the problems above may occur. Sometimes there are lesions at two totally separate levels affecting the two sides of the body differently.

In teaching students with spinal cord injuries, it is best to *ask* them what they can do and encourage them to help plan their own physical education and recreation activities. Most important is motivation, optimal involvement with peers, and group problem solving in regard to architectural barriers and transportation. Their problems are similar to those of other persons confined to wheelchairs: a tendency for the hip, knee, and ankle flexors to become too tight, with resulting contractures (abnormal shortening of muscles) from extended sitting; ulcers or pressure sores from remaining in one position too long; bruises and friction burns from rubbing body parts that lack sensation and give no pain warnings; and tendency toward obesity because of low energy expenditure.

Because the sacral level of the spinal cord supplies innervation for bladder and bowels, persons with spinal cord injuries lack control of these organs. Consequently, they use catheters or wear urinary bags at all times, including in swimming. Defecation is managed by scheduling time and amount of eating as well as regulating time of bowel movements. If defecation becomes too great a problem, surgical procedures (ileostomy or colostomy) are performed, creating an opening in the side. A tube inserted in this opening connects the intestine with a bag that fills up with fecal matter and must be emptied and cleaned periodically. These bags are not worn during swimming; the opening is covered with a water-tight bandage. Persons with spinal cord injuries have a high incidence of urinary and kidney infections. Should the physical educator notice signs of infection (flushed face, elevated temperature, or other signs), he or she should insist on no exercise until symptoms disappear.

Many paraplegics become superb athletes. Weight lifting and strength exercises for the upper extremities are extremely important not only for athletics but also for mastering crutch walking and transfers in and out of the wheelchair. A well-rounded exercise program for all usable parts of the body should include flexibility (range of movement) activities, cardiovascular work through arm pedaling of bicycle ergometer or distance wheelchair dashes, and agility maneuvers.

Poliomyelitis

In 1915–1917, 1944, and again in 1952, major epidemics of poliomyelitis left thousands of persons paralyzed. The most famous of these was Franklin D. Roosevelt, who in 1938 organized the National Foundation for Infantile Paralysis and the memorable March of Dimes campaigns. Until the late 1950s, when the Salk vaccine was introduced, polio was the leading crippler of children in the United States. Now, most of these persons have graduated from high school or college, and the physical educator seldom sees the residual paralysis left by polio.

Polio is caused by a virus that attacks the anterior horn of the spinal cord. The inflammation affects the motor cells in the spinal cord, which in turn affects the muscles. The Greek prefix *polio* means gray and refers to the fact that nerve cell bodies are gray matter.

Three stages are detectable in the course of the disease: (a) *acute,* which lasts a week to 10 days and is characterized by sore throat, fever, nausea, vomiting, and muscle stiffness; (b) *convalescent,* which lasts anywhere from a few weeks to several months, during which muscles improve in function or return to normal, depending upon the extent of damage; and (c) *chronic,* which begins about 18 months after the onset of the disease and continues for years. Tendon transplants and arthrodesis are common during the chronic stage. Aproximately 6% of the persons who contract polio die, 14% have severe paralysis, 30% suffer mild after-effects, and 50% recover completely.

Implications for Physical Education

Many orthopedic deformities are not handicaps in the sense that movements are restricted. Children learn quickly to compensate for the inconvenience of a deformed or absent foot or arm. At the elementary school level, such children, if so inclined, can achieve considerable success in athletic activities. Many participate in Little League baseball and Pee Wee football, deriving most of their childhood satisfactions through sports. Unfortunately, as they progress to the middle grades, and competition for a position on the team increases, the disability influences speed and accuracy just enough to prevent selection.

Adolescents with a disability often content themselves with intramurals or warming the bench as members of the B interscholastic team. They may gradually lose interest or channel their energies into such compensatory activities as athletic trainer, team manager, sportswriter, photographer, broadcaster, scorekeeper, or official. Regardless of their role, inclusion on out-of-town trips, practice sessions, and extracurricular activities meets social and emotional needs more fully than that of substitutes. The other alternative is wheelchair sports. Ideally, students are provided opportunities for both integrated and wheelchair activities.

Learning Activities

1. Invite the local wheelchair basketball team to play a demonstration game at your university and/or attend several of their regularly scheduled games. Become acquainted with the sports classification and playing ability of each team member.

2. Hold a track and field meet at your university for persons with orthopedic disabilities. Use the official classification systems of NWAA and USAAA in planning events. If persons with cerebral palsy plan to compete, use the NASCP classification system (see Chapter 23) in planning their events.

3. You and your classmates simulate (role play) assigned disabilities and practice sports skills. Use official NWBA, NWAA, or USAAA rules to guide the playing of the games. If possible, employ an OI athlete to serve as a consultant in guiding this experience.

4. Check that your university library has up-to-date official rule books of NWBA, NWAA, USAAA, and similar organizations and that it subscribes to *Sports 'N Spokes* and *Palaestra,* the two magazines that best feature sports.

5. Obtain information about winter sports and other activities conducted by the National Handicapped Sports and Recreation Association (NHSRA) and attend such events. If your climate does not support snow activities, review films that cover this content.

6. Request your kinesiology/biomechanics professors to become involved in filming and analyzing the movement patterns of persons with different OI problems. Create a library of such films and videotapes for individual study.

7. Given films, videotapes, and slides of different OI conditions, practice assigning classifications and noting sports most appropriate for each person.

8. Devote 1 to 2 hours a week to engaging in sports and/or coaching persons with OI conditions.

9. Invite a consultant in orthopedic medicine or rehabilitation to class to explain common surgical procedures (osteotomy, arthroplasty, arthrodesis, and tendon transplants) mentioned in this and subsequent chapters. Ask how these operations affect physical education participation.

References

Davis, G., Kofsky, P., Kelsey, J., & Shephard, R. (1981). Cardiorespiratory fitness and muscular strength of wheelchair users. *Canadian Medical Association Journal, 125*(12), 1317–1323.

Epps, Jr., C. H., & Vaughn, H. H. (1972). Training the child with an acquired lower-limb amputation. In National Academy of Sciences (Ed.), *The child with an acquired amputation* (p. 129). Washington, DC: Author.

Federal Register, August 23, 1977, PL94–142, the Education for All Handicapped Children Act.

Gass, C., & Camp, E. (1979). Physiological characteristics of trained paraplegic and tetraplegic subjects. *Medicine and Science in Sports and Exercise, 11,* 256–259.

Kofsky, P., Shephard, R., Davis, G., & Jackson, R. (1985). Fitness classification tables for lower-limb disabled individuals. In C. Sherrill (Ed.), *Sport and disabled athletes* (pp. 147–156). Champaign, IL: Human Kinetics Publishers.

Kofsky, P., Shephard, R., Jackson, R., & Keene, C. (1983). Field testing: Assessment of physical fitness of disabled athletes. *European Journal of Applied Physiology, 51,* 109–120.

Richard III. In W. A. Wright (Ed.). (1944). *The complete works of William Shakespeare* (Cambridge Edition Text) (p. 113). Philadelphia: Blakiston.

Rothenberg, M., & White, M. (1985). *David.* Old Tappan, NJ: Fleming H. Revell Company.

White House Conference on Child Health and Protection, Committee on Physically and Mentally Handicapped. (1933). *The handicapped child* (p. 3). New York: Appleton-Century Co.

Winnick, J., & Short, F. (1984). The physical fitness of youngsters with spinal neuromuscular conditions. *Adapted Physical Activity Quarterly, 1*(1), 37–51.

Winnick, J., & Short, F. (1985). *Physical fitness testing of the disabled: Project UNIQUE.* Champaign, IL: Human Kinetics Publishers.

Zwiren, L. D., & Bar-Or, O. (1975). Responses to exercise of paraplegics who differ in conditioning level. *Medicine and Science in Sports and Exercise, 7,* 94–98.

Bibliography

Adams, R. C., Daniel, A. N., McCubbin, J., & Rullman, L. (1982). *Games, sports, and exercises for the physically handicapped* (3rd ed.). Philadelphia: Lea & Febiger.

Anderson, E. M., & Plewis, I. (1977). Impairment of a motor skill in children with spina bifida cystica and hydrocephalus: An exploratory study. *British Journal of Psychology, 68,* 61–70.

Barclay, V. (1979). Competition for physically handicapped children. In L. Groves (Ed.), *Physical education for special needs* (pp. 49–80). London: Cambridge University Press.

Bauer, J. J. (1972). *Riding for rehabilitation: A guide for handicapped riders and their instructors.* Toronto, Ontario, Canada: Canadian Stage and Arts Publications Limited (49 Wellington Street East).

Bigge, J., & O'Donnell, P. (1982). *Teaching individuals with physical and multiple disabilities* (2nd ed.). Columbus, OH: Charles E. Merrill.

Bleck, E., & Nagel, D. (1982). *Physically handicapped children—a medical atlas for teachers* (2nd ed.). New York: Grune & Stratton.

Brunt, D. (1980). Characteristics of upper limb movements in a sample of meningomyelocele children. *Perceptual and Motor Skills, 51,* 431–437.

Brunt, D. (1981). Predictive factors of perceptual motor ability in children with meningomyelocele. *American Corrective Therapy Journal, 35,* 42–46.

Brunt, D. (1984). Apraxic tendencies in children with meningomyelocele. *Adapted Physical Activity Quarterly, 1*(1), 612–667.

Cameron, B., Ward, G., & Wicks, J. (1977). Relationship of type of training to maximum oxygen uptake and upper limb strength in male paraplegic athletes. *Medicine and Science in Sports and Exercise, 9,* 58.

Cowart, J. (1979). Sports adaptations for unilateral and bilateral upper-limb amputees. *AAHPERD Practical Pointers, 2,* 1–13.

Crase, N. (1977). Wheelin' softball. *Sports 'n Spokes, 3,* 5.

Crase, N. (1978). Horseshoes. *Sports 'n Spokes, 4,* 21.

Crase, N. (1979). Amputee sports. *Sports 'n Spokes, 5,* 11–12.

Cratty, B. J. (1969). *Developmental games for physically handicapped children.* Palo Alto, CA: Peek Publications.

Davis, G., Tupling, S., & Shephard, R. (1985). Dynamic strength and physical activity in wheelchair users. In C. Sherrill (Ed.), *Sport and disabled athletes* (pp. 139–146). Champaign, IL: Human Kinetics Publishers.

Emes, C. G. (1973). A comparison of wheelchair and nonwheelchair athletes on specified tests of physical fitness. (Doctoral dissertation, University of Oregon). *Comprehensive Dissertation Index, 1973–1977, 34,* 12A.

Emes, C. G. (1977). Physical work capacity of wheelchair athletes. *Research Quarterly, 48,* 209–212.

Freeman, J. (Ed.). (1974). *Practical management to meningomyelocele.* Baltimore: University Park Press.

Goldberg, R. (1974). Rehabilitation of the burn patient. *Rehabilitation Literature, 35,* 73–78.

Goodwin, G. (1978). Outward bound. *Sports 'n Spokes, 4,* 5–7.

Guttman, L. (1976). *Textbook of sport for the disabled.* England, Aylesbury, Bucks: HM & M Publishers Ltd.

Hedrick, B. (1985). The effect of wheelchair tennis participation and mainstreaming upon the perceptions of competence of physically disabled adolescents. *Therapeutic Recreation Journal, 19*(2), 34–40.

Hopper, C. (1985). Socialization of wheelchair athletes. In C. Sherrill (Ed.), *Sport and disabled athletes* (pp. 197–202). Champaign, IL: Human Kinetics Publishers.

Kegel, B., Webster, J., & Burgess, E. (1980). Recreational activities of lower extremity amputees: A survey. *Archives of Physical Medicine Rehabilitation, 61,* 258–264.

Labanowich, S. (1975). *Wheelchair basketball: A history of the national association and an analysis of the structure.* Unpublished doctoral dissertation, University of Illinois.

Labanowich, S. (1979). The psychology of wheelchair sports. *Therapeutic Recreation Journal, 12,* 11–17.

Loiselle, D. (1979). Sport and the physically disabled. *Leisurability, 6,* 3–6.

Lorber, J. (1971). Results of treatment of myelomeningocele. *Developmental Medicine and Child Neurology, 13,* 279–303.

McBee, F., & Ballinger, J. (1984). *The continental quest.* Tampa, FL: Overland Press.

McCowan, K. (1972). *It is ability that counts: Therapeutic riding for handicapped.* Olivet, MI: Olivet College Press.

McDaniel, J. W. (1976). *Physical disability and human behavior.* New York: Pergamon Press.

McLaurin, R. L. (Ed.). (1977). *Myelomeningocele.* New York: Grune & Stratton.

Molnar, G. E., & Taft, L. T. (1977). Spina bifida and limb deficiencies. *Current problems in pediatrics, 7,* 2–55.

Nilsson, S., Staff, P., & Pruett, E. (1975). Physical work capacity and the effect of training on subjects with long-standing paraplegia. *Scandinavian Journal of Rehabilitative Medicine, 7,* 51–56.

Pomeroy, J. (1964). *Recreation for the physically handicapped.* New York: Macmillan.

Price, R. (1980). *Physical education and the physically handicapped child.* London: Lepus Books.

Savitz, H. (1978). *Wheelchair champions: A history of wheelchair sports.* New York: Thomas Y. Crowell.

Smith, E. D. (1965). *Spina bifida and the total care of spinal myelomeningocele.* Springfield, IL: Charles C. Thomas.

Smith, M. L. (1976). Competitive swimming. *Sports 'n Spokes Reprint Series.* (Includes articles from 6 issues [Sept./Oct. 1976 to Sept./Oct. 1977]).

Sosne, M. (1973). *Handbook of adapted physical education equipment and its use.* Springfield, IL: Charles C. Thomas.

Stein, J. (1978). Weight training for wheelchair sports. *AAHPERD Practical Pointers, 2,* 1–19.

Stein, J. (1979). Principles and practices for championship performances in wheelchair track events. *AAHPERD Practical Pointers 2,* 1–23.

Szyman, R. (1980). The effect of participation in wheelchair sports. *Dissertation Abstracts International, 41,* 804A–805A. (University Microfilms No. 8018209).

Weininger, O., Rotenberg, G., & Henry, A. (1972). Body image of handicapped children (spina bifida). *Journal of Personality Assessment, 36,* 248–253.

Weisman, M., & Godfrey, J. (1976). *So get on with it: A celebration of wheelchair sports.* New York: Doubleday.

Weiss, M., & Beck, J. (1973). Sport as part of therapy and rehabilitation of paraplegics. *Paraplegia, 2,* 166–178.

Wicks, J., Oldridge, N., Cameron, B., & Jones, N. (1983). Arm cranking and wheelchair ergometry in elite spinal cord injured athletes. *Medicine and Science in Sports and Exercise, 15,* 224–231.

Zwiren, L. D., Huberman, G., & Bar-Or, O. (1977). Cardiopulmonary functions of sedentary and highly active paraplegics. *Medicine and Science in Sports and Exercise, 5,* 683.

22 Les Autres Conditions

Figure 22.1 Boy in stage 5 of muscular dystrophy has such limited strength that bowling must be with a light ball and close to the pins.

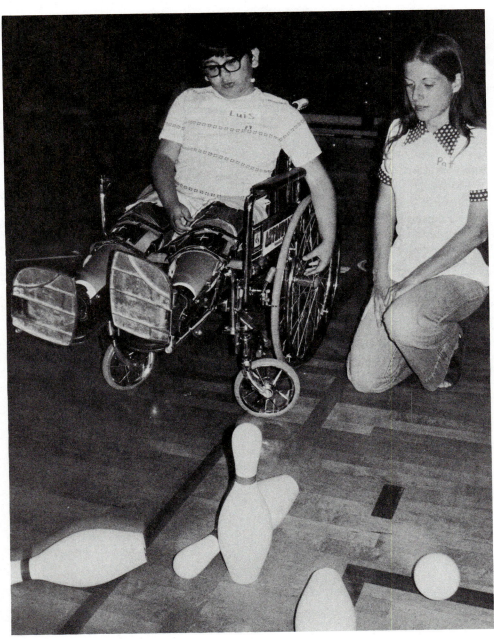

Chapter Objectives

After you have studied this chapter, you should be able to

1. Define *les autres,* cite examples of common les autres conditions, and discuss physical education programming for each.

2. Identify three types of muscular dystrophy, discuss stages of functional ability, and suggest physical education activities for each level. Relate these levels to NASCP sports classifications (see Chapter 8 or 23) and discuss appropriate sports competition for each.

3. Describe and discuss each of the following conditions: multiple sclerosis, arthritis, arthrogryposis, osteogenesis imperfecta, Ehlers-Danlos syndrome, Friedreich's ataxia, Charcot-Marie-Tooth syndrome, Barre-Guillain syndrome, spinal muscle atrophies, and progressive muscle weakness conditions of middle and old age. Indicate physical education programming for each. Be able to recognize and name such conditions in films, videotapes, slides, or real life.

4. Differentiate between achondroplasia, Morquio syndrome, and Turner's syndrome. Describe each and discuss physical education programming.

5. Discuss short stature and growth disorders and indicate why such terms as *dwarf* and *midget* are not favored by the Little People of America. Suggest applications in physical education assessment and programming to meet needs of persons with chondrodystrophies.

6. Given age, gender, syndrome or condition, and description of psychomotor functioning of hypothesized students, write the physical education IEP. Substantiate physical education placement as integration, partial integration, or separate.

7. Discuss available and needed research on physical education and athletics for les autres students.

Les autres, the French term for *the others,* is used in sports to denote the *other locomotor disabilities,* meaning those not eligible to compete in NWAA wheelchair sports or in NASCP cerebral palsy sports. Among the conditions specified as les autres are muscular dystrophy (see Figure 22.1), arthritis, multiple sclerosis, short stature and growth disorders, osteogenesis imperfecta, arthrogryposis, Friedreich's ataxia, and numerous little-known syndromes that affect movement.

Sports competition for les autres has been conducted in the United States by the National Association of Sports for Cerebral Palsy since its founding in 1978. Internationally, sports competition for les autres is governed by the International Sports Organization for the Disabled (ISOD), which uses a different classification system from that adopted by the United States. In 1985, the first National Les Autres Games was conducted in Detroit, Michigan, in conjunction with the fifth National Cerebral Palsy Games. Les autres athletes also compete in NWBA wheelchair basketball.

The 1984 International Games for the Disabled were largely responsible for progress in this country in the development of les autres sports competition. Twenty countries brought les autres athletes who competed in air pistol, air rifle, archery, field, lawn bowling, swimming, table tennis, track, sitting and standing volleyball, and weight lifting. ISOD representatives also described the success of les autres athletes in such winter sports as alpine and nordic skiing, biathlon (10k, track, and air rifle), and various sledge (sled) activities. In the past, United States physical educators have been aware of the importance of regular exercise in conditions of progressive muscular weakness; they now realize that students with les autres conditions can learn and subsequently compete in almost any sport.

Thus, new role models are appearing, and attitudes about physical education for les autres students are rapidly changing. Physicians should be informed that their medical colleagues were involved in the conduct of the 1984 International Games for the Disabled and that enforcement of a classification system ensures competition against others with the same functional abilities.

Not all les autres persons have progressive muscular weakness and/or a disabling condition. Persons with skeletal growth disorders, for instance, are normal in every respect except for their short stature and disproportionate body parts, which put them at a decided disadvantage in sports activities against persons of average height. Over the years, their national organization (Little People of America) has conducted golf tournaments, basketball games, and other contests in conjunction with its annual meeting. A bowling tournament, as well as other sports events specifically for little people, was held in 1985 as part of the first National Les Autres Games.

Sports and Age Classifications

Les autres sports in the United States use the same eight sports classifications as cerebral palsy sports. In most sports, les autres and cerebral palsied persons can compete in the same heats, but separate awards should be made available within each class (i.e., it is not fair to permit a les autres person to win over a cerebral palsied person or vice versa). Until more participants are involved, age classifications cannot be initiated in les autres sports. Generally, children 8 years and older are welcome to compete; most regional and national competitions have qualifying standards that all athletes, regardless of age, must meet.

Physical Education Implications

If instruction in the regular physical education setting can be adapted so that les autres students can fully participate, they should be integrated part of the time with nondisabled peers. Part of their physical education, however, should be separate and focus on competence in wheelchair sports and/or activities in which they can compete equitably with persons having comparable disability. Regular exercise is more important for these students than for the able-bodied.

Some les autres conditions may be complicated from time to time by respiratory and other infections. It is important to remember that persons running an elevated temperature and showing other signs of acute infection should not engage in vigorous exercise.

Should students evidence chronic, long-term infection of any kind, the physical educator should confer with the physician concerning the best type of activity to prevent loss of motion range and contractures. When students are assigned to physical therapy, the exercises done in that setting should not be substituted for physical education and recreation activities that facilitate peer group involvement and social growth. Particular emphasis must be given to maintenance of good mental health, enjoyment of each day, and motivation to live life (however limited) to its fullest.

Muscular Dystrophies

The muscular dystrophies are a group of genetically determined conditions in which progressive muscular weakness is attributed to pathological, biochemical, and electrical changes that occur in the muscle fibers. The specific causes of these changes remain unknown. Several different diseases have been identified since 1850, many of which are rare. The three muscular dystrophies having the highest incidence are Duchenne, facio-scapular-humeral, and limb girdle types. Approximately 250,000 persons in the United States have muscular dystrophy. Of this number, 50,000 are confined to a wheelchair or bed. Most persons with muscular dystrophy fall between the ages of 3 and 13 and attend public school. Of these, few live beyond early adulthood. Specifically, 1 of every 500 children in our schools will get or has muscular dystrophy. Boys are affected five or six times more often than girls.

Muscular dystrophy in itself is not fatal, but the secondary complications of immobilization heighten the effects of respiratory disorders and heart disease. With the weakening of respiratory muscles and the reduction in vital capacity, the child may succumb to a simple respiratory infection. Dystrophic changes in cardiac muscles increase susceptibility to heart disease. The dilemma confronting the physical educator is how to increase and/or maintain cardiovascular fitness when muscle weakness makes running and other endurance type activities increasingly difficult. Breathing exercises and games are recommended.

Duchenne Muscular Dystrophy

The Duchenne type of muscular dystrophy is the most common and most severe. Its onset is usually before age 3, but symptoms may appear as late as age 10 or 11. Males are affected more frequently than females. The condition is caused by a sex-linked trait that is transmitted through females to males. The sister of an affected male has a 50% chance of being a carrier and will pass the defective gene on to 50% of her sons. Persons with muscular dystrophy seldom live long enough to marry. Characteristics of Duchenne muscular dystrophy include

1. Awkward side-to-side waddling gait.
2. Difficulty in running, tricycling, climbing stairs, and rising from chairs.
3. Tendency to fall frequently.

Figure 22.2 Walking posture and Gower's sign in muscular dystrophy. Gower's sign refers to the peculiar method of rise to stand.

4. Peculiar way of rising from a fall. From a supine position, children turn onto their face, put hands and feet on the floor, and then climb up their legs with their hands. This means of rising is called the *Gower's sign* (Figure 22.2).

5. Lordosis.

6. Hypertrophy of calf muscles and, occasionally, of deltoid, infraspinatus, and lateral quadriceps.

This hypertrophy (sometimes called pseudohypertrophy) occurs when quantities of fat and connective tissue replace degenerating muscle fibers, which progressively become smaller, fragment, and then disappear. The hypertrophy gives the mistaken impression of extremely well-developed healthy musculature. In actuality, the muscles are quite weak.

The initial areas of muscular weakness, however, are the gluteals, abdominals, erector spinae of the back, and anterior tibials. The first three of these explain the characteristic lordosis and difficulty in rising while the last explains the frequent falls. Weakness of the anterior tibials results in a foot drop (pes equinovarus), which causes children to trip over their own feet. Within 7 to 10 years after the initial onset of symptoms, contractures begin to form in the ankle, knee, and hip joints. Contractures of the Achilles tendons force children to walk on their toes and increase still further the incidence of falling. Between ages 10 and 15 most dystrophic children lose the capacity to walk, progressively spending more and more time in the wheelchair and/or bed. This enforced inactivity leads to severe distortions of the chest wall and kyphoscoliosis.

Facio-Scapular-Humeral Type

This is the most common form of muscular dystrophy in adults. It affects both genders equally. Symptoms generally do not appear until adolescence and often are not recognized until adulthood. The prognosis is good, compared with that of the other dystrophies, and life span is normal. The disease may arrest itself at any stage. Characteristics include

1. Progressive weakness of the shoulder muscles beginning with the trapezius and pectoralis major and sequentially involving the biceps, triceps, deltoid, and erector spinae.

2. Progressive weakness of the muscles of the face, causing drooping cheeks, pouting lips, and inability to close the eyes completely. The face takes on an immobile quality since muscles lack the strength to express emotion.

3. Hip and thigh muscles are affected less often. When involvement does occur, it is manifested by a waddling side-to-side gait and the tendency to fall easily.

Limb Girdle Type

The limb girdle type may occur at any time from age 10 or after. The onset, however, is usually the second decade. Both genders are affected equally. The earliest symptom is usually difficulty in raising the arms above shoulder level or awkwardness in climbing stairs.

Weakness manifests itself initially in either the shoulder girdle muscles or the hip and thigh muscles, but eventually both the upper and lower extremities are involved. Muscle degeneration progresses slowly.

Stages of Functional Ability

Daily exercise slows the incapacitating aspects of the disease. As long as the child is helped to stand upright a few minutes each day and to walk short distances, contractures do not appear. Once confined to the wheelchair, fitness seems to deteriorate rapidly. Stretching exercises become imperative at this point, as do breathing games and exercises.

Eight stages of disability are delineated by the Muscular Dystrophy Associations of America, Incorporated:

1. Ambulate with mild waddling gait and lordosis. Elevation activities adequate (climb stairs and curbs without assistance).
2. Ambulate with moderate waddling gait and lordosis. Elevation activities deficient (need support for curbs and stairs).
3. Ambulate with moderately severe waddling gait and lordosis. Cannot negotiate curbs or stairs, but can achieve erect posture from standard-height chair.
4. Ambulate with severe waddling gait and lordosis. Unable to rise from a standard-height chair.
5. Wheelchair independence. Good posture in the chair; can perform all activities of daily living from chair.
6. Wheelchair with dependence. Can roll chair, but need assistance in bed and wheelchair activities.
7. Wheelchair with dependence and back support. Can roll the chair only a short distance, need back support for good chair position.
8. Bed patient. Can do no activities of daily living without maximum assistance.

Even in Stage 8 some time each day is planned for standing upright by use of a tilt table or appropriate braces. Children should attend regular public school and engage in adapted physical education as long as possible, with emphasis upon the social values of individual and small group games, dance, and aquatics. In the later stages they may attend school only a small part of each day. Since they are not being educated for a future, they should be allowed to engage in school activities that give the most pleasure and allow the

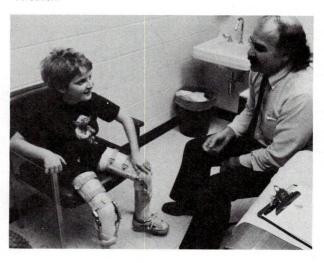

Figure 22.3 The muscular dystrophy child needs much individual counseling in regard to physical education and recreation.

greatest socialization. The following illustrative case study describes a child in the early stages of muscular dystrophy (see Figure 22.3).

Case RS: Duchenne Muscular Dystrophy

RS's walk is characterized by a marked lordosis, with weight carried on the balls of the feet, arms slightly abducted for balance, and head held erect. RS is 9 years old and a member of a third-grade section in the regular wing of the school. He comes to the special education wing daily for mathematics and for physical therapy.

Medical Report

There is hypertrophy of the calf muscles, some shoulder involvement, winged scapulae, and a quadriceps weakness in addition to the hypertrophy of the gastrocsoleus group. The school physician has recommended a program of active exercise, muscle education, gait training, and hydrotherapy. RS has therapy sessions 5 days per week for 30 minutes each day with a group of three other boys. Four of these sessions are held in the pool and the other in individual activity.

Psychological and Social Status

Intellectually, RS ranks in the average group. In the classroom RS is sometimes a leader and sometimes a follower. When working with others he seems to resent correction. His general temperament is outgoing and his emotional outlook quite healthy. When faced with a frustrating situation, however, he angers easily, saying, "I can't," or quits trying.

RS is the second of three boys in his family. His brothers are 22 and 3 years old. The father is a building contractor and the mother a homemaker.

Physical Education Experience

RS's mobility is adequate for daily activities. He can walk and run, though somewhat more slowly than most of the boys in his class. He runs holding his head erect and swinging each leg out to the side as he moves it forward. He cannot squat or stoop well because of the difficulty of recovery from these positions. Arm movements are practically normal. He throws, catches, and bats with average skill and enjoys hanging and swinging in the flying rings. His kicking is limited because of only fair balance. In kickball, a teammate kicks for him and RS does his own running. He plays in the infield when his team is on the defense. School records indicate that RS participates in regular physical education classes. RS's mother indicates that she thought he needed more physical exercise. His teacher believes that he is carrying as full a schedule as is desirable for a child with progressive muscular dystrophy. While his program should be as active as possible, RS should also be developing sedentary recreational interests for the future (Spragens, 1964).

Implications for Physical Education

In the public schools, the physical educator most often encounters Duchenne multiple dystrophy. Until confined to a wheelchair, these children are entirely normal and should participate in regular physical education. They may fatigue more easily than their classmates, but specialists concur that they should be allowed to play as hard as they wish. Normal fatigue from vigorous physical activity is intrinsically good, and the dystrophic child should be withdrawn from a game only when he or she appears totally exhausted. Should this occur, several *normal* children who are also showing signs of exhaustion should be excused at the same time. At no time should the dystrophied child be sitting alone on the sidelines! It is hoped that full participation in games and athletics while the disease is in the early stages will enable the child to form close friends who will stick by as he or she becomes increasingly helpless. It is imperative, therefore, that the dystrophied child and his or her friends receive instruction in some sedentary recreational activities that will carry over into the wheelchair years. Rifle shooting, dart throwing, archery, bowling, fishing, and other individual sports are recommended. The parents may wish to build a rifle or archery range in their basement or backyard to attract neighborhood children in for a visit as well as to provide recreation for their own child. Unusual pets such as snakes, skunks, and raccoons also have a way of attracting preadolescent children. Swimming is recommended, with emphasis upon developing powerful arm strokes to substitute for the increasing loss of strength in the legs.

Dystrophied children are learning to adjust to life in a wheelchair just when their peers are experiencing the joys of competitive sports. They are easily forgotten unless helped to develop skills like scorekeeping and umpiring, which keep them valued members of the group. The physical educator should not wait until disability sets in to build such skills, but should begin in the early grades to shape the image of dystrophied children, congratulating them on good visual acuity, knowledge of the rules, decision-making skills, and other competencies requisite to scorekeeping and umpiring. These mainstream physical education activities should not, however, substitute for adapted physical education.

Dystrophied children tend to show lowered motivation for achievement, withdrawal of interest in their environment, emotional immaturity, and low frustration tolerance. These traits are not surprising when one considers that children probably suspect their prognosis of early death, no matter how carefully guarded. Why should they study? Why should they consider different careers? Why should they care about dieting and personal appearance? Who wants to date them? The emphasis in academic studies, physical education, and social learnings must be upon the present, for they will not have a tomorrow.

Arthritis

Over 12 million Americans suffer from some form of arthritis and other rheumatic diseases. The terms *rheumatism* and *arthritis* are sometimes used synonymously, but technically they are separate entities. Rheumatism refers to a whole group of disorders affecting muscles and joints. It includes all forms of arthritis, myositis, myalgia, bursitis, fibromyositis, and other conditions characterized by soreness, stiffness, and pain in joints and associated structures. Arthritis means, literally, inflammation of the joints. Rheumatoid arthritis is also completely different from rheumatic fever, although it is a side effect of the rheumatic fever.

Over 100 causes of joint inflammation have been identified, but the majority of cases fall within seven major categories: (a) rheumatoid arthritis; (b) degenerative joint disease (osteoarthritis); (c) nonarticular rheumatism, including those of psychogenic origin; (d) arthritis resulting from known infectious agents; (e) arthritis resulting from fractures, torn ligaments, and abnormal joint stresses and/or traumas; (f) arthritis resulting from rheumatic fever; and (g) gout.

The first three of these seven categories account for two thirds of all arthritis. Rheumatoid arthritis, which affects 30 to 40% of all cases, may strike at any age. Degenerative joint disease, which accounts for 25 to 30%, is a natural outcome of aging. Nonarticular rheumatism, which afflicts 10 to 20% of the cases, is primarily an adult problem of psychogenic origin. It appears in the wake of an unusually stressful situation with which the person is coping poorly.

Rheumatoid arthritis is the nation's number one crippler and is the type that is found most often in school-age children. Approximately 30,000 children and adolescents in the United States suffer from rheumatoid arthritis, with 16,000 a year requiring medical care. This discussion is limited, therefore, to rheumatoid arthritis as it may affect students enrolled in school physical education.

Juvenile Rheumatoid Arthritis

The average age of onset is 6 years, with two peaks of incidence occurring between ages 2 and 4 and between ages 8 and 11. Rheumatoid arthritis affects three to five times as many girls as boys. The specific etiology is generally unknown. Because young children seldom complain of pain, a slight limp is often the only manifestation of the condition.

Mode of Onset

The onset of juvenile rheumatoid arthritis is capricious, sometimes affecting only one joint and other times involving several joints. In about 30% of the initial episodes, only one joint, usually the knee, is involved, but within a few weeks or months many more joints may swell. The onset of arthritis may be sudden, characterized by severe pain, or progressive, with symptoms appearing almost imperceptibly over a long period of time. In the latter situation, joint pain is not a major problem.

Rheumatic arthritis may be *systemic,* affecting the entire body, or *peripheral,* affecting only the joints. When the disease is systemic, the joint inflammation is accompanied by such symptoms as fever, rash, malaise, pallor, enlargement of lymph nodes, enlargement of liver and/or spleen, and pericarditis. Systemic rheumatic arthritis in children is known as *Still's disease,* deriving its name from George F. Still, a London physician who first described the condition in 1896.

Joint Problems

Affected joints have the following characteristics: (a) swelling, (b) heat, (c) redness, (d) tenderness, (e) limitation of motion, (f) crepitation (sounds when joints are moved), and (g) muscular atrophy. Tenderness to palpation is common, while the presence of pain is variable. Acute episodes of intense pain have been known to last from 1 or 2 days to several weeks, but generally pain occurs only with motion or not at all.

Knee

The knee is involved more often than other joints, causing a slight limp as the child walks. The characteristic swelling gives the appearance of knock-knees. Swelling makes knee extension difficult or impossible. Knee flexion deteriorates from its normal range of 120° to 80 or 90°. Flexion contracture usually develops.

Ankle

Involvement of the ankle joint results in a ducklike, flat-footed gait similar to that of the toddler. Muscles of the lower leg tend to atrophy, and the Achilles tendon becomes excessively tight. Limitation of motion and pain occur most often in dorsiflexion.

Foot

Swelling within the joints of the foot makes wearing shoes uncomfortable. Characteristic arthritic defects are pronation, flatfoot, valgus of the calcaneous, and a cock-up position of the metatarsal phalangeal joints. Later manifestations are muscular rigidity because of flattening of the longitudinal arch, peroneal muscular spasm resulting from talonavicular joint involvement, and a flattening of the entire posterior foot. The cock-up toe position may eventually lead to a cavus deformity.

Wrist, Hand, and Arm

Extension is limited by a combination of synovial involvement (see Figure 22.4), tenosynovitis of associated tendon sheaths, muscular atrophy, and weakness. A common late manifestation is *ankylosis.* This is an abnormal union of bones whose surfaces come into contact because the interjacent cartilages have been destroyed. Normal grip strength is lessened by the combination of muscular atrophy, contracture, and pain on motion.

Hip

Over one third of the children favor an affected extremity. All ranges of movement are limited, but the flexion contracture is most troublesome.

Figure 22.4 Swollen fingers and hands require special attention.

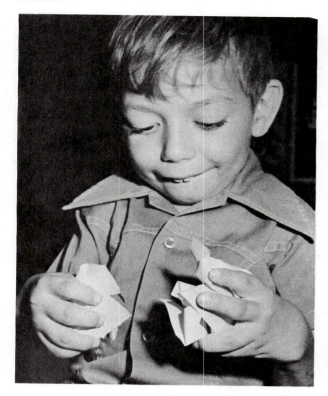

Figure 22.5 First half of log roll demands all out effort.

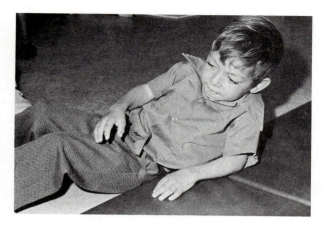

Figure 22.6 Execution of log roll shows characteristic flexion.

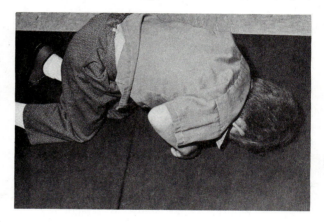

Spinal Column

Juvenile rheumatoid arthritis tends to limit motion in the cervical spine (see Figures 22.5 and 22.6). There may be spasms of the upper trapezius muscle and local tenderness along the spine. The thoracic and lumbar spine are seldom involved. In young males, a form of rheumatoid arthritis, classified as *rheumatoid spondylitis,* affects the posterior intervertebral articulations, causing pain and stiffness in the back. This condition is also called *Marie-Strumpell disease.*

Course of the Disease

In spite of enlargement of the liver and spleen, pericarditis, and other side effects, rheumatoid arthritis is rarely fatal. It does cause severe disability in about 25% of the cases and mild to moderate disability in 30%. Complete functional recovery is reported in approximately 30 to 70% of the cases. When the disease affects the entire body, the period of acute illness lasts from 1 week to several months. During this time, children may be confined to home with their education guided by an itinerant teacher. They require frequent rest periods and daily physical therapy. When significant reduction of joint swelling is evident and other symptoms disappear, the disease is said to be in partial or total remission. Unfortunately, periods of remission are interspersed with weeks of acute illness and maximum joint involvement. The course of the disease continues in this way for an unpredictable duration.

Implications for Physical Education

The purposes of movement for the child with rheumatoid arthritis are (a) relief of pain and spasm, (b) prevention of flexion contractures and other deformities, (c) maintenance of normal ranges of motion for each joint, and (d) maintenance of strength, particularly in the extensor muscles. *Daily exercise* is perhaps more important in rheumatoid arthritis than in any other disability. It must begin as soon as the acute inflammation starts to subside. At this time, even gentle passive movement may be painful, but every day of inactivity increases joint stiffness and the probability of permanent deformity. The physical educator and/or physical therapist should work with parents in establishing a home exercise program. In addition, children should participate in a school physical education program adapted to their needs.

The deformities that develop in rheumatoid arthritis bear out the following kinesiological facts: (a) flexors are stronger than extensors, (b) adductors are stronger than abductors, and (c) external rotators and supinators are stronger than internal rotators and pronators. It is essential, therefore, that the physical educator plan exercise sequences that will strengthen the extensors, the abductors, the internal rotators, and the pronators. *Most authorities agree that flexion exercises are contraindicated.* The activities of daily living provide adequate flexion, and there is no danger that the joints will stiffen in flexion.

In the early stages of remission, most of the exercises should be performed in a lying position to minimize the pull of gravity. When exercise tolerance is built up sufficiently, activities in a sitting position can be initiated. Riding a bicycle or tricycle affords a means of transportation as well as good exercise. Sitting for long periods of time, however, is contraindicated since it results in stiffness.

Some children, such as the 8-year-old boy depicted in Figure 22.7, are left so disabled that they cannot walk. The gait of the severely involved arthritic child is slow and halting. The child has difficulty ascending and descending steps. Any accidental bumping or pushing in the hallway or while standing in lines is especially painful. Older pupils who change rooms should be released from each class early so they can get to the next location before the bustle of activity begins. Occasionally, their schedule of courses must be adjusted so that all classrooms are on the same floor and/or in close proximity.

Occasionally, the physician may prescribe mild, moist heat as a preliminary to exercise. This is accomplished by immersing the extremities in warm (92 to 102°) or hot (102 to 110°) water or by using compresses for a period of 20 to 30 minutes. Heat should not be applied longer than 30 minutes.

The physical educator should know the normal range of motion in degrees for each joint and be proficient in the use of the goniometer. The number of degrees through which each body part can move is recorded and serves as an index against which progress can be measured. Each body part, even the individual fingers and toes, should be taken through its full range of motion two or three times daily.

Figure 22.7 Cortisone and other drugs used in arthritis tend to inhibit normal growth. This 8-year-old boy is so disabled that he uses a quadricycle in lieu of walking.

Contraindicated Activities

The following activities are contraindicated because of their trauma to the joints:

1. All jumping activities, including jump rope and trampoline work.
2. Activities in which falls might be frequent, such as roller skating, skiing, and gymnastics.
3. Contact sports, particularly football, soccer, and volleyball.
4. Hopping, leaping, and movement exploration activities in which the body leaves the floor.
5. Diving.
6. Horseback riding.

Recommended Activities

During periods of remission the child who can participate in an activity *without pain* should be allowed, but not forced, to do so. Because of the weeks and/or months of enforced rest during acute attacks, the child's circulorespiratory endurance is likely to be subaverage. Hence, the child will need more frequent rest periods than his or her peers.

Swimming and creative or modern dance are among the best physical education activities. The front crawl and other strokes that emphasize extension are especially recommended. Water must be maintained at as warm a temperature as is feasible for other swimmers. Creative dance also stresses extension in its many stretching techniques and affords opportunities for learning to relate to others. Group choreography and performance can provide as many of these positive experiences as the team sports that are denied arthritic youngsters. Quiet recreational games include croquet, ring or ball tossing, miniature golf, horseshoes, shuffleboard, and pool. Throwing activities are better than striking and catching activities.

Other Factors

Cortisone and its derivatives (steroids) appear to be the most effective medications at this time. Unfortunately, one of their major side effects is the inhibition of normal growth, causing children to look several years younger than they really are. Alterations in body growth occur as the direct result of severe rheumatoid arthritis. This stunting of growth, coupled with the overprotection of parents, may contribute to serious problems in peer adjustment.

Changes in weather are known to correlate with arthritic flare-ups. Attacks seem to occur most often prior to cold rain or snowfall.

Morning stiffness is characteristic of the arthritic child as well as of the arthritic adult. It may be so severe that the child cannot rise from the bed alone.

Any prolonged inactivity, such as an afternoon nap or simply sitting in the classroom for an hour, results in a return of this stiffness. It can be relieved by a few minutes of moving about and/or a warm bath.

Multiple Sclerosis

Approximately 500,000 persons in the United States have *multiple sclerosis* (MS), a progressive neurological disorder that ends in total incapacitation and death. It is caused by *demyelination,* the disintegration of myelin covers of nerve fibers throughout the body. Its name is derived from the Greek word *sklerosis,* which means hardening, and refers to the scar tissue that replaces the disintegrating myelin. The resulting lesions throughout the white matter of the brain and spinal cord vary from the size of a pinpoint to more than 1 centimeter in diameter. The cause of the demyelination is unknown.

Since multiple sclerosis characteristically affects persons between the ages of 20 and 40, the college physical educator may be called upon for counsel. Early symptoms of demyelination include numbness, general weakness, partial or incomplete paralysis, staggering, slurring of speech, and double vision. The disease is characterized by periods of relative incapacitation followed capriciously by periods of remission.

Case Study

The following description of multiple sclerosis over an 8-year period was written by Sherry Rogers, who developed MS while a junior physical education major in college.

Now with the diagnosis starts the story of the most demanding years of my life. The pain I experienced was tremendous. It was more localized now. It was mostly on my right side and the lower part of my back, especially the sciatic nerve of my right leg.

After about a month of getting one or two bottles of ACTH intervenously every day, I could see some improvement. Then the physician started me on cold showers to stimulate my circulation. All of this and my prayers worked for me. Physical therapy, mainly to exercise my legs, was given me also. I had not moved much of my body for about a year, and the therapy was designed to stimulate the muscles. I continued to progressively get better control of myself.

Then blindness, seeing only a narrow vision of light, appeared, lasting for about three weeks. Seeing double lasted for about another month. Then my vision progressively got better until it seems normal at present except that I now need glasses to read or do any close work.

I went to Gonzales Warm Springs for a short time, where I lost my voice for a while. I was told that the only thing to do for my disease was to rest and walk very much. Because of this, I rest each day for about an hour or more. I walk some distance each day depending upon how I feel.

The effects of multiple sclerosis on me can best be described as weakening. There are days when I need crutches to walk and other days when I feel fine and can walk without any assistance. The muscle groups affected the most were all of the voluntary muscles of my right side. The most noticeable to me has been my right hand, which feels like it is asleep all of the time. I again was fortunate because I am left handed. Endurance was the most noticeable change in fitness. I have to rest after any strenuous exercise. My strength is about one-fourth of what it used to be before I was stricken. My posture has been very much affected. I bend forward from my waist some days when I stand. This is more apparent on some days than others depending upon my strength. I was paralyzed for about a year. Gradually I improved until now I walk almost normally.

My handwriting is not as legible as it was, and there are times when MS recurs slightly and affects portions of my right side. This sometimes lasts for days but always returns to what is now normal for me.

In spite of my handicap, I returned to college and received my Bachelor of Science degree in physical education in the spring of 1972 and was presented the most representative woman physical education major award from Delta Psi Kappa. All of this has impressed upon me the fact that the bodies of men are truly temples of God and should be cared for as such. If there is one thing I could tell you it is that nothing is certain in this life and it is not to be taken for granted. Make certain that you live to the fullest because you never know what the future holds for you.

Course of Disease

In the most advanced stages of multiple sclerosis, loss of bladder or bowel control occurs as well as difficulties of speech and swallowing. Progressively severe intention tremors interfere with writing, using eating utensils, and motor tasks. The prognosis for multiple sclerosis varies. Many patients have long periods of remission during which their lives are essentially normal.

Implications for Physical Education

Most physicians recommend breathing exercises, gait retraining, gross coordination activities, stretching exercises, and hydrotherapy. Swimming is helpful. Therapeutic exercises such as walking between two parallel bars are easier in water than on land. College students with MS should engage in as normal a physical education program as possible. After graduation, they should find an exercise group and continue regular activity as long as possible.

As MS progresses and ambulation is lost or becomes increasingly difficult, special therapeutic exercises will be needed. The stationary bicycle is recommended.

Arthrogryposis

Approximately 500 infants are born with *arthrogryposis* each year. The incidence is 3 per 10,000 births. Arthrogryposis multiplex congenita (AMC) is a nonprogressive congenital contracture syndrome usually characterized by internal rotation at the shoulder joints, elbow extension, pronated forearms, radial flexion of wrists, flexion and outward rotation at the hip joint, and abnormal positions of knees and feet. This birth defect varies tremendously in severity, with some persons in wheelchairs and others only minimally affected. The contracture syndrome is characterized by dominance of fatty and connective tissue at joints in place of normal muscle tissue. Some or all joints may be involved.

The major disability is restricted range of motion. Many AMC persons involved in les autres sports seem to be in Class 1, with almost no arm and shoulder movement available. They can, however, excel in track activities in a motorized chair. The opposite condition, only lower limb involvement, is illustrated by Ron Hernley, President of the National Handicapped Sports and Recreation Association, who participates in many wheelchair sports.

Figures 22.8 and 22.9 depict two boys, ages 11 and 7, from the same school system who have arthrogryposis. Although both boys have some limb involvement, their greatest handicap is the fixed medial rotation of the shoulder joints (Figure 22.10). Both have normal intelligence, as is almost always the case in arthrogryposis. Until recently, the older boy walked without the use of crutches. His present reliance on them is believed to be somewhat psychosomatic, although articular surfaces do tend to deteriorate with age.

Major physical education goals are to increase range of motion (flexibility) and to teach sports and games for leisure use. Activities discussed under arthritis are appropriate in most cases, as are those in the chapter on cerebral palsy. Programming depends, of course, upon sports classification. Swimming is particularly recommended in that it fulfills both goals: it teaches a leisure skill and stretches muscle groups.

Dr. Jo Cowden, at the University of New Orleans, reports movement work with a 4-year-old AMC child over a 2-year period and emphasizes the importance of early intervention. Periodic videotapes show that levels of mobility have been obtained that were once not believed possible. When the child (see Figure 22.11) began the program, she used her chin to pull herself across the mat, rolled from place to place, or used a wheelchair. Now she can crawl and creep through obstacle courses and walk using reciprocal braces with a walker. Like many spina bifida children, she was taught first to use a parapodium with a walker and then progressed to reciprocal braces. Surgery, casting, and bracing have characterized much of her early life. As a potential Class 1 or 2 les autres athlete, this child can swim competitively with flotation devices and engage in slalom, track, and soccer activities in a wheelchair. As important as increasing range of motion is developing attitudes and habits favorable to physical recreation.

Osteogenesis Imperfecta and Related Conditions

Closely related to arthrogryposis are congenital disorders of bones and connective tissue like osteogenesis imperfecta and Ehlers-Danlos syndrome. *Osteogenesis imperfecta* (OI) is an inherited condition in which bones are abnormally soft and brittle and therefore break easily. These breaks peak between 2 and 15 years, after

Figure 22.8 Arthrogryposis, overweight, and poor fitness combine to make batting a real chore for this 11-year-old. Arms show the characteristic increase of subcutaneous fat and loss of skin flexion creases, which result in a tubular appearance sometimes described as wooden and doll-like. Despite the awkwardness of joint positions and mechanics, no pain is felt.

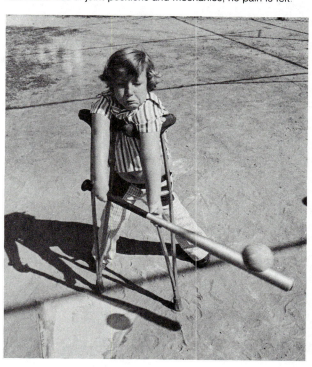

Figure 22.9 Lively 7-year-old with arthrogryposis demonstrates his best posture.

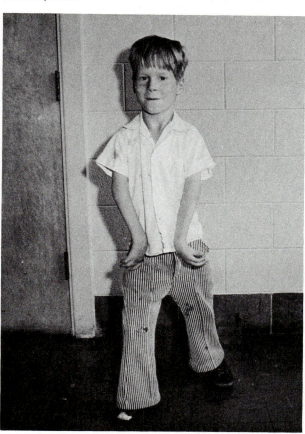

Figure 22.10 Medial rotation at the shoulder joints complicates fine muscle coordination.

Figure 22.11 Water activities provide range of motion exercises for young child with arthrogryposis.

Figure 22.12 Seventeen-year-old student with osteogenesis imperfecta awaiting his swimming competition at National CP/LA Games.

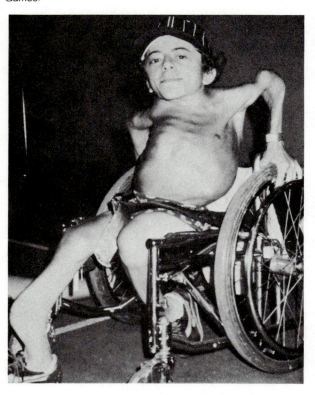

Figure 22.13 Wayne Washington, international OI competitor in weight lifting, visiting with coach before a recreational swim.

Figure 22.14 Bill Lehr, international OI competitor in swimming, with coach Kathi Rayborn.

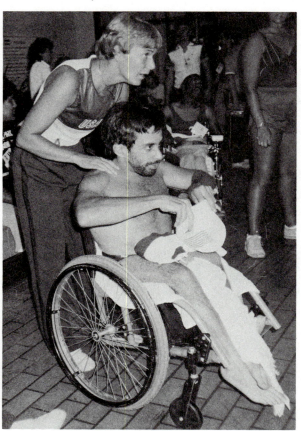

which the incidence of fractures is reduced. Characteristics include short stature and small limbs that are bowed in various distortions resulting from repetitive fractures. Joints are hyperextensible with predisposition for dislocation. Most athletes with OI are in wheelchairs. *Ehlers-Danlos syndrome* is an inherited condition characterized by hyperextensibility of joints with predisposition for dislocation at shoulder girdle, shoulder, elbow, hip, and knee joints. Other features are loose and/or hyperextensible skin, slow wound healing with inadequate scar tissue, and fragility of blood vessel walls; risk sports are therefore contraindicated.

Many les autres athletes have OI. The incidence of this condition is 1 in 50,000 births for congenital OI and 1 in 25,000 for a later appearing, less serious, form called OI tarda; it is possible that these medical statistics lack accuracy in that OI students can easily be spotted in every large school system.

Figures 22.12 to 22.14 depict OI persons of various ages who participate in les autres sports. By the age of 7 or 8 years, most OI children become wheelchair users since weight-bearing itself is often sufficient stress to break leg bones. Swimming and other Class 1 and 2 les autres events are the best physical education activities until the condition arrests itself, usually in late adolescence. Motorized chairs permit the challenge and thrill of track and slalom events. Use of a 5-ounce soft shot (bean bag) or discus seldom causes fractures, whereas regulation balls might. Shuffleboard and ramp bowling add variety.

After the condition arrests itself, the OI person can engage in almost any sport. Wayne Washington (Figure 22.13), who weighs 112 pounds, is a world class weight lifter with a 290-pound record; he began weight lifting at age 18. Bill Lehr (Figure 22.14), a world class track and swimming star, also plays wheelchair basketball and has completed the Boston marathon in 2 hours and 50 minutes. He has done the 100 meters in 18.8, the 400 in 1:16.8, and the 800 in 2:34.

About his childhood, Bill says,

I was born with a broken collar bone, my knees were bent in a way a baby's knees aren't supposed to bend and in the first 12 years of my life, I must have spent half the time in surgery. . . . When I was growing, I could walk and even run a few yards at a time. Then a bone would break in one of my legs and they'd have to put a cast on me. I'd be laid up for a few weeks, get out of the cast, but that would only last a week or two before I'd break another bone and have to be put back in a cast again.

Before Bill's condition arrested itself, he had over 40 fractures. From age 7 onward, he was a wheelchair user; he began wheelchair basketball and track at age 12. Telling OI children about world class athletes like Bill Lehr and Wayne Washington and showing them photos and videotapes opens new horizons; this is an important part of the physical educator's job.

Friedreich's Ataxia

Friedreich's ataxia is an inherited condition in which there is progressive degeneration of the sensory nerves of the limbs and trunk. The most common of the spinocerebellar degenerations, Friedreich's ataxia first occurs between ages 5 and 15 years. The primary characteristics are ataxia (poor balance), clumsiness, and lack of agility. Many associated defects (slurred speech, diminished fine motor control, discoordination and tremor of the upper extremities, vision abnormalities, and skeletal deformities) may also develop and affect sports performance. Degeneration may be slow or rapid. Many persons become wheelchair users by their late teens; others manifest only one or two clinical signs and remain minimally affected throughout their life cycle. The incidence of Friedreich's ataxia is about 2 per 100,000.

Charcot-Marie-Tooth Syndrome

Also called peroneal muscular atrophy, this relatively common hereditary disorder appears between ages 5 and 30 years. It begins as weakness in the peroneal muscles, which are on the anterolateral lower leg, and gradually spreads to the posterior leg and small muscles of the hand. Weakness and atrophy of the peroneal muscles causes foot drop, which characterizes the *steppage gait*. The condition, which is caused by demyelination of spinal nerves and anterior horn cells in the spinal cord, is progressive but sometimes arrests itself. Persons with Charcot-Marie-Tooth syndrome may be active for years, limited only by impaired gait and hand weakness.

Barre-Guillain Syndrome

A transient condition of muscle weakness, this results from degeneration of approximately the same area as Charcot-Marie-Tooth syndrome. Its symptoms and progress are similar to polio except that there is usually complete recovery. Rehabilitation may require months of bracing and therapy. Some persons are left with muscle and respiratory weakness. The incidence of Barre-Guillain syndrome is 1 per 100,000.

Spinal Muscle Atrophies of Childhood

Several spinal muscle atrophies (SMA) have been identified and named: Werdning-Hoffman disease (Figure 22.15), Kugelberg-Welander disease, and Oppenheim's disease, among others. In school settings, however, these are usually called the floppy baby syndromes or congenital hypotonia since the major characteristic is flaccid muscle tone. Most of these atrophies are present at birth or occur shortly thereafter. They are caused by progressive degeneration of approximately the same CNS parts as in polio.

The conditions vary in severity, with some leveling off, arresting themselves, and leaving the child with chronic, nonprogressive muscle weakness. Others are fatal within 2 or 3 years of onset. Typically, in severe cases there is a loss of muscle strength followed by tightening of muscles, then contractures, and finally nonuse. SMA is sometimes impossible to distinguish from muscular dystrophy. It can be differentiated from cerebral palsy because there is no spasticity, no ataxia, no seizures, and no associated dysfunctions. Sensation remains intact.

Deteriorations of Middle and Old Age

Several similar conditions in which the main characteristic is progressive muscle weakness occur in adulthood. Among these are amyotrophic lateral sclerosis (ALS), also known as Lou Gehrig's disease, Huntington's disease, made famous by singer Arlo Guthrie, and Parkinson's disease.

Figure 22.15 Ten-year-old boy with spinal muscular atrophy, Werdnig-Hoffman type. He has normal intelligence and attends a special school for orthopedically handicapped children. Note how scoliosis limits breathing.

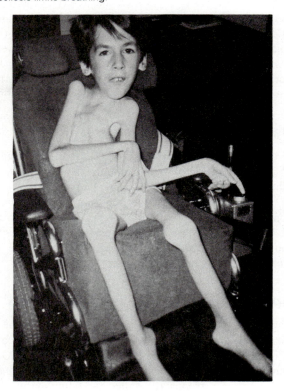

Figure 22.16 Individual differences in stature and body proportions in three children, age 10 years. (*A*) Normal. (*B*) Achondroplasia. (*C*) Morquio's syndrome.

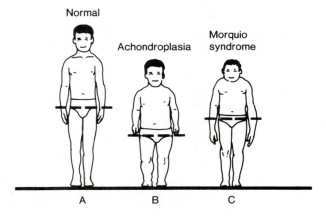

Normal

Achondroplasia

Morquio syndrome

A   B   C

Short Stature and Growth Disorders

Over 100 syndromes are characterized by short stature, which medically is defined as retarded physical growth that is more than three standard deviations from the mean for the age group. There are many reasons for growth disorders. Most relate in some way to the growth hormone (GH) secreted by the pituitary gland in response to stimulation from the hypothalamus, the part of the brain that regulates growth. Failure of the skeleton to convert cartilage (chondro) within its growth centers into bone is broadly termed the *chondrodystrophies* or *skeletal dysplasias*.

Whereas the general public persists in using such terms as *dwarf* and *midget*, persons with the chondrodystrophies prefer to be called *little people*. Their organization is Little People of America (LPA), and much of its work entails educating the public not to use slang like dwarf and midget (words historically associated with carnivals, circuses, and courts entertained by jestors). Criteria for membership in LPA is height of 58 inches or less. Medical literature more and more is using such simplified terms as skeletal growth disorders (chondrodystrophies) and short stature syndromes (other conditions caused by metabolism, chromosomal, or unknown problems).

By far the most common chondrodystrophy is *achondroplasia* (Figure 22.16B), which occurs about once in every 10,000 births. Achondroplasia is a condition of short stature, disproportionately short limbs, relatively large head, and normal intelligence. Associated problems are lumbar lordosis, waddling gait

Figure 22.17 Little people illustrating different syndromes. Each is an excellent athlete.

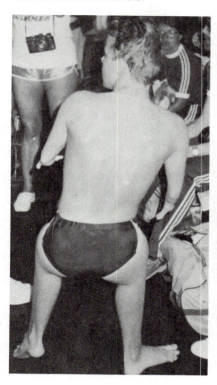  

caused by abnormally short femoral head, and restricted elbow extension. The shape of the femoral head makes hip joint dislocation and/or defects relatively common.

Achondroplasic little people can participate in regular physical education instruction with adaptations made for their short limbs (relatively inefficient leverage system in activities with balls, bats, and racquets) and short stature (a disadvantage in sports like volleyball and basketball). This entails changing game rules, equipment (smaller balls and shorter handles on hitting implements), and grading systems when grades are based on motor performance and fitness tests with norms. These adaptations should be made routinely for all short children, not just little people. Class teams, formed to practice basketball and volleyball skills, rules, and strategies, should be equated on heights or a system instituted whereby the shorter team starts with a set number of points. No one likes to feel he or she is a handicap to one's team; the teacher's role is to prevent such feelings by adapting the rules.

Like wheelchair users, some achondroplasic individuals are more naturally athletically inclined than others. Those who love sports eventually will wish to join sports leagues of little people as well as become involved in the annual national les autres competitions (see Figure 22.17).

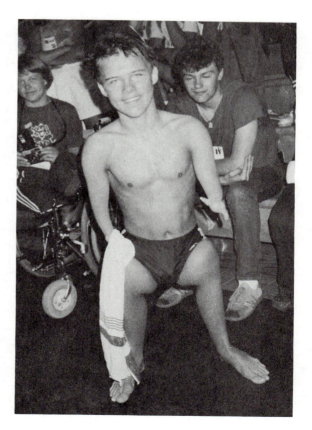

Two other growth disorders, in which intelligence is also normal, occur often enough to merit mention. *Morquio syndrome* (Figure 22.16C), caused by a metabolism disorder rather than a chondrodystrophy, is a short stature condition characterized by a disproportionate short neck and trunk, severe kyphosis, and knock-knees. Sometimes, joint laxity or restriction occurs, and cardiac complications are common. *Turner's syndrome,* caused by a chromosomal disorder, is a short stature condition characterized by a disproportionately short and often webbed neck, broad chest with widely spaced nipples, sexual sterility, and congenital heart disease; trunk and limbs have normal proportions. It occurs only in females. Many embryos with this syndrome spontaneously abort in the first prenatal months. Nevertheless, the incidence is variously stated as 1 per 5,000 and 1 per 10,000 (about the same as achondroplasia).

Individuals with these syndromes need the same physical education adaptations as other little persons. Additionally, cardiac and respiratory problems merit consideration. Morquio syndrome is characterized by late onset of aortic regurgitation, whereas heart defects in Turner's syndrome are usually coarctation of aorta (see chapter on cardiovascular problems for adaptations).

Several mental retardation syndromes are characterized by short stature. These include Down's syndrome (1 per 2,000 incidence), Cornelia de Lange syndrome (1 per 10,000 incidence), cri-du-chat syndrome (1 per 20,000 incidence), fetal alcohol syndrome (3 to 6 per 1,000 incidence), Hurler's syndrome (1 per 100,000 incidence), Noonan syndrome (1 per 1,000 incidence), and rubella syndrome (1 per 10,000 incidence). These conditions obviously are relatively common and require physical education adaptations for short stature and short limbs. They are discussed more fully, however, in the chapter on mental retardation since the primary adaptations relate to mental functioning (i.e., task analysis and behavior management).

Learning Activities

1. Identify the organizations and/or agencies related to each les autres condition and write or telephone national, state, or local offices for additional information. Ask if they have an official position statement on sports participation and what sports events they sponsor or recommend.

2. Identify persons with les autres conditions in your university or community. Get acquainted and find out if they would like your coaching and/or companionship in sports, dance, or aquatics activities. Ask if they will speak to your class.

3. Ask the local special education director and/or adapted physical education specialist if they have les autres students in their classes. Ask permission to assist with and/or observe the physical education of these students.

4. Get acquainted with parents of les autres students. Ask them about the exercise, diet, and leisure aspects of their children's lives.

5. Find out about the medications that persons with les autres conditons take. What are the side effects? How do these medications affect motor performance and fitness?

6. Assist your kinesiology/biomechanics professors in developing a film library of les autres persons in sports, dance, and aquatics activities.

7. Attend and/or assist with NASCP sports meets and events in which les autres athletes are often integrated. Ascertain that you can distinguish les autres from cerebral palsied athletes. If CP sports events do not encompass les autres in your community, find out what organization does.

References

Cowden, J. (1985). *Arthrogryposis: A case study approach for adapted physical education.* Manuscript submitted for publication.

Spragens, J. (1964). *A study of the physical education needs and interests of a selected group of orthopedically handicapped children with recommendations for planning and conducting physical activities.* Unpublished master's thesis, Texas Woman's University, Denton.

Bibliography

Basmajian, J. (Ed.). (1984). *Therapeutic exercise* (4th ed.). Baltimore: Williams & Wilkins.

Bleck, E., & Nagel, D. (Eds.). (1982). *Physically handicapped children: A medical atlas for teachers.* New York: Grune & Stratton.

Bowker, J. H., & Halpin, P. J. (1978). Factors determining success in reambulation of the child with progressive muscular dystrophy. *Orthopedics Clinical North America, 9,* 431–436.

Brewer, E. J. (1970). *Juvenile rheumatoid arthritis.* Philadelphia: W. B. Saunders.

Carroll, J. E. (1979). Bicycle ergometry and gas exchange measurements in neuromuscular diseases. *Archives of Neurology, 36,* 457–461.

de Lateur, B. J., & Biaconi, R. M. (1979). Effect on maximal strength of submaximal exercise in Duchenne muscular dystrophy. *American Journal of Physical Medicine, 58,* 26–36.

Downey, J., & Low, N. (1974). *The child with disabling illness.* Philadelphia: W. B. Saunders.

Drennan, J. (1983). *Orthopaedic management of neuromuscular disorders.* Philadelphia: J. B. Lippincott.

Edwards, R., Round, J., Jackson, M., Griffiths, R., & Lilburn, M. (1984). Weight reduction in boys with muscular dystrophy. *Developmental Medicine and Child Neurology, 26*(3), 384–390.

Eickelberg, W., Less, M., & Engels, W. (1976). Respiratory, cardiac, and learning changes in exercised muscular dystrophic children. *Perceptual and Motor Skills, 43,* 66.

Gershwin, M., & Robbins, D. (1983). *Musculoskeletal diseases of children.* New York: Grune & Stratton.

Ghezzi, A., Manara, F., Marforio, S., & Rocca, M. (1978). Multiple sclerosis in childhood. *Acta Neurology, 33,* 157–169.

Greenblatt, M. H. (1972). *Multiple sclerosis and me.* Springfield, IL: Charles C. Thomas.

Hageman, G., & Willemese, J. (1983). Arthrogryposis multiplex congenita: Review with comment. *Neuropediatrics, 1,* 6–11.

Harris, S. E., & Cherry, D. B. (1974). Childhood progressive muscular dystrophy and the role of physical therapy. *Physical Therapy, 54,* 4–12.

Jamero, P., & Dundore, D. (1984). Three common neuromuscular diseases: Considerations for vocational rehabilitation counselors. *Journal of Rehabilitation, 48*(1), 43–48.

McAlpine, D. (1972). *Multiple sclerosis: A reappraisal* (2nd ed.). Baltimore: Williams & Wilkins.

Millar, J. G. D. (1971). *Multiple sclerosis, a disease acquired in childhood.* Springfield, IL: Charles C. Thomas.

Pozer, C. (1979). Multiple sclerosis, a critical update. *Medical Clinics of North America, 63*(4), 729–743.

Rusk, H. A. (1972). *Rehabilitation medicine.* St. Louis: C. V. Mosby.

Schaller, J., & Wedgwood, R. J. (1972). Juvenile rheumatoid arthritis: A review. *Pediatrics, 50,* 940–953.

Schneitzer, L. (1978). Rehabilitation of patients with multiple sclerosis. *Archives of Physical Medicine Rehabilitation, 59,* 430–437.

Siegel, I. M. (1972). Pathomechanics of stance in Duchenne muscular dystrophy. *Archives of Physical Medicine and Rehabilitation, 53,* 403–406.

Swaiman, K., & Wright, F. (1970). *Neuromuscular diseases of infancy and childhood.* Springfield, IL: Charles C. Thomas.

Vignos, P. J., & Watkins, M. P. (1966). The effect of exercise in muscular dystrophy. *Journal of the American Medical Association, 197,* 843–848.

Williams, P. (1978). The management of arthrogryposis. *Orthopedic Clinics of North America, 9*(1), 67–88.

Ziter, F. A., & Allsop, K. G. (1975). Comprehensive treatment of childhood muscular dystrophy. *Rocky Mountain Medical Journal, 72,* 329–333.

23 Cerebral Palsy

Figure 23.1 Cerebral-palsied children are introduced to the concept of partner ball play via a ball suspended by string from ceiling. Note how mirror provides additional visual reinforcement.

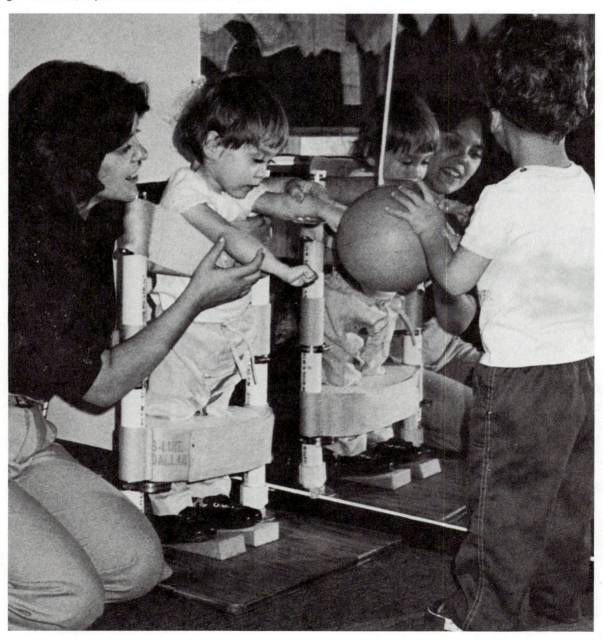

Chapter Objectives

After you have studied this chapter you should be able to

1. Explain the NASCP classifications and discuss their relevance for physical education assessment and instruction.

2. Discuss the dysfunctions commonly associated with cerebral palsy and state implications for physical education.

3. Discuss the motor development (normal, abnormal, and delayed) of persons of different ages, types, and severity of cerebral palsy. How does this affect physical education programming?

4. Identify the 10 primitive reflexes most common in cerebral palsy, describe each, and state the problems caused by retention.

5. Discuss each of the following: (a) inhibition or suppression of abnormal reflex activity, (b) normalization of muscle tone, and (c) facilitation of righting, parachute, and equilibrium reactions. Indicate specific techniques in relation to each.

6. Describe each of the following medical classifications: (a) spasticity, (b) athetosis, (c) ataxia, (d) rigidity, (e) tremors, and (f) mixed type. Shown examples of these on film or in real life, recognize each.

7. Indicate physical education techniques for working with students who exhibit spasticity and/or athetosis.

8. Discuss sports (including aquatics) programming for CP students. Keep in mind the eight NASCP classifications and the activities best for each.

9. Discuss existing and needed research concerning cerebral palsy and physical education.

10. Review chapter 8 and determine which types of wheelchairs and assistive devices are most appropriate for specific conditions and sports described in this chapter. In writing PE-IEPs, remember to designate types of wheelchairs and assistive devices needed to implement instruction.

Cerebral palsy is a group of neuromuscular conditions caused by damage to the motor areas of the brain. About 90% of such brain damage occurs before and during birth. Anoxia, infection, and injury to the brain during childhood account for the other 10%. Over 750,000 persons in the United States have been diagnosed as cerebral palsied, one third of whom are under 21 years of age. The condition is more common among the white race than the black, among males than females, and among the firstborn. The incidence is 3.5 cases per 1,000 births. Cerebral palsy, to most persons, implies moderate to severe motor involvement (see Figure 23.1). Mild cases often are not identified, but the careful observer of movement will note that many awkward children display characteristics described in this chapter.

Sports for cerebral palsied persons are governed by the National Association of Sports for Cerebral Palsy (NASCP), which was founded in 1978. This organization conducts a national meet during odd-numbered years and participates in international games conducted by Cerebral Palsy-International Sports and Recreation Association (CP-ISRA) during even-numbered years. Each quadrennial year since 1980, CP athletes have been represented in the International Games for the Disabled. Most large cities in the United States now have sports clubs specifically for individuals with cerebral palsy.

NASCP membership is for persons with average or better intelligence. Coaches estimate that perhaps 10 to 20% of their athletes are mildly mentally retarded; they do, however, all understand competition and game strategy. Multiply handicapped CP persons who are mentally retarded participate in Special Olympics rather than NASCP. It is obviously essential that physical educators understand the difference between these two organizations, prepare students specifically for events for which they are eligible, and enter them in the appropriate meets.

Table 23.1
Sport Classifications for Persons with Cerebral Palsy

Class	Description	Class	Description
1	Uses motorized wheelchair because almost no functional use of upper extremities. Severe involvement in all four limbs, limited trunk control, has only 25% range of motion. Unable to grasp softball.	5	Ambulates without wheelchair, but typically uses assistive devices (crutches, canes, walkers). Moderate to severe spasticity of either (a) arm and leg on same side (hemiplegia) or (b) both lower limbs (paraplegia). Has approximately 80% range of motion.
2	Propels chair with feet and/or very slowly with arms. Severe to moderate involvement in all four limbs. Uneven functional profile necessitating subclassification as 2 Upper (2U) or 2 Lower (2L), with adjective denoting limbs having greater functional ability. Has approximately 40% range of motion. Severe control problems in accuracy tasks, generally more athetosis than spasticity.	6	Ambulates without assistive devices, but has obvious balance and coordination difficulties. Has more control problems and less range of motion in upper extremities than Classes 4 and 5. Moderate to severe involvement of three or four limbs, with approximately 70% range of motion in dominant arm.
3	Propels chair with short, choppy arm pushes, but generates fairly good speed. Moderate involvement in three or four limbs and trunk. Has approximately 60% range of motion. Can take a few steps with assistive devices, but not functionally ambulatory.	7	Ambulates well, but with slight limp. Moderate to mild spasticity in (a) arm and leg on same side or (b) all four limbs with 90% of normal range of motion for quadriplegia and 90 to 100% of normal range of motion for dominant arm for hemiplegia.
4	Propels chair with forceful, continuous arm pushes, demonstrating excellent functional ability for wheelchair sports. Involvement of lower limbs only. Good strength in trunk and upper extremities. Has approximately 70% range of motion. Minimal control problems.	8	Runs and jumps freely without noticeable limp. Demonstrates good balance and symmetric form in performance, but has obvious (although minimal) coordination problems. Has normal range of motion.

NASCP Classifications

The NASCP classifications were introduced in Chapter 8 as a helpful system for use by public school teachers in describing the functional abilities of all students. Although designed as a method of equalizing abilities for sports competition, the classifications in Table 23.1 are applicable to all age groups and all activities. Use of these eight descriptions to classify students is recommended as the initial assessment approach for physical educators. Decisions are based on such movement exploration challenges as, "How high can you raise your arms? How far apart can you spread your legs? How high can you kick? How high can you throw?" Once a classification is assigned, the description of present level of performance on the IEP can be satisfied by simply writing the class number. For students ages 7 years and over, goals and objectives can be derived from NASCP official sports and events.

This chapter presents many of the activities described in the NASCP *Classification and Sports Manual*. For additional information, consult the manual, which is published by United Cerebral Palsy Associations, Incorporated, 66 East 34th Street, New York, NY 10016, or the training guide edited by Jones

(1984). Another method of obtaining help is to telephone UCPA national headquarters (212–481–6359) and ask for the sports coordinator, Mr. Rafael Bieber. Still another method is to contact the American Cerebral Palsy/Les Autres Coaches Association, which was formed in 1984. Its address is 5 Beachwood Drive, North Kingstown, RI 02852.

Throughout this chapter, persons with CP are described as athletes. This reflects adherence to expectancy theory: if we treat our students as athletes, they will perceive themselves that way and act accordingly. This chapter is based largely on knowledge gained by close association with NASCP athletes and coaches. Their philosophy is *sports by ability . . . not disability*. Every child, regardless of severity of disability, has the potential of becoming either a CP athlete (if intelligence is average or above) or a Special Olympian (if IQ is below 70 and other criteria for mental retardation are met).

Multiple Handicaps

Almost all CP persons have multiple handicaps. Estimates of prevalence of these conditions vary widely in the professional literature. In placement, persons with

Table 23.2
Associated Dysfunctions of General CP Population as Compared to NASCP Athletes

Associated Dysfunctions	General CP Population %	NASCP Athletes %
Mental retardation	30–70	10–20
Speech problems	35–75	25–35
Learning disabilities	80–90	45–55
Visual problems	55–60	20–30
Hearing problems	6–16	10–20
Perceptual deficits	25–50	60–70
Seizures	25–50	25–35
Reflex problems	80–90	65–75

Note. Estimates for the general population come from published sources (Bleck & Nagel, 1982; Thompson, Rubin, & Bilenker, 1983). Estimates for NASCP athletes come from the author's research.

both mental retardation and cerebral palsy are typically classified as multiply or severely handicapped, whereas those with mostly motor and speech dysfunctions are classified as cerebral palsied (i.e., as orthopedically impaired, under the PL 94–142 categories). Table 23.2 presents differences in associated dysfunctions between the general CP population, on which most medical research is based, and the NASCP membership, on which research is just beginning.

Mental retardation was once believed to characterize almost all persons with cerebral palsy. Today, books can be found that cite prevalence rates anywhere between 30 and 70%. New sources, however, focus more on learning disabilities than mental retardation. Difficulties in speech, language, and motor function make valid evaluation of intellectual functioning impossible in many students.

Electronic communication devices like the Canon communicator depicted in Figure 23.2 and the use of computers to teach language have demonstrated that many CP persons, previously believed to be mentally retarded, have intact intelligence. The speech of many Class 1, 2, and 6 (i.e., quadriplegic) CP athletes who qualify for international competition cannot be understood without much practice. Interpretors are often used with CP persons just as with individuals who speak in sign or a foreign language. It should never be assumed that a person without intelligible speech is mentally retarded.

Almost all CP children need speech therapy. Even with intensive training, however, only about 50% improve to a point in which they communicate primarily by talking. Many use communication boards with

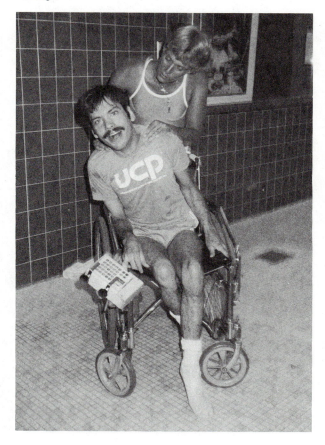

Figure 23.2 Bill Reilly, Class 2 international athlete with master's degree, often uses Canon communicator instead of talking. Swim coach Kathi Rayborn notes absence of sideways parachute reaction as Bill loses balance during shoulder massage.

Figure 23.3 Different types of communication boards and pointing systems.

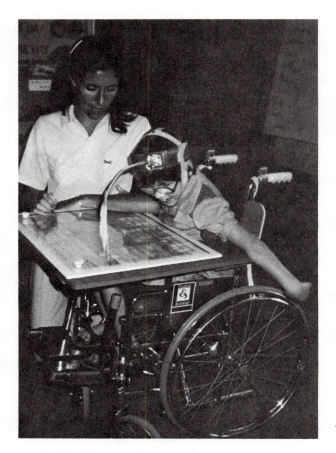

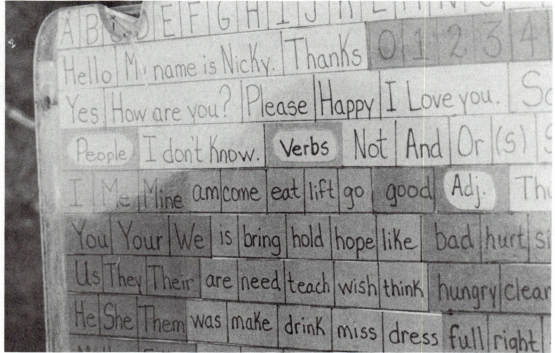

words, as depicted in Figure 23.3, or symbols. Others learn sign language. It is vital that teachers take the time to let CP students talk and make as many of their own decisions as possible. As with deaf students, language may be a greater problem than motor functioning. Inadequate communication skills lead to problems in socialization and delays in social development.

Consider the leisure activities of able-bodied persons. Almost all require ability to use the hands (cards, board games, arts and crafts, cooking), to converse and/or sing, and to drive a car. About 50% of persons with cerebral palsy do not have these abilities; their leisure and social functioning is therefore very different from that of peers. They can, however, excel in NASCP sports designed for their specific ability classification.

It is estimated that 55 to 60% have visual defects. *Strabismus,* the inability to focus both eyes simultaneously on the same object, is the most common problem—not a surprising fact when one remembers that eye focus requires the coordinated action of six muscles of the eyeball. Imbalances in strength cause squinting, loss of binocular vision, and inefficiencies in depth perception, pattern discrimination, and figure-background detection. These deficits naturally affect motor learning and success in sports.

Many persons with cerebral palsy exhibit *soft signs* of brain damage similar to those shown by LD persons: lack of concentration, hyperexcitability, perseveration, distractibility, emotional lability, conceptual rigidity, hyperactivity, and motor awkwardness. They are called *soft* because they cannot be substantiated neurologically. Nevertheless, these characteristics often result in a vicious circle of underachievement, lowered self-esteem, and lack of motivation. *Emotional overlay* is said to be present when the soft signs and/or self, parent, and sibling attitudes seem to evoke emotional disturbances.

Abnormal Retention of Reflexes

Figure 23.4 Different manifestations of the asymmetrical tonic neck reflex. Activated by turning the head, the ATNR causes increased extensor tone in the arm on the face side and increased flexor tone in the arm on the scalp side.

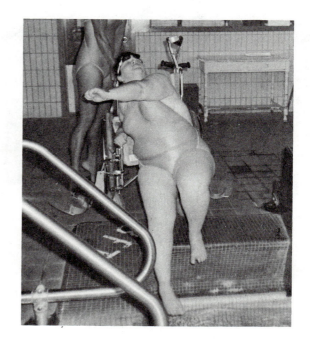

In order to understand the motor behavior of CP students, teachers should learn as much as possible about primitive reflexes. Basic information on reflexes was presented in Chapters 5 and 10. Whereas the primitive reflexes are typically integrated by age 2 years, many persons with CP are dominated by reflex activity throughout their lives. Nonambulatory persons are naturally affected more by abnormal reflex activity than ambulatory persons. In fact, it is the retention of reflexes that prevents their learning to crawl, creep, sit, and walk.

The five reflexes covered in Chapter 10 in relation to the Milani-Comparetti assessment system interfere with the motor control of almost all nonambulatory and some ambulatory CP persons. These are the hand grasp reflex, asymmetrical tonic neck reflex (Figure 23.4), moro reflex, symmetrical tonic neck reflex, and foot grasp reflex.

Five additional reflexes commonly dominate the motor behavior of nonambulatory CP students classified as severely disabled. Their description follows, with the most debilitating reflexes presented first.

Tonic Labyrinthine Reflex—Prone

Description
Increased flexor tone in response to any change in the position of head and/or body. Visualize the newborn infant in prone; the TLR is responsible for this position.

Normal Time Span
Normal, but gradually decreasing, during first 4 months.

Persistence
Results in abnormal distribution of muscle tone and inability of body segments to move independently of one another. Prevents raising head, which, in turn, prevents development of symmetrical tonic neck reflex and Landau extensor reaction. Characteristic shoulder protraction (abduction) results in inability to move arms from under body. Infant or severely handicapped person dominated by TLR is virtually helpless.

Tonic Labyrinthine Reflex—Supine

Figure 23.5 Six-year-old with cerebral palsy exhibits disturbance in reciprocal innervation which results in abnormal muscle tone (domination of flexor tone), poor head control, and limited trunk rotation. This child is still dominated by the tonic labyrinthine reflex and thus has little voluntary muscle tone.

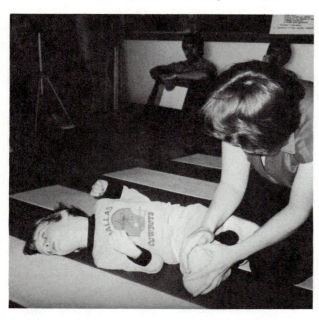

Figure 23.6 The opisthotonic or wind-swept position caused by severe muscle rigidity. Exercises for this girl are done on a moonwalk (pictured), waterbed, or in a hammock.

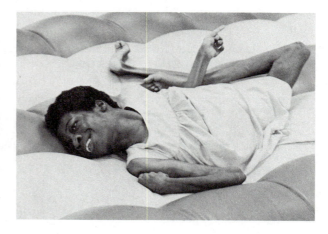

Description
Increased extensor tone in response to any change in position of head and/or body.

Normal Time Span
Normal, but gradually decreasing, throughout first 4 months.

Persistence
Domination by extensor tone, which holds shoulders in retraction (adduction) and prevents or compromises head raising, bringing limbs to midline, and rotation (turning) of body. In severely handicapped persons, may contribute to wind-swept (opisthonic) position (see Figures 23.5 and 23.6).

Crossed Extension Reflex

Description
Fluctuation in muscle tone and/or movement of one leg reflexly affects the other. Evidenced when one leg cannot flex (as in kicking a ball) without associated extension of the other leg. Also evidenced when medial surface of upper legs touch or rub against one another; this stimulus contributes to scissoring. Correct positioning in a wheelchair, with bolster between thighs, prevents this.

Normal Time Span and Role
Normal during first 2 to 3 months of life when it helps to break up dominant symmetrical flexion and extension patterns.

Becomes integrated with positive supporting reflex between 3 to 8 months of age, during which time it facilitates development of extensor tone to stand on one leg while the other leg flexes (i.e., permits reciprocal leg movements needed for creeping and walking).

Persistence
1. Prevents coordinated leg movements needed to crawl, creep, and walk.
2. Sometimes serves as substitute for absent positive support reflex in athetosis and ataxia. Child can stand only on stiffly extended legs and raises legs too high in walking.

Persistence in Conjunction With Positive Supporting Reflex
1. Affects kicking in a standing position. When leg is lifted to kick ball, a strong extensor spasm affects support leg and causes loss of balance. Child loses balance because he or she pushes reflexly against ground with ball of support foot (positive supporting reflex thereby reinforcing extensor spasm); this is accompanied by knee hyperextension and clawing of toes. To prevent falling backward, reflex activates flexion of trunk at hips and brings kicking leg down and forward, leaving weight-bearing foot, leg, hip, and shoulder behind. This rotatory movement prevents straight follow-through in the kick.
2. Affects walking pattern. Results in hyperextended knees, clawing of toes, and hip flexion in support leg to prevent falling. This is typically compensated for by forward flexion of head and lordosis.

Extensor Thrust Reflex

Description
Increased extensor tone throughout the body evoked by stimulus of sudden pressure to soles of feet. Most often mentioned in conjunction with sitting postures, a common problem in nonambulatory persons with cerebral palsy. In first 2 months, sometimes mistaken for early standing ability.

Normal Time Span and Role
Normal during first 2 to 3 months of life. Strengthens extensors, thereby promoting balance between flexor and extensor postural tone.

Persistence
Inability to maintain proper sitting position; entire body stiffens so that student slides out of wheelchair unless strapped into one that is specially made. Usually occurs in conjunction with positive supporting reflex of legs and/or tonic labyrinthine-supine reflex or symmetrical tonic neck reflex. Often, the abnormal movement produced by one or both of these is called an *extensor thrust* (i.e., the term is not limited to action of the extensor thrust reflex alone).

Positive Supporting Reflex

Description
Increased extensor tone (plantar flexion at ankle joint) caused by soles of feet touching floor or foot rests of wheelchair.

Normal Time Span and Role
Normal from 3 to 8 months of age; contributes (along with Landau extension of trunk) to strengthening hip and leg extensors needed for straight-back sitting and standing.

Persistence
1. When fully present, prevents independent standing and walking; creates difficulty (along with extensor thrust reflex) in wheelchair posture adjustments and/or wheelchair transfers because sensory input from foot plates stimulates soles of feet, which, in turn, increases extensor tone.
2. When partially present, affects walking gait by causing toe walking (prevents placing heel on floor), contributing (with crossed extension reflex) to scissoring, narrowing base of support, and producing backward thrust of trunk with compensatory lordosis and arm out to assist with balance.
3. Also interferes with kicking a ball (see crossed extensor reflex).

Figure 23.7 Incorrect handling of child dominated by tonic labyrinthine reflex—supine causes increased extension.

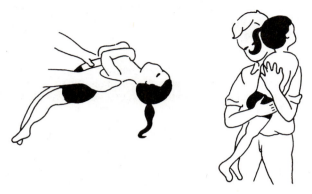

Figure 23.8 Correct handling of child dominated by TLR-supine inhibits extensor tone.

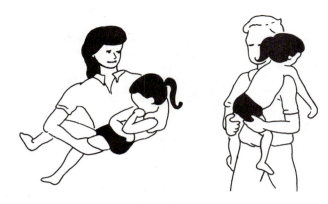

Figure 23.9 Two correct ways of carrying nonambulatory spastic cerebral-palsied child with *dominant flexor tone* (i.e., dominated by tonic labyrinthine reflex-prone). Both ways

emphasize keeping the limbs, head, neck, and back extended. Note importance of child facing outward so she can see where she is going.

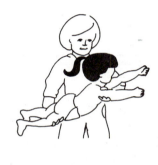

Coping with Reflexes

Guidelines to follow in regard to reflexes vary with age. The emphasis until about age 7 years is on integration of reflexes, primarily so that the child can learn to sit, walk, and run independently. Most young children with cerebral palsy need both physical therapy and physical education. Since the development of ambulatory skills is delayed, play focuses upon body image, movement exploration, and object control activities that can be done from a lying or sitting position. Ways should be devised also to move the child through space in many and varied ways: go carts, specially designed wagons and wheel toys, rugs pulled across the floor, and loco-motor activities of the teacher with child in arms or in backpack.

In devising early childhood activities, the physical educator should adhere to the same principles as do therapists. These are (a) inhibition or suppression of abnormal reflex activity, (b) normalization of muscle tone, and (c) facilitation of righting, parachute, and equilibrium reactions. The best way to learn these is

Figure 23.10 The position of the teacher can activate or inhibit primitive reflex action. (*A*) Correct position is working at eye level. (*B*) Wrong position (speaking to student from above) activates the extensor thrust.

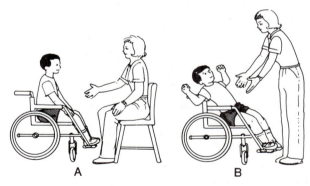

by working in a multidisciplinary setting in which therapists and physical educators share goals and techniques. There is nothing mysterious or especially difficult about implementing these principles. They are not owned by any profession. They do require knowledge of kinesiology, exercise physiology, and neurology,

Figure 23.11 Methods of inhibiting primitive reflexes. *Top left,* strapping the thighs and lower legs to wheelchair prevents extensor thrust from causing student to slide out of chair. *Top right,* a hard roll or bolster between the thighs maintains the legs in abduction and inhibits scissoring. *Bottom left,* large ball that keeps fingers in extension inhibits hand grasp reflex, which is activated by clutching small balls. Hyperextension of the wrist should be avoided since it also activates hand grasp reflex. Striking activities performed with open hand are better than throwing activities. *Bottom right,* apparatus to help CP children stand is built with straps to keep body parts centered in midline and thus inhibit ATNR.

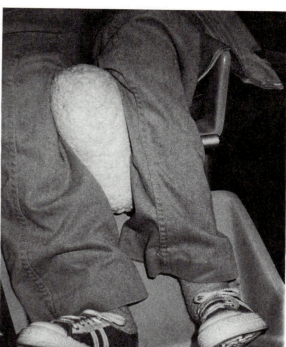

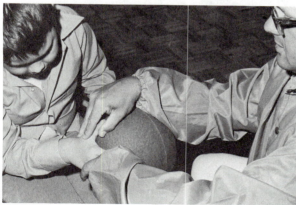

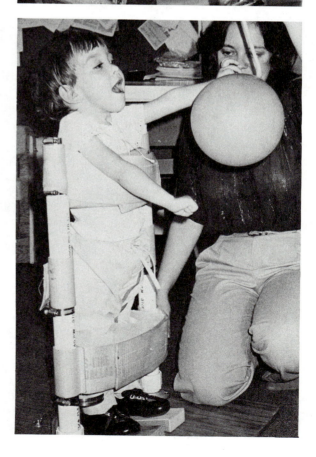

all areas in which adapted physical education specialists should be well trained. Regular physical educators assigned to work with severely disabled young CP children should request the assistance of such a specialist.

Inhibition or suppression of abnormal reflex activity is achieved by proper positioning and avoidance of activities that elicit reflexes. See Figures 23.7 to 23.11 in this regard. Most young severely handicapped CP students are in manual wheelchairs specially designed

Figure 23.12 Correct positioning of the nonambulatory child is extremely important. (*A*) Use of bolster. (*B*) Use of foam rubber wedge. (*C*) Use of padded inclined board with safety straps for the child unable to push down at the shoulders.

A   B   C

Figure 23.13 Spasticity in some students may be so great that limbs need to be strapped down during physical education. Here, Tom Cush, international Class 2 CP athlete, has both arms strapped to chair while he competes in wheelchair soccer. In throwing and striking activities, only one arm is strapped down.

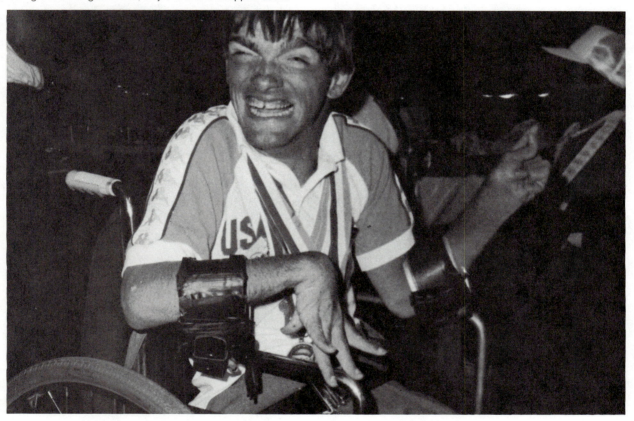

to keep their bodies in correct alignment. The teacher needs to know how to lift such children from their chairs and carry them to the bathroom and/or mats for physical education activity. When placed on mats, the prone position is usually best, as illustrated in Figure 23.12. When students remain in their chairs for physical education, strapping is an effective means of inhibiting reflexes (see Figure 23.13) and preventing falls caused by extensor thrust action. A bolster between thighs inhibits the crossed extension reflex that helps to cause scissoring. Students with adequate muscle tone to stand with assistance (see Figure 23.11) should have some play activities in this position, but care should be taken not to activate the asymmetrical tonic neck reflex (i.e., the head should not have to turn in order to see the target or visually track the ball). Whereas throwing and striking patterns can be practiced from a standing position, kicking is taught best from a sitting position if the student exhibits either the crossed extension or the positive supporting reflex.

Normalization of muscle tone is facilitated by activities that help break up domination of flexor tone in prone position and extensor tone in supine position (i.e., TLRs). This is done by passive movement of limbs, two at a time or one at a time, so as to facilitate the ability to flex or extend body parts independently, without associated movements of other parts. If students have the ability to move body parts without help, then active rather than passive exercises should be used. Rolling activities are also helpful, whether rolling on a mat or being gently rocked while on top of a large ball. Crawling, creeping, and swimming (i.e., activities entailing reciprocal leg action) also help. Passive patterning of limbs is used if students cannot move independently.

Righting, parachute, and equilibrium reactions are facilitated by emphasizing dynamic balance work on vestibular boards, playground apparatus, scooter boards, and related equipment. Remember, this work is done primarily in a lying or sitting position when students are nonambulatory.

After age 7 or 8, many physicians believe that physical therapy should no longer be directed toward loss of reflexes and learning to walk, but should focus on increasing range of motion and strength so that students have a better chance for success in sports, aquatics, and dance (Bleck & Nagel, 1982). Physical educators may work alone or in association with physical therapists to achieve the same goals of fitness and motor performance in CP students as in able-bodied students. When it appears that reflexes are enduring and will probably remain throughout life, it is advantageous to explore ways that students can use reflexes to their advantage.

Bleck and Nagel (1982) state that the type of motor performance that the CP child will have as an adult is most likely to be the same as that at the age of 7. Most CP children who are going to learn to walk have done so by the age of 7. From that age onward, current pedagogy seems to be to disregard reflexes per se and emphasize optimal positioning for successful sports performance. Regardless of the severity of the physical condition and the retention of primitive reflexes, there are many sport, dance, and aquatics activities that CP persons can learn and enjoy. These are discussed later in this chapter.

Extent of Involvement

1. *Paraplegia,* involvement of the lower extremities only.
2. *Hemiplegia,* involvement of the entire right side or left side.
3. *Triplegia,* involvement of three extremities, usually both legs and one arm.
4. *Quadriplegia,* involvement of all four extremities.
5. *Diplegia,* lower extremities much more involved than upper ones.

Use of these terms permits teachers to describe and program for the functional abilities of students. Descriptions like mild and severe are also used to indicate degree of involvement in each limb.

Medical Classifications

Six neuromuscular classifications are recommended by the American Academy for Cerebral Palsy: (a) *spasticity,* (b) *athetosis,* (c) *rigidity,* (d) *tremor,* (e) *ataxia,* and (f) *mixed.* The specific motor impairment indicates the anatomic localization of the brain injury. For instance, when there is spasticity, the lesion is usually in the cerebral cortex. Athetosis, rigidity, and tremors are caused by pathology in the basal nuclei, whereas ataxia is a sign of cerebellar damage. Review Chapter 5 for illustrations of parts of the brain and additional information (see Table 5.2).

Spasticity

Approximately 66% of the diagnosed cases of cerebral palsy are spastic. *Spasticity is characterized by exaggerated stretch reflexes, a marked decrement in ability to perform precise movements, and increased hypertonicity.*

The exaggerated stretch reflex is responsible for jerky movements (see Figure 23.13). It is caused by the failure of antagonistic muscles to relax when the prime movers initiate an action that opposes gravity. The antagonists resist any stretching by an explosive recoil sort of action, which is sometimes called the *clonus phenomenon.* When the arm reaches forward or upward, for instance, it is often jerked back toward starting position by the antagonists. Likewise, when the student strives to maintain good posture with head, neck, and spinal column in extension, the antagonists contract reflexly and cause undesired flexion postures.

Hypertonus is greatest in the flexors of the upper extremities and the extensors of the lower extremities. Contractures occur in these muscles if range-of-motion exercises are not performed daily. A *contracture* is a shortening or distortion of a muscle or group of muscles caused by prolonged hypertonicity and/or contraction against weak or flaccid muscles.

Athetosis

From 20 to 30% of persons with CP have some degree of athetosis manifested in continuous *overflow* movement of involved body parts. The motion is slow, involuntary, uncontrollable, unpredictable, and purposeless. The muscles of the fingers and wrists are affected most often, rendering handwriting and similar coordinations almost impossible. Facial expression, eating, and speaking are major problems. The head is usually drawn back, but may roll unpredictably from side to side; the tongue may protrude, and saliva drool down the chin. This lack of head control results in problems of visual pursuit and focus. Some athetoid children cannot move their eyes unless they simultaneously move the head.

Persons with athetosis exhibit fluctuating muscle tone, sometimes hypertonic and sometimes hypotonic. Athetoid children who have enough muscle control to stand usually exhibit lordosis. To compensate for this postural problem, they may hold their arms and shoulders forward. Their legs are hyperextended, and they lead with their abdomen as short, stiff steps are taken. They fall backward more often than forward.

Ataxia

Disorders of balance and proprioception constitute the major problems for approximately 8% of cerebral palsied individuals. Ataxia is a widely used word that denotes poor motor coordination stemming from vestibular and kinesthetic inadequacies. Thus, *ataxia* can be alcoholic, autonomic, cerebellar, choreic, or hysterical. Ataxic cerebral palsy is believed to originate from cerebellar damage, and probably many more persons have ataxia than are diagnosed. If motor awkwardness and problems of balance are not inherited from parents, it can be assumed that mild ataxia is present.

Ataxic cerebral palsy is usually not detected until the toddler begins to walk. The child appears normal except for a somewhat awkward gait. In mild cases, such children are simply labeled *clumsy* and resign themselves to Cs in physical education and the occasional embarrassment of missing a step or upsetting a dinner glass. With concentrated effort, they may become good in a particular sport and make the varsity team. Nevertheless, they are acutely aware that they must practice twice as hard as most of their friends. Seldom are they able to expend the time and energy required to maintain their athletic skills over a period of years.

In more severe cases of ataxia, such as those seen frequently among LD children, pupils may seem lost in space. The defective proprioceptive sense gives the children inadequate information about their center of gravity, postures, and relationships to the objects about them. When they reach for an object, they are inclined to overshoot the mark. When climbing stairs or stepping over an obstacle, they tend to lift their feet too high. In ducking under and/or between obstacles, they misjudge the distance. They bump into things, knock them over, and seem to stumble over their own feet. They may walk and run fairly well on level ground, but on an uneven surface or downhill grade they fail to make the necessary postural adjustments to avoid loss of balance.

Rigidity

Rigidity in cerebral palsy is associated with severe mental retardation. Approximately 4% of all cerebral palsy falls within this category. Brain damage causes rigidity in both the contracting muscles and their antagonists, but most strongly affects the antagonists. The result is a tendency toward diminished rather than abnormal motion. It is manifested as a generalized inelasticity or stiffness. Because the stretch reflex is decreased or absent, hyperextension of body parts occurs.

In extreme cases, the child lies helpless in an opisthotonic, or *wind-swept,* position as depicted in Figure 23.14. The cervical, thoracic, and lumbar spine is hyperextended, and the hypertonicity of affected muscles makes moving body parts difficult.

Figure 23.14 Boy with severe rigidity enjoys scooter board activities.

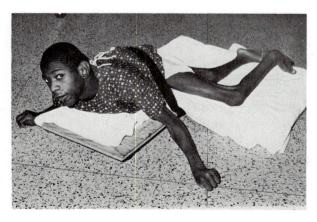

Tremors

Tremors are involuntary vibrating movements that are usually regular and rhythmic. They account for about 2% of cerebral palsy. When caused by cerebellar damage, the tremor is accentuated by voluntary movement, increasing in severity as the body part approaches the end of the movement. This type of tremor is called intentional, action, or terminal. It occurs more often in the arms than in the legs. When caused by damage to the basal ganglia, the tremor decreases in severity and/or disappears during sleep and certain motor tasks that require concentration. This type of tremor is called nonintentional, rest, or passive. It mostly affects the cranial and digital muscles.

In their most severe form, tremors produce a condition of dystonia. In its generic sense, *dystonia* refers to abnormally heightened or lessened states of muscle tone.

Mixed Type

Most persons with cerebral palsy exhibit characteristics of several types. Spasticity and athetosis almost always coexist, with some body parts more involved spastically than others.

The child is classified into one of the five types according to the symptoms that seem to predominate. When no one type predominates, the cerebral palsy is designated as mixed. This category is used infrequently. Persons classified as having mixed cerebral palsy are usually severely involved and multiply handicapped.

Coping with Spasticity

Most persons with cerebral palsy have some degree of spasticity. This hypertonic condition keeps muscles abnormally tight and sometimes causes contractures; therefore, stretching exercises, especially before all-out game play or competition, are especially important. These may be active or passive and are similar to those used in warm-ups by able-bodied persons. Remember, however, the exercise principles in Chapter 13, which emphasize that active stretching (i.e., that done by the student without assistance) is more effective than passive stretching.

Children with spasticity so great that it forces body parts into abnormal postures (see Figures 23.15 to 23.17) should not be allowed to freeze in such positions. Therapists and teachers within the school district should adapt the child's wheelchair and devise a strapping system that minimizes scissoring and abnormal arm and head positions. There are times, however, when body parts go into spastic spasms, and teachers need to know handling techniques for reducing spasticity. Figures 23.15 to 23.17 present some of these techniques. Two principles underlie handling techniques. The first is to *maintain symmetry* (i.e., avoid rotation, thereby keeping body parts in midline). Remember that symmetry of the head, neck, and spine is essential since positions of these parts affect the rest of the body. The second principle is to *work from designated key points* in correcting abnormal postural reactions. As indicated in Figures 23.15 and 23.16, these key points are the shoulder joint for abnormal arm positions and the pelvis and hip joints for scissoring.

Figure 23.15 Correcting the position of the spastic child's arms. (*A*) Typical hemiplegic arm position with shoulder joint adducted and flexed, elbow flexed, forearm pronated, wrist and fingers flexed, and thumb lying across palm. (*B*) and (*C*) To straighten the arm, lift it first by rotating it outward at the shoulder and elbow joints; then straighten the wrist and fingers. (*D*) Another typical flexion/adduction pattern. (*E*) Grasp lateral aspect of elbows and/or upper arms. (*F*) Simultaneously lift and outwardly rotate the arms.

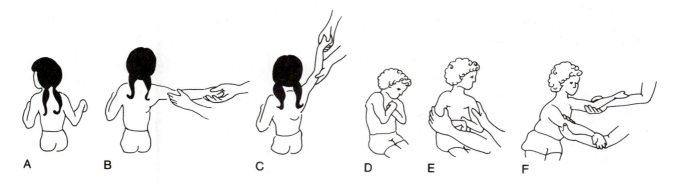

A B C D E F

A   B   C

Figure 23.17 Correcting the standing position of the spastic child to facilitate walking. (*A*) Typical position with limbs adducted, flexed, and inwardly rotated. The scissored legs narrow the base of support, and the pronated feet make it difficult to transfer weight sideways to take a step forward. (*B*) Stand behind the child, holding her at the elbows. Extend and outwardly rotate the arms at the shoulder joint while pushing the shoulders forward and up.

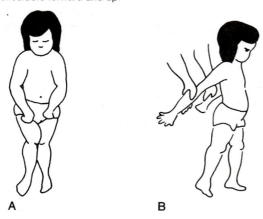

A   B

The best way to learn these is hands-on practice with spastic children. Only by experience can one become used to the resistance offered by spastic limbs. Do not equate hypertonus with pain; just think of it as a different way of moving. An excellent beginning book for increasing knowledge about handling and positioning is one written specifically for parents:

Finnie, N. R. (1974). *Handling the young cerebral palsied child at home* (2nd ed.). New York: E. P. Dutton & Co., Inc.

Particular caution should be taken with hip joint movement because nonambulatory CP children are at high risk for hip dislocation. In approximately 25% of such children, the head of the femur becomes displaced in an upward and posterior direction. The average age of dislocation is 7 years, but it may occur at any time. Hip dislocation is corrected by surgery.

Most persons with severe spasticity undergo several surgeries. The most common of these is surgical lengthening of the Achilles tendon to allow normal dorsiflexion at the ankle joint, thereby eliminating toe walking. Surgery performed to prevent scissoring is called a *tenotemy* or *myotomy*. In these operations the hip adductors are lengthened and one of the nerves innervating the spastic adductors is cut. While this reduces spasticity, it also weakens the muscles. Adapted physical education must be planned for the weeks following surgery.

Bracing is also used to control spasticity. Illustrations of different kinds of orthoses are presented in Chapter 8.

In selecting physical education activities for persons with spasticity it is important to remember the tight muscle groups (flexors, adductors, and inward rotators of both shoulder and hip joints and flexors of both knee and ankle joints) and to avoid activities that might contribute to further tightening. Movement exploration challenges calling for walking on toes or toe pointing, for instance, are contraindicated, whereas walking up inclined surfaces and tap dances stressing heels and flats are recommended. Activities like swimming, horseback riding, and dance, which emphasize extension and good postures, are especially desirable.

Sometimes spasticity is so great that the person simply has to learn to live with it. Class 1 CP athletes fall into this category. When a student cannot use a manual wheelchair in obstacle races (i.e., the slalom) and sprints, then activities should be devised for motorized chairs. For students who find grasping and releasing difficult, bean bags (soft puts) are thrown instead of regulation balls. For those who find grasping easy but releasing impossible, games are created in which impetus is imparted to the ball by means of a mouth or hand stick. Croquet, miniature golf, hockey, shuffleboard, and boccia are among the games that can be easily adapted. When both grasping and releasing are impossible (as is the case with Class 2 Lower CP athletes), then kicking events are substituted for throwing ones.

Learning relaxation and stress control techniques is especially important for persons with spasticity. An outdated practice is protecting such children from conditions and situations that cause excitement, which in turn contributes to increased hypertonicity. Such protection violates the normalization principle. CP students should have the same opportunities to learn and participate in competitive sports as their able-bodied peers.

Coping with Athetosis

Athetosis is usually combined with spasticity. Within the NASCP sports classifications, for instance, Class 2 and 6 athletes exhibit more athetosis than spasticity, but both conditions are usually present. Although Class 6 persons are ambulatory, their locomotion is very unsteady. Those with severe athetosis fall often, making track and running games a challenge for even the stouthearted. For this reason, Class 6 athletes have a choice between wheelchair and ambulatory soccer. Many Class 6 persons, as they grow older—especially if they become overweight—rely more and more on wheelchairs. Class 6 athletes tend overall to have more problems with speech and motor control than those in Classes 3, 4, and 5.

Warm-ups are not needed by persons with athetosis whose muscle contractions keep them in a state of never-ending readiness. Instead, the emphasis should be upon relaxation and tension reduction. It is generally believed that athetosis ceases during sleep. During waking hours, the ever-present overflow of movements fluctuates with the level of stress. Often the harder the person tries to relax, the more troublesome the movements become.

Hellebrandt and her colleagues (1961) report cinematographical and electromyographic research in which a 50-year-old athetoid woman was taught bowling, tennis, and golf. The woman's chief problems were difficulty in walking and in the use of the hands. Bowling with a 10-pound ball was executed from a sitting position. To develop sufficient strength for bowling, the number of throws attempted was increased each day until 100 throws in a single practice session no longer produced undue fatigue. The less affected of the two arms was used in bowling, and it was found that involuntary motions did not distort the throwing pattern. Throwing the bowling ball seemed to suppress all overt manifestations of athetosis on the same side.

The forehand drive in tennis and the drive in golf were executed from a standing position. As in bowling, swinging the sports implements suppressed all overt manifestations of athetosis in the body parts directly involved in the motor task. The application of force was surprisingly smooth. The movement abnormalities included prominence of tonic neck reflexes, exaggerated

postural adjustments, and problems with balance before the stroke was initiated and during its follow-through. The findings of the two studies led the Wisconsin researchers to conclude that moderately involved athetoid persons can learn individual sports that demand accuracy in aiming and swinging. More research of this nature is needed.

Sports and Aquatics

The first international games for persons with CP were held in 1968 in France. Sports groups have been testing activities and identifying those in which CP persons have the most opportunity for success for almost 20 years. NASCP sports were derived largely from those used in Europe. In general, CP students perform better in individual sports than in team activities. This book tends to emphasize skills to be taught to severely disabled students rather than those in Classes 7 and 8, who can be taught easily in the mainstream setting even though they cannot compete equitably with able-bodied peers.

Only two team sports are recommended for CP athletes: soccer and boccia. Students in Classes 6 to 8 are eligible to compete in ambulatory soccer, which is played (with only a few exceptions) according to the rules of able-bodied soccer. The game is coed, with seven players on a team; these must include at least one Class 6 and no more than four Class 8 athletes. The game consists of two equal periods of 25 minutes each.

Wheelchair soccer is a unique combination of soccer and basketball designed for persons in Classes 1 to 6. Nine players are on each team; these must include four persons from Classes 1 to 3 and 6. The remaining players are made up of any combination of Classes 4 to 6. The game is played with a 10-inch playground ball (1985 rule change) and soccer-type goal that is 5'6" in height, 9'0" in width, and 4'0" in depth. Protective headgear is recommended. The playing area should be on a floor or concrete slab not smaller than a regulation basketball court. The game is coed, with all players required to stay in their chairs for the 25-minute halves. Only Class 1 athletes can use motorized chairs.

Boccia, played with leather balls of about baseball size, can be either a team or an individual sport. Balls can be given impetus by throwing, rolling, kicking, or assistive device. Figure 23.18 illustrates this game. Although popular in Europe, this game is just beginning to be known in the United States. Indoor adapted boccia sets, with game rules, can be ordered through Flaghouse, Incorporated, 18 West 18th Street, New York, NY 10011. All balls except the target ball (which is smaller) weigh 275 grams and are 26.5 cm in diameter.

Figure 23.18 Boccia is a bowling-type game specifically for Class 1 and 2 athletes. A team is comprised of three members, one of whom must be Class 1. The object is to give impetus to the ball so that it lands as close as possible to the white target ball. Each player has two balls per round. A team game is six

rounds. *Left,* Class 1 athlete with no functional use of arms or legs uses head pointer to give impetus to the ball. *Right,* Class 2 athletes either kick or throw the ball into play, depending upon whether they are 2L or 2U.

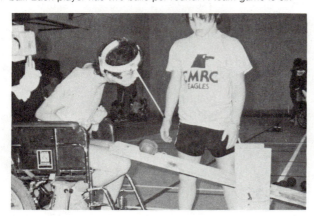

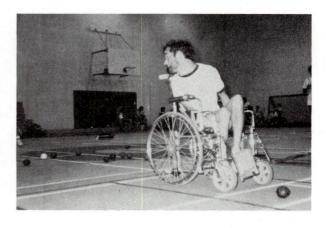

Table 23.3
Swimming Events for Cerebral Palsied Persons 1985 Rules

Event	Nonambulatory Classes				Ambulatory Classes			
	1	2	3	4	5	6	7	8
25-m freestyle	X	X	X			X		
25-m backstroke	X	X	X			X		
50-m freestyle			X	X	X	X	X	X
50-m backstroke				X	X		X	X
50-m breaststroke								X
100m freestyle				X	X		X	X
100-m backstroke							X	X

Note. A 3 X 25-m medley relay is conducted for swimmers from Classes 1 to 4; a 3 X 50-m medley relay is conducted for swimmers from Classes 5 to 8. Only one swimmer per class is allowed.

Figure 23.19 Class 1 and 2 CP athletes can use personal flotation devices in swimming competition. *Top,* Class 1 athlete has almost no use of arms; note flexion of all four limbs. *Bottom,* Class 2 athlete can extend arms and legs, but has only about 40% range of motion.

Individual sports in which CP persons do well include archery, bowling, bicycling and tricycling, track and field, horseback riding, swimming, rifle shooting, slalom, table tennis, and weight lifting (Jones, 1984). The following pages illustrate and describe adaptations in these sports.

Official competitive swim events are specified in Table 23.3. Unlike swimming instruction with able-bodied students, use of personal flotation devices (PFDs) is recommended when teaching CP students to swim. Most Class 1 and 2 athletes, because of severe spasticity, will need PFDs throughout their lives, regardless of how well they learn to swim (Figure 23.19).

Table 23.4
Boccia, Bowling, and Field Events for Cerebral Palsied Persons
1985 Rules

Event	Nonambulatory Classes				Ambulatory Classes			
	1	2	3	4	5	6	7	8
Boccia	X	X						
Chute bowling with assistant	X	X						
Chute bowling, no assistant			X			X		
Regulation bowling				X	X		X	X
Soft discus	X							
Precision soft shot[a]	X							
Distance soft shot	X							
High toss	X							
Distance kick		X						
Thrust kick		X						
Shot put	X	X	X	X	X	X	X	X
Club throw		X	X	X	X	X		
Discus	X	X	X	X	X	X	X	X
Javelin				X	X	X	X	X

[a]Soft shot is a 5-ounce bean bag.

Figure 23.20 Two kicking events are offered for Class 2 athletes with no functional use of arms. *Top,* athlete performs distance kick with 13-inch rubber playground ball. *Bottom,* Rick Resa, international competitor, performs thrust kick with 6-pound medicine ball.

A few internationally ranked swimmers are exceptions to this generalization, but independence from PFDs is not a realistic goal for most Class 1 and 2 athletes. *Speed* is the goal rather than good form, although increasing range of motion improves form as well as speed. Flippers are not allowed. Team relays, with three persons on a team, are conducted.

Field events are entered by more CP athletes than any other activity. Table 23.4 indicates all official field events that involve throwing as well as boccia and bowling events. Only Class 2 Lower athletes compete in the two kicking events; this is because their arms are functionally useless for throwing. Success in throwing and kicking events (see Figures 23.20 and 23.21) depends largely on the size and weight of the projectiles: Table 23.5 presents these. Students with the ATNR need to be positioned so that the head does not need to be turned during the throw.

Slalom, track, and cycling events are depicted in Table 23.6. Until 1985, a 20-m motorized chair dash was used for Class 1 athletes. Although no longer a NASCP event, 20 meters represents a good beginning distance for teaching students about competition. The

Figure 23.21 Throwing events for Classes 3–4 are the same as for Classes 5–8 except for the javelin, which is inappropriate for Class 3. *Top,* Class 3 athletes, Alfred Dore and Manyon Lyons, international competitors. Note that Class 3 athletes need waist and leg straps for support and hold onto their chairs during the release. *Bottom,* Class 4 athletes Rene Rivera and Joan Blalark, international competitors, do not need straps or arm support.

Table 23.5
Official Equipment for Cerebral Palsied Sports
1985 Rules

Event	Implement	Weight or Design
Soft shot distance, precision, and high throws	Bean bag	5 ounces (150 grams)
Thrust kick	Medicine ball	6 pounds (3 kg)
Distance kick	Playground ball	13 inches
Club throw	Club	1 pound, 14 inches long
Discus	Standard women's discus	2 pounds (1 kg), 180 mm diameter
Shot put	Shot put	4, 6, or 8 pounds depending on classification
Javelin	Standard women's javelin except for Class 8 males	
Boccia	Leather-covered boccia ball	275 grams, 26.5 cm diameter
Ambulatory soccer	Regulation soccer ball	14 to 16 ounces
Wheelchair soccer	Playground ball	10 inches
Weight lifting	Universal weight machine, nonprogressive bench	
Bowling	With or without retractable handle chute (ramp)	Varies; 10 pounds for Classes 1 and 2

Note. The soft shot *precision throw* uses a ground target with eight concentric rings. The athlete has six throws from a distance of 6 feet from the center of the bullseye. The bullseye counts 16 points. Each ring away from it counts 2 points less than the previous. The soft shot *high throw* uses high jump standards with the bar set at 3 feet and raised 6 inches at a time. The competitor stands 1 mm from the bar and has three throws per height.

Table 23.6
Slalom, Track, and Cycling Events for Cerebral Palsied Persons
1985 Rules

	Nonambulatory Classes				Ambulatory Classes			
Event	1	2	3	4	5	6	7	8
Slalom	X	X	X	X				
60-m motorized chair dash/weave	X							
60-m manual chair or ambulatory; see note.		X	X			X		
100 m				X	X		X	X
200 m		X	X			X		
400 m		X	X	X	X	X	X	X
800 m			X			X	X	
Cross country, 1500 & 3000 m						X	X	
Long jump						X	X	
Tricycle, 1500 m		X	X	X	X	X		
3000 m					X	X		
Bicycle, 5000 m							X	X
10,000 m							X	X

Note. Beginning with 60 m, manual chairs are used for Classes 2–4; Classes 5–8 ambulate in individual, unique styles.

60-m motorized chair race incorporates weaving around pylons at set intervals; otherwise, it is in a straight line. Each competitor has two track lanes in this event; practice in the school setting should use lanes and stress staying within the assigned distance.

The slalom (see Figure 23.22), a race against time in which athletes follow a clearly marked obstacle course, is discussed in Chapter 8. Class 1 athletes use a motorized chair, whereas Class 2 to 4 athletes use manual chairs. Specifications for the official slalom courses appear in the *NASCP Classification and Sports Manual.* Teachers without access to this book can create their own courses, using ramps, traffic cones, and lines. Unlimited possibilities for fun exist in this event.

Tricycles, bicycles (see Figure 23.23), and horses offer students a chance for freedom not possible in wheelchairs. Stationary tricycles and bicycles should be available in adapted physical education resource rooms and for winter use. Three-wheeled adult cycles are available through Sears and other popular chain stores. Like able-bodied students, every CP child should own his or her cycle and master this means of locomotion. Often adaptations must be made to tricycles for Class 2, 3, and 6 athletes; an occupational therapist or physical therapist can make these.

Figure 23.22 Classes 1–4 athletes compete in slalom, moving around a set course in the fewest number of seconds possible. *Top left,* Class 1 athlete has almost no use of arms and legs, so must use a motorized chair. *Top right,* Class 2 athlete typically uses feet for power. *Bottom,* Class 3 and 4 CP athletes are difficult to distinguish from spinally paralyzed athletes. Class 3 uses short, choppy arm pushes, whereas Class 4 uses forceful, continuous arm action.

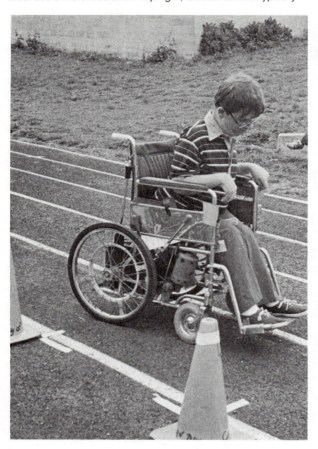

Figure 23.23 Class 6 athletes have more motor control problems than Classes 4–5. Class 6 ambulates without assistive devices, but typically has much athetoid movement, which causes balance and accuracy problems. *Top left,* Class 6 athlete throwing discus. *Top right,* Class 6 athlete putting shot. *Bottom,* Class 6 athletes in 1500 meter tricycle race. Note that Classes 7–8 athletes compete on bicycles.

Figure 23.24 Classes 5, 7, and 8 in 100 meter dash. *Top left,* Class 8 athletes run freely without a noticeable limp. *Top right,* Class 5 athlete uses assistive devices. *Bottom,* Class 7 athletes run with slight limp; have mild to moderate spasticity, either all on one side or affecting all four limbs.

In assessment and programming for CP students, ages 7 years and up, the emphasis should be on learning and using functional sports skills for enrichment of leisure and maintenance of optimal fitness. Some activities can be taught in mainstream physical education, but most CP students need part-time instruction by an adapted physical education specialist who can teach wheelchair sports and offer knowledgeable coaching.

Dance and Rhythmic Activities

Little information is available in this area, but CP students need the same kinds of dance instruction available to able-bodied peers. All forms of dance are easily adaptable to wheelchairs. See Chapter 15 on adapted dance and be creative! As important as motor skills are the opportunities for socialization that confidence in dance provides.

Learning Activities

1. Contact local, regional, or national offices of United Cerebral Palsy Associations, Incorporated, and other organizations that serve physically disabled persons to find out if CP sports are conducted in your community and how you can help. Act as a volunteer 1 or 2 hours each week.

2. Invite a physical or occupational therapist or someone knowledgeable about reflexes to your class to give a lecture-demonstration. Ask this person also to cover transfer and handling techniques for nonambulatory CP persons.

3. Identify persons in your university or community who have cerebral palsy and invite them to your class to discuss physical education and recreation.

4. Attend several sports events (integrated or separate) in which CP persons participate in sports. Analyze movement patterns and, if the opportunity exists, help coach these persons.

5. Conduct a debate or panel discussion, with at least one CP person participating, on the pros and cons of separate sports organizations like NASCP, NWAA, and NWBA vs. all physically disabled persons belonging to the same organization and using the same sports classifications.

6. Attend workshops on cerebral palsy conducted by other university departments or community agencies. Design a multidisciplinary plan for education and treatment.

7. Arrange for a salesperson to demonstrate various electronic and computer aids used by persons with severe communication and/or mobility problems.

References

Bleck, E., & Nagel, D. (Eds.). (1982). *Physically handicapped children: A medical atlas for teachers* (2nd ed.). New York: Grune & Stratton.

Finnie, N. R. (1974). *Handling the young cerebral palsied child at home* (2nd ed.). New York: E. P. Dutton & Co., Inc.

Hellebrandt, F. A., Waterland, J. C., & Walters, C. E. (1961). The influence of athetoid cerebral palsy on the execution of sports skills: Bowling. *Physical Therapy Review, 41,* 106–113.

Hellebrandt, F., & Waterland, J. C. (1961). The influence of athetoid cerebral palsy on the execution of sports skills: Tennis and golf. *Physical Therapy Review, 41,* 257–262.

Jones, J. A. (1984). *Training guide to cerebral palsy sports.* New York: National Association of Sports for Cerebral Palsy. (2nd ed. to be published by Human Kinetics Publishers, Champaign, IL.)

National Association of Sports for Cerebral Palsy. (1983). *NASCP: USA classification and sports rules manual* (2nd ed.). New York: United Cerebral Palsy Associations, Inc.

Thompson, G., Rubin, I., & Bilenker, R. (Eds.). (1983). *Comprehensive management of cerebral palsy.* New York: Grune & Stratton.

Bibliography

Abercrombie, M. L. J., Gardiner, P. A., Hansen, E., Jonckheere, J., Lindon, R. L., Solomon, G., & Tyson, M. C. (1964). Visual, perceptual, and visuomotor impairment in physically handicapped children. *Perceptual and Motor Skills: Monograph Supplement 3-V18, 18,* 561–625.

Berg, K. (1970). Effect of physical training of school children with cerebral palsy. *Acta Paediatrica Scandinavica, 204* (Supplement), 27–33. (This source includes seven other articles on fitness and cerebral palsy.)

Berg, K., & Isakasson, B. (1970). Body composition and nutrition of school children with cerebral palsy. *Acta Paediatrica Scandinavica, 204,* 40–47.

Bobath, K. (1974). *The motor deficit in patients with cerebral palsy.* London: Spastics International Medical Publications.

Bobath, K. (1980). *A neurophysiological basis for the treatment of cerebral palsy.* Philadelphia: J. P. Lippincott.

Brown, A. (1975). Review: Physical fitness and cerebral palsy. *Child: Care, Health and Development, 1,* 143–152.

Chee, F. K., Kreutzberg, J. R., & Clark, D. L. (1978). Semicircular canal stimulation in cerebral palsied children. *Physical Therapy, 58,* 1071–1075.

Compton, D., & Price, D. (1975). Individualizing your treatment program: A case study using LMIT. *Therapeutic Recreation Journal, 9*(4), 127–139.

Connor, F., Williamson, G. G., & Siepp, J. M. (1978). *Program guide of infants and toddlers with neuromotor and other developmental disabilities.* New York: Teachers College Press.

Cooper, M., Sherrill, C., & Marshall, D. (In press). Attitudes toward physical activity of elite cerebral palsied athletes. *Adapted Physical Activity Quarterly.*

Cruickshank, W. (1965). *Perception and cerebral palsy* (2nd ed.). Syracuse, NY: Syracuse University Press.

Cruickshank, W. (Ed.). (1976). *Cerebral palsy: A developmental disability* (3rd ed.). New York: Syracuse University Press.

Davis, R. (1985). *Backward wheelchair propulsion during the sprint start by elite class 2 cerebral palsied athletes.* Unpublished doctoral dissertation, Texas Woman's University, Denton.

Ekblom, B., & Lundberg, A. (1968). Effect of physical training on adolescents with severe motor handicaps. *Acta Paediatrica Scandanavica, 57,* 17–23.

Finnie, N. (1970). *Handling the young cerebral palsied child at home.* New York: E. P. Dutton & Co., Inc.

Gillette, H. (1969). *Systems of therapy in cerebral palsy.* Springfield, IL: Charles C. Thomas.

Horgan, J. (1980). Reaction and movement-time of children with cerebral palsy. *American Journal of Physical Medicine, 59,* 22–29.

Hourcade, J., & Parette, H. (1984). Cerebral palsy and emotional disturbance: A review and implications for intervention. *Journal of Rehabilitation, 50*(3), 55–60.

Huber, C. (1979). Coming of age . . . cerebral palsy sports. *Sports 'n Spokes, 5,* 17–18.

Huberman, G. (1976). Organized sports activities with cerebral palsied adolescents. *Rehabilitation Literature, 37,* 103–106.

Kanda, R., Yuge, M., Yamori, Y., Suzuki, J., & Fukase, H. (1984). Early physiotherapy in the treatment of spastic diplegia. *Developmental Medicine and Child Neurology, 26*(4), 438–444.

Levitt, S. (1977). *Treatment of cerebral palsy and motor delay.* Oxford: Blackwell Scientific Publications.

Lundberg, A. O. (1975). Mechanical efficiency in bicycle ergometer work of young adults with cerebral palsy. *Developmental Medicine and Child Neurology, 17,* 434–439.

Lundberg, A. O. (1976). Oxygen consumption in relation to work load in students with cerebral palsy. *Journal of Applied Physiology, 40,* 873–875.

Lundberg, A. O. (1978). Maximal aerobic capacity of young persons with spastic cerebral palsy. *Developmental Medicine and Child Neurology, 20,* 205–210.

Lundberg, A. O. (1984). Longitudinal study of physical working capacity of young people with spastic cerebral palsy. *Developmental Medicine and Child Neurology, 26*(3), 328–334.

Lundberg, A., Ovenfors, D., & Saltin, B. (1967). Effect of physical training on school-children with cerebral palsy. *Acta Paediatrica Scandinavica, 56,* 182–188.

McCubbin, J., & Shasby, G. (1985). Effects of isokinetic exercise on adolescents with cerebral palsy. *Adapted Physical Activity Quarterly, 2*(1), 56–64.

Robinault, I. (1973). *Functional aids for the multihandicapped.* New York: Harper & Row.

Robson, P. (1968). The prevalence of scoliosis in adolescents and young adults with cerebral palsy. *Developmental Medicine and Child Neurology, 10,* 447–452.

Robson, P. (1972). Cerebral palsy and physical fitness. *Developmental Medicine and Child Neurology, 14,* 811–813.

Sherrill, C., & Adams-Mushett, C. (1984). Fourth national cerebral palsy games: Sports by ability . . . not disability. *Palaestra, 1,* 24–27, 49–51.

Short, F., & Winnick, J. (1985). The performance of adolescents with cerebral palsy on measures of physical fitness. In C. Sherrill (Ed.), *Sport and disabled athletes* (pp. 239–244). Champaign, IL: Human Kinetics Publishers.

Templin, S., Howard, J., & O'Connor, M. (1981). Self-concept of young children with cerebral palsy. *Developmental Medicine and Child Neurology, 23,* 730–738.

Thompson, G., Rubin, I., & Bilenker, R. (Eds.) (1983). *Comprehensive management of cerebral palsy.* New York: Grune & Stratton.

24 Deafness and Hearing Impairments

Figure 24.1 The Rome School for the Deaf has their own way of sideline conversation.

Chapter Objectives

After you have studied this chapter you should be able to

1. Explain hearing loss in terms of the three attributes of sound.
2. Identify and describe five classes of hearing handicap. What are the implications of each for physical education instruction?
3. Discuss problems of the following: (a) congenitally deaf, (b) adventitiously deaf, and (c) deaf-blind individuals. How is speech affected in each? Why is the deaf-blind condition typically covered in units on deafness rather than blindness?
4. Differentiate between conductive and sensorineural hearing loss and state implications of physical education for each.

5. Discuss how physical education programming can be used to ameliorate various problems of persons with hearing loss.
6. State eight guidelines for physical educators in teaching deaf students. Discuss each.
7. Discuss the American Athletic Association for the Deaf and opportunities for competition.
8. Discuss existing and needed research concerning hearing loss and physical education.

Deaf and hearing impaired students often excel in physical education. At Gallaudet College in Washington, DC, the only liberal arts college in the world for the deaf, student interest in athletics is so high that men and women engage in several intercollegiate sports. The Gallaudet Modern Dance Group has performed in Europe and throughout the United States. Says Peter Wisher, founder of the group, "The majority of audiences are composed of hearing people, but they soon forget the dancers are deaf. They become tremendously involved with the kids, especially during the numbers using abstracted sign language" (Carney, 1971, p. 21).

Other deaf persons, like Penn State halfback Gary Klingensmith and Sam Oates at Hardin-Simmons in Texas, have gained recognition as outstanding members of hearing teams. Gary and Sam agree that a deaf athlete must try harder than a hearing one, but success is possible if the motto *100% all the time* is followed.

The adapted physical educator may choose to work in a school for the deaf (see Figure 24.1) or may wish to integrate one or two deaf or hearing-impaired children with his or her regular classes. He or she soon realizes that many children have hearing losses and/or problems of auditory perception.

Attributes of Sound

Hearing loss can be discussed in terms of the three attributes of sound: intensity, frequency, and spectrum, or timbre. Classifications of hearing impairment for educational purposes are made only in terms of intensity (see Table 24.1). *Intensity* refers to the perception of loudness and softness. The unit of measurement that expresses the intensity of a sound is the *decibel* (dB). Normal hearing is established as the zero level in decibels. A sound at 0 level is barely audible. For normal conversation to be heard from a distance of 10 to 20 feet, the loudness may vary from 35 to 65 dB, depending upon the highness of the pitch. This is the normal threshold of hearing for daily living activities. When the intensity of sound ranges above 100 decibels, the sound may become painful.

Frequency refers to the perception of high and low pitch. It is measured in terms of Hertz (Hz). Most human beings with normal hearing can perceive frequencies from about 20 to 20,000 Hz. It should be noted, however, that the audiogram includes only the frequencies between 125 and 8000, since these are the most important in daily communication.

Three of these frequencies—500, 1000, and 2000 Hz—are emphasized in relating hearing loss to speech and vice versa. For instance, persons who do not hear frequencies above 2000 Hz have difficulty in recognizing such *high frequency* sounds as the letters *s, z, sh, zh, th* as in think, *th* as in that, *ch* as in chair, *j* as in Joe, *p, b, t, d, f, v,* and *h.*

Spectrum, or *timbre,* encompasses the different tonal qualities ranging from *pure tone,* which has a single frequency, to the *complex tones,* which comprise

Table 24.1
Classes of Hearing Handicap

Hearing Threshold Level dB (ISO)	Class	Degree of Handicap	Average Hearing Threshold Level for 500, 1000, and 2000 Hz in the Better Ear[a]		Ability to Understand Speech
			More Than	Not More Than	
	A	Not significant		25 dB (ISO)	No significant difficulty with faint speech
25					
	B	Slight handicap	25 dB (ISO)	40 dB	Difficulty only with faint speech
40					
	C	Mild handicap	40 dB	55 dB	Frequent difficulty with normal speech
55					
	D	Marked handicap	55 dB	70 dB	Frequent difficulty with loud speech
70					
	E	Severe handicap	70 dB	90 dB	Can understand only shouted or amplified speech
90					
	F	Extreme handicap	90 dB		Usually cannot understand even amplified speech

[a]Whenever the average for the poorer ear is 25 dB or more greater than that of the better ear in this frequency range, 5 dB is added to the average for the better ear. This adjusted average determines the degree and class of handicap. For example, if a person's average hearing-threshold level for 500, 1000, and 2000 Hz is 37 dB in one ear and 62 dB or more in the other, his or her adjusted average hearing-threshold level is 42 dB and his or her handicap is Class C instead of Class B.
From Davis & Silverman, 1978.

normal speech sounds. Timbre includes all the qualities besides highness, lowness, loudness, and softness that enable the listener to differentiate between sounds. Inability to hear sounds at certain frequencies affects the perception of tonal qualities. It is doubtful that anyone with normal hearing can be *tone deaf;* yet, widespread individual differences exist within abilities to perceive speech sounds. In general, vowels and diphthongs are most easily perceived. Children with mild to moderate hearing losses have the most difficulty in perceiving the following high frequency sounds: *th* as in think, *f, p, d, b, th* as in that, *v, k, g, t, s, z,* and *zh.*

Classification of Hearing Loss

Table 24.1 presents the most widely used system for classifying hearing loss. Children with 30dB or more loss are generally fitted with hearing aids.

They *cannot* hear conversational speech from a distance further than 3 feet and may miss as much as 50% of class instruction if they cannot see the lips of the speaker. If the loss is of high frequency type, they may exhibit a slight speech defect.

Children within the *mild* classification can hear *loud* conversation within a 3-foot range, but often misunderstand meanings. For this reason, they may be wrongly labeled as *slow* or a *behavioral problem.* They

generally have defective speech, especially with *s, z, sh, ch,* and *j* sounds. Their language usage and vocabulary are deficient also. Children with moderate loss often do not hear clearly even with the amplification provided by hearing aids. They require special training in speech reading and are often placed in special education.

Children within the *marked* classification are considered partially or educationally deaf. Although they retain *residual hearing,* special training is needed for them to learn language. With a hearing aid, they can hear loud noises such as an automobile horn or a dog barking. With amplification, they may also hear words spoken several inches from their ear. If the hearing loss is congenital, they need special training in order to learn to talk. They can enjoy music, but their pleasure is derived largely from its rhythm.

Children within the *severe* classification cannot hear words even with the amplification of a hearing aid. They may be able to distinguish some noises from others if they are close by. They respond reflexively to loud sounds close to the ears, but the sounds themselves are meaningless. Children born deaf must receive specialized help very early in order to learn to speak and communicate with others. They may be fitted with a hearing aid at age 2 or 3 to enhance their awareness of loud sounds, thus improving their ability to interpret the environment. The hearing aid does not enable them to discriminate between speech sounds. They respond to music by recognizing the presence or cessation of vibrations.

Because communication skills are related to the age at which deafness occurs, children are classified further as either *congenitally deaf* or *adventitiously deaf*. The former are born deaf, whereas the latter are deafened through illness or accident. The terms *prelingual* and *postlingual* deafness are used also to specify whether deafness occurred before or after the development of speech and language.

Etiology and Incidence of Hearing Loss

Approximately 62% of all severe and profound hearing losses are congenital, while the other 38% are acquired. The National Foundation estimates that there are over 300,000 children in the United States who were born deaf or with a hearing loss. This condition shares second place in prevalence among the common birth defects: congenital blindness or visual loss, genitourinary malformations, and congenital heart and circulatory disease.

Of the hearing losses designated as congenital, some are hereditary; some are idiopathic; and others can be traced to diseases. Rubella (German measles) in the mother is the most frequent cause. The novel *In This Sign*, by Greenberg (1970), tells the story of Abel and Janice Ryder, both born deaf. As is often the case, both of their offspring as well as their grandson could hear and speak normally. In most cases, congenital deafness seriously impairs language development. Even with excellent instruction, many deaf infants grow into adulthood unable to speak intelligibly.

Acquired hearing losses vary in severity, depending upon the degree of loss and age of onset. Among the many persons with acquired hearing losses are Ludwig van Beethoven, Bernard Baruch, and Thomas Alva Edison. The last 25 years of Beethoven's life were spent in almost total deafness. His famous Ninth Symphony, the *Missa Solemnis*, and many of his piano sonatas and string quartets were composed after he became totally deaf. At his last appearance at a public concert, in 1824, Beethoven was completely oblivious to the applause of the audience acclaiming his ninth and final symphony.

Prevalence

Approximately 5 to 7% of all school-age children in the United States have auditory disorders. For government reports, the prevalence for deaf, hard of hearing, and deaf-blind children are all reported separately. The latest OSE figures indicate that 74,249 hard of hearing

and deaf students are receiving special education services. Many, however, remain unserved. For the total population, the prevalence is approximately 3.2% hard of hearing and .87% deaf.

Deaf-Blind Individuals

Persons with combinations of handicaps that prevent their profiting satisfactorily from educational programs provided for the blind or the deaf individual are called *deaf-blind*. This condition may be hereditary or acquired through such diseases as rubella, scarlet fever, and meningitis. In the hereditary category, *Usher's syndrome* is the leading cause. It is a genetic condition resulting in congenital deafness and a progressive blindness known as retinitis pigmentosa, which first appears in the early 30s.

It was not until the widespread rubella epidemic of 1963 to 1965, however, that large numbers of children were identified as deaf-blind and receiving inadequate educational services. Estimates revealed that 2,000 to 2,500 children and 5,000 to 7,000 adults were deaf-blind.

To cope with this problem, the federal government in 1968 authorized the development of 10 (now 11) regional deaf-blind centers scattered throughout the 50 states. A grant was awarded also to the University of Iowa to develop the *National Institute on Program Development and Training in Recreation for Deaf-Blind Children, Youth, and Adults*. Information on the delivery of recreation and leisure services can be obtained by writing to Dr. John Nesbitt, National Institute on Recreation for the Deaf-Blind, University of Iowa, Iowa City, Iowa 52242.

The best known of deaf-blind persons is Helen Keller (1880–1968), who was disabled by an illness at 19 months of age. Helen Keller graduated *cum laude* from Radcliffe, mastered five languages, and wrote three books. Her beautifully written biography (Keller, 1965) is among the classics that everyone should read. Less well known is Laura Bridgman (1829–1889), the famous deaf-blind pupil of Samuel Gridley Howe, the founder of Perkins Institution, now located in Watertown, Massachusetts. Laura, who became deaf-blind at age 2 from scarlet fever, was described by Charles Dickens in his book *American Notes*. Only by reading Dickens's book were Helen Keller's parents in Alabama made aware of the existence of Perkins Institution and the availability of her famous teacher, Anne Sullivan Macy.

Still another deaf-blind person, Robert J. Smithdas, who suffered cerebral spinal meningitis at age 5, has gained recognition through the publication of an autobiography and success in his work as a public

Table 24.2
Comparison of Conductive and Sensorineural Hearing Losses

Conductive	Sensorineural

Dysfunction of outer ear or middle ear
a. Tympanic membrane
b. Ossicles
c. Eustachian tubes
	Dysfunction of inner ear (labyrinth)
	a. Cochlea
	  Organ of Corti
	  Basilar membrane
	b. Semicircular canals

Air conduction loss only	Air conduction and bone conduction tests show equal threshold losses.
Results only in partial loss never exceeding 55 to 60 decibels	Varies from partial to total losses
Tends to have about the same loss of sensitivity for sounds of all frequency; called a *flat* hearing loss. Largely unaware of noise; benefits by speaker shouting.	Tends to have greater loss of sensitivity for sounds of high frequency than of low. Shouting does not help. Noise is frustrating.
Main problem is amplification of sound; discrimination of speech sounds is normal.	Main problem is discrimination among speech sounds; can usually hear but unable to derive meaning from high frequency sounds.
Hearing aids generally helpful. May hear well over telephone because of bone-conduction of sounds. Speech development and acquisition of language are not impaired seriously.	Hearing aids of limited value. Development of speech, understanding of language structure, and articulation are limited. Mispronounces words with high frequency sounds.
Can hear own voice through bone-conduction; tends to speak too softly.	Tends to speak with excessive loudness.

relations counselor and lecturer at the Industrial Home for the Blind in Brooklyn, New York. At age 32, after completing a Master of Arts degree at New York University and working at IHB for several years, Smithdas wrote,

Loneliness was continually present in my life after I became deaf and blind. And even now, in adulthood, I find it with me despite all my adjustments to social living. Loneliness is a hunger for increasing human companionship, a need to be part of the activity that I know is constantly going on about me. . . . To share my moments of joy with someone else, to have others sympathize with my failures, appreciate my accomplishments, understand my moods, and value my intelligence—these are the essential conditions that are needed for happiness. (Smithdas, 1958, p. 259)

Types of Hearing Loss

The major types of hearing loss are described in Table 24.2. Acquired hearing losses are generally conductive, while congenital losses are usually sensorineural.

Conductive Hearing Losses

Some dysfunction of the outer or middle ear prevents the vibrations of sound waves from reaching the inner ear. Figure 24.2 depicts the *external ear,* the *middle ear,* and the *inner ear. External otitis,* an inflammation of the outer ear caused by bacteria or fungi, causes temporary loss of hearing. Persons who swim a lot seem more susceptible to this condition than others. It results in swelling and partial closing (stenosis) of the external meatus, severe pain, persistent itching, and a thin watery discharge. Pupils with external otitis should not swim, nor should they be allowed in the swimming pool or any other moist area.

The middle ear, a tiny cavity only 1 to 2 cubic centimeters in volume, is where most conductive hearing losses occur. The middle ear is actually an extension of the *nasopharynx* by way of the *Eustachian tube,* and any malfunctioning of this tube affects hearing. Enlarged adenoids around the opening of the tube in the nasopharynx and allergic swelling of the tube cause malfunctioning, as does the common cold. The beginning of almost all middle ear infections is the Eustachian tube. Any blockage of the Eustachian tube lowers the air pressure within the middle ear. The resulting unequal pressure on the two sides of the tympanic membrane causes retraction, or a sucking inward, of the membrane, which in turn interferes with the vibration of sound waves. Artificial tubes are often inserted in the young child's ears to allow adequate healing of the middle ear. During the months that these tubes are worn, swimming is contraindicated.

Infection or inflammation of the middle ear, regardless of the cause, is known as *otitis media* and accounts for more conductive hearing losses than any other condition. Chronic inflammation may result in adhesions (very fine tears) between the tympanic membrane and the three tiny bones in the middle ear, which

Figure 24.2 Diagram of the human ear.

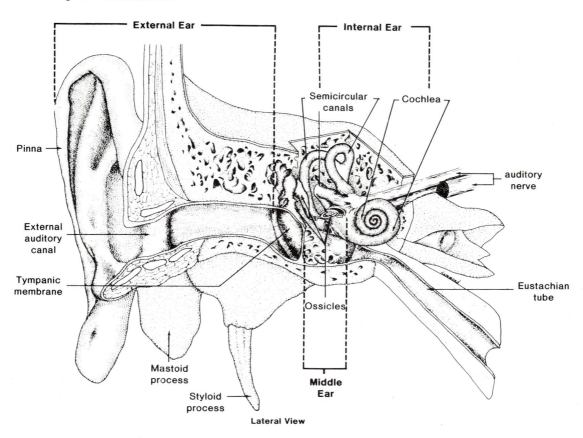

External Ear

Internal Ear

Semicircular canals

Cochlea

Pinna

auditory nerve

External auditory canal

Tympanic membrane

Eustachian tube

Ossicles

Mastoid process

Styloid process

Middle Ear

Lateral View

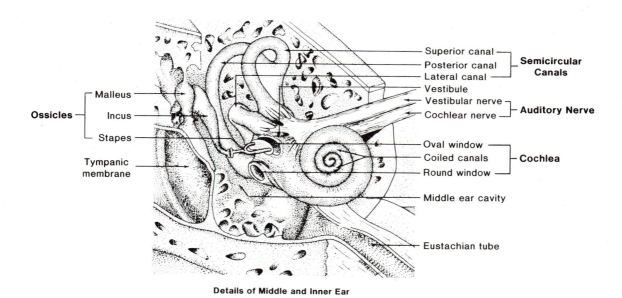

Superior canal

Posterior canal

Lateral canal

Semicircular Canals

Ossicles

Malleus

Incus

Stapes

Vestibule

Vestibular nerve

Cochlear nerve

Auditory Nerve

Tympanic membrane

Oval window

Coiled canals

Round window

Cochlea

Middle ear cavity

Eustachian tube

Details of Middle and Inner Ear

in turn prevent the normal transmission of sound waves. Even though the adhesions heal, their scar tissue makes it impossible to regain normal mobility of the ossicles. Active infection in the middle ear is especially dangerous since it may spread backward into the air cells of the mastoid process of the temporal bone, causing *mastoiditis.* Prior to the 1940s, this was one of the most deadly conditions to which children were susceptible. The discovery of antibodies has significantly reduced the number of mastoidectomies once performed as well as the incidence of hearing loss. Chronic otitis media, however, remains a potential killer in that infection in the mastoid area can easily find its way to the meninges of the brain and cause *meningitis.* Among the many side effects of meningitis is severe sensorineural hearing loss.

Sensorineural Hearing Loss

These hearing losses are more serious than are conductive hearing losses because they interfere with the transmission of sensory impulses to the brain. A hearing aid cannot compensate adequately for such losses, and no cures are known. By far the most common cause of sensorineural hearing loss is normal aging, in which sensitivity for higher frequencies gradually diminishes. Progressive loss of hearing related to aging is called *presbycusis.* Along with hearing loss, the aged tend to experience a deterioration in balance.

Relationship between Hearing Loss and Balance

The inner ear governs the functions of both hearing and balance. A hearing loss, therefore, often affects balance. Specifically, the sensory receptors for sound are within the *organ of Corti,* which is located within the *cochlea* and surrounded by endolymph.

The sensory receptors for balance are located within the *vestibular apparatus,* which consists of the three semicircular canals, the utricle, and the saccule. The vestibular, or labyrinthine, sense enables the body to relate to the gravitational field by detecting changes in both static and dynamic balance. *Static balance* is governed primarily by changes in head position, which are detected by hair cells within the utricle (also called the otolith organ) and perhaps the saccule. Changes in *dynamic balance,* including the body righting reflexes, are detected by hair cells within the fluid-filled ducts of the semicircular canals. The hair cells within the vestibular apparatus connect with thousands of nerve fibers which form the vestibular branch of the auditory nerve. Sensory impulses reporting changes in position

are transmitted to the cerebellum via the vestibulospinal tract. Disorders of balance, therefore, can be traced to approximately four anatomical sites: (a) the cerebellum, (b) the vestibulospinal tract, (c) the vestibular branch of the auditory nerve, and (d) the inner ear.

Individual Differences

Widespread individual differences exist among persons with hearing losses. Only those children who are born with severe losses or who lose their hearing before they develop speech and language are significantly different from their normal peers. The characteristics discussed here apply only to such children.

Socialization Problems

The greatest problems experienced by deaf persons are in the social domain, specifically in the acquisition of speech and language. Even with superior training, their vocalizations tend to have a distorted tonal quality. The voice is monotonous, guttural, and highly fluctuating in pitch range. Most persons cannot easily understand what deaf people are trying to say, and communication is often impossible because the listener does not care enough to try to extract meaning from their best efforts at speech. As a result, deaf persons suffer almost the same problems as a foreigner whose language is not understood.

Deaf children are likely to be left out of the spontaneous neighborhood play activities. The problem is intensified as the low organized games of childhood become increasingly structured and governed by complex rules. Without special help, deaf children do not grasp the intricacies of such team games as baseball, football, and soccer that are usually acquired in spontaneous play. The rare exception to this generalization occurs when a deaf child exhibits such superior skills that the neighborhood team cannot afford to ignore his or her potential contributions. These motor skills may have been developed through practice alone, with a parent or sibling, or with a special friend. The important point is that they are developed *before* group acceptance occurs rather than in the everyday give-and-take of neighborhood play. For every superior deaf athlete who is accepted by the group there are hundreds who are not integrated. These children may be inordinately lonely. Many withdraw and develop solitary play interests and hobbies. Thus the vicious circle begins. With few or no playmates, there are fewer opportunities for practicing speech and learning to lipread. With little practice, the child's speech worsens, as does ability to understand that of others.

Implications for Physical Education

The primary purpose of physical education for deaf students in an integrated setting should be socialization. When the physical educator welcomes a deaf child into the class, the curriculum for all students must be modified somewhat for a few days or weeks. The instructor must consider, What physical education activities require the least verbal communication for success? In which activities can a *different* child make friends the quickest? It is extremely important that deaf children not be integrated into a hearing team until they are accepted and liked by the team members. The other players must be willing to give them the ball, to create opportunities for them to score, and to help them understand team signals, the calls of the official, and the suggestions of the coach. Deaf children's motor skills seldom compensate for the inconveniences in team communication that their presence creates. Only when they are genuinely liked and wanted by the team members will their integration on the team be mutually satisfying. Neither the physical educator nor any other adult can rush this process.

The physical educator who agrees to accept a deaf child in the class should be committed to providing individual and dual sports, dance, and aquatics. Swimming, all forms of dance, archery, golf, rifle shooting, bowling, tennis, and badminton are among the many activities that deaf individuals most enjoy playing with the hearing. In these activities, they can wear a hearing aid and derive maximum social benefits from communication with others. Ideally, they can be introduced first to individual sports and dance. Then, as their ability to communicate and make friends grows, they can progress to dual and team sports.

Language Problems

Difficulty in learning to speak is often greater than learning to use residual hearing and/or to read speech. The terms *deaf mute* and *deaf and dumb* are not only repugnant, but inaccurate as well. With good training, most deaf persons can learn to speak, although the speech of some will be more intelligible than that of others.

Deaf infants babble normally in infancy, producing the same sounds as others of comparable age. Whereas the child who hears continues to make sounds for his or her own pleasure as well as to communicate, the child with no auditory sense to reinforce these verbalizations tends to produce fewer and fewer vocal sounds. Normal children, for instance, enjoy growling when doing the bear walk and barking when doing the dog walk. They may talk incessantly to an imaginary

Figure 24.3 Abstractions like the dog walk make sense to a deaf child only after he has seen a dog and has a model to emulate.

playmate. In contrast, deaf children are capable of making sound, but seldom do so except to attract attention or to convey a need.

Deaf persons compensate for their inadequate speech through various modes of nonverbal communication: They use eye contact, facial expressions, and gestures.

The expression of intense emotions in socially acceptable ways is difficult when speech is inadequate. When angered, the deaf person may resort to physical violence. Instead of trying to tell someone to stop annoying him or her, the deaf person is likely to shove or push back. Whereas many persons *work out* problems of grief, insecurity, and misunderstanding by talking to a trusted friend, deaf individuals find the sharing of emotions difficult. Likewise, the normal channels of individual and group psychotherapy, which are based largely upon vocalization, are denied them. Dance and movement education can often meet their needs.

Deaf persons whose inner language is that of signs and gestures have great difficulty in coping with abstractions (see Figure 24.3). Unless a word, idea, or feeling can be conveyed *visually* or *kinesthetically*, deaf children may be unable to comprehend its meaning until they receive instruction in oral language. Expressive language, or the ability to speak and/or to use signs and gestures for communication, develops only after inner language is established. The slowness with which deaf children develop inner and expressive language skills is often mistaken for mental retardation. The physical educator who works with deaf children must acquire as much knowledge as possible about nonverbal communication.

Implications for Physical Education

Physical education, using a guided discovery or motor creativity approach, can contribute substantially to language development in young deaf children. Lubin and Sherrill (1980) demonstrated that deaf children ages 3 to 5 exposed to only 20 sessions of guided movement exploration on the London trestle tree apparatus improved significantly over the controls in learning *I CAN* (Wessel, 1976) associated words and in motor creativity as measured by the Torrance test of Thinking Creatively in Action and Movement. The recommended approach is using *total communication* (both signs and spoken words) in posing such challenges as, "How many different ways can you move across the room?" and "Who can show me a new way to climb the ladder?" As children respond with movements, the teacher helps them find the word (or sign) to describe what they are doing. With this approach, physical education and language proceed concurrently (see Figure 24.4).

The role that physical education, especially dance, can play in enhancing the development of expressive language is unparalleled. When the physical educator teaches in a school for deaf students, the primary purpose may be instruction in the use of movement as a means of nonverbal expression. Modern dance, synchronized swimming, and free floor exercise in gymnastics offer opportunities for communicating ideas and feelings.

The physical educator must ascertain that the learning environment is conducive to the reception of symbolic language. The lighting must be adequate for lip reading, and the person giving instructions must be close enough so that minute movements of the lips and tongue can be perceived. When instruction occurs out-of-doors, care must be taken that the deaf child is not facing the sun when trying to read lips.

In games like soccer and football, which cover many yards of distance, players and teacher should be ever aware that deaf children cannot read lips from across the field, nor can they hear a whistle. Large hand signals should accompany all verbal instructions and whistle blows. The teacher should position himself or herself to be always within the deaf child's view.

Many authorities recommend that hearing aids be removed during physical education. This generalization seems appropriate only for team sports with body contact. In dance and individual and dual sports there appears to be no reason for removing the hearing aid. It should be remembered, however, that a hearing aid amplifies *all* noise, not just word sounds. As a result, deaf children may react negatively to prolonged noise and have frequent tension headaches.

Figure 24.4 Language concepts are reinforced through movement education challenges given through sign.

In physical education, deaf children should not be expected to enjoy exercises that demand postures in which the body is bent over and the vision limited. There is a tendency, for instance, for deaf children to keep their head up while touching their toes or performing the various animal walks. In aquatics, for the same reason, many deaf children prefer swimming with the head, or at least the eyes, out of the water. Underwater lights can be used for signaling when deaf children learn standard strokes and synchronized stunts.

In most deaf education settings today, total communication is used. This is the combination of signing and spoken words. To function optimally in such settings, physical educators must learn sign language. Eichstaedt and Seiler (1978) have devised 45 signs specific to physical education for the new teacher to learn. These signs have been found helpful in teaching nonhearing impaired persons also.

Hyperactivity

Deaf children may appear hyperactive. They must move frequently to maintain visual contact with the action. Knowing that they are expected to follow instructions although unable to hear them, they feel compelled to watch the teacher's mouth as he or she moves about the room. Often this is at the expense of completing assigned work at the desk. Deaf children's restlessness often stems from boredom. Unable to hear or comprehend, they may wiggle, shuffle their feet, or grit their teeth. Since they cannot hear, they are often completely unaware of these disquieting activities. If their pronunciation is poor and sometimes evokes laughter they may use movement as an attention-getting device rather than risk speaking.

Balance

Impairment of balance occurs most frequently when the hearing loss is caused by meningitis. In such cases, the destruction is primarily in the semicircular canals rather than in the cerebellum. When deafness and loss of balance are present simultaneously, the convalescent often finds the loss of balance to be the greater problem. In some instances, he or she must learn to walk again.

Myklebust (1964), Long (1932), and Morsh (1936) in separate studies each compared deaf and hearing students on several motor tasks. Each investigator found significant differences between their two samples only on balance. Of the six motor abilities measured by the Oseretsky motor proficiency test, deaf students made their lowest scores on general static balance and on speed. Deaf children have also been found inferior on locomotor coordination (dynamic balance) as measured by the Heath rail walking test. Furthermore, *meningitic deaf students with semicircular canal impairment* made significantly lower scores on the rail walking test than did other deaf children. Lindsey and O'Neal (1976) and Boyd (1967) also found deaf children inferior to hearing ones on balance. When data were analyzed by etiology, the prenatal deaf group was found poorest in performance and slowest in motor development.

Implications for Physical Education

When children, deaf or otherwise, have known balance problems, they should be given special instruction on the kinesiological principles of equilibrium. Movement exploration sessions may be developed around the following themes:

1. Center of gravity. What is it? How do your movements affect it? In what movements can you keep the center of gravity centered over its supporting base? Can your hands be used as a supporting base? What happens when your center of gravity moves in front of the supporting base? In back of it? To the side of it? What activities lower your center of gravity? Raise it?

2. Broad base. How can you adapt different exercises so that the supporting base is larger than normal? In what directions can you enlarge your base, i.e., how many stances can you

Figure 24.5 Some, but not all, deaf children have difficulty with balance. Activities like walking on tin can stilts provide practice in learning to use vision and kinesthetic cues as compensatory measures.

assume? In which direction should you enlarge your base when throwing? Batting? Serving a volleyball? Shooting baskets?

The child quickly learns to compensate for poor balance by maintaining the body in a mechanically favorable position. Games and relays performed with the eyes closed or blindfolded are contraindicated for deaf children. Activities should be planned to enhance vision and kinesthesis. All forms of dance increase body awareness. The increasingly popular Oriental exercise systems and martial arts—karate, kung fu, and Tai Chi—contribute to this objective also.

The use of perceptual-motor activities planned specifically to improve balance is controversial. Myklebust (1964) has stated that such training may be ineffective and even unwise since semicircular canal dysfunction is irreversible. No research has been reported that shows that the balance of deaf children can be improved by specific activities. Myklebust (1964) did observe that over a long period of time victims of meningitis gradually acquired good balance, apparently through compensatory use of vision and kinesthetic cues (see Figure 24.5). This occurred naturally rather than through prescribed balance activities.

Pennella (1979), who has taught physical education to deaf students for over 15 years, has recommended a well-rounded physical education program with specific programming in tumbling, gymnastics, and trampoline for children who need special help (see Figure 24.6). For additional ideas on teaching and testing balance, refer to Chapter 11, Perceptual Motor Functioning, Games, and Sports.

Motor Speed

The relationship between deafness, speed, time, and motor behavior is clearly indicated. Myklebust (1964) reported that speed was one of the two greatest deficits of deaf children taking the Oseretsky motor proficiency test. Boyd (1967), using the same test, found deaf students equal to or significantly better than the

hearing on motor speed. More research is needed before generalizations can be made on whether the deaf child is slow or fast in motor tasks. Neurologically, there is some evidence that the senses of time and temporalness are dependent upon the same areas of the brain as is auditory perception.

Gait

Persons with severe hearing losses may walk with a shuffling gait. This characteristic is not limited to those with semicircular canal deficits. Hence, it is assumed that the inability to hear the sounds of movement, not brain or ear damage, is the cause of a shuffling gait. When needed, heel-toe gait practice should begin at the preschool level, and methods of reinforcing the correct walking pattern must be found since the child cannot hear the difference between picking the feet up and dragging them. The heel-to-toe walk can be reinforced visually by practicing walking toward mirrors or by watching a videotape monitor. Visual training, however, tends to result in the habit of watching the feet.

Proprioceptive training, with emphasis upon the difference in the *feel* of walking on heels (dorsiflexion) and on toes (plantarflexion), is recommended. *Tap dance offers perhaps the best training of this type.* The teacher may tap the rhythm lightly on the child's head so that he or she can perceive it via bone conduction while moving the feet. Another possibility is positioning the child so that his or her hand is on the record player, piano, or drum. A system of flashing lights can also be devised to convey rhythmic patterns.

Physical Fitness

Since no evidence exists to the contrary, it can be assumed that deaf persons are more like the hearing in physical fitness than unlike them. Like most children in our society, the deaf are likely to have low cardiovascular endurance, poor arm and shoulder strength, and poor abdominal strength. The most recent work on fitness of deaf students is that of Winnick and Short (1985).

Approaches to Communication

There are three approaches to learning communication skills: (a) the manual method, which includes finger spelling and signing, (b) the oral method, and (c) total communication. Most school systems today combine the best of oral and manual methods. In many schools that serve the deaf, *all teachers* are expected to complete courses in signing and finger spelling. In schools that use only the oral method, signing may be prohibited.

Signing can be viewed on several national television stations when church services for deaf persons are broadcast in signs. It is used also by the National Theatre of the Deaf, which has toured both Europe and the United States since its establishment in 1967. Most of the company's professional actors are alumnae of Gallaudet College, where both manualism and oralism are used. The National Theatre of the Deaf is housed at the Eugene O'Neill Memorial Theatre Center in Waterford, Connecticut.

Deaf students tend to achieve academically below their normal peers (see Figure 24.7). In a study of 93% of all of the deaf students over age 16 in the United States, 60% were at grade level 5.3 and below and 30% were functionally illiterate. This seems to result from language deficits rather than retardation. The average nonverbal IQ of most deaf children is about 100.

Figure 24.7 Games should be invented to reinforce classroom learnings in such subjects as geography and social studies. "How fast and how accurately can you trace the boundaries of the states I call out (sign)?" is the challenge issued by the teacher.

Athletics

Because of their unique communication problems, deaf and hard of hearing individuals tend to mix socially with persons like themselves. Although many are superb athletes and could certainly compete on integrated teams, most belong to sports organizations specifically for deaf athletes. Furth (1973) alludes to this behavior in describing the deaf community:

Of all physical disabilities, deafness is the only one that makes its members part of a natural community. Therefore, although we do not find blind or crippled subgroups in society, we are justified in referring to a deaf community as a societal subgroup. This major difference between deafness and other disabilities must never be forgotten. In the United States deaf persons are perhaps better organized than in other parts of the world, but regardless of country, deafness creates an underlying community that provides for all but a few individuals a social-psychological basis of belonging. This belonging to a community is probably the single most important factor working in favor of the deaf individual. (Furth, 1973, pp. 1–2)

Table 24.3
Summer Sports in which Deaf Persons Compete Internationally

Individual	Team
Cycling (men)	Soccer (men)
Wrestling, greco roman and freestyle (men)	Water Polo (men)
	Handball (men)
Swimming (men and women)	Volleyball (men and women)
Track and field (men and women)	Basketball (men and women)
Tennis (men and women)	
Table tennis (men and women)	
Badminton (men and women)	
Shooting (men and women)	

Gaining entrance into the sports aspect of the deaf community may constitute a real challenge to the physical educator who does not sign. With increasing emphasis on physical education mainstreaming, this trend may change—at least for young deaf students whose physical education teachers take a special interest in them.

World Games for the Deaf, like the Olympics, are held every 4 years. Summer Games are held on a schedule that runs 1985, 1989, and so on, and Winter Games are held on a schedule that runs 1987, 1991, and so on. Pan American Games are also held. In 1985, the Summer Games were conducted in the United States for the first time; over 2,500 athletes from 42 nations competed in 13 different sports. The United States team has won more medals than any other team in these quadrennial games since 1977.

To be eligible for participation in sports for the deaf, students must have a hearing loss of 55 decibels or greater in the better ear (three frequency pure tone average at 500, 1000, and 2000 Hz). Deaf athletes are not placed in classifications according to severity of hearing loss.

Table 24.3 presents the eight individual and five team sports in which deaf athletes can compete internationally in summer sports. Competition in the Winter World Games includes alpine and nordic skiing and speed skating. Additionally, United States deaf athletes have regional and national competition in basketball, softball, football, and other sports. News about sports for deaf individuals is regularly published in a magazine called *The Deaf American*.

Among the sports organizations for deaf athletes are the International Committee of the Silent Sports, organized in France in 1924, the American Athletic Association for the Deaf (AAAD), founded in 1945, and the United States Deaf Skiers Association, founded in 1968. The AAAD, with approximately 20,000 members, promotes state, regional, and national basketball and softball tournaments and prepares athletes for participation in the World Games for the Deaf and activities of the International Committee of the Silent Sports. Over 160 local groups are affiliated with AAAD.

General Guidelines for the Physical Educator

Physical educators who work with deaf students should seek orientation concerning whether oral, manual, or combined methods are preferred by their administration. The following guidelines may help them establish rapport with deaf children:

1. Always position yourself where the deaf child can see you.
2. Do not talk or give directions while writing on the blackboard or facing away from the deaf child.
3. Do not raise your voice when speaking to a person with a hearing aid.
4. When outdoors, position yourself so that you rather than the deaf child face the sun.
5. When a child indicates that he or she did not understand your instructions, rephrase your sentences so that the child can perceive sounds of a different frequency or letters more visible on the mouth than those originally used.
6. Allow children with hearing losses to move freely about the gymnasium in order to be within seeing and hearing range.
7. If your school favors the oral method of teaching, avoid gestures. The child who is accustomed to watching hands forgets to follow the lips.
8. Whether or not you understand a child's attempt to speak, give the child some response to reinforce his or her efforts at the mastery of speech.

Figure 24.8 Standard fingerspelling and number signs.

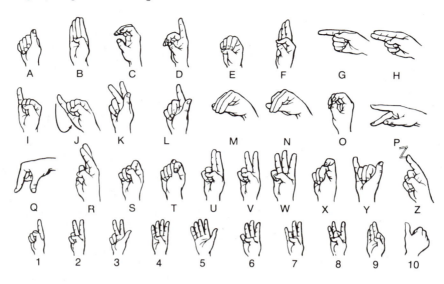

Learning Activities

1. Enroll in a sign language course and practice communicating in sign with deaf persons.

2. Learn different methods of communicating by telephone with deaf persons.

3. Attend several performances by choirs and/or a theatre for the deaf. Choirs that use sign can often be found through churches.

4. Become involved in the sports program of AAAD.

5. Make a field trip to a residential facility for deaf students and observe physical education classes. Most states have one facility of this nature.

6. Arrange to take a hearing test through the appropriate university department and learn how to interpret yours and other persons' audiograms.

7. Invite a speech and hearing therapist to lecture to your class concerning working with deaf students.

8. Simulate a hearing loss by using earplugs. Attempt to learn a new dance or exercise routine through speech reading alone.

9. Arrange to have a salesperson or other knowledgeable individual explain the different kinds of hearing aids to your class.

10. Participate in a debate concerning the best physical education placement for selected deaf students with varying strengths and weaknesses.

11. Memorize the standard finger spelling and number signs (see Figure 24.8) and devise games that use them. See Figure 24.4 for an illustrative game in which students match signs with alphabet letters on a ground canvas.

12. Read the article by Eichstaedt and Seiler (listed in the References) and learn signs for words and commands specific to physical education.

References

Boyd, J. (1967). Comparison of motor behavior in deaf and hearing boys. *American Annals of the Deaf, 112,* 598–605.

Carney, E. (Ed.). (Spring, 1971). Beat of a different drum. *Gallaudet Today,* p. 21.

Eichstaedt, C. B., & Seiler, P. (1978). Communicating with hearing impaired individuals in physical education. *Journal of Health, Physical Education, and Recreation, 49,* 19–21.

Furth, H. G. (1973). *Deafness and learning: A psychosocial approach.* Belmont, CA: Wadsworth.

Greenberg, J. (1970). *In this sign.* New York: Holt, Rinehart & Winston.

Hallahan, D., & Kauffman, J. (1978). *Exceptional children.* Englewood Cliffs, NJ: Prentice-Hall.

Keller, H. (1965). *The story of my life.* New York: Airmont Publishing Co.

Lindsey, D., & O'Neal, J. (1976). Static and dynamic balance skills of eight-year-old deaf and hearing children. *American Annals of the Deaf, 121,* 49–55.

Long, J. (1932). *Motor abilities of deaf children.* New York: Teachers College, Columbia University.

Lubin, E., & Sherrill, C. (1980). Motor creativity of preschool deaf children. *American Annals of the Deaf, 125,* 460–466.

Morsh, J. (1936). Motor performance of the deaf. *Comparative Psychological Monographs, 13,* 1–51.

Myklebust, H. R. (1964). *The psychology of deafness.* New York: Grune & Stratton.

Pennella, L. (1979). Motor ability and the deaf: Research implications. *American Annals of the Deaf, 124,* 366–372.

Smithdas, R. J. (1958). *Life at my fingertips.* New York: Doubleday.

Wessel, J. (1976). *I CAN: Locomotor and rhythmic skills.* Northbrook, IL: Hubbard.

Winnick, J., & Short, F. (1985). *Physical fitness and testing of the disabled: Project UNIQUE.* Champaign, IL: Human Kinetics Publishers.

Bibliography

American Alliance for Health, Physical Education, and Recreation. (1976). *Physical education, recreation, and sports for individuals with hearing impairment.* Washington, DC: Author.

Ammons, D. (1985). World games for the deaf. In C. Sherrill (Ed.). *Sport and disabled athletes* (pp. 65–72). Champaign, IL: Human Kinetics Publishers.

Auxter, D. (1971). Learning disabilities among deaf populations. *Journal of Exceptional Children, 37,* 573–577.

Beggs, W., & Breslaw, P. (1982). Reading, clumsiness, and the deaf child. *American Annals of the Deaf, 127*(1), 32–37.

Berges, S. A. (1969). The deaf student in physical education. *Journal of Health, Physical Education, and Recreation, 40,* 69–70.

Birch, J. (1975). *Hearing impaired children in the mainstream.* Reston, VA: The Council for Exceptional Children.

Bronstein, J. (1983). *Body image of young hearing impaired children: Changes during a movement exploration program.* Unpublished master's thesis, Texas Woman's University, Denton.

Brunt, D., & Broadhead, G. (1982). Motor proficiency traits of deaf children. *Research Quarterly for Exercise and Sport, 53,* 236–238.

Brunt, D., & Broadhead, G. (1983). The use of discriminant analysis in the assessment of deaf children for physical education. *American Corrective Therapy Journal, 37,* 43–47.

Brunt, D., Layne, C., Cook, M., & Rowe, L. (1984). Automatic postural responses of deaf children from dynamic and static postures. *Adapted Physical Activity Quarterly, 1*(3), 247–252.

Butterfield, S. (1985). A comparison of the fundamental motor and balance skills of deaf and hard of hearing children ages three through fourteen (Doctoral dissertation, Ohio State University, 1984). *Dissertation Abstracts International, 45*(7), 208A.

Carlson, R. B. (1972). Assessment of motor ability of selected deaf children in Kansas. *Perceptual and Motor Skills, 34,* 303–305.

Curtis, W., & Donlon, E. (1984). A ten-year followup study of deaf-blind children. *Exceptional Children, 50*(5), 449–455.

Darbyshire, J. (1977). Play patterns of young children with impaired hearing. *Volta Review, 79,* 19–26.

Davis, H., & Silverman, R. (1978). *Hearing and deafness.* New York: Holt, Rinehart, & Winston.

Delgado, G. (1982). Beyond the norm—Social maturity and deafness. *American Annals of the Deaf, 127*(3), 356–359.

Effgen, S. K. (1981). Effect of an exercise program on the static balance of deaf children. *Physical Therapy, 61*(1), 873–877.

Galloway, H. F., & Bean, M. F. (1974). The effects of action songs on the development of body-image and body-part identification in hearing-impaired preschool children. *Journal of Music Therapy, 11,* 125–134.

Geddes, D. (1978). Motor development profiles of preschool deaf and hard-of-hearing children. *Perceptual and Motor Skills, 46,* 291–294.

Ladd, G., Munson, H., & Miller, J. (1984). Social integration of deaf adolescents in secondary-level mainstreamed programs. *Exceptional Children, 50*(5), 420–428.

Lubin, E., & Sherrill, C. (1980). Motor creativity of preschool deaf children. *American Annals of the Deaf, 125,* 460–466.

Nearing, R. (1985). *Gait analysis of selected hearing impaired subjects through the use of biomechanical cinematography and dynamography.* Unpublished doctoral dissertation, Texas Woman's University, Denton.

Nesbitt, J., & Howard, G. (1975). *Proceedings of the national institute on recreation for deaf-blind children.* Iowa City, IA: University of Iowa Press.

Padden, D. A. (1959). Ability of deaf swimmers to orient themselves when submerged in water. *Research Quarterly, 30,* 214–226.

Pennella, L. (1974). XII world games for the deaf. *Journal of Health, Physical Education, and Recreation, 45,* 12–14.

Potter, C., & Silverman, L. (1984). Characteristics of vestibular function and static balance skills in deaf children. *Physical Therapy, 64*(7), 1071–1075.

Reber, R., & Sherrill, C. (1981). Creative thinking and dance/movement skills of hearing impaired youth: An experimental study. *American Annals of the Deaf, 26*(9), 1004–1009.

Robbins, N., & Stenquist, G. (1967). *The deaf-blind "rubella" child.* Watertown, MA: Perkins School for the Blind.

Schmidt, S. (1981). *The relationship between hearing impairment and motor proficiency in selected school age children.* Unpublished doctoral dissertation, Oregon State University, Corvallis.

Schmidt, S., & Dunn, J. (1980). Physical education of the hearing impaired: A system of movement symbols. *Teaching Exceptional Children, 12,* 99–102.

Shapira, W. (1975). Competing in a silent world of sports. *The Physician and Sports Medicine, 3,* 99–105.

Stewart, L. (1978). Hearing impaired/ developmentally disabled persons in the United States: Definitions, causes, effects, and prevalence estimates. *American Annals of the Deaf, 123,* 488–495.

Wisher, P. (1979). Dance for the deaf. In C. Sherrill (Ed.). *Creative arts for the severely handicapped* (pp. 105–111). Springfield, IL: Charles C. Thomas.

25 Blindness and Visual Impairments

Figure 25.1 Charles Buell gives a blind child and his sighted opponent a first lesson in wrestling.

Chapter Objectives

After you have studied this chapter you should be able to

1. Differentiate between legal blindness, travel vision, motion perception, light perception, and total blindness. Discuss physical education programming for each.
2. Identify some of the characteristics/behaviors associated with blind persons. Remember individual differences as you do this. Discuss implications for physical education.
3. Discuss the following in relation to assessment and instruction: (a) haptic perception, (b) spatial awareness, (c) trust and courage, (d) sound usage, (e) physical fitness, (f) orientation and mobility, and (g) adaptations of equipment and facilities.

4. Contrast public and residential facilities in the education of blind students.
5. Discuss the United States Association for Blind Athletes and opportunities for competition.
6. Explain the three USABA classifications and discuss similarities and differences in the sports events recommended for each.
7. Describe the games of goal ball and beep baseball.
8. Discuss existing and needed research concerning vision loss and physical education. Review the contributions of such researchers as Charles Buell, Joseph Winnick, and James Mastro.

Never check the actions of the blind child; follow him, and watch him to prevent any serious accidents, but do not interfere unnecessarily; do not even remove obstacles which he would learn to avoid by tumbling over them a few times. Teach him to jump rope, to swing weights, to raise his body by his arms and to mingle, as far as possible, in the rough sports of the older students, and do not be apprehensive of his safety, and if you see him clambering in the branches of a tree, be sure he is less likely to fall than if he had eyes. Do not too much regard bumps upon the forehead, rough scratches or bloody noses, even these may have their good influences. At the worst, they affect only the bark, and do not injure the system, like the rust of inaction.

—Samuel Gridley Howe

Blind and visually impaired children in the United States have benefited from the leadership of persons interested in their physical education from the very beginning. The often quoted statement above was made by the first director of Perkins Institution in Boston, the earliest residential school for blind students in this country. Perkins is known for its training of Anne Sullivan Macy, the teacher of Helen Keller. Perkins is recognized also as the leader in physical education for blind students throughout the 19th century.

Prior to 1948, almost all blind children were educated in residential schools. This fact helps to explain why the history of physical education for blind persons parallels the growth of residential schools and reflects their leadership. This history, from 1934 to 1984, has been recorded by Charles Buell (1984), a versatile physical educator (Figure 25.1). Another book by Buell (1982) includes an annotated bibliography of 23 books

and 88 articles on physical education, recreation, and camping for blind persons. Of this number, Buell wrote 6 books and 29 articles. Legally blind himself, Buell holds a doctorate in educational psychology from the University of California. His enthusiasm, perseverance, and leadership have contributed immeasurably to a growing understanding of the physical capabilities of blind persons. No other handicapping condition, with the exception of mental retardation, has such an abundance of literature to guide the physical educator.

Definitions

Visual handicaps are defined in terms of visual acuity as measured by a Snellen chart. The lines of progressively smaller letters are read by a person sitting or standing at a distance of 20 feet from the chart. Sharpness or clearness of vision is designated as a numerical ratio. One of the following classifications may appear on a student's school record:

20/200—*legal blindness*. The ability to see at 20 feet what the normal eye can see at 200 feet. This classification makes the student eligible to receive assistance under state and federal programs.

5/200 to 10/200—*travel vision*. The ability to see at 5 to 10 feet what persons with normal vision see at 200 feet.

3/200 to 5/200—*motion perception*. The ability to see at 3 to 5 feet what the person with normal vision sees at 200 feet. This ability is limited almost entirely to motion.

Less than 3/200—*light perception*. The ability to distinguish a strong light at a distance of 3 feet from the eye, but inability to detect movement of a hand at the same distance.

Lack of visual perception—*total blindness*. This is the inability to recognize a strong light that is shown directly into the eye.

Since most legally blind persons have some usable vision, these classifications often result in confusion. Buell laughingly describes the disbelief of his colleagues when he uses a pocket magnifier to look up a telephone number in the city directory. "But you are blind," they say. He corrects them by stating that he may be legally blind, but he is nevertheless partially sighted. Most persons with 10/200 or better vision, like Buell, prefer reading print over using braille readers. Most blind persons have some *residual vision*. A few can read both print and braille, but the large majority read large-print books.

Prevalence

Blindness and visual impairment are largely problems of old age. Approximately a half-million persons in the United States are legally blind, and countless others have serious visual problems. At least two thirds of these persons are over 65 years of age.

The statistics concerning visual impairment among school-age children vary with the definition used. OSE estimates that 31,576 visually handicapped children between ages 3 and 21 are receiving special education services. The United States Department of Education does not break these figures down into the blind vs. the visually impaired. It should be noted, however, that visual impairment affects fewer children than any other handicapping condition, with the exception of the multihandicapped and deaf-blind classifications.

Causes of Blindness

Most blindness in school age children is attributed to birth defects. Rubella (German measles) in women during the first 3 months of pregnancy continues to be the cause of most birth defects because many persons still do not avail themselves of the rubella vaccine. Many rubella children are multiply handicapped, with their visual impairments complicated by mental retardation, deafness, cerebral palsy, or heart disease. Many adolescents and older persons have *retrolental fibroplasia*

(RLF), a condition occurring in premature infants exposed to poorly regulated oxygen in their incubators before such apparatus was refined in the 1960s. Malfunctioning incubators still occasionally cause RLF. These persons often have, in addition to blindness, mild brain damage from the excessive oxygen.

Infectious diseases, tumors, and injuries are minor causes of blindness. In older persons, cataracts and diabetes are leading causes. *Cause of blindness does not affect physical education programming.*

Concerns and Aspirations

The child who is totally blind has few, if any, restrictions in physical education. Nothing can worsen the vision, and the child can participate fully in any physical activity. The child who is gradually losing visual acuity constitutes a much greater problem. Such visually impaired children may fear falling, being hit in the eye by a ball, or other accidents that can rob them of their remaining vision. These fears are generally unfounded.

Often, visually impaired children are pushed to master academic and vocational skills that will be needed in the future. Many local agencies for the blind provide such instruction during summers and afterschool hours, but few offer opportunities for engaging, in physical recreation and developing lifetime sports skills. Unless partially sighted children develop recreational skills that will help them to remain a part of the neighborhood play group, they are likely to become increasingly lonely. No amount of academic success and vocational independence can substitute for the social values derived from informal play. Special instruction should be provided in such activities as swimming, horseback riding (see Figure 25.2), skating, bowling, dance, and gymnastics so that children who are losing their sight can keep up with their classmates socially as well as academically.

The autobiographies of such persons as Harold Krents (1972), Tomi Keitlen (1960), and Harry Cordellos (1981) emphasize the importance of sports participation in making friends and gaining self-confidence. Krents's book recalls step by step how his brother taught him to catch a regulation football and to bat a 10-inch playground ball—skills he could have been taught by a physical educator but was not. In high school physical education he was allowed to play touch football with his sighted classmates, but was admonished to "Keep out of the way." The anecdotes leading to his acquisition of the nickname *Cannonball* make the book well worth reading. Tomi Keitlen's book describes in detail her first attempts at swimming, golf, horseback riding, fencing, and skiing after becoming totally blind at age 33. In addition to valuable accounts of how such

Figure 25.2 Horseback riding is one of many lifetime sports which the blind can enjoy with the sighted.

sports can be learned and enjoyed without sight, Keitlen describes the problems of adjusting to blindness. The greatest battle, she stresses, is to avoid being segregated and labeled as different from sighted persons.

Buell (1982) has pointed out that many of the excellent physical educators in residential schools are partially sighted. According to him, only 20/200 vision is necessary to conduct the physical education program.

General Characteristics

Although widespread individual differences exist among blind persons, certain characteristics appear more often than in the sighted population. Foremost among these are stereotyped behaviors (previously called *blindisms*), defined broadly as mannerisms resulting from repression of the innate need to move. The most

common of these are rocking backward and forward; putting fist or fingers into eyes (Figure 25.3); waving fingers in front of face; whirling rapidly round and round; and bending the head forward. These same behaviors may be observed among sighted persons with emotional problems or limited opportunities for release of normal tensions. They can be prevented or at least minimized in both blind and sighted persons through the provision of vigorous daily exercise. Other characteristics have implications for physical education:

1. Posture is often poor since they have no visual ideal to emulate. The position of the head is a particular problem.
2. Physical growth and maturation are often retarded because of inadequate opportunities to move.

Figure 25.3 Rubbing the eye is a stereotyped behavior that should be called to the child's attention and extinguished.

3. There is a definite tendency toward overweight caused by the sedentary quality of life and paucity of interests.

4. Proprioceptive awareness is frequently poor. There is no evidence that any of the senses are heightened to compensate for loss of vision. Special training is required for optimal development of touch, hearing, taste, smell, and proprioception.

5. Blind pupils are often highly verbal, giving the appearance of being tense and high strung. It should be remembered that lulls in conversation and periods of quiet are tolerated less easily by blind persons than the sighted because of their inability to perceive the many nonverbal cues by which others communicate.

6. Blind persons often seem insensitive to the needs of others, primarily because they cannot modify their behavior in response to facial expressions, gestures, subtle exchanges of eye contact among group members, and other nonverbal cues taken for granted in the sighted world.

7. Whereas the sighted show more expression with age, the face of the blind person may become increasingly expressionless. Games and creative dramatics should be designed to teach facial expressions appropriate to different emotions and settings.

8. Although blind children may excel in folk and square dance, they experience difficulty with modern dance and spontaneous creative movement. Since they have never seen gestures and movements of others, the communication aspects of dance are hard to teach. The concept of good form in gymnastics, diving, and other sports lacks meaning when different motor performances cannot be compared visually.

9. Partially sighted persons often profess to see more than they actually do, so strong is the desire for normalcy. Many partially sighted persons, although legally blind, are very sensitive about being called *blind*.

10. Blind persons who adapt successfully to the environment seem particularly skilled in memorization. The physical educator should reinforce this strength by calling upon the blind child to review instructions given in previous lessons.

Haptic Perception

Perhaps more than any other disability group, blind children need extensive experiences in creative dance and spontaneous movement. The traditional visually oriented instructional approach should be adapted to the predominantly haptic perception of most blind children. Creativity in movement is elicited in blind children through discussions of muscular sensations, kinesthetic experiences, touch impressions, and cognitive considerations of the self rather than the environment as the central reference point. The blind haptic child's choreography is subjective rather than objective. He or she tends to invest movement with feeling rather than to concentrate upon such visual outcomes as good form, proper space relationships, and group composition. No experimental research concerning methods of teaching creative dance to blind children has been reported. Lowenfeld's (1952) suggestions for developing creativity in the blind through sculpture and painting can be adapted by the dance teacher. Distinctly different methods of teaching should be used with predominantly haptic and visual perceptual types.

When planning movement exploration activities for blind students, the physical educator must realize that space is interpreted unconventionally by haptic minded persons. Whereas the visually oriented child perceives distant objects as smaller than those nearby, the blind child does not differentiate between foreground and background. The size of objects is not determined by nearness and farness, but rather by their emotional significance to the child attempting to imagine how something might look.

Blind children experience difficulty in conceptualizing boundaries. Having no visual field to restrict them, their space is as large as their imagination. They tend, however, to think in parts rather than wholes since realistic conceptualization is limited to the amount of surface they can touch at any given time. In order to familiarize themselves with the gymnasium, they may move from one piece of apparatus to another, feel the walls, discover windows and doors, and creep on the floor, but never are they completely certain how the unified whole feels or looks. Make available to blind children three-dimensional models (similar to doll houses) of the gymnasium, swimming pool, playground, campsite, and other areas of space. Miniature figures can be arranged on the simulated playground to acquaint the children with playing positions, rules, and strategies. Dolls can be used also to teach the children spatial relationships between dancers in a group composition, cheerleaders in a pep squad demonstration, and swimmers in the assigned lanes of a meet. Unless small dolls with movable joints are taken through such movements as forward rolls, cartwheels, and skin-the-snake on a parallel bar, the blind child has no way of conceptualizing the whole prior to attempting a new activity.

Spatial Awareness

Cratty (1971) makes the following observations about the body image of blind children:

1. Among populations of blind children who have normal IQs and who are free from emotional and motor problems are children as proficient as sighted youngsters of a similar age in the verbal identification of body parts, the left-right dimensions of their bodies, and similar judgments.

2. Among populations of blind children whose mean IQs are below normal (i.e., 80), the deficiencies in body image, as identified by

verbal tests, are similar to those that would be expected in populations of sighted youngsters with similar IQs.

3. Clinical experience has taught us that through training, the verbal identification of body parts may be significantly improved in both blind children and in children with vision.

4. The body image of blind children may be reliably measured.

Other topics discussed by Cratty are manual identification of objects, the orientation to stable and moving sounds, spatial orientation, the improvement of movement efficiency, complex spatial orientation, and mobility training. Cratty, among others, emphasizes that blind children need special training in recognizing the right-left dimensions of objects that are facing them. Not capable of seeing, they have never received a mirror image and hence the concept of someone facing them is especially difficult. The art products of blind persons reveal that they conceptualize another person's body from behind rather than reverse the features, as would occur normally.

Blind children must be provided with opportunities for learning about their own body parts as well as those of animals and other human beings. This can be accomplished, at least partially, by tactual inspection. Three-dimensional figures must be available to teach similarities and differences between ectomorph, mesomorph, and endomorph builds; stereotypes of male and female physical characteristics; and appearances of various postural deviations. Movement exploration based upon modifications of the dog walk, seal crawl, mule kick, and others, is meaningless unless the blind child can feel, smell, hear, and perhaps taste (lick) the animal about to be imitated. Tactual inspection of persons, animals, and objects is called *brailling*. Thus, the child may say he or she *brailled* a dog before doing the dog walk.

Other activities that will help the blind child to organize and learn about space include

1. Practice walking a straight line. All sightless persons tend to veer about 1.25 inches per step or walk a spiral-shaped pathway when attempting to traverse a straight line. The 10-year-old, however, should not veer more than 10 feet when attempting to walk forward for 50 feet, or more than 30 feet when moving forward 150 feet.

2. Practice facing sounds or following instructions to make quarter, half, three-quarter, and full turns. Blind adults tend to turn too much (100 to 105°). Full turns are the most difficult, with the average person moving only 320 to 325°.

3. Practice reproducing the exact distance and pathway just taken with a partner.

4. Take a short walk with a partner and practice finding the way back to the starting point alone.

5. Outside, where the rays of the sun can be felt, practice facing north, south, east, west. Relate these to goal cages and the direction of play in various games.

6. Practice determining whether the walking surface is uphill or downhill or tilted to the left or right; relate this to the principles of stability and efficient movement.

7. Practice walking different floor patterns. Originate novel patterns and then try to reproduce the same movement.

These and many other space explorations offer fun and excitement for sighted youngsters who are blindfolded as well as for the blind child in their classroom. It should be remembered, however, that the blindfolded child is at a greater disadvantage than the sightless youngster, who has had several years to cope with spatial problems.

Trust and Courage

Blind children and their blindfolded friends should be provided with a *guidewire* stretched from one end of the playfield or gymnasium to the other to enable them to meet such challenges as "Run as fast as you can," "Roller skate as fast as you can," or "Ride a tricycle or bicycle as fast as you can." The children can hold on to a short rope looped around the guidewire or follow the guidewire with their fingers. Window sash cord stretched at hip height is probably best for this purpose. A knot at the far end of the rope warns the runner of the finish line. Residential schools for the blind erect permanent guidewires on their tracks. It is possible, of course, for blind children to improve their running efficiency or master a new locomotor skill by grasping the elbow of a sighted partner, but the ultimate goal should always be self-confidence in independent travel.

Sound Usage in Locomotion and Sports

Blind children can be grouped with LD children who have auditory perception deficits for special training in recognizing and following sounds. A continuous sound is better than intermittent ones. Whenever possible, the sound source should be placed in front of the pupil so that he or she is moving directly toward it. The next best position is behind the child so that he or she can proceed in a straight line away from it. Most difficult to perceive and follow are sounds to the side of a person or those moving parallel to his or her intended line of travel. A progression from simple through difficult must be developed so that children can learn to capitalize on all kinds of sounds. When they can cope with a single sound source, they must be exposed to several simultaneous sounds, with instructions to pick out and follow only the relevant one.

They must develop such competencies as the following:

1. Discriminate between the bouncing of a small rubber ball for playing jacks, a tennis ball, a basketball, and a cageball.

2. Judge the height of the rebound of a basketball from its sound and thus be able to catch a ball bounced by themselves or by another.

3. Perceive the direction of a ground ball and thus be able to field or kick one being rolled toward their left, right, or center.

4. Discriminate, in bowling, the difference between sounds of a ball rolling down the gutter as opposed to the lane; the difference also between one bowling pin vs. several falling.

5. Recognize, in archery, the sound of a balloon bursting when it is hit by an arrow or of an arrow penetrating a target made of a sound-producing material (Figure 25.4).

6. Recognize the difference between the center of the trampoline and its outer areas by the sound of a ball attached to its undersurface.

7. Walk a nature trail or participate in a treasure hunt by following sounds from several tape cassettes located about the area.

8. Follow a voice or bell as they swim and dive in an open area.

9. Perceive the rhythm of a long rope alternately touching the ground and turning in the air so that they know when to run under and can learn to jump the rope.

Physical Fitness

Blind and visually handicapped persons, for the most part, are inferior in physical fitness to their sighted peers. Performance of partially sighted students tends to exceed that of the totally blind. The primary source concerning fitness for the blind is Buell, who authored an AAHPERD book (1982) giving fitness norms for the blind. Buell has stated that the AAHPER youth fitness test can be used for blind pupils except for items involving running and throwing. Project UNIQUE (Winnick & Short, 1985) is another source of fitness data on blind students ages 10 to 18.

Figure 25.4 Balloons attached to the target enable the blind child to hear a bull's eye.

Studies on cardiovascular fitness of blind persons have shown them to be equal to sighted persons or to have low fitness and significantly improve as a result of treadmill and bicycle ergometer training. Harry Cordellos, blind marathon runner and AAHPERD Honor award recipient, has such outstanding fitness that he is the subject of an ongoing longitudinal study at the Cooper Aerobic Institute in Dallas. A film featuring Cordellos, entitled *Survival Run,* is available (Media Marketing, 1983).

Orientation and Mobility (O and M) Training

Units on orientation, travel, and locomotion are included in a comprehensive physical education program for blind children. Many children are overprotected prior to entering school and hence need immediate help in adjusting to travel within the school environment. Illustrative of objectives for young children are the following ones devised by Charles C. Young, physical educator and principal at the Texas School for the Blind at Austin.

1. Select a partner and take a short, safe, and enjoyable walk on the campus under the direction of the teacher.
2. Be able to give a general description of the campus.
3. Show evidence of using sounds, landmarks, smells, and wind currents as aids in traveling alone.
4. Walk with good posture free from all tics.
5. Be able to go from cottage to gymnasium, athletic field, and hospital unassisted.

The physical educator must also orient young blind children to the use of playground equipment. Bells may be attached to the supporting chains of swings to warn children of the danger. Blind children often excel in climbing and hanging feats. Unable to see their distance from the ground, they seem fearless in the conquering of great heights and enjoy the wonder and praise of their sighted classmates. Illustrative objectives for a unit on the use of playground equipment are

1. Demonstrate how to play safely on all equipment.
2. Tell safety rules and reasons for each.
3. Display a cooperative attitude and express a willingness to learn.
4. Walk a hand ladder.
5. Pump self (sitting) while swinging.
6. Climb to top of both 8- and 14-foot slide alone and slide down feet first.
7. Perpetuate tilted merry-go-round by swinging out on downside and leaning in on upside.
8. Play simple games on the jungle gym.
9. Use seesaw safely for a short period with a companion.

Adaptations of Equipment and Facilities

Teachers and parents of visually impaired children should write to the American Foundation for the Blind for catalogs of special equipment that can be ordered. Each year improvements are made in sound-source balls and audible goal locators that facilitate the teaching of ball skills. Electronic balls with beepers are gradually replacing balls with bells (see Figure 25.5). *Balls should be painted orange or yellow for the partially sighted students.* In most elementary school activities, bean bags with bells sewn inside are preferred over balls, which are harder to recover.

Outside softball diamonds should be of grass with mowed baselines or have wide asphalt paths from base to base and from the pitcher's mound to the catcher. Inside, guidewires can be constructed from base to base. Boundaries for various games are marked by a change in floor or ground surfaces that can be perceived by the

Figure 25.5 Electronic balls with beepers make basketball a possibility.

soles of the feet. Tumbling mats, for instance, can be placed around the outside periphery of the playing area to mark its dimensions.

Braille can be used on the swimming pool walls to designate the changing heights of the water. It can be used also on gymnasium floors and walls as aids in determining the colors, shapes, and sizes of targets.

Portable aluminum bowling rails 9 feet long and 3 feet high are available through the American Foundation for the Blind. These rails are easily assembled and broken down for transportation to different bowling alleys.

For the most part, however, equipment does not need to be adapted to the special needs of the blind. The play area should be quiet enough to facilitate use of sound and well lighted to enhance use of residual vision.

Patterns of General Education

Since World War II the number of blind and visually impaired children who remain at home and attend public schools has steadily increased. The public school physical educator will find that only about one of four visually handicapped children is totally blind. If limitations are not imposed, the partially sighted youngster often has learned to compensate well enough to engage in the regular physical education program. In contrast, over half the children served in residential schools are totally blind. The other half have vision ranging from the ability to see hand movements up to 20/200 acuity. A growing number of children in residential schools are multihandicapped. Yet, for the most part, state schools for blind students have outstanding physical education and athletic programs.

Residential Schools

Buell (1984) offers comprehensive coverage of physical education and athletics in residential schools. The activities he recommends most highly are wrestling, tumbling, gymnastics, bowling, swimming, weight training, judo, relays, dance, roller skating, ice skating, shuffleboard, horseback riding, tandem cycling, hiking, camping, fishing, rowing, water skiing, and surfing. Little or no adaptation in these sports must be made in order for blind students to participate with the sighted (see Figure 25.6).

Wrestling seems to be the only sport in which blind athletes can compete with the sighted on a comparatively equal basis. About four fifths of the schools for blind students have interscholastic wrestling teams, and many blind pupils excel over their sighted opponents in state and national events.

Figure 25.6   Blind persons can enjoy many sports with their sighted friends.

In the 1970s, special ball games for blind students, such as *beep baseball* and *goal ball,* became popular. Kickball with tandem running around the diamond gives children a chance to identify with big league baseball. A study of blind adults' memories of and opinions about physical education (Sherrill, Rainbolt, & Ervin, 1984) found that their favorite childhood outdoor sport was baseball/softball. Respondents did not mention adaptations. Tying for second place were swimming, football, and horseback riding. Two thirds of the sample had been reared in residential schools. These persons expressed positive opinions about school-based physical education, but negative feelings about both past and present community, church, and family physical education and recreation—indicating usually that there were none.

Public Schools

Two of three visually handicapped students in public schools are not being offered programs of vigorous physical activity. This statistic stems not from lack of physical ability among blind students, but from the unconcern and/or ignorance of the sighted.

Implications for Physical Education

Physical education with sighted classmates is recommended. Except for ball handling activities, blind children can participate with few adaptations. Their success depends in large part upon the ability of the physical educator to give precise verbal instructions. Like any other children, blind children strive to fulfill the expectations of their teacher. Falls, scratches, and bruises should be disregarded as much as possible so blind persons are allowed the dignity of recovering without oversolicitous help. Physical assistance should not be given unless requested. In tandem walking, for instance, the blind child should hold onto the upper arm of the sighted partner, not vice versa. Sighted persons, of course, bear the responsibility for making their presence known and should state their name when initiating a verbal exchange rather than assume that the other has an infallible auditory memory. When activities are practiced in small groups, the leader should ascertain that blind pupils know the names of their classmates, the approximate space allocated to each, their place in the order of rotation if turns are being taken, and the direction of movement. Sight is not required for success on the trampoline, parallel bars, and other pieces of apparatus; for tumbling, free exercise, and dance; for weight lifting, fitness activities, swimming; or for many other sports.

Athletics

An understanding of national and international athletic opportunities gives insight into programming for the one or two blind students in the physical education mainstream. While blind children can participate in many integrated activities, they should be given optimal training in areas where they are most likely to excel.

While athletics have been well organized within the residential school network for years, the movement gained new impetus with the formation of the United States Association for Blind Athletes (USABA) in 1976. The first official act of the group was to enter 27 athletes in the 1976 Olympiad for the Physically Handicapped in Canada in response to the first invitation ever issued for blind athletes to participate in this competition. In 1977, USABA sponsored its first national championships. These are now held every year, with international competition occurring every fourth year in conjunction with the Olympic Games. Sanctioned sports for the national games include power and weight lifting, swimming, track and field, wrestling, goal ball, women's gymnastics, winter sports (downhill and cross-country skiing), tandem cycling, speed skating, and others as selected by the USABA board. Under consideration are crew rowing, sailing, archery, and competitive diving. The rules for these sports are based upon those used by such organizations as the United States Gymnastics Federation (USGF), the National Collegiate Athletic Association (NCAA), and the National Federation of State High School Associations (NFSHSA).

Sports Classifications

In competition (except wrestling), blind athletes compete against others with similar visual abilities. Table 25.1 shows the classifications used. All measurements pertain to the better eye after correction.

Table 25.1
Sport Classifications for Blind Persons

Classification	Description
B1	No light perception at all in either eye up to light perception and inability to recognize objects or contours in any direction and at any distance.
B2	Ability to recognize objects or contours up to a visual acuity of 2/60 and/or a limitation of field vision of 5°.
B3	2/60 to 6/60 (20/200) vision and/or field of vision between 5 and 60°.

Note. In 1982, this system was adopted in place of the system that used Classes A, B, C.

Track and Field Events

Track events include 60 or 100 meter, 200, 400, 800, 1500, 3000, and 10,000 meter runs conducted separately for B1, 2, and 3 athletes. In the shorter runs, guidewires and individual lanes are used. Beginning with the 800 meter run, Class B1 athletes run with partners and Class B2 and B3 athletes can run with or without partners. The contact between partners may be a nonelastic rope or cloth no more than 50 centimeters in length as a contact tether. In such partner runs, the blind person must always precede the sighted.

Field events include the standing or running long jump, standing triple jump, high jump, shot put, javelin, and discus. Special events include the pentathlon and the 10,000 meter road run. The previously popular tandem running was eliminated from United States events because it is not in international competition.

Gymnastics

Events in which blind persons compete are floor exercise, balance beam, uneven bars, vaulting, and all round. They are expected to have achieved a level of competence in which the aid of a coach or spotter is not necessary. Such persons may, however, be present for any move considered a risk. A 0.5 deduction is made for aid by a coach or spotter during competition. Added safety is provided by an extra layer of mats and padding covering all exposed metal parts of apparatus. Gymnastics competition, while presently for females only, will be sanctioned for males when sufficient numbers express interest. Currently, most men seem to prefer wrestling.

Goal Ball

A game created in Europe especially for blind veterans of World War II, goal ball is played under the rules of the International Sports Organization for the Disabled (ISOD) (Kearney & Copeland, 1979). The only required equipment for the game is a bell ball. Each team consists of three players wearing helmet, mouth piece, elbow pads, and blindfold.

The playing area has slightly different dimensions for boys and girls (see Figure 25.7). Very important is the regulation that all field markings be 5 centimeters in width and made of a distinctive texture for easy player orientation.

Games are 10 minutes in duration, with 5-minute halves. Each team tries to roll the ball across the opponent's goal while the other team tries to stop them (see Figure 25.8). A thrown ball may bounce, but it must be rolling before it reaches the opponent's throwing area or it becomes an infraction. The entire team helps with defense. The arriving ball can be warded off in a standing, cowering, kneeling, or lying position with any body part or the whole body (Figure 25.9).

Because all team members are required to wear a blindfold, goal ball places blind children on equal terms with their sighted peers and thus can be used in mainstream physical education. Rules are available through USABA, the September 1979 *Journal of Physical Education and Recreation,* or from most physical educators at residential schools. Many adapted games and drills of this nature can be designed to give mainstream students a novel experience as well as excellent training in auditory perception. Goal ball is suitable for all age groups, beginning at about the third or fourth grade.

Figure 25.7 Playing area for goal ball.

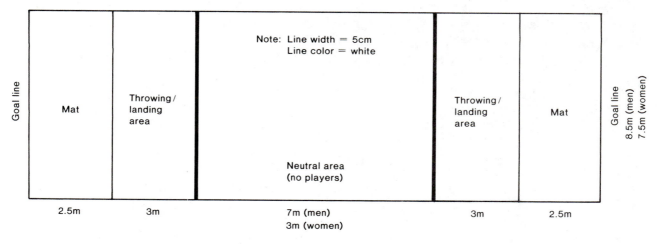

Figure 25.8   Starting positions for the offensive team in goal ball.

Figure 25.8   Starting positions for the offensive team in goal ball.

Figure 25.9   In goal ball any part of the body or the whole body can be used to prevent the bell ball from rolling across the goal line.

Figure 25.10 Playing field for beep baseball. The circular foul line between 1st and 3rd bases is a constant distance of 40 feet from home plate. A batted ball must travel over this line to be considered *fair*. The pitcher stands 20 feet from home plate. The distance between home plate and each base location is 90 feet. The base is 5 feet outside the baseline.

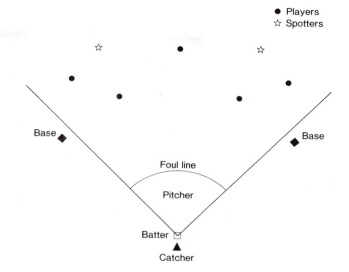

Beep Baseball

Although not a USABA regulation sport, beep baseball is played by blind persons throughout the United States and supported/facilitated by the Telephone Pioneers, an association that can be contacted through the local telephone company (Montelione & Mastro, 1985). Its rules are governed by the National Beep Baseball Association, which was founded in 1976. These rules are different from the original game, invented by Charlie Fairbanks in 1964 and played with seven players in the field, each in a different lane.

Current rules call for a regulation-size baseball diamond with grass mowed to an approximate height of 2 inches (Figure 25.10). Grassy areas are used because they affect sound distribution and make the ball easier to locate. The ball, which is available through the Telephone Pioneers, is a regulation softball 16 inches in circumference, with a battery operated electronic sound device inside. A regulation bat is used. Bases are 48 inches tall, with the bottom part made of a 36-inch tall pliable plastic cone and the top part made of a long cylinder of foam rubber. A speaker is installed in each base. Players with a visual classification of light perception or better must wear blindfolds.

A team is comprised of six totally blind or blindfolded players and two sighted players who act as pitcher and catcher when their own team is up to bat and act as spotters when their team is in the field. As spotters, their role is to call out the fielder's name to whom the hit ball is coming closest. Only one name is called, for obvious safety reasons.

Batters are allowed five strikes at pitched balls. Except on the last strike, fouls are considered strikes. Batters must attempt to hit all pitched balls, with the option of letting two go by without penalty. When a fair ball is hit, the umpire designates which one of the two buzzing bases shall be activated. A run is scored if the batter gets to the buzzing base before being tagged out. Games are six innings in duration with three outs per inning. The teams are comprised of both males and females.

For more information about beep baseball, write Dr. James Mastro, National Beep Baseball Association, 512 8th Ave. NE, Minneapolis, MN 55413.

Figure 25.11 Standard English Braille alphabet.

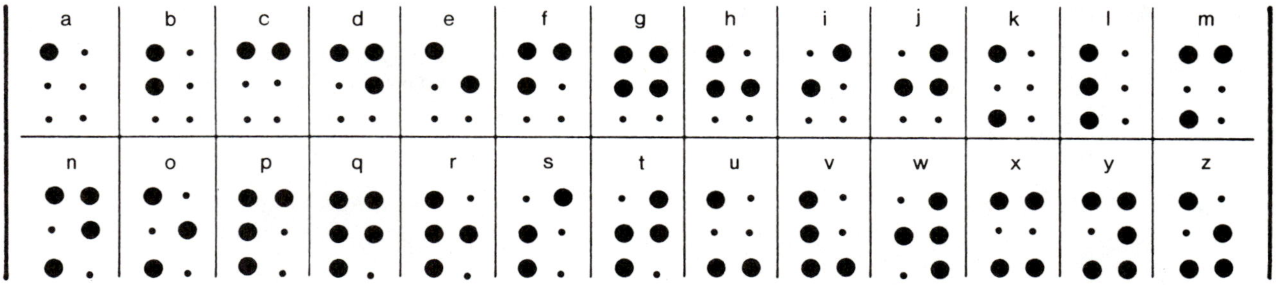

Learning Activities

1. Contact various organizations and agencies that serve blind persons and find out what kind of recreation and sports activities they sponsor. Offer to serve as a volunteer.

2. Invite a blind person to lecture to your class concerning orientation, mobility, and sports participation and/or attend a lecture by a blind person like Charles Buell, Harry Cordellos, or James Mastro at a conference.

3. Role play and/or simulate the condition of blindness. Try such physical education activities as (a) goal ball or beep baseball, (b) track and field, (c) archery, and (d) dance and such daily living activities as (a) eating a meal, (b) using a strange bathroom, and (c) dressing and applying makeup.

4. Become involved in USABA and the National Beep Baseball Association by serving as coaches, umpires, and assistants for various events.

5. Support USABA, NBBA, and similar groups as a spectator who attends their sports events. Encourage friends to attend also.

6. Visit a residential facility for blind students and observe physical education classes.

7. Obtain illustrative materials in braille and experiment with learning the braille alphabet (see Figure 25.11). Develop games that reinforce learning braille.

8. Arrange for a salesperson or other knowledgeable individual to demonstrate computers and other electronic devices available for use by blind persons.

9. Contact the American Foundation for the Blind, 15 West 16th Street, New York, NY 10011, for a copy of their equipment and supplies catalog, which includes information pertaining to sports and recreational activities.

10. Contact the Telephone Pioneers of America, 195 Broadway, New York, NY 10007, for additional information about beep baseball and the loan or purchase of electronic balls and bases.

References

Buell, C. (1984). *Physical education for blind children* (2nd ed.). Springfield, IL: Charles C. Thomas.

Buell, C. (1982). *Physical education and recreation for the visually handicapped* (2nd ed.). Washington, DC: AAHPERD.

Cordellos, H. (1981). *Breaking through*. Mountain View, CA: Anderson World Inc.

Cratty, B. (1971). *Movement and spatial awareness in blind children and youth*. Springfield, IL: Charles C. Thomas.

Howe, S. G. (1841). *Perkins report*. Watertown, MA: Perkins Institute for the Blind.

Kearney, S., & Copeland, R. (1979). Goal ball. *Journal of Physical Education and Recreation, 50*, 24–26.

Keitlen, R. (1960). *Farewell to fear*. New York: Avon Book Division.

Krents, H. (1972). *To race the wind*. New York: G. P. Putman's Sons.

Lowenfeld, V. (1952). *Creative and mental growth*. New York: Macmillan.

Media Marketing. (1983). *Survival run.* This 16 mm film can be ordered from Media Marketing, W-STAD, Brigham Young University, Provo, UT 84602.

Montelione, T., & Mastro, J. (August, 1985). Beep baseball. *Journal of Physical Education, Recreation, and Dance,* pp. 60–61, 65.

Sherrill, C., Rainbolt, W., & Ervin, S. (1984). Attitudes of blind persons toward physical education and recreation. *Adapted Physical Activity Quarterly, 1*(1), 3–11.

Winnick, J., & Short, F. (1985). *Physical fitness testing of the disabled: Project UNIQUE.* Champaign, IL: Human Kinetics Publishers.

Bibliography

Adelson, E., & Fraiberg, S. (1974). Gross motor development in infants blind from birth. *Child Development, 45,* 114–126.

Arnhold, R., & McGrain, P. (1985). Selected kinematic patterns of visually impaired youth in sprint running. *Adapted Physical Activity Quarterly, 2*(3), 206–213.

Barraga, N. (1976). *Visual handicaps and learning.* Belmont, CA: Wadsworth.

Beaver, D. P. (Ed.). (1983). *Official National Sports Development Committee Athletic Handbook.* Beach Haven Park, NJ: United States Association for Blind Athletes.

Cordellos, H. (1976). *Aquatic recreation for the blind.* Washington, DC: American Alliance for Health, Physical Education, and Recreation.

Cordellos, H. (1981). *Breaking through.* Mountain View, CA: Anderson World Inc.

Cratty, B., & Sams, T. A. (1968). *The body-image of blind children.* New York: American Foundation for the Blind.

Dawson, M. (1981). A biomechanical analysis of gait patterns of the visually impaired. *American Corrective Therapy Journal, 35,* 66–71.

DePauw, K. (1981). Physical education for the visually impaired: A review of the literature. *Journal of Visual Impairment and Blindness, 75*(4), 162–164.

Duehl, A. N. (1979). The effect of creative dance movements on large muscle control and balance in congenitally blind children. *Journal of Visual Impairment and Blindness, 73*(4), 127–133.

Fraiberg, S. (1977). *Insights from the blind: Comparative studies of blind and sighted infants.* New York: New American Library.

Freedman, S. (1973). Realities and misconceptions. *Therapeutic Recreation Journal, 7,* 10–13.

George, C. & Patton, R. (1975). Development of an aerobics conditioning program for the visually handicapped. *Journal of Physical Education and Recreation, 46,* 39–40.

Head, D. (1979). The stability of self-concept scores in visually impaired adolescents. *Education of the Visually Handicapped, 11,* 66–74.

Jankowski, L. W., & Evans, J. (1981). The exercise capacity of blind children. *Journal of Visual Impairment and Blindness, 75,* 248–251.

Kratz, L. E. (1973). *Movement without sight.* Palo Alto: Peek Publications.

Krebs, C. S. (1979). Hatha yoga for visually impaired students. *Journal of Visual Impairment and Blindness, 55,* 209–216.

Lowenfeld, B. (1973). *The visually handicapped child in school.* New York: John Day Co.

Lukoff, I. (1972). *Attitudes toward blind persons.* New York: American Foundation for the Blind.

Mastro, J. (1985). *Psychological characteristics of elite male visually impaired athletes and sighted athletes.* Unpublished doctoral dissertation, Texas Woman's University, Denton.

Mastro, J., & French, R. (1985). Sport anxiety and elite blind athletes. In C. Sherrill (Ed.). *Sport and Disabled Athletes* (pp. 203–210). Champaign, IL: Human Kinetics Publishers.

McGowan, H. (1983). The kinematic analysis of the walking gait of congenitally blind and sighted children: Ages 6–10 years. *Dissertation Abstracts International, 44,* 703-A. (University Microfilms No. DA 8318095).

Nezol, A. J. (1972). Physical education for integrated blind students: Its relationship to sociometric status and recreational activity choices. *Education of the Visually Handicapped, 4,* 16–18.

Norris, M. S., & Brody, R. H. (1957). *Blindness in children.* Chicago, IL: University of Chicago Press.

Oliver, J. (1970). Blindness and the child's sequence of development. *Journal of Health, Physical Education, and Recreation, 41,* 37–39.

Olson, M. (1983). A study of the exploratory behavior of the legally blind and sighted preschoolers. *Exceptional Children, 50*(2), 130–138.

Pope, C., McGrain, P. & Arnhold, R. (1985). Running gait of the blind: A kinematic analysis. In C. Sherrill (Ed.). *Sport and Disabled Athletes* (pp. 173–180). Champaign, IL: Human Kinetics Publishers.

Resnick, R. (1973). Creative movement classes for visually handicapped children in a public school setting. *New Outlook for the Blind, 67,* 442–447.

Scranton, P., Clark, M., & McClosky, S. (1978). Musculoskeletal problems in blind children. *Journal of Bone and Joint Surgery, 60-A*(3), 363–365.

Sherrill, C., Pope, C., & Arnhold, R. (In press). Sport socialization of blind athletes: A preliminary study. *Journal of Visual Impairment and Blindness.*

Siegel, I. M. (1966). *Posture in the blind.* New York: American Foundation for the Blind.

Sonka, J., & Bina, M. (1978). Coming out ahead in the long run. *Journal of Physical Education and Recreation, 49,* 24–25.

Stamford, B. A. (1975). Cardiovascular endurance training for blind persons. *The New Outlook, 33,* 308–311.

Tait, P. (1972). Behavior of young blind children in a controlled play session. *Perceptual and Motor Skills, 34,* 963–969.

Winnick, J. (1985). The performance of visually impaired youngsters in physical education activities: Implications for mainstreaming. *Adapted Physical Activity Quarterly, 2*(4), 292–299.

Prevalence and Incidence Statistics

Prevalence and Incidence of Handicapping Conditions

Statistical information on the prevalence and incidence of handicapping conditions in the United States lends insight into the competencies a physical educator must develop in order to work with all children and youth. *Prevalence* refers to the total number or percentage of existing cases in the population at a given time. *Incidence* refers to the number or percentage of new cases occurring each year. For example, the prevalence of mental retardation in the United States is over 6 million. The incidence is approximately 100,000 mentally retarded infants born each year. The orthopedic impairment with the highest prevalence is cerebral palsy. It is estimated that 750,000 individuals with cerebral palsy are living in the United States. The incidence is 3.5 cases per 1,000 live births.

United States Population Estimates

Total population	232,000,000
Students in public schools	44,333,000
Probable number of disabled students	8,000,000
Documented number of disabled students served under PL 94–142 and 89–313 (see Table A.1 for details)	4,298,327

Most prevalent documented handicapping conditions in school-aged children in order of prevalence

Learning disabled	1,745,871
Speech impaired	1,134,197
Mentally retarded	780,831
Emotionally disturbed	353,431
Hard of hearing and deaf	75,337

Prevalence of selected handicapping conditions for all age groups

Hearing impaired, one or both ears	14,491,000
Chronic obstructive pulmonary disease	14,000,000
Chronic heart conditions	10,291,000
Orthopedic impairments other than paralysis and absence of limbs	8,018,000
Rheumatoid arthritis	5,000,000
Paralysis, complete or partial	1,392,000
Severely visually impaired	1,306,000

Table A.1
Report of Handicapped Children Receiving Special Education and Related Services, 1982–1983

Handicapping Condition	PL 94–142				PL 89–313	Combined
	Ages 3–5	Ages 6–17	Ages 18–21	Total	Total	Total
Mentally retarded	18,693	585,387	73,974	678,054	102,777	780,831
Hard of hearing and deaf	5,108	39,686	4,325	49,119	26,218	75,337
Speech impaired	172,035	942,381	5,760	1,120,176	14,021	1,134,197
Visually handicapped	1,703	17,289	2,306	21,298	9,798	31,096
Emotionally disturbed	5,884	293,224	14,768	313,876	39,555	353,431
Orthopedically impaired	6,793	36,380	3,286	46,459	11,047	57,506
Other health impaired	3,764	40,659	3,681	48,104	3,922	52,026
Learning disabled	20,090	1,643,201	60,468	1,723,759	22,112	1,745,871
Deaf-blind	248	986	149	1,383	1,170	2,553
Multihandicapped	7,795	37,647	4,925	50,367	15,112	65,479
Total	242,113	3,636,840	173,642	4,052,595	245,732	4,298,327

Note. PL 94–142 figures include handicapped children and youth served by public schools; PL 89–313 figures include persons served by residential and other state-supported schools

Table A.2
Incidence of Selected Handicapping Conditions

High Incidence Conditions (based on 1,000 persons)		Moderate Incidence Conditions (based on 10,000 persons)		Rare Incidence Conditions (based on 100,000 persons)	
Anorexia nervosa	4[a]	Achondroplasia	1	Apert's syndrome	.5
Arthritis	20	Arthrogryposis	3	Blindness	21.6
Asthma	3–6	Autism	5	Cri-du-chat	5
Cancer	250	Blindness	2	Friedreich's ataxia	1.8–2
Cerebral palsy	3.5	Cooley's anemia	9	Galactosemia	2.2
Cleft palate and/or lip	1	Cornelia de Lange syndrome	1	Guillain-Barre	1
Club foot	1.5	Cretinism	1.7	Huntington's disease	6.5
Congenital heart defects	6–10	Down's syndrome	5	Hurler's syndrome	1
Congenital hip dislocation	1–3	Hemophilia	1	Marfan's syndrome	1.5
Convulsive disorders	5	Klinefelder's syndrome	2[b]	Multiple sclerosis	6
Cystic fibrosis	1	Neurofibromatosis	3	Muscular dystrophy	3
Deaf	9	Rubella syndrome	1	Osteogenesis imperfecta	3
Depression	120	Tourette's syndrome	1–5	Perthes disease	4
Diabetes	10	Trisomy 18	3	Phenylketonuria	7
Down's syndrome	.5	Turner's syndrome	1[a]	Prader-Willi	.5
Fetal alcohol syndrome	3–6			Reye's syndrome	1
Hard of hearing	32			Tuberous sclerosis	1
Learning disabilities	3–20				
Mental illness	166				
Mental retardation	30				
Noonan syndrome	1				
Obesity	150				
Schizophrenia	10				
Sickle cell anemia	2[c]				
Spina bifida	1–3				

[a]Females only   [b]Males only   [c]Blacks only

Causes of Activity Limitations in Children under Age 17

Cause	Percent
Asthma and hay fever	20.0
Lower extremity impairments	8.3
Paralysis, complete or partial	7.4
Chronic bronchitis and sinusitis	5.5
Mental and emotional problems	3.8
Heart conditions	3.7

Leading Causes of Death in Childhood and Adolescence

Childhood	Adolescence
Accidents	Auto-related accidents
Cancer	Other accidents
Congenital anomalies	Homicide
Homicide	Suicide
Influenza and pneumonia	Cancer
Heart disease	Heart disease

Figure A.1 Percentage of population using drugs by age and type of drug: 1979.

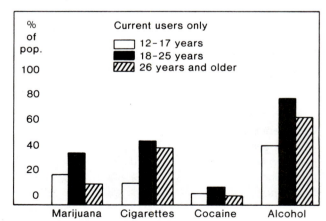

Table A.3
Risk Factors Associated with Major Causes of Death

Cause	Percent of All Deaths	Risk Factor
Heart disease	37.8	*Smoking, hypertension, elevated serum cholesterol (diet),* lack of exercise, diabetes, stress, family history
Cancer	20.4	*Smoking, worksite carcinogens,* environmental carcinogens, alcohol, diet
Stroke	9.6	*Hypertension, smoking, elevated serum cholesterol,* stress
Accidents other than motor vehicle	2.8	*Alcohol,* drug abuse, smoking (fires), product design, handgun availability
Influenza and pneumonia	2.7	Smoking, *vaccination status*
Motor vehicle accidents	2.6	*Alcohol, no seat belts, speed,* roadway design, vehicle engineering
Diabetes	1.7	*Obesity*
Cirrhosis of the liver	1.6	*Alcohol abuse*
Arteriosclerosis	1.5	*Elevated serum cholesterol*
Suicide	1.5	*Stress,* alcohol and drug abuse, and gun availability

Major risk factors appear in italics.
Source: *Health United States,* 1980, p. 274.

Medications

Management of health problems and handicapping conditions through medication is becoming increasingly common as new, more effective drugs are created. School personnel, including physical educators, must be knowledgeable about the prescribed medications that they routinely administer as well as those which students take on their own. Often, little is known about the side effects of medication in relation to strenuous exercise and specific motor ability and fitness factors. Each teacher must therefore assume responsibility for observation and reporting of side effects.

This appendix lists the medications most commonly used in today's society. In most instances, both the *generic* (medical) and *trade* (sales) names are given. The major reference book on medications and side effects is the *Physician's Desk Reference,* commonly called the *PDR,* published annually by Medical Economics Co., Oradell, New Jersey. Side effects described in this reference are typically medical rather than exercise-related. Research is needed to determine the influence of various medications on physical education performance and classroom/gymnasium behavior.

I. Anticonvulsants: for control of seizures
Diphenylhydation (dilantin) for grand mal
Ethosuximide (zaronthin) for petit mal
Paramethadione (paradione) for petit mal
Phenobarbital (luminal, stental) for grand mal
Primidone (mysoline) for grand mal, psychomotor

II. Medications for management of hyperactivity
Dextroamphetamine (dexedrine)
Methylphenidate hydrochloride (ritalin)
Pemoline (cylert)

III. Medications for management of asthma
B2-adrenergic agents like epinephrine, ephedrine, iso-
proterenol, terbutaline (brethine, bricanyl),
albuterol, metaproterenol
Theophylline and its derivatives like slophyllin
Bronchodilator inhalers like ventolin, vanceril,
alupent
Prednisone and other corticosteroids
Cromolyn sodium

IV. Medications for reducing inflammation and managing such conditions as arthritis, severe chronic asthma, some types of cancer
ACTH (corticotrophin)—given by injection
Cortisone
Dexamethasone
Hydrocortisone
Prednisone
Triamcinolone

V. Medications for fighting infections (remember, exercise is contraindicated whenever a student has an infection)
Aminoglycosides
Cephalosporins
Macrolides
Penicillins
Polypeptides
Sulfonamides

VI. Medications for managing allergies and hayfever
Antihistamines like benadryl
Desensitization injections
Corticosteroids like prednisone

VII. Tranquilizers (i.e., antianxiety agents)
Barbiturates like phenobarbital
Chlrodiazepoxide hydrochloride (librium, valium)
Hydroxyzine (vistaril)
Meprobamates (milltown, equanil)

VIII. Antidepressants: Three types for management of depression
Tricyclic antidepressants
Amitriptyline (elavil, endep)
Desipramine (pertofrane, norpramin)
Doxepin (sinequan, adapin)
Imipramine (tofranil, imanate, presamine)
Nortriptyline (aventyl)
Protriptyline (vivactil)
Monoamine oxidase (MAO) inhibitors
Isocarboxazid (marplan)
Phenelzine (nardil)
Tranylcypromine (parnate)
Lithium for manic-depressive states, sometimes used in recurrent depressions

IX. Antipsychotic drugs for management of schizophrenic reactions, manic disorders, and other severe conditions
Chlorpromazine (thorazine)
Fluphenazine (prolixin)
Haloperidol (haldol)
Thioridazine (mellaril)
Thiothixene (navane)
Trifluoperazine (stelazine)

X. Medications for management of selected other conditions
Insulin for diabetes
Diuretics for prevention or elimination of edema
Amphetamines for appetite-suppression
Antitumor drugs for cancer

Additional Sources of Information for Term Papers and Research Reports

Because adapted physical education is a relatively new area of specialization, much ingenuity is often needed in finding information on selected topics. Students should be acquainted with traditional library search methods that utilize such reference books as *Education Index* and *Index Medicus*. This section includes the newer systems for identifying related information.

1. **ERIC, Educational Resources Information Center**

   This computer-based information network, established in 1966, is sponsored by NIE, the National Institute of Education, and comprised of several collaborative components. Among these are the United States Government Printing Office and a network of 16 subject area clearinghouses. Of most value to the adapted physical educator is the *ERIC Clearinghouse on Handicapped and Gifted Children,* operated by the Council for Exceptional Children (CEC).

   Your own university library can conduct an ERIC computer search for you, thereby identifying almost everything published on a particular topic. Abstracts of theses and dissertations, as well as other materials, can be found in *Resources in Education* (RIE), the monthly journal published by ERIC. For additional information, write to ERIC Processing and Reference Facility, 4833 Rugby Ave., Suite 300, Bethesda, MD 20014.

2. **MEDLARS, Medical Literature Analysis and Retrieval System**

   This computer-based information network is sponsored by the National Library of Medicine in Bethesda, Maryland. Many university libraries can conduct MEDLINE searches, thereby using the computer to identify articles pertinent to your selected topic in over 2,300 worldwide biomedical journals. When MEDLINE searches are not available, students generally rely upon reference books entitled *Index Medicus* to find articles related to their topics.

3. **IRUC, Information and Research Utilization Center in Physical Education and Recreation for the Handicapped—AAHPERD**

   This center, as part of the AAHPERD Unit on Programs for the Handicapped at the national headquarters, 1900 Association Dr., Reston, VA 22091, was directed by Dr. Julian Stein until 1981 and was closed in 1982. Many publications produced by the Center can be found in your library, listed under AAHPERD.

4. **Theses and Dissertations**

   Theses and dissertations are reports of research conducted by graduate students in partial fulfillment of their degree requirements. They vary in size from a few to several hundred pages and often reflect the quality of the graduate program. Theses and dissertations are excellent sources of information since they generally include new research findings, reviews of related literature, and comprehensive bibliographies. If your university offers a graduate program in physical education and/or recreation, it may be helpful to ask your professors about the theses and dissertations they have directed. These volumes can be found in your university library.

   This textbook lists several outstanding theses and dissertations in its chapter bibliographies. Many of these, especially the dissertations, can be found in the microfilm and microfiche section of your library. Ask your university librarian for assistance in finding them. If these studies are not available locally, your university librarian can obtain them for you through *interlibrary loan* or you can purchase copies through *University Microfilms International,* 300 North Zeeb Road, Ann Arbor, MI 48106, or *Microfilm Publications,* College of HPER, University of Oregon, Eugene, OR 97403.

   In order to identify additional theses and dissertations in physical education and recreation for the handicapped, the reader should become familiar with the following sources: DATRIX II, a computerized service available in most university libraries, that provides a computer print out that includes title, author, degree, year, university, location in *Dissertation Abstracts International,* the price, and information for ordering a copy from University Microfilms International, Ann Arbor, MI.

   Completed Research in HPER, a paperback book published annually by AAHPERD, is a compilation of titles and abstracts of theses and dissertations written by graduate students in universities throughout the United States. These reference books are available in your university library and can be purchased also through AAHPERD Publication Sales.

5. **Major Journals and Magazines in Adapted Physical Education and Sports for Disabled**

Ability, official publication for the United States Amputee Athletic Association, PO Box 5311, Mission Hills, CA 91345.

Able Bodies, official newsletter of the American Alliance for Health, Physical Education, Recreation, and Dance, 1900 Association Drive, Reston, VA 22091.

Adapted Physical Activity Quarterly, Human Kinetics Publishers, Incorporated, Box 5076, Champaign, IL 61820.

The Deaf American, 814 Thayer Avenue, Silver Spring, MD 20910.

NWAA Newsletter, 2107 Templeton Gap Road, Suite C, Colorado Springs, CO 80907.

Palaestra, Challenge Publications, Ltd., PO Box 508, Macomb, IL 61455.

Sportsline, official newsletter of the National Association of Sports for Cerebral Palsy, UCPA, Incorporated, 66 East 34th Street, New York, NY 10016.

Sports 'N Spokes, 5201 North 19th Avenue, Suite 111, Phoenix, AZ 85015.

USABA Newsletter, Jim Duffield, Managing Editor, RD #3, Box 495, Felton, DE 19943.

Appendix D

Addresses of Selected Governing Bodies in Sports for Disabled Athletes

National Wheelchair Athletic Association (NWAA)
Pat Karman, Chairperson
Andy Fleming, Executive Director
2107 Templeton Gap Road, Suite C
Colorado Springs, CO 80907
(303) 632–0698

National Association of Sports for Cerebral Palsy
(NASCP)
Raphael Bieber
66 East 34th Street
New York, NY 10016
(212) 481–6359

United States Association for Blind Athletes (USABA)
Art Copeland
55 West California Avenue
Beach Haven Park, NJ 08008

United States Amputee Athletic Association (USAAA)
Richard Bryant
Route 2, County Line
Fairview, TN 37062
(615) 670–5453

National Handicapped Sports and Recreation Association
(NHSRA)
Ron Hernley, President
Capitol Hill Station
PO Box 18664
Denver, CO 80218

Special Olympics, Incorporated (SO)
Eunice Kennedy Shriver
1350 New York Avenue NW
Suite 500
Washington, DC 20005

American Athletic Association of the Deaf (AAAD)
Richard Caswell
3916 Lantern Drive
Silver Spring, MD 20902
TTY: (301) 942–4042

Note. Each of these organizations has two representatives
on the Committee on Sports for the Disabled of the
United States Olympic Committee. Eligibility for this
representation is sponsorship of two or more sports that are
included on the programs of the Olympic or Pan American
Games.

Addresses for Purchasing Supplies and Equipment

Flaghouse, Incorporated
18 West Street
New York, NY 10011

Front Row Experience
540 Discovery Bay Boulevard
Byron, CA 94514

GSC Athletic Equipment
600 North Pacific Avenue
San Pedro, CA 90733

Jayfro Corporation
PO Box 400
Waterford, CT 06385

J. A. Preston Corporation
71 Fifth Avenue
New York, NY 10003

Wolverine Sports
745 State Circle
Ann Arbor, MI 48104

Appendix F

Addresses of Other Organizations

Academic Therapy Publications
200 Commercial Boulevard
Novato, CA 94947

Adapted Sports Association, Incorporated
Communications Center
6832 Marlette Road
Marlette, MI 48453

Alexander Graham Bell Association for the Deaf,
Incorporated
3417 Volta Place, NW
Washington, DC 20007

The Allergy Foundation of America
801 Second Avenue
New York, NY 10017

American Academy for Cerebral Palsy and Developmental
Medicine
PO Box 11083
2405 Westwood Avenue
Richmond, VA 23230

American Alliance for Health, Physical Education,
Recreation, and Dance
1900 Association Drive
Reston, VA 22091

American Association for the Blind
1511 K Street, NW
Washington, DC 20005

American Association on Mental Deficiency
5101 Wisconsin Avenue, NW
Washington, DC 22016

American Blind Bowling Association, Incorporated
150 North Bellaire Avenue
Louisville, KY 40206

American College of Allergists
2117 West River Road North
Minneapolis, MN 55411

American College of Sports Medicine
1440 Monroe Street
Madison, WI 53706

American Dance Guild
1133 Broadway, Room 1427
New York, NY 10010

American Dance Therapy Association
Suite 216–E
1000 Century Plaza
Columbia, MD 21044

American Diabetes Association
2 Park Avenue
New York, NY 10016

American Foundation for the Blind
15 West 16th Street
New York, NY 10011

American Heart Association, Incorporated
7320 Greenville Avenue
Dallas, TX 75231

American Instructors of the Deaf
5034 Wisconsin Avenue, NW
Washington, DC 20016

American Lung Association
1740 Broadway
New York, NY 10019

American Occupational Therapy Association, Incorporated
600 Executive Boulevard
Rockville, MD 20852

American Physical Therapy Association
1156 15th Street, NW
Washington, DC 20005

American Psychological Association
1200 17th Street, NW
Washington, DC 20036

American Red Cross National Headquarters
17th and D Streets, NW
Washington, DC 20006

American Thoracic Society
1740 Broadway
New York, NY 10019

American Wheelchair Bowling Association
N54 W15858 Larkspur Lane
Menomonee Falls, WI 53051

The Arthritis Foundation
1212 Avenue of the Americas
New York, NY 10036

An Association for Children and Adults with Learning
Disabilities (ACLD, Incorporated)
Resource Library
4156 Library Road
Pittsburgh, PA 15234

Association for Retarded Citizens
2501 Avenue J
Arlington, TX 76011

Association for the Education of the Visually
Handicapped—Bulletin for Physical Educators
919 Walnut Street
Philadelphia, PA 19103

The Association for the Severely Handicapped (TASH),
formerly AAESPH
Garden View Suite
1600 West Armory Way
Seattle, WA 98119

Asthma and Allergy Foundation of America
19 West 44th Street
New York, NY 10036

Braille Sports Foundation
730 Hennepin Avenue, S
Suite 301
Minneapolis, MN 55403

Breckenridge Outdoor Education Center
Programs for Handicapped
PO Box 697
Breckenridge, CO 80424

California Association for Neurologically Handicapped
Children
PO Box 61067
Sacramento, CA 95860

Canadian Amputee Sports Association
18 Hale Drive
Georgetown, Ontario
Canada L7G4C2

Canadian Wheelchair Sports Association
333 River Road
Ottawa, Ontario
Canada K1L8B9

Congress on Research in Dance (CORD)
Dance Dept., Education 675 D
New York University
35 West Fourth Street
New York, NY 10003

The Council for Exceptional Children
1920 Association Drive
Reston, VA 22091

Council of Organizations Serving the Deaf (COSD)
PO Box 894
Columbia, MD 21044

Cystic Fibrosis Foundation
6000 Executive Boulevard
Suite 309
Rockville, MD 20852

Dalcroze School of Music
161 East 73rd Street
New York, NY 10021

Dance Horizons
1801 E 26th Street
Brooklyn, NY 11229

Dance Notation Bureau, Incorporated
8 East 12th Street
New York, NY 10003

Disabled Sportsmen of America, Incorporated
PO Box 5496
Roanoke, VA 24012

Epilepsy Foundation of America
1828 L Street, NW
Suite 406
Washington, DC 20036

Gallaudet College
Office of Demographic Studies
Annual Survey of Hearing Impaired Children and Youth
7th Street and Florida Avenue, NE
Washington, DC 20002

Handicapped Flyers International
1117 Rising Hill
Escondido, CA 92025

Handicapped Scuba Association
1104 El Prado
San Clemente, CA 92672

The Institute for Aerobics Research
12200 Preston Road
Dallas, TX 75230

Institutes for the Achievement of Human Potential
8801 Stenton Avenue
Philadelphia, PA 19118

International Medical Society of Paraplegia
E and S Livingstone
43–45 Annandale Street
Edinburgh, EH7 4AT
Scotland

International Sports Organization for the Disabled (ISOD)
Stoke Mandeville Sports Stadium
Harvey Road
Aylesbury, Bucks
England

Joseph P. Kennedy, Jr. Foundation
1350 New York Avenue, NW
Suite 500
Washington, DC 20005

Laban Institute of Movement Studies
Institute of Movement Studies, Incorporated
133 West 21 Street
New York, NY 10011

Learning Disabilities Research Institute
164 Rugby Road
Charlottesville, VA 22903

Little People of America
P.O. Box 633
San Bruno, CA 93901

Minnesota Outward Bound School, Courses for the
Handicapped
308 Walker Avenue
South Wayzata, MN 55291

Muscular Dystrophy Association
27 Floor
810 Seventh Avenue
New York, NY 10019

National Association of the Deaf
814 Thayer Avenue
Silver Spring, MD 20910

National Association of Sports for Cerebral Palsy
United CP Associations, Incorporated
66 East 34th Street
New York, NY 10016

National Beep Baseball Association
512 8th Ave. NE
Minneapolis, MN 55413

National Center for Health Statistics
Public Health Service, HRA
Rockville, MD 20852

National Consortium on Physical Education and
Recreation for the Handicapped Membership Chairman
Dr. John Hall
Physical Education Department
University of Kentucky
Lexington, KY 40506

National Council of YMCAs
291 Broadway
New York, NY 10007

National Dance Association
1900 Association Drive
Reston, VA 22091

The National Easter Seal Society for Crippled Children
and Adults
2023 West Ogden Avenue
Chicago, IL 60612

The National Foundation/March of Dimes
1275 Mamaroneck Avenue
White Plains, NY 10605

National Foundation of Wheelchair Tennis
4000 MacArthur Boulevard
Newport Beach, CA 92660

National Handicapped Sports and Recreation Association
4105 East Florida Avenue
Denver, CO 80222

National Hemophilia Foundation
25 West 39th Street
New York, NY 10018

National Inservice Network
Indiana University
2853 East Tenth Street/Cottage L
Bloomington, IN 47405

National Multiple Sclerosis Society
205 East 42nd Street
New York, NY 10017

National Rehabilitation Association
1522 K Street, NW
Washington, DC 20004

National Society for Autistic Children
Suite 1017
1234 Massachusetts Avenue, NW
Washington, DC 20005

National Society to Prevent Blindness
79 Madison Avenue
New York, NY 10016

National Spinal Cord Injury Foundation
369 Elliot Street
Newton Upper Falls, MA 02164

National Therapeutic Recreation Society
3101 Park Center Drive
Alexandria, VA 22302

National Wheelchair Athletic Association
2107 Templeton Gap Road
Suite C
Colorado Springs, CO 80907

National Wheelchair Basketball Association
110 Seaton Building
University of Kentucky
Lexington, KY 40506

National Wheelchair Softball Association
PO Box 737
Sioux Falls, SD 57101

North American Riding for the Handicapped Association
Box 100
Ashburn, VA 22011

Office of Special Education (OSE), formerly Bureau of
Education for the Handicapped (BEH)
400 Maryland Avenue, SW
Donahoe Building
Washington, DC 20202

Ontario Wheelchair Sport Association
585 Tretheway Drive
Toronto, Ontario
Canada M6M 4B8

Paralyzed Veterans of America
4330 East-West Highway
Suite 300
Washington, DC 20014

People-to-People Committee for the Handicapped
1522 K Street, NW, #1130
Washington, DC 20005

Physical Activities Report
171 Saybrook Industrial Park
Old Saybrook, CT 06475

The Physical Educator
Publications Office
9030 Log Run Drive, North
Indianapolis, IN 46234

President's Committee on Employment of the Handicapped
1111 20th Street, N.W.
Washington, DC 20036

President's Committee on Mental Retardation
Washington, DC 20201

Quebec Association for Children with Learning Disabilities
6338 Victoria Avenue
Montreal 252
Quebec, Canada

Rehabilitation International USA
20 West 40th Street
New York, NY 10018

Royal Institute for the Blind
224 Great Portland Street
London, WIN 6AA
England

The Seeing Eye, Incorporated
Morristown, NJ 07960

Ski for Light, Incorporated
Skiing for Visually Impaired and Physically Handicapped
1455 West Lake Street
Minneapolis, MN 55408

Special Olympics
Joseph P. Kennedy, Jr. Foundation
1350 New York Avenue, NW
Suite 500
Washington, DC 20006

Spina Bifida Association of America
343 South Dearborn
Chicago, IL 60604

Telephone Pioneers of America
Beep Ball Information
195 Broadway
New York, NY 10007

United Cerebral Palsy Associations, Incorporated
66 East 34th Street
New York, NY 10016

United States Association for Blind Athletes
55 West California Avenue
Beach Haven Park, NJ 08008

United States Department of HEW
Public Health Service
Office of Health Research, Statistics, and Technology
National Center for Health Statistics
3700 East-West Highway
Hyattsville, MD 20782

Wheelchair Motorcycle Association
101 Torrey Street
Brockton, MA 02401

Wheelchair Sports Foundation
c/o Benjamin H. Lipton
40-24 62nd Street
Woodside, NY 11377

Wheelchair Pilots Association
11018 102nd Avenue, N
Largo, FL 33540

Important Events in the History of Disabled Persons

1817 The first residential schools to be established in the United States were for deaf students: the American School for the Deaf in Hartford, CT, and the New York School for the Deaf in White Plains, NY, founded in 1817 and 1818, respectively. Thomas Hopkins Gallaudet is credited with founding the school in Connecticut. In 1856, the institution now known as Gallaudet College, Washington, DC, evolved through the efforts of philanthropist Amos Kendall.

1830 The first residential schools for the blind were founded between 1830 and 1833 in Boston, New York, and Philadelphia. Only one of the early residential facilities, the Perkins Institution in Boston, provided physical education for its students.

1847 *The American Annals of the Deaf,* first published in 1847, is the oldest educational journal in the United States still in existence.

1848 The first residential institution for mentally retarded persons in the United States was organized in Massachusetts in 1848.

1863 The earliest residential facilities for orthopedically handicapped persons in the United States bore such names as Hospital of the New York Society for the Relief of the Ruptured and Crippled (1863) and the Children's House of the Home for Incurables in Philadelphia (1877).

1864 Edouard Seguin's classic book *Idiocy and Its Diagnoses and Treatment by the Physiological Method* was translated into English. This book provided the framework for the earliest attempts to train mentally retarded persons. Seguin was a student and protégé of Jean-Marc Itard, known for his work with Victor, "the Wild Boy of Aveyron," in the early 1800s.

1876 Establishment of the American Association on Mental Deficiency (AAMD). First president was Edouard Seguin. One of its original goals was to promote the development of residential facilities. During the first decade of AAMD's existence, 20 states created residential schools for retarded persons.

1885 Formation of the Association for the Advancement of Physical Education, the forerunner of AAHPERD. First president was Edward Hitchcock, MD. Almost all the early members were physicians.

1895 The National Education Association (NEA) organized a Department of Physical Education.

1899 Public schooling for handicapped persons had begun, with the earliest documentation citing 100 large cities with special education classes. Among these were Boston, Chicago, Cleveland, Detroit, New York, and Milwaukee.

1902 The National Education Association organized a Department of Special Education. Alexander Graham Bell, pioneer in deaf education, spearheaded this recognition.

1906 Formation of the Playground Association of America, the forerunner of National Recreation and Parks Association (NRPA) of which the National Therapeutic Recreation Society (NTRS) is a subdivision. First president was Dr. Luther Halsey Gulick.

1912 Establishment of Children's Bureau in Washington, DC, to promote the welfare of children and to prevent their exploitation in industry.

1917 Origin of the National Society for the Promotion of Occupational Therapy, the forerunner of the American Occupational Therapy Association (1921).

1919 National Easter Seals Society for Crippled Children and Adults founded.

1920 The National Civilian Vocational Rehabilitation Act, a forerunner of the Social Security Act.

1921 Origin of forerunner of American Physical Therapy Association. First president was Mary McMillan, who strongly influenced early leaders in corrective physical education who were also physical therapists, George Stafford and Josephine Rathbone.

1922 Establishment of Council for Exceptional Children (CEC), the first organization to advocate for all handicapped groups. First president was Elizabeth Farrell.

1928 First textbooks to use the term "corrective physical education" were published:
Stafford, G. T. (1928). *Preventive and corrective physical education.* New York, A. S. Barnes.
Lowman, C., Colestock, C., & Cooper, H. (1928). *Corrective physical education for groups.* New York: A. S. Barnes.

1930 Historic White House Conference on Child Health and Protection. The Committee on the Physically and Mentally Handicapped wrote the often quoted Bill of Rights for Handicapped Children (see p. 492).

1935 Social Security Act passed.

1938 National Foundation for Infantile Paralysis founded by Franklin Delano Roosevelt; the memorable March of Dimes campaigns began. (See 1958 also.)

1939 Social Security Act, Title V, Part 2, as amended, authorized a program of services for every state for (a) locating all crippled children and maintaining a state register, (b) providing skilled diagnostic services by qualified surgeons and physicians at state clinics, and (c) providing skilled medical, surgical, nursing, medical-social, and physical therapy services for children in hospitals, convalescent homes, and foster homes.

1943 PL 78–113, the amended Vocational Rehabilitation Act, provided federal aid to enable State Boards of Vocational Education and State Agencies for the Blind to furnish disabled persons ages 16 and over with all services necessary to render them employable.

1944, 1952, also **1915–17** Major epidemics of poliomyelitis, which left thousands of persons paralyzed. In 1952 alone there were 57,628 cases of polio reported.

1945 Formation of the American Athletic Association for the Deaf (AAAD). This was the first special population in the United States to form its own sports organization.

1946 Association for Physical and Mental Rehabilitation (APMR) established, the forerunner of American Corrective Therapy Association (ACTA). Name changed to ACTA in 1967.

1949 Formation of the National Wheelchair Basketball Association (NWBA).

1950 The National Association for Music Therapy, Inc., (NAMT) was formed.

1950 The National Association for Retarded Citizens (NARC) founded. Name changed in 1979 to Association for Retarded Citizens (ARC).

1952 First International Wheelchair Games held at Stoke Mandeville, England.

1955 Salk vaccine recognized as 80 to 90% effective against paralytic polio.

1956 Formation of National Wheelchair Athletic Association (NWAA).

1958 National Foundation for Infantile Paralysis became The National Foundation-March of Dimes and turned attention to birth defects and genetic counseling.

1958 PL 85–926 was passed, authorizing grants to universities and colleges and to state education agencies for training personnel in mental retardation. This legislation represents the beginning of the federal government's commitment to the rights of handicapped persons, which culminated in 1975 with the passage of PL 94–142.

1960 First Paralympic Games held in Rome. This was the first time that the International Stoke-Mandeville Games were held in conjunction with Olympic Games.

1961 Kennedy appointed the first President's Panel on Mental Retardation.

1963 PL 88–164 amended 1958 legislation to encompass all handicapped groups that required special education.

1964 Civil rights legislation (PL 88–352) passed.

1964 Association for Children with Learning Disabilities (ACLD) formed. Name changed in 1980 to ACLD, Inc., (An Association for Children and Adults with Learning Disabilities).

1965 PL 89–10, the Elementary and Secondary Education Act (ESEA), was passed. Included Titles I to IV. Many innovative public school physical education programs, now nationally well known, were funded under Title III (now IVC). Among these programs were Vodola's Project ACTIVE in New Jersey and Long's Project PEOPEL in Arizona.

1965 The AAHPER Project on Recreation and Fitness for the Mentally Retarded was formed with a grant from the Joseph P. Kennedy, Jr. Foundation. This project was the forerunner of the present Unit on Programs for the Handicapped, which was established in 1968.

1966 American Dance Therapy Association, Inc., (ADTA) founded in New York City.

1966 Bureau of Education for the Handicapped (BEH) was created by PL 89–750 within the Office of Education of HEW. BEH, which became the Office of Special Education (OSE) in 1980, has been the agency that funds university training programs in physical education and recreation for the handicapped.

1967 Formation of the National Handicapped Sports and Recreation Association (NHSRA), which governs winter sports.

1967 ESEA amended under PL 90–170, Title V, Section 502, to support training, research, and demonstration projects specifically in physical education and recreation for the handicapped. This was part of the Mental Retardation Amendments originally supported by Senator Edward Kennedy and signed by President Lyndon B. Johnson.

1967 National Therapeutic Recreation Society (NTRS) created as a branch of the National Recreation and Park Society.

1968 AAHPER Unit on Programs for the Handicapped approved. This replaced Project on Recreation and Fitness for the Mentally Retarded.

1968 PL 90–480, Elimination of Architectural Barriers to Physically Handicapped, passed. This was the first federal legislation pertaining to architectural barriers.

1968 First Special Olympics; AAHPER—Kennedy Foundation Special Fitness Awards were established.

1970 Title VI, Public Law 91–230, Education of the Handicapped Act (EHA), passed. This was the first major legislation leading to the subsequent passage of PL 94–142 in 1975.

1970 Series of institutes sponsored by BEH held on the Development of AAHPER Guidelines for Professional Preparation Programs for Personnel Involved in Physical Education and Recreation for the Handicapped. Report published by AAHPER in 1973.

1972 Information and Research Utilization Center (IRUC) in Physical Education and Recreation for the Handicapped funded by BEH and established in conjunction with AAHPER Unit on Programs for the Handicapped.

1972 Title IX legislation (PL 92–318) passed.

1972 AC/FMR (Accreditation Council for Facilities for the Mentally Retarded) issued standards, including recreation services, which all residential and intermediate care facilities must implement in order to receive accreditation. New *ACFMR* standards, issued in 1978, are available through the Joint Commission on Accreditation of Hospitals (JCAH), 875 North Michigan Avenue, Chicago, IL 60611.

1973 Rehabilitation Amendments (PL 93–112) completely recodified the old Vocational Rehabilitation Act and placed emphasis upon expanding services to more severely handicapped clients. Section 504, the "nondiscrimination clause," which specified that no qualified handicapped person shall be excluded from federally assisted programs or activities, is the best known part of the law. PL 93–112 was not implemented, however, until 1977, when its rules and regulations were agreed upon and published in the May 4, 1977, issue of the *Federal Register.*

1973 National Ad Hoc Committee on Physical Education and Recreation for the Handicapped formed by BEH project directors at Minneapolis (AAHPER) conference.

1974 At the annual conference in Anaheim, California, AAHPER was reorganized as the American Alliance for Health, Physical Education, and Recreation with seven independent associations. Three of these included programs for the handicapped: ARAPCS (Association for Research, Administration, Professional Councils and Societies); NASPE (National Association for Sport and Physical Education); and AALR (American Association for Leisure and Recreation).

1974 The National Diffusion Network (NDN) was created by the United States Office of Education. This system facilitates optimal use of programs like Project ACTIVE through a network of state facilitators and developer/demonstrators. For additional information, contact Division of Educational Replication, USOE, ROB3 Room 3616, 400 Maryland Avenue, SW, Washington, DC 20202.

1974 Formation of the American Association for the Education of the Severely/Profoundly Handicapped (AAESPH). In 1980 the name of this organization changed to the Association for the Severely Handicapped (TASH) and the title of its journal became *JASH, Journal of Association for Severely Handicapped.*

1975 National Consortium on Physical Education and Recreation for the Handicapped (NCPERH) evolved from National Ad Hoc Committee. First president was Leon Johnson, University of Missouri.

1975 PL 94–142 enacted. Called the "Education for All Handicapped Children Act," it stated specifically that *instruction in physical education* shall be provided for all handicapped children.

1976 Formation of the United States Association for Blind Athletes (USABA).

1976 The Olympiad for the Physically Handicapped (formerly Paralympics) was held in Canada in conjunction with the Olympic Games. This was the first time that blind athletes and amputees were recognized and allowed to participate.

1976 White House Conference on Handicapped Individuals (WHCHI) was held with delegates chosen from governors' conferences in each state. The final report included 420 recommendations, several of which pertained to recreation and leisure. For further information on implementation of these recommendations, contact Robert H. Humphreys, Commissioner, Rehabilitation Services Administration (RSA), 330 C Street, SW, Room 3006, Washington, DC 20201.

1977 International Federation of Adapted Physical Activity founded. First symposium held in Montreal.

1977 First National Championships, United States Association for Blind Athletes.

1977 Regulations to implement Section 504 of PL 93–112, the Rehabilitation Act of 1973, were signed by the Secretary of HEW, Joseph Califano. This is the first civil rights law guaranteeing equal opportunities for disabled Americans. As a result of Section 504, compliance committees are being established in universities and agencies throughout the country.

1977 Regulations to implement PL 94–142 were published in the August 23 issue of the *Federal Register.* (See Chapter 3.)

1977 First Annual National Wheelchair Marathon was held in conjunction with the Boston Marathon (26.2 miles). This event is now sponsored annually by the National Spinal Cord Injury Foundation.

1978 Formation of the National Association of Sports for Cerebral Palsy (NASCP).

1978 PL 95–602, the Developmentally Disabled (DD) Assistance and Bill of Rights Act was passed, updating DD legislation of 1970 and 1975.

1978 PL 95–606, the Amateur Sports Act, recognized the sports organizations of disabled athletes as part of the United States Olympic Committee structure.

1979 The American National Standards Institute (ANSI) published the revised ANSI standard A 117.1 (Specifications for Making Buildings and Facilities Accessible to and Usable by Physically Disabled People). This standard replaced the one established in 1961 and reaffirmed in 1971. ANSI is the governmental agency responsible for, among other things, setting standards for wheelchair accessibility. For more information, contact ANSI, 1430 Broadway, New York, NY 10018.

1979 AAHPER's name was officially changed to AAHPERD (American Alliance for Health, Physical Education, Recreation and Dance), thereby giving recognition to dance as a discipline separate from physical education.

1979 AAHPERD held a national conference entitled "The Consumer Speaks: An Evaluation of Physical Education, Recreation, and Sports by People with Special Needs." Consumers in attendance included persons who were deaf, cerebral palsied, ambulatory disabled, and blind.

1979 The United States Olympic Committee (USOC) organized a Committee for the Handicapped in Sports, with Kathryn Sallade Barclift elected as its first chairperson. This committee brought representatives from the five major sports organizations for handicapped athletes together for the first time.

1979 PL 96–88 changed the status of the old United States Office of Education within HEW to a Department of Education. Shirley M. Hufstedler was appointed its first Secretary. HEW was disbanded.

1980 Reorganization was completed for the two new departments replacing HEW. These new structures are the Department of Education (ED) and the Department of Health and Human Services (HHS). Within ED's seven principal program offices, the Office of Special Education and Rehabilitative Services (OSERS) relates to the handicapped. Principal components of OSERS are Office of Special Education (OSE), which replaces BEH; Rehabilitation Services Administration (RSA); and National Institute of Handicapped Research.

1981 Declared the "International Year of the Disabled" by the United Nations.

1981 January 19 issue of *Federal Register* (Vol. 46, No. 12) devoted to IEPs, including clarifications for physical education.

1981 Formation of the United States Amputee Athletic Association (USAAA).

1982 First UNESCO-sponsored international symposium on physical education and sport programs for physically and mentally handicapped persons.

1984 International Games for the Disabled (blind, cerebral palsied, amputee, and les autres) held in Long Island, NY, with approximately 2,500 athletes competing. Seventh World Wheelchair Games (spinally paralyzed) held in England.

1984 *Adapted Physical Activity Quarterly* first published. This was first professional journal to be devoted specifically to adapted physical education.

1984 The International Association for the Research of Sport and Exercise for the Disabled (IARSED) founded at the Olympic Scientific Congress in Eugene, OR. First president was Robert Steadward of University of Alberta, Canada.

1985 *Sport and Disabled Athletes,* the proceedings of the Olympic Scientific Congress, published by Human Kinetics Publishers, Champaign, IL.

1986 First World Congress on Research of Sport and Exercise for the Physically Disabled held in Banff, Canada.

1986 Merger completed within AAHPERD of NASPE Adapted Physical Education Academy and ARAPCS Therapeutic Council. The new structure is called the *Adapted Physical Activity Council* and is housed within ARAPCS.

Glossary of Abbreviations

AAAD American Athletic Association for the Deaf

AAESPH American Association for the Education of the Severely/Profoundly Handicapped; now TASH

AAHPER American Alliance for Health, Physical Education, and Recreation; now AAHPERD

AAHPERD American Alliance for Health, Physical Education, Recreation, and Dance

AALR American Association for Leisure and Recreation

AAMD American Association on Mental Deficiency

AB able-bodied

ABC achievement based curriculum

AC/FMR Accreditation Council for Facilities for the Mentally Retarded

ACLD Association for Children and Adults with Learning Disabilities

ACTA American Corrective Therapy Association

ACTH adrenocorticotrophic hormone

ACTIVE All Children Totally Involved in Exercise (Vodola's project)

ADL activities of daily living

ADTA American Dance Therapy Association

AKOs ankle-foot orthoses

ALS amyotrophic lateral sclerosis

ALT academic learning time

AMC arthrogryposis multiplex congenita

ANSI American National Standards Institute

APAC Adapted Physical Activity Council, new AAHPERD structure

APAQ *Adapted Physical Activity Quarterly*

APERR adapted physical education resource room

APMR Association for Physical and Mental Rehabilitation, now ACTA

ARAPCS Association for Research, Administration, Professional Councils and Societies

ARC Association for Retarded Citizens

ARD admission, review, dismissal

ASD atrial septal defect

ASV aortic stenosis, valvar

ATNR asymmetrical tonic neck reflex

BCP Behavioral Characteristics Progression (test)

BEH Bureau of Education for the Handicapped; now OSE

BGMA Basic Gross Motor Assessment (Hughes)

BMPP Basic Movement Performance Profile (Fait, Ness)

BOTMP Bruininks-Oseretsky Test of Motor Proficiency

bpm beats per minute (heart rate)

CARIH Children's Asthma Research Institute and Hospital

CB center of buoyancy

CCBD Council for Children with Behavioral Disorders

CCW counterclockwise

CDH congenital dislocation of the hip

CEC Council for Exceptional Children

CG center of gravity

CNS central nervous system

COA coarctation of aorta

COPD chronic obstructive pulmonary diseases

CORD Congress on Research in Dance

COSD Council of Organizations Serving the Deaf; also Committee on Sports for the Disabled

CP cerebral palsy

CSCS Children's Self-Concept Scale

CW clockwise

D deaf

db decibel

DB deaf-blind

DD developmental disabilities

DDST Denver Developmental Screening Test

DS Down's Syndrome

DSM-III *Diagnostic and Statistical Manual of Mental Disorders*

DTR Registered Dance Therapist

ECD endocardial cushion defect

ED emotionally disturbed

EHA Education of the Handicapped Act

EIA exercise-induced asthma

EMG electromyographical (response)

EMR educable mentally retarded

ERIC Educational Resources Information Center

ESEA Elementary and Secondary Education Act

EST electric shock therapy

FES functional electrical stimulation

FEV₁ forced expiratory volume for 1 second

GAPES Goals of Adapted Physical Education Scale

GH growth hormone

HEW (Department of) Health, Education, and Welfare; now Department of Education (ED) and Department of Health and Human Services (HHS)

HH hard of hearing

HKAFOs hip-knee-ankle-foot orthoses

Hz Hertz

ICFMR intermediate care facilities for the mentally retarded (standards)

IED Inventory of Early Development (Brigance)

IEP individualized educational programming

IGD International Games for the Disabled

IPPB intermittent positive pressure breathing

IRUC Information and Research Utilization Center

ISO International Standard Organization (determines classifications for hearing loss)

ISOD International Sports Organization for the Disabled

ITP interval training prescription

ITPA Illinois Test of Psycholinguistic Ability

JCAH Joint Commission on Accreditation of Hospitals

JOHPER *Journal of Health, Physical Education and Recreation*

JOPER *Journal of Physical Education and Recreation*

KAFOs knee-ankle-foot orthoses

KR knowledge of results

LAB Leisure Activities Blank

LD learning disabilities

LDB Leisure Diagnostic Battery

LEAP Leisure Education Advancement Project

LH left high

LPA Little People of America

LRE least restrictive environment

LSS Leisure Satisfaction Scale

LT left tilt

MCB maximal breathing capacity

MC Milani-Comparetti (assessment system)

MD muscular dystrophy

MEDLARS Medical Literature Analysis and Retrieval System

MIC mitral insufficiency, stenosis

MM myelomeningocele (a form of spina bifida)

MPAP Movement Patterns Achievement Profile (Evans)

MR mentally retarded

MS multiple sclerosis

MZSC Martinek-Zaichkowsky Self-Concept Scale

NAMT National Association for Music Therapy

NASCP National Association of Sports for Cerebral Palsy

NASPE National Association for Sport and Physical Education

NBBA National Beep Baseball Association

NCAA National Collegiate Athletic Association

NCAH National Committee, Arts for the Handicapped

NCPERH National Consortium on Physical Education and Recreation for the Handicapped

NDN National Diffusion Network

NEA National Education Association

NFSHSA National Federation of State High School Associations

NHSRA National Handicapped Sports and Recreation Association

NIE National Institute of Education

NIMR National Institute on Mental Retardation (Canada)

NINDS National Institute of Neurological Diseases and Stroke

NPRM normal postural reflex mechanism

NRPA National Recreation and Parks Association

NTRS National Therapeutic Recreation Society

NWAA National Wheelchair Athletic Association

NWBA National Wheelchair Basketball Association

OCR Office of Civil Rights

OHI other health impaired

OI orthopedically impaired, also osteogenesis imperfecta

OSE Office of Special Education

OSERS Office of Special Education and Rehabilitation Services

OSU-SIGMA Ohio State University—Scale of Intra Gross Motor Assessment

OT occupational therapy

PASSING Program Analysis of Service System's Implementation of Normalization Goals

PDA patent ductus

PDMS Peabody Developmental Motor Scales (Folio & Fewell)

PDR *Physicians Desk Reference* (for medications)

PEAC physical education adapted counseling

PEOPEL Physical Education Opportunity Program for Exceptional Learners

PFD personal flotation device

PKU phenylketonuria

PL Public Law

PNF proprioceptive neuromuscular facilitation

PNRR primitive neck righting reflex

PRE progressive resistance exercises

PREP Preschool Recreation Enrichment Program; also preschool motor and play program in Canada

PSV pulmonic stenosis

PT physical therapy

PTA Parent-Teachers Association

PWC physical work capacity

RH right high

RIE *Resources in Education*

RLF retrolental fibroplasia

RSA Rehabilitation Services Administration

RT right tilt

SATPA Simon and Smoll Attitude Toward Physical Activity Scale, also known as CATPA

SCI spinal cord injured

SCPMT Southern California Perceptual-Motor Tests (Ayres)

SCPNT Southern California Postrotary Nystagmus Test

SD standard deviation; also σ

SEA state education agency

SELF Special Education for Leisure Fulfillment

SFE slipped femoral epiphysis

SIV single ventricle

SMA spinal muscle atrophies

SO Special Olympics

SPMTPE Sherrill Perceptual-Motor Tasks for Physical Education

STR symmetrical tonic reflex

TAPE test, assess, prescribe, evaluate

TASH The Association for the Severely Handicapped

TAT tricuspid atresia

TGMD Test of Gross Motor Development (Ulrich)

TGV transposition

TLR tonic labyrinthine reflex

TMR trainable mentally retarded

TNR tonic neck reflex

TOF tetralogy of Fallot

UCPA United Cerebral Palsy Associations, Inc.

USAAA United States Amputee Athletic Association

USABA United States Association for Blind Athletes

USGF United States Gymnastics Federation

USOC United States Olympic Committee

VH visually handicapped

VI visually impaired

VKT vestibular, kinesthetic, and tactile

VSD ventricular septal defect

WHCHI White House Conference on Handicapped Individuals

Appendix I

Competencies Needed to Perform Tasks Required of Adapted Physical Education Specialists

Tasks Associated with Roles of Assessment and Counseling

1.1 Utilize effective procedures for collecting information about present level of psychomotor performance and play/game/leisure preferences and practices of handicapped students and their families.
    1.11 Make effective use of informal assessment procedures: observation, interviews, oral questionnaires, preferences and practices inventories, checklists, anecdotal records, school files.
    1.12 Utilize criterion-referenced and norm-referenced standardized instruments, as appropriate.
    1.13 Utilize videotape and film techniques in recording and analyzing movement.
    1.14 Construct new instruments or modify and/or adapt old ones to performance levels.
1.2 Integrate guidance and counseling processes with assessment and teaching and extend counseling models to include such physical education parameters as fitness and leisure.
    1.21 Adapt values clarification processes to physical education.
    1.22 Utilize normalization/socialization models to facilitate peer acceptance.
    1.23 Facilitate interpersonal communication and appreciation of individual differences.
1.3 Assist student and significant others (including family members) in understanding and appreciating self and psychomotor potential.
    1.31 Cooperatively explore psychomotor potential through participating, discovering, feeling, sharing, and creating in movement.
    1.32 Cooperatively explore potential for attending, observing, enjoying, appreciating, understanding, and criticizing psychomotor performance of others.

1.4 Work effectively with specialized services and resources.
    1.41 Participate in multidisciplinary assessment and IEP processes.
    1.42 Encourage school 504 committee[a] and offices/committees for handicapped student affairs to facilitate physical education and athletic opportunities for handicapped students.
    1.43 Encourage community recreation and health/fitness personnel to share resources and conduct integrated programs.
    1.44 Encourage civic organizations to help with volunteer tutoring, coaching, transportation, etc.

Tasks Accepted with Individualized Educational Programming Role

2.1 Participate in school district's IEP process (see Chapter 3).
2.2 Write psychomotor portion of IEP.
    2.21 Include in IEP a statement of present level of psychomotor performance.
    2.22 Include in IEP a statement of annual goals for psychomotor domain, including short-term specific behavioral objectives.
    2.23 Include in IEP a statement of the instructional services to be provided, including adaptations of content, teaching styles, and equipment.
    2.24 Include in IEP the projected date for initiation of physical education services and anticipated duration of such services.
    2.25 Include in IEP the evaluation procedures for determining discrepancy between objectives and actual performance after set periods of instructional intervention.

[a]Section 504 of the Rehabilitation Act of 1973 resulted in most schools and agencies establishing "504 committees" to monitor compliance with the law. See Chapter 2 for further information about this law.

Tasks Associated with Roles of Developmental/ Prescriptive Teaching and Coordination of Resources/Services

3.1 Apply principles of growth and development, biomechanics, and exercise physiology to physical education instruction.

    3.11 Recognize psychomotor prerequisites to physical education participation: Head and neck control, sufficient muscle tonus; grasp and release mechanisms; fine muscle coordination.

    3.12 Adapt physical education equipment and facilities accordingly.

3.2 Plan teaching-learning physical education situations in accordance with principles of learning.

    3.21 Provide for effective and continuing motivation and/or reinforcement.

    3.22 Analyze activities and skills into learning progressions appropriate to individual needs.

    3.23 Apply behavior management and/or appropriate group dynamics processes in classroom organization.

    3.24 Avoid activities/environmental conditions that are contraindicated by disability or psychomotor weaknesses.

    3.25 Maintain appropriate balance between safety and risk in facilitating movement confidence.

    3.26 Utilize teaching strategies that facilitate socialization and peer group acceptance.

    3.27 Adapt content (movement challenges, game rules and strategies, and the like) to each student's developmental level.

    3.28 Help student apply school physical education learnings to varied home and community settings.

3.3 Demonstrate professional level in instructional competence.

    3.31 Provide evidence that instruction changes student's level of psychomotor performance.

    3.32 Provide evidence that learning experiences facilitate normalization and socialization.

    3.33 Provide evidence that learning carries over into self-actualizing fitness and leisure practices/ habits.

3.4 Provide physical environment that facilitates psychomotor learning.

    3.41 Adapt equipment, supplies, materials to learner.

    3.42 Control heat, light, ventilation, and the like.

    3.43 Provide adequate structure and eliminate irrelevant stimuli.

    3.44 Eliminate architectural barriers.

3.5 Evaluate continuously as an integral part of the instructional process.

    3.51 Involve students and significant others in evaluation.

    3.52 Use resulting data to improve psychomotor learning processes.

3.6 Use community resources to enhance and reinforce psychomotor learnings.

    3.61 Involve handicapped persons in community (as well as in books, television, and films) as role models in fitness, athletics, and the like.

    3.62 Take advantage of psychomotor expertise of persons in other disciplines; also of volunteers in community.

    3.63 Solicit help from parent-professional organizations, civic groups, and various agencies.

    3.64 Ascertain that students have direct access to physical education/fitness resources in community.

    3.65 Develop in students responsibility for caring for and protecting physical education/athletic facilities/equipment in school and community.

    3.66 Help students acquire value systems that cherish movement, fitness, and other physical education parameters as an essential right of all American citizens.

Tasks Associated With Role of Community Leadership/Citizen Involvement/Advocacy

4.1 Participate in the definition and solution of community problems relating to handicapped persons.

4.2 Interpret to others legislation, and possible litigation, that protects rights of handicapped persons.

4.3 Act as advocate for handicapped persons and their families.

4.4 Work closely with the press and other media in presenting and interpreting physical education and leisure needs and potentials of handicapped persons to the public.

4.5 Engage in research and continuously examine alternative ways of translating adapted physical education theory into practice.

Credits

LINE ART, TABLES, TEXT

Preface

Poem on p. xviii From Dave Compton, "On Being Different," in *Proceedings of Special Populations Institute,* March 28–29, 1974. Ogleby Park, Wheeling, West Virginia: Northern Community College, 1974.

1

Poem on p. 9 From James Kavanaugh, *Will You Be My Friend?* Copyright © 1971 by James Kavanaugh. Los Angeles, CA: Nash Publishing Company, 1971.

4

Excerpt, pp. 74–75 Leo Buscaglia, *The Disabled and Their Parents: A Counseling Challenge,* (Thorofare, New Jersey: Charles B. Slack, Inc., 1975), pp. 19–20.

5

Figure 5.2 Adapted from Patten, *Human Embryology.* Copyright 1933 by McGraw-Hill Book Company.
Figures 5.3(a), 5.3(b), 5.6, 5.19, 5.20, 5.21(a), 5.21(b) From Hole, John W., Jr., *Human Anatomy and Physiology,* 2d. ed. © 1978, 1981 Wm. C. Brown Publishers, Dubuque, Iowa. All Rights Reserved. Reprinted by permission.
Figure 5.7 From Shirley, M. M., "The First Two Years," in *Child Welfare Monograph 7,* 1933. © 1933, renewed 1960 University of Minnesota Press, Minneapolis.
Figure 5.9 From Mader, Sylvia S., *Inquiry Into Life,* 2d. ed. © 1976, 1979 Wm. C. Brown Publishers, Dubuque, Iowa. All Rights Reserved. Reprinted by permission.

6

Figure 6.3 Concept from M. Wild, *Research Quarterly,* AAHPERD, 1938; redrawing from C. Corbin, *A Textbook of Motor Development,* 2d. ed. Copyright © 1980 Wm. C. Brown Publishers, Dubuque, Iowa. All Rights Reserved. Reprinted by permission.
Figure 6.11 From *The Cerebral Cortex of Man,* by Penfield and Rasmussen. © 1985 by MacMillan Publishing Company, Inc.

7

Figure 7.3 From *Fundamental Movement: A Developmental and Remedial Approach,* by Bruce A. McClenaghan and David L. Gallahue. Copyright © 1978 by W. B. Saunders Company.
Figure 7.6 From Muska Mosston, *Teaching Physical Education—From Command to Discovery.* Columbus, Ohio: Charles E. Merrill Books, Inc., 1966, 1981, p. 230.

9

Figure 9.5 Source: Wessel, J., *I CAN—Sport, Leisure and Recreation Skills.* Northbrook, IL: H. Hubbard, 1979.
Table 9.4 Source: Wessel, J., and L. Kelly, *Individualizing instruction: Quality programs for all students.* Philadelphia: Lea & Febiger, 1985.
Tables 9.8, 9.9, and 9.10 From G. S. D. Morris (1980), *How to Change the Games Children Play,* 2d. ed. Minneapolis: Burgess.

10

Figures 10.2 and 10.18 Reprinted by permission of A. Milani-Comparetti and E. A. Gidoni, Italy. Reproduced by permission from Norris G. Haring, *Developing Effective Individualized Education Programs for Severely Handicapped Children and Youth* (Columbus, OH: Special Press, 1977, p. 79). Available for purchase from Crace Rossa Italiana, Comitato Provinciale De Firenze, Centro Di Educazione Motoria, "Anna Torrigiani," via Di Comerata 8, 50133 Firenze.
Figure 10.27 Tracings are from cinematographic research by Dr. Barbara Gench and Dr. Marilyn Hinson, Texas Woman's University, Biomechanics Research Center.
Figure 10.31 From *Fundamental Movement: A Developmental and Remedial Approach,* by Bruce A. McClenaghan and David L. Gallahue. Copyright © 1978 by W. B. Saunders Company.
Figure 10.32 Concept from M. Wild, *Research Quarterly,* AAHPERD, 1938; redrawing from C. Corbin, *A Textbook of Motor Development,* 2d. ed. Copyright © 1980 Wm. C. Brown Publishers, Dubuque, Iowa. All Rights Reserved. Reprinted by permission.
Excerpt, pp. 254–55 Printed by permission of Counselor Recordings and Tests, Box 6184 Acklen Station, Nashville, Tennessee 37212. Test manual can be purchased from this company for $3.50.

13

Figures 13.3 and 13.4 Illustrations from Kirkendall, D., et al., *Measurement and Evaluation for Physical Educators.* © 1980 Wm. C. Brown Publishers, Dubuque, Iowa. All Rights Reserved. Reprinted by permission.
Table 13.4 From Carl C. Seltzer and Jean Mayer, "A Simple Criterion of Obesity," *Postgraduate Medicine 38* (August, 1965): A101–107.
Table 13.5 Table adapted from Per-Olaf Astrand, *Experimental Studies of Working Capacity in Relation to Sex and Age* (Copenhagen: Munksgoaard, 1952).
Table 13.6 From Brian J. Sharkey, *Physiology of Fitness,* Champaign, Illinois: Human Kinetics Publishers, 1977, p. 37.

17

Figure 17.2 and Table 17.2 Source: Bar-Or, O., *Pediatric Sports Medicine for the Practitioner.* New York: Springer-Verlag, 1983.
Figures 17.7, 17.8, 17.18, 17.20, and 17.21 From Hole, John W., *Human Anatomy and Physiology,* 2d. ed. © 1978, 1981 Wm. C. Brown Publishers, Dubuque, Iowa. All Rights Reserved. Reprinted by permission.
Figure 17.12 From Hole, John W., Jr., *Human Anatomy and Physiology,* 3d ed. © 1978, 1981, 1984 Wm. C. Brown Publishers, Dubuque, Iowa. All Rights Reserved. Reprinted by permission.
Table 17.7 Reprinted by permission from Catherine A. Neill, M.D., and Lulu M. Haroutunian, M.D., ''The Adolescent and Young Adult with Congenital Heart Disease,'' in *Heart Disease in Infants, Children and Adolescents,* ed. Arthur J. Moss, M.D., Forrest H. Adams, M.D., and George C. Emmanouilides, M.D. (Baltimore, MD: Williams & Wilkins Company, 1977), p. 720.
Figure 17.22 (a and b) From Mader, Sylvia S., *Inquiry Into Life,* 4th ed. © 1976, 1979, 1982, 1985 Wm. C. Brown Publishers, Dubuque, Iowa. All Rights Reserved. Reprinted by permission.

19

Table 19.1 Source: *The Problem of Mental Retardation,* U.S. Department of Health, Education and Welfare, Office of the Secretary, Secretary's Committee on Mental Retardation, Washington, D.C.: Government Printing Office, 1969.
Figures 19.2 and 19.13 From Hole, John W., Jr., *Human Anatomy and Physiology,* 3d. ed. © 1978, 1981, 1984 Wm. C. Brown Publishers, Dubuque, Iowa. All Rights Reserved. Reprinted by permission.
Table 19.2 Adapted from The President's Committee on Mental Retardation, ''Facts on Mental Retardation,'' Washington, D.C.: President's Committee on Mental Retardation, 1970.
Table 19.6 Adapted from Ruth C. Webb, ''Sensory-Motor Training of the Profoundly Retarded,'' *American Journal of Mental Deficiency* 74 (September, 1969): 287.

21

Figure 21.23 From Hole, John W., Jr., *Human Anatomy and Physiology,* 3d. ed. © 1978, 1981, 1984 Wm. C. Brown Publishers, Dubuque, Iowa. All Rights Reserved. Reprinted by permission.

23

Figures 23.7, 23.8, 23.9, 23.15, 23.16, 23.17 From *Handling the Young Cerebral Palsied Child at Home,* Second Edition, by Nancie R. Finnie. Copyright © 1974 by Nancie R. Finnie, F.C.S.P.; additions for U.S. edition, copyright © by E. P. Dutton and Company, Inc.
Table 24.1 From *Hearing and Deafness,* 4th ed., by Hallowell Davis and S. Richard Silverman. Copyright © 1947, 1960, 1970 by Holt, Rinehart and Winston, Inc. Copyright © 1978 by Holt, Rinehart and Winston, Inc.

Appendix A

p. 600, lower left corner Source: Adapted from ''Children and Youth—Selected Health Characteristics,'' *Vital and Health Statistics,* series 10, no. 62 (United States, 1958 and 1968, p. 18).
Figure A.1 Source: Statistical Abstract, 1980.
Table A.3 Source: Health United States, 1980, p. 274.

PHOTOGRAPHS

1

Figure 1.3 Cosom Games and Athletic Goods Company, Minneapolis, MN
Figure 1.4 M. Marsallo and D. Vacante, ADAPTED GAMES AND DEVELOPMENTAL ACTIVITIES FOR CHILDREN
Figure 1.5 B. Cadden, Valdez Public Schools in Alaska

2

Figure 2.1 (left and top right) Dr. Lane Goodwin, University of Wisconsin at LaCrosse, Special Populations Programs
Figure 2.1 (bottom right) Adapted Dance Program, Texas Woman's University
Figure 2.2 Rich Faverty
Figure 2.4 Curt Beamer, *Sports 'n Spokes*

3

Figure 3.1 (top left) Adapted Sports Program for Blind Students, Texas Woman's University
Figure 3.1 (bottom left) Dr. Ernest Bundschuh, University of Georgia

4

Figure 4.11 (all) Beneficial Designs, Inc., Santa Cruz, CA
Figure 4.12 Dr. Lane Goodwin, University of Wisconsin at LaCrosse, Special Populations Programs
Figure 4.13 Barron Ludlum, *Denton Record Chronicle*

6

Figure 6.8 Cosom Games and Athletic Goods Company, Minneapolis, MN

7

Figure 7.1 Rae Allen
Figure 7.5 Dr. Garth Tymeson, Northern Illinois University
Figure 7.9 DeKalb Public Schools, Georgia
Figure 7.14, Figure 7.15 Dr. Lane Goodwin, University of Wisconsin at LaCrosse, Special Populations Programs

8

Figures 8.5–8.10 Dr. Horst Strohkendl, Universidat Koln, W. Germany
Figure 8.12 (left) Nancy Crase © *Sports 'n Spokes*/Paralyzed Veterans of America
Figure 8.12 (right) Candy Jackson, Courage Center, Golden Valley, MN
Figure 8.13 Nancy Crase © *Sports 'n Spokes*/Paralyzed Veterans of America
Figure 8.20 National Academy of Sciences, National Research Council, Washington, DC

10

Figure 10.26 Steve Edmonds

11

Figure 11.1 Creative Playground by Sharon Schmidt
Figure 11.2 Contributed by Dr. Ernest Bundschuh, University of Georgia

12

Figure 12.3 Reprinted by permission of Reedco Incorporated
Figure 12.7 Denton State School

13

Figure 13.2 Provided by Dr. George Jurcisin, corrective therapist and recreation specialist at Veterans Administration Medical Center, Chillicothe, Ohio
Figure 13.3 (top), Figure 13.4 (top), Figure 13.5 From Don R. Kirkendall et al., *Measurement and Evaluation for Physical Educators,* Wm. C. Brown Company, Dubuque, IA

14

Figure 14.3 Barron Ludlum, *Denton Record Chronicle*

16

Figure 16.1 (both) Judy Newman
Figure 16.10 Longview, WA YMCA

17

Figure 17.1 Rae Allen
Figure 17.3 Fonda Johnstone
Figure 17.5 Lester V. Bergman & Associates, Inc.

19

Figure 19.2 (left), Figure 19.3 (right) Redding, A. and Hirschhorn, K.: *Guide to Human Chromosome Defects,* In Bergsma, D. (ed.): Birth Defects: Orig. Art Ser., vol. 4, no. 4. Published by The National Foundation—March of Dimes, White Plains, NY 1968
Figure 19.10 Paul Emert, Denton State School
Figure 19.11 (both) Recreation Center for the Handicapped, Inc., San Francisco, CA

20

Figure 20.2 Ross Photos
Figure 20.3 Jim Estes

21

Figure 21.3 Paralyzed Veterans of America/*Sports 'n Spokes*
Figure 21.10 National Academy of Sciences, National Research Council, Washington, DC
Figures 21.11–21.13 University of Texas SWMS–Dallas, Department of Medical Art
Figure 21.14 National Academy of Sciences, National Research Council, Washington, DC
Figure 21.21 (both) *Sports 'n Spokes*

22

Figure 22.3 Muscular Dystrophy Association
Figure 22.11 Dr. Jo Cowden, University of New Orleans
Figure 22.15 (both) Marilyn Butt, adapted physical education consultant from Ontario, Canada

25

Figure 25.1 Steve Edmonds
Figure 25.2, Figure 25.4 Christian Record Braille Foundation. Photo by Robert L. Sheldon
Figure 25.5 Steve Edmonds
Figure 25.6 National Camps for Blind Children, Lincoln, Nebraska
Figure 25.8, Figure 25.9 Provided by Rosanna Copeland, Parkview School for the Blind in Oklahoma

Name Index

Subject Index